THE LIBRARY OF
RICHARD E. ROSE

Exposition of The Psalms

EXPOSITION OF

The Psalms

by H. C. Leupold, D.D.

PROFESSOR OF OLD TESTAMENT EXEGESIS
THE EVANGELICAL LUTHERAN SEMINARY
OF CAPITAL UNIVERSITY
COLUMBUS, OHIO

BAKER BOOK HOUSE
Grand Rapids, Michigan

Reprinted, 1969, by
Baker Book House Company

Eighth printing, September 1984

Copyright 1959, The Wartburg Press
Assigned to Augsburg Publishing House, 1961
Library of Congress Catalog Card Number: 59-9289
ISBN: 0-8010-5521-0
Printed in the United States of America

TO MY CONGENIAL COLLEAGUES

of the Evangelical Lutheran Theological Seminary

Columbus, Ohio

Foreword

It is now some time since a thorough-going conservative commentary on the Psalms has appeared. Much scholarly work in this field has been done but the results of such study need to be sifted and carefully revised. This is in part what the present exposition attempts to do.

Besides, it is necessary that a commentary be provided that the intelligent layman can use as well as the busy pastor, for the Psalter still is the Prayer Book of the people of God. We hope that by moving the grammatical and critical Notes to the end of the treatment of each psalm we may have helped both the lay users of the book and the pastors.

Brevity of treatment has been one of our major concerns. To prepare a book several times as large as the present volume would in the last analysis have been much easier.

The Psalms have been widely used in worship and in public and private devotions. New hymnals published by several denominations encourage such continued use. The Service Book and Hymnal of the Lutheran Church (1958) includes more than one hundred psalms. We hope that the increased use of the Psalter may result in the more diligent study of this sacred book. This exposition hopes to satisfy this need.

On the anniversary of the Presentation
of the Augsburg Confession, June 24, 1959

H. C. Leupold

Introduction

NAME

THE BOOK is frequently designated merely by the title "Psalms." *KJ* calls it the "Book of Psalms." Luther and most German Bibles designate it by the name *Psalter,* which is thoroughly familiar also in English usage. Both names are traceable to the Greek word *psalmoi,* which strictly speaking designates poems that are sung to the accompaniment of music played on strings. This term is, in turn, expressed by the Hebrew word *mizmor,* a word which occurs 57 times as a designation in the title of certain psalms. Strangely, the Hebrew Bible uses the title *sepher tehillim,* Book of Praise-Psalms. At first glance this Hebrew title might seem to be more to the point as an accurate description; but on closer reflection it will appear that the element of praise, though prominent in the Psalter, is not so prominent as to warrant thus describing the majority of the poems commonly called "psalms." It is true that especially toward the close of the book the element of praise swells forth more emphatically. But for all that, praise is only one of many elements that stand forth in the book. Praise is an incidental feature in psalms.

DIVISION INTO FIVE BOOKS

THOUGH it is plainly printed in many English Bibles, the division of the Psalter into five books is scarcely observed by the average Bible reader. These five divisions are as follows: 1—41; 42—72; 73—89; 90—106; 107—150. Many attempts have been made to explain how this fivefold division came into use and why, but the only factor involved that seems to be of any moment is that some sort of agreement with the fivefold division of the Pentateuch was intended. Yet no commentator seems to be able to say wherein this correspondence consists. Explanations are usually about as fanciful as is that of Gregory of Nyssa, who, according to *Delitzsch,* maintained that "the Psalter in its five books leads up as it were by five stages to moral perfection." Rather more to the point is the observation that the five books are very closely associated with the gradual growth and development of the whole book, as we shall soon show.

Here may be the most appropriate place to indicate how the more prominent versions differ in the numbering of the psalms. The *Septuagint,* followed by the Latin, differs from the Hebrew (and for that matter, the English) style of numbering as follows:

Hebrew	*Greek*
1–8	1–8
9–10	9
11–113	10–112
114–115	113
116:1–9	114
116:10–19	115
117–146	116–145
147:1–11	146
147:12–20	147
148–150	148–150

This difference must be borne in mind when one is reading books by Roman Catholic authors or when consulting the *Vulgate* or the *Septuagint.*

ORIGIN OF THE BOOK

HOW THE BOOK came to assume its present form and arrangement, that is to say, how it grew by various stages into the fivefold book we now have has been a matter of much and learned conjecture. No definite information is obtainable. Conjectures and deductions are admissible up to a certain point, but they do not help us to arrive at certainty. We shall attempt to present only so much of what is usually offered under this head as seems to be pretty well established.

The usual point of departure is the remark appended after the conclusion of Ps. 72, that is, 72:20: "The prayers of David, the son of Jesse, are ended." This remark apparently indicates some editorial activity and voices the conviction of him who appended it to the psalm that whatever "prayers" (another word for "psalms") "of David" were available had been included in the collection of the psalms up to this point. There is the added possibility that, since in the group of psalms 1–72, psalms by David, according to the headings, far outnumbered all others, the collection was designated by the name of the majority. It is also apparently quite reasonable to assume that he that appended this notice to the psalm knew of no further prayers of David, in fact, believed he had collected all that were to be found. In that as-

Introduction 3

sumption he was mistaken, for in the remaining books of the Psalter about 17 more appear that are ascribed to David.

The second step in trying to trace the gradual composition of the book through successive stages is the noticeable fact that these first two books are in a certain contrast with one another inasmuch as the second book (42–72) uses the divine name *Elohim* much more frequently that any other name, especially the proper divine name *Yahweh,* the ratio being 164 to 30, whereas in the first book the ratio was the reverse, *Yahweh* being used 272 times and *Elohim* 15. Commentators have long been at a loss to explain this difference, especially since it can be shown that in the second book the name *Yahweh* was frequently changed to *Elohim,* even where the former was originally in the text. It may be claimed with the *Westminster Dictionary of the Bible* that the name *Elohim* was substituted "for the purpose of meeting a felt need in the worship" inasmuch as this name lends itself more to the "adoring contemplation of God in the fulness of that conception." Be that as it may, the use of the divine names as well as other factors indicate that at the time this subscription (Ps. 72:20) was made two distinct books were already in existence, and presumably of the same scope and compass that they now have.

Book III could have then been added. But from this point onward material informing us as to its origin is practically nonexistent. Since Book III contains eleven psalms by Asaph, four by Korah, one by David (Ps. 86), and one by Ethan, a simple assumption (but one for which we could offer no positive proof) would be that some persons, competent and authorized to do so, made a collection of psalms by several prominent authors who had written psalms that seemed worthy to be added to the psalmbook that already contained 72 psalms. When and by whom this could have been done we have no way of ascertaining. Writers on the subject are not at all agreed as to the origin of Book III.

Evidence of various efforts at collection is indicated by the duplications that appear within the Psalter: Ps. 14 equals Ps. 53; 40:13ff. equals 70; 57:7–11 and 60:5 make up 108. What bearing these repetitions have on the question of the origin of the book is answered differently by each writer.

It may be remarked that Book II and Book III may have been united into one before they were added to Book I. On questions of this sort there is room for much speculation.

As we come to Book IV we should remark that any one of the five Books may have had later additions or withdrawals made before it was incorporated into the whole Psalter. What is at least beginning to become evident is that different collections were quite obviously made by different persons in successive periods spread over quite a space of time. In Book IV we find two psalms that are ascribed to David, one to Moses, ten that have no title, and four that have headings but no ascription of authorship. By reaching back as far as Moses the collector seems to indicate that he was intent on preserving whatever still existed anywhere within this field as he knew it.

Since Book V gives evidence of a similar trend (there are fourteen by David, one by Solomon, and the rest are nameless) there is, of course, the possibility that Books IV and V may have been combined before they were added to the complete book. In any case, by a gradual process of some sort of accretion Book was added to Book until the whole was complete.

The fact that some kind of final editorial activity must have taken place is indicated in part already by the incident that the round number of 150 psalms was chosen to make up the entire Psalter. For some unexplainable reason the *Septuagint* has a supernumerary psalm which it lists as such and thus has a total of 151. It may also be noted that some principles of arrangement can be detected as one looks through the successive psalms. Oftentimes psalms by the same author are grouped together as nearly as possible. Thus we note the psalms of David in several such groups here and there. Besides, similar situations or contrasting situations often lead to putting two psalms side by side. Quite frequently similar words and phrases that occur in two psalms seem to have led to placing them side by side whatever their character may have otherwise been. This similar use of words and phrases strikes us as having been one of the most common factors in determining the placing of two psalms side by side.

Beyond this, little that is reliable can be said about the origin of the book as a whole.

THE USE OF THE PSALTER AMONG THE JEWS AND IN THE CHRISTIAN CHURCH

IT CAN BE SHOWN that the Jews made ample use of the Psalter in the early centuries of our era. From the Mishnaic period (ca.200) dates certain evidence that already then certain psalms were assigned to certain days of the week (Ps. 24, 48, 82, 94, 81, 93, 92). Even modern Jewish prayer books have a generous measure of material from the psalms.

It is of special interest to Christians that the New Testament quotes more liberally from the Psalter than from any other Old Testament book. *Kirkpatrick* claims there are 93 such quotations; *Delitzsch,* 70. The difference in number is obviously due to the fact that it is diffi-

Introduction

cult to determine whether certain statements or phrases merit the designation of a quotation. Jesus, our Lord, was apparently quite familiar with the Psalter, for on the cross he quoted from Ps. 22 (Matt. 27:46 and parallels), and in controversy with the Pharisees He quoted from Ps. 110 (Matt. 22:43f. and parallels). Cf. also Luke 24:44. In the writings of the apostles statements such as Col. 3:16 should be noted. Psalm singing apparently constituted a greater part of the singing of the early church.

As we advance through the centuries, the singing of psalms continues, and the Psalter is a very popular book that is much in use. The best writers among the church fathers wrote commentaries on this book. Outstanding are those of Chrysostom and Augustine. When the canonical hours came into use in monasteries, portions of the book were assigned to the various hours, and in many instances the entire Psalter was chanted regularly in the course of each week, as is still said to be the custom among Benedictine orders. There was even a time when as a prerequisite for admission to the priesthood it was mandatory that the candidate be able to recite the entire book.

The Reformers encouraged the use of the Psalter, and Luther was particularly known for the love that he bore to the book and the faithful use that he made of it on all occasions as well as for the high praise that he bestowed upon it. In the church of the Reformation psalm-paraphrases constituted many of its hymns, quite aside from those Reformed churches where the singing of only psalms or psalm-paraphrases was permitted in public worship. Perhaps we are safe in saying that no Biblical book has seen more use throughout Christendom than has the Psalter.

AUTHORSHIP

As ONE pages through the psalms, it becomes quite obvious that many psalms bear headings which in a considerable number of instances indicate authorship. These headings were once regarded as substantially correct. After a measure of critical treatment had been given them, they were more and more disregarded. Today they are usually regarded as being practically worthless. *Schmidt* (p. V) perhaps expresses the view that is most commonly held in our day: "In our day the view . . . is quite generally accepted that the notations [in the headings] concerning the author, which by the way are more numerous in the Septuagint, are not to be regarded as a matter of reliable historical record but as conjectures made by the collectors [of the psalms]— venerable indeed as early attempts in the field of literary studies but of no moment for the understanding of the psalms." Commentators are ready, for that matter, to substitute in a rather positive tone another possibility on the score of authorship. *Mowinckel* advances the claim: "The conclusion is inescapable (made previously already by *Gunkel* at least for the oldest psalms): the psalms originated in the circle of the Temple attendants (*Tempel personal*)."

Far more sober and very much to the point are remarks such as those offered by the *Westminster Dictionary of the Bible:* "In many cases . . . sufficient reason does not exist for denying the authenticity of the title; or the outcome of the inquiry, stated positively, may be that the contents of the psalm are suitable to the occasion attested by the title." We believe the restraint of a writer like *Noetscher* deserves commendation when he says: "The headings are apparently old and are therefore not to be set aside without sufficient ground. But they do not belong to the text."

The fact that they do not belong to the text every student of Hebrew has long known. However, they were in their day inserted by men in Israel who belonged to her trustworthy leaders. This could have been done by men like Ezra who ventured by this insertion to preserve a valuable and well-authenticated tradition, which they felt should not be lost and could be of use to readers of the psalms in centuries to come. Concerning these titles, it is hardly fair when the sweeping demand is made that, unless the contents of the psalm *prove* authorship as claimed by the heading, the heading must be regarded as unreliable. By such canons of literary criticism no claim of authorship under comparable circumstances could ever stand. We rather venture the claim that the correctness of the title dare be questioned only then when an actual contradiction to known facts of David's life appears between the title and the contents of the psalm. This demands that allowance be made for the fact that our knowledge of the events of David's life is quite limited, and that much supplementary information may be culled from the psalms.

The following Biblical evidence has further bearing upon the question of authorship. We begin by answering the question: Is there good evidence in the Scriptures for the assumption that David may have been a writer of sacred poetry? The Biblical evidence on this matter is very helpful. We know that David had poetic ability, for certain poems of a more secular nature are clearly ascribed to him: He wrote a touching lament concerning Saul and Jonathan (II Sam. 1:19–27). He also lamented the tragic end of Abner in the brief poem which is recorded either in part or in whole in II Sam. 3:33f. The historical books, whose validity on this score is not open to doubt, indicate that David was active in the field of sacred poetry, see particularly II Sam. 23:1–7, which incidentally indicates that David enjoyed some reputation as a

Introduction

writer of psalms at the time he wrote the words there recorded, for he describes himself as "the sweet psalmist of Israel," almost in the manner of one accepting a tribute which men had quite commonly begun to bestow upon him, and which he deemed had bearing on the importance of the particular utterance that he was about to commit to writing.

The chapter immediately adjoining the one just referred to, II Sam. 22, is, as is immediately apparent to even the casual reader, Ps. 18 with minor changes. The historical book of Samuel attributes the psalm to David. That this involves a tradition which is validated by other writers appears from the fact that the casual reference of Amos 6:5 clearly points in the same direction. And so at least a number of writers have again dared to advance the claim that at least some of the psalms whose headings claim that the psalm stems from David must be ascribed to him. One of the strongest claims along this line stems from *Koenig,* who cheerfully attributes the following psalms to this good king of Israel: 3, 4, 6–8, 11, 15, 18, 23, 29, 30, 32. We feel he might well have gone farther and accepted the whole number that have the words "of David" in the superscription.

Two other factors could be said to have bearing upon the case. One is a matter, pointed out by *Delitzsch,* that David, being closely associated with Samuel as he was in his early years, may have also had contacts with the bands of the prophets who were assembled in the schools of the prophets at that time, and where studies of such subjects as sacred poetry may have flourished. Though this lies entirely in the field of conjecture, there is another factor that must not be made light of, and that is the claim that "the Spirit of the Lord came mightily upon David from that day forward," I Sam. 16:13. The day referred to is that of David's anointing. We regard the unction of the Spirit as a major prerequisite for the writing of inspired poetry. In addition it may be pointed out that David, as is well known, had many admirable qualities. He was a personable youth, discreet in his conduct at court, of a friendly disposition, endowed with notable virtues such as the forgiving spirit that he manifested over against Saul, and certainly deserving of the friendship of a true man like Jonathan. The psalms reflect these virtues.

As we are ready to accept the claim of the title for all the instances where it appears to the effect that certain psalms stem from David, so we in like manner feel that the validity of the claim of other such titles stands. We are ready to accept the claim that Moses wrote Ps. 90; that 72 and 127 stem from Solomon, that others come from the sons of Korah, and Asaph composed certain others. Nothing in these psalms actually conflicts with the claim of the title.

Here we may briefly insert a reference to an issue that will appear frequently in the following pages. It is the question whether there are not obvious Aramaism in some of these psalms; and are not Aramaisms an indication of a late date, possibly the Persian era? Without going into the matter in any detail, let us merely point to an insight that is growing upon not a few writers at the present time and is well expressed by *McCullough* at the conclusion of his investigation into the matter in the introductory material of the *Interpreter's Bible:* "To cite 'Aramaisms' as evidence of the late date of a psalm is therefore a highly questionable procedure." Or as *Weiser* puts it (p. 13): "Even late forms and expressions here and there prove at the most that the final form arrived at [*Endgestalt*] is late."

HISTORICAL SITUATIONS REFLECTED IN THE PSALMS

Certain historical incidents and events could easily have given rise to the composition of psalms. We mention a few of those which could have stirred individuals or the whole nation to break forth into praise or petition. The rebellion of Absalom roused many a mind and heart, especially David's. Though it was intensely personal in character as far as David was concerned, the Bathsheba incident could have led the king to compose a psalm of warning and instruction. When the Assyrians under Sennacherib were forced to beat a retreat, the national consciousness may well have been stirred to the point where it sought public expression in psalms. The Exile and the return from the Exile furnish equally valid occasions for outbursts of sacred poetry.—We arrive at the conclusion that, when a heading claims that the psalm in question is associated with some such event, that possibility dare not be lightly thrust aside but may be accepted as long as there is no conflict between the claim and the contents of the psalm. By way of illustration we may refer to the following psalms as involving such situations: 3, 46–48, 51, etc.

DATE OF THE COMPLETION OF THE PSALTER

COMMENTATORS will invariably determine this date according to the date that they accept with regard to the completion of the entire canon, because there is no distinct evidence of date as to completion in the entire book of Psalms. Since we hold that the Old Testament canon was complete by the year 400 B.C. or shortly thereafter we find nothing in the psalter that would lead us to conclude that it was brought to a conclusion later than this date. We have referred to Aramaisms.

Introduction

Related to this issue is, of course, the question concerning Maccabean psalms (date: near the middle of the second century B.C.). Whereas *Calvin* already in his day voiced the assumption that Ps. 44, 74, 79 should be assigned to this period, nothing is to be found within even these psalms that compels us to accept this suggestion. For a time the trend ran strong in the direction of regarding almost all psalms as being composed in the Maccabean period. Now this approach has largely been given up.

MUSICAL NOTATIONS AND TECHNICAL TERMS

ASIDE FROM the matter already mentioned as appearing in the titles of the psalms, there are certain technical terms and expressions that are now commonly regarded as being of a musical nature. We refer first of all to those terms which occur more or less commonly, such as "chief musician," "a psalm," "a song," "a maskil." It is quite commonly conceded that the first of these may be correctly translated "choirmaster" (*RSV*) or even "choir director" or "chief musician" (*KJ*). But even after this is posited, the question still remains, Why should these psalms have been assigned to him? For the present we offer only one suggestion, which to us seems the most reasonable of all, that the author of the psalm, usually David, put the psalm into the hands of the choirmaster with the intent and purpose that he might rehearse it with the Levitical choirs and so introduce it to Israel for public worship. Compare in this connection I Chron. 15:16ff.

"Selah," which comes from a root "to lift up," may indicate one of two things: either an increase in volume of the music or of the singing, or else the setting in of a musical interlude. It may, therefore, be indirectly regarded as marking a pause for reflection. But it is quite apparently a musical notation of some sort.

Terms like "psalms" and "song" may have in their day marked a very clear-cut distinction. If so, we have no idea as to what the actual difference was, nor have we any way of finding out.

Terms like "maskil" and "miktam" are equally puzzling. The former may mean a "didactic poem," the latter could mean a "treasure." The contents of the psalms involved agree to some extent with the possibility here stated; but we must freely confess we cannot be too sure if we have fully captured the significance of these technical terms.

There are also certain other difficult terms in the headings. We list a few: "Muth-labben" (Ps. 9), "The Sheminith" (Ps. 12), "The Hind of the Dawn" (Ps. 22). These terms have been much discussed. Some commentators have thought that they indicate in a subtle way the contents of the psalm. *Muth-labben* means "the death of the son"; *Shem-*

inith could mean the "eighth"; "the hind of the dawn," being interpreted as Luther does: The hind that is hunted early, could in some way refer to Christ, of whose passion the psalm treats. But all this is again somewhat fanciful. We incline toward the opinion prevailing in our day that these terms are the opening words of tunes or songs, according to which the psalm in question is to be rendered.

CURRENT TRENDS OF INTERPRETATION

IT CAN SCARCELY be expected that at this point we could give every trend that is in evidence in our day. But it is clear that certain trends stand out sufficiently and claim so much attention that they simply dare not be ignored.

Perhaps the most distinctive feature of psalm interpretation in our day is the recognition that there are certain *types* of psalms, and that these types are clearly recognizable. Very solid work has been done in this field, and tangible results have been achieved, especially since Gunkel-Begrich published the famous work, *Einleitung in die Psalmen* (1933).

However, one should not assume that total ignorance of the possibility of classification of psalms prevailed in earlier days. In his *Summarien* Luther listed five classes of psalms as being outstanding. There were in his opinion first of all those psalms that were prophecies about the Christ; then there were doctrinal psalms; then psalms of comfort; then also prayer psalms; and lastly psalms of thanksgiving. Almost every writer that commented on the psalms after him had his own particular pattern of classification. In our day form criticism brought this issue more prominently to the fore until Gunkel made his exhaustive studies in this field. Though he speaks with too much finality and practically submits his classification as the last word on the subject, it cannot be denied that what he has written has tended to clarify the problem immensely. As Gunkel sees it, there are seven classes to be observed. They are 1) hymns, 2) enthronement of Yahweh psalms, 3) national laments, 4) royal psalms, 5) laments of the individual, 6) psalms of individual thanksgiving, 7) lesser categories. In this last class are to be found six subheads: a) words of blessing and cursing, b) pilgrimage songs, c) hymns of victory, d) hymns of thanksgiving, e) the legend, f) the law. No one writer could, even if he were deeply in sympathy with Gunkel, arrive at quite the same classification. The last word can never be spoken on subjects like this. But since Gunkel has written, commentators have been classifying psalms pretty much after the pattern he developed. Nor can it be doubted that many an issue has been clarified as a result.

Introduction

Some disadvantages of giving too much emphasis to this approach are already beginning to appear. Some writers seem to assume that the ancient Israelites made similar psalm studies and operated consciously with this type of form criticism. Others seem to have a feeling that, as soon as they have properly classified a psalm, that is to say, put it into its proper pigeonhole, the last word about the nature of the psalm has been spoken. It is frequently being overlooked that the pattern or type involved is not so much a matter of traditional form as it is a purely natural procedure that is bound to be followed whether the types involved are clearly in the mind of the writer or not. There is a kind of natural logic about some of these procedures. When a man is in trouble and gives poetic vent to his emotions in a literary production or, for that matter, in a free outburst of prayer, it may well happen that without any reflection or without being conscious of any pattern he describes his situation in detail to the Lord. After this a lament might quite naturally follow, laying bare his inmost feelings and bitter pain. Such a lament might be repeated or dwelt on at greater length, depending on the extremity of the situation in which the man is involved. Then quite naturally could follow petitions for relief from the great distress. This prayer might be long or short as the feelings of the moment dictate. There could then follow more lament, if the prayer had failed to raise the petitioner above the level of his distress. Or there might follow a note of restored confidence and even a word of thanksgiving for the comfort and help received from the Lord.

No one would deny that the sequence of parts in such a psalm could be arranged in almost any order. One and the same man might be praying in one fashion this year and in quite another fashion three years hence. In other words, the rigidity of pattern has been stressed too much. We still insist that to attempt careful classification of psalms according to the types involved is necessary and very helpful, even if the terms currently in use are not always rigidly followed.

A second trend that is very much in evidence but has far less to commend it than the trend just described is the effort to determine that there must have been Enthronement of Yahweh psalms associated with a New Year's Festival. The prominent name in this area is *Mowinckel,* whose voluminous *Psalmenstudien* appeared in 1921. To try to present the issues involved briefly, it should be noted that comparative studies in the field, particularly of Babylonian literature, had convinced Mowinckel that the festival of the annual enthronement of Marduk, chief divinity of the Babylonians, played so important a part in Babylonian life that it was unthinkable that the lesser nation, Israel, should not have been deeply influenced by it and should not have had a similar festival. The total silence of the sacred writings of Israel on this subject did not deter this writer from assuming that he could prove his point. By manifold and involved deductions Mowinckel finally builds up conclusions that supply all the needed background. The New Year's Festival becomes virtually the most prominent of all of Israel's festivals. Numerous psalms are claimed to be associated with this celebration, in fact, this view assumed tremendous proportions. On every possible and impossible occasion the enthronement of Yahweh, so called, was read into the picture. Without attempting an extensive refutation, we draw attention to the fact, which is quite basic and has been so well expressed by *McCullough:* "The idea that the Hebrew God could in any real sense be enthroned annually was poor theology, and could hardly have been seriously held by the nation's religious leaders." Perhaps never has so elaborate a superstructure been built on so minimal an amount of evidence.

Another trend of interpretation which claims less attention in our day than it previously did is the trend to make the "I" of the psalms refer to the congregation of Israel—the "collective I" as it has been called. This trend grew out of an overemphasis on community thinking, which, to tell the truth, has often been too little regarded. It will have to be admitted that there are times when the pronoun I (my or mine) does seem to refer to the entire nation. That nations feels itself to be a unit. It is in such cases the nation that prays, not the individual. But when such a possibility assumes major proportions and dominates interpretation so that the pronoun "I" is thought of as always referring to Israel, a possibility has been exaggerated far beyond what the facts of the case warrant.

Then there is the trend which goes on the assumption that the whole of the Psalter was designed for cultic use, or, to word it differently, that the psalms are liturgical literature. After it had been recognized that there were more liturgical elements in the Sacred Scriptures than men had previously supposed, this approach was pressed to the point where the liturgical was being discovered everywhere. *Mowinckel* went to this extreme. Others have followed him. But a sober reaction is beginning to set in. *Gunkel* has contributed to a more normal approach, though the claim that the whole of the Psalter is liturgical is still being advanced. Without going into much detail, it will be readily seen that psalms like 1 and 23 would never occur to average readers as having any possibilities along this line. Or for that matter, to overlook the sensible possibility that psalms could easily have originated in all manner of situations in life is to overlook the obvious. In other words, there is ground for viewing with suspicion the approach that, as soon as a psalm is being approached, seeks to find some liturgical situation into which it might fit. Such an approach deserves, in our humble opinion,

Introduction

to be classified among the obsessions. Proofs to the contrary that have been attempted are open to too many objections.

Allied with this approach is the attempt to make the psalms reflect highly dramatic procedures which to some extent serve to cover up the weakness of this approach but are too stilted and unnatural to be accepted with conviction. When the assembled congregation is represented as breaking forth into thunderous acclaim, when incense and levitical choirs and solemn processions are gratuitously injected into the scene to make the interpretation effective, when divine theophanies and high-strung emotionalism are frequently assumed as common occurrences—this strikes us as forced and unnatural.

In addition it has become a commonplace procedure to make extensive textual alterations in the Masoretic text, often with numerous or at least major alterations of the text, correcting into the text the very element that is required for a certain approach of interpretation. When this is done, such a procedure becomes reprehensible. Added to this there is the partitioning out of the psalms to various individuals and groups for responsive rendering to make interpretations more striking. No one would deny that such responsive arrangements may indeed have been very common, but seldom can commentators agree as to the precise limits of the reponsive element, and too often they here, too, resort to textual alterations in order to make their approach plausible.

To try to sum up our approach under this head, we are of the conviction that better justice is done to the book when it is said that "the Psalter is the Hymnal and the Book of Devotions (*Gesang-und Erbauungsbuch*) of the Jewish congregation." How much was at first designed to be liturgy and later frequently became material for private devotions, and how much was at first the outgrowth of private devotions and was later adapted to liturgical use, no man will ever know. Both trends must be reckoned with and will have been much in evidence. The other familiar designation could appropriately be used, "the hymnal of the second Temple," if it be understood that it was intended for public and private use. To close with a quotation from *Noetscher* (p. 4): "The cultus in any case is not the sole source of these hymns, perhaps not even the oldest. The *Sitz im Leben,* the situation out of which a psalm grew, frequently cannot be determined at all, or with any degree of certainty."

HEBREW POETRY, PARALLELISM, AND POETIC STYLE

IT HAS BEEN long recognized that parallelism is the distinctive mark of Hebrew poetry. Two statements are yoked together, rarely even three.

These statements may stand in various relations to one another. Of the many classifications of these relations that have been attempted with a good measure of justification three still appear to be basic. The parallelism may be a) synonymous, which involves that the second statement says much the same as the first. Or it may be b) synthetic, which involves that the second statement adds to the first and goes beyond it. Third it may be c) antithetic, which involves that a contrast to the initial statement is offered by the second. This classification is, of course, an oversimplification but is quite useful as far as it goes in that it helps the reader to detect quite readily whether a portion of Scripture is poetic or not. All the Psalms are poetry and should be printed as such as the *ARV* and the *RSV* have consistently done.

More difficult is the matter of meter, for it is clear that in this field Hebrew poetry is quite different from the patterns familiar to us. The Hebrew mind was not concerned about long and short syllables as was Greek and Roman poetry; it had no interest in accented syllables. It was concerned about accented *words* in a given line (lines are also called "stichs"). By way of example: according to *Schmidt,* the following is the pattern of Ps. 23: vv. 1, 2, and 3:4 3, 3 2, 3 2; v. 4: 2 2 2, 2 2 2; v. 5:3 2, 3 2; v. 6:3 2, 3 2. There is also a 4 4 pattern and a 4 3 pattern. It becomes immediately apparent from the example offered that any one set pattern of accented words does not seem to prevail throughout any psalm, so that Hebrew meter from our point of view amounts to little more than a kind of rhythmic speech pattern in a higher strain of diction. Some interpreters have called this the *dialectus poetica.* Any verse may depart from the pattern of the preceding verse. The stichs may be longer or shorter. To demand that, because a certain pattern has been followed at a given point, therefore a particular length of stich is demanded at a given point means drawing conclusions that cannot be warranted. In other words, the critical approach that claims that the meter at a given point demands a certain number of accented words and then to attempt to correct the text to obtain the required number of words, must be viewed with a very critical mind. Yet in our day numerous corrections are made on this score and obviously with insufficient warrant. For that matter, rhyme does occur in Hebrew occasionally, but it would appear that it is a matter of accident or coincidence (see Ps. 146).

However, something of a more positive nature may be detected in the general area of poetic style. There are certain words and constructions that have been listed especially by *Koenig* (*Die Psalmen,* pp. 6-9) which are distinctive of Hebrew poetic usage and may be indicated here in brief for the Hebrew scholar. Aside from the fact

Introduction 15

that the article is not used in poetry with the same consistency as in prose, there are the following terms: *zeh* serves as a relative pronoun; the verbal suffix *mo* is used for simple *m; ath* appears as the feminine absolute ending; old case endings are retained; older and more resonant nominal suffixes appear (*ki* for *k; yehu* for *yo; mo* for *hem,* etc.); frequent use of *bal* as the negative; the use of lengthened prepositions (*minni* for *min; kemo* for *ke; 'eley* for *'el; 'alay* for *'al*); the conjunction *'aph* for *gam;* omission of the article to make a noun a proper noun; *waw* consecutive separated from its verb by several other words; occasional different spelling of words tending toward the Aramaic form. This is a sizable array of poetic peculiarities that have for the most part been noted all too little by commentators. But they do confirm the claim that there are certain earmarks of Hebrew poetry as to the form used, as is the case in many languages.

THE STATE OF THE HEBREW TEXT

THIS BRINGS US to a related subject on which we have to some extent already indicated our position. It may safely be maintained that the Hebrew text of the Psalter has come down to us in a rather good state of preservation. There is always room, of course, for sound textual criticism, for there are instances where the text is obscure. That does not mean that some error or defect of transcription is involved. It often implies only that our knowledge of Biblical Hebrew has its limitations. To resort to quick emendations as soon as a difficulty or an obscurity is encountered is not warranted. In some instances the problem will be a *hapax legomenon* (a word occurring only once in the Hebrew Bible). If we are uncertain as to the meaning of such a word, that does not immediately make that word suspect. Or there may be a translation of the Septuagint, or the Targum, or the Vulgate that does not seem to agree with the Hebrew text. That in itself may indicate nothing more than that these early translators had their difficulties with the word in question, for their knowledge of Hebrew had its limitations. It is unwise at once to start emending according to the versions. Almost the whole world of scholarship in the field of the Hebrew needs the admonition to stay patiently with the Hebrew text when difficulties are met with and to seek to determine what the text really says and if, what it says, may not agree well with what went before and what follows. Such possibilities are explored too little, and scholars proceed to make conjectures and emendations which display more ingenuity than wisdom. By such means much can be read into texts, material that would have astonished even the original writers.

BABYLONIAN AND EGYPTIAN PARALLELS TO THE PSALMS

COMPARATIVE MATERIAL would be such as that offered by Pritchard, *Ancient Near Eastern Texts,* pp. 365-393. Quite a bit of material is now available to indicate to us what other nations had in days of old that was comparable to what the Scriptures present in the psalms, and in many cases this material is also older.

However, as one reads at length these non-Israelitish hymns and prayers one is struck, not so much by their similarity to the Biblical material, but by the striking differences that are in evidence. One Babylonian prayer addressed to Marduk repeats 16 times the plea. "Be appeased." When Amon, the Egyptian deity, is addressed as the sole God, only a select number of the stanzas of the prayer are given, among them the 300th and the 600th. What "vain repetitions" these must have been! In a prayer addressed to the goddess Ishtar there is a wearisome enumeration of attributes even to the number of 25. The views that are reflected concerning these gods outside of Israel are often cheap and trivial, to say the least. Flattery is often obviously resorted to in the attempt to enlist the good will of a god. The view of religion that underlies these prayers is on the whole often very externalistic.

In view of these differences it strikes us as being more than farfetched to try to establish the relationship of these extra-Israelitish prayers to the Book of Psalms as being one of dependence of the latter upon the former. It is not very likely that literature of this sort outside of Israel had any influence on Israel whatever. It may even be questioned whether the psalm writers of Israel were acquainted with these foreign productions.

This much is true, that traditionally they may both be traced back to some common source, which could have been the prayers of the early patriarchs, even Noah, for all we know. What modifications in this tradition were made on both sides and to what extent the one tradition influenced the other can now scarcely be determined. Somewhere in this field lie the few uses of old, perhaps mythological material (cf. Ps. 89:10) that appear in the Psalms. But the attempt to discover frequent allusions in the psalms to this type of material is quite superficial, and a better explanation of what is actually said can be devised.

Quite another matter is the observation that some psalms have in their vocabulary a striking percentage of words or roots that are Ugaritic, as can be learned by comparing them with Ras Shamra material. Some comparisons have been made in a rather extensive way by Helen Jefferson (JBL, 1954, III, p. 152ff.) where the almost exact percentage of correspondence of roots is determined, a correspondence which runs surprisingly high. One need not be alarmed by such discoveries if one bears in mind that two slightly different types of the Canaanite (or Hebrew) language are involved. Least of all, is the dependence of the Hebrew production in such a case established. Perhaps, to sum up the issue involved, it may be sufficient to give a pertinent statement by *Noetscher* (p. 2): "Very few traces point to poetic productions in Canaan prior to the time of Israel." With so very little material available, it will be difficult to establish dependence of the one on the other.

SPECIAL PROBLEMS

a) SAINTS AND SINNERS IN THE PSALMS

This is a problem that has long engaged the attention of Bible students, a problem the solution of which seems still to be far off. Especially in the first half of the book certain evildoers appear who are the opponents of the writer. They are called by various names, the "wicked" being apparently the most common designation. They are also called "evil" or "evil men." They are also described as the "enemies" of the writer. In this opposition group one individual usually seems to stand out as the leader. The psalms attributed to David have this feature rather commonly. What astonishes the thoughtful reader is the fact that the historical books of the Bible do not give us the same picture of the days of David. At times, indeed, certain groups were in opposition to David. But in the cases referred to the writer speaks as though this had been one of the most common experiences of his life. It is difficult even to determine whether these persons are to be thought of as being within the nation Israel, or whether they are foreigners and outsiders.

The most original attempt to solve the problem is that offered by *Mowinckel,* who took the noun '*awon,* meaning "transgression or guilt" and appearing in expressions like "doing transgression" (the noun derived from it being "evildoers") and imputed a rather sinister meaning to it, namely, that it referred to sorcery, which he claims was very commonly practiced. So the "wicked" became "sorcerers." Very few have ventured to follow this unduly bold interpretation, and the problem before us remains as difficult as ever. We shall simply have to arrive at the conclusion that in his day David had many more open and private enemies than we had hitherto supposed. They caused him much grief, and he on his part laid the matter before the Lord in prayer, for it was more than he could cope with.

Over against the evildoers are placed the saints, who are also mentioned quite commonly in the psalms, though not always by this title. They appear particularly also as the "righteous." With them the psalmist is closely associated; he loves their company; they are of great comfort to him in his affliction. They, too, constituted a group though sometimes only an individual among them is referred to. We know too little about either group.

b) IMPRECATORY PSALMS

Perhaps even more difficult is the matter of the imprecatory psalms, a term used to designate those psalms in which the writer prays that God may afflict the evildoer and punish him according to his deserts. Some interpreters put this issue into the category of curses and magic and go on the assumption that the imprecations involved are nothing else than curses that are pronounced against enemies. But this solution is as much beside the point here as in the question of determining who the "evildoers" are. The issue will be dealt with separately in practically every psalm where it occurs. Therefore we here confine ourselves to a summary treatment.

Sometimes there are brief statements of this sort. Again there are lengthier portions in certain psalms. The following psalms have the longest portions: 35, 69, 109. Of course, the whole question of retribution is involved. In this area it dare not be overlooked that there are some clear-cut words on the subject dating back to the days of Moses. In Deut. 32:35 Moses presents the Lord as saying: "Vengeance is Mine." In words dating back to the time of Solomon a similar sentiment finds expression when a man is exhorted to show kindness to his enemies: "If your enemy is hungry, give him bread to eat; and if he is thirsty, give him water to drink; for you will heap coals of fire on his head, and the Lord will reward you," Prov. 25:21f. So in this field the express doctrine of the Old Testament is exactly the same as that of the New (cf., Rom. 12:19, 20). Besides, the man David, to whom many of these sharp utterances are attributed, in the course of his lifetime showed an exemplary spirit of tolerance and forgiveness, especially over against Saul, the very man who persistently wronged him and sought his life. See I Sam. 24 and 26 in particular. Also note the charitable tone of the elegy written upon the death of Saul (II Sam. 1:17-27).

It must also be noted that the writer of the psalms that embody the imprecations appears in all the other utterances of the psalm involved as a man who was eminent for true piety and fear of the Lord. That alone should induce us to use all possible charity in judging such a case. Then it should be borne in mind that in each case it is apparent that

Introduction

more than personal enmity on the part of the opponent is involved: the man in question is seen to be an avowed enemy of God's people and God's cause. Besides, we are all ready to admit that, when difficult problems assail us, prayer is an effective counteragent to employ. By this very prayer the psalmist takes the matter out of his own hands and consigns it to God.

Not every instance involved will bear all the distinguishing features that we shall enumerate, but it should be noted in addition that in some instances the psalm writer is concerned about the ultimate conversion of the evildoers (Ps. 2:10-12). Other objectives that control the writer's thinking are indicated. He should not be judged apart from what he himself claims is his purpose. He may have in mind the vindication of God's cause (see Ps. 79:10). He may be concerned about not having the wicked despise God (see Ps. 10:12f.). He may be concerned about having the righteous take courage at what they see (see Ps. 35:26f.). He may have a concern that the wicked be taught to fear God (see Ps. 64:7-9). If these objectives be sincerely voiced they should be taken at their face value. (Much of this material was taken from *Hengstenberg*).

Noetscher has a fresh approach to the problem, which incorporates some of the views expressed above but deserves special note. This approach appears in connection with his comments on Ps. 79. He admits that these "curses" leave something to be desired from the Christian point of view and indicates that the evil that is wished upon the enemy is something that the enemy has fully deserved both on the score of just retaliation as well as on the score of prevailing rules of warfare. The Oriental, he remarks, when emotionally aroused, employs commonly accepted forms of picturesque speech and dearly loves to portray things in brilliant colors, especially as he gives vent to what pains him or to that which he deeply desires. His own existence and the welfare of the nation being at stake, it appears to him that the only way to get relief is to have the enemy completely humbled or even utterly destroyed. "But more particularly," says Noetscher, "the faith in Yahweh is endangered if the ungodly, Yahweh-defying opponent wins out." In the light of the then-prevailing views on retaliation, which definitely had their limitations, disaster was regarded as proof of the impotence of their God. In this terrible dilemma "the godly believer in Yahweh resorts to impassioned wishes as the way out. It is not mere thirst for revenge that dictates these utterances; it is a sort of spiritual emergency where a man is fighting for his honor and his very existence." Lastly Noetscher indicates the rather noteworthy fact that the psalmists in no wise minimized or overlooked their own guilt but confessed it and cast themselves on the mercy of God.

Not without bearing on the case is an observation that *Gunkel* has made (*Einleitung,* p. 226): "It is rather striking that the *wishes* [*Wuensche*] against the enemy outnumber the *prayers* against him about two to one."

Therefore we arrive at the conclusion that the sharp pronouncements against the writers of imprecatory passages that are encountered are quite out of place ("spirit of vengeance," "incandescent hate," and many others). It is rather surprising that the New Testament has striking points of similarity in the conduct of exemplary individuals, whose course of conduct has always been regarded as being model. What Paul says about Alexander the coppersmith in II Tim. 4:14 comes under this head (an alternate reading makes this optative rather than future). Paul before Annas (Acts 23:2) speaks rather sharply in the vein of the psalmists. What Peter speaks against Simon Magus (Acts 8:20) is no benediction.

Certainly, imprecations should be resorted to with the utmost of discretion in our days. *Sampey's* remarks (ISBE, 2494) have much of wisdom in them: 'We ought to use the imprecatory psalms in the light of our Lord's teaching. We cannot pronounce curses on our personal enemies. This heavy artillery may be turned upon the saloon, the brothel, and the gambling hell, though we must not forget to pray for the conversion of the persons who are engaged in these lines of business."

c) MESSIANIC PSALMS

It is true that altogether too much was read into the psalms under this head in times past. When St. Augustine in his *Expositions on the Psalms* regarded practically all psalms as Messianic he was, indeed, carrying a New Testament approach beyond the limits that the facts warrant. The same tendency is found even down through the age of the Reformation. But the reaction that has set in in our day has veered over to the other extreme. Several quotations may make clear what we have in mind. As *Gunkel* sums up the situation (*Einleitung,* p. 330) he surely goes beyond what we can accept when he claims: "At the same time it becomes apparent that the eschatology of the psalms offers no Messianic features of a sort such as bygone generations have erroneously sought to find." If he had meant this only in the sense that the psalms which are clearly eschatological often or commonly describe the Messianic age without making specific mention of the Messiah Himself, we could have accepted the statement. But a further statement of his (p. 361) eliminates this possibility: "Furthermore, the hope for a Messiah is unknown. The psalms know nothing

Introduction

of a human deliverer-king [*Heilskoenig*]. Their ultimate expectation knows only of acts of Yahweh, only of a future kingdom of the God of Israel." *McCullough* (*Interpreter's Bible,* p. 13) has summed up the more commonly accepted opinion of our day when he says: "The older view that the psalmists refer to an anointed personage [the Messiah] who would have a share in bringing in Israel's future blessedness, has had to be abandoned, for it is now generally recognised that the anointed one of the psalms (2:2; 18:50; 20:6; etc.) is a reigning Hebrew king. This salvation of Israel may be connected with the destruction of the wicked . . ." Though we are ready to grant that the reference to the Lord's "anointed" is, indeed, to the reigning king of Israel, that matter is not disposed of by this mere claim. For the New Testament sees something Messianic, e.g., in Ps. 8, 16, 22, 31:5; 69: 21; 110. This factor cannot be lightly disposed of by assuming that the New Testament writers merely used suitable expressions that they happened to find in the psalms as fitting expressions of the truth they were attempting to put into words. They themselves attribute the prophetic element to the writers of the old covenant.

What, then, becomes of some of these psalms in the light of such modern interpretation? Ps. 45 becomes a wedding hymn; Ps. 72 is a psalm composed on the occasion of the accession of a king. But the language is then seen to be all too colorful. Kings are spoken of in terms that are all too extravagant. Yes, and this is condoned as being patterned after the prevailing court style of court poets of that time as Babylonian and Egyptian models indicate. However, such an interpretation poses far more problems than it solves, especially in the area of the inspiration of the Scriptures.

We cannot accept this approach, especially since such definite indications of the great hope placed into the Davidic line by the Lord were well known in Israel and would, no doubt, have found definite reference made to them in the psalms. Ps. 110 (cf., 132) would have to be put into this category. Furthermore, the thought of a Suffering Servant could easily have arisen and found expression in the days of David, when he, God's faithful servant, was made to suffer so much, in spite of his innocence, under Saul. Ps. 22 gives expression to this aspect of Messianic truth. For the features of this psalm far transcend the actual experiences of David.

It is true that some psalms are prophetic only by way of type (8 and 118). It is true that some words are used in the New Testament by way of accommodation (Ps. 31:5). But the strictly prophetic element we believe finds expression in Ps. 22, 45, 72, 110.

All of this still leaves us with the net result that the Messianic element is by far not as common in the Psalter as we might have supposed. It is also true that the royal psalms (like 93–99) do have a feature of the eschatological in them and do describe the ultimate kingdom of Yahweh. Surely they posed a problem for their day. For how could an Old Testament reader recognize at this early date that what Yahweh did would be done by Him who was co-equal with Him—the Lord's Christ? But the same feature appears very frequently in the words of many of the prophets who refer to the Messianic age without specifically bringing the Messiah into the picture. We venture to say that to some extent the Messianic age so obviously involved the Messiah that this fact often went without saying in the prophetic pronouncements.

And lastly, is it not obvious that so deep and involved a subject would before the breaking of the day of the Messiah be fraught with innumerable problems?

THE DOCTRINES OF THE PSALMS

UNDER THIS HEAD we should like to discuss certain doctrines of the psalms that have in one way or another become a problem, either already from the earliest times or else because of more recent theological developments.

a) OTHER GODS

There is, first of all, the question, Do the psalms concede the *existence of other gods?* This problem is raised by the form of statement used in the psalms, e. g., 77:13, "What god is great like our God?" or 86:8: "There is none like Thee among the gods, O Lord." On the face of it the statements could be interpreted either way. They could mean: There is none like the Lord among those commonly designated as gods; or they could actually give expression to the view that the other gods had existence but were far inferior to the Lord in power and in influence. In the popular belief of Israel the latter view would quite likely sometimes have been held. But our concern is with the revealed religion as it was held by true prophets and the body of the faithful in Israel. That the view prevailed that "gods" meant the entities that the heathen thought had real existence whereas in reality they did not exist appears most clearly from a passage like Ps. 96:4b, 5. Where the familiar form of statement appears first: "He [the Lord] is to be feared above all gods," the next line states with utmost clearness what the actual facts of the case are: "For all the gods of the peoples are idols," a term being used that involves the root "worthless."

Introduction

b) SACRIFICIAL WORSHIP

Do the psalmists accept and approve of it? Or are they enemies of sacrificial worship? An array of passages can be rallied in support of either side of the question. The fact that sacrifices may on occasion be very proper and pleasing to God appears from statements like 4:5; 20:3; 50:8; 51:19. Again there are words that seem to support the contrary opinion such as, 40:6; 50:13; 51:16f; 69:30f. This is obviously one of those cases where there are two sides to a matter. What makes the difference is the spirit and attitude of the man that brings sacrifice. If the proper attitude of the heart is in evidence—true humility and reverence for God, true devotion, utter sincerity—and where the sacrifice then expresses what the heart truly feels, there sacrifices may be brought by a man, and they will be entirely acceptable to the Lord. They are visible tokens of deeper things. But where the sacrifice is given in a perfunctory spirit, where it is offered in an attempt to pacify God by externalistic acts that are devoid of the spirit of true penitence and devotion, there sacrifice may become an abomination to the Lord and be classified as "the sacrifice of fools," Eccles. 5:1. The prophets and the psalm writers do not condemn sacrifices outright. They do not attribute true validity to all sacrifices that are offered. They know that in this field right and wrong attitudes have been in evidence since the days of Cain and Abel. Perhaps no statement went more nearly to the root of the matter than the declaration of David: "The sacrifice acceptable to God is a broken spirit, a broken and a contrite heart, O God, Thou wilt not despise," 51:17.

c) YAHWEH AS THE CREATOR OF NATURE

Over against current opinions abroad in our day attention should at least be drawn to a distinctive position that the Israelite took over against Yahweh as far as the forces operative in nature are concerned. Whereas men of our day take a somewhat mechanistic view of nature and regard it as the play of forces that are at work of themselves according to what we are pleased to call the laws of nature, producing and regulating everything of and by themselves and often leaving God entirely out of the picture, the writers of Sacred Scripture with one accord regard the Lord as operative in all things great and small that transpire in the broad realm of what we call nature. Perhaps nowhere does this thought find clearer expression than in Ps. 65:9f. where even the watering of the earth, the settling of the ridges and their softening with rain are attributed to direct action of God. In this respect the view that the psalms hold of nature is all of one piece. The marvel of God's work is that it covers even areas such as these and is vast and comprehensive beyond our boldest thoughts. The psalms abound in this approach to the realm of nature.

d) YAHWEH THE GOD OF HISTORY

In this broad field with its many ramifications we should like to stress one aspect of the case only, and that is the fact, commonly found in the Psalter, that what happens in history is attributed to the doing of Yahweh, particularly the constructive achievements that are of historical importance. It is well known from the historical books that Israel dispossessed the Canaanites and took their land. There is an obvious point of truth in that statement. But the deeper approach says that the Lord with His "own hand" did drive out the nations and plant His people; it was not "their own sword" that proved effective; it was His right hand and arm that did it (Ps. 44:1–3). There is a greater force at work in history than mighty armies and armaments. The same approach is to be seen in 111:6 on the same issue, for it was the Lord who was at that time "giving them the heritage of the heathen." As one of the deeper truths of history a fact like this should not be overlooked. It belongs to the things that are prominent in the Psalter. Many more passages could be cited.

e) UNIVERSALISM

Is there a sound and wholesome universalistic outlook in the psalms or are the people of God so preoccupied with themselves that their thoughts never turn in the direction of what God may mean for the nations or what His plans and purposes for them are? Quite obviously the truth that Israel stands in a covenant relation with God receives due attention and is properly appreciated. We need cite no proof for this fact. But for the true Israelite this singular preferment and unique blessing that Israel enjoys do not make for selfishness and indifference toward the lot and destiny of the other nations on the face of the earth. Of the abundance of material that might be cited under this head we would draw attention to a few typical utterances. In Ps. 66 the nation is exhorted to sing the praises of the God who delivered His people from the bondage of Egypt, doing mighty works in the process (vv. 5–7). But the opening word of the psalm already bids the whole earth take part in this glorification of the God. Again in v. 8 the "peoples" are admonished to give praise for what God has done in behalf of His people. There is implied the thought that what God did do for the good of Israel will somehow work out for the good of the other nations on the face of the earth. Therefore by way of anticipation they are to begin to praise even before it becomes apparent how they, too, will profit by

Introduction

what was done. A similar note is struck in Ps. 67, except that the approach is the reverse: God is asked to bless Israel in order that His "way may be known upon earth, [His] saving power among all nations." Ps. 100 may also be noted in this connection.

f) THE DOCTRINE OF SIN

Nowhere does a fully developed doctrine of sin appear in the psalms as must be obvious to all who read them. But there are indications of a deep sense of sin as appearing at certain times and under certain circumstances. What is at issue under this head is best indicated by reference to the so-called "penitential psalms." These usually include the following: 6, 32, 51, 106, 130, 143. In not every instance in these psalms is there an express confession of sin. A deep sense of being under the wrath of God, however, appears to be common to all. There is also the conviction that only God, who has been sinned against, can deliver man from the serious situation into which he has plunged himself. Each of these psalms has something distinctive about it as the exposition shall attempt to show. Unique about the group of psalms as a whole is the manner in which sin is seen to bring a man under the wrath of God. That wrath is to the psalmist a terrible reality. Attention is drawn to this matter chiefly because from time to time the reality of sin and its damning results are treated all too lightly—a mistake that Biblical revelation, also in the psalter, is not guilty of.

g) REWARDS AND PUNISHMENTS

On this subject there is quite a bit of confused thinking at the present time. It all seems to be the indirect outgrowth of the fact that interpreters have begun to understand a bit more clearly the aim of the book of Job. The book of Job is among other things also a protest against a narrow doctrine of retribution as it sometimes appears in its applied form. The view protested against is to contend that the good that is done by a man invariably leads to obvious rewards and tokens of divine good pleasure; on the other hand, the sin that is done brings down upon the head of the sinner divine retribution. The particularly vicious result is the conclusion that may in everyday living be drawn from this view. A man may conclude that, because one prospers, he must have done what is right; again, because of what he suffers he must be adjudged as having done wickedly, no matter how righteous his life may appear. This last conclusion can be particularly wrong. Now comes the erroneous conclusion drawn from all that precedes; even the principle formerly held by many that God rewards them that do His will and punishes all who fail to do it must be regarded as wrong if not even vicious.

There is abundant evidence that, for all that, God does still to a very large degree deal thus with His children: as a general rule He rewards the good that is done and punishes the evil. Our mistake is to make this general observation *absolute*. But we are not the ones to determine how God in individual instances applies the principle as such.

Therefore two truths must be held fast: a) the general validity of the rule as such; b) the application of the principle to specific instances, which is, however, God's prerogative alone and will be exercised by Him at times in ways that we are not able fully to understand. Ps. 16:9–11 is a beautiful statement of the application of this principle as we frequently see it applied in the course of the lives of godly men. Ps. 17 indicates that a man may rightly anticipate that this rule will be followed by God, especially v. 15. Ps. 39:6f. shows that a man may rightly hope that God will deal graciously with him who has put his trust in Him. The thought of rewards that have been earned and deserved is, however, not to be found in a passage like this. Ps. 49 considers one angle of the case and develops it at length. It shows that the seeming prosperity of the wicked is not to be thought of as final, for the decision lies in God's hand, and it is well known according to what rule he works. Ps. 73 deals quite thoroughly with an aspect of the case that particularly disturbed the psalmist at one time in his life—"the prosperity of the wicked" (v. 3). Vv. 23–28 are a glowing description of the ultimate rewards that a righteous man may confidently anticipate. Ps. 112 is a statement of the case that is wholly on the positive side of the ledger. It is true that a self-righteous man may look to the reward rather than to the Lord, and so the whole principle involved may be degraded. But an important truth is expressed by this psalm also, one which even Jesus Himself underscored in various ways in the course of His teaching (see Matt. 19:29).

THE AFTERLIFE

WHAT THE PSALMS have to offer on this score may prove both difficult and disappointing to the average reader as he begins to reflect on the matter. The difficulty is that from one point of view the passages involved seem to indicate that there is no hope for the time after death: there is no future life. That will naturally prove disappointing because we usually approach the Psalter with the expectation that it is rich with comfort for every situation, including the comfort of life after death. Incidentally, the material involved is quite meager. But passages like 6:5 will disturb men—"In death there is no remembrance of Thee, in Sheol who can give Thee praise?" That seems to annul the hope of life after death. Of the same sort are passages like 88:10; 30:9; 115:17.

Several thoughts should be noted in coming to grips with this issue. First of all, it must be admitted that the revelation concerning the hereafter did not burn half as brightly in the Old Testament as it does in the New. Therefore it could well happen that, when doubt and distress dragged a man's hope down, he gave utterance to thoughts which do not always express the normal hope of Israel. If, then, that hope is not as clear as is ours, statements will be made that are unsatisfactory. Apparently in the passage quoted above the writer was thinking only in terms of that dead body that was laid into the grave before his eyes. When we are such we can no longer remember God. Such a dead person cannot sing God's praises from the grave. This is not so much a denial of the hope of everlasting life as a failure to see things that cannot be seen any too well even by the most enlightened faith of that day. In other words, grief sometimes momentarily deprived men of the little light that they had on this subject. But the utterance of sad bereavement is not always the utterance of normal faith.

But fortunately there are in the psalms better words than these. Sometimes men grappled with their doubt and grief and held fast to the hand of the Lord and came through their difficulty with a pronouncement of faith which, for that age, is downright amazing. One of these instances is recorded in Ps. 16:9–11. Keeping close to the Lord and realizing that God will not forsake him if he does not forsake God, the writer carries the logic of faith through to a brilliant conclusion, every part of which is valid. He anticipates that God cannot abandon his body (v. 9). He further concludes that it is contrary to the nature of God simply to give His child over to Sheol (v. 16). There is a "path of life" which must be the very antithesis of the path of death; there is an abiding in the presence of God which involves "fullness of joy" and "pleasures for evermore."

This is the Old Testament faith in the hereafter at its best. Similar are the triumphant conclusions of 73:23–26. Whether all of Israel in the Old Testament always lived on this high level of hope is quite another question. But, for that matter, does the New Testament Christian always hold the faith in its fullest implications?

THE ENDURING VALUE OF THE BOOK OF PSALMS

WHO CAN sufficiently extol the merits and the value of the Psalter? Many eloquent words have been written on the subject. Let us try to summarize some of the good things that have been said.

Luther, in a manner typical of him, asserted that these hymns enable us to look directly into the heart of God's saints. Every man who has sought to expound the psalms agrees with this testimony.

One may well waver between the use of two descriptive terms: in the psalms we certainly have a hymnal, but we just as certainly have a prayer book. Which deserved the preference at the time of composition and which in the course of later usage of the book has not yet been fully determined. But it is certain that we have here a large collection of formulated prayers, almost every one of which is calculated to be used as such (with the obvious exception of psalms like Ps. 1). This might give pause to those who advocate the exclusive use of free prayers as alone being acceptable in the sight of God.

There does not seem to be any situation in life for which the Psalter does not provide light and guidance. Thus we are struck by the fact, oft noted in other connections, that there is really nothing that is new to life under the sun. We have yet to hear of men who have turned for guidance to the Psalter and have not found it. This may be partly due to the fact that the tone of this book is always stimulating. Or it may be because the insights and the comforts of the psalms are always so much to the point. They are not the fruit of abstract meditation. They did not grow out of the study of the scholar. They were born out of real-life situations. They are often wet with the tears and the blood of the writer.

Then they have a peculiarly enduring quality. Frequent use does not wear them thin. The more familiar they become, the more they are loved. That is, of course, the mark of all true literature, but doubly the mark of the psalms.

This again may be due to the fact that the psalms continually carry the reader into the immediate presence of God. They do not refer to Him in the abstract. God is not a God of the distance to the psalmist. All the psalms were prayed on the steps of the throne of mercy. The light that emanates from that presence somehow gives light to them that sit in darkness and in the shadow of death.

Besides, the psalms have the happy faculty of stimulating our own private prayers and of fructifying them to an unusual degree.

Oftentimes the psalms become the superlative utterance of our deepest needs. This may sometimes work in such a fashion that psalms that have long lain dormant suddenly break into life and become meaningful for us. At such times they strike us almost as if they had been providentially created for our own individual use by the wise providence of God.

Bibliography

1. COMMENTARIES

Augustine, *Expositions on the Book of Psalms,* Nicene and Post-Nicene Fathers, edited by Philip Schaff, The Christian Literature Company, New York, 1888.
Butterwieser, Moses, *The Psalms,* The University of Chicago Press, Chicago, 1938.
Briggs, Charles Augustus and Emilie Grace, *The Book of Psalms,* The International Critical Commentary, Charles Scribner's Sons, New York, 1909.
Calvin, John, *In Librum Psalmorum Commentarius* (Latin), Gustav Eichler, Berlin, 1836.
Creager (Harold L.) and Alleman (Herbert C.) *The Psalms,* Old Testament Commentary, The Muhlenberg Press, Philadelphia, 1948.
Delitzsch, Franz, *A Commentary on the Book of Psalms* (3 vols.), translated from the 1883 edition by David Eaton and James Duguid, Funk and Wagnalls, New York, (no date).
Hengstenberg, E. W., *Kommentar ueber die Psalmen* (4 vols.) 2. edition, Ludwig Oehmigke, Berlin, 1849.
Kessler, Hans, *Die Psalmen,* Strack und Zoeckler Kommentar, C. H. Beck, Munich, 1899.
Kirkpatrick, A. F., *The Book of Psalms,* Cambridge Bible for Schools and Colleges, University Press, Cambridge, 1906.
Kittel, Rudolf, *Die Psalmen,* Sellins Kommentar zum Alten Testament, Deichert, Leipzig, 1914.
Koenig, Eduard, *Die Psalmen,* Bertelsman, Guetersloh, 1927.
Leslie, Elmer A., *The Psalms,* Abingdon-Cokesbury Press, New York, 1949.
Leslie, Elmer A., Psalms I–LXXII, Shelton, W. A., Psalms LXXII–CL, *The Abingdon Bible Commentary,* Abingdon-Cokesbury Press, New York, 1929.
Luther, Martin, *Auslegungen ueber die Psalmen,* Walch, reprinted by Concordia Publishing House, St. Louis, Vol. IV, 1895.
Maclaren, Alexander, *The Psalms,* in the *Expositors' Bible,* Hodder and Stoughton, New York, (no date). An admirable commentary; keeping an open mind on critical issues, but not too readily swayed by new and novel opinions. It penetrates deeply into the spirit of the Psalms.
McCullough, W. Stewart, *The Book of Psalms,* Interpreter's Bible, Vol. IV, Abingdon Press, New York, 1955.

Moll, Carl Bernhard, *Der Psalter,* Velhagen and Klassing, Lange's homiletisches Bibelwerk, Bielefeld and Leipzig, 1869.
Oesterley, E.O.E., *The Psalms, S.P.C.K.,* London, 1953.
Schmidt, Hans, *Die Psalmen,* Eissfeldt's Handbuch zum Alten Testament, Mohr, Tuebingen, 1934.
Noetscher, Friedrich, *Die Psalmen,* Echter Bibel, Echter, Wuerzburg, 1953.
Vilmar, A.F.C., *Der Psalter,* Collegium Biblicum, Bertelsman, Guetersloh, 1882.
Weiser, Artur, *Die Psalmen,* Goettinger Bibelwerk, Vandenhoeck and Rupprecht, Goettingen, 1950.

2. OTHER HELPS

Gunkel, Herman, *Einleitung in die Psalmen* (completed by Begrich) Goettingen, 1933.
Mowinckel, Sigmund, *Psalmenstudien,* Kristiania, 1921.
Walker, Rollin H., *The Modern Message of the Psalms,* New York, 1938.

3. ABBREVIATIONS

ARV—American Standard Version, 1901.
BDB—*Hebrew and English Lexicon* of the Old Testament, by Francis Brown, S. R. Driver, and C. A. Briggs, Boston and New York, 1907.
Buhl—*Hebraeisches Woerterbuch,* Gesenius, Edited by Frants Buhl. Leipzig, 1905.
GK—Gesenius Kautzsch, *Hebr. Grammatik,* 27th Edition, Leipzig, 1902.
JBL—Journal of Biblical Literature.
K (or KB)—*Lexicon in Veteris Testamenti Libros,* 1951, by Ludwig Koehler and Walter Baumgartner.
KJ—King James Version.
KS—*Lehrgebaeude der hebraeischen Sprache,* II Syntax, Eduard Koenig, 1897.
KW—*Hebraeisches und aramaeisches Woerterbuch zum Alten Testament,* Eduard Koenig, Leipzig, 1922.
RSV—Revised Standard Version, 1952.
ZATW—*Zeitschrift fuer Alttestamentliche Wissenschaft.*

4. NOTE FOR THE READER

The verses of the Psalms are always numbered according to the numbering of the English and the American Versions.

BOOK ONE

Psalm 1

THE TRULY HAPPY MAN

THE Book of Psalms opens with two psalms without headings. Judging from their general character, it would appear that they were prefixed to the book with the specific purpose of emphasizing certain fundamentals that are of importance in approaching this book. It is plain to those who read the Old Testament Scriptures that law and prophecy are fundamental to the spiritual life of Israel. One is the basis, the other is the essential superstructure. One lays the foundation, the other builds on what is thus laid.

The first two psalms touch respectively on these two points, emphasizing what the essential attitude on both issues ought to be. Psalm 1 can rightly be said to exemplify the proper attitude toward the law of the Lord. Psalm 2, as it were, gives the essence of prophecy and indicates what place it plays in the life of the true Israel. He who has grasped these two issues aright is well on the way that leads to a right reading of the Psalter.

It is true that the authorship of the second psalm can be determined by a New Testament reference—Acts 4:25. This passage scarcely refers to the Book of Psalms by an inaccurate metonomy which substitutes David for the book of which he wrote the major part, inasmuch as David is specifically referred to as "our father." But to base any further conclusions on this fact in trying to determine the authorship of the first psalm is quite unwarranted. Just as problematical is the claim that this psalm must be dated somewhere in the Greek period. This claim is based on the unprovable contention that the whole collection of psalms was first completed in the Greek era, and that this first psalm was prefixed after the rest of the collection had been finished. Besides, as *Taylor* reminds us: "It is not necessary to suppose that the psalm was written to supply an introduction to the Psalter."

With at least as much propriety it may be contended that the psalm could have been written in the days of Solomon. Had that wise king made a collection of psalms composed by his godly father he might well have written a preface such as the first psalm, embodying in it the godly instruction received from his father. The figures employed would be like those employed by Solomon in Proverbs; the didactic character of the psalm is like the tone of Proverbs; and Solomon certainly had the literary qualifications for such a work. But all such claims rest on too little evidence. With a far greater show of reason it may be contended that our psalm must have been written before Jer. 17:8 or Ezek. 47:12. For these two verses employ the figure of the tree planted by the side of streams of water in a manner so closely akin to that of this psalm that the conclusion is almost inevitable that one is quoting the other. Usually, however, the quotation becomes more detailed by further usage, rather than being abbreviated in the process. So we might with some show of reason contend for the priority of the psalm. But even this conclusion is not binding. An interesting Egyptian parallel is found in *Pritchard, Ancient Near Eastern Texts*, p. 422.

We need not be afraid of this psalm as though it opened the venerable Book of Psalms with a distorted statement of the nature of true happiness, as not a few interperters contend (*Briggs, Kittel, Buttenwieser et al.*). Since the initial statement has to do with a strong aversion to sin in all its forms and counsels that the individual consciously shun the companionship of all ungodly persons, that counsel may, indeed, be carried out in a spirit of self-righteousness and lovelessness; but certainly Psalm one never taught anyone such an attitude.

Again the charge has been raised that the study of the law, as here advocated, savors of a narrow-minded bookishness, which esteems the life of the student of the law as the only true life and despises all other occupations as inferior and the common people, who know not the law, as accursed (cf., John 7:49). Such a charge, however, first distorts what is a sober and sound counsel and then brands the distortion as unwholesome. The Jews did, indeed, at a later time take such unreasonable attitudes and advocate such extreme positions. But this is not the position of this harmless and beautiful psalm.

So much is obviously true: this psalm does not attempt to say *everything* that can be said on the subject of the truly happy life. It does not give an exhaustive treatment of the case. Its presentation may rather be regarded as suggestive; and, if the author only be given the benefit of the doubt, no one would venture to treat this little gem of a psalm critically. *Oesterley* covers the case when he remarks that such omissions are "in what is in the nature of a preface, a matter of common sense."

Again the truth pointed out by the psalm is not to be pressed with such extreme emphasis as though some invariable criterion of godliness had been presented to enable men to classify all human beings

Psalm 1

conveniently as to whether they stood right in the sight of God or not, and this criterion—mere outward prosperity or success. For in the first place, it is a misinterpretation of the psalm to assume that it taught such a purely external view of religion and godliness. Prosperity certainly involves more than visible success. But on the other hand, as *Hengstenberg* aptly points out, when a man, in spite of his faithful adherence to the Word of the Lord, discovers that prosperity still seems to be far from him, let the observation that he makes call him to repentance. For there are none who are so wholly devoted to the Word and the will of the Lord as to be able to claim that a full measure of prosperity is due to them as their reward. Our best endeavors in this respect are marked by manifest imperfections; and so we ourselves, by our very shortcomings, prevent the full measure of divine favor from becoming ours. *Weiser* says very aptly: "It means a strong, optimistic faith when one believes that a godly man cannot fail to meet with success in all that he undertakes . . . but it is a dangerous thing when a calculating doctrine of retribution grows out of this approach."

Though we rightly regard the Psalter as a prayer book we need not be alarmed by the observation that this psalm is not specifically a prayer. Though it lacks the formal characteristic of direct address to God it may yet be regarded as a prayer in the broader sense in that it presents reflections made, as it were, in the very presence of God. Most readers of this psalm would not notice that it is not strictly a prayer, unless this fact were specially drawn to their attention. It must, therefore, be freely conceded that, from one point of view, this is a didactic poem in the finest spirit of the Book of Proverbs.

The theme of the psalm may be stated as above, The Truly Happy Man.

The attitude of the author is one of true enthusiasm for his subject. He feels keenly about the qualities that he here describes and about the fortunate position and the goodly prospects of a godly man.

1. *O how happy is the person who has not shaped his conduct after the principles of the ungodly,*
   Nor taken his stand in the way of sinners,
   Nor taken his seat in the assembly of scoffers!
2. *But it is in the law of the Lord that he takes his delight;*
   And on His law he keeps pondering day and night.
3. *And he will be like a tree planted by the side of streams of water,*
   That yields its fruit in its season;
   Its leaves also do not wither;
   And whatsoever he undertakes, succeeds.

4. Such is not the case with the ungodly,
   But they are like the chaff which the wind scatters.
5. On this account the ungodly shall not be able to maintain themselves when the judgment comes,
   Nor sinners, in the congregation of the righteous.
6. For the Lord knows the way of the righteous;
   But the way of the ungodly is headed toward destruction.

(Note: For the benefit of the student using only the English text we number the verses according to the English version.)

1. The very happy state of the man whose life has the right roots is about to be described. The Hebrew expresses the superlative by a plural of intensity: "happiness of the man." This gives the statement the force of an exclamation, which would be very nearly approximated by our: "O how very happy is the man!" For the plural (*'ashrey*) literally means the full measure of the happy circumstances. Very obviously the word "man" that follows lays no emphasis whatever on the gender of the word as some mistakenly claim. To remove all possibility of misunderstanding, we have ventured to render the word "person."

It need not strike us as strange that this happiness is first pictured in terms of negatives—what such a man will not do. For, as has been rightly observed, wrong conduct in most manifold forms surrounds us on every hand, and we are continually under necessity of taking a position over against it. In other words, sins abound and must be shunned. For the same reason the Ten Commandments are primarily negatives. This, however, in no sense lessens their value.

Three types of sinners, three forms of expression of sin, and three places of such expression are now specified. It is true, these three clauses are presented in an ascending climax. But no particular importance is to be attached to this climax. It does briefly indicate that, when a man once begins to live in the company of men who are separated from God, both will find themselves becoming involved ever more deeply. But far heavier emphasis is laid on the fact that in his aversion to sin a godly man shuns every form of it at all times and in all places. Obviously, strong attachment to the law begets a correspondingly strong aversion toward evil. He who cannot sturdily hate the bad will not have much love for the good.

The word that we have translated "shaped his conduct" is really the Hebrew word for "walked." But since *'atsath* follows, literally "counsel" as *KJ* has it, but actually meaning the "plan" or the "principles" according to which men live, we had to translate the Hebrew verb accordingly. The wicked go under the name of *resha'im,* a word coming from a root which means those who are "loose" and so "abnormal" or "wicked." This is a telling description of wickedness: getting loose from God and falling into evil.

"The way of sinners" obviously means their manner of living. The "sinners" themselves are *chatta'im,* men who have "missed the mark" which they should have reached, which mark is outlined in the law of their God. When a man "takes his stand" in such a "way" he is committed to the nefarious way of life that marks all who are walking in it.

The third class of manifest sinners alluded to are "the scoffers," the men who have rejected whatever the Word of God had to offer and who now seek to fortify themselves in their own thinking by openly deriding what they rejected—a self-defense mechanism. Besides, since they seek the moral support of those who are of one mind with them they associate with what may be classified as "the assembly of the scoffers." Birds of a feather flock together. Mockery and ridicule of that which is holy have often drawn men together in this unholy cause. Indeed, the original calls it "the seat" (*moshabh*) of these mockers, but obviously this term signifies their assembly rather than a chair. Of the three classes referred to, this last has plainly advanced farthest away from God. Also, in the case of this last class the necessity of parting company with this group requires no further demonstration.

2. The positive statement of the case now presents the worth-while content of the life and character of the man who is being described. The strong adversative (*ki-'im*) sets this aspect of the case into bolder relief. The inversion of terms in the Hebrew word order places the thought of the law into the emphatic position. We have sought to retain this emphasis in our translation by the arrangement: "But it is in the law of the Lord that he takes delight." *Torah* ("law") must, however, be carefully analyzed as to its meaning. Our familiar understanding of this word misleads us. We think first of the Ten Commandments. But the word obviously refers to at least the whole Pentateuch, in which both words of law as well as words of gospel content abound. So "law" is closely synonymous with the "Word of God." For this usage see: Josh. 1:7; II Kings 17:13; 21:8; Ps. 78:5; etc.

In this law the man that is being described "takes his delight." It is to him not a troublesome and unwelcome fetter; it is not a set of hard restraints. It is a joy for him to learn and to do the demands of the law. For with emphasis the second half of the verse repeats that it is upon this same law that "he keeps pondering day and night." Obviously not an unwholesome absorption with the law is under consideration but a healthy interest in it and a knowledge of its real content, which continually influence and affect the man so devoted to this holy treasure. The verb "ponder" (*yehgeh*) does, indeed, mean "moan, hum, utter, speak, muse," but all meanings involve the same process. For the man is pictured as reading over texts of this law to himself. This half-aloud reading and rereading are really the process of musing or meditating as it may be practiced in the Orient. But to make such meditation an unhealthy absorption lays unintended meaning into the words. Or to have it signify pure meditation that has no practical results is equally unnatural and an obvious distortion of the intended meaning.

Thus far the true root of the godly man's life has been viewed. Now in vv. 3 and 4 the fruits of such a life are vividly shown.

3. We have departed from the familiar "and he shall be" of this verse and rendered "and he will be." For nothing in the original indicates that a promise is intended as to future success. The verb embodies a mere statement: Such a man, so rooted in the law, will be fruitful. The common Scriptural figure of a flourishing tree is employed (cf., Job 8:16, 17; Ps. 52:8; 92:12, 13; Is. 44:4; etc.). There is something monumental about thriving trees that have stood long and regularly borne their fruit. To the Oriental the idea of being planted near abundant supplies of water is more impressive because of the almost universal desiccation of these lands. The chief point of the comparison involved is that such a tree is healthy ("its leaves do not wither") and yields fruit. Such a man's life yields something worth while, of use to himself and others. But essential for the good works produced was the basic relation to the Word of God.

The figure used is abandoned in the last clause of the verse when it is said: "and whatsoever he undertakes succeeds." This is meant absolutely only in so far as the devotion to the Word is absolute. But generally speaking, it will be obvious in such a life that God is crowning the man's endeavors with success. Tokens of divine favor abound. The man is blessed and is a blessing. This tree stands, therefore, as a monument to God's faithfulness. *Weiser* deserves to be quoted here: "At this point the poet is simply standing before the fundamental principle of divine theology: 'A good tree *cannot* bring forth evil fruit.'"

4. By way of contrast the description might have continued with reference to a scrawny, crippled, blasted tree that is in every way the reverse of the one just pictured. Instead, a stronger contrast is obtained by selecting the most useless of the elements to be found in the vegetable world and generally known as such in times of old—chaff. For the same figure see Ps. 35:5; Job 21:18; Is. 29:5; 41:2; Hos. 13:3; Matt. 3:12.

Of the various names employed above for the wicked man, the first is chosen—"the ungodly"—the man who is loose and flaccid and, therefore, wicked. It may seem that the verdict is a bit too harsh when throughout the psalm separation from God and wickedness are viewed as synonymous. But experience has shown the correctness of the observation. If patent wickedness does not result from such a separation sooner, it usually comes later. Of these ungodly ones the verse says very tersely, in literal translation: "not so the ungodly." This very brevity seems to indicate a kind of reticence about saying too much regarding persons whose fate is bound to be most unfortunate. This brevity was not appreciated by the Greek translation which repeats the "not so." This repetition is followed by the Vulgate. Our rendering merely attempts to make idiomatic English: "Such is not the case with the ungodly."

The scattering of the chaff involves a more picturesque figure than the average reader supposes. In the Holy Land the threshing floors are on elevated ground, and the mixture of straw, stubble, chaff, and grain is taken off the heap left by threshing and tossed into the steady breeze of the moonlit night. The breeze does the winnowing, and the regular practice of the husbandman thereafter was either to burn the chaff with fire, if it was a sizable heap, or to let the wind dispose of it without further concern on his part. What a drastic picture of futility when life yields nothing more substantial than useless remains scattered so completely as not even to be found when sought! That this is ultimately the fate of the life divorced from God is not always apparent in every case in outward and tangible results or the lack of them. But to the eye of faith there is no other outcome possible or discernible. The brevity of the statements of the verse would seem to indicate that the author is not minded to dwell at any length on the unpleasant subject. But there is certainly not a trace of "spiteful spirit" here (*Weiser*).

In each of the two preceding sections of the psalm the two types of life were contrasted. The same procedure is followed in the third section which shows how a life that has the proper roots eventually ends.

5. The opening words "on this account" are significant. A basic principle has just been presented, a principle that is operative continually and works itself out in history on every hand. Because this principle prevails, "on this account" the end of the ungodly man must be what it is.

The familiar phrase of the *KJ,* "shall not stand in the judgment," is most plainly a Hebraism. Its meaning is made clear by our translation: Such a one "shall not be able to maintain himself" or stand his ground when the judgment comes. Keeping the same figure, he shall be obliged to sit down or to retire in shame or confusion as one convicted of guilt.

But what "judgment" have we here? Though it may be true that throughout life those who have turned from God must experience many a setback and defeat in which they are not able to maintain themselves, even as in a broader sense the proverb has it: *Die Weltgeschichte ist das Weltgericht* ("The history of the world is the judgment of the world"), nevertheless, this word seems to refer primarily to one outstanding judgment which is the climax of them all, and whose verdicts are ultimate, the final judgment. By referring chiefly to the last great judgment the psalm merely cites the most outstanding example of how the ungodly will be dealt with. This judgment is the most drastic demonstration of their overthrow.

Parallel with this runs the statement that the sinners shall not be able to maintain themselves "in the congregation of the righteous." This brings another angle of the case into the picture. The "sinners" are, therefore, not to be thought of only as such who grind the ordinary standards of decency under their heel and live in flagrant shame and vice, but, it would almost seem, they are more frequently to be sought among men who try to maintain their place in "the congregation of the righteous." They are the group known as hypocrites. So strange are the manifold aspects of wickedness. But when the true congregation of the righteous is at the last established in the final judgment—of this also Ezek. 34:10-24 and Joel 2:32 speak—then the purge of the judgment will have removed these pretenders, and not a wicked one will be left in the assembly. Matt. 13:36-43, 47-50 describe this from the New Testament point of view.

6. Something was implied in v. 5 but was not stated because it was so very obvious. It was the fact that the Great Judge who removes the evil elements from His congregation was none other than the Lord. The sixth verse elucidates this implication by showing why it was that the Lord did this. Thus the initial "for" is to be explained.

The "knowing" that is here spoken of obviously involves more than "knowing of or about." It must be more than an act of the intellect. It does involve interest in, and care for, the person known. Some interpreters, therefore, render the word, *als einen Bekannten anerkennen,* i.e., to recognize one as an acquaintance (*K.W.*) or, "take notice of, regard" (*BDB*). "Cares for" would be good colloquial English. This would then yield the thought: God regards with favor the course of such a one's life. And such favor on God's part is no empty thing. God Himself goes with such a one through life—so we might paraphrase the Hebrew idiom.

The other side of the matter is that "the way of the ungodly is headed toward destruction." We might think of the course of the wicked as a path that becomes increasingly less clearly defined and

Psalm 1

finally loses itself in a swamp and morass. The psalm certainly ends on a sober note.

By standing first in the book and by depicting the character of a certain type of man at that point, this psalm certainly serves another purpose. Since throughout the Psalter it is the man of prayer who speaks, we are reminded at the very outset that such a man has very definite moral qualifications: he is pre-eminently a righteous man after the pattern of the one here described. It is as though the psalm said: Prayer involves definite moral obligations, and these obligations are what we are now about to outline.

NOTES

1. The noun 'etsah, from the root ya'ats, does primarily mean "counsel," then the "assembly" where such counsel is formulated; then it comes to mean in a more general way the "tendency" displayed by any given counsel, and so ultimately can come to mean "principles" as we have rendered it.

By a rather unusual device this verse conveys the thought that the virtues depicted in vv. 1 and 2 are to be thought of as embodying the whole course of a man's life. In the first verse three perfects are used: halakh, 'amadh, and yashabh. Being perfects, they convey the idea that a fixed mental attitude on the issues here involved is under consideration. Then, continuing the same description, we encounter the imperfect yehgeh ("he keeps pondering"). That brings the description up to the present and may be said to involve all of the future of a man's life as well.

3. The opening construction (wehayah) has been faulted as being wrong, or a late construction, or a mere mechanical quotation from Jer. 17:8. But it appears that KS has demonstrated that we have here the conversive "and" in the explicative sense, i.e., "and so," (K.S. 369g). V. 3 merely unfolds what is involved in the supreme happiness that is claimed for the righteous man in v. 1.

Shathul need not be taken in the exclusive sense of "transplanted." All planting of trees involves a transplanting. Therefore "planted" is not inaccurate. Of a similar nature is the translation of pelegh, which some interpreters claim dare be understood only in the sense of artificial watercourses because the root palagh means "to cut." But natural watercourses also cut their way and so meet the requirements of the root involved. And surely, a tree that stands by a natural stream or group of streams meets the requirements of the picture as fully as does the one that stands by the side of irrigation ditches or canals. Therefore "streams of water" is an adequate translation.

Yatsliach, being Hifil, is pressed by some commentators as though only the meaning "he makes to succeed" were here permissible. But that translation emphasizes what the statement in question did not want to put into the foreground at all—success resulting from *human* initiative. By using the simple meaning "succeeds," in which the distinctive *Hifil* feature is lost, the emphasis on the divine causality is made to appear the stronger. A similar use of the word is found in passages like Gen. 39:2; Judg. 18:5; I Kings 22:12.

5. The basic meaning of *tsaddiq* is to be entirely "normal." Nothing, of course, is quite so normal for a man as to walk in the precepts of the Lord.

CRITICAL ISSUES

Several textual changes are suggested rather generally. But when they are offered on the basis of improving the Hebrew meter, we are strongly of the opinion that mistaken notions as to what constitutes Hebrew meter are abroad, especially in all those cases where more or less extensive changes of the Hebrew text have to be made so that the psalms may conform to the metrical principles of the critic. On this score we reject the removal of the second *torah* in v. 2 as well as the repetition of *lo-khen* in v. 4. The other emendations suggested are trivial.

The suggestions to examine the psalm critically in the light of the higher truth of the New Testament, as they are offered at some length by *Kittel,* result chiefly from attributing a certain bias to the author of the psalm and then claiming that this bias is unwholesome. We insist that in each case the unwholesome meaning imputed to the writer does not actually lie in the statements as offered by the psalm.

Wholly inadequate are the reasons upon which the entire third verse is bracketed as a later interpolation. It neither breaks the Hebrew construction, as we have indicated above, nor interrupts the flow of thought; nor can it be demonstrated to have been taken over from Jeremiah at a late date. The reverse might rather be the case.

The sharpest criticisms come from *Buttenwieser.* He charges the editors who set this psalm as a preface to the Psalter with having shown "poor judgment." For in his opinion religion consists for the author "in minute observance of the law—moral and ceremonial alike." This position he rightly designates as a "barren view." But he seems unaware of the fact that the "law" may be taken in a much more constructive sense, and that delight in the law in that sense is anything but barren. Then to contrast the author's idea of religion with that of Jeremiah, as though Jeremiah had a much deeper insight into the true inwardness of religion, would certainly be a mistaken criticism, if, as we maintain above, Jeremiah (17:8) may well have been quoting from this psalm, giving his stamp of approval by his quotation, and adding the note of faith in his quotation as a note definitely implied in the word.

This has always been a psalm that was known and dearly beloved by the church of God. God's children have understood its fine truth and have guided themselves by its holy instruction. It fully merits its place as a fine portal through which we enter into the Psalter.

Psalm 2

THE ULTIMATE VICTORY OF THE LORD'S ANOINTED

WITH THE FULL confidence of faith this psalm sets forth the basic truth concerning the Messiah and His kingdom. Standing almost at the beginning of the Psalter, this psalm gives due prominence to the Messianic truth, which looms large in the psalms. So the truth about the man who is acceptable in the sight of the Lord (Ps. 1) as well as the truth concerning the Savior (Ps. 2) get well-deserved emphasis at the very beginning of the entire book.

Men have waxed enthusiastic with the enthusiasm of faith in their admiration of the excellent truth set forth by this psalm as well as the way in which this truth is formulated. Only a few of those who are more critically minded venture to speak belittling words.

The theme of the psalm deals with victory so plainly that we have been moved to select the above caption: The Ultimate Victory of the Lord's Anointed. This thought is presented in four strophes of three verses each, each strophe being a very distinct unit in itself. Not often is the outline of the thought of a psalm presented in so clear-cut a fashion.

The first strophe describes the bitter opposition of the enemies of the Lord's anointed. The second describes the calm assurance of the Lord Himself in the face of this opposition. The third presents the glorious divine ordinance appointed for the Lord's anointed. The last consists of an exhortation to the rebels to submit discreetly to Him who is their Lord.

In the highly dramatic presentation of the subject matter that this psalm offers the person speaking changes rather rapidly and without being formally introduced. At first the author-king himself speaks and sketches the situation. In the third verse the rallying cry of the rebels is offered without being formally introduced as such. The poet goes on to show how the Almightly reacts to the rebellion staged against Him by man. His actual utterance closes the strophe even as the declaration of the rebels closed the first. This utterance of His, however, also is not formally introduced.

In the first line of the third strophe the author-king speaks only as king and in the first person, revealing a decree by virtue of which he holds his present prominent position. The actual words that the Lord spoke to him begin to be offered at the conclusion of the second line. The divine decree is then given as a quotation down to the end of the strophe. In the last strophe the author falls back into his role of poet and teacher, instructing the rebels how to escape from the fate impending over them. The very last line is still spoken by the same teacher but appears in the form of a general observation that applies to those who are rebellious as well as to all men.

One fundamental question must be definitely settled before the interpreter can proceed with any measure of assurance. This is the question whether the psalm is directly Messianic, or typically Messianic, or a mixture of both, beginning with some theocratic king and gradually expanding in thought until it has transcended the narrow bounds of the earthly type. From this approach it will appear clearly that we cannot go along with those who insist that "the Messianic interpretation cannot be sustained" (*Taylor*).

By a psalm that is "directly Messianic" we have in mind one that is from beginning to end an out-and-out prophecy about the Christ. He would then be the one against whom the rebels bestir themselves in v. 2. And about Him v. 6 would speak. He Himself would be the speaker in v. 7, and to Him the decree following would be addressed; and to Him finally the submission counselled in the closing portion should be offered.

By a psalm that is "typically Messianic" we have in mind one that refers to an actual situation which obtained in the days of some theocratic king of Judah, whose identity is to be established, if possible. He is the one who experiences the antagonism of the nations; he is the one about whom the Lord has proclaimed a decree; he publishes this decree, which guarantees him great success; finally submission is to be offered to the Lord by submitting to this king who is God's appointee to his high office. He that submits to him thereby submits to the Lord. Throughout the psalm this earthly king would then serve as a type of Christ, not accidentally but by virtue of divine appointment. He would

Psalm 2

have experienced something on a lower level which is closely analogous to what the Messiah encounters on the higher level. He is not an accidental type but a divinely ordained type. He in his own person portrays the truth concerning the Messiah and knows that he does, and the writer presents him with this very thought in mind. This does not exclude the possibility that the author himself is this king.

We definitely hold that this second type of Messianic presentation is found in this psalm. The third we discard as an unsound mixture of the two just described. The human experience of the king prepared him for the higher truth which his own experience reflects. Humanly speaking, it would seem as if the initial experience that he had with rebellious nations brought to his attention the deeper truth as to the attitude of the nations the world over against the Lord and His Christ. What his reflections suggested, the Holy Spirit directed and clarified and raised to a higher potentiality so as to make it revealed truth of the highest sort concerning the Messiah. But this revelation had a natural background and foundation in human experience and so came to the author of the psalm at a time when he was prepared to receive this result and apprehend it as something which fitted into his thought-life, and for which he had been prepared sufficiently to appreciate what was involved.

We deem this matter of sufficient moment to pause to evaluate the arguments advanced in favor of the directly Messianic interpretation. Not that we deem such a type of prophecy impossible. We shall encounter a notable example of it in Ps. 22 and elsewhere. But in this instance it behoves us to note that the arguments advanced in its support are inadequate.

Hengstenberg, who espouses the idea of a directly Messianic psalm most strongly, in this instance advances first of all in support of this theory the argument that a superhuman dignity is ascribed to the person referred to in v. 12. We readily grant that part of the statement, but we claim that He to whom the superhuman dignity is ascribed is not the Messiah Himself but the Lord who stands behind and upholds His anointed one.

It is next claimed in support of this view that vv. 1-3 as well as vv. 8 and 10 indicate that the ruler under consideration has dominion over the *whole* world, which has been given him or is to be given him for a possession. But just that point on which the argument hinges is the point that happens to be noticeably absent. Those that revolt against the king in question in vv. 1-3 are indeed peoples, nations, kings, and rulers; but not all of them, nor are they said to come from and represent the *whole* world. The same situation obtains in vv. 8 and 10. It is just not said that the *whole* earth shall be given to this king upon his demand; nor are *all* the kings of the earth bidden to submit to him. World-wide dominion may ultimately result from all this, but that is not said.

Next the claim is raised that rebellion against the anointed one is treated like rebellion against the Lord Himself. We grant that freely but refuse to draw the conclusion that is claimed. For the situation is still the same when the anointed one is appointed to his office by the good Lord and has the full support of the Almighty. To refuse to submit to him definitely involve refusal to submit to the God who gave him his rank and standing.

Then lastly the claim is raised that the same arguments that support the directly Messianic character of Ps. 45, 72, and 110 substantiate the Messianic character of the psalm before us; they all stand or fall together. We are far from sure that such is the case. The other psalms referred to will remain Messianic whether one particular type of the Messianic character or another happens to be the type involved in each instance.

Let it also be understood that the psalm that is Messianic by type is in no sense Messianic in an inferior sense. The providence of God is most manifestly displayed in this class of prophecies also. For in them the Spirit of prophecy so worded the things that the God of history had in His wisdom controlled that the lower level of experience of man expressed the higher level which would become reality in Chirst. The whole Old Testament thus became a shadow of the things to come.

All of which brings us to the issue of the authorship of this psalm. The psalm itself gives no direct indication as to who wrote it. The time before the division of the kingdom seems to meet the needs of the case far better than does any situation that arose after the division. The high sense of Messianic truth that prevails throughout the psalm leads us definitely to the point where we have before us an age in which the appreciation of the truth concerning the Christ to come was lively and correct. Again, a later age meets the needs of the case less appropriately. The age of the Maccabees is least suited for such a production as this is.

The problem is removed out of the realm of the conjectural by the statement found in Acts 4:25, where a passage from this psalm is quoted. The author of Acts, speaking by divine inspiration, tells us that David was the author. Even so good a commentator as *Kirkpatrick* misses the point at issue when he claims in this connection: "The language of Acts 4:25 does not decide the question, for 'David' in the New Testament may mean no more than 'the Psalter' (Heb. 4:7) or 'a psalmist.'" What he claims regarding the passage Heb. 4:7 we believe is correct. But the situation is quite different in Acts 4:25, which reads thus: "who by the Holy Spirit by the mouth of our father David, didst say." Granting that a common metonomy would allow for the use of the word "David" for "the Psalter," we cannot allow that the case is parallel when the "mouth of our father David" is referred to, and he is further designated as "Thy servant." Such a statement is an unquestionable allusion to a person. We may not know how the author of Acts came into possession of this knowledge. But we believe that he has rendered a verdict on the problem of the authorship of this psalm.

Several other facts agree with this presupposition: first, David's well-known ability as an author of psalms; then his intimate connection with Messianic truth; also his experience with the hostility of the kingdoms of this world; then, too, his high sense of his theocratic position (cf., I Chron. 29:23, which indicates that for David the throne of Israel was "the throne of Jehovah" as much as it was for Solomon— cf. also I Chron. 28:5); and lastly the strong faith of which David was a notable exponent more so than many another, the same faith which is so sturdily reflected in this psalm.

a) "The First Strophe" (vv. 1–3)
1. *Why did the nations stir up riots*
   And the peoples devise futility?
2. *Why did the kings of the earth take a stand together*
   And the dignitaries counsel together
   Against the Lord and against His anointed?
3. *"Let us rend their bonds asunder,*
   And let us cast from us their cords."

1. The first two verses are a unit. It refers to some particular event in which the hostility of the nations displayed itself. At least, so our translation would indicate. (We shall justify this translation later in the Notes below.) What occasion was this? Almost any one of the later wars of David might serve as a starting point for an experience of this sort. We believe that the events recorded in II Sam. 8 or 10 would seem to agree best with the situation before us. It is even possible, for that matter, that several such occasions are before the writer's eyes simultaneously.

As far as the king's personal experience was concerned, he may have learned from this incident that the world and the hostile forces in the world hate the people of God with a hatred that is stronger than that which usually grows out of national antipathies or purely racial or nationalistic feelings. Knowing that this strong opposition was directed against him just because he was a sturdy exponent of the cause of

46   *Exposition of the Psalms*

Jehovah, he does not regard himself as a notable martyr but rather reflects on the vanity of the hostility involved. For the interrogative "why?" expresses both wonder and the thought of the futility of it all.

First, the turbulent disorders of the children of this world are described. "Nations" (*goyim*, a word usually bearing a hostile connotation) are involved in this; so are "peoples," that is to say, persons of various nationalities. They may differ from one another and have little in common otherwise, but in matters of religion they have the common bond of hatred against the Lord. The activities they have engaged in are variously described. On the one hand, they "stir up riots," or "rage," or "assemble tumultously." The verb *ragash* designates any noisy or riotous assembly that practically seethes in its antagonism. On the other hand, they are said to "devise futility." They meditate on it in the same manner in which a godly man is said to meditate upon the law of the Lord; the same verb is used in both instances. But the fact that the plan under consideration will come to naught is indicated in advance by the word *riq*, which means "emptiness" or "futility."

2. The efforts of the ruling spirits among these rebels are described, "kings" and "dignitaries." The expression "kings of the earth" is not an uncommon one (cf., Ps. 76:12; 89:27; 138:4; 148:11). It includes all rulers of kingdoms apart from the kingdom of God. As *Luther* rightly remarks in this connection, they are usually the ones who are so self-sufficient that they are not minded to let anybody instruct them. Besides, they are the ones who are usually the guiding spirits of any concerted efforts to oppose the good Lord. These are said to "stand together" or to "take their stand" consciously as opponents of the cause of Yahweh. Before they took this stand they had "counseled together."

Adding all this together, all sorts of groups and all sorts of individuals are indicated as having engaged in all manner of hostile activity against the Lord. By listing these persons and these activities the author indicates how manifold and strong are the currents of opposition that he had observed. A very beehive of unholy industry is pictured. All this is directed "against the Lord and against His anointed." First of all, it is aimed at the one whose very name spells gracious and faithful love, Yahweh. Never were grief and opposition more causeless. Never were men more in the wrong than when they opposed him who was their salvation.

And in the same breath the writer says that this activity was directed against the "anointed" one of the Lord. Saul was the first among the rulers of Israel to be thus designated (cf., I Sam. 24:6; II Sam. 1:14). How David became the next one to receive this title appears from I Sam. 16:13 (cf. also II Sam. 19:22; II Chron. 6:42; Ps. 18:50, 20:

6; etc.). Since we found good reasons for designating David as the author of this psalm, the "anointed one" that is here referred to would most aptly be David himself. The nations round about Israel cannot have been ignorant of the unusual dignity that was claimed by Israel for its king, and that this position involved a direct relationship to Yahweh, the true God. By opposing God's representative they were opposing Him. David felt and understood this situation full well.

3. Without formally introducing the sentiments of these God haters, the author gives an insight into the inmost reflections of these men when he records the thinking that prompted their opposition: "Let us rend their bonds asunder, and let us cast from us their cords." As far as the historical occasion of it all is concerned, it was when the nations conquered by David had staged a rebellion in order to shake off the unwelcome yoke of Israel from their necks. Such an effort might seem entirely just and right. For what nation is there that would not gladly attain its freedom? However, if David's wars are examined, it will become apparent, as *Hengstenberg* rightly claims, that these wars were not waged in the spirit of aggression or as the outgrowth of an unwholesome imperialism. All of David's wars were defensive. He took no pleasure in subjugation. Conquest had become a stern necessity in order that the serious threats raised by the enemies of Israel might be met. David had most certainly not made Israel's yoke upon the neck of the subdued enemies any heavier than was necessary. Yet his opponents speak as though he had sought to enslave them. In fact, any relations to Israel and Israel's God are pictured as things that are hard and grievous to be borne, as though the service of Israel's God had been bondage and slavery.

To sum it all up, this strophe presents a scene of riotous preparations against Yahweh and Israel's king, preparations made in the spirit of the strongest hostility. All this reflects how the nations and their mighty leaders have for the most part felt throughout the course of history. Christ's yoke was not esteemed easy and light by them. All this explains why we cannot agree with those who suppose that the unrest that accompanies the rise of a new king was the occasion thought of in this psalm (*Oesterley, Weiser*).

b) "The Second Strophe" (vv. 4–6)

4. *He who sits in the heavens laughs,*
   The Lord of all derides them.
5. *Then will He speak with them in His anger;*
   In His hot indignation He will terrify them.
6. *"Yet, as for Me, I have inducted My king*
   Upon Zion, My holy hill."

4. Various remarks have been made by writers on the contrast between the tumultuous scene of the first strophe and the heavenly calm of the second. Some see these bold rebels as ready to confound heaven and earth, yet all their efforts are little more than the idle jumping of grasshoppers. Others picture the rebellious ones as so bold that they might be expected any minute to leave the earth behind them as they leap boldly out into space in defiance of the laws of gravity. Others speak of a child defying an army. Correct as all these reflections and comparisons are, they are not as effective as is the original presentation of the psalm.

In a bold figure the Lord is represented as being amused at the foolish endeavors of His enemies: He "laughs," He "derides" them. He has not been moved even to rise from His throne. A title is here given Him, "the Sitter in the heavens," *yoshebh bashshamayim*. The expression naturally involves the thought of the calm and serene dignity that characterizes Him who is so infinitely removed from the frailty and littleness of man. Cf. also Ps. 113:4-6; Is. 40:12ff; 66:1ff.

The boldness of the figure employed in ascribing laughter and derision to the Almighty is a safeguard in itself. It calls for an immediate recollection of the fact that this is the One whose sympathies with the frailties of mankind pass our boldest belief. We recall at once that He is also known as the One who "beheld the city and wept over it." But to tell the truth, opposition against God, all thoughts that in effect culminate in the defiant: "We will not have this man to rule over us," are most absurd and ridiculous.

5. He will not always be so tolerant. Wicked opposition calls for action. When His hour has come, He will let His anger blaze forth. He is first represented as speaking forth in tones of righteous indignation. His rebukes are well interpreted by *Calvin* to mean "the demonstration of divine wrath," that is to say, the acts whereby He brings His opposition low and hurls it to the ground. The other side of the matter is that, when He finally waxes indignant, "He will terrify them." Till then they will have been deceiving themselves as to what they amount to and as to who He is. When He but speaks severly with them, unspeakable terror will take hold on them. Just when that will take place is but vaguely indicated by a general "then." This, of course, means, when His hour has come. The very vagueness of the term carries something ominous in it: you can never tell when His anger will flash forth.

Just as the first strophe brought the thoughts and purposes of the rebels boldly to the fore by concluding with a statement that revealed how they felt, so this second strophe closes with a summary statement bearing on the case in hand and coming from the lips of the Almighty. Neither of these two statements is formally introduced.

The emphatic "I" is set into bolder relief by the adversative conjunction, *waw* adversative. The statement is really an ellipsis. Its introductory thought is unexpressed. This would have been something like: "You may rebel and make plans to overthrow my anointed one; but all I have to say is." In fact, all He does say is surprisingly simple: His king, that is the present writer or the ruling monarch of Zion, holds office by divine appointment. Already that settles the case: God appointed him. Inasmuch as Zion was already in David's day recognized as the site selected for the central sanctuary, Zion is here described as God's "holy hill" (for the literal "hill of My holiness" means just that). The meaning of *nasakh* as "appoint" or "induct" is established by the corresponding Assyrian *nasaku*.

One may well inquire at this point, whence did the writer get the information about God's supreme assurance and the certainty of victory derived from the divine appointment of the monarch on Zion? Was this vouchsafed to the writer as a revelation? Was he a prophet? Apparently that was not the case in the psalms. The holy poets of Israel or her psalmists merely restated in manifold ways the truth granted to the prophets by direct divine revelation. Only in a secondary sense were the psalmists prophets. The truth expressed here and in still fuller measure in the third strophe is a poetical restatement of the contents of the divine oracle that came to Nathan the prophet in II Sam. 7, especially in vv. 5–17. V. 16 of Nathan's prophecy might be said to be under consideration in v. 6 of this psalm.

A good practical comment by *Luther* that applies to this whole strophe may well be offered here. He says: "What a great measure of faith is necessary in order truly to believe this word: For who could have imagined that God laughed as Christ was suffering and the Jews were exulting? So, too, when we are oppressed, how often do we still believe that those who oppose us are being derided by God, especially since it seems as if we were being oppressed and trodden under foot both by God and men?"

The Messianic application of this strophe is not difficult to make. As the "Lord of all" (*'adhonay*) was not alarmed by what David's enemies did in their day but met the challenge to His authority by the firm assertion that the king assailed held office by His appointment, so in a higher sense will He vindicate His Messiah, threaten His opponents with dire disaster, and support Him, who in the truest sense holds office by direct appointment from God on high.

c) "The Third Strophe" (vv. 7–9)

7. *"Let me declare an appointment: the Lord has said unto me:*
   'You are my son, I have this day begotten you.

8. Ask of Me, and I will give you nations for your inheritance
And for your possession, the ends of the earth.
9. You shall break them with a rod of iron;
As a potter's vessel you shall shatter them.' "

V. 7 is a poetic restatement of II Sam. 7:14; vv. 8 and 9 reflect vv. 10, 11, 15, 16 of the same chapter. The whole of II Sam. 7 is practically the "appointment" spoken of. For this "appointment" is a *choq,* an "ordinance," a matter divinely ordained. The noun is derived from the root *chaqaq,* which means "to engrave." Nathan's word has about it something of the nature of such an unalterable decree. How very appropriate, too, is the statement by David himself: "Yahweh hath said unto me"! Regarding any other incumbent of Israel's royal throne this statement was only relatively true. But on David's part it is also an assertion to the effect that he had not rashly thrust himself into a position of responsibility: God had set him on high, and he was well aware of the rare nature of the honor that had been bestowed upon him.

The first part of this divine decree, as David restates it, is given in a parallelism. The first half of the statement runs thus: "You are My son." We can well understand how this statement prompted some commentators to find here the chief support for a directly Messianic interpretation. However, they overlooked the fact that this was also the statement in II Sam. 7:14 in direct reference to David, and that it must, therefore, be interpreted in the light of this basic statement. It may be of help to accept for the moment the rendering, "You are My child." We see at once that, since the Hebrew readily permits this meaning, the statement can very properly apply to any man. *Hengstenberg* has a very helpful comment here. He says: "Whenever in the Old Testament God is designated as Father, or where sons of God are spoken of, there . . . in every case reference is being made by means of an abbreviated comparison to the intimate love which He has for men, a love like unto that of a father for a son." He cites numerous examples, all of which quite plainly substantiate his point: Ps. 103:13; Exod. 4:23; Deut. 14:1, 2; 32:6; Isa. 63:16; Hos. 11:1; Mal. 1:6. It is well to remember that in the Old Testament the statements involved stay within these limits. So David asserts nothing more than that he knew himself to be the object of God's paternal love. This personal relation was basic.

The parallel statement reinforces this thought and indicates when this relationship of intimate love began: "I have this day begotten you." *A.V.* loses the required emphasis of the statement when it renders: "This day have I begotten thee." The initial "I" is, as usual, emphatic. This is as much as to say: It is not you who inaugurated this very special relationship; I did it; take comfort from that fact. Of course, the verb "begotten" is here used in an indirect or figurative sense even as we find the word used thus in Jer. 2:27. It means, therefore, This day have you entered into this relationship with Me.

But all this still leaves the question, In what sense is the word "this day" used here? Since the king quotes this statement as it was spoken to him when the unique promise came to him from the lips of Nathan the prophet, that greatest day in the life of David is the day that was referred to. On that day God was pleased to advance David to the exalted position of being the object of God's love in the most direct sense of the word. This the statement recalls and nothing more.

In the very nature of the case there just cannot be a reference to the eternal generation of the Son by the Father even though the words as such, apart from their connection, could easily convey such a meaning. But such an interpretation of these words would be dogmatic construction in an unwholesome sense.

But what about Acts 13:33, where it is specifically said that this word was fulfilled in the resurrection of Jesus Christ from the dead? The explanation should not be difficult. If the psalm is a type of Christ as we strongly maintain, then even as there was a day in David's life when he was admitted to a close relation to God and classified as God's child, so there would, of course, be a corresponding day in the life of Christ when His unique relation to the Father was declared in a most significant way. If anyone asks, "When in the life of Christ was such a declaration most plainly made?" we cannot but answer, "By His resurrection." This is Paul's inspired interpretation in the passage in Acts just mentioned as well as in another form in Rom. 1:4.

The *Targum* gives a rather good interpretation of the verse as a whole when, with a measure of paraphrase, it offers the following: "I will relate the decree of Yahweh: He said: 'Beloved as a son of his father art thou of men, righteous art thou, even as if I had on this day created thee.'" However, this rendering has made one combination of words that is not so commendable. It does as do many modern writers on the subject; it connects "decree" and "Yahweh" by putting the first into the genetive relation: I will declare the decree of Yahweh. Nothing of value is gained by this alteration.

8. When the grace of the Lord singled out David above all others and gave him, first of all, a unique position in regard to his God, it also made provision for the eventualities that would arise in David's relation to the nations round about him. For the favor bestowed upon David would naturally arouse the enmity of all kings and nations on every side of Israel. As far as David was concerned, this new relation involved also dominion over all whom he should desire to overcome. All this might for the moment sound as if David had imperialistic aspira-

tions and had been promised that they would be realized. But if we consider, as was remarked above, that all of David's wars, according to the Biblical record, were defensive wars, and that he never aspired to achieve greatness by the conquest of others, all that is here meant (vv. 8, 9) is that, of conquest becomes imperative, let him ask for dominion over his foes, and he shall prevail over them by the grace of God.

To insert the example of the Babylonian Empire into the picture and have David or whoever the author may be dream of making his realm as great as this mighty Babylonian Empire was, distorts the issues and sanctions ideas of unwholesome greatness. Or merely to assume that world dominion was here being thought of, again fails to do justice to the issues involved. All that had reference to this case in the basic passage was that Israel was assured security and peace (II Sam. 7:10, 11). Some interpreters leap at this conclusion of world dominion because they believe the supreme rule of Christ requires this. We concede that the words of the psalm are poured into a big mold so as to reach beyond what was actually realized in the reign of David. But basically we have here a measure of hyperbole even as this same figure appears elsewhere in the Scriptures with proper restraint. As examples of hyperbole in the psalms see Ps. 30:2 and 18:5.

The nature of the statement indicates how highly favored by God the speaker actually is; if he for one reason or another desires nations, as a free, unearned gift ("inheritance"), let him ask, and God will freely give them. Should he go so far as to make a request of regions or kingdoms that lie at the "ends of the earth," these, too, shall be his unrestricted possession.

9. The ease with which this beloved son shall shatter all opposition is the only thought that is more fully illustrated in order that it might be made clear that God's giving of these nations was not a questionable boon. This aspect of the case happens to be under consideration throughout the psalm. For this psalm deals with the problem of the rebellious nations who arise against the Lord's anointed.

It is first stated that he shall be much stronger than any opposition that may arise when it is said: "You shall break them with a rod of iron." Since *shebhet* means primarily "rod" or "staff," and that for smiting or beating, we may well ignore the second meaning, "sceptre." To demonstrate the effectiveness of his punitive efforts, he is pictured with an iron rod that utterly smashes all opposition. This thought is then presented with added color by representing the foes as being as fragile as potters' vessels would be. Such complete defeat of all that opposed him was guaranteed to this man who was dearly beloved by God from the very outset.

Commentators make unnecessary difficulties for themselves when they expect every side of the matter to be touched upon, or when they think at once or exclusively in terms of the Messianic import of it all. Essential in the light of the situation depicted in the first three verses was some statement as to whether God's anointed could prevail over all his foes. As long as this side of the matter is under consideration, there is no immediate call for a statement of the more kindly and gracious aspects of his reign. Neither need the kindly conquests of the souls of men by the Messiah be brought into this picture. Other holy writers were on proper occasions given opportunity to treat of this subject. Whatever balance of treatment may be required will be taken care of by the last strophe. Here the things demanded by the crucial situation pictured in the first strophe are still being effectively disposed of.

This approach helps us get our bearings in regard to those interpretations that would derive from vv. 8 and 9 thoughts about the propagation of the gospel or of some other beneficent work of the Lord. So *Luther* comments on "break them": "For he slays our will in order to establish His own will in us. He puts to death the flesh and its lusts in order to make alive in us the Spirit and the things that he desires." Or *Calvin* remarks: "The meaning is that the Father denies the Son nothing that bears upon the extension of His kingdom even unto the uttermost parts of the earth." This comment is made on, "Ask of Me." These are certainly wholesome Scripture truths, but they do not happen to be expressed *here*. The psalm offers no occasion to deal with this aspect of the Messiah's work. Nothing is gained by forced interpretations.

If one then asks, What aspect of the work of the Christ is portrayed in this type? the answer is, His punitive work; the manner in which He deals with refractory foes; that which John the Baptist put into the words: "The chaff He will burn with fire unquenchable."

d) "The Fourth Strophe" (vv. 10–12)

10. *And now, O you kings, act discreetly;*
    Suffer yourselves to be instructed, you judges of the earth.
11. *Serve the Lord with fear*
    And exult with trembling.
12. *Kiss the son, lest he be angry, and you perish from the way;*
    For soon will his wrath be kindled.
    Blessed are all they who take refuge in Him.

The royal author now expresses his own sentiments. If there was any danger of misunderstanding statements such as, "He who sits in the heavens laughs," or, "You shall break them with a rod of iron," we must understand these remarks in the light of this closing exhortation. The author has no desire to see men suffer. He does not gloat over the destruction of his foes. He was merely expressing in strong terms the certainty of the victory of the cause of the Lord. His personal sentiments on this score are disclosed in this last strophe. He, too, would have all men to be saved and to come to the knowledge of the truth.

10. He addresses his exhortation to the kings and judges because, in the last analysis, the rabble would hardly be as hostile as they are but for the leadership that directs them into this dangerous course. The kings are advised to "act discreetly." For there is no higher folly than to oppose God and no better discretion than to submit to Him. The author futher pleads with the "judges" to "suffer themselves to be instructed." He implies that men in high position find this difficult to do. "Judges" are practically synonymous with "rulers" in the Old Testament language as is indicated by the two basic meanings given for the word "judge, govern" (*BDB*).

11. That particular instruction which the author desires to impart is now offered, first briefly and pointedly in this verse, then at greater length in the last verse. *Kirkpatrick* rightly says: "The context indicates that political submission to Jehovah in the person of His representative is primarily intended." As instances of such political submission he cites Ps. 18:43 and 72:11. Then he adds: "But the wider meaning must not be excluded. 'Serve' and 'fear' are words constantly used with a religious meaning . . . Cf., 97:1; 100:2; Hos. 3:5."

There are always two sides to any man's relationship to the Almighty, especially when we consider the fact that we all were by nature rebels against the Most High. Heb. 12:28 speaks of the same matter. The one side is humble service, the other is exultation with becoming reverence. Neither rules out the other. The exulting is, perhaps, best understood as a reference to the shouts of jublilation with which a monarch is to be greeted: *Koenigsjubel* says *Hengstenberg* in reference to Num. 23:21.

All this does not yet say that the person under consideration as the Lord's anointed and Yahweh are identical because here Yahweh alone is to be submitted to. The thought, as above indicated, is that Yahweh is served by submission to His chosen representative on the throne of Israel.

12. The statement which we have rendered, "Kiss the son," has been the subject of much controversy. Some interpreters utterly reject the possibility of such a translation and usually admit after they have done so that the substitutes they offer are not very plausible or meaningful. Some few adhere to the traditional translation with certain

misgivings. A small group still holds to the traditional rendering of the versions that are familiar to most of us as entirely certain and correct. We find ourselves in this class.

The Hebrew reads *nashshequ-bhar*. We shall discuss the critical aspect of the case below. As to its meaning the "son" here referred to must be the same one who is so called in v. 7. Because the close fellowship between Yahweh and the man of His choice was indicated by this term in the most eminent way, this term here becomes a sort of title. Those that rebel against his authority and seek to overthrow him are counselled to offer as token of submission the kiss of fealty. According to some interpreters this was in days of old bestowed upon the hem of the ruler's garment, according to others upon his hand, or upon one's own hand or the hem of one's own garment. Unless this is done, he, powerfully supported by Yahweh, may let his anger flash forth against these opponents of his, and they shall be overthrown— "perish from the way" says the Hebrew, which may be construed as meaning: "blasted from their course." Though ordinarily the Bible reader's thoughts upon hearing about the kindling of such a powerful anger might be moved to think of the Lord Himself, it must be remembered that here the person in question is backed by the strength of the Almighty. As a closing word in the warning we hear: "For soon will his wrath be kindled." The opposition is warned: the patience of the offended ruler can bear little more. His being a just wrath in a just cause, it is not to be trifled with.

Lest this last verse seem to have made too much of the rare dignity that this servant of God enjoys, it recalls to our mind that in the last analysis whatever attitude they take to God's appointed representatives, the all-important thing is that they make Yahweh Himself the object of their trust and confidence. This is a kind of missionary invitation that these Gentiles come and share in the privileges of Israel. The words are: "Blessed are all they who take refuge in Him." Yahweh is not mentioned by name since He was referred to in the preceding verse. The verse serves as a kind of conclusion to the psalm.

NOTES

1. The sequence of tenses in the first two verses has called forth all manner of explanations, most of which do not satisfy. We believe no approach to this problem is better than that of *Koenig,* who makes these two verses dependent upon the initial "why" and indicates that the imperfects should be regarded as dependent upon the *waw* conversive, from which they happen to be separated by an intervening word. So both *yehgu* and *yithyatstsebhu* are converted into perfects by

the *waw* before *le'ummim*. Consequently all verbs are reduced to the tense of *rageshu* and are to be treated as perfects, and, therefore, all actions referred to have already taken place, and in regard to all of them the author asks with wonder: Why have men and rulers done these things? *Nosedhu* returns to the tense of *ragheshu,* not converted. This matter of the rather common separation of the verb from the *waw* conversive is discussed at length in *K.S.* 368 h-v.

2. Regarding the word *mashiach,* from which "Messiah" is derived, it is important to note that, though it refers to priests (Lev. 4:35, etc.) and the patriarchs (Ps. 105:15) and to the kings of Israel (I Sam. 2:10, etc.) and also to Cyrus (Is. 45:1), it also refers to the Messiah of God Himself in Dan. 9:25, 26. So the New Testament use of the term in John 1:42 and 4:25 is based on Old Testament usage and not only on the Book of Enoch (48:10).

3. The halves of the verse close with nouns having pronominal suffixes that present an assonance, a kind of rhyme: *moserothemo* and *'abhothemo.* It will help little to have the first of these nouns refer to means whereby the yoke is bound to the beast and the second to the rope by which it is attached to the wagon, even though the basic idea of the one is "bonds" and of the other "ropes." Enslavement is the general idea connoted by these terms.

5. The arrangement of the clauses is chiastic: "He will speak in His anger; in His indignation He will terrify."

7. No special emphasis attaches to the *'el* used after "let me declare." Though the preposition means "in reference to," the sense would have been no different if a direct object had been used instead. Ps. 69:27 is similar.

The verb form *yelidhtikha* is the perfect of action completed at the time of the speaker. The first "i" is explained by *G.K.* 69s as being caused by a striving after a more euphonious form.

9. The initial verb *tero'em* was read with different vowels (*tir'em*) by the Septuagint and also by Jerome. The motive for reading thus apparently sought to introduce something of the gentler nature of the Messiah, to whom these words were directly referred, and so the translation "thou wilt feed them" resulted. The parallelism of the members of the verse points, however, to the correctness of the original Masoretic text.

10. The *niphal hiwwaseru* is to be classified as a *niphal tolerativum;* found also in Is. 55:6 and Prov. 13:10.

12. The bone of contention in this verse is the noun *bar,* which is the Aramaic noun for "son." That this did create a difficulty—this Aramaism at this early date—is apparent in the major versions. The Septuagint rendered: "Accept correction." Jerome: *adorate pure*

("worship sincerely"). But several substantial arguments may be presented for maintaining the translation we have given above. In the first place, the same word is used in Prov. 31:2, to which passage a late date is assigned partly because of the use of this word—the argument in a circle. In the second place, a Phoenician inscription of the ninth century uses the same word; and Phoenician is not Aramaic but practically Hebrew (cf., Koenig's *Commentary* on this fact). Then it must be admitted to be a rarer word such as the poetic writers are wont to use; a select term for a select thought. Since the exhortation is addressed to groups which are largely Aramaic (note: Damascus and all the region toward the Euphrates) a word that is well known to them is used. Lastly, the choice of the word may have been motivated in part by the effort to avoid the dissonance of *ben pen*.

The expression *kim'at* is best rendered "soon" (cf. also *A.R.V.* and practically all the versions). *A.V.* has "when His wrath is kindled *but a little.*" But the point at issue is not how much of the wrath of God it takes to consume the wicked, but how precarious their position is. Therefore "soon" deserves the preference.

The *Catholic Biblical Quarterly* (1943, No. 1, pp. 63-67) presents an article by Albert Kleber, in which he points to the fact that vessels have been discovered on which execration texts were copied out denouncing or threatening mishap to some person or groups, and then the vessel would be shattered by a heavy rod. There is the possibility that v. 9 could contain a reference to some such familiar custom though, as Kleber also maintains, no magic would be implied in the form of statement that the psalm makes. The title of the essay is: "Ps. 2:9 in the Light of an Ancient Oriental Custom."

CRITICAL ISSUES

In every verse of this psalm some change is proposed either on the basis of the manner in which the Greek translators rendered it, or on the basis of pure conjecture as to how the critical writer thinks the text must have read, a mode of procedure which can never lay claim to scientific validity where so good a text as the traditional Hebrew text is the basis.

None of the proposed changes are of particular moment or particularly substantiated. Here are a few typical ones. A *Selah,* is to be added to v. 3. In v. 4 *Yahweh* is substituted for *'adhonay*. In v. 7 the words "my son art thou" are to be deleted. In v. 12 the text is so amended as to yield the meaning "kiss his feet."

Then there are many attempts that make this psalm apply to some later king of Israel as though the idea of Davidic authorship were too preposterous even to entertain seriously as a conjecture.

Buttenwieser is most pronounced in his critical attitude. He argues that there is a spiritual kinship between this psalm and Ezekiel and arrives at the conclusion that, since the tone of the prophecies is reflected, the psalm is equally "narrow-souled and void of vision" and obviously postexilic as Ezekiel himself is. We feel such verdicts require no refutation.

Psalm 3

A MORNING HYMN
OF A GODLY MAN IN DISTRESS

AFTER CERTAIN fundamental issues such as the importance of the law of the Lord in the life of a man of God (Ps. 1) or the ultimate victory of the Messiah (Ps. 2) have been set into the foreground, it is very proper that a prayer book offer a morning hymn (Ps. 3) and an evening hymn (Ps. 4). We shall presently indicate that there are ample reasons for thinking that this is a morning hymn.

This psalm is commonly called "a lament of an individual." The thought of the psalm runs as follows: In vv. 1 and 2 the psalmist briefly voices his cry of distress; in vv. 3 and 4 he sets over against this his sure ground for hope; to this he adds in vv. 5 and 6 a statement of the courage that animated him when he took his stand on this sure ground of hope; then in vv. 7 and 8 he concludes his prayer with a petition for complete deliverance.

In the title we meet for the first time the term "a psalm" (Heb. *mizmor*). It seems best to accept as the root meaning of the word *zamar* the idea of plucking strings rather than to sing; and it is better to understand *mizmor* in the sense of a poem that is to be rendered with musical accompaniment (*K.W.*) than as "melody" (*BDB*). The latter term would result in a misleading meaning; for the psalm is not a "melody" but a poem sung to a melody or accompanied by some melody. The word as such appears in fifty-seven psalm titles.

The heading carried by the psalm in the Hebrew text and, for that matter also in the Septuagint, is: "a psalm of David when he fled before Absalom his son." Though this is rather generally brushed aside by commentators in our day as worthless and negligible, upon closer investigation it may be seen that this heading agrees in a substantial number of items with the subject matter of the psalm. Note that the opponents of the author are numerous (vv. 1, 2, 6); note the same situation in II Sam. 15:13. Again, the attitude of some of David's opponents was that he had forfeited all right to hope for divine aid; cf., II Sam. 16:8. V. 2 of our psalm says the same thing. That David directs his prayer to the holy hill (v. 4) agrees well with the situation as outlined in II Sam. 15:25, where David had taken steps to have the ark, which marked the presence of God on the holy hill, returned to Jerusalm rather than to have it taken along with him on his flight. Lastly, the thought that the issues of this whole experience rested with God (cf., v. 9) is the very thought expressed in II Sam. 15:25. Besides, the author is a man of some eminence. Nothing of moment can be adduced to remove any of these points of correspondence between the history of David and the contents of the psalm. The headings to the psalms rest upon a sound tradition. Yet we can subscribe to *Weiser's* comment that Davidic authorship can neither be fully proved nor disproved on the basis of the psalm itself.

If one should try to be more specific and to determine at what point during this rebellion David may have composed this psalm, the probability is that it was about the second night after the rebellion was staged. For II Sam. 17:22 leads to the conclusion that the first night was spent inducing the whole group that had attached itself to David to effect a fording of the Jordan. The next night would then have been best suited for the situation involved in this psalm. For the opposition is very strong and the danger still very acute; the issues have in no sense been settled. A major battle is about to be fought.

Interpreters who are ready to concede this as well as those who reject the authorship of David find it difficult to understand that there is no more specific allusion to the situation here involved, least of all any direct references to Absalom, the instigator of it all. Here thoughts such as *Hengstenberg* develops at length are in place. For it must be remembered that a feature commonly found in the psalms is that they strip off those elements which would be highly individualistic and would apply only to the author in his peculiar predicament but retain such items as could be of moment to any man who might find himself in a similar situation. This mode of writing may well be attributed, on the one hand, to the didactic purposes which authors like David may consciously have carried through; and on the other hand, it may be thought of as having been carefully directed by the Spirit of inspiration, who taught men what could be of moment for the church of God of all times, and so gave them much needed guidance.

A Bible student who probes more deeply into the problems here involved may well recall that the position in which David finds himself may have called for at least some reference to his own guilt and sin. For it is unquestionable that, according to II Sam. 12:10, the whole train of evil consequences that befell his house had been set in motion by his own sin in the matter of Bathsheba and Uriah, the Hittite. If, then, David's own sin is the primary cause of all these calamities, how can this king take so cheerful an attitude and ignore the whole matter? Apparently the answer is that other psalms had adequately portrayed what David did in the question of getting into the clear with his God. For in historical sequence psalms such as 51 and 32 must have preceded the one before us. Only on the assumption that the king had sought the face of his God in true repentance and received the full assurance of forgiveness can he again be confident of the grace of his God. These are such obvious presuppositions, because every Christian knows that the full assurance of faith that finds such exemplary expression in this psalm is impossible except in the case of those whose sins have been pardoned by the grace of God. *Oesterley* remarks "that for the expression of sublime trust in God this psalm is not surpassed in the Psalter."

1. *O Lord, how many have my foes become!*
   There are many that rise up against me.
2. *There are many that say of me,*
   There is no help for him in God. **Selah.**

1. As we shall presently show (v. 5), this psalm was written to describe the situation of the author on the morning of a given day, just after he had risen. The whole unhappy grief rushes with fresh impact upon his soul the moment he rises. What could have been a dismal complaint becomes a trusting prayer the moment all is laid before the Lord. Perhaps the chief element of David's distress was the fact that of a sudden his foes had multiplied so enormously. Three times we have in Hebrew the root "many." First of all, these persons are described as "foes," which means in the original men who cause him distress by crowding him into a narrow place. Then they are referred to as men that "rise up against" him. For it was obviously a rebellion that had been staged; and, no matter who a man is, he always feels keenly when opposition is encountered. This is all the more the case when such opposition is causeless.

2. Since the first two instances of the use of the term "many" referred to enemies, it seems imperative to let the third "many" refer to enemies also. These men speak words that are calculated to wound him in his inmost being, that is, in his very "soul." For so the Hebrew expresses it, though our English idiom would prefer, "They say *of me.*"

What they say is enough to wound any man, especially one of finer

Psalm 3

spiritual sensibilities: "Nothing of help for him in God" (so more literally). The assumption is that all men are agreed that David has himself done things whereby he forfeited the right to expect help of God, and so God will not consider his petitions. David attempts no defense in self-justification. He has gotten into the clear with his God and so is not unduly disturbed by what men may say of him. By the way, the participle "saying" here suggests: They keep on making this assertion. "God" is used rather than "Yahweh" because help in the most general sense is thought of.

The "Selah" occurring here for the first time in the psalms may be rendered "forte" after the example of *Koenig's Commentary*. Practically all modern writers on the subject are agreed that this "is indeed first of all a musical notation" (*Hengstenberg*). But most of them concede also that it is inserted at those points where a pause is desirable for the singer or the reader of the psalm in order that the statement last made or the thought as a whole just developed may be reflected upon before the next turn of the thought appears. As musical term, it may have one of several meanings, none of which can be determined with absolute certainty. Our view of the term suggest that it marks the place where the orchestra or the musical accompaniment should set in more loudly. So it might be said to mark a musical interlude or even also the point where a chorus makes a repetition.

3. *But Thou, O Lord, art a shield about me,*
   The source of my glory and He that lifts up my head.
4. *Loudly did I cry unto the Lord;*
   And He answered me with help from His holy hill. Selah

3. The note of confidence now comes to the fore in the psalm. Not any of his own resources but what God is and does give the singer strength. Bold enough would be any statement to the effect that the Lord held a shield round about this servant of His. Much bolder is the concept of God Himself as this shield, especially when this shield is "about" him, affording all-sided protection.

More difficult is the interpretation of the expression, which in the original reads: "my glory." This could mean: He in whom I glory. But the statement immediately following speaks of that which God has done for the psalmist. Therefore the word had better be taken to mean, as we have translated above: "the source of my glory"—a metonomy. Whatever glory David had achieved and even, humanly speaking, his fame and reputation were not slight. These the good king attributes solely to his God. Obviously parallel is the expression, "He that lifts up my head." Looking back at the expression just used, this suggests that what is meant is, God is the source of any dignity that belongs to the king. But the expression has a broader meaning. The head drops when a man is discouraged and disappointed. When God lifts up the head He delivers a man from all those things that depress. So often has He done this for David that a kind of title grows out of this expression: the Lifter-up of my head the participle in the original.

4. Continuing his record of the experiences that give him reason for hope, David speaks of another matter that had regularly taken place: He had cried again and again in the past, with a measure of urgency or loudly, and the faithful covenant-Lord had always been wont to hear him. (See note below on the tense involved.) This help had come "from His holy hill." This is the constant viewpoint of the Old Testament saints of the kingdom days or thereafter: since Yahweh was pleased to establish His dwelling place among His people in a central sanctuary, they on their part would speak to Him as being where He had said He would be, and He on His part would answer them from this same place. In all this there were no unworthy conceptions of God and His omnipresence involved. Cf. also Ps. 2:6; 15:1; 43:3; 99:9. In order to indicate more clearly that the "answering" here spoken of is not something merely conversational but an effective answer, we have translated the verb "answered with help."—The Selah invites a pause for reflection.

5. *As for me, I laid me down and slept;*
   I awoke again, for the Lord sustained me.
6. *I am not afraid of ten thousands of people*
   Which have set themselves against me round about.

5. The psalmist is telling how he feared under the present circumstances when he again put his trust in the Lord. Though many, e.g., *Smith,* are still inclined to render v. 5 as describing something habitual in the present, this interpretation does violence to the tense of the Hebrew verbs, which, being perfect, must first be construed as naturally referring to the past unless other considerations compel one to depart from this construction. It seems that some commentators feel they have such weighty considerations when they point to the fact that to say: I laid down, slept, and awoke again, is altogether too prosy and commonplace to be the meaning intended. But rightly construed, the thought involved is anything but ordinary. In fact, this is the high point in faith reached by the psalm. The emphatic "I" at the beginning of the verse begins to give our thoughts the right direction, for it means: In the grave extremity in which I found myself (see vv. 1 and 2) I was, nevertheless, enabled by my God to rest safely and securely in Him, so much so that I had an untroubled slumber in the midst of these grave perils. So this is a historical perfect, whose distinct sense could

have been caught by a translation such as: "As for me (last night) I laid down and slept; (this morning) I awoke again" This experience is, however, in no sense set down as a personal achievement of this individual, for he plainly ascribes it to his God: "for Yahweh sustained me," that is, the God of covenant grace, whose mercies are new unto His own every morning.

6. This verse is to be read almost in one breath with the preceding; it represents David's feelings the moment he awoke and recalled the huge multitude of his foes as v. lf. said he did. If the conclusion of v. 5 had not read as it did, v. 6 would be idle boasting, cheap heroics. But as it is, having been furnished with courage by his Lord, the author now faces the dangers of the day, knowing full well that there are "ten thousands of people, who have set themselves round about." The numeral is really more vague than our translation indicates, for it may equally well be rendered "myriads." It is the boldness of true faith that speaks here. This is an utterance like unto a goodly number of others that date from David and are spoken in moments when his faith was nothing less than truly heroic. The tense has obviously changed from v. 5, although the two verses are to be regarded as having been spoken in the morning after David rose. In brief he says: I slept calmly through the night; now I am not afraid of the terrors that this new day brings.

Some interpreters note that the strophe ends without the "Selah" that marked the conclusion of the two preceding verses. This omission can scarcely have been an oversight. *Delitzsch* has best explained the case: (the Selah) "is wanting because the clause 'I am not afraid' is not spoken in a tone of triumph but is only a humble, quiet expression of believing confidence." A Selah here would have savored of proud boastfulness.

7. *Arise, O Lord; help me, O my God.*
For Thou hast always smitten all my enemies upon the cheek,
Always broken the teeth of the wicked.
8. *Help belongs to the Lord;*
Upon Thy people be Thy blessing. Selah.

7. This bold summons "arise" is common enough in the psalms (Ps. 7:6; 9:19; 10:12; 17:13; 74:22) and is obviously derived from the old prayer that Moses was wont to use (see Num. 10:35) when the ark of the covenant was taken up to lead the children on Israel on their march to the Land of Promise and against their many foes. Since the present rebellion is against the established theocracy and thus is tainted by the spirit of heathenism, the same summons is quite in place. David, knowing full well that his cause is that of the theocracy

under the present circumstances, implores God's intervention on his own behalf: "help me, O my God." The Lord is appealed to in both capacities, as Yahweh and as God, for the king has natural as well as covenant claims upon the Most High.

As a motive for the appeal to God to help him is the psalmist's reminder that He has always in the past up to this very present (so the perfect is here used, cf., *K.S.* 125) been wont to shatter the power of the adversary. Only that person could venture to speak thus who was entirely sure of the fact that he and his cause are the Lord's, and that, on the other hand, the cause of the enemy is beyond question that of the forces that are openly hostile to Yahweh. Because the enemies were of that category they are likened to ravenous wild beasts. Their overthrow is like a breaking of their teeth by a blow of the Almighty. Smiting on the cheek has always and everywhere been regarded as the height of insulting treatment; cf., I Kings 22:24; Job 16:10; Lam. 3:30; Mic. 5:1. This touch of the figure treats the enemies as men whom the Lord openly disavows with every show of indignity. Since David's earlier experiences (cf., I Sam. 17:34) had suggested the likeness of the wicked to ravenous beasts, carrying this figure through to its natural conclusion, the breaking of their teeth would display how such persons will be rendered utterly harmless by a stroke of the Almighty. This word involves a prophecy as to how the present uprising will terminate.

8. At the conclusion of a psalm there very frequently is found a substantial statement which supplies a weighty conclusion. Here we have the clause, "Help is Yahweh's." The word order puts Yahweh first, as much as to say: With Yahweh alone are deposited all resources of help, and how they shall be bestowed rests exclusively with Him. But equally significant is the second half of the verse, which is a prayer of this godly monarch in behalf of his people, who are being sadly confused and harmed by the rebellion the king's son has instigated. Selfish concerns do not blot out the true and faithful king's sense of responsibility although he later erred somewhat in this respect (cf. especially II Sam. 19). Only God's blessing can cancel the disastrous harm that may result to Israel from the threatening disorders.

NOTES

1. The participles *qamîm* and *'omerîm* (v. 3) are, of course, durative (men are continuing to rise up on every hand, and they keep reaffirming) and are the equivalent of relative clauses (cf., *Driver,* Par. 135).

2. The noun *yeshu'athah* here has an old case ending (*thah*) which

has lost all significance but still gives a sort of venerable dignity to the word when it is used, being an archaism. *Selah* can well be derived from the root *salal,* 'to raise'; Imv. *sal,* deflected to *sel* when *ah* is added.

3. The *we* in *we'attah* is adversative, and the pronoun is emphatic. *Merîm* is *Hifil* participle from *rum.*

4. If it seems strange that we translate *'eqra',* an imperfect, "I did cry," it should be noted that the verb following, being a converted imperfect, marks the whole statement as lying in the past. Consequently *'eqra'* expresses continued or oft-repeated action in past time (*K.S.* 157).

Har qodhshô, though literally translated 'hill of His holiness,' must, like all kindred expressions, mean nothing other than "His holy hill."

6. The verb *shatû,* though almost universally translated as a reflexive, 'they have set themselves,' had, perhaps, better be regarded, with *Hengstenberg,* as a plural verb with an indefinite subject, making it equivalent to the passive, and translated 'whom men have set against me round about.' Though Is. 22:7 is cited as a parallel, it would appear that this passage can be construed after the same manner.

7. *Qûmah* is an imperative hortative, the hortative ending *ah* often being added to the imperative.

The attempts to correct the standard Hebrew text are, as usual, based upon critical opinions, upon the versions, and upon conjecture. The fact that the *Septuagint* renders v. 2: "hope for him in his God" scarcely seems significant enough to regard this reading as the original. It might be one more of the instances where the Septuagint translated inaccurately. The same is true in regard to v. 3, where, instead of "the lifter up," the Septuagint has ἀντιλήμπτωρ, that is to say, He who receives me.

Buttenwieser states that such exultant trust as this psalm manifests was "the fruit of the preaching of the prophets." Since he assigns a late date to the prophets he concludes that this psalm must be of a late date. All the evidence regarding the correspondence of the contents of the psalm with a situation in David's life is brushed aside as nonexistent. This may be called shutting one's eyes to facts that one does not care to consider.

Psalm 4

AN EVENING HYMN
OF A GODLY MAN IN DISTRESS

THE HEADING of the psalm suggests nothing about the situation that gave occasion for it. So, too, the contents of the psalm reveal little along this line. Yet there are enough significant points of contact between this psalm and the one that precedes to give warrant for the supposition that the condition in which David found himself is the same in both psalms. Note: "Many there are that say" (3:2; 4:6); the division of the psalm by Selahs; "my glory" (3:3; 4:2); "I cry, and He answers" (3:4; 4:1); "I laid me down and slept" (3:5; 4:8). Nothing in Ps. 4 indicates the high position of its author except the superscription itself. In v. 3 there are clear indications of the author's rank and station. To refer the psalm to the days when David fled before Absalom certainly fits the words of the psalm in a number of striking ways: the author is obviously in distress; his honor is assailed; he seeks to set his erring son and those that err with him aright; a paternal type of admonition is used such as David might well have used over against the rebel son; and lastly, the author manifests a courageous faith such as is often noted in the life of David.

Particular attention should be given at the very outset to the calm expostulation that the writer uses over against those that are hostile to him. This feature of the psalm is rather unusual. Throughout this part of the psalm the tone is one of wise and considerate restraint. If enemies could be reasoned with, this kind of reasoning ought to win them.

The following line of thought runs through the psalm. First an urgent plea for help is uttered. Then follows the remonstrance addressed to the foes (vv. 2-5). This portion begins with a warning to desist from iniquity against the psalmist, for Yahweh is wont to set apart godly men as the objects of His particular care (v. 2f.). Then these evildoers are exhorted to reflect upon their state and to offer proper sacrifices (v. 4f.). The last part of the psalm is an expression of security in Yahweh, addressed first of all to those who have grown hopeless because of the present confusion (v. 6f.) and then voicing the psalmist's own confidence in the very present help of his God.

Psalm 4   67

1. *When I call, answer me, O my righteous God.*
   Whenever I was in distress, Thou didst always set me free.
   Be gracious unto me and hear my prayer.

1. Men speak thus when they are in great anxiety and trouble, and when it seems as though God were not lending an ear and were not going to answer prayer. Petitions seem to bound back from heaven. As a fulcrum to gain leverage for his prayer the psalmist voices his conviction that his God is his "righteous God." The adjective implies that He is a faithful God who can be depended upon. All the experience of the author's past confirms this thought. The author's confession of this conviction is an argument that he brings to bear upon God: God's own well-known attitude toward His saints.

The next line expresses the same thought at greater length: "Whenever I was in distress, Thou hast always set me free." The last verb is also translated "set me at large" (*A.R.V.*), the idea being that he had been pressed into a tight place; that now the confining influence has been removed, and he has ample room: he is "set free." Again the note of petition is struck in a double plea: "Be gracious unto me and hear my prayer." This is not an asking that is based on conscious merit or desert but wholly on the free grace of the Giver. So clear in their thinking were God's saints of the Old Covenant that it was not by works of righteousness which they had done that they could expect a hearing from God. This first verse is still permeated by the note of anxiety.

2. *You brave men, why should my glory be turned into dishonor?*
   Why do ye love sham?
   Why do ye seek out lies? Selah.
3. *Know, furthermore, that God has always set apart for Himself*
   a godly man.
   The Lord will also now hear me when I call unto Him.

2. This address to the foes of the psalmist begins with an expression that can be literally translated, "O ye sons of men." But the Hebrew word for "men" here used implies brave men as it does in I Sam. 4:9; 26:15; cf. also Ps. 49:3. Here the expression appears to be used a bit ironically: they may be brave enough, but their bravery is showing itself in bearing down hard on an unfortunate foe; their deeds, to say the least, are not very brave deeds. The author's charge against them in particular is first of all that they are turning his glory into shame. Only a man who is conscious of his innocence could dare to raise an issue of this sort. Slanderous devices are being resorted to

in order to make an honest man appear dishonorable. II Sam. 15:2ff. gives an example of the methods that had been employed.

The trouble lies deeper; it is a character defect that leads to this sin of defamation. These men "love sham," and, therefore, they can so freely advance hollow and empty charges against an innocent man. The second question drives this barb of truth into the conscience of the opposition. The third remonstrance calls to their attention the fact that they industriously "seek out" and fabricate the very "lies" that they utter against the man whom they oppose. Their whole venture is thus described as being built on falsehood. Positive as all this is, the author, nevertheless, states his case against the opposition with considerate kindness. He appears to be trying to win men from the error of their way. The *Selah* or "forte" that follows here does not appear so much to mark a division of strophes, as is so frequently the case, but a pause in the development of the thought that would allow his warning to sink home.

3. The "furthermore," which we have used as a translation of the simple Hebrew *waw,* goes on the assumption that there is in v. 2 a veiled exhortation. The exhortation continues with express words in our verse. It amounts to this, that those who are thus manifestly wronging a man are thus sinning against the Lord, who obviously has always set apart as in a class by himself and as deserving special care and attention any and every man who honestly deserves to be called "godly." As in the sight of God, who loves the truth and hates the lie, the author obviously classes himself among men whom God puts into this class. To say "know, therefore," means: I am calling to your attention a solemn truth. He then draws another conclusion from the position that he occupies. "Yahweh will hear me now." The "now" is not found in the original. But it serves to show the connection of thought that is implied in the original, as much as to say: If I, therefore, now present my cause before my God, He will hear me, which is a favor that you cannot in good conscience expect from the Most High.

4. *Tremble and sin not;*
   Speak with your hearts upon your bed and be still. Selah.
5. *Bring true sacrifices and trust in Yahweh.*

4. The first verb means "to tremble" or "to fear." "Stand in awe" is also a good rendering in that it implies that a wholesome fear of God should take possession of these men: let them learn to stand in awe of Him. Such true reverence will naturally compel those who have it to depart from any sin that they may be contemplating. This

Psalm 4

conveys the thought: All the wicked devices that you harbor should be abandoned, for God is against you in all of them. It must be admitted that the warning is put very calmly and without a trace of the heat of passion.

What about the more familiar rendering: "Be ye angry and sin not," especially since this has the apparent support of the New Testament (Eph. 4:26)? This is the translation of the verse given in the Greek version. Must we, then, translate the word in a sense which it could well have "tremble with rage"? Not necessarily. For the thought that Paul desired to express about being righteously indignant against wrong without being carnally angry he happened to find in the familiar Greek version and used this handy form of words. His use of it, however, does not in itself answer the question whether this is a correct rendering of the verb *raghaz*. In fact, why should evildoers, whose entire course of conduct is reprehensible, be admonished to display righteous indignation? But they may very aptly be reminded that it behooves them to stand in fear of God and to avoid all wrongdoing.

That is the first part of the admonition, which then continues to advise them to practice a bit of introspection and "speak" with their own "hearts upon their bed and be still." Addressing some wholesome warnings like this to their own hearts in the quiet of the night hour as they lie upon their bed, and the stillness of the night invites reflection, might well make them "be still." The turmoil of their unwholesomely agitated thoughts might cease, and they might begin to feel the wrong of their whole procedure. The Selah appropriately marks the place for a pause and reflection as do the words themselves.

5. Their outward conduct also should be made right. For the whole venture that Absalom had inaugurated had been launched under the auspices of a solemn sacrifice. The holiest rite had been debased by making of it a cloak of maliciousness. One's blood boils at the thought of the treachery that had been involved. Such iniquity could not go on. That basic piece of hypocrisy had to be disavowed. David's plea to make such a disavowal is found in the words "bring true sacrifices," in the sense: substitute for your unholy act a sacrifice brought in a spirit without guile and for the purpose of expressing your own contrition for your wrongdoing. Only when men are motivated by such a spirit dare they "trust in Yahweh" and feel assured that His favor rests upon their enterprise. Again the admonition was conveyed graciously but withal in such a manner as to strike at the root of the wrong that was to be righted.

6. *Many are they who keep saying: Who will help us to find some good?*
   (But I say) *Lift up upon us the light of Thy countenance, O Lord.*
7. *Thou hast always been wont to put joy into my heart,*
   More than these people have when their grain and wine abound.

6. In the course of his prayer the psalmist has now recovered his godly assurance; he speaks in a note of true confidence which rests in the Lord. His words are addressed, first of all, to the disheartened among his followers who keep reiterating their pessimistic conviction that things are never going to turn out right. For when they say: "Who will help us to find some good?" they intend to say, No one can ever bring this present sorry mess into any semblance of order. They voice their despair of God's ability to stem the tide of the evil that is abroad. Unfortunately, those who are thus minded are "many," and equally tragic is the fact that they "keep saying" this (durative participle *'omerîm*). Over against these halfhearted supporters of his cause the psalmist must take a definite stand.

He does this in the prayer that he utters in their hearing. For the words that follow their complaint are to be taken in an adversative sense. For this reason we inserted the explanatory, "But I say." Dramatically the psalm omits everything that might have introduced his prayer as set over against the despairing utterance of his timid friends.

His prayer is an allusion to Num. 6:26. He asks to be blessed with the blessing that God has commanded to be pronounced upon His people. He can be sure that He is praying according to the will of God. "Lift up upon us the light of Thy countenance" means: Let us bask in the sunshine of Thy favor; let Thy kindliness be directed toward us. No more is needed, for as long as one can be sure of the favor of the Almighty, all things else can be borne until the time when it pleases Him to set men free from their distress. Put still more briefly:
If God be for me, who or what can be against me? This trait of the character of God is embodied in the divine name used—"Yahweh."

7. The joy that grows out of this assurance of God's favor leads the author to reflect upon the many other kindred instances where the Lord has let him experience this same joy: "Thou hast always been wont to put joy into my heart," again the perfect tense that expresses the customary experience of the past (*nathatta*). This joy he contrasts with the joy that his enemies have when they experience the highest joy of which they are capable—the joy because of an abundance of food and drink.

The mode of statement of the case is so very elliptical, as *Perowne* pointed out, that the Hebrew omits three things: the adjective "more"; the noun "gladness"; the relative adverb "when." Inserting all these, which are definitely implied, We get the thought: "More than these people have when their grain and wine abound." We used the subject "these people" because the pronominal suffix (*"their* grain," etc.) actually referred to the psalmist's enemies; and English usage hardly warrants the use of pronouns with antecedents that are so entirely vague. A historical background of this statement of the case may be the fact that David and his men stood in need of provisions (II Sam. 16:1ff.) whereas the enemy appeared to have seized all the stores they needed. The reference to grain at this point hardly allows for the supposition that there had been a failure of harvest, which had disappointed many but not the psalmist.

> 8. *And so in peace I will both lie down and sleep,*
> *For Thou, Yahweh, alone art He who will make me to*
> *abide in safety.*

8. Here, as so often, the Hebrew does not employ the transition of words, which are implied in the connection. We have inserted them: "and so." Because of the assurance that David has again gained from his God's merciful care he makes bold to say that he shall go to sleep calmly and unafraid. His reason, as expressed, is that Yahweh alone is the one who can grant a man such a sense of security. So the psalm comes to a close on a high level of faith. The mood has undergone a decided change from the cry of distress which was uttered in the first verse. This verse, like v. 5 of the preceding psalm, is nothing short of heroic in its childlike confidence in the Lord.

NOTES

1. Though many translators prefer the rendering, "God of my righteousness," and though this seems a stronger translation than the one we offer, "my righteous God," nevertheless, the latter is the usual meaning to be given a phrase such as this even as "Thy holy hill" in the original usually reads "the hill of Thy holiness." This means: since He has done the right thing for the author, therefore He has always proved Himself dependable or faithful. This is our interpretation above.

The heading of this psalm reads thus: "To the Director, upon stringed instruments; a psalm of David." The word "to the Director" is *lamenatsé (a) ch*. Though recent efforts have sought to cast doubt upon this meaning and to substitute for it the idea that psalms of this sort are to be thought of as "the means of propitiating God by sacred song and instrumental music" (*Oesterley, A Fresh Approach to the Psalms*, p. 78), such an interpretation contains a thought that is not in harmony with the truth of Scriptures. The Old Testament nowhere else presents propitiation as being wrought by song and music. Besides, the meaning noted above is quite in keeping with the etymology of the word. *Natsach* means "be pre-eminent, enduring" (*BDB*); in the Piel the meaning "act as overseer, superintendent, director" is accepted by *BDB* and *KW*. The *A.V.* intended to convey about the same idea by its rendering "to the Chief Musician." Luther, who indeed wavered in regard to the meaning of this word, finally offered a different interpretation by his *vorzusingen,* by which he may have meant "to sing publicly" or "to lead in the singing" (cf. the German *Vorsaenger*). This latter meaning would have been very close to our accepted English translation, "Chief Musician" or "Director." The uncertainty of the versions in regard to the meaning of the term merely indicates that it has its difficulties, which we are free to admit.

Hirchábtha is one of those perfects which may be called the equivalent of a gnomic aorist, that is, a perfect form that expresses what is found to be habitual practice. Therefore such forms are best translated with an "always" or the like, thus: "Thou hast always set me free."

Chonnéni, "be gracious," or, as it is sometimes rendered, "have mercy," suggests "the free bestowal of favor rather than the exercise of forgiving clemency" (*Kirkpatrick*). Consequently the word does not imply the forgiveness of sins.

2. The expression '*adh meh,* though usually rendered, "how long?" is more naturally translated in all instances where it occurs as: "to what end?" or "why?"

3. Luther took quite a different view of this verse in his familiar rendering: *Erkennet doch, dass der Herr seine Heiligen wunderbar fuehrt* (Know, I pray, that the Lord leads His saints in a marvelous manner). He arrives at this translation by taking the verb to come from the root *pala*' rather than from the root *palah.* Though the two classes of verbs involved often exchange forms, there is no particular indication that such is the case here. This part of the verse means that God has always set godly men apart for Himself as the objects of His particular care. That is a thought to hold over against an ungodly opposition so that their enmity might feel restrained from doing harm to such saints. *Luther's* thought, good as it is in itself, and a possible translation, would be more suitable as a word of comfort addressed to the godly man himself.

Chasidh, "a godly man" is a term that has been much discussed as to whether it means "one who shows mercy" or "one who receives mercy" (*Chasîdh* being of the same root as *chésedh,* "mercy"). Apparently the former meaning deserves the preference; and so the term means "the pious or godly one."

6. The verb *nesah*, spelled with *samekh*, is here apparently used for the form written with *sin* and so is the regular verb for "lift up."
8. The word *yachdaw*, when used with an "and," has the meaning "both . . . and" (see *K.S.* 375 h for a goodly number of examples).

CRITICAL ISSUES

Textual changes are proposed in v. 1, largely as a result of attempts to remove the sequence of a request followed by a historical statement, i.e., imperative followed by perfect. But since the text as it stands makes perfectly good sense, such changes are unnecessary. In fact, the proposed changes make a lively cry for help a tame historical report.

In v. 2 the lead of the *Septuagint* is followed by some interpreters who alter "glory" and what follows into "hardhearted" by a slight consonantal change. But the text as it stands in the Hebrew makes fully as good sense as does the meaning that the Greek translators extracted from it.

In v. 3 an alteration of the text is suggested which results in the meaning: God has made His kindness marvelous toward me. Though that would fit smoothly into the context, it cannot be denied that as the text stands the sequence of thought involved is also very good.

As *Kittel's* footnotes indicate, all these textual emendations are suggested as possibilities or probabilities, and in no case do they offer any decided advantage of interpretation.

Psalm 5

PRAYER FOR GUIDANCE
AND FOR THE OVERTHROW OF THE UNGODLY

We have no indication whatsover as to any particular occasion which may have caused the composition of this psalm. Its tone is intentionally general, as it would seem, in order to make it serviceable for all manner of occasions. The heading merely indicates that the psalm is to be put into the hands of "the Director" (on this term see the heading of Ps. 4), and is a psalm of David (nothing in the text is in conflict with this claim of authorship) and lastly is to be rendered "according (to the tune of) 'the inheritances.'" Though this last term is most commonly understood to refer to some tune that was familiar in the music of David's day, another interpretation offered in this connection dare not be brushed aside lightly. This interpretation points to the other possible translation of the word *hannechîlôth,* namely, "the lots." With this meaning in mind, we might regard the term as an indication in a meaningful sort of way of the substance of the psalm, which does, indeed, contrast the distinctive lot of the godly with that of the ungodly. It must, however, be admitted that there is too little material available on these headings of the psalms to allow us to arrive at results of interpretation that are entirely incontrovertible.

The general tone of this psalm is much like that of the two that preceded it. It may be classified as the lament of an individual. The meter is largely the *qinah* measure, $3+2$.

In line with the general tone of the psalm, which we have just indicated, is the complete absence of any statement of the personal trouble that the author may have experienced at the time he was writing. Since the personal note is absent from this poem, and, in fact, in the last two verses the reference to godly men in general disregards the thought of an individual case, we are quite in harmony with those interpreters who suggest that this is a psalm that was designed rather for congregational than for personal use. In other words, thus the church might well pray at all times though the use of the psalm by the individual need not be excluded.

As to the general classification of this psalm, we soon note that it belongs to those psalms that voice a deep sense of the need of moral integrity in the sight of God. A tone of moral earnestness prevails throughout.

If this leads among other things to a prayer against the ungodly that they may be put out of the way, the critical spirit should not pass judgment upon this part of the prayer, as is so commonly done, as though such a prayer must needs always be spoken in a tone of vindictiveness, or as though some unholy emotions must motivate the man who prays thus. Commentators ought rather to catch the spirit of Old Testament writers generally on this subject, namely, the spirit which feels God's will in this matter very keenly and prays that God may act in conformity with His holy will. Indeed, there can be no doubt about it that it is the good and perfect will of God utterly to overthrow the stubbornly impenitent; and it was just this latter class of men against whom prayers of this sort are directed.

The outline of this psalm is as follows: it first expresses a plea to be heard (vv. 1, 2); it then gives expression to the general principle that is involved, the clear principle that the wicked may not abide in the presence of God, but God's true children may come into His presence (vv. 3–7); then follows the prayer based on this principle, which prayer

Psalm 5

petitions: Guide me but condemn the manifestly wicked—a result because of which all godly men will rejoice (vv. 8–12).

Prayers of this kind may have more value than our age is inclined to admit. They are surely born out of a deep sense of the sinfulness of sin and out of the conviction that the only one who can stem the tide of sin is the Almighty. Viewed thus, these psalms that are prayers against wickedness and the wicked may, indeed, be prayed with great profit, at least by the true children of God. These are psalms that express what the Lord Jesus Himself taught us to pray: "Thy will be done on earth as it is in heaven," which includes that "God break and hinder every evil counsel and will."

a) A plea to be heard (vv. 1–2)
1. *Hear my words, O Lord;*
   Consider my sighing.
2. *Hearken unto the voice of my cry, my King and my God,*
   For unto Thee do I present my prayer.

1. This initial plea is marked by a certain urgency, which is in the spirit of the reminder that "the effectual fervent prayer of the righteous man availeth much." We have "hear," "consider," and "hearken." The prayer is first described in general as "words" (a poetic word reserved for special prayers like these) and "sighing," to describe how it issues from the deep feeling of the heart; and also as "the voice of my cry," to remind that help is eagerly sought. The word *shaw'i* means basically "cry for help." If, as seems to be the case, it is Israel's king offering up this prayer, there is a fine confession in the fact that he calls the Lord his "king," for he acknowledges that Yahweh is the true King of kings. But higher is the title which follows: "my God." So men speak who stand in a personal relation to God. For all such, *i.e.*, for the church, is this prayer designed. The only plea added as to why this prayer should be heard is the simple statement: "For unto Thee do I present my prayer." The mere fact that God's children have the confidence which moves them to present their prayer to their God is thought of as a plea that carries weight with God. If men trust Him enough to cry unto Him, that will please the Almighty so much as to make Him inclined to hear their petition.

b) The wicked may not abide in the presence of God, but God's true children may abide (vv. 3–7)

3. *O Lord, as soon as morning comes, do Thou hear*
   my voice;
   As soon as morning comes, I shall set (my prayer) in order
   for Thee and keep watch.

3. The author intimates that he is going to offer up his prayer promptly in the morning. This ties in with the preceding statement that he purposed to "present his prayer." It is true that the original says no more than "in the morning" (*bóqer*), beginning the two successive clauses with this adverbial accusative. But in this connection this means what we have tried to capture by the use of the explanatory clause, "as soon as the morning comes." We do not believe that the expression here used indicates, as so many assume at this point, that this is a morning prayer as such. In this prayer the author merely asserts that day by day he purposes to lose no time in offering his petitions to the Lord, his God; as soon as the dawn breaks, his own first task shall be to offer up his prayers. Cf., Ps. 59:17; 88:14; 92:3; 55:18. The word used to express this thought ("set in order") is borrowed from the terminology of sacrifice, having as its object such things as the wood of offerings or the offerings themselves. The psalmist expresses the thought that what he is presenting is also a sacrifice though it is the "offering of the lips." Cf. also Job 32:14: "words" as the object of the verb. We have felt free, therefore, to add the object that is implied: "my prayer." At the same time the author intends to "keep watch," that is to say, look up unto the Lord, His God, until the help desired by him comes. In manifold ways God gives tokens to His own that He has heard their cry if they would but keep watch or look out for them. A kindred thought is found in Mic. 7:7.

4. *For Thou art not a God that is pleased with wickedness, not Thou;*
Neither may an evil man sojourn with Thee.
5. *Boasters may not take their place in Thy sight;*
Thou hatest all workers of iniquity.
6. *Thou wilt destroy all them that speak lies;*
The Lord will abhor the man of blood and deceit.

4. Now begins the statement of the principle involved. It is stated negatively at first: God is opposed to all those that do evil. No wicked man may dare to hope to keep company with Him, for He takes no pleasure in wickedness. This is a mild litotes, that God takes no pleasure in wickedness, but it becomes stronger at the end of the verse, where the "Thou" stands out—an arrangement which results in a thought that is somewhat like the one we have reproduced by the "not Thou." Should any one, therefore, nevertheless presume to seek the company of the Almighty he would be promptly thrust out.

5. The manifold terms that are used to describe wicked men simply add up to this, that no form of evil may dwell with the Lord. He abhors wickedness in all its ramifications. The verbs used grow increasingly

Psalm 5

stronger in expressing God's aversion as this is innate in His very nature: from "sojourn" to "take their place in Thy sight" to "hate" to "destroy" in an ascending climax. After He has destroyed them He will turn away from them as from a thing that is to be utterly abhorred.

6. The culmination of the evil persons is reached in those who are men "of blood and deceit." A "man of blood" is not necessarily a bloodthirsty man but rather one who is spotted with the blood of those whom he has slain.

It must be noted that all the thoughts that are expressed in reference to the wicked are not as yet prayers spoken against them but primarily expression of confidence that the Lord will deal with all such after a given pattern, and that one and the same lot awaits them all. This fact has led us to draw attention repeatedly to the principle that is here being set forth.

7. *But as for me, I may come into Thy house because
of the greatness of Thy mercy;
I may worship toward Thy holy temple in awe of Thee.*

7. The psalmist (note the emphatic "as for me") contrasts himself with those whom he has just described as being immersed in evil and addicted to it. Because he is conscious of being opposed to evil in every form and of being in the company of those who have a good conscience in the sight of the Lord he knows that God is minded differently toward him. Yet he does not base this different attitude of God toward him on any merit of his own. He distinctly sets forth his exclusive reason for hope in the words "because of the greatness of Thy mercy." In the presence of God men of God have always taken their stand on His mercy. There is no other adequate reason for hope. In that respect this man is utterly different from those whom he has just described. Much more is involved in the expression "I may come into Thy house" than merely making bold to step into the Temple building at Jerusalem. For that would be a matter that is purely external in character. The higher privilege is under consideration, that of venturing into the personal presence of God in true fellowship, be it in thought or in prayer. Since this privilege is under consideration, it is better to translate as we have, "I may come," rather than, "I shall come" (A.R.V.); likewise, "I may worship."

This understanding of the verse disposes of a difficulty that some interpreters have in that they feel that the buildings referred to had not yet been erected in the days of David, and, therefore, that the words "Thy house" and "Thy holy temple" conflict with the claim made by the heading that this is a psalm of David. But since the heavenly abode is primarily under consideration, this objection is invalid. Even if the holy edifice in Jerusalem had been referred to, the words here used would not have been inappropriate, though we well know that the Ark of the Covenant was still housed in a tent (II Sam.7:2). For men would involuntarily think of the high and holy habitation of the Lord and use terms descriptive of its greater dignity. Even *Kessler* says: "Only he who will not allow for any freedom of expression in poetry would draw conclusions against Davidic authorship from the fact that words such as *báyith* (house) and *heykhal* (palace) are here used, and emphasize that in David's day the sanctuary was still an *'ohel* (tent)."

Besides, it can be amply demonstrated that the expression "house of the Lord" is used with reference to the ancient Tabernacle; see Exod. 23:19; Deut. 23:18; Josh. 6:24; I Sam. 1:24; 3:15. It is also used with reference to the tent which David pitched for the ark on Mount Zion (II Sam. 12:20). There is good reason for saying, *"toward* Thy holy temple," inasmuch as all worship would very naturally be directed in thought toward the place where God had promised to manifest His presence, so that even a physical turning toward this place came to be customary in the course of time (Dan. 6:10). The expression usually rendered "in Thy fear" means, of course, "in awe of Thee," the suffix in the original being the equivalent of an objective genetive.

c) **A prayer for guidance, and condemnation of the wicked (vv. 8–12)**

8. *O Lord, lead me in Thy righteousness because of them that lie in wait for me;*
Make level the way that Thou leadest me.

8. The arrangement of the thoughts is chiastic. In the first section of the psalm the wicked were described first, then the righteous man was referred to. Here the prayer of the righteous man comes first. In fact, he appeals to Yahweh, the faithful covenant God, because he knows that he stands in a covenant relationship with Him. To be led "in Thy righteousness" means according to that faithfulness which has always prompted Him to do that which is right and just toward those who have proved faithful to Him. Were God to fail such a man, this failure would give occasion "to them that lie in wait" for him to resort to mockery of him and blasphemy of God.

A man may well express concern about having so unfortunate a thing happen to him. The expression "make level" may be rendered "make straight," depending on one's viewpoint. The Hebrew says: Make straight before my face Thy way. This must mean what we have indicated above. God's own have this confidence in Him, that they are always being led along a path of God's choosing and not without plan and purpose. But so fully is God in control of every situation that He not only is the one that determines the road that is to be taken but is capable

Psalm 5

also of making that road—life's pathway—level or straight if it would seem that the going is about to be somewhat difficult.

9. *For there is nothing dependable in the mouth of every such a one;*
   Their heart is full of treachery;
   Their throat is an open grave;
   Their tongues (indeed) utter smooth words.
10. *Declare them guilty, O God;*
    Let them fall by their own counsels;
    Because of the multitude of their transgressions thrust them out;
    For they have rebelled against Thee.

9. When an entire psalm is directed against certain evil men, these men must of necessity be very evil, otherwise such an issue could not be made of what they are and do. The psalmist owes us the description that v. 9 gives. We have no reason to doubt the correctness of what he says, for there is no touch of personal enmity manifested anywhere in the psalm. This description then being true, we are practically compelled with *Delitzsch* to contend that there is something Satanic about their sin, and that therefore it is unpardonable. This factor must be evaluated carefully; and to it must be added the further fact that the inspired writer was not giving merely his own personal verdict in the case but was writing unimpeachable truth. Surely, over against such perversity man must take a positive stand.

These are the elements of the description offered: Not a statement issuing from the mouth of these evildoers is "dependable," and they are strangely all alike in this respect; besides, "their heart is full of treachery." How, then, could their mouth utter good things! Expressed in a figure: "their throat is an open grave." As the vilest stench of death issues forth from open graves, so every utterance of theirs is tainted to the highest degree and utterly repulsive. They may usually cover up this fact by making their words smooth and seemingly harmless. But their words are in contrast with the actual sentiment of their hearts. This the Hebrew renders: "They make their tongues smooth."

10. An aggressive prayer follows the description in the preceding words. Since these statements of the Old Testament have not been understood rightly by our age, which is unduly tolerant of evil and has largely forgotten God's righteousness and gratuitously goes on the assumption that these Old Testament men never did a thing to set these evildoers right and never prayed for them, it will be in place to offer the following very sober suggestion of *Maclaren's*: "The vindication of such prayers for the destruction of evil-doers is that they are not the expression of personal enmity ('they have rebelled against Thee') and that they correspond to one side of the divine character and acts, which

was prominent in the Old Testament epoch of revelation, and is not superseded by the New." Since the Old Testament bears such ample testimony to the fact that godly men like David encountered a rare measure of diabolical and unrelenting hostility to Yahweh and to the representatives of His church in those days, and since we see a similar spirit rearing its ugly head in the time of Christ and not resting until it had brought Him to the cross, we had better not flatter ourselves in our day that wickedness is the pale and innocuous thing that men often claim it is.

All of which makes it perfectly obvious that we are not to confuse personal opposition and enmity with stubborn and unrelenting enmity against the Lord and against His Anointed and are to be very careful to what use we put these psalms. The church, however, can and should use them in the spirit of the petition: "Thy will be done on earth as it is in heaven."

"Declare them guilty" is another way of saying, Let them be dealt with as they have so richly merited. No one, except the hardened criminal, would venture to pray thus unless he were sure as to what the divine verdict would ultimately be. The Spirit who inspired this prayer enlightened him that prayed it to see its necessity. Falling "by their own counsels" involves the common Scriptural thought of having divine justice act in such a manner as to let the very evil that had been devised for others fall back upon the originators of it (cf., Ps. 7:15; 9:15; 35:8). The only reason they are to be "thrust out" is that they have been guilty of a "multitude of transgressions"; their sins make a very sizable heap. The chief of all their misdeeds, however, is that they "have rebelled against the Most High." That may well be considered as the Old Testament equivalent of the sin against the Holy Ghost and so substantiates our interpretation as to the spiritual state of the persons described. This whole prayer does not savor a spirit of unkindness but the desire to see necessary divine justice done.

11. *But let all those that take refuge in Thee be glad;*
    Forever may they rejoice, and then Thou wilt protect them;
    Let those exult in Thee that love Thy name.
12. *For Thou wilt bless all righteous ones, O Lord;*
    Thou wilt surround them with favor as with a shield.

11. Here a class of men is under consideration who are as radically different from those just spoken of as they can be. They are given the title "those that take refuge in Thee," and those "that love Thy name," and also "the righteous." These descriptive names indicate how true and close their communion with God is. Prayer is made for them that "they may be glad," that they "may rejoice and exult." This joy will

Psalm 5

scarcely be joy because of the overthrow of the ungodly but rather joy over their own deliverance from all that the ungodly may have designed for their hurt. At the same time we cannot rule out the thought of the true joy and happiness which are always the lot of those who have peace with God. For that reason, too, the prayer is to the effect that such may have this joy "forever," for it is the mark of God's people. But as they thus go on living in the joy which God has put into their hearts, God will add new cause for joy to their lot—"then Thou wilt protect them." So they will go from joy to joy. Those that "love His name" are the ones who delight in that revelation of His character which He has at all times and in all places given of Himself.

12. At the close the psalm broadens out into what might be called a statement of principle, which is here offered as a reason why the righteous may hope that He will hear this prayer. God is a God who always "will bless all righteous ones" or, to use a figure, He will "surround them with favor as with a shield." On this note of confident assurance, which only the righteous have, the psalm closes.

NOTES

1. It is somewhat difficult to render the word for "sighing" correctly, for it means either "murmering" or "musing" and is in somewhat of a contrast with "words" which are spoken aloud. Readers will do well to compare the expression found in Rom. 8:26, "groanings that cannot be uttered."

3. We feel it is quite a bit better to render the imperfect *tishma'* as an optative than as a future, "Thou shalt hear," therefore, "Do Thou hear." The psalmist is not informing God as to what he purposes to do; he is praying.

4. The imperfect *yegurekha* is likewise rather a potential imperfect than a future. For even as v. 7 expresses a privilege that right-minded men exercise, this verse expresses the thought that evil men may not do so. Compare here Ps. 15:1; 61:5; 120:5a.

9. A whole class is being spoken of. Yet when the singular suffix appears in *pîhû,* "*his* mouth," the effect of that singular possessive is distributive. Therefore we translated freely, "in the mouth of every such a one." See *K.S.* 348 u-y.

10. The Hebrew for "let them fall *by* their own counsels" is "*from* their own counsels." But the "from" (*min*) is either the *min* separative or the *min* causal. We believe the latter is the more natural.

11. We also believe that the imperfect *yismechû* fits better into the sequence of thought when it is regarded as a precative rather than as an assertion or prediction. In v. 10 the psalmist prayed in reference to the ungodly; here he prays in reference to the godly.

In *wethasekh* we believe the imperfect, without *waw* conversive, is used to indicate the next step in what is to be expected even as we have translated: "and then Thou wilt protect them." See *K.S.* 364 l.

12. Since *tsaddiq* is used without an article it stresses the quality as such and may, therefore, be translated "all righteous ones."

There is no confusion of the text in vv. 11, 12, calling for a realignment of clauses (*Oesterley*). The text makes very good sense as it stands.

When *Leslie* claims that this "is the prayer of one who has been falsely accused" who then "pays a visit to the Temple in the hope of being decisively vindicated" and further adds, "He has arranged an omen sacrifice," even using this word in his translation of v. 3, we cannot go along with his approach—it is too much of a pressing of a particular presupposition which is not in the text.

CRITICAL ISSUES

V. 3 closes with the words, "and will keep watch." It has been surmised that this must refer to some kind of activity which has to do with divination or prognostication of the future and would then here mean as much as "to watch the entrails for omens." This approach would press the level of the Sacred Scriptures down to the acknowledged level of heathen culture. The Scriptures are very clear as to what is heathen practice and what is not, and, as *Koenig* has well shown, the vocabulary of divination is a vocabulary all its own and does not include this term. Therefore the meaning must be retaining of waiting or watching for a token of God's answer to prayer.

V. 10, it is claimed, gives evidence of an occasional naive self-righteousness of some of old Old Testament saints, who suppose themselves to be above reproach and feel free to ask God to condemn their opponents. But, as the above exposition has shown, the opposition involved is not ordinary opposition, nor is there a smug complacency about the men who venture to come into God's presence merely on the basis "of the greatness of His mercy," v. 7.

In this verse "Elohim" appears as the divine name in a Yahwistic psalm because, according to the meaning of these names, Elohim is the God of judgment.

Psalm 6

A PSALM OF PENITENCE

THIS TITLE is not quite to the point, but the point involved cannot be stated so very briefly. This is really the prayer of a man beset by enemies whose opposition has made him feel God's anger to such an extent that his health was badly impaired.

The psalm may be divided into the following sections, which again can scarcely be designated as strophes, for as *Maclaren* rightly says: It "has four curves or windings, which can scarcely be called strophes without making too artificial a framework for such a simple and spontaneous gush of feeling." We can divide as follows:

a) A plea that God may desist from His rebuke, which plea is motivated by the author's extreme weakness and fear (vv. 1-3a).

b) A further plea for deliverance, motivated by the thought that, only if the author survives, can he praise God (vv. 3b-5).

c) The extremity of the author's grief and its devastating effect (vv. 6-7).

d) Sudden assurance of having been heard makes the psalmist bid all enemies depart and makes him predict their utter defeat (vv. 8-10).

A rather unusual feature of this psalm is that it is truly a psalm of penitence, which, however, strangely does not happen to mention sin.

Enemies are in the picture, men who antagonize the psalmist, and they are evildoers whereas he has a clear conscience over against them. The connection with the idea that this is a psalm of penitence seems to be this: The enmity of the ungodly on this occasion awakens in this man David a sense of his being under the wrath of God. This conviction then weighs so terribly upon his mind that he fails in health and becomes physically much distressed. The physical ailment seems definitely to be the outcome of his spiritual pain.

The rather startling feature about the psalm is the extent of the pain that this godly man feels at being under God's anger. The confession that he makes is mostly one of weakness and utter helplessness unless God pardons his inquity. If a deeper sense of guilt is not expressed in this psalm, there is at least a great measure of grief in evidence over having lost God's favor.

a) A plea that God may desist from His rebuke, which plea is motivated by the author's extreme weakness and fear (vv. 1–3a)
1. O Lord, do not rebuke me in Thine anger;
Do not correct me in Thy wrath.
2. Have mercy upon me, O Lord, for I am weak;
Heal me, O Lord, for my bones are terrified.
3a. In particular, my soul is terrified exceedingly.

1. Translated very literally, the verse would read: "Not in Thine anger rebuke me, etc." That would seem to imply, as not a few interpreters construe it, that the author welcomes correction as long as it is not administered in God's anger. The thought would then be like that voiced in Jer. 10:24f. The author seeks correction in love. Though there is such a thing, the sequence of the thought in the next verses does not suggest love-rebuke vs. anger-rebuke but rather a complete removal of the correction because the correction is an evidence of God's anger. In other words, the negative is not to be taken as modifying the adverbial phrases "in Thine anger" and "in Thy wrath" in the second half of the verse. The negative modifies the whole thought, or more particularly the verbs "rebuke" and "correct."

The correction that God makes of His children is always motivated by His love. But in so far as they are still carnal and controlled by the old Adam, God's anger is manifested against this element of their being, and the correction gets to be a correction in anger. In his distress the author of the psalm feels no indication of his being in a state of grace. He has, in fact, fallen from it and seeks to enter it again. As long as this sense of loss is upon him, just so long must the rebuke of God be felt as anger. So in this instance the plea made involves the plea for a reinstatement into God's grace and so is the equivalent of a free and full confession of sin and utter unworthiness even though these thoughts are not expressed in the customary form.

The second member of the verse marks an advance upon the first. "Rebuke" involves merely an indication that wrong has been done, and that it should not have been done. "Correct" involves positive efforts to set the person in question right. So also "wrath" is more than "anger," being in reality what the *A.V.* has labelled "hot displeasure." The word means "heat" or the "heat of anger."

Both halves of the verse taken together are in reality a plea for forgiveness and a practical admission that the wrong done is of so serious a nature that it must be disposed of, which disposal can be effected only through forgiveness.

2. A noteworthy feature of this confession is that it wisely offers no plea of merit on the part of the writer. He does not seem to be aware

Psalm 6

of the fact that he had anything of merit that God should consider in granting forgiveness. In fact, all thoughts of merit are strictly ruled out in the plea "have mercy upon me." This, added to the request to let "lovingkindness" prevail (v. 4), causes the author to cast himself wholly upon the goodness of his God and shows this Old Testament saint to be a one that understands well the true gospel of pure grace without merit or worthiness on his part.

His plea is reinforced by three considerations that set forth his misery: "I am weak," "my bones are terrified," "my soul is exceedingly terrified." It speaks well for David that he regards his God as one who is moved by even the weakness of His children. More so is He touched when their pain at being under His displeasure mounts to the point where the very bones are terrified. See a parallel expression in Prov. 16:24. Cf. the feelings of the body in Ps. 19:8; 35:10; 84:2. How keen must pain over sin be as it was felt by these Old Testament saints when it must be described as a terror felt in the very bones! Paralyzing fear might be a good commentary on what was felt. All who take sin lightly may well weigh what true children of God have felt when God's Spirit wrought repentance in their heart. The peak of suffering is expressed by, "My soul is terrified exceedingly." This was not a morbid state of mind but a true realization of what a dreadful thing sin is. One can well understand why this psalm struck a responsive note in *Luther's* heart, and why he claimed that it dealt with the "high spiritual temptation," *i.e.,* those temptations in which men wrestle with their God over their soul's salvation and are much concerned whether their God will be merciful to them or not.

The petition "heal me" does not necessarily refer to physical healing but may well include every restorative work that God does upon body and soul.

b) A further plea for deliverance, motivated by the thought that, only if the author survives, can he praise God (vv. 3b–5)

3b. *But as for Thee, O Lord, how long . . . ?*
4. *Return, O Lord, deliver my soul;*
   Save me for Thy lovingkindness' sake.
5. *For in the state of death men do not remember Thee;*
   In the realm of the dead, who will give Thee thanks?

3b. Distress is resting so heavily upon him that the author continues his cry for help. From himself he shifts the thought emphatically to God when he says, "but as for Thee," in Hebrew merely the emphatic personal pronoun with the adversative. More impressive than an utterance is the unfinished statement, an aposiopesis: "How long — — — —?" The thought must obviously be something like: How long wilt Thou remain inactive? or, How long must I suffer thus? Other instances of aposiopesis: Ps. 90:13; 35:25 (margin); 75:6.

4. When the thought continues, "return," the speaker implies that God has gone from him, turned his back upon him, and shunned him (cf., 10:1; Zech. 1:3). The fact that his very existence is at stake is indicated by the plea: "Deliver my *soul*," i. e., My life. The parallel plea is motivated, as it was in v. 2, by an appeal to God's "lovingkindness." Again there is no thought of personal worth that deserves recognition. Such appeals reach into the very depth of God's heart and being. Beyond that there are no depths of appeal that can be reached. But the more extensive motivation for all this is given in a new form in v. 5.

5. The average Bible reader is greatly puzzled by statements like the one found here. It would seem as though the writer of them did not believe in the life after death. Or, on the other hand, the statement might make the impression that the author's praise is highly esteemed in the sight of God. Strangely, there is a measure of truth in each of these views. Both require further elucidation, and these considerations alone do not make the issues entirely clear.

On the one hand it is true that the Old Testament saints did not have that clear revelation of the life after death that the New Testament saints have been granted. They were, however, not left utterly in the dark on the subject. They had some knowledge of a good hereafter ever since Enoch's departure which is recorded in such a significant way in the first book of the Bible (Gen. 5:24). Sometimes the Old Testament Scriptures indicate no more of this existence than that departed spirits enjoyed a great measure of rest in the realm of the hereafter. We cannot always tell, when the weaker utterances under this heading are considered, whether the words spoken, especially in the psalms, are words that were spoken when doubt and despair lay heavily upon men. These passages especially 88:10; 115:17; Is. 38:18 must be used with care when deducing what the normal doctrine in Israel was on this subject. Frankly expressed misgivings are not good bases for proving doctrine (*sedes doctrinae*). It is this latter thought that we would dwell on with special emphasis in considering our verse. It cannot be denied that the soul of the author was deeply afflicted when he wrote this verse. A truth that was but partially revealed seems to have faded momentarily from his view. Even then he does not deny existence in the hereafter. It seems to be such a dim, shadowy existence (cf., 88:12; Job 3:13ff.) that he feels he would not be able there to remember God's goodness and praise Him for it.

In all this there is certainly an element of truth. It cannot be denied that, after the soul has departed and the body has not yet been raised in the general resurrection from the dead, man's salvation is not yet full and perfect. Somehow men of old may have dimly felt some of this truth.

We shall particularly bear in mind that this statement was made in a very trying situation which had caused some of the truth known to recede from consciousness for the moment. From another point of view this statement may be regarded as expressing a very good and substantial thought, such as was characteristic of many of the Old Testament saints. They loved to praise God here on this earth. When death overtook them, they felt that this particular privilege would come to an end. This man pleads that he might not be denied it. None of the godly men of the Old Covenant had advanced to the point of longing to depart and be with the Lord. Their hope was not so strong nor their revelation so clear. To judge them from the standpoint of New Testament revelation does them a grave injustice and ignores the increasing clearness that is to be noted as God's unchanging truth became more and more distinct from age to age.

Lest, however, we leave a wrong impression in regard to the light that had been revealed on this subject in the days of the Old Testament, those clearer passages should also be considered which constitute a valid part of the Old Testament revelation. We refer to Ps. 16:8–11; Is. 26:19; Dan. 12:2, 3. Nor will it do to assign a late date to all these passages because of the dogmatic belief that this doctrine emerged late in the revelation of the Old Covenant. There is ample evidence for considering Ps. 16 Davidic, even as there is for attributing Is. 26 to none other than Isaiah. When speaking, therefore, of the normal faith of the Israelite of days of old, these important statements dare not be ignored.

We shall also not let ourselves think too lightly of the idea that the praises of God's saints are acceptable unto Him. Heb. 13:15 clearly expresses this thought on the New Testament level.

c) The extremity of the author's grief and its devastating effect (vv. 6–7)

6. *I have toiled over my groaning;*
I made my bed, so to say, to swim all night long;
I have practically dissolved my couch with my tears.
7. *My eye is dimmed because of grief;*
It has grown old and weak because of all my foes.

Whereas the preceding plea was centered in Yahweh and based on His mercy, this plea centers in man and his attitude. This is in effect an expression of the thought that the author is deeply pained because of his sins. Surely, it is not a light and trivial repentance which languishes so deeply under the feeling of divine displeasure. Neither is this merely a feeling of wretchedness, which morbidly and selfishly regards only the fact that a feeling of wretchedness is upon one. These tears are wept in the sight of God, they are a part of the earnest prayer unto God. They are then in effect an earnest confession of sin and misery. Not without reason the author believes that God hears men when they cry thus.

6. First of all, the author asserts that his groaning is something over which he has actually "toiled." The other translation "am weary" merely expresses the effect that is produced by such toiling. Obviously employing a hyperbole, he says that his tears have been so numerous that they have all but made his bed to swim all the night long. Few men have taken their sins so seriously. The third statement added to the parallel members of the verse—and such tristichs are not at all uncommon—has a hyperbole that is equally strong when it says: "I have practically dissolved my couch with my tears." We have sought to indicate, after the manner prevalent in our day, that the statements made pass the bounds of literal exactness by adding 6b "so to say" and 6c "practically." It will be observed that our translation adds such touches rather frequently, for what we express in words was supplied in thought by the reader of the original.

7. Since the eye in particular would show the marks of such excessive grief, the author indicates that this has actually come to be the case. The lasting "grief" that is upon him has made his eye lose its luster. In fact, the grief that his foes have caused him has made the eye "become old and weak." We have used a double expression for the single verb in the original because both ideas are implied. Any such plea of grief and wretchedness may well be thought of as rousing the pity of the Almighty, who is not pleased to see His faithful ones who cry unto Him abandoned to their misery.

d) Sudden assurance of having been heard makes the psalmist bid all enemies depart and makes him predict their utter defeat (vv. 8–10)

8. *Depart from me, all ye workers of iniquity;*
For the Lord hath heard the sound of my weeping.
9. *The Lord hath heard my entreaty;*
The Lord hath accepted my prayer.
10. *All my enemies shall feel shame and terror;*
Suddenly shall they turn back and feel shame.

8. A sudden change of mood appears in the psalm at this point. Parallel instances are found in 22:22ff.; 16:8f.; 28:6f.; 31:21ff.; 69:32ff. We can readily understand how one who has gone into the divine

presence with his particular trouble and has freely unburdened his heart before the throne of the Almighty may be mightily comforted by having gotten the matter off his chest and by having deposited his burden with God. Such moods are not, however, to be forecast or anticipated. They break upon good men of God, without their being able to account for them. Here, of a sudden the grief, the vexation, the uncertainty, and the feeling of the divine displeasure disappear as a flock of scavenger birds. Instead comes the dove of God's peace.

When all those that disturb the psalmist are bidden to "depart," the thought is practically, he has felt all his enemies to be clustered round about him, whether they were as a lot near to him physically or not. In his thinking they were always present and intent upon his harm. He suddenly becomes so sure of having been heard by God that he feels that the machinations of the enemies have come to nought. And since they must sooner or later depart, he dismisses them now in the certainty that they must go whether they will or not. Admirable courage of faith lies in this "depart." The psalmist is very clearly not slandering his foes but is describing them objectively as what they are when he designates them "workers of iniquity." This title, appearing also in the *A.V.*, signifies that all such opponents are men who habitually practice iniquity, hollow, empty worthlessness. For the fundamental characteristic of "iniquity" (*'awen*) is that it is basically worthless as far as lasting, constructive results are concerned. To practice such things is certainly indicative of a useless and misspent existence.

The reason advanced for this bold dismissal is stated in the following three clauses, the substance of which is, "Yahweh hath heard." Only the heart that has experienced the assurance that comes from the certainty of being heard can understand why this man is so bold. Nothing may have been done by the Lord as a visible and tangible deed, yet the heart is certain. With becoming modesty the author ascribes to himself nothing more than this, that he had laid before the Lord "the sound" of his "weeping." It was not because he had prayed so excellently, but because the Lord had been so compassionate.

9. Again he calls his prayer "entreaty" or "plea for mercy" as some commentators render the word. In the last instance he calls it only "prayer." In these three parallel clauses the emphasis lies on the certainty of acceptance, and the statements as such constitute one of the finest instances of anaphora found in the psalms.

10. But just as certain as he is that his prayers have been accepted, just so assured is he of the complete overthrow of his enemies. His own acceptance is an absolutely accomplished fact (perfect tense in the Hebrew); their discomfort is yet to come (imperfects in the Hebrew). The lot of all of them will be the same, he is sure. The familiar

translation of the Hebrew verb *bush,* "be ashamed," is scarcely forceful enough in our day. It seems to convey the mild idea of embarrassment whereas the fate implied is "to be utterly disgraced," *zu Schanden werden,* as *Luther* regularly renders it. Our translation "feel shame" must be taken in the strongest sense of the word as its parallel expression, "feel terror," also indicates. The second line of the verse plainly conveys the thought that their fate will have about it something of the catastrophic: "suddenly shall they turn back and feel shame." Utter defeat and overthrow are involved in this adversity of theirs. *Luther* seeks to express something more than even the Hebrew imperfects allow when he renders: *muessen zurueckkehren und zu Schanden werden,* "*must* turn back," etc. This would involve the thought that the psalmist had said that in all such cases a drastic overthrow is inevitable. The psalmist rather reflects only on what he is sure will befall them in this instance in answer to his prayer to God.

NOTES

2. It seems somewhat difficult to determine whether '*umlal* is a participle Pual, written without the customary *m* as a prefix, or whether it should be classified as a Pual Perfect from '*amal;* we believe the former deserves the preference.

3. All such expressions as the initial "in particular" are not literally found in the Hebrew, which in this case has only a *waw* ("and"). However, *Koenig* seems to be quite correct in classifying the *waw* in question as a *waw augmentativum*—a new classification not previously recognized by grammarians.

5. For what we have rendered "state of death" the Hebrew has only the plain *maweth,* usually rendered "death." Here, however, the parallel element is *she'ol,* "the realm of the dead." This parallelism makes our translation desirable.

7. The rendering offered by some interpreters of *bekholtsoreray,* "in the midst of all mine enemies," has less to warrant it than the familiar "because of all mine enemies." There seems to be no reasonable motivation for telling *where* the eye has failed, but there is reason for revealing *why.* The lead of the *Septuagint* is in this instance not satisfactory.

8. The familiar *qol* does mean "voice," but its secondary meaning "sound" is a bit more suitable here.

The perfect *shama'* illustrates the difficulty involved in the translation of the Hebrew tenses. We render it, as is common enough for perfects, "hath heard." *Koenig* seems to regard it as a prophetic perfect and so renders, "will hear." Neither his rendering nor *Luther's* present tense *hoert* expresses quite so well the full assurance found in the perfect, and there is surely a full measure of confidence at the close of the psalm. The translation should be in harmony with this fact.

CRITICAL ISSUES

Criticism sometimes leads interpreters to extreme claims. This becomes apparent when what is really a statement of doubt felt in the extremity of trial about not being able to praise God in the state after death is pressed as though it contained the doctrine that the dead are beyond the reach of God according to the express teaching of the Old Testament. Such a thought has obviously been inserted into the passage, not extracted from it.

Kittel does not judge soberly the issues involved in this psalm when at the conclusion he ventures the surmise that a priestly oracle or blessing may originally have been attached to this psalm after what seems to have been a Babylonian precedent (*so scheint es in Babylon gewesen zu sein*). Why must Israel have imitated all Babylonian precedents? Or why make doubtful precedents normative in interpretation? The psalm comes to a well-rounded conclusion.

Psalm 7

A PRAYER THAT YAHWEH MAY OVERTHROW THE OPPRESSORS OF THE RIGHTEOUS

IT HAS BEEN aptly said that Ps. 6 "wailed like some soft flute" but that, on the other hand, Ps. 7 "pealed like the trumpet of judgment" (*Maclaren*). There is a certain vehemence of feeling in this psalm, which may, perhaps, account for the title that appears in the original where this psalm is called a "Shiggaion." According to its root this word might mean "a wild, passionate song with rapid changes of rhythm" (*BDB*). But one may well have misgivings regarding this etymology, for the passionate element is scarcely as pronounced as this explanation claims. In view of this difficulty we may have to content ourselves with the somewhat colorless translation "ode." The Assyrian root *shegu* could suggest that this is a "complaint."

The heading found in the original would then read: *An ode of David, which he sang unto Yahweh concerning the words of Cush, the Benjamite.* The second difficulty encountered is that we cannot positively identify this "Cush." To regard this as another name for Doeg, Edomite (I Sam. 22:9) is precarious, if not impossible. The situation presented in this psalm is so much like that described in this chapter of I Samuel or more particularly that found in I Sam. 24 (see particularly v. 9) that we are much inclined to think in terms of this period of David's life. *Delitzsch* has rightly said: "We need only to read I Sam. 24-26 in order to see how rich in unmistakable allusions to this period of David's life our psalm is."

Others, including *Luther,* have seen in the title "Cush" a reference to the dark hue of the character of this bitter enemy of the author, as though David sought to mark him as a man of black character or as "a black-hearted man" (*Kirkpatrick*). This, though possible, seems less likely. This seems to be a man concerning whom the historical record of the Scriptures conveys no further information. From the Greek version down attempts have been made to read *kushi* in the heading, identifying this man according to II Sam. 18:21ff.

It may disturb some readers to notice that the writer ventures to call upon Him who is the Judge of the universe to act in his own particular interest as though such weighty matters as his personal difficulty would be considered by Him who has matters of so much greater moment to consider. But this writer is apparently a man who sees in himself an exponent of the cause of the righteous generally. *Hengstenberg* says very properly: "David's conflict with Saul was not a struggle between individuals but between parties—one single phase of the wickedness and the righteousness which are in evidence throughout all periods of the history of the church." Without a doubt, the author was keenly aware of his position and of its importance for all in the church who would in the course of time find themselves in situations analogous to his own. We also trust that our interpretation will demonstrate that the statement is not true that we have here "a vivid picture of the hatred engendered by religious strife, a hatred which is mutual" (*Oesterley*).

a) A Plea for Help (vv. 1–2)

1. *O Lord, my God, in Thee have I taken refuge;*
   Save me from all my pursuers and deliver me.
2. *Lest they tear my life like a lion,*
   Who drags away his prey with none to deliver.

1. The author is in grave danger. He is not engaged in calm meditation upon theoretical difficulties. In this plea for help he first of all casts himself upon the mercy of his God and hides himself in Him: "in Thee have I taken refuge." Such a course of action constitutes a strong plea: the Lord cannot forsake those who make Him their refuge.

2. A whole host of bitter enemies is in pursuit and hot on his

Psalm 7

trail. This is one indication of the fact that the struggle involved is not
between man and man as it might appear on the surface. David's
chief opponent is backed by many who are of the same mind with
him. At the moment it is apparent that, if David were to fall into the
hands of the pursuers, they would tear his very "life" (*nephesh* often
has this meaning in Hebrew) like a "lion, who drags away his prey with
none to deliver." The pursuer is bent on full and final destruction.
So this plea is the outcry of a soul in grave extremity.

b) **A Protestation of Innocence, asking that God may punish the
writer if he is guilty (vv. 3–5)**

3. O Lord, my God, if I have indeed done this;
   If there be any injustice upon my hands;
4. If I have dealt out evil unto him that was at peace with me—
   But I delivered him that was my enemy without cause—
5. Then let the enemy pursue my soul
   And let him overtake me and trample my life to the earth
   And lay my soul in the dust. Selah.

3. This is surely the protestation of a man who is definitely aware
of his innocence, at least in so far as the charges advanced against
him are concerned. At first he calls the thing or things charged merely
"this." He at once, however, defines what this is, namely, the unjust
treatment that he is said to have dealt out to his opponent. V. 4 particularly defines the charge made: doing evil to a man who had been
utterly without guile over against David. Such an act would have made
stains upon David's hands, the stains of iniquity. The same figure is
found in I Sam. 24:12; 26:18; Is. 1:15; 59:3, 6. The use of it here
suggests that, as we have rendered above, the iniquity is to be thought
of as a stain "upon the hands," not as something that he carries about
with him hidden "in his hands" (*A.R.V.*).

4. There is always something particularly dastardly about committing injustice against a man who lives at peace with one. This appears
to have been the charge raised against David. One almost gets the
impression that he is referring to a slander which had just been freshly
devised and had just come to his ears. The "this" seems to have some
such emphasis. With strong indignation the writer interrupts himself.
Not only had he not done the evil charged, he had even done the very
opposite: he had delivered his enemy, who had no cause for the enmity
that he harbored against David. This half of the verse could also have
been translated: "Yea, I have delivered him," etc. (*A.R.V.*).

5. David brings his sentence to a conclusion with a strong malediction upon himself: May his enemy continue his persecution; may he
succeed in catching his prey; may he, like some cruel brute, trample

his very life to the earth—trample him to death as it were; and may he thus inflict upon him a most ignominious death—"lay my soul in the dust." This last expression "in the dust" does not mean "the dust of death" merely because this expression happens to be found in Ps. 22:16. The figure "in the dust" is complete in itself and signifies the most shameful sort of defeat.

Only the man who is sure of his innocence in the sight of God would venture to call for such a doom upon himself in case he had been guilty of the thing wherewith he is charged. David, therefore, represents the cause of the righteous who are unjustly persecuted, as the church always is.

c) **A Plea That God may curb the Enemies and Vindicate the Writer (vv. 6–7)**

6. *Do arise, O Lord, in Thy anger;*
   Lift up Thyself because of the outbursts of fury of my foes and awake for me;
   Thou Thyself hast commanded to exercise judgment.
7. *A multitude of peoples may indeed surround Thee;*
   But triumphing over them do Thou return on high.

6. The author feels rather keenly that the situation is one that calls for the exercise of divine judgment. With strong forms of the imperative like our English, "Do arise," he calls upon God to take the present case in hand and dispose of it. The fact that the misdeeds of his ungodly opponents are such as to cause God to be justly angered is entirely clear to him. This divine anger is to manifest itself over against the "outbursts of fury" of the foes. Even that bold imperative found elsewhere in the psalms which bids God "awake" is here resorted to as though God were at the moment asleep. Yet surely no irreverence is intended, it is only the Lord's seeming inaction that is reflected upon. The final plea advanced is that God himself "has commanded to exercise judgment." No particular command seems to be under consideration. The author is rather thinking of the fact that whatever justice or judgment is exercised, God's sovereign will and manifold injunctions in Israel's law indicate that He is the Author of all true judgment upon earth since Gen. 9:6. All general precepts as well as all individual laws have their source in Him. How very proper it is, therefore, that He Himself act as He has commanded men to act!

7. This verse indicates what a situation He may meet were He to come down to judgment, for the opponents that the psalmist has encountered are indeed many. A veritable "multitude of peoples" may appear, as it were, arrayed against the Almighty, for to the writer

Psalm 7

his present enemies are but a few of the many who harbor hostile sentiments against God and His people. The rendering that we have given makes the imperfect of the Hebrew a potential imperfect, one of the manifold shades of meaning involved in the imperfect. Besides, we have substituted for the more formal rendering "congregation" a "multitude."

The second half of the verse is difficult. It may be best to interpret it as follows: God is called upon to return after the obvious victory which He will gain to His throne of majesty and judgment on high and to uphold again as before and as in this specific manifestation of His firm and strong rule that impartial and just administration of the government of the world that has always been characteristic of Him. Literally all that is said is, as *A.R.V.* has rendered it: "And over them return Thou on high." But the expression "over them" is rather pregnant with meaning, implying, as we have rendered, "triumphing over them." Or stated differently, the thought is: Give just one brief demonstration of Thy just government and then resume Thy regal throne.

d) A Plea for the Just Verdict of the Righteous Judge (vv. 8–10)

8. *The Lord will judge the nations;*
   Do me justice, O Lord, according to my righteouness;
   And according to my integrity may my verdict be.
9. *May the iniquity of the wicked be no more;*
   But do Thou establish the righteous and so prove Thyself a righteous God, Thou who triest hearts and minds.
10. *My safety lieth in God,*
    Who saveth the upright of heart.

8. In pleading that justice may be done to him the writer puts two items into a strange juxtaposition: the judgment of the nations and his own vindication. It might seem presumptuous for him to speak thus, yet two thoughts should be borne in mind. On the one hand, faith knows that He who governs the nations, holding them in the hollow of His hand, has a concern for the welfare of the individual saint. On the other hand, David and all who are in a similar position are not individuals in the abstract, they represent a whole category, and what they ask for themselves they desire for all others who are in a like position, and desire it with equal earnestness. It is to be regretted that some commentators call this juxtaposition of the nations and the individual something that borders on the "comic."

We have translated the verb involved in the second member of the verse "do me justice," for though it could be rendered in the Hebrew idiom "judge me"—as many versions read—the peculiar genius of the Hebrew language involves the idea of securing an individual's rights for him. We too readily associate punitive judgment with the verb "judge." The phrases indicating the norm of judgment to be followed in no sense argue for an unwholesome self-righteousness. When the writer refers to his "righteousness" and his "integrity" he has in mind the particular situation in which he finds himself, charged with some wrong of which he is innocent. He knows that his life will bear scrutiny in regard to the charge raised against him and calls for a divine verdict.

9. The fact that the psalmist's thoughts are not confined to the narrow circle of his personal interests appears in the broader aspects of the case that he at once takes in hand when he asks that in the process of his own vindication "the iniquity of the wicked" may also be put away, all this iniquity that cruelly persecutes and wrongs God's children. Equally much he desires that all truly righteous men be established by this same Just Judge, who is well able to judge righteously because He discerns the thoughts and intents of the heart, or, as is said here, He is a trier of "hearts and minds." We have made bold to rearrange the sequence of words slightly in order to express the contrast between the treatment of the wicked and the righteous more strongly and have then let the appositional participle ("the trier") follow. We take it that the words which stand last in the Hebrew sentence for emphasis are best given that needed emphasis if we render them: "and so prove Thyself a righteous God," rather than to offer a merely literal ellipsis which the original has, "a righteous God."

To tell the truth, these big issues which have just been enumerated are here and always at stake when God's children are unjustly oppressed by the wicked. This is not a case of an exaggerated sense of one's own importance.

10. Summing up briefly, the author declares that the issues lie wholly with the Lord or: "My safety lieth in God." This is a rather free rendering of the Hebrew idiom: "My shield is with God." Since a shield can become a synonymn of safety, we are free to translate as we have done. In the second member the Hebrew again differs slightly from our rendering in that it uses what may be regarded as a title of God, calling Him the "Saver of the upright of heart." All this is a sturdy utterance of faith.

e) **A Prediction concerning the Overthrow of the Evildoers by the Almighty (vv. 11–13)**

11. *God is a just Judge,*
    A mighty God, who displays indignation every day.
12. *He will surely whet His sword again,*
    Bend His bow and aim it.

Psalm 7

13. *He will prepare for Himself deadly weapons;*
    He will make His arrows fiery.

11. The tone of the psalm grows more confident from this point onward; it no longer pleads or petitions, it confidently predicts.

The things predicted are intimately tied up with the very nature and character of God Himself. He is both a "just Judge" and "a mighty God" who on His part never discontinues His activity against evil and evildoers, for He "displays indignation every day." We prefer this translation to "hath indignation" (*A.R.V.*) because it conveys the thought that God's indignation is not an idle feeling, like a kind of impotent rage. His being indignant expresses itself in acts, acts such as those described in the following verses.

12. This translation (discussed in detail below) is more in harmony with the picture of the activity of the God who is indignant against evil. As He has often done, so He will now once "again whet His sword" to be ready for its use at any moment. He is, in fact, to be regarded as having already bent the bow and as having taken aim. So directly imminent is the punishment of the evildoer. We often fail to realize how perilous the position of the impenitent really is.

13. That feature of the description is left with the arrow that is ready at any moment to take its flight. The account continues with a moment's reflection on the weapons, which are of the "deadly" sort, and the arrows in particular are "fiery" in the sense of being wrapped with readily combustible materials, which make them more destructive.

As the account continues in this vein it makes an issue of the fact that he for whom evil is designed by the hands of the Almighty is fully deserving of it—a note which is rather heavily rung throughout the psalm. We have not before us a psalm in which a private grudge controls the writer's feelings.

f) The Unhappy End of the Man Who Plots Evil (vv. 14–16)

14. *See, a man conceives perversity;*
    He is pregnant with mischief;
    He brings forth a lie.
15. *A pit hath he dug and excavated;*
    And he fell into the trap that he was making.
16. *The mischief that he plotted shall recoil on his own head;*
    Upon his own crown shall his violence descend.

14. Not a particular deed so much as a man's general course of conduct is first described. In its conception it is "perversity." While it is being nursed along it is "mischief." When fully matured it is all a "lie" or falsehood. See Jas. 1:14f. Observe that the current

translations of this verse mar the fine sequence that it expresses by having the individual "travail" already in the first member. Though the verb involved usually means something like "to writhe" it may also represent the cause as such, by metonomy, as *KW* shows.

15. The description of the kind of activity that such a one delights to engage in continues by presenting him as engaged in the activity of digging and excavating a pit—two verbs to mark the man as engaged heart and soul in this unholy business—and this with the purpose in mind of showing that the pit is here as so often (see Ezek. 19:4; Ps. 57:6; Eccles. 10:8) dug with the intent of trapping—in this case trapping some enemy. With a sudden turn the description pictures this wicked fellow as suddenly falling into his own pit. He experiences the harm that he designed for another, and this happens while he is still in the process of preparing the evil for his enemy. V. 16 expresses this as a kind of general principle, which experience has proven to be only too true. History and experience abound in illustrations of this truth.

g) A Resolve to Praise God for His Deliverance (v. 17)

17. *I will praise the Lord for His righteousness*
And sing praises unto the name of the Lord, the Most High.

17. Confidence finally grows so strong in the faith with which God fills the psalmist's heart that he resolves to begin to offer his praises to the Lord now in the full assurance that He will manifest His righteousness in due season and in such a manner that the righteous cannot but praise and be jubilant that the well-known character ("name") of Yahweh has again been so significantly manifested. This verse might have been combined with the preceding section (f) as the most confident part of its confident conclusion. We have placed it under a separate heading (g) to mark the unusually high point of assurance at which it arrives.

NOTES

2. The Hebrew has the verb, rendered above "they tear," as a singular, *yitroph*. But "pursuers" had just been mentioned. When the Hebrew then continues with the singular of the verb it actually has in mind the indefinite subject: "lest one tear," etc. We felt that the English idiom preferred the plural in such a case, and that the change of number seems too harsh for legitimate English.

4. The Hebrew has a double object following the verb "dealt out," namely, both the direct and the indirect as two direct objects.

5. The first word of this verse has a Hebrew pointing which inserts the vowels of both the Kal and the Piel—take your choice. Noth-

Psalm 7

ing in the verse distinctly indicates that the apodosis begins here, yet it is very obvious that such is the case; *K.S.* 415c.

6. Though we preferred to translate: "Thou Thyself hast commanded to exercise judgment," we cannot deny the possibility that this statement could be construed as a relative clause, the relative being omitted, thus: "to the judgment which Thou hast commanded." Our first rendering retains the abruptness of the original. Yet cf., *K.S.* 172b.

7. It will be noted in our interpretation above that we do not regard the nations, as some commentators do, merely as onlookers or witnesses of the judgment that God exercises. Nor, on the other hand, is the full judgment upon the nations here brought into the picture. As our rendering of the second member of the verse showed ("triumphing over them") the author thinks in terms of that measure of opposition that the nations are manifesting in his particular case, and he anticipates that God will overcome this opposition effectively.

8. Our translation, "Yahweh will judge the nations," does not fully catch the force of the imperfect, which rather expresses a continuous attitude as explained in *G.K.* 107f.

9. The "righteous" in the clause, "but do Thou establish the righteous," is, indeed, a singular, but being without an article, it conveys the idea: "every righteous man," and so may be used for the plural (*K.S.* 256d). The verb preceding this word (*tekhonen*), being connected with the preceding sentence only by an "and," may rightly be construed: "and (thus) do Thou establish." See *K.S.* 360f.

When, as here, "hearts and reins" (kidneys) are mentioned together, the heart is regarded chiefly as the seat of man's thinking (cf., Gen. 6:5; 8:21, etc.) or even of the will (cf., Jer. 3:17; Ps. 51:10); the kidneys are the seat of the deepest feelings (e.g., Jer. 17:10; 20:12). This is not effectively rendered in any translation, and our rendering "hearts and minds" has chiefly this merit, that it at least speaks English.

10. In the expression "upright of heart" the word "heart" is an accusative of specification.

12. In the translation we offer, "He will surely whet His sword again," we have, first of all, regarded the compound particle *'im lo'* as an "emphatic affirmative" (*BDB*), and we have taken *yashubh* as denoting repetition (see *G.K.* 120dg).

Psalm 8

GOD'S GLORY REVEALED IN MAN'S DIGNITY

FROM ONE POINT of view this psalm in one of the "nature psalms" (cf., Ps. 19, 29, 65, 104). What it does say in reference to nature is consistent with the usual Scriptural approach, namely, nature reflects God's glory, is His handiwork, and is entirely under His control.

Primarily, however, this is a hymn of praise. It aims to set forth one particular aspect of the glory of God, chiefly in so far as this glory is revealed by the very creation and position of man, the chief of the creatures of God. In a striking way the psalm indicates how high an estimate revealed truth puts upon man. The true dignity of man is taught nowhere as effectively as in the Scriptures.

Yet we do not have two subjects running parallel with one another in this psalm as the *A.R.V.* states: "Jehovah's Glory and Man's Dignity," a theme which would be glaringly deficient in unity. But rather, as our title above indicates, the second of these items serves to make clear the first: Jehovah's glory is being set forth primarily by a consideration of the dignity with which He has invested man.

As soon as this issue becomes clear, we are confronted by the other major problem associated with this psalm—In how far and in what sense is it Messianic? It is the New Testament which gives us our full authorization for classifying this psalm as Messianic by the consistent use which it makes of it, particularly of v. 5 and secondarily of v. 2 (Heb. 2:6-8; Matt. 21:16).

This New Testament use of the psalm does not at once state in what sense the psalm is Messianic, and it must be the serious concern of everyone who expounds this psalm not to identify *his own conception* as to how the New Testament employs the psalm with the actual use itself. In other words, to conclude that, because the psalm is Messianic, therefore it must apply directly and exclusively to Christ alone—this conclusion, we say, must be designated as a hasty solution of the question, In what sense are certain psalms to be classified as Messianic?

To tell the truth of the matter, had it not been for the clear testimony of the New Testament, commentators might readily have contented themselves with interpreting the whole psalm in such a manner that the Messianic thought would have had no part in it. But upon

Psalm 8

deeper reflection, following the clear indication of the New Testament writers, we are compelled to make an approach which allows for the following fact, that the "first Adam" (I Cor. 15:45) prefigures much of that which becomes vital in the life of the "last Adam." The true character and essence of the original Adam are manifested most effectively in the life of Jesus Christ. Therefore, if the true dignity of the first Adam is strongly set forth, the whole description obviously finds its fullest realization in Jesus Christ.

In other words, the idea of the *types* of the Old Testament enters into the picture, however, only in a general and basic sort of way: Adam prefigures what Christ is; or again: the psalm is Messianic by type. It has, first of all, a clear-cut subject as is conveyed by our title, "God's Glory as Revealed in Man's Dignity." The God of history so shaped the details of history that the man originally created is a clear foreshadowing of all the excellencies and marvels of the life of Jesus Christ, our Lord. What was said of the one may well be claimed for the other. It may well be that the author of the psalm did not himself realize clearly this particular aspect of what he wrote. He was being led to express certain higher elements of truth, of which he himself was not at the time aware. But what the Spirit of God had thus laid into the words employed He later disclosed to others so that they were able to convey the Spirit's intended use of these words to their fellow men. All this comes under the head of divine providence.

In summary then: man as created reflects God's glory. But the Son of man, in whom the original pattern is more fully realized, reflects this same glory far more perfectly. The New Testament use of these words is not, therefore, mere homiletical adaptation of them but a disclosure of an appropriate meaning, which was intended at the time of the original writing. The typical nature of the words employed was a result of the clear design of the Spirit of inspiration.

> *To the Choir Director*
> *After the tune of the treaders of the winepress*
> *A psalm of David*

This heading is the first verse of the text according to the Hebrew notation. On "choir director" see 4:1. "After the tune of the treaders of the winepress" is a translation of the words *'al gittith*.

The fact that this is a "psalm of David" in this case adds nothing to the interpretation, nor does it clear up any difficult issues. It merely shows by its close correspondence with the creation account of Gen. 1 that David was thoroughly familiar with this account. There is no particular period in David's life into which this psalm would fit more closely than it does into any other.

1. O Lord, our Lord, how majestic is Thy name in all the earth;
   Whose praises have always been sung above the heavens!
2. Out of the mouth of babes, and even infants, hast Thou established a stronghold because of Thine enemies,
   To still every enemy and revengeful person.

1. The thought of these verses is that the Lord's name is superabundant in majesty, requiring no stronger defense than the praise of children.

Since "the name of God" is any and every revelation of Himself that He has given, the particular point at issue is that, wherever God has in any wise revealed Himself at any time, there is one respect in regard to which this revelation is always entirely consistent, and that is that God is always found to be "majestic." For this revelation is the same "in all the earth." Impressed by this fact, the author casts his reflection in the form of a strong exclamation. But that observation need not surprise anyone, for it is also thus "above the heavens," where the stars and the angels voice the praises of God, each in their own way; cf., Ps. 19: Job 38:7; also Is. 6:3; Ps. 103:20f. This obvious majesty of the name of the Lord is, therefore, in evidence everywhere upon earth as well as in the heavens.

2. So secure is the honor of the name of the Lord that in the full consciousness of His great glory He has let the defense of His honor be committed to babes. There are other forces that can and do take up the defense of His name, but as far as the Lord is concerned, He can be content with what the mouth of babes can utter. In fact, the statement made does not even specify the praise that infants lips may try. Any and every utterance of theirs is apparently conceived of as constituting a part of the great defense that God has thus provided. The mere fact that infants can speak and can praise is all the "stronghold" that God's honor requires. When the Greek translators, as they are also quoted in the New Testament, Matt. 21:16, rendered this word "praise" they were translating freely and staying well within the meaning of the passage. Whatever an "enemy and revengeful person" may say by way of a bitter attack upon the honor of God's name, in the eyes of all dispassionate observers such opponents are refuted by what children may in their own way say or do. Here, too, applies the word of the Savior about our becoming as little children. Or as *Noetscher* states it: "Dropping the hyperbole, unbiased and uncorrupted minds recognize God without difficulty from His creation."

Vv. 3 and 4 constitute the next section of the psalm. Their thought is this: When the heavens, the chief visible revelation of God's glory, are viewed, one might well wonder why He took note of man. The transition from the "our" of v. 1 to the "I" of v. 3 merely indicates that the writer at first thought of himself together with others of like mind.

> 3. *Whenever I look at Thy heavens, the work of Thy fingers,*
> *The moon and the stars, which Thou hast prepared;*
> 4. *What is mortal man that Thou didst consider him?*
> *And the son of man that Thou didst care for him?*

3. To many interpreters this verse seems to offer conclusive evidence of the fact that this is a night hymn, for the moon and the stars and the heavens are mentioned. However, it will be observed that these heavenly bodies appear only in the second half of the verse. Furthermore, the word rendered "when" in A.V. could more fittingly be rendered "whenever." The conclusion, therefore, drawn by the psalmist in v. 4 is in reality suggested each time the heavens are viewed. Now, as *Hengstenberg* in particular has pointed out, the most obvious glory of the heavens is the sun. This fact is so evident that the writer does not even specifically mention it. In any case, it might well be asked whether the conclusion drawn is more readily suggested by the starry heavens at night than by the heavens, whether viewed by day or night. It will then be seen that the emphasis upon the possibility of a night hymn is misplaced.

Any and everything that is so majestically displayed by the heavens suggests one and the same conclusion: How is it possible that He who made the vast heavens and all that appears on the face of them, whether it be by day or night, should ever have busied Himself with the little being called "mortal man," so as either to "consider" him or even in any way to "care for him"? Of the many terms that the Hebrew might have used a word is chosen that suggests the weakness and frailty of the being called "man." As the tense of the verb in the original suggests and as the verses following explain in detail, a particular historical event is under consideration, man's creation. Not something that God does now as most of the versions suggest; cf., *A.V.,* "That Thou *art* mindful of him . . . and *visitest* him." Our suggested rendering does not warrant the conclusion that God now no longer cares. In fact, a conclusion to the effect that God still cares could very fittingly be drawn from the evidence submitted. But that does not happen to be the matter that the author talks about here.

The next section extends from vv. 5 to 8 and develops the thought: God invested man with a dignity that is second only to His own and made him ruler over the world which He had just created.

5. *And Thou didst make him lack but little of God,*
   With glory and honor Thou didst crown him.
6. *Thou madest him to have dominion over the works of Thy hands;*
   Everything hast Thou put under his feet.
7. *Sheep and oxen—all of them,*
   And also the beasts of the field;
8. *The birds of the heavens and the fish of the sea,*
   Whatsoever traverses the paths of any seas.

5. The creation of man and his investment with honors and responsibilities are being reviewed. Details are cited verbatim from Gen. 1. First a comprehensive statement which asserts man's rare dignity with almost breath-taking emphasis: "Thou didst make him lack but little of God." The statement is so bold that the early translators, beginning with the *Septuagint* and continuing up to the *A.V.,* have substituted the word "angels" for "God" (*'elohim*). Though this translation, commonly found in older versions is remotely justifiable, the context would definitely have to indicate that such beings are meant, and then it would at best be but a dubious statement. (For a fuller discussion of the issues involved see the Notes appended.)

In any case, the writer views the account of the creation of man as asserting that man was placed so high on the scale of created beings (for he is himself the very image of God) that man "lacks but little of God"—as *BDB* renders the phrase. The reference is obviously to the primordial man, the first Adam before the fall, in the fullness of his powers and attributes, the very reflection of the majesty of the Almighty, who had patterned man after Himself. If someone might object that angels stood much higher in the scale than man, it must be remembered that they were from the outset "ministering spirits" (Heb. 1:14) whereas man, as the words following (vv. 6-8) in our psalm indicate, was assigned a position of rule and authority over all things in the world. Nowhere is man's dignity asserted more clearly and boldly than in this passage. But we again remind the reader that the reference is to man before the fall.

The second half of v. 5 is very aptly worded when it asserts that God did "crown" this chief among His creatures. His high position was the equivalent of having a regal crown set upon his head or, still more exactly, the "glory and honor" that were his crowned him.

6. The separate items that are now enumerated as being under the dominion of man give a comprehensive picture of the extent of his dominion. V. 6a says by way of a summary that, generally speaking, "the works of Thy hands" come under man's control. How much that involves neither this statement nor Gen. 1 specifies, but it certainly

cannot indicate a mere nominal control, for the parallel statement of v. 6, on the one hand, extends man's authority to "everything" and, on the other, claims that these things may be said to have been "put under his feet." Angels may have greater power than does man, but in his own realm man was sole authority quite apart from them. It may be due to the fact that we know comparatively little about the power and sphere of the activity of angels that from the geocentric viewpoint of this account the angels are not considered. One can readily understand how the above-mentioned translation of v. 5 came into the thinking of the earliest translators.

7, 8. As the writer thinks back on these things, the very words of the account of creation as the first chapter of the Bible offers them seem to suggest themselves naturally to him. So he mentions that man's dominion included the domesticated animals as well as the beasts that roam about wild, the birds as well as the fish. For that matter, he reminds the reader that even the manifold and mighty creatures that inhabit the seas are also included as man's subjects, mighty and manifold though they be and wherever they may roam. The statement just made would be an obvious and legitimate inference drawn from Gen. 1:28 and is a good illustration of the very proper way in which the later writers of the Scriptures interpreted the Scriptures they had.

9. *O Lord, our Lord, how majestic is Thy name in all the earth!*

Since the psalmist has now fully demonstrated the original thesis which he set out to prove, he reiterates this thesis by way of a summary and conclusion. It also is now perfectly obvious that the author's object was not to dwell primarily on the dignity of man but on this dignity in so far as it was one of the most striking demonstrations that can ever be offered of the greatness of our God. The God who can create such a being as man is must indeed be superlatively great.

NOTES

We rendered *'al haggittith* "after the tune of the treaders of the winepress." This rendering is based on the more likely meaning of the root *gath* in this connection. For *gath* may mean "winepress," or it may refer to the Philistine city of Gath. It is less likely that the Hebrews would have used tunes originating in the heathen city of Gath for sacred hymns than that they might have adopted a tune used by those that trod out the winepress. To be still more exact, *'al* does not necessarily mean "according to the *tune* of," for we do not know whether these musical notations referred to tunes or to particular types of chanting.

1. *'adhonénu* is the plural of abstraction. Yet it is without a doubt to be construed as a singular, *K.S.* 263f, g.

Though *'addir* originally means "wide, lofty," here something like "glorious, majestic" must be intended.

1b. A notable crux from days of old is the form *tenah*. We have based our rendering on the root, acknowledged by grammarians generally, that has the meaning for the verb *tanah* "recount, rehearse," (*BDB*) or *besingen* (KW). Following *Koenig's Commentary,* we prefer to regard this as a *pual,* "have been sung." At the same time the idea of a gnomic aorist as best explaining the perfect form is in order. The thought of the verse then flows very smoothly: God's praise, much in evidence upon the earth, has always been sounded in heaven.

The objections to be offered against other renderings are briefly these. *Tenah* could be infinitive construct from *nathan*. This would result in the clumsy rendering: "Thou in reference to whom the giving Thy glory is above the heavens." So *Hengstenberg* and others. The thought could scarcely be expressed in a more cumbersome way, even after efforts at explanation have been added.

Tenah could be an imperative from *nathan,* for this form occurs 56 times elsewhere. However, there is an obvious harshness about a statement which begins with an exclamation: "How majestic is Thy name!" and continues with an imperative, entirely unmotivated: "Put Thy glory above the heavens," a note which is never again struck in the psalm.

Tenah could be an incorrect form or a copyist's error for *nathátta*. But then the difficulty is to be met as to why so obvious a form was so badly written. The versions, for the most part, render as though this were the form. In the translation no reader notices that a problem exists. In rendering thus the versions have followed the path of least resistance.

2. We have rendered the word *'oz* "stronghold." It means, first of all, "strength." The next step in the development of the meaning of the word was to have it connote a stronghold. We may well stop at that point, for a development frequently noted has occurred: the meaning has advanced from the abstract to the concrete. KW goes one step farther in suggesting the meaning *maechtiger Chor* ("a mighty chorus"), but that goes on the assumption that what the children do is primarily to praise, and so Koenig suggests *strong* praise.

When we rendered *'oyebh* "every enemy" we did so because the absence of the article suggests the idea of whatever may be called "enemy." The same applies to *mithnaqqem,* "every revengeful persons." For this reason the suggestion of *Stoeckhardt* is unacceptable, namely, that this is a reference to the archenemy of mankind, the devil. The rest of the approach that this author then builds on this interpretation must also be rejected.

5. The reason for regarding the two verbs *thizkerennu* and *thiph-*

Psalm 8

qedennu as equivalents of an English past tense "didst consider" and "didst care for," is chiefly the context as it follows this verse. For the events of creation are pointed to: they are the particular instances when God "considered and cared for" man. Or, as it might just as aptly be stated, Gen. 1 relates what the author has in mind. Cf., *KS* 366f.

In regard to the expression "the work of Thy fingers" we feel that those interpreters are correct who maintain that no special emphasis attaches to the word "fingers" as though a special type of handiwork of a finer sort were to be indicated by this word. Are the "works of His *hands*" which are referred to in v. 6 to be regarded as being less finely wrought than the heavens were because the word "fingers" is not there used?

We are strongly of the opinion that *'elohim* should here be translated in its plain and regular meaning "God," a meaning which it has almost without exception. For all the instances cited even by *BDB* for the meaning "angels" are more than dubious. The word may refer to superhuman beings as it does in I Sam. 28:13. It does also refer to judges in passages such as Ps. 82:1, 6 and, perhaps, in passages like Exod. 22:7f., but in the latter instances the plain meaning "God" can readily be maintained. Aside from that, there is the meaning "gods" in reference to heathen divinities. Consequently there is little to commend the rendering "angels" from any point of view.

On what basis does Luther's rendering of the Hebrew rest when he offers the translation: *Du wirst ihn lassen eine kleine Zeit von Gott verlassen sein?* It is a fact the *me 'at,* "littleness," could refer to time, and that Luther interpreted the psalm as being primarily Messianic, not by way of type but directly Messianic. Then the resultant translation seemed to agree well with the suffering of Christ in His *passio magna*.

Though the Greek version renders "angels" at this point, the New Testament does not find the rendering out of keeping with the general tenor of the passage and so does not brand it as erroneous—the usual attitude of the New Testament on the question of the exact rendering of the familiar versions of those days.

8. As in v. 2, the participle *'obher,* standing without an article, is best rendered "whatsoever passes"—as the *A.V.* has translated it. The same principle applies to the last word of the verse *yammin,* which, without an article, is best taken as meaning "any seas."

Psalm 9

PRAISE, THE BASIS OF AN EARNEST PLEA FOR DELIVERANCE

THERE IS MUCH debate on the question as to whether this is a psalm of praise or a psalm of petition. Both elements of prayer are so blended into one another that it seems unwise to say it is either the one or the other. It is both; and as our heading indicates, the element of praise constitutes the basis for a plea for deliverance.

From the time of the Greek translation onward there have been versions that regard this psalm and the tenth to be of one piece. That they have a kinship cannot be denied. That they have obvious differences is equally clear. The issue is complicated by the fact that both psalms are acrostic to some extent—successive verses in groups of two beginning with successive letters of the alphabet. In this respect Ps. 9 is fairly regular, Ps. 10 less so. Certain letters of the alphabet are not considered. Though we shall give the needed details below we feel that it is sufficient to point out for the present that "the two psalms present an unsolved literary problem" (*Kirkpatrick*). Furthermore, each deserves to be considered an independent psalm.

In determining the time of the composition of the psalm we indicate that there is no valid reason for questioning the correctness of the heading of the psalm, which claims that this is a psalm of David. However, we are not in a position to determine exactly into what time of David's life it falls. The time must be fixed as being rather well along in the life of this king because a notable overthrow of the enemies of the nation lies at the basis of the psalm; and it is well known that David had to undergo many years of hard fighting before he decisively overcame his many external foes. Besides, as v. 11 reminds us, this psalm must have been composed after the ark of the covenant had been brought up to Jerusalem, for Yahweh is being regarded as the one "who dwelleth in Zion."

Looking a bit more closely at the question, Who are the enemies of whose overthrow the psalm speaks? we must in the nature of the case think first of all of David's particular enemies, the nations round about him on every side who assailed him again and again until they were decisively defeated. But when verses like 5 and 15 are considered, we infer correctly that also the early Canaanite nations that were overcome by Israel enter into the thinking of the author, though secondarily. Vv. 12b and 18b, where the "poor" and the "meek" are considered as having experienced deliverance, suggest the idea that internal foes are being thought of as well, ungodly Israelites who have been guilty of injustice and oppression.

If one considers the foes who have been overthrown one is driven to the conclusion that the speaker is not so much the king alone as the nation as such. Yet this theory of the collective "I" of the psalm is not to be pressed to the point where the personal sentiments of the godly king are to be ruled out. He does, indeed, speak in the name of the nation, but his own experience blends so completely with that of the nation that he describes both in one.

Oesterley very properly reminds us that "in its present form" this psalm was hardly "used in the temple worship."

As to the outline of the thought of the psalm, we believe the following to be fairly exact:

Praise, the basis of an earnest plea for deliverance
a) Praise for a mighty deliverance (vv. 1–12).
b) A plea for the continuation of this deliverance (vv. 13–20).

The details of the development of the thoughts are as follows:

vv. 1, 2. I will praise what God has done.
vv. 3, 4. He has turned back the enemy and thereby upheld my cause.
vv. 5, 6. His overthrow of the enemy has been complete.
vv. 7, 8. But Yahweh rules supreme as Judge.
vv. 9, 10. This will lead His own to take refuge in Him.
vv. 11, 12. For this God is to be praised; He has remembered His own.
vv. 13, 14. Consider my still remaining distress that I may praise Thee.
vv. 15, 16. The nations are caught in their own devices.
vv. 17, 18. The wicked shall perish, but the needy shall not be forgotten.
vv. 19, 20. Judge the nations that they may know their fraility.

On the term "to the choir director" see 4:1.

More difficult is the phrase "after the manner of 'Die for the son.'" All efforts to have these words give some kind of summary preview of the contents of psalm are farfetched. To shift the consonants so as to have "for the son" read "Nabal," is precarious. The safest course to follow is to regard this as a musical direction, either to sing the psalm according to the melody of a song or hymn by that name, or to render it after the manner of this hymn. There might be some kind of reference to II Sam. 18:33 or to a piece of poetry that David or another might have composed on the occasion of Absalom's death. All this, however, is purely conjectural.

In its praise of the Lord this psalm is ardent and warm; in its petition it is fervent. It breaks forth into a kind of torrent of praise in its opening words.

a) **Praise for a mighty deliverance (vv. 1–12)**

1. *I will praise the Lord with all my heart;*
   I will tell all Thy marvelous works;
2. *I will be glad and exult in Thee;*
   I will sing praise to Thy name, O Most High;

1. Throughout the psalm the verses appear in groups of two. These first two express the resolve to praise God for the marvelous deliverance Israel has experienced. Mere lip service is not adequate to render due praise to God; therefore, "with all my heart," cf., Deut. 6:5. Quite naturally the words spoken about Yahweh, by an easy transition merge into direct address to Yahweh in v. 1b. The "marvelous works" under consideration are the deliverances that Israel experienced in its past, particularly since the time David became the king of God's chosen people. So manifold are the emotions struggling for utterance that in addition to the resolve to praise and tell there is the deep emotion of the heart, "be glad" and "exult," and the added resolve to "sing praise," which implies the use of musical accompaniment of some sort.

3. *Because my enemies turn back,*
   Stumble, and perish at Thy presence.
4. *For Thou hast maintained my cause and my case;*
   Thou hast seated Thyself upon Thy throne, a righteous Judge.

3. A semicolon was placed after the conclusion of the second verse, to indicate that v. 3 brings the conclusion of the sentence in that it specifically states the special cause for the glad praise that the first two verses are anxious to give. The fate of the "enemies" is described in three successive stages of their overthrow: first they "turned back," then they "stumbled," and lastly they "perished." And all this happened at the sight of the presence of the Lord, who as a mighty Judge flashed the glory of His majesty upon them as He did upon the Egyptians at the Red Sea (Exod. 14:24). In a dramatic way the psalmist visualizes the discomfiture of the enemies as if God had appeared to them as an assembled host, had made His glory blind them, and they on their part had not only dropped back but had actually perished. By all this the psalmist's (or Israel's) cause, which was virtually up for trial, was "maintained," as if God Himself had spoken a favorable verdict for His people. For this reason the added figure of a judge taking his place for judgment upon the bench or "throne" is also used.

Psalm 9

5. *Thou hast rebuked the nations, destroyed the wicked ones;*
   Their names hast Thou blotted out forever and ever.
6. *The enemy are come to an end—ruins forever;*
   And cities hast Thou uprooted, the very remembrance of them
   is perished.

5. This is still a portion of that for which God is praised: His overthrow of the enemy has been complete. The fact that hostile nations are the foe that is referred to is obvious. The fact that wickedness characterized their hostility is equally obvious. The omission of the conjunctions lends a certain intensity to the successive remarks in v. 5. All that the Almighty did may be regarded as an effective rebuke from His holy lips, a rebuke so strong that the enemy withered away at the force of it. In fact, they passed off the scene, never to reappear: "their name hast Thou blotted out forever and ever." This was actually the case in regard to the Canaanite nations that were overthrown by Israel: they never revived; they had passed off the stage of history. Vividly picturesque is the description that likens them to perpetual ruins ("ruins forever"), to "cities uprooted," that passersby are no longer able to identify. Surely, the Almighty is here viewed as having done a thorough and effective piece of judgment. One cannot help but think in this connection of the Amalekites as a typical fulfillment of this statement, for of them it was said that their remembrance would be blotted out forever (cf., Exod. 17:14; Deut. 25:19).

7. *But the Lord will sit enthroned forever;*
   His throne is prepared for judgment.
8. *And He it is that will judge the world in righteousness;*
   He will govern the people with equity.

7. The result of the judgment previously described is that Yahweh is now presented as ruling supreme as the heavenly Judge that He is. There is quite a contrast between the two scenes in vv. 5, 6 and vv. 7, 8. On the one hand, every indication of judgment and overthrow and ruins; on the other, a King enthroned in serenity to rule with equity forever and to handle effectively any similar situation that may arise. Whereas the Hebrew seems to say only that Yahweh will "sit," the meaning "sit enthroned" is well established by 29:10 and Exod. 18:14, where the same verb is obviously used in this higher sense. Puny nations in their wicked opposition may come and go; Yahweh is perpetually enthroned, ready for any judgment that the needs of His people may require. But this judgment will always square with the highest standards of "righteousness" and "equity." With emphasis it is said that He Him-

self will administer judgment after this pattern. Surely, such an insight is well suited to kindle praise on a godly man's lips.

> 9. *Thus the Lord will be a secure height for the oppressed;*
> *A secure height for times of trouble.*
> 10. *And they that know Thy name will trust in Thee;*
> *For Thou hast not forsaken those that seek Thee, O Lord.*

9. After the picture of the sovereign Judge enthroned forever there follows the effect that this truth will have on His own: they will be moved to take refuge in Him. In fact, by the very overthrow of the enemy He will make Himself a refuge. Though the "thus" that we used by way of introduction of this verse does not appear in the Hebrew, this seems to be the connection in thought. It will be "oppressed" persons in particular who shall bethink themselves of what Yahweh has done, especially when they are in "times of trouble." Or those who already "know His name" will be moved to anchor their trust in Him more securely than ever before. For they will have new proof of the fact that God is not one to "forsake those that seek Him." Thus we have a description of the increase in confidence that grows out of the larger national experiences.

> 11. *Sing praises unto the Lord who dwelleth in Zion;*
> *Tell among the peoples His mighty works.*
> 12. *For as an avenger of blood He hath remembered them;*
> *He hath not forgotten the cry of the poor.*

11. The section closes as it began—with a summons to praise on the part of the poet. In this summons He does not so much incite himself as he does his people to sing the praises that are due unto Yahweh. Thus the section vv. 1–12 is enclosed in praise. It is already obvious that the Lord has chosen the city of David as His earthly dwelling place for Old Testament times. Therefore He is described as the one who has bestowed this rare honor upon the city of Jerusalem, this honor of coming into the very midst of His chosen people: He is the one who "dwelleth in Zion." v. 12 gives two telling descriptions of the manner in which He may have been said to have done His work. The first is "as an avenger of blood." This figure must be purified of all earthly and carnal dross that we might be inclined to attach to it. "Avengers of blood" were oftentimes actuated by nothing less than a most bloody zeal for vengeance and followed up all clues to capture their enemy with an assiduity that was relentless. But with an unrelenting faithfulness Yahweh avenged His own and procured true justice for them.

The second description is touching in its simplicity: "He hath not forgotten the cry of the poor." No matter how high and great the

Psalm 9

Almighty is, the cry of the poor is highly regarded by Him and never forgotten just because such criers are poor. For He is no respecter of persons. When v. 11 said that all these things were to be "told among the peoples," that does not imply that the psalmist expected any far-reaching results from such a proclamation. The true people of God were never jealous of their spiritual treasures. They proclaimed them in the days when men outside their own nation of Israel gave scant heed, and they did such work of sowing their seed in the hope of a better day that might bring a more generous response.

b) A plea for the continuation of this deliverance (vv. 13–20)

13. *Have pity on me, O Lord, see my affliction from them that hate me;*
    Thou that liftest me up from the gates of death;
14. *That I may tell all Thy praises;*
    That in the gates of the daughter of Zion I may rejoice in the salvation that Thou bestowest.

13. The fundamental motif of this second section of the psalm is petition: it begins and ends with prayer even as the first section began and ended with praise. Though there was praise for deliverance already experienced, that does not imply that the psalmist waited until every last trouble was removed before he began to think in terms of praise. Therefore, though there was good reason for praise, there were also griefs that would lead men to make earnest pleas. Consequently this plea has the sense: Consider my still remaining distress. Those commentators who fail to note this obvious explanation hold that plea must necessarily mar the tone of praise that prevailed at the beginning of the psalm. Haters are abroad; affliction still presses painfully. Since God has so often lifted up His own in the past, therefore this is called to mind by the use of a new title for God, for the original says practically, "my Lifter-up." The fact that the danger involved was not slight appears in the circumstance that the one crying out had already gotten so far as to be practically at the point of passing through the "gates of death."

In v. 14 the psalmist motivates his prayer by indicating that the deliverance which he so earnestly seeks will give him occasion to sing new praises unto God, for he purposes to make mention of them all, as many as there are. A strong contrast is introduced in the statement that these praises will be rendered in that delightful place which is the very antithesis of the "gates of death," namely, "the gates of the daughter of Zion." This refers, of course, to the place in Jerusalem where the concourse of people is the heaviest, where there will be as many as possible to hear this glad thanksgiving. The term ordinarily rendered "Thy salvation" is here translated "the salvation that Thou bestowest" in order to render the term as we might express it.

15. *The nations have plunged into the pit they made;*
    In the net which they hid is their own foot caught.
16. *It is made known that the Lord has executed judgment;*
    The wicked one is snared in the work of his own hands.
                                                    Higgaion, Selah

15. After the summons to praise, the first half of this psalm at once made mention of the overthrow of the enemies. The second half follows the same pattern but introduces a new thought, that Yahweh made it plain that this was His doing by following a pattern of punishment that had often characterized his judgments: He let the wicked fall into their own pits and nets. By letting the outcome be thus, the justice of His doings was made most obvious. For what could be more just than to have men fall into the very evil that they had secretly prepared for others?

Higgaion is a word that we have left untranslated because its meaning is uncertain. It may be a musical term calling for an interlude of "resounding music" (*BDB*). *Selah* (forte) apparently reinforces this.

17. *The wicked shall return to the realm of the dead;*
    All the nations that forget God.
18. *For the needy shall not always be forgotten;*
    Nor the hope of the meek perish forever.

17. By way of a summary as he approaches the conclusion of his psalm the holy writer contrasts the respective fortunes of the wicked nations that were overthrown with those of the poor and needy who put their trust for help in God. The nations perish; the poor shall not always be forgotten. This, too, is the work of the Lord and is to be proclaimed to His praise. When v. 17 presents "the wicked" and "the nations" as synonymous, it becomes clear that the nations were guilty of an inexcusable hostility against the people of God, namely, that hostility which the world has always had toward the church, and which grows out of the fact that they "forget God." When such men are said to "return" to the realm of the dead, that does not mean that they once came from there but involves a loose but perfectly natural use of the idea "return." The "needy" and "meek" here mentioned, together with the "poor" of v. 12, are the same, namely, the persons who are in reality the godly but suffer oppression for the Lord's sake. They bear their affliction in a godly spirit. They will throughout history seemingly be "forgotten," their "hope" will always seem to be at the point of perishing. But they are the ones who will endure.

Psalm 9

19. *Do arise, O Lord, let not man prevail;*
    Let the nations be judged in Thy presence.
20. *Appoint terror for them, O Lord;*
    Let the nations know themselves to be but men. Selah.

19. In a bold concluding prayer the psalmist beseeches God to bring the pending issues to a definite termination, in which the rebellious nations who oppose God are put down once and for all. If this is not done, man would seem to "prevail." So he calls for this judgment in the very presence of God, for He is known as a God who is absolutely just, and it is His intervention that is here sought. The psalmist prays for no more than God Himself has in mind for the ungodly when he asks that "terror" be appointed for all such. Vindictiveness has not dictated this prayer but a strong conformity to the will and purpose of God. The self-intoxication of man or even his self-deification is reflected upon when the purpose of this prayer is said to be that the nations may "know themselves to be but men." Throughout all history man has so often given evidence of the most audacious pride. The church's defense against all such is her prayer.

NOTES

A very ingenious textual alteration suggested by the conservative *Hengstenberg* in regard to the heading of the psalm would change the word *labben* to *Nabal* by a mere rearrangement of the consonants. Though this might yield a point of contact in the life of David, the device is so purely conjectural as to be utterly unreliable.

3. The expression *beshubh* means literally "in the turning back." Since this follows a verb of rejoicing, and these verbs regularly introduce the object of their rejoicing by *be,* this *be* may here rightly be classified as a *be* causal.

4. Our rendering "cause and case" is intended to translate the words *mishpat* and *din,* which nouns are closer to one another than are "right and cause" (*A.R.V.*). It is difficult to express the difference between the two words. *Koenig* renders: *Gerichtsakt und das Rechtsprechen fuer mich.*

It should also be noted that when the sentence begins with the infinitive construction it, as is often the case in Hebrew, soon continues with the imperfect or the finite verb.

5. The first two clauses of v. 6 are a close parallel as to structure, being built exactly alike. The suffix on *shemam* refers back farther than the *rashaʻ*.

6. The sentence structure of this verse is unusual but easily understood. The singular, *ha'oyebh* ("the enemy") is used with the plural

verb *tammû* ("they are come to an end"). This construction has the effect of individualizing: each one has come, etc. See *K.S.* 346m. The second clause is elliptical: "ruins forever," which literal translation we have retained. It means, of course, "being completely ruined." "Cities" may refer by metonomy to the inhabitants of the cities (*K.S.* 249c). It is well-nigh impossible to reproduce the distinctive force of the pronoun *hemmah,* which really emphasizes the suffix on *zikhram.* We could reproduce this emphasis by italicizing thus: *"Their* very remembrance is perished," a contrast being implied with Yahweh of the next verse.

7. The *waw* adversative before *hu'* serves to make this contrast more pronounced.

8. *Tébhel,* "world," meaning the inhabited world, is used without an article, which makes it the practical equivalent of a proper noun (*K.S.* 293b).

9. The connection between v. 8 and v. 9 is closer than the *A.R.V.* rendering would suggest when it reads: "Jehovah also will be a high tower." The "and" (*we* and not *wa*) here practically conveys the idea of an "and thus." His judgment, mentioned in v. 8, is the thing that makes Him a refuge. "Times of trouble" though literally "times in trouble" may be classified among instances of the construct state (*K.S.* 336w).

12. The familiar *A.V.,* "maketh inquisition for blood," could, indeed, be misunderstood. Therefore we have preferred the literal "as an avenger of blood." *Luther* inverts the order of the two verbs and says very clearly: *Denn er gedenkt und fragt nach ihrem Blut.* The suffix on *'otham* appears to be best taken proleptically, anticipating the plural noun "the poor." *K.S.* 11b.

13. *Chonnéni,* though regarded by *G.K.* 20b as Piel, may be regarded as an uncontracted Kal imperative with a suffix.

15. *Zu* is used as a relative, not a demonstrative.

16. The beginning of the verse is most likely to be construed so that "Yahweh" is taken into the first clause by anticipation, for, "It is known that Yahweh, etc." the Hebrew likes the construction: "Yahweh is known that He, etc." See *K.S.* 414e.

18. The *'anaw* of this verse is analogous to the *'anay* of v. 12. These two words are usually identified so nearly with one another that *BDB* suggests "poor, afflicted, humble, meek" for the one and "poor, afflicted, humble" for the other. Yet it would seem that those interpreters are more nearly correct who claim that the latter means "afflicted" and the former "humble." In other words, the one (*'anay*) expresses the condition, the other (*'anaw*) the frame of mind resulting from such

a condition. The Jewish marginal reading often suggests the one for the other, perhaps without sufficient warrant.

20. The word for "terror" seems to be rendered more nearly correct than Luther's translation *Meister* even as that of some of the versions (*LXX*). Nine manuscripts write the word with a final *aleph* rather than with an *h* even as do *Theodotion,* the *Targum,* and *Jerome.* The root would then justify our translation, which certainly fits more suitably into the picture.

In addition, we should like to round out the presentation on the similarity between Ps. 9 and Ps. 10, especially as far as language is concerned. The briefest summary is that of *Kirkpatrick:* " 'in times of trouble' (9:10; 10:1) is a peculiar phrase found nowhere else: the word for 'oppressed' or 'downtrodden' (9:10; 10:18) . . . ; 'mortal man' is mentioned at the close of both psalms in the same connection (9:20, 21; 10:18). Comp. further 9:13a with 10:4, 13; 9:13b with 10:12 and 9:19 with 10:11: 'for ever and ever,' 9:6; 10:16: the appeal to 'arise' 9:20 and 10:12: and other points of thought and expression."

It is a quite hopeless task to attempt to reconstruct some so-called original version of Ps. 9 and 10 on the basis of the sequence of the letters of the alphabet in the acrostic which the two psalms constitute. Several letters do not have sections of the psalm begun by them; several others are out of sequence. Attempts to reconstruct an original is the veriest guesswork and not deserving of serious attention. Those interpreters who delight in clever manipulations of this sort may play with them to their heart's content. The results of such efforts, however, are neither exegesis nor an unfolding of the oracles of God.

One may get somewhat of an idea as to how far the acrostic arrangement is carried through in the two psalms in question by examining the following list of the Hebrew letters used: *a, b, g,* (*d* skipped), *h, w, z, ch, t, y, k,* and Ps. 10:1, (*m* skipped), *n,* (*s* skipped), *p* and *'ayin* (order reversed), (*ts* skipped), *q, r, sh, t.*

Psalm 10

A CONFIDENT PRAYER
AGAINST THE WICKED OPPRESSORS IN ISRAEL

THIS IS obviously an independent psalm as we have indicated in connection with the interpretation of the preceding psalm. One difference between the two becomes very noticeable: in this psalm foes within the kingdom are under consideration. In Ps. 9 it had been enemies who were in the nations round about Israel.

In regard to the many obvious points of similarity between Ps. 9 and 10 we refer to the list given under Ps. 9.

Because of the many points of kinship between these two psalms, it would be very reasonable to assign also this psalm to David. Another possibility cannot, however, be ruled out entirely: that some writer who had absorbed the spirit of the former of the psalms had himself composed a psalm that had many points of correspondence with the model after which he patterned. In any case, there is nothing in the psalm that points to the time of Nehemiah as the time of composition of the psalm although, of course, at that time, too, there were inner foes aplenty within the nation of Israel. In fact, this psalm would agree less obviously with the time of Nehemiah inasmuch as the group of foes who are under consideration seem to be rather few in number, vexatious as they may be for all that.

Luther approaches the psalm from this angle: he claims that we here have an exhaustive description of the wicked in their opposition to the kingdom of God. Godlessness as it typically manifests itself is here being portrayed, he claims. In this view he follows the lead of *Augustine*. On this basis he concludes that it is really Antichrist who is being described. This seems to us to be too pointed an interpretation that is built on the basis of evidence that is a bit scant.

Since the prayer of the psalm practically asks God to dispose of the wicked man, it will scarcely do to conclude with some interpreters that this is a typically shortsighted Old Testament approach in that it never even thinks in terms of the possible conversion of evildoers. There is still the likelihood that such a result is not necessarily excluded. The persons involved do not seem to have been very likely prospects for conversion. Had they turned unto the Lord from their evil ways, no one would have been happier than the psalmist himself. This is a psalm of lament.

This psalm obviously has a different approach to the problem than do certain other psalms like the 37th and the 92nd, both of which teach that the prosperity of the ungodly is short-lived. That is, no doubt, often the case. Often, too, the ungodly must be committed into the hands of the Just Judge.

The theme of this prayer is offered above in the caption of the psalm. We submit the following subdivisions:

a) A bitter complaint because of the oppression of the poor and innocent by the wicked (vv. 1–11).
b) A prayer for divine intervention (vv. 12–15).
c) Assurance that Yahweh has heard (vv. 16–18).

a) A bitter complaint because of the oppression of the poor and innocent by the wicked (vv. 1–11)

The situation that prevails comes clearly into view in the opening verses.

1. *Why dost Thou stand afar off, O Lord;*
   Why hidest Thou Thyself in troublous times?
2. *Because of the pride of the wicked the poor is seared;*
   They [the poor] *are caught in the schemes which they* [the wicked] *have devised.*

1. The times are very disturbed. The wicked push on in their ungodly pride. The poor, who have no resources or friends, become the victims of the deeds of the wicked and are so painfully afflicted that they may be said to be "seared" by these ungodly tactics. Nor are they merely the victims of circumstances. The wicked have actually laid their schemes in such a way as to ensnare the poor. But in the meantime the good Lord stands "afar off" like one who cares little as to what happens to those who have only Him as their Helper.

The wicked man is now described as to his character and his attitudes.

3. *For the wicked, in spite of the desire of his soul, joins in singing hallelujahs;*
   The greedy getter blesses—rather, spurns the Lord.
4. *The wicked in his arrogancy thinks: "His wrath will not search it out."*
   "There is no God" is what all his schemings amount to.
5. *His ways are always prosperous;*
   Thy judgments are far above, out of his sight;
   As for all his foes, he snaps his fingers at them.

6. *He has always said and still does: "I shall not be moved;
Forever and ever I am a man who is not in adversity."*

3. "The wicked" very obviously represents a class of men. A rather extensive description of this class is given. The psalmist knows them well. He has evidently studied their motives and character. He has discerned how deep-seated their iniquity is. This may well be incorrigible wickedness. This may explain why the author does not think in terms of conversion of these persons.

First of all (v. 3) the relation of men of this class to the Lord, as far as public worship is concerned, is described. Black as the devices of the wicked man may be ("in spite of the desire of his soul"), he, nevertheless, appears among those that sing praises to the Lord, more particularly "hallelujahs." This he may do, either because religion is something purely habitual to him, or else because he is attempting to create the impression of piety. But the writer describes him as he really is by the term "greedy getter." Blessings of God are, indeed, upon his lips, but all who know him are aware of the fact that in his heart he actually spurns God. Therefore the first verb tells what this man's worship sounds like ("blesses"); the second tells what it actually is ("spurns").

4. We are afforded a glimpse into the heart of this man and see how he disposes of the problem of eventual punishment. He is arrogant enough to imagine: "His wrath will not search it out." The second half of the verse may be paraphrased thus: He goes about his schemings as though there were no God. He knows there really is, but he acts as though there were not. *Schmidt* very correctly points out that the persons involved do not deny the existence of God (as *Gottesleugner*); they merely despise Him (as *Gottesveraechter*).

5. How secure this man is, and how confidently he behaves are portrayed at this point. Every course he follows ("his ways") turns out successfully. God's judgments are apparently so far removed from him that they are out of sight. One gains the impression that this sinner and God's judgments will never come together. This man has enemies, but he treats them with contempt as persons that may well be disregarded ("he snaps his fingers at them"); they cannot harm him, upon whom fortune smiles so benignly.

6. So sure is this man of himself that he actually believes that his success must go on forever: "I shall not be moved." Thus godly men have spoken in confidence in the Lord, their God (16:8; 30:6). Thus this man speaks in superb trust in himself. The rest of his statement amounts to this, translating a bit more freely: "I am the kind of man whom adversity cannot touch." Such pride may be obnoxious, its very audacity may seem to call forth God's judgment. But these sentiments are actually in the heart of such men.

Psalm 10

We are now given a sketch as to how this man deals with others whom he encounters in the course of his life.

7. *With cursing his mouth is filled, also with deceit and violence;*
   Under his tongue are toil and trouble.
8. *He lies in wait in the lurking places of villages;*
   In hiding places he slays innocent men;
   His eyes spy out the helpless ones.
9. *He lurks in secret as a lion in his thicket;*
   He lurks to catch the poor;
   He catches him by drawing him into his net.
10. *He crushes* (his victim) *and again crouches down;*
    And the helpless fall by his strength.

7. Attention is first centered on what the tongue of such a wicked man utters: it is all of such a sort as is calculated to harm others. Since "deceit and violence" are what comes forth from his mouth over against others, "cursing" must be understood in the sense of curses that he wickedly utters against others, not as referring to imprecations that he rashly utters against himself. About all that his mouth or tongue yields over against others is "toil and trouble." When these are said to be "under his tongue," that means nothing other than that his mouth is full of them: there they are stored for ready usage. This interpretation fits better into the context than does the idea that he turns these things over in his mouth as sweet morsels.

8. There follows an account of the manner in which this evildoer practices wickedness against his fellow men. Like a highwayman he bides his time in ambush, waylaying innocent men. He chooses the unwalled "villages" or as some interpreters render this word, "settlements," where men are relatively less able to be defended. There he slays innocent men in his "hiding places" where he is comparatively safe from detection. There he spies out others that may also be overcome by violence when the occasion is ripe in the eyes of the murderer. Deeds of this sort had, no doubt, been done, and men had wondered who the author of them was. But the psalmist knows that it was these wicked men whom he is here describing.

9. The wicked is now likened to a lion who lurks in his thicket. Cowardly as he is though likened to a lion, he singles out the "poor" as his victims, such as have few resources for their defense. With a quick change of figure the evil man is described as a hunter who catches his victim by drawing him into his net.

10. The description quickly reverts to the former figure, that of a lion, or it may be thought of as changing to that of a thug, who crushes his victim and then swiftly crouches down, ready to seize upon and

crush another. So the evil man described uses the great strength that he happens to have.

In the whole of this description we need not regard the various items as being literally exact. It may well be possible that these are but figurative descriptions of the various forms of oppression and iniquity that these rascals engage in.

11. *He has always said in his heart and still does:*
"God has forgotten; He has hidden His face; He has never seen."

The description of the evildoer concludes with a summary statement of the attitude of this man on the subject of ultimate punishment by the Almighty that is destined sooner or later to catch the evildoer. This man simply believes that he is outside of the confines of the righteousness of God. God has forgotten to take vengeance upon him or has turned aside so as not to see what is being done. The fact that such an attitude is pure self-deception is quite obvious.

b) **A Prayer for Divine Intervention (vv. 12–15)**

12. *Arise, O Lord;*
    O God, lift up Thy hand;
    Do not forget the poor.
13. *On what ground has the wicked always spurned God?*
    (Or) has said in his heart: "Thou wilt not search it out"?
14. *(But) Thou hast seen, for Thou art wont to note trouble and vexation to deal with them;*
    To Thee the hapless one commits himself.
    As for the orphan, Thou hast always been his helper.
15. *Break Thou the arm of the wicked and evil man;*
    Thou shalt search out his wickedness, not shalt Thou find it.

12. The evil seems to be of the kind that men are powerless to correct. Therefore God is appealed to. In short, eager petitions the psalmist cries out, bidding God to cease from His inaction, and he does this in the boldness of faith. "Arise" involves the thought that God has sat by passively. "Lift up Thy hand" involves the thought that He should bring it down with a stroke of punishment. "Do not forget the poor" reminds the reader of the fact that He is a God who is known to have been wont to champion the case of the poor.

13. This verse emphasizes what the wicked have generally done. The question really demands the answer: Never have the wicked had any good reasons for the position that they take. They seem to be so sure of themselves, one might suppose that they had reason for saying that God will let these things that they do pass by unavenged.

14. This verse stands in obvious contrast to the tacit assumption of the wicked. We have, therefore, inserted into the translation the

Psalm 10

adversative "but." Over against the assumption of the evildoer is pitted the clear knowledge of the righteous: "Thou hast seen." By an obvious change of tense the Hebrew indicates that it is habitual for God to observe matters of this sort: "Thou art wont to note trouble and vexation." The fact that such noting is not an idle observation is indicated by the concluding statement of the verse: "Thou art wont to note . . . to deal with them."

In the second member of the verse the translation might also indicate that what the hapless one does is also habitual, the same tense being employed in the original. It might read: "The hapless one is wont to commit himself." The assumption included in this thought is, of course, that those who thus commit their case into the hands of the Almighty have not done so in vain. The third member of the verse expresses this thought by the strong claim that in the case of the orphan God has always been his helper.

15. The prayer now asks that drastic punishment may overtake the wicked one. The writer is obviously more interested in having the evil that such a person does thwarted than he is in seeing the wicked suffer. After God shall have taken such a case in hand He will have effectually disposed of it: if He "search out his wickedness" He shall not find it. The thought is not that the wicked devices of ungodly men are not discernible to the Almighty, but that He will have so completely disposed of them that no trace of them will be left. *Hengstenberg* reminds us that a subtle irony is involved in this statement. The wicked had thought God could not find out what he was doing. True, He shall not find it, but for quite a different reason.

c) **Assurance that Yahweh has heard (vv. 16–18)**

16. *The Lord is king forever and ever;*
    The nations have perished out of His land.
17. *Thou hast heard the desire of the meek, O Lord;*
    So dost Thou establish their hearts, dost hearken with Thine ear,
18. *In order to do justice to the orphan and the oppressed.*
    Not shall man who is of the earth terrorize any longer.

16. In the course of this prayer the assurance of the writer grew step by step until it finally rings out boldly and strongly. God's universal control of all things is asserted in the statement that He "is king forever and ever." One striking proof of this kingship, as far as His people Israel are concerned, is offered in the fact that "the nations [i.e., the old Canaanites of every sort that had once possessed the land] have perished out of His land."

17. At this point the assurance of the psalmist shines forth most clearly; he knows that God has heard his own prayer as well as the

cry of all those who have suffered affliction at the hands of the wicked. By thus giving ear to their cry He "establishes their heart," that is, gives them new courage and a brighter outlook for the future. This thought runs over into the first part of the 18th verse, where it is asserted that this is merely a part of His general work of "doing justice," a characteristic for which He is justly famous in the case of the "orphan and the oppressed." The psalm closes with a reflection upon the evildoers who were so prominently in the foreground throughout the psalm: their doom is sealed. Proud though they were and seemingly successful, they were still only "man who is of the earth." It is scarcely seemly that such men should terrorize the helpless. So the psalm which ran its course in a minor key ends in a major key.

A somewhat unique feature of the psalm is the very colorful description of the wicked men abroad at that time, found in vv. 7–10. It might seem like an overstatement. But, as *Oesterley* remarks, "If one reads such passages as Is. 1:4–6, 21–23; Mic. 3:10, 11; Jer. 5:1–9, 25–28, among many others, it becomes evident that there is no overstatement here."

Psalm 11

THE RIGHTEOUS LORD IS A REFUGE FOR THE RIGHTEOUS

DAVID IS being wickedly antagonized by ruthless enemies, who have apparently succeeded so well in their machinations that David's own friends counsel him to flee: nothing can avail against these enemies. David, who in bold faith recognizes that God's providence watches most carefully over those who put their trust in Him just as He carefully keeps an eye on the evildoers—David, we say, has taken his refuge in the Lord, and there He proposes to stay. Flee he will not. We have here a psalm of trust, cf., 7:1; 16:1; 31:1; 71:1.

Something can be said in favor of the suggestion that David may well be speaking in the name of the whole body of those who fear the Lord. David is not voicing only his own feelings and attitude. So this would become a hymn of the congregation.

Though authorship by David is considered impossible by quite a few writers on the subject, we cannot help but feel that it is quite feasible. Situations such as the one here described are certainly not at all unthinkable in the days when David was at Saul's court. What such enemies did to David was fraught with all sorts of peril for him, the very foundations of the state seemed to be torn apart. Or the days of Absalom's rebellion could be thought of. Here, as in Ps. 12, a measure of hyperbole may enter into the description of the perilous situations created by the enemies. But surely, the case is not pictured in any more dreadful terms than David actually felt it to be. There are two sections in this psalm.

a) **The Cowardly Advice to Flee before Treacherous Foes (vv. 1–3)**
   To the Director. By David.
   1. *In the Lord I have taken refuge.*
      How can you say to me:
      "Flee to your mountain like a bird?
   2. *For, lo, the wicked bend their bow;*
      They have fitted their arrow on the string
      To shoot in darkness at the upright in heart.
   3. *When the foundations* [of society] *are torn down,*
      What can the righteous do?"

1. For the term "Director" see Ps. 4. "By David" is part of a reliable heading which indicates David as the author of the psalm.

Though almost the whole of this section is, indeed, the cowardly advice to flee before treacherous enemies it opens with a basic note which will be struck again in the second section and be the essence of it. Here is a man who has "taken refuge in the Lord." If he had not, the statements made later would have been boastful claims without solid ground to stand upon. The words spoken to David appear to come from the mouth of well-being but timid friends. Having put his trust in the Lord, the writer cannot but reject as unseemly the counsel they offer: "How can you say to me, etc.?" The essence of their advice is quick flight. They speak in the figurative language that is characteristic of the Orient. Birds flee to the forests when they are in danger. The forests of Palestine were on the mountains. Therefore: "Flee to your mountain like a bird." The verb is plural, *nudhu,* "flee *ye*"; the plural suffix "*your* mountain" agrees with this form. This led us to say above that the psalmist speaks for a group who are associated with him. As is so often the case, David and the true members of the people of God are making common cause. So the psalm has more than a personal note.

2. The reasons advanced for immediate flight follow. They are that the wicked have already "bent the bow" and have already "fitted the arrow on the string." This figure may imply any form of threatening

danger. It certainly describes the readiness of the foes to take bloody measures to dispose of their opponent. The danger cannot have been small. Their purpose is stated as being "to shoot in darkness at the upright of heart." If the writer's estimate is correct—and there is no reason to question it—then the opposition are "the wicked," and his own party are "the upright of heart," as was so often the case in David's life. If the intention of the foes is to shoot "in darkness," then they must have been engaged in underhanded devices to dispose of David and his followers. That these devices were magic and, perhaps, slander (*Schmidt*) is mere surmise.

3. Further reasons for flight are stated. The enemies have apparently done so much damage that it can be claimed that because of their opposition to the righteous "the foundations [of society] are torn down." The parenthesis "of society" does not appear in the text. It was added by way of interpretation. It might have substituted "of the state" or the like or even "the basic principles of justice and righteousness"—all of which amount to practically the same thought. In Saul's time the bitterness of the party opposing David could surely be charged with having done such devilish work. But is it not true that at such times a feeling of futility comes upon those who espouse the cause of righteousness? Therefore his friends were saying: "What can the righteous do?" You cannot change the situation; you cannot stop them; they sweep everything before them.

b) **The Righteous Lord Is a Refuge for the Righteous (vv. 4–7)**

4. *The Lord in His holy temple,*
   The Lord, whose throne is in the heavens—
   His eyes behold, His glances test the children of men.
5. *The Lord tests the righteous;*
   But the wicked and the lover of violence He hates.
6. *On the wicked He rains slings [of destruction];*
   Fire and brimstone and a heavy gale will be their lot.
7. *For the Lord is righteous;*
   He loveth righteous deeds;
   His countenance beholds the upright.

4. When the psalmist evaluates who the Lord is and what He does, the writer must be conscious of his own right attitude toward the Lord, otherwise he could not have spoken thus. He begins with a consideration of the exalted nature of the God who sits enthroned in His sanctuary in the heavens—no thought here of an earthly temple. But this conception of the high and holy God does not imply remoteness on His part or unfamiliarity and indifference toward what is going on upon earth. Just because He is so high, therefore nothing escapes

Him. Each man is under His surveillance. Each man's actions are under continual scrutiny. In the light of what was just said about the ungodly schemes of the opposition this means that God is well aware of what is being done and has the right appreciation of it though it be clothed, let us say, with the mantle of royal sanction. For the present the claim is merely that *all alike* are under this continual scrutiny.

5. When the first result of this inspection by God is said to be: "The Lord tests the righteous," the thought implied is, of course, that He finds them to be what they claim and aim to be. That implies that His divine approval rests upon them. The case of the "wicked" is stated a bit more precisely. They are, first of all, more clearly defined as being "lovers of violence," implying that God recognizes them to be just that. Saul obviously claimed that his persecutions of David were measures that were necessary for the welfare of the state. For all that, they were deeds of violence, and he was a man who loved violence. Sharp and blunt is the conclusion reached with regard to this class of men: He "hates" them. Strong language, growing out of the correct conception of the vigor of the divine character in its opposition to all forms of evil!

6. The lot of the wicked man is a perilous one, not his own, says the psalmist in effect. For "on the wicked He rains slings." So the Hebrew. The term slings (*pachim*) would imply some evil that catches and holds the evildoers and so brings them low. So for the sake of explanation we added to the word the parenthesis "of destruction." Textual changes are quite unnecessary here. It would seem that at this point the analogous case of the destruction of Sodom and Gomorrah came to the writer's mind, for he borrows terms that were characteristic of that calamity only when he says: "Fire and brimstone and a heavy gale will be their lot." When He takes the wicked in hand, there is no trifling, there are no halfhearted measures. The punishment is commensurate with their crime, and their crime was not a light one. "Lot" is "the portion of their cup," which certainly is a far more picturesque way of stating it. God gives a man a cup in hand; in it is found what God in His justice has appointed for him, either an abundance of good ("my cup runneth over," Ps. 23:5), or a bitter potion, as here, where it means the drink of God's wrath. "Heavy gale" (*Koehler*) could be translated literally "winds of wraths" as *Hengstenberg* contends. *Taylor* suggests rightly that "such language is more than an expression of Hebrew vindictiveness. It reflects . . . the belief that evil is in hopeless conflict."

7. To build this contention on a solid basis and to sum up effectively, the psalmist now says: "The Lord is righteous." Only a man who is convinced of the justice of his cause and the injustice of the

opposition would dare to appeal to the righteousness of God. That, after all, is a broad base on which to stand at all times. From this truth follows the next: "He loveth righteous deeds." Of this love in his own case the psalmist is assured, otherwise he would not have dared to pray as he does and take his refuge in God as he did in v. 1. Since the whole emphasis lies on what God does and is, and that alone constitutes the solid basis of comfort, we have translated the last clause: "His countenance beholds the upright," implying that same watchful care that was stressed above. The words could have been translated: "The upright shall behold His face." But *panemo,* which equals *panaw,* His countenance, being a plural, can readily take the verb in the plural, *yechesu,* which is easier to construe than to regard the singular *yashar* as a collective plural and so make it the subject of the verb.

NOTES

1. *Tsippor* (a bird), a kind of adverbial accusative, involves a comparison. Cf., *KS* 3321.

2. *Qesheth* (bow) without an article, involving the idea of the customary. *KS* 294f. *Konenu* (they have fitted) is a case of the omission of a conjuction, asyndeton, in the consecutive use of the verb. *KS,* 368g.

3. For emphasis *tsaddiq* (the righteous) even precedes the interrogative pronoun "what." *KS* 339e.

4. *Yahweh* (the Lord) is clearly a nominative absolute. *KS* 341h.

6. *Yamter* (He rains), though it looks like a jussive and not like a plain hiphil imperfect is yet to be treated like the latter. *GK* 109k cites many instances where this happens. Cf. also *KS* 194f.

Psalm 12

THE LORD A HELPER
AGAINST MAN'S TREACHERY

THIS PSALM is a complaint and a plea for mercy against treachery which is encountered on every hand but at the same time an expression of confidence that the Lord, as He has promised, will effect the deliverance of His own in due season.

The Hebrew heading indicates that David committed the psalm into

Psalm 12

the hands of the choir director with the direction that it be sung *'al-hasnsheminith,* which may mean "by the basses," cf., I Chron. 15:20, where a corresponding expression may refer to the sopranos.

There is no good reason for removing the composition of psalm from the age of David, which the heading suggests. It may well have been written while David was at the court of Saul or during the time when David was in perpetual flight before Saul's jealousy. There were men who were poisoning Saul's mind against him as *Kirkpatrick* points out (cf., I Sam. 26:19). The city of Keilah proved treacherous (cf., I Sam. 23:11). The Siphites were equally faithless (I Sam. 23: 19ff.). The attempt to make a late exilic or postexilic date fit the contents of the psalm suffers chiefly from the inadequacy of not agreeing with the type of men who are here depicted as causing grief to the psalmist: they were men of "smooth lips and a double mind," which is surely not a good description of the people who dominated Israel in exilic times or thereafter. At this later date violence and highhanded oppression were the order of the day.

The position that we take does not yet answer the question as to whether the enemies referred to were compatriots or foreigners. From the references given above there may well have been some foreigners among them. But the lament that "the godly have ceased to be" would seem to reflect definitely upon members of the covenant people. For the *chasidh* (v. 1) is primarily a man who is faithful to the covenant in which his people stand. Cf. also *Oesterley, The Psalms,* p. 56ff.

It must become obvious on closer examination of the psalm that it sounds nothing of a strictly personal note; there is no "I" and "my." Though a personal experience may have been at the bottom of all that David says, it seems quite likely that he broadened his thinking to the point where he saw that his complaint was the complaint of the people of God of all times though the situation becomes more painful and acute only from time to time. *Hengstenberg* rightly contends that "without a doubt this psalm is not personal in tone but was composed at the very outset for the needs of the congregation." This is one of the many instances when the psalms rise above the purely personal and local and look to the later needs of the church of God.

Related to this question is the one as to whether this is a strictly liturgical piece (*Leslie*). To make it such is plainly an overstatement of the case and an excessive use of the principle of the prevalence of the liturgical element in the psalms. *Leslie* says: Ps. 12 is a solemn liturgy prepared for a regularly recurring service of petition. He assigns the first part as a petition to the congregation, vv. 4 and 5 to the "officiating priest," and vv. 6–8 to the congregation. An examination of the psalm will reveal that it simply cannot support such far-reaching conclusions. A pet theory dominates the interpretation. *Schmidt* quite unfairly makes it the embittered utterance of an old man who cannot get over his bitterness.

One further issue should be disposed of in advance: Is the section vv. 5–8 a prophetic utterance in which the poet turns prophet and speaks by divine inspiration? The words could be interpreted thus, but nothing in the psalm makes such an interpretation compulsory. Though we cannot agree with those interpreters who assert (like *Koenig*) that the psalmists never speak as prophets, we feel that in this instance all the needs of the case are met if we assume that the writer offers a summary of statements of God that he has heard or read—a free, comprehensive summary of sound prophetic thoughts in poetic fashion.

a) **A prayer for deliverance from the men who speak in hypocrisy and treachery and have become very boastful (vv. 1–4)**

1. *Help, O Lord, for the godly have ceased to be,*
   For faithfulness has disappeared from among the children of men.
2. *(But rather) they speak deceit, every man with his neighbor;*
   With smooth lips and double mind do they speak.
3. *May the Lord cut off all smooth lips,*
   The tongue that talks big;
4. *The ones who have said:*
   "With our tongues we shall do heroic things;
   Our lips are under our control.
   Who is lord over us?"

1. Dark is the picture that is presented: Loyal members of the covenant people are hard to find, have all but disappeared from the nation. Basic virtues like "faithfulness" are no longer in evidence. The situation is so bad that it presses a strong cry from the psalmist's lips—"help," a common cry when a situation is desperate, without necessarily requiring that an individual state from what he desires help. The situation as such makes the need obvious. It is clear that the form of statement used is a hyperbole. But that is all the more evidence as to how keenly the writer feels the existing corruption. His complaint, as has been well pointed out by *Hengstenberg,* is not so much about the universal corruption of his time but about the suffering that this has caused the godly. "The psalmist has been brooding over the black outlook till his overcharged heart relieves itself in this single-worded prayer ('help')."

2. By prefacing the verse with the words in parentheses ("but rather") we seek to indicate words of transition that the Hebrew usually takes for granted. The sins that have brought about the fact that "the godly have ceased" and that "faithfulness has disappeared" are primarily sins of the tongue—"they speak deceit," "with smooth lips and double mind they speak." In other words, treachery and flattery and duplicity are inherent in all that one hears. The hyperbole used in v. 1 continues, for these sins are charged against "every man" in relation to "his neighbor."

3. Since there is little that man can do about this state of affairs, the situation is laid before the Lord with the implied request that He may remedy it. By a typical synecdoche—part for the whole—the destruction of the lips implies the destruction of those whose they are, the lips being mentioned as the particular source of harm. An added feature in the description of these evildoers is that they have a "tongue that talks big." This somewhat colloquial rendering of the Hebrew uses the same idiom, except that the original employs the plural "big things," which plainly means boastful and proud utterances. Since all pride of sinful man is offensive to the Almighty, He is rightly appealed to put an end to such irregularities.

4. Three proud claims are specifically ascribed to these sinners: a) "With our tongues we shall do heroic things," in which statement it dare not be overlooked that these tongues were resorting to flattery and deceit. Yet they promise themselves great success from these unholy pronouncements. b) "Our lips are under our control." This would imply that they will suffer no man to interfere with the wicked utterances by which they hope to achieve success. Deceitful tongues are joined with stubborn self-will. c) "Who is lord over us?" They acknowledge no superior, whether it be on earth or in high heaven. Pride and arrogance plus full confidence in their evil use of the tongue are earmarks of these men.

We need not be too worried about the prayer of vv. 3 and 4, as to whether it implies a spirit of vengeance or the absence of a spirit that would rather see an evil man recover from his sinful ways than be punished and destroyed. David's life gives ample evidence of a conciliatory and forgiving spirit so that we are well justified in taking for granted that he would rather see sinners saved than destroyed. A helpful remark of *Maclaren's* should not be lost sight of: "But the impatience of evil and the certainty that God can subdue it, which make the very nerve of the prayer, should belong to the Christian yet more than to the psalmist."

b) Reassured by promises of God that he recalls, the psalmist rests secure in the confidence that God will sustain His own in the midst of their ungodly enemies (vv. 5–8)

5. (Therefore) *because of the violence done to the poor, because of the whimperings of the needy,*
Now will I arise, says the Lord;
I will set in safety him who so eagerly pants for it.
6. *The words of the Lord are pure words,*
Silver refined in a smelter in the ground,
Purified seven times.
7. *Thou, O Lord, wilt regard them,*
Thou wilt guard them from this generation forever,
8. *Who on every side strut about as wicked men,*
As if the wickedness of sons of men were exalted.

Over against the heaven-storming pride of those who were just described God is introduced as speaking. What he says (see above) is an effective summary of such godly sentiments as the writer recalls as bearing on the case, perhaps not one of them a quotation but a free paraphrase of what those who know God may rightly expect him to say under the circumstances. Amos 8:4–7 and Is. 3:14ff. would be analogous statements which men of a later generation might have remembered under similar circumstances.

5. What stirs Him to action is the violence that the proud manipulators of smooth and deceptive words have done to the "poor" and the "needy" whose "whimperings" He has heard (cf., Exod. 3:7). The Lord is represented as forming a resolve: "Now will I arise," and as promising deliverance: "I will set in safety him who so eagerly pants for it." The picture unfolds naturally as we go along. All the harm done, especially to God's saints, by the evil men who were first described was not immediately apparent. *Schmidt's* peculiar criticism to the effect that the quotation recalled by the psalmist in the second half of the psalm does not quite agree with the situation depicted in the first half is refuted by this simple observation. Nothing further is sketched at this point than the resolve of the Lord to help the needy. That is a guaranty of the fact that it will be achieved.

6. David reassures himself that this will take place by recalling the general nature of God's words as he and all of God's saints know them: they are "pure words," which expression removes the alloy of undependability. Man may often intend to do well and may promise help but may fall short of keeping his promise because of human frailty. Not so God. Therefore His promises may be likened to "silver refined in a smelter in the ground, purified seven times," the very purest of the precious metal.

7. Since God may rightly be described in reference to His words as just indicated, the psalmist draws proper conclusions with regard to the situation in which he and other godly men like him find themselves. Addressing God in prayer, he expresses the confidence that God will keep His watchful eye on those that have suffered oppression ("Thou wilt regard") and will go farther in that He will keep His protecting hand over them. The psalm here takes on a note of the more personal feelings in that the writer includes himself ("Thou wilt guard *us*"). This protection is offered in the face of this wicked class of oppressors above described (in this sense the word "generation" is here used), and this protection of God will be exercised for all times to come.

8. The description of the men against whom this prayer for protection is directed continues in the last verse. The last sentence may be construed as having omitted the relative pronoun, a construction as common in Hebrew as it is in English. Therefore we freely inserted a "who" by way of beginning v. 8. No matter where you turn, "on every side," in emphatic position in the Hebrew, these persons are found strutting about as the wicked men that they actually were, making no pretense at being good men, quite content to be known as practicing wickedness. But their brazenness might well create the impression "as if the wickedness of sons of men were exalted," which plainly means that these persons act as if by common consent and popular vote wickedness had been set on a throne as the dominant force ruling in that generation—an extreme that surely had not yet been reached under any circumstances. But all this shall not prevail, for God guards His own. On this note of confidence the psalm closes, for v. 7 is still the chief clause of the final statement.

NOTES

1. *'emunim,* though plural and though as to form could well mean "faithful ones," because of the contrast with the deceit mentioned in v. 2 is best regarded as one of the plurals used for abstract qualities, *KS* 235d.

2. What we have rendered "double mind" is "heart and heart" in the Hebrew. Since the heart is the seat of thinking, we believe our rendering is justified.

5. *Mishshodh* is an example of the *min* causal, *KS* 403e. So is *me-'enqath. Yaphiach lo* presents some difficulty, none, however, that warrants textual changes. Again the relative has been omitted. Opinion is just about evenly divided as to whether the relative refers to "safety" which immediately precedes or is to be understood as a masculine as we have translated.

6. There is no valid reason for having misgivings about *ba 'alil* in the sense of "in a smelter" or "smelting pot." Though the word appears no-

where else, the *Targum* gives it this meaning, which makes good sense. *La'arets* allows for another translation. Instead of "in the ground" attached to "smelter" it may be construed with the verb thus: "silver, refined in a smelter (poured out) to the earth." Either seems admissible.

8. *Libhney* is to be regarded as having the *le* which expresses the genitive relationship, *KS* 280n. *Kerum* is the infinitive with *ke*.

In *Pritchard, Ancient Near Eastern Texts,* pp. 405–7 (110) there are a few sentiments in which the person in question speaks of the prevalence of evil men much as the psalmist does in this psalm, but with the significant difference that, as the title of the piece shows ("A Dispute over Suicide"), the Egyptian feels driven to take his own life, cf., *Taylor, Interpreter's Bible.*

Psalm 13

YEARNING FOR HELP FROM GOD

A BEAUTIFUL PSALM—brief, helpful, and very instructive. It is obviously born out of a life situation such as many must face. Its tone is highly individual—one man tells what he experienced, tells, that is to say, indirectly through his prayer, which has been preserved for us. There is no good reason for doubting the validity of the heading, which ascribes the piece to David. Thus David may well have cried toward the end of the days when he was being persecuted by Saul and had been hounded day after day through the wilderness of Judea (cf., I Sam. 27). But fortunately the manner of referring to the experience is such that any individual may pray this prayer after the original sufferer. It is to be classified as the lament of an individual.

> *To the Choir Director. A Psalm of David.*
> 1. *How long, O Lord, wilt Thou completely forget me?*
>   *How long wilt Thou hide Thy face from me?*
> 2. *How long shall I devise plans in my soul, grief in my heart all the day?*
>   *How long shall my enemy triumph over me?*
>
> 3. *Look, answer me, O Lord, my God.*
>   *Lighten my eyes lest I sleep the sleep of death;*
> 4. *Lest my enemy say, "I have overcome him,"*
>   *And my foes exult that I am shaken.*

Psalm 13

5. *But as for me, I have trusted in Thy faithfulness;*
   May my heart rejoice in Thy deliverance.
6. *I will sing unto the Lord*
   Because He will deal bountifully with me.

The psalm opens with a pitiful complaint that expresses the earnest yearning of the soul for deliverance (vv. 1, 2). It continues with the prayer proper (vv. 3, 4). It concludes on a note of reassurance (vv. 5, 6—one verse in the original). At first feeling runs high; gradually it subsides; at the end of the prayer calm has been restored. Even so has many an experience gone in the course of men's lives.

1. The fourfold "how long" indicates the extremity of this poor man's misery. His strength is well-nigh spent. His patience can hold out no longer. Why has God not intervened this long while? It seems as though God had "completely forgotten." It appears besides as if He were intentionally letting His face be hid from the poor suppliant. Behind this statement lies the vital use of the expression "the face of God." That signifies the experience of His gracious goodness, His divine presence. There has been no tasting of the divine comfort that comes from the reassurance that He will stand by a man and help him. The word that we have translated "completely" (*netsach*) originally means "forever." To translate it thus in the same sentence with a "how long" does not make sense—*Buttenwieser* rightly calls this "nonsense." To devise elaborate explanations to reconcile such inconsistency as being due to the bewildered writer's confusion is farfetched. "Forever" is used very loosely, as *Luther* already saw, who translated it as we have done (*so gar*).

2. The period of waiting has long been filled with plans that were devised for self-deliverance. The verb used implies putting plans into a place where they are stored up. Always new plans are being projected, every night as it were. Night is the time for planning. Day the time for trying to carry them out. But when they are attempted, it is found that they are futile, for God will not grant success, and so the experience of "all the day" is "grief in my heart all the day." If this pattern is kept in mind, it will be seen that the expression "all the night" is presupposed for the first member of the verse. Naturally, then, if all plans have miscarried, it is but natural that the enemy has been successful day after day, and therefore we have as the last complaint: "how long shall my enemy triumph over me?" Here and in v. 4 the enemy appears to be a single individual, a situation which fits well the case of Saul vs. David. One feels keenly that this fourfold cry is uttered out of the depth of the grief of heart and soul.

3. If the first two verses are complaint, the next two are petition pure and simple. It is as though God had averted His face and refused to con-

sider what was befalling His child: "Look, answer me." God had done nothing to indicate that He had heard what His child had said or noted what he had done. But the poor man still regards himself as God's child and God as his God—"O Lord, my God." The next petition, "lighten my eyes," implies that he is in danger of having the lamp of life within him go out entirely. When the vital powers grow dim, a Hebrew says his eyes are darkened. When he is refreshed and vitalized he says his eyes are "lightened." Cf. on this usage I Sam. 14:27, 29; Ezra. 9:8. Here the psalmist feels that, unless God intervenes, his life's lamp may go out completely, perhaps because he would fall entirely into the power of his enemy.

4. The enemy's triumph is the motive urged for hearing this petition. There is more involved here than merely having one foe exult over his opponent. The writer has identified his cause with God's and knows that it is truly that. *Maclaren* very wisely remarks in this connection: "God's honor is identified with His servant's deliverance, a true thought, and one that may reverently be entertained by the humblest lover of God, but which needs to be carefully guarded. We must be very sure that God's cause is ours before we can be sure that ours is His."

5. Some interpreters view the last two verses as giving reasons for being entitled to expect deliverance (*Koenig*), others call them "a joyous hope of ultimate deliverance" (*Kirkpatrick*). We prefer to describe them as bringing the note of reassurance. Calm confidence has returned to the heart. Deliverance has not yet come, but trust ("I have trusted") has returned and has as its basis God's "faithfulness" (*Chesedh*— which always implies His covenant faithfulness). The writer does not know when help will arrive, but when it does come, his sentiment is: "May my heart rejoice in Thy deliverance," meaning, of course, impending deliverance.

6. Not only shall gladness fill his very heart, but his praise will become vocal at that time—"I will sing unto the Lord." Expressing the sentiment of the preceding verse that this help is still future, he says: "Because He will deal bountifully with me." Faith has climbed out of the lowest depths of despair where it had well-nigh perished into the full sunlight of godly hope. It can wait for the help to come, for it is sure that it will not fail him.

NOTES

Heading: *lammenatseach,* cf. the heading of Ps. 4, "Notes."
2. There is no reason for changing the Hebrew text of the word *'etsoth* ("plans"). The traditional text makes perfectly good sense. Because of the absence of a reference to the night after "day" has been

mentioned is not sufficient reason for adding the word. Note the explanation above.

3. The Hebrew says, "lest I sleep death." In our idiom this must be expanded into "sleep the sleep of death." *KS*, 329h.

4. On *yekhaltiw* note that it takes an object suffix though it is usually construed with a dative object. This is not an adequate reason for textual correction; cf. especially *KS*, 211b.

5. *bishu 'athékha* ("Thy deliverance") is obviously a subjective genitive implied in the suffix and means: the deliverance that I expect from Thee.

6. Though *gamal* means "render," it is so obviously taken in the good sense here that the translations quite regularly render accordingly, like "deal bountifully with me."

Psalm 14

GOD'S REACTION TO THE UNIVERSAL
CORRUPTION OF MANKIND

THE SPECIAL DIFFICULTY in the interpretation of this psalm is the perplexity of the reader in regard to the situation described. If he knows Rom. 3:1–12 he is aware of the fact that v. 1 of our psalm is cited in support of Paul's contention that all mankind is under the taint of sin. He then tries to make the first verse of the psalm a general truth and is inclined to translate the perfect tenses of these verses as presents. So do *Luther, Hengstenberg, Maclaren, Delitzsch, Oesterley,* etc. Delitzsch has the strongest presentation of the claim that *'amar* and the rest of the perfects are to be translated as an "abstract present." Still it seems so much more natural to let the perfect be a past tense, "The fool *hath* said" (*AV, ARV* etc.).

As soon as this view is accepted and the whole psalm translated thus, as *Koenig* very correctly contends it must be done, one immediately tries to think of a historic situation which would fit this description. No interpreter has attempted this more consistently that has *Kirkpatrick,* who offers the ingenious suggestion that the author has in mind such situations as the times of the Flood, of the Tower of Babel, and of Sodom and Gomorrah, instances of history when human wickedness was very much in evidence. He then claims that v. 3 is offered as an illustration as to how the same situation appeared also in Israel in the psalmist's day in that the meek and lowly were oppressed by those who had influence and power. But God proves Himself the defender of His people, and the closing prayer drives home the hope of absolute deliverance, which will finally come from God.

But here again, as the text of the psalm is reread, one feels keenly that nothing in the contents of the psalm warrants being so specific about the historical situations that are referred to. Yet on the whole much of the approach mentioned above may be retained. True as it is that the writer did not set out to furnish proof for Paul for the universal depravity of mankind, he is definitely thinking along these lines. In the first section (vv. 1–3) he has a situation of prevailing wickedness in mind, that is to say, throughout the world by and large, time and again when we view mankind critically we must get the impression that those who dwell upon the earth are "fools," and that they deny the existence of God, and as a result degenerate morally. The psalmist sees a similar depravity rearing its ugly head also in Israel (v. 3). But he knows full well that God cannot tolerate such iniquity (v. 5f.) and prays that Israel in particular may be restored to its ideal state.

There is no serious reason for claiming that David could not have written this psalm as the heading claims. What he may have seen and heard about neighboring nations may have instructed him as to their depravity. The sad oppression of good men under Saul's rule have furnished the needed illustration of a similar corruption in Israel. The certainty of the overthrow of wicked oppressors in Israel may well have come from David's pen as a suitable conclusion of his prayer.

To the Director. By David.

1. *The fool said in his heart, There is no God.*
   They have acted wickedly, made their doings abominable;
   There was none that did good.
2. *The Lord looked down from heaven upon the children of men*
   To see if there was a man of insight,
   One who sought after God.
3. *All have gone astray;*
   They have altogether become spoiled;
   There was not one that did good, not even one.

4. *Have they become aware of this, all these evildoers,*
   Who devour My people to feed themselves?
   On the Lord they do not call.

5. *Then they were greatly terrified,*
   For the Lord is in the midst of the righteous generation.

Psalm 14

6. *Ye shall be put to shame as far as your plans against the*
   poor are concerned,
   Because the Lord is his refuge.

7. *Oh, that the deliverance of Israel would come out of Zion!*
   When the Lord completely restores His people,
   Then may Jacob rejoice, and Israel be glad!

On the "director" see 4:1.

The fool (*nabhal*) is without an article and is to be taken in the generic sense. To some extent the verb "has said" (*'amar*) is a gnomic aorist—"has always said." Fools have always said there is no God. What is described is more largely practical atheism rather than theoretical atheism. Both may be included. When men deny God's existence or live as though He were not, then wickedness prevails: men "have acted wickedly, made their doings abominable." Atheism bears its proper fruit in rotten conduct. Many have been the times when such utter degeneracy of mankind has been all but universally in evidence, but it always has its beginning in severing the connection with God. That the fools as a class are meant, though the singular is used, appears from the fact that the verbs unconsciously become plurals—"*they* have acted wickedly." As further proof note that, when God views what is going on, He is said to behold the "children of men," not an individual.

To cover the whole realm of human conduct and to show that it is to be regarded as being infected by the defection from God, the author offers three statements: "They have acted wickedly, made their doings abominable, there was none that did good." The first two of these statements are without a connective. Asyndeton is sometimes to be regarded as merely one mode of statement resorted to in poetry (*KS* 357h). If the concluding statement seems somewhat too general, it must at least be admitted that those who are less flagrant in their attitude may very often in a practical way deny God and so really fall under this condemnation if closely scrutinized.

2. The matter is now viewed from the divine perspective. God subjects men to an inspection, "looked down from heaven upon the children of men." The verb actually says "bent over" to look. All "the children of men" are made to pass in review before Him. Basic essentials are the rule by which he judges: is there "a man of insight?" (the participle is used, "a discerning one" or "one who sought after God"). Certainly if God is not in all their thoughts, they cannot be good men. So the divine inspection aims at the things that count.

3. The result is summarized. The initial "all" is emphatic: The Almighty, the Judge of mankind, finds them all infected with the same virus of sin. That theory and practice lie close together is indicated by

the fact that the inevitable issues of ungodly theory immediately result in ungodly living: "All have gone astray; they have altogether become spoiled." The second verb starts from a root that implies souring of milk. Apart from divine grace this is the way mankind looks to the Lord on high. By way of summary comes the statement, refrain like, looking back to the conclusion of v. 1: "There was none that did good, not even one."

4. The sense of this verse is not immediately connected with that of the former. It has nothing to do with men in the world at large. Indeed, those "who devour My people" could be men of a nation outside of Israel. It seems more likely that a situation is being thought of like that which is encountered in quite a number of other passages in the Scriptures where an ungodly element in the population of Israel preys upon the meek and the lowly, taking cruel advantage of their defenceless position; cf., Isa. 3:12; Amos 2:6f.; Mic. 2:2; 7:3; Ezek. 34:8. Besides, though a prophet or psalmist could, indeed, refer to Israel as "my people," since in the two preceding verses God had been introduced, it is quite likely that He still speaks here. He is so often introduced as the father of the widow and the fatherless children. These unfortunates are indirectly addressed by the question: Have they never become aware of how God regards the evildoer and speaks His sentence against him? So for the verb "become aware of" we have supplied the object "this," referring to the two preceding verses. The specific sin the "fools" are charged with is that they devour God's people to feed themselves. This reads literally: "eaters of My people they eat bread." We believe this means that they live by means of ungodly preying upon their victims as *Kessler* has well rendered it. We believe we have caught most of that thought in the translation, "who devour My people to feed themselves." Quite obviously such persons would not be men who are regularly given to prayer. Therefore the further indictment, "on the Lord they do not call." As *Maclaren* remarks: "Practical atheism is, of course, prayerless." *Oesterley* gets priests into the picture by translating: "They eat the bread of God." Clearly priests are not in this picture.

Note the omission of the logical object in the case of the verb *yadhe'u*, a common occurrence; cf., *KS*, p. 342, 1. Also, that *'okheley*, though a participle, is the equivalent of a relative clause, *KS*, 411i.

5. There is an intentional vagueness about the initial "there" (*sham*). Some interpreters translate it "there"; others "then." It may have both meanings. But it is here intended to refer to that situation or that time when the Almighty, the Just One, who cannot tolerate iniquity forever, begins to vent His wrath upon those of Israel who oppress the Lord's true children (cf. v. 4). When He took them in hand, then or there they were always greatly terrified (Hebrew, "trembled with trem-

bling"). They had failed to see that the meek and lowly who have put their trust in the Lord are the objects of His special care; "the Lord is in the midst of the righteous generation." "Generation," as so often, has here gone over from the meaning of people of a given period to a special class of people even as we also use this word. Since the whole verse is cast into the past tense it obviously refers to all those instances in the past when the oppressors were overthrown even as were Ahab and Jezebel who preyed upon defenceless Naboth (I Kings 21).

6. In a solemn prediction the psalmist states the fate of all who thus oppress the poor: "Ye shall be put to shame as far as your plans against the poor are concerned." This is not the usual meaning given the words of this verse. But since the parallel form *hobhish* is usually an intransitive, it is more in keeping with usage to take *tabhishu* as an intransitive and to regard *'atsath* as an accusative of specification with the noun dependent upon it treated as the objective genitive: "plans against the poor" (*KS*, 336e). Parallel with the second half of v. 5 is the thought, "because the Lord is his refuge."

7. Having been reminded by the issue on which the three preceding verses have dwelt of the unhappy conditions that prevail in many other directions among God's own people, the writer quite naturally turns to prayer that God may heal the grievous hurt of His people. Since Zion was even then the site of the sanctuary, it was to be expected that he would think of God as going forth from His holy place where He dwelt among His people in order that He might deliver them. Therefore the statement: "O that the deliverance of Israel would come out of Zion!" Since a thoroughgoing restoration alone could help, therefore this is thought of as coming to pass. "When the Lord completely restores His people" means, of course, He will in due time most assuredly do this. The form of the prayer, however, asks that, when this comes to pass, Israel may not be remiss, but "Jacob may rejoice, and Israel be glad." For too often God's mercies have been received, and He has not been fittingly thanked for them. *Shubh shebhuth* in the sense of bringing about a thoroughgoing change, cf., *KS* 329i.

Ps. 53 has almost the same contents as this psalm. The relation between the two can be discussed after Ps. 53 has been studied.

The simplest explanation for the double occurrence of the psalm in the Psalter seems to be that it appeared in each of two earlier collections, which were later combined.

The tendency to make a part of the psalm (v. 4) an invective against corrupt priests is feasible on the score of extensive textual changes, all of which are quite subjective. *Weiser, Taylor, et al.,* refuse to go along with this approach.

Psalm 15

THE MARKS OF A TRUE WORSHIPER

The detail of the heading that reads, "A Psalm of David," may not be brushed aside lightly. It cannot be disproved. It certainly fits into the life and activity of David. Its time may be fixed more precisely as being that period of his life when he manifested an interest in the restoration of the ark and thus the establishment of public worship. Any man who has lived close to God recognizes the pitfalls of formalism and ritualism that continually tend to corrupt any worship that is cast into some kind of fixed form. David may, therefore, well have seen that, after public worship is instituted, the nation should be instructed not to be content with the externals of worship, in other words: What are "the marks of the true worshiper"? This psalm is, of course, didactic in character.

There is a measure of propriety in having this psalm follow Ps. 14. Ps. 14 may be said to have described the typical ungodly man; Ps. 15 describes the typical man of God.

One cannot help but be struck by the fact that this psalm does not seem to have any depth of piety. It would appear to move on the surface of things. Homely basic virtues are listed. Rightly viewed, this approach has distinct merit without condemning any other approaches that psalmists and prophets may make elsewhere. For surely, if the basic virtues that are here listed are not in evidence in the life of a worshiper, his worship cannot be effective and his attitude toward his God right. The author is apparently listing basic essentials, which *Noetscher* says "give examples but do not exhaust the case." Other statements of the case by the same author may be thought of as being supplementary to this treatment of the subject, such as Ps. 24.

There may be some merit in the contention of those interpreters who say that this psalm seems to be directed against the hypocrites; and since it is characteristic of such individuals to fall short of practicing the most common virtues, it is just these virtues that must be stressed. Besides, it dare not be overlooked that the psalm may in no sense be described as stressing only a sort of externalism. For the fact that more than ordinary morality is demanded appears in phrases such as "speaking the truth from the heart" and "honoring those that fear God"; as also from the fine regard for the sanctity of the oath so clearly emphasized in v. 4.

The thought pattern followed by the psalm is as follows: an opening question is addressed by the author to God which sets forth the theme of the psalm; this is followed by a detailed answer spoken by the author himself as standing in the sight of God. In this answer there are found, first of all, three broad principles of conduct and then a number of basic virtues, all of which together equal ten commandments of conduct; to which is appended the reassurance that he who meets these requirements shall be able to stand firm.

Maclaren's explanation may well be appended to the effect that the things here required are not "the impalpable refinements of conduct." He adds that "lofty emotions, raptures of communion, aspirations which bring their own fulfilment and all the experiences of the devout soul, which are sometimes apt to be divorced from plain morality, need the ballast of the psalmist's homely answer to the great question."

A Psalm of David.
1. Lord, who may sojourn in Thy tent?
   Who may dwell in Thy holy hill?

2. He who walks blamelessly, and does right,
   And speaks the truth from his heart.
3. He does not slander with his tongue
   And does no wrong to his fellow man,
   Nor takes up a reproach against his neighbor.
4. He despises the man who deserves to be rejected
   And honors those that fear God.
   He swears to his own hurt and does not change it.
5. He does not put out his money on interest
   And does not take a bribe against an innocent man.

He who does these things shall never be moved.

1. The form of the psalm indicates that it is more than an abstract dissertation on the question, Who is a true worshiper? It does this by addressing a question to God, as much as to say, Of whom, Lord, dost Thou approve? In the answer to the questions asked the speaker is still the psalmist, and he is still standing before God as he did when asking the initial question. The two parts of the question are two figurative expressions. There is obviously no thought of any man's trying to take up permanent residence in the tent which David had raised to house the ark; nor does anyone presume to take up perpetual residence on the

holy hill on which the tent was erected. The true children of God or, what amounts to the same, the true worshipers in a certain sense dwell in God's tent and so enjoy the rights commonly associated with Oriental hospitality—protection and sustenance. In a sense they also share the same dwelling with God and "dwell with Him." The question would have this issue defined. Therefore it seems most proper to translate the Hebrew imperfects with the auxiliary "may" as most recent translations do. The "shall abide" and the "shall dwell" of the *A.V.* shift the emphasis slightly, reflecting on, Who shall in the long run be able to stay there? "Sojourn" (*gur*) does mean temporary residence but not necessarily brief residence (cf., 61:4). Paraphrased, the question amounts to this: Whom, O Lord, wilt Thou accept when he comes to Thy house?

2. The answer lists broader principles of conduct as the marks of a true worshiper. The first of these is all-inclusive, "He who walks blamelessly." The original *tamim* covers a broad area. Though it is sometimes translated "perfect" or "perfectly" it signifies completeness of moral conduct, that is to say, a many-sided, well-rounded-out pattern of living which leaves no important area uncultivated. Stated more concisely, this means, he "does right," for which the Hebrew again has the stronger expression—the noun "righteousness." But to blameless conduct and to the idea of always doing the right thing may well be added the most obvious expression that such an attitude finds through the words of the mouth, therefore: "and speaks the truth from his heart." This expression looks at the root of the utterances heard: they emanate from the heart and do not lie superficially on the tongue. The last phrase could also very properly be translated "with his heart." A man who lacks the attributes enumerated would scarcely prove acceptable to his fellow men, therefore quite obviously not to God. Isa. 33:15 presents much the same thought as does this verse.

3. From this point onward to the concluding statement of v. 5 the *RSV* attaches the successive clauses to v. 2 by the use of the relative "who." This very properly binds all ten demands together as constituting a unit. We have not done this because the Hebrew sentence structure does not do so. It begins with three participles in v. 2, thereby expressing the thought that these attributes must be enduring qualities. In v. 3 the construction changes to the finite verb (*KS* 413 1) and uses perfects, expressing that which is habitual (*KS* 125).

Specific instances of sins avoided are now given. The verse has only negatives. Acceptable lives have the element of what is done as well as the element of what is avoided. The first of these is, "he does not slander with his tongue." No mouth can bless God in worship and slander a fellow man in the next breath. Nor can such an individual be guilty of

Psalm 15

doing "wrong against a fellow man." Lastly he would always refuse to "take up a reproach against his neighbor." This appears to imply taking up for the sake of gossip anything that may be uttered by way of defaming another's character.

4. The fine balance of such a person's judgment is then effectively described. Since his behavior is consistent, he knows whom to reject—for some deserve our wholehearted contempt—and he also knows who deserves to be respected and honored. Those whom God and man reject—the consistent evildoers—are rightly despised by those who truly love God (cf., 1:1). If a man truly honors God, we cannot but honor him. Those interpreters who render this verse: "Who is displeasing in his own eyes, worthy of contempt"—thus emphasizing the almost abject humility that should be found in worshipers—first of all offer a dubious translation and then introduce a contrast into the text that does not fit it. They also overstate the nature of true humility.

5. One check on a righteous man's conduct is: What is his attitude toward oaths? One of the best tests of this attitude would be, What does a man do when he has sworn an oath and then finds that it is going to be to his disadvantage to carry out what he has sworn? In such a case he must have a high regard for the binding character of the oath if he still abides by it. It is this attitude that is described in the words, "He sweareth to his own hurt and does not change it." Stated a bit more at length, this would be: He takes an oath which has as a result that he gets into a bad situation, but he still does not tamper with the oath but holds it to be binding in an irrevocable sense. This obviously implies that the original oath was not made rashly or inadvisedly. It is just a case where things take an unexpected turn to his disadvantage.

6. Two instances from the area of the use of money conclude the examples cited. The first is, "He does not put out his money on interest." This reflects passages like Exod. 22:25; Lev. 25:36f.; Deut. 23:20, where the taking of interest from a man in need is forbidden. The ethical nature of this demand is obvious. If I enrich myself at my poor neighbor's expense, when he is in financial straits, I certainly have the wrong attitude on the matter. In Israel the other situation that we find commonly in our day when a man lends money to expand his business or the like was not considered in the passages referred to. True charity repudiates the idea of personal gain as a result of usury. Though the second instance mentioned in this verse is too obvious to call for comment, in Israel in days of old bribery was as common an offense in the courts as it is in any modern nation (cf., Exod. 23:8; Deut. 27:25; Is. 1:23; Ezek. 22:12). True impartiality, true fairness is always a basic virtue.

Having completed the listing of ten fundamental virtues, the psalmist has completed his answer to the original question. He now offers a concluding comment: "He who does these things shall never be moved." "To be moved" scarcely means never to be visited by any calamity. That would give the worshiper's virtues too mercenary a cast. A higher result is envisioned: Such a one will never be shaken from the fine position of godliness that he now occupies, either by temptation or by adversity. On this note of high encouragement the psalmist rests his case and concludes his portrayal.

One recent approach to the interpretation of this psalm seems to us to be quite fanciful and to have netted nothing that is either sound or helpful. This is the approach which regards the psalm as "a temple liturgy which was used at the moment when a company of pilgrims was at the point of entering the holy place" (*Leslie*). This approach takes two forms. It either has the psalm rendered by the priests before such a pilgrim group, or it gives the pilgrims some share in it, letting the priests offer the response. The chief objection to such an interpretation would appear to be that, as hundreds of groups approached the Temple area, this psalm would have been rendered hundreds of times per day to the point of deadening monotony. Besides, nothing indicates such liturgical use.

Psalm 16

THE LORD—THE PSALMIST'S PORTION IN LIFE AND HIS DELIVERER IN DEATH

THE SUPERSCRIPTION ascribes this psalm to David. This may well be correct. For on the one hand, when David was obliged to flee from Saul and thus was separated from his portion among the people of God he may have given earnest thought to the fine expedient of making the Lord Himself his portion. And again, whereas in I Sam. 26:19 we find evidence that David had been taunted with the prospect that he might as well cast in his lot with other gods and serve them, here he emphatically denies any such temptation. Aside from these two items, certainly the warmth of personal relation to God that characterizes this psalm agrees well with what we know of David's personal faith life.

The other detail of the heading, which in Hebrew reads, "A Mik-

Psalm 16

tam," may be rendered "a mystery poem" in the sense of a poem that treats of a mysterious issue in life, like the deep mystic relation to God. Absolute certainty cannot be claimed for the interpretation of this word.

The theme of the psalm has been rather well caught by the heading which the *ARV* has, "Jehovah—the Psalmist's Portion in Life and His Deliverer in Death." There is, perhaps, no statement of prophet or poet that more beautifully and consistently traces down to its final consequences what it means when a man commits himself fully into the hands of God and abides in Him.

The line of thought running through the psalm may be outlined as follows: The writer first states what attitude he has taken toward God, and what God means to him (vv. 1, 2); he then shows how this basic attitude of his determines his or, for that matter, any man's position over against the two groups found in mankind (vv. 3, 4); he next describes the present blessedness that he enjoys as a result of having taken the position that he has over against his Lord (vv. 5–8); and lastly he outlines the possibilities for the future that lie latent in his basic position (vv. 9–11).

A mystery poem. Of David.

1. *Preserve me, Thou strong God, for in Thee have I taken refuge.*
2. *I have said to the Lord, "My Lord art Thou;*
   I have no good beyond Thee."

3. *As for the saints that are in the land,*
   They are the noble; all my delight is in them.
4. *Many shall be the sorrows of those who woo another god;*
   I shall not pour out libations of blood for them,
   Neither will I take their names upon my lips.

5. *The Lord is my choice portion and my cup;*
   Thou wilt make my portion of land broad.
6. *The allotted piece of field has fallen to my lot in pleasant places;*
   Yea, I have a goodly heritage.
7. *I will bless the Lord who has counseled me;*
   Yea, by night my inmost thoughts have instructed me.
8. *I have kept the Lord continually before me;*
   Because He is at my right hand, I shall not be moved.

9. *Therefore my heart has always been glad,*
   And my soul has rejoiced;
   Also my flesh shall dwell securely.

10. *For Thou wilt not surrender my soul to Sheol;*
    Thou wilt not permit Thy godly one to see destruction.
11. *Thou wilt make known to me the path of life;*
    Fulness of joy is in Thy presence;
    In Thy right hand are pleasures for evermore.

1. Some commentators have made altogether too much of the force of the first petition here voiced—"preserve me"—as though it necessarily implied that the speaker was in the greatest of peril, even in danger of death, from which he hoped to be rescued by the Lord. That some measure of peril may be involved is obvious. But according to the context nothing more is involved than that the psalmist has taken refuge in the Lord and now prays Him to help him stay in that close communion with his God and not slip from it. Quite appropriately he calls God 'el in the Hebrew, which means "the Strong One," implying that according to the import of that name God is well able to do what His suppliant asks.

2. The unique feature about this psalm is the fact that the writer has taken this step with deep and thoroughgoing conviction. He really made the Lord his refuge. He drew as close to Him as he could. This second verse evaluates the full force of the degree to which he drew near to God. The emphasis lies on the interpretation that the writer himself gives to the words "My Lord art Thou." To him that means, "I have no good beyond Thee." In other words, "Thou art my highest treasure." Nothing can ever mean anything to me as you do. This is the attitude from which he prays God that he may never be shaken.

3. This determines his position over against those persons that dwell in this world, who are obviously divided into two classes. They are either minded as the writer is—and these are called "the saints"—or they are individuals who fail to take this attitude and thus become persons contact with whom is to be shunned. In reference to these saints the writer indicates that he has a high regard for them, for he knows himself to be of one mind with them. To him they are the true nobility of mankind, not by virtue of accident of birth but as a result of free allegiance to God. Since these are in the nature of the case Israelites, he adds the words, "that are in the land," meaning Palestine. He cannot help but take pleasure in them and in their attitude—"all my delight is in them." This is simply one of the many aspects of the communion of saints: they do delight in godly fellowship with one another. This statement does not conflict with v. 2 ("I have no good beyond Thee") which in a sense defines what the psalmist's true treasure is.

4. As much as David delights in the fellowship of the one group,

so much he utterly detests association with the other. All of this must be viewed in that enlightened sense of opposition of which Ps. 1 speaks, where a strong conscious aversion to sin is one of the characteristic marks of a true man of God. For by departing from the living God—this is implied in "woo another god"—such persons create for themselves painful and distressing situations: "Many shall be the sorrows of those who woo another god." That such a position is completely abhorrent to him the writer declares by saying that he could not do such a thing as offer sacrifices for such wicked men, asking God to bless them. That is the meaning of the statement, "I shall not pour out libations of blood for them."

This somewhat difficult statement is, perhaps, best rendered as we have translated it. *Nésekh* (libation) appears to be used in a broader sense than is customary. Ordinarily it means a libation of wine. It may here be used to designate the pouring out of the blood of a victim at the base of the altar in a regular sacrifice and so could refer to the sacrifice as such. The suffix "*their* libation" would then mean a libation which is offered *for them.*

In like manner, without unkindness or prejudice in what he says, the psalmist tries to express his utter abhorrence of the attitude of those who have forsaken the true God for another by saying that he refuses to "take their names upon his lips." Though this could easily be misunderstood it means that these persons have rendered themselves so vile by what they did in their apostasy that the very mention of their name would seem to be a contamination. *Gunkel's* reconstruction of vv. 3, 4 is as brilliant as it is unreliable.

5. Now the description of the present blessedness growing out of the position taken with conviction and firm resolve. He first once again defines his position. This is a restatement of the substance of vv. 1 and 2. "The Lord is my choice portion and my cup." Though the Hebrew uses two words—"the portion of my portion"—it really implies a superlative. This means: I have no treasure that I value more highly than my Lord. Synonymous is the thought that He is "my cup," which figure signifies that he is the satisfying draught that refreshes and invigorates the soul, a thought developed quite forcefully by Jesus in John 4.

In the second half of the verse the description of the present blessedness begins. The first descriptive clause reads thus: "Thou wilt make my portion of land broad." A figure that is taken from the allotment of the land of Canaan to the Twelve Tribes in the days of Joshua is used. Whereas each man had hoped for a choice and roomy portion for himself so that he would have ample space for house and home and tillable acreage, the writer says: spiritually speaking, that is my happy lot since I have made the Lord my refuge. All confining and crippling cares are removed.

6. The same figure is carried a bit farther in this verse. This man views his life as being like that of a godly man of Joshua's time, whose inheritance was situated in a very pleasant place in the land. So his is "a goodly heritage." It may strike the uninformed Bible reader as a very curious circumstance that this verse could be translated by *AV*, "The lines are fallen unto me in pleasant places," and we now venture to say, "The allotted piece of field has fallen to my lot, etc." The facts are that *chabhalim* may and does mean "measuring lines" and by metonymy may designate the tracts that are measured off by the surveyor's lines. That is how *Koehler* arrives at the meaning "the allotted piece of field." All in all, one should not miss the almost exuberant note that pervades this passage.

7. The psalmist is still on the subject of how happy his lot is. He regards the decision that he made to make the Lord his refuge (v. 1) or his highest good (v. 2) or his choice portion (v. 5) as one that was made at the Lord's own suggestion: so the Lord counseled him, and he thanks Him for having done so. Whenever he thinks his situation over in the quiet of the night when all distracting influences are silenced, his "inmost thoughts" instruct him that he has done the right thing. In other words, his present position in reference to the Lord is one that he has taken and cannot and will not disavow. He knows with fullest certainty that it was the right thing and the one and only course for him to follow. The Hebrew expression for "inmost thoughts" is "reins," i.e., old English for "kidneys." But here as always the inmost part of a man's make up, the very core of his being is meant. We have rendered this "inmost thoughts"—"conscience" would not have been inappropriate.

8. Since such deeply spiritual issues are not easily expressed, the writer, by way of summing up, now chooses another formulation as to what his attitude toward his God really is when he says: "I have kept or set the Lord continually before me." It is as though by a conscious effort of the will he tried to make real to his thinking that which was a reality above all realities, namely, the fact that God is always present with His own. Still another statement of the case would be: I am keeping Him always before my mind's eye. But since the exact wording is not the all-important thing, the psalmist at once substitutes an equivalent clause for the expression just used when he says: "Because He is at my right hand," which is the position of honor. The concluding statement sums up all the benefits that he enjoys as a result of this right relation to his God. They are: "I shall not be

Psalm 16

moved," or shaken or dislodged or overthrown. Here is security at its best! But it is not inherent in us but the outcome of the vital relation to the living God. Thus ends the description of the present blessedness that the author enjoys.

9. The last verses indicate the future possibilities that are latent in his fortunate position. He begins, however, by once again summarizing what it all means to him for the present. Ever since this attitude has consciously been his, his "heart has been glad." And if in Hebrew conception the heart is the center of one's thinking, then this is the equivalent of saying: Glad thoughts have been coursing through my mind. The perfect used here is the gnomic aorist, so to say, which expresses what is constantly true. Besides, his "soul has rejoiced." Soul may well signify the whole inner being of a man.

Now, looking more to the future, he also asserts that his "flesh shall dwell securely." Implied is the thought that his whole being shall enjoy security, for David is here apparently speaking somewhat after the manner of Paul in I Thess. 5:23, "May your spirit and soul and body be kept sound and blameless." The three parts of man emphasize that every part of his being shall share in the security which is his. "Heart" and "soul" could well signify the two aspects of his inner being; "flesh" could designate the physical part of him. In this verse there does not appear to be a reference to death and the grave, and so "my flesh shall rest securely" does not mean "in the grave." That turn of thought begins to appear in the next verse. So the thought of this verse may well include total security of the whole being. And again the verse may well be said to be spoken in a somewhat exuberant tone.

10. With beautiful consistency of the logic of faith, the writer develops still more fully what possibilities are latent in this close fellowship with his God that has come to be a reality in his life. Is there any power stronger than this bond whereby he is tied to God, or the strength wherewith God holds him? The answer is a definite No. Death and the grave are being thought of in particular. Though "Sheol" generally refers to the afterlife as such, to the realm into which one passes as he leaves his present form of existence, it can in a practical way be equated with the grave. Or it may simply be thought of as what we call the hereafter.

Sheol is commonly pictured as a huge, relentless monster, standing with mouth wide open, ready to swallow all the children of men as they are swept along toward it. Though the psalmist has never seen a man escape the fate of being swallowed by death, yet the writer is sure that the power of the living God to whom he stands closely bound in faith is such that, as long as he retains his hold on Him, Sheol will not obtain the mastery. God will prevent his passing into Sheol's power. This is what the statement must mean: "Thou wilt not surrender my soul to Sheol." All visible evidence to the contrary, faith still makes this confident assertion. Though the verb '*azabh* means "forsake" or "abandon," that meaning is obviously caught quite well by the idea of "surrender." The writer does not express the thought that he hopes merely to escape from death but rather the bolder thought that death shall never get dominion over him. Never did faith wax bolder in dealing with this problem.

The parallel statement is equally bold, "Thou wilt not permit Thy godly one to see destruction." The subjective condition to be met by man finds stronger expression; a man must be one who may be classed as a "holy one," (*AV*) or "godly one," according to our translation. That means one who is set apart unto the Lord. Surely, God's care for us is so great and His power so strong that this result may rightly be expected. One cannot help but marvel at the boldness of this faith which holds to this valid conclusion, all evidence to the contrary notwithstanding.

11. Having gotten past the grave in his thinking, what does the rest of the future hold in store for a saints of God? Three things. First, "Thou wilt make me to know the path of life," meaning, of course, the path that leads to life, and the traveling of which is life. "Make to know" is the equivalent of tasting and experiencing the reality of all that is involved. Whereas some individuals see only death in prospect after life's candle is snuffed out, this man sees life. Second, "fulness of joy is in Thy presence." The central point at issue was that the psalmist had firmly grasped God in faith and would not let go. In that sense is he in the "presence" of God. But that reality is "joy" and "fulness of joy" without end. Here lies the secret of a truly happy life. Third, "in Thy right hand are pleasures for evermore." Gifts are held in readiness by God to give to those that abide in Him. They are described as "pleasures" or "raptures" and as being available "for evermore." Having reached this point, the psalmist breaks off abruptly as though the highest point of advance had been reached, and as though any further attempt to picture the utmost of felicity must result in an anticlimax.

The boldness of it all almost leaves the reader breathless. How can a man see all men dying and note that all the children of men before him have died without exception and still say: God cannot let that happen to me! It appears like sheer being carried away into rhapsody of bold assertions. But still, in the last analysis, must not faith draw the conclusion that, if you hold to God, God will take care of you perfectly? We seem to face a hopeless dilemma: experience teaches one

Psalm 16

thing; faith holds the very opposite to be true in the face of inescapable evidence.

The statement involved seems to reach beyond itself and have something of the prophetic element in it. How much the psalmist knew about the element that reached beyond the horizon of his thinking we may never be able to ascertain.

Peter, making effective use of this passage in his Pentecost sermon (Acts 2:25ff.) points out that, having said he would not die, David did lie down and die, and so in a sense this statement was never fulfilled in regard to him. But in Christ it was fulfilled; and the best statement of the case is offered by Peter (v. 31): David "foreseeing this spake of the resurrection of the Christ." Again, to what extent he did this consciously we are unable to fathom. Shall we say with *Hengstenberg*: "David in Christ could very properly speak as he here does"? Rightly understood, this could be the case. Better, however, seems to be the approach which says in effect that in the providence of God it pleased Him so to guide the spirit of the writer by His own Holy Spirit that he gave shape and form to his utterance in such a way that what he concluded in the logic of faith reached a marvelous fulfilment in the resurrection of Christ for every believer. For those that are "in Christ" do most assuredly share in the fruits of His resurrection. Christ's resurrection has vindicated David's bold assertions of faith, and though to all intents and purposes he died, yet he did not die but lives forevermore. This result was not accidental but the outcome of the work of the Spirit, whose modes of working are marvelous and wonderful. For sheer boldness few passages in Holy Writ can equal this utterance. It ranks on a par with Rom. 8:31ff.

NOTES

2. We have translated *'amart* as though it were a defective way of writing *'amarti*, "I have said," rather than to supply "*O my soul,* thou hast said, etc." *GK* 44i cites a number of instances of the same sort. *'adhonay* had better be rendered here, as in 35:23, "*my* Lord"—not just Lord, which is the far more common meaning. *'al* has the sense of "in addition to" or "beyond," cf., *KS* 308d.

3. In *liqdoshim* the initial *le* serves to introduce the subject in the sense "*as for* the saints." Our translation of this difficult verse removes the *we* before *'adhirey* (on the authority of the margin in *Kittel's* text) and so places this word in a sort of apposition to *qedhoshim*.

4. *Maharu,* which could mean purchase, is construed after the meaning of the derivative *mohar* (the price or dowry paid by the bridegroom) and so may be construed in the sense of "woo."

5. *Kos* ("cup") in Hebrew becomes synonymous with "lot" or "fate" (*KW* says *Schicksal*).

10. "Thy godly one" is *chasidhekha,* without the *yod* before the suffix and so is a singular. An ancient marginal reading suggests the plural form, "Thy godly *ones.*" The plural would be the more difficult form and should from that point of view be accepted. But the verdict of the versions unanimously points to the singular. Many interpreters insist that *sháchath* must mean "pit." However, those commentators seem to be in the right who see two roots at work in this form, and so it may well be translated "destruction" after the lead of the *Septuagint*.

Psalm 17

A PLEA FOR VINDICATION AND PROTECTION

THIS PSALM bears many striking resemblances to Ps. 16, in its conclusion and as to the situation of the suppliant and as to words employed. Its major difference from the former psalm seems to be the nature of the danger which threatens; in this psalm it is more immediate. Nor can it be denied that this psalm is more aggressive in its tone: it rumbles with a threatening note. Constructions seem more difficult and the thought a bit more involved. Difficulties of interpretation are a bit more numerous. All of this does not, however, warrant resorting to manifold textual changes as though the state of the text were quite corrupt. The compactness of utterance constitutes a part of the difficulty.

The psalm is to be classified as the lament of an individual. The author may well be David as the traditional heading indicates. Saul is the leader of those who oppose him. I Sam. 23:24ff. fits the situation of the psalm rather well. Surely, the proofs adduced to deny Davidic authorship are not of a substantial sort. It may be a bit difficult to determine whether the tone of the Psalm is strictly personal and individual or whether it is spoken in the name of a group of godly men of those times. The evidence points in the direction of a purely personal plea growing out of David's situation.

As to the note of self-righteousness charged against the writer, this is, in the last analysis, nothing more than the claim: I am not guilty of the things with which I am charged; besides, I have sought to live a blameless life and am not to be charged with insincerity. If this

claim is maintained rather stoutly, it should not be overlooked that
the writer had apparently been slandered rather viciously. Such an attack naturally calls for an indignant disavowal. *Delitzsch's* remark
may be recalled at this point: "In all such assertions of the pious self-
consciousness, what is meant is a righteousness that has its basis in the
righteousness of faith." So also *Maclaren's* reminder is much in place:
"The modern type of religion which recoils from such professions,
and contents itself with always confessiong sins which it has given up
hope of overcoming, would be all the better for listening to the psalmist and aiming a little more vigorously and hopefully at being able to
say, 'I know nothing against myself.' "

a) An earnest plea for help by a man innocently accused (vv. 1–5)

   A Prayer of David.
1. *Hear, O Lord, a just cause,*
   Give heed to my outcry,
   Give ear to my prayer, which does not come from deceitful lips.
2. *From Thee let my verdict come forth;*
   Let Thy eyes behold the right.
3. *When Thou triest my heart and visitest me by night,*
   When Thou purifiest me, Thou shalt find nothing;
   I have resolved: My mouth shall not transgress.
4. *As for the works of men, I for one, according to the word of Thy*
      lips,
   Have shunned the ways of the violent.
5. *Inasmuch as my feet have held to Thy prescribed path,*
   My feet have not slipped.

1. The Psalm launches into eager petition: "Hear . . . give heed
. . . give ear." Being wrongfully accused, the singer at once vigorously asserts his innocence. He describes his case with one word,
tsédheq—the "right" or "a just cause." He makes an issue of this
cause of his in the first five verses. "Outcry" usually has the connotation of jubilant outcry; here it is obviously painful. In pleading
for a hearing he at once strongly asserts that there is no hypocrisy in
what he says: his prayer "does not come from deceitful lips."

2. Vindication rests with God alone. Only the verdict of the Most
High is of moment to this poor petitioner. Therefore the word order:
"From Thee let my verdict come forth." "Verdict" (*mishpat*) has
connotations like "justice" and "judgment." Here it must mean "a
just decision." God's beholding of the right in this case implies very
definitely that He is being thought of as hearing the prayer of His
faithful follower with distinct favor. It is worth much to a man to be so

sure of the justice of his cause. David certainly merits such a description in the period when he was continually in flight before Saul.

3. Self-assurance grows bolder. It must naturally be understood that the psalmist refers only to the things with which he is charged. In reference to them he is ready to maintain his total innocence. Whether he is otherwise a sinless man was not under consideration at the time. Therefore he is ready to submit to God to being "tried" and "visited" and "purified." Surely, this means the very closest inspection on God's part. It is a wonderful thing to be able to maintain one's innocence so sturdily as to be able to say with confidence, "Thou shalt find nothing." The added statement, "I have resolved. My mouth shall not transgress," must apparently be limited to the present situation and must mean, I have resolved to keep my mouth from any hasty or unseemly utterance—to which we are so prone when we are strongly and wrongfully accused.

4. One of the major charges raised against the psalmist is apparently being mentioned. He had been accused of violence. But he could with a good conscience repudiate the charge: "I have shunned the ways of the violent." In doing that he had consciously kept in conformity with the "Word of God's lips." Men in his condition—he and his followers were fugitives from justice because of the unreasoning persecution of Saul—are so apt to fall into a type of "works of men" that are marked by little regard for the rights of others. David could assert with emphasis that he was innocent of the charge raised against him.

5. Still viewing his life in the light of divine precepts and before the very judgment of the Almighty, the writer claims that he has been able to keep from slipping with his feet, "inasmuch as my steps have held to Thy prescribed path." Literally he says only "Thy paths," but he certainly means that in the sense of: the paths Thou hast prescribed. God indicated the way His servants are to follow. This servant has followed these prescriptions. That made for firm, correct going and blameless conduct. No trace of self-righteousness is to be detected in these claims. But they are strongly made because the writer knows that God will not heed the prayers of the evildoer.

b) **The Plea Reinforced by a Sketch of the Wickedness of His Assailants (vv. 6–12)**

6. *I indeed have called upon Thee, for Thou, O God, art wont to answer me;*
   Incline Thy ears to me; hear my words.
7. *Give a marvelous display of Thy steadfast love,*
   Thou Savior of those who seek refuge from those that rise up against Thy right hand.

Psalm 17

8. Protect me as the apple of Thy eye;
   Hide me under the shadow of Thy wings,
9. From the wicked who have done violence to me.
   From my enemies who viciously encircle me.
10. They are enclosed in their own fat;
    Their mouth has always been wont to speak arrogantly.
11. As for our steps—already they have surrounded us;
    They have set their eyes to cast us down to the ground.
12. Each one is like a lion ready to tear,
    Like a young lion lurking in ambush.

6. After making a strong claim of innocence the writer again utters a plea which continues through the next four verses. When men cry so persistently, trouble lies heavy upon them. In contrast with the wicked dealings of his opponents the writer emphatically mentions himself (*'ani*), "I indeed," stressing, without sanctimoniousness, that he has been engaged in calling upon God (*'el,* the "Strong One" who is able to deliver), and he has some experience of what God is ready to do for His own: "Thou art wont to answer me." Brief and urgent are the two additional pleas for help: "Incline Thy ear to me; hear my words."

7. Faith grows bolder as the prayer advances. The psalmist ventures to ask that God may do something out of the ordinary. This is not presumption but a clear insight into the fact that God's children are important to Him. Therefore: "Give a marvelous display of Thy steadfast love." The thing that is to be outstanding is God's steadfast love. To pray for its display can come from the worthiest of motives. Beautiful is the title given to God in this connection, "Thou Savior of those that seek refuge."

Those individuals from whom the godly seek refuge are described in such a manner that one cannot regard them as mere personal enemies of the writer. They are "those that rise up against Thy right hand." When a man says that in the sight of God he must know that God is the one who will most readily detect whether one merely imagines that they are God's enemies, or whether they actually are such. If we grant the sincerity of the psalmist as we do, we cannot but accept this description as a correct characterization. His opponents are men who are in rebellion and defiance against God. Their reason for so viciously assaulting the writer is that they know that he openly espouses the cause of God. As soon as one recognizes that this is consistently the situation in the psalms of David, one can begin to understand why his prayers so insistently call for the overthrow of his opponents.

8. The two figures employed to reinforce the next petition reveal more of the insight that the author has of the importance of God's saints in His eyes. Ae we tenderly guard the "apple of the eye," so

may he be guarded. As a bird shelters its young so may he be sheltered. For God's love is more than a mother's love. It scarcely seems likely that the figure is exactly that employed in Matt. 23:27, for hens were apparently not known before New Testament times.

9. The sentence then describes those against whom protection is sought as "the wicked who have done violence to me." He is only too keenly aware of the fact that his enemies have ridden roughshod over his rights. He feels it every day that they are "enemies who viciously encircle" him. For the expression *benephesh* most evidently means "against my life," a common meaning of *nephesh*. Since they encircle him with murderous intent, this action may well be termed "viciously" or even murderously. Too often we have failed to catch the extremity of danger which led David to plead for divine help as strongly as he does. I Sam. 23:24 is but one of many such instances in which David found himself involved. Quite remarkably David never once mentions Saul, his chief assailant—a notable instance of the fine restraint exercised in these so-called imprecatory psalms, and a factor too little noted.

10. Now comes a further description of those who deal so unfairly with the writer, a description which continues to the end of v. 12. "They are enclosed in their own fat" indicates their extreme carnal-mindedness; cf., 73:7 for a parallel and especially 119:70. This is better than *RSV:* "They close their hearts to pity," implying that the fat is thought of as the seat of emotions and therefore rendered "heart." A clear instance of such usuage cannot be cited. "Their mouth has always been wont to speak arrogantly" indicates that whatever arrogant things they have asserted with regard to themselves and against their foe in this case is but the same pattern they have always followed. Condemning their enemies and exculpating themselves is a vile habit of theirs.

11. "Our steps" stands first in the Hebrew as a nominative absolute. The reference to I Sam. 23:24 is most appropriate, for on that occasion David was all but trapped by an encircling movement. The goal on which these men have relentlessly fixed their eyes is, says he, "to cast us to the ground." The "us" is not in the text but grows out of the connection and implies furthermore that the writer did not live through this experience alone. Complete overthrow of him and his followers was the avowed plan of the wicked opposition. It is not as though the psalmist were trying to inform God about things that he thought the Almighty had not noted. It is rather a case of making vocal that which is the particular danger that besets our heart continually.

12. The description concludes with comparing the spirit animating these enemies to that of ravenous beasts, who on their part cannot be

Psalm 17

blamed for being so bloodthirsty. But such traits on the part of man testify to the utter degradation of those that manifest them.

c) **The Plea for the Complete Confusion of His Enemies Reinforced by a Lively Hope (vv. 13–15)**

13. *Arise, O Lord, confront them, bring them low!*
Deliver my life from the wicked one with Thy sword,
14. *From men by Thy hand, O Lord, from men of the world, whose portion is in this life.*
Do Thou fill their belly with what Thou hast in store for them;
May their children have their fill; may they leave their surplus to their babes.
15. *As for me, I would behold Thy face in righteousness;*
Let me be satisfied with beholding Thy form when I awake.

13. The prayer grows more insistent. The psalmist would have God act and delay no longer. Therefore strong forms of the imperative are employed, "arise . . . confront . . . deliver." The fact that such prayers do not exclude the thought of a possible repentance and restoration of the ungodly enemies appears, for example, in 83:16. However, since such an outcome is scarcely likely, it is seldom expressed in the psalms; cf. also Ps. 2:10ff. With strict consistency the opponent is again described as what he actually is, "the wicked one," whose wickedness consist in part in this that he actually aims to take the writer's "life." It is not unseemly to describe the Lord Himself as being like unto a mighty warrior who also wields a "sword."

14. The sentence begun in v. 13 continues into v. 14—a very difficult verse, but not to be thought of as presenting an utterly corrupt and unusable text. The opponents are first described merely as "men," a term frequently used when the insignificance in numbers is to be emphasized. So here in the last analysis they are a meagre host over against the Lord, no matter how numerous they may be otherwise. From these God will deliver His saint "by His hand," implying, as so often, the omnipotence with which the hand of the Lord is so regularly associated. The fact that these opponents are further described as "men of the world, whose portion is in [this] life" again reminds us how little understanding of God and His own they had if they found righteousness in the life of the opponent they were hunting down.

The prayer now becomes really aggressive, more so than we would dare to make our prayers. But it must be remembered that the writer had an unusually clear call from God to be the leader of God's people and in following the ways of his calling was encountering an opposition that he saw was fanned by all the forces of evil. How could he do other than work and pray for the total and drastic overthrow of those who clashed with the purposes of the Almighty? This can surely be interpreted as a very wholesome attitude on his part. Continually to find fault with it often results from refusing to allow that the psalmist's motives could have been noble and enlightened.

Believing that God has punishment in store for those who maliciously oppose Him, he asks God to give them a strong dose of the medicine that is due them, "Do Thou fill their belly with what Thou hast in store for them." Surely, the spirit of the next statement is the same as that noted in Exod. 20:5, which definitely states that the children are in danger of the same judgment as their fathers if they persist in going in the same evil ways as their fathers. Therefore "may their children have their fill" means: of the same punishment, and obviously would not apply to them if they had broken with the ways of their fathers. And in almost inescapable reference to Exod. 20:5 the third generation is also brought into the picture, for "may they leave their surplus to their babes" takes up the "children" of the preceding clause. In one sense it may be said: "This sounds heartless," but no more heartless than God Himself is when He speaks as he does in the Decalogue.

15. As so often, also here the troubles that completely surround a man are conceived as likely to continue as long as one lives; so complete deliverance from them will be possible only when this present life has run its course. From that point of view it should seem quite natural that the hope of the great deliverance that all saints cherish comes to the forefront here. If affliction has caused the flame of hope to be kindled more brightly in this instance, that would be in line with what has often been found to be the experience of God's children. The time will come when he hopes to see God face to face "in righteousness," which here implies total vindication and surely is but a short step removed from the clear concept of justification by faith as found in the New Testament. Then will he truly "be satisfied" when he "awakes" from the slumber of death to the experience that he shall be "beholding" His form. That sight puts an end to all troubled doubts and is the perfect and final answer to prayer. *Oesterley* summarizes the issue well: "How can communion with the ever-living God be broken by death?"

Many interpreters do not venture to find here so clear a statement of the hope of the resurrection and of life eternal with God. Their chief reason is that it has been claimed that at this point in their history God's people could not have had a clear conception of the blessedness of the hereafter. But it can be demonstrated that that hope had always been a part of godly faith, dimmer, indeed, in patriarchal days and still much in need of clarification in the early days of the monarchy. But both Ps. 16 and Ps. 17 offer clear-cut testimony as to how faith practically postulates such a solution, and how saints grew in experience to see that on the premises of true trust in God hope of complete fruition of His presence is a logical necessity. A very unsatisfactory interpretation is that which dreams of the singer's spending the night in the Temple of God and waking up in the morning with his doubts allayed (*Schmidt, Leslie,* etc.) Such an interpretation scarcely does justice to the statements made. This view was originally projected by *Mowinckel* (*Psalmenstudien,* I, 155).

NOTES

2. "The right" appears in the Hebrew as a plural noun, in conformity with the principle that *KS* (262f) has pointed out that abstract nouns are frequently found in the plural.

3. The Hebrew has three coordinated clauses in the perfect, which could be translated: "Thou hast tried . . . hast visited . . . hast purified." Yet it should be noted that it is frequently the context which indicates that such clauses are to be regarded as the equivalents of conditional sentences although *Hengstenberg* strenuously opposes such an approach. See *KS* 390r. "I have resolved" (*zammothi*), though variously interpreted as to form, is most likely a perfect from *zaman;* see *KS* 231a.

4. "As for the works"—the introductory *le* is used as a means for placing a term prominently into the foreground; *KS* 271b. The *be* in *bidbar* indicates the sphere or the norm; *KS* 332r.

5. The somewhat unusual construction *tamokh* is best construed as an absolute infinitive used as noun in the construct with *'ashuray* dependent upon it, literally "as for the holding fast of my steps." See *KS* 225d.

7. The phrase "from those rising up" as well as the phrase *biminékha* have been construed as modifiers of the verb "deliver," necessitating the translation of the second phrase as "by Thy right hand." However, since verbs implying attack or warfare are usually construed with a *be,* it would be better in this instance to make the second phrase depend upon the first and translate "against Thy right hand."

8. "The apple of the eye" really reads: "pupil, daughter of the eye," "daughter" being used as a mere relation word. But since in English "apple of the eye" has become well-nigh proverbial, it seemed better to translate thus than to render it "pupil." Stranger still, the word for "pupil" really means "little man."

10. The first verb is not a passive. Rendered literally, we should translate: "(with) their fat (adverbial accusative) they have closed." The object to be supplied is "themselves." But the simplest English rendering seems to be to use a passive: "They are enclosed in their

own fat." Similarly the second half of the verse omits the preposition before "mouth" and should be rendered literally: "With their mouth they have always spoken arrogantly." For a smoother rendering we have made *pimo,* though singular, the subject of the plural verb. We regard *dibberu* as a kind of gnomic aorist. The ending *mo,* twice used in the verse, equals *am* and is poetic.

11. "As for our steps" is one of several instances within the psalm where a noun is moved forward for emphasis. Here the word may be regarded as an accusative of specification; see *KS* 328f.

12. We have translated *dimyono,* not as "his likeness," but as "the likeness of each one of them." This was smoothed out to read: "Each one is like," etc. The pronominal suffix often has a distributive force like "of each one of them." See *KS* 380 c.

13. Practically all of the imperatives have a specially reinforced form, stressing the urgency of the prayer.

15. The verbs could be translated "I shall behold" and "I shall be satisfied." However, the second has a *qametz he* hortative appended and is, therefore, better rendered "let me be satisfied"; then the parallelism suggests a similar form for the first verb; therefore, "I would behold."

The word rendered "form" reminds the reader of the similar expression found in Num. 12:8. But even as in that passage an actual beholding of God of some sort is under consideration, so it appears to be here. And that further supports our interpretation that the writer thinks in terms of a beholding of God after the awakening from death. *Koenig,* reluctant to concede a reference to a physical resurrection, has it refer to the great "day of the Lord" so frequently mentioned by the prophets and to the event of the great and final restoration of God's people (the *shubh shebhuth*), and thus he arrives at almost the same result.

Psalm 18

DAVID'S PSALM OF PRAISE AND VICTORY

THERE is every reason for accepting the heading of this psalm as correct, whether it originated with David or with some editor who merely recorded a well-established tradition. Many features point to Davidic authorship—the general tone of the psalm, its note of confident faith, its poetic fervor, its agreement with the facts of David's life as they are known to us. To this must be added the propriety of having a man like David sum up in one paean of praise his feelings of gratitude, which he must have experienced in unusual strength at the time when he had already been granted many remarkable deliverances by the Lord his God in the course of a life crowned with victories. It might, indeed, seem as if this psalm had been penned before David's great lapse into sin because its mood might well have been toned down considerably after that tragic event. Even *Weiser* concedes the possibility of Davidic authorship.

It is also fitting that the heading speaks of all deliverances but specifices those that were granted him from the persecutions of Saul, which did, indeed, constitute a major experience during David's life. It is with this in mind that we translated the "and from the hands of Saul" as "especially from the hands of Saul," a translation of the "and" that is quite permissible in Hebrew syntax.

Though this psalm strikes a distinctively personal note, it need not be restricted to David's personal thanksgiving. There were so many who shared in David's experiences and were involved in his deliverances almost as much as he was. To call this a psalm to be used by the congregation would, therefore, be most appropriate. It is a hymn of thanksgiving (*Gunkel*).

There is scarcely a poem from the pen of David that is better attested historically than is this psalm because it appears also in the historical books—II Sam. 22. This double recording also testifies to the importance of the piece. But this double transmission raises an unusual question. How are these two versions of the poem related to each other? The question is by no means easy to answer. The interpreter who is convinced that there are many poor copies of the Hebrew text of the Old Testament Scriptures will appeal to this basic fact to provide an answer to our question and will label the one the poorer copy and the other the better text. Since, however, in almost every instance it is never a group of words or a phrase that are changed but only single words, and these again seem to differ according to a fixed pattern, it may well be that our psalm is the original text, which abounds in somewhat unusual words and forms. This leads to the opinion that the version of the poem found in Samuel may have been consistently altered by an editor, who for purposes of clarification substituted the simpler and more common forms for the more difficult, abstruse, and more highly poetic wordings. Such is the contention of *Hengstenberg,* who has made as good a case for this view as has any writer. As to the differences involved, commentators frequently list them all. *Koenig* has done this as completely as has any interpreter.

Another issue that looms unusually large in regard to this psalm is the question of the tenses, so called, of the Hebrew verbs. Imperfects are rather common, so much so that *Buttenwieser* felt impelled to make a drastic change from the traditional interpretation of the psalm, calling it not a prayer of thanksgiving but "A Cry of the Depths." However, if the tenses are evaluated a bit more carefully as *Koenig* has done, in his *Commentary* and *Syntax,* quite a different impression is gained, and the traditional interpretation is seen to have been entirely correct. Grammatical details will be given below. When *Schmidt* states that this is a story of recovery from sickness he loses almost all of the distinctive elements in the psalm.

The following may constitute a workable outline of the psalm:
a) What God now means to the psalmist as a result of his experience (vv. 1–2).
b) The story of the psalmist's deliverance (vv. 3–19).
c) Why God condescended to deliver him (vv. 20–24).
d) The basic principle involved (vv. 25–27).
e) The story of deliverance retold, with applications to the future (vv. 28–45).
f) A concluding note of praise (vv. 46–50).

a) **What God now means to the psalmist as a result of his experience (vv. 1–2)**

To the Choir Director. By the servant of the Lord—David—who addressed the words of this song to the Lord at the time when the Lord had delivered him from the hand of his enemies, especially from the hand of Saul. He said:
1. *I dearly love Thee, O Lord, my strength.*
2. *The Lord is my rock and my fortress and my deliverer;*
   My God, my rock on which I take refuge, my shield and the horn of my deliverance, and my high tower.

1. An unusual word, used only here, opens the first verse. Since it does imply a love of a very tender sort, we follow *Luther's* lead in translating: "I dearly love Thee." Who would not love God after having experienced so many and strong tokens of His favor? Then follow terms that are expressive of the rich understanding of God and the richness of His being, terms which a loving ingenuity loves to multiply, still feeling that it cannot exhaust the wealth of the divine Being.

2. The first word rendered "rock" might have been rendered "crag" as it is by some interpreters since a prominent single portion of rock is meant, on which a man may take refuge and stand far above the reach of his enemies. Among the many figurative terms there is one that is nonfigurative—"my deliverer." All expressions used convey the

thought of safety, protection, and deliverance, with varied shades of color. All these again have as a central core the ancient title of God *'el*, "the Strong One." This is obviously a case where the mouth speaketh out of the fulness of the heart.

b) **The story of the psalmist's deliverance (vv. 3–19)**

3. *I called on the Lord, who is deserving of praise,*
   And I was delivered from my enemies.
4. *The pains of death had overtaken me,*
   The torrents of destruction had terrified me.
5. *The snares of Sheol had closed me in,*
   The traps of death had confronted me.
6. *In the distress that was upon me I called upon the Lord;*
   Unto my God I cried for help.
   From His temple He heard my voice, and my cry to Him reached
      His ears.
7. *The earth shook and quaked;*
   And the foundations of the mountains trembled and were shaken
      because He was angry.
8. *Smoke arose from His nostrils,*
   And fire from His mouth devoured—coals were kindled by it.
9. *And He bowed the heavens and came down;*
   Thick darkness was under His feet.
10. *He rode upon a cherub and flew;*
    He soared upon the wings of the wind.
11. *He made darkness His covering round about Him;*
    His pavilion was the darkness of waters—thick masses of clouds.
12. *Because of the brightness before Him the clouds about Him*
       passed away;
    Hailstones and coals of fire.
13. *Then the Lord thundered in the heavens;*
    And the Most High uttered His voice—hailstones and coals of
       fire.
14. *And He shot His arrows and scattered them;*
    He hurled His lightnings and confounded them.
15. *Then the bed of the waters could be seen;*
    The foundations of the earth were laid bare because of Thy re-
       buke, O Lord, and because of the blast of the breath of Thy
       nostrils.
16. *He reached down from on high and took me;*
    He drew me out of the great waters.
17. *He delivered me from my strong enemies*
    And from those that hated me, for they were mightier than I.

18. *They overcame me in the day of my calamity;*
    But the Lord became my stay.
19. *And He brought me forth where there was ample room;*
    He delivered me, for He took pleasure in me.

3. The psalmist composes a highly poetic description of what he experienced at the hands of his God. All deliverances are described as *one* deliverance. This one experience is again stated as having been an instance when he was drawn out of dangerous waters that threatened to engulf him. It may be, and has been, called a magnificent "theophany." It is as though the Lord actually appeared to His servant and extricated him from his dangers. This is certainly an emphatic way of ascribing all to God. But the whole description is correct psychologically. For in a man's recollection many experiences may telescope themselves together into one whole, and consequently this description is accurate in every way. That the literal meaning of the psalmist's words dare not be pressed is obvious. David may never have been in danger of drowning in deep waters. It is the poet who speaks here.

The opening (v. 3) is again a summary of the whole of the following experience. It all amounted to this: "I called on the Lord, and I was delivered from my enemies." Quite appropriately already here the author intimates that such a God indeed "is deserving of praise." Besides, what may afterward be described as grievous dangers threatening from deep waters is in the last analysis danger threatening from persons—"my enemies."

Then the extremity that was upon him is described as having been imminent death with its pains, torrents of destruction, snares, and traps. All terms used are indicative of forces of evil closing in on a man, threatening to overwhelm him (vv. 4, 5). But what could a man of God do under such circumstances other than call upon the Lord and cry for help, v. 6? The heavenly temple is thought of in this instance (see 11:4; 29:9; Mic. 1:2; Hab. 2:20).

The description now becomes colorful. God is pictured as being angry because a faithful follower of His has been unjustly assaulted, and terrible is the anger of the Almighty. It causes the very earth and the mountains to tremble before Him: *they* sense the terribleness of anger even if *man* should fail to do so. He Himself is pictured in terms that are almost startling in their force: smoke emanates from His nostrils; blasts of fire that issue from His mouth devour all that stands before them; coals are even kindled by a single blast.

But his anger does not remain static. He comes in person to deliver His saint. The picture is that of a violent storm—a figure so frequently used in the Scriptures to furnish the accompaniment of God's approach, He Himself being as it were housed in the storm. From the time of Sinai onward these figures become standard (cf., Exod. 19:16–18; Judg. 5:4, 5; Ps. 68:7, 8; 77:16–18; Is. 29:6; 30:27ff., etc.). As the storm sweeps near, He is in it. The thick storm clouds are the material upon which He rides.

A cherub, the heavenly being embodying and representing all the forces and powers of nature, bears up this throne of His.[1] Deep as the darkness in which He is enshrouded is on the one hand (vv. 9–11), just so bright may it become with overwhelming brightness when His lightnings flash forth before Him (v. 12). These lightnings dispel the darkness, and masses of hail and lightning are vomited forth by the enshrouding cloud—"hailstones and coals of fire"—twice repeated for emphasis. Then to cap the climax God's mighty thunder rolls. This is most appropriately called, "He uttered His voice." But since all this is an attack upon His enemies or those that beset the writer these lightnings become arrows that He shoots forth at them; and they become utterly confounded (v. 14).

The waters of trouble into which the psalmist had sunk are blasted aside. The very beds of the ocean are disclosed (v. 15). It was as though a man could see the very foundations of the earth and the mountains laid bare since the waters receded from before Him or receded at the blast of His mouth. Then with personal solicitude the Almighty reached down and took His own distressed child out of the dangerous waters (v. 16) or, to change the figure, He "delivered me from my strong enemies," men who "hated" him and at the same time could have prevailed against him, for "they were mightier" than he (v. 17). Though they had already gained the upper hand they had to relinquish their hold and yield up their prey because the Lord was his sure and invincible defender (v. 18). To complete the description, the poor, afflicted soul was brought out of all his troubles and set in an open and secure place "where there was ample room." The description closes most aptly by pointing out that, whatever escape or deliverance there was, it was God who delivered him that trusted in Him and called upon Him. That which prompted Him was nothing other than His free sovereign good will that led Him "to take pleasure" in His follower (v. 19).

c) Why God condescended to deliver him (vv. 20–24)

20. *The Lord rewarded me in accordance with my righteousness;*
    In accordance with the cleanness of my hands He requited me.
21. *For I have kept the ways of the Lord;*
    I have not dealt wickedly in departing from my God.

---

[1] This scarcely leads to the conclusion that cherubim are the personification of the storm cloud as Eichrodt claims, *Theologie des Alten Testaments*, Leipzig, Hinrichs, 1935, II, p. 108.

22. *For I kept His ordinances before me;*
    And His statutes I have not thrust away from me.
23. *And so I was blameless with Him;*
    And I guarded myself against my iniquity.
24. *And so the Lord requited me because of my righteousness;*
    Because of the cleanness of my hands in His sight.

20. We obviously have an explanation as to why God condescended to deliver the writer. In one word, it was because of his righteousness. Emphasis on this point would seem to have been in the mind of the psalmist lest persons who have not lived a life worthy of the people of God derive unwarranted comfort from what was previously written about God's readiness to help those that call upon Him.

Interpreters who sense here a note of self-righteousness and therefore speak of the lower level of ethical insight in the Old Testament may well take note of the fact that such a misconception is offset, among other things, by the fact that at the conclusion of the psalm the writer ascribes all that God did for him to His own "steadfast love" (cf. also v. 32). Besides, the tone of this section is in no sense proud or haughty. *Hengstenberg* drew attention to the fact that what is here asserted about David's righteousness is not set in contrast to human frailty but in contrast to outright iniquity. Frailty the author could not deny, iniquity he could.

The general thought is that there is an eminent propriety about having one who does the will of his God experience the help of his God in adversity. It is still true that, generally speaking, God delights in standing by those that serve Him. The following points are stressed: David has kept himself from obvious infractions of God's law: his hands are clean, he dealt righteously with others. Besides, he has known what God's laws demanded, what way they outlined for a man to walk in, and he has carefully walked in these "ordinances" (v. 20). But such obedience was not a mere outward observance of the letter of the law but a conscious attempt to keep from "departing from God" (v. 21). Whatever ordinances and "statutes" he knew he kept continually before his eye, never thrust them away from him, and so he can maintain that he has with steadfast purpose tried to do what God has required to be done (v. 22).

It cannot be denied that what he has just outlined can be described as living with a holy purpose in mind, and no man can deny that such living may achieve some measure of being "blameless with Him." All the while David was not ignorant of certain sins that beset him, and so he guarded himself against these as carefully as possible. Sins that he is liable to commit he calls "my iniquity" (v. 23). And so he may well claim by way of a summary: "And so the Lord requited me because of my righteousness; because of the cleanness of my hands in His sight" (v. 24).

Some writers have remarked that in portraying this situation somewhat at length David may well have intended to encourage others to walk in the way of the Lord's precepts and thus in perfect holiness in the sight of the Lord. The element of indirect instruction often enters into the psalms. No forced or unwholesome construction is put upon a section such as this when it interpreted in this manner.

d) The basic principle involved (vv. 25–27)
25. *With a faithful man Thou keepest faith;*
    With a blameless man Thy conduct is blameless.
26. *With a pure man Thou dost act purely;*
    And with a crooked man Thou dost prove Thyself astute.
27. *For Thou wilt deliver humble folk;*
    But haughty eyes Thou wilt bring low.

25. The psalmist reduces what he is saying to a broad, basic principle. He has made the observation, and it is quite correct, that God very appropriately deals with every man as that man deals with Him. God lets man, as it were, choose the pattern after which he will be dealt with. The complete fairness of such a procedure can scarcely be questioned. If a man keeps faith with God he will find that God "keeps faith" with him (v. 25). If a man's conduct is blameless—and it should be noted that this is a typically Biblical mode of speaking also in the New Testament (Luke 1:6)—he will never find a thing that he can blame God for. The same holds true with regard to a "pure" man (v. 26) or, as we might say, a sincere man. God is found to meet him with an approach that is in turn entirely pure.

But then there is also the opposite tendency to be reckoned with—and here the writer is content with one example, for his intention was primarily to illustrate the positive—"and with a crooked man Thou dost show Thyself astute." The pattern followed cannot be strictly adhered to, ascribing a similar ungodly trait to the Holy One. So the verb changes in reference to God, and we believe it is a bit precarious to give to the verb used with reference to Him a meaning such as "froward." For the root involved merely means "to twist or be tortuous." In God's case that must have a good sense; therefore "be astute." Nothing more is said than this: since man insists on going devious ways in his dealings with God, God outwits him, as that man deserves. On the whole this is a deep and far-reaching observation.

One general application must still be made in a practical way, which can be of special help to God's people (v. 27), and that is that God delights in delivering "humble folk," but on the other hand continually brings low the "haughty eyes." When the writer says this he must in all humility class himself among the humble. We cannot help but feel that arrogance would be ascribed to him only by a very uncharitable interpretation.

Having summarized the whole situation for purposes of godly instruction, the psalmist continues much in the spirit of the first major section of the psalm.

e) **The story of deliverance retold, with applications to the future** (vv. 28-45)

> 28. *For Thou wilt light my lamp, O Lord;*
> *My God will lighten my darkness.*
> 29. *For by Thee I will overrun a troop;*
> *And by my God I shall leap over a wall.*
> 30. *As for God—His way is perfect;*
> *The word of the Lord is tested—He is a shield to all that take refuge in Him.*
> 31. *For who is God but the Lord?*
> *And who is a rock save our God,*
> 32. *The God who girded me with strength*
> *And made my way blameless;*
> 33. *Who made my feet swift like a doe's*
> *And made me to stand on my heights.*
> 34. *Who taught my hands to war,*
> *So that my arms drew a bow of bronze?*
> 35. *And Thou hast given me Thy shield of safety;*
> *And Thy right hand has sustained me, and Thy condescension has made me great.*
> 36. *Thou didst provide ample room for my steps;*
> *My ankles have not turned.*
> 37. *I pursued my enemies and overtook them;*
> *And I did not turn back until they were consumed.*
> 38. *I shattered them, and they were not able to rise;*
> *They fell under my feet.*
> 39. *And Thou didst gird me with strength for war;*
> *Thou didst subdue under me those that rose against me.*
> 40. *Thou didst make my enemies turn their back;*
> *And them that hate me I have destroyed.*
> 41. *They cried, but there was none to deliver;*
> *Unto the Lord, but He did not answer them.*
> 42. *And so I pulverized them as dust in the face of the wind;*
> *As the mire of the streets I poured them out.*

Psalm 18

43. *And Thou didst deliver me from wars fought for the people;*
    Thou didst set me as head of the nations;
    People that I knew not serve me.
44. *As soon as they heard of me they submitted to me;*
    Foreigners fawned upon me.
45. *Foreigners faded away*
    And came trembling out of their strongholds.

One can well see the propriety of telling twice over so wonderful a story as the psalmist had to tell. For this section (vv. 28–45) is the story of deliverance retold. But it immediately becomes obvious that we are not dealing with an idle repetition. In fact, in the first three verses of this section the author's purpose is not at once apparent. For, basing his thoughts on what the first half of the psalm had presented, he begins to draw conclusions as to the future and how God's steadfast love, which was so strongly manifested in his life heretofore, will, no doubt, continue to show itself in the future.

The first of the things that God will do for His servant is that He "will light his lamp." Though this can in a general way signify that God will as time goes on remove every danger and evil that threatens, the use of this phrase in I Kings 11:36 and similar passages indicates that it has the specific meaning of giving him an heir to follow him on the throne. But the second half of v. 28 would rather convey the meaning we first suggested. Then (v. 29) the writer grows superlatively bold in the confidence of faith, employing two illustrations that immediately captivate the imagination—with God at his side he is able single-handedly to encounter a "troop" and vanquish it; with God at his side, though he be confined by a wall, he can overleap any wall. The old confidence of true faith that was so remarkably manifested in the days of the conflict with Goliath here speaks again by the mouth of David. Cf., I Sam. 17:45ff.

Once again reducing his entire experience to a general truth, David summarizes by saying that no one who has cast himself on the mercy of God can arrive at any other conclusion than that there is never a flaw in God's dealings with His own—"His way is perfect." Since He keeps His promises, "the word of the Lord is tested." In fine, "He is a shield to all that take refuge in Him" (v. 30).

The retelling of the story of God's deliverance begins most appropriately (v. 31) by ascribing to God, the Lord, His utterly exclusive character. None can be what He is; none can be a refuge such as He is. Among the things that He did there are listed, first of all, a number of personal blessings that He has bestowed on David by way of equipping him for the manifold conflicts in which he had to engage (vv. 32–36). Among these favors bestowed upon him are: He gave me strength

(v. 32); for what can a warrior engaged in conflict do unless he is physically able successfully to encounter his foes? Besides that, a basic requirement for felicitous conduct in every walk of life is to be enabled to live blamelessly. Note how absolutely this result in his own life is attributed to God's gracious dealings with him.

Or again (v. 33) when swiftness of feat was essential for flight or pursuit or for successful combat, God made his feet swift like those of a doe. Or if the psalmist was enabled to rise to certain heights in life, that is, achieve outstanding fame, it was again God who bestowed that ability. Still more (v. 34), when personal conflict with foes took place —and David seems to have been engaged in the thick of the fray almost to the end of his days (II Sam. 21:15–17)—it was the Lord who gave skill and success in the manipulation of the instruments of war. In addition, in a beautiful figure David ascribes to Yahweh the lending of His shield to His servant so as to keep him utterly safe; and whenever he stumbled, it was the hand of the Lord that sustained him. In fact, throughout all his experiences God condescended to serve him, and this it was that made the writer great (v. 35)—a telling description of the true source of his success. One more figure is employed (v. 36) to convey the same impression: God always gave him sufficient room to walk and move and never suffered his ankles to turn on rough ground.

Since David's enemies were so many, it is not to be wondered at that he has some remarks to make on the subject of how he was enabled to deal with them. But the same undercurrent of thought appears also here: the Lord gave me strength to overcome what would without Him have been an invincible opposition. In regard to his dealing with these his opponents (vv. 37–42) David at once strikes a note of victory in a summary account: "I pursued my enemies and overtook them; and I did not turn back until they were consumed." In still more drastic language (v. 38) he describes his effort as being a shattering of them so that they were not able to rise. Well aware of the fact that he fought the wars of the Lord, he claims that God gave him whatever strength he needed to conquer in these wars (v. 39); and the claim that he was not the aggressor he makes with a good conscience, as in the sight of God. *They* "rose against" *him,* and God enabled him to subdue them.

After further describing the victory that was given him which forced his enemies to turn their back, he characterizes them as persons that had hated him, the implication being that he had given them no occasion for such hatred, and thus the hatred was unjust (v. 40). It is this fact that determines the interpretation of the next verse (v. 41). For if "they cried, and there was none to deliver," if they directed their petitions "unto the Lord, but He did not answer them," then it must be true that they had no just plea to present. A man must be thoroughly sure of the full justice of his cause before he makes assertions such as these, otherwise he lays himself open to the charge of a very unwholesome self-righteousness. Concluding this part of his resumé (v. 42), the writer describes the defeat which he administered to his foes in these terms: "And so I pulverized them as dust in the face of the wind," total destruction and removal from the scene being implied. The parallel statement presents the same thought with still more color.

The conclusion of this account very properly speaks of the nature of the victory he secured in the process just described. Since this was written at a time when all David's wars had been successfully concluded, he could well state: "Thou didst deliver me from wars." Step by step his success is ascribed to the Lord. As a further indication of the fact that the wars were wars that were thrust upon him and not begun by him we find the expression "wars of the people," which we have rendered "wars fought for the people," for '*am* quite regularly refers to the people of God. A further unplanned and unsought outcome was that by God's help David became "head of the nations," and people about whom he had concerned himself little, in fact, had not even known, now served him (v. 43).

In some instances (see II Sam. 10:9ff.) David's campaigns were dangerous and extremely difficult. But the result was always such a total overthrow of the enemy that the submissiveness of the enemy was most surprising: "As soon as they heard of me they submitted to me; foreigners fawned upon me" (v. 44). Some measure of hyperbole is evident here. But now in retrospect it seems as simple as it is here described. Such is also the nature of the last statement (v. 45): "Foreigners faded away and came trembling out of their strongholds." But not for a moment can the reader get the impression that there is some unseemly self-glorification involved in what is here said. Here is grateful acknowledgment of mercy received.

f) A concluding note of praise (vv. 46–50)

46. *The Lord lives, and praised be my rock,*
    And exalted be the God of my salvation,
47. *The God that executed full vengeance for me*
    And subdued peoples under me
48. *And delivered me from my wrathful foes*
    And raised me up above those that rose against me;
    From the man of violence He delivered me.
49. *Therefore will I give thanks unto Thee among the gentiles, O Lord;*
    And I will sing praise unto Thy name;

50. *Who gives great victories unto His king
And shows steadfast love to His anointed,
To David and to his seed forever.*

This concluding paean of praise very appropriately closes the psalm. In addition to having ascribed all success to God, David ventures into extended praise and thanksgiving. To begin with, he has arrived at a new understanding of the fact that his "Lord lives" (v. 46). This is a triumphant assertion of a truth which has taken on new vitality for the psalmist. Reverting to the words of the beginning, David describes the Lord as his "rock and the God of [his] salvation." The threefold description of the enemy that follows—"wrathful foes . . . those that rose against me . . . the man of violence"—shows how manifold was the opposition, and how many types of deliverence were experienced (v. 48). David also gives expression to a vow to the effect that he intends to make known the marvelous deeds of his God "among the gentiles," implying that he will make a public proclamation that will reach the nations subdued and other nations as well, that it was the Lord, Yahweh, who wrought such great things for him (v. 49). This was the least that he could do, for even among nations like the Moabites victories would be publicly ascribed to the power of the god of the nation (cf., the Moabite Stone).

In the last statement (v. 50) David brings a new thought into the picture, which it must be said gives a touch of the Messianic to the whole. Well aware of the fact that the victories achieved were God's gift and tokens of His "steadfast love," David recalls the unique position that his own seed has attained in the providence of God (II Sam. 7) and thus freely claims that God's mercies were granted him because his own seed has been promised so high a destiny, and that, therefore, God must have had this goal in mind: David was given victory to make possible the greater victories of his Greater Son.

Heading: That David is styled the "servant of the Lord" agrees with the same title in the heading of Ps. 36. Cf. also II Sam. 3:18; 7:5, 8; I Kings 8:24; Ps. 78:70; 89:3, 20; 132:10.

2. *metsudha* is a mountain fastness. In the expression "horn of my deliverance" we have a genitive of apposition (*KS* 3371) and so: the horn which is my deliverance or works deliverance. In *"high tower," misgabh,* the height and inaccessibility are the chief points of emphasis. An "and" (*u*) may well have fallen out before *misgab* as this frequently happened before *m* (*KS* 330 p).

3. *Mehulal,* strictly meaning "praised," was originally used in the past; but when it is related to the present and the future it gains the meaning "deserving to be praised" (*KS* 236 b).

Psalm 18

In *'eqra'* as well as in numerous instances throughout this psalm (cf. especially 36 and 38) the imperfect is used as a means of presenting the various acts described as transpiring before the writer's eye, in what may well be called a sort of "historical present"; and that the past is really involved appears from the constructions with *waw* consecutive which appear in v. 7, or the perfect at the beginning of v. 8; cf. also the first verbs in vv. 9 and 10. *KS* 158.

6. *Batstsar li* does not mean "my distress"—the simple suffix on *tsar* could have secured that result—but rather "the distress that was upon me" (*KS* 281 o).

"His sanctuary" need not refer to the Temple at Jerusalem as some interpreters maintain but may well describe the heavenly dwelling place of the Most High.

13. "Uttered" may rightly be regarded as one of those numerous instances when the imperfect is used even though another word has been inserted between the *waw* consecutive and the imperfect. (See *KS* 368 h).

16. In "he drew me out" the very root of the verb used (*mashah*) makes this a hidden reference to the parallel case of Moses, whom God also had drawn out of the waters.

17. "My strong enemies"—literally: he that is my enemy with might.

21. The expression "in departing from my God" is the familiar *constructio praegnans,* for the Hebrew says merely: "I have not dealt wickedly from my God." (*KS* 213 c.)

23. "And I was blameless" we have translated, "And so I was blameless" because in giving the result the Hebrew often omits little words like "so." The same holds true in the next verse: "And so the Lord requited me."

24. Though some commentators translate *kebhor yaday* literally: "according to the cleanness of my hands" (*RSV*), nevertheless, the cause rather than the norm is being stressed (*KS* 403 a); therefore: "because of the cleanness."

30. *Ha'el* offers an instance of a nominative absolute—best translated "as for God." See *KS* 341 h.

32. *Wayyitten* offers one of those instances when the Hebrew passes over from the participial construction to the finite verb (*KS* 413 l).

33. *Ya'amidhéni* (cf., v. 13) imperfect with *waw* consecutive though another word has been inserted.

The Hebrew says "feet like a doe's," omitting the point of comparison in a shortened expression (*KS* 319 g).

35. *'anawah* is the German *Demut, Herablassung* and thus "condescension." This is better than a pale "help" (*RSV*).

36. The use of the imperfect *tarchibh* is to be explained as a reference to an act that is not yet concluded (*KS* 158).

38. "I shattered them" is another instance of the historical present. "They fell" is the same.

40. The Hebrew has: "As for my enemies, Thou didst give them to me, in reference to the back," *'oreph* being an accusative of reference (*KS* 328 h).

41. "They cried" is another instance when the *waw* consecutive was dropped after *m* (*KS* 330 p).

42. "And *so* . . . ," cf. v. 23.

44. *Waw* is lost as it was in v. 41. It is also lost before, "Thou didst set me."

47. *Neqamoth,* plural of intensity; therefore *"full* vengeance."

48. "Man of violence" is used generically. Therefore *RSV:* "men."

50. The final *h* of the preceding verse should apparently be attached to the initial word of v. 50 as the article before the participle, which is then to be thought of as carrying over to the second participle *'oseh.* See *KS* p. 283, N. 1.

The basic and original unity of the psalm can be defended in spite of the strong prevailing tendency which claims that two originally distinct psalms are welded into one.

Cross and Freedman, *Journal of Biblical Literature,* vol. LXXII, part 1, March, 1953, offer an excellent study of the relation of this psalm to II Sam. 22 and support an early date for its composition.

Psalm 19

THE GLORY OF THE LAW OF THE LORD

THIS IS A PSALM of eloquent praise of the law of the Lord. This view can be maintained in spite of the fact that the first impression it creates is that it treats of the glory of God in *nature*. The usual interpretation given to the psalm, therefore, runs something like this, "Two Witnesses of God" (*Kessler—Zwei Herolde Gottes*). In other words, it is asserted that the subject is God's glory as it is manifested first in the book of nature and second in the book of God's law. Such an approach makes the glory of God the chief subject and certainly subordinates

Psalm 19

the eloquent praise of the law, which stands out as the most prominent feature of the psalm. Besides, such an approach denies the unity of the psalm.

The best solution is that offered by *Hengstenberg,* who subordinates the first part to the second by having it present the praises of the great Giver of the law and thus prepares for the unique glory of the law which comes from the hand of so great an Author. It is true that such an approach seems to overlook the fact that in the first six verses the glory of the Lawgiver seems to be regarded as an independent subject, and thus the introduction to the main subject becomes unusually long. However, it may well be claimed that the author is swept along by the magnitude of his subject as he describes the glory of Him who is the Author of the law. But this is an issue which deals with the subject matter of the psalm.

A structural problem looms rather large in the treatment of the psalm, and that is the problem as to whether it may justly be maintained that the psalm was originally a unit. The differences between parts A and B seem too prominent to allow one to think of the two parts as having from the outset constituted one piece. However, several strong considerations may be urged in support of the original unity. In the first place, if some later writer, familiar with these two fragments (or two independent poems, for that matter) saw that they might effectively be joined into a unified piece, why could not the original author just as readily have seen such a possibility?

Others, like *Kessler,* point to the obvious symmetry of the two parts. When the abruptness of the transition from the first part to the second is stressed as an obstacle to original unity, *Maclaren* rightly points out that this constitutes rather an argument for the opposite point of view inasmuch as a compiler, in putting the two parts together, might well have striven to smooth over the transition. Though *Schmidt's* position agrees with the majority of writers on the subject, his approach borders on arrogance when he asserts that the two parts cannot originally have belonged together "as is apparent without further argument" (*ohne weiteres*), though he does for good measure submit a few arguments. Also the change of rhythm and meter is no more pronounced than is that found between sections of Schiller's *Glocke.*

That David is the author is claimed by the Hebrew heading. Though this is again challenged on the ground that the law had not achieved a position of such prominence in David's day, such a negative claim is based on an artificial reconstruction of Israel's development. The valid historical record attributes just this kind of regard for the law to David (I Kings 2:1–4). This would then determine the time of composition.

When we use the approach indicated by the title we give the psalm we indicate clearly that we place it in the category of didactic psalms which glorify the Word of the Lord from one or another viewpoint. Only incidentally can it be claimed that this is a nature psalm. In this connection several unfortunate approaches must be discarded like the claim that this is a kind of hymn to the sun. *Schmidt* claims that in this psalm the heavenly spheres sing the praises of the most glorious planet of their number, admitting, however, that in the process of so doing their song almost incidentally becomes a song of praise of a greater One. This scarcely squares with the facts of the case. *Kittel,* too, claims that at least vv. 5c–7 are a hymn to the sun. Then all interpreters of this school of thought state that it becomes quite obvious that the material of the psalm is in the process of transition from mythological lore to the distinctive type of Israel's literature.

The following outline can be traced through this psalm:

a) The glory of the Lawgiver (vv. 1–6).
b) The glory of the law in its manifold uses (vv. 7–10).
c) The law in relation to the psalmist (vv. 11–14).

a) **The glory of the Lawgiver (vv. 1–6)**

> *To the Choir Director. A Psalm of David.*
> 1. *The heavens are telling the glory of God;*
>   *And the firmament is declaring the work of His hands.*
> 2. *One day pours forth speech to the next day;*
>   *And night to night proclaims knowledge.*
> 3. *There is no speech, nor are there words,*
>   *Where their voice is not heard.*
> 4. *Through all the earth their influence has gone forth;*
>   *And to the ends of the earth their words.*
>   *In them He has set a tent for the sun,*
> 5. *Which is like a bridegroom leaving his chamber*
>   *And rejoices like a strong man about to run a race.*
> 6. *Its starting point is from one end of the heavens;*
>   *And its circuit to the other end thereof;*
>   *And there is nothing hid from its heat.*

1. The glory of the Lawgiver is being declared. "Heavens" are in an emphatic position in the Hebrew as much as to say: The very heavens declare, or even, The heavens in a very distinct sense declare. Since the participle follows and expresses continuous action, we must render the verb "are telling," for they do it continually by day or by night. Downright majestic is the "glory" which these heavens advertise. Since this is a truth which is apparent even to the heathen (cf., Rom. 1:19ff.),

one of the most general names of God is used—'*el,* "the Strong One." We might begin the second half of the verse thus: "And especially the firmament . . ." which, according to Gen. 1, seems to refer to the lower realm of the heavens immediately above the earth. By its very beauty and magnitude this firmament declares clearly that it, too, is the work of none other than the omnipotent Creator and is fashioned by His hands.

To think here and in the next two verses of something like the hymn of the heavenly spheres as they run their course through the heavenly regions is a bit fantastic. "Telling" and "declaring" are used in that figurative sense so commonly found elsewhere in the Scriptures (cf., Is. 14:8; Ps. 35:10; 50:6; 96:12; 148:2–4; 98:8, etc.). The approach is like that of Ps. 8: it is as though the word "glory" were written in capital letters across the very heavens and the firmament.

2. Day and night are now thought of as conveying the same truth about God's glory, but in their own way. They "pour forth" or literally "bubble forth" their information. As someone has rightly remarked, it is as though their eloquent testimony bubbled forth at every crack and cranny of the universe. In fact, the very existence of day and night in the form in which they function is so remarkable as to tell about their Maker. So each day is poetically envisioned as informing the next of this glory, and thus the uninterrupted tradition has gone down through the ages.

3. "Speech" and "language" (*AV*) convey the thought of the verse exceedingly well. That is to say, in all languages, or to be more precise, among all nations where these languages are spoken this testimony has been noted: not one is exempt. The point is the universality of the testimony referred to in v. 2. The translation of this verse has long been an issue on which interpreters showed little agreement, except that perhaps the majority reject the translation we offer. But our translation is defensible. It shows the progression from the long history of this testimony (2) to its universal character. The terms "speech" and "words" may by metonymy refer to the nations using them. All that is required is to supply the relative before "their voice," the relative being omitted in the Hebrew about as frequently as it is in the English. So the lead given by the *Septuagint* may still be safely followed. The customary translations emphasize the silent testimony of the witnesses named: "There is no speech, nor are there words; their voice is not heard" (*RSV*). But this approach necessitates a change of the text of the next verse to secure the desired contrast: "Yet their voice goes out." (*RSV*).

4. The thought expressed in v. 3 is reiterated. The influence of the testimony of the heavens has gone out through all the earth. We believe this to be the easiest way to capture the thought of the very

unfamiliar Hebrew idiom, which had been retained, for example, by *AV:* "Their line is gone out through all the earth." "Line" (*qaw*) is "measuring line." By a simple figure the thought may substitute the territory measured for the line that does the measuring. So some interpreters understand the *qaw,* "the extent of territory" (*Hengstenberg*) or "The measuring line marks the limits of possession" (*Kirkpatrick*). Our idiom would seem to require "their influence," which is certainly not difficult to understand. This also agrees well with the second half of the verse: "And to the ends of the earth their words (have gone forth)."

From the third member of this verse onward through two more verses attention centers on the greatest of the heavenly bodies, the sun, which is introduced in the statement: "In them [that is, the heavens] He has set a tent for the sun." The idea is: the sun has its place of residence in the heavens. Some writers are so intent on noting a supposed resemblance to heathen lore that they write: "The sun-hero (*Sonnenmann*) has his heavenly tent in the sea" (*Schmidt*) quite a far cry from what David wrote!

5. The glory of this heavenly body which has awed all nations from days of old may well be delineated at this point, for it reflects the glory of its Maker. Two figures are employed. The first likens the sun to a "bridegroom leaving his chamber," the point of comparison being the fresh, lusty strength of the young man, happy in his youthful love. The second likens the sun to "a strong man about to run a race." The thought stressed is obviously the same.

6. Abandoning these figures, which are colorful enough, the writer dwells on the vastness of the course traversed by the sun. The point of departure ("starting point") is the one end of the heavens; the point of its turning around ("circuit") is "at the other end" of the heavens. Though the ancients could scarcely have had a conception of what happens astronomically they all noted that a great distance had to be covered and a repetition of the same course had to be run with unwearied strength. Quite naturally the writer speaks according to what the eye sees and not in an attempt to make statements that square with the findings of the astronomer as *Louis Harms* clearly preached when he explained this psalm. The last member of the verse could be translated: "And there is nothing hid from its light," as *Koenig* suggests, inasmuch as heat and light are so closely associated. Some interpreters determine the time of composition of the psalm by remarks such as: "It is a testimony to the antiquity of this psalm that the hero covers the vast distance afoot" and not like Apollo in his chariot. If this is exegesis, make the most of it! The author of the statement (*Schmidt*) chooses a date that is later than the time of Ezra!

Psalm 19

b) **The glory of the law in its manifold uses (vv. 7–10)**

7. *The law of the Lord is perfect—restoring the soul;*
   The testimony of the Lord is sure—making wise the simple;
8. *The precepts of the Lord are right—rejoicing the heart;*
   The commandment of the Lord is pure—enlightening the eyes;
9. *The fear of the Lord is clean—enduring forever;*
   The verdicts of the Lord are true—and righteous altogether;
10. *More to be desired are they than gold—even much fine gold,*
    Sweeter also than honey—and the droppings of the honeycomb.

7. It should be rather obvious that the singer has now mounted to a higher level and speaks with greater eloquence as he touches upon the higher theme—the excellencies of the law in its manifold uses. Quite appropriately he ascribes this law to the Lord (*Yahweh*), the covenant God of Israel, who has revealed Himself in it. Furthermore, it must be equally obvious that David does not use the term law in the Pauline New Testament sense. Though the root meaning of *torah* is "instruction," it is noted immediately that the term is here almost the equivalent of what we commonly call the Word of the Lord. It is well known that it soon became the term for the Pentateuch. It must be equally clear that gospel elements are included in the law. To the writer it has become a means of grace—all of which could in no sense be a criticism of Paul's approach, who thinks of the law quite generally in Romans and Galatians as that which makes unconditional demands upon men and so is harsh and unrelenting. The use made of this term in this psalm is more like that called the Third Use of the Law in the Confessions (FC. Epitome VI).

A fixed pattern is followed in the next three verses: first a distinctive name for the law; then an appropriate adjective; then a beneficial effect or some other encomium.

Note first the distinctive names in addition to law. It is "testimony," perhaps chiefly in the sense of "reminder" (*Koehler*) reminding man both of what he should do and of where he has failed to do it. It is then designated "precepts"—also to be translated "orders," for these words claim attention as words that the authority of the Almighty has uttered, and which we cannot do other than obey. "Commandments" is even more specific. "Fear" is strictly not a synonym for law but rather emphasizes a reaction that it calls forth, namely, a wholesome reverence for the will of the Lawgiver, emphasizing that no one who deals with the law dare regard it merely as an abstraction or in a spirit of absolute objectivity but should rather feel the need of his submitting to it. It may also be described as "verdicts" in that God's law does pronounce a verdict on many difficult issues and so speaks with final authority.

The following descriptive adjectives are then used. This law is first "perfect" in the sense of being all-sided so as to cover completely all aspects of life. It is "sure" in the sense of being a foundation on which a man can unhesitatingly build. It is "right" in that it maps out a straight course for any man that would be guided by it. It is "pure" insofar as it may well be conceived as a product that has been thoroughly purified and is thus unadulterated; there are no unwholesome elements in it. "Clean" expresses practically the same thought; it is used, e.g., with reference to metals. "True" is particularly strong, being the only noun used as adjective in the series. It implies utter dependability.

The beneficial effects are, first, the restoration of the soul, not to be thought of in the sense of conversion but rather as a beneficial reviving effect that permeates the very life and soul of a converted child of God. "Making wise the simple"—that is to say, imparting true heavenly wisdom to all who will keep their soul open to its effects. "Simple" is not a derogatory term; it is not *albern* ("foolish") as Luther renders it. It is also said to "rejoice the heart" which surely implies deep and satisfying joys. It "enlightens the eyes," for it imparts a freshness and joy to the very looks of the eye. Nor does it offer a mere chance opinion that may lose its value shortly: it "endures forever." If the last virtue ascribed to the law is its "righteous" character, that signifies that it is the essence of true normalcy, a meaning which this root regularly has.

True, these are all more or less abstract concepts, lacking some of the lustre that marked the figures employed in the description of the sun. But that is due to the nature of the words used and does not make this section less poetical. He that knows the value of the Word of God will find his heart ringing with responsive vibrations of joy and will scarcely say of this section that it "has been commonly overrated" (*Buttenwieser*).

10. Abandoning the fixed pattern followed throughout three verses, the author closes his words of praise of the law by showing its absolute desirability and sweetness. As for true value, there is no gold that can be compared with it; and the sweetest of the honey is inferior to the attractive taste of the law that God gives to His people.

c) The law in relation to the psalmist (vv. 11–14)

11. *Furthermore by them has Thy servant been warned;*
    In keeping them there is great reward.
12. *Who can discern his errors?*
    Absolve Thou me from hidden faults.
13. *Keep back Thy servant also from presumptuous sins;*
    Let them not rule over me.

Psalm 19

> Then I shall be blameless;
> And I shall be absolved of manifold transgressions.
> 14. Let the words of my mouth and the meditation of my heart be
> acceptable before Thee,
> O Lord, my rock and my redeemer.

11. The author is now speaking of the law in relation to himself. He thinks first of this past experiences. He has often (niphal participle) been warned by the law and kept from evil ways. Quite modestly he refers to himself merely as God's servant. But he has also found that whenever he has kept the course the law prescribes, God has given tokens of His pleasure—"great reward." This, as has been correctly observed, was scarcely written to promote the spirit of selfish observance of the law for the reward's sake but is part of the manifold praises of the law offered here. It is a law that brings this added blessing of a reward from God.

12. But as for the future, there are still further blessings that the law can convey. Its bright light can help a man detect and remove "errors," which are in reality sins of weakness inadvertently committed. They are the sins that we ordinarily do not even discern as being committed by us. They may also for that reason be called "hidden faults." When we become conscious of them, it is our most earnest desire that God may "absolve" us of them. Note what a wholesome attitude the faithful use of the law has begotten in the writer. But more of this.

13. There is another less insidious but, perhaps, more damaging type of sin, the "presumptuous" that one might commit in defiance of the Lord. He, therefore, prays that God may guard him from such, for if one once begins to slip into them, they may, like all other sins, "rule over" a man. Only so, by God's enlightenment wrought through His law and by His protecting grace, can a man be kept "blameless and be absolved of manifold transgressions." It must be very obvious that the writer's relation to the law is not one of abstract and fruitless meditation. He is not content with mere theory about the excellence of the law. He has felt its beneficent effects and desires to have more of them.

14. Well aware as to how imperfect our best efforts are, the psalmist very appropriately closes his prayer with a humble plea that that which his mouth has uttered and his heart devoutly meditated on may be well pleasing in His sight, who is his "rock" on which he builds and his "redeemer" who delivers him in his many needs.

NOTES

3. The words *beli nishma'* may be construed as a clause of circumstances—"without their being heard"—as is most generally done; but

when the relative is supplied, we get a rendering that fits better into the context. For the first view see *KS* 412 w. In his *Commentary Koenig* changed to the view we advocate.

10. The initial participle, attached to a noun that does not immediately precede, becomes the equivalent of a relative clause, a fact that is completely obscured by our translation, which is still very much to the point. See *KS,* p. 283, Note. The article before this participle carries over to the adjective "sweet."

12. The agent is introduced by *be* in *bahem;* see *KS* 106.

13. *Zedim* could, of course, be translated "the proud ones," but in the connection in which it appears it is much better to regard it as referring to one of the various types of sin that are to be shunned—therefore "presumptuous sins."

The claim commonly made in our day that this psalm dates from the time of Ezra because in that age the interest in the law of the Lord is supposed to have become strong is a viewpoint that grows out of the late dating of the so-called sources of the Pentateuch. There is much historical evidence pointing to the fact that in the age of David the distinctive importance of the law was rather clearly understood (cf., I Kings 2:1–4; 9:4ff.).

Psalm 20

A PRAYER FOR THE KING

THE GENERAL PURPOSE of the psalm is rather obvious. The nation is offering a prayer for its king. We have, therefore, a psalm of intercession. The course of its thoughts is as follows:

a) The prayer is presented (vv. 1–5).
b) Expression given to the assurance of the king's success (vv. 6–8).
c) A summary petition by way of conclusion (v. 9).

Is the heading found in the Hebrew text, which ascribes the psalm to David, reliable? There is ample reason to believe that it is. The major problem would then be: Is it reasonable to suppose that a king like David would himself have composed a prayer in which he is the object of his people's petitions? Why should such a thought be incongruous?

The king is aware of his God-given responsibility as the head of the Lord's people. He knows the efficacy of believing intercession on the part of the people of God. Any enlightened king may serve as a spiritual leader of his people on such issues. David and Solomon repeatedly functioned as teachers of Israel (cf. especially Ps. 122 and 127); and surely, in the case of a king of Israel it cannot be regarded as an undue preoccupation with one's self when he instructs his people to pray for him. Other objections to authorship by David stem from nebulous arguments based on taste and style and seem to be of little moment.

An issue challenging special attention in connection with this psalm is the question as to whether we have here a strictly liturgical piece. Some interpreters go so far in their claims that the poem bears just such a character that they specify that it is designed to be prayed at the very moment when the sacrifices for victory are being offered; or they say that the section (vv. 6–8) was to be spoken by the priest; or they distribute the verses of the psalm over a responsive pattern that covers the whole; or they even place the king at the entrance to the Temple court when the first strains of the psalm begin to be spoken; or they insist that it was a hymn that was used so frequently as to bear evidence of being a bit worn and prosy. All such approaches give evidence of reading something into the psalm that is not there. In general it is one of those instances when a pet theory, like the liturgical interpretation, comes to be an obsession that must be maintained at all costs.

We should concede that the psalm bears a half-liturgical stamp. When it was composed it could well have been used by the assembled congregation on a special occasion (perhaps a situation such as the one described in II Sam. 8 or 10) or at any time thereafter, when Israel's monarch stood in special need of divine assistance. But it certainly could have been part of the prayer of any devout Israelite at any time when he felt impelled to invoke the blessing of the Almighty upon his government and its king in times of trouble. So much may safely be claimed without going beyond the evidence offered by the psalm. Offering up prayer especially for victory is met with in a number of Scripture passages; cf., I Sam. 7:9; 13:9; II Chron. 14:11; 20:4ff.

Ps. 21 is a companion piece to our psalm as will appear when we examine this psalm.

a) **The prayer is presented (vv. 1–5)**

To the Choir Director. A Psalm of David.
1. *The Lord answer you in the day of distress;*
   The name of the God of Jacob protect you!
2. *May He send you help from the sanctuary;*
   And may He from Zion uphold you!

3. May He remember all your offerings;
   And your burnt offerings may He regard with favor!
4. May He grant you your heart's desire;
   And your plans may He fulfil!
5. May we exult over the victory granted you;
   And in the name of our God may we unfurl our banner;
   May the Lord fulfil all your petitions!

1. It seems a little too definite to label this the beginning of a prayer for the king in time of *battle* or on the eve of battle. For though v. 5 may be translated as we have rendered it ("victory"), the word there used is basically "salvation." And since this verse calls the situation one of "distress," we had best let that term stand. Here again we may have one of those instances when a prayer that is born out of a very special situation reflects the nature of that situation somewhat less definitely, so as to be usable in all manner of similar situations. In other words, the prayer may be used in all kinds of emergencies.

The burden of the petition, however, is that the Lord may answer the prayers that the people know that their king is making. For they have confidence in him that he is a man who prays. The expression "the name of the God of Jacob" means: the revealed character of the Lord as His people know Him in so far as this character is summed up in His holy name. The expression "God of Jacob" appears to be used in distinct reference to the experiences that Jacob had of the faithfulness of his God in the days when he called upon Him.

2. Since Israel had been taught to think of God as being enthroned in its midst, graciously present above the ark of the covenant, what could be more natural than to think of His help as emanating from that very sanctuary as the parallel expression "from Zion" clearly suggests? To speak thus means to look for the Lord and His help where He has taught His people that they should look. He is envisioned, not as a remote God, therefore, but as One who is near.

3. For people to pray as they do in this verse implies that they are aware of the fact that their king has been wont to fulfill his religious obligations as these are expressed in sacrifices regularly and faithfully. They would also know that in the case of a faithful king such as they had such a fulfilment of religious obligations would not have been a matter of mere form but a truly devout service of God in a manner ordained by Him and pleasing to Him, outward form and inner spirit being in fullest harmony with one another. Since the sacrifices were prayers incarnate, the nation may well refer to them and express the desire that God "may regard them with favor." It is uncharitable criticism of the psalm and its author to speak of "utilitarian motives. In return for their offerings, the king and his army expected

Psalm 20

God to grant them victory over the nation's enemies" (*Buttenwieser*).

4. So thoroughly is the nation in sympathy with the king's objectives and so completely convinced that they are right and good that it cannot but desire that God may grant whatever the king's heart desires under the circumstances (literally: "according to your heart"). It surely bespeaks a strong confidence when the people can pray: "and all your plans may He fulfil." This is surely much more than cheap chauvinism.

5. One might be inclined to prefer the rendering, "we will triumph" and "we will set up," (*ARV*) which are expressive of the resolve to rejoice when God grants the petitions previously expressed. However, the Hebrew syntax suggests that, since all the forms involved in vv. 1–5 are of the same pattern (regular imperfects used as optatives), it is much better to consider the verse as a part of the prayer which the psalm began and to let the expression of assurance begin with the following verse. The prayer, therefore, asks that those who pray may be granted the privilege of exulting over the victory when it comes as well as for the privilege of unfurling the victory banner on the great day. Summarizing all the petitions, the last one, like v. 5b, asks: "May the Lord fulfil all your petitions." Very aptly stated, for they know that their king is the kind of man who not only teaches others to offer prayers but himself faithfully offers them.

b) Expression given to the assurance of the king's success (vv. 6–8)

6. *Now I know that the Lord has helped His anointed;*
   He has answered him from His holy heaven with mighty deeds of
   deliverance by His right hand.
7. *Some make their boast of chariots and some of horses;*
   But we shall make our boast in the name of the Lord our God.
8. *They have always bowed down and fallen;*
   But we have risen and stand firm.

6. The "now" marks a new point in the development of the prayer. On the basis of what has been asked the conviction has strongly grown upon the people who pray that God has in the past given victories to their king, who is anointed by God's appointment, and, therefore, "His anointed." It is unnatural to translate the verb found here in the past tense "has helped" as though it implied a present "saveth" or a future "will help." The obvious meaning is that we here have a reference to things that God has done in the past. This is expressed more fully in the second member: "He has answered him from His holy heaven." It is the nation that speaks in the collective singular, which quite naturally broadens out into a "we" in v. 7b. It is rather artificial to assume that in this verse the voice of some individual is being heard,

that of a prophet or priest or even of the king himself. The natural unity of the psalm is maintained by our interpretation. Those many instances of the past when God saved David "by mighty deeds of deliverance by His right hand" form the basis for a mighty assurance of being heard in the present instance.

7. The prayer gives a broader statement of the case, almost in the form of a basic principle that motivates the thinking of God's people now and at all times. In their attitude the people of God are radically different from the heathen way of thinking, which amounts to this: "Some make their boast of chariots and some of horses." By the omission of the verb the original makes the statement more striking: Some in chariots; some in horses. The basic error of the unbelieving mind is here scored: warlike equipment is the source of victory. But God's people have a higher and safer ground of confidence: "We shall make our boast in the name of the Lord our God." Again that mighty and saving power, the "name" of the Lord (cf., v. 1)! With it could be equated the idea of the character, the well-known character of the Lord.

8. Being on the subject of the contrast between the heathen and the people of God, the psalm presents it from another point of view, namely, the ultimate outcome. In the area defeat has always been the lot of the one group, victory and confidence the lot of the other. The assurance expressed is striking and clearly marked with the note of a sturdy faith. It is as though the psalmist understood very well that when you ask *"believing* you shall receive."

c) A summary petition by way of conclusion (v. 9)

9. *O Lord, help;*
May the King answer us when we call!

Since the burden of the psalm was prayer, it is most appropriate that a petition, by way of a summary, addresses one last plea to the Almighty. A note of tense earnestness is thus struck. It is also very proper in this connection to consider how the prayer for the king of Israel is addressed to the King of the whole world. So the Hebrew text has it, and there is no good reason for departing from this approach as *RSV* does. The balance of the parallelism is a further argument for retaining the familiar rendering.

NOTES

1. To maintain full consistency with the manner of rendering the verbs in the first five verses it would have been better to begin: "May the Lord answer you . . . may he protect." The *AV* apparently suggested the approach we have used above as the more familiar.

2. This verse and the next two have a chiastic arrangement of the members: a) verb–object; b) object–verb. We have tried to keep that pattern by the wording of our translation even though the English style is less inclined to favor this pattern.

3. The Hebrew verb "remember" (*zakhar*) is suggestive of a term used in connection with sacrifices in Leviticus, '*azkarah*) (Lev. 2: 2, 9, 16), which terms implies that sacrifices offered for individuals bring them up in remembrance before God. It may well be questioned whether *minchah* ("offerings") should be rendered, as the German versions prefer, "meal offerings" even though it may seem to be in contrast with "burnt offerings." *Minchah* is the broadest term available, signifying all manner of gifts—which meaning is most appropriate here. The verb "regard with favor" (*dishshen*) literally means "regard as fat." For the suffix on the verb—*eh* for *ah*—see *GK* 48 d.

5. The rendering "the victory granted to you" expresses more clearly the import of the suffix, which in the Hebrew reads merely: "your victory."

6. The verb *ya'anehu* seems to be a future. But when it is thus construed it comes into conflict with *yadha'ti*. So this is apparently an instance when the final *waw* of *meshicho* is written but once but must serve also as the *waw* consecutive for the verb following (haplography); cf., *KS* 368f. For "mighty deeds of deliverance by His right hand" the Hebrew has a unique construction: "by heroic deeds of salvation of His right hand."

8. The perfects *kare'u* and *naphelu* are best regarded as the equivalent of gnomic aorists (*KS* 126). Since synonyms are involved, the usual arrangement with *waw* consecutive is not used (*KS* 370 f).

9. Though the Hebrew has "in the day when we call," the expression "in the day" has no emphasis; therefore "when." *Schmidt* makes this a reference to some special day.

It should yet be remarked that the psalm has a somewhat general tone so that it could well be employed by Israel as well as by Christian people of all times when they know their ruler to be engaged in espousing a just cause or even, for that matter, whenever they know their government to be in distress.

That raises the further question: Is the psalm Messianic? It can scarcely be claimed that it was intended to be this. *Luther* said that such an interpretation seemed to him to be "too remote." *Hengstenberg,* however, claimed that the psalm "ultimately points to Christ and His kingdom." The truth seems to be that, being a prayer for a godly kind in a just cause, it may fitly be adapted to a Messianic use by any pious soul.

Psalm 21

THE NATION'S THANKSGIVING
AND HOPE FOR ITS KING

As INDICATED above, this psalm is a companion piece to the preceding psalm. The latter was primarily a prayer of intercession; this one is dominated by the note of thanksgiving. That will, however, scarcely warrant putting the two so close to one another as to describe the first as offering the petition and the second as offering praise for the answering of the petition just offered. It cannot be demonstrated that the two psalms grew out of one and the same situation and offer two different reactions to this situation.

In fact, it has become quite common to designate our psalm as a prayer of thanksgiving for victory. That theme is not quite broad enough. The psalm may include thanksgiving of such a type. But a wider possibility must be considered.

But another issue must first be disposed of: Is this a psalm of David? The claim which the heading of the psalm offers under this head may well be maintained—"a Psalm of David." Davidic authorship cannot be brushed aside by a mere verdict such as *Koenig* offers, "The author cannot be David." Why not? The arguments we offered in connection with the preceding psalm hold good in this instance also. David, aware of his unique position as the king of Israel, confident of his people's interest in his position and success, and mindful of their prayers and the value of such prayers, may well have written a psalm that embodied in acceptable petition the deep needs of the kingdom of David, which was then the earthly manifestation of the kingdom of God. Only a selfless king who was well aware of his theocratic importance could have ventured to do such a thing; and David was just such a king.

If he was, then the question arises as to what particular event occurred in the life of David that called for the nation's thanksgiving in a special sense. Certainly, his eminent success on the field of battle against the many foes that he had to encounter may well be thought of. But there was one event that must be regarded as the crowning climax of all that he experienced, and that is the event recorded in II Sam. 7, where David is apprised of the fact that God shall bless him in such a measure that his kingdom shall be an everlasting kingdom, to be ruled by One of the line of David who shall reign eternally. Ps. 89 and Ps. 132 show how profoundly the people had been impressed by this promise. Vv. 4 and 6 emphasize in particular the eternal character of the blessings that had just been bestowed on David. It is true that no part of the sacred record that we have states what is mentioned in v. 2, namely, that David had desired this blessing from his Lord. But what is unnatural about assuming that such a desire may have arisen in the heart of David though it is not specifically mentioned in the record as such? Did David not know and understand Gen. 49:10? On the assumption that he did alone we may rightly suppose that it had been the deep yearning of his heart to have his own line of descent honored by God in this significant way.

And what would be unseemly about the prayers offered in vv. 7–13; or for David to lay such prayers on the lips of his people? The situation is far different from that of any ambitious earthly monarch when a godly king of Israel teaches his people to pray thus. He has godly desires in so doing, and so have his people in following his suggestions. Authorship by David is, therefore, both reasonable and possible.

a) **Thanksgiving for mercies granted to the king (vv. 1–6)**

To the Choir Director. A Psalm of David.
1. *O Lord, in Thy strength the king rejoices;*
   And in Thy help how greatly he rejoices!
2. *Thou has given him what his heart desires;*
   Thou hast not refused him what his lips ask.
3. *For Thou dost come to meet him with rich blessings;*
   Thou settest a crown of fine gold upon his head.
4. *He asked life of Thee, and Thou didst give it,*
   Length of days forever and ever.
5. *His glory is great through Thy help;*
   Honor and majesty Thou dost lay upon him.
6. *For Thou dost render him most blessed forever;*
   Thou dost make him glad with joy in Thy presence.

1. God has done something for Israel's king. The nation is aware of it. The people are vitally interested in it. The psalmist king, though himself involved, teaches the people to express their thanksgiving in these words. It must have been something notable. The word we have in v. 1 translated "help" could be rendered "victory" if there were a direct indication of such a victory. On the meaning ascribed to this one word *yeshu'a* hinges the whole direction of the interpretation. We feel that "help" is broader and allows for all the issues that may be involved. That it comes from God is most obvious. That it made the re-

cipient very glad cannot be denied. It was (v. 2) a matter of such great concern to the author that he had previously prayed for this gift. As indicated above, that could well have been the case with regard to the promise of the greatness of his house given him by God.

Moreover, regarding this blessing it could be said most appropriately (v. 3) that God came "to meet the king with rich blessings," or even that He had set "a crown of fine gold upon his head." This second statement is not out of keeping with the fact that David was definitely crowned king before this time. The grace that God granted him set the regal crown upon his head a second time; or this grace instated him in his great office more effectually than ever.

The promise of an everlasting dynasty may also be called "life" (v. 4) in a most eminent sense. For it may well have been David's prayer that God might grant him to *live* in the sight of his God. Thereupon God gave him this promise as an answer. In fact, He gave "length of days forever and ever." II Sam. 7:13, 16 agree so perfectly with this thought as to make this interpretation most apropos.

It is also quite obvious that a blessing like the one promised to David on that great and auspicious occasion could most properly be described as "glory" (v. 5) and as "honor" and "majesty." All this became David's lot "through the help" of the Lord. It was certainly not merited and achieved by the king. Besides, all this may be summarized as a case where God had "rendered him most blessed forever." Or again, this was an experience that made "him glad with joy" in the presence of God. For it must be recalled that according to II Sam. 7:18 David immediately went into the sanctuary of God and voiced his heartfelt thanks. Since this involves the nation's greatest welfare, Israel as a whole may well be invited to praise God as is here done.

b) The hope of future victories for the king (vv. 7–12)

Though some of the expressions used may seem to point to the possibility that God is being addressed, and that this is a prayer, yet on closer inspection it will become apparent that the nation is thought of as expressing these pious wishes in behalf of its king.

7. *For the king trusts in the Lord;*
   And because of the steadfast love of the Most High he shall not be moved.
8. *Your hand shall dispose of all your enemies;*
   Your right hand shall dispose of those who hate you.
9. *You shall make them like a blazing oven at your appearing;*
   The Lord in His anger will consume them;
   Fire shall devour them.
10. *Their fruit you will destroy from the earth,*

And their offspring from among the children of men.
11. *When they have planned evil against you or devised mischief,*
They shall not prevail.
12. *For you will drive them away in flight;*
With your bow you will aim at their faces.

7. Since the people cherish good wishes for their king, and rightly so because of his rare destiny, the king composes godly wishes for their use as they express their hopes for his future success. It must first be stressed that the king is not a man who trusts in his own strength and abilities, his trust is in the Lord. It is only because the Lord is so faithful to His covenant that the king will not be moved or brought to fall.

It is to be hoped that the following instances of success shall be the lot of their king. First that (v. 8) "his hand shall dispose of his enemies." The verb employed is "find" the enemies. This means something like "dispose" of them. Since they hate a king who has so high a destiny as this one has, it is but proper that the wish also be expressed that his right hand dispose of such ungodly haters. To make the opponents like "a blazing oven" implies that they may be cast into such an oven and be consumed. However, any such act of judgment must be left to the Lord. Therefore (v. 9b) this thought is expressed. For already in the Old Testament the truth was known that vengeance is the Lord's.

In v. 10 the word "fruit" refers to the plans and undertakings of the wicked or also to their achievements. It is hoped that Israel's good king will destroy what the wicked produce and also dispose successfully of their children ("offspring") if they continue in the evil ways of their parents. Such a condition, though not expressed, must quite naturally be assumed. For the Lord would reject all prayers that are prompted by a spirit of vindictiveness.

The hope expressed for the king becomes more positive in v. 11. Whatever evil or mischief may be devised, it is positive that these things "shall not prevail." And so the section closes with the picture of the enemy in precipitate flight before the victorious king (v. 12), and the king himself as a victorious hero who aims his lethal bow at their very faces to cause their overthrow.

c) **Praise of God for His goodness to the king (v. 13)**

In one pregnant prayer of utmost brevity the nation or any individual in it is taught to pray to the Almighty as the only One who can achieve what they so earnestly desire, and that the glory for it all may be His. Those who pray thus are not asking for trivial or selfish blessings but understand right well that what they seek is the very welfare of the kingdom over which God Himself is the omnipotent Ruler and David

His humble appointed servant. For all success that may come they say: "We shall sing and praise Thy might." On this lofty note the psalm closes.

13. *Be Thou exalted, O Lord, in Thy strength;*
    We will sing and praise Thy power.

NOTES

One could regard this psalm as a liturgical piece as follows: "Ps. 21 is a king's song, sung by the royal choir in the presence of the reigning monarch of Judah. The occasion is the anniversary of the enthronment" (*Leslie*). Two considerations make this dubious: Was there a "royal choir"? and, Was the "anniversary of the enthronment" observed?

Again, to state that there was "an oracle or a sign of the divine favor" between the two halves of the psalm lets the imagination play rather freely.

Psalm 22

THE VICTORIOUS SUFFERER

To GIVE a somewhat more precise formulation for a title of this psalm we might have said: A Prophecy concerning the Messiah's Sufferings and Victory. This is the noblest of the passion psalms. It is sanctified in a singular sense by Christ in that He used its opening words in the extremity of His agony on the cross.

The most difficult problem seems to be to characterize the exact nature of this psalm, that is to say, just how it is related to the Christ. *Kirkpatrick* has the most exact statement of the four possibilities involved. They are: Is this psalm to be interpreted in the personal, the ideal, the national, or the predictive sense? A brief review of the meaning of each of the four terms here used will clarify issue.

If the personal interpretation is to be adopted, the basis of approach is the supposition that some individual, David or some anonymous person, lived through the experiences here described and now recounts them.

The ideal interpretation claims that this is not a record of the experiences of any one man but a statement of the things that would befall the ideal righteous man; a sort of composite picture of all the sufferings that would befall a man if he were entirely righteous. *Hengstenberg* is the chief exponent of this approach.

The national approach would refer the experiences here detailed to the nation of Israel, particularly in the Exile. Among modern interpreters *Buttenwieser* is the most notable exponent of this view, with the exception that he refers the psalm to the national crisis of 344 B.C.

The predictive approach regards the entire psalm as pure prophecy concerning the Christ Himself and assumes that the author was conscious of the fact that he was prophesying. This is the oldest of the four types and is in reality the one that was predominant in the Christian Church from days of old and to a very large extent still is.

We believe that this last type of interpretation is the one that deserves the preference but do not deny that an element of some of the others may be detected here and there. For to tell the truth, some of the experiences related here are duplicated in the life of David. It may also be maintained that these sufferings are a kind of composite picture of what righteous men have endured throughout the ages; but such an abstraction has too little flesh and blood to be located in this psalm. Some of Israel's experiences could be said to be remotely set forth here although that is only incidentally the case. The psalmists could on occasion turn prophets, witness Ps. 110 (cf., Matt. 22:43); and so this poet may be placed by the side of Isaiah, the great author of the prophecy of chapter 53.

We do not hesitate to ascribe the psalm to David as the heading maintains. For only if the position is taken that the psalm must recount only such experiences as lay within the limit of the events recorded in Scriptures concerning David can this poem be denied to David. Or one must take the position, also not warranted by fact, that psalmists could not function as prophets.

The heading reads thus: "To the Choir Director. According to 'the Hind of the Dawn.' A Psalm of David." Much ingenuity has been expended to make this expression "the Hind of the Dawn" a kind of mystical reference to Christ and thus a sort of summary of the contents of the psalm. The approach of *Luther* is usually followed who found in "the dawn" a reference to the fact that that is the time when hinds are hunted; and so he translated, "Concerning the hind which is hunted in early morning." Though many interpreters still advocate this interpretation, we cannot help but feel that it is a bit fanciful.

The other major approach just as insistently claims that "the Hind of the Dawn" must be a poem or piece of music and thus find here a reference to the tune or manner according to which this psalm is to be rendered. In other words, we have here a musical direction. Neither of the approaches can be validly established, and so our verdict must be: We cannot tell with any finality what this part of the heading means.

We offer, in a sort of preview, the following outline:

a) *Forsaken of God* (vv. 1–21).

v. 1f. A pitiful cry for help.
vv. 3–5. The fathers' experience—never an appeal in vain.
vv. 6–8. The scornful treatment experienced at the hands of the enemy.
vv. 9–11. A plea for help to the God who has always been a Helper.
vv. 12, 13. The danger threatening from the enemies.
vv. 14–18. The extremity of this manifold misery.
vv. 19–21. The last desperate plea for help, which suddenly bursts into the assurance of having been heard.

b) *Delivered by God* (vv. 22–31).

vv. 22–25. Praise on the part of the sufferer and of the godly for this deliverance.
vv. 26–31. The various kinds and classes of men sharing in the resultant blessings.

Looking at the first division of the psalm as a whole, we observe a strange wavelike movement, a vacillation between wretchedness and hope. As soon as one mood has found expression, the poor sufferer enters into the other, being unable to come to rest until of a sudden in the midst of the last verse of this division (21) a positive note of assurance is struck, which comes like one of those sudden changes of mood that all of us have at one time or another experienced in life.

a) Forsaken by God (vv. 1–21)

1. *My God, my God, why hast Thou forsaken me?*
   Why are the words of my groaning so far from obtaining my help?
2. *O my God, I cry unto Thee by day, and Thou answerest not,*
   Also by night, and still there is no silence for me.

1. No one can read this first verse without at once thinking of Jesus Christ on the cross and the use He made of this outcry. Men may have had analogous experiences in their life. In no case was their experience quite as acute as was that of Jesus. Pages could be written on the import of this cry. Suffice it to say that in the case of Christ there must have been far greater suffering than that experienced by any mortal man, otherwise, from the standpoint of faith, men would in some cases have manifested greater courage in enduring their lot than did this great Sufferer. It must also be noted that the "why" is not so much an attempt to find the deepest reason for it all as it is a complaint as

to the incomprehensibility of it all (*Kessler*). Surely, God had forsaken Him who utters this complaint, but the reason was that He had made Him to be sin for us who knew no sin (II Cor. 5:21). No man can fathom the mystery of this outcry and what it meant in the experience of Christ. But of this we can be assured: the God-forsakenness was real.

The more familiar translation of the second member of this verse, "*Why art Thou so* far from helping me?" must insert four auxiliary words to express this thought and two more in the statement, "*and from* the words of my groaning, "namely, the italicized words. This procedure points out the weakness of this translation. The rendering we have given, "Why are the words of my groaning so far from obtaining my help?" is what the words say. Restated, this would mean: much as I have cried, why is it that my words have not obtained the help I seek? God has withdrawn Himself. In every sense of the word He is the *deus absconditus*.

2. This is a reiteration of the thought of the preceding verse. Though he is not heard he lets his cries continually ascend to his God whom, here and in the preceding verse, he designated "my God," so giving proof that, though he is forsaken, he refuses to cast away his hope in God. That is the very essence of faith. It should, however, be noted that the two expressions for "my God" are not the same in the two verses. V. 1 has *'eli* (my Strong One); v. 2 has the most common designation of God, *'elohay* (the One to be feared by me).

Two objections have been raised against the direct Messianic character of this verse. The one claims that Jesus did not pray to be helped out of His trying situation but willingly took all suffering upon Himself. But it should not be overlooked that Gethsemane surely reflects the spirit of this verse.

The other objection (by *Koenig*) is that it can scarcely be maintained with any show of reason that Jesus cried thus for days and nights on end. But prophecy cannot be interpreted too literally, otherwise all prophetic utterances would have their inadequacies. In His great Passion Christ did, without a doubt, cry by day and by night as long at it lasted. For though the Gospel records do not report the continuous sequence of prayers that welled up from His heart, who would doubt that they flowed without interruption?

The second half of this verse, "and still there is no silence for me," means nothing other than, since God does not answer, I cannot become silent but must keep crying until He hears me.

3. *But Thou art holy,*
   Enthroned on the praises of Israel.

> 4. *In Thee did our fathers trust;*
> *They trusted, and Thou didst deliver them.*
> 5. *To Thee did they cry and were freed;*
> *In Thee they trusted and were not disappointed.*

3. Hope reasserts itself in this section, it finds an anchorage in the holiness of God. For in this case "holy" means "exempt from the shortcomings of man." It would be an obvious defect in the character of God if He could simply abandon one who had put his trust in Him. The thought is reinforced by the rest of the verse, "enthroned on the praises of Israel," a highly poetic statement and an exceptionally beautiful one, signifying in plain prose: One who has so faithfully delivered His own in times past that they, to use another figure, have enshrined Him in their praises. The figure is built on the fact that in the Tabernacle and the Temple God was enthroned (Hebrew: "sitting") above the mercy seat, which was His throne. So the praises of the faithful for blessings received are the new throne above which He resides.

4. The experiences of the fathers that gave rise to their praises are now described more fully. Fundamental to any such experience is trust on the part of the individual. Therefore: "in Thee did our fathers trust." Whenever they pinned their hopes on Him, He "did deliver them." Sometimes at a time they had not appointed. Sometimes in a manner other than they had expected. It is still true: "I have never seen the righteous forsaken."

5. The experience is so great that it deserves ampler statement. It can be put into these words: "To Thee did they cry and were freed." Or again: "In Thee they trusted and were not disappointed." One would have expected that on this platform faith would find a secure footing and fearlessly face the future. But this sufferer's extremity is too great; and so he relapses into his previous mood.

> 6. *But as for me, I am a worm and not a man,*
> *An object of the derision of men and despised by the people.*
> 7. *All who see me mock at me;*
> *They gape with open mouth and shake their head.*
> 8. *"Commit all issues to the Lord! let Him help him to escape!*
> *Let Him rescue him, seeing He delighted in him."*

6. We see in the figure of a "worm" used here (also Is. 41:14; Job 25:6) a reference to utter helplessness and frailty. It seems to be going too far to suppose that the worm had already been crushed by a hobnailed boot as some interpreters do. Such an extremity might befall the sufferer unless God intervenes. Much in the spirit of Is. 53 this Sufferer describes Himself as "the object of the derision of men" (for

Psalm 22

which it suffices in the Hebrew to say, "the derision of men") and "despised by the people." Ridicule hurts and produces a peculiar diffidence in men.

7. The description continues in the same vein. It is the universality of the mockery that is especially high lighted as was actually the case in the sufferings on Golgotha: all men present seemed to share in the scoffing that began with the high priests. For what we have rendered, "they gape with open mouth," the original has: "they make an opening with the lip," which is close to the rendering of the *RSV,* "they make mouths at me." As that is an obvious gesture of derision, so is the further action, they "shake their head." This is, no doubt, to be thought of as a plain gesture that expresses hopelessness in a derisive way.

8. The whole verse is a direct quotation which is not formally introduced. The opposition seems to quote from remarks that their victim had previously made. In all situations his watchword seemed to be, "Commit all issues to the Lord!" With obvious ridicule they suggest his own word to him as happened in striking fulfilment when the Jews all but quoted these words when they had their enemy affixed to the cross. On this motto they build the further suggestion: "Let Him help him to escape," implying, however, in this instance that this man was too far gone in wretchedness to be capable of deliverance. Still in the spirit of utter mockery they continue: "Let Him rescue him, seeing He delighted in him." The baseness of it all consists in this, that a man's faith in God is the point at which he is attacked.

9. *Yea, Thou art He that took me from the womb;*
   Thou didst make me to feel safe at my mother's breast.
10. *Upon Thee was I cast from birth;*
    Thou hast been my God since I was born.
11. *Be not far from me, for distress is near;*
    For there is no helper.

9. Faith and hope begin to reassert themselves. At the same time the poor sufferer does exactly what his opponents have just recommended to him to do, to commit all issues to God. He recounts what God has meant to him in the past, and what He has done for him from earliest infancy. In the process of birth it was God who held a protecting hand over him and delivered him. In the tender years of extreme infancy it was He again who gave to the infant's heart that assurance of safety that comes when the little one can nestle close to its mother's breast. Though he may not have understood it at that time, yet he now knows that he was cast upon God from his birth (v. 10), yea, since that time God has been his God and given evidence of this fact. Summing it up,

it is as though he had said: During every moment of my life till now Thou hast been my God and hast sustained me.

11. This leads quite obviously to the inference that He can and will help in the present extremity. Therefore the petition to be near as He always was. For there is no other helper. But somehow assurance does not come to the troubled heart with this prayer. Again the poor sufferer relapses into distress at the thought of those who are against him.

12. *Many bulls have surrounded me;*
    Strong bulls of Bashan have encircled me.
13. *They have opened their mouth wide at me—*
    A ravening and roaring lion.

Again the critics of our interpretation insist that such statements cannot refer to Christ directly inasmuch as He was not surrounded by His enemies, who had not yet gotten Him into their power. However, all that is stated here is purely figurative language. It surely represents one aspect of the case. He was certainly hemmed in by His foes. They on their part were certainly anxious to wreak their vengeance on Him.

12. These enemies are likened to vicious bulls or to strong bulls from the grassy plains of Bashan, where they found ample pasturage and were well fed, who are thought of as being ready to dash in on this poor victim whom they have encircled, making escape impossible. Imagine what fear must come to a man in such a case! Figuratively, Christ's enemies continually hovered around Him, shutting off every avenue of escape. And He as a man felt the danger and horror of His situation.

13. The figure of the bulls is dropped. There is substituted the one of ravenous wild beasts who are anxious to devour their victim. In the second member of the verse the figure again changes—one of the number of the enemy, perhaps their most aggressive member, is compared to a ravenous and roaring lion. *Gunkel* offers the fantastic suggestion that we should at this point think of the "Babylonian demons in animal form."

We might have added the next three verses to the preceding two to make one stanza of five verses. Yet v. 13f. describe the enemy; vv. 14–16 describe the sufferer's wretched plight.

14. *I am poured out like water, and all my bones are out of joint;*
    My heart has become like wax, it is melted within me.
15. *My strength has dried up like a potsherd,*
    And my tongue cleaves to my jaws;
    Into the dust of death Thou layest me.

16. *For dogs have surrounded me;*
 A gang of evildoers have encircled me;
 They have pierced my hands and my feet.

14. Though the expression is variously understood, to be "poured out like water" may well be a symbol of the feeling of utter helplessness and weakness that overwhelms this poor individual. He can scarcely mean the statement literally that all his "bones are out of joint." He may imply that his pain is as extreme as if all bones were thrown out of joint. The distorted position into which the body of a crucified person was thrust may have brought about something analogous to this. In addition, his "heart has become like wax" and is melted within him. Surely, this is a description of being utterly without courage.

15. The extremity of misery includes the fact that he has as little strength as moisture that might be found in a potsherd—which is obviously nil. It furthermore seems that when men are in great physical suffering the dryness of the tongue as it cleaves to a man's jaws seems to be one of the chief elements of discomfort. The man is all but dead. That is what he means by the words, "Into the dust of death Thou layest me." But it must be noted that even in this grave crisis, God is still the One who controls all things that may befall him—strong evidence of a persistent faith.

16. This is not another description in the spirit of v. 12, which likens the opposition to vicious beasts. For dogs come under the head of scurrilous creatures, especially when one thinks of the packs of them that run wild through the streets of Oriental cities as scavengers. The parallel statement reinforces this thought by likening the same persons to a "gang of evildoers," not a "congregation" of them as older versions translate, which invests the description with too much dignity. The very last line of the verse brings the famous words, "They have pierced my hands and my feet." This translation can safely be retained (see the Notes at the conclusion) and is the one statement of the psalm that most obviously points to the crucifixion.

17. *I can count all my bones;*
 But they gaze, they feast their eyes on me.
18. *They apportion my garments among them;*
 And for my raiment they cast lots.

17. This is the last section in which the poor victim recounts his suffering. Looking first at his physical condition, he notes that some sort of emaciation has set in that makes the entire bony framework visible. This could scarcely be applied literally to the Crucified One,

for His suffering was not protracted long enough to produce such complete emaciation. But the extremity of cruel treatment could have produced some results that were analogous to this. In any event, He was reduced to a state of such misery that it should have produced some pity in the heart of the onlookers. Instead "they gaze" heartlessly and with some measure of satisfaction. They may even be said to "feast their eyes" on Him. This verse may well be said to sum up the enemies' cruelty and his own wretchedness.

18. One last action of theirs is described, a sort of rude horseplay (as *Luther* also interpreted it) on the part of the soldiers, by which they wanted to dramatize their conviction that this pretender's ambitions were at an end. His garments can have meant little to them, but by partitioning them and casting lots over them they emphasized the thought that this man was completely done for. The parallelism of the verse aims at nothing more than to restate the thought with emphasis. It needed not to be fulfilled to the letter. But so strange are the ways of divine providence that even the second member of the verse was literally fulfilled.

19. *But Thou, O Lord, be not afar off;*
    Thou source of my strength make haste to help me.
20. *Deliver my life from the sword,*
    My one treasure from the power of the dog.
21. *Save me from the lion's mouth—*
    Yea, from the horns of the wild oxen Thou hast answered me.

19. In these verses we have the last eager cry for help. With emphasis the "Thou" addressing God is placed first, contrasting Him with the heartless behavior of those who are attempting to dispose of the sufferer. The separation from God, of which the first verse of the psalm complained, is still a matter of concern. Nearness of God is what he wants to be assured of. For that matter, he seeks quick relief, for he cannot survive much longer. Therefore: "make haste to help me." He addresses God as "my strength," which, like similar expressions, is always best regarded as signifying, "Source of my strength."

20. Since the issue is actually one of life and death, the one of whom the psalm speaks prays for the deliverance of his "life," (Hebrew, "soul"), which, in the parallel expression, he designates as his "one treasure," sometimes rendered the "only one," an obvious reference to the soul or life. For man has but one, and it is, in the last analysis his chief treasure. In the figure used the sword is to be thought of as drawn and poised above his head, ready to descend. So imminent is the danger. Or again, the "dog" has thrown his soul to the ground and is about to begin to tear it to pieces.

Psalm 22

21. From one figure that is expressive of extreme danger the author proceeds to another. It is the powerful lion that is about to sink his fangs into his poor victim.

Then of a sudden, in the very middle of this verse as indicated above in the outline, the assurance of help breaks through, and the complaints and pleas are at an end. The tense of the verb suddenly becomes the historical perfect, "Thou hast answered me." How extreme the peril was is indicated by the last figure, "from the horns of the wild oxen." This could well mean that the victim envisions himself as being caught up on the oxen's horns and about to be further tossed or gored to death when he is suddenly snatched away and set beyond the pale of danger. There is some dispute as to whether the creature referred to is the white antelope or the wild ox. In either case it must have been a singularly ferocious beast, a thought that is best expressed by the second name for the creature.

If the first half of the psalm could be captioned, "Forsaken by God," the second half could quite properly have the title, "Delivered by God." The tone is so notably different. Whether v. 21b should have been included in the second half may be left as an open question. The tone now becomes so jubilant, the blessings recounted as resulting from the experience are so many and so illustrious that one cannot help but realize that the sufferings involved must have been different from those endured by any other of the sons of men. All this, too, points to the great redemption that was here achieved.

b) Delivered by God (vv. 21–31)

22. *I will proclaim Thy name to my brethren;*
    In the midst of the assembly I will praise Thee.
23. *You that fear the Lord, praise Him;*
    All you, the descendants of Jacob, honor Him;
    And stand in awe of Him, all you descendants of Israel.
24. *For He has not despised or abhorred the affliction of the afflicted;*
    And He has not hidden His face from him, but He hearkened
        when he cried to Him.
25. *From Thee comes my praise in the great assembly;*
    My vows will I pay before them that fear Him.

There is even a formal difference between the first half of the psalm and the second. In the first half the statements of the individual verses are shorter, like gasps breathed in distress. Now they are longer, for the speaker is delivered and free from pain.

It must also be plain that the marvelous results that are here enumerated are to be thought of as being fruits of the experience through which the sufferer has just gone.

The emphasis is now on the thought that such a deliverance calls for praise on the part of the one delivered as well as on the part of all the godly. Naturally, as we now see in the light of the fulfilment, the basic thought is not that the speaker was kept from suffering but rather that he passed through the extremest form of it and was yet delivered. True, there is no mention of the resurrection from the dead as there is in Is. 53. But what prophetic Scripture can cover every possible aspect of a case?

22. Though we do not usually think of Christ's reaction to His deliverance from death and His Passion as being one of gratitude to His Father, it is that, too. He will declare to His brethren what God has done for Him. It must be told that God was not appealed to in vain. John 20:17 may contain an allusion to this verse in that Christ there calls His disciples "brethren." Of course, as the second member of the verse shows, the basic thought is that this is an experience that is to be discussed in the company of like-minded souls, who will appreciate what it means.

23. But not only He Himself will praise God. As a result of this experience others will have ample occasion to share in this praise. Different classes are called upon as being vitally interested. First, those "that fear the Lord." Then all who are truly "descendants of Jacob." Lastly all who "stand in awe of Him," implying that persons other than the offspring of Jacob shall have a vital concern in these matters.

24. Again we have an instance which demonstrates that prophetic passages cannot cover every aspect of the fulfilment. In His Passion Christ's major concern was our salvation as the Gospels testify in so many ways. But it can well have been a matter of grave concern to Him to be delivered from the extremeity of suffering in which He found Himself, and after He was raised above it all, thanksgiving for this deliverance may also have had a place in His praise. That is what this verse indicates. Viewed thus, it requires no further comment.

25. The Great Sufferer likens Himself to any other person in Israel who might have been in distress in days of old. He here speaks the language of the faithful in Israel in Old Testament times. These would have wanted to praise God "in the great assembly," and sincerely pay any "vows" that they may have made in time of trouble, and do that "before them that fear Him." Viewed thus, this verse does not require the interpretation that Christ must have made some vows during the time of His suffering.

26. *The meek shall eat and be satisfied;*
They that seek the Lord shall praise Him.
"May your hearts live forever!"

27. All the ends of the earth shall bear this in mind and return to
    the Lord.
    All the families of the nations will bow down before Him.
28. For the kingdom is the Lord's;
    And He is the Ruler among the nations.
29. All the weighty personages of the earth will eat and worship Him;
    Before Him will bow down all who go down to the dust, and the
    man who cannot keep himself alive.
30. Posterity shall serve Him;
    Men shall tell concerning the Lord to that generation.
31. Men shall come and declare to a people yet to be born
    That He hath done justice.

26. This section indicates that every class and kind of men shall share in the blessings of the experience which the psalm has reported. Those listed first as expressing their gratitude are "the meek" and the ones "that seek the Lord." These two groups might be put under the head of the more earnest and devout among mankind. They will rejoice especially in the redemption that Christ secured for mankind. The "meek," however, are spoken of as those who "eat and are satisfied." The language is borrowed from a typical Old Testament mode of expressing thanksgiving to the Lord, the peace offering (Lev. 3), in connection with which a feast was prepared (Lev. 7:15f.) to which a man would invite poor friends of his that they might share in his joy and deliverance. It could be possible that v. 25 and v. 26 are connected in thought in that the vows spoken of may include the vow to sacrifice such a peace offering if the sufferer was delivered. The concluding benediction is one that at such a meal the guest, perhaps, spoke in reference to his host: "May your heart live forever"—another way of saying, May God be your reward, or the like. Such unintroduced exclamations are found elsewhere in the Scriptures; cf., Ps. 104: 24; 87:6b; 31:14a; 45:6a.

27. Turning from the truly devout, the writer directs attention to persons all over the world. That is to say, the effects of this experience will be world-wide. "All the ends of the earth" is synonymous with the remotest corners of our globe, or as the parallel expression states it, "all the families of the nations." The first member says literally that "all the ends of the earth shall *remember*." This last verb is not used in the sense of recalling a thing previously known but rather in the sense of the German *eingedenk sein* (*KB*), i.e., retain in mind. And as they thus keep revolving this matter in their mind, it will induce many of mankind who have been long drifting about far from the Father's house to bethink themselves "and return to the Lord." We need not be as

literal as *Koenig* is, who believes that, strictly speaking, only those can return who have consciously departed. And so he prefers the somewhat forced meaning "the outlying district of the land" for "ends of the earth" and mentions that the outlying regions were more exposed to idolatry than was the core of the land. The second member of the verse indicates that world-wide results are being considered. What is echoed is in essence the blessed gospel, which induces men to "bow down before Him" in faith and adoration.

28. All who thus return and find their God recognize at the same time the sole sovereignty of Jehovah; and so, leaving their idolatrous misconceptions behind them, they offer the confession that "the kingdom is the Lord's; and He is Ruler among the nations." If anything had convinced them of this fact it was the signal victory that the Great Sufferer had won.

29. The effects of this experience will be felt not only among those who are far distant, but another group is also singled out by two contrasting expressions: "weighty personages" and "all who go down to the dust," that is to say, men in the prime of their strength and influence as well as those about to perish, "who cannot keep their soul alive." Not persons already dead are referred to, for the parallel clause asserts that they cannot keep themselves alive for any length of time. In other words, the weak and the strong will alike glory in what He experienced.

30. The last two verses round out the picture that tells that the effects of this great deliverance shall be universal. For they state that also the generations yet to come are to hear of and rejoice in that which happened. This class is described by the terms "posterity," "that generation," "a people yet to be born." That the influence of what they hear shall be of tremendous importance to those yet to be born is indicated by the fact that they "shall serve Him," and that one group shall declare it to the next, for this is a truth worth perpetuating. The truth that shall be thus handed down from generation to generation is "that He has executed justice." That is to say, God Himself has carried out that which was the proper thing for Him to do, namely, the saving of mankind. We prefer this translation of *Koenig,* for the customary approach to the last clause allows everything to remain suspended in midair because the last verb lacks an object, even more so than the customary English translations indicate. For the Hebrew reads: "that He hath done." No textual emendation needs to be made to secure our translation. It is merely a case where, as so often in the Hebrew, one term of an object clause is in advance taken into the preceding clause (like Gen. 1:4, etc.): "they shall declare His righteousness to a people to be born, that He hath executed it."

So the psalm closes by pointing out the many classes and kinds of men who shall benefit by what was suffered.

NOTES

1. "Why hast Thou forsaken me?" *Luther,* unaware of the fact that Christ spoke Aramaic, changes the transliteration of the Aramaic in the Gospels back to the Hebrew and writes *lama 'azabhtáni. Rachoq,* though the predicate of *dibhrey,* is singular according to the Hebrew rule to begin with the singular if the number is as yet uncertain. Cf., *GK* k45r.

3. "Thou" is emphatic and adversative; *KS* 360b. For "enthroned" the Hebrew has *yashabh,* here used transitively (*KS* 211d).

5. "Were freed" lacks the *waw* consecutive and has two successive *perfects* connected by *waw* copulative, as is done in actions that are parallel and belong together (*KS* 370e).

8. It may well be that *gol* is the absolute infinitive (*KS* 217b). We have, nevertheless, translated it as an imperative for convenience' sake. A literal rendering might read as follows: "To commit things to the Lord (that was his motto)." The object of the verb is not expressed. We thought it to be in harmony with the spirit of the verb to add, "all issues."

15. *Wehithparedhu* omits the *waw* consecutive as above, v. 5.

16. For a full defense and explanation of the translation given above for *ka'arey,* construct of the participle kal of *kur,* we refer to *Koenig's Kommentar* and *KW.* The translation "like a lion" cannot be made to yield sense, no matter how the issue is turned. There is no need to resort to textual changes. The *Septuagint* and the *Vulgate* support this translation. The participle, of course, if derived from *kur,* would have no *'aleph* unless it were written after the Aramaic fashion as is sometimes the case in Hebrew (cf., Hos. 10:14).

29. The first verb, *'akhelu,* is obviously to be regarded as a prophetic perfect. Therefore we have translated "will eat" and "will worship," *KS* 147. Though in the Hebrew the subject is "fat ones of the earth," we felt that it would come closer to our idiom to render the word "weighty personages." The suffix on *naphsho* is distributive.

30. We feel that the last word, *laddor,* is a case where the article has a kind of demonstrative force.

The approach used in the above interpretation, namely, the predictive, meets with scant favor in our day. The historical meets with some favor. It supposes that the psalm is the record of the sufferings of an individual, which Jesus found rather helpful in His day and applied to Himself. However, the weakness of this approach is that the results expected from the deliverance of the sufferer involved are far in excess of what any human sufferer dared claim as the outcome of his experience.

The other rather popular approach is the assumption that in the first half of the psalm the author was a very sick man and had been in such a state for a long time. This scarcely does justice to the statements of the psalm.

Psalm 23

"THE LORD IS MY SHEPHERD"

EXPOSITORS vie with one another in describing the rare beauty and charm of this psalm. Perhaps none has stated it better and simpler than *Maclaren:* "The world could spare many a large book better than this sunny little psalm." Commentators stress the strong note of faith that rings through the poem. Others claim that it is pitched on too high a level to be in any real sense attainable by any saint of God. Some interpreters read things into the psalm that are not warranted by the material available. Since they are rather liturgically minded they claim that a sacrifice must have been offered, and that this psalm was its accompaniment. Others almost insist that it is a psalm of praise after recovery from severe sickness.

Then there is the matter of the unity of the psalm or the unity of the figure employed by the psalmist. Some, the majority, perhaps, find only one figure, that of the shepherd. Of a slightly more recent date is the interpretation that finds two figures, that of the shepherd and that of the host. Others insert a third between the two, the guide. Others, giving special thought to v. 6, devise some kind of a fourth figure. By this time one is compelled to admit that the beautiful little psalm has been pretty sadly fragmentized.

In the face of these diverse approaches it seems best to let the opening statement serve as a theme sentence and stick to the one figure, that of the shepherd. However, though attempts have been made to have the total imagery, excepting, perhaps, v. 6, derive from actual shepherd usage as it is still witnessed in the Orient (cf., Knight, *The Song of Our Syrian Guest*), it would seem a bit more appropriate to insist on the unity of the figure but at the same time to allow for a bit of exuberance in the use of the figure, so that its limits are not too sharply observed. (Morganstern, *Journal of Biblical Literature,* vol. LXV, pt. 1, pp. 13–24, arrives at practically the same conclusion.)

The chief defect of the two-figure interpretation (shepherd and host) is that the use of it would involve a strange conception of the work of the shepherd: he does everything except feed his sheep; that task is performed by the host. Such a weakness in the first figure is nothing short of fatal. For a further validation of our argument note especially the interpretation of v. 2.

Then there is the question as to whether the speaker in the psalm is to be thought of as an individual, or whether we have a collective subject. This latter interpretation was presented already in days of old by the Talmud. Though it cannot be denied that the idea of the Lord as a shepherd of His people Israel is found frequently in psalms and prophecy (Ps. 74:1; 77:20; 78:52, 70ff.; 79:13; 80:1; Is. 40:11; Jer. 31:10; Ezek. 34:12–14; Mic. 5:4), the tone pervading this psalm seems to strike almost all readers as being so thoroughly personal in its warmth as to make the collective idea of the subject seem quite artificial.

It must also be pointed out that no really valid argument against authorship of the psalm by David has yet been advanced. Yet it is far less likely that "the sweet psalmist of Israel" (II Sam. 23:1) wrote this piece in his youthful days while he was still tending his father's flock. Romantic as that thought may seem, it would be far more in keeping with what the Scriptures reveal elsewhere concerning him, when they tell us that after his anointing the spirit of God came upon him (I Sam. 16:13), to assume that the spirit-filled servant of the Lord composed such helpful songs as these. Details found in v. 2 especially indicate that it was, perhaps, even the older David who composed the psalm. For if the first virtue stressed in reference to a good shepherd is the fact that he gives rest, then men must have begun to know what weariness is.

We offer the following outline of the psalm:
The Lord Is My Shepherd
He provides:
a) Rest and guidance (vv. 2, 3).
b) Protection (v. 4).
c) Food (v. 5)
  (a parenthesis in which all figures are abandoned, v. 6a).
d) Fellowship with God (v. 6b).

A Psalm of David.

1. The Lord is my shepherd;
   I shall not suffer any want.
2. He will make me to lie down in grassy meadows;
   He will lead me beside waters of resting places.
3. He will restore my soul;
   He will lead me in the paths of righteousness for His name's sake.
4. Even though I should walk through the darkest valley I shall fear no evil;
   For Thou art with me, Thy rod and Thy staff—they will comfort me.
5. Thou wilt prepare a table before me in the sight of my enemies;
   Thou hast already anointed my head with oil, my cup overflows.
6. Surely, goodness and mercy will follow me all the days of my life.
   And I shall dwell in the house of the Lord forever.

One grammatical item must be noted in determining the whole pattern of the translation. Practically all versions from the *Septuagint* down very properly begin with the future in v. 1, "I shall not want." *Mir wird nichts mangeln,* etc. From this point onward all the verbs till v. 5a have the same form of the Hebrew verb—the imperfect. Consistency demands that these imperfects be rendered either as futures or presents. Though the Hebrew verb allows for either, the future deserves the preference, for on the basis of the fact that the Lord is the shepherd, the psalmist looks confidently toward the *future.* This plain fact, though noted already in the Prayer Book Version *(Book of Common Prayer)* has not been observed in any of the familiar versions, not even in the *RSV. Koenig* has it in his *Kommentar* on the psalms.

1. The opening statement is characterized by utter simplicity. Old and young can grasp its import, all the more so in lands where sheep and shepherds are commonly found. The great name of God, *Yahweh,* is used most appropriately, for this name always connotes God's absolute faithfulness to His people. If God is one's shepherd, it cannot be denied that one could conclude with regard to the future that under His care one shall never "suffer any want." Note our form of translation. Though the idiom is now sanctioned because of its usage in this psalm, we do not ordinarily use the verb "to want" absolutely. For that reason we supplied the object "any want" somewhat as *Luther* did, *Mir wird nichts mangeln.* Though this statement is one of absolute trust, it should not be objected that this is too elevated a position to ascribe to David. For there are many times in life when the faith of men rises to this level, at least for a time.

2. Emphasis is now placed upon the rest which the shepherd knows how to provide for his sheep at proper times. For it is characteristic of the everyday task of most Oriental shepherds that, with but scanty pasturage available, they must spend a good bit of time moving from one spot where a bit of grass is available to another. This verse actually starts with noonday, when the flock has already covered quite a bit of ground in thus moving about and is in need of rest lest it be overdriven (Gen. 33:13). When the shepherd makes the sheep to lie down, it is in a place where there are "grassy meadows." We have translated thus because sheep do not graze when they lie down, and the verb also does not mention grazing but only resting. So "green pastures" (*KJ,* etc.) is a little less to the point. So the first prospect held before the eyes of faithful followers of the good Lord is that, when rest becomes imperative, He will supply it.

The parallel thought is very similar. When the place for relaxation is to be furnished, He will so guide His own that they find themselves "besides waters of a resting place." Though the Hebrew uses the plural ("resting places"), this refers only to such water as is commonly found at resting places. The best interpretation of this much disputed expression that we have been able to find is that of *KB,* who offers: "resting place with water (on river, brook, well, lake)." We may well think of the resting places that are customarily used by shepherds for their flocks and have become traditional because they are safe, and the water supply is sufficient. That could in some instances include even the water found at khans or caravansaries, the typical Eastern inns, bare, but open to caravans. For caravansaries are "resting places" as *Koenig* interprets. But the concept must be kept broader and include all that we have mentioned above. So the emphasis is on places where, in addition to rest, also an ample water supply is to be found. "Still waters" does not quite meet the force of the expression. The literal use of the Hebrew expression, "waters of rest," is unsatisfactory because it is not understood. Nor does "quiet waters" express the precise idea. The "waters" are brought into the picture merely to supplement the concept of rest, which is to be thought of as being in every sense adequate.

3. The shepherd also furnishes guidance. It is certainly very artificial to forget that shepherds, especially Oriental shepherds, must guide their sheep and to insist that at this point the new figure of the guide is introduced. To tell the truth, the first part of this verse, strictly speaking, does not continue the shepherd figure or any other. It introduces momentarily a nonfigurative statement of spiritual values, reminding us for the moment that it is not only physical well-being that the true Shepherd provides for His own. It savors of pedantry to press

this statement, "He restores my soul," to the level of what sheep can experience and to stress, what is true enough that *néphesh* can also mean "life," and so arrive at the meaning: He revives me or my life. One must allow for deeper values and not insist on purely mechanical procedures.

The second member of the verse has also provoked much discussion, especially as to the precise meaning of "paths of righteousness." Following the lead of *Luther* who rendered this expression, *auf rechter Strasse,* many interpreters insist on translating, "in the right way," citing passages like Lev. 19:36 (*"just* balances," etc.) where the same noun for "righteousness" appears, viz., *tsédheq.* But some of the richer content of the Hebrew word is squeezed out of it by rendering it merely "right" or "just." We cannot but agree with men like *Hengstenberg, Kessler,* etc., who prefer to retain "in the paths of righteousness." There is an emphasis on God's righteousness, which manifests itself in the way in which He leads men, which emphasis here calls to mind that He faithfully fulfils the demands that His covenant obligations to His people impose on Him. This larger thought plainly includes the much lesser thought that the individual will then always be guided on the right path.

All this He does "for His name's sake." Since "name" is the equivalent of "character" or "reputation," this beautiful little phrase means: He does all this because He has a reputation among His saints for faithful dealings with them, a reputation which must be cautiously upheld.

4. The author now emphasizes the feature of protection. The shepherd figure may still be involved. In the course of the late afternoon dark defiles may have to be entered. The sheep, a timid creature, may manifest a certain reluctance about passing through the dark spot, where beasts or robbers may lurk. But the very presence of the shepherd gives it strong reassurance. Besides, the sheep may have noted that in previous instances the shepherd's staff stood him in good stead, and wild and dangerous beasts were beaten off or even killed—"Thy rod and Thy staff, they will comfort me." But without a doubt the all-important thing is the presence of the Shepherd Himself—"Thou art with me."

Two things call for special comment here. The first is the word which we have rendered "darkest valley," which is literally "valley of deepest darkness." The Hebrew word is *tsalmáveth,* which could, indeed, be broken up into its component parts: *tsal,* "shadow," and *maveth,* "death," except for the fact that the Hebrew almost never forms compound nouns except in the case of proper names. This has led to the very proper claim that a kind of popular etymology is involved, one that, perhaps, originated after the Hebrew had begun to fade out as a spoken language, and which operated with the idea of the "shadow of death." The Hebrew word used contains no reference to death as such but does refer to all dark and bitter experiences, one of which may be death. So in the common use of the passage the thought of death need not be excluded, but the reference is certainly much broader.

Again in interpreting the double expression "rod and staff" a number of differing meanings are offered. Some interpreters have observed Syrian shepherds carrying but one staff. Others have seen a shepherd equipped with a typical shepherd's crook and with a small but heavy club besides, whose heavy end may have been reinforced with nails driven into it or with a ball of bitumen which had hardened to rocklike consistency. Etymologically the interpretation can scarcely be determined, for the two words used, *shébhet* and *mish 'eneth,* have such a multiplicity of uses. Observed usage also does not quite warrant the claim that every shepherd went about equipped with two separate implements. Perhaps, then, those interpreters are nearest the truth who claim that the one commonly observed shepherd's crook could be used for purposes of defense as well as to guide and direct sheep that stray from the road, an approach which *Kirkpatrick* expresses thus: "The shepherd's crook is poetically described by two names, as the *rod* or club with which he defends his sheep . . . and the staff on which he leans." To the last statement we would add the idea of occasional use for guidance.

The pronominal subject which recapitulates—"*they* comfort"—has an emphasis somewhat like: *They,* if nothing else, would quite reassure me. In the middle of this verse the thought quite naturally turned from speaking about God to direct address of Him.

5. The thought turns to the food and sustenance that the shepherd provides. The limits of the figure are not strictly maintained, for it might seem to come closer to the figure of an Oriental banquet when the second member of the verse speaks of the anointing with (perfumed) oil, a courtesy shown guests at a banquet in early times. The "enemies" are introduced for the moment as looking on helplessly while the guest enjoys the sanctity of the home of the host even as at an Oriental banquet onlookers were often permitted to observe everything from without. However, without attempting to be too literalistic, it is not going too far to point out that all may still be strictly within the figure of the shepherd's activity if he is a faithful man. For, in the first place, the "table" (*shulchan*), as dictionaries point out, was in days of old a large piece of leather on which food was set or, in this case, on which some supplementary reserve fodder might be spread by the shepherd on days when forage was scarce. In like manner shepherds are still known to

carry a little flask of oil to anoint the scratched face of the sheep that was obliged to seek its food among thorns and brambles. And even the last factor need not exceed the limits of the figure employed. For when the sheep is overtired and out of sorts, it would not be beneath the dignity of a faithful shepherd to carry a drinking vessel of some sort to refresh the poor creature that needed it.

We would not insist that everyone reading the psalm interpret everything strictly according to the letter of the figure. Who in everyday life is so strict about the use of figures? A bit of mixed metaphor is not unwholesome, except in the eyes of the pedant. This much is sure, the verse conveys the thought that every last want of the hungry sheep will be adequately supplied.

A bit of change of tense creates an unusual emphasis when the second member of the verse introduces the first perfect tense in the psalm, a fact which we tried to catch by inserting an "already" into the translation. For the thought is: not only will my wants be provided for, but Thou hast already given indication of Thy feelings toward me by anointing my head. *Luther* caught the force of the last statement very beautifully when he rendered it: You fill my cup brimful—*Du schenkest mir voll ein.*

6. At this point, perhaps, every figure is abandoned and a kind of parenthetical summary is given shortly before the end of the psalm. We say "perhaps" because one may still contend that we here have a kind of personification of "goodness" and "mercy." This scarcely deserves to be made an issue. A worthier question is whether these two graces that follow a man are to be thought of as a kind of abstraction, or whether they are the goodness and mercy of God. The latter seems more feasible, for all the blessings enumerated thus far are thought of as growing out of the care of the heavenly Shepherd. The new emphasis of the verse is partly on the enduring nature of the relationship involved, for we have the two terms "all the days of my life" and "forever."

The very last line brings a new blessing, which may well be the concrete summary of them all—fellowship with God, expressed in the words, "And I shall dwell in the house of the Lord forever." It will be conceded, we believe, that the broader thought is not physical presence in the Temple or sanctuary but rather actual communion with God. Therefore the claim that these words require a Temple built at Jerusalem and therefore point beyond the days of David misses their deeper import. True, deep, and real fellowship with God, that is the climax of all the blessings enjoyed when a man is under the protecting care of this true Shepherd.

NOTES

4. For "shadow of death" (*KJ*) the Hebrew has, at least according to the pointing of the Masoretic text, *tsalmáweth*. As Oesterley remarks, it "has long been recognized [that] the word should be pointed *tsalmuth*, from *tsélem*, 'shadow' . . . with the noun termination *-uth*" (*GK* 86k).

6. One is almost compelled to accept the correction, found in the versions, *weyashabhti*, i.e., "and I shall dwell."

Now as for the psalm as a whole. Is there anything Messianic about it? Some interpreters feel that they cannot begin to do justice to the psalm unless they think of it in terms of the Messiah, who said of Himself that He was the good shepherd. Yet we feel that the psalm does not expressly point in this direction. If a reader desires to make a practical application of the facts set forth in the psalm and raises the claim that in Christ all reaches a perfect climax, he is entirely correct. But the psalm does not say that. Our application of the thoughts of the psalm suggest that as a further and devout consideration that need not be overlooked. The psalm is not Messianic, but it suggests thoughts that point in the direction of the Messiah.

Psalm 24

A SONG AT THE RETURN OF THE ARK TO ITS PLACE

A GREAT MAJORITY of writers on the subject will concede that this psalm may have been written on the occasion of the return of the ark to its position of honor and dignity in the city of Jerusalem after it had been captured by the Philistines in the days of Eli and had then for a long time under Saul and in the beginning of David's reign been all but entombed or at least consigned to comparative oblivion. II Sam. 6:12ff. relates the consummation of this purpose by David after an abortive attempt had previously been made with somewhat disastrous results. The people had not apparently yet learned the proper spirit of respect and humility at this first attempt, and so they were in need of sober correction. After this had been administered, and it was obvious that wholesome instruction might well be in place, David himself may well have written this psalm further to instruct the nation. Nothing in the psalm conflicts with this view; all things in it strongly substantiate such an approach.

It will serve a good purpose to submit an outline of the contents of the psalm. It has the following three major parts:

a) The Lord's rulership of the world established by creation (v. 1f).
b) The conditions upon which men may come before the Lord (vv. 3–6).
c) The coming of the Lord to His holy place (vv. 7–10).

If this outline is examined closely, and if one keeps in mind that David was endeavoring to instruct Israel as to the holy nature of the Lord and of the symbol of His presence, the ark, it would seem quite logical to suppose that the third part, which describes the coming of the Lord and His ark into its place, will constitute the core of the psalm and its obvious climax. This section describes the event around which everything centers. It would seem highly desirable to prefix to this section a statement of the conditions that one should meet who desires to come into God's presence after the place of the ark comes to be known as the one place where His presence among His people was guaranteed. In other words, part c) requires as an obvious prelude part b). But more than this is required. Any effort to localize God, as it were, for the purpose of public worship may readily lead to gross misconceptions as experience has amply proved. Localizing often becomes synonymous with confining Him to one place in a manner in which it is actually impossible to confine Him. David, therefore, found it highly desirable to append some wholesome instruction on the subject of God's omnipresence over against His localized presence which He has seen fit to promise His people. Therefore part a) becomes such instruction and a protest against narrow and unwholesome views of the living God.

Viewed thus, the psalm is its own refutation of the critical claim that it originally consisted of two, if not three, separate poems or portions of poems, which at some later date were finally smelted together. To refute that ungrounded opinion we need merely remember that, if some later compiler saw how two portions, related in thought to one another, could be effectively combined, equal insight of the relevance of the two parts to one another could also have been in the mind of one original composer of both parts. Biblical writers were not so sadly afflicted with one-track-mindedness.

Another issue in connection with this psalm is the question as to whether it should in part or in its entirety be assigned to different individuals or groups for liturgical rendering. Quite a number of different patterns would be possible such as assigning the whole to be sung by the Levites as they bore the ark from the house of Obed-edom to the holy hill of the Lord, reserving the last section till the time when they had finally arrived before the city gates. Others again let the questions of

v. 3, v. 8, and v. 10 be spoken by individuals and the answers either by individuals or by groups. How successful such an assignment of roles may be depends largely on the ingenuity of the interpreter who contrives it. It must, however, always be borne in mind that we have nothing more than surmises as to how this liturgical rendering may have been done. The very divergence of the answers given shows how much of conjecture is involved. Since, especially in our day, the liturgical approach is being sadly overworked with the injection of theories such as the one concerning the New Year's Festival of the enthronement of Yahweh, great caution is advisable, and it must always be clearly borne in mind that there are such devices as rhetorical questions, which any writer may resort to, which together with the answers here given may be all that the holy writer intended. It surely avails little to have surmises, conjectures, and mere possibilities regarded as though they were irrefutable proofs of what took place. Consult these subjects as treated under this head in the Introduction.

a) **The Lord's rulership of the world established by creation (v. 1f).**
Of David. A Psalm.
1. *The earth is the Lord's and whatever is in it,*
The world and they that dwell in it.
2. *For He Himself founded it by the side of the seas;*
And by the side of the rivers He established it.

b) **The conditions upon which men may come before the Lord (vv. 3–6)**
3. *Who may ascend into the hill of the Lord?*
And who may stand in His holy place?
4. *The clean of hands, the pure of heart;*
He who has no delight in what is false
And does not swear deceitfully.
5. *He will receive a blessing from the Lord*
And righteousness from the God who saves him.
6. *This is the generation that seeks Him,*
They that seek Thy face are Jacob. Selah.

1. Though in the first two verses, the emphasis might seem to be on the sovereignty of the Lord, it appears to be much more to the point to regard what is said as a protest against the idea that God is or can be limited to a certain area like Jerusalem or like the sanctuary in which He is thought by some to be confined. The vast world is His domain, and since it is His, He is ever present and in full control, and any notion that would limit this broad truth is to be rejected. He is master of the world as a whole and of the many things that fill it. More particularly

of the "world," i.e., the inhabitated and cultivated part of it, and of those beings who are His chief creatures, namely, "they that dwell in it." This is a broad and sweeping confession of God's unchallengeable dominion.

2. In proof of the claim just advanced the writer with good logic points to the other accepted fact, that God made it. What I make is mine if I am working of my own choice and volition. The writer, however, offers the much richer thought that He made it in àn incomparable manner which still challenges attention: "He founded it by the side of the seas" so that it overtops the waters, and they, greedy as they sometimes seem to be to swallow up the land, are restrained so as not to be able to overstep their boundaries. We may oftentimes be too dull to note it, but there is a marvel involved here. The parallel statement suggests: "And by the side of the rivers He established it." The thought added is that the smaller areas of water like the rivers are also parts of the well-planned and well-functioning system that He originally established.

The greater number of present-day commentators translate the preposition involved in such a way that the thought is, "founded *upon* the sea . . . established *upon* the flood or rivers." By way of explanation these writers usually introduce some primitive ideas that were supposedly held by the Hebrews to the effect that the world, at least the dryland part of it, in some mysterious manner floated on the waters and yet was stable. This would, indeed, be rather marvelous. By way of proof, passages from Genesis are cited, (1:9; 7:11), and Ps. 136:6. The meaning advocated by these writers is arrived at by choosing the more difficult force of the preposition involved (*'al*). But this preposition can also have the meaning "by" or "by the side of," and KB gives as its first meaning, "higher than." So there is no compelling necessity to translate it in such a way as to find in the thought expressed remnants of some "primitive Semitic cosmology" (*Leslie*) and then to claim that "ethical theism has here triumphed over Semitic mythology," and to add other features which make the original material which is supposed to have been reworked in this psalm still more primitive and fantastic.

In any case, the opening words remind the reader of this psalm not to cherish any thoughts of God that are unworthy of Him.

3. Furthermore, the situation as it obtained at the time of the writer called for careful evaluation of motives and attitudes. Fresh in the memory of David and the nation was the calamity of the death of Uzzah (II Sam. 6:6ff.). Surely, a punishment such as that would never have been visited upon an individual by way of warning to the nation if the people had not entertained some very unwholesome attitudes regarding the worship of the Lord. We can now understand better why God

Psalm 24

had let the nation be deprived of the ark: it had been unworthy of its presence and of what it signified. To remedy the evil, David offers a concise digest of demands that God would naturally make of all those who aspire to come into His presence. It is, indeed, a privilege to appear before the Lord God Almighty. For that reason it is better to translate the imperfect tense of the verbs of this verse as permissives, "Who *may*," etc. The implied supposition in connection with this verse is: Who may come and who may stand as one who is *acceptable* in God's sight? This means "stand" in the common sense of "stand one's ground unashamed and unafraid." One might paraphrase the verse thus: What are the requirements of proper worship of the Lord?

4. The answers have a sharp conciseness in the original which is completely lost in our versions. A literal rendering can capture quite a bit of it. It is just a brief as we have stated it: "The clean of hands and the pure of heart." This is followed by complete statements. This is obviously not a complete catalogue of the requirements of true worship. The author means something like this: Here are typical ethical qualities that a true worshiper would manifest. The spirit is like that in Ps. 15, where the most obvious requirements are listed, for if even such requirements could not be met, what claim has a man to being accepted by the Lord? Therefore first the outward virtue of not being tainted by foul deeds—"clean of hands." As a warning against the spirit that might be content with externals the next phrase emphasizes a corresponding attitude of heart—"pure of heart." Another typical requirement that should be met—"he who takes no delight in what is false." When one lifts up or directs the soul toward an object, as the original idiom views it, that means in our language to take delight in such a thing. Therefore our translation, patterned after *Luther's* more popular rendering. In brief, utter sincerity marks such an individual. And lastly again a type of deed that goes deeper in that it defines a man's attitude toward the Eternal One Himself—"he does not swear deceitfully." He has a sincere reverence for things holy. These are typical virtues to be found in true worshipers.

5. Such persons God will accept. They will come from His presence with a "blessing." More than that, He will impute to them "righteousness," which they so earnestly desired and came into His presence to seek. To interpret *tsedaqah* in this manner catches the deeper significance of the term and of the spirit of Old Testament worship. The reason this greater gift is sought and expected is that the worshiper knows from previous experience how often God has saved Him in other situations in life. For "God of his salvation" means just that: "the God who saves Him."

6. Summarizing his description, David says: "This is the generation

that seeks Him," for true worship always involves a measure of earnest seeking after God. In fact, it involves seeking to penetrate into the very presence of God; therefore the parallel expression: "seek Thy face," another of the many instances when the contemplative mood suddenly turns to direct address of God. Two different verbs are used for "seek," but any attempt at a valid distinction between the two would be futile. However, the new feature about the second member is that those who seek to come into the very presence of God deserve to be compared to Jacob of old, from whom stems the memorable utterance, "I will not leave Thee except Thou bless me," Gen. 32:26. Therefore David says: "They . . . are Jacob." This is a perfectly valid and satisfactory statement, and, therefore, the text requires no such emendation as inserting "God" before Jacob and translating, "O God of Jacob," as the Greek version did. It is unthinkable that the word "God" could have been so carelessly dropped by a scribe. The KJ rendering, "that seek thy face, O Jacob," just does not make sense.

Note that we have not translated 6a: "This is the generation of them that seek Him," for that would necessitate a textual change which is unnecessary. *Doresho,* kal active participle singular, "seeking Him," makes perfectly good sense as a modifier of *dor,* "generation."

c) The coming of the Lord to His holy place (vv. 7–10)

7. *Lift up your heads, O gates!*
   And be lifted up, O ancient doors!
   That the glorious King may enter in.
8. *Who is this glorious King?*
   The Lord, strong and mighty, the Lord mighty in battle.
9. *Lift up your heads, O gates!*
   And lift them up, O ancient doors!
   That the glorious King may enter in.
10. *Who then is this glorious King?*
    The Lord of hosts, He is the glorious King.

7. Though this is a psalm which has a partly didactic purpose and could later have been used at the sanctuary, for Jewish tradition has it that it also was the stated psalm for the day after the Sabbath, we are not averse to an interpretation that would allow for its having been sung by Levites on the occasion of the transfer of the ark from the house of Obed-edom. There would then have been a fine propriety in its being sung for the first time before the gates of the new capital city. Yet one and the same chorus of Levites could have sung both the questions found here as well as their answers with as much propriety as we in our day may answer a rhetorical question appearing in the hymnal. With

Psalm 24

equal propriety it may be assumed that one chorus of Levites stood within the gates about to be opened, and that another chorus stood outside.

In any case, the ark was the God-appointed symbol of His presence; therefore, where it was, there He was also. When the ark, therefore, for the first time stood outside the "ancient doors" of Jerusalem, which in their day had witnessed the entrance of the old priest-king Melchizedek, it was, indeed, a memorable occasion. We can well understand the poet's holy imagination and his thinking in terms of the much greater One about to enter and trying to express the thought that these gates are far too small to permit such a One to enter and so crying out: "Lift up your heads," that is, enlarge yourself vastly, for here comes One who is not cast in the small pattern of mortal beings; here is a truly "glorious King." The double summons to the gates becomes quite dramatic, to say the least. *Luther's* rendering of the first member has still not been equalled: *Machet die Tore weit,* "Open wide the portals." But the second member of his translation cannot be accepted: *und die Tueren in der Welt hoch. Luther* resorted to the post-Biblical force of the word *'olam,* "world," whereas in Biblical usage it can mean only something like "very ancient," scarcely "everlasting" (KJ).

8. To obtain an occasion to state fully and emphatically who it is that on the present occasion deigns to enter the holy city for the first time as a type of a gracious presence never before met in this place, the question is propounded: "Who is this glorious King?" Since this is the meaning of the phrase traditionally rendered "king of glory," we prefer this form of statement. It is cheerfully conceded that He must be a glorious king, but who is He? The answer comes—rich, strong, and sonorous: "The Lord, strong and mighty, the Lord, mighty in battle." Why should Israel not cheerfully acknowledge particularly His strength and victorious character when the Philistines had been compelled to make free admission concerning His great power (I Sam. 5:6ff.)? Since He had sustained His people in the conquest, during the days of the judges, and now again in a striking manner through the great victories granted to David, such an emphasis on the Lord's power to direct the course of battles is most appropriate, without necessitating the supposition that this was an inferior conception on the part of Israel to the effect that Yahweh was a "God of war" (*Buttenwieser*). Not every aspect of God's being must be mentioned at each reference to Him to prove that we know all His attributes.

9. No one can deny that so weighty a question may well bear repetition for emphasis' sake. It appears with a slight variation: for "be lifted up" it substitutes "lift them up," requiring that the object of the verb *se'u* be supplied. So also the answer (10) is almost the same, except

that is uses the most glorious of all the names of the Old Testament for the full identification of the glorious King, the title "the Lord of hosts." The full form of this name, by common consent, is "Yahweh (the God) of hosts," as it appears in II Sam. 5:10. We believe that those commentators are right who refer this name to God's rulership over the entire host of created things, including the heavenly armies and even the armies of Israel. In some instances the last factor may get special emphasis; but the name is one of unusual scope and so most appropriate on this occasion. For if the whole host of created things is His, who could venture to deny Him entrance into a city where He deigns to dwell? So the psalm comes to an unusual climax in a blaze of glory.

NOTES

The most popular approach to the psalm as a whole at the present time is that it graced the New Year festival, the importance of which is exaggerated; and that it commemorated the enthronement of Yahweh, a festival which is pure assumption, no trace of it appearing in the Scriptural record. *Taylor* states the case thus without committing himself: "Some scholars, therefore, assume that the psalm is a processional hymn which was used at the annual feast when the Lord's enthronement as king of men and of the world was celebrated."

Oesterley brushes interpretations like our own aside with the verdict, "There is not the slightest justification for regarding the gates as those of the city." Since he states that all the action must take place at the Temple gates, nothing else is even possible.

5. One possibility must at least be reckoned with, namely, that "righteousness" could mean "due reward" as *Taylor* suggests.

Psalm 25

A PRAYER FOR HELP AND FORGIVENESS

THIS IS A PSALM with an acrostic arrangement (see below on the peculiarities of this acrostic). As a result of being bound by this somewhat artificial device the sequence of thought does not flow as freely as is ordinarily the case in the psalms. Yet it would be unwarranted to claim that each verse stands in a kind of aphoristic isolation. Furthermore, the psalm is not a conglomerate of sententious proverbs, nor is it removed from life and its actual problems ("It was worked out at the desk"—*Hans Schmidt*). Though it may be difficult to prove that it was the outgrowth of some specific experience that we can now describe, it still throbs with life and vitality.

Whatever heading is given the psalm will needs have to be somewhat general. Yet it can be rightly claimed that there are three discernible divisions of equal length, that is to say, of seven verses each, with a "supernumerary" attached. There is first an eager petition for help from some distress; then follows a confession of God's goodness in helping in the past; and lastly the note of petition is sounded a second time. There is nothing that stands in the way of accepting the claim presented by the heading that David was the author. Nor is there any need of departing from a purely personal interpretation of the whole and claiming that the individual speaks in the name of the whole congregation of Israel though he, without a doubt, belongs to it very intimately.

> *By David.*
> 1. *To Thee, O Lord, do I lift up my soul.*
> 2. *(O my God) in Thee do I trust;*
> *Let me not be put to shame;*
> *Let not my enemies exult over me.*
> 3. *Yea, none that trust in Thee shall be put to shame;*
> *They shall be put to shame who deal treacherously without cause.*
> 4. *Help me to know Thy ways, O Lord;*
> *Teach me Thy paths.*
> 5. *Guide me in Thy truth and teach me,*
> *For Thou art the God who helps me,*
> *On Thee do I wait all the day.*
> 6. *Be mindful, O Lord, of Thy tender mercies and steadfast love,*
> *For they have been from of old.*
> 7. *The sins of my youth and my transgressions—be not mindful of them;*
> *According to Thy steadfast love be Thou mindful of me for Thy goodness' sake, O Lord.*

Considering the section as a whole, the first thought noticeable is the longing that the author has for the Lord. There are enemies in the picture who would gloat over his downfall (v. 2). A principle is at stake— a man is in distress who trusts in the Lord. Such individuals can never be abandoned by Him (v. 3). What he needs to understand better is the way in which God is leading him. He is the only one who can give him this understanding, for He is the God who has always helped heretofore, and for that reason His faithful one waits unwaveringly on Him (vv. 4, 5). One of the pleas that God's saints often presented was the appeal to the mercies and love of God, which had been so marvelously manifested in the past. So here (v. 6). One dark cloud is in the sky—sins—both the careless ones of the days of youth and the more deliberate ones of more mature years ("transgressions" is "rebellions"). Therefore the plea that God may graciously not take note of them but recall His "steadfast love" which has been the refuge of all His saints.

Throughout the psalms the terms "way" or "ways" and "paths" keep recurring. Opinions differ sharply as to whether these mean the way man should go or the way in which God is leading man. There appears to be no necessity of insisting on a uniform interpretation of the term. In this first section it seems most natural (v. 4) to think of the psalmist as praying that he may understand the way in which God is leading him. In v. 8 and v. 12 it seems a bit more likely that the way is meant in which man should walk, the path of duty and of God's commandments.

It is obvious that the note of confession of sins comes into the picture as a subordinate one. The sense of wrongdoing is not overwhelming, and, as has been rightly observed, it does not seem to grow out of the chastisement which God has inflicted. Yet for all that this is a psalm that has rightly found much use among believers and seems to fit many situations. The title, "The Hunger for Intimacy with God," (*Leslie*) is not broad enough.

8. *Good and upright is the Lord;*
   Therefore will He teach sinners as to the right way.
9. *He will guide the meek in what is right;*
   He will teach the meek His way.
10. *All the ways of the Lord are steadfast love and truth*
    For those who keep His covenant and His testimonies.
11. *For Thy name's sake, O Lord, pardon my iniquity,*
    For it is great.
12. *Who is the man that fears the Lord?*
    Him will He teach the way he should choose.
13. *He himself shall dwell at ease;*
    And his offspring shall possess the land.
14. *Intimate association with the Lord is for those that fear Him;*
    And His covenant aims to give them understanding.

From contemplating his personal needs and distress the writer turns to the contemplation of the Lord and the manner in which He deals with the children of men, especially with those who are His own.

One great favor that flows from the goodness and faithfulness of the Lord is that He guides men in the way of good conduct. For the word "way" used in v. 8b seems to dictate that interpretation, and we have, therefore, ventured to render "the right way." This thought is developed more fully in v. 9: the "meek" are the ones for whom He does this; He guides and instructs them as to what He would have them do. But a man must show teachableness; therefore: "He will guide the *meek*."

When the next verse asserts that "all the ways of the Lord are steadfast love and truth," it is almost imperative, we believe, to think of these "ways" as being the ways in which He leads men. So v. 10 marks an advance upon v. 9: not only what He demands of men does He teach them, but He also instructs men as to how He guides them. But to share in the privilege of being thus led by the Lord, it must be borne in mind that His covenant and His testimonies must be dutifully observed. That is another form of the meekness recommended in v. 9.

Quite naturally personal inadequacy is again felt, and so a petition for pardon again appears. The sin involved is felt to be more than a trifle. The only hope of pardon is the character of God, which has always been marked by mercy and grace. Therefore the plea: "Pardon . . . *for Thy name's sake.*" But the negative note is not sounded for long. For the individuals that enjoy God's gracious help have already been defined as "the meek" and "those that keep His covenant." There is now added the further definition, they "that fear the Lord." The interrogative form of the statement merely means: "Whoever fears the Lord, Him will He teach." But here again it seems quite obvious that the "way" referred to is the way of conduct, the way of keeping the Lord's commandments. That is why the versions render, "the way he *should* choose."

Now the blessings are described that God is wont to bestow on those that walk in the way He has outlined for them. First, he "himself shall dwell at ease." (For "at ease" the Hebrew says "in good.") "His offspring shall possess the land" as was promised so often to the fathers in the days of the wilderness wanderings. The more spiritual blessings are these: first, he will have intimate association with the Lord, and second, the covenant relation in which he stands to his God increases his understanding of godly truth. All these are marks and testimonies of the goodness of God which His saints have enjoyed in all ages. All together they constitute the "name" of the Lord.

15. *My eyes are ever toward the Lord,*
    For He shall draw feet out of the net.
16. *Turn unto me and have mercy upon me,*
    For I am lonely and afflicted.
17. *The troubles of my heart have grown vast;*
    Bring Thou me out of my distresses.
18. *Consider my affliction and my trouble*
    And forgive all my sins.
19. *Consider how many my enemies are,*

       And that they hate me with hatred ready to burst into violence.
20. *O keep my soul and deliver me;*
     Let me not be put to shame,
     For in Thee have I taken refuge.
21. *Let integrity and unrightness preserve me,*
     For I hope in Thee.

As prayers for deliverance are again uttered, it becomes apparent that the situation of the psalmist is more desperate than his first set of petitions would have led us to believe. Quite naturally the view of God's mercies often cannot be kept before our eyes for a great length of time. After they have been beheld, the sense of our miserable situation often comes home to us the more painfully.

The grave character of the writer's situation appears from the fact that he may describe himself as having his feet caught in the "net." Only the Lord can extricate him from that difficulty. Again he makes a plea of his loneliness and affliction (v. 16). Again the troubles of his heart have grown vast; he is in "distresses" from which God's strength alone can deliver him. Besides, he has "affliction" and "trouble." Here it is that the sense of his sinfulness comes upon him, not overwhelmingly, but as a stern reality from which the Lord alone can free him.

In addition to all this there are "enemies," and they are "many" (v. 19), and they hate him "with a hatred ready to burst into violence." Who would not in the face of such and so many dangers cry out (v. 20): "O keep my soul and deliver me; let me not be put to shame; for in Thee I have taken refuge"? But more keenly than some individuals he still feels the obligation of unimpeachable conduct and so pleads that God may also grant him the favor that he may be a man who is marked by "integrity and uprightness." Characteristic of the saints of God have been such motivating pleas as "for in Thee I have taken refuge," and "for I hope in Thee." Thus end his personal petitions.

22. With an appropriate afterthought the writer recalls that he is not the only person who is in a difficult situation. Many of God's people are in equal distress. Unselfishly he remembers them all: "Redeem Israel, O Lord, out of all his trouble." This is certainly no trivial appendage, nor a loose and inappropriate addition. We are never to become so immersed in our own problems as to forget the needs of all of God's saints.

NOTES

Listing the irregularities of the acrostic arrangement of this psalm, we note that the *beth* (v. 2) has one word that has been inserted before what should be the initial letter—"my God." This could be omitted without altering the thought of the verse, but it has likely been inserted for emphasis rather than by accident. The verse beginning with *waw* between v. 5 and v. 6 is not to be found. Two verses beginning with *peh* occur, v. 16 and v. 22. There is no verse beginning with *qoph,* but two begin with *resh.* Strangely, the absence of the verse beginning with *waw* and the introduction of a second verse beginning with *peh* as a supernumerary at the close also appear in Ps. 34. Therefore these irregularities seem to be rather designed than an accident or due to carelessness on the part of copyists. No satisfactory explanation for these strange departures from the regular pattern is to be offered.

V. 3 is frequently rendered as a petition, "Yea, let none that wait on Thee be ashamed, etc." It seems better in this case to render the imperfect as a regular future: "None . . . shall be put to shame." In any case, it is a far stronger rendering.

V. 9 is analogous, only the reverse. The initial verb *yadhrekh* is strictly precative and should be rendered, "May He guide the meek in what is right," etc., as *KS* (195) points out.

In v. 13 the subject of the first member of the verse is literally "his soul." But this is in contrast with his "offspring" and is, therefore, best rendered "he himself."

In v. 17 there is no need of changing *hirchibhu* to the singular and have it mean "relieve" (RSV). As *KS* well points out, the form may be rendered "have grown vast" (*haben einen hohen Grad erreicht,* 339r).

The claim that this psalm must be regarded as postexilic is based on two factors: first, the acrostic form, second, the presence of wisdom motifs which are mixed with the hymnic strains. These wisdom motifs are vv. 4, 5 and 12–14. The fact that wisdom literature had nct been developed in the days of David and Solomon is one of many unproved assertions. Besides, we know too little about the acrostic form to ascribe only late dates to it.

Psalm 26

A PLEA FOR VINDICATION AND PROTECTION

IT IS, INDEED, strange to note how differently this psalm has been interpreted. Some commentators dispose of it brusquely with the charge, "Nor does it even ring true" (*Buttenwieser*). More commonly the criticism is voiced that it is a composition that is distinctly self-righteous, some, like *Koenig,* class the writer with those who are referred to by Christ when He said, "They that be whole need not a physician," Luke 5:31. *Kittel* writes it off in the same spirit and offers a lengthy explanation that is designed to mitigate the sharpness of the criticism and stresses particularly that the psalm has its Old Testament limitations. Some mention the possibility of the psalmist's being carried away by sickness in a time of pestilence—a very remote possibility, to say the least (*Gunkel*). Somewhat better is the approach which states that the psalm deals with the "Love of God's House and its Rituals" (*Leslie*). But why the "rituals" should be made so prominent is far from obvious, except for the fact that one strong trend of the present is to include everything in the psalms under the category of the liturgical. But the love of God's house is an incidental thought in the psalm; scarcely its theme. A unique level of misinterpretation is reached when the claim is voiced that the whole psalm is practically a prescribed ritual procedure for a man who is charged with witchcraft and with taking part in a conspiracy (*Hans Schmidt*). *Noetscher* very properly suggests that the writer is concerned about being vindicated before he passes off the scene.

We believe that it must be quite obvious that the writer is a man who has been falsely accused and is on the defensive, pleading with God that He may take his case in hand, vindicate, and protect him.

Since the charge of self-righteousness raised in connection with the author of the psalm is so strong and so commonly repeated, this issue has to be dealt with in some detail. The writer is not to be thought of as coming to the Temple, or sanctuary for worship in a calm frame of mind, untroubled by difficulties, and then, Pharisee—like, reciting this proud catalogue of his virtues. According to the evidence of the psalm itself, he is not placing himself over against God but over against certain accusers. He has been roundly defamed; he rises in protest.

Within such a situation, with the limitations just described, the man is naturally not saying everything about his relation to his God that can be said. He is on the defensive, and as *Weiser* has most fittingly pointed out, must be judged from this point of view and in the light of v. 11, which definitely cancels out the spirit of self-righteousness. It is unfair in view of the whole content and spirit of the psalm to compare its author with the Pharisee in the Temple (Luke 18:9ff.). We feel that a theme like "A Plea for Vindication and Protection" is far more suitable in catching the spirit of the psalm.

Nothing very definite can be stated on the question as to whether the psalmist speaks purely for himself or in the name of the whole congregation (the collective "I"). We feel that the psalm has a distinctly personal note.

It seems feasible to divide the psalm into two parts:

a) A plea for vindication, adducing proof of blameless conduct (vv. 1–8).
b) A plea to be spared the fate of evildoers (vv. 9–12).

We see no valid reason for denying the Davidic authorship of the psalm which the heading claims. Though there is not too much material available for or against this view, yet during the days when David was fleeing before Absalom he may well have uttered sentiments like v. 8 as II Sam. 15:25 shows. There certainly were men who at that time consistently maligned David; and what is more natural than that David should have placed his case into the hands of the Lord as this writer certainly does.

It should be noted that there are several points of resemblance with the preceding psalm, points such as those men who compiled the book of psalms seemed particularly to observe. Compare the claims of integrity in v. 1 and v. 11 with 25:21; the claims of trust in the Lord v. 1 with 25:2; also the prayer for deliverance v. 11 with 25:16, 21, 22; also v. 3 with 25:5, 6, 7, 10 on the subject of the love of God.

a) **A Plea for vindication, adducing proof of blameless conduct (vv. 1–8)**

1. *Vindicate me, O Lord, for I have walked in my integrity;*
   And I have trusted in the Lord without wavering.
2. *Examine me, O Lord, and test me;*
   Tried is my heart and my mind.
3. *For Thy steadfast love is before my eyes;*
   And I walk in fidelity to Thee.
4. *I have not sat with false men;*
   Neither do I mingle with dissemblers.

5. *I have hated the company of evildoers;*
   And I will not sit down with the wicked.
6. *I wash my hands in innocence*
   That I may go about Thy altar, O Lord,
7. *Giving utterance to praises with a loud voice*
   And recounting all Thy wondrous works.
8. *O Lord, I love the refuge that Thy house offers,*
   And the place where Thy glory dwells.

1. Much depends on catching the tone and meaning of the first verse. "Judge me" (*KJ*) could be construed as a proud and self-satisfied utterance. *Luther* indicated a different and correct approach when he rendered, *Shaffe mir recht,* "vindicate me." David means, "Prove me to be right." This is said in the face of charges, spoken or assumed, that the writer has been a hypocrite, and that the ills that now befall him are proof of this fact. But the man has served God in sincerity to the very best of his ability; and he knows well that ordinarily God is not wont to let His faithful followers go unrewarded. The integrity that he claims (*tummi*)—a word that is sometimes rendered "perfect"—really implies conduct from which no essential element is missing. It is not far removed from utter sincerity. But that the type of conduct involved is not self-righteousness at all appears in the second member of the verse, "and I have trusted in the Lord without wavering." His need for dependence on God is quite obvious though it is also clear that the speaker especially emphasizes the fact that this conduct toward God has been consistent—"without wavering." Any truly consistent Christian might still speak thus without becoming guilty of pride.

2. He has lived his life as in the sight of God in all sincerity and still does so. It is God's verdict that counts; that he knows right well, and so he appeals to the Supreme Court for an inspection. But at the same time, since he has been living his life as before God's eyes, he can say with assurance: "Tried is my heart and my mind." This second statement may appear to be a bold claim, but the writer is about to offer evidence for what he claims. It must be remembered that he always claims that he is not what his opponents claim he is.

3. The proof of blameless conduct that he submits begins with a definition of his attitude toward his God. He keeps his eyes fixed on the polestar of all faith and godly living, the "steadfast love" of his God. The very idea involved is that the basis of all steadfastness is God's steadfast love. Surely, this is not self-sufficiency. That this attitude does not imply an idle gazing at God is made clear by the second member: "And I walk in fidelity to Thee." This is the better rendering of the

phrase "in Thy truth." He looks for divine approval, and he walks so as to keep divine approval.

4. A few additional instances of godly conduct are listed, and it may well be possible that they are chosen to indicate that the writer is not guilty of certain types of misconduct of which his opponents are obviously guilty. The first of these is negative, "I have not sat with false men." He is of so radically different a spirit that he cannot consort with such men. Implied is the idea, of course, that, if one has sat with such, some kind of iniquity was being planned. But the verse implies more by its use of the perfect and the imperfect. The first clause uses the perfect; the imperfect that follows means as much as: neither do I now mingle with dissemblers. I have not kept fellowship with such either in the past or do so now. If he had mingled with "dissemblers" he would have been of the same ilk with them. The term implies such as use craft in an underhand way, *hinterlistig* (*KW*).

5. By the same use of tenses in the two members of this verse the same result is obtained: I have always hated the company of evildoers, neither will I now sit down with the wicked as a friend and companion of theirs. Of course, behind all this lies the assumption: Tell me with whom you associate, and I will tell you what you are. This need not be construed as a self-righteous assertion any more than is the analogous pronouncement of the first psalm: "Blessed is the man that walketh not," etc.

6. Aside from shunning evil associates, this man aims to preserve a blameless type of conduct, such that he may claim that his hands are not stained with evil deeds. Figuratively expressed, the claim is stated thus: "I wash my hands in innocence." It would appear that from days of old the rite of washing the hands was used as a "solemn attestation" that a man was guiltless (*Leslie*) as is indicated by the passages Deut. 21:6; Ps. 75:13; Matt. 27:24. It was required also on the part of priests that before they apprached the altar they engage in ceremonial ablutions (Exod. 30:17–21). This thought may also have been in the psalmist's mind. For this was one goal that he had in mind when he cultivated blameless behavior. The expression "that I may go about" does not seem to involve a solemn procession as is so commonly claimed. Neither do the passages cited proved this point. For Ps. 42:5 and 118:27 (*Kittel*) can be made to refer to ceremonial processions only after a change in the text has introduced this feature—a rather unwarranted way of securing proof for a contention! *Kirkpatrick* goes far enough when he asserts the meaning to be, "take my place in the ring of the worshippers around it." *Luther* seems to come even closer to the meaning when he translates, *und halte mich, Herr, zu deinem Altar,* i.e., I resort to Thy altar.

7. The thought, beginning with v. 6, is as follows: I abstain from iniquity that I may be accounted worthy to appear at Thy sanctuary, "giving utterance to praises with a loud voice." Not mere appearance in the sanctuary but the praising of God after one has arrived there and being fit to praise worthily—that is his wholesome objective. In addition, like many another saint of the Old Testament, he desires to "recount all of God's wondrous works." When such ambition activates a man's deeds, he surely does not deserve to be classed with evildoers and may call on God to vindicate him.

8. The last item in his solemn protestation of innocence is the claim that he loves to take refuge in the very presence of God: "O Lord, I love the refuge that Thy house affords." This means more than loving to resort to the sanctuary in public worship, though according to our familiar versions this is the thought usually associated with this verse. Here, as in Ps. 23:6, the "house of the Lord" is His immediate presence, whether it be experienced in the public sanctuary or anywhere else. It means actual fellowship with God. That always affords a place of "refuge" for men. As far as the earthly sanctuary is concerned, this is also "the place where God's glory dwells." For the Tabernacle and later the Temple were marked by the coming of God's glory to this sacred spot in the visible cloud. So it is clear that this man does not seek fellowship with God apart from the earthly place of His manifestation; but the personal fellowship is still his chief concern.

It would seem that this man had adduced sufficient proof that his conduct is above reproach, and that he does not deserve the calumny of his opponents. Neither was there any unseemliness about any of the claims that he made, nor any self-righteousness.

Having offered a basis for his petition, he now proceeds to

b) A plea to be spared the fate of evildoers (vv. 9–12)

9. *Do not gather me up together with sinners,*
   Nor my life together with bloodthirsty men,
10. *In whose hands are dastardly deeds;*
    And whose right hand is full of bribes.
11. *But as for me who walk in my integrity,*
    Redeem me and be gracious unto me.
12. *My foot stands on level ground;*
    In the congregations I will bless the Lord.

9. Only when a man has thoroughly and consistently shunned the ways of evil and completely detests them can he speak as this man does. This is another proof of his innocence. He shrinks from the thought of a fate like that which awaits the sinners. This does not imply that there is some judgment abroad which threatens the good and the evil alike

as some interpreters conclude from the verb "gather," which some render in German *raffe*, which seems to imply "snatch" or "sweep" (*RSV*), which is, however, altogether too strong a rendering. Paraphrased, the thought of vv. 9 and 10 could well be: May I never drop to the level of these whose fate is such a terrible one. Yet these were apparently the ones who strongly opposed and threatened the psalmist.

11. He throws himself completely upon the mercy of God, for he has no other refuge. Though he can and does consistently claim that he is one "who walks in his integrity," yet his deliverance cannot come from any other source than the goodness of his God. This is the thought expressed in "redeem me and be gracious unto me." It is true that "redeem" (*padhah*) does not primarily have a spiritual connotation such as we are wont to associate with the term "redemption." It includes any and every form of deliverance from ills that beset us. But *God* is the liberator, not the goodness of the speaker. "Be gracious" involves more of the same thought for the root involved stresses the fact that the benefactor inclines of His own volition to the one to whom He shows mercy. He delivers because He is kindly disposed and of a gracious disposition. When the psalmist, therefore, utters the petition, "redeem me and be gracious unto me," he certainly entertains no thought of self-sufficiency and superior personal merit, and this verse must without a doubt be taken into account when an estimate is made of his frame of mind.

12. The calmness of faith comes upon the petitioner. He becomes certain of his being heard and delivered and sees all the rough places of the path on which he has been walking smoothed out. The perfect of the verb '*amedhah* has something of the prophetic element in it. As so often, the faithful believer feels the urge publicly to praise the Almighty for His gracious help "in the congregations" whenever in times to come he may find himself in the midst of groups of the faithful. Gracious deliverance calls for public acknowledgment.

NOTES

1. Though the last clause could be translated, "therefore I shall not slide," it is preferable to render it as a circumstantial clause, somewhat thus, "so that I do not waver." Therefore "without wavering," according to *GK* 156 g.

2. *Tsorephah*, as the margin suggests, would be an imperative as it is most commonly rendered. The consonants call for *tseruphah*, feminine of the passive participle, a form which makes good sense and fits well the author's claim of integrity. For "heart and mind" the Hebrew has "kidneys" (seat of emotions) and "heart" (seat of mental activity).

3. The older versions render *ba'amittekha* "in Thy truth," but regarding the suffix as an objective genitive, the newer renderings deserve the preference when they translate, "in fidelity to Thee," or the like.

4. "False men" are literally "men of vanity," men whose moral fibre is quite insubstantial.

6. The *waw* consecutive introduces a final clause when it is joined to an optative form in the second member of the verse (*KS* 364 g). Therefore, "that I may go about" and not, "and go about" (*RSV*). *KJ* seems to be closer to the right approach: "so will I compass."

8. "Refuge of Thy house" means "refuge that Thy house offers," subjective genitive covered by the suffix.

Psalm 27

"THE LORD IS MY LIGHT AND MY SALVATION"

A BETTER TITLE than this could scarcely be found. It at least expresses in a positive way what echoes throughout the psalm.

Aside from this note of confidence the second most prominent feature of the psalm is its obvious change of mood: the first half (vv. 1–6) being on the very heights of supreme confidence in God, the second section (vv. 7–12) being on the lower level of plaintive petition. The last two verses may be regarded as a formal conclusion that brings the second section back into the spirit of the first. However, many interpreters assume that the first two sections are so radically different from one another that they refuse to believe that any one man could have spoken or written the two consecutively as one piece without having the one flatly contradict the other. However, it should be noted that in actual experience men may find moods undergoing a swift transition, like Goethe's *himmelhoch jauchzend, zum Tode betruebt.* Why should religious experience be exempt from such fluctuation? Greater difficulty arises if the two parts are ascribed to two authors or to the same author writing of two different experiences. Who would have dreamt of combining things that are so much at odds with one another and presenting them as a unit? Besides, the same situation is reflected in both of these major parts. In spite of the strong confidence voiced in part one there are even then "evildoers" who are called "adversaries and foes" (v. 2); dangers are obviously threatening (v. 3); triumphing over enemies is thought of (v. 6). Only at the beginning is the writer able to rise victoriously over all things that threaten. The exuberance of faith later dies down, but he still trusts in the help of the Living God.

The correctness of the ascription of the psalm to David according to the heading need not be questioned. This could have been what David felt at the time when he fled before Absalom (cf., Ps. 3:5 for similar sentiments). Again, v. 10 may refer to the situation described in I Sam. 22:3, 4.

Another issue that disturbs commentators is the question as to whether the actual sanctuary at Jerusalem is referred to as the asylum to which the writer would love to repair, or whether the thing he desires is the spiritual fellowship with God that is the object of his heart's desire. We believe the latter unquestionably to be the case. No one ever ventured to aspire to dwell in the visible sanctuary "all the days of his life" (v. 4). Nor would a man seek refuge there from trouble (v. 5). As so often, especially also in 23:6, dwelling in the house of the Lord means personal spiritual fellowship with Him, being assured of His favor and loving-kindness.

a) **Confident trust in God in the midst of danger (vv. 1–6)**
1. *Of David. The Lord is my light and my salvation, whom shall I fear?*
   The Lord is the refuge of my life, of whom shall I be afraid?
2. *When evildoers approached to slander me—my adversaries and foes—*
   It was they who stumbled and fell.
3. *Though a host encamp against me, my heart shall not fear;*
   Though war arise against me, nevertheless I will be confident.
4. *One thing I have asked of the Lord, that I will seek after—to dwell in the house of the Lord all the days of my life;*
   To behold the kindness of the Lord and to inquire in His Temple.
5. *For He shall hide me in His shelter in the day of trouble;*
   In the hiding place of His tabernacle He shall hide me;
   He shall set me up upon a rock.
6. *And then shall my head be lifted up above my enemies round about me;*
   And I will offer in His tabernacle sacrifices with shouts of joy;
   I will sing, and I will make music to the Lord.

1. Any Christian might well wish that he could in times of trouble always occupy as lofty a ground as do these verses. This is as we should always be minded if the Lord is truly our "light and salvation." "Light"

means more than intellectual insight, and "salvation" obviously means deliverance from every form of evil. "Light" includes joy (cf., 97:11), life, and hope. If an individual's heart is thus truly established in God, what or whom could he fear? If one continually takes refuge in Him as the "refuge of one's life," what reason is there for ever being afraid? This is a certainty that faith has often spoken to our hearts. We fail to carry through on the obvious logic of this position.

2. The psalmist cites past experiences in support of his contention. He has again and again found it to be true that, when "evildoers approached to slander" him, they were the ones that fell, not he. The expression found in many versions (*e.g., KJ*), "to eat up my flesh," in the Aramaic means slander as appears from Dan. 3:6; 6:25. To translate the verse as referring to the present as even *RSV* does overlooks the rule that infinitives (*biqrobh*) derive their connotation of time from the main verb on which they depend (here *kashelu wenaphalu*) as *KS* 216 demonstrates. The "adversaries and foes" could well be the opposition party at the time of Absalom's revolt.

3. It would be unwise to press the literal statement about a "host encamping" and "war arising" and insist that all this must have transpired at the time of some war. It would also be unwise to insist that the psalm does not voice the thoughts of a single person but is to be referred to the collective "I," the congregation. For this psalm is poetry as *Kittel* rightly points out. Reduced to prose, this statement means: No matter how great and threatening a danger may arise against me, I refuse to be afraid; I shall still be confident. It is a statement made in the exuberance of faith.

4. We now come to the roots of this bold faith. The psalmist had kept in closest communion with his God. He knew that God had made his courage strong, and he thus ardently voices his desire for the continuance of this communion as the one great goal of his life. But he also knows that such fellowship cannot be continued unless it is continually fed by prayer. The idea of fellowship may be variously expressed. One may speak of the *unio mystica;* one may speak of living with God. The psalmist uses the latter figure. In such fellowship one has certain experiences. Here in particular the psalmist hopes to recapture what he has experienced before, namely, "to behold the kindness of the Lord" for one thing, and second, "to inquire in His temple." The "kindness" of the Lord, *no'am,* is a term that is difficult to render. It means "pleasantness," "graciousness" and the like. *Luther* thought too much in terms of worship in the sanctuary when he rendered the word "beautiful services of the Lord." It means nothing more than to discover anew how gracious and merciful the good Lord really is.

So also the verb "to inquire" (*baqqer*) has its difficulties. In the light of the several instances of its use in Scripture the meaning "inquire" may well be retained. *Wellhausen's* conjecture that the consonants should be pointed *"in the morning"* was not a happy one. God's kindness is not to be noted more readily in the morning.

5. The thought of seeking the close presence and fellowship of God continues. The psalmist draws his conclusions as to what will grow out of such fellowship. For one thing, he who abides with God is safe. Utilizing the figure a bit more fully, David claims that it is as though God were to hide such a person in a shelter in the day of trouble until the danger is passed. Or, slightly changing the figure, it is as though God hid His child so that the adversary could not find him. Or, again changing the figure, it is as though He set him up on a high rock that is well out of the reach of danger.

6. The ultimate outcome of such close fellowship is depicted. For one thing, the enemies of a man who kept close to his God will be brought low; he himself will, however, stand with head uplifted, confident and safe in the keeping of his Lord. Such experiences will give him occasion to repair to the public sanctuary and "offer sacrifices" before the Lord with "shouts of joy." Such outward formal tokens of true appreciation will be accompanied by his personal songs and the music that he makes unto the Lord—a point that corresponds well with things that David was wont to do.

b) **Anxious plea for help in the midst of danger (vv. 7–12)**

7. *Hear, O Lord, I am crying aloud;*
   Have mercy upon me and answer me.
8. *Of Thee my mind has always thought; my face has always sought*
      Thee;
   Thy face, O Lord, I will continue to seek.
9. *Hide not Thy face from me; turn not Thy servant away in anger;*
   Thou hast been my help; thrust me not aside, neither forsake me,
      O God of my salvation.
10. *For my father and my mother have left me;*
    But the Lord will take me up.
11. *Teach me Thy way, O Lord,*
    And lead me on a level path because of my adversaries.
12. *Deliver me not to the will of my enemies,*
    For false witnesses have risen up against me,
    And one who breathes out violence.

7. The full, resonant tone of the first half has disappeared. We now hear the plaintive cry of the second. Petitions for help and mercy ring out. The psalmist has lost his assurance of being heard and helped. But faith is not prostrate; he still knows that God can be appealed to.

8. This verse has its obvious difficulties. The problem may be solved by supplying a clause. So *Luther* does, beginning: "My heart holds up before Thee Thy word: 'Seek ye . . .'" The *KJ* approach is almost the same: "When Thou saidst, 'Seek ye. . . .'" The conciseness of the expression seems to allow for either. But *Koenig* has ventured to strike out in a different direction, which we have followed in part. The perfects are to be regarded as gnomic aorists, describing what has always been done in the past. "Heart" (lebh) is the center of the intellect rather than of the emotions, therefore "mind." The verb *'amar* often means "to think." "Face" is always a plural noun and is more frequently construed with a plural of the verb. Therefore the second clause reads: "My face has always sought Thee." Then quite appropriately the imperfect is used in a future sense, indicating that the writer intends to continue following this course: "Thy face, Lord, I will continue to seek." The verse, thus translated, fits well into the picture and is unambiguous. It supports the preceding plea, saying in effect: In the past I have always thought on Thee and sought Thee; and I shall continue to seek Thy presence in every time of need.

9. Faith grows timid and fearful. Doubts assail the writer: Will God hear him? So he pleads that God may not turn His face away, nor turn His servant away in anger. His past experience affords him a footing: Thou hast been my help. Then follows the moving plea: "Thrust me not aside, neither forsake me, O God of my salvation," which means, O God, who hast been wont to save me. Whether all this argues for a sense of guilt on the writer's part or merely reflects the uncertainty which men feel in time of trouble cannot be easily determined.

10. The incident referred to above, of which we read in I Sam. 22: 3, 4, may here be under consideration. David took his parents to the Moabites. In a sense they had left him as *'azabh* may indicate without having the harsher meaning "forsake" (*KJ*). To speak of their going thus involves no criticism of them: they had to leave. No one could stand by him except the Lord. Of this fact he strongly reminds himself. It is true, on the other hand, that the half-proverbial meaning usually associated with this verse in the familiar versions has much to commend it: "When my father and my mother forsake me, then the Lord will take me up." The verse would then mean: When all earthly props give way, the Lord can still be depended upon, and on Him I rest. The difficulty cannot be solved by a reference to the original because the initial *ki* can mean either "for" or "if." Either interpretation has about the same sense.

11. The first clause, "teach me Thy way, O Lord," is usually understood in an ethical sense. It then means, show me what line of conduct I shòuld follow to be well-pleasing to Thee. Because of the

second member of the verse, this interpretation is not acceptable. The "way" corresponds with the "level path." "Teach me Thy way" then means: Show me a road to follow where there are no troubles or dangers. When this is asked for "because of adversaries," this means, because the psalmist knows that in the sight of the Lord his adversaries are wicked, but he is not; for he has sought to walk in the ordinances of the Lord blameless. They on their part would love to see him brought low; let them not have that satisfaction.

12. This plea closes with the prayer not to be given into the will (Hebrew: *nephesh,* which here means greedy desire; German: *Gier*) of his enemies. For the writer well knows that their desires are relentlessly cruel. Besides, they are false witnesses, which does not refer to witnesses in a public trial but means about the same as slanderers. Among them is one in particular who breathes out violence.

There is no question about it, the writer is in imminent peril of losing his life. He feels that this very threat to his existence will move his God to give heed to the petition of an innocent petitioner.

c) **Self-reassurance (vv. 13, 14.)**

13. *Unless I had believed to see the goodness of the Lord in the land of the living—!*
14. *Wait thou for the Lord!*
    Be strong and let your heart be of good courage;
    But wait thou for the Lord!

The petitions are at an end. The last two verses contain a kind of reminiscence of the first part of the psalm and seek to reassure the writer. Because of its very incompleteness v. 13 attracts attention. *Maclaren* appropriately calls it "an abrupt half-sentence." Its very silence as to the conclusion to be strong is the equivalent of a strong declaration. Though some thought his life was forfeit, the psalmist virtually declares that he confidently believes to see proof of the "goodness of the Lord," that is to say, His mercy and kindness, while he is still in the "land of the living."

14. So "his faith rebukes his faintness," as *Kirkpatrick* so aptly says; and in so doing he uses admonitions that are reminiscent of Joshua in days of old, whom God addressed in these very words (Josh. 1:6). It may require a bit of waiting. God has not always answered His saints on the second; therefore, "Wait on the Lord"—repeated doubly to impress it on the faint heart.

NOTES

2. In the expression "they stumbled and fell" it will be observed that we have an instance to show how the use of the *waw* consecutive grew

less common in the course of time, especially with synonyms; see *KS* 370f.

6. This verse seems to begin "and *now*" (*KJ et. al.*). But it is merely a term that marks *logical,* not temporal sequence and is best translated "and *then.*" *Teru'ah* is an adverbial accusative, and though it is in the construct relationship, it may not be translated "sacrifices of shouting" or the like, for such sacrifices were not known in Israel.

7. The fact that certain psalms (*e.g.,* 55:1; 61:1; 64:1) begin, "Hear, O Lord," is not yet a sufficient reason for regarding this portion as a separate psalm. The correspondence is purely formal and external.

Psalm 28

A PRAYER FOR HELP
AND PRAISE FOR ITS ANSWER

THIS PSALM follows an inverse pattern to that of the one preceding. There, exultant praise first, then eager petition; here, first the prayer for help, then the praise for its answer. In fact, the heading given the psalm in *ARV* is as appropriate as any: "A Prayer for Help and Praise for Its Answer." It also has several points of similarity with Ps. 26.

If the superscription is taken seriously, that the psalm was written by David—and there is no reason for questioning this—then its composition would be assigned to the time when Absalom rose in rebellion against his father. David's son's followers could well be described in the words of vv. 3 and 5. Then v. 1 in no sense exaggerates the danger involved, and v. 4 describes the fate the rebellious deserve. The prayer made for the people and the king (v. 8) is also most appropriate.

On the other hand, it cannot be denied that the psalm does not more closely specify the nature of the danger that threatened its writer. The individual characteristics are not stressed so that many saints may use the psalm in analogous situations. It is, therefore, unwarranted to make this the "petition of an invalid" (*Schmidt, Leslie*); in fact, this conclusion requires rash changes in v. 7. Equally unsuited, or at least one-sided, is the position of *Briggs,* "a prayer for help in time of war." Or also of *Kirkpatrick,* who thinks of a season of pestilence. When

Taylor speaks of "sickness for which he holds certain godless and deceitful persons responsible," that involves crude superstition.

The collective I does not appear in this psalm though it cannot be denied that the author prays for his people as well as for himself, for he sees that they share the affliction that has befallen him.

a) **Prayer for help (vv. 1–5)**
1. *Of David. Unto Thee, O Lord, do I cry;*
   My Rock, do not ignore me;
   Lest if Thou be silent to me, I become like those who go down into the pit.
2. *Hear the voice of my supplication when I cry unto Thee for help;*
   When I lift up my hands unto Thy holy oracle.
3. *Do not dispose of me with the wicked and with the workers of iniquity,*
   Who speak friendly words with their neighbors, but evil is in their minds.
4. *Repay them according to their work, according to the evil of their doings;*
   According to the works of their hands repay them;
   Requite them what they have perpetrated.
5. *Because they regard not the doings of the Lord nor the work of His hands,*
   He will tear them down and not build them up.

The cry for help is prompted by an unusual fear that has taken hold of the writer: God might not deign to hear him, He might "ignore" him or "be silent" to him. These saints of God had their manifold misgivings even as we do in our day. How these doubts originate is hard to say. If the Lord should fail to answer, the psalmist realizes that his doom is sealed; death will overtake him or, expressed poetically: "lest I become like those who go down into the pit." "Pit" is merely another word for Sheol or the afterlife. The term scarcely refers to a separate "deep dark dungeon in Sheol" as *Briggs* states, a view that is certainly not warranted by a reference to Is. 14:15 or kindred passages. It is clear that the author considers himself in peril of death.

2. So the petition continues. The writer feels that the earnest pleas for help made by God's children are not a matter of indifference to the Father. Therefore he enumerates what his desperate situation is driving him to do: he makes "supplications" (in the Hebrew a plural of potency); he "cries for help"; he lifts up his hands toward God's "holy oracle"—the *debhir* of the sanctuary, where he knows God is enthroned, and to which place God's saints have directed their peti-

tions (cf., I Kings 8:29, 31, 33, 35, 38, 42). This term is best thought of as being derived from the root *dabhar,* "to speak," inasmuch as God did from days of old utter His voice from this place as is shown by Num. 7:89. For this reason *AV* very properly renders the word "oracle," which we have retained. The tendency inaugurated by *Gesenius* to render it "backroom of the Temple" (Koeh. Baum.), basing this translation on a parallel Arabic or Coptic root, still appears to us as *Hengstenberg* states it, *Scheu vor der Tiefe,* which might be rendered: a dread of anything that has depth. *KW's* reference to I Kings 8:6 does not cancel this view. The *debhir* has rightly been likened to the "audience chamber of a regent." Cf. also Exod. 25:22. The "lifting up of the hands" (cf., Ps. 63:4; Lam. 2:19) is, perhaps, best regarded as "an outward symbol of an uplifted heart."

3. There seems to be some possibility in the mind of the psalmist, occasioned, no doubt, by the misgivings which prompted v. 1, that God might ignore his plight and sweep him away in the judgment that properly befalls evildoers. He prays especially that this may not be his lot. That *they* deserve such a fate is obvious, for they make a practice of dissembling; they are out and out hypocrites. Friendly greetings may fall from their lips, "but evil is in their minds." How much of this damnable hypocrisy must have been current in the days when Absalom's rebellion was in the making!

4. If the prayer is uttered that these dissemblers may be repaid "according to their works, according to the evil of their doings," and two additional statements of the case follow in parallel phrases, then surely there is nothing wrong about this request. God always judges all men according to their works. To desire that God do as He has always done and must of necessity do is not asking for an unseemly thing. Nor is the man that utters the prayer giving evidence "of the unhappy traits of partisanship, revenge, and gloating over another's misfortunes" (*Kittel*). There have been cases when one man had done the other absolutely no harm. All the wrong was on one side. In those cases the innocent man may give utterance to prayers like these with a pure heart. Note that the added phrase always indicates: as they have deserved.

5. The writer gives evidence of deeper insight into what was wrong with the whole group of those whose ultimate fate he hoped to escape. They left God out their thinking, or, as it is here stated: "They regard not the doings of the Lord nor the works of His hands." *Kirkpatrick* very concisely labels them "atheists in practice, if not in profession." It is well known how God deals with such: "He will tear them down and not build them up."

Psalm 28

b) **Praise for its answer** (vv. 6–9).

6. *Blessed be the Lord,*
   For He has heard the voice of my supplication.
7. *The Lord is my strength and my shield;*
   My heart has always trusted in Him, and I received help;
   And my heart exulted, and with my song I praised Him.
8. *The Lord is the strength of His people;*
   He is the saving refuge of His anointed.
9. *Help Thy people and bless Thine inheritance*
   And feed them and lift them up forever.

Some time obviously elapsed between the first part which is petition and the second which is praise. This fact need not lead to the conclusion that the last four verses are another poem. Nor does one need to speak of "the sudden, almost violent transition" from the one to the other (*Kittel*). Parallels could easily be adduced from familiar hymns. Suddenly all misgivings are at an end, all fears conquered. The writer can praise the Lord again, and he does it with vigor. He feels that the change of attitude on his part is due to answered prayer. "He has heard the voice of my supplication."

7. A sturdy confidence now steals over him: "The Lord is my strength," a statement which usually means: the source of my strength. A feeling of invulnerability becomes his: the Lord is "my shield." But all this is so much in line with previous experiences that the author gives a resume of them all in the words: "My heart has always trusted [perfect equal to a gnomic aorist, expressing what is always true] in Him, and I received help." This is no new experience for a man like the psalmist. And whenever he had such an experience, the sequel always was: "And my heart exulted, and with my song I praised Him." Both these statements are retrospective, a fact lost sight of by the current translations, also *RSV*, yet demanded by the forms of the Hebrew verb (cf. the Notes).

8. As one might rightly expect of a true monarch, this man has a due regard for the welfare of His people. And here, when they and he were involved in like danger, he reminds them that now that the deliverance has come, the Lord is their "strength" even as "He is the saving refuge of His anointed." According to the standing usage of the term the Lord's anointed is the true king of Israel. This is another way of saying: people and king have been saved by their Lord, and He is still their strength and help. Saying that God *is* these things implies that both parties should *let Him be* "strength" and "refuge" to them.

9. With a very proper prayer and benediction the author of the

psalm closes his poem. What v. 8 reminded the readers of is turned into a prayer that people and land may be blessed, the land and the people being called God's "inheritance," a synonym for a delightful possession. He is further implored to play the part of a shepherd over them and to continue to exalt them or lift them up time and again as He has in the past. "Lift up" is a richer rendering than "carry," *RSV*, though the latter is reminiscent of Is. 40:11. Some commentators call this beautiful close an extraneous liturgical addition. Its propriety is its best defense.

NOTES

1. The *'eqra'* is best taken as an emphatic present (*Briggs*) rather than a future. The desire to delete *Yahweh* because it seems to disturb the metrical pattern grows out of the failure rightly to evaluate the freedom of Hebrew poetry which allows for plain rhythm rather than for strict metrical rules.

3. "Friendly words" is literally, "who speak peace," but this may well be referred to greetings, which were conveyed by the word *shalom*.

7. If *batach* is like a gnomic aorist ("has always trusted"), then the form *wene'ezárti,* which does not follow the pattern of the *waw* consecutive construction, is to be regarded as another gnomic aorist, or as *KS* 367i states, it expresses the iterative. The last word of the verse, *'ahodénnu,* is one of the many instances where the *waw* consecutive is omitted. *Koenig's Kommentar,* (p. 8 of the Introduction (1)) gives many illustrations of this omission.

8. The opening words are literally: "Yahweh is strength for them." In the light of v. 9 "for them" can mean only "for His people." This correction is actually offered by eight manuscripts, the *Septuagint,* and the *Syriac*. Though this correction is not necessary it is in full keeping with the meaning of the passage.

Psalm 29

THE GLORY OF GOD IN THUNDER

A TYPICAL nature psalm if the expression "nature psalm" is admissible, for the Scriptures never regard nature as an independent agency moving and acting according to its own laws—as we so often do—but rather as a creature of God, which He still controls, and in which His

Psalm 29

operation is discernible, especially in violent disturbances of nature such as the storm or more particularly as the thunder. The one feature of a storm on which this psalm focuses attention is thunder. In the original this is a far more effective term than is our somewhat lame "thunder," for the very resonance of the term— *qol Yahweh*—is most sonorous, especially with the arrangement of anaphora, as a result of which successive statements keep beginning with the term. *Qol Yahweh* means "the voice of the Lord."

Letting their imagination play, some writers suggest that this poem was suggested by a storm that was witnessed. They then trace the storm as it takes its violent course over the land. The truth of the matter is rather that a picture of an ideal storm is painted. Striking features, instances of what a storm may do, are grouped together without necessarily claiming that all of them will be in evidence in each storm.

Again it is not the physical storm as such which claims attention, but that which it reflects. Therefore we are inclined to accept the following statement of what constitutes the theme of the psalm: The Glory of the Lord in Thunder. We submit the following division:

a) A summons to the angels to praise the Lord because of the majesty of thunder (vv. 1, 2).
b) What thunder can do (vv. 3–9).
c) The Lord has always controlled such forces, as He still does, for the good of His people (vv. 10, 11).

In the material found in the psalm no positive clue to authorship can be discovered. *Kessler* is correct when he claims that the authorship by David can be neither proved nor disproved. Certainly a shepherd, tending his flocks, would have had ample opportunity to observe what things a storm does. Besides, David had the ability to put into adequate words what he saw. On the subject of the possible derivation of this psalm from Ugaritic originals see the Notes below.

a) **A summons to the Angels to praise the Lord because of the majesty of thunder (vv. 1, 2)**

A Psalm of David.
1. *Give unto the Lord, O heavenly beings,*
   Give unto the Lord glory and strength.
2. *Give unto the Lord the glory due unto His name;*
   Worship the Lord in holy array.

1. Introductory to the description of the majesty of the thunder is a summons to the holy angels to praise the Lord. For what they are to praise the Lord we and they are not told till the body of the psalm

(vv. 3–9) informs us. The original addresses them by the title "sons of God." Since this expression is construed so differently by commentators, we have preferred to use the term which is sanctioned also by *RSV et.al.*, "heavenly beings," which is certainly more readily understood than, "O ye mighty" (*KJ*). For a full discussion of the term see the *Notes*. No reader will misconstrue the imperative "give," which certainly cannot connote, when used in connections such as these, that we could give strength to God. Every interpreter knows what limitations to put upon the term, and that it signifies something like "ascribe" or "acknowledge." So the thought suggests: recognize the glory and the strength which He manifests.

The unusual structure of vv. 1 and 2, especially v. 1b viewed in connection with v. 2a, as *Albright*, e.g., suggest in *Old Testament Commentary (Alleman* and *Flack)* p. 157f., is described as involving the pattern *a-b-c, a-b-d,* the item *d* being over and above what the parallelism of the first half suggests. This structure reappears also in Ugaritic parallels and elsewhere in the paslms.

2. Another way of describing the Lord's glory is that it is "the glory due unto His name," which is an effective translation that appears in *KJ* for (literally): "the glory of His name." "His name" is the reputation that He has acquired among His saints. No matter which being it is that gives glory to God, it is still most fitting that it prostrate itself before the divine majesty. This is the connotation of the verb "worship." The expression "in holy array" borrows the picture from earthly ministrants, who were, according to Old Testament regulations (cf., Exod. 28:2; II Chron. 20:21), to appear for service in God's sanctuary only when properly vested. The idea is transferred to the area of heaven where the thought becomes this: They, too, should appear before the Lord in proper array. "In the beauty of holiness" may be a beautiful phrase, but it does not convey what the Hebrew suggests. *Luther's, in heiligem Schmuck,* is a much better rendering.

Without a formal transition the holy writer now states what it is that should move these heavenly beings to utter their devout adoration before their Lord. It is thunder, which is so majestic and overwhelmingly impressive. He describes what it may do in the second chief part of the psalm.

b) **What thunder can do (vv. 3–9)**

3. *The voice of the Lord was above the waters;*
   The God of glory thundered;
   Yahweh above many waters.

4. *The voice of the Lord in its might;*
   The voice of the Lord in its majesty;

5. *The voice of the Lord which breaks cedars;*
   And the Lord broke the cedars of Lebanon.
6. *And He made them skip like a calf;*
   Lebanon and Sirion like a young wild ox.
7. *The voice of the Lord which hews out flames of fire.*
8. *The voice of the Lord shakes the wilderness;*
   The Lord shakes the wilderness of Kadesh.
9. *The voice of the Lord makes the hinds to calve*
   And stripped the forests bare;
   And in His temple all cry, "Glory!"

The display of God's glory in the thunder is so magnificent that man feels he cannot do justice to its proper praise. So the angels have been invited to do so for him.

3. A peculiar change of tenses, which few commentators have noted and even *Koenig* not fully, is found in this description. The past tense is consistently used through vv. 3–7. Then v. 8 and v. 9a appear in the imperfect, here the present, but v. 9b goes back to the past. The versions ignore the difficulty and render all verbs in the present tense. The perfects and the imperfects are, perhaps, to be construed as follows: The perfects describe what thunders have been known to do. The presents or imperfects might record what is actually going on in a storm at the moment the writer is composing this psalm.

A brief comment on "the voice of the Lord." The term is still most appropriate though we may be able to give an explanation of the physical phenomenon in terms of well-known natural laws. For to the devout mind there is nothing known that could so aptly convey to human feeling the power of the voice of God as could thunder.

The chief difficulty, apart from this in the present verse, is whether the expression "above the waters" has in mind the waters of the storm clouds that are gathering, black and heavy, before the storm breaks; or whether, as the parallel expression "above many waters" might indicate, this refers to the storms arising out over the vast stretches of the Mediterranean, to which the Scriptures do apply the expression "many waters," as in Ezek. 28:26, which fact agrees well with the observation that in Palestine storms do originate out over the Sea. Still, since this second usage is not so common, the first deserves the preference. The rolling of the thunder before the storm, seemingly above the storm clouds, is referred to. The "God of glory" causes this thunder to roll: there are no independent natural forces at work anywhere.

4. There follows an apposition, not a statement, which further describes the phenomenon just named, "the voice of the Lord." It always resounds in the might that is characteristic of it—note the article before

"might" and "majesty"—it always manifests the majesty of Him that uses it. Both terms are singularly appropriate; there is something grand and imposing about thunder.

5. Seldom has this been felt more keenly by man than when he has stood before a shattered tree of the forest, cast down and blasted to bits, as the mighty cedars sometimes were. The parallel statement specifies that the cedars referred to are the mighty "cedars of Lebanon," the more precise statement being held in reserve for the second member. The Germans call this "the parallelism of *Aufsparung*" (holding in reserve). Besides, we observe here again what first appeared in v. 3c and will reappear in v. 8b, namely, that "the Lord" becomes the subject in the parallel statement in place of the chief subject, "the voice of the Lord." This fluctuation could be due to the seeking for variety of expression. It may also be due to the fact that the "voice of the Lord" is not to be regarded as an independent agency; therefore the true agent is referred to repeatedly. Some interpreters make all these instances where the subject becomes "the Lord" later insertions, liturgical responses, in fact, for a kind of antiphonal rendition. Such interpretations are conjecture and offer little toward an understanding of the psalm.

6. Another thing that the writer has observed the thunder do is: he has seen a violent shaking of these mighty giants of the mountains, so violent that with a certain exuberance of imagination he likens it to the gambols of a calf—a figure that is not half as inappropriate as it might seem, especially to folks of rural background, who were quite familiar with the sight. For that matter, it was not only the trees of the forest that trembled as he had often observed; it was the very range of "Lebanon" itself and its mightiest peak "Sirion"—here called by its ancient Sidonian name. Lacking imagination, some writers regard an earthquake as the cause of the commotion—a very uncalled-for suggestion. Thunder can take care of what is here described.

7. Another manifestation of the power and the majesty of the thunder is offered in an appositional statement, in the shortest verse of the psalm, short because it seeks to represent "the jagged explosion of the lightning" (*Hengstenberg*). Thunder and lightning are regarded as twin manifestations of one and the same force. "Hewing out flames of fire" seems to have in mind that, as fire issues forth from flint when it is struck, so the thunder emits its fire when it strikes. All these are things that the writer has observed here and there in the past. He offers a composite picture.

8. The writer now seems to move forward to a scene as his eyes behold it, being part of a storm that he is witnessing as he writes. He uses another parallelism that holds the more precise formulation of the idea in reserve till the second thought has been presented (cf. v. 5).

The scene has shifted to the "wilderness" (*midhbar*), the steppe-like plain lying around Palestine to the east and the south. Here it is the wilderness of Kadesh. Though the wilderness by this name that is most commonly known is the one through which the children of Israel passed after they left Mt. Sinai (cf., Deut. 1:19), it seems more likely at this point that another such wilderness lying to the north by the side of the Lebanon range is meant because of the use of the same term in the Ras Shamra poem. Cf. Albright's suggestion noted on v. 1. So after viewing what storms or thunders have done in forests he studies what he observes out in the open wilderness, how the whole area is made to shudder at the thunderclaps. It is usually observed here or elsewhere that the Palestinian storm is so much more violent than are the ones we are familiar with.

9. Itemizing a few more of the effects of God's mighty thunder, the psalmist mentions first that "hinds" have been observed to have been hastened into the process of parturition by the fright that thunder caused; and also that forests may present the spectacle of leaves stripped off branches and bark off trunks after the violence of the storm has subsided. But leaving all these details, the writer suddenly summarizes by stating what the total effect is on beings who view all these things with more perfect reactions than those of man. For God's holy angels, who serve Him continually in His heavenly sanctuary, are moved to cry with one accord, "Glory"! for that it is that is displayed to their view. The reference to the heavenly temple is the more appropriate here, since such usage of the term *hekhal* is found in Ps. 18:6; Mic. 1:2; Hab. 2:20. To translate *kabhodh* as Schmidt does, *O der Glanz!* which practically means, "O what a bright light!" really borders on the trivial. This interpretation of ours also agrees well with v. 1. So ends the account of what the storm can do.

c) **The Lord has always controlled such forces, as He still does, for the good of the people (vv. 10, 11)**

10. *The Lord sat enthroned over the Flood;*
    And the Lord sat enthroned as king over the ages.
11. *The Lord will give strength to His people;*
    The Lord will bless His people with peace.

The conclusion aims to emphasize the thought that behind all such elemental forces as the ones just described stands the Lord, always in full and perfect control. The most notable instance of His perfect power was the Flood. The word here used (*mabbul*) refers invariably and exclusively to the great Deluge. When it occurred, never for a moment was it out of control. The vast cataclysmic forces unleashed remained obedient to His will: "He sat enthroned over the Flood."

The parallel statement broadens the thought to a certain universality: "He sat enthroned as king over the ages." To keep the same construction in *b* as in *a* of this verse demands this translation. The noun *'olam* is really a singular and is often rightly translated eternity, but it actually means the dim and hidden time of old as well as of the future. Therefore "the Lord sits enthroned *forever*" is not an incorrect translation, but it does not include enough. The psalmist's statement really takes all past time into consideration: through all these dim ages the Lord held the reins firmly and still does. For that reason, too, it is not entirely wrong to translate the verb as a present. It really means that all through the ages He has mounted His throne and sits there enthroned ever since. So *GK* 111r interprets the verse.

11. Now comes the practical climax to which all this has been consistently building up. The same Lord, whose control of the forces of nature is absolute, wields this control for the good of His people. He will grant them "strength" whenever they need it; "He will bless His people with peace." On this note of reassurance the psalm closes. Conclusions such as these every true member of the people of God reaches when he reflects upon a storm that occurs with its resounding thunders. We can well understand why the church in days of old used to instruct her children to read this psalm during the time of a storm. The classic remarks of *Delitzsch* may well be recorded here: "*Gloria in excelsis* is the beginning, and *pax in terra* ['peace on earth'] the close."

NOTES

1. As indicated above, we translated *beney 'elim* "heavenly beings." It means literally "sons of gods" (*RSV* margin). At first glance one might arrive at the conclusion that gods of an inferior rank could be referred to, for the term seems to allow for the existence of gods other than the true God. Some interpreters assert this and so have the writer of the psalm stand on a polytheistic or at least half-polytheistic level. This level of the psalm is to be offset by glowing descriptions of the rare poetic beauty of the whole conception. The truth of the matter is that we have here a kind of double plural, such as *KS* describes at length (267b-g), also *GK* (124q), which seems to be formed as a parallel expression to the familiar *beney 'elohim,* "sons of God," found in reference to the angels in Job 1:6; 2:1; 28:7. Ordinarily the term would read *beney 'el.* A similar case found in Ps. 89:7 also refers to the angels. As *Koenig* has shown at length in his commentary, the translation "sons of the gods" is not warranted by Hebrew usage, and, therefore, there is no trace of polytheistic conceptions on the part of the writer. In fact, the very idea as such that divine beings of an inferior sort are under

consideration is to be classed as an instance of "mythologizing misinterpretation (*Umdeutung*) of the Old Testament."

3. If the first member of the verse, a nominal clause, is translated, "The voice of the Lord *was* . . ." this is due to the fact that the verb of the second clause is in the past, and all such nominal clauses take their tense from the context in which they appear.

Now the subject of Ugaritic parallels. There is in fact a Ugaritic original that runs parallel to this whole psalm, with the difference that it has, in place of the name Yahweh, the name of the god Hadad, as stated by *Albright, Weiser,* et. al.

Psalm 30

PRAISE OF GOD ON THE OCCASION OF THE CONSECRATION OF THE SITE OF THE TEMPLE

TO A GREATER degree than is usually the case the interpretation of this psalm depends on determining its occasion. The question is answered in the heading which is now found in the Hebrew text, chiefly in the words: "a song at the dedication of the house." But here again the issue is not at once clear. This could refer to the dedication described in II Sam. 24 and I Chron. 21; then the "house" would be the Temple site. It could refer to the building of David's own palace, mentioned in II Sam. 5:11. Or thirdly, this part of the heading could be a later addition, referring, perhaps, to the event which later gave rise to the Feast of Dedication, which dedication is described in I Macc. 4:52ff. and II Macc. 10:1ff., and which dedication festival is referred to in John 10:20.

Certain writers (*Koenig, Kessler,* etc.) maintain that David wrote the psalm, but scarcely one since *Hengstenberg* dares to regard the heading as original and reliable and actually decribing the occasion of the psalm. Yet, it seems to us, that no explanation fits better or gives a better approach to the understanding of the psalm.

Examining the events recorded in the two chapters referred to above (II Sam. 24 and I Chron. 21), we note that the particular incidents that led to the choice and dedication of the site of the Temple at Jerusalem were the census and the subsequent plague, together with the termination of the plague at the place where David saw the angel of the

Lord with drawn sword, that is, at the threshing floor of Araunah.

Note, first of all, that in speaking of the site thus marked I Chron. 22:1 uses the very term that is used in the heading of the psalm, the word *bayith*: "Here shall be the house." The dedicatory offerings made on that site on that occasion are the *chanukhah* ("dedication") referred to in the heading. Note also a number of points of agreement between the event and the text of the psalm. To begin with, the whole psalm is a thanksgiving for the deliverance which the Lord granted to David and to the nation in consequence of David's intercessory prayer. David's description of his recovery is most appropriate, for he may, like many others, especially since he was the instigator of the deed that brought on the plague, have thought himself all but dead as a result of the pestilence then raging and about to strike Jerusalem. Besides that, the plague lasted "from morning till the appointed time," which may well be the time of the evening sacrifice (cf., I Kings 18:36); and this agrees with the time limit set in v. 5. V. 6 of the psalm would then indicate the spirit which animated David when he appointed the taking of a census, a spirit of pride and carnal security. Also the satisfaction that David's enemies might have gained from a more extensive plague is the matter referred to in v. 1. We feel that the psalm fits this historical situation as a glove fits the hand.

a) **The first part of the psalm is a resolve to thank God for deliverance from grave peril (vv. 1–3)**

A psalm—a song at the dedication of the house—by David.

1. *I will extol Thee, O Lord, for Thou hast drawn me up
And hast not let my enemies rejoice over me.*
2. *O Lord, my God, I cried unto Thee for help;
And Thou didst heal me.*
3. *O Lord, Thou hast brought up my soul from Sheol;
Thou hast preserved my life so that I was not among those that go
down to the pit.*

The heading of the psalm is a part of the Hebrew text. We have given it as a heading in order to preserve the numbering of the verses as it is usually found in the English versions; in the Hebrew it is v. 1.

1. Grave peril is past, a peril that will in a moment be described in all its intensity. At the moment of its coming to an end the need of extolling the Deliverer is strong. Reflecting on the situation of the termination of the dangerous pestilence described in II Sam. 24 and I Chron. 21, one can well understand the great relief of the people when the plague that had begun to rage so furiously was terminated so suddenly. David himself could describe his feelings as being like unto those of a man who had stumbled into a deep cavity and had thought he

Psalm 30

would perish, and now, unexpectedly, the Lord has "drawn him up"—the same verb that is used for drawing water out of a well. Coupled with that thought is the other, how greatly his enemies would have gloated over his mishap had the pestilence raged longer and claimed many lives, perhaps even his own.

2. As the writer reflects on his experience, the one thing he seems to recall most vividly is how earnestly he fell back upon prayer in his extremity, and how effective prayer proved on this occasion. The entire experience may be said to be summed up in this one verse.

3. The writer was keenly aware of the enormity of the danger that threatened to engulf him. Since so many were dying in Israel, and since he knew himself to be the chief sinner that had brought on the entire mishap, he felt his doom as good as sealed. Regarding this verse there is considerable debate as to whether David was actually in sickness and at the point of death, or whether the expressions used are more or less figurative. In the light of what we have just said it appears that David could speak as though he were sure to die even if the plague had not yet struck him. Biblical writers were wont to use terms like these when they were close to death; see 9:13; 88:4ff.; cf., also Is. 38:10. "Sheol," which, strictly speaking, refers merely to the afterlife, is here practically the same as "death." The "pit" is merely another synonym for the same idea. David felt that he was as good as in the realm of the dead, practically at the point of those who are laid into the grave. Then God stayed the hand of the avenging angel (II Sam. 24:16) and thereby "brought up [his] soul from Sheol." Thus the resolve to praise and the occasions for praise are given in brief form.

b) **A summons to godly men to join in this praise (vv. 4, 5)**

One need not be so pedantic as to demand that this involves that in the midst of his thanksgiving David turned about and addressed godly worshipers in the Temple who stood behind him. That may add color to an interpretation but is not sufficiently warranted by the evidence.

4. *O sing unto the Lord, O you His saints,*
   And give praise to His holy memorial name.
5. *For a man stays in His wrath but for a moment*
   but in His favor for a lifetime;
   Weeping may lodge in the evening, but joy comes in the morning.

4. It is rather natural to expect others to share one's joy and to summon them to take part in the thanksgiving, cf., 9:11; 22:23. "His saints" are really those who are loyal to the covenant; the term could be translated "His holy ones," which would come closer to the New Testament expression. Giving "praise to His holy memorial name" is

the parallel expression. The original says, "give praise to His holy remembrance." The passages Exod. 3:15; Ps. 97:12; 122:4 show that this means the name of God. *RSV*, in fact, translates the expression thus, interpreting rather than translating. We feel that our rendering of it catches both elements. His "name" connotes the remembrance of all His mighty works.

5. Referring again in thought to the deliverance just experienced, the holy writer describes it with rare insight. For one outstanding element of this experience of his was the fact that help came so swiftly. From this he generalizes correctly that, in the last analysis, God's help always comes swiftly: "a man stays in His wrath but for a moment." On the other hand, equally true and very far-reaching is the observation that a man stays "in His favor for a lifetime." So the statement must be translated. By their very position "a moment" and "a lifetime" are in strict parallelism with one another. It is best to supply an indefinite subject, "a man," for these two clauses. The *RSV* rendering "for His anger is," etc., ignores the preposition before the word "anger."

One is very reluctant to abandon the classic translation of *AV* of the rest of the verse, for it has caught the emphasis of the verse remarkably well. We have departed from it merely to show that there is a slight touch of the original which was thereby lost. For the Hebrew does not say "may endure" but rather "lodges" or "may lodge," the thought being: In comes weeping as a guest for the night; by the time morning has come, it becomes apparent that weeping has disappeared, and joy has come in its place. Analogous are the passages Exod. 34:6f.; Ps. 103:8ff.; Is. 54:7f.; Mic. 7:18; John 16:20.

c) **A fuller account of the deliverance referred to in v. 1–3 (vv. 6–10)**

It is a common procedure on the part of writers to refer first in brief to a given situation, then to expand the issue involved at greater length, especially if significant and instructive features are involved.

6. *But as for me, I said in my security:*
   I shall never be moved.
7. *O Lord, according to Thy good pleasure Thou didst make my*
      mountain to stand strong;
   Thou didst hide Thy face, I became dismayed.
8. *To Thee, O Lord, I cried;*
   And unto the Lord I made supplication.
9. *What profit is there in my blood if I go down to the pit?*
   Will the dust praise Thee? Will it tell of Thy faithfulness?
10. *Hear, O Lord, and have mercy upon me;*
    O Lord, be Thou my helper.

Psalm 30

6. Whereas the historical accounts of the event recorded in II Sam. and I Chron. leave us in the dark as to the thoughts that prompted David to order a census, v. 6 instructs us in his own statement of the case as to what motivated the undertaking—a sense of pride or carnal security: "I said in my security, I shall never be moved." At whatever point in David's life the census was taken, it was after he had enjoyed a period of prosperity. Uninterrupted success had bred a spirit of "security." He felt: things will now continue as they are. The census was an expression of this feeling. Prov. 1:32; Deut. 8:10ff.; 32:15; Dan. 4: 27ff. offer good parallels.

7. The truth of the matter, which he had at the moment overlooked, was that the Lord according to His "good pleasure" had made his "kingdom" (here described as "mountain") to "stand strong." That fact David failed to consider at the time. His prosperity was all undeserved favor from God. David apparently ascribed it to his capable government. Then God turned away: "Thou didst hide Thy face." Immediately the psalmist experienced how frail and weak he was: "I became dismayed." This was the situation out of which the Lord drew him, v. 1. The Lord must needs resort to corrective measures in the treatment of His saints; and when He does, they soon sense what He is seeking to teach them.

8. Feeling his utter helplessness in the situation that developed—for who can stay a pestilence?—he cried unto the Lord as his only hope, and unto the Lord of all (*'adhonay*) he "made supplication."

9. In the next two verses David is very likely quoting what he said to the Lord. Suppose David does die during the pestilence (figuratively: his "blood" is spilt); suppose he does go down into the grave ("pit" means practically that); what would be gained? By a startling line of argumentation the writer points out that there would then be no further opportunity to sing the praises of the Almighty, and so God would be the loser. All this is spoken with due reverence and utter sincerity, and it must flow out of the conviction that the praises of God's saints are precious to Him. The following are parallels: Ps. 6:5; 88:10ff.; 115:17, and Hezekiah's prayer in Is. 38:18f. Only on this level of enlightenment could men of the Old Testament pray thus when the truth concerning the resurrection of the body was not yet fully revealed or grasped, and the glorious life in the hereafter was not sufficiently understood.

10. How thoroughly the writer abandoned all confidence in himself and how earnestly he cast himself upon the Lord's mercy appear from the earnest petitions that he here utters. One feels that at this point God's chastisements had fully achieved their purpose, and the man was shaken out of his unwholesome "security."

d) A suitable conclusion, which both summarizes the whole experience and is praise in itself (vv. 11-12)

11. Thou hast turned my mourning into dancing for me;
Thou hast put off my sackcloth and hast girded me with joy
12. In order that my soul may sing unto Thee and not be silent,
O Lord, I will praise Thee forever.

11. So complete and total is the deliverance that from the depth of "mourning" when one beats his breast in despair he is of a mind to engage in "dancing," when one whirls about for the very ecstacy of joy (*Reigentanz*). A further point of literal correspondence with the narrative of the case is found in the fact that I Chron. 21:16 reports that David and the elders actually wore "sackcloth" at the time when they saw the angel of the Lord hovering over the city. So, though the expression could have been used figuratively, as a symbol of penitence and grief, it is here a reminiscence of an actual occurrence. The Hebrew says: "Thou hast loosed my sackcloth," indicating that God is the one who loosens the belt that holds the garments together, removes them, and substitutes "joy," as it were, for them. Who can estimate the relief that came to David when the angel's sword was stayed!

12. All this, according to David's statement of the case, had the purpose that the author might find opportunity to "sing unto" the Lord "and not be silent." God's deliverances are designed to be occasions for abundant thanksgiving. Moreover, it is the writer's earnest intent to let the praise for this deliverance ring on "forever." The mercy bestowed was great; the praise should keep pace with its magnitude. So the psalm closes, as it began, with the voice of praise and thanksgiving.

NOTES

1. The two terms used in the heading to describe this poem are *mizmor*—the term that has become the technical designation of psalms —and *shir*—a word that signifies that the piece is designed to be sung. The fact that an appositional statement is inserted between the words that usually appear together (psalm of David) is not an indication of a late time of composition. David himself could have placed the words thus. Assumptions to the contrary are subjective and unwarranted.

3. "So that I was not among those that go down to the pit" in the Hebrew consists of only two words, *miyyoredhey-bor*, literally, "away from those going down," etc. This is a concise way in the Hebrew of expressing a negative result clause. Nor is there any need of the other reading (the infinitive) that the *keri* offers.

12. The Hebrew reads: "In order that *my* glory [so the Greek] may sing." There are quite a few passages in which "glory" is used as an

equivalent for "soul," the soul being, as it were, the more glorious part of man, see Ps. 7:6; 16:9; 57:9. Consequently this rendering is most appropriate here. To trace the term back to the root "liver" and thus arrive at the meaning "soul" is far-fetched.

Psalm 31

A STRONG PLEA FOR HELP BY A MAN SORELY BESET

VILMAR very properly calls this "a magnificent psalm of confidence" -*ein grossartiger Vertrauenspsalm*. It seems difficult to cast it into the mold of a piece in which the nation speaks rather than the individual. It savors too much of a purely personal experience though it could, no doubt, be adapted by the congregation to its use if so desired. In hymnals it appears in the form given it by Adam Reusner -*In dich hab ich gehoffet, Herr*. *Kittel* artificially makes it "a liturgy of prayer" (*Gebetsliturgie*). This is part of the trend that continually tries to press psalms into the liturgical pattern. Quite unacceptable is the division of the psalm into two parts, regarded separately, as though they had no connection with one another, without even justifying the separation (*Schmidt, Leslie*). *Oesterley* believes such an approach "to be unnecessary."

It will be worth our while to determine the exact situation of the psalmist according to his own statements, for the case is often overstated. He claims that a net has been laid for him by his enemies (no doubt, a figurative expression) in v. 4; he is in affliction and distress of soul as a result of the experiences that have befallen him (v. 7); over against him is an enemy who stands out as such (v. 8); his physical condition is miserable: eyes fail, the whole body is sick, life seems to be concluded, and his years cut short, his strength fails, his bones are wasted away (vv. 9, 10); he does not indicate whether this physical condition is the result of the rest of his distress, or whether it is its cause; he is scorned and avoided by friends and neighbors (v. 11); he is brushed aside so that he feels he has already completely passed out of mind like a dead man (v. 12); plottings against him abound (vv. 13–20); he was at one time reduced to a kind of panic by the many things that rushed in upon him (v. 22). To draw further conclusions from all this is scarcely warranted, such as that long-drawn out sickness had made him repulsive to his acquaintances, etc. Least of all is there warrant for the conclusion that at the sanctuary he was charged with wrong because his sickness was thought to offer proof of guilt and then confined to prison after some kind of ordeal performed at the Temple. That is fictitious imagination on the part of *Hans Schmidt et al.* But it cannot be denied that a multitude of afflictions have beset the poor man.

The heading ascribes the psalm to David. The facts of the case as just described are in agreement with this heading if they are compared with I Sam. 23, where David is in flight before Saul, delivers Keilah, is about to be betrayed by the inhabitants of the city, and must again betake himself to flight. Note especially that in I Sam. 23:7 David was in a city (cf., Ps. 31:21), and that in v. 9 Saul "was plotting" (cf., v. 20), etc. Since David was not physically ill at the time, the afflictions spoken of are to be thought of as being the distress of mind which seemed to break his physical strength and shorten his days. Such an interpretation is in keeping with the facts of the case.

Note the attitude of the writer over against this mass of afflictions. V. 1 serves as a summary: "In Thee, O Lord, do I take refuge." Note how his chief hope and treasure is the living God: He is his "rock" and "citadel" (vv. 2, 3), and his "refuge" (v. 4); into His hands he has committed his life (v. 5); he puts his trust consciously in God (v. 6b); in at least one instance in this experience the Lord had extricated him from grave danger (v. 8); he puts his trust unreservedly in the Lord (vv. 14, 15); he continues to offer his earnest pleas to his God (vv. 16–20). What more can a man do?

It is true that there is no sharply defined line of thought that runs through the psalm just as the reverse is true that the psalm is not hopelessly confused. The following outline given in connection with the text will show the nature of the psalmist's thought.

a) **Plea for help reinforced by a statement of the psalmist's attitude (vv. 1–8.)**

By this we mean that, after the psalmist has uttered his pleas for help, he indicates that he may rightly expect help, and that God has good reasons for giving it because he has taken refuge in Him. In other words, God cannot fail the man who casts himself upon His mercy.

To the Choir Director. A Psalm of David.

(On "choir director" see Ps. 4.)

1. *In Thee, O Lord, do I take refuge;*
   Let me never be ashamed;
   In Thy righteousness deliver me.

2. *Incline Thy ear to me, deliver me speedily;*
   Be Thou a rock of refuge for me, a citadel to save me.
3. *For Thou art my rock and my citadel;*
   And for Thy name's sake Thou wilt lead me and guide me.
4. *Pull me out of the net which they have laid for me,*
   For Thou art my refuge.
5. *Into Thy hand I commit my spirit;*
   Thou hast redeemed me, O Lord, Thou faithful God.
6. *I hate those that pay regard to vain idols;*
   But I myself put my trust in God.
7. *I will rejoice and be glad over Thy steadfast love,*
   For Thou hast seen my affliction and hast noted the distress of my soul,
8. *And hast not delivered me into the hand of the enemy;*
   Thou hast set my feet where there is ample room.

1–4. Adding a few brief comments to what has been said above, we again note that v. 1, as so often, is in the nature of a theme-sentence for the psalm. When the Hebrew says: "Let me not be put to shame forever," that is obviously, according to our idiom, "never." "Citadel" (v. 2) is literally "a house of places of refuge," which refers to any place where abundant safety of refuge is available. These opening verses are almost identical with Ps. 71:1–3.

V. 5 has been made sacred by the Savior's use of it (Luke 23:46), where at least the first half of the verse is quoted. It appears that those interpreters are correct who claim that in this case "spirit" is the equivalent of "life" (*Lebensodem*). Why should a distinction be made between the two constituent parts of man, and only one be entrusted to God's care? That is neo-Platonic undervaluation of the body. The second half of the verse, though, perhaps, spoken while David's trouble still lay heavy upon him, may well reflect the strong confidence that returns when faith is on the upsurge as happens so often during prayer. "Thou hast redeemed me" is the perfect of confidence. It does not seem as though this cry is made for help from "impending" trouble (*Taylor*).

6. Whereas older versions give somewhat different renderings such as "lying vanities," (*KJ*), literally, "the vanities of emptiness," it is well known that the first word is often used with reference to the heathen idols, see Deut. 32:21; I Kings 16:13; II Kings 17:15; Jer. 2:5; 8:19; 10:3, 15, etc. So we have translated "vain idols." Many interpreters render the first words of the verse, "Thou Lord hatest," a translation which is possible if the final letter is regarded as an abbreviation of *Yahweh,* which it often is. The second member of the verse is then in

the sharp contrast with the first, which the initial "and I" demands. But that contrast is still there over against the latter part of the first half of the verse if it is translated as we have rendered it above.

b) The psalmist's pitiful situation (vv. 9–13)

When the psalmist describes the misery in which he finds himself he does so because he rightly believes that the Lord is much interested in the well-being of His children. A statement of their wretchedness will touch His heart. There may be something naive about this—the assumption that the Lord does not know what the situation is unless we tell Him. But if one carries that approach through logically, a person would never present a petition to God: why tell Him; He knows? Here the trusting confidence of the child of God speaks out of the necessity that is upon men to get relief of their distress by uttering it.

9. *Be gracious unto me, O Lord, for I am in trouble;*
   My eyesight fails because of grief, my soul and my body also.
10. *For my life is finished because of sorrow, and my years because of sighing;*
    My strength fails because of my iniquity, and my bones have wasted away.
11. *I have become an object of reproach to all my enemies and to my neighbors exceedingly*
    And an object of fear to my acquaintances;
    They that see me on the street have run away from me.
12. *I am forgotten like a dead man out of mind;*
    I have become like a broken vessel.
13. *For I have heard the whisperings of many—terror on every side;*
    As they take counsel together against me, they plot to take my life.

9, 10. Allowing a bit for exuberance of grief when a man is in great distress, vv. 9 and 10 describe the case of a man whose troubles have begun to weigh too heavily on his mind. He must unburden himself. A part of his distress is caused by the fact that he knows that his conduct has not been blameless. He asserts that his "strength fails because of [his] iniquity." Many interpreters alter that concept by changing the word '*awoni* to '*oni*, "misery" instead of "iniquity." They follow the lead of the *Greek* version, which, however, is noted for trying to remove difficulties rather than for faithful rendering. There is no good reason for this alteration.

11. The Hebrew says: "I have become a reproach" whereas we should say: "I have become an object of reproach" and "an object of fear."

Psalm 31

12. The rendering "a lost article" (*J. M. P. Smith*) for "a broken vessel," though possible as a meaning of *keli,* loses some of the richer color of the more familiar rendering.

13. The expression "terror on every side" seeks to give a kind of apposition to "whisperings of many" or better, the content of these whisperings. The writer has the feeling that in every instance where he observes men putting their heads together and whispering, a new plot of evil is afoot against him, a new cause of terror, for, as the second half of the verse says, "They plot to take my life," an attitude on the part of the people of Keilah that is amply supported by I Sam. 23:12. Jeremiah spoke similar words, 20:7–10.

c) **The psalmist's trust urges him to further cries for help (vv. 14–18)**

14. *But as for me, in Thee have I trusted, O Lord;*
    I have always said, "Thou art my God."
15. *My times are in Thy hands;*
    Deliver me from the hand of my enemies and persecutors.
16. *Make Thy face to shine upon Thy servant;*
    Save me for Thy mercy's sake.
17. *Let me not be put to shame, O Lord, for I have called upon Thee;*
    Let the wicked be put to shame and utterly silenced in Sheol.
18. *Let the lying lips be dumb,*
    That speak insolently against the righteous in pride and contempt.

From the plots and calumnies of men the psalmist consciously seeks his refuge in God, the initial "and I" being strongly adversative: no matter what my enemies do against me, *I* trust in my God. This section contains the immensely comforting 15th verse: "My times are in Thy hands," meaning, of course, whatever happens in the course of my life is under the providential care of my God. In a statement that is reminiscent of the blessing of Aaron (Numb. 6:25) the writer prays for the sunshine of God's beneficent blessing (v. 16) and also appeals to the divine "mercy," the well-known covenant love of God.

The last two verses of the section offer what is commonly described as an imprecation or curse upon the enemies of the author. To pray for the overthrow or the just punishment of the wicked is not wicked. It is generally a vigorous desire that the iniquity of evil men might be brought to an end. A number of arguments could be offered to show that these Old Testament saints would have far preferred to see the conversion of these their enemies (cf. the close of Ps. 2); but since, in most cases, this was out of the question, they prayed earnestly that God would put an end to their ungodly career and so to the harm that they sought to bring upon the godly. Certainly v. 18 can be regarded as a perfectly harmless prayer, yea, even as a desirable one.

d) **Praise of the goodness of God toward those that fear Him (vv. 19–22)**

Seldom do the psalmists become so immersed in their own difficulties as to compose psalms that are only petition and complaint. Prayer lifts the burden off the soul and gives broader perspectives so that in the midst of trouble the ability to praise God and bless His name is often recaptured. That is the case in this section of the psalm.

19. *How great is Thy goodness which Thou hast laid up in store for them that fear Thee,*
    Hast wrought for them that trust Thee openly before men!
20. *Thou dost hide them in the safety that Thy presence affords from the plottings of men;*
    Thou dost hide them in a shelter from the strife of tongues.
21. *Blessed be the Lord,*
    For He has displayed a marvelous steadfast love toward me in a fortified city.
22. *But as for me, I said in my consternation: I am cut off from before Thy eyes!*
    Surely Thou wilt hear the voice of my pleas when I cry unto Thee for help.

19. A beautiful picture is unfolded in this verse: God accumulates treasures, His goodness, which He lays up in store for His children against the time when they need it. He has prepared it or "wrought" it for those whose adherence to His cause is vouched for by the sincerity with which they openly confess Him as their God in the sight of all men. They are not secret followers. Open confession is the test of sincerity.

20. What is familiarly known as "the secret of His presence" is "the safety which His presence affords." Near Him all are safe. He is fondly thought of as a haven, a special "shelter" (Hebrew "booth") in which He hides men from "the strife of tongues." The wounds that sharp words inflict are among the most painful experiences of men.

22. A plaintive note, more by way of reminiscence, is now sounded. The writer had been at the point where panic had come upon him. He had felt for a moment that he might somehow have been cut off from contact with God. He had actually in "consternation" voiced this thought. Now, though he is not yet delivered, he has again won the assurance that the "voice of his pleas" will not go unheard. That hope is enough for him.

e) A closing exhortation to all of God's saints to trust in Him (vv. 23, 24)

Hengstenberg describes the content of these verses as being "the instruction that should grow out of this experience for the congregation." It could also be said that this is the practical application to be made by others. It amounts to this: Don't ever lose faith in Him.

23. *O love the Lord, all ye His saints!*
    The Lord keeps faith;
    And He abundantly repays him who acts proudly.
24. *Be strong and let your heart be of good courage,*
    All you who wait for the Lord.

23. More is involved than merely the exhortation not to lose faith in Him. Faith will not be lost if love keeps burning. Though most of the versions render the next line as does *KJ*: "The Lord preserveth the faithful," yet the plural word which is translated "faithful" can well be an intensive plural for an abstract noun, and the statement can, therefore, be rendered even more appropriately: "The Lord keeps faith." All the more reason for loving Him. But it dare not be overlooked that "He abundantly repays him who acts proudly."

24. To doubt is unwholesome weakness. In a statement that calls to mind God's exhortations to Joshua and Israel in the days of the occupation of the land (Josh. 1:6, 7) the writer encourages God's saints to cultivate firmness and courage. But the last expression ("all you who wait for the Lord") also indicates that God's help is seldom immediately forthcoming. Strength consists in being able to wait till the time comes when it pleases God to send His help.

Psalm 32

THE BLESSEDNESS OF FORGIVENESS

THIS IS THE SECOND of the psalms customarily known as penitential psalms, having, as *Vilmar* particularly emphasizes, a character all its own as the heading given above sufficiently indicates. With equal propriety it may be designated as a doctrinal psalm (*Veit Dietrich: ein ausbuendiger Lehrpsalm*), not, of course, in that obnoxious sense which makes all doctrine cold and lifeless, but in that good Biblical sense, that regards doctrine as vital, dynamic, saving truth.

The vibrant note of a living faith can scarcely be missed by even a casual reading of the psalm. *Weiser* does not exaggerate when he says that it was written with the very blood of its author. Deep, searching, personal experience lies at the root of this confession. To this day many find it a most illuminating guidance on the way of peace with God.

The newer criticisms that are made of its contents are scarcely warranted. *Kittel* thinks it savors too much of a rigid adherence to the doctrine of inevitable retribution, according to which already on this earth, the righteous are regularly rewarded for their good works and the wicked are regularly punished for their iniquity. Of course, as a general principle that rule of retribution stands if Exod. 20:5, 6 still stands as it indubitably does though all men recognize that such laws do not operate with unyielding rigidity, nor must their operation always be clearly in evidence during the course of this earthly life.

Altogether unwarranted conclusions are drawn from the text when it is claimed on the basis of vv. 6 and 10 that forgiveness is made available only to the righteous. The truth of the matter is that such brief psalms cannot exhaust every aspect of a given doctrine or situation; and here the righteous are exhorted as the ones who will be most likely to hear without even a thought that a poor sinner would be excluded if he presumed to come with a plea for pardon. The universality of the first two verses cover this aspect of the case sufficiently to answer adverse criticism. Men should rejoice over this gem of psalmody rather pick trivial and inconsequential flaws.

The claim advanced in the heading that this psalm is "of David" may not be brushed aside lightly. Against the background of II Sam. 12, everything stated here fits excellently into its place: a grievous, conscience-burdening sin; a state of impenitence when it was thought that the deed could be ignored; the obvious uneasiness of conscience though the record passes this by as being only too obvious; the day when the frank confession was elicited; the unequivocal confession; the total absolution. And who would be better qualified than David himself to write the record of it all for the abiding instruction of generations to come?

To go on the assumption that religious experience was not so deep and thorough at that time is to fly in the face of a plain historical record. Or to approach the matter from the angle of form criticism, claiming that the blend of these various literary types—"blessing, the lamenting narrative of experience, admonition, address, general observation of the law of retribution, and hymn" (*Leslie*)—was hardly possible before 500 B.C., is to lay down canons of criticism that have certainly not been proved and to ignore the richness of literary forms that appear in the

Psalm 32

psalms of David times without number. It is also quite arbitrary to claim that at a time such as that of David wisdom literature could not yet have been developed (aimed at vv. 8–11).

By this approach we have also indicated that the psalm must be regarded as personal in character and not one that features the "collective I."

The view which would make almost every one of the psalms liturgical in character must yet be briefly considered. There is an obvious injection of preconceived ideas when it is claimed that in this psalm the saint who offers a sacrifice in the Temple must present his confession as a vital part of the service. Sick unto death as he is (this feature is freely injected), the worshiper drags himself to the Temple and confesses that the hand of the Lord was laid heavily on him. The "songs of deliverance" of the assembled multitude burst forth on every side. The attendant priest, a venerable old man, absolves and admonishes the worshiper (*Hans Schmidt*). Such an interpretation obviously seeks to make the whole action of the psalm liturgical in character whether the evidence warrants this or not.

The heading calls this a *maskil*, i.e., a didactic psalm.

We offer the following outline of the contents of the psalm:
a) The theme: the blessedness of forgiveness (vv. 1, 2).
b) The wretchedness of impenitence, recorded as a personal experience (vv. 3, 4).
c) A summary statement of the entire experience (v. 5)
d) An exhortation to the godly to avail themselves of this privilege (vv. 6, 7).
e) A divine exhortation not to continue in impenitence (vv. 8–9)
f) An exhortation to all who have shared in this experience to rejoice over it (vv. 10, 11)

It is at once evident from this outline how well integrated the line of thought is that runs through the psalm. Few of the critical writers (except *Buttenwieser*) have attempted any rearrangement of the verses.

> *Of David. A Maskil.*
> 1. O how happy is he whose transgression is forgiven,
>   Whose sin is covered!
> 2. O how happy is the person to whom the Lord does not impute iniquity,
>   And in whose spirit there is no insincerity!
> 3. When I tried to cover it up with silence, my very bones wasted away
>   Through my grieving all the day long.
> 4. For day and night Thy hand was heavy upon me;

My marrow was turned into the drought of summer.
5. *My sin did I confess to Thee; and my iniquity did I not cover up;*
   I said, I will confess my transgression unto the Lord;
   And Thou forgavest the iniquity of my sin. Selah.

1. The psalm opens on a jubilant note. How utterly wretched the impenitent king, who had previously basked in the sunshine of God's grace, must have been that he expresses his relief in such almost exultant tones! One hesitates to abandon the classical rendering of the first word, "blessed." But to try to catch a bit of the force of the original which uses a plural construct, we have rendered, "O how happy!" The wrong done is variously designated as "transgression" (Hebrew: rebellion); "sin" (missing the mark); and "iniquity" (guilt). All this means as much as: no matter what form of sin you are caught in, the pardon of it is a blessed experience. Quite obviously this does not mean that God simply ignores sins of certain individuals when He is so minded. But it does say that, when a man is truly penitent—that is the point of the whole experience of David—God grants him an official verdict of pardon. This is a forensic act, a judgment from the throne of heaven. The man is still a sinner, but God consents to liberate him.

The verbs used ("forgiven, covered, not imputed") demonstrate the effectiveness of this forensic act on God's part. It should also be noted that this is a statement of universal applicability, for v. 2 says "the person" (Hebrew, "man"), that is to say, any man who will avail himself of the mercy of God.

2. The closing statement of v. 2, "and in whose spirit there is no insincerity," indicates an essential prerequisite of forgiveness. This is inserted first of all over against all who, like himself, the singer, seek to cover up or ignore their sin. Such individuals are wanting in sincerity. It is then directed against all others who suppose that forgiveness is easily obtained and thus regard God's pardon lightly. A formal admission of guilt, and all's well—so they think. They are lacking in sincerity, and for them there is no forgiveness.

Interpreted thus in its context, the statement is very pertinent to the psalm as a whole. Quite out of line with the obvious intention of the words is the view that regards this as an indication that the psalm teaches that forgiveness is for good people, sincere souls who have done no wrong. Construed thus, the words insert a confusing note into the picture. Forgiveness was first portrayed as being free and unmerited; it is now characterized as being held in reserve only for deserving persons. No misunderstanding could be more fatal.

3. Having plunged into the very heart of the matter in the opening statement, the writer now goes back to give the case history that led to

this glad and exultant claim. Without going into any details regarding the sin committed—the whole nation knew only too well what had been involved—he indicates that there had been a season of impenitence. Man is naturally reluctant to admit sin, especially in situations like those of David, who had enjoyed a reputation for unsullied character in the eyes of the whole nation so many years. One effect of his unnautral silence was, figuratively speaking, that his "very bones wasted away." It seemed as though a withering away of his strength took place that penetrated into the core of his being. Besides, his wretchedness weighed so heavily upon him that he could not but give expression to it in frequent groans, whether they were audible to others or repressed within his own heart.

4. Now that release has come, he recognizes clearly what at that time he sought to hide from himself, that God's hand was all the while pressing him down, a figure of speech used to describe whatever wretchedness he felt at the time. His total being seemed to wither away under God's displeasure. This seems to be the force of the statement, "My marrow was turned into the drought of summer."

5. Now comes the all-important key statement, made in one verse and of greater length than the rest to convey a sense of its importance. Again the writer does not go into detail as to how he was brought to the point where he was ready to make a confession. By this time the nation knew the story only too well. Therefore the simple statement, "My sin did I confess to Thee," which is followed by the parallel that reminds the readers regarding what it was that had delayed the confession, "my iniquity did I not cover up." A third statement follows, which is designed to show particularly how the forgiveness followed hard on the heels of the confession. It might, in fact, almost be paraphrased: As soon as I said, I will confess, Thou forgavest. It was as simple as that. The writer is still filled with wonder. He had not believed that sincere penitence and confession would meet with such a direct response from God.

We cannot but point out how thoroughly this statement of the case agrees with the doctrine of salvation by free grace. Certainly, no merit of the writer entered into the case. That is why Paul could use this passage so effectively in Rom. 4:7f. in corroboration of the doctrine of free grace as he was wont to present it. How marvelously all this is summarized in the New Testament, I John 1:8f., but also in the form of a striking proverb in Prov. 28:13!

6. *Therefore let every godly man pray to Thee at a time of finding;*
Only in the flood of great waters they shall not reach him.
7. *Thou art a hiding place for me;*

*From trouble Thou wilt deliver me;
With jubilant songs of deliverance Thou wilt surround me.*

6. There follows an exhortation that is based on the experience which David has had. He recognizes that to a certain extent God let all this befall him in this form that he might share his better insight with others. In effect, he teaches them not to repeat his mistake. Since, generally speaking, "godly men" are the only ones who in the nature of the case will give heed to this exhortation, he addresses all such not to delay when they have been overtaken by sin but speedily to pray for forgiveness. For there is the further consideration that God will not extend the period of grace indefinitely. As Is. 55:6 also shows, there is a time "when the Lord may be found," implying that there is also a "too late." When pardon has been granted—this is added as a further motivation—it will not be necessary for the Lord to use corrective measures, that is, great tribulation (here typified by the "flood of great waters") in order to make a man aware of the fact that he has incurred divine displeasure. For "waters" used thus see Ps. 18:16; 69:1, 2; 144:7.

7. What a confident attitude a man may assume when he is sure of the pardon of God that is reflected in this verse! To him God is a "hiding place." He knows God as the One that delivers "from trouble." For trouble is usually a corrective agent employed by the Lord regarding the erring and evildoers. In fact, so great is the goodness of the Lord toward those who take refuge in Him also from their sins, that they may well say: "With jubilant songs of deliverance Thou wilt surround me."

8. *I shall instruct you and teach you the way which you shall go;
   I will counsel you with my eye upon you.*
9. *Be not like a horse or a mule without insight,
   Whose mouth must be filled with bit and bridle,
   Else one cannot approach them.*
10. *Many are the sorrows of the wicked;
    But he that trusts in the Lord, steadfast love shall surround him.*
11. *Be glad in the Lord and rejoice, O righteous,
    And exult, all you who are upright in heart.*

8. The exhortation contained in the next two verses may be regarded as coming from the mouth of the psalmist. But as one reads on, it becomes apparent that there is some measure of incongruity about having a teacher say to his pupil or any listener, "I will counsel you with my eye upon you." Therefore it is better to regard these two verses as offering *divine* admonition. This involves the thought that what the

Psalm 32

writer lays upon the lips of the Almighty is the admonition that *God would have men take to heart* in the light of David's experience. The import of the exhortation is much the same as that of the two preceding verses, with this added thought: It is God's counsel to you, O man, to walk the road of prompt repentance when you have sinned. The idea of being counselled with God's "eye upon you" is best thought of in the light of Luke 22:61, where the Lord looked upon Peter. Besides, this statement involves the idea of gracious, kindly watching over the soul's welfare of one who is in danger of straying.

9. Refusal to let oneself be guided by the Lord's kindly direction puts one in the class of the brute beasts that must at times be controlled by forcible and harsh means when they refuse gentle guidance, a thought found elsewhere in Sacred Writ, cf., Jer. 10:4; Ps. 49, 10, 12, 20; 73:22.

10. As the psalm began on the note of high joy, so it closes with an exhortation to be joyful because of the experience of forgiveness each time it is granted, such exhortation being well in line with the didactic character of the psalm (cf. also the superscription "a Maskil," i.e., a didactic poem). Carrying over the thought of the preceding verse, v. 10 thinks of those as the wicked who have many sorrows, who refuse to be led into the blessed experience of forgiveness. God will indeed, as a general rule, be obliged to resort to disciplinary means to bring such to their senses. By their own impenitence and hardness of heart (Rom. 2:5) they store up wrath for themselves. But the other group referred to are obviously those who follow the course this psalm so strongly advocates, for that is what the statement "he that trusts in the Lord" means in this connection.

11. This last verse quite obviously stays within the limits of what has been under discussion throughout the poem. The "righteous" are men whose sins are forgiven. They gave evidence of true sincerity by their free and frank confession ("all you who are upright"). They have every reason to "be glad" and "rejoice" and to "exult."

So David instructed Israel and summarized his own experience for his guidance after his deep fall into sin. We agree wholeheartedly with those interpreters, like *Hengstenberg,* who hold that, whereas Ps. 51 may well have been written under the impact of the forgiveness that was bestowed upon David soon after the event, our psalm gives the impression of being the fruit of longer reflection, in the course of which the more general statement of the issues involved is developed. This psalm could, therefore, be regarded as the fulfilment of the vow contained in Ps. 51:13: "Then will I teach transgressors Thy ways, and sinners shall be converted unto Thee."

NOTES

4. The verb *tikhbadh* is an imperfect as part of the narrative which expresses that the thing narrated was of some duration; and so *KS* calls it an imperfect *durans* (*"yaqtul durans"*) 157b. The word *lashadh*, which we have translated "marrow" (according to *Buhl*) actually means "fat" or "cakes baked in fat." So it could be translated, "My fat is turned." That is about what *KJ* intends with its "my moisture." Since neither of the two are quite our idiom, we have preferred Buhl's rendering. There is no call for any revisions of the text, all of which are quite problematical. The word could also have been rendered "life sap."

5. For "confess my transgressions" the Hebrew has "confess with reference to (*'al*) my transgressions," the object being expressed by the use of a preposition (*KS* 327 g).

6. The initial phrase (*'al zo'th*), rendered by *KJ* "for this," is stated better by the expression "therefore," introducing a conclusion drawn from the preceding verses.

The word "only" that introduces the second member is to be joined to the phrase "to him." But the English word order seems to make this virtually impossible. The German seems to be able to do this effectively: *Beim Heranfluten grosser Wasser werden sie nur zu ihm nicht hinanreichen* (Koenig). That means that the penitent soul is the only one who will not be reached by the floods of adversity.

8. "With my eye upon thee" is a very much contracted expression in the Hebrew: literally, "I will give counsel, upon thee my eye." This is not quite the same as *AV*, "I will guide thee with my eye."

9. The word rendered "mouth" (*'adhi*) is difficult. It originally means "ornament"; then in Ps. 103:5 perhaps "cheek"; then in this instance by metonymy "mouth," following the lead of the *Septuagint*. The clause "else one cannot approach them" is much condensed in the Hebrew: "no approaching for thee." It is better to construe this as we have translated it rather than as *KJ* renders: "lest they come near unto thee." *RSV* is vague.

One matter must yet be disposed of. *Taylor* remarks: "The psalm does not reach the higher spiritual levels of the Psalter since it reflects the common opinion held throughout the ancient Near East with reference to the relation of all sickness to sin." First of all, the sickness involved is less physical than mental. In the second place, there is a great measure of truth in the view that there is often a relation between sickness and sin. The writer of the psalm does not give evidence of a rigid doctrine on this subject and, therefore, should not be faulted. Lastly, since this psalm deals with justification, and since its opening verses are quoted with such strong approval by St. Paul (Rom. 4:7, 8), it would be much better to regard this psalm as moving on the highest levels of spiritual discernment, especially by all those who love and appreciate the heritage of the Protestant Reformation.

Psalm 33

A PSALM OF PRAISE FOR THE PEOPLE OF GOD

To ARRIVE at a proper approach to the psalm it must be noted that it lays down a basic principle that is always to be borne in mind by God's people, namely, that God's people are always to put their trust in Him, not in arms, resources, generals, equipment, national defenses, and the like. Though this is instruction, the psalm is not primarily didactic. It moves on the higher plane of praise of the Lord, who is all that Israel needs for her strength and security.

Efforts to determine the occasion that gave rise to the psalm are fruitless. In fact, we may take the position that the sacred writers often intentionally ignored the distinctive historical occasion that led them to a given line of thought, knowing that the truth set forth was more important than the historical occasion that gave rise to it. Some find a possibility for determining the occasion in the defeat of the Assyrians under Sennacherib in the days of Hezekiah, a reasonable possibility. Others date it in the Maccabean period, scarcely a likely date. It is still possible with a good show of reason to attribute the psalm to David though its anonymity is quite obvious. In case it was composed in the time of David, the historical occasion would, perhaps, be the obvious antithesis between the spirit it seeks to inculcate and the general attitude that Saul developed in the later years of his rule.

The points of contact with Ps. 32 are mostly on the surface, such as the almost accidental fact that Ps. 32 ends on the note on which our psalm begins; or the fact that both inculcate trust in the Lord (cf. 32: 10 with 33:21) and similar points.

It is interesting to note the more recent turn in the approach to the interpretation of this psalm that was inaugurated largely by *Mowinckel*. It was formerly regarded almost exclusively as a national hymn of praise suggested by some historic occasion, *Briggs* being one of the last notable exponents of this approach. Almost without exception (see

Schmidt, Leslie, Weiser, etc.) it is now worked into the pattern of the New Year's festival of the enthronement of Jahweh, which is supposed to represent "the renewal of creation." The singing of the song is supposed to be "the congregation's cooperation with the energies of God." There is a strange insistence that this obscure Babylonian festival must needs have a counterpart in Israel's life and worship in spite of the fact that it is never mentioned by name in all the Scriptures, and no indubitable instance of its use and observance has yet been discovered. Such unscientific exegesis must be rejected.

The psalm may be outlined as follows:
a) Introduction: a summons to praise the Lord (vv. 1–3).
b) A special reason for praise—what God is, and what He has done, understood in the broadest sense (vv. 4–9).
c) More particularly that He makes the counsel of the heathen of none effect (vv. 10, 11).
d) A momentary reflection upon Israel's happy lot in having the Lord as God (v. 12).
e) God's sovereign rule and control of all things (vv. 13–17).
f) More particularly of those who fear Him (vv. 18, 19).
g) Conclusion: Therefore we wait on Him to bless us (vv. 20–22).

a) **Introduction: a summons to praise the Lord (vv. 1–3)**

1. *Rejoice in the Lord, O you righteous;*
   Praise befits the upright.
2. *Praise the Lord with the harp;*
   Play to Him on the lute with ten strings.
3. *Sing to Him a new song;*
   Play well on the strings, uttering jubilant shouts.

In this introductory summons to praise the Lord it is quite obvious that six separate calls to engage in this task are presented. This means that God is at all times deserving of our very best praise, when special occasions are to be considered as well as when nothing special has taken place. It is the "righteous" and the "upright," that is to say, God's people as such, who are well qualified for such praise and thus are specially addressed.

Various instruments may be enlisted in the service of such praise to enhance its beauty. In fact, as occasion demands, it may become necessary to compose new songs to fit the new occasions for praise which the Lord affords His people though, to tell the truth, any old hymn becomes new and fresh when it is sung with true devotion. In the third verse the emphasis is more on the "jubilant" character of the praise offered than upon the more external character that it is "loud" (*KJ* and *RSV*).

b) A special reason for praise (vv. 4–9)
4. For the word of the Lord is right,
And all His work is done in faithfulness.
5. He loves righteousness and justice;
The earth is full of the steadfast love of the Lord.
6. By the word of the Lord were the heavens made,
And by the breath of His mouth all their host.
7. He gathered the waters of the sea as in a bottle;
He lays up the deeps in storehouses.
8. Let all the earth fear the Lord;
Let all the inhabitants of the world stand in awe of Him.
9. For He spoke, and it came to pass;
He commanded, and it stood fast.

4. Praise always concentrates on some specific object. Here as the first reason for praise mention is made of what God is, and what He has done, both statements being understood in the very broadest sense. Certain attributes of His are lifted out above others, all of them calculated to move men to praise, attributes such as faithfulness, righteousness, justice, and steadfast love. His faithfulness expresses itself primarily in His "word," which is here thought of in the widest sense —whatever words He is known to have spoken for the good of the children of men, or for the creation of the world, or laid down for man's use in sacred Scriptures. All these are always "right," that is to say, just what they should be and, therefore, normative and dependable. These attributes are also expressed in His "work," where His "faithfulness" appears, if anything, still more tangibly.

5. Since works and attributes of God are under consideration, the "righteousness" and "justice" that He loves are not so much these virtues as practiced by men but as manifested in His own dealings with the children of men. The one quality that particularly stands out, so much so that it may be said to have filled the earth, is His "steadfast love," a term which usually signifies God's covenant faithfulness toward His chosen people.

6. Showing further what a marvelous thing the "word" is that was referred to in v. 4, but also demonstrating the Lord's omnipotence, this verse reminds us that the magnificent "heavens" in all their vastness and splendor were made by nothing more than the mere word or command of God. To catch a further glimpse of what that involves, we are reminded that it required no more than "the breath of His mouth" —in which, without a doubt, God's Holy Spirit was potently at work— to bring into being "all their host," that is to say, all the heavenly bodies

that adorn the skies by day or by night. Devout contemplation of these notable divine attributes cannot leave us cold but must impel us to tell forth the praises of Him, whose these attributes are.

7. The author says, as it were: "Let a few more of His mighty works pass in review before your minds eye. Consider the mighty ocean. God keeps its turbulent waves under control with the ease with which a man pours water into a leathern bottle"—a customary sight in the Orient. The vast resources of water involved are to be thought of as laid up in store by Him in special places of deposit. ("Bottle" -*nodh*- is the reading of practically all the ancient versions, beginning with the *Septuagint;* "heaps" -*nedh*- of grain, though this is the vowel pointing of the Hebrew text, seems less suitable.) Behind all this we may see a contrast with the Babylonian Creation Myth, which has these works done only after a violent struggle between the gods, good and bad, had taken place. Here there is the consummate ease of the Almighty. However, we cannot know whether the average Israelite was acquainted with the Babylonian Creation Myth in those days. It also seems rather doubtful whether the reference to water is reason enough for concluding that the psalm is a prayer for rain in the autumn season.

8. Since the last works mentioned are discernible by all who dwell on the face of the earth, and men can from them recognize something of the power and deity of the Creator (Rom. 1:20), the writer addresses himself to all men, inviting them to give the tokens of praise that are due unto the Lord, which are first of all due "fear" and "awe." Man's littleness and weakness must always lead him to due reverence for the One who is so much greater than himself.

9. The point that should thus influence men is summed up concisely: "He spake, and it came to pass" -*fiat* creation in its superlative form. Nothing that man can attempt will come remotely near to this type of divine activity. The second half of the verse could be translated: "He commanded, and there it stood." Who would not fear such a Lord? The writer has said enough on the subject of the occasion that should move men to praise.

c) He makes the counsel of the heathen of none effect (vv. 10, 11)

10. The Lord brings the counsel of the heathen to nought;
He annuls the devisings of the peoples.
11. The counsel of the Lord stands forever,
The thoughts of His mind to all generations.

10. It is at this point that a historic occasion for the psalm might be detected. Perhaps the Lord had just done some such work of making the schemes of surrounding heathen nations, which had been devised

against Israel, fall to the earth, whether in David's time (cf., II Sam. 8 and 10), or in Hezekiah's, or in any other. By making the statement general the author reduces the statement he makes to a truth that always obtains. To this end he uses the perfect tense, which in the Hebrew is also used to express facts that are universally true (gnomic aorist as it were, *GK,* 106k). His statement could also be translated: "He has always brought the counsel of the heathen to nought." But if He does this, and if it is a great work, that is certainly a valid reason for praising the Lord.

11. In direct contrast to the preceding statement is v. 11, which sets "the counsel" of the Lord over against those that were frustrated, and His "thoughts" over against theirs, indicating that His will stand "to all generations." How often God's people have had occasion to praise the Lord for this manifestation of His steadfast love!

d) Israel's happy lot in having the Lord as God (v. 12)

12. *How happy is the nation whose God is the Lord,*
    The people He has chosen for His own heritage!

This verse is imbedded in the very core of the psalm as a kind of hub about which the whole psalm revolves. The nation of which this can be predicated is, of course, Israel. The whole psalm has been building up to this point in enumerating the reasons for praising God, and from this verse as a vantage point it proceeds to unfold the claim just made more fully. The verse, therefore, has a sort of exultant note. This fact is a perfectly natural and proper point of view and need not be faulted as though it were extreme nationalism without the necessary moral connotation as *Kittel* does in an uncalled-for and unwholesome way. The moral qualifications that accompany such claims as these are implied in terms such as "righteous" and "upright" (v. 1).

e) God's sovereign rule and control of all things (vv. 13–17)

13. *The Lord looks down from heaven;*
    He sees all the children of men.
14. *From the place where He is enthroned He looks forth*
    Upon all the inhabitants of the earth,
15. *He who fashions the hearts of them all,*
    He who observes all their deeds.
16. *There is no king saved by a great army;*
    A mighty soldier is not delivered by great strength.
17. *A horse is a vain thing for safety,*
    And he does not deliver by his great strength.

13. Another area is considered as a special basis for praising the Lord—God's sovereign governance of all things. He controls matters

so well that His children, whose interests are also thereby being safeguarded, ought to be continually praising Him. First he considers the matter of His general providence. From the high vantage point of heaven He can have His eye upon all those that dwell upon the face of the earth. To reinforce that thought the next statement reminds the readers that heaven is the place of His enthronement (v. 14). Though this could be regarded as the place where He dwells, the verb used (*yashabh*) is so frequently employed in connection with the sitting of a king upon his throne that *Luther's* lead in his translation may well be followed (also *RSV*).

15. To the Lord must also be ascribed the work of influencing the thinking of the children of men more than is ordinarily supposed, not in arbitrary ways that would nullify the freedom of man in his decisions, but for both man's good and God's glory. "For He fashions the hearts of them all," which, since the heart is primarily the seat of mental activity, means more by way of directing man's thinking than man is aware of. Num. 16:22; 27:16; Prov. 21:1 give a bit more of the thinking of the Scriptures on this subject. The added thought is that it is "He who observes all their deeds." There is nothing that man does on the earth which could escape God's notice. That alone is so stupendous a thought that no man could grasp the full scope of it. All this is a part of that great divine providence that we extol. "He fashioneth their hearts alike" (*KJ*) does not mean that He makes them all the same, rather that he fashions the one as well as the other, that is to say, all.

16. A more practical turn is now given to the thought involved: human resources are not the important things in settling issues and outcomes. Dependence on them is frequently, if not always, futile in the long run. So for example, the size of the army of a king is no guaranty of victory. The fact that "a mighty soldier" (Hebrew: *gibbor*, a "hero") has great strength is no guaranty of victory to him. Man says it is. Human reason again and again comes to the same conclusion. Yet this is not true. In like manner, if men put confidence in seemingly superior equipment such as cavalry (v. 17) they will find that it is "a vain thing (Hebrew: "a lie") for safety." This then leaves the Lord as the only recourse of the children of men. It is this thought of the psalm that should with special emphasis be recaptured as a very necessary and practical lesson for our unbelieving age.

f) God's sovereign rule of those who fear Him (vv. 18, 19)

18. *Behold, the eye of the Lord is on them that fear Him,*
    On those that hope in His steadfast love.
19. *To deliver their soul from death,*
    To keep them alive in famine.

Psalm 33

The preceding verses were the negative side of man's sure basis of confidence. There follows the positive side. If men know these things and "fear Him" and "hope in His steadfast love," then "the eye of the Lord is upon them," in the sense of ceaselessly watching over them to guard them. When death threatens, that is sudden death and disaster, He delivers them. When others perish in famine, He miraculously sustains His own, even to the point of working miracles as He did in the case of Elijah. The contemplation of such a Lord and His providential care should surely call forth our warmest praise.

g) Conclusion: Therefore we wait on Him to bless us (vv. 20-22)

20. *Our soul waits for the Lord;*
    He is our help and our shield.
21. *For our heart is glad in Him,*
    For in His holy name we trusted.
22. *Let Thy steadfast love be upon us*
    According as we hope in Thee.

20. The psalm has a formal and an appropriate conclusion of three verses even as it has a similar introduction. The conclusion gives expression to an attitude that is precisely the one that the psalm had advocated in the preceding section (vv. 13–19). It may be regarded as a holy resolution: What we have advocated that we ourselves will also do, in fact, that we are doing. First of all, our hearts are, as it were, anchored in faith in Him, for we know that He is "our help and our shield." But such confidence also naturally leads to the joyfulness of faith. The presence of gladness in the heart (v. 21) is regarded as proof of the presence of faith. The second member of the verse, introduced by "for," shows that the trusting in His holy name was the basis for the gladness of heart that resulted.

22. Some interpreters regard this verse as a useless liturgical addition. It is obviously more than that. Rather than close upon the subjective note of asserting that we practice what we preach and so trust in the Lord with glad hearts, the psalm concludes on the more modest note of prayer: We pray that the Lord may manifest His goodness toward us, which is for His people always His "steadfast love." But the measure of favor that we may thus receive is conditioned by the measure of the hope we place in Him.

Since *Kessler,* as nearly as we are able to ascertain, it has become quite customary to regard the presentation of the providence of God as presented in this psalm under three heads: a) the word of God (vv. 6–9); the counsel of God (vv. 10–12); and the eye of God (vv. 13–19). We believe our outline embodies the values that lie in this approach and yet goes somewhat beyond it.

Psalm 34

A HYMN OF PRAISE AND INSTRUCTION

THE HEADING claims that the psalm was written at the time when David was in the land of the Philistines, was staying at the court of the king, and was under suspicion for his pro-Israelite attitude, as recorded in I Sam. 21:10–15. He resorted to the dubious expedient of feigning madness ("changed his behavior" says the Hebrew idiom) in the presence of the king. It is quite obvious that the contents of the psalm neither prove nor disprove this claim. Yet it is scarcely likely that the editors that attached this heading to the psalm will have done so without some good reason. In fact, we need only the following two assumptions: 1) that the psalm was not composed until a reasonable time had elapsed to allow David to produce a well-balanced, objective treatment of the case; and 2) that the vv. 13ff. indicate that the deception practiced was not what helped the author, in fact, such efforts are to be thoroughly discountenanced. We, therefore, have more in this heading than "an interesting example of the character of Jewish exegesis" (*Taylor*).

Besides, it must be stressed that the very questionable course that David followed was certainly not sanctioned by God when He delivered David from his grave danger. Nor does the whole heading belong in the category of the inaccurate because in I Sam. 21 the king is called Achish. As has been amply demonstrated by many commentators, Abimelech was the dynastic name, like Pharaoh among the Egyptians, Achish was the personal name.

A peculiarity that appears only in the original is that the poem is an acrostic, like Ps. 25, with the additional similarity that here as there the letter *waw* is bypassed, and that a supernumerary *pe* is appended. Such an arrangement always entails a certain artificiality of order in the development of the thoughts of the psalm, yet not of so serious a nature as to mar it. It may also be mentioned that there is reason for believing that the original order of the letters ʻ*ayin* and *pe* was the reverse of that which we now have, so that vv. 15 and 16 should be inverted in order to arrive at the original order, as we shall presently indicate. Note, for example, that in Lamentations, chapters 2–4, which are acrostic, the *pe* precedes the ʻ*ayin*.

Psalm 34

Those commentators who stress the liturgical use of the Psalter overmuch think that this psalm was designed for public thanksgiving in the Temple on the part of its author after a signal deliverance from great danger or sickness (*Schmidt*). There is nothing in the psalm that warrants making that its specific purpose. The psalm may indeed be put to such a use but also, with equal propriety, to many other uses.

This very devout poem, marked by deep piety and religious insight, scarcely deserves the reflections of those, who like *Kittel,* find in it a "naïve theory of retribution" and an inadequate concept of the highest good. Devout readers have always found a much deeper religion in it than that. Besides, the desire for a long life as the possible highest good removes one piece of the whole as though it had no broader setting. Furthermore, it will always be true that, generally speaking, those individuals who are true to the Lord do receive His blessings, and those who sin against Him experience evident tokens of His displeasure.

a) **Praise of God for His gracious help, inviting others to share in this experience (vv. 1–10)**

Of David; when he feigned madness before Abimelech so that he drove him away, and he departed.

1. *I will bless the Lord at all times;*
   His praise shall continually be in my mouth.
2. *Of the Lord shall my soul make her boast;*
   The meek shall hear and be glad.
3. *Magnify the Lord with me,*
   And let us together exalt His name.
4. *I sought the Lord, and He answered me*
   And delivered me from all my fears.
5. *Men look to Him and stream toward Him;*
   And their face is not red with shame.
6. *Here is a poor man who cried, and the Lord heard;*
   And He rescued him from all his trouble.
7. *The angel of the Lord encamps round about those that fear Him*
   And delivers them.
8. *Taste and see that the Lord is good.*
   How very happy is the man that takes refuge in Him!
9. *Fear the Lord, you His holy ones;*
   For those who fear Him suffer no want.
10. *Young lions may lack and suffer hunger;*
    But they who seek the Lord shall not lack any good thing.

1. In vv. 1 and 2 the resolve on the part of the writer to praise the Lord at all times is expressed. His kindly deeds may loom up before us in their full magnitude so that we feel that a lifetime of praise is all

that can begin to do justice to them and Him. Or restated, there is no time in life when His praises cannot or should not be on our lips. All such praises will center, not in the mercy bestowed upon us so much as in the Lord Himself, "of the Lord" being placed first for emphasis. Whenever that takes place, "the meek," who have been brought low in their own esteem by life's adversities, take note of what an individual does who truly praises God, and they rejoice with such a one and over him, that he has found his chief business and duty in life.

3. Praise would share its experience with others. Therefore the call: "Magnify the Lord with me." Truly, we cannot make Him great, but our praises can exalt Him. When this is done "together," then praise grows richer and deeper.

4–7. At this point a statement is most aptly in order regarding what it was that gave rise to the psalmist's desire to praise. Stated briefly, it was: "I sought God, and He answered me." That statement might include almost any type of experience. The seeking referred to is the seeking done in prayer. Deliverance was sought, and deliverance was granted. David's vision may have been a bit blurred when he resorted to pretence and deception to gain immunity. Nevertheless, in his inmost heart he was earnestly seeking the Lord. The imperfection of his search God overlooked and helped him "and delivered [him] from all [his] fears." This experience leads the author to generalize. The perfect tense used in v. 5 is the well-known gnomic aorist, which is expressed most simply by the present: "Men look to Him and stream toward Him; and their face is not red with shame." Countless thousands can testify to the correctness of this assertion.

Coming back to himself, the author again summarizes his whole experience. Remembering how desperate his plight, and how weak he himself was, he designates himself, "Here is a poor man who cried." The next step was that "the Lord heard and delivered him from all his trouble." Still another statement of the case (v. 7) is this: "The angel of the Lord encamps round about them that fear Him and delivers them." That great and mighty divine being of days of old, who so often dealt with the patriarchs and figured so prominently in the history of Israel (see Exod. 23:20ff.) but is mentioned only here and 35:5, 6 in the Psalter, He deigned to provide complete protection by merely encamping round about those that fear Him. The writer may well have had Elijah in mind (II Kings 6:14–17). Higher agencies were, no doubt, at work in David's deliverance from grave peril, and we know these to be angelic in character or the very Angel of His Presence Himself.

8–10. There follows an invitation to put God to the test in any similar situation. For those that do so can "taste and see" for themselves

Psalm 34

"that the Lord is good" (quoted in I Pet. 2:3). They will also realize "how very happy are all those that take refuge in Him." This is merely another way of saying, "Fear the Lord." For the practical side of the fear of God is such reverence for Him that we trust Him implicitly to deliver us from any danger that may arise. You can, in fact, lay it down as a general principle, "those that fear Him suffer no want." Those who are naturally strong and self-sufficient like "young lions" do not have the guaranty of safety that is characteristic of those who "seek the Lord." A title used for such in v. 9 is "His holy ones." They are the ones whom His grace has set apart for Himself. That is implied in the title. The various titles used for them in the psalms are "the meek" (vv. 2, 6); "fearers of God" (vv. 7, 9); "holy ones" (v. 10); "righteous" (vv. 15, 19, 21); "God's servants" (v. 22).

b) Instruction as to what leads to such heartening experiences; chiefly, living in the fear of the Lord (vv. 11–22)

11. *Come, children, listen to me;*
    I will teach you the fear of the Lord.
12. *Who is the man that delights in life,*
    Who loves length of days that he may see good?
13. *Keep your tongue from evil*
    And your lips from speaking deception.
14. *Turn away from evil and do good;*
    Seek peace and follow after it.
15. *The eyes of the Lord are directed toward the righteous,*
    And His ears toward their cry.
16. *The face of the Lord is against those who do evil,*
    To cut off the memory of them from the earth.
17. *They* [the righteous] *cry, and the Lord hears;*
    From all their troubles He delivers them.
18. *The Lord is near the brokenhearted;*
    He saves those who are crushed in spirit.
19. *Many are the afflictions of the righteous;*
    But the Lord delivers him out of them all.
20. *He always guards all his bones;*
    Not a one of them is broken.
21. *Evil may slay the wicked;*
    And they that hate the righteous shall pay the penalty.
22. *The Lord redeems the life of His servants;*
    And all who take refuge in Him will not pay the penalty.

11, 12. The singer turns teacher and offers instruction, not in a prosy way, but still in the spirit of a true poet. He gives instruction by which men may be enabled to have heartening experiences such as he has had. With commendable skill he immediately summarizes the point he wants to make: it is to live in the "fear of the Lord." After the manner of other godly men in Israel he as a teacher addresses his hearers as "children," indicating that there is a certain intimacy involved in the teacher-student relationship: the teacher stands in the place of the parent (cf., Prov. 1–9). Before his instruction begins, the teacher injects another summary statement as to what the fruits of the fear of the Lord are. They are "life" in the richest and fullest sense, not mere living; and "length of days"—a gift naturally valued highly by all mankind; and "good"—which is obviously synonymous with blessing. The idea implied is that the fear of the Lord usually, all things being equal, yields fruits such as these.

13. In the following the writer does not attempt to give a summary of all the items that belong to a life that is lived in the fear of the Lord. He mentions a few typical ones that stand out and bear emphasizing, at least in the light of his recent experience of deliverance. They are: Watch your tongue; seek the good; seek peace with your fellow man. He could have spared himself much grief if he had kept his tongue under control, seeing that he resorted to "deception" in his dealings with Achish. Whether this deception was put precisely into words or acted out is of secondary moment in this application. In fact, this rule is merely a subhead under the broader rule of seeking the good, which is always a two-sided attitude, involving as much the shunning of evil as the doing of the good itself. The "peace" here advocated is not the peace of heart that a man should seek in relation to his God. In this connection it must be some *expression* of such a proper relationship, and it, therefore, is in the category of the things the Savior inculcated in Matt. 5:9, peaceful relations with our fellow men. The double statement ("seek" and "follow after") indicates that all such virtues must be cultivated, not halfheartedly, but with a certain assiduousness.

15–17. We deviate from the order of these verses and consider them in this succession: vv. 15, 17, 16. We retained them in the familiar order in our translation above, but we sought to get the same result by inserting in parentheses "the righteous" at the beginning of v. 17, as a number of older translations do for the sake of clarity.

When an individual sets out to follow the psalmist's instruction to cultivate the "fear of the Lord," particularly in the three areas indicated, he will encounter trouble and tribulation. But this should in no wise disturb him. For "the eyes of the Lord are directed toward the righteous." He keeps faithful watch over them, having become responsible for them by recommending to them that they follow this course. When their difficulties mount to the point where they must cry

Psalm 34

out unto the Lord, His "ears [are directed] toward their cry." All this is emphasized by the beautiful statement in v. 17: "They cry out, and the Lord hears; from all their troubles He delivers them." The other side of the matter is that His attitude is the diametrically opposite with reference to those "who do evil." If they persist in their course, it is His intention "to cut off the memory of them from the earth."

18–20. This approach, especially as far as God's taking note of His faithful children is concerned, is developed a bit more fully. For as one follows the course of cultivating the true "fear of God," it may also happen that he meets with experiences that well-nigh break his spirit or crush the very life out of him. God has not promised His own exemption from these disappointments. The thing to be borne in mind, however, is that "the Lord is near," and "He saves." The disappointing experiences, for that matter, are not to be thought of as being rare or isolated occurrences. Just as the ungodly have many troubles, so in the classic statement of our good writer, "Many are the afflictions of the righteous." But more important is the phrase that balances this statement: "But the Lord delivers Him out of them all." Or, a rather unique way of stating the same case: "He always guards all his bones" (the idea "always" lies in the durative participle) "not one of them is broken." This passage as well as Exod. 12:46 may well have been in the evangelist's mind when he wrote John 19:36.

21. Since a broad principle is involved, the writer offers a summary of the situation by way of a conclusion. In the course of the working out of the principles involved, when the ungodly are the unrelenting foes of the godly, the outcome for the former will always be this: "Evil shall slay the wicked; and they that hate the righteous shall pay the penalty." On the other hand, those that seek to live in the "fear of the Lord," who are here designated by a new title, "His servants," have this assurance: "The Lord redeems the life of His servants; and all that take refuge in Him shall not pay the penalty." So closes the poet's instruction with reference to the godly life that he earnestly recommends to all who would serve God in all sincerity.

NOTES

5. Though a few manuscripts have the imperative (*habbitu*), this does not seem to fit the context as well as does the indicative. The verb is used with an indefinite subject, "men." The verb *naharu* can mean "be radiant" or "stream toward"—the latter being somewhat more common. *Luther* rendered it very popularly: *die ihn anlaufen*.

6. "This poor man" (*AV*) would require a different word order. *Buttenwieser* calls this the "interjectional use" of the demonstrative. So also *KS* 334u.

10. Though the *Septuagint,* which was followed by *Luther,* interpreted in its own way rather than translated and suggested "the rich," it is far better to retain the clear Hebrew "young lions" here used, not figuratively, but by way of illustration and comparison.

13. Note the change of person. In relation to v. 12 it could have continued quite naturally thus: Let him keep his tongue . . .

21. "Pay the penalty" is difficult to render. The verb *'asham* means basically "be guilty." *RSV,* "be condemned," is better than *AV,* "be desolate."

Sclater (*Interpreter's Bible*) points out that this psalm was "sung by the church of Jerusalem at the time of Communion," and that it "was on the lips of martyrs as they faced the arena."

Psalm 35

A PRAYER FOR RESCUE FROM ENEMIES WITHIN THE NATION

THIS TITLE indicates the distinctive feature of this psalm. There are men within the nation, people close to the psalmist, who have developed an intense enmity against him. With reference to these he prays to his God. It is quite obvious that this note is struck in many of the psalms. Some interpreters have listed the following as having kinship with this psalm: 36, 39, 71, 109; also 7, 22, 31, 54, 55, 56, 140, etc.

It plainly becomes more difficult to find such an array of dangerous foes against the king in the days when he was already on the throne, except in the days of Absalom's rebellion, for by that time men, for the most part, courted the favor of the king. Many points of correspondence between the statements of this psalm and the experiences of David in Saul's day can be suggested if one compares I Sam. 20, 23, 24, 25, 26. There was someone seeking his life; there were slanderers; David himself pointedly appealed to God as judge, I Sam. 24:12, 15. Though these points of correspondence do not conclusively prove Davidic authorship they show at least that the superscription "of David" is reasonable and possible. The counterargument that the psalm lacks the vigorous language of David is subjective opinion. Not everything Shakespeare wrote had the same degree of vitality. We are content to think of the psalm as coming from David's pen.

Some newer approaches to the interpretation of this psalm are not particularly helpful. Its writer was not a sick man as *Schmidt* by rather devious reasoning concludes. The whole piece does not turn about the issue of a lawsuit (v. 1a.), for then, strangely, the first figure used is taken literally without further proof for this approach; all the rest are allowed to remain as figures. Again, it is not a "national prayer" (*Briggs*), for no reader would get that impression after several readings if he were not strongly minded to use the "collective I" approach. Nor is the poem lacking in "originality" as *Kittel* claims who supports his contention by pointing to *six* verses which have a close affinity with verses in other psalms. That still leaves better than twenty verses that do not come under that category. Similarity with a number of passages in Jeremiah could well be due to the fact that Jeremiah was much given to quoting from earlier writers.

Further light on the subject of the imprecatory element as it finds expression in this psalm might be gained from an explanation that *Kessler* offers: what certainly played into cases of this sort is the fact that the enemies of the psalmist were so obviously "unjust and ruthless as to prove by their attitude that they were foes of God Himself." To desire earnestly the overthrow of such is not mere personal vindictiveness. All this may, of course, not quite approach the level of New Testament thinking, but it cannot be branded as ungodly as is done by many commentators.

We suggest the following outline for the psalm:
a) Prayer that God may arise in the singer's behalf and repay those who have wrongfully attacked him (vv. 1–10).
b) The singer's true sympathy for the misfortune his foes once suffered which is but poorly rewarded by them now (vv. 11–18).
c) Prayer that God may bestir Himself against these false friends and vindicate the psalmist's righteousness (vv. 19–28).

This outline indicates that the psalm has a certain unity. Though we might concede that "these three sections may relate to three separate episodes in the life of the psalmist" we are not ready to grant that "more probably they are of independent authorship" (*Taylor*).

a) **Prayer that God may arise in the singer's behalf and repay those who have wrongfully attacked him (vv. 1–10)**

Of David.
1. *Take up my case against those who contend with me;*
   Fight against those who fight against me.
2. *Take hold of shield and buckler*
   And arise for my help.

3. Draw the spear and build a blockade against my pursuers;
   Say to my soul, I am your help.
4. Let them be put to shame and dishonor who seek after my life;
   Let them be turned back and made ashamed who devise evil against me.
5. Let them be as chaff before the wind,
   While the angel of the Lord thrusts them aside.
6. Let their path be dark and slippery,
   While the angel of the Lord pursues them.
7. For without cause they have laid for me this net-pit;
   Without cause they have dug a pit for my life.
8. Let destruction come upon them unawares;
   May each one's net which he has laid catch him;
   Let them fall into it to their ruin.
9. But my soul shall rejoice in the Lord;
   It shall rejoice in His help.
10. All my bones say: O Lord, who is like unto Thee?
    Who deliverest the poor from him that is too strong for him,
    The poor and the needy from him that would rob him.

1. The trouble in which the writer is involved is as vexatious and disturbing as is a lawsuit. This the figure used implies, and the writer asks God to fight his case for him, in the language of our day, to become his lawyer. *Oesterley*, too, says that these words "must not be taken too literally." From another point of view the writer is involved in war as it were. He pleads with his Lord to fight his battle. This figure is developed at greater length in that, in the first place, God is asked to take hold of "shield" and "buckler" (a larger shield) to protect His faithful follower who finds the struggle too much for his strength. Varying the figure a bit, God is then called upon like a mighty warrior to "draw the spear" from its protective enclosure and stand there to block any attempt of the pursuers to pass. The figure then takes on a most comforting touch: as the Lord stands there holding off the bitter attackers He turns to His faithful friend, whom He is shielding, and says, "I am your help." The foes are still there, as ferocious as ever, but the Lord has them under full control. All this is colorful language but not "unedifying."

4–8. It is scarcely going too far when we say that the imprecation which follows remains within certain limitations. The first statement asks only that, as far as their present iniquitous plans against him are concerned, they may be "put to shame and dishonor." The clause immediately following suggests this. In like manner the prayer asks that they may be turned back from the evil that they devise against him. Some interpreters have injected a note of purely personal and selfish vindictiveness, a view which is scarcely supported by the devout tone of the rest of the psalm. These pursuers are still being thought of as being on the psalmist's trail. That path of theirs, prays David, is to be made "dark and slippery," there it is that they are to be made "as chaff before the wind." There it is that the "angel of the Lord" is to "thrust them aside" and "pursue" them. This is the same great Deliverer who worked so mightily in behalf of His people in the days of the Exodus and earlier in the days of the patriarchs, foreshadowing the great spiritual deliverance that He would work in days to come. Only in this psalm and the preceding one is He referred to in the entire book.

That the writer is thinking only of the miscarriage of their present iniquitous plans against him appears still more clearly from v. 8, where their plans are to backfire upon them, and they are to fall into the very destruction that they planned for him—a very just retribution. If the statements appear somewhat strong at times, it becomes evident that the psalmist is thinking in terms of a total and effective overthrow of these men and all that they devise.

9, 10. Each of the three sections of the psalm quite appropriately closes with the resolve to give thanks to God when the deliverance has been effected. All this is, however, not stated conditionally but quite confidently, as an experience which he has every reason to anticipate. The "help" prayed for in v. 9 can refer only to the present emergency. That is what *AV* obviously meant when it employed the term "salvation," a word which is in this context largely without spiritual connotation. This anticipated experience will produce a new understanding of the greatness of the Lord—"Who is like unto Thee?" For the foes were too many and too strong for him; but God is the one who delights in helping such individuals, especially the poor, the weak, and the needy. That is a distinguishing characteristic of His. "Bones," cf., Ps. 51:8, means the "entire being."

b) **The singer's true sympathy for the misfortune his foes once suffered (vv. 11–18)**

11. *Men who bear witness concerning violence kept rising up;*
    They kept asking me about things that I knew not.
12. *They repaid me evil for good;*
    My soul is quite forlorn.
13. *But as for me, when they were sick, my clothing was sackcloth;*
    I afflicted my soul with fasting, and I prayed most earnestly.
14. *I went about as though it were my friend and brother;*
    As in sorrow for a mother I was bowed down with grief.

15. But now when I fall, they are glad, and they assemble, they assemble against me;
    Ready to smite without my knowledge, they rend without ceasing.
16. As profane men, cheap table-jesters,
    They gnash upon me with their teeth.
17. O Lord, how long wilt Thou look on?
    Rescue my soul from their lies, my one treasure from the lions.
18. I will thank Thee in the great congregation;
    Amid the great throng I will praise Thee.

11. The calm that was attained in the course of the prayer at the conclusion of the first section departs. The mood changes. So prayer has its manifold colorings. The psalmist returns to a remembrance of what his enemies had done. For one thing, they were "witnesses concerning violence," that is, concerning violent deeds that he was supposed to have done. They kept raising questions as though he had done these deeds whereas they were in reality questions "about things that he knew not." Trumped-up charges seem to have been a favorite stock in trade among the Jews then and in Christ's time. What made it worse was that there were good deeds on record that the psalmist had done for them (v. 12). No wonder he says: "My soul is quite forlorn"! The Hebrew has "childlessness of my soul," which may be reproduced as we have rendered it; similarly *RSV*.

13, 14. There comes the record of how sympathetically he once dealt with these men. Their sickness grieved him to such an extent that in deep feeling for them he wore sackcloth. He even fasted in his prayers for them as did Bible men in days of old in many instances. He would at such times go about as though his closest of kin, friend, brother, or mother, had been sick. This friendship was of importance at least to himself in days of old.

15, 16. If this kindly relationship had ever meant anything to these men it certainly does not mean anything now. Any mishap that he may experience makes them glad. Time and again they assemble together to plot some new mischief. They are "ready to smite without his knowledge," which seems to mean that they are always ready for more contention. "They rend without ceasing" implies that they rend his good name to tatters and would tear him to pieces if they could.

The first half of v. 16 is difficult for us to understand because an unfamiliar idiom seems to be involved. Literally it would read "as profane men, mockers for cake," which *BDB* renders quite aptly "cheap table-jesters." This makes good sense and does not immediately call for alterations of the text after the example of the *Septuagint* or for fol-

Psalm 35

lowing other conjectures. To conclude the story—in impotent rage—they hate him so much—"they gnash upon [him] with their teeth."

17. This is such obvious injustice that it calls for divine intervention. So the writer pleads with God not to delay any longer in delivering him from this unhappy situation. The soul or life, which he calls on God to deliver, he calls his "one treasure" as in Ps. 22:20.

18. Again, as the section closes, the writer takes comfort in the prospect of praise, which he shall be privileged to offer to God when God has brought this sorry mess to an end. "In the great congregation" and "amid the great throng" he will speak his due praise, for David was always a man who thought carefully as to how his own experience might be made profitable for his people. Critics, failing to see the symmetry of the conclusion of the several parts of the psalm, in a number of instances call this verse misplaced and move it to a place that is supposedly better suited to its meaning.

c) **Prayer that God may bestir Himself against these false friends and vindicate the psalmist's righteousness (vv. 19–28)**

19. Let not those who are wrongfully my foes rejoice over me;
    Let not those who hate me without cause mock me.
20. For they do not speak peace;
    But against those that are quiet in the land they devise deceptive words.
21. And they opened their mouths wide against me;
    And they said, "Aha, Aha! our eye has seen it."
22. Thou hast seen, O Lord, be not silent;
    O Lord, be not far from me.
23. Bestir Thyself and awake to secure my right,
    To settle my case, my God and my Lord.
24. Judge me according to my righteousness, Lord, my God;
    Let them not rejoice over me.
25. Let them not say in their heart, "Aha, our desire is fulfilled!"
    Let them not say, "We have swallowed him up."
26. Let them all be ashamed and red of face who rejoice in my calamity;
    Let them be clothed with shame and dishonor, who boast over me.
27. Let them rejoice and be glad who delight in my vindication;
    And let them say continually, "Great is the Lord, who delights in the welfare of His servant."
28. My tongue shall tell of Thy righteousness
    And of Thy praise all the day.

The singer is not yet out of his difficulty. Once more he resorts to vigorous petition that the Lord may bestir Himself, suppress these false friends who are at the same time such bitter enemies, and may vindicate the psalmist.

19–21. The writer first presents his case as being one in which men who are wrongfully his foes might rejoice if the Lord did not take it in hand. He offers reasons why this ought to happen, such as, they hate him without cause; and also they are not men who speak words that tend to the peace and wellbeing of all; besides, they agitate against the "quiet in the land" of whom he is one: the least offensive persons are made the object of attack; lastly, they had made proud boasts of having been witnesses of the evil that they charge against him. Men guilty of such practices should certainly be curbed in their actions.

22–24. The plea grows more urgent; the psalmist prays with the confidence of faith. He contrasts with what they have said the fact that God, who knows and sees all, has seen what has transpired and knows how utterly false the charges raised against him are. When men slander thus, it is enough for him if only the Lord remains near to him. Having suffered long, the writer wants prompt action and makes bold to implore God to bestir Himself and to awake to secure his right, which has so long been denied him. He feels it is high time "to settle his case." And all the while he can claim with a good conscience that the Lord is His God. V. 24 has no trace of self-righteousness, for it reflects only on the issue at stake, in regard to which the author feels his absolute innocence. According to this righteousness he would be judged. What a pity if the wrong should triumph and his foes rejoice when their iniquity succeeds!

25–28. One last plea presented to the Lord in support of his cause is to the effect that each of the parties involved may receive its just dues: that the wicked may not be able to boast that they have achieved what their hearts plotted, but rather that they may leave the scene ashamed and red of face, burdened with the dishonor and disgrace which they so well merit. On the other hand, since there were many righteous men who know of the justice of his own cause and would have been bitterly grieved if he had not prevailed, the prayer is to the effect that all such may have the satisfaction of seeing true justice done, which satisfaction they will after the pattern of godly men express in terms of praise to God, whom they know as One "who delights in the welfare of His servant."

Calmness and confidence breathe from the last utterance, which is the third conclusion that promises due praise to the Lord. The theme of this praise shall be God's righteousness, of which the psalmist will have a new proof, and the praise will not be meagre but ring out "all the day long."

NOTES

3. We have rendered the word *seghor,* which means literally "close" or "shut," "block off" or "build a blockade." Since this is a reasonable meaning which fits well into the thought, it is unnecessary to regard the word as a noun, representing an old Scythian battle axe, σάγαρις, a word that is unknown in Hebrew usage.

7. We regard the expression *shachath rishtam* as a sort of compound noun with a suffix: "their net-pit," which term would designate a pit made doubly effective for capture by having also a net used in connection with it. So the text would require no alteration. But the verb "dig" in the second member requires *shachath* as the object understood.

8. This verse suddenly swerves from the plural of the preceding verses to the singular. As so often, this is intended to particularize—a feature that we have sought to make plain by using the distributive "each one."

11. The first verb of v. 11 and the first of v. 12 are apparently used as frequentative imperfects in the past, for in v. 13 the perfect *'innethi* is used as the narrative continues. The last verb of v. 13, *thashubh,* appears to be the usual imperfect that is used with the *waw* consecutive, in this case separated from the *waw* (see *KS* 368i).

13. There is no denying the difficulty of the statement that we have rendered, after Luther's example, "I prayed most earnestly." That seems to convey the sense that most writers prefer. The literal rendering is: "and my prayer returned to my bosom." That might mean, as *RSV* suggests, "I prayed with my head on my bosom," which rendering offers no help by way of interpretation of the unusual expression. Many writers refer to I Kings 18:42 as a comparable attitude of prayer, which seeks to make plain the intensity of the prayer on that crucial occasion. Our interpretative rendering removes at least some of the difficulty.

25. The quotation given is elliptical in the original, "Aha, our desire!" *Nephesh,* usually translated "soul," is, without doubt, to be thus rendered here. See any Hebrew dictionary. This interjective use of the word is apparently to be taken in the sense we have indicated by adding "is fulfilled." Another rendering, more colloquial, would be: "Aha, this is what we wanted!"

Psalm 36

THE WICKEDNESS OF MEN
AND THE STEADFAST LOVE OF GOD

THERE IS so little material that may be used to determine the date or the authorship of this psalm that we must freely admit the difficulty. At the same time there is nothing that definitely conflicts with authorship by David. Therefore we are ready to let the traditional claim of the heading—"of David"—stand. The rest of the heading, "the servant of the Lord," would serve to indicate that the writer is not speaking for himself, nor as the king of Israel, but rather in an official capacity as a leader and instructor of his people, whom he serves by serving the Lord.

Two sharply contrasted pictures are presented by the psalm. A blending of the materials offered is presented in the last three verses. The first of these pictures shows the wicked man in his inmost thinking and his general attitude toward life. With this is contrasted the mighty mercy of God. For the wicked man in his wickedness is dangerous, but the godly have recourse to the Almighty and His clearly known attributes and take their refuge in Him. The speaker is at least a man who has tasted how good the Lord is. True personal fellowship with the Lord is more than theory to him. In his thinking the gentle alkali of the mercy of God neutralizes the acerbity of the ungodliness that he has encountered. So the concluding prayer asks for nothing more than that this mercy of God may prevail as it safeguards him against any threat that lies concealed in the attitude of the wicked, whom the Lord will dispose of in due season.

The following outline covers the line of thought:

a) The sorry infatuation of the wicked (vv. 1–4).
b) The abundant mercy of God toward mankind (vv. 5–9).
c) Prayer that God's mercy may prevail (vv. 10–12).

The outline of thought just suggested would serve as an ample refutation of claims such as: "The literary relationship between the two parts is so weak that it seems obvious that originally they were independent compositions" (*Taylor*).

This psalm has labored under the unusual handicap of having its first verse translated so ambiguously, at least into English, that no man could have a reasonable conception of what it meant. *KJ* renders: "The transgression of the wicked saith within my heart that there is no fear of God before his eyes." *Luther* allowed himself quite a bit of freedom but at least arrived at a simple and clear meaning, much like *RSV*, when he translated: "I am speaking from deepest conviction with reference to the ungodly that there is no fear of God before their eyes." All translators have wrestled with the problem, showing that they were in difficulties, either by making slight alterations in the text, or by giving unusual meanings to the first two words. If a slight alteration, which was adopted already by the *Septuagint* is allowed, then one may render as does *RSV*, which at least makes very good sense and fits well into the context: "Transgression speaks to the wicked deep in his heart; there is no fear of God before his eyes." However, more detailed discussion must follow after we have the whole section before us in what we trust is a helpful translation.

a) **The sorry infatuation of the wicked (vv. 1–4)**

To the Choir Director. Of David, the servant of the Lord.

1. *A divine oracle about transgression has been heard in my heart with reference to the wicked:*
There is no dread of God before his eyes.
2. *For he flatters himself in his own thinking*
That his iniquity will not be found out or hated.
3. *The words of his mouth are falsehood and deceit;*
He has abandoned acting wisely and doing good.
4. *He devises falsehood upon his bed;*
He sets himself in a way that is not good;
He spurns not evil.

1. Now to examine the problem presented by v. 1 more carefully. The first word is *ne'um,* meaning "a divine oracle." It is used hundreds of times with the word Yahweh or its equivalent dependent upon it— "oracle of Yahweh." The noun following it usually indicates the source of the oracle. This does not always hold true. In a few cases like Num. 24:3, 4, 15; II Sam. 23:1; Prov. 30:1 it can be followed by a noun which indicates the medium through whom the message was transmitted. Our passage is in a class by itself. It reads literally: "a divine oracle of transgression." The genitive may be either subjective or objective. If it is subjective, the expression would mean that transgression, speaking like a kind of evil genius within a man, inspires him, ironically speaking, as the Lord did His prophets. That is what *RSV* and kindred translations seem to have in mind: "Transgression speaks to the wicked deep in his heart." But in order to arrive at a consistent thought the

textual change noted above must be resorted to: "my heart" is changed to "his heart." Now textual emendations should not be resorted to lightly in order to avoid difficulties. Nor must this one be made. The genitive may be regarded as an objective genitive: "a divine oracle about transgression." The psalmist means that deep down in his heart insight was granted to him about what really is wrong with the wicked. He saw the roots of the thinking of the ungodly laid bare, not by reasoning out what they were; nor by intuition; but by divine revelation, even as the enormity of any or all iniquity can be discovered only by divine revelation.

What did this divine disclosure reveal? Answer: "There is no dread of God before his eyes." The word for "dread" is *páchadh,* which can mean fear of God in the wholesome sense, but here more likely refers to restraining dread of the power of God that could serve to check the impulses of wickedness. The wicked man has completely lost that wholesome check.

2. The consequences of this basically wrong attitude are now shown. They are: "He flatters himself in his own thinking that his iniquity will not be found out or hated." Here again the text has its difficulties. These are not so insuperable as to warrant the device resorted to by not a few interpreters who pass the verse by and use a series of dots as though it were utterly impossible to get any tolerable sense out of the text. This verse produces evidence of the result of the basically wrong attitude of the wicked man. It is not God flattering him as some interpreters suppose; or his sin as others suggest. He flatters himself regarding the finding and hating of his iniquity, which quite obviously can mean "That his iniquity will not be found out or hated." Such an idea may grow out of the practical observation made by many that iniquity is not always punished at once. It is seemingly not punished at all if by punishment one means swift and immediate punishment. God's mills grind slowly. The wicked fail to see that fact. So the poor wicked man labors under the delusion that there is no retribution: that he can get away with what he does, and he shapes his course accordingly.

3. Such wickedness always bears certain fruits and always has its obvious manifestations. Typical ones are listed: You cannot depend on what he says: "The words of his mouth are falsehood and deceit." He has lost all worth-while objectives: "He has abandoned acting wisely and doing good." He is totally committed to the practicing of evil so that even those quiet night hours, when reflection is most sober, and man sees himself as he is, are spent in "devising falsehood upon his bed." He does not drift into evil ways; he follows them by design: "he sets himself in a way that is not good." Lastly, a broad negative closes

the description: "he spurns not evil." It is dangerous to have such persons around. They are atheists in action.

b) **The abundant mercy of God toward mankind (vv. 5–9)**

5. Lord, Thy steadfast love dwells in the heavens;
   Thy faithfulness reaches to the clouds.
6. Thy righteousness is like the mountains of God;
   Thy judgment is the great deep;
   Man and beast dost Thou save, O Lord.
7. How precious is Thy steadfast love, O God!
   The children of men take refuge under Thy wings.
8. They may drink their fill of the rich gifts of Thy house;
   Thou givest them to drink of the stream of Thy delights.
9. For with Thee is the fountain of life;
   In Thy light do we see light.

5. With obvious intent of presenting a striking contrast the writer places God in all the glory of those attributes that mean so much to man over against the sinner in his sorry state. What if men, bad men, are as they are and do the depraved things that they do? There is a quality of His called "steadfast love," which is His covenant faithfulness (*chésedh*), which is not only seen everywhere on earth but also towers into the very heavens. Parallel with it is the other attribute of "faithfulness," God's absolute dependability. It reaches to the very clouds. These are the verities that confront man's depraved action.

6. There is in addition His "righteousness," which has never suffered Him to treat a single person on the earth wrongly. It stands firm and unshaken as the very "mountains of God," a Hebrew superlative (*KS* 309 1) that is not adequately rendered by *KJ:* "the great mountains." In speaking of another attribute that He manifests, "judgment," the psalmist refers to the most striking instance of divine judgment known in all history, "the great deep," that is to say, the historic Deluge, which demonstrates how God can bring judgment upon evil in the mass so effectively that it is obvious that God has done it. A little sidelight on that remarkable judgment is brought into the picture by way of a brief reminiscence: "man and beast dost Thou save, O Lord," Noah and the beasts in the ark. The one striking instance is recalled when iniquity was rampant but God's well-tempered and righteous judgment was able to cope with the situation.

7. Coming back to the "steadfast love" of God, it is as though the writer said: All these divine attributes that we have listed add up to this one, which he now designates as "precious" in the eyes of God's children. The conviction that it exists induces "the children of men" every-

where "to take refuge" under the wings of God. He is at this point most appropriately designated by the general name *'elohim* because He is regarded as the Father of all children of men and not Israel's only.

8, 9. Much in the spirit of Ps. 1, the happy lot of those who have taken refuge in Him is now pictured in deep and rich colors. The words breathe the universalism of the New Testament. Since not all the children of men feast on the rich things offered by God but only a goodly number of them do, we avoid exaggeration by translating the imperfect of the verb potentially: "they *may* drink their fill." The Hebrew speaks of the things received as "the fatness of Thy house" (*KJ*), the thought being, partaking of the rich portion of a well-fed sacrificial victim that is being eaten by the worshipers at a solemn feast. The verb means "to drink one's fill," but since two figures are blended, it matters little whether one translates as we do: "they may drink their fill of the rich gifts of Thy house"; or as *RSV* renders: "they feast on the abundance of Thy house." Another figure takes the place of this one, that of quenching one's thirst at a cool fountain whose waters satisfy: "Thou givest them to drink of the stream of Thy delights."

But that it is, in the last analysis, God Himself who is the fountainhead of all that His own receive must also be indicated. He is the ultimate source of all they receive and enjoy. How could that be said more trenchantly than in the words, "For with Thee is the fountain of life"! This surely refers to life in every sense, not merely in the sense of being alive physically. And since in this psalm certain basic insights into life and motives are involved, quite appropriately along the same line of thought the writer says: "In Thy light do we see light." "Light" is here used in the rich sense of Ps. 27:1 and according to the usage of John in the New Testament (8:12) as embodying the fulness of salvation.

When contemplating the rich meaning of vv. 5–9 some writers grow quite enthusiastic about what they term "Old Testament mysticism at its best" (*Leslie*). Well they may, for the emphasis is plainly on the personal, living relation to God and not on the externals of sacrifice. In fact, the latter are blended into the picture as the symbols and types that they are. But to regard such mysticism as a late product in the spiritual life of the Old Testament saints, or to claim that David would have been incapable of such deep mystical experience, or to state that the age of Abraham was ignorant of these things, are extremes that are strongly to be guarded against.

c) **Prayer that God's mercy may prevail (vv. 10–12)**

10. *O continue Thy steadfast love to those that know Thee*
    And thy righteousness to the unright in heart.

Psalm 36

11. *Let me not be trampled under the foot of pride;*
    Let not the hand of the wicked push me aside.
12. *There the evildoers have fallen;*
    They are thrust down, they shall not be able to rise again.

10. By setting the two pictures thus far offered sharply over against one another without comment the writer has made each stand out more clearly. The last section (vv. 10–12) relates them to one another in a prayer. And what could a man pray for more appropriately than the continuance of God's mercy and protection against the unscrupulousness of those who have "no dread of God before their eyes"? In the prayer for the continuance of God's "steadfast love" the author asks for it only in reference "to those that know" the Lord, "know" being used in that more intimate sense which borders on "love." Only they are receptive to it; only they may have it, even as the Lord's "righteousness" will be manifested in its saving aspects "to the upright in heart." For God's own would bask in the warm sunshine of His gracious attributes.

11. Having experienced, on the other hand, that godlessness may become militant, the godly have recourse in their prayers to the same Lord, asking "not to be trampled under the foot of pride" on the one hand (for the wicked have often ridden roughshod over God's saints); and on the other they desire that "the hand of the wicked may not push them aside," which is a mild statement for the extremes of cruelty to which the wicked may resort. Our best defence against violence is still prayer.

12. Whereas the first picture drawn presented the ungodly in the full flush of their seemingly successful activity, strongly entrenched in their wickedness, that feature of the picture calls for some modification. None know better than God's own that such seeming strength and prosperity are but for the moment. If, therefore, an adequate picture is to be drawn, another feature must be inserted, and that now follows. With a strong Hebrew perfect tense, almost prophetic in its character, the "evildoers" are described as having already "fallen," "thrust down . . . and not able to rise again." All this shall happen "there" or "then" as some interpreters translate. The adverb leaves the thought vague but all the more ominous. The time and the place are held in reserve for the drastic and calamitous overthrow. So the psalm rounds out what it began to say about wickedness, its nature, and its ultimate destiny.

Psalm 37

FRET NOT BECAUSE OF EVILDOERS

A "didactic psalm" says *Briggs*. A "comfort psalm" says *Veit Dieterich*. Both are correct. It offers instruction for the purpose of comfort, and does this more in the way of the book of Proverbs than in the manner of Psalms, for it has to reckon with the problem of the seeming prosperity of the wicked and the difficulty this causes the observant righteous man. It is often enough to irritate any man to see that the evildoer thrives and no punishment seems to overtake him. It is for this reason that *Koenig* puts the psalm into the category of those that offer a protest against pessimism.

As to form our psalm is in the group of those that are called acrostics. It has two verses beginning with each letter of the alphabet, except that for some reason no longer discernible the '*ayin* is bypassed. Yet, as we shall point out in connection with v. 28, '*ayin* may be restored without too much difficulty after the manner of the *Septuagint*. This fetter on the form of the poem has, as is usual in such cases, the result of interfering somewhat with the clearly articulated development of the thought. A certain lack of connection of verses as well as a certain repetitiousness result. However, this defect is only relative; movement and progression of thought can in a general way be easily detected by any reader or hearer.

Again, as far as authorship is concerned, writers differ widely. In regard to the time of composition their views range from the Maccabean age to a definitely preexilic date. It is obvious that as far as the type of experience is concerned that is requisite for dealing with a subject such as this, David certainly had seen ample indications of the seeming prosperity of the ungodly whereas he, though innocent of the things that they did, was the victim of their harsh persecutions. We are content to let the claim of the heading stand—"of David."

What does the psalm instruct a man to do when divine governance seems to fail to adjust things that seem to cry out for intervention? Basic is the directive that recurs repeatedly in the psalm, "trust in the Lord" (see vv. 3, 4, 5, 7, 34, 39) which is offered in various modulations. Coupled with this is the reminder that ethical responsibility is as binding as ever on all true followers of the Lord (see vv. 3, 27,

Psalm 37

34, 37). To this is added the counsel of patience, bearing up under the strain of what looks like divine inaction. Two other reminders are clearly stressed: one is that the godly are in due season blessed by the Lord in obvious ways; the other, that punishment will overtake the wicked. This scarcely merits *Kittel's* criticism that the psalm is marked by "a naive religious optimism." For without a doubt this is advice that even the New Testament stresses and experience corroborates again and again, not invariably but often enough to establish the general principle.

It cannot be denied that more can be said on this matter than our psalm offers. Seldom does one section of Scripture present the whole counsel of God on a given subject. *Hengstenberg* has made quite a bit of the point that *future* rewards and punishments are not even reflected upon in this psalm but points out that the Old Testament cannot in the nature of the case be as clear on such a subject as is the New. Besides, the writer of this psalm does not make much of the fact that the rule about rewards and punishments has its exceptions. That item is covered by the fact that God's retributive justice is seen to delay its execution.

The practical insight that this psalm offers has been of substantial comfort to many an individual who was irked by what he saw regarding the prosperity of the wicked. It would be sheer blindness to overlook the fact that this psalm has many a nugget of pure gold in it, verses that have been of untold comfort to those that used the psalm and precious memory verses that have been recalled again and again. Most notable of these in the Lutheran tradition is v. 5, on which Paul Gerhardt based the hymn, *Befiehl du deine Wege.*

If further light on the subject that engages our writer's attention is sought, there are the classic treatments of the matter offered by Ps. 49 and 73 as well as the whole book of Job. We may even thank God for the fact that some of these treatments of the subject in hand limited themselves to a few aspects of the case, lest a man's thinking be overburdened by more material than he can effectually assimilate. *Munch* (ZAW, 1, 2, p. 37ff.) contrasts Ps. 37, 49, and 73 in an interesting fashion.

No two outlines agree, but here is one after the analogy of those commonly presented.

Fret not because of Evildoers
a) Counsel against irritation over evildoers (vv. 1, 2).
b) The need of trust in the Lord (vv. 3–7).
c) Further reasons for avoiding irritation (vv. 8–11).
d) The futility of the wrongdoer's activity (vv. 12–15).
e) The righteous and the wrongdoer contrasted (vv. 16–22).

f) The blessings enjoyed by the righteous (vv. 23–28).
g) Further marks of the righteous (vv. 29–34).
h) A concluding contrast of the righteous and the wicked (vv. 35–40).

a) **Counsel against imitation over evildoers (vv. 1, 2)**
   Of David.
   1. *Fret not yourself because of the wicked,*
      Neither be envious because of evildoers.
   2. *For like the grass they shall soon fade away;*
      And like the green herb they shall wither.

   These two verses present both the problem and a summary solution (cf., Prov. 24:19). It is not said that the prosperity of the wicked and the seeming inaction of God are the issues that give rise to the fretting that is discouraged. But that is implied as the rest of the psalm indicates. The solution suggested is that soon or late these persons shall fade away and wither, which figure always has a little more emphasis in the Holy Land, where vegetation dries earlier and more completely than it does with us.

b) **The need of trust in the Lord (vv. 3–7)**
   3. *Trust in the Lord and do good;*
      Dwell in the land and practice faithfulness.
   4. *Take your delight in the Lord;*
      And He shall give you the things your heart desires.
   5. *Commit your way unto the Lord*
      And trust in Him, and He will act.
   6. *And He will bring forth your righteousness as the light*
      And your sight as the noonday.
   7. *Be still before the Lord and wait patiently for Him;*
      Fret not yourself over him who succeeds in his way,
      Over the man who resorts to evil scheming.

   3. The two opening verses (1, 2) were negative in character. They offered a suggestion of what not to do and also a motivation. The author follows these with a positive, and his point is: There are things that a man must leave in the hands of God while he himself performs his normal duties. The second half of the third verse might suggest that men were tempted to flee the land because of the persecution that the wicked were conducting. That conclusion must not necessarily follow from the statement, "Dwell in the land." This statement might mean nothing more than: Stay in the place where God has put you and fulfil your duty there, as *Weiser* rightly suggests. And whereas the vexation that has been referred to could take all the joy out of life, the further positive suggestion is to "take delight" in the Lord, let Him

be your joy, for He is wont to give those that leave all issues in His hands such things as are good for them and "their heart desires."

5. More is, however, required than a mere passive letting things take their course. Therefore: "Commit your way unto the Lord." The original says, "Roll your way," the figure being: dislodge the burden from your shoulders and lay it on God, who has bidden you follow this course. All of which comes back to the basic idea expressed in v. 3, "And trust in the Lord, and He will act." That delayed action on God's part is what we find so difficult to believe. The familiar *AV,* "and He will bring it to pass," is not quite as forceful as is the original. Luther's familiar *Er wird's wohl machen* did not intend to have *wohl* understood as "well" but in that looser sense, common enough in German usage, "eventually."

This thought is further developed in v. 6. When God does this, His action will result in the vindication of His own, who have lived blamelessly. For both their "righteousness" and their "right" will obviously come to light.[1] So v. 7 stresses the same thought of trust from the point of view of quiet submission and patient waiting. When fretting is counseled against, we are reminded that the wicked over whom men were inclined to fret had, as was suggested above, also been successful in their undertakings and had wickedly plotted against the righteous.

c) **Further reasons for avoiding irritation (vv. 8–11)**

8. *Leave off from anger and forsake wrath;*
   Fret not yourself, this merely leads to evil.
9. *For the wicked shall be cut off;*
   But the ones who trust in the Lord, they shall posses the land.
10. *For yet a little while and the wrongdoers shall be no more;*
    And if you look sharply at his place, he will not be there.
11. *But the meek shall possess the land*
    And shall delight themselves in abundant prosperity.

Here are further reasons for avoiding irritation. Summed up, they amount to a twofold assertion: the wicked shall be cut off, shall be no more, shall not be there; but those who trust in the Lord shall possess the land and shall delight themselves in abundant prosperity. These are basic truths that, generally speaking, will stand the test as long as the world endures, though exceptions are always possible.

d) **The futility of the wrongdoer's activity (vv. 12–15)**

12. *The wrongdoer schemes against the righteous*
    And gnashes his teeth at him.

---

[1] For, as *Eerdmans* remarks, "One of the shades of meaning [of the word] is 'a thing one is entitled to.'"

13. *The Lord laughs at him,*
    For He sees that his day will come.
14. *The wrongdoers draw their sword and bend their bow*
    To bring the meek and the poor to fall,
    To slaughter those of upright conduct.
15. *Their sword shall enter into their own heart;*
    And their bows shall be broken.

The futility of the wrongdoer's activity is well pictured here. This counterbalances the seeming success that he has. He is presented first as gnashing his teeth at the righteous in impotent wrath. Or again, figuratively or literally speaking, as drawing his sword and bending his bow with nothing less than the most cruel result in mind. But all this wicked endeavor miscarries, for the Lord laughs at His impotence— one of the strongest statements as to why wickedness must fail (cf., 2: 4)—and their sword shall pierce the heart of him that drew it, and their bows shall be broken. One notable statement should not be overlooked. With regard to the wicked the Lord knows (v. 13) "that his day will come." This is the obvious day of judgment, the fixing of which lies entirely in the hands of the Lord.

e) **The righteous and the wrongdoer contrasted (vv. 16–22)**

16. *Better is the little that a righteous man has*
    Than the riches of many wrongdoers.
17. *For the arms of the wicked shall be broken;*
    But the Lord sustains the righteous.
18. *The Lord knows the days of the upright;*
    And their heritage shall continue forever.
19. *They shall not be put to shame in the time of evil;*
    And in the days of famine they shall have plenty.
20. *For wrongdoers shall perish;*
    And the enemies of the Lord are like the pastures of the sheep;
    They shall vanish away, like smoke they shall vanish away.
21. *The wrongdoer borrows but does not pay back;*
    But the righteous is always generous and gives.
22. *For they that are blessed by Him will possess the land;*
    But they that are cursed by Him will be cut off.

16. In this section the righteous man and the wrongdoer are contrasted. This contrast is itself a refutation of the idea of the prosperity of the wicked. How can they be said to flourish when their arms shall be broken, and they perish? In each comparison the advantage is definitely on the side of the righteous, and the Lord is viewed as sustaining them. It is equally plain that He is against the wrongdoer.

Points of interest are these: A righteous man's more meagre substance outweighs the riches of many wrongdoers. In the Hebrew "riches" means "noise or tumult" because of the confusion attendant upon the acquisition and possession of riches. Or this: the arms of the wicked with which they practice their iniquity will be broken; but the Lord's arms are under the righteous man to uphold him.

18. When v. 18 says that the Lord "knows the days of the righteous," that intimate, rich meaning of "knows" is involved which indicates the loving concern on the part of Him who follows the things that are happening in the lives of His children. Out of this knowledge grows the fact that (v. 19) "they shall not be put to shame in the time of evil, and in the days of famine they shall have plenty." And this in spite of the fact that they seemed to have far fewer resources. But if, on the other hand, the wicked are said to be like "the pastures of the sheep," the figure is again a reference to the brief continuance of vegetation in this land; thus shall the wicked wither quickly and die.

21. We can agree with those commentators who interpret v. 21 not so much as a contrast between the lack of moral responsibility on the part of the one and the conscientiousness of the other, but rather as an indication that the one borrows and has not the wherewithal to repay, but the other is so well blessed by God that he can always repay his honest debts. In v. 22 in the expression "they that are blessed of Him" the "Him" can refer only to the Lord Himself. So also in the parallel expression "cursed of Him." The possessing of the land which is repeatedly referred to in the psalms (9, 11, 29) is the standing phrase from the time of the Conquest for the holding of the land of promise. The statement, therefore, involves God's fidelity to His covenant promise made to Israel. Therefore "shall inherit the earth" (AV) is to be rejected. Though v. 11 furnishes the reason for this statement in the Beatitudes (Matt. 5:5), the broader application of the thought that Jesus makes beyond what applies to Israel certainly demands the translation, "shall inherit the *earth*."

f) The blessings enjoyed by the righteous (vv. 23–28)

23. *The steps of a man are made firm by the Lord,*
    That is to say, of one whose way pleases Him.
24. *Though he fall he will not be cast off,*
    For the Lord upholds his hand.
25. *I have been young and now am old;*
    Yet have I not seen the righteous forsaken,
    Nor his descendants begging bread.
26. *He is always generous and ready to lend;*
    And his descendants are blessed.

27. *Depart from evil and do good;*
    So shall you abide forever.
28. *For the Lord loves justice and will not forsake His saints;*
    They shall be kept forever;
    But the descendants of the wrongdoers shall be cut off.

Though the good man and the evil man have repeatedly been contrasted in the psalm, there is still more to be said on the matter of the blessings enjoyed by the righteous. That is the main subject under consideration in this section. We list these blessings: God makes his steps firm because He delights in him; though he may fall, it is but for the moment, for he is not cast off; God never really forsakes him so that his children go abegging for bread (thus a long life of close observation testifies); his life is marked by generosity in the field of helping others, and as he helped them, so others will help even his descendants. From all this the practical conclusion is drawn (v. 27) that any temptation to depart from the path of righteousness that may have momentarily assailed a man should be promptly dismissed and the path of rectitude should be followed, for then men "continue forever." For such the Lord loves, and He approves their conduct and will not forsake them as He does the wicked.

g) Further marks of the righteous (vv. 29–34)

29. *The righteous shall possess the land*
    And shall dwell upon it forever.
30. *The mouth of the wise utters wisdom;*
    And his tongue speaks of justice.
31. *The law of his God is in his mind;*
    His steps will not slip.
32. *The wrongdoer spies upon the righteous*
    And seeks to slay him.
33. *The Lord will not abandon him into his hand;*
    And when he is brought to trial he will not be found guilty.
34. *Wait for the Lord and keep His way;*
    And He shall exalt you to possess the land;
    You shall be witnesses how the wrongdoers are cut off.

If this section may be described as offering further marks of the righteous, the thought in the mind of the writer is that in spite of his disappointment at the way things are going with regard to the wrongdoer a man is, nevertheless, not to let down the bars or forget certain basic requirements that are still to be expected of the righteous. Coupled with those things that are ethical demands there are listed certain advantages that he has always possessed. Under the latter head come things such as possessing the land and dwelling upon it; or not being abandoned into the hand of the wicked. Under the former duties are to be mentioned matters such as: "The mouth of the wise utters wisdom; and his tongue speaks of justice." How much to be regretted, therefore, are ill-advised words that he might let fall from his lips if he allowed his irritation over the wicked to get the better of him! Or again: "The law of his God is in his mind; his steps will not slip." Since "law" is basically instruction, he already has basic truth by which to guide his steps in all such trying situations as the one in which he now finds himself.

When the wicked man is casually referred to in this connection, it is for the purpose of providing, as it were, a dark background against which the brighter picture of the normal character of the righteous man is to be painted. And since the whole psalm has something of the hortatory in it, it is most appropriate that an exhortation should round off this section: "Wait on the Lord and keep His way." The emphasis met with several times before is rightly again brought to the forefront: dependence on the Lord always goes hand in hand with the faithful observance of His commandments, here called "way."

h) A concluding contrast of the righteous and the wicked (vv. 35–40)

35. *I have seen a wicked man given to violence;*
    And he spread out like a green tree in its native soil.
36. *And he passed away, and, behold, he was no more;*
    And when I sought him, he could not be found.
37. *Note the blameless man and behold the upright,*
    For there is a future for the man of peace.
38. *But the transgressors shall altogether be destroyed;*
    The future of the wicked shall be cut off.
39. *The help of the righteous comes from the Lord;*
    He is their refuge in time of trouble.
40. *And the Lord has always helped them and delivered them;*
    He will deliver them from the wrongdoers and will help them,
    For they have always sought refuge in Him.

The contrast between the righteous and the ungodly, which was but touched upon in the preceding section, again comes prominently into the forefront. It is basic for the solution of the problem that is being treated. Examine the lot of these two carefully in many instances and over a long period of time, and the pragmatic proof will appear that in the long run their very fate, rather, the outcome of their lives, provides the answer. Beginning with the wicked, the writer says, "I have seen a wicked man" who gave evidence of being in the class under consideration by being "given to violence." He seemed to flourish as a healthy tree. But it was only for a time, "and he passed away." You could neither find him anymore nor any fruits or results of his life. He just simply "could not be found." But now fasten attention on the blameless man, that is what the term "mark" (*KJ*) implies. That man's life is not futile: "there is a future for the man of peace."

After asserting that the wrongdoer's fate is from every point of view bound to be the very opposite of all that has been described, the writer traces the righteous man's success to its proper source. It is not a case of moral laws working themselves out with unabating regularity. Rather: "The help of the righteous comes from the Lord; He is their refuge in time of trouble." That rather than the misgivings expressed in v. 1 is the real truth of the matter.

And so with fine propriety the last verse reduces the whole problem regarding the Lord and His care for the upright to a general rule by the use of what we sometimes designate as the gnomic aorist, a type of the Hebrew perfect: "And the Lord has always helped them and delivered them." So much for the past. The statement then looks toward the future: "He will deliver them from the wrongdoers and will help them, for they have always sought refuge in Him." On this positive note the instruction and comfort of the psalm come to a close.

NOTES

3. For the expression which we have rendered "practice faithfulness" *Luther* offers: *naehre dich redlich,* i.e., support yourself honestly. The verb *ra'ah* means literally "tend" or "pasture." Of course, that can come to mean "sustain" or "support"; and from that may be derived the interpretation "practice faithfulness," which is all the more to be accepted inasmuch as nothing in the context indicates the adverbial use of *'emunah*.

23. In the clause, "whose way pleases Him," the customary relative is omitted, and the introductory *waw* is an example of the *waw explicativum* (*GK* 154 n.b and *KS* 360d). That means that the *waw* is to be translated "namely" or "that is to say."

35. For "like a green tree in its native soil" the Hebrew has "like a green native." Though the phrase is difficult, it would seem that as a native is to be regarded as a person who lives rooted in his own soil, so a tree could be thought of as doing the same. That relieves us of the necessity of altering the text though the alteration offered by the *Septuagint* and many translators is harmless enough and amounts to about the same thing as our translation—"like a cedar of Lebanon."

36. The first natural meaning of the first verb is "pass over." This needs merely be taken in the derivative sense of "pass away," and we

have a very simple and natural meaning, which eliminates the necessity of altering the text to read, "*I* passed by," a change which was adopted by the earliest versions but is not necessary.

37. Since the two nouns *tam* and *yashar* occur most commonly as masculines, i.e., "the blameless man" and "the upright," there is much to commend the approach that understands the verb *shamar* in the sense of "watch" or "mark." Thus the rendering given by *AV* is to be preferred to *Luther's* translation: *Bleibe fromm und halte dich redlich*, i.e., Stay godly and observe uprightness.

The word *'acharith* means "end, issue" (*BK*) and more commonly, "the end to which somebody has to come," (*BK*), which, we think, is well covered by the use of the word "future" used abstractly. Though many dictionaries also give the meaning "posterity," we feel that this meaning is included in the much broader "future."

40. The second *yephalletem*, without a conjunction, is rendered much better as a future, "He will deliver them," than as an optative (*Koenig*).

To secure a verse beginning with *'ayin* omit the *le* of *le'olam* in v. 28 and read the form *'awwalim*, "the wicked ones," as the *Septuagint* did.

Psalm 38

A PENITENT SINNER'S CRY

IN OUR DAY this psalm would be classified as a lament. Traditionally it is one of the penitential psalms. It is ascribed to David as its author in the heading. Since these headings reflect a sound tradition of the Jewish church, even if they may not be dated back to the original writer himself, we dare not brush the possibility of Davidic authorship aside lightly. The usual reason for not accepting it is that a situation such as that described in the psalm, involving a very sorry physical state of health on the part of David, does not happen to be recorded in the historical books. This position almost amounts to an expectation that the historical books of the Bible owe us an account of every instance when David was seriously ill in the course of his life. It is true that during the first year or two after his grievous lapse into sin he seems to have been well and active. Thereafter the miserable state described by the psalm may have come upon him physically, and he may have still been troubled by the sins concerning which Nathan had pronounced an absolution in the name of the Lord. For it is the nature of the conscience and of the weak faith of man to raise the question of the finality of absolution, especially in the case of more grievous sins. So it is quite possible that the historical sequence may be this: Ps. 51, 32, 38, each reflecting a new phase of the writer's experience.

The psalm is different from the others just referred to in several respects. In the first place, it dwells at gearter length on the physical consequences of the sin or sins committed. There is first a tacit admission of sin (v. 1) and then an open confession (v. 18). It cannot furthermore be denied that no deep sense of guilt is expressed. Penitence takes on various shades and forms, and the deeper sense of guilt has found expression in the other two psalms mentioned. The fact that those who were formerly friends had turned against him is obvious especially from the story of the rebellion of Sheba (II Sam. 20) as well as from the revolt of Absalom (II Sam. 15–19).

Some interpreters, who are impressed overmuch by the objection that the book of Job raises against the old axiom that suffering is always punishment for sin, state that the author was suffering from a misapprehension. But in this case it is most obvious that the writer *knows* that he has sinned and rightly attributes his suffering to the wrath of God because of his sin. He is not being falsely judged by enemies. His thinking is perfectly clear and correct on this point, cf. vv. 1, 3, 18.

Or again, it scarcely goes to the root of the matter when some commentators describe the psalm as being the "complaint of a sick man" (*Schmidt*), for this approach puts secondary matters first. The title should rather be like the above, or as *Kittel* words it, "the Penitential Hymn of a Sick Man." The attempt to be more specific than the writer is and to label his sickness as leprosy or some more acute form of eczema is rather futile. Or to picture the poor wirter as he pantingly makes his way up the Temple hill to address his prayer to the Lord, overlooks the obvious possibility that such prayers may have been made by the faithful anywhere in days of old; and there is no need to make every psalm a liturgical piece enacted at the Temple.

The heading: *A psalm of David. To make a memorial*. Jewish tradition has it that the second half means that this prayer liturgically accompanied the offering of the *Azkara* (cf., Lev. 24:7). The words could also be translated, "to express praise"—a thought that does agree with the spirit of this psalm and with 70:1.

We suggest the following outline:

a) David pleads his wretched state as a reason for deliverance from God's wrath (vv. 1–10).
b) He pleads particularly the attitude that false friends have taken over against him (vv. 11–14).
c) He expresses confidence to be heard on the basis of several additional arguments (vv. 15–20).
d) He utters a final cry for help (vv. 21–22).

1. *O Lord, do not rebuke me in Thy anger;*
   Do not correct me in Thy wrath.
2. *For Thy arrows have sunk deep into me;*
   Thy hand has pressed down hard upon me.
3. *There is nothing sound in my flesh because of Thy indignation;*
   There is no health in my bones because of my sin.
4. *For my iniquities have gone over my head;*
   Like a heavy burden they have become too heavy for me.
5. *My wounds have grown foul and festered*
   Because of my folly.
6. *I am bowed down and brought very low;*
   All the day I go about mourning.
7. *My loins are badly inflamed;*
   And there is no soundness in my flesh.
8. *I am benumbed and utterly crushed;*
   I roar because of the disquietness of my heart.
9. *O Lord, all my longing is before Thee;*
   And my groaning is not hid from Thee.
10. *My heart throbs, my strength has left me;*
    As for the light of my eyes, it also is gone from me.

1. The structure of this section is as follows: the double plea of v. 1 is supported by all the arguments advanced in vv. 2–10. These last nine verses give reasons as to why God should spare him who prays. As already remarked on Ps. 6:1, which is almost identical with our verse, the negative is not to be construed merely with the modifying phrases "in Thy anger" and "in Thy wrath" but with the whole thought. The writer does not ask for a different type of correction, namely, the correction of love. He prays to be delivered from the entire experience that he is now undergoing, that of being taken severely to task by God. The anger and wrath of God are rightly a reality to the writer as they are throughout the whole Old Testament. It has remained for our age to make light of the terrible reality of God's wrath as being a delusion.

Describing God's wrath figuratively, the writer (v. 2) likens it to having arrows shot at one and sticking in him; or, varying the figure, it is like unto having the heavy hand of God pressing down hard and cruelly upon one. He feels that he may plead such a miserable experience as one that would arouse God's pity. We have here that famous paradox of appealing to God who is merciful against God who is angry—a procedure which can never be logically explained, but which is the peculiar privilege of faith. It is true that v. 2 may also be interpreted to mean that the arrows and the hand represent God's punishments (cf., Deut. 32:23; Ezek. 5:16; Deut. 32:4). Both interpretations belong together.

3. There comes a description of the writer's wretched state of health in vv. 3, 5, 6, 7, 8. Briefly summarized, it involves a total affliction that seems to leave no part of the body without infection. It feels to him as though it had penetrated down to the very bones. It seems most natural to take "wounds" (v. 4) in a literal sense in the light of what v. 3 had said. These wounds "have grown foul and festered." The man is unable to assume an upright posture (v. 6). Luther translates very aptly: *Ich gehe krumm und sehr gebueckt*.

The second half of this verse describes the inner pain involved: he "goes about mourning all the day." He feels keenly that all is not right between him and his Lord. One of the symptoms of his ailment is that "his loins are badly inflamed" (v. 7), certainly no trifling affliction. He reiterates the thought expressed in v. 3 that there is no soundness left in his flesh: all is diseased. A kind of physical apathy has already set in, for he is "benumbed and utterly crushed." Whatever ailment or better combination of ailments it was that brought about all this misery we may never determine, nor is it important. But we can well understand how his feelings sought expression in that he was roaring "because of the disquietness of his heart" (v. 8).

Even as all this has been spoken as though he were in the presence of the Lord—not as though God did not know of it, but rather that His faithful ones feel free to cast their burden upon the Lord—so he now again naturally addresses God directly (v. 9). What he has not been able adequately and perfectly to state before his God in his complaint he knows God understands: "all my longing is before Thee; and my groaning is not hid from Thee." There is comfort in the thought that God does not abhor or despise our groanings. A kind of summary of his physical state closes this section of the psalm (v. 10): "My heart throbs, my strength has left me; as for the light of my eyes, it also is gone from me." This last statement may mean that his very eyesight is impaired or at least blurred.

Imbedded in this lament is one verse that points to the underlying cause of it all and shows that the writer was deeply conscious of the basic spiritual issues involved. For v. 4 assigns as a reason for it all, his sin: "For my iniquities are gone over my head; like a heavy burden they have become too heavy for me." The figure implied in the first member is that of deep waters in which a man is sinking; and in the second that of a load which is too heavy to be carried any farther. This may not be strict confession, but it is certainly frank admission.

In the second section of the psalm, vv. 11–14, the approach of the first is continued: the writer still pleads his sufferings as a reason for deliverance. But now it is the attitude of his friends or pseudo-friends that is under consideration.

11. *My friends and companions would stand aloof from my plague;*
    My kinsfolk have taken their place at a distance.
12. *And they that seek my life lay snares for me;*
    And they that seek to harm me discuss my overthrow;
    They devise treachery all the day.
13. *But as for me, I am like a deaf man who does not hear*
    And like a dumb man who keeps his mouth shut.
14. *Yea, I was like a man who hears nothing;*
    And in whose mouth there is no defense.

At this point *Hengstenberg* strangely makes the attitude of the writer's friends the chief and primary affliction that besets him. His physical afflictions are then secondary results. There is nothing in the context that suggests the subordination of vv. 1–10 to vv. 11–14. It could, for that matter, be even the opposite: his friends withdraw from him because of his affliction of the body, which makes him more or less repulsive to them. Since the psalm does not indicate this relationship, it appears better to let both types of grief stand side by side without attempting a subordination of the one to the other.

The unique change of tenses in v. 11 has usually been disregarded. The first statement represents the friends as still debating as to what to do regarding him; they are inclined to withdraw from him: "My friends and companions would stand aloof from my plague." The second statement represents them as having reached a decision: "My kinsfolk have taken their place at a distance." But there are others that are wicked and plot evil. Some go even so far as to "seek his life." Then there are those who "seek to harm" him. Lastly there are those who "devise treachery" (v. 12). It is difficult to endure such experiences. David lays them before the Lord.

For reasons best known to himself the writer resolved to make "no defense." He played the part of a deaf and dumb man, as though he had heard nothing of what they said and could not answer if he tried.

Perhaps he recognized the futility of any type of defense at the time. Perhaps the sense of his being guilty before God made him to feel that this was the only proper attitude.

In the third section there are presented further arguments for being heard by the Almighty God, the Deliverer.

15. Yea, for Thee, O Lord, do I wait;
    Thou wilt answer me, O Lord, my God.
16. For I have said: "If only they do not triumph over me;
    When my foot slipped, they boasted against me."
17. For I am ready to fall;
    And my grief is continually before me.
18. For I confess my iniquity;
    I am sorry for my sin.
19. But my enemies keep on living, and they are strong;
    And they that hate me wrongfully are numerous.
20. And those who render me evil for good are my opponents
    Because I follow after good.

15. The structure of this section seems quite clear. The first verse expresses the confidence that God will answer. In the meantime the writer waits for the Lord. Each of the following verses can be construed as a separate plea as to why God should answer. To indicate this, vv. 16–18 are introduced by "for." The first reason is that the psalmist's downfall would give the enemies an occasion for boasting, which would be, in effect, a boasting that God had failed him. When once his foot did slip, they boasted over him (note the Hebrew perfect). The second plea that could well move the Lord to answer is the fact that the writer is on the very brink of ruin. "I am ready to fall." His "grief is continually before him," staring him in the face. Such a plight of His children touches the Almighty, the psalmist correctly assumes.

17. The third plea (v. 17) has special emphasis: this man freely confesses his iniquity and is "sorry for his sin." He makes neither too little nor too much of his wrong. His penitence is wholesome. To this is added a further reference to the enemies, whom we have already met in v. 11f. In spite of their wicked attitude they "keep on living, and they are strong." It is not right that they should go unpunished, although this aspect of the matter the writer distinctly leaves in the hands of God, not even suggesting intervention. The matter clearly troubles the author as it often did other men in the Old Testament. V. 20 could be regarded as the further unfolding of the attitude of the enemies. It may also be regarded as a separate plea, chiefly in view of the second half of the verse. Since the writer is in his inmost heart clear as to his purpose, namely, that he is "following after good," he

feels that it is very unjust that his enemies should be his "opponents" just because he does what is right. He feels that this constitutes a valid plea in the sight of his God.

Having as yet experienced no deliverance from his galling situation, the author concludes his psalm with a final cry for help.

21. *Forsake me not, O Lord;*
    O my God, be not far from me.
22. *Make haste to help me,*
    O Lord, my salvation.

The whole issue is put into God's hands. The petitions are brief and urgent. The psalmist's lot is very difficult, and so he cries out that God may "make haste." The closing title he uses for God is a beautiful one, "O Lord, my salvation."

Though this whole psalm could be regarded as the voice of the congregation (the "collective I"), there is nothing in its contents that seems to indicate this directly, though this view is strenuously maintained by *Hengstenberg* and a few others. To us the psalm seems to breathe a very personal note.

NOTES

1. The negative, expressed but once, must also be supplied with the second verb. Cf. *KS* 352u.

6. The usual mode of connecting verbs, the second having the *waw* consecutive, is not followed here because this construction is often ignored when synonymns are used. Cf. *KS* 370h.

8. A similar situation obtains here with regard to the first two verbs, with this difference that the second verb has *waw* but not the imperfect. Cf. *KS* 370f.

10. The pronoun *hem* agrees in number with "eyes" rather than with "light." The first may be stressed as well as the second. *KS* 349i.

11. On the tense of the verbs, indicated above, see *KS* 187 and 155.

13. The forms that would be used with *waw* consecutive are sometimes used when the *waw* is lacking. See *yiphtach* and cf. *KS* 368i.

19. The expression "enemies keep on living" has its difficulties. Many interpreters change the word *chayyim* to get the meaning "without cause" (*RSV*). It could mean "the enemies of my life" (*KS* p. 236, N. 1). Our rendering seems acceptable. For "keep on living" *AV* renders "lively."

20. "Because I follow after good" is an infinitive that expresses cause. *KS* 403g.

Psalm 39

THE PRAYER OF A MAN SORELY AFFLICTED

THIS PSALM opens, as none have heretofore, with a dedication to the "choir director, to Jeduthun." There is some information concerning this person in the historical books. *Delitzsch* has summed up this information concisely. Referring to Jeduthun, he writes: "The name of one of David's three musicians, the third after Asaph and Heman (I Chron. 16:41f.; 25:1ff.; II Chron. 5:12; 35:15) undoubtedly the same person as Ethan (I Chron. 15:19), a name which after the appointments at Gibeon (I Chron. 16) was changed to Jeduthun." Further details as to why this psalm should have been put into Jeduthun's hands are lacking.

Authorship by David is also claimed in the heading even though further details as to the specific situation in David's life that was referred to are missing. Much of David's rich life is not related in detail in the Biblical record.

A unique feature of the psalm is that it is difficult to assign it to one of the usual categories into which the psalms have been divided, *Weiser* claiming that it cannot be classified under any of the accepted groupings.

Another unusual feature of the psalm is the fact that it tells the story of a resolution that was not kept. Its author had vowed to keep silence in a given situation. He failed to do so. He faithfully tells the story of his failure without embellishment, with utmost candor. Equally unusual is the fact that the author finds little, if any, comfort in the hope of a better hereafter. This does not warrant the hasty conclusion that such hopes did not exist, or for the other, that at other times in his life he was entirely without hope. His present affliction had apparently crowded this hope so far into the background that it was for the present actually lost sight of. Yet we must readily grant that on the whole this hope burned far more dimly in Old Testament days than it did at a later time. But in this case it is impossible to draw sweeping conclusions from the momentary depression in which the writer found himself.

Out of what experience did this psalm grow? The question is not

Psalm 39

easily answered. To insist that it must have been sickness, although no sickness is mentioned, is unwise. But when two verses are held side by side, the truth of the matter may become apparent. In v. 10 the psalmist prays for the removal of God's "stroke" which has fallen upon him. That allows for any heavier affliction. In v. 1 he resolves in the light of the difficulty that is upon him to "muzzle his mouth as long as the wicked are before him." Combining these two thoughts, we are certainly justified in assuming that one feature of the silence that the writer lays upon himself is that the wicked may not hear him as he gives vent to his feelings over his trouble and so may be deprived of an opportunity of scoffing such as the ungodly love to engage in when they see the affliction of the children of God. At the same time the ungodly were apparently not afflicted as the writer was. Consequently those commentators who say that a part of the grief of the writer was due to the prosperity of the wicked may be very correct. For if the wicked were also in affliction they would not be under temptation to scoff at the godly. We would, therefore, state the theme of the psalm a bit more fully in the following formulation: The prayer of a man sorely afflicted, yet careful not to give the ungodly an opportunity to scoff.

The following outline may reveal the line of thought developed in the psalm:

a) The resolution to keep silent in a painful situation (vv. 1–3).
b) The prayer of impatience uttered at the time (vv. 4–6).
c) A trustful prayer for deliverance from sin and from the stroke of the Almighty (vv. 7–11).
d) A repeated cry for relief (vv. 12–13).

> *I resolved: I will guard my ways so that I may not sin with my tongue;*
> *I will muzzle my mouth as long as the wicked are before me.*
> 2. *I held my tongue and was silent;*
> *I kept still even about good things;*
> *But my grief was stirred the more.*
> 3. *My heart became hot within me;*
> *As I was musing the fire burned;*
> *Finally I spoke with my tongue.*

1. Supplementing what has been said above about the state of the writer, we readily see that with v. 1 we are plunged into the midst of a given situation. The psalmist is concerned about unstraining the tongue which, in any event, is all too ready to speak unwarranted things. So he "resolved" (the Hebrew "said" is often used in this sense) to watch

carefully the utterances of his tongue; or, to state the case even more strongly, to "muzzle his mouth" ("bridle" is less to the point). But the major controlling factor in this self-imposed silence is that "the wicked are before" him. It is not said what they would do, but it may well be inferred that they would gloat over the lack of faith or of self-restraint on the part of a godly man and would thus be led to make remarks that would not tend to the glory of God.

2. The repetition of the words describing this silence ("held my tongue," "was silent," "kept still") shows what restraint the man laid upon himself. But the modifying phrase added to the last statement—"even about good things"—indicates that an unwholesome factor was involved. Good things that might have been said were suppressed. He felt the compulsion that the situation involved, but his inmost being was not wholly in sympathy with what God was allowing to happen. Some interpreters have characterized this silence as "unevangelical" or "legalistic." It involved too much repression. It requires little insight into the psychology involved to discover that such restraint could well lead to an aggravation of the evil as the next verse indicates.

3. The writer's thinking on the whole subject became more and more inflamed ("heart" is the center of thinking in the Hebrew rather than of the emotions). It is at this point that we sense that the writer must have had a feeling of some kind of injustice that might have been involved, such as the flourishing of the wicked and the languishing of the writer. Such observations really irritate. The more he mused, the more inflamed his mind grew. This is the meaning of the statement, "As I was musing the fire burned." This does not refer, as some commentators surmise, to the kindling of some noble thoughts within a man. The internal pressure finally became too great. It was impossible to exercise repression any longer—"Finally I spoke with my tongue." Though the Hebrew has no word for the "finally" we have inserted, yet the addition of the word makes the English statement of the case clearer. Nor is it redundancy of expression to add "with my tongue" to "spoke." For this was the very member that he had resolved to keep muzzled.

4. *Lord, let me know my end, and what the measure of my days is; Let me know how transient I am.*
5. *Behold, Thou hast made my days as only a few handbreadths; And my lifetime is as nothing before Thee; Surely, every man stands there as a mere breath. Selah.*
6. *Surely, as a mere shadow man walks about; Surely, he is in turmoil over vanity; He heaps up things and knows not who will gather them in.*

4. At this point of the interpretation much depends on how we regard this section. Is it what was spoken when the writer said (v. 3): "Finally I spoke with my tongue," or is what he said at that time not recorded, thus making vv. 4–6 another prayer? It seems most natural to view vv. 4–6 as the impatient utterance referred to in v. 3. The words involved could, indeed, have been spoken in a tone of impatience, and then the words, "Lord, let me know my end," could easily be construed as the equivalent of the unwholesome demand, How soon am I going to die? the sooner the better. This is all the more possible in the Hebrew since the verb "let me know" can well mean cause me to know. And since in the Hebrew the verb "know" so frequently involved the idea of experience, "cause to experience" can well mean: bring about my death. Unfortunately, the statements of vv. 4–6 have often been divorced from their context and can, indeed, if given a milder interpretation, yield the thought that the author asks to be impressed with a sense of the brevity of human existence. But then the question arises, Why does the author not pen his impatient utterance but substitutes another prayer at this point?

The threefold prayer of v. 4 can obviously be interpreted in the sense of impatient utterance. Even when the Hebrew verb is changed in the third member, it is only a change of stem, not of the verb proper, and can still mean: Let me experience how transient I am.

5. Then, of course, v. 5 will be regarded as a complaint rather than as a sad observation. So much depends on the tone in which a statement is spoken, and this verse can be spoken in a tone that is far from respectful toward the Almighty, somewhat in the sense of: Let me die, life is rather short in any case. Interpreters who regarded the words of the writer as a godly prayer for insight into life's brevity toned down their translation accordingly. The statements of the verse are spoken much in the spirit of the book of Ecclesiastes. What is said is only too true and can be repeated by any godly man in a purely wholesome sense and tone.

6. The same is true in regard to v. 6. Man does walk about as a "mere shadow" ("mere" again being inserted to catch the unique emphasis in the Hebrew). Again it is only too true that man is "in turmoil over vanity." What strenuous endeavors to acquire things that are mere breaths of vapor! And then the tragedy of it all! "He heaps up things and knows not who will gather them in." This can be spoken with a measure of sadness. We believe that the writer said it in a spirit of bitterness.

At this point there is a distinct change of tone and attitude. Having spoken what irritated him, the writer has unburdened his mind, and a wholesome reaction now sets in. What follows is a "trustful prayer." The "now" marks the transition.

7. And now, Lord, what wait I for?
   My hope is in Thee.
8. Deliver me from all my transgressions;
   Make me not the scorn of fools.
9. I held my tongue (at first), I did not open my mouth;
   For it is Thou who hadst done it.
10. Remove Thy stroke from me;
    I am well-nigh spent as a result of the attack of Thy hand.
11. When Thou dost chasten a man with rebukes because of iniquity,
    Then Thou dost consume his precious things like a moth.

7. Everything depends on the place where our hope and trust are fixed, and thus, since the psalmist had for a time lost his moorings, he now bethinks himself as to where the anchor of his hope should hold, asking himself the rhetorical question, "What wait I for?" addressing it, of course, to the Lord Himself. The concise statement, "My hope is in Thee," is merely a formulation of the new and better attitude that he has now attained after his unseemly outburst. Basic issues can usually be stated very briefly and simply.

8. From this vantage point he now takes issue with the difficulties that confronted him. With clear insight he puts his "transgressions" first. From them he asks to be delivered. This means, on the one hand, forgiveness of these transgressions and, on the other, strength to desist from any wrong course that may have been momentarily followed. Since such lapses into sin so often involve the fact that the sinner becomes the "scorn of fools," the writer prays to be delivered also from this result. There must have been a particular situation involved in this case that made this part of the prayer necessary.

9. At this point our interpretation, with *Koenig*, departs from the commonly accepted understanding of this verse, chiefly because the tense of the Hebrew verbs points in this direction. Since a purely historical perfect is apparently involved, this verse contains a reference to the situation described above, vv. 1–3. For this reason we have inserted the parentheses ("at first"). We could have said something like "previously." The experience related in vv. 1–3 was not soon forgotten by the writer. The second statement ("I did not open my mouth") is reminiscent of this same section where the same idea is repeated about four times. He mentions in addition what had not been alluded to in the initial statement of the case that he strongly felt that the hand of the Lord was involved in what had befallen him ("for it is Thou who hast done it"), for the consciousness of that fact had been a contribut-

ing factor that persuaded him that he ought to keep silent. Verse 9 seems to add this fact to v. 8: that, though he might have become the scorn of fools by rash speech, his chief reason for silence was after all the fact that he knew his grief could not have befallen him without the consent of the Lord, and that thought was one of the controlling features of his silence. The customary interpretation of the verse renders it as though it were written in the present tense, describing the new and better silence that the writer has learned as a result of his experience.

Having reckoned with his sin as the deepest of his troubles (v. 8), he now comes to the more obvious difficulty, the affliction that the Lord had laid upon him—"Thy stroke." Though it is not specifically described it cannot have been a light matter as the effect mentioned indicates—"I am well-nigh spent as a result of the attack of Thy hand." It seems as though the vagueness of the psalm writers about their particular trouble is calculated to allow any man with an analagous affliction to use their psalms.

11. David now indicates that he has been mindful of such lessons as the Lord may have desired to impress upon him when he voices the insight expressed in this verse: When the Lord makes His correction felt to draw a man away from his sin, then a new realization of the vanity of the things formerly regarded as precious becomes overwhelmingly clear: they are as though they had already been consumed by moths, worthless like a moth-eaten garment. Not only the vanity of the *things* man holds dear on this earth but also a sense of the vanity of purely earthly existence becomes apparent—"Surely every man is a mere breath." The "selah" suggests a pause for reflection.

The last section repeats the cry for relief previously uttered.

12. *Hear my prayer, O Lord, and give ear to my cry for help;*
    Hold not Thy peace at my tears,
    For I am a passing guest with Thee, a sojourner like all my fathers.
13. *Turn Thy look from me that my face may brighten*
    Before I go hence and be no more.

12. The light of hope, which was kindled in v. 7, has thus far burned but dimly in this man's heart. He has not extricated himself entirely from his difficulty. He must resort to still further prayers for deliverance. So there are three short petitions that breathe a sort of eagerness. One motivation for these petitions is his "tears" which have not yet ceased to flow. The more extended motivation that he offers draws attention to a truth that seems to have dawned upon the writer with new force, that, namely, his stay on earth is but brief, and he is but a stranger here as all true children of God (his "fathers") were in days of old. In fact, the

expression, "a passing guest with Thee," implies that in their homeless state all men live under the special care of God, as guests for the moment under His roof. Besides, the "sojourner" is the stranger from another land, who must needs dwell among other people for a time and can never feel quite at home though he is treated well and kindly. The emphasis is, therefore, on that feeling of strangeness that God's people sometimes develop amid adverse conditions, a feeling that we are strangers here below. Though this prayer could advance to the next step that could well follow, "heaven is my home," this thought is somehow not expressed though it is certainly implied to some extent.

13. The psalm ends on the subdued note of the hope that God may turn His glance, expressive of His displeasure, away from this poor sufferer before, as he says, "I go hence and be no more." Though we should have preferred a ringing declaration of hope as the closing note of the psalm, as noted above, this aspect of the truth appears to be momentarily subdued in the consciousness of the psalmist even as it does not always burn with such brightness in our own hearts as we might well wish.

On closer inspection it will appear that this psalm has obvious points of similarity with Ps. 62 as well as with the book of Job.

NOTES

1. Though we have construed "the wicked" as a plural, it is the singular without an article, meaning "any wicked man."

2. "Even about good things" is in the Hebrew a simple "from good." Many interpretations of the phrase have been given. Such phrases with *min* are oftentimes the equivalent of negative result clauses. We have interpreted it thus. Cf. *KS* 406 o.

5. "A few handbreadths" is one of those uses of the plural which condense or summarize so that we are obliged to supply the adjective "few"; see *KS* 265 a.

6. *Kol* before *hébhel* is used adverbially; "mere" covers this or the adverb "entirely," see *KS* 332 k.

11. An instance where the plain perfect introduces a conditional clause. "Thou didst chasten" is, therefore, to be rendered, "when Thou dost chasten." *GK* 159h.

12. *Ger* is usually translated "stranger." But such a translation would create a wrong impression. If one takes in a stranger he treats him as "guest." That is what God is thought of as doing in this case. The emphasis is, however, on the entirely transitory character of all of this present life. We, therefore, consider it an apt phrase when *RSV* translates, "passing guest."

13. "That my face may brighten" is in the Hebrew, "and I shall

cause to be bright." This is scarcely our idiom. Besides, the coordinate conjunction here introduces a result clause. *KS* 364 n.

The above interpretation of the psalm is accepted by very few commentators. The difficulty experienced by those who do not adopt this approach is seen in the case of *Gunkel,* who feels that he must rearrange the verses thus: 1–6, 11, 7, 12cfab, 8–10, 13. Such a procedure is an indictment of the whole approach used.

Psalm 40

THANKSGIVING AND PRAYER

THERE ARE no serious reasons for questioning the Davidic authorship of this psalm. The psalm would then most logically fit into the earlier time of David's life, when he was an outlaw fleeing from Saul. It would at the same time reflect a lesson which was underscored in a very emphatic way for Saul and all men living in those days, the lesson recorded in I Sam. 15:22, of which David must have heard in his day, and which he took to heart.

Many Bible students may be disturbed by the rather vigorous assertions that are made to the effect that this psalm cannot be of one piece, nor be attributed to a single author. For with minor changes vv. 13–17 appear as a separate writing, as Ps. 70. The objection raised against the unity of our psalm is further supported by what is claimed to be the psychological unlikelihood of having a psalm begin with thanksgiving and then to find that the writer is still deeply in trouble. However, upon closer reflection it will appear entirely possible to have a man thank for a partial deliverance that has been his or for deliverance from one of many evils that afflict him and then to proceed to ask that God may deliver him from whatever evils still beset him. In fact, *Weiser* had made a very sturdy defense of the situation as the psalm depicts it when he says: "The tension between having and striving for the certainty of faith, which tension covers the whole psalm down to the very last verse, dare not be interpreted away by assigning the psalm in its two halves to two different authors; but it belongs to the very essence of faith and is a distinguishing mark of the true, living piety of a man who prays after the biblical manner, to march along the way over the heights and depths of the life of faith from experience to hope." Or to cite *Vilmar's* brief but very helpful remarks: "He who has slipped away from God cries out of the depths; he who has kept close to God begins his prayer with praise and thanksgiving." *Gunkel* is of the same mind: he finds two factors blending into one another, thanksgiving and lament.

The suggestions that the author may have composed the second half of the psalm on a previous occasion and later added it to his new psalm, or that the original unity is maintained, are not too important. To us it seems far more likely that the entire psalm is a unit, composed as such from the outset, and strictly reflecting a life situation that may easily be duplicated in the experience of many of the saints of God.

In what sense the psalm may be Messianic is a question that becomes acute as a result of the use of vv. 6–8 in Heb. 10:5–9. That it cannot in its entirety be intended as a direct prophecy of the Messiah is made clear by v. 13, where the writer refers to his manifold iniquities. To relieve this difficulty by thinking of imputed sins is an evasion. Even *Hengstenberg* admits that the psalm is not directly Messianic. That means that certain statements in it are found to be applicable to the life of Christ and are so used as a kind of type of the Christ which was prefigured in the life of a saint of the Old Covenant.

Quite a bit is made of the suggestion by more recent writers that the psalm is a liturgical piece. Though a kind of liturgical construction may be put upon it (for example, v. 4 may be regarded as a response of a priest present at the Temple at the time of the writer's thanksgiving), very few who are of this school of thought agree as to how the liturgical arrangement is to be made. Soberly evaluated, v. 4 may be nothing other than a purely natural exclamation such as writers make on every hand under the impulse of strong feeling.

Most students of the psalm will rather feel that the piece carries a very personal note and is not to be thought of as a song of the congregation.

a) **A joyful account of a deliverance from trouble (vv. 1–4)**

In the Hebrew text the heading reads: "To the Choir Director. A psalm of David."

1. *I waited patiently for the Lord,*
   And He inclined unto me and heard my cry.
2. *And He brought me up out of the awesome pit and from the miry slime*
   And set my feet upon a rock, enabling me to take firm steps.
3. *And He put a new song in my mouth, a song of praise to our God;*
   Many will see and fear the Lord and trust in Him.

4. O how very happy is the man who has made the Lord his trust
And has not turned to the proud, to those who turn aside to false idols!

1. The Hebrew says, "waiting did I wait for the Lord." This is rather well rendered by the *KJ*, "I waited patiently." This does not quite catch the note of tenseness that lies in the root of the original. The help received while he was waiting and crying is described by the psalmist in the words: "He inclined unto me and heard my cry." He must have been in some major distress, and, therefore, the deliverance is notable. The next verse describes how precarious his situation was. It was like unto that of a man who had slipped into an "awesome pit" (Hebrew, "pit of tumult") at the bottom of which was only deep slime (Hebrew, "mud of slime") after the water had been used up. It is scarcely necessary to refer the figure of the pit to deep waters of the sea. Since "pit" is often synonymous with the grave or the hereafter, the expression can well be construed to mean that the writer was brought close to the gates of death. From all this the Lord delivered him, and, to continue the figure, after he had been brought up out of the pit, set his feet upon a rock, the very antithesis to slimy mud that sucks a man's feet down. He is now enabled "to take firm steps."

3. So patently did the Lord work this deed of deliverance that the writer has material for a "new song" in which he will celebrate what his God has done for him. Whether by the "new song" he meant that he would add fresh color to old hymns that were extant; or whether he meant singing the old with deeper understanding; or whether he implied the composition of a song that was entirely new, is quite immaterial. It could well mean any of the three possibilities suggested. A new experience was always felt by the psalm writers to put them under obligation to their God to confess before others what the Lord had done. David envisions the result: "many will see" (i.e., experience, which the verb often means) and as a result "will fear the Lord and trust in Him." Thus do the graces experienced by an individual become the blessings of others. What one member has is thus felt and shared by all.

4. It is quite natural at such a point to generalize and to try to sum up the whole experience in a broad statement. This the writer does, being in a state of exultation, in the form of an exclamation: "O how very happy is the man who has made the Lord his trust!" He has known this right along. He has now experienced it afresh. He might have sought help from men, "the proud," the self-sufficient, the arrogant, as we all so often do in the day of trouble. They would have been the individuals who "turn aside to false gods" (Hebrew, "to lies"). But they,

like the gods in whom they trust, would have been a complete delusion. There may have been some particular situation involved on which we are not able to shed any more light at the present time.

b) A record of the thanksgiving offered to the Lord (vv. 5–10)

5. *Many are Thy wondrous works which Thou hast wrought,*
   O Lord, my God, and Thy thoughts toward us;
   There is none to compare with Thee;
   I will declare them and tell them; yet they are more than can be numbered.
6. *Sacrifice and offering Thou dost not desire;*
   But Thou hast given me open ears;
   Burnt offering and sin offering Thou dost not require.
7. *Then I said: Lo, I come;*
   In the roll of the book it is prescribed for me.
8. *I delight to do Thy will, O my God;*
   Thy law is in my inmost heart.
9. *I have proclaimed the good news of righteousness in the great assembly:*
   Lo, I have not shut my lips; O Lord, Thou knowest.
10. *Thy righteousness have I not concealed within my heart;*
    Thy faithfulness and Thy salvation have I declared;
    I have not concealed Thy steadfast love and Thy faithfulness from the great assembly.

5. This is a transcript of the praise offered in the presence of others, no doubt at the sanctuary of God. This may well have been informal praise without a fixed liturgical procedure. His own experience reminds the psalmist of the many other wondrous works that the Lord is known to have wrought for His people and of His "thoughts toward us." What happened to the writer is not without parallel. Every such experience teaches us afresh that "there is none to compare with" Him. Yet the psalmist is resolved "to declare them and tell them," knowing full well that "they are more than can be numbered." The best praise we offer is inadequate also from the point of view of being incapable of telling all that the Lord has done.

6. The statement that follows suggests an alternative course that he might have followed, perhaps, for that matter, he did offer the requisite sacrifices that the law of that time demanded. But a new insight was his, and he wanted to share it with others. In connection with this whole experience this insight came home to him with new force. Samuel had stressed it in an unusual connection (I Sam. 15:22f.). It was the truth that the externals of worship are secondary. Or expressed in an absolute statement for a relative one—a type of statement often resorted to by

Biblical writers of the Old Testament and the New—"sacrifice and offering Thou dost not desire." This is a truth that all men can readily discern and easily understand except when they are momentarily making the mistake that could be involved; then they do not see that it applies to them.

The psalmist has nothing against sacrifices as such. They embody beautifully what the heart feels under various conditions but are meaningful only when done in a spirit that corresponds with the nature of the sacrifice offered. Priest and prophet are not poles apart, nor are they at odds with one another. There is room for both and need for both. But the aspect of the case that required special stressing in David's time on the strength of the fresh statement of the case that Samuel had made was a truth that David had absorbed. This is what he refers to when he says: "Thou hast given me open ears" (Hebrew, "ears hast Thou dug for me"). He means: You have made me heedful of the truth involved. He then repeats with variations what he had just said: "Burnt offering and sin offering Thou dost not require." He means, There is something else that Thou desirest first. *Friederichsen* (ZATW, 1922 3–4, p. 315) arrives at much the same conclusion about the expression, "ears hast Thou dug for me."

7. It will be noted that the progression of thought has been logical and natural throughout this section. It still is. For the words, "Then I said: Lo, I come," must in this connection refer to his going to the Temple or sanctuary to pay his vows before the Most High. In doing so he was following the procedure that the Lord had prescribed for him, whether one thinks in terms of sacrifice, which he naturally brought in spite of his protestations in v. 6, or whether one thinks in terms of the more important "sacrifice of the lips" and the doing of the Lord's will at all times and under all circumstances. All these procedures are in one form or another clearly prescribed in God's law or, as he here calls it, "the roll of the book." We obviously here have a reference to the law of Moses which was in existence at that time as numerous passages indicate. This had been "prescribed for" him as it had been for all the people of God as this leader of Israel well recognized with unusually clear insight. This happens to be one of the clearest testimonies to the importance of the Word or law of the Lord for the people of the Old Covenant.

8. Continuing in the same vein, the writer indicates that such conformity to the law and will of the Lord was not a hard and bitter thing for him, for he can say with sincere conviction: "I delight to do Thy will, O my God." Or going a bit deeper, he indicates how this compliance with the will of God has penetrated into his inmost being—"Thy law is in my inmost heart" (Hebrew, "bowels," like the New Testament

usage). One might feel for a moment that the limitations of the Old Testament have been ignored, for Jer. 31:33 indicates that it is characteristic of the "new covenant" to have the law inscribed on the heart. However, achievement of the higher purposes of God is relative before the great consummation; and there are several passages that indicate that the core of the matter, deep, heartfelt obedience to the law, was understood to be essential at all times. See Deut. 6:6; also Prov. 3:3; 7:3.

9. It is in this spirit that the psalmist has told what God did for him, and told it "in the great assembly" where God's people congregated in the holy city for public worship. It is of interest to note how he describes these acts of public confession and thanksgiving. He calls them "proclaiming the good news" (one word in the Hebrew, like "evangelize"), in fact, "good news of righteousness." For God's righteousness is that marvelous attribute of His which leads Him both to deal graciously with those who faithfully serve Him and seek His countenance as well as to punish the evildoer. Whenever God helps us, we are in duty bound, in the language of the Scriptures, to extol His righteousness. Conscious that his confession was in no sense halfhearted or concealed, he adds: "Lo, I have not shut my lips, O Lord, Thou knowest."

10. Continuing in the same strain, he adds: "Thy righteousness have I not concealed within my heart." He would remind both himself and others that it may be cowardice to claim to feel duly grateful but to fail to give an open indication of this feeling. The rest of his confession points up what attributes of God have taken on new meaning for him. He recognizes as he never did before the "faithfulness and the salvation of God" and has "declared" this openly. He has also been made aware that the "steadfast love" of God, which moves Him to keep all the covenant obligations that bind Him to His people, is far greater than he has supposed and makes confession of this fact publicly. This is a fine Old Testament passage on the subject of bearing witness to the things that the Lord has done for us, especially as such witness finds expression among fellow believers and worshipers.

c) A prayer for deliverance from ills still impending (vv. 11–17)

11. *Do not Thou, O Lord, withhold Thy mercies from me;*
    May Thy steadfast love and Thy faithfulness ever preserve me.
12. *For innumerable evils have shut me in;*
    My iniquities have overtaken me so that I cannot see;
    They are more than the hairs of my head;
    My courage fails me.
13. *Be pleased, O Lord, to deliver me;*
    O Lord, make haste to help me.

14. May they be put to shame and confounded altogether who seek
    to destroy my life;
    May they be driven back and put to shame that wish me evil.
15. May they be appalled by reason of their shame,
    Who say to me: Aha, Aha!
16. May all they that seek Thee rejoice and be glad in Thee;
    May they who love Thy salvation say continually, Great is the
    Lord!
17. Though I be poor and needy, yet the Lord cares for me;
    Thou art my help and deliverer; do not tarry, O my God.

11. A major difficulty has been overcome, others are yet to be overcome. Having thanked for deliverance from the first, the writer continues to pray for help from the second.

The section can naturally be divided into several parts. First there is the extended petition for help (vv. 11–13). Then follows a prayer that is directed against those that oppose him with evil intent and purpose (vv. 14, 15). In contrast to this God's blessing is asked upon the head of those that help him or that take the same attitude that he does (v. 16). A closing plea for help rounds out the whole. As he began his prayer with emphasis on his waiting for the Lord's help, so he closes it.

12. In an extended petition for help the writer (v. 12) makes mention of his sins, "My iniquities have overtaken me." He apparently intends to say that the consequences of his iniquities, that is, the logical punishments that follow, have begun to catch up with him. More must be intended than merely an acute sense of sinfulness. These saints were not greater sinners than are others, nor were they too keenly aware of their sins in a somewhat morbid sense, so to speak. The full weight of what sin is had merely taken hold upon them under the enlightening influence of the Spirit. It was this that led the psalmist also to say: "They are more numerous than the hairs of my head." Nothing can so unman one as this deep sense of sin. Therefore he also says: "My courage (Hebrew, "heart") fails me."

14. It will be noted that in the prayer directed against those that oppose him (v. 14f.) his intention is in no sense the destruction of his opponents, but rather that they may meet with such experiences as may bring them to their senses. This should be noted carefully in trying to evaluate the so-called "imprecatory" psalms. That his opponents are not merely personal enemies who are animated by a certain ill will is apparent from the fact that they both wish him evil and seek to destroy his life. They are intent on nothing less than murder. Where the line of demarcation is so sharply drawn as it is in this psalm, the other group are the ones who "love the salvation" of the Lord. To pray that they may be made glad is but a natural and proper prayer.

The closing verse has a poignancy all its own. The form into which it was cast by the *A.V.* has a pleasant flavor, especially the clause, "Yet the Lord thinketh upon me."

NOTES

3. "Many will see and fear." This sentence has an unusual play upon words in the original: Many will *yir'u* and *yira'u*.

4. "The proud" has this meaning only in this passage. Whether the word has any connection with the chaotic ocean that existed at primeval creation is hard to determine. The meaning "proud" is well enough assured in this instance. In apposition with this word is *satey khazabh*, literally: "turners aside of lie," which must mean, those "who turn aside to false idols." The same use of "lie" appears in Amos 2:4.

6. The clause that we have rendered, "Thou hast given me open *ears*," appears in Heb. 10:5 as, "But a *body* Thou hast prepared for me." How this change in text came about in the Greek is hard to determine. But the writer of the letter to the Hebrews apparently felt that the basic import of the verse had not been changed (the whole body for a part), and he was thus content to quote the text as he found it.

7. This verse is usually translated as *RSV* renders it: "In the roll of the book it is written of me." But the Hebrew idiom involved *(kathubh 'alay)* can also very properly be rendered "prescribed for me" as II Kings 22:13 shows.

12. Some interpreters feel that the words "so that I cannot see" should be rendered so that an object is supplied: "so that I cannot see them all" (so *Koenig*). But there is such a thing as being overwhelmed by the perplexity that sin causes to such an extent that one finds his sight waning in his distress—not an unworthy thought.

17. Though the Hebrew says, "But I am poor and needy," it may be noted that many clauses that are thus coordinated have a concessive meaning in certain connections. That meaning is found here.

On the relation of this psalm to Ps. 70 it may be added that the latter need not be regarded as presenting a slightly corrupted text in the instances where Ps. 70 differs from the latter part of Ps. 40. The theory is advanced by *Hengstenberg* that David himself may have prepared the second half of Ps. 40 as a separate piece for those who especially feel the need of immediate help but have not recently been delivered from some notable distress. In separating it thus the writer may have made some minor changes with the freedom that any writer has under the circumstances. Whether we are able at this late date to tell exactly what motivated these changes is difficult to say.

Psalm 41

THE PRAYER OF A SICK MAN
BESET BY CRUEL ENEMIES

THE CLAIM of the Hebrew text that this is a psalm of David can be maintained on the basis of the correspondence between the statements of the psalm and the known facts of David's life. One major factor involved in this prayer is that its author writes concerning a sickness of his. We admit freely that we find no such instance in the material reported in the historical books of the Old Testament. Yet it must be quite obvious that the Sacred Record did not attempt to record all such minor details. However, if we place this psalm into the time of the rebellion of Absalom, it would fit exceptionally well. The "bosom friend" could well be Ahithophel. The period of illness would have led to the omission of the carrying out of many duties in David's administrative work, which would explain how Absalom was able to claim that men were not getting just treatment under David's administration (II Sam. 15:2–6). The fact that the father makes no special reference to his son can easily be explained.

A more recent trend in the interpretation of this and similar psalms is to make much of the possibility that such a psalm could be a section of a liturgy that was regularly used by men when they recovered from illness or on one particular occasion when this one man recovered after an unusual experience. We have our serious misgivings regarding this approach. In the first place, if this psalm is liturgical, then there must have been many occasions for the use of it. Yet a situation exactly like that of the writer involved is hard to duplicate. But if the piece was used but once, such isolated use scarcely warrants calling it liturgical. Besides, the mere possibility that some parts may be assigned to certain individuals (like v. 1 to a priest or v. 13 to the assembled congregation) does not yet prove that such a possibility was a reality. Different commentators usually offer different possibilities, which are far from agreeing with one another. Even if remotely parallel pieces from the literature of Babylon, Egypt, and Canaan, or Ugarit, are usually construed as being liturgical in character, that does not warrant casting many psalms into the same molds. At best we can admit the possibility of liturgical use in some instances, but the liturgical approach is not so surely established as to allow it to dominate the interpretation.

The fact that in John 13:18 Jesus quotes part of v. 9 from this psalm and refers it to Judas has led some interpreters to regard the entire psalm as Messianic. This is scarcely permissible. What David experienced with regard to Ahithophel was duplicated or fulfilled in an analogous way in Christ's experience with regard to Judas. Christ could scarcely have meant more than that when He quoted this psalm. For in it, as in the one preceding, there is an admission of sinfulness on the part of its author, cf. v. 4. This psalm may at best be regarded as being *indirectly* Messianic.

Two experiences afflict the writer grievously: he is sick, and he has vindictive enemies. Whether the treatment suffered at the hands of his enemies brought on his sickness, or whether the one affliction was more grievous than the other, it is almost impossible to determine.

We suggest the following outline of the psalm:

a) A reflection on how God deals with the compassionate (vv. 1–3).
b) A complaint of a sick man because of cruel enemies (vv. 4–9).
c) A prayer to be upheld by God (vv. 10–12)

> *To the Choir Director. A Psalm of David.*
> 1. *O how very happy is the man who has consideration for the weak!*
>   *In the time of trouble the Lord will deliver him.*
> 2. *The Lord will protect him and keep him alive;*
>   *He shall be called blessed in the land;*
>   *And mayest Thou not give him up into the will of his enemies.*
> 3. *The Lord will sustain him on his sickbed;*
>   *Thou hast changed his whole lying down in sickness into health.*

It has long been a source of great difficulty to determine what the relation of this first section is to the rest of the psalm. There are two types of interpretation. One group regards this section as an indirect admonition to the *readers* to show "consideration" for the weak, that is to say, for the psalmist, who was one of the "weak" in his affliction. By this they mean (*Weiser*) that the readers are to take note of what befell him and share in his joy over the deliverance which he experienced. This seems rather involved and difficult to follow.

The other group regards the whole section as an objective statement, in which the psalmist states what sounds like a general truth but implies that he himself is one of those who followed the principle involved, of having consideration for the weak; and then, since he did this, he may expect the recompense that the Lord grants to those who act thus. Modesty prevents his saying directly that he is in this class.

Nevertheless, since he once practiced this virtue, he hopes to receive the reward granted such an individual—an unusual approach to be sure, but not an unwholesome one. It would be nothing more than to expect to see the promise of the Lord realized in your own case: "Blessed are the merciful, for they shall obtain mercy."

There is, it is true, one other major approach, which states that the verse should be translated: "Blessed is he that judges wisely of the weak," that is, who does not let himself be misled by the afflictions of a lowly man so as to conclude that, because his sufferings are many, therefore he must be an exceptionally guilty person, as Job's friends judged with regard to him (*Calvin*). But the verb involved (*maskil*) scarcely has this meaning whereas the meaning that we have given it above is well supported by passages such as Ps. 101:2; Prov. 16:20; Neh. 8:13. We accept the first of the above interpretations. We admit that it lays a heavy emphasis on a promised reward, but it must not be overlooked that in Matt. 5:7 and elsewhere the Lord Himself promised such a reward. Our passage may be the first instance where the issue is formulated as concisely as we have it here. But it certainly makes sense to expect the Lord to deal with men as they have dealt with others.

The reward expected is broken down into six different statements. There is first the over-all statement, "In the time of trouble the Lord will deliver him." Since he presumably delivered others (this is implied in "having consideration for") the Lord will do as much for him. Then, "the Lord will protect him and keep him alive." This implies largely keeping evils away from such a person. Then, his lot shall be so fortunate that men shall point to him as an example: "He shall be called blessed in the land."

At this point the psalmist involuntarily turns directly to God, addressing Him as the Scriptures so often do in unexpected ways, "And mayest Thou not give him up into the will of his enemies." Such a prayer was doubly motivated in a psalm which has much to say about the "will" or fury of unreasonable foes. Lastly also quite an issue is made of the fact of deliverance from sickness because the writer himself had gone through this experience or was still in process of going through it (v. 3): "The Lord will sustain him on his sickbed." Then follows a rather positive statement in the perfect tense, "Thou hast changed his lying down in sickness into health." The reason for the change of tense could well be that the writer here drops the purely objective statement and speaks of his own experience: he has experienced a complete recovery.

The efforts to escape the difficulty posed by the first verse by changing the text are unwholesome. Such are: "Oh, the happiness of him who takes account of God" (*Leslie*); "Blessed is the man who is delivered out of great distress" (*Schmidt*)—an obvious and inspired platitude.

The second section is in the nature of a historical account which offers the prayer that the psalmist uttered in the day of his trouble. The bulk of it has to do with his enemies.

4. *As for me, I said: O Lord, be gracious unto me;*
   Heal my soul, for I have sinned against Thee.
5. *My enemies speak against me maliciously:*
   When will he die and his name perish?
6. *And if one comes to me to see me he speaks lies;*
   His heart gathers wicked slanders;
   He goes outside and tells it abroad.
7. *All that hate me whisper together against me;*
   They devise evil against me.
8. *(They say): Some dastardly thing has fastened upon him;*
   He who has lain down will not rise up again.
9. *Even my bosom friend in whom I had full confidence,*
   Who ate my bread, has lifted up the heel against me.

4. His prayer may be summed up in the topic sentence, "O Lord, be gracious unto me." He motivates it by a statement that is expressive of deep understanding, "Heal my soul, for I have sinned against Thee." Whenever troubles befall us, there is some element of sin and guilt involved on our part. In David's case this petition was all the more appropriate because he had but recently committed his very grievous double crime. We always merit fully whatever punishment or correction is involved in God's laying His hand upon us. The plea "heal my soul" should not be reduced to a pale "heal me." "Soul" is the entire person including what we call "body and soul." Though this could obviously be rendered "me," the simple pronoun fails to express the richer connotation of the Hebrew idiom.

5. In regard to the "enemies" involved it may well be noted that, since David was the leader of the group that worshiped the Lord, the enemies were godless and unprincipled men. More than personal enmity was involved in all cases such as this. During the psalmist's sickness they gave utterance to malicious words, for what else but malice is it when men say: "When will he die and his name perish?" This implies that they would welcome nothing more gladly than his early death.

6. The singular of the verb that follows aims to cite a particular instance—"and if one comes to see me." The enemies apparently observed the common courtesies of the day: in his sickness they did come

to see him, but their visit was hollow sham: "He speaks lies," that is to say, in the words of comfort that he utters. His mind (Hebrew, heart) is busy gathering wicked slanders on the basis of the observations he makes in the sickroom with reference to the patient. Then "he goes outside and tells it abroad."

7. More than that, these false friends, here rightly described as "all that hate me," go so far as "to whisper against" him, and "they devise evil against" him. This may well explain how the plotting of Absalom was possible. David sensed that something was afoot but discovered too late what it was. This may also explain why David seemed so little able to forestall the scheming of his son. Physical incapacity weakened his usually active administration of affairs. *Mowinckel's* suggestion that "whisper" means *Beschwoerungen murmeln* ("mutter curses") is not well grounded.

8. One of the direct slanders resorted to was: "Something dastardly has fastened upon him." Note the vagueness of the statement. Some of the most effective slanders have been characterized by such vagueness. The Hebrew phrase, "a thing of wickedness," is unusually difficult to translate, witness the many different renderings by commentators. It seems more likely that some physical disability is hinted at than some moral obliquity. Therefore *KJ* may not be too far from the truth of the matter with its rendering, "an evil disease." Though the last part of their statement is cast in an almost proverbial form, "He who has lain down will not rise up again," yet only one person could be in their thoughts: he whom they detest so much that they will not even speak his name.

9. But the "most unkindest cut of all" was what his "bosom friend" did (Hebrew, "the man of my peace"), one in whom he had fullest confidence (cf., II Sam. 16:23), one who had been intimate with the king and had eaten at his table as one of the regular attendants at court. He "lifted up the heel against" David. Whatever the precise import of the phrase is, it seems to get its color from the doings of a beast of burden that kicks out at its master unawares. The phrase is the epitome of vile dealing.

It would appear, according to v. 4, that this entire complaint was spoken in prayer before the Lord, and we may justly assume that such an approach tempers extreme statements, so that all that is spoken in these words is free from unseemly exaggerations and from excess of passion. The picture of the enemies is not overdrawn.

The trouble is not yet over, therefore the prayer continues, asking that the one who prays may be upheld by his God in the danger and necessity that are upon him.

10. *But Thou, O Lord, be gracious unto me and raise me up
That I may requite them.*
11. *By this I know that Thou delightest in me,
In that my enemy does not triumph over me.*
12. *But as for me, Thou upholdest me in my integrity;
Thou dost set me before Thy face forever.*

10. Many readers of this psalm have wished that v. 10 might have ended with the words, "be gracious unto me and raise me up." The purpose for which the writer asks to be raised up is stated in the words, "that I may requite them." *Kittel* cites this as an instance of "hot, glowing vengeance" and speaks of "carnal passion." He admits that we can understand how it came about but claims that we can never sanction it. Most recent writers take a similar attitude. But it may be pointed out that a wholesome explanation has been offered. No one has phrased it quite so soberly as has *Kirkpatrick:* "The words have a vindictive ring which is startling and seems inconsistent with Ps. 7:4; Prov. 20:22. Yet if the speaker was David, conscious of his divine appointment to be king, he might well pray that he might be restored to punish traitors as they deserve. For the most part he would leave vengeance to Jehovah (I Sam. 25:33; II Sam. 3:39)." It may be added that punishment of treason is among the duties of a faithful ruler. Our soft age has largely overlooked this responsibility in its overly sympathetic attitude toward all miscreants.

11. If the enemy is not permitted to overthrow him, the writer will see in that fact a token of God's approval of him. This is virtually a prayer that the outcome desired might become a reality.

12. The last part of the prayer is by far not as self-righteous as may appear on the surface. *Koenig* says very properly that "integrity is merely a comparatively high measure of virtuous conduct." It is the least that could be expected of any faithful follower of the Lord. Though the verse could be translated, "Thou upholdest me because of my integrity" (as *Septuagint, Luther,* etc. render it) and though such a translation could be defended on both grammatical and moral grounds, yet we prefer the old *AV* approach, which is equally defensible. It also agrees well with the second member of the verse, which has the ring of calm assurance. So the psalm closes with a statement of certitude that all is well between the psalmist and his God, and if that is the case, then all is well.

13. *Blessed be the Lord God of Israel from everlasting to everlasting.
Amen and Amen.*

This appears to be a liturgical addition that was, perhaps, inserted by those who gave final form to the arrangement of the Psalter. Each of the five books of the Psalter closes with some such addition (cf., 72:18f.; 89:52; 106:48).

NOTES

1. The word *dal*, rendered "poor" by *KJ*, is rather the weak or lowly.
3. We should have liked to retain the *KJ* rendering, "Thou wilt make all his bed in his sickness," which is dependent on the interpretation of the verb *haphakh* "to change," implying the changing of the rumpled state of his bedclothes. The verb apparently has greater force and involves completely changing a man's situation.
8. On the unusual use of *debhar* see *KS* 306p. It here includes the whole category.
11. The *ki* introduces, not a clause of cause but of evidence, see *KS* 389b.

BOOK TWO

Psalm 42

LONGING FOR GOD

THIS PSALM is marked by rare poetic beauty and deep feeling. A plaintive cry runs through it—deep thirst of a soul for God.

Since it is placed first in the second book of the Psalter, it should at once be noted that the psalms in this group are distinguished in part by the fact that the name of God that predominates throughout the book is *Elohim,* no longer *Yahweh,* as was the case in the first book.

If the heading is construed as were those that preceded, then the authorship of the psalm must be ascribed to the sons of Korah—a group. Why individuals of this group are not mentioned must forever remain a secret. Regarding the sons of Korah we know that they were of the tribe of Levi as may be gathered from I Chron. 6:7, 22; Num. 16:1; 26:8ff. That they were a kind of guild of singers at the Temple appears from II Chron. 20:19. But a peculiar feature will be observed as the study of the psalm progresses that there is no man to whom the things written in it would apply more clearly than they do to David himself. To harmonize these two possibilities, some interpreters arrive at the conclusion that what really happens in the course of the poem is that a sympathetic Levite of the Korah family so vividly transports himself into David's situation that he virtually writes out of the very soul of David. That construction, however, may seem a bit forced.

So there is the other possibility that a Korahite actually wrote the psalm and described an experience of his own, and the similarity of what he lived through and that which David experienced results from the fact that this man accompanied David on the occasion of his flight from his son Absalom (II Sam. 15:30ff.). This view is most ably presented by *Delitzsch*. The author may well have been a prominent Levite of the Korahite group, and so the position of leadership, demanded by v. 4, would be taken care of. The question that is raised by the geography indicated in v. 6 will be discussed when this verse is interpreted.

Some commentators find in this psalm a longing for the sanctuary of God. Others emphasize the fact that the longing for God Himself is stressed. Both apparently, go together though the longing for God Himself is paramount as v. 1 clearly indicates. Love for the sanctuary without the love of the God of the sanctuary is meaningless. Love for God which does not result in love for His house is unnatural.

Then there is the question of the relation of this psalm to the one that follows. That there is a connection between the two is clear from the fact that the refrain of Ps. 42 (viz., vv. 6 and 12) appears as the conclusion of Ps. 43, whether exactly in the same form in each case or not is immaterial for the present. Besides, Ps. 43 brings the unresolved issues of Ps. 42 to a conclusion so that the latter practically makes the former necessary. Also the fact that Ps. 43 has no heading whereas practically all others in this book of the Psalter have indicates that it must be tied up very closely with the preceding one. This much must at least be claimed: the two psalms belong together. Whether they originally constituted one psalm is a question that cannot now be answered with any measure of certainty. It seems to be the case that from earliest times they appeared separately, for the *Septuagint* offers them as two distinct poems.

a) **The painful experience of being separated from God (vv. 1–5)**

To the Choir Director. A maskil (didactic poem) *by the sons of Korah.*

1. *As the deer longs for streams with water,*
So my soul longs for Thee, O God.

2. My soul thirsts for God, for the living God;
   When may I come and appear before God's face?
3. My tears have been my food day and night,
   While men are saying to me all day long: Where is your God?
4. These things will I remember and so pour out my soul by myself:
   How I went along with the throng, how I served as leader for them going to the house of God
   With the sound of rejoicing and praise, a multitude keeping the festivals.
5. Why are you cast down, O my soul; and why are you disquieted within me?
   Hope in God, for I shall again praise Him who is the help of my countenance.

1. The psalmist feels himself separated from God. It is an inner separation which greatly disturbs him. God does not seem to answer or respond when He is approached. Some barrier seems to intervene between himself and his God. It is a feeling that is as strong or stronger than physical thirst. It recalls to the writer's mind a parallel that he has seen at one time or another: a deer going about in search of water in a dry and barren land. Such an experience may be very real and anything but an illusion. *Luther's* classical description may be offered here: "Here a man must make a distinction, for God is of two kinds. At times He is a hidden and covered God. He appears to be such a one at times when a man feels his sins during a season of temptation, or feels other shortcomings, whether they are spiritual or physical. These things claim one's attention so much so that a man can take no comfort from the fact that God will be gracious and merciful to him. They now who draw their conclusions on the basis of this hidden type of God fall into despair and damnation without any hope whatsoever. . . . The other picture or concept of God is that He is openly manifested and not a hidden God, that is to say, He is the picture of a kindly, gracious, merciful, and reconciled God. . . . Even as the sun is of two kinds . . . sometimes covered with clouds, and sometimes shining out of a clear sky" (St. Louis ed., IV, 1584). The illustration employed by the psalmist forcefully conveys the thought of the deepest possible longing for God as it is felt by the godly man in times when the normal relation to God has been disturbed. The reason the writer says "streams with water" is that there are so many runlets or wadis in the Holy Land, which are utterly devoid of water during the greater part of the year.

2. As the psalmist reiterates the thought of his thirsting for God he

describes Him as "the living God," apparently for the reason that he feels that, in the last analysis, God is the only source of the life of his soul. Having life, He can impart life. It now becomes apparent what brought about this state of acute wretchedness. For when the psalmist asks: "When may I come and appear before God's face?" the very form of expression implies going to the sanctuary. Therefore something has happened to prevent him from going to the sanctuary of God as he had been wont to do in times past. This situation has brought about a feeling of separation from God. The thought is not that the writer could not have felt the nearness of God without going to the sanctuary, but under the present circumstances these two things go together. That might well agree with David's experience or that of any man who accompanied him at the time. For in David's case in particular the flight from Absalom could not but recall to David how his own sin had been the root of all the tragic happenings connected with Absalom's rebellion.

3. In the type of emotional expression characteristic of the Oriental the writer's grief has sought relief and found expression in tears, so much so that he has done more weeping than eating. He practically says: "Instead of eating I weep" (*Hengstenberg*). What at the same time puts a sharp barb into his heart is the taunt of men who keep saying to him continually, "Where is your God?" that is to say, "Why does He not give heed to your extremity and prayers and tears to deliver you from the sad lot that has befallen you?" One need not venture the claim that the individuals who spoke thus must have been heathen. The opposition that David and men like him continually encountered would explain the attitude of the persons involved. They may well have been men of Israel without being in any sense devout and godly men. Most men have found the taunts of their fellow men the most bitter of human experiences.

4. The psalmist manfully resolves to recall a helpful and pleasant experience of the past, both to cheer himself because it was pleasant and to strengthen himself because it may again become his. He recalls what a blessed experience the great festivals at the sanctuary of God were in former times. Corporate worship has rewards all its own. The writer envisions how throngs of worshipers went to the holy place, he himself according to the position that he held leading them as they went. Jubilant shouts and words of praise filled the air as the throng drew nearer and nearer to the sanctuary. He remembers how real it all was, and how it helped him personally to draw near to God. What God did for him at that time seems to be what he especially recalls though he speaks chiefly of that which he and the multitude did.

5. He now bestirs himself in an effort to throw off the wretchedness

that is upon him. As some interpreters state it: His spirit addresses a challenge to his lagging soul: "Why are you cast down, O my soul, and why are you disquieted within me?" as much as to say: All your past experience adds up to this, that God has not withdrawn from you nor abandoned you. In fact, the positive side of his self-admonition charts a very helpful course for him to follow: "Hope in God." That is to say, Build on Him, rest on Him even though for the present He gives no tokens of accepting you or even of hearing you. You know that your past experience gives you full warrant for such an attitude. In fact, for the moment he grows quite confident: "I shall again praise Him who is the help of my countenance." Though he may be thinking chiefly of public worship, his statement surely points to the certainty of again being at one with God in due time. The expression "help of my countenance" apparently means: the help to which my countenance turns (*Koenig*).

b) **Assurance partly restored by earnest prayer (vv. 6–11)**

6. *O my God, my soul is cast down within me;*
   Therefore will I remember Thee from the land of Jordan and the
      Hermon hills, from Mount Mizar;
7. *Where deep calls to deep at the sound of Thy cataracts;*
   All thy waves and Thy billows have gone over me.
8. *Yet by day the Lord commands His steadfast love;*
   And by night His song is with me, prayer to the God of my life.
9. *I will say to God, my rock, Why hast Thou forgotten me?*
   Why go I mourning because of the oppression of the enemy?
10. *As with a grievous wound in my bones my enemies taunt me*
    While they say to me all the day: Where is your God?
11. *Why are you cast down, O my soul, and why are you disquieted*
       within me?
    Hope in God, for I shall again praise Him who is the help of my
       countenance and my God.

6. The first half of the psalm was largely complaint, and there is still some undercurrent of the same sort here, but it would be safe to say that the spirit of prayer pervades all a bit more prominently. As a result a larger measure of assurance is in evidence though it cannot yet be said that full assurance has been restored.

That heavy depression resulting from God's hiding His face has not yet been overcome. The psalmist frankly lays this issue before the Lord Himself. He is on the way to recovery in the very moment he does so. His words are: "O my God, my soul is cast down within me." The remedy in such a case is not to try to forget God. Rather: "Therefore will I remember Thee." The fact that he at this point mentions the very place where this experience occurred, as it were identifying it geographically, is not as *Schmidt* states it "a case of prosaic preciseness . . . utterly without parallel." It may rather be thought of as one of those instances when the very locale where an experience came to us impresses itself so strongly upon our remembrance that we cannot think of the one without thinking of the other. There is, therefore, no need of rearranging the text till it says what we think it should say under the circumstances.

The descriptive terms used are "from the land of the Jordan and the Hermon hills, from Mount Mizar." Although *Dalman* found some places in the very area of Mt. Hermon that bore names almost like Mizar, that may not yet be accepted as positive identification. We are inclined to accept the interpretation of *Hengstenberg* and *Delitzsch et.al.* who refer the expression "the Hermon hills" (Hebrew, plural of the word Hermon) to the Anti-Libanus range which is the continuation of the range which is crowned to the north by old Mt. Hermon itself. The "Hermon hills" would then be the range that runs down to the east of the Jordan, which is the very area to which David went in his flight before Absalom. Mizar remains an unidentified hill.

7. The writer may have stood on the bank of the Jordan or some other stream where cataracts were visible. Though these may not have been cataracts that would seem impressive to the traveller from outside of Palestine they may have seemed much more so to the native Palestinian, who most likely never saw any bigger stream of water than the Jordan, which in its downward course has cataracts here and there. Besides, it must be noted that the meaning of the term employed (*tsinnor*) is uncertain. "Cataracts" is the rendering employed by the *Septuagint*. In any event, as the psalmist saw one fast wave rolling over the other; one, as it were, calling to the one succeeding it ("deep calls to deep"), this seemed to him a vivid picture of the griefs that had befallen him, which led him to address himself involuntarily to God: "All Thy waves and Thy billows have gone over me."

8. Some basic truths give anchorage to this troubled soul. One factor is God's "steadfast love." The psalmist knows that God has given command that this shall always stand by him and help him. Another factor that he earnestly believes in is that during the watches of the dark night God will give him such assurance that he will be enabled to voice his confidence in God in "song" and make "prayer" to the God of his life. The distance between himself and God is diminished appreciably when a man can speak thus. He is well on the road to the recovery of the full assurance of faith.

9. This verse and the next offer the prayer that this man resolves to

make. There is no question about it that God is and will forever remain "his rock," the firm ground on which his whole life rests. What perplexes him for the moment is the fact that his feelings do not reflect this fact as they should. But it is not only a matter of subjective impression. God has in His wisdom done something that has brought about this situation. The writer feels that questions concerning what the Lord is doing with us can be best answered by the Lord Himself. He, therefore, purposes to lay the issues before Him: "Why hast Thou forgotten me? Why go I mourning because of the oppression of the enemy?" In his inmost heart the writer, no doubt, knows that God cannot forget a man. Yet for the present it would seem as though He had. The psalmist is confident that God will in due time clear these matters up for His saints.

10. The author reverts to a matter that is alluded to in v. 3, the taunts of the enemies. These taunts are so painful that he describes them as being the equivalent of "a grievous wound in my bones." The Hebrew has even a sharper word than "wound," it says "killing" as *Luther* retains this in his translation: *Es ist als ein Mord in meinen Beinen*. The taunt that must have been often repeated is stated again: "Where is your God?"

11. Cf. v. 5. By being repeated as a refrain the thought expressed in this verse becomes an emphatic keynote of the psalm.

NOTES

The other psalms attributed to the sons of Korah are 44–49, 84f., and 87f.

1. The word for dear *'ayyal,* is masculine though the verb used with it is in the feminine. This does, indeed, point to the hind rather than the hart, but the Hebrew is apparently doing what all languages do, it is using the masculine form for the feminine as we have also done in our translation.

2. Further examples that the nifal of the verb "see" has the meaning "appear" are the following: Exod. 23:15, 17; 34:23f.; Deut. 16:16. The correction suggested by the margin, the *kal,* "see," overlooks the fact, so emphatically stated in Exod. 33:20, that man cannot see God and survive, a fact that is frequently stated elsewhere in the Scriptures.

4. "These things" refers, of course, to the things about to be mentioned. Some commentators suggest that the root of the verb *'eddaddem* may be *dadah* (so *KB*), others, that it may be *dawah* (so *KW*). The hithpael is here used. *BDB* regards the form as a piel, "lead slowly."

5. It cannot be denied that the first word of v. 6, "my God," may be joined to v. 5 and thus the refrain made to correspond literally with

v. 11 and with 43:5. However, it is equally plausible to let "my God" stand as it does in the Masoretic text, a vocative that begins v. 6.

It cannot be denied that there are difficult forms in this psalm and a number of unfamiliar terms. But it is still far better to make the best of the text as it stands than to resort to the vague uncertainties of conjectural emendations.

Psalm 43

PRAYER FOR VINDICATION AND RESTORATION

THE RELATION of this psalm to the preceding one has been discussed in the introduction to Ps. 42. It may be indicated in addition that this psalm furnishes the proper conclusion to its predecessor. The whole experience has not been terminated till Ps. 43 has concluded. When the two are regarded as a whole as is done by most present-day commentators, there are three stages through which the thought runs. The tension and pain are most severe in the first section (42:1–5); as our division of the psalm indicated, the rest of the psalm may be considered under the heading, "Assurance partly restored by earnest prayer"; by the time the end of Ps. 43 has been reached the waves have subsided, and the speaker is all but restored to the very steps of the sanctuary.

Two petitions are offered: one for vindication, the other for restoration. Each consists of two verses. The refrain concludes the thought, but in its new setting it breathes a more restrained and hopeful note.

1. *Vindicate me, O God, and plead my case against an ungodly people;*
   From deceitful and wicked men deliver me.
2. *For Thou art the God who is my refuge;*
   Why hast Thou cast me off?
   Why go I about mourning because of the oppression of the enemy?

1. The vindication asked for has to do with clearing the name of the writer, which has been sullied by criminal attacks. He is sure of his innocence in regard to the charges that have been directed at him. He is ready to stand before the bar of divine justice and submit to the inspec-

tion of the all-seeing eye of God. Or, changing the figure, he invited no one less than God himself to argue his just case even as we engage a competent lawyer to take our case in court. If we consider concrete possibilities we may think of the writer as being associated with David in the flight before Absalom and sharing the vile defamations that were heaped upon the head of the king at that time.

The antagonists are described as "an ungodly people." Though the term *goy* is used, which commonly refers to hostile Gentiles, the psalmist seems to be thinking rather of their great numbers and the fact that their attitude is ungodly. They are further described as "deceitful and wicked men." Though the singular is written ("man"), it is, no doubt, used collectively in the sense of deceitful and wicked men generally. Slanders upon our good name always affect us painfully, all the more so when we are innocent.

2. In approaching God the writer practically claims that this is the normal and natural thing for him to do, for God is the God who is his refuge. The why of it all, as is so often the case, eludes him, so the painful why is committed to the Lord Himself. It appears as though God has cast him off. The second painful question is repeated from Ps. 42:10b—another indication of the fact that both psalms belong together.

3. *Oh, send out Thy light and Thy truth;*
   They shall lead me and bring me to Thy holy hill and to Thy dwelling.
4. *Then will I go to the altar of God, to God, my exceeding joy;*
   Then will I praise Thee upon the harp, O God, my God.
5. *Why are you cast down, O my soul, and why are you disquieted within me?*
   Hope in God, for I shall again praise Him, who is the help of my countenance and my God.

3. "Light" is best thought of as a figure of God's mercy or His "steadfast love." Darkness seems to have settled upon us when we are deprived of the assurance of God's mercy. Light seems to shine into our life when we know ourselves to be in God's favor. "Truth" is appropriately combined with light, for truth implies absolute steadfastness and thus indicates the continuance of God's mercy. Both may have been envisioned by the writer as guardian angels of a sort who are walking along at his side. This is, then, another way of saying: Let me again become assured of Thy gracious favor, O Lord. With emphasis, which is indicated by the use of the personal pronoun, the Hebrew says: "*They shall lead me,*" as much as to say: I seek no lesser guides than these.

The writer rests assured that, being guided thus, he will again attain what he had so earnestly sought in the first part of this double poem (42:2, 4): he will be guided to God's holy hill, where the established sanctuary is to be found. The all-important thing for him is not the visible sanctuary as such but the assurance of being received and accepted by God. The visible approach and the invisible were of one piece to this man, as should be the case for all. Then the rare joys of sacrifice and public praise of God will again be his as he here vows to make them his (v. 4).

5. On v. 5 see 42:5.

NOTES

1. The verb *ribhah* has an unusual accent on the ultima. See *GK* 72s.

3. The word for "dwelling" appears in the plural, which some grammarians call the "amplificative plural." See *KS* 260f. Such a plural expresses the rare dignity of the structure.

4. For "my exceeding joy" the Hebrew uses a form of expression which is the equivalent of a superlative (literally "the joy of my exultation"). Cf. *KS* 309b.

Psalm 44

"WHY DOST THOU HIDE THY FACE?"

ACCORDING to *Gunkel's* classification this psalm is very properly designated a lament.

Authorship of this psalm is ascribed to the sons of Korah as was also Ps. 42. The time of the writing of the psalm causes much trouble for commentators. Though it had almost become a commonplace to set the time as the age of the Maccabees, especially since *Calvin* advocated such a date, many have had serious misgivings about this dating, in fact, today they even claim more frequently that such a date is impossible (e.g., *Leslie*). It appears to us that it makes good sense and is in full harmony with the matters that are written about the reign of David to ascribe this psalm, as we did Ps. 42, to his age. The precarious military situation that the psalm reflects—a very seroius military setback and a people greatly disturbed thereby—seems to be met by what is recorded in II Sam. 8:13, 14, where David was severely beset by the Syrians to the north and the allied Edomites, Ammonites, etc., to the south. An indication of the serious nature of the situation may be gathered from I Kings 11:15, which indicates that the issue was so grave that Joab had to bury the slain secretly lest the enemy discover how greatly his forces had been weakened.

Furthermore, that higher level of faith which the nation here manifests in being able to claim an adherence to the covenant of the Lord fits best into the picture that the Scriptures give us of the reign of David. The age of Jehoiachin could advance no such claim with any measure of sincerity. Neither could the Israel of the days of the Maccabees as I Macc. 1:15 clearly shows.

The effort to regard this psalm as a cultic piece, or a liturgy, or a liturgical piece for use in days of national lamentation as one modern school of thought is inclined to do necessitates too many assumptions before it becomes feasible. The lack of agreement among the advocates of this approach is additional testimony to its weaknesses.

One point utilized by this approach is the fact that the "we" and the "I" alternate throughout the psalm, the "I" being found in vv. 4, 6, 15. It is claimed that a solo voice speaks in the midst of the liturgical rendition. However, it must appear quite obvious that the shift from plural to singular comes so naturally that it presents no problem to the casual reader; and for the close student the needs of the case are fully met by the assumption that the nation sometimes quite naturally refers to itself by the plural pronoun first person and occasionally collectively by the singular pronoun first person. Both types of usage appear frequently in the psalms. Here they appear side by side.

A strikingly simple and helpful summary of the contents of the psalm was given by *Hengstenberg* in the following words: "The thought pattern stands out very clearly: Thou hast helped us, Thou must help us, but Thou art not helping us, and yet we are not being excluded from Thy help because of guilt on our part, therefore do Thou help us."

We suggest the following outline:

a) God is Israel's king on the basis of past experience (vv. 1–8).
b) The sad plight of Israel as of the present (vv. 9–16).
c) The problem of the psalm: Israel had remained faithful (vv. 17–22).
d) An eager prayer for help (vv. 23–27).

The problem of the psalm is embedded in its very midst and may be restated thus: Israel has not been unfaithful to the Lord, yet affliction has come upon her. Greatly disturbed by the seeming discrepancy, the psalmist lays the whole issue before the Lord with earnest prayer for help.

> *To the Choir Director, of the Sons of Korah.*
> *A Didactic Poem* (Maskil).
> 1. *O God, we have heard with our ears, our fathers have told us*
>   *Of the work which Thou didst perform in their days, in days of old.*
> 2. *Thou with Thy hand didst drive out the nations and didst plant them;*
>   *Thou didst afflict peoples, but them Thou didst spread abroad.*
> 3. *For not by their sword did they gain possession of the land;*
>   *Nor did their arm win the victory for them;*
>   *But Thy right hand and Thy arm and the light of Thy countenance;*
>   *For Thou didst delight in them.*
> 4. *Thou art my king, O God;*
>   *Command deliverance for Jacob.*
> 5. *Through Thee we will push down our assailants;*
>   *Through Thy name we will plunder them that rise up against us.*
> 6. *For not in my bow will I trust;*
>   *Neither will my sword save me.*
> 7. *But Thou hast saved us from our assailants;*
>   *And them that hate us hast Thou confounded.*
> 8. *We have made our boast of God continually;*
>   *And we shall praise Thy name forever.*

1. This section clearly has two divisions: vv. 1–3 and vv. 4–8, as the greater length of the members of vv. 1–3 also indicates. The first division offers a record of the past experiences of Israel that have a bearing on the present situation. The present generation has heard from its fathers of a particularly great work which God performed for the fathers in days of old—the expulsion of the inhabitants of Canaan followed by the planting of Israel in their stead. One group was afflicted, the other was "spread abroad," a verb that is applied to the spreading and growth of a plant or bush. And the success of this venture of the occupation of the land of Canaan by the Israelites was to be ascribed, so the nation well knew, to nothing other than the right hand of the Almighty, to His arm, and to the light of His countenance, which in its superb divine splendor scattered Israel's foes (cf., Exod. 14:24). And the Israelites further understood and confessed that all this happened to them, not because of any merit or worthiness in them, but because in His free sovereign grace He did delight in them. The expression

"light of Thy countenance" may also refer to God's "gracious favor" (*Taylor*).

In the division that follows (vv. 4–8) Israel expresses the faith that it as nation has as a result of God's manifestation of His mighty power and grace. Almost the whole of this section is a confident note of assurance that the nation will be able to prevail in the strength of the Lord, its God. Only one brief note of petition in regard to the prevailing trouble is injected in v. 4b, where the later petitions are anticipated. But the keynote of the whole (vv. 1–8) is given in v. 4a: "Thou art my King, O God." God's effective rule of Israel is confessed. The brief petition, "Command deliverance for Jacob," employs the figure that deliverance is a holy messenger of the Lord, who stands at His beck and call and will, if He so directs, bring such help to the nation as it needs.

To this is added the strong assurance (v. 5) that no foe can hold its own against a nation that rests on the Lord, its God. All opponents will be put down and plundered. The weapons of the warfare of God's people are not carnal. Though bow and sword are used, it is not these that give the victory, and, as Israel has now abundantly experienced, it is God (v. 7) who has saved His people and confounded her foes in the past. This gives a reason (v. 8) for the glorious confidence that the true people of God have always had: they have made their boast of Him continually and already now praise His name for all the future victories which, they are sure, His mighty strength will secure for them.

9. *Yet Thou hast cast us off and put us to shame*
   And hast not gone forth with our armies.
10. *Thou hast made us turn back from our assailant;*
    And they that hate us took spoil for themselves.
11. *Thou hast given us over as sheep for the slaughter*
    And hast scattered us among the nations.
12. *Thou hast sold Thy people for a mere trifle;*
    And Thou hast not increased Thy wealth by their price.
13. *Thou hast made us a taunt to our neighbors,*
    A mockery and derision to those round about us.
14. *Thou hast made us a byword among the nations,*
    A shaking of the head among the people.
15. *All the day long my disgrace is before me;*
    And the shame of my face has covered me;
16. *Because of the words of the mockers and scoffers*
    By reason of the enemy and the avenger.

This is a picture of the sad plight of Israel as it appears at the time of the writer. This picture is offered as a prayer to God, not as though He were not aware of what is transpiring, but because God's people always cast their burden upon the Lord. The "Thou" that is the subject of the first six verses of this section clearly ascribes all the present affliction to God's agency. Things like this do not just happen. The Almighty sits on the throne and rules effectively. It is because of His sovereign disposition that these calamities have come about.

We list Israel's troubles briefly. Shame has come upon the nation because the Lord has not gone with its forces as He did in days of old. A disastrous defeat must have occurred. David's initial efforts against the Syrians (cf., II Sam. 8:3ff.) may have been marked by reverses. This psalm may have been written during the time they occurred. The description continues (v. 10) by indicating that Israel was turned back and plundered. The loss of troops suffered at the time must have been alarming (v. 11), for Israel is spoken of as having been like sheep for slaughter (Hebrew: "sheep for food"), and captives taken on the field of battle were sold into slavery "among the nations." This last statement does not necessitate thinking of the whole nation as having been led away into a captivity like the Babylonian captivity. With a note of complaint rather than of mild irony the whole incident which the Lord allowed to take place is likened to a poor bargain that He made (v. 12), selling "for a mere trifle" and not "increasing one's wealth" by it all. Neighboring nations would naturally gloat over the disaster that befell an envied nation. But when the writer refers to this he apparently has in mind that such aspersions are at the same time cast upon the God of the derided nation.

This section closes with a sorrowful complaint (vv. 15, 16) which shows the feelings that overwhelmed the nation at that time. Its disgrace and shame weighed heavily upon it, and the words of the enemy and revengeful opponent were harsh and bitter.

17. *All this has come upon us though we had not forgotten Thee*
    And had not been traitors to Thy covenant.
18. *Our heart had not turned back;*
    Nor had our steps turned aside from Thy way.
19. *Yet Thou hast crushed us in the place of jackals*
    And covered us with deep darkness.
20. *If we had forgotten the name of our God*
    And spread forth our hands to a strange god;
21. *Would not God search this out?*
    For He knows the secrets of the heart.
22. *Yea, for Thy sake we are slain all the day long;*
    We are accounted as sheep for the slaughter.

Psalm 44

This is the suffering that pained the people almost more than did the actual affliction that had befallen them: Israel had remained faithful. Before the details of the statement are examined, it should be noted that this claim of the psalmist is not to be regarded as an instance of blameworthy self-righteousness. If the individual statements are weighed carefully, it will become clear that the nation does not claim to be sinless. Yet it is asserted that God had not been forgotten; His covenant had not been dealt with treacherously; the people had not turned away from God. A fair estimate of such statements reveals that the people had been relatively without fault. Claims that this is reprehensible pride lay things to the charge of these people of which they were not guilty. For that matter, v. 20f. indicate that the persons involved are well aware of the fact that God searches the hearts of men, and treachery on their part would, therefore, have been discovered by Him. These statements are virtually an appeal to God's just judgment.

God's numerous promises in the Old Testament (see especially Lev. 26 and Deut. 28 and parallels) made it very plain that God would reward fidelity to Him with success and even victory in time of war. Now the opposite has taken place. V. 19 seems to refer figuratively to a crushing defeat suffered in some desolate spot, a defeat that David may have suffered in the early stages of his Aramean campaign, above referred to. Dark despair had settled upon the nation for the moment. We lack information to understand exactly what v. 22 included. "Slain all the day long" and to be "accounted as sheep for the slaughter" implies that many lives were lost, and that the life of the Israelites was regarded cheap. Yet it is clearly understood that this did not happen without the will of the Lord; in fact, it was He who laid it upon His people as the phrase "for Thy sake" indicates. The suffering was therefore, in the nature of a cross. There are many such situations in life when God's people are unable to understand the way of the Almighty and the course He is following with them.

23. *Bestir Thyself! why sleepest Thou, O Lord?*
    Awake, cast us not off forever!
24. *Why dost Thou hide Thy face?*
    Why hast Thou forgotten our wretchedness and oppression?
25. *For our soul is bowed to the dust;*
    Our body cleaves to the ground.
26. *Arise and help us!*
    Deliver us for the sake of Thy steadfast love!

In this earnest prayer for help the language is strong but not reprehensible. Some interpreters fault the author for manifesting unseemly boldness. This is certainly the boldness of faith. But questions like "why sleepest Thou?" are meant only in the sense: To us it would seem as though Thou wert asleep. This is certainly a strong plea for action and intervention. Since a tone of absolute reverence pervades the psalm, these unusual expressions dare not be charged too heavily against their writer. If the psalmist did not know that God does not forget our wretchedness and oppression he would never have pleaded with God as he does. So also the description of the nation as "bowed to the dust" and "cleaving to the ground," utterly prostrate is based on the clear conviction that the wretchedness of His people is a matter of deep concern to the Lord. The whole of this last prayer for help is well summed up in v. 26: "Arise and help us; deliver us for the sake of Thy steadfast love." This is obviously an appeal to something that is in God and not to merit that is inherent in the nation.

NOTES.

1. The second half of the verse begins with a relative clause that omits the relative particle *'asher*. *GK* 155h.

5. "Through" in the second member of the phrase "through Thy name" is used as the preposition *be* is basically used, in the sense of "in connection with Thy name" and thus could not be misconstrued to have magical connotation. "They that rise up against us" is the participle with a suffix ("risers up of us") which is merely a concise way of saying the same thing without the use of a preposition; *KS* 23.

9. Beginning at this point and continuing with the beginning of the vv. 10–14, we have what may be called the consecutive use of the verbs without the *waw* consecutive. See *KS* 368f. Note that in at least three instances a final *waw* of the preceding verse is involved, which may merely have been written once but was designed to be read twice. In v. 9 the conjunction is separated from the verb by the negative; *KS* 368i.

17. In the expression "come upon us" the Hebrew attaches the pronoun to the verb without a preposition. *KS* 22.

19. The connective *ki* here has a concessive meaning. This is due to the connection; *KS* 394g.

20. The last part of this section reads more smoothly when vv. 20 and 21 are regarded as a parenthesis. The initial *'im* introduces a condition that is contrary to fact; *KS* 390t.

26. "For our help" is expressed by a kind of accusative of purpose by attaching an ending *ah* with a very modified locative meaning; see *KS* 287b.

Psalm 45

THE MARRIAGE OF THE KING

MUST WE agree with those commentators who regard this as a purely secular ode and the only instance of such material in the Psalter? To say the least, such use of a psalm would be most unique. Nor do we believe that the Jews who were the jealous guardians of the canon would have permitted such elements to appear in this book. Neither can we be content with that mediating position which makes this psalm secular in origin but having an allegorical meaning that was assigned to it at a later date. We still have too high a regard for the processes of inspiration of the Scriptures to believe that such procedures were in keeping with the manner of operation of the Spirit.

There is a tradition of long standing both in the synagogue and in the church of Christ that this psalm deals with the King Messiah and His bride, the synagogue of days of old and in later times the church. Is such tradition to be brushed aside? Has it been invalidated by solid research which makes such an outmoded approach quite untenable, in fact, to be regarded with a mildly amused tolerance where it is still defended? Though a commentator stands quite alone at the present if he supports the traditional interpretation, it appears to us that too many fatal weaknesses mark every other approach. So much has been written on the subject that much must be passed by due to our somewhat limited treatment.

To begin with, we believe that we must forego trying to discover the personage that may have been in the mind of the writer of the psalm as the hero whom he glorifies. Among those who have been suggested at one time or another are Solomon, Jehoram of Judah who married Athaliah, Jehoshaphat, Ahab, Jehoiachin, Jehu, Jeroboam II, not to mention men outside of Israel or those who were living in the period of the Maccabees. None of the persons proposed has all the features stressed by the psalm. This lack is then usually reconstrued in some more or less violent fashion in order to make the text available agree with the theory advanced. The hero of the psalm has not been successfully identified with any one of these earthly kings.

Almost equally difficult is the attempt to advance some theory regarding the mechanics of the composition of the poem, that is to say, to establish what the writer was actually trying to do. A theory that to the best of our knowledge was first proposed by *Kessler,* at least in the form we are about to describe, seems to some extent to meet most of the needs of the case. This writer states that some godly author found a purely secular marriage ode that had been composed for one of the kings of Judah and saw the possibilities of superimposing an allegorical interpretation upon it after making a few necessary changes such as inserting the vocative "O God" after "Thy throne" in v. 6. Thus an ode that had never been intended to be sacred in its association was lifted above the level for which it was intended and carried a religious meaning ever after. Though the process described strikes us as being unworthy of the purpose of the poem, we, nevertheless, feel that something remotely analogous to this took place. For the ancient marriage customs that would be involved in such an approach see *Gaster,* JBL 74, IV, p. 239ff., not in reference to a Jewish king but in reference to simple villagers, who are regarded as "king for a day" and "queen."

The writer may have been familiar with the type of poetic effusions that court poets wrote as marriage odes and was moved to think on the level of prophets like Hosea of the relation of Jehovah to His bride, the nation of Israel, as being a topic of a related sort and deserving of a spiritual ode. He then wove together various features that he had heard stressed by various poets in the lives of the better of the kings of Judah. The resultant description does not portray any one king but is obviously composite in character. All the qualities that the poet can assemble in his highly idealized painting find their fulfilment in the Messiah. Into that picture he painted two of the more notable features of the Messiah as these are offered by prophecy: the everlasting nature of His throne and realm (cf., II Sam. 7:12ff.) and the divine character of His being, for which he found warrant in Is. 9:6 ("Mighty God"). He did not need to attach the label of a godly allegory to his ode, for all Jews who knew their Scriptures and the rich colors in which Messianic prophecy had been presented could not but recognize what he intended to portray, as the traditional interpretation of the Jews and also of New Testament times very clearly indicates (cf., Heb. 1:8, 9).

But even then we must warn against trying to extract a specific meaning from every feature in the portrait. Some elements seem to have been included merely because they lent color to the painting as a whole. Pedantic application of detail is scarcely required, in fact, is to be warned against. For even in the parables of Jesus, which are a sort of allegory, there are features which, if interpreted and applied in a specific way, would only distort the point the Savior tried to make

Omne simile claudicat (Every comparison limps). We, therefore, arrive at the result that this psalm is prophetic in character. Whether its writer is to be regarded as a primary prophet like the great valid prophets of Israel or as a secondary prophet, who reworks the message of the great leaders in this field and popularizes it, is a question that it is difficult to answer. On this distinction compare *Koenig's Kommentar* on the Psalms, Intro. 19, 3. Simply to deny the possibility of prophecy to the writers of the psalms fails to square with the facts. For Ps. 22 obviously contains a great prophecy, and so does this psalm.

The two chief characters in this divine allegory are Christ, the bridegroom, and His church (whether of the Old or of the New Testament), the bride. A beautiful description of both is given, and the occasion is thought of as in the nature of a wedding celebration.

Since on the basis of v. 6 we feel compelled to accept the divine character of the Bridegroom we have adopted the device of capitalizing the pronouns that refer to Him wherever they occur in the psalm. Those commentators who label our interpretation a misconception of the nature of Messianic prophecy have, perhaps, first advanced their theory as to what Messianic prophecy ought to be and have then made their treatment of a psalm like the present one conform to the theory. All we need to postulate in regard to the time of composition of the psalm is that it may well have been written later than Is. 9:6, and that in dwelling on the divine character of the Messiah it develops a thought that had been clearly taught by the prophets.

a) **Introduction (v. 1)**

> *To the Choir Director. According to "Lilies." By the sons of Korah. A didactic poem. A song concerning the lovely.*

1. *My heart is stirred by a good subject;*
   I speak my poem concerning a king;
   My tongue is the pen of a skilled scribe.

The heading, "according to 'Lilies,' " may refer to the melody according to which the psalm is to be rendered. Most writers regard it thus. According to the older interpreters it could be a sort of mysterious indication of the contents of the poem. On "didactic poem" see the heading of Ps. 44. It is clear that something of the didactic element appears in vv. 10ff. where instruction is offered to the bride. "A song concerning the lovely" indicates the nature of the subject matter: it is something lovely, a feminine plural used for the abstract in the Hebrew.

1. The writer voices his personal feelings about the subject he is treating and the poem in which he treats it. If any court poet might have warmed up to his subject when he was called upon to sing the

praises of the king as a bridegroom, that was more true in the case of this man. With all sincerity he can claim that he "is stirred" by what engages his thoughts. With fine propriety he claims that all he says centers about the "king" even though quite a number of things are said about the queen. Still the king is in a special sense the prominent figure. The writer's subject matter caused him to grow eloquent. He speaks with some emotion of his great theme even as the pen of a skilled writer moves along rapidly over the page. His sacrifice, so to speak, was, indeed, kindled upon his lips. *Mowinckel* says the writer here claims inspiration. This introduction, in which the writer tells what his subject did to him and how it took hold on him is without parallel in the Psalter. In view of the exalted nature of the subject involved this might well be so. *Gunkel* renders the verse, *Mein Herz wallt ueber von begeisterten Worten* (My heart overflows with inspired words).

b) **The words addressed to the king, the bridegroom (vv. 2–9)**

2. *Fair, fair indeed, Thou art above the children of men;*
   Grace is poured out upon Thy lips;
   Therefore God has blessed Thee forever.
3. *Gird Thy sword upon Thy thigh, O hero,*
   Thy glory and Thy majesty.
4. *In Thy majesty ride forth successfully for the cause of truth, meekness, and righteousness;*
   And Thy right hand shall teach Thee wondrous things.
5. *Thy arrows are sharp—may people fall under Thee—*
   In the heart of the enemies of the King.
6. *Thy throne, O God, is forever and ever;*
   The sceptre of Thy kingdom is a righteous sceptre.
7. *Thou hast loved righteousness and hated wickedness;*
   Therefore God, Thy God, has anointed Thee with the oil of gladness above Thy fellows.
8. *Myrrh and aloes and cassia are all Thy garments;*
   From the ivory palaces stringed instruments have made Thee glad.
9. *Kings' daughters are among Thy ladies of honor;*
   At Thy right hand the queen has taken her stand in gold of Ophir.

2. This verse offers a description of the King's beauty as he appears on his wedding day. This beauty is more than purely physical, which is proverbially only skin deep. It is the attractiveness of His person and His character that is under consideration. The fact that this beauty is superlative is made evident by the repetition: "Fair, fair indeed, art Thou," as well as by the contrasting of Him with the "children of

men" generally speaking. It would be putting too much into the expression if we were to make it mean that He is contrasted with the children of men because He is another type of being. So also the statement, "Grace is poured out upon Thy lips," is surely intended to involve more than beauty of lips as such. It rather involves an ability for speaking graciously as in their day both David and Solomon were known to have spoken and written, and as Christ Himself was distinguished from the moment of His first public appearance among men in His capacity as Savior (see Luke 4:22). The "therefore" that follows serves to indicate, not that He is blessed because of His beauty and gracious utterance, but rather that these qualities are proofs that God's blessing has been laid upon Him.

3. The fact that the qualities with which He is endowed are to be used in strenuous combat and are not for personal embellishment and gratification only is evident in the summons that follows. The tone becomes martial. The description is that of a warrior who is well armed and is challenged to gird on His sword and do mighty things. We need not be more specific in an endeavor to determine exactly what the sword stands for (the figure employed in Rev. 19:15 is somewhat different, as is also Eph. 6:17). "Thy glory and Thy majesty" could, as some interpreters have pointed out, be his glorious armor. In any case, He is to ready Himself for energetic action.

4. His victorious course is described as He now rides forth for the battle for which He is in a singular sense destined. His is not the agent of bloody, cruel conquest, but he does battle in the interest of "truth, meekness, righteousness." Since He champions these godly causes, the writer is sure that He must have success, and so he inserts the adverb "successfully." (On the problem here involved see *Notes*). The writer is further certain that the great power with which this hero is equipped will manifest "wondrous things" in the course of the victory that He achieves. The figure used ("teach") implies that capabilities that are even beyond what He Himself thought of will be discovered, humanly speaking.

5. This verse is designed to give color to the account of the victorious conquest of this hero. It might even be possible that before his mind's eye there lived a portrait like that which Egyptian and Assyrian rulers left of themselves in monumental carvings, showing how they advanced victoriously in their chariots, the ground being littered with the bodies of enemies whom their arrows had slain. These representations on the monuments help us at least to visualize the picture here presented. The sentence, however, that makes up this verse is broken into by a wish that is parenthetically inserted: "May people fall under

Thee!" A certain dignity is added to the statement of the verse by having the noun *"king"* take the place of the possessive pronoun, *"your* enemies."

6. At this point a note of devotion is inserted into the apostrophe regarding the king because He is understood by the writer to be divine. The psalmist addresses his hero as "God." If the writer lived after the time of Isaiah he might well have done this, by basing his statement on Isaiah's clear pronouncement (9:6). That the translation we, too, have offered is very natural and proper appears from the fact that all the older versions render this verse in the same manner by construing "God" as a vocative. The grammatical issues involved are dealt with at length in the *Notes*.

The reference to the King as divine is only incidental as far as the purpose of the verse is concerned. Its major emphasis is on the fact that the throne of the King is an everlasting one. That this also denotes divine character is obvious. The concept as such is based on the famous historical passage II Sam. 7:12ff. This King is, therefore, regarded as the one in whom the great things predicted by Nathan of old find their fulfilment. If one combines this verse with the preceding verses, its thought is: Such a king as is there described, battling in the spirit in which He does and equipped as He is, cannot but achieve results that shall establish His throne "forever and ever."

The second half of the verse amplifies this thought by stressing the fact that the King's rule is absolutely just. For "sceptre" is synonymous with rule. The thought as such is so closely akin to that in Is. 9:7 that one is forced to think this passage must have been known to the psalmist.

7. This verse continues in the same strain and gives a more subjective touch to the thought. Not only does this Great Champion uphold the cause of righteousness and suppress wickedness, he also personally loves the one and hates the other. For who can remain personally neutral when he is confronted by such forces? We believe that those interpreters are correct who regard the second half of the verse as a clause that offers evidence rather than result. One rightly concludes that, if this Hero loves righteousness and hates iniquity, it is because God has given Him an anointing with the oil of gladness, rather than that the case should be reversed. God has given Him this quality of rare gladness of heart, for the genitive "of gladness" is an apposition: the oil is gladness. An ineradicable joy is inherent in the entire being of this Hero. This confident, victorious attitude leads to His gaining victory upon victory. Besides, never was there such a cheerful, joyous, buoyant personality even though at one point in His life there were those who esteemed Him "a man of sorrows."

Psalm 45

8. At this point the psalm becomes a marriage ode, for vv. 3–9 obviously think in terms of a bridegroom. His wedding garments are poetically described. He is so richly and attractively perfumed that it may be metaphorically said that these precious odors constitute his very garments: "Myrrh and aloes and cassia are all Thy garments." Myrrh is an aromatic resin that is used mostly in powdered form. Aloes is a sweet-smelling wood from India. Cassia is a dried cinnamon blossom that is used for incense. As the king moves to the place where the wedding is to occur, "stringed instruments" sound from within the ivory palace as a fit accompaniment.

9. It would appear that, though the wirter set out to write a marriage ode, he became so enraptured by the thought of the person and the destiny of the bridegroom that he dwelt on that subject rather at length until he reached this point where the basic picture emerges quite clearly. The scene portrayed seems to catch the very moment when the bridegroom steps forth for the nuptials. The verse is at the same time preparatory for the remarks that are to be made with reference to the queen. She appears at the right hand of the king with ornaments of the best Ophir gold. She has a retinue of noble attendants: kings' daughters are among the ladies of honor though the latter, strictly speaking, are in this verse described as *his* ladies of honor. In this portrayal everything is made to center about the bridegroom—rather than about the bride as is so often the case in modern weddings.

c) **The words addressed to the queen, the bride (vv. 10–16)**

10. *Hear, O daughter, and consider and incline your ear*
    And forget your people and your father's house.
11. *And the King will desire your beauty;*
    Since He is your Lord, bow down before Him.
12. *The daughter of Tyre shall be there with a gift;*
    The rich ones among the people shall seek your face.
13. *All glorious is the king's daughter in her chamber;*
    Her garment is embroidered with gold.
14. *In raiment of needlework she is brought to the King;*
    The virgins, her companions, following after her are brought to you.
15. *They are brought with joy and gladness;*
    They enter the palace of the King.
16. *In the place of your fathers shall be your sons;*
    You shall make them princes in all the earth.

10. The figure that describes God's relation to His people as being

like unto the relation of husband to wife or, for that matter, of bridegroom to bride is common enough in the Old Testament, not to mention the New (see Hos. 1 and 2, the Song of Solomon, and Ezek. 16). That figure appears in this section. It is apparently based on a remembrance of, let us say, Solomon's marriage to a foreign princess, an Egyptian. The bride, Israel, is in a sense in such a situation. Coming to the Lord as His own, she must forget and disavow her former connections and concentrate on the blessings of her new association. The opening words of this section are an exhortation definitely to break with her inferior past.

The writer, assuming the role of an old and experienced teacher, addresses the bride on her nuptial day as a fatherly counselor well might: "O daughter." Such a form of address is analogous to that employed by the teachers of wisdom (see Prov. 2:1; 3:1, etc.). By multiplying terms that call for close attention ("hear and consider and incline your ear") the exhorter makes it clear that his lesson should be carefully heeded. The essence of his good counsel is: "Forget your people and your father's house." The church must ever continue to learn that lesson: forget her worldly attachments and associations.

11. Even as a king would love his bride the more for having put thoughts of her father's house and of her people away and having found full compensation in the true love of the king, so will the Lord love His people the more as a true reward for their wholehearted attachment to Him: "The King will desire your beauty." Such absolute devotion on the part of the church is all the more natural for her since He is her "Lord." She owes such devotion and attachment to Him. It should be total submission: "Bow down before Him." This profitable lesson the church of the Old Testament needed as much as does the church of the New. It is always the first requirement of the church.

12. Such devotion and submission have their rich rewards or compensations. The bride may miss her former family. New associates will take the place of the old. In the figure, there will be the "daughter of Tyre." According to a familiar idiom this means the nation of Tyre, which is here thought of as offering gifts as tokens of friendship and alliance through her chosen emissaries. The rest of the figure speaks of "the rich ones among the people" as "seeking her favor" (literally, "stroking her face" in an effort to conciliate). Such gestures of goodwill may well serve to recompense the new queen for what she had to sacrifice. In seeking an interpretation of these statements we can scarcely dare to attach special meanings to "gifts" and "favor" or "the daughter of Tyre" or the "rich ones among the people," yet the general and satisfactory meaning is clear, that whatever sacrifices are made

because of true allegiance to the King will be richly compensated for by the rewards that His own presence and providence bring.

13. There follow two verses (13f.) that give a description of the manifold beauties of the bride on her wedding day, all of which symbolize the rich beauty and glory of the church of the Lord in Old or New Testament. The picture presented is one of glory and honor. We can easily visualize the queen as she is about to issue forth from her chamber. "Her garment is embroidered with gold; in raiment of needlework she is brought to the King." Magnificent Oriental splendor is in evidence. Part of her retinue naturally consists of "the virgins, her companions, following after her." At this point the description becomes an apostrophe of the king when it is said that they "are brought to You." Specific interpretation of the details is again out of the question. But the general truth remains that the bride of the Lord, His church, has a beauty and glory all her own. The figure as a whole is such that the Lord Himself, in speaking His parables, did not disdain to use it (see Matt. 25:1–13). When the attempt is made to extract a specific meaning from the idea of the virgin attendants of the queen, absurdities may be the result (cf. *Hengstenberg,* who makes them other brides, representing the converted heathen nations).

15. This last verse of the description of the wedding procession merely rounds out the picture by depicting bride and bridesmaids as "they enter the palace of the King" in a mood of gay festivity, that is to say, "with joy and gladness." For in Biblical days weddings were in a special sense regarded as occasions for rare happiness. All of which portrays nothing more than the general truth that it is a most blessed thing for the church to enjoy the privilege of becoming the Lord's own.

16. The admonition, which began to remind the bride to break with her past and forget it, gradually merged into a description of the bridal procession. It closes with a tone of instruction by again reminding the queen of a few of the compensations that she may hope for if she devotes herself wholly to the King. She may miss the persons of her father's house; she may instead expect to have sons of her own. She may miss those of princely blood with whom she may have associated; she shall instead be able as time goes on to train up her own sons to be "princes in all the earth." This feature of the allegory lends itself to no special interpretation.

d) **Conclusion (v. 17)**

17. *I will cause Thy name to be remembered in all generations;*
    Therefore the people will praise Thee forever and ever.

This conclusion can scarcely refer to the queen, especially since the praise of the one addressed is to endure "throughout all generations" and is also to be "forever and ever." This thought agrees well with the everlasting dominion of Him who sits on the throne of His father David. So the psalm closes on the fine note that He who is being commemorated deserves to be extolled forever and ever and is deserving of His people's praises as long as the sun and the moon endure.

NOTES

The word in the heading that we have translated "concerning the lovely" is to be understood in the sense of "concerning that which is lovely," referring, of course, to the whole subject of the poem. The word *yedhidhoth* is a feminine plural used as an abstract noun as *KS* 245c explains.

2. The "therefore" can be regarded as introducing a clause of evidence. See *KS* 373i.

3. By a kind of zeugma "sword" in the first member and "glory and majesty" in the second are regarded as objects of the verb "gird," the latter two nouns being in apposition to "sword."

4. The two unconnected imperatives, "prosper, ride," are rendered best if we regard the former as a kind of adverb and translate it "successfully." See *KS* 361p and *GK* 120g. There is a difficulty in "truth, meekness, righteousness," which we have tried to indicate by letting the three nouns stand unconnected. The Hebrew would seem to connect the last two as if they were written "meekness-righteousness." Only fanciful explanations are given of this supposed close connection. The Greek translators ease themselves out of the difficulty by inserting *and's:* "truth and meekness and righteousness," which may still be the most helpful approach. The great hero champions these three causes in particular.

5. On the use of "king" instead of the personal pronoun to stress the title of dignity see *KS* 5.

6. We now come to the issue which has been discussed at very great length and in some form or other by practically every commentary: Is *'elohim* a vocative? Most writers take the attitude: It could scarcely be, considering the limitations of Messianic prophecy, or considering, as they say, that the divine character of the Messiah had not yet been clearly revealed. *Koenig* alone, as far as we have noticed, takes the position: It *cannot* be the vocative. His arguments appear quite inconclusive to us. We may be pardoned for not refuting them as he seems to stand almost alone in his outright disavowal of the possibility of a vocative. Most writers argue rather for the possibility and correctness

of the translation: "your divine throne" (*RSV* by way of illustration). In other words, Can the construction, which reads literally, "Thy throne of God," be construed to mean: "Thy divine throne," harsh as the expression seems in the Hebrew? We must answer that such a construction is grammatically possible. Passages like Num. 25:12 show that such a construction was used. Yet cf., *GK* 128d. But to prove possibility does not demonstrate necessity. The procedure by which this result is determined seems to us to be consciously or unconsciously the following. Commentators first determine that a confession of the deity of the Messiah is *per se* impossible or never occurs (in spite of Is. 9:6). Then the simple and obvious translation, upheld by all the prominent versions down to the *ARV,* which offers a marginal alternative, is rejected and an argument in support of a far less natural translation is sought. Critical bias can determine the course that translation takes equally as much as does conservative bias.

The alternate offered by the margin of the *ARV,* "Thy throne is the throne of God," is equally difficult to defend and would scarcely suggest itself as an easy and natural rendering. It is an obvious attempt to avoid what almost any translator would regard as the first possibility. *Koenig's* contentions in support of this second possibility do not impress us. See *KS* 277f.

8. The perfect "have made Thee glad" could be a sort of gnomic aorist, "have always made Thee glad." That would make the king appear as a known lover of music. Cf. *KS* 126.

9. The literal translation of this verse could be this: "daughters of kings are among Thy precious ones." This would give an unnecessarily polygamous touch to the thought. We have followed *RSV* in its more happy phrasing: "are among Thy (your) ladies of honor."

12. Quite a few interpreters insist that the expression "daughter of Tyre" must, because it is the singular, refer to a Tyrian princess. Any dictionary will indicate that the collective use of *bath* in the sense of "inhabitants," that is to say, used collectively, is very common. Cf. "daughter of Zion" in the sense of the inhabitants of Zion. So we are in no sense under necessity of thinking in terms of a prince who wed a Tyrian princess.

13. The somewhat puzzling "within" of the *KJ* is far clearer if it is rendered "in her chamber" (*RSV*).

17. When the same noun is repeated as *dor wador* is here, it signifies "very many" or "throughout all generations." *KS* 88.

Psalm 46

GOD IS OUR REFUGE AND STRENGTH

THE FIRST impression created by the psalm is that it is born out of an event which is still quite vivid in the minds of those for whom it was first composed. Yet other approaches are attempted. Some interpreters believe that the psalm looks out into the far distant future and is thus quite eschatological in character—an approach that is advanced by *Gunkel*. Others feel that it is best understood when it is placed against the background of the festival of the enthronement of Yahweh, when the dramatic liturgy made the congregation aware of what a great helper it had in the Lord. This is clearly an overevaluation of the effects that the liturgy is wont to produce. In the face of such attempts at a re-evaluation the traditional approach, which found in the psalm a reference to a recent historical event, still proves most satisfactory.

But to which historical event should we attempt to relate the psalm? Late dates are suggested such as the reign of Josiah or even the times of Artaxerxes II, the Persian monarch. But whatever deliverances were wrought for the people of God during the reigns of these kings, they were certainly not so outstanding as to call forth the strong reaction that characterizes this psalm. The great deliverance that took place in the days of Jehoshaphat (II Chron. 20) could well be thought of here. But the city of Jerusalem was apparently too indirectly involved to make this event suitable. Nothing meets the needs of the case quite so well as does the great deliverance that took place in the days of Hezekiah (701 B.C.) when Sennacherib's forces were disastrously destroyed after having directly threatened the city of Jerusalem, and when the omnipotence of the God of Israel was underscored as it was on few other occasions.

Whether the slaughter of the Assyrian forces by the angel of the Lord (Is. 36, 37) took place at Lachish or nearer Jerusalem is very difficult to determine. Yet the results could have been witnessed by the inhabitants of Jerusalem as v. 8 of the psalm invites them to do. Besides, the impression that the event created was such that men are to be thought of as being confronted by it most forcibly at a recent date. In addition, the terms used by the poet agree in so many instances with the very words Isaiah used in this connection, as we shall point out in the exposition.

So the psalm invites the choice of a theme which is either the opening statement of the poem as such or one that is commonly used by those who are familiar with the hymn that Luther in part based on this psalm, "A mighty fortress is our God." Few psalms breathe the spirit of sturdy confidence in the Lord in the midst of very real dangers as strongly as does this one.

The heading reads thus: *To the Choir Director. By the sons of Korah. According to Alamoth. A song.*

On "choir director" and "sons of Korah" compare previous instances of the use of these expressions. "According to Alamoth," since *alamoth* can mean "young women," could have a meaning something like, "to be sung by the sopranos." But there appears to be no good reason why the sopranos should render this psalm. Its sturdy character would seem to be better rendered by the basses. The designation "a song" could have had some technical meaning that we are also unable to detect in our time.

a) **The sure confidence of those who trust in the Lord in the face of physical dangers (vv. 1–3)**

1. *God is our refuge and strength,*
   A well-proved help in troubles.
2. *Therefore we will not fear though the earth change;*
   Though the mountains totter into the midst of the sea;
3. *Though its waters roar and foam;*
   Though the mountains sway with its violence.

1. The order of the words in the Hebrew places emphasis on the word "God"—He, nothing else, is our refuge in the face of calamities of every sort. The statement really reads thus: "God is for us refuge and strength," the important thought being that God is on our side. But the traditional form in which this verse has become familiar also has much to commend it. "Refuge and strength" involve two aspects of the help that He renders: He is first like a strong fortress into which a man may flee and be absolutely safe; He is at the same time an unfailing source of strength, enabling one to cope manfully with the dangers that assail him. The second half of the verse scarcely stresses the fact of His nearness ("a very present help in trouble") but rather what experience has amply demonstrated with reference to Him; therefore: "a well-proved help in troubles." This is the basic assertion on which the whole psalm rests. It can scarcely surprise us, therefore, that Luther concentrated his famous hymn exclusively on this thought and ignored the rest of the psalm.

2. If one really appropriates the truth embodied in the first verse, his attitude cannot be any other than one of complete fearlessness. For the present the poet emphasizes this only over against physical dangers or, to be more specific, over against a most violent earthquake. For that is what is described in this verse and until the end of v. 3. It is, indeed, a mild expression when the first feature of the description refers only to the fact that "the earth changes" in such a happening. But to have what seemed to be this firm and immovable earth tremble and shake, that is a complete change from its usual nature and appearance and can be extremely terrifying. The parallel statement presents mountains as tottering into the midst of the sea. We need not think of more than huge masses of rock breaking off, let us say from a promontory as *Briggs* suggests, a promontory such as Mt. Carmel, jutting out into the Mediterranean. Since earthquakes are frequently associated with tidal waves and serious unrest of the sea, we may find the further concessive clause ("though its waters roar and foam") very much in place. The last clause of v. 3 takes us back to the land— "though the mountains sway with its violence." It is no light matter to remain confident and fearless in the midst of such manifestations of the forces of nature. But he who has fully grasped what God is for His people may well remain unmoved.

The question may be raised whether the author is at this point thinking in terms of actual physical dangers in the realm of nature, or whether he has in mind other dangers that may be symbolized by these natural disturbances. The most feasible answer is that he actually has in mind physical dangers of the sort described. We may encounter them; they may put our faith to the test; we may be able to remain fearless under the test. That does not exclude the application that everyone may make for himself from the suggestion offered, namely, that He who thus safeguards His own against harm in physical distresses can guard them equally well from all other assaults that may threaten their safety.

The suggestion is commonly met that the refrain which will appear as vv. 7 and 11 may have been omitted at this point. The insertion of it after v. 3 surely does not alter or change the basic emphases of of the psalm. But it is still an emendation, the necessity of which cannot be fully proved.

b) **The security that comes from God's presence in the face of the dangers of war (vv. 4–7)**

4. *There is a river whose channels make glad the city of God,*
The sanctuary which is the dwelling place of the Most High.

5. God is in the midst of her, she shall not be moved;
   God shall help her when the morning dawns.
6. Heathen have often raged, kingdoms have been shaken;
   He has uttered His voice, the earth melted.
7. The Lord of hosts is with us;
   The God of Jacob is our refuge. Selah.

The original Hebrew places the river more abruptly into the forefront as an absolute nominative, which might be translated, "Lo, a river!" Not to make the construction too abrupt, we have retained the *AV* rendering. The thought seems to have been taken directly from Is. 8:6–8 and only been recast somewhat in more poetic fashion. In contrast with the mighty and turbulent river mentioned by the prophet, which symbolizes the mighty world power Assyria, stands a quiet and insignificant streamlet which runs from the fountain of Siloam to the east of the holy city. Trivial as it seems in contrast with the mighty Euphrates or Tigris, it may, nevertheless, in its own way well symbolize the insignificant appearance of the kingdom of God in the eyes of the world. What the world despises makes glad the people of God, "the sanctuary which is the dwelling place of the Most High." God's city has a quietness and joyful confidence all its own. Though Luther's paraphrase of the verse is not a translation in the ordinary sense of the word it catches the spirit of the verse beautifully: "Yet for all that the city of God shall maintain its marvelous cheerfulness with its little wells, for there are the holy dwelling places of the Most High." The "channels" are the little runlets used for irrigation purposes, which, insignificant though they seem, nevertheless serve their purpose. Similar figures appear in Is. 17:12; Jer. 47:2; 46:7. And in Dan. 7:2, 3 groups of nations are symbolized by turbulent waters rather than a single nation as is the case in the other passages.

5. That which makes the difference between the mighty nations and the seemingly insignificant one is the indwelling of God in the latter. It is this that makes her inviolable and unassailable. When the night of danger and distress is past, then the morning of God's help regularly dawns. This is the meaning of the statement, "God shall help her when the morning dawns." He can offer His help so effectively because He is in the very midst of His people.

6. The most natural construction to put upon this verse is the one that grows out of the consideration that the first three verbs are in the past tense. This is best construed to mean that in the past the thing that has regularly happened is that "heathen have raged," etc. To indicate that this has generally been the rule we have inserted the

word "always" in our translation. We might have repeated it in the next two clauses. For kingdoms have always been shaken, and God has been the one who has regularly controlled the situation: He has always uttered His voice, and as a result all that men and kingdoms devised collapsed before Him. He controls the raging of the nations and their tumults.

7. The reason that God's people could remain unmoved when world-shaking calamities transpired was, as v. 5 had already indicated, "The Lord of hosts is with us." The same positive note that breathed in v. 1 finds utterance here again though in a slightly different form. Still more in keeping with v. 1 is the second member of the verse, "The God of Jacob is our refuge." Isaiah, too, has a fondness for using "Jacob" in place of "Israel," for he does this about forty times. This refrain is dictated by a sturdy faith.

c) **A summons to consider visible evidence of all this in a recent disaster of the enemy (vv. 8–11)**

8. *Come, behold the works of the Lord,*
   What astounding things He has done in the earth,
9. *Who makes wars to cease to the ends of the earth;*
   Who breaks the bow, shatters the spear, and burns the chariot with fire.
10. *Desist and know that it is I, God;*
    I will be exalted by the nations, I will be exalted in the earth.
11. *The Lord of hosts is with us;*
    The God of Jacob is our refuge. Selah.

8. The psalm has thus far been cast in general terms that give no indication that there was any particular occurrence that roused the holy sentiments expressed. The writer now indicates that there is tangible evidence of all that he has claimed for the Lord. Whether this evidence is directly visible from the city walls or on the part of those who go forth a short distance from the holy city; or whether the writer is asking men to visualize the scene that has been reported to them as being actually visible down in the vicinity of Lachish, is of little moment. For when you consider the matter rightly, it is clear that there are some great "works of the Lord" in evidence. It is superlatively clear that the Lord hath done what has been done. These are "astounding things" that were wrought, not in some secluded corner of the world, but out in the open where the facts as such can be readily checked by any investigator. The world learned soon enough what had befallen the hosts of mighty Assyria when they grew presumptuous against the Lord God of Israel. But even this verse with its seemingly

specific reference to a recent event is, as is usually the case in the Psalter, cast in such general terms that it might express what men can and should behold continually, for the world is full of testimony to His "astounding works."

9. Here are the particulars the psalmist had in mind. And surely Sennacherib's setback furnished colorful evidence of the psalmist's previous claim. A war had been made "to cease." The very manner in which this was done was proof and token of the interference of the Lord. To make the sketch more drastic, it is stated that the deserted field of battle looks very much as if the God of Israel had gone out in person and had broken the bows of war, shattered the spears, and burned the wagons of war (whether chariots or baggage train) in the fire. For the field and the adjoining territory were still littered with the weapons and supplies of war, and the only way that the wreckage could be disposed of was by consigning it to the fire. On the very day the psalmist wrote, the smoke of these fires has been hanging all over the area. If this does not prove that the Lord controls the destinies of war, what does? If this is not a sufficient token that "God is our refuge," what is?

10. As a result of all that has been depicted thus far a bit of instruction is addressed to those who set themselves in unreasoning and hostile opposition to the Lord of hosts. It is, first of all, the summons to "desist" from all the hostilities that have been stirred up against Him and His people. It involves, in the second place, that all such should not seek to evade the obvious conclusion that He who has done these things is in this instance none other than the God of Israel, who had so clearly foretold that He would bring these things to pass. See especially Is. 37:21–35. He has determined that He shall so govern the affairs of His people Israel that the nations, if they are honest with themselves, will be compelled to admit that it was His doing. And so He "will be exalted among the nations," in fact, He "will be exalted in the earth." For events like this one shall make the renown of His name resound to the ends of the earth.

11. The refrain clinches the point with fine emphasis.

NOTES

2. In *behamir* the "in" is neutral, yet, as *KS* 405b shows, in a negative context this becomes the equivalent of a concessive clause. The imperfects in v. 3 then continue this concessive emphasis.

3. The suffix expressing the possessive in "its violence" refers to "waters." But these are regarded as a singular. Therefore the singular suffix.

4. What *KJ* has rendered, "the holy place of the Tabernacles of the Most High," we have construed as an appositional genitive. This conveys at the same time something of the thought of a superlative. See *KS* 305d.

6. Especially in the original this verse has something of the famous *Veni, vidi, vici* as some writers have remarked. The key points are marked by perfects; the attendant or resulting circumstances are expressed by the imperfect. *KS* 155. *Mowinckel* (II, 3, d. p. 127) regards all the perfects as references to a cultic drama which has just been enacted before the eyes of the worshipers.

8. There has been needless debate about *shammoth*. According to its root meaning it signifies "desolations" (*KJ*). But desolations may quite obviously be of so remarkable a character that they may be described as "astounding things."

9. The term *'agaloth* refers to anything that has wheels. This could be baggage wagons as well as chariots. We have let the traditional "chariots" stand.

10. The translation, "know that I am God," misses the point at issue. In connection with the preceding verse the point to be made is that "it is I, God," that am doing this (*Briggs*). Whether God was God or not was not involved here.

Psalm 47

GOD IS KING OF ALL THE EARTH

It is quite likely that the occasion that called forth this psalm is the same as that which gave rise to the preceding psalm, the astounding defeat of the Assyrians before or near Jerusalem in the days of Hezekiah. Again the victory recorded in II Chron. 20 over Moab and Ammon would not be inappropriate, but it lacks some of the elements that make the previous occasion more outstanding.

Yet the emphasis is quite appropriately a different one from that which the preceding psalm suggested. Ps. 46 presents the subjective reaction of the people of God, the reassurance they gained from God's mighty work in their behalf. Here the outlook is broader: the writer speaks in terms of what the whole world may well think as a result of

Psalm 47

the news of the event involved. This psalm makes it obvious that the one who displayed such power in one instance is none other than the King of all the earth, and as such He should be praised.

The distinctive emphasis discovered in the psalm by the individual commentator will vary according to his basic position. There are some who will be content to state that there was an obvious historical occasion which agrees with the facts recorded in the psalm. There are those who, because of a trend to reduce every possible psalm to eschatological terms, will cast the whole piece into the eschatological mold. Those again who in our day make the cultic element all-important will regard the psalm as reflecting the impression that the observance of the festival of the covenant so called with its imposing ritual made on the sympathetic observer or worshiper. Since the last two tendencies referred to have become extreme views, which are forced into the picture by almost violent means, we prefer to stay with the first one mentioned—this is a psalm with a historical background. *Eerdmans* very properly remarks, "The psalm is a reflection of recent events."

In the later Jewish tradition this was the distinctive psalm for the New Year festival which was observed about the beginning of October. The traditional Christian use of the psalm is for the festival of the Ascension because of the words: "God is gone up with a shout." This raises the question as to whether the psalm is to be regarded as a prophecy of the ascension. On closer inspection it will appear that this can scarcely be claimed. Yet it must be admitted that it will arouse in the New Testament believer thoughts of Christ's ascension and so may appropriately be used on the commemoration of that occasion. For quite obviously there are an association and a similarity involved: He who came down to earth in Israel's day, won a victory, and returned triumphantly to His throne made a similar outstanding and dramatic return on high after a still greater victory. One event of necessity recalls the other, all the more so because of v. 5.

The psalm may be outlined as follows:

a) A call to the nations to praise God for what He has done for Israel (vv. 1–4).
b) A call to Israel to praise God, who has demonstrated that He is King (vv. 5–8).
c) The heeding of this call by some heathen rulers is a token of the submission of the Gentiles to the God of Abraham (v. 9).

The heading reads thus: *To the Choir Director. A psalm of the Sons of Korah.* Compare the three preceding psalms.

1. *O clap your hands, all peoples;*
   Shout unto God with jubilant cry.
2. *For the Lord, the Most High, is awe-inspiring,*
   A great King over all the earth.
3. *He subdued peoples under us*
   And nations under our feet.
4. *He chose our inheritance for us,*
   The pride of Jacob whom He loves. Selah.

1. It is to be noted that the general tone of the psalm is exuberant without quite rising to "passionate enthusiasm" (*Weiser*). In a dramatic apostrophe the writer addresses himself to no less an audience than "all peoples" on the face of the earth. He is deeply impressed with the fact that what God has just done for His people is of such importance to every last nation on the face of the earth that, if the nations could but be made aware of it, they would gladly respond by a loud and sturdy acclaim of the power and majesty of the Most High. One must be sure to catch the uniqueness of the thought, which is found also in Ps. 66 and 117, that Gentiles everywhere ought to praise the Lord for what He did in behalf of *Israel*. A sense of the mediatorship of Israel between the Lord and the Gentiles was never lost by her leaders who were sent here by God. In this case the fealty of the nations should find expression in clapping of hands and in jubilant outcries, both of which were traditional at the time of the accession of a new king (cf., I Sam. 10:24 and II Kings 11:12).

2. The fact that should produce allegiance and submission is that "the Lord, the Most High, is awe-inspiring," first of all. "Terrible" (*AV*) has a misleading connotation in our day. Not something repulsive but something most marvelous and attractive, which calls forth our richest praises, is what is involved, "awe-inspiring," therefore. Or to phrase it differently, He is not like the tribal and national gods the world over in those days limited to some definitely prescribed area that is marked by national boundaries but the true "King over all the earth." The hosts of Assyria and of every other great empire are entirely under His dominion as He has just now so drastically demonstrated. For the children of Israel proof of this fact was furnished in days of old (v. 3), for then did He "subdue peoples under us and nations under our feet," Israel might say. The reference is to the conquest of the land of Canaan in the days of Joshua. For despite all the odds against them, the children of Israel undertook a task that bordered on the impossible and did conquer many nations that were stronger and mightier than themselves even

though the complete conquest took longer than the book of Joshua might at first glance suggest.

4. That the writer is actually back in that period of Israel's history appears from the fact that he goes on (v. 4) to speak of the acquisition of the "inheritance," a term that was commonly used for the land of Canaan when it was thought of in this connection (see Exod. 15:17; Deut. 4:21, 38; Jer. 3:19, etc.). When it is also called "the pride of Jacob," this term clearly means that this is the object of the nation's pride. The closing clause is best regarded as a modifier of "Jacob" rather than as of "pride," for the Lord loved the nation rather than the land. A reference to the recent defeat of Sennacherib's forces may well be thought of at this point. The nations who did, indeed, know Israel's earlier history in the days of the Conquest would have this new fact to note, namely, that by subduing more peoples under Israel God had, as it were, confirmed the choice of the inheritance for them and given fresh tokens of His love for Jacob. A Selah at this point suggests a musical interlude which gives pause for reflection.

5. *God went up with a shout;*
   The Lord with sound of a trumpet.
6. *Sing praises unto our God, sing praises;*
   Sing praises unto our King, sing praises.
7. *For God is King of all the earth;*
   Sing praises with a psalm.
8. *God has become King over the Gentiles;*
   God has taken His seat upon His holy throne.
9. *The willing ones among the people have assembled as the people*
      of the God of Abraham,
   For the rulers of the earth belong to God;
   He is greatly exalted.

5. To say that "God is gone up" is to use a figurative mode of speech to signify that He had, as it were, first come down to take a certain task in hand (cf. passages like Gen. 18:21; Is. 31:4), then, having completed what He came to do, He goes up again to His throne on high. This approach is made the more dramatic by describing Him as going aloft like a triumphant conqueror who is Himself glad over what He has achieved, for He goes up "with a shout." The figure changes when the modifying phrase is added, "with the sound of a trumpet." As an earthly ruler's victory might be celebrated by fanfares of trumpets, so to give more color to the picture this Ruler's ascension is described in similar terms.

6. God's people do not stand idly by as all this transpires: they re-

joice and would express their joy. Therefore the psalmist with a fourfold summons, "sing praises," calls upon them to participate. The verb used implies to sing a song in the nature of a psalm, for the typical word for psalm has the same root as the verb that is here used. The theme of the praises to be sung is indicated by the substitution of the "King" for "God." For this is the point that God's people understand more clearly as a result of the recent and great victory achieved, that God's authority is not circumscribed. He is "King of all the earth." This is a truth that is downright glorious when it is grasped in its full magnitude and in its full implications. The last summons, which reads, "Sing praises with a psalm," is only partly correct as to its translation. That there is difficulty involved appears from the fact that from the time of the Greek translation onward men felt that the term used might be rendered, "with understanding" or as *ARV* has it, "every one that hath understanding." The term employed (*maskil*) appeared as a title of Ps. 45 and elsewhere. It would appear to be a special type of psalm, whose exact character we may not fully understand, but which could still be as indicated above, "a didactic psalm." In any case, our translation is permissible and, perhaps, the most suitable. *BDB* suggests: "a contemplative poem."

8. The truth just set forth calls for fuller and more emphatic statement. Therefore, dwelling on the matter a bit longer, the psalmist expresses this truth thus: "God has become King over the Gentiles." By this he would not say that He was not King previously, but rather that it has become obvious that He is King. We might have ventured to render: "God has proved Himself King." And rounding out more fully the thought begun with v. 5 ("God went up") the writer envisions the final act in the great drama: "God has taken His seat upon His holy throne." There He sits as the victorious Monarch that He really is. So this part of the psalm comes to an effective conclusion by emphasizing in a new and colorful manner the truth of God's kingship, which is taught so abundantly in many other passages of the Scriptures.

9. This last verse stands apart from the preceding summons in order to picture what effects this ascension of the Lord may be thought of as having had upon at least some of those that dwell upon the earth. This verse may rightly be interpreted in a historical manner as *Koenig* so strenuously maintains. There are certain individuals among the children of men who have always kept an open mind for the truth of God, who could properly be described as "the willing ones," who accepted the excellent proof of the true kingship of Yahweh and were willing to be numbered as part of the "people of the God of Abraham." True, they were not many; but we do read of occasional individuals like Uriah, the

Hittite, and "the Cushite" (II Sam. 18:21) who were non-Israelites and had yet united with God's people. It is true that there may not have been many. But the eye of faith may see in them forerunners of a great host. We do not possess sufficient material from the days of Hezekiah to indicate more clearly just how many of such were to be found in Israel in those days.

On the other hand, whoever the mighty ones on the earth may be, here called "rulers of the earth," they "belong to God," are under His control, whether they know it or not, whether they acknowledge it or not. So all things are under His absolute dominion. On this positive note the psalm closes: "He is greatly exalted." And so this psalm shares something of the strong conviction that marked the preceding psalm.

NOTES

1. The "jubilant cry" (*teru'ah*) is the typical shout that voiced the homage due to Yahweh as King as appears from Num. 23:21.

3. In determining whether the first verb of this verse and the next is to be rendered as a present or future, on the one hand (*AV*), or as a past (*RSV*), it must be remembered that the imperfect in the *waw consecutive* construction often appears without the *waw* (*KS* 194f) as the *Septuagint* already understood these forms and as fits best into the whole connection, "He subdued."

9. The word "willing ones" (*nedibhey*) may, indeed, be rendered "noble" (*BDB*) or "princes" (*AV*), but the former is the primary meaning and fits better into the present connection. On the other hand, the word we have rendered "rulers" does read in the original, "shields" (*KJ*, etc.). By metonymy the defensive weapon, shield, is substituted for the shield-bearers, in this case quite obviously men of some importance.

Psalm 48

THE GREATNESS OF THE GOD OF ZION

THE SIMILARITY between this psalm and Ps. 46 is rather obvious. No commentator has traced it better that has *Maclaren* who writes: "In both we have the same triumph, the same proud affection for the holy city and sanctuary, the same confidence in God's dwelling there, the same vivid picturing of the mustering of enemies, and their rapid dispersion, the same swift movement of style in describing that overthrow, the same thought of the diffusion of God's praise in the world as its consequence, the same closing summons to look upon the tokens of deliverance, with the difference that, in the former psalm, these are the shattered weapons of the defeated foe, and in this the unharmed battlements and palaces of the delivered city."

We should not fail to note that it is the proper psalm for Whitsunday. It is most appropriate for this festival, for if God's indwelling in His holy city is her safety, then what brings home this thought more effectively than does the perpetual indwelling of His Holy Spirit, who has also as in days of old again and again driven off the foe and delivered His holy church?

A historic event of major importance that involved a striking deliverance of the holy city apparently lies at the basis of this psalm. The deliverance wrought in the days of Hezekiah (see II Kings 19:35ff.) which involved the dramatic overthrow of Assyrian forces meets the needs of the case best. Even *Buttenwieser* concedes this. The event recorded as having happened in the days of Jehoshaphat (II Chron. 20) might qualify, though not quite so well as does the one first noted.

A more modern type of interpretation may be examined with more detail as to its inadequacy, namely, the interpretation that has everything in the psalms represent liturgical procedures, and that also brings into the picture the very problematic enthronement-of-Yahweh festival. Rather than to seek the occasion of this psalm in a striking and helpful historical event, something that you can really sink your teeth into, this type of exegesis substitutes for it a bit of pageantry that was enacted in the Temple court at Jerusalem, a pageant that was so effective that it moved the psalmist to produce this stirring psalm. This pageant or cultic drama is described somewhat as follows (see *Leslie*): first kings assemble who represent the pagan rulers; they band together against Zion; they see Zion and are filled with confusion and take to their heels in precipitate flight; they are somehow destroyed by the mysterious power of the Lord who dwells in Zion.

Imagine substituting such pageantry for the stirring realities of history and expecting it to produce a greater impression on the minds of men than do the great lessons of history, which God on occasion thunders into the ears of the world! The exponents of this type of interpretation mysteriously hint at something more. They would seem to be trying to create the impression that, when this cultic drama was sincerely enacted, the Lord may as a kind of climax to it and re-enforcement

Psalm 48

of it have added a glorious appearance of Himself; and they hint at such theophanies as being quite a common occurrence in Jerusalem. We cannot but point out that fancy plays a major role in discovering the needed evidence for such interpretation.

Though at a later date in Judah's history some political enthusiasts put a nationalistic interpretation upon historical occasions such as the one we believe to be the background of our psalm and dreamed of Jerusalem as being invincible, come what may, the conclusion that this psalm draws is that the God who dwells at Zion is immeasurably great and will be a sure defense of all who put their trust in Him as Ps. 46 had already pointed out with emphasis.

The psalm presents the following pattern of thought:

a) Zion's greatest glory is the indwelling of the Lord (vv. 1–3).
b) a recent instance of God's protection of Zion (vv. 4–8).
c) an exhortation to praise the Lord for His judgments (vv. 9–11).
d) the glories of Zion to be transmitted to posterity (vv. 12–14).

The heading: "A song. A psalm of the sons of Korah." Compare the heading of Ps. 42 and others that follow it.

1. *Great is the Lord and greatly to be praised*
   In the city of our God, in His holy mountain.
2. *Eminently beautiful, the joy of the whole earth is Mount Zion in the far north,*
   The city of the great King.
3. *God in her citadels*
   Has become known for a refuge.

1. Something has apparently transpired which has in a marvelous way again underscored the greatness of the Lord and the fact that He is deserving of praise. But since God's people had instruction to worship Him in the sanctuary that He had appointed, the writer quite naturally mentions Zion as the place where such praise should become vocal and appropriately calls the famous old citadel "the city of our God" and the sanctuary "His holy mountain." This thought calls to mind (v. 2) the uniqueness of the holy city which, because of these sacred associations, the psalmist believes to be "eminently beautiful."

But he is not ignorant of the parallel truth that Israel's advantages are ultimately to be shared with the other nations on the face of the earth; so he quite properly calls this city "the joy of the whole earth" by using a title which carries with it something of the prophetic. When he uses the descriptive phrase "in the far north" he seems quite definitely to be making an allusion to another hill which traditionally was a kind of Olympus for the Near Eastern nations even as the Greeks were wont to think of their whole pantheon as dwelling on Olympus. This mount of the gods is referred to also in Is. 14:13, 14. The writer seems to use the expression as one that is generally known and by the use of it implies that what the fables of the Gentiles imagined was a reality in Zion: God really dwelt there.

3. Building up on the thought previously expressed and preparing for the allusions that follow, the writer stresses that in the palaces of the holy city an old truth had become fresh and new, the truth that the God of Israel can be depended on as being a true refuge in the day of trouble. When he says, "has become known," he refers to a historical incident, namely, the one we have indicated above. In her palaces or "citadels" that was the subject of sanctified conversation. Each man was reassuring the other that it was so.

4. *For, behold, the kings assembled;*
   They crossed over (the boundaries) together.
5. *They saw (Zion), then they were dumbfounded;*
   Confusion seized them; they fled in panic.
6. *Trembling took hold of them there;*
   Pain as of a woman in travail.
7. *By means of the east wind*
   Thou breakest the ships of Tarshish.
8. *As we have heard, so have we seen,*
   In the city of the Lord of hosts, in the city of our God,
   God establishes her forever. Selah.

4. That recent instance of God's protection which called forth this jubilant outburst of the psalm is now described, not in a prosy, literal fashion, but with rare dramatic skill. "Kings" were aligned against Zion. They were Sennacherib's vassals. He himself had described them as kings (Is. 10:8) in a passage that revealed his practice of using conquered kings in his army. Cf. also Ps. 2:2. They met by coming to the point of rendezvous from different vassal states. Then began the invasion of Israelitish territory: "they passed over." Since in Judg. 11:29 and II Kings 8:21 the same verb is used in the sense of crossing boundaries, we have inserted this object parenthetically in our translation.

Then comes a verse that is outstanding for its pregnant brevity in the Hebrew. It consists almost entirely of four verbs, long antedating Caesar's famous three-word report and just as effective, except that it marks an anticlimax. With the first verb all kinds of objects have been supplied, even a complete theophany such as the Egyptians

saw at the Red Sea (Exod. 15), or some nameless thing that struck
fear into their hearts. Most natural would be the assumption that
what they beheld was the city of Zion itself—which we have also inserted in the translation. It was quite obviously not literally the city as
such which caused the startling effects that are now enumerated. But
since Zion is so important in the Lord's eyes, the poet describes the
whole experience as growing out of the mere beholding of the holy city.
The resultant effects of this beholding were: "then they were dumbfounded; confusion seized them; they fled in panic." Their consternation
grows until it results in wild flight. In the Hebrew the concise verse reads
thus: *rá'u, ken thamáhu, nibhhalú, nechpházu.*

6. In an effective comparison, one that appears frequently in the
Scriptures in one form or another, the whole experience is summed
up: "Trembling took hold on them there," on these mighty warriors
of Assyria who were famed for their iron courage and great strength,
"pain as of a woman in travail." By a choice metaphor (v. 7) the
whole disaster is well portrayed: "By means of the east wind Thou
breakest the ships of Tarshish." The east wind was known for its destructive strength. Ships of Tarshish represent any man's proud structures also in Is. 2:16. At another time one of the kings of Israel experienced such a disaster (II Chron. 20:36f.). All this becomes more
vivid when we realize that "ships of Tarshish" were the mightiest of
the sea going vessels of those days.

The whole experience is now summed up from the point of view
of faith (v. 8). Many were the mighty instances of God's protective
power and providence that the children of Israel had heard of from
the mouth of their fathers. They now saw recent confirmation of the
old truth: "God establishes her forever," and all this "in the city of
the Lord of hosts, in the city of our God." Her ancient renown was
enhanced.

9. *O God, we have pondered Thy steadfast love*
   In the midst of Thy Temple.
10. *As Thy name, O God, so is Thy praise unto the ends of the earth;*
    Thy right hand is full of righteousness.
11. *Let Mount Zion be glad;*
    Let the daughters of Judah rejoice because of Thy acts of judg-
    ment.

9. This exhortation to praise begins with a prayer that reviews the
recent great event and meditates upon it in the presence of God Himself in His holy Temple, where praise is most appropriately voiced.
Properly summed up, this was a manifestation of God's "steadfest

love" (*chésedh*) or of His covenant faithfulness. The dimensions of this love become more obvious as a result. A further conclusion (v. 10) is drawn from these observations. God has a name or reputation the world over for mighty acts of deliverance; His praise will now be heard after what He has done for His people. The substance of this praise can be summed up in the statement: "Thy right hand is full of righteousness." God's righteousness is two-sided: it punishes the wicked according to their deserts; it rewards and delivers the godly according to God's marvelous faithfulness. Here both aspects of this great attribute of God came to the fore and are to be remembered.

11. If, therefore, men the world over, wherever they hear of what the Lord has done for Israel, break out in praises of Him, how much more appropriate is it that God's church, here designated "Zion," should be glad of heart? In a sense in this connection the designation "Zion" had in mind the holy city, and so the "daughters of Judah" signifies the smaller cities surrounding the mother city. They are bidden in the same spirit to "rejoice" because of the "judgments" of the Lord. This latter word, as our translation indicates, in cases like this signifies "acts of judgment." The Assyrians were judged according to their pride and had received the due reward of their arrogance. It is not unseemly to thank God for such great deeds of His.

12. *Walk about Zion, go round about her;*
    Count her towers.
13. *Note carefully her ramparts;*
    Walk through her citadels
    That you may give an account to the next generation:
14. *That such a one is God, our God, forever and ever;*
    He will be our guide—in spite of death.

12. Mighty works of God are to be remembered for days to come; they are to be transmitted to the future. This section appropriately relates how this may be done. The inhabitants of the land, particularly of Jerusalem, are addressed and exhorted to make good use of their newly won freedom. For during the time the enemy infested the city they were closely confined within her walls. Let them now freely walk about, in fact, let them go to the trouble of going completely around the holy city—these cities of old were very compact, and a man might encircle the city conveniently in half an hour. This city had taken on a new sanctity and meaning for them all. Since God was "in the midst of her," and she was not to be moved, her very towers had become the symbols of impregnability. So her people might well be bidden to "count her towers." Everything that was indicative of strength could, in fact, be

Psalm 48

regarded as exemplifying this very attribute in a new and better sense because God sustained her.

13. Therefore the people are admonished to "note carefully her ramparts," the outermost points of her strongly built walls, and to "walk through her citadels," the high and fortified structures that figured so mightily in her defense. All this, of course, was not strength in itself; but by His deliverance the Almighty had invested it all with new dignity and meaning. This latter importance was the matter of which they were to "give an account to the next generation." The remembrance of great works that God has done dare not die out. Nor could one generation do justice to what God had wrought by way of praising it. The remembrance and the praise were to carry on to the next generation.

14. What form this transmitted truth was to take is specifically stated. It was to be an emphasis, not on invincible bulwarks, not on walls, towers, citadels, or bastions, but on the fact regarding what kind of God this God is: namely, "that such a one is God, our God, forever and ever." For that matter, he has always been such though men were aware of it only faintly or not at all; and He always will be, come what may. And He stands in direct relation to His people, in fact, will guide their destinies whenever the need arises. "He will be our guide." So the church maintains stoutly through the ages, and experience verifies her assertion again and again. The last statement stresses one often difficult feature about this experience, and that is that those who are being mightily delivered by Him often seem to be passing through nothing less than death itself. But somehow, He is there, mighty to deliver, and though the church seems to be at the point of death she it is of whom the words are truly spoken: "dying, behold we live."

NOTES

1. The words "greatly to be praised" could be rendered more correctly "most praiseworthy," but if they are translated thus they would not fit in quite so aptly with the following phrases.

2. The verse begins literally: "beautiful for elevation." No translator seems to have caught the force of the words better than did *Koenig,* whom we have followed. The expression is a kind of superlative. In his translation of this rare word (occurring only here) *Luther* followed the Aramaic meaning, which is poorly established, and rendered: *ein schoen Zweiglein* (a pretty little branch).

Yarkethey tsaphon would be literally: "on the sides of the north." But, as most dictionaries agree, that should mean, "in the remotest parts of the north." For this the simplest rendering would seem to be "in the far north" as we have given it.

5. After "they saw" the logical object is omitted as being one that can readily be supplied. The four verbs of this verse are not given in sequence with *waw* copulative because in the case of synonymns this construction is often bypassed (*KS* 370h).

14. The concluding phrase, which we have rendered "in spite of death," (on this meaning of *'al* see *BDB* 574 (f) and *KB* 704) is quite commonly rejected as being quite out of place. By means of a textual change *RSV* substitutes another phrase for it. *KJ* renders: "even unto death." It may properly be objected that, if this phrase is understood to refer to personal reassurance for the individual that God will not forsake him in the hour of his death, such a thought is out of keeping with the objective thoughts that are prominent in the psalm on the subject of God's guidance of His church. But the phrase need not be construed thus. The sense which we have given it may very appropriately refer to God's saving guidance in the face of seeming death. The phrase deserves to be retained. *Luther* renders the statement: *Er fuehret uns wie die Jugend,* (He guides us as the youth) following the lead of the *Targum,* which also required a textual emendation.

Psalm 49

THE PROBLEM OF THE PROSPERITY OF OPPRESSORS

"This psalm is of the wisdom type." Thus many writers rightly begin the treatment of it (*Oesterley et.al.*)

The character of the psalm is indicated by the title that we placed at the head of it. Some interpreters list the poem under the head of psalms that combat pessimism. It is without a doubt didactic in character. Its chief concern is that wicked men so obviously thrive in this life. It is indicated but briefly and indirectly in v. 5 that those who have wealth are using the power that they have to "take advantage" of the psalmist, but we are offered no further details as to just how this was done or how grievous the oppression practiced was. This led *Kirkpatrick* to say: "The rich . . . are not expressly condemned as tyrannous and oppressive, though no doubt they tended to become so." On the whole much the same problem is met with here as that found in Ps. 37 and 73. The psalm prays the problem through in the sight of God and is, therefore,

Psalm 49

deserving of a place in the Psalter. *Mohwinckel* misses the point in remarking: "The author of this didactic and boastful psalm" ... (I, 132).

It need not trouble us unduly that there are certain phases of the subject which are not touched upon, or that more could have been said from one angle or another. The writer imparts what insight the Lord has given him, and imparts it for what it is worth. Basically his argument boils down to this, that death is the great leveller: what is not adjusted in this life and world is adjusted in the next. We also have no good reason for assenting to the claim of *Kittel* that the solution offered does not measure up to the high expectations that the somewhat elaborate introduction would lead us to expect. What the writer says is a very potent antidote to the misgivings that are occasioned by the injustice that seems to prevail in this area of life.

Many writers make quite a bit of the seeming state of corruption in which the text of the psalm is to be found in our day. This must be viewed as an exaggeration of the actual situation. The *Kittel* text, for example, has about one third of a page of critical suggestions or emendations on this psalm. Very constructive suggestions have been offered to relieve by far the greater number of these difficulties. Yet it cannot be denied that the translation of parts of the psalm is fraught with difficulties, and that difficult constructions appear here and there. But it must also be admitted that much constructive work has been done by many more recent writers, notably *Koenig,* in the direction of showing how a reasonable translation of the text may be obtained, and how the text may be reasonably construed.

It is practically impossible to make any safe pronouncement on the identity of the author and the time of composition. For beyond the bare "the sons of Korah" we have nothing to guide our thinking on this score; and as to the other matter there is a certain timelessness of the issue involved. Because some have wealth and others not, *Briggs* argues for a late Persian or early Greek date as though rich and poor offered a contrast only at that late date.

The reference to immortality, found particularly in v. 15, is commonly evaluated either too high or too low. Some brush it aside as being purely incidental and unimportant; others would deduce from it a full-blown doctrine of immortality. The truth lies somewhere between these extremes. We shall attempt to indicate where, when we interpret v. 15.

We suggest the following outline of the psalm:

a) the solemn introduction (vv. 1–4)
b) the futility of wealth, consisting in this that it cannot buy off death (vv. 5–12)

c) the end of those who trust in wealth contrasted with the end of the man who trusts in the Lord (vv. 13–15)
d) the seeming injustice involved further discounted by the fact that the rich cannot take their wealth with them (vv. 16–20)

To the Choir Director. By the sons of Korah. A Psalm.

On this heading compare the preceding psalms.

1. *Hear this, all peoples;*
   Give heed, all who dwell in the world,
2. *Both low and high,*
   Rich and poor together.
3. *My mouth shall speak of wisdom,*
   And the meditation of my heart of understanding.
4. *I will incline my ear to a parable;*
   I will expound my riddle to the music of the harp.

1. The formal character of the introduction to this psalm is unique. It is apparently the outgrowth of the writer's conviction of the importance of the instruction he is about to offer. Parallels are offered by the following passages: Deut. 32:1; Ps. 50:1; Mic. 1:2; I Kings 22:28, especially regarding v. 1. For to address a vast audience and bid it hear, even, for that matter, heaven and earth, was merely a figurative way of saying that the words about to be spoken were of vast importance. This audience is made all-inclusive by a peculiar device, which the Hebrew frequently resorts to, mentioning two extremes and automatically including all that lies between such as "root and branch," etc. Here "low and high" includes all that are between these extremes; and "rich and poor" does likewise.

3. A description is given in advance regarding the nature of what the psalmist is about to announce: it is "wisdom," implying by the use of the plural: wisdom of the highest sort. Besides, when it was being meditated upon in the heart it deserved to be characterized as "understanding"—another plural—synonymous with deep insight. The writer makes lofty claims for the truth that he is about to set forth. To question as some interpreters do, whether he succeeded in setting forth an adequate treatment of the subject in hand makes the writer a pompous boaster.

4. It is most difficult to render the word "parable" adequately. Basically it signifies what is in wisdom literature also called a "proverb" as the title of the Book of Proverbs indicates. Here it signifies that the form that his poem is going to take is somewhat in the nature of a "prover-

Psalm 49

bial saying" as some interpreters render the word. However, the still more significant things about the statement is that the writer claims that he "inclines his ear to" this pronouncement. This means that he was inspired and gave close heed to what was imparted to him in the process of inspiration. Since his poem furthermore aims to help settle a vexatious question, the writer designates it a "riddle" which he is about to expound or help to explain. The closing phrase, "to the music of the harp," seems to indicate nothing more than that he expected this psalm to be rendered to musical accompaniment even as we know of many hymns that have a largely doctrinal content but are yet to be rendered to music. He himself rendered it thus.

A further unique feature of this introduction is that it gives no intimation whatsoever as to the subject matter that is to be treated in the psalm that follows.

5. *Why should I fear in days when evil prevails,*
   When the iniquity of those who would take advantage of me surrounds me,
6. *Of those who trust in their own wealth*
   And boast in the abundance of their riches?
7. *A man cannot by any means ransom a brother,*
   Nor give to God a price for him;
8. *(For the ransom of his life is too costly*
   And can never suffice.)
9. *That he should continue to live on*
   And not see corruption.
10. *But he will see wise men die,*
    The fool and the brutish alike perish
    And leave their wealth to others.
11. *Their inward thought is that their homes shall last forever*
    And their dwellings to all generations;
    They call their lands by their own name.
12. *But man in spite of his honor cannot abide;*
    He is like unto the beasts that perish.

5. One test is applied to wealth and thus to the possessors of it, as to whether it has any real validity, and that test is: Can it ward off death? The outcome of the test is that death is known to march on relentlessly and sweep all its victims before it, whether they possess wealth or not.

But the whole case as such does not rest on an abstraction. The writer is directly involved. He finds himself to be living in a time "when evil prevails," for that is, no doubt, what the expression "days of evil" means. There are men "who would take advantage" of him, and under the circumstances their iniquity "surrounds" him. He does not actually say that harm has been done to him, but he admits that he is in danger. Those who thus oppose him are further to be described as "those who trust in their own wealth and boast in the abundance of their riches." They have means, and their means are their hope and confidence. In fact, it must have been their wealth that made them so dangerous. But the writer has already arrived at the conclusion that, viewed from the lofty point of view of faith, the situation is such that he must ask, "Why should I fear?"

7. He has made the very correct observation that this money in which these opponents put their trust fails completely when it is subjected to certain tests, especially one great test—death. Suppose a man were to see his very "brother" (placed first in the Hebrew sentence for the sake of emphasis) in danger of death by sickness or from any other cause, what sum of money would make an impression on death to have it pause? Money just does not suffice at all for that kind of price of ransom even if it were offered to God, in whose hands the issues of life and death are known to lie. The explanation is inserted parenthetically that this is one of the things money cannot buy. In fact, no matter how much of it a man may have, it "can never suffice." In other words, the case is unthinkable that after the payment of a sufficient price a man "should continue to live on and not see corruption" such as those see who are laid into the grave (v. 9). A case like Exod. 21:30 is obviously in his mind, and in this instance the word *nephesh* ("soul") means "life." Salvation or redemption of the soul is not even remotely thought of.

10. But when such an individual looks out upon the children of men he observes that there is a certain relentless impartiality, which impels death to sweep away even such worthy characters as "wise men," and in addition such unworthy persons as "the fool and the brutish alike." All travel the same course and leave this wealth that seemed so vastly important "to others."

11. All the time that they lived, they labored under the peculiar misapprehension that the houses that their wealth had been able to purchase "shall last forever and their dwellings to all generations." Not that they really thought this impossible thing to be likely, but they lived as though they did. And they made much of such gestures as "calling their lands by their own name," as though calling estates formally their own would insure the permanence of their possession of them. But there is a certain plain, blunt summary of the whole situation: "But man in spite

of his honor cannot abide, he is like unto the beasts that perish." He may have seemed to have so many advantages, it may have seemed such a pity that, all such honors as he possessed should come to nought. But so it was. Wealth, honor, reputation could not avail. Death swept him away. And so whatever persecution of righteous men he may have initiated or threatened to initiate, "Why should I fear?" (v. 5). Death, the great leveller, has disposed of the problem involved.

In the next section of the psalm (vv. 13–15) the writer looks down the same road a little more intently and observes that there is more to it than he has already said, in fact, there is a certain notable contrast to be noticed in this business of dying.

13. *This is the lot of those who are marked by stupidity,*
    Also the latter end of those who delight in their talk. Selah.
14. *Like sheep they were appointed for Sheol, death pastures them;*
    The upright have dominion over them in the morning;
    And their form is appointed for the decay of Sheol so that no
        dwelling is left for it.
15. *But God will ransom my soul from the power of Sheol,*
    For He will receive me.

13. Reflecting a bit more intently on the role that death plays in this problem, the writer now points up a little more sharply how those are to be judged who, being wealthy and influential, were thus swept away by death. They are persons "who are marked by stupidity." But there is a second class that is also involved and shares the same "lot" or "latter end." They are the ones who without, perhaps, having wealth and power themselves may yet be said to "delight in their talk." For when the rich spoke proudly and presumptuously, these persons approved what they said and flattered them as being right. Such hangers-on share the same lot.

14. The helplessness and unhappy lot of all who thus go down in death are stressed at this point. At this juncture in life these once so wealthy and influential persons become as helpless as sheep that are herded together. "They were appointed for Sheol," and unto Sheol they go. "Death pastures them"—such a very strange character to have as a shepherd. In fact, a peculiar reversal of lot is sometimes seen to take place: "the upright shall have dominion over them in the morning." No peculiar deductions are to be drawn from this statement. It would seem to imply nothing more than that a strange reversal of role has taken place. When "the morning" comes, that is to say, when the night that threatened disaster to the godly is past, they will still be found on the scene when their wealthy oppressors or would-be oppressors have

passed off the scene and are no more. For even the body that walked about so proudly and impressively has a rendezvous with death: "their form is appointed for Sheol so that no dwelling is left for it." This final outcome gives a proper perspective to all this and makes values appear in their true light.

15. With startling insight the writer suddenly notes the very antithesis to this tragic and drastice overthrow of ungodly men of wealth. It is the lot that he anticipates for himself. It is an outcome that rests with God and can be received only as it is bestowed by His gracious goodness. It is this: "God will ransom my soul (or life) from the power of Sheol, for He will receive me." If that is true, then, in the last analysis, the wealthy man without God, the proud oppressor, is seriously to be pitied. But he, the oppressed poor man without means but with the fear and love of God in his heart, is to be regarded most fortunate. Death will not carry the day as far as he is concerned. Just how this outcome is to be visualized is not stated in further detail. The essence of it, however, is this: "He will receive me." The same verb is used that was employed in the case of godly Enoch (Gen. 5:24). Strangely, it can be translated, "will receive me" or "will take me hence." The net result is the same. To claim that the verse refers only to "deliverance from the premature and penal death of the wicked" scarcely does justice to it.

The offhand way in which this deep and comforting truth is mentioned surprises us. Why the writer does not dwell on this matter longer is difficult to determine. It must be that the hope of life with God was more real in Old Testament days than many commentators would allow for. The truth as such flashes up for a moment, and the writer goes on with the matter in hand. He apparently had no intention of developing this side of the matter at this point.

16. *Be not afraid, therefore, if a man becomes rich,*
    When the glory of his house increases.
17. *For he will not take anything with him when he dies;*
    His glory will not go down after him.
18. *Though he counts himself happy while he lives;*
    And men will praise you when you do well for yourself;
19. *A man will only come to the generation of his fathers,*
    Who will nevermore see light.
20. *Man that is in honor and has no understanding*
    Is like the beasts that perish.

16. We are still on the subject of the futility of wealth. This is now demonstrated by the fact that wealth must be left behind. That such would be the case had been briefly intimated in v. 10c. At the same time

Psalm 49

what now follows is a conclusion, especially as far as v. 16 is concerned, that is drawn from the preceding. We have sought to indicate the connection involved by inserting a "therefore" into the translation, a word which does not appear in the original.

The point that is being made is, first of all, this, that in spite of the imposing and threatening character of the rich men that are in power over against the righteous, there is still no actual reason to "be afraid when a man becomes rich, and when the glory of his house increases." Wealth has so little real and lasting value, especially in view of the fact that it cannot stem the tide of death. Or to stress the other aspects of the matter (v. 17), "he will not take anything with him when he dies." "His glory," which is his wealth, "will not go down after him." He arrives in the hereafter as naked as do the very poorest as far as material wealth is concerned. And it is the ultimate issues that count, not momentary possessions somewhere along the line.

8. The thought is expanded a bit more. The rich man may take quite another view of the situation as long as he lives and his riches seem to be in his power. "He may count himself happy" or as some interpreters render it, he may "congratulate himself." His own attitude, moreover, seems to be re-enforced by the attitude of others on this same question: "Men will praise you when you do well for yourself," generally speaking. In other words, as with one united voice, during the lifetime of the individual in question, all agree as to how fortunate he is. But all are deceived as the sequel proves. And the sequel is this: "A man will only come to the generation of his fathers and will nevermore see the light." The "only" that we have inserted is implicit in the nature of the case though the original does not express it. The rather dim view of the hereafter, especially as regards the men alienated from God, is the one that is here reflected. Everyone knows that the generation of the fathers has gone the way of all flesh, has relinquished all wealth, and is now to be found stripped and bare of all material possessions. The "light" of happiness that wealth once seemed to shed on their path is permanently dimmed.

20. Almost refrain-like—cf. v. 12—this verse sums up the whole matter, a fact which led Luther to introduce the verse with an appropriate "in short" (*kurtz*). The verse begins like v. 12, but we have not translated the first phrase "in spite of his honor" in order to make smoother reading with what follows. The issue is pointed up a little more sharply as befits a summary: If a man is in honor *and has no understanding,* then he "is like the beasts that perish," that is to say, if he puts unseemly confidence in earthly possessions; if he fails to consider that wealth must fail a man in the end; if he leaves God out of the picture and does not make Him his confidence.

Such a lesson on the vanity of earthly possessions, so aptly put and so well reinforced by sound argument, is a most important bit of wholesome instruction that well deserved the strong introduction which the author gave it. This is basic insight that men the world over need very badly if they are ever to come to the elements of true insight into values.

NOTES

2. How the mention of two extremes commonly occurs in the Hebrew to designate all that lies between and so becomes synonymous with "all" or "many" is illustrated by *KS* 92 at length.

3. On these intensive plurals "wisdom" and "understanding" see also *GK* 124e.

6. "Of those who trust" is a plural participle with the article referring to an antecedent which is slightly removed from it. See *KS* 411e.

7. The sentence is marked by an inversion of the regular order. The object "brother" stand first for the sake of emphasis. In this way we feel that a clearer thought is obtained, and one that is more in keeping with the progression of thought.

8. If we construe this verse parenthetically as we have done, it is best to regard the initial *waw* as a "for."

10. Those commentators who make "brother" the subject in v. 7, here keep the same noun as the subject of "will see," which yields a very strange and forced meaning.

11. At this point it is quite common to suppose that the text is so corrupt as to warrant a change, namely, *qirbam* (their inward thoughts) becomes *qibhram* (their graves), following the lead of the *Septuagint*. There is no need for this. The text makes good sense.

13. The translation "latter end" is arrived at by some interpreters by resorting to a textual emendation, *'acharitham* for *'acharehem*. But *'acharey* can mean that which comes last as II Sam. 2:23 shows.

14. "So that no dwelling is left for it," i.e., for their form, appears in the Hebrew as a very condensed expression, in which the *min* introduces a negative clause of result though it is followed only by a noun (literally "apart from a dwelling"). *KS* 406p.

18. In "when you do well" the "you" is not direct address so much as what grammarians call the "ideal" second person. See *KS* 324b. The same holds true with regard to the first word in v. 20 (*tabho'*) which we have translated more freely: "a man will come," for this is also that ideal second person and may be translated "a man" or "one."

Volz (*ZAW*, 1937, p. 235ff.) has a very thought-provoking article on this psalm. He calls v. 16 *die voellige Erschliessung des Raetzels* (the final solution of the problem), and adds the significant remark: "We stand here at the beginning of the belief in immortality . . . as at the beginning of the belief in hell."

Psalm 50

TRUE WORSHIP

VARIOUS TITLES could be given to this psalm. We are almost tempted to call it a thundering indictment of formalism. Though the negative is clearly stigmatized, the ultimate purpose and statement of the psalm are positive, and so we are inclined to choose a caption like the above, after the pattern of other writers on the subject.

We could wish that we knew more about the writer "Asaph." According to passages like I Chron. 15:17, 19; II Chron. 29:30; I Chron. 25:1, he could be the singer who did significant work by way of beautifying the Temple services in David's day. But details of information are lacking, and we shall be equally at loss in trying to determine the time when the psalm was written. It must be said at least that in the light of I Sam. 15:22 it would have been quite reasonable for a man of David's day to have written statements like those contained in the psalm on the subject of true and false worship.

In any case, the writer furnishes us a fine abstract of the doctrine of the prophets on worship in general and on the relative merit and importance of sacrifice in worship. The following passages from various prophets reflect the spirit of the psalm: Amos 5:21–26; Hos. 6:6; 8:13; Is. 1:11–15; Mic. 6:6–8; Jer. 7:21–23, in addition to the one previously referred to. Had the writer been influenced by all these he would, of course, have been a writer at a comparatively late date.

What seems to trouble the casual reader or even the one who reflects at length on the matter is the nature of God's appearance as described in vv. 1–6. When *did* He come as here described? Or if one follows the *KJ* text with its future tenses one may be inclined to ask: When *will* He thus come? Or when one takes note of the present tense used by some versions (*RSV* and *Luther*), the question is: When and how *does* this take place? A certain measure of poetic fancy is involved, something to the effect: If He came, thus would He speak and act. But there is more to the matter than that. The whole scene is pictured as a theophany that has taken place: God has come; God has spoken; He has rendered a verdict. All that His word has spoken through the prophets by way of indictment of hypocrites is summed up dramatically and emphatically in this striking portrayal that vv. 1–6 offer.

Those writers who like to pit prophet against priest, or who note an unresolved contrast between true spiritual worship and sacrifice arrive at extreme conclusions and are inclined to call this psalm something like the abrogation of sacrifice. Quite obviously when these two elements of worship are under consideration, it must be maintained that one should be done, and the other not left undone. They can go hand in hand and always did in the case of the faithful and true worshipers in Israel. The kind of sacrifice that this psalm condemns is that which is without spirit and truth. The writer maintains the need, not of an "either-or," but of a "both-and."

That the psalm is didactic can scarcely be questioned. To associate it with the festival of Yahweh's enthronement or with the festival of the making of the covenant (both festivals of very dubious validity) can be done only by stretching slim evidence in favor of pet theories beyond the point where they carry conviction.

a) God's appearance for judgment (vv. 1–6)

A Psalm of Asaph.

1. *The Mighty One, God the Lord, has spoken*
   And has called the earth from the rising of the sun unto its setting.
2. *From Zion, the perfection of beauty,*
   God has shined forth.
3. *Our God came and could not keep silence;*
   Fire devoured before Him, and round about Him a mighty storm raged.
4. *He called to the heavens above*
   And to the earth in order to judge His people.
5. *"Gather My saints to Me,*
   Who make a covenant with Me by sacrifice."
6. *Then the heavens declared His righteousness;*
   For God, He is judge. Selah.

1. The nature of this introduction has been discussed above. In this visionary description of God's preparing for judgment the Judge is first described with unusual dignity by three successive titles. He is "the Mighty One" (*'el*), and He is "God" (*'elohim*), and He is "the Lord"

Psalm 50

(*Yahweh*). The second title stresses the reverence and fear that are due Him. The last title connotes His unchangeable being and His covenant faithfulness. This One is to be thought of as having called "the earth" as a witness to a judgment scene. This scarcely refers to the inanimate earth as such but rather to its inhabitants, that they may profit by the instructive experience that they shall gain as God proceeds to exercise judgment on His people. Summoning a vast audience as is done here from the rising of the sun to its setting shows the solemnity and importance of the transactions which are about to follow. See Ps. 49:1 and the parallels there cited. It should also be noted as *Oesterley* remarks, "though Israel alone is addressed, all men are to be listeners."

2. In this entirely visionary scene the point from which God appears to His people is Zion. Not as on the occasion of that other memorable appearance when He gave the law—Mt. Sinai. For since David's day Zion was the place of His choice. God's dwelling in this place exalted it so in the thinking of Israel that this holy hill was even called "the perfection of beauty." Cf. Ps. 48:2 and Lam. 2:15. After others had appeared because they were summoned, He Himself puts in His appearance. "He came" (v. 3) and "could not keep silence," for the issue involved was of such moment that it impelled Him to assert Himself. But no one would venture to suppose that this was a colorless and tame vision. A correct tradition had it, that when God appeared in days of old, the impression He made upon men was overwhelming and terrifying. The description here pictures Him as being One before whom fire flashes forth that consumes all that lies in His path, and the elements as being in violent disturbance as a result of His appearance. Cf. Exod. 19:16–18; Deut. 33:2; Dan. 7:10, etc.

4. The Almighty summons not only all men upon the face of the earth but also the heavens above and the earth beneath, for the importance of the scene and transaction must be properly enhanced. The thought is not that heaven and earth are to do any judging. He does that. They serve as witnesses of the solemn transaction. Neither are they to be the agents who execute the command that follows. In fact, no one is specified as being responsible for gathering those who are to be judged. When He commands, it is certain that it will be done. But those individuals who are specifically to be gathered are first described as His "saints." The term could be rendered "My loyal ones." It implies that they are, or at least should be, devoted to Him. The fact that they stand in a special relation to Him appears also from the description that indicates that they are those "who make a covenant with Him by sacrifice." This last statement implies no more than that they have made sacrifices

and have thereby confirmed that they know themselves to be in covenant relationship with the Lord and have accepted the responsibilities of such a relationship.

6. The scene that the writer envisions as being preparatory to God's pronouncements that are about to follow involves one last event: "The heavens declared His righteousness" after He summoned them to be in attendance. This is a poetic form of statement that, perhaps, involved no more than that, after the heavens were called to stand by, a peal of thunder was heard, whose subtle meaning, the writer suggests, is that God, the Judge, is absolutely righteous in any trial which He conducts. That seems to be embodied in the statement "For God, He is Judge." Or else this is merely a poetic way of saying that the judgment about to follow is bound to be absolutely just.

b) Rebuke of Israel for its formalistic worship (vv. 7–15)

7. *Hear, O My people, and I will speak;*
   O Israel, and I will testify against you, I God, your God.
8. *Not because of your sacrifices do I chide you;*
   Your burnt offerings are continually before Me.
9. *I will accept no bull from your house,*
   Nor rams from your folds.
10. *For every beast of the forest is Mine*
    And the cattle upon the hills by the thousands.
11. *I know every bird of the mountains;*
    And all that moves in the field is Mine.
12. *If I were hungry I would not tell you,*
    For the world is mine and all that is in it.
13. *Should I eat the flesh of oxen*
    Or drink the blood of goats?
14. *Offer unto God thanksgiving*
    And pay your vows to the Most High.
15. *And call upon Me in the day of trouble;*
    I will deliver you, and you shall glorify Me.

7. Some writers call this a rebuke of hypocrites in the nation. According to the opening statement of the section it is the whole nation that is addressed, no doubt because it was predominantly hypocritical in its attitude. The poison of this sin had infected all inhabitants more or less. What makes the sin the more reprehensible is the fact that they are God's own people. Therefore, to whom much is given, of him much shall be required. But the verse as such is a summons to give heed to what God is about to say. He purposes to "testify." As most writers remark on this issue, the Lord is both the judge and the prosecuting attorney. In the case of men such a dual function of those who take part

in trials is not permissible. Not so in the case of the Judge of all the earth, who does right (Gen. 18:25) and is absolutely impartial.

8. A possible misapprehension is first removed from this trial. The thought is not that the required sacrifices have not been forthcoming. This was a time when the Temple, the sacrifices, the priestly functions, and the participation of the people in all this, in other words, the fulfilment of the outward requirements of sacrificial worship, was clearly in evidence. Early and late all manner of sacrifices were to be seen burning upon the altar as prescribed. "Burnt offerings" only are mentioned as an example of the rest, and most appropriately, too, because this kind of sacrifice typified total self-surrender. But it was just this feature of the sacrifice that was lacking. So this statement admits that Israel meticulously performed all that the law required of it.

9. Now in five verses a kindred factor is stressed at length in order to remove it from consideration in this trial. The issue is not that God needs physical sacrifices in a literal or figurative sense. It may well be that the author is taking issue with one of the strange but typical heathen misconceptions with regard to sacrifice, as though it were something on which the god feeds, and by the use of which he sustains himself. The language by which this misconception is rejected is rather strong and colorful in order to impress the facts at stake more deeply on Israel's consciousness. But it must be borne in mind that this rejection by God is involved only in the case where the materialistic conception of sacrifice prevails, as though the things required were the beast, the fire, and the altar. God obviously has no interest in bulls and rams as such. To state it still more bluntly: He is not a cattle buyer. For, moving to the higher level (v. 10), in the highest sense of the term, "all the beasts of the forest are His," and the cattle, too, no matter whose they are, are, in the last analysis, His, even the thousands that dot the hills of Palestine and every land. For He is the omnipotent Creator and Maker of them all. His providence and rights, for that matter, extend so far (v. 11) that there is no "bird of the mountains" of whose existence He is ignorant. That is much more than man can claim. But, of course, birds were also involved in certain types of sacrifices.

To round out the statement of total ownership on the part of the Almighty of all that belongs to the realm of creatures that could be sacrificed one last statement includes the remainder: "all that moves in the field is Mine." Basically man can give nothing to God, for God has given everything as a loan to man and has never withdrawn His claim to it all. This thought is offered in v. 12b: "For the world is Mine and all that is in it." With a noble divine irony God injects what all must readily grant as being true: "If I were hungry I would not tell you." This is a part of the *reductio ad absurdum* that the Lord makes of the whole issue and of the attitude of His people. For some such thoughts as these were, after all, involved in the attitude that they were taking. The strongest statement of all concludes this vigorous assault that the Lord makes on the nation's unwholesome thinking in all its folly: "Should I eat the flesh of oxen and drink the blood of goats?"

14. A certain divine indignation pervades the preceding passage. It destroys a misconception at length. One senses that this divine utterance cannot end on the note that has prevailed throughout the last five verses. The positive as it now follows is highlighted very effectively by being written without a conjunction or a transitional word (asyndeton): "Offer unto God thanksgiving." True thanksgiving is a truly spiritual matter. It is worship on a higher level. When a man can thank and praise he has learned the lesson as to what true worship is. The technical term "offer" is used in this connection to indicate that all such terms have spiritual overtones, all such acts have a spiritual connotation. Since the psalmist is offering concrete examples by way of illustration he presents another: "Pay your vows to the Most High." Vows, though nowhere commanded in the Old Testament, are a true test of the attitude of the heart. They can be forgotten quite readily. No precept seems to be violated by such an omission, for nothing was commanded. But the individual to whom God is real and worship real cannot under any circumstances ignore what he had vowed to pay to the Lord.

15. Another rather striking example of the kind of acts of worship that please God is now offered. We might place it on the lower levels of worship, for it could be thought of as lying in the area of things that are more or less selfish or as an outgrowth of preoccupation with self. The example has to do with our cries for help in the day of trouble. The reason they may be more acceptable may be the thought that trouble is very apt to make us feel our utter helplessness and our total dependence on Him, and so in the evil day a man may cry with complete self-abandon and cast himself wholly on God's mercy in the prayer of faith.

To say the least, it is a source of great comfort to many that their pleas for help are valued so highly by our Lord. The writer lets God speak further along this line. To encourage God's people to pray freely in evil days, God adds a divine promise: "I will deliver you, and you shall glorify Me." So one act of true devotion (calling on Him) produces an act of deliverance, and that, in turn, leads to glorification of the Deliverer; and thus a kind of godly chain reaction has set in. This positive feature in the first section of the treatment of the subject is so much to the point that the psalm lets the matter rest there.

c) **Rebuke of the definitely wicked among His people (vv. 16–21)**

16. *But to the wicked God has said:*

> What business have you to recite My statutes
> Or to take My covenant on your lips?
> 17. Seeing you hate discipline
> And cast My words behind you.
> 18. When you saw a thief you liked his company,
> And you had fellowship with adulterers.
> 19. You gave your mouth free rein for evil;
> Your tongue framed up deceit.
> 20. You sat down and spoke against your brother;
> You slandered your own mother's son.
> 21. These things you did, and I kept silence;
> You supposed I was just like yourself.
> I will correct you and set things right before your eyes.

16. As the initial statement indicates, the words here recorded are addressed to the "wicked." In trying to reach a conclusion as to how these verses (16–21) are related to the preceding section, we should note that there is apparently a deeper connection than appears at first blush. The group addressed in the preceding section and this present group cannot be thought of as being quite identical, nor are they to be regarded as being absolutely diverse. They apparently overlap somewhat. If men are to be charged with formalistic worship, then, unless this evil is corrected, they become definitely wicked. Formalism cannot be cultivated with impunity; progressive degeneracy is the outcome.

When this verse asserts that God "has said" something to the wicked, namely, what immediately follows, the past tense refers, not to what He is thought of as saying in the theophany described in vv. 1–6, but to a kind of summary of well-known precepts and ordinances that were known to the people of God from the days of Moses. The writer merely regroups the thoughts and sentiments of divine revelation with regard to the godly life in a free fashion, stressing rather the negative side, namely, things that God's ordinances had clearly forbidden. Sins that were current on every hand among the people of Israel are apparently under consideration. The first sin that is rebuked comes pretty close to the sin of formalism in that it represents an Israelite as being rather careless in reference to statutes, perhaps even the statutes that regulate sacrifices. A man may know these, talk about them at length and in a familiar way. He may refer to the covenant, that holy covenant in which Israel stood with God since the days of Moses. The type of speaking thought of is the kind that is lacking in reverence. For the statements that follow (vv. 17–20) indicate that there is no real respect of God and His ordinances in the heart of him who speaks so freely of these matters.

17. How the man in question actually feels about what God has commanded is revealed by the fact that, whatever correction or "discipline" the Word of the Lord might seem to demand, he hates so much as to refuse to let himself be corrected by it. True respect for the Word means ready submission to its corrections. In fact, in this attitude alone it already becomes apparent that the Word of the Lord is being despised, or to speak the language of the psalm: you "cast My words behind you."

18. There follows a list of typical misdemeanors of which these despisers of the Word of the Lord are guilty. They are listed according to the Seventh, Sixth, and Eighth Commandments, the last of these being treated at greater length (vv. 19, 20). The first item touched on involves the proverb: "Tell me with whom you associate, and I will tell you who you are." This nominal Israelite likes the company of thieves. He also has fellowship with adulterers. He may be able to claim that he himself is not guilty of the sins of which they are guilty, but he is very close to guilt on any score.

19. The sins of the tongue, being no overt act and often so difficult to trace, seem to be the type of evil these men, who are supposed to be among God's loyal saints, are most prone to engage in. They actually seem to remove all restraint from their tongue in regard to "evil." They plan evil, they delight in it, they speak it. That is as good as doing it. As one of the most heartless sins of the tongue there is mentioned that sort of attitude which allows one freely to slander those who are closest to him by ties of blood (v. 20).

21. A factor that bears upon the practical problem involved is brought into the picture by the Judge, the factor that God oftentimes for a long season seems to do nothing about irregularities of which men are guilty. The evildoer had not been corrected by the Lord, in fact, it seemed as if He absolutely "kept silence." It shall not always go on thus. For under such circumstances men suppose that God is as they are, quite indifferent to the issues of right and wrong. But His threat is that He will not go on thus forever: "I will correct you and set things right before your eyes." That is to say, these men shall yet be witnesses of God's concern about the injustices that men practice upon men.

All this leads up to the closing admonition, which follows.

d) The closing admonition (vv. 22–23)

22. *O consider this, you who forget God;*
Lest I tear in pieces, and there be none to deliver.
23. *He that offers thanksgiving glorifies me;*

> *And to him that orders his conduct aright I will show the salvation of God.*

22. God takes no pleasure in the death of a sinner who is perishing in his sins. So He admonishes him betimes. The chief fault of which such sinners have been guilty is that they "forget God." This is another way of saying that God is not a reality to them; they have no awareness of His holiness and greatness. If they continue to be thus self-satisfied and self-sufficient, there is only one prospect for them, which is stated in an almost fierce tone. God will come upon the impenitent evildoer as a lion upon a defenceless man and rend him, and no one will be able to do a thing about it. Only when the wrath of God has been watered down to the point where it is a mild and spineless reaction on His part will men take exception to the vigor of the statement of the case or be inclined to regard this as a gloss by some later writer.

23. That is the end of the warning. As is so often the case in the psalms, the treatment of the matter in hand ends on a very positive and constructive note. Since it was worship that was under consideration, especially in the first half of the psalm, and the neglect of worship as the cause of the misdeeds was specified in the second half, we might well expect a brief definition of true worship. An all-sided statement of the case reads as follows: "He that offers thanksgiving glorifies Me." "Thanksgiving" is so wholesome a matter that it is the mother of all the other phases of true worship. Thus it may very rightly be said that he who is thankful truly "glorifies" God; and what is worship but the true glorification of God? But worship that is wholesome affects the life of the worshiper so that out of very reverence for the God whom he worships he will observe the ordinances of the Lord and will "order his conduct aright." Persons who interpose no obstacle between themselves and the Lord, who delights to bless the children of men, will be the recipients of the fullest favor of the Lord in all its manifold aspects. That is the truth contained in the statement, "I will show him the salvation of God."

NOTES

3. It is a bit bewildering to find the versions differing so widely regarding the tense of the initial verb, *yabho'*: "will come," (*KJ*), "comes" (*RSV*), and "came" (our translation). It can, however, be said in favor of our translation that the imperfect is often used to express the minor attendant circumstances of an event that is being described (see *KS* 186c). The same holds true with regard to v. 4. *KS*

calls this imperfect *yaqtul concomitans*. In addition the verb *yecheresh* may be considered as expressing potentiality, "could not keep silence."

8. In his *Commentary, Koenig* defends the translation of *'okhichékha*, "I shall justify you." Even the one instance from Job (13:15) that he cites as supporting this meaning is dubious. The familiar "reprove" (*AV*, etc.) still deserves the preference.

10. The familiar "the cattle upon a thousand hills" reads in the Hebrew: "on the hills of the thousands." This is best understood to mean: "upon the hills by the thousands." It is not the hills that are so numerous but the cattle.

14. It is true that in the language of Leviticus *zébhach todhah* is used for the bringing of a thankoffering. See Lev. 7:12; 22:29, etc. But that is not quite the same as the expression used here, which is a verb (imperative) with an object, not a noun in the construct state. So the claim that this expression regularly refers to a type of Hebrew sacrifice is not exact. In fact, in this psalm the primary meaning of the word ("thanksgiving") alone fits the context. Cf. also v. 23.

15. Some commentators prefer to translate *thekhabbedhéni,* "you shall glorify Me" rather than "will glorify." The Hebrew, of course, allows either rendering.

21. It must be admitted that *wehecheráshti,* though a coordinate clause, could well be translated: "If I had kept silence." See *KS* 390r. But coordinating the clauses also makes good sense.

22. We feel that in a case like this the hortative particle *na'* can effectively be rendered by an introductory "O."

23. The participle *sam* is the equivalent of an abbreviated sentence, "he who orders," as *KS* 408a indicates.

Psalm 51

"GOD BE MERCIFUL TO ME, A SINNER"

A PENITENTIAL psalm, deeply moving in character. In contrast with the others of this type that have been considered (Ps. 6, 32, 38) this psalm bears the marks of deep inner grief over sin. It strikes a note that is so intensely personal that one is led to wonder how the interpretation that makes the psalm the expression of the feelings of the nation of Israel could ever have originated.

Psalm 51

The well-known heading points to David as the author of the psalm. The wording of the heading points to the likelihood that it is an editorial addition of a later date. In our day the validity of the heading is dismissed rather lightly. It is even claimed that the authorship by David is absolutely out of the question. Very few of the more recent writers venture to defend it. Yet there is so much to be said in its favor that we cannot but believe that the editors who captioned the psalm with these words were well aware of what they were doing and how correct their statement was.

Examining the chief objections to Davidic authorship, we find the fact pointed out that the psalm makes no express mention of the two great crimes that preceded—the adultery and the murder of Uriah; instead it seems to deal in generalities. However, we believe that this objection can be completely answered if we but note the fact that David knew that all the nation knew of these crimes: they are the tacit assumption behind all that is spoken. We can well understand how David would have refrained from mentioning the events which were so intensely painful to him. He was glossing nothing over. The obvious was just not dragged out into the open. It was too sordid for mentioning.

Another objection is built on the statement of v. 4, "Against Thee, Thee only have I sinned." This is said to be utterly unreconcilable with the great wrong done both to Bathsheba and to Uriah. Yet on the other hand, it is quite thinkable that the fact that all sin is, in the last analysis, sin against the Holy One Himself had hit David's conscience so hard that he voiced his conviction in this absolute statement. Words like this, born out of intensity of feeling, are not to be measured as to their technical correctness from the point of view of dogmatic formulation.

Furthermore, there are writers who advance the opinion that, if the writer were David, he would be far in advance of the insight of his time as to the guilt and misery of sin. However, does insight grow in a regular progression only, or is it not also to be seen from time to time as advancing by rapid leaps and bounds when some great and shaking experience comes upon a man? No man had sinned quite so miserably against God as had this man; no man had been so dramatically reclaimed and brought to repentance: few had ever had the spiritual insight and susceptibilities that this great king manifested. Considering all these facts, we may well conclude that they form the needed groundwork for a great spiritual experience and insight.

Lastly it is claimed, almost universally, that the last two verses could not by any stretch of the imagination be ascribed to the situation in which David found himself: walls of Jerusalem destroyed and in need of rebuilding. When we come to interpret these verses we shall attempt to show that, without doing violence to sound interpretation, these words do fit well into the days of David, and that there is no need for the current assumption that they are a later addition.

Attention must yet be drawn to the fact that the more recent trends of interpretation fit this psalm deeply into the ritualistic pattern. By assigning unusual meanings to the more difficult words of v. 6, meanings which are purely conjectural, and by assuming that symbolic acts were performed in connection with some type of Temple ceremonial, a certain ordeal was enacted which could proclaim the divine verdict of the guiltlessness of the author, to whom various crimes had been imputed, and who resorted to these manipulations at the Temple in order to secure a divine verdict. We regard such interpretations as vagaries that are based on the assumption that never in the past did the church, whether of the Old or of the New Testament, sense the true interpretation of key psalms like this one.

Equally beside the point is the view of those commentators who find the chief element in the interpretation of the psalm in the claim that the writer is a sick man (*Krankheitspsalm*) and is concerned chiefly about getting well.

Very much to the point is *Oesterley's* statement: "For the realization of the sense of sin, set forth with unflinching candor, it has no equal."

Note the following outline:
a) the basic plea for pardon (v. 1f.)
b) the reasons on which this plea is built (vv. 3–6)
c) the plea renewed in manifold detail (vv. 7–12)
d) the resolve to offer grateful service to God (vv. 13–17)
e) a prayer for the welfare of the holy city (vv. 18f.)

Quite obviously a regrouping of these expressions could find in the psalm a twofold division: vv. 1–12, a prayer for what God is to do for the author; vv. 13–19, a vow of what the writer will do thereafter.

The heading found in the Hebrew is translated thus: *To the Choir Director. A psalm of David. When the prophet Nathan came to him after he had gone in to Bathsheba.*

In the latter part of this heading two thoughts stand out. One is that the psalm, if it is the outgrowth of this very sordid experience, now becomes a sort of public penance that the great king of Israel did, in which, without morbid introspection and without undue dwelling upon the part that he personally played in this whole event, David gives wholesome warning and instruction to his people, both by his belated admission of guilt and by making the spiritual insights that he has gained accessible to other children of God. It should be noted further that, if the encounter with Nathan precedes, the psalm becomes an indication of what a struggle it cost this great sinner to appropriate the assurance of forgiveness, and how he wrestled with God and with himself before full assurance came to his troubled heart. We believe those writers to be correct who regard both this psalm and Ps. 32 as the outgrowth of the same experience, Ps. 51 having been written while some of the keen anguish of a conscience in turmoil was still with the writer, Ps. 32 having been written after reflection had grown calmer, and the whole matter is viewed in a more distant perspective.

1. *Have mercy upon me, O God, according to Thy steadfast love,*
   According to Thy great pity wipe out my transgression.
2. *Wash me completely from my iniquity*
   And cleanse me from my sin.

1. From the great sin that David committed he takes refuge in God. As *Maclaren* states it: "The psalm begins with at once grasping the character of God as the sole ground of hope." All the great truth about God's readiness to pardon the penitent, from Exod. 34:6ff. onward, is the foundation upon which this entire psalm is built. This implies a true knowledge of God that is aware of the fact that He can pardon sin no matter how black it is. The two phrases used indicate with remarkable clarity that pardon has its base, not in the merit or worthiness of man, but in the fact that God is so good; we refer to the phrases: "according to Thy steadfast mercy" and "according to Thy great pity." Reasons for forgiveness are found in God. The chiastic arrangement of the members of the verse make this feature stand out more prominently. The same thought is conveyed by reflecting upon the attributes of God that are made prominent in these phrases: "steadfast love" and "pity." Quite clearly all men are here being taught to take refuge in God's mercy when the thought of their sins lies heavily upon them. The whole tenor of the psalm is, therefore, seen to be indirectly didactic. Without undue obtrusion of himself David makes his experience serviceable to the rest of God's saints.

2. V. 2 brings the boon prayed for more closely home to him who prays, for when God's mercy becomes operative, then the guilty man is both "washed" and "cleansed." Equally helpful is the thought which stresses that the washing is done "completely" (on "blot out" cf. Exod. 32:33 and Is. 43:25). For one whose sin seems of a deep scarlet dye nothing less than total cleansing can suffice. The three terms used for sin underscore what a wretched thing it is. As "transgression" it is nothing less than "rebellion" (*pésha‘*); as "iniquity" it connotes perversion and twisting of moral standards (*‘awon*); and as "sin" it implies that the divinely appointed goal that has been set for us has been completely missed (*chatta’th*). Strong terms for an ugly thing are intentionally employed.

3. *For I recognize my transgression;*
   And my sin is ever before me.
4. *Against Thee, Thee only, have I sinned and done that which is evil in Thy sight,*
   That Thou mightest be just when Thou speakest and pure when Thou judgest.
5. *Lo, I was brought forth in iniquity;*
   And in sin did my mother conceive me.
6. *Lo, Thou hast always delighted in truth in the inmost heart;*
   And in the inner man Thou teachest me wisdom.

3. When we labelled this section, "the reasons on which this plea (i.e., that of vv. 1 and 2) is based," we meant this only in the relative sense, for the true basis of forgiveness is God's amazing mercy and pity. We are here thinking in terms of prerequisites on the part of man that in the very nature of the case have to be met, otherwise all penitence is sham, and all prayer for pardon, hypocrisy. Of the terms for sin employed above the strongest is used and in the original is placed first for the sake of emphasis: "For my rebellion I recognize." By stating it thus, the remark becomes the equivalent of: I know how grievously I have sinned, and the thought of it clings to me night and day. Or again this might be paraphrased: I am not unaware of the enormity of my deed. True penitence does not make sin appear light but freely admits that it is grievous.

4. This verse must be understood as part of the statement that emphasizes how great this sin committed is. All sin is seen to be great when it is understood as having been directed against none less than God, no matter how much man may have been wronged by it. The conclusion which the writer draws from this fact testifies to the sincerity of his penitence. It is expressed in the form of a result clause, and the result involved is that, since sin is directed against God only, any indictment of man that God presents, as Nathan did against David, makes it very plain that God's charges are entirely just, and His judgments are quite unimpeachable. A truly penitent man in no wise belittles his wrong, nor does he, on the other hand, unduly exaggerate it. He simply admits that over against God he is entirely in the wrong, and that over against him God is entirely in the right. When excuses are offered, penitence is not sincere.

5. After the total vindication of God there follows a statement of the total indictment of man. Or it might be thought of as explaining to some extent why man does such things as he, the writer, did. Not, indeed, in the sense of minimizing his guilt, or in the sense of claiming for himself a kind of unfortunate determinism which victimized him.

The statement, "Lo, I was brought forth in iniquity," is a classic formulation of what we commonly designate as the doctrine of original sin. In effect it says, How can I or any other man do anything other than sin, seeing that from the very moment of the origin of our life the taint of sin is upon us? Mark, this is not spoken by way of excuse or palliation of his grievous misdeed but by way of a matter of fact explanation.

The same holds true of the parallel statement: "And in sin did my mother conceive me." The writer does not intend to blame his mother for his sinful state. It never entered his mind to express a thought such as: the very act that led to my conception was a sin. The psalmist is rather, merely indicating that he is in that common stream of mankind where all, from the moment of birth, are sinners. Or to reformulate the thought, the writer is bewailing his own sinfulness, not that of his parents. The mother happens to be mentioned instead of the parents because of her obviously more prominent part in the matter of birth. This statement is in line with other classic utterances of the Old Testament such as: Gen. 8:21; Job 14:4; 15:14; 25:4.

6. The writer now sets over against that which is in his heart that which ought to be there. His statement has a somewhat remorseful cast. The first statement is in the nature of a general principle which always holds true with regard to God: "Lo, Thou hast always delighted in truth in the inmost heart." As the parallelism shows by the repetition of two kindred phrases, the emphasis lies on the fact that God wants men to be upright down to the very core of their being. The writer feels this the more since the taint that strains the roots of his being has come home to his consciousness as never before. By the use of the present tense, the parallel statement seems to underscore the fact that even at that moment God is by His Spirit imparting this deep insight to him. It might help to catch the spirit of this statement to note, as *Koenig* indicates, that vv. 5 and 6 were spoken in a hesitating and halting fashion; not bodly but with a deep sense of personal shortcoming.

7. *Purge me with hyssop, and I shall be clean;*
   Wash me, and I shall be whiter than snow.
8. *Let me hear joy and gladness;*
   Let the bones which Thou hast crushed rejoice.
9. *Hide Thy face from my sins;*
   And all my iniquities do Thou blot out.
10. *Create for me a clean heart, O God,*
    And restore a steadfast spirit within me.

11. *Cast me not away from Thy presence
And take not Thy Holy Spirit from me.*
12. *Restore to me the joy over Thy salvation
And sustain me with a willing spirit.*

7. The psalm began with a plea of deepest earnestness. This plea was interrupted by an attempt to find needed reasons for any and every plea that was offered. The idea is now renewed in manifold detail; or one might say, it breaks forth with renewed intensity. The man needs much help before he can resume the old tenor of his life. His chief concern is still to be cleansed completely from the horrible stain that his sin has put upon him; therefore he pleads: "Purge me . . . wash me." The first verb used has in it the root of the word for sin, the thought being something like, "Desin" me, a thought that is happily rendered by the German verb *entsuendigen*.

Two notable instances were familiar to his readers from the Jewish ceremonial in which hyssop was used in cleansing: the case of the man who had been healed of leprosy (Lev. 14:4ff.) and the case of the man who had touched a dead body and defiled himself by so doing (Num. 19:18). If *God* were to undertake such a cleansing, it would, indeed, be effective. The verb for "wash" is more vigorous than the translation might suggest, for it includes pounding, stamping, and vigorous rubbing in order to loosen the dirt. But there again, if *God* does it, the effect will be an adequate cleansing, in fact, he shall become "whiter than snow," a phrase that is reminiscent of Is. 1:18, which statement of the prophet could well be based on this passage.

8. As the Lord had, by the word of His prophet, created a deep sadness of repentance in the writer's heart, so it is now He who can bring about the further result of not letting the sinner be overwhelmed by the sense of deep guilt. So the prayer continues, asking for the assurance which brings "joy and gladness," a standing expression for deep joy; cf., Is. 22:13; 35:10; 51:3, 11. We remark parenthetically that the point of similarity between our psalm and Isaiah can at any event be readily explained on the assumption of Davidic authorship and the acquaintance of Isaiah with this early psalm. The reference to the "bones" that follows is, of course, by synechdoche to the whole man. He has been utterly crushed by Nathan's indictment. This was a result that God sought to bring about for his good. Only God can make him find a sense of gladness over the pardon bestowed.

9. As the prayer becomes more importunate (in the good sense of the word!) the speaker in the original turns from optatives to imperatives. The first prayer asks that God may totally disregard what

the sinner is guilty of. The second that He may do away with his sins so that they are as completely disposed of as is the writing on a slate that has been gone over with a wet sponge. Then follows the strongest plea of them all (v. 10) in which the author implores that God may put His creative power into operation (like Ezek. 36:25–27) and make his old heart free from stain. It must be remembered that the "heart" is in the Hebrew the center where thoughts and plans originate. This is to be redone, as is also the spirit of the man himself, which had wavered in uncertainty and vacillated between hope and despair. What he needs and prays for is a "steadfast" spirit that rests assured on God's grace and a total pardon.

When *Luther* seems to render this *freudigen Geist,* this is, as *Vilmar* has shown (in *Collegium Biblicum*) a misprint for *freidigen,* an old German expression which means as much as resolute or *tapfer,* which is again only a synonym for "steadfast." Furthermore, the emphasis that lies in the verb "restore" is not so much in the area of bringing one back into a state that was formerly enjoyed as it is in the direction of letting a new state take the place of an undesired old one.

11. One thought that may have engaged the contemplation of the poet rather seriously in connection with his foul misdeeds after repentance had begun to set in was the consideration that he might experience what Saul experienced, whom God cast off, and from whom He withdrew His spirit (I Sam. 16:1, 7). That would at the same time involve to be excluded from the presence of God and from free access to His throne. So the prayer goes on: "Cast me not away from Thy presence and take not Thy Holy Spirit from me." One can scarcely escape the conclusion that this passage comes close to Is. 63:10, 11, where not a principle but a personal divine Spirit is under consideration. But in the mind of the writer the loss of the Spirit means the total loss of God's grace.

12. After this one negative element in the prayer the psalmist returns to the positive by expanding the thought of v. 8 more fully. The fact that he so urgently prays for a joyful heart indicates how seriously depressed he must have been, and how well aware he was of the fact that the state of grace is a state of joyfulness of heart and mind. He had once known well what it meant to be glad over the salvation which the Lord bestows on His own in such manifold forms. To this he adds the boon of a "willing spirit," remembering, no doubt, how enslaved he had been to fear, to an evil conscience, and to sin itself; and knowing that in the state of grace a spirit of willing service to the Lord is one of the manifold gifts that a man enjoys.

The fact that the psalmist prays for so many things (vv. 7–12) indicates how many things he knew he had lost when he plunged into sin. His prayer is that all this tragic loss may be covered by God's grace.

13. *Then will I teach transgressors Thy ways;*
    And sinners shall return to Thee.
14. *Deliver me from blood-guiltiness, O God, Thou God of my salvation;*
    My tongue shall exult over Thy righteousness.
15. *O Lord, open Thou my lips;*
    And my mouth shall declare Thy praise.
16. *For Thou hast no delight in sacrifice—else, I would give it—*
    Thou desirest not burnt offering.
17. *The sacrifices of God are a broken spirit;*
    A broken and a contrite heart, O God, Thou wilt not despise.

Though the note of resolution predominates in this section, there is also injected a further plea for pardon (v. 14) and a reflection on the value of formal sacrifices (v. 16). As *Luther* reminds us: "Here the prophet begins to speak of his own good works."

13. This verse commences rather abruptly: there is no introductory "then" in the Hebrew. Yet the hortative ending of the verb form has the same force as our adverb "then." A vow is clearly involved. Having had a deep and moving experience of God's mercy, the writer realizes that such experiences are not to be kept selfishly to oneself. He realizes, bitter as the whole series of events was, that he now has values that he may pass on to others. The king is proud to become a teacher of his people though all the events involved do him no honor. Other sinners and transgressors after him may profit by what he lived through. Man cannot estimate the amount of rich, comforting instruction this psalm may have conveyed to others. David's object is primarily the conversion of sinners: "and sinners shall return to Thee."

14. Again overwhelmed for a moment by the thought of his own deep-dyed guilt, he beseeches God to remove him from the danger that threatened to engulf him. It is quite obvious that he regards his misdeed in anything but a light manner. The term employed to describe his deed, "blood-guiltiness," reflects this fact. Though the Hebrew merely has the noun "blood" in the intensive plural, this term excellently describes one aspect of this grievous sin. David now sees that he shed Uriah's blood. Such guilt is not easily erased. But immediately the thought veers over to the praise that he vows to give for the pardon bestowed: "My tongue shall exult over Thy righteousness." And having sounded the note of the praise which is due to God, he continues in this vein by asking for ability to speak and vowing that, when

he is enabled, he will declare the Lord's praise. Whereas he had previously used the word "righteousness" to describe the quality of God that he desired to extol, he now refers to that two-sided attribute in God which motivates Him both to punish the evildoer and also to show favor to the penitent and to reward the doer of good. Quite obviously this praise that is vowed is being thought of by the psalmist as a worthy kind of sacrifice of the lips that gratitude should offer.

16. The last thought expressed in this section shows what induced the writer to speak of the subject of sacrifices. This is another area in which he has gained new and deeper spiritual insight. It is this: sacrifices that fulfil the letter of the law and express mere conformity to that letter but are accompanied by no inner feeling of which the sacrifice is a kind of visible embodiment are futile. It is this formalistic type of sacrifice against which the psalmist inveighs. Mere oxen, rams, and sheep may be a very undesirable thing if the spirit of sacrifice is absent. In this sense the pronouncement is meant: "Thou hast no delight in sacrifice—else would I give it." Also the parallel statement: "Thou desirest not burnt offering."

17. This is one of the statements of deepest spiritual insight found in the whole of the Old Testament. It is akin to Is. 57:15. A pardoned sinner alone knows what it means. It is not a disparagement of sacrifices that are offered after the pattern of the Mosaic ritual. But it does indicate what true spiritual sacrifices are. It seems unbelievable, yet it appeals to one's inmost heart as being absolutely true. For when a man has sinned, and the hammer of God's law has crushed his heart in true repentance, and he really has, as the explanatory terms state it, "a broken and a contrite heart," the man is ready for God's further work upon his heart which results in the full restoration that only grace can accomplish. To say that God "will not despise" such sacrifices, is a mild understatement. By stating the case thus the writer implies, of course, that he is even here and now bringing to God his own sacrifice of a broken heart.

18. *Do good in Thy good pleasure unto Zion;*
    Build Thou the walls of Jerusalem.
19. *Then wilt Thou have delight in proper sacrifices, in burnt offerings and whole burnt offerings;*
    Then shall men offer bullocks upon Thy altar.

18. Though many interpreters claim that the psalm could end very effectively, in fact, more effectively with v. 17, and that these last two verses must be an addition by some later hand, we feel compelled to reject both claims. For it must be remembered that the psalm, if it at all agrees with the things that David experienced, has said noth-

ing as to the possible effect that David's sin may have had upon the whole nation. Yet it is unthinkable that after his recovery David should not have felt what his wicked example might do to his people. It is equally unthinkable that he should not have prayed to God to turn aside the evil effects of his bad example. That is exactly what these last two verses reckon with.

Nor do we regard it as being in any sense farfetched if David, using a figure, looks upon the spiritual entity, Jerusalem, as being reduced to ruins by his sinful deeds. The prayer then follows quite naturally that God would bless the city of His habitation by building again what sin had torn down. David can plead no merit of his own, but he can appeal to God's "good pleasure." If God then again turns His favor upon the holy city, there will be many who, profiting by David's newly gained insight, will also (v. 19) offer the sacrifice of a humbled spirit and a broken heart, and so ultimately, to some extent at least, a more spiritual worship may result at Jerusalem. For the things that were written above (v. 16f.) were not intended to make light of the formal sacrifices previously offered in the Old Testament cultus. Since the two preceding verses might have led to misunderstanding, this last verse restores the balance between formal and spiritual worship. The psalmist's hope is that both shall flourish better side by side from this time onward. Thus the psalm closes on a hopeful note and gives evidence of actually being what *Luther* claimed for it: "here the doctrine of true repentance is set forth; two parts constitute true repentance: first that a man recognize sin, then that he recognize what grace is."

Many commentators declare that the last two verses are a later addition, which was perhaps, made during the time of the Babylonian Captivity, or they date the psalm as such in this period and thus conclude that the whole psalm is of one piece. The fact that these verses may be a later addition does not necessarily invalidate the preceding part of the psalm. For even to *Luther's* hymn, "Lord, keep us steadfast in Thy Word," several verses were added, and the expanded hymn continued in use in many circles. But the evidence available on this psalm in no wise makes necessary the assumption that the psalm had verses added to it. As it now stands, the psalm is a fine and complete unit.

NOTES

2. There seems to be no good reason why the form that originally appeared in the text (*harbeh*) should not be retained with that peculiar adverbial use of the finite verb that is characteristic of this verb. See *GK* 120g.

4. Whereas *KJ* renders, "and done this evil, etc." the Hebrew has:

"and done that which is evil," the latter being slightly more in the nature of a verdict pronounced upon the deed.

5. Most commentators and versions render the verb *yechemáthni* as plain "conceive," many German translations render *bruenstig geworden,* implying a kind of heat of evil passion. This latter rendering is less appropriate because it would seem to describe the writer's sin as originating in his mother, an emphasis which is foreign to the tone of the passage.

6. The perfect *chaphatsta* is in the nature of a gnomic aorist.

16. Though many interpreters prefer to render the second half of this verse like *RSV:* "were I to give burnt offering," etc., there are ample reasons for regarding this clause as being in the nature of an apodosis introduced by a *waw explicativum.* See *KS* 201c and 360d.

Psalm 52

GOD'S FAITHFULNESS ENDURES FOREVER

To the Choir Director. A didactic poem. Of David. When Doeg the Edomite came and told Saul and said to him: David has come to the house of Ahimelech.

This heading of the psalm, though commonly regarded as being unfactual, is to be retained as being historical and in full harmony with the historical evidence available. However, it does not aim to create the impression that the statements of the psalm that follow are directed against Doeg as one might at first be inclined to suppose. *Hengstenberg,* though alone in the defense of the position that we are taking, offers the most constructive approach. If his approach is retained, most of the difficulties that are usually pointed to as standing in the way of the acceptance of the heading are met.

In the first place, Doeg is a secondary figure in this psalm. He merely gives occasion to consider the historical setting. All the sharp things said in the psalm against a particular individual scarcely fit the man Doeg. What he said and did according to I Sam. 21:7 and 22:6ff. was not spoken with a lying tongue. Furthermore, he had apparently not gone to Saul with the express intent of informing against David. I Sam. 22:22 implies merely that through Doeg the facts of the case would surely come to Saul's ears. Furthermore, Doeg does not seem to have been overly eager to destroy the priests; only when Saul explicitly commanded him to slay the priests did he rise up against them. But every one of the sharp words spoken in the psalm does apply to Saul, the man with whom David had so many dealings in those early days of his residence at court after the slaying of Goliath.

One objection raised against the validity of this heading is the fact that it makes no reference to the bloody purge of the priests of Ahimelech's house. That, it is claimed, is an inexcusable silence. However, it must be borne in mind that David had made a very clear-cut pronouncement on this subject at the moment when Abiathar, the only priest who had escaped, brought the news of the slaughter to David (I Sam. 22:22f.). Who will lay down the rules as to what a man must say in a poem such as this? Is the prose statement in the passage just referred to to be disregarded, and must the contention be upheld that there must be another reference to the situation in this poem? These are arbitrary canons of subjective judgment that carry little weight.

Another reference in the psalm, which is considered damning evidence against the correctness of the heading, is found in v. 8, in the words: "in the house of the Lord." This is claimed to be a distinct reference to the Temple at Jerusalem, which, of course, had not yet been built in David's day. Yet it is commonly known that the word "house" is used with reference to the Tabernacle in pre-Davidic days. Besides, it is commonly admitted by not a few writers that the reference in this passage is not at all to a visible house as such, but that the phrase refers to fellowship with God as parallel passages also indicate (note the interpretation of the verse in the following exposition).

Finally, the heading is arbitrarily disposed of by the claim: "This reference was not made with the view that the Psalm was actually composed at that time; but it might be conceived as expressing the emotions of David under the circumstances" (*Briggs*). We regard this statement as a glaring instance of making a passage say what we should like to have it say.

As to the general approach to the psalm and its purpose we would yet point out how prepossession with certain types of interpretation can lead to strange results. Those interpreters who force almost all psalms into the pattern of liturgical exposition are inclined to classify this psalm as a "song of thanksgiving" (*Dankgebet-Hans Schmidt*). Yet they must resort to the strange expedient of claiming that "it must have made a strong impression when one who has been delivered out of extremity begins with a curse instead of with the thanksgiving that was anticipated"—strange indeed! In its general tone this psalm resembles Ps. 58 and may be compared with Is. 22:15–19.

Psalm 52

We feel that the first verse is the theme of the psalm. It states both the situation and the attitude which the writer proposes to maintain in the face of it. Therefore we suggest the following outline:

a) **The denunciation of Saul (vv. 1–5)**

1. *Why do you boast of evil, O mighty man?*
God's covenant faithfulness endures all day long.
2. *Your tongue devises very wickedness*
Like a whetted razor, you worker of treachery.
3. *You love evil rather than good*
And lies rather than the speaking of right. Selah.
4. *You love destructive words,*
O you deceitful tongue.
5. *God shall likewise break you down forever;*
He shall remove you and snatch you from your tent;
He shall uproot you from the land of the living. Selah.

1. "It is exceptional to find a psalm not beginning with words addressed to God" (*Oesterley*).

Saul apparently showed no remorse after the slaughter of the priests of Nob but acted presumptuously as though the wicked deed done deserved applause, as though it had been righteous and absolutely defensible. For this reason David addresses Saul as he here does: "Why do you boast of evil, O mighty man?" The word used by way of address is *gibbor,* which does, indeed, mean "hero" or "mighty man" and is apparently here not used in a sarcastic sense. Yet there is an undertone of rebuke, for heroic men should not seek honor in the slaying of the defenceless. David applies the same title to Saul in his elegy in II Sam. 1:19. Men of Saul's political and social standing were regularly referred to as being in the class designated as *gibbor.* The term would hardly have fitted Doeg.

Over against the presumption of a cruel man, which was at the same time a most dangerous presumption, the writer places a sturdy fact in which he puts his trust: "God's covenant faithfulness endures all day long." The attribute of God referred to is *chésedh,* which *RSV* usually prefers to translate "steadfast love." "Covenant faithfulness" is in some respects a better translation, for the fidelity that God shows because He has by a covenant bound Himself to Israel is really the quality that is under consideration. That quality affords sure ground to stand on when the tyranny of men threatens. By stating it at once the author sets it in high relief. For the unsatisfactory nature of the *RSV* translation of this fine verse see "Notes."

2. The cruel king is denounced for what he is. He has maliciously used his tongue against David and against his own son by preferring

a very wicked charge against both and setting it forth in a self-righteous manner but with utter distortion of facts. He is here charged with having devised "very wickedness." We have used this expression because the Hebrew uses an intensive plural, which is not too well rendered "destruction." Since it is a form of wickedness that is calculated to harm and destroy men, the writer likens the tongue to a "whetted razor" and labels the individual who uses it thus as a "worker of treachery." What more serious distortion of facts could a man have been guilty of than Saul was when he harangued his soldiers (I Sam. 22:6ff.)! Such a man must be basically distorted in character (v. 3). Therefore David describes him as loving "evil rather than good and lies rather than speaking of right." Evil lies deeper in the case of such a person than it does in the case of others. He not only *does* wrong; he *loves* it. This is particularly true in the area of words spoken (v. 4): his words must needs be "destructive."

5. There follows the heart of the denunciation, which pictures a drastic overthrow in successive steps by the use of a number of colorful expressions. How absolutely true this prediction—for that is what it ultimately amounts to—proved to be when the tragic close of Saul's life came! "Breaking down" is the first word used. The author is, perhaps, thinking in terms of a sturdy fortress. "Remove" is the verb used for carrying away coals from the hearth. "Snatch" implies sudden removal from a place of safety. The climax is reached when the man is "uprooted from the land of the living."

The "Selah" appearing here marks what we believe to be a clear-cut division of thought. Above, at the end of v. 3, we fail to see how this term fits the situation.

b) The fortunate lot of the righteous (vv. 6–9)

6. *The righteous shall see it and feel reverent awe;*
   But at him they shall laugh, saying:
7. *Look, there is the man who did not make God his refuge*
   But trusted in the abundance of his riches and made his wickedness his refuge.
8. *But as for me, I am like a green olive tree in the house of God;*
   I trust in the covenant faithfulness of God forever and ever.
9. *I will thank Thee, for Thou hast done it;*
   And in the presence of Thy saints I will proclaim that Thy name is good.

6. This verse begins the description of the happy lot of the righteous. True, the last two verses of the psalm are most distinctly in the nature of such a description whereas vv. 6 and 7 treat of the same subject only by way of contrast, by placing the good man's lot over against

that of the presumptuous man described in vv. 1–5. That which the righteous man is said to "see" is, of course, the drastic overthrow of the proud boaster referred to in the first section of the psalm. The verb is without an object, not even an "it," for the Hebrew often takes such logical objects for granted.

When the righteous man does see how mightily God acts in such an overthrow, the first reaction will be a feeling of reverent awe at what God has done. The Hebrew calls this "fear." So as not to be misunderstood we called it "reverent awe." Coupled with this deep insight into the fact that God has acted will be a feeling of a sort of amusement, rather of the ridiculousness of the behavior of the insolent boaster. For this was a case that was bigger than mere personal animosities. In opposing an innocent man of God's choice Saul had set himself against God, and all such efforts are ridiculous. Old *Johann Arnd* remarked on this passage: "There are two kinds of laughter." In connection with passages such as this one should note that the New Testament expresses similar thoughts; cf., Rev. 18:20; 19:1ff. Nor do we feel that under these circumstances this passage is a violation of the spirit of Prov. 24:17.

7. The words placed on the lips of the righteous man lay bare the very root of the foolish behavior of the proud boaster. The chief defect that marked him was that he "did not make God his refuge" but substituted two other objects of confidence for Him: "abundance of riches" and "his wickedness." Tragic as that is, it cannot be denied that it is also purely absurd and laughable.

8. Enough of that. In contrast with such an unhappy lot David claims for himself far better things. It should, however, be noted that he that makes this claim is a hunted refugee, a man with a price on his head, and a man who would have seemed to have every justification for bitter complaints. Note, therefore, to what heights of bold confidence this psalm rises.

First of all, the writer likens himself to "a green olive tree in the house of God." One need not think of the Temple courts at Jerusalem where to this day certain trees grow. To be "in the house of God" means to enjoy closest fellowship with Him and to be accepted by Him. The olive tree seems to have been a standing symbol of a healthy, flourishing life; cf., Jer. 11:16; Ps. 92:13. Such a statement is not boastful but merely descriptive of what the Lord can do for those individuals who lean on Him. The second half of the verse puts the emphasis on this inner relationship: "I trust in the covenant faithfulness of God forever and ever." The same quality in God that was stressed in v. 1 is the one on which the psalmist postively builds.

9. The closing verse of the psalm mounts still higher in that it rises

to the level of praise and confession. Since the overthrow of the presumptuous man was the deliverance of the writer, we can well understand how this experience would stir him to thanksgiving, which he on his part vows shall never end. Besides, he feels that in the company of other like-minded men such gracious acts of deliverance should be proclaimed over and over again. *Luther's* translation of the second half of the verse cannot be justified.

NOTES

1. Apparently acting on the presupposition that the second half of the verse strikes too high and positive a note, many commentators of our day resort to a number of textual corrections, which eliminate the reference to God's covenant faithfulness. They, it is true, in part follow the lead of the *Septuagint*. But when the Greek version differs from the Hebrew, that is far from being proof that the Hebrew text is corrupt. The Greek version frequently mistranslates.

5. The imperfects are synonyms, therefore no *waw* consecutive is used. *KS* 370k.

6. This verse offers a play on words in the first two verbs: *yir'u* and *yirá'u*.

7. The imperfect in the form *yasim* presents some difficulty. Interpreters waver between making it an imperfect of habitual action or the imperfect of attendant circumstances which is subordinate to a verb expressing past time. The former may have the preference. See *KS* 366n.

9. "Proclaim" as a translation of *'aqawweh* is fairly well substantiated by *KW,* who bases it on a parallel Assyrian root.

The approach which offers as a heading for this psalm, "Pattern for Revolution" (*Poteat*), overlooks the fact that nobody is being stirred up to violent opposition; the decision is left in the hands of God (v. 5). The same writer does, indeed, later offer the remark, "This is not to advocate revolution; it is to describe it." This latter type of revolution must be described by a different term; it is no longer revolution.

Psalm 53

THE UNIVERSAL CORRUPTION OF MANKIND AND GOD'S REACTION TO IT

No BIBLE STUDENT would care to claim that this psalm is a different psalm than the fourteenth. Only one verse presents appreciable differences. So the question arises as to how these two different versions of one and the same psalm are to be accounted for.

Two theories aside from the one mentioned in connection with Ps. 14 claim attention in giving the answer to this question. One is the theory that a writer discovered an imperfect or defective copy of Ps. 14 and tried to restore the text as best he could, not knowing or not being able to read the original too well. Result, Ps. 53. The other theory has it that a man, having the familiar text of Ps. 14 before him, desired under certain circumstances so to change the psalm as to make it applicable to a situation that was prevailing at his time. He made a few minor alterations and gave an entirely different cast to v. 5. As a result the similarity of the two psalms is apparent as well as their differences. Yet the new version had so much to commend it that it deserved a separate place in the psalter.

We offer a translation of v. 5:
There were they greatly terrified; yet there was no fear, For God scattered the bones of those arrayed against thee. Were you put to shame? No, for God rejected them.

For the course of the thought followed by vv. 1–4 of this psalm consult our interpretation of Ps. 14. After the sketch of universal depravity has been presented and Israel has been included in this picture as being like all the rest of mankind, the writer expostulates with all these evildoers for their senseless behavior. In v. 5 he then moves forward a step to the point where he declares that sudden and great destruction has come upon them. Driven by a guilty conscience and, perhaps, their own superstitions, they have experienced great and unspeakable terror. It all reads like a reference to a well-known event in which the evildoers met with drastic reverses. A situation may be referred to such as that which confronted Israel at the hands of the Assyrians in the days of Hezekiah and Isaiah (II Kings 18:9ff.).

Yet there was a group who would have seemed to have every reason to be afraid and were not: "Yet there was no fear." When one considers the dramatic and sudden overthrow of the Assyrians in that one memorable night one can understand the propriety of the description, "for God scattered the bones of those arrayed against thee"—words that are addressed to the nation of Israel as such. This address continues: "Were you put to shame?" The utter defeat of Israel had seemed inevitable, for overpowering odds were arrayed against Israel. Yet, as Isaiah had promised, the utter defeat of the superior Assyrian force came to pass, or, to use the words of the psalm in answer to the question just posed: "No" we were not put to shame, "for God rejected them."

Interpreted thus, the psalm becomes a poem that is applicable to a new situation that arose long after the days of David and becomes virtually a new psalm. The interpretation and translation offered above are not original with us but stem very largely from *Koenig's* commentary.

The remaining differences in the text of the two psalms are the following: for the words "made their doings abominable" our psalm says: "made their doings utterly perverse." It uses a stronger term. Again in vv. 2, 4, 5, 6 "God" is substituted for "Lord" as is to be expected in this Elohistic book of the psalter. In v. 3 the word "all" has a suffix: "all of them," and "fallen away" is used for "going astray." These are obviously minor differences.

An entirely new approach to the interpretation of this psalm is to be found in *Schmid* and *Leslie*. By clever conjectures as to how the text may once have read these interpreters arrive at the conclusion that the persons specifically under consideration are priests. So *Leslie* gives the psalm this caption: "Toward a Nobler Priesthood." Such approaches build an interpretation on a very insecure subjective foundation. A psalm may be made to mean almost anything if the text is sufficiently altered.

Psalm 54

GOD IS MY HELPER

To the Choir Director. On stringed instruments. A didactic poem. Of David. When the Ziphites came and told Saul: David is hiding among us.

Though there is nothing in the psalm that compels us to accept the above heading as being necessarily true, there is also nothing in the psalm that disproves its correctness. We accept it, therefore, as quite likely being correct. The episode referred to is possibly recorded in I Sam. 23:19ff. or in I Sam. 26:1ff. Both incidents are equally fitting and are a case in point to show how historic events may repeat themselves in almost identical fashion.

When the heading further suggests that this is a "didactic poem," we can accept that as being quite suitable. The writer, David, may have had in mind to suggest that all such extremities, when one seems hopelessly caught by circumstances, are to be met in the spirit of trustful submission to the Lord. He tells how God gave him grace to meet the emergency. He records the experience without in any wise putting himself into the forefront so that others may learn how God at such times helps in giving a bold and courageous spirit to those that put their trust in Him.

Though Davidic authorship of the psalm is rejected quite commonly, this seems to be due to a general mistrust of the traditional headings, a mistrust that is supported by the contention that the psalm cannot be proved to have grown out of the situation described—an unreasonable claim. On the rest of the heading see the *Introduction*.

There is nothing particularly unique about the psalm. It reflects a rather common situation; it meets this situation in a way that is almost stereotype. But still the frequent occurrence of this kind of situation may help the distressed person to recognize that this is a common experience in life. The general pattern is, therefore, the common one of a prayer for deliverance (vv. 1–3), and confident assurance of help (vv. 4–7). As a theme we suggest: "God is my Helper," though we are well aware of the fact that this really covers only the second half of the psalm.

a) A prayer for deliverance (vv. 1–3)
1. *O God, by Thy name save me,*
   And by Thy might vindicate me.
2. *O God, hear my prayer;*
   Give ear to the words of my mouth.
3. *For strangers have risen up against me;*
   And ruthless fellows seek my life;
   They do not keep God in mind. Selah.

A fine instance of how a man in trouble casts himself wholly on the mercy of God. A key phrase is the unusual "by Thy name save me." The phrase involved is readily understood if we recall that God's name is His character or reputation. He has a well-known reputation among His saints as being one who delights to save. To this well-established fact this phrase appeals.

"Vindicate me" implies that some unjust accusations have been directed against him; but God can clear his name. One partly unique feature of the psalm is that the opponents are designated as "strangers." This does not necessarily imply that they are persons of another nation. It seems quite reasonable to suppose that they were, indeed, members of the writer's own nation, but that they had behaved in such a way that an outsider could not have behaved more cruelly. Also in this respect they are like the typical non-Israelite: "They do not keep God in mind."

b) **Confident** assurance of help (vv. 4–7)
4. *Lo, God is my helper;*
   The Lord is the one who guards my life.
5. *The evil shall return upon my enemies;*
   Put an end to them in Thy faithfulness.
6. *Freely will I sacrifice to Thee;*
   I will praise Thy name, O Lord, for it is good.
7. *For it has delivered me from all trouble;*
   And my eye has looked in triumph upon my enemies.

4. Having laid the burden of his affliction upon the Lord, the psalmist now speaks in a mood of confident assurance. What he had believed right along now again becomes a certainty to him. Simple as the statement is, it ranks among the classic utterances of the Scriptures: "God is my helper." Though the Hebrew says in the next statement that He guards my "soul," the emphasis is not at all that which our modes of speech associate with the words. "Soul" means "life." So the second member is a paraphrase of the first. That being the situation with regard to himself, the writer also knows what the situation of his wicked and unjust opponents is: "The evil" that they planned to bring upon his

Psalm 54

head "will return" upon the enemies according to the well-established principle: He that digs a pit shall fall into it himself. Since His faithfulness leads God to be faithful to those who have proved faithful to Him, it is but just to ask of Him to "put an end to them," for they were and are wicked, and wickedness deserves an overthrow.

6. The vow that is now made concerning sacrifices to be offered is not at all expressed in the spirit of bringing some selfish pressure to bear upon the Lord or to tempt Him with some kind of unworthy bribe. We do well to credit the writer with a nobler spirit than that. He is confident that the desired outcome will be met with and says in effect, When that takes place, then will I have the joy of a goodly sacrifice presented to the Lord in His sanctuary. I shall have further joy: "I will praise Thy name, O Lord, for it is good." Since the term "name" here has the same connotation it had in v. 1, this statement implies that by that time God will have vindicated His character.

7. The particular grace that the writer anticipates is that God's deliverance will have been complete—"from all trouble." But the deed that God does has two sides even as the prayer that was uttered had two objectives: deliverance of him who prays, and the overthrow of those who plotted evil against God's saints. To see the latter overthrown may well constitute a part of the triumph of the godly, not in an attitude of gloating in unholy glee but in a feeling of holy sympathy for what God's righteousness prompts Him to do. This prospect is stated confidently as though it had already transpired; therefore the use of the perfect tense. The name of God is given almost a personal character here as so often in the Scriptures, "for *it* has delivered me."

NOTES

We reject as unnatural and quite untenable the view that this is "a prayer for *national* victory" (*Briggs*). The psalm has too personal a tone to allow for such an interpretation.

Equally inadequate is the interpretation that makes everything revolve around the point that the author is charged with some crime and seeks to have his name cleared. Though that issue is found in v. 1, it is not the dominant one in the psalm.

Equally unsatisfactory is the approach which says that the psalmist gives evidence of a fine spirit of trust in the first part of his poem, then spoils it all by the nasty note of personal vengeance. *J. M. P. Smith* states it: "My eye has gloated over my foes."

3. For the word "strangers" some manuscripts and the *Targum* offer "proud ones"—*zedim* for *sarim,* in the Hebrew the change of one letter. This change of the text seems to have crept in from Ps. 86:14. But there is no proof that the latter passage was the original. We have translated

the Hebrew idiom a bit freely in the last member, for whereas it says: "they have not set God before them," we gave the more idiomatic: "They do not keep God in mind."

4. As a translation for the form *besomechey* AV offers: "The Lord is *with them that uphold* my soul." That is a very literal rendering, but it yields the rather unacceptable thought that the Lord is one among many who sustain him—which can scarcely be the meaning. It is better to regard the participle as an example of an intensive plural referring to God. Cf. *GK*. 119i.

5. The consonants of the first word suggest *yashubh*, "it shall return." That is a better approach than the own indicated by the vowels inserted in the Masoretic correction *yeshibh:* "may He turn back."

Psalm 55

PRAYER IN THE FACE OF A WICKED CONSPIRACY INVOLVING A FORMERLY TRUSTED FRIEND

THE UNIQUE feature of this psalm is indicated in the title we have chosen above: some friend has turned traitor and so caused the writer a particularly cutting grief. Quite naturally the person involved is a sort of type of the traitor Judas. It could have been Ahithophel (cf., II Sam. 16:20ff.).

However, this view hinges on the question of authorship of the psalm, at least in part. For if we accept the heading as being correct, David wrote the psalm. When we try to fit the material of the psalm into the life of David as it is known to us from the Biblical books, quite a number of difficulties at once suggest themselves. But as a number of writers point out, our present-day difficulties may arise chiefly from the fact that we know altogether too little about the issues involved, for they are reported in the Scriptures only in their major outlines. Against the identification of this man with Ahithophel is the fact that he scarcely ranked as a man who was David's "equal" and his "partner" and "intimate acquaintance." But, as *Maclaren* remarks, Davidic authorship "has at least as much to say for itself as any of the [other] conjectures" that have been offered.

Psalm 55

To the Choir Director. On stringed instruments. A didactic poem. Of David. (See Introduction on this heading).

1. *Give ear to my prayer, O God,*
   And hide not Thyself from my plea.
2. *Attend to me and answer me;*
   I toss about in my anxiety.
3. *I am quite distracted by the voice of the enemy, by the pressure of the wicked,*
   For they tumble trouble upon me, and in anger they antagonize me.
4. *My heart is in anguish within me;*
   And the terrors of death have fallen upon me.
5. *Fear and trembling have come in upon me;*
   And shuddering has covered me.
6. *And I said, Oh, that I had wings like a dove!*
   I would fly away and dwell somewhere.
7. *Lo, I would wander far off;*
   I would lodge in the wilderness. Selah.
8. *I would hasten to some shelter for myself*
   From the stormy wind and the tempest.

1. A psalm of lament by an individual.

This first section of the psalm is a complaint about the anguish caused by enemies. Only the first three lines are a prayer; the rest is a complaint, but obviously in the framework of a prayer. So the psalmist's experience becomes more than idle grief. It is as though a man began to pray but found his situation so overpowering that he had first to unburden his heart of the grief that was upon him. There is an urgency about the initial prayers: the writer wants to be sure that he is being heard.

He admits freely (vv. 2–5) that he is much disturbed. His trouble has made him very restless and distracted. The enemies, who are wicked men, have brought the pressure of distress upon him. They have made trouble to fall upon him in huge portions and have vented their anger upon him. His heart feels nothing less than anguish because of this kind of treatment. Even the very "terrors of death," the most formidable kind of distress, have become his lot. The whole outcome is so fraught with dangers that he admits freely that fear and trembling and shuddering have practically covered him. Such, for example, must have been the feelings of David when the plot of Absalom was revealed and broke upon his head.

Some brave men may delight in facing danger in its various forms and may almost enjoy the rough and tumble combat that results. Not so this man. If he was David, his fairly recent experiences in the matter of his adultery and the murder committed, followed by the prophet's rebuke, had rendered him weak and unaggressive because of a sense of his own wrong. So in this case he was anxious to get away from it all (vv. 6–8). His wish was: "Oh, that I had wings like a dove! I would fly away and dwell somewhere." For even in those days the dove must have been known for her ability to cover a great distance in her flight. The greater the distance the psalmist could have put between himself and the present distress, the happier he would be. Some quiet place of refuge like a cleft in the rock would have been such a welcome shelter against the "strong wind and the tempest" that were, figuratively speaking, raging around him. Such flight is not cowardice but a natural desire to escape from that which is most painful.

9. *Destroy or, at least, divide their tongues, O Lord,*
   For I have seen violence and strife in the city.
10. *Day and night they go around it on its walls;*
    And toil and trouble are in the midst of it.
11. *Calamity is in the midst of it;*
    Oppression and deceit do not depart from her market place.
12. *(For it is not an enemy who taunts me—then I could bear it;*
    Nor is it one that hates me who magnifies himself against me—
    then I could hide from him.
13. *But it is you, a man who is my equal,*
    My partner, my intimate acquaintance.
14. *We enjoyed intimate fellowship together;*
    We went to the house of God in processions.)
15. *May death overtake them,*
    For wickedness is in their dwellings, yea, within them.

9. This second section of the psalm is a prayer for judgment upon the evildoers and conspirators. It is combined with a further description of the mischief the conspirators have caused in the city. The first and the last verse of the section before us invoke God's judgment upon these wicked men. It cannot be denied that there are propriety and justice about having wicked devices and those that devise them overthrown and cancelled. There might be higher things to pray for, like the conversion of the evildoer. But it also seems that the wicked men involved were of such a type that there could be no legitimate hope of their conversion. They certainly were not just ordinary personal enemies. All the evidence of the psalm indicates that they were wicked men (cf., v. 15c, also vv. 19b–23).

Since most of their mischief had thus far been brought about by the wrong use of the tongue, the first prayer of the psalmist is that that tongue be destroyed (implying, of course, the destruction of him whose tongue it is) or at least that it be "divided" as was done in days of old when God confounded the arrogant builders of the tower of Babel (Gen. 10:25). The last verse of the section goes so far as to ask that "death may overtake them," thus putting a complete stop to all the evil they have devised. In fact, the prayer goes so far as to call down upon them the very end that befell Korah and his rebellious crowd (Num. 16:32).

The description of the confusion caused in the city by these rebel leaders is typical of what intestine strife has been known to cause. "Violence and strife" are the order of the day. These instigators themselves go about "day and night on its walls" and stir up "toil and trouble in the midst of it." The net result is nothing short of "calamity," and "oppression and deceit" stalk about in the very market places. This was nothing short of a major calamity.

12. Parenthetically imbedded in this section is the allusion to the false friend who became involved in these machinations (vv. 12–15). One cannot help but feel that the writer's heart bled for the man whom he had so completely trusted, and with whom he had been so completely of one mind. Surely, we have here a description of a hot friend grown cold. It was not "an enemy" nor a man who had hated him who became associated with the conspirators. That could have been borne; against such a one a man would know what steps to take. Here was a man of the same rank and standing as the speaker—"my equal." Here was a close associate and intimate acquaintance. Sweet had been the fellowship that had been enjoyed on occasion, even in the area of like-minded pursuits in the matter of religion: arm in arm they went to the sanctuary in festal processions. To think that such a one had turned traitor, that was the thing that hurt. Note that the writer calls down no maledictions upon the head of this former friend—a fine indication that passions had not become unleashed in the writing of the psalm.

16. *As for me, I called upon God,*
    And the Lord helped me.
17. *Evening and morning and at noon I uttered my complaint and*
    moaned;
    And He heard my voice.
18. *He delivered my soul in peace from the battle against me,*
    For in great numbers men stood by me.
19. *God will hear and answer them, He who sits enthroned from of*
    old. Selah.
    They change not, and they fear not God.

20. *Each one of them put forth his hands against such as were at peace with him;*
   He violated his covenant.
21. *The flatteries of his mouth were smooth, but war was in his heart;*
   His words were softer than oil, yet they were drawn swords.
22. *Cast your burden upon the Lord, and He will sustain you;*
   He will never let the righteous be shaken.
23. *But Thou, O Lord, wilt bring them down into the pit of destruction;*
   Bloodthirsty and deceitful men will not live out half their days;
   But I will trust in Thee.

16. This last section is an expression of confidence in the Lord's help. It is combined with a further description of the ingrained wickedness of the opponents. If several elements seem to be commingled in each section at the expense of a purely logical development, it must be remembered under what stress the writer's soul labored.

The reasons for rendering vv. 16–18 as we do, in reference to the past, will be given in the Notes. According to this approach they describe what the psalmist consistently did under the adverse circumstances pictured above. While his enemies secretly plotted against him and wrought confusion, he "called upon God." Early and late he kept laying the issues before God, and help came. God delivered his soul from the battle against him and gave him peace, that is, that full measure of blessings when one lacks nothing. And as He has heard the psalmist's prayer, so He will hear what their evil deeds clamor for and will answer them with punishment even as they deserve (v. 19). For He is that kind of God who has from of old sat as judge and king, watching over the deeds of the children of men (see Ps. 29:10).

19. The description of the character of the opponents is now rounded out more fully (vv. 19b–21). The first statement indicates the reason we had for claiming that there seemed to be no hope of the conversion of these men. "They change not" means just that; and the respect in which they do not change is that "they fear not God." The singular used in v. 20f. is used collectively in reference to each one of the opposition; therefore we ventured to insert the expression "each one" at the outset (see Notes below). These evildoers had no provocation. Men who "were at peace" with them were attacked. Men who stood in covenant relationship found that solemn covenants counted for nothing. Flatteries and deceptive words were the subtle tools employed whereas their words were in reality like drawn swords.

22. Admonishing and encouraging himself and others, the writer makes the classic statement of v. 22a, a statement that has guided many

Psalm 55

a man in trying times: "Cast your burden on the Lord, and He will sustain you." It is also important to reiterate the old truth that "bloodthirsty and deceitful men" go down to destruction and die before their time. The psalm closes on a note of confidence: "But I will trust in Thee."

NOTES

3. "I am quite distracted." By putting this verb into the third verse we follow the lead of the *Kittel text*. It also appears that 'aqath, taken in the sense of "pressure" (*BDB*), makes very good sense and requires no emendation into "outcry" or the like.

6. "Dwell" is used vaguely. Like *Luther* we have supplied an adverb.

7. "Wander far off." This is one of the many instances where the hiphil form is reduced to an adverb (*KS* 399o).

9. We have inserted an "at least" in the translation to indicate that the second verb somewhat limits or modifies the thought of the first.

12. We would scarcely construe *we'essa'* as a result clause. It marks a kind of apodosis as in Ps. 51:16.

15. *Yashshimaweth* is best regarded as two words as it is pointed in the Masoretic text, "May death overtake." In *'alémo* the ending represents the suffix, third person plural, masculine, a poetic form. The expression "go down alive into Sheol" is nothing more than allusion to the incident of the Korah's rebellion. To render Sheol "hell" as *KJ* does is not warranted.

16. In justification of "I called" as a translation of *'eqra'*, which by far the majority of translators render as a future, note that in v. 18 the form *wayyishma'* occurs, which casts the whole thought into a past setting.

17. The mention of three periods of prayer which this passage lists is not yet proof that such formal periods were observed at the time the psalm was written.

18. "He delivered my soul in peace" is an example of a "pregnant construction." It is a brief statement for: He delivered my soul so that it was in peace. *Hayyu 'immadhi* cannot be translated "are arrayed against me" (*RSV*). The preposition "with" does not mean "against."

19. "Hear" makes good sense; there is no need to change to "humble." *Chaliphoth*, from a root signifying to change garments, can, without forcing the issue, mean changing the pattern of life.

20. The fact that the singular may be used in the distributive sense of "each one of them" is abundantly illustrated in *KS* 348u, v.

22. *Yehabhekha* may mean, "what he has given you" (*RSV*), or it may be derived from the Aramaic word *yehaba'* (burden) *KW*.

Psalm 56

A PLEA FOR DELIVERANCE
IN THE SPIRIT OF GRATEFUL TRUST IN GOD

SOME FEATURES mark this psalm as unique even though it presents the familiar pattern of a godly man who is beset by bitter foes and cries out unto God for deliverance as in Ps. 52–54. The unusual features are the statement in v. 8, "Put my tears in Thy bottle," and then the helpful and touching statement (v. 3): "What time I am afraid I will trust in Thee" (*AV*). Nor should the refrain be overlooked (vv. 4 and 10f.) which conveys a note of remarkable insight into the nature of the Word of God.

The heading of the original is a bit cryptic in its reference to the "Silent Dove among the Strangers," which appears to be, first of all, a tune after the pattern of which our psalm is to be rendered. This could at the same time be intended as a hidden reference to David, who was obliged to flee far away as a dove might and take refuge among strangers, that is, the Philistines, from the bitter hostility of Saul as we read in I Sam. 21. As the heading also indicates, the psalm is to be attributed to David. The reasonableness of this claim is still admitted by *Kessler et.al.* even though full and conclusive proof for it may not be offered.

Thinking, then, of the historic occasion alluded to, we may reflect on David's situation as he felt that he was no longer safe within the borders of the kingdom of Israel from the implacable wrath of Saul. The enemies who kept assailing him and seeking his life are Saul and all that were on his side as well as the Philistines who recognized and thought him a threat to the safety of their kingdom.

The heading, which is unusually long, reads thus:

To the Choir Director. According to "The Silent Dove among Strangers." By David. A mystery poem. When the Philistines seized him in Gath.

On "mystery poem" see the heading of Ps. 16.

The psalm may be divided into sections after several patterns. Some interpreters find groups of two verses throughout the psalm, with the exception of the last section, which has three verses. To us that pattern of outline seems most appropriate which has the twice-repeated refrain mark the end of a section, at v. 4 and at vv. 10, 11. Then follows a conclusion of two verses.

a) **A confident plea for help in the face of bitter adversaries (vv. 1–4)**
1. *Have mercy upon me, O God, for men have snapped at me;*
   All the day long foemen crowded in upon me.
2. *Adversaries always snapped at me all the day long,*
   For many were they who fought against me proudly.
3. *Whenever I am afraid*
   I put my trust in Thee.
4. *God makes it possible for me to praise His Word;*
   When I have put my trust in God I am not afraid;
   What can flesh do to me?

The psalm opens with a plea for help. The writer is in grave peril. He describes this situation which has gone on for some time. The enemies are, indeed, mere mortals (*'enosh*—man in his frailty), but they have been like curs that keep snapping at a man, nor do they let up as the day goes on. They are further described as "foemen"—men who make war on the one whom they antagonize. They keep crowding in on their victim continually. All of them are marked by pride in their attitude.

Practically the only instance on record that mentions the fact that David experienced fear in an extremity is a reference to the dangers encountered at Gath, the city of the Philistines (I Sam. 21:12). V. 3 agrees with this statement. It at the same time records the proper attitude to take in such an emergency, trust in the Lord. There is something touching about the simplicity of this statement. It has a helpful proverbial form. Immediately, as it were, all dangers and fears leave him who has thus fixed his hope in the Lord, and he gives beautiful expression to his experience in the classic statement: "God makes it possible for me to praise His Word."

He is thinking, of course, of every word that God had given to His people up to that time: the helpful words of Sinai and the rest of the Mosaic collection, the promises heard from the lips of Samuel, and such other words as God's Spirit may have caused to live in the consciousness of His chosen servant. The touching thing about any such experience is that the Lord can be absolutely depended upon when He speaks a word to His children. That word then becomes glorious and the object of the praise of God's children. But God is the one who creates those situations which enable us to understand the glorious nature of His words. Added to this praise of the Word in the refrain is a reiteration of the fine thought of v. 3: true trust in God drives out fear. Or to make the thought more concrete for the current situation: "What can flesh (i.e., any man whose arm is mere flesh) do to me?"

b) **The same confident plea stated more fully (vv. 5–11)**

5. *All the day long they troubled my affairs;*
   All their thoughts were against me for evil.
6. *They banded together, they lurked, they watched my steps;*
   As they have watched for my life.
7. *Unto trouble set them free;*
   In wrath cast down the people, O God.
8. *Thou hast kept count of my wanderings;*
   Put my tears in Thy bottle;
   Are they not in Thy book?
9. *Then shall my enemies retreat in the day when I call;*
   This I know, for God is for me.
10. *God makes it possible for me to praise His Word;*
    The Lord makes it possible for me to praise His Word.
11. *When I have put my trust in God I am not afraid;*
    What can man do to me?

5. The higher ground that had been reached in the prayer of vv. 3 and 4, is held only momentarily. The thought of the bitter opposition that the enemies offered again comes crowding in on the writer. He recounts what they did in the past. Without letting up, throughout the day, they kept disturbing his life. Not a kindly thought ever entered their mind. Terms borrowed from military situations describe how they continued their hostilities: banding together, lurking, spying out weaknesses. They aimed at nothing less than his very life. The psalmist cannot but utter a prayer that they may be checked. Half-bitterly and half-ironically he prays for their deliverance "unto trouble." And since more than individuals were arrayed against him and his men, he prays that "the peoples" may be cast down by God.

8. The thought which gives him confidence that God will hear his prayer in the present extremity is the remembrance that God has noted all that he as an exile was compelled to suffer in times past. It is his conviction that God "has kept count of all [his] wanderings." It was not due to any selfish ambitions that David had become involved in his grave struggle with Saul. Therefore he dared believe that God had taken note of what he had suffered. He bases the unique prayer on the conviction that God might gather the tears that he shed in His bottle, which is to say, to take intimate note of each of them. Of course, in the Hebrew "bottle" is a large wineskin (unless the tiny bottles referred to by archaeologists are meant) and so more than a tiny receptacle, for his

Psalm 56

tears have been so many. Or to vary the figure: "Are they not in Thy book?" Cf. Ps., 139:16. In the Hebrew the question is often the equivalent of a strong assertion as *Luther* also translates. The utterance of confidence grows as it moves on. Thus the next verse (v. 9) quite confidently asserts the final outcome: "Then shall my enemies retreat when I call; this I know, for God is for me." One must have a thoroughly good conscience to be able to speak thus. All this makes it possible for the writer once more to repeat the special refrain which he composed for this psalm as he had done in v. 4, with this one difference that the first line of the refrain is reiterated with the single change of "Lord" for "God." This repetition is purely for the sake of emphasis.

c) A note of gratitude and full assurance (vv. 12–13)

12. *The vows I have made to Thee, O God, are upon me;*
    I will render thank offerings to Thee.
13. *For Thou hast delivered my soul from death, my feet from falling;*
    That I may walk before God in the light of the living.

When a writer like David speaks of the vows that he will pay after deliverance, this is scarcely an attempt to influence God by the prospect of the sacrifices offered but rather an expression of confidence that the time will come when such obligations may be paid. Vows have been the frequent expression of religious feeling everywhere, and they have their propriety even as they have a very binding character. The very sincerity of one's religion is tied up with the spirit in which vows are regarded. The closing verse gives marvelous expression to the confidence referred to. The man is not yet delivered from death, nor are his feet stayed from falling, nor has he as yet walked out of his trouble into the light of the living. But he claims that he has achieved all these deliverances by a sturdy faith, which rests assured that the Lord will not fail him. This last verse is quoted in Ps. 116:8 with a slight alteration.

NOTES

1. For the word "men" the Hebrew uses the collective singular, *'enosh*. In like manner the collective *lochem* stands for "foemen."

3. The concise expression of this verse which omits the relative "when," translated literally would read: "A day I fear" meaning: In the day when I fear. Cf. *GK* 1551.

4. *KJ* which renders: "In God I will praise His Word," is either meaningless or at least very difficult to decipher. The opening phrase seems to be understood in the sense of "through God" or "with the help of God." This we believe leads to a meaning such as that which *Kautzsch* offers in the *Textbibel*, which we have sought to follow: "God makes it possible for me to praise His Word."

We believe that the whole pattern of the psalm is determined by the fact that the initial verb which relates what men have done to the writer is in the perfect, a plain historical perfect, *she'aphani*, "They have snapped at me." The imperfects that follow are the imperfects of attendant circumstances. These same imperfects occur again in vv. 5 and 6. Cf. *KS* 154.

8. In the Hebrew a pun appears in that "wanderings" and "tears," though different words, are pronounced alike (*nodh* and *no'dh*).

12. For "the vows I have made to Thee" the Hebrew uses the objective genitive "Thy vows."

We see no reason for thinking that this psalm is not to be regarded as that of an individual but as that of the congregation (*Briggs*) even though the *Septuagint* and the *Targum* regard it thus. Nor does the fact that vows and sacrifices are mentioned give sufficient warrant for considering the psalm as the liturgy that was used in the sanctuary on the occasion of the final thanksgiving.

Psalm 57

PRAYER OF A MAN ASSAILED BY CRUEL FOES

IT IS AMAZING to note how often godly men of Old Testament times encountered bitter and relentless foes, who already at that time attempted character assassination. This psalm is an example of such calumny. It has distinctive features. Outstanding is the fact that the matters that distress the writer disappear as soon as he betakes himself to prayer; also quite original is the thought expressed in v. 10: "Thy steadfast love is as high as the heavens, and Thy truth as the clouds."

It should also be noted that there are formal points of resemblance with the preceding psalm, such as the initial "have mercy," the use of the same word to express the hostility of the enemy, v. 3, and a refrain at the close of the two major sections. The situation of the writer is much the same in this psalm as it was in the preceding psalm. Somewhat distinctive rhetorically, however, is the use of emphatic repetitions (vv. 1, 3, 7, 8). Besides, one should note that vv. 7–11 are used at the beginning of Ps. 108. They were apparently borrowed from this psalm.

The heading designates David as the author of this poem. The general trend in modern interpretation of the psalms is to reject the statements of the headings unless the psalm compels their acceptance. Many

Psalm 57

interpreters recognize that in this instance the heading may be regarded as being historically valid. The question arises as to which of the two caves in which David took refuge may be referred to, Adullam (I Sam. 22) or Engedi (I Sam. 24). There is not sufficient evidence available to permit us to reach a final decision. Besides, there is nothing in the psalm that directly indicates that an experience in a cave is involved.

In arriving at an outline we are again guided by the refrain which closes each of the two sections. The first section, vv. 1–5, is a confident cry for deliverance from cruel enemies; the second section, vv. 6–11, is a resolve to praise God for deliverance. We reject as bordering on the fantastic the suggestion that v. 4 indicates that it was a custom, when one was charged with a wrong, that perhaps both parties to a quarrel lay down to sleep in the sanctuary, there to hope for some reassuring experience in a dream, and then went home imbued with a sense of divine vindication (*Schmidt*).

The heading: *To the Choir Director. "Destroy not." Of David. A mystery poem. When he fled from Saul, in the cave.*

The "destroy not" may be a sort of keynote that indicates the dominant thought of the psalm. The very phrase occurs in Deut. 9:26 when Moses intercedes for Israel. So David may have been thinking of the harm Saul's savagery had done to Israel and was praying to God to overrule these evil results. The *Septuagint* and the *Targum* support the use of this statement. This is also a "mystery poem" or *mikhtam* as is the preceding psalm. The only comment still called for regarding the expression, "when he fled from Saul, in the cave," is that here, as so often, it is most amazing to note that in the midst of such trying experiences a man should have been able to maintain such a firm confidence and to think such devout and courageous thoughts.

1. *Have mercy upon me, O God, have mercy, for in Thee my soul has taken refuge;*
   Yea, in the shadow of Thy wings I take refuge until the calamity pass by.
2. *I cry unto God Most High;*
   To the Mighty God who does things for me.
3. *He will send from heaven and save me, whom they that snap at me despise;* (Selah)
   God will send His steadfast love and His faithfulness.
4. *In the midst of lions I must lie, of persons who greedily devour the sons of men;*
   Their teeth are spears and arrows and their tongue a sharp sword.
5. *Be Thou exalted, O God, above the heavens;*
   Let Thy glory be over all the earth.

1. The danger is great, and the cry to be delivered is urgent, for it is twice uttered. Beautiful is the oft-repeated approach that, because one has taken refuge in the Lord, therefore he must inevitably be safe: God cannot fail a man. The change of tense is important. At some point in the past the writer cast himself upon God; he continues to do so until the rescue is complete. It is much more satisfactory to find a thought like that expressed in Matt. 23:37, where Jesus likens His activity to that of a hen with her chickens, in the phrase "in the shadow of Thy wings," than to think that this is an allusion to the wings of the cherubim in the sanctuary, where one takes refuge in time of trouble, figuratively or literally. The word "these" before "calamities" (*KJ*) is an interpretative insertion, but is not necessary.

2. Already in the second verse confidence begins to assert itself. It seems to grow in part out of the recognition that God is the "Most High" and, therefore, the One who ultimately and completely controls man's destiny, or out of the similar title "the Mighty God" (*'el*), for the writer can venture the assertion: He "does" things for me. The object of the verb is not expressed in the Hebrew, but "things" seems to convey the desired emphasis. "*All* things" (*KJ*) seems to insert a little too much by way of interpretation. Dwelling on the conclusion that his faith is arriving at, the psalmist (v. 3) feels bold to anticipate that God will intervene from high heaven by sending some sort of help, perhaps even His holy angels to work deliverance from those who snap at him like curs and despise him (cf., 56:1). But for the helping angels he at once substitutes other guardians who are even more powerful than angels, God's "steadfast love" and "His faithfulness."

He is not completely out of the morass of his troubles. Confident though he is of help, he still finds himself compelled to lie down, practically each time he retires at night, "in the midst of lions," (cf., Dan. 6:16) powerful and ferocious foes, who have no compunction about "greedily devouring the sons of men," in fact, they seem to have formed the habit of disposing thus of their enemies figuratively speaking. This is another way of saying that they are implacable foes. Their cruelty is further described by the statement that "their teeth are spears and arrows and their tongue a sharp sword."

5. This verse is praise rather than prayer. It is not to be understood in the sense that God might do something whereby He would become exalted, but rather in the sense that He deserves to be exalted for what He has done. The note of confident assurance predominates. Of course, the added phrase "above the heavens" means: as high as any man can conceive. The parallel statement prays that the glorious deliverance that He has manifested may become recognizable the wide world over, that all men may see it and come to know God.

Psalm 57 433

6. *They have spread a net for my steps; this has bowed down my
    soul;
    They dug a pit before me, they have fallen into it themselves.
    (Selah).*
7. *My heart is resolute, O God, my heart is resolute;
    I will sing and make music to Thee.*
8. *Awake, my soul;
    Awake, lyre and harp;
    I myself will awake the dawn.*
9. *I will praise Thee among the peoples, O Lord;
    I will make music to Thee among the nations.*
10. *For Thy steadfast love is as high as the heavens
    And Thy truth to the clouds.*
11. *Be Thou exalted, O God, above the heavens
    And Thy glory over all the earth.*

6. Some fluctuation of feeling on the part of men who are in trouble and are calling upon the Lord is to be anticipated. Seldom do men stay unwaveringly on so high a level as v. 3 or v. 5 has attained. But the troubling thought of what the enemies are capable of doing recurs only briefly (v. 6). They had thought to bring their victim to fall by some "net" that was cunningly spread before him. He knew of their activity, and it bowed down his very soul, for no man likes to be the victim of deadly plots. Or, to vary the figure, they had on occasion "dug a pit before him." But the sight so commonly witnessed in history was granted to the psalmist. The wickedness of the enemies fell back upon them, or they fell into the pit of their own making—a common Biblical thought. This is a juncture in the development of the thought that is sufficiently important to be marked by a *Selah*.

7. Though these calamities are not entirely overpast, the writer feels that their end is so near that he may resolutely forget them and give attention to the prayer and thanksgiving that God ever richly deserves. This is about the force of his statement: "My heart is resolute," twice uttered. When God's praise is to be exalted, this is best done to the higher strains of music. We added the phrase "to Thee" at this point, for it is obviously music that is to be made to God. In addition the writer seeks to rouse himself to a sufficiently high level of activity by the cry: "Awake, my soul," and by the added cry: "Awake, lyre and harp." That is to say, such a task as he is about to undertake deserves his worthiest efforts. He also uses the beautiful figure that he "will awake the dawn." Before it has roused men, he will rouse it with the sound of praises to the Almighty and Faithful One. "My soul" reads literally "my glory," i.e., the glorious part of me.

9. Resolutions like the one that is made in this verse are not to be taken literally in the sense that the poet went out from one nation to another singing the praises of the God of Israel with the harp. But they do imply at least two things: one, that God's praises deserve to be made known among all the nations, for they are so great; and second, that wherever an opportunity presented itself in his contacts with the nations or their representatives David was not slow in attributing his deliverances to the faithful God of Israel. This brings him to a climax of exalted utterance (v. 10), for he has learned anew the comfort of two of the basic attributes of his God, His "steadfast love" (*chésedh*) and His "truth." How deeply God loves His people, and how true He is to His word—these are experiences that keep growing on God's children as long as they draw breath here on earth. Surely, both are as "high as the heavens" or "as high as the clouds."

The refrain fits well into this development of the psalm, for it is the most exuberant feature of the praise that is here offered.

NOTES

1. For the word "calamity" the Hebrew uses an intensive plural (*hawwoth*), which word could be translated by some stronger term such as "engulfing ruin" (*BDB*) or "storms of destruction" (*RSV*). A singular verb stands first in the sentence as is so often done in the Hebrew (*KS* 348i).

3. This verse is difficult, especially the clause *chereph sho'aphi*, which is best regarded as a relative clause from which the relative *'asher* has been omitted. It refers to the object of the preceding verb, "me." We translated the clause as though it had a plural subject because the subject does seem to be collective—there was more than one such foe. One gets the feeling that the "selah" is out of place in the middle of the sentence.

4. The verb *'eshkebhah* with an otiose hortative ending expresses merely a modal idea like, "I *must* lie down." (*KS* 199b). *Lohatim* must be construed with the preceding construct *bethokh*. It is to be attributed to poetic or rhythmic license that "spear" appears in the singular collectively and "arrows" in the plural.

6. The subject of *kaphaph* seems to be the idea of the preceding clause: the spreading of nets has bowed him down (*KS* 323f.).

7. The Hebrew frequently omits the obvious, like, "I will make music *unto Thee*." See also v. 9.

On the whole we lack evidence for claims such as: "While it is true that portions of two psalms have here been combined. . . ."

Psalm 58

JUDGMENT ON UNJUST COUNSELLORS

ONE NEED only compare this psalm with the preceding psalms to notice that the theme is much the same in all of them. There are enemies; the writer is being unjustly opposed; he puts his trust in the Lord and prays for deliverance, always with a note of more than ordinary confidence. Yet each of these psalms has its distinctive features. In this psalm the extremely colorful language and the striking comparisons are exceptional. This indicates, of course, a certain originality of thought.

It cannot be denied that the language also presents unusual difficulties. Some expressions are rather concise. Certain words are not too clear as to their import. But that does not furnish a reason for the assumption that the state of the text is particularly corrupt or even damaged beyond repair. Nor does it give warrant for the typical present-day conjectures and emendations.

Since the heading ascribes the psalm to David, it should be noted that the contents of the psalm agree with known situations in the life of this man of God. David is known to have committed the issues that were at stake between him and his opponents into the hands of God and not to have taken vengeance into his own hands, as we read in I Sam. 26:10 and as can also be noted in I Sam. 24:13. The fact that David was the victim of grievous unrighteousness that made him cry out in protest against Saul and his associates is only too obvious. Although we cannot find some one incident in his life into which all the details of the psalm fit, that does not make Davidic authorship impossible. The contention of *Delitzsch* that the event in David's life reflected in the psalm is the rebellion of Absalom has this argument against it: David was not at all sharp in his denunciation of the wicked deed of his son, as this psalm is, but was rather far too lenient.

The concluding verse of the poem is memorable: "Surely, there is a reward for the righteous; surely, there is a God that judges on earth." This conclusion that faith arrives at is among the unique features of this psalm.

To the Choir Director. "Destroy not." Of David. A mystery poem.
For an interpretation of the unusual features of this heading see the preceding psalm.

a) **Reproof and rebuke of the wicked enemies (vv. 1–5)**
1. *Do you, indeed, by silence speak righteousness?*
   Do you judge the sons of men uprightly?
2. *Nay, in your hearts you devise perverse things;*
   In the land you deal out the violence of your hands.
3. *The wicked go astray from the time they are born;*
   They err from their birth, these speakers of lies.
4. *They have poison like the poison of a serpent;*
   Like a deaf adder that stops its ear,
5. *That does not listen to the voice of the charmer*
   Or of him who cunningly weaves cunning spells.

1. The peculiar difficulties that are presented by the first verse will be examined in detail in the *Notes*. We shall merely unfold the meaning as it is indicated in the translation we have offered.

The trouble question addressed to some group is the equivalent of a direct charge. Men are being addressed whose business it is to reach verdicts and make decisions. They are as *Calvin,* we believe rightly, points out, the advisors or counselors of Saul. As the same writer also indicates, by laying his case before them David gives evidence of the total justice of his cause. However, when they were in a position in which their office demanded of them a clear-cut verdict they were keeping silence. Thus their very silence had become an obstacle to their speaking righteousness. In certain cases silence may be the equivalent of an unjust verdict.

Since more than David's own rights were, no doubt, involved, he further questions whether persons generally ("the sons of men") had been judged uprightly by these counselors. He at once goes on to say what their refusal to give a clear verdict in an issue in which his own justice was so clear has in reality accomplished. They had (v. 2) devised perverse things in their hearts, for on questions of injustice one cannot remain neutral. One inequity had apparently led to another, and they practiced their injustice throughout the land so that instead of distributing fair dealings they had dealt out "the violence of their hands"; one injustice after the other had been committed. Saul may have been the moving spirit behind it all; these counselors were his willing tools and accomplices.

3. There is a close connection between vv. 2 and 3. The gap is bridged when the assumption is made that, whereas he first addressed his enemies as men who were open to reason, seeing their stubborn

Psalm 58

perversity in evil, he now desists from attempting to influence them further and speaks of rather than to them. There are depths of depravity into which men may sink. These men have arrived at the depths which are here described. As is the case with all men who are born after the common course of nature, their perversity starts "from the time they are born." They then begin to "go astray," i.e., wander about without a fixed and good goal. They are already then in the wrong as to the whole tenor of their life. Some interpreters would limit this statement as though it were an integral part of the description of these evildoers. It is more than that: it is a generalization that describes what all men generally and these men in particular do from the very beginning of their earthly career. It is, therefore, a confirmation of the old divine dictum expressed in Gen. 8:21 as well as of the old doctrine of the total depravity of the natural man.

4. These men have a further distinctive feature that they have developed by their refusal to listen to the truth, a certain imperviousness to all good effects that any honest approach may have on them. They have degenerated so far that they produce evil as naturally and as regularly as does the serpent that has poison beneath its tongue. They do not care to change, and they cannot change. When truth hits their ear, they stop it up so as to shut out all beneficent effects. These men are to be likened to serpents that somehow succeed in shutting out the effects of the words of those men who are skilled to charm serpents or cast a spell upon them.

These are not merely, in fact, not at all spiteful words that speak things that are derogatory to the personal foes of the writer. This is an enlightened description of an extremely dangerous spiritual condition into which enemies of truth have fallen again and again, especially in certain ages of departure from the truth.

b) **A prayer that God may take them in hand (vv. 6–11)**

6. *O God, break their teeth in their mouth;*
   Tear out the fangs of the young lions, O Lord.
7. *They shall flow away like water that runs off;*
   Such a one shall shoot his arrows as if they were blunted.
8. *They shall be like a snail that melts away as it goes,*
   Like an untimely birth that never saw the sun.
9. *Before your pots can feel the thorn,*
   Something like hot anger shall sweep it away before it is burned.
10. *The righteous shall be glad when he sees the vengeance;*
    He will bathe his feet in the blood of the wicked.
11. *And men shall say: Surely, there is a reward for the righteous;*
    Surely, there is a God that judges the earth.

6. Imbued with a true sense of the justice of his cause and of the utter injustice of the attitude of Saul and his followers, David ventures to pray that God may deal with the wicked as He is known to have done, and as they fully deserve. We can rest assured that, if there had been any hope of turning these men from their evil ways, no one would have been happier than David to see them turn. As matters now stand, they must be made incapable of doing further harm. They are likened to ravening lions whose teeth are to be broken in their mouth or whose fangs are to be torn out.

From this point onward a gentler tone may be given to the prayer than some interpreters are wont to attribute to it. Though the verbs allow for the precative rendering, "May they flow away," they allow equally well for the purely predictive translation, the note of certainty of the overthrow of the enemies. We prefer the latter. Thus the prayer indicates that their opposition shall melt or flow away like water when it runs off. Or the futility of their actions may be described by likening any one of them to a man shooting blunted arrows from his bow, arrows that cannot hurt their victims.

8. Again the failure of the lives of those that feed on iniquity may be likened unto the gradual melting away of a snail as it drags along its slimy course. Most effective of all is the comparison that likens them to an untimely birth that never saw the sun. Such a life is not marked by achievement.

9. The last figure has special color and effectiveness in describing how little lives that are given to ungodliness can achieve. The figure is that of setting a pot to boil on an outdoor fire of thorns. Before the pot actually feels the heat of the just-kindled fire, along comes a sudden gust of wind ("something like a hot anger") and sweeps away, not only the fire, but the very fuel. That is the epitome of an unsuccessful life. All the comparisons used indicate the strong sense of the total uselessness of the lives that are directed against God's saints.

10. Since the outcome shall be as described, the righteous man shall witness what happens and thank God for the vindication of his cause, which was and is God's cause. That the singer knew full well otherwise he could not have had the confidence that he manifested. He shall rejoice over the vengeance of God, for it was absolutely deserved. Note again the same spirit as that manifested in I Sam. 26:10; 24:13. When the righteous man is said to "bathe his feet in the blood of the wicked," it is a total misunderstanding of this statement to assume that there is some kind of unwholesome gloating, an ungodly bloodthirstiness, involved. "Bathe" is meant in the sense of getting one's feet wet. This may be quite accidental. But when it takes place, the

total defeat of unrighteousness is brought home in the most forceful manner possible.

11. This verse is a practical summary of the whole experience. It is written with epigrammatic brevity. "Men shall say"—for they all see the truth of what took place—"Surely, there is a reward for the righteous." This may often seem questionable; it may be long delayed. But God does encourage His own by rewarding their faithfulness to Him. But the greater truth is that "surely, there is a God that judges on earth." God keeps things in hand and under full control. This is not clearly apparent at all times, but it is so at least on crucial occasions. The prayer closes on this note of a sturdy confidence that is based on the living God.

NOTES

1. One may be bewildered by the wide divergence of the translations that are offered for the first verse. *KJ* renders: "Do ye indeed speak righteousness, O congregation?" *RSV* translates: "Do you indeed decree what is right, you gods?" Our rendering is: "Do you, indeed, by silence speak righteousness?" The nub of the difficulty is the word *'élem,* which, as most lexicons admit, comes from a root which would give the word the meaning "silence." We need merely construe it as an adverbial accusative, "by silence," to arrive at the meaning we have chosen above, and which is far from being too complicated to accept. *Luther,* using a bit more freedom in his translation, arrives at practically the same result in a statement that every reader could at once grasp: *Seid ihr denn stumm, dass ihr nicht reden wollt was recht ist?* The statement is a rebuke for the inadmissible silence of men in high position as councillors. The *KJ* translation perplexes all who read it. It is based on a conjectured meaning of the word *'elem,* which the Jewish rabbi, Kimchi, offered in the twelfth century. By "congregation" *KJ* seems to refer to a body of advisors that counselled Saul. Almost all modern efforts at translation grow out of a slight change of the text. By a slight change of vowels the word *'elem* is read *'elim,* which does mean "gods" and is then understood in the sense of Ps. 82:1b, where, because of an office which God upholds, judges are regarded as His representatives and are actually denominated "gods" as His substitutes on earth. But the fact that makes this approach impossible is that elsewhere in the Scriptures this name for judges is *'elohim,* not *'elim.* The interpretation becomes preposterous when some commentators (*Schmid, Weiser, Leslie, Taylor*) state that the Israelites had assumed that at the time of the conquest of Canaan the Canaanite divinities were demoted to a governing council under Yahweh, where they still had the

power to rule the various nations of the earth. This their obligation they had performed so wickedly that they are remonstrated with for their inadequacy. This is supposed to be the thought that the Israelites of old found expressed in this psalm!

We may mention one last interpretation which follows the old versions (*Septuagint* and *Latin*) and renders *'elem* "indeed." So *Briggs:* "But do ye indeed speak justice?" Aside from what seems like a guess of the early translators, this approach has little support.

Even as *'elem* is used as an adverbial accusative, so is *mesharim,* "uprightly." See *KS* 332p.

3. "From the time they are born" is expressed more concisely in the Hebrew as "from the womb."

5. The expression "cunningly weaves spells" has a cognate accusative: "spelling spells cunningly." The Scriptures do not enter upon the question as to whether charms and spells of snake charmers are real or pure deception. It seems to be admitted that snakes can be charmed.

9. *KJ* translates the expression *chay kemo charon* "both living and in His wrath," and many other translators such as *RSV,* "whether green or ablaze." We believe our rendering (following *Koenig*) has much to commend it. *Chay* means "fresh" in the sense "before they are burned." *Kemo charon,* "like wrath," is meant in the sense of "something like hot anger."

Psalm 59

A PRAYER FOR HELP
AGAINST UNPRINCIPLED FOES

SINCE Ps. 54 the general subject of the succeeding psalms has been the same as that of this psalm: a saint of God is being antagonized by wicked men. If one adds to this group the many psalms in which the same issue was at stake one may appreciate what *Kirkpatrick* suggests: "The constant recurrence of this note in the Psalter is doubtless intended to provide a large measure of comfort and encouragement for the various circumstances of trial to which the godly were exposed." The psalm is the complaint of an individual.

When we seek to find a statement that might cover the subject of the two sections of the psalm (vv. 1–10 and vv. 11–17) we find that the same pattern of thought appears in reference to these "unprincipled foes": May God overthrow them—He assuredly will. It is quite obvious that in each section the writer prays that God may take these men in hand and comes to the quiet assurance that He will do so, and so the writer closes each of the two sections on a note of confidence.

Like a number of the preceding psalms, this one not only has a similar heading, at least as far as the chief distinctive terms are concerned, but it is also marked by refrains, two in this instance, for vv. 6 and 14 which introduce the second half of each major section are in the nature of a refrain; and also vv. 9 and 17, though in them a few minor differences appear.

The distinctive problem that this psalm offers has reference to "the nations" that are referred to in vv. 5 and 8 and indirectly in v. 11 (by the remark "my people" over against "them.") This reference to nations seems entirely unmotivated since it has nothing to do with the unprincipled foes who are apparently members of the nation of Israel. Various attempts have been made to remove this difficulty; none is quite satisfactory. *Hengstenberg* understands the statement, "Awake to visit the nations" in the sense: "O Thou, whose work it is to visit the nations." This seems a bit strained. *Kirkpatrick* assumes that originally there was no reference to the outsiders, the psalm being the prayer of an individual who did not look beyond his own special need; later, by additions for the liturgical use of the poem, the psalm was broadened beyond its original purpose. *Schmid* develops this in detail by making a clean division between the original and the additions but leaves his readers in the dark as to what should have motivated such extensive reworking of the psalm. This seems to make the understanding of it more difficult.

We venture an explanation of our own in regard to this problem. Since we accept the heading as being correct when it states that the psalm grew out of the experience of David "when Saul sent men, and they watched the house in order to kill him," it does not seem farfetched to us to assume that at that very time outside enemies of the nations, especially the Philistines, were harassing the nation in one way or another. As a result, when David reflects on his own distress he felt that, when God took his case in hand, He would at the same time work deliverance from the distress into which the nation had been brought by attacks from the heathen. This thought is not developed at length, for it did not at the time have the same pressing need that his personal problem did. From that point of view the psalm is a good example of how private concerns did not make a man like David indifferent to matters of national import.

By what we have just said we have indicated that we give full credence to the heading as being historically reliable and as actually reflecting the situation out of which the psalm grew. Certainly, not every last bit of the poem must have direct bearing upon the particular incident in question. Some of the elements may merely reflect the general situation and the antagonism which David experienced at the hand of Saul and of all his followers.

To the Choir Director. "Destroy not." Of David. A mystery poem. When Saul sent men, and they watched the house in order to kill him.

Compare the preceding psalms for an interpretation of the first four notations. The historical reference takes us back to I Sam. 19:11ff. The fact that the danger was not slight is quite obvious.

1. *Deliver me from my enemies, O my God;*
   Protect me from them that rise up against me.
2. *Deliver me from evildoers*
   And save me from bloodthirsty men.
3. *For, lo, they have lain in wait for my life;*
   Being mighty, they made an attack upon me for no fault or sin on my part, O Lord.
4. *Without provocation of mine they come arunning and get themselves ready.*
   Rouse Thyself and meet me and see!
5. *Since Thou art the Lord, the God of hosts, the God of Israel, awake to visit all the nations;*
   Do not show mercy to those who are treacherous in wickedness. Selah.

1. Cries like these may have risen to the lips of David when Saul's soldiers surrounded the house, and it was announced to him by his wife that he must flee. Note how the verbs pile up: "Deliver, protect, deliver, save"—all brief sentence prayers. Note the characterization of the opponents: "enemies, those that rise up against me, evildoers, bloodthirsty men." Verse 3 is certainly not an exaggeration: the house was encircled, and David was to be taken alive when he ventured forth. Power was on their side ("being mighty"). What could one lone individual presumably avail against an armed troop? But the writer is keenly aware of his innocence of the things wherewith he is charged. It seems as if in those early days at Saul's court, as the writers of I Samuel indicate, David was particularly circumspect in his conduct so that he was actually innocent of all the things that Saul's jealousy charged him with (cf., I Sam. 18:14, *KJ*). For once this protestation on the part of David ("for no fault or sin on my part") was absolutely

correct. In the case of most men it is not, nor was it in David's later life. "Fault" is the particular transgression; "sin" is the general attitude.

4. A third time the protestation of innocence is uttered. As the reference to the soldiers sent to take him is made, you can almost see them marching up on the double-quick and taking their assigned stations. Since David cannot help himself in this dilemma he again appeals to the Lord, who might be regarded as having been inactive throughout all that transpired: "Rouse Thyself and meet me and see!" As they came from one side, so may He come from the other. If only one can rest assured that God "sees" what is transpiring, that is quite enough.

5. In order to gain strength in faith to face the present danger the writer recalls God's unique power by employing the various most familiar names by which He was known in Israel—"Lord, God, Lord of hosts, God of Israel." Since the Lord bears such titles of universal import, it may not seem too strange to think of the author as feeling impelled to call upon God to take in hand all wicked nations as well as the wicked men who were at that moment threatening his own life. To him God is the kind of God who sets things right upon the earth throughout His vast domains. Thought of thus, the petition that He might "awake to visit (i.e., punish) all nations" is very much in place, nor does it impute to David a breadth of insight and interest to which he was a stranger. Since the pressing issue is these gangsters that have encircled his own home, it is but natural that David should concentrate his attention upon them. Allied with them were, of course, those who had sent them, Saul and his counsellors. The plea, therefore, that God may "not show mercy to those who are treacherous in their wickedness" is much in order. Such a prayer is an indirect request that God may deal with them as they deserve. Their harassed victim, David, cannot restrain them. May God do so.

6. *In the evening they keep howling again like dogs;*
And they prowl about in the city.
7. *Lo, they pour forth words with their mouth;*
Swords are in their lips—"For who hears?" they say.
8. *But Thou, O Lord, shalt laugh at them;*
Thou shalt have all nations in derision.
9. *My strength, for Thee will I watch;*
For God is my fortress.
10. *As for my God, His steadfast love shall come to meet me;*
God will let me look in triumph on my enemies.

6. The psalmist's opponents are characterized first as what they are so as at the same time to indicate how deserving they are of the judgment of God which is being called down upon them. The Oriental

dogs are mongrel curs of a very unsavory sort who serve as the city's scavengers. They keep more or less under cover by day, but at night they rove about through the city to satisfy their greedy appetites. This seems to be the point of the comparison: the writer's enemies work in the dark and are voracious to destroy good men. The writer obviously reflects on more than the soldiers who were sent to capture him on this occasion. Besides (v. 7), they resort to abundant slanders ("pour forth words with their mouth") like a bubbling fountain. But their words are of so pernicious a sort that it may be said rightly that "swords are in their lips." Having no knowledge and fear of God in their hearts, their inmost thoughts are that there is none that observes them when they set a rumor afoot with regard to this hunted man.

8. From the contemplation of the enemies' tactics the psalmist turns to the Lord, and what He must needs think of such vile deeds. To the Lord such efforts to overthrow His saints are downright ludicrous. For an instant the writer's thoughts turn to those hostile nations round about who are at the moment manifesting the same attitude and tactics toward Israel that his personal foes are directing at him, and so he injects the thought that He shall in like manner "have all nations in derision" when they wantonly assault His people. But here, as in v. 5, the thought as to how the nations shall be dealt with is not developed more fully because it was injected only casually, by way of analogy.

9. But as far as he himself is concerned, being unable to cope with the danger that has arisen with his own strength, he makes the Lord his "Strength" and takes refuge in Him as in an unassailable "fortress." Having declared this intention and acted upon it, a calm assurance of help now steals into his heart (v. 10). Since God is his God He will not fail him but will assuredly "come to meet" him or, what amounts to the same, "His steadfast love"—the obligation under which He has put Himself by the covenant that He has made with His people—will come to his help. The day will yet come when David will see his enemies overthrown and his own just cause vindicated. Men can speak thus only when they have a full conviction of the justice of the cause they espouse and of the utter vileness of the opposition.

11. *Slay them not lest my people forget them;*
    Make them to totter by Thy power and bring them low, O Lord, our shield.
12. *The sin of their mouth is the word of their lips;*
    They shall be caught in their pride and for cursing and lying which they speak.

13. *Destroy them in anger, destroy them that they be no more;*
    So that men to the ends of the earth may know that God rules
    over Jacob. Selah.

11. Though for a moment quiet assurance had taken hold of his mind, the victory of faith is not yet final. The writer again turns his thoughts to petitions that his enemies may be thwarted in their wicked designs upon him. He would not have them destroyed at once but rather have them live on under the judgment of God as a warning to all evildoers and to his own people as a whole. God is at least implored to make them totter and to bring them low so that they may not execute their evil intentions. To motivate this prayer (v. 12) the psalmist asserts that these men cannot speak without uttering a fresh sin: every pronouncement of theirs is wicked. He at the same time expresses the conviction that they that speak thus—"cursing" and "lying"—must be caught in their pride, without defining any more fully what "be caught" implies.

13. This verse seems to contradict the plea made above in v. 11: there, "slay them not"; here, "destroy them." *Kirkpatrick's* approach is most helpful. He states: "Burning indignation does not study logical consistency." We may also think of those other suggestions that have been made such as that the writer would have individual evildoers of this group meet with their just punishment but the class of them as a whole not destroyed at once. And when just punishment does strike the individual according to the counsels of the Almighty, then "men to the ends of the earth may know that God rules over Jacob." Such must have been the impression made when not too long after these events Saul perished so miserably on Mt. Gilboa. God's just judgments had finally overtaken him. We may insert in passing that all these so-called "imprecatory" psalms leave the issues in the hand of God, to whom alone judgment belongs.

14. *In the evening they keep howling again like dogs;*
    And they prowl about in the city.
15. *They stray about for food;*
    If they are not satisfied they growl.
16. *But as for me, I will sing of Thy power;*
    I will exult over Thy steadfast love in the morning,
    For Thou hast been a fortress for me and a refuge in the day of
    trouble.
17. *O my strength, I will sing unto Thee;*
    For God is my fortress, the God who shows me steadfast love.

14. The fact that so unusual a verse as v. 14 should serve as a refrain (cf., v. 6) indicates that this characteristic, their curlike character,

must have been rather prominent. The picture is now unfolded with a bit more detail (v. 15). The insatiability of the wicked in finding new wicked morsels for them to devour, i.e., the opportunity to do new mischief, seems to be the point of the comparison. In obvious contrast to what "they" do the writer's sets what *he* does ("but as for me"). The contrast then appears to be between their unholy growling and his joyful singing (v. 16). The "power of God to deliver him becomes the theme of his song." Like so many before him, he delights to dwell exuberantly on the "steadfast love" (*chesedh*) of Israel's covenant God. For whether the danger is completely over, or whether this section of the psalm was written in retrospect after the danger had passed, or whether calm assurance stole over him and lifted him above the danger, he can speak in utter trust: "Thou hast been a fortress for me and a refuge in the day of my trouble."

17. In full-throated praise the psalm comes to a sonorous conclusion. The psalmist felt so utterly weak; God proved Himself to be his "strength." That calls for a song. He was in danger; God was found to be a strong "fortress." A new proof of the "steadfast love" of God is now on record and will not be forgotten.

NOTES

4. The verb "get themselves ready," *yikkonánu,* is a Hithpael form, the *taw* being assimilated before the *kaph* (*GK* 54c). This verse and the last part of v. 3 as well as the first part of v. 5 could be rearranged as the *Kittel* text indicates.

5. This verse begins literally: "And Thou, O Lord." This can also be translated: "And Thou art the Lord," and thus would be a clause that is coordinated with the following. As so often in the Hebrew, correlation of clauses is best translated by subordination as the connection seems to demand.

A bit unique in this verse is the form *'elohim tsebha'oth,* whereas usually a construct is found—*'elohey.* KS explains this as a case where the noun *tsebha'oth* has become a complete new name in itself (*Verselbststaendigung*) KS 285b. This also occurs in 80:5, 20; 84:9.

6. In the expression "howling again" the "again" is represented by the verb *shubh* which is used adverbially. KS 361m.

7. "For who hears?" is one of the many instances when direct discourse suddenly appears without an introductory statement. We have added "they say" for the sake of clearness.

9. Following many manuscripts and the versions, we read *'uzzi*. The verb does not need to be changed to make this verse read exactly as does v. 17.

10. In like manner in this verse also the first word should be sup-

plied with a different final vowel, viz., *'elohay,* as the *Septuagint* did.

12. This verse could be translated, "For the sin of their mouths" (*RSV*), following *KJ*. We believe that the translation we have offered is simpler and meaningful. The relative is omitted before the last verb.

13. The obvious object of the verb "destroy" is omitted in the Hebrew. It may be supplied from the clause that follows.

15. "They growl" reads literally: "and they growl," for the *waw* consecutive construction often expresses the logical sequence, like: *then* they growl. *KS* 366p.

17. For "the God who knows me steadfast love" as we have translated, following *RSV,* the Hebrew has: "the God of my steadfast love," a very un-English form of statement.

Psalm 60

CONFIDENT PRAYER
IN A GREAT NATIONAL CRISIS

THE HEADING of this psalm, which consists of two verses, is a very helpful guide in the interpretation of this prayer. It again deserves to be accepted as being correct as the headings of all the psalms are. It is quite commonly regarded as being accurate by commentators ancient and modern. The only score on which it would seem to be out of accord with facts is that II Sam. 8 and I Chron. 18, which give a summary report of the military action involved in this connection, make no mention of a severe setback which had been suffered, perhaps by the incursion of the Edomites, which setback is reflected in this psalm. It need merely be noted that the chapters just referred to speak of David's successes in war, not of his defeats, and they are besides merely summary accounts of military action throughout the reign of David. With only such fragmentary accounts at our disposal, it is ill-advised quickly to speak of contradictions or discrepancies.

We interpret "testimony is a lily" as a reference to a tune or a manner of rendition of the psalm. It cannot be denied that it could in this instance be a mystical designation of one aspect of this psalm, for the phrase as such could mean: God's testimony (i.e., His law) is pure as a lily and free of all defects; and it is true that vv. 6–8 are such a testimony on the part of God on which the nation bases its confidence.

But these interpretations of the heading seem a bit too whimsical. The phrase "to teach" seems to imply that this was intended to be a poem that was to be taught to the nation and committed to memory (cf., Deut. 31:9).

In a general way the situation that obtains in Ps. 44 is the same as that with which we are confronted in this psalm. It may also be indicated that vv. 7–14 appear again in Ps. 108, in which they are joined to a section that is taken from Ps. 57, viz. vv. 8–12.

As for the rest of the heading, it must be noted that the exact location of Aram-Zobah has not yet been determined. A minor difficulty is the fact that the victory that is here ascribed to Joab is credited to David (II Sam. 8:13) and to Abishai (I Chron. 18:12). David was the commander-in-chief in charge of all operations; Joab was very likely delegated to take care of the Edomite campaign; Abishai served under him. From all this it becomes quite obvious that the crisis involved consisted in this that, while David was busily engaged in warding off a dangerous attack in the extreme north, the Edomites made capital of the situation and staged a surprise invasion.

The psalm is obviously a prayer of the congregation and not that of an individual, a sort of liturgy. Thus the nation was taught to pray by her good king David. Outstanding are vv. 11 and 12, both as being striking in thought and as deserving to be remembered by the church in times of danger. As to the whole psalm, a most valuable thought is this that the Word of God (vv. 6–8) is made the basis of its faith in a very direct and pointed way. Thus faith should always seek the foundation of the Word of God.

Certain features of interpretation that are less reliable and quite unacceptable are these: the effort to make the psalm liturgically dramatic by assuming that in the rendition of it in the sanctuary a prophet suddenly appears with an appropriate divine oracle (vv. 6–8). Such an interpretation gives free play to an overactive imagination and is not based on solid fact. (*Schmid* and to some extent *Weiser*). Or to make the psalm a lament that was spoken by the congregation just before the fall of Jerusalem (587 B.C.) in a kind of fanatical upsurge of hope of deliverance, which, unfortunately, was quite a delusion (*Gunkel* and *Leslie*). Or to claim to have discovered two original psalms which were skillfully (?) woven together into what we now have (*Briggs* et.al.).

a) **God has allowed the present calamity to befall His people, therefore they turn to Him (vv. 1–5)**

1. *O God, Thou hast cast us off and hast broken us;*
   Thou hast been angry.—oh, restore us!

Psalm 60

2. Thou hast made the land to quake and hast caused rents in it;
   Heal its cracks, for it totters.
3. Thou hast made Thy people experience hard things;
   Thou hast made us drink wine that made us reel.
4. Thou hast given a banner to them that fear Thee,
   That it may be displayed because of the truth. Selah.
5. That Thy beloved may be delivered
   Help us by Thy right hand and answer us.

1. The spirit of faith and of prayer predominates in this section; it is, however, colored by a certain lament. A severe defeat must have been suffered by the nation, a defeat that made it feel that God had cast it off and had "broken" it. This last verb may have in mind the figure of the breaking of the walls of a city or that of the breaking of the lines of the army. In either case the situation is precarious. But at the bottom of this disaster lies the wrath of God, which cannot become operative unless men sin against their God. So there is an implied confession of guilt at this point. But to flee from the God who afflicts to the God who alone can heal has ever been the attitude of God's people, and so they cry: "Oh, restore us!"

2. The second verse follows the same pattern. Yet it does not refer to the military issues but to an earthquake which seems to have visited the land simultaneously with war. So the prayer is that the open cracks that appear in the earth may close up, for recurring earthquake shocks seem to have caused continuing alarm—"for it totters." The earthquake may be a figurative description of the disaster that is referred to in v. 1, although this is less likely.

3. The total disaster is now described (v. 3). The people had to pass through distressing experiences by the will of God, or, to employ a figure, they were obliged to drink a powerful potion that makes one reel, the point being that the nation was rendered helpless and utterly confused by this distressing experience. The figure certainly does not mean that God confused them and is to be blamed for their staggering, but rather that they brought down upon themselves the evil that befell them.

In the midst of these calamities the writer teaches the nation to bethink itself of what had been given it for such eventualities. Without for the present identifying what he means by the "banner" he reminds the people that they are like a nation that in the time of national disaster raises up a significant banner as a rallying point for all. This banner is to be displayed "because of the truth," which means, of course, the truth and fidelity of God. On God's truth they are to bank until these calamities are overpast. A "Selah" calls for reflection.

5. The note of prayer and petition which pervades the whole section now breaks out into more powerful volume (v. 5) in that God is called upon to grant His help: "Help us by Thy right hand and answer us." The double petition is obviously urgent. This petition is reinforced by a statement of the purpose that motivates it. In this case the subordinate clause is placed first in the sentence: "that Thy beloved may be delivered." God is being asked merely to do what His interest in His "beloved" ones would naturally prompt Him to do. The whole section is an instance of obedience to the command: "Call upon Me in the day of trouble."

b) **His ancient promises of possession of the land and of hostile neighbors are recalled (vv. 6–8)**

6. *God has spoken by His holiness;*
   I will exult; I will divide up Shechem; I will measure off the Valley of Succoth.
7. *Gilead is mine, and Manasseh is mine;*
   And Ephraim is my helmet and Judah my ruler's staff.
8. *Moab is my washbasin;*
   On Edom I throw my shoes;
   Philistia, tender me your shouts!

6. One is at once tempted to ask, When did God make this pronouncement? Is this some mysterious oracle that was given in days of old? That is not impossible. It seems a bit more feasible to assume that this is free adaptation of God's promises to the nation which He made in various forms and ways throughout the whole of the Pentateuch. The substance of these promises is such as to make Israel exclaim: "I will exult; I will divide up Shechem; I will measure off the Valley of Succoth." Speaking more accurately, the substance of these promises is that the whole land east and west of the Jordan as well as the surrounding territory from the river of Egypt to the great river, the Euphrates, was to be Israel's possession (cf., Gen. 15:18). That pronouncement of God stands secure; no one can invalidate it. Therefore by way of exemplification the nation confidently asserts its possession of the various parts of the country.

Shechem was the place at which Jacob stayed after his return from Mesopotamia after having crossed the Jordan (Gen. 33:18). Succoth was his trans-Jordanian stopping place prior to this (Gen. 33:17). So by metonymy these two places represent the territory west and east of the Jordan, respectively. Gilead and Manasseh then represent larger areas of the East-Jordan area and are claimed by virtue of the divine promise. Ephraim, as the most powerful tribe west of the Jordan, next to Judah, the ruling tribe under David, must represent the West-Jordan area, and full control over it is expressed as well as its strategic importance when it is called the "helmet" or literally "the strength of mine head" (*KJ*). To Judah, from which David came, rule and leadership are quite naturally ascribed—"my ruler's staff" apparently a quotation from Gen. 49:10. So much for the land of Israel proper.

The extent of territory held in prospect for Israel since Gen. 15 included the surrounding nations insofar as they had to be subdued to make Israel's position safe against attack. Therefore those nations which had of late been particularly troublesome are now assigned their place in the scheme of things. Moab, the frequent ally of Edom, is given a very inferior position by being described as Israel's "washbasin." This becomes all the more humiliating when it is recalled that a vessel for the ablution of the feet is very likely being referred to. There is no reference to the Dead Sea, in which, since it is adjacent to Moab, the giant, God, washes His feet.

"On Edom I throw my shoes" implies: I consider Edom as very menial, perhaps like a slave to whom one tosses dusty shoes for cleaning, or like a mean piece of furniture on which dusty shoes are thrown after they are removed. But cf. also Ruth 4:7–9. Philistia, the ancient and troublesome enemy of Israel, is told that she must tender her shouts of allegiance to the victor, like, "Hail to the conqueror."

The whole section is an expression of exuberant confidence that God will fulfil His ancient promises to His people and will give them the land in possession. Therefore the present threat brought about by Edom's invasion must collapse as soon as Israel penitently seeks her help from God.

c) **Confidence of achieving the impending conquest of Edom is expressed (vv. 9–12)**

9. *Who will bring me into the fortified city?*
   Who will lead me into Edom?
10. *Is it not Thou, O God, who hast cast us off*
    And hast not gone forth, O God, with our armies?
11. *Give us help from the foe,*
    For vain is the help of man.
12. *With God we shall do valiantly,*
    For He it is that shall tread down our enemies.

9. Edom must be beaten back and conquered. Her almost impregnable city, Petra (cf., II Kings 14:7), also called Sela, must be occupied. Halfway measures against Edom such as beating back the invader to the border would be futile. Thus the writer desires to give expression to the thought that the humanly impossible is to be achieved. The fact that God can help His people and make the campaign a success

is expressed by the use of the questions asked in v. 9. Only when a man is clearly aware of the fact that complete conquest of a foe who made continual incursions in the land is utterly imperative dare he seek God's help in battle.

But the writer has not shut his eyes to the fact that the present experience seems to remove all hope of success, for God has "cast off" His people and has not gone forth with their armies when they at the time of the invasion attempted as much defense as they were able to muster. Yet in the face of such apparent disavowal of His people by God the psalmist has the assurance that God is the One who will grant success, for the promises just recited (vv. 6–8) give a reason for such confidence.

11. Since help always rests in the good pleasure of God it must be sought humbly in prayer, and to such prayer David, therefore, addresses himself (v. 11). Seldom has the futility of the help that man can render in emergencies been more aptly expressed than it is in this verse—"for vain is the help of man." But "with God," that is to say, with His help, mighty deeds can be done, for which fact the classic expression is: "With God we shall do valiantly." For even when they feel themselves empowered by Him and are assured of success, it will be so entirely the work of God Himself that the enemy is overpowered that it can well be said: "For He it is that shall tread down our enemies." In fact, that is the only strictly correct form of the statement. So the psalm closes on a strong note of confidence which was engendered by the promises of God, which were grasped in faith. True faith rests on the Word.

NOTES

1. "Oh, restore us!" regards the verb as an imperfect that expresses a prayer. There is the possibility that the last letter (*taw*) of the preceding word and the first letter of *teshobhbhebh* may have been written twice by mistake (dittography). Then *Shobhbhebh* would be a perfect like the other verbs in the verse and would have to be translated, "Thou hast turned us back." But the analogy of the next verse, which closes with a prayer, supports the translation we offer.

4. *Lehithnoses* ("that it may be displayed") is a difficult verb. It could be derived from *nus,* "to flee." *RSV:* "to rally to it," which certainly makes very good sense. The rendering of *KJ* has just as much to be said in its favor. It regards the verb in question as a denominative from *nes* ("banner") and so establishes the meaning "to be displayed." Evidence seems to be a bit stronger for regarding *qóshet* as "truth" rather than as "bow."

6. "By His holiness" deserves the preference over "in His sanctu-

ary." For it is largely fiction that, apart from a few strictly historical instances when God appeared and spoke in His sanctuary (Num. 7: 89; Exod. 33:7–11), God was wont periodically to speak in the sanctuary. But to say that "God hath spoken by His holiness" means as much as: He has sworn by His inviolate, holy character.

8. The last verb (*hithro'a'i*) does not have to be corrected into a verb in the first person because the preceding statements had the first person. It may well have the meaning "tender me your shouts," implying that they will be shouts of acclaim of the king to whom they submit.

9. When we translate: "Who *will* lead me?" we accept the suggestion offered by the *Septuagint* that the final *yodh* of the interrogative should be read twice (haplography), making *nacháni* read: *yanchéni*. The parallel verb of the first member confirms this construction.

10. The rendering, "Is it not Thou?" (*KJ:* "Wilt not Thou?") requires only the insertion of the relative after "God," which insertion is most natural since the Hebrew omits the relative about as frequently as the English does. Since the note of confidence becomes stronger toward the end of the psalm, we feel that this rendering is much more in keeping with the spirit of the psalm than: "Hast not Thou rejected us, O God?" (*RSV*), a translation which is otherwise perfectly admissible.

11. Either "From the foe" or "from trouble" (*KJ*) is correct. Though the Hebrew says "and vain," coordinating the clauses, the sequence of the thought demands subordination in the sense of "for vain."

Psalm 61

THE EXILED KING PRAYS FOR RESTORATION

ON READING this psalm of lament one soon becomes aware of the fact that its writer is in some form of banishment. Since the heading attributes the psalm to David, the possibility that David is the exile deserves consideration first of all. A historical situation comes to mind as it is reported in II Sam. 17:27ff., where David had to take refuge in Mahanaim in his flight before his own son Absalom. There is nothing in the psalm that is out of harmony with the situation there described or with the possibility that a man like David would have composed a psalm like this on such an occasion. Whether we dare go so far as to pin-point the exact time of the composition of the psalm at the moment when David's men had gained the victory over the insurrectionists, and David was still at Mahanaim before the people recalled him, may well be left as an open question.

On first reading, vv. 6, 7 may be regarded as extraneous material, for why should a prayer for the king be injected into a prayer that David makes for himself? We agree with all those interpreters who regard this prayer for the king as a section that was also composed by David who based his whole approach on the fact that unusual promises had been made to David and his house in II Sam. 7. The Messianic hope had there by the prophetic promise been associated with the line of David. So David makes prayer for that promise and teaches his people also to pray thus, for his royal office had an unusual destiny as they and he well knew.

In this light the psalm has Messianic implications, not in so far as it might be said to refer directly to the Messiah's reign, but at least in so far as it revolved around the hope of the house of David that God had implanted in it, that the Messiah should come from his line.

The traditional use of the psalm, also in the hymn paraphrases that have been built upon it, makes it a psalm that teaches how God's people pray for their rulers and government.

We find the following present-day approaches unsatisfactory as being out of harmony with the express statements of the text: this is the prayer of a sick man (*Schmid, Leslie*); this is the prayer of the nation (*Briggs*); this is a liturgical prayer on the occasion of the festival of the covenant, when the allotment of tribal territory was commemorated (*Weiser*).

The psalm appears to be built up of three petitions:
a) An exile's prayer for help (vv. 1–3)
b) His plea to dwell with God forever (vv. 4, 5)
c) His prayer for the king (vv. 6–8)

To the Choir Director. On a stringed instrument. By David.

The one new feature in this heading, "on a stringed instrument," seems to have less meaning for us than it may have had for people of the day when it was added.

a) An exile's prayer for help (vv. 1–3)

1. *Hear, O God, my cry;*
   Give ear to my prayer

Psalm 61

   2. *From the end of the earth will I call unto Thee when my heart is faint;*
      Lead me to the rock that is otherwise too high for me.
   3. *For Thou hast always been a refuge for me,*
      A strong tower against the enemy.

The structure of this section is the same as that of the following two sections of the psalm: first the petition itself, then its motivation (v. 3). The plea is not very distinct as to what the specific situation of the writer is; he does utter a "cry" (scarcely a "yell"—*Briggs*) and a "prayer." Only in the second verse does it begin to become apparent that his heart is faint from the prolonged anguish that has come upon him, and that he needs to be led out of the dangerous situation in which he finds himself to a place of safety, which is unattainable for him in his own strength. God must lift him on high. The phrase "from the end of the earth" is usually and, we believe, rightly interpreted to mean that the intensity of his feeling measures the distance that he is removed from the beloved sanctuary rather than the actual number of miles involved. The phrase could be rendered "from the border of the land," but this translation is a bit precarious.

The reason the writer advances for being heard is that his past experience warrants falling back upon God: God has never failed him when he needed a refuge. Rather expressive is the added figure, "a strong tower against the enemy" (cf., Prov. 18:10), when describing what the name of the Lord means to His people.

b) His plea to dwell with God forever (vv. 4, 5)

   4. *Let me dwell in Thy tent forever!*
      Let me take refuge under the shadow of Thy wings. Selah.
   5. *For Thou, O God, hast heard my vows;*
      Thou hast given me the heritage of those that fear Thy name.

4. This petition makes us aware of the fact that the writer is by force of circumstances separated from the sanctuary. It does not do so by direct statement but by implication, for, as in Ps. 42, it was the separation from the sanctuary that made him aware as never before of what the sanctuary meant. Though a man might pray to "dwell in Thy tent forever" even when he still had access to the presence of God, yet when the petition is compared with the statement, "from the end of the earth will I call," our interpretation makes necessary the assumption that the psalmist was debarred from the physical sanctuary. Yet his prayer may be for the spiritual reality of continuous communion with God more than for participation in public worship even as this

is the emphasis in Ps. 23:6 and in many another instance where dwelling in the house of the Lord is spoken of. "Forever" gains a special emphasis from the fact that an intensive plural is used in the Hebrew. The fact that the personal relation to God is the chief issue is clear when one considers the parallel statement: "Let me take refuge under the shelter of Thy wings." He seeks the privilege of keeping as closely as possible in the shelter of God's presence. Cf., Exod. 19:4; Deut. 32:11; Ps. 17:7; 36:7.

5. The psalmist advances as the first reason for the granting of his petition the assurance that God has "heard (his) vows," which term must in this instance include both the prayers and the vows that were made simultaneously. He has apparently experienced what is in many instances the fortunate lot of those who pray: the assurance steals over them that God has heard, and that their prayer is answered. Part of that assurance is in this case: "Thou hast given me the heritage of those that fear Thy name." Since the writer does not for the moment define closely what this "heritage" is, the reader of our day is inclined to place into the expression whatever meaning best suits his need. However, since in every other instance of the occurrence of the word it refers to the occupation of the land of Canaan by the children of Israel, it would seem to apply to any gift that is by analogy the fulfilment of God's promise to His people. That leads us to accept that interpretation which suggests that the two verses that follow are a definition of what the "heritage" meant in this instance: the fulfilment of the distinctive promise given to David by Nathan in II Sam. 7, the eternal continuance of the throne of David and of one of his seed who is to sit upon it.

Viewed thus, vv. 6f. pray precisely for the realization of this divine boon and fit into the total picture of the psalm most intimately. This also explains more fully what we indicated above and shows why it is perfectly proper for David to pray for himself objectively in the third person. For it was not strictly only for himself that he prayed but also for that seed to whose continuance upon his throne the promise pointed. So David in effect taught his people in this psalm to pray for the coming of the Messiah, at least for the fulfilment of the promises made with reference to that coming.

Note in this connection especially that the emphasis rests upon the eternal aspect of the promise even as it does in the original chapter, II Sam. 7:13, 16 (2x) and I Chron. 17:12f. The second half of v. 7 is a freer adaptation of the thought and is stated more poetically. For if "steadfast love and faithfulness" are appointed to guard him, that will insure the eternal endurance of his throne and his kingdom. These two are thought of as guardian angels of a sort who were specially sent by God for this purpose. This prayer moves on a high plane, for it prays with fervor for nothing less than the high things that God has promised. Thoughts such as these stirred the mind of David when his kingship trembled in the balance before the assault of his wicked son Absalom.

We now offer the third petition, most of which we have already interpreted.

c) His prayer for the King (vv. 6–8)
> 6. *Mayest Thou prolong the days of the king*
> *And his years as many generations.*
> 7. *May he be enthroned before God forever;*
> *Appoint steadfast love and faithfulness to guard him.*
> 8. *So will I sing praises unto God forever,*
> *That I may daily pay my vows.*

By way of supplementing the interpretation of v. 6 above it may be noted that the Hebrew idiom for "prolong" is: "Mayest Thou add days to the days of the king." And in v. 7, "enthroned" is only the verb "sit" which, however, is used with reference to royalty sitting on the throne and so fully warrants this translation (see also *RSV*).

Surely, the praises that are to be offered in the future when God has answered the psalmist's prayer are not offered for the purpose of inducing God to answer him. They are rather the expression of the confidence that the day will come when the prayers uttered will have been heard, and the psalmist sees himself as at that time praising his God and paying the vows which he made to his God in the day of his distress. As is so often the case in the psalms, also this psalm closes on a note of confidence.

NOTES

2. We have inserted an "otherwise" in the interest of clarity, and we believe that this is the sense in which *KJ* intended its translation. *Luther* leaves out a part of this statement.

3. We regard "hast always been" as a perfect that is used as a gnomic aorist.

4. The translations waver between, "Let me dwell," and, "I shall dwell." One is as permissible as the other. The analogy of the structure of the psalm induced us to use the precative.

Psalm 62

CALM ASSURANCE IN THE MIDST OF DISTRESS

THERE IS SCARCELY another psalm that reveals such an absolute and undisturbed peace, in which confidence in God is so completely unshaken, and in which assurance is so strong that not even one single petition is voiced throughout the psalm. Men who were in distress have often longed that they might manifest a spirit of undismayed calm such as this writer possessed.

There is nothing in the psalm that makes it difficult to accept the authorship of David that is presented in the heading. But to assign the psalm to some period or to some particular situation in the life of this king of Israel is absolutely impossible.

It is not very likely that the speaker is a sick man as it has become quite popular to characterize him. Nor is it very likely that the text of the psalm is in a state of sorry confusion because of poor transmission or because of extensive tampering with it. Nor is there such a difference between the first section (vv. 1–8) and the remainder that the first is to be described as pulsating with warmth and vitality whereas the second voices a cold and stern tone that estranges the reader.

Divided by "Selahs," the psalm appears to consist of three sections of four verses each, which present a progression of thoughts somewhat after the following pattern:
a) Resigned to God, though cruelly assailed (vv. 1–4)
b) Resigned and inviting others to do the same (vv. 4–8)
c) The futility of all help other than the Lord's (vv. 9–12)

The heading: *To the Choir Director. According to Jeduthun. A psalm. Of David.*

The only feature calling for comment is the phrase "according to Jeduthun." Compare the introductory remarks on Ps. 39 for the identity of Jeduthun. In that connection the psalm was apparently transmitted to Jeduthun that he might take care of its public singing. Here the phrase has a different force, implying, perhaps, that the psalm should be sung in a manner that was characteristic of Jeduthun.

a) Resigned to God, though cruelly assailed (vv. 1–4)

1. *Only as it looks to God is my soul utterly resigned;*
   From Him comes my deliverance.

Psalm 62

2. *He only is my rock and my deliverance,*
   My fortress, I shall not be greatly shaken.
3. *How long will you storm in upon a man or thrust at him, all of you,*
   Like at a leaning wall, a tottering fence?
4. *Only from his high position have they planned to thrust him aside;*
   They delight in lies;
   With their mouth they bless, but inwardly they curse. Selah.

1. The first verse is almost untranslatable, for the Hebrew says: "Only unto God silence my soul." This explains the wide variation among the versions: "Truly my soul waiteth upon God" (*KJ*); and: *Meine Seele ist stille zu Gott* (*Luther*), just to mention a few. "Silence," of course, means absolute composure. The word for "truly" more frequently means "only." Therefore we have ventured to translate: "Only as it looks to God is my soul utterly resigned." For the spirit of the utterance Is. 30:15 and Exod. 14:14 may be compared.

Opposition of cruel and wicked men could have embittered this man's life, but since he turned wholeheartedly unto his God in total submission he found that peace and quiet in the inmost soul were still possible—but only in this way. Turning unto God alone brought him deliverance. This fact he underscores (v. 2) by ascribing all the help received only to his God. God, changing the figure, is the firm "rock" on which he stands. He has delivered him. He is the impregnable fortress behind whose walls he can flee and be secure. Assaults may be made upon him; they may cause him some disquietude; but he "shall not be greatly shaken," that he knows with supreme confidence. One notices that the tone is one, not of self-confidence, but of God-confidence.

3. From that which constitutes his strength he now turns to the trouble that has assailed him, rather to the troublesome persons who might well have driven him to despair. He addresses them in a kind of expostulation: perhaps they will listen to reason when they see their vile deeds characterized as they deserve to be. They "storm in upon him" with threatening gestures. *BDB* suggests that in the Arabic of Damascus this verb still implies coming with "cries and raised fists." They "thrust" at him in an endeavor to overthrow him. That is why he likens himself to "a leaning wall, a tottering fence." In the estimation of his proud enemies it will take only a sturdy push, and the man will collapse. The enemies had apparently continued this type of attack for a long time (note: "how long?"). But trying to touch the consciences of men such as these is hopeless. So he turns from addressing them to a further objective evaluation of what these men are really like. Something like envy or jealousy must have been an impelling motive in

their attitude toward him, for they were planning to thrust him "only from his high position." If this one objective can be attained, they will be well content.

This section of the psalm agrees well with the possibility that this is a psalm that was composed by David, and that, perhaps, his royal station was not as yet completely established. But the methods pursued by the adversaries in gaining their ends are utterly despicable: "They delight in lies; with their mouth they bless, but inwardly they curse." Such type of treatment is always utterly galling. Yet in the midst of it all the poet was able to maintain a perfect composure by directing his soul exclusively unto God. A "Selah" calls for further reflection upon this point.

b) **Resigned and inviting others to do the same (vv. 5–8)**

5. *My soul, be resigned, looking only to God;*
   From Him comes my hope.
6. *He only is my rock and my deliverance;*
   My fortress, I shall not be shaken.
7. *On God rest my deliverance and my glory;*
   My mighty rock, my refuge is in God.
8. *Trust in Him at all times, O people;*
   Pour out your heart before Him;
   God is a refuge for us. Selah.

5. The same spirit of peace and rest pervades this section. The first two verses are practically the same as the first two verses of the preceding section. The minor changes are, nevertheless, significant. Whereas in the first section complete resignation to God's will was asserted, in this section it is prayed for. This does not imply a weakening of the former position but rather that whatever vantage ground we hold we must continually recapture by prayer. Faith's battles are never finished, nor does struggle depart from our life.

Another slight change is that "hope" is now substituted for "deliverance" as a treasure that comes "from Him." Hope marks a lesser degree of possession but is still very positive. Yet if some shift of position has been indicated by these two terms, the other notable change indicates that there have been fresh advances. New ground has been gained, for he can now say: "I shall not be moved," leaving out the word "greatly." That implies: not moved at all. Confidence and peace grow with prayer.

7. This verse is an attempt at an evaluation of what God means to him in his present situation: "deliverance . . . glory . . . rock . . . refuge" —all are in Him. We are reminded of the manner in which descriptive names are heaped up in Ps. 18:1f. One glories in God when he speaks thus, for God is his all in all. He supplies his every need.

Psalm 62

8. A man like David could not help but feel that each new spiritual experience put him under obligation to share as much of it as he could with his people, especially the godly among them. Thus his exhortation to the people is: "Trust in Him at all times." But since true trust leads to voicing one's needs before Him in the day of trouble, he adds as a second suggestion: "Pour out your heart before Him." For we shall again and again need a refuge in times of trouble, and God is just the refuge that our manifold needs require. Selah again marks a pause for reflection.

Five significant "only's" have marked these two sections of the psalm so that among the purely stylistic features this is the most unique mark of the psalm.

c) The futility of all help other than the Lord's (vv. 9–12)

9. *Men of low estate are merely a breath;*
   Men of high estate are untrustworthy;
   Weighed in the balances, they are bound to go up;
   Altogether they are less than a breath.
10. *Trust not in oppression; set no vain hopes on robbery;*
    If riches increase, set not your heart on them.
11. *Once has God spoken, twice have I heard this,*
    That power belongs to God.
12. *And unto Thee, O Lord, belongs steadfast love;*
    For Thou dost requite every man according to his work.

9. This section is in obvious contrast with the two that preceded. This is the negative of that in which men should put their trust in time of trouble or ever. Yet these are the values that men seek first and trust in most. First of all, there is man himself, whether he is a person of some standing or without such a distinction. Man is "breath" or vapor. When you need his help most, then it is seen how untrustworthy he is. When man's actual worth as the dependable helper in distress is computed, the balances are "bound to go up," for man lacks ability for coping with the many ills that may arise. Taken collectively, they are still "less than a breath." These utterances are not to be evaluated as though the writer of them were quite misanthropic. As *Maclaren* well remarks: "The singer is not cynically proclaiming man's worthlessness, but asserting his insufficiency as the object of man's trust." Jer. 17:9; Ps. 82:7; 118:8; 146:3 may be compared.

10. Evaluating another category of things that men put their trust in, the singer advises men not to have recourse to "oppression" or "robbery," for the hopes that are engendered by efforts in these fields are vain hopes. These particular words seem to be directed at those who are

showing hostility to the writer. Equally unsatisfactory are riches, and it is quite foolish "to set one's heart" upon them if they should happen to increase. For in the final test there is not much that they can do for you.

11. Pointing to God as the ultimate, only, and completely dependable source of help, the writer sums up the wisdom acquired in his recent experience as a kind of word spoken by God, at least a truth that God has impressed upon his heart. Repeatedly (that is the meaning of the "once" and "twice" in the proverbial saying cf., Prov. 30:18ff.) it has been borne in upon him that "power," that is, true ability to help in every time of need, belongs to God. Coupled with that power is the readiness of mind to use it to help men in need, which thought is expressed in the words: "And unto Thee, O Lord, belongs steadfast love," that loving-kindness which keeps Him true to the clear promises that his free love caused Him to make to His people. As *Weiser* has rightly said: "In the union of power and steadfast love the essence of the Old Testament faith in God lies summed up; for power without mercy does not beget confidence, and mercy without power is devoid of sincerity." But in practice this combination of attributes in God results in this "that Thou dost requite every man according to his work." The faithful will not be forgotten. The wicked will not be left unpunished. So in a word that is reminiscent of the words of wisdom literature (cf., Ps. 37, 49, 73, 130) the psalm concludes with solid instruction, having begun with the notes of solid confidence.

NOTES

1. The restrictive use of *'akh* in the sense of "only" deserves the preference since it applies in almost every instance of its use in the psalm. *Dumiyyah,* being a noun used for an adjective, requires a somewhat stronger equivalent than a mere adjective. This led us to offer the translation "utterly resigned."

3. The difficult verb form *teratstsechú*. if it is derived from the verb commonly in use, would have to mean something like: "you murder him" (see *Luther*). *KW*'s suggestion that the word may have a meaning that is suggested by the parallel Arabic root, "to kick at a one," seems to merit attention. Then the verb is a sort of apposition to the less familiar verb "storm in upon a man." The Hebrew shortens the comparison in "like at a leaning wall," etc., by leaving out the preposition (*KS* 319g).

9. A comparison with Ps. 49:2 on the use of *'ish* and *'adham* will indicate that such a distinction is to be made here as most versions indicate in part or in whole, especially *KJ,* which we have retained: "men

of low estate" and "men of high estate." The *le* before the infinitive dare not be ignored and means something like "bound to" do a thing. See *KS* 399z.

12. Though *'ish* means "man," here the connection obviously demands the sense "every man" as the *Septuagint* and *Latin* indicate.

Psalm 63

THE THIRSTING SOUL FINDS RELIEF IN GOD

FROM DAYS of old this was the morning psalm of the church. This usage was due to the fact that the major translations had rendered the first verb as *KJ* does: "early will I seek Thee." But more exact investigation has shown that the second root of the verb involved does not apply, and that the verb means merely "to seek" or "to seek diligently." Still in the light of v. 6 there is a propriety about regarding this as a psalm for use in the morning.

The psalm as such may well be said to reflect David's experience when he fled before his son Absalom. For when the heading says, "When he was in the wilderness of Judah," this may be understood as referring to those northern parts of this wilderness that he had to cross in his flight (see II Sam. 15:23, 28; 16:2, 14; 17:16). This psalm also emphasizes the facts that absence from the sanctuary is implied (v. 2); the writer is a king (v. 11); and the high degree of faith manifested throughout is to be found particularly in the king after God's heart.

It is this faith in particular that characterizes the psalm. It has been asserted that the faith that marks Ps. 61–63 finds its greatest height in our psalm. At the same time the following feature is prominent: The cultus of the sanctuary as such, though beloved by the writer, is not all-important; he is able to have fellowship with God apart from the outward aids to worship. This is a fine instance of discriminate worship: loving the forms that God appointed—regarding God rather than these forms as essential.

The difficulties encountered in trying to make a clear outline of the psalm are more than average. But when the heart speaks with a strong gush of emotion, we should not expect the coldly reasoned arrangement of thought that characterizes a scientific treatise. Yet a theme like the

one we have given above seems to meet the needs of the case: "The Thirsting Soul Finds Relief in God." For our part, we find in the psalm the following development of thought:
a) The writer seeks close fellowship with God as in former days (vv. 1–4).
b) His satisfaction in such fellowship (vv. 5–8).
c) The unhappy lot of cruel foes (vv. 9–11).

We find it necessary to reject the following approaches of interpretation as failing to do justice to one or the other major factors of the psalm. It is not a psalm composed by a sick man (*Leslie*), for the words "my flesh pines for Thee" fail to support such a contention. Nor is it primarily a lament, nor can it be termed a song of thanksgiving, though both elements are present in it. It is not a psalm which calls for an ingenious rearrangement of the verses in order to discover its original form (*Schmid:* 2, 3, 7, 8, 9, 5, 6, 4, 10, 11, 12b, 12a; or *Briggs:* 2, 3, 7, 5, 9, with 10, 11 appended, also 12a, b, and glosses: 4, 6, 8, 12c). For such purely subjective readjustments allow each individual to find exactly what he desires to find. Nor is it a psalm that outlines some cultic procedure in order to experience some form of theophany by way of vindication of the writer and the condemnation of his accusers (*Weiser et al.*). *Oesterley's* attempt to identify the writer with Jehoiachin will not find many supporters; but he rightly rejects the rearrangement of verses.

The heading: *A Psalm of David. When he was in the Wilderness of Judah.*

a) **The writer seeks close fellowship with God as in former days (vv. 1–4)**

1. *O God, my God, Thou art He whom I seek;*
   My soul thirsts for Thee, my flesh pines for Thee in a dry and weary land where no water is.
2. *So have I looked for Thee in the sanctuary,*
   To see Thy power and Thy glory.
3. *For Thy steadfast love is better than life;*
   My lips shall praise Thee.
4. *So will I bless Thee as long as I live;*
   In Thy name will I lift up my hands.

1. The needs of the case are completely met if we think of David's situation in flight through the wilderness of Judaea: he has not lost his hold on God. He seeks Him in this hour of need as ardently as he ever did. He feels his need of him with a thirst and a longing that possess his whole being ("soul . . . and flesh"). The "dry and weary land where no water is" is an apt description of the wild, inhospitable region between Jerusalem and the Jordan. But the fact that having God and seeking

Him go hand in hand is well expressed by Maclaren: "In the region of the devout life the paradox is true that we long precisely because we have." The physical aspect of the land may have suggested as a kind of parable the utterly dry and arid state of the soul that is deprived of God.

2. The same longing that now has hold of the writer, had filled his being often when in the past he sincerely sought fellowship with God "in the sanctuary." What he sought to see was not necessarily a manifestation of God's presence over and beyond what is a possibility for the saints of God in all ages: the seeing with the eyes of faith. But the particular objectives in mind were: to become aware of God's "power" to help and the "glory" that is manifested whenever such help is experienced.

3. In the last analysis such a vision of the power and the glory is nothing other than an experience of the "steadfast love" (*chésedh*) of God, to become aware of which "is better than life." Though life is commonly regarded as being almost our chief treasure it is far surpassed by the realization of how great God's faithfulness in His dealings with His children actually is. The realization calls for some acknowledgment. Therefore: "My lips shall praise Thee." Religious experience and the grateful expression of God's greatness realized afresh go hand in hand. In fact, the theme is so great (v. 4) that the writer vows: "So [in conformity with what insight I have gained] I will bless Thee as long as I live." To this God (or "in Thy name") he determines to lift up his hands both in gratitude and in petition. The experience has made a lasting impression upon him. His whole life shall bear the mark of it.

The whole section bears the mark of a rich and deep communion with God, the need of which has been more deeply felt than ever, and the enjoyment of which in all its richness has made the heart glad again with a joy that shall never die.

b) His satisfaction in such fellowship (vv. 5–8)

5. *My soul is satisfied as with marrow and fatness;*
   And my mouth praises Thee with joyful lips.
6. *Whenever I remember Thee upon my bed,*
   Then will I meditate on Thee in the night watches.
7. *For Thou hast been my help;*
   And in the shadow of Thy wings will I exult.
8. *My soul clings to Thee;*
   Thy right hand upholds me.

5. The poet now expresses at some length what deep satisfaction this fellowship with God, which has become increasingly real to him as he recalls what it once meant to him, imparts to his inmost soul. It is a

satisfaction to be likened to that of a hungry man who has sat down to a feast of rich things that completely met his needs and now rises from the table. There is no deeper satisfaction. The writer is again moved to say that for such a gracious gift his mouth shall praise God with joyful lips. Since the earthy flavor of the Hebrew comparison might appeal less to our way of thinking when we visualize the remnants of bones and bones that have been broken to get at the marrow littering the table, *Luther* sought to get the essence of the figure: *Das waere meines Herzens Freude und Wonne, wenn ich dich mit froehlichem Munde loben sollte,* allowing himself further freedom in adjusting the relation of the clauses to one another. But even such a rendering bespeaks deep satisfaction because of the experience involved.

6. We believe this to be a separate thought and not the continuation of the preceding verse as *KJ* has considered it. Since the deeper realization of what God means for him is so rich, the writer anticipates that whenever the thought of it all, particularly of God Himself, comes to him by night, the very watches of the night shall pass in pleasant reflection upon this happy theme.

7. Besides, God merits such devout contemplation of His mercies, for in many instances He had in the past been the psalmist's help so that the impression that fills the writer's mind is that he is continually walking about under the protection of God's sheltering wings, and that thought fills the very soul with exultation. The figure has varied, but the thought of a deep-seated satisfaction is still under consideration.

8. For a good summary of this mutual relationship no statement could, perhaps, be more attractive than is this one. On his own part his relation to God is: "My soul clings to Thee." The Hebrew tried to combine two ideas into one by saying: My soul cleaves after Thee, a thought that is aptly, if a bit archaically, rendered by *KJ:* "My soul followeth hard after Thee." Both a holding fast and a following are involved. But the *divine* side of the action is this: "Thy right hand upholds me." As man struggles along he will always find great comfort in the experience that the hand of One who is stronger than himself will not let him fall. This is not a quietistic enjoyment of God but a practical relationship which helps a man to ride victoriously over the dangers he will without a doubt encounter.

c) **The unhappy lot of cruel foes (vv. 9–11)**

9. *But they on their part seek my soul to their own hurt;*
They shall go into the depths of the earth.
10. *They shall all be delivered into the power of the sword;*
They shall be a prey for jackals.

Psalm 63

11. *But the king shall rejoice in God;*
    All that swear by Him shall glory;
    For the mouth of those that speak lies shall be shut.

9. It is not an unnatural attitude in a situation like the one indicated in this psalm to think in terms of the ultimate defeat of the wicked opposition who seek to defeat the royal dynasty that has God's approval in a unique sense. It must not be forgotten that those who oppose the psalmist are fighting God. Issues like this are not to be left to continue indefinitely. To look for a final solution is but natural. It is in this spirit that the writer describes or, one might say, confidently predicts the unhappy lot of his cruel foes.

His first assertion is that, though they seek his soul, they do so to their own hurt. For they are bent on nothing less than cruel murder, an act that God avenges. He feels quite correctly that, like the wicked rebels of days of old, Korah and his fellows (Num. 16:31–34), these men, too, shall come to an untimely end. "The depths of the earth" seems to be merely a paraphrase for "the hereafter" or Sheol itself. The expression employed does not predict the ultimate destiny of those whom God shall snatch away out of this life.

10. It is anticipated that the end of the opponents will come on the field of battle as it obviously did in this case, for there is where the "power of the sword" most generally makes itself felt. Then their slain bodies are visualized as lying on the deserted field of battle, and the jackals, the customary beast of prey in those areas, come to feed on the slain. "Foxes" was simply an erroneous translation of earlier days.

11. With that objective approach which is characteristic of other psalms (cf, vv. 61:6) the psalmist goes on to speak of the victory of the king, whose status has been made unique by the Lord Himself (II Sam. 7). He does not say "I" since the promise is to his "house" and includes far more than himself. When he sees the outcome of the present struggle he shall find great joy in the fact that God has wrought such an outcome. Of the same mind and sharing the same joy are all those who swear by and thereby acknowledge the true God of Israel. This is in clear contrast to all those who have recklessly been using lies to further their cause. The mouths of all such shall be forcibly closed.

NOTES

1. The literal translation of the beginning of this verse is: O God, my 'el, meaning "the Strong One." In man's weakness the divine attribute that often comforts him is strength. The words may also be translated: "O God, Thou art my God; early, etc." (*KJ*). We prefer our rendering, which would involve the omission of the relative.

The word for "weary" is *'ayeph,* which we regard as a masculine form that modifies *'arets,* feminine, that is written as a masculine because it is farther removed from its noun and a preference for the masculine prevails. Cf. I Kings 19:11; and see *GK* 145t. Cf. also Ps. 143:6 and Is. 32:2, where the same adjective is used with this noun.

2. Without sufficient reason *KJ* has inverted the order of the two clauses of this verse.

5. The Hebrew does not really say "marrow and fatness" but uses two words that signify "fat." *KJ* made the expression more attractive by the use of "marrow." In the expression "joyful lips" the Hebrew has "lips of joys," where apparently the second plural is caused by the first (*KS* 267b).

6. The initial *'im* may be used as particle of time in the sense of "whenever." See *GK* 164d.

7. To find here an allusion to the wings of the cherubim because the singer is supposed to be spending the night in the sanctuary, where the ark is, which is shielded by the wings of the cherubim, is highly fanciful.

10. The singular suffix of the first verb is apparently used in the individualizing sense of "each one," which we have sought to express by the word "all." *KS* 348v.

11. Many interpreters prefer to render the expression "swear by Him," "swear by him" (singular, i.e., the king). For that an oath sworn by the king was known at least in Egypt is indicated by (Gen. 42:15). But that fact does not guarantee such a usage by the Israelites. In fact, passages like Deut. 6:13 and 10:20 rather point in the direction of an oath sworn by God. Such proper swearing is in one sense a distinctive mark of those who faithfully serve the Lord.

Psalm 64

AN INSTANCE OF DELIVERANCE FROM TREACHEROUS FOES

THERE IS NOTHING very unique about this psalm. A man in distress cries to the Lord for deliverance from foes who work insidiously. Perhaps it does not even reflect a particular situation in which the writer found himself at a given time but is in effect a general prayer that was prepared for the use of individuals who encounter unprincipled foes. But it is quite obvious that the writer had abundant experience in such situa-

Psalm 64

tions and so prepares a general prayer for all who face this particular problem.

One feature should, however, be noted about the psalm. It is not a prayer which reflects a serious situation in the midst of which the writer struggles, hoping for deliverance. It is rather in the nature of a historical account which begins with the prayer that was once uttered but relates also how that prayer was answered. In other words, we are taking issue with practically all the more recent versions from the days of the Reformation onward to the present and are going back to the approach of the *Septuagint* and the *Vulgate,* which find in v. 7 a reference to an event that has already passed, not a reference to a hoped-for future deliverance. See *Notes* for justification of this approach grammatically.

The foes who are mentioned are men who are characterized by treachery, particularly in the wicked use of the tongue. Their plots are slanders that they put into circulation, or shoot like poisonous arrows, or hide like insidious snares.

One feature is, after all, perhaps distinctive of the psalm, and that is, as *Vilmar* remarks, the fact that the overthrow of the ungodly opposition is ascribed exclusively to the operation of God and not to the ingenuity of man—a feature that well bears stressing.

We offer the following outline of the psalm:
a) A description of the wicked machinations of wicked enemies (vv. 1–6).
b) A description of their sudden overthrow (vv. 7–10).

This could be broken down into greater detail, for the first section is introduced by a prayer for help, and the second section closes on a note of exultation. So we could discover the following sequence: 1) prayer; 2) lament; 3) deliverance; 4) exultation.

As the many commendable translations of the psalm that have been offered show, we have here a text that is, as usual, in a good state of preservation. There is no indication that the psalm is a specifically liturgical piece. Nor does it reflect the party strife of postexilic days: narrow-minded bigots who claim to be the blameless against a more liberal-minded party (*Kittel* reads modern situations back into the psalm without warrant). Nor are the words that fly about like dangerous arrows to be regarded as words of sorcery as some commentators, following *Mowinckel's* lead, have surmised.

The heading reads: *For the Choir Director. A psalm of David.*

a) A description of the wicked machinations of wicked enemies (vv. 1–6)

1. *Hear my voice, O God, in my complaint;*
   From fear of the enemy protect my life.

2. *Hide me from the secret counsel of the wicked,*
   From the raging of the evildoers;
3. *Who whetted their tongue like a sword;*
   Who aimed their arrow—a bitter word—
4. *To shoot from hiding places at the blameless;*
   Suddenly they shot at him and fear not.
5. *They established for themselves an evil plan;*
   They discussed the laying of snares; they said: "Who can see us?"
6. *They devised unjust deeds;*
   "We are ready; the plot is well devised;
   The mind of man, yea, his heart is deep."

It is obvious that no mere phantoms of danger were involved. The psalmist was in danger of his life. The plots that had been projected were deadly in character. But what made them all the more threatening (v. 2) was their secret nature: they were all deeply hidden, dangerous like traps (v. 5). Calumny apparently had been resorted to—character assassination (v. 3). V. 6 reflects the confidence with which they viewed the plots that had been so cleverly conceived. Direct discourse (6b), not directly introduced but obvious from the context, reflects their proud thinking after their plans had been completed. They believed that their plots had been so well conceived that no one would be able to detect or counteract them. For the words, "The mind of man . . . is deep" signify: No man can fathom or discover what we have devised.

b) **A description of their sudden overthrow (vv. 7–10)**
7. *But God shot an arrow at them;*
   Suddenly blows came upon them.
8. *Each one was ruined; their tongues overcame them;*
   All that saw them shuddered.
9. *All men were awed and declared that God had done it;*
   And they considered His work.
10. *Let the righteous rejoice in the Lord and take refuge in Him;*
    And let all the upright in heart glory.

The tables are suddenly turned. What they intended to inflict on others befalls the wicked themselves. This led *Leslie* to give the psalm the caption, "The Boomerang of Malicious Speech." God suddenly intervenes. They had aimed to shoot (v. 4), but God shoots first. They had aimed to act suddenly; God's sudden action anticipates theirs (v. 4). They whetted their tongues for evil (v. 3); their own tongue overcame them (v. 8). This is clearly divine retribution. So the emphasis of v. 7 may well be caught by stressing the last word thus: "Suddenly blows came upon *them*."

The effect was so striking that "all who saw them shuddered." Or, as v. 9 very properly interprets this, "all men were awed." They could not help but see that a greater hand than that of man had been at work. For the rendering: "They considered His work" we might have substituted: "They gained insight into how He works." Thus the general effect of God's intervention is a wholesome awe and fear on the part of the wicked and a realization on the part of all men that God had acted. A different kind of reaction is to be expected from the "righteous" and the "upright." They already knew about these other reactions that have just been recorded. For them it was fitting that, on the one hand, they rejoice; then also that they take refuge in Him anew over against all exigencies that may arise; in fact, it was most appropriate for them to glory in God's marvelous and holy works.

6. The verb *tamnu* presents a difficulty. It is not the usual form for the first person plural but may well be construed thus (*GK* 67e).

NOTES

7. This verse is in a sense the key to our approach to the psalm which views it as being primarily the record of a historical experience. For here we clearly have a case of an imperfect with *waw* consecutive, which construction is the usual manner of continuing a narrative concerning past events. The fact that all that preceded, apart from the opening prayer (vv. 1, 2), occurred in the past is apparent from the use of the perfect *shanenu* (v. 3), which is followed by another perfect, *darekhu*. The imperfects that follow indicate the subordinate features of the narrative (cf., *KS* 154). The perfect appears again in v. 5 (*'ameru,* "they said"). When *wayyorem* introduces v. 7, the most natural way to translate is: "but God shot," the conjunction being a *waw* adversative, setting God in contrast with what the writer's foes had been contriving.

The second half of the verse has its difficulties. It might read literally: "suddenly they became *their* blows," which *J. M. P. Smith* has rendered: "Suddenly their wounds are there." The Hebrew text draws "suddenly" to the preceding clause.

8. The beginning of the verse reads literally: "and they (here used impersonally) caused him to stumble." The "him" refers to each individually and separately; therefore: "each one."

Psalm 65

IT IS ALWAYS FITTING TO PRAISE GOD

THE ESSENCE of this psalm is thanksgiving for a harvest that still stands unreaped in the fields, but this thanksgiving is built up on a broader basis than this one great gift of God.

The unusual poetic beauty, especially of the concluding section, is obvious. The fact that the tone of this psalm is quite different from the common run of Davidic psalms that have preceded it is not in itself proof that David could not have written it as is claimed by the heading. In fact, on the basis of the material found in the psalm Davidic authorship can be neither proved nor disproved. That brilliance and freshness of style, which are common to David's psalms, can also be detected here. So we are content to let the heading stand as being correct. It should be noted in this connection that this psalm in common with the two that follow has a somewhat universalistic note, and thus these three psalms constitute a little triad of kindred spirit.

In connection with this psalm, perhaps more than in many others, the danger of elevating a mere possibility of interpretation to the level of clearly accepted fact is most readily discernible. We offer illustrations. The psalm might have been written after a threatening drought had been averted; but it reads just as well if all thoughts of a drought are dismissed. It could have been written for some great festival (opinions differ very widely as to which); but it is readily understood apart from such a supposition. It may have been used as a liturgical piece by the congregation; it is just as fitting if it was used by an individual or by any group that loves its sentiments. By some stretch of the imagination v. 3 may be referred to a case of sickness from which the writer had recovered; it is far more likely that no thought of sickness is to be associated with the poem. One may assume that the vows referred to in v. 1 were those that were regularly made by farmers as they sowed their grain and then at harvesttime paid their vows, though this savors too much of an unhealthy emphasis on vows in Israel's religious life. Though all these approaches have been offered, we feel that they stand on too insecure a footing and dare not dominate the trend of the interpretation.

The universalistic outlook of the psalm finds expression in vv. 5

and 8 and has some measure of similarity with passages such as Mal. 1:11; Is. 2:2ff.; Mic. 4:1ff.; Jer. 16:19; Is. 45:24; 66:23; Ps. 22:27; 86:9; 94:10.

One approach that we reject more emphatically than others is the one that associates this psalm with the festival of the annual enthronement of Yahweh. This is thought of as involving a procession of the ark of the covenant through the city to the Temple, analogous to II Sam. 6:3–5, and reference to which is supposed to be found in the expression used in v. 11, "Thy tracks," which is supposed to refer to the tracks of the cart on which the ark was borne. Such superstition and magic after the Babylonian pattern were scarcely characteristic of Israel's religion.

The heading reads thus: *To the Choir Director. A psalm of David. A song.* This has been discussed in part. We are not sufficiently aware of the distinction between "psalm" and "song" to offer very constructive comments.

1. *It is fitting that men praise Thee, O God, in Zion
   And pay their vows to Thee.*
2. *O Thou, that hearest prayer,
   To Thee all flesh may come.*
3. *My iniquities are too much for me;
   As for our transgressions—Thou wilt forgive them.*
4. *O how very happy is the man whom Thou dost choose and receive to dwell in Thy courts!
   Let us be sated with the excellence of Thy house and the holiness of Thy Temple.*

1. The Hebrew reads: "Praise befits Thee." We felt that the thought involved could be most clearly expressed by translating: "It is fitting that men praise Thee." The poet's statement stresses the propriety of praise on the part of those who frequent the house of the Lord in Zion. God always deserves praise. That thought may safely be regarded as the keynote of the psalm. Analogous to prayers are vows. It is in like manner fitting that these be paid in the sanctuary at Zion. Whether special vows are to be thought of may well be questioned. The writer has stated the broad principle that it is most fitting to offer both prayers and vows to the Lord in His sanctuary.

2. Since a broad program of thanksgiving is being presented, the author reflects for a moment on the thought that in His very nature God is One who hears all such prayers of His children, in fact, He may be designated the "hearer of prayer." The Hebrew does just that by using the participle. It should besides be borne in mind that Israel has no exclusive option on prayer. "All flesh," that is, all mankind, is

accepted by Him, if it will but turn to Him. This is an obvious protest against an unwholesome exclusivism, into which Israel might in days of old have been in danger of falling. The statement need not be translated, "To Thee shall all flesh come," for that would be a universalism that is nowhere taught in the Scriptures. See *Notes*.

3. If praise is not to be offered superficially, a man must reckon with his sins. For he is a sinner, and his sins may interpose themselves between him and his God. In order to help men take this circumstance into account, the writer prays for himself and teaches others to pray and confess that the sins that lie upon them are more than they can dispose of. But there is still hope, for these transgressions of men, which are far from being a light matter, will be forgiven by God to every true penitent who confesses them. Thus, in effect, the writer proceeds to address himself to thanksgiving by the way of confession and absolution. Being thus prepared, he can approach God in the right spirit and be accepted in his gratitude.

4. The author goes on to rejoice in the fellowship to which he feels restored now that his sins are removed by divine grace. He dwells with rapture on the blessedness of that wholesome personal relationship which he knows he enjoys with his God. All who dare to approach God thus and trust that they shall be accepted by Him base this procedure on the sovereign freedom of God to choose men and deign to receive them (here not thought of in a predestinarian sense). For God is under no compulsion to receive sinners unless it be the free compulsion of His love. Those who are accepted by pardon are His house guests. They "dwell (as it were) in His courts." Continual spiritual fellowship is being thought of rather than outward presence in a public sanctuary.

The description of this happy lot is for a moment interrupted by a petition that the rich blessings involved may be granted, and that the blessed satiety which only those experience who live in fellowship with God may become a reality. Whether "the excellence of (His) house and the holiness of (His) Temple" are thought of as involving the visible sanctuary in Zion or the invisible courts of God's spiritual presence is immaterial as far as the writer is concerned. Fellowship with God is the thing.

These first four verses may be regarded as a preparation for the praise that is to follow.

5. *In awe-inspiring manner Thou wilt answer us in righteousness,*
   O God of our salvation,
   Who art the confidence of all the distant ends of the earth and the sea.

Psalm 65

6. *He who by His strength has established the mountains,*
   Who is girded with power,
7. *Who stilled the roaring of the seas,*
   The roaring of the waves, the tumult of the peoples.
8. *So that they who dwell at the ends of the earth were afraid at*
   Thy signs;
   Thou didst make the outgoings of the morning and the evening
   to rejoice.

5. Whereas the first section (vv. 1–4) dwelt on the propriety of praise in spite of sin, especially praise for the fellowship with God, the present section sets forth this truth: The works done for His people and in nature give assurance for the future. This section recounts the works of the Almighty in a spirit of praise. The tense of the first verb is important. From the approach made in the opening verses assurance for the *future* is gathered. God will respond and help in times to come, whenever His own appeal to Him. But this will not be done in some commonplace fashion. When God redeems His own, this will always be done in an "awe-inspiring manner." It will always be "in righteousness," which leads Him to deliver His own whom He has promised to help. It is, therefore, right for Him to do so.

Besides, because of the many instances of help which He rendered in the past He has obtained the rare name of "God of our salvation." But He is the object of the confidence not only of Israel, His chosen ones. He is the same for "all the distant ends of the earth and the sea." Those who dwell in these remote parts may not know that such is the case, but it is still true: He is their only help.

6. Certain works of the Almighty are now recounted (v. 6f.). These furnish the evidence for the fact that God is the true Helper of all. The very recounting of these works is again praise of Him who did them. There is first the reference to the impressive establishment of the mighty mountains. They did not set themselves into place or become firm and immovable, *God* established them, giving proof thereby that He is girded with power.

Another work of His that points in the same direction: He "stilled the roaring of the seas." That includes every instance of the calming of the waves of a disturbed sea. They never composed themselves; God calmed them. In like manner it was He who stilled "the tumult of the peoples." The agitations in nature remind the author of the disturbances of nations, which are analogous. These, too, did not merely subside. God calmed them. A graphic instance of what is last referred to might well be the event of the crossing of the Red Sea, when God restrained the waters for the deliverance of Israel but overcame the tumult of the Egyptians by letting them be overwhelmed by these same waters.

8. Whenever God did mighty works such as these, men were apprised of what had happened. The report of them penetrated to "the ends of the earth," and all who heard of what He had done were filled with reverent awe at His "signs" and so in a measure acknowledged Him. And they were to some extent made to rejoice, especially those who knew the true God and how He works. This mighty result was apparent in a manner that was world-wide, or as here stated: "Thou didst make the outgoings of the morning and evening to rejoice," which would seem to mean: those persons who dwell in the remote regions where the sun seems to rise or to set.

9. *Thou hast* (again) *visited the earth and watered it, greatly hast Thou enriched it;*
The river of God is full of water;
Thou hast prepared their grain, for thus hast Thou prepared it.
10. *Its furrows Thou hast watered abundantly, hast settled its ridges;*
With showers hast Thou watered it, hast blessed its growth.
11. *Thou hast crowned the year with Thy goodness;*
Thy tracks dripped with fatness.
12. *The pastures of the wilderness dripped;*
The hills girded themselves with joy.
13. *The meadows were clothed with their flocks;*
The broad valleys were covered with grain;
Men shout for joy, yea, they sing.

There follows that section of the psalm for which all that preceded prepared the way. As *Weiser* beautifully points out: the first section (vv. 1–4) provides depth for the praises to come; the second section (vv. 5–8) provides breadth of outlook; the last section, built on this groundwork, makes it possible to see the bounteous crops that stand in the fields in the light of all of God's munificence and mercy.

9. This verse begins by recounting what notable works God has once again done—the "again" being implied, not expressed. Crops grow because He comes and gives them. It is not thought to be beneath the dignity of the Lord to picture Him as personally even watering the earth and so enriching it, that is, enabling it to produce endlessly. In Palestine and adjacent lands the value of the gift of water was appreciated the more because of its being found in such scant measure. So the poet underscores this fact by the statement, "The river of God is full of water," referring, of course, to the rain. To Him must be attributed both the preparation of the grain, which is about ready to be reaped, and the preparation of the soil. This member of the

verse ("Thou hast prepared their (i.e., man's) grain, for thus hast Thou prepared it") is clearer in the original because of the gender of the pronouns there employed.

10. The account of what God has done in making the impending harvest possible continues. God is pictured as watering "furrows" and settling the "ridges" after plowing, as watering the growing crops with "showers" and blessing their growth. The poet obviously attempts to ascribe each successive step in the process to direct divine action. In the Bible nature does not work autonomously.

11. If God's "goodness" is in evidence, this is the result of one major act, which may poetically be phrased thus: "Thou hast crowned the year with Thy goodness." Or it may be rephrased: "Thy paths dripped with fatness." He passed through—whether this is to be thought of as being done afoot, or perchance on His divine chariot, or by the passing overhead of the clouds—He passed through and made the land fertile and productive. In fact, even those portions of the land with which fertility is less likely to be associated—"pastures of the wilderness" or steppes and "the hills" themselves—were made to produce, "dripping" with fertility on the one hand and "girding themselves with joy" on the other. What an eloquent description, here and throughout, of God's blessing upon a land!

13. A few touches may yet be added that lend color and life to the picture, stressing features of the daily common life of Israel that were important to all. What a pretty sight to see the flocks peacefully pasture in a meadow! The poet says: "The meadows were clothed with flocks." And who has not been impressed with the sight of fields of ripening, waving grain, especially when the broad valleys are thus covered and ringed with mountains for a scenic background? When man's sensibilities are not too dulled, he cannot but do as is here described: "Men shout for joy, yea, they sing." We venture the claim that this is the most eloquent and beautiful description of the blessings that God bestows on field and meadow to be found anywhere in such brief compass.

NOTES

1. The word *dumiyyah,* as here pointed, does mean "silence." But to attempt to work it into a translation that has an unforced meaning is well-nigh impossible. Even the ancient versions (*Septuagint* and *Vulgate*) did not do that. They regarded the form as an active participle from *damah* ("the be like") and rendered it "be fitting," the form being *domiyyah. RSV* can be understood on the basis of this change: "Praise is due Thee."

2. The final verb, *yabho'u,* is best construed as a permissive im-

perfect; and if it is regarded thus, there is no need of adding the next two words as an object, or of making any other changes in the text. The point is that God is far more ready to hear than men are to ask.

3. In the Hebrew "iniquitous deeds" are "things of iniquities."

4. After the interjection *'ashrey* ("O how very happy") both the pronoun and the relative (he and who) are understood. Therefore in our translation we supplied "the man who." See *KS* 337v.

8. In the Hebrew this verse merely begins with another verb that is attached by an "and." It would be quite permissible to make this clause a subordinate clause of result. But the translation should quite obviously read: "So that . . . they *were* afraid," thinking, perhaps, of some historical event like the passage of the Red Sea. *Tarnin* is an imperfect with *waw* consecutive not expressed, a common construction; see *KS* 368i. So also is *ta'sherénnah* (v. 9).

10. "Hast watered" and "hast settled" are infinitives absolute in place of the finite verb. See *KS* 217b.

11. "Dripped" is a further case of an imperfect that is separated from the conversive "and," as found above in v. 8.

Psalm 66

"MAKE A JOYFUL NOISE TO GOD, ALL THE EARTH"

THIS IS a stirring hymn of praise. It is marked by repeated summonses that are addressed to various groups to come and praise the Lord God of Israel (see vv. 2, 5, 8, 16). Some deliverance had apparently come to the children of Israel, the magnitude of which made them feel that they alone could not offer sufficient praise to the Lord for His goodness. They felt besides that others would be impressed by what they had experienced to such an extent that they, too, would not be disinclined to praise. Thus the psalm, like the one that precedes and the one that follows, sounds something of a universalistic note. Israel was not oblivious of the fact that the things that were done to her were to be made known among all peoples.

Though no particular occasion is indicated by the heading or the statements of the psalm as such, there is one situation which seems to meet the needs of the case better than does any other, the occasion of the deliverance of the children of Judah from the threat of the Assyrian conquest in the days of Hezekiah (II Kings 18, 19; Is. 36, 37). Add to this event the personal experience of the king who was delivered from sickness about the same time, and some of the references of the last section of the psalm would be explained, in which an individual addresses God in the spirit of the first section of the psalm. None of the other occasions which have been pointed out with reference to the psalm particularly recommend themselves.

The understanding of the psalm is not furthered by the assumption that various choirs, half-choirs, and solo voices must have rendered the successive parts of the psalm, quite apart from the precariousness of such an interpretation. The claim that the psalm is a liturgical piece which is expressly designed for those occasions when vows were paid in public worship by various groups who had had some common experience obviously goes beyond the limits of what the evidence offers. Or again to bring the annual so-called enthronement festival of Yahweh into the picture as the obvious occasion of the poem presses available evidence far beyond its actual weight. The psalm is of the mixed type: personal and corporate praise blend in it.

To the Choir Director. A song. A psalm.

In this heading the unique feature that it shares with the next psalm only is the fact that after the phrase "to the choir director" the name of the author is not appended as is usually the case.

1. Shout in triumph to God, all the earth.
2. Sing the glory of His name;
   Make His praise glorious.
3. Say to God: "How awe-inspiring are Thy works!
   Because of Thy great power Thy enemies cringe before Thee.
4. All the earth worships Thee;
   And men sing unto Thee, yea, they sing the glory of Thy name."
   Selah.

1. The opening words of the psalm are in the nature of a theme sentence. We have, therefore, placed them at the head of the psalm in the words of the familiar version: "Make a joyful noise unto the Lord, all the earth." Familiar though this sentence is, it is not quite adequate to call praise "noise." The point at issue is that the deliverance that God's people experienced is so great that they would be unable to offer praise in a volume such as the occasion requires. Therefore let all the earth do her part. This thought is developed in the first four verses.

2. The verb used implies that poetry accompanied by musical instruments is to be the medium of expression, which we have tried to

indicate by the use of the verb "sing." Since God has expressed His character or "name" in the mighty work that He has just done, and this was a work that was marked by glory, it is "the glory of His name" that should be celebrated in song. Nor is tame praise sufficient under the circumstances. Praise should be made "glorious." Playing the part of a helpful instructor, the writer lays the very words on the lips of those who would follow his summons. These words extend through two verses (3 and 4). The natural effect of beholding with unbiased mind what God has done is to make men tremble with awe at what they behold. Such is always the nature of God's works. Those who oppose Him are made to feel again and again what "great power" He displayed, and so, though unwilling to offer homage, they must yet "cringe" before Him.

In some measure (v. 4) "all the earth worships" Him. For there are many even among those who do not profess to be followers of His who are, nevertheless, struck with admiration by what they behold, and they tell freely the "glory of His name." It may not be perfect praise. It may not be done as well as God's own people could do it. Yet in a manner not to be despised they, too, sing unto the Lord.

Though there seems to be a specific occasion behind the whole picture that is presented, the writer draws his conclusions in the form of what sounds almost like a generalization. Psalm writers consciously wrote in such a manner as to make their psalms serve all manner of future occasions that might seem to be of a similar character.

The second section of the psalm lists the mighty works that inspire such praise as the opening summons called for.

5. *Come and see the works of God;*
   Awe-inspiring are His doings among the children of men.
6. *He turned the sea into dry land;*
   Men crossed the river on foot;
   Therefore let us rejoice in Him.
7. *He rules by His power forever;*
   His eyes watch the nations;
   Let not the rebellious exalt themselves. Selah.

5. One must take time to consider what God has done otherwise he will not be impressed by the Lord's works. The writer in spirit invites men to view a few choice examples of the Lord's mighty workings. The things that are in evidence, obvious so that all men can see them, are "awe-inspiring" in character. In our day "terrible" has the wrong connotation (*KJ*). The thought is rather that an overpowering majesty dwells in every work that God does.

6. It is as though the writer said in v. 6: Let us examine some typical

instances that show how He works. He once turned the sea into dry land on the occasion of the crossing of the Red Sea by the children of Israel. On another occasion men crossed the river on foot when an entrance into the Promised Land was made across the Jordan. Such things still carry their message to us. "Therefore let us rejoice in Him."

7. And now, to bring our thoughts down to present issues, says the writer (v. 7): God "rules" actively "by His power forever." Especially in the matter of the governing of the nations does His government manifest itself. He "watches the nations" continually so that they cannot attempt to do any harm to His people without His detecting what they have in mind; and thus He is always ready to check them in their endeavors. From this fact the writer draws the obvious conclusion: "Let not the rebellious exalt themselves." They will not prosper in the things that they undertake against those over whom the Lord is watching. A "Selah" marks an obvious break in the thought.

The next section (vv. 8–12) refers to a special deliverance which is the present occasion for praise in this psalm.

8. *Bless our God, O ye people;*
   Let the sound of His praise be heard,
9. *He that keeps our soul alive*
   And has not allowed our foot to slip.
10. *For Thou hast put us to the test, O God;*
    Thou hast refined us as silver is refined.
11. *Thou hast brought us into the net;*
    Thou hast laid distress upon our loins.
12. *Thou didst let men ride over our heads;*
    We went through fire and through water;
    But Thou didst bring us forth and refresh us.

8. As indicated above, the tone of this description is so general that it appears to be designed for any possible eventualities that may arise. Psalm writers, moved by the Spirit of God that inspired them, were thus serving their day and also times to come. In harmony with the tone of the psalm which we have indicated above "all peoples" are invited to engage in this work of blessing the name of the Lord. Not without good reason emphasis is placed on the desirability of making God's praise vocal ("Let the sound of His praise be heard"), for praise unexpressed seldom grows to its full stature.

9. The deliverance wrought in Hezekiah's day would furnish a suitable background for every figure used in the next four verses. The very existence of the nation was at stake; but God kept the people's "soul alive." They were in danger of a fatal fall; but He did "not allow their foot to slip." They were "put to the test" in a most searching way and

felt keenly the gravity of the situation. They were cast into the hot furnace of affliction that they might be refined "as silver is refined," and that always implies extreme pain. Again, while the crisis prevailed, they were like a creature "brought into the net"; but God provided an unexpected way of escape. For a time they felt crushed in their very loins by the "distress" that was laid upon them (cf., Is. 37:3).

12. It is quite obvious when comparison follows comparison that Biblical writers are not merely letting an exuberant imagination run riot. They are trying to convey a sense of the extreme character of the danger in which they were caught. Thus also v. 12 adds two vigorous figures. The first implies that the nation had been dashed to the ground, was wounded, perhaps, and helpless, and that, while they lay thus prostrate, the chariots or the cavalry of the enemy rode roughshod over them. What an extremity of danger and fear! The next figure, having become so common, seems to have lost some of its attractiveness. Is. 43:2 offers a good parallel. Both fire and water may represent deadly hazards, and that is what the writer would emphasize.

The last member of v. 12 is the final outcome which applies to the deliverance from all the dangers described in the large assortment of figures previously employed. In regard to each of these it may be said: "But Thou didst bring us forth and refresh us." The conclusion of this statement seems to us to have been rendered best by *Luther,* following the lead of both *Septuagint* and *Vulgate,* rather than by the more literal English tradition, "into a wealthy place" (*KJ*) or "to a spacious place" (*RSV*). *Luther* translates: *Aber du hast uns ausgefuehrt und erquicket,* Thou hast brought us forth and hast refreshed us.

The next major section of the psalm (vv. 13–20) presents the grateful response of an individual who has experienced personal help from God when he, too, was in distress. It is introduced by an unexpected "I." To make this the collective "I" in which the congregation of Israel speaks is unsatisfactory. No good reason can be adduced for first using the "we" for this purpose and then suddenly veering over to the "I." To assume that an individual was confronted by some special danger about the same time that the nation was threatened by a general calamity seems to meet all the needs of this section.

13. *I will come into Thy house with burnt offerings;*
    I will pay Thee my vows,
14. *Which my lips have uttered,*
    And my mouth has spoken when I was in trouble.
15. *Burnt offerings and fatlings will I offer to Thee*
    Together with the sweet odor of the sacrifice of rams;
    I will offer bulls and goats.

16. Come, hear, all you who fear God,
    And I will declare what He has done for my soul.
17. I cried to Him with my mouth;
    And praise was upon my tongue.
18. —If I had had evil intentions in my heart,
    The Lord would not have heard me—
19. But verily God has heard me;
    He gave attention to the voice of my prayer.
20. Blessed be God who has not rejected my prayer
    Nor turned away His covenant faithfulness from me.

13. Above we suggested the possibility that Hezekiah may be thought of as the one who originally spoke these words. In such dangerous times any number of persons in Judah could have had a kindred experience that called for praise such as this though statements like v. 16 would come with better grace from the lips of a man of some prominence.

14. The person in question vows to offer his praise to the Lord in public in the traditional manner. In this instance his resolution is reinforced by vows that were made in the time of distress. "Burnt offerings" symbolized complete self-consecration to the will of the Lord and were most appropriate after life had been restored to an individual at a time when its very existence had been threatened (vv. 14, 15). He dwells with some pleasure on the various types of sacrifices that he purposes to bring, each one more or less costly and the sum total of them quite expensive but gladly given in this case, for his heart was truly grateful.

16. The desire to have like-minded people share in one's personal paying of vows and sacrifices is but natural when one has once experienced that God's people rejoice in the joy of every other member of the body (I Cor. 12:26). It will then be quite natural for one to invite others to take part: "Come, hear, all you who fear God." What he would like especially to tell them is what the Lord has done for his soul. This does not suggest, as we in our day are inclined to interpret it, spiritual benefits in a special sense. Since "soul" is so often used to refer to the whole personality, the psalmist is thinking in terms of the totality of the blessings received.

V. 17ff. may well be regarded as a summary statement of that which God did for his soul: "I cried to Him with my mouth," and (v. 19) "verily God heard me; He gave attention to the voice of my prayer." The manner in which v. 17b follows upon the initial statement suggests that already at the time when the cry for help was being uttered praise was ready to be offered, for the certainty of being heard was so great. This is the way it should always be but usually is not.

18. For some reason not immediately discernible a parenthetical statement is inserted. Was it done because someone had questioned the writer's sincerity? Was it for purposes of general instruction? In any event, the writer stresses his sincerity, without which he knows that he would never have been heard. This is not necessarily a note of self-righteousness. It could be described as such only if there were definite evidence to indict him. The statement certainly serves as a reminder that God will not hear the evildoer. The writer's experience served both as reassurance and as vindication—"but verily God has heard me." Thoughts similar to those stated in v. 17 are expressed in Prov. 15:29; Is. 1:15; Is. 59:2, 3.

20. With a well-rounded statement of full-toned praise the author brings his psalm to a close (v. 20), for this statement is one in which the whole congregation could join with perfect propriety; and thus both halves of the psalm are brought to a conclusion. God could even, in spite of the sincerity of the man who prayed, have refused to grant His prayer, for His will is sovereign. But in this case He did not do so. Thus the statement: "Blessed be God, who has not rejected my prayer." If the last source of His willingness to hear is sought, for the writer it lay in God's "covenant faithfulness" which led Him to have regard to this poor man's need.

NOTES

3. "Awe-inspiring," *nora'*, appears in the singular as a predicate to the plural subject following. This usage follows a trend to prefer verbs in the singular when they precede their subjects. See *GK* 145, 5.

7. "Exalt themselves" is the reflexive pronoun (*lamo*) appearing in the dative, a dative of advantage.

8. Though the word for "peoples" sometimes refers to the tribes of Israel, that would seem unnatural here in view of the universalistic outlook of the psalm.

11. It is true that the meaning "net" is a bit doubtful for *metsudhah*. The figures used follow in swift succession, and the thought is by no means difficult. Also the second half of the verse has its difficulties. *Me'uqah* seems to mean "restraint." Besides, the other possible meaning, "burden," may be objected to on the score that burdens are not laid upon the loins. The loins, as *Briggs* points out, "are the seat of pain (Is. 21:3; Nah. 2:10) and weakness (Ps. 69:24)." Therefore the noun in question will have to be understood in a more general sense such as "distress."

12. The last word, *rewayah*, does mean something like "a spacious place" (*RSV*). *Fuelle an Getraenk, Ueberfluss* (KW). That this may

be rendered *erquicket* (*Luther*) is so obvious a solution that there is no reason to change the word to *rewachah*.

17. It conflicts with the spirit of the psalm to have part *b* of this verse mean: I had scarcely uttered my petition when the relief was already there. "Why so quickly? Because he is a righteous man" (*Kittel*). Kittel then finds fault with the self-righteousness which he has imputed to the poor writer.

20. This verse involves a zeugma. The only verb used, "rejected," can scarcely have as its object "covenant faithfulness." So another verb must be supplied in the second member. It is the word *chesedh* that we have rendered "covenant faithfulness." *RSV* generally translates "steadfast love."

Psalm 67

MAY THE PEOPLES PRAISE THEE, O GOD

THIS PSALM does not center about the harvest. Its scope is very broad. It is nothing less than a prayer that the nations may learn to know and praise Yahweh, the true God. That its purpose is universal appears from the fact that those prayed for are referred to by a variety of terms ("peoples, nations, nationalities"), which, taken together, are surely designed to include all the groups that dwell upon the face of the earth.

One might say that this psalm is one of the clearest expressions of the thought that Israel is to be God's priest to the nations, a thought that is offered already in Exod. 19:5, 6. The nation Israel as a whole was not always clear as to its destiny nor mindful of it. But this is one of the psalms that expresses this noble destiny most directly and enters into the spirit of it.

One difficulty, reflected very clearly in the various versions, is the fact that the Hebrew imperfect may be translated as a present, as a future, or in the precative sense, voicing a prayer. It matters little whether the predictive sense or the precative is employed, for "aspirations . . . may tremble on the verge of being prophecies" (*Maclaren*), but to regard these imperfects as prayers yields by far the better sense.

The structure of the psalm reveals rather clearly what is central to its thought. It may be divided as follows:

a) A prayer that Israel may be blessed so that God's gracious dealings may become known the world over (vv. 1, 2).
b) The same prayer expressed more emphatically (vv. 3–5).
c) The immediate occasion for this prayer (vv. 6, 7).

The second section of the psalm is longer than the other two sections, which indicates that it is the place where the chief emphasis is to be placed. The repetition of v. 3 in v. 5 makes this verse, which is practically the keynote, a refrain.

As to the particular historical occasion, if any, of this psalm we can only conjecture. Some interpreters feel that a major national deliverance is at the background of the words spoken (*Kirkpatrick*), and that this could have been the deliverance from the Assyrian, Sennacherib, in the days of Hezekiah. Though it is not inappropriate, this supposition is not backed by sufficient evidence. Nor dare we be positive about the time of composition. If all deeper insights came late to Israel, then the postexilic period would have to be suggested. But many of the deeper truths known were clearly understood from Mosaic times onward.

To the Choir Director. On stringed intruments. A psalm. A song.
The heading is much like that of Psalm 4.

a) **A prayer that Israel may be blessed (vv. 1, 2)**

1. *God be merciful unto us and bless us*
   And cause His face to shine with us; (*Selah*)
2. *That Thy way may be known on the earth,*
   Thy saving help among the nations.

In this instance the "selah" seems inappropriately placed in the middle of a sentence, and thus it certainly does not mark a division of the thought. Still, if it indicated a *fortissimo,* a louder blast of music, it may have ushered in the second half of the thought quite effectively. The writer would have the nations recognize that they are under the guidance of the God of Israel, and that "the way" in which He leads them as well as Israel is good and wise. It is, in fact, a way of "saving help" for all. For He is the only God, and His dealings with the children of men are good and kind. The only way in which Israel can communicate this thought to the nations of the earth is by herself receiving God's blessing. For when the writer says: "God be merciful unto us and bless us," he is not praying for the ability of utterance, or for the ability to put the message into moving and impressive words, but for material blessings upon God's people. For when God's people fare poorly, their lot leads the nations to believe that their God cannot provide for them. If, on the other hand, they are blessed, this fact serves as an indication to the nations round about that He is well able to provide for His people's wants. The writer prays, however, in terms that were sanctioned from of old

Psalm 67

and were given by God Himself as a worthy expression of how God's blessing is to be invoked or imparted when he uses the words of the blessing of Aaron as they are given in Numb. 6:24f. One minor change in wording appears. The psalm says "shine *with* us" rather than "upon." The blessing is thought of as being in the midst of rather than over the nation. To ask to be blessed in order that others might be won from the error of their way is unselfish prayer. It tends to the glory of the Lord.

b) The same prayer expressed more emphatically (vv. 3–5)

3. *May the peoples praise Thee, O God;*
   May all the peoples praise Thee!
4. *May the nationalities be glad and sing for joy,*
   For Thou rulest the peoples righteously
   And guidest the nationalities upon the earth! Selah.
5. *May the peoples praise Thee, O God;*
   May all the peoples praise Thee.

3. The fact that Israel only is not referred to, as *AV* might seem to indicate by the use of the singular "people," is apparent from the plural form of the word used. The prayer (v. 3) means: may the various nations on the face of the earth come to the point where they recognize the futility of their own gods and the supremacy of the only God, the God of Israel. This is a psalm in the second book of the psalter in which the divine name almost always appears as or has been changed to "God." It may, therefore, well be possible that the proper name *Yahweh* was originally used in this verse. Thus knowledge of the one true God is involved. For He cannot be rightly praised unless He is known.

4. To know Him and His gracious purposes would make any one among the various "nationalities" "be glad and sing for joy." For as Israel well knows, of Him it can be said: "Thou rulest (judgest, says the Hebrew) the peoples righteously." And for any group to know itself to be under the sovereign care of one who administers the affairs of all justly is great cause for rejoicing. For there is a God who is mighty and great enough to control the affairs of all the nations on the face of the earth. That is expressed by the parallel statement: (Thou) "guidest the nationalities upon the earth." (The "selah" again does not mark a major division of thought.)

5. The repetition of the verse marks this as the key thought of the psalm. For this reason we chose it as a heading.

c) The immediate occasion for this prayer (vv. 6, 7)

6. *The land has yielded its increase;*
   God, our God, has blessed us.
7. *God has blessed us;*
   May all the ends of the earth fear Him.

6. There may again have been a successful harvest. Since the statement, "The land has yielded its increase," is a quotation from Lev. 26:4, and also because the writer cannot know whether harvests have been successful the world over, the word *'erets* must refer to the land of Israel and not to the "earth" (*KJ, RSV*). When crops fail in Israel, she becomes a reproach among the nations (Joel 2:17, 19). But when God's people are blessed, the nations round about take note. See Jer. 33:9; Zech. 8:20ff.; Is. 9:9. For that matter, it may not have been the intention of the psalmist to restrict this verse to a particular harvest. The psalmist may be expressing a general truth of which he was again reminded by the harvest of the current year. But the land never yields its increase without the blessing of God. Therefore the parallel statement stresses this latter fact.

7. The last verse deems the importance of the blessing of God so great as to think it worthy of repetition. Then suddenly the basic thought of the psalm comes to the fore again in a prayer for the nations (here: "the ends of the earth"). When the thought is voiced that they may learn to "fear Him," the idea is obviously that they may learn to reverence Him as He deserves to be reverenced, and do that on the basis of a true knowledge of Him. This is a prayer for the conversion of the heathen. Thus already in days of old God's people understood that truth was given both to save them and to have them spread it abroad among those that had it not.

NOTES

6. The perfect *nathenah* is historical. The imperfect that follows is the imperfect of attendant circumstance as *KS* 155a explains, and as *RSV* rightly renders the tense of the second verb: "God has blessed us." To give the same verb, when it is repeated in v. 7, a precative sense as *Koenig* does in his commentary is scarcely feasible. The last verb is clearly a resumption of the previous prayers.

Psalm 68

BLESSED BE THE GOD WHO MARCHES ON TO VICTORY!

THERE IS SOMETHING triumphant about this psalm as the theme stated above indicates. *Maclaren* can scarcely be charged with exaggeration when he writes: "This superb hymn is unsurpassed, if not unequalled, in grandeur, lyric fire, and sustained rush of triumphant praise." *Vilmar* insists that it is a "hymn of victory of the church militant," whose notes dare never die out among God's children. Many other eloquent and enthusiastic comments in the same vein could be offered.

Over against this approach stands the other which deplores the "very imperfect" state of the text; or the claim that "no other piece in the psalter offers the student difficulties so great as those presented" by this psalm; or the hopelessness of discovering a sequence of thought in the various sections. To call it a "Libretto of Songs for the Sanctuary" is too vague (*Taylor*).

It is our strong conviction that the positive approach is the correct one in this instance. No one ventures to deny the obvious difficulties of interpretation. No one would be so bold as to claim that he can fully elucidate every line of the poem with complete assurance of being correct. However, even when this is admitted, two considerations should be borne in mind. One is that poetry, done in rich colors and exuberance of the imagination, cannot be restated in an exposition that is capable of the strictest precision of correct formulation. The other is that though here as so often in the Scriptures some things have become blurred as a result of the span of time that separates us from the original readers, that does not imply that everything is blurred. So much of the original brilliance is still discernible that to refuse to see the light because of certain shadows is an unwholesome attitude. It should again be said that poetry was never intended to be cast into the precise formulations of the Pauline epistles.

As we shall indicate in the course of the exposition, the psalm abounds in references to older portions of the Sacred Scriptures, and many later writings refer to it. Which writing deserves the priority in point of time is not always easy to determine. This is particularly true concerning the instances of correspondence with the second half of Isaiah. In addition the psalm may have incorporated many poetic passages of one sort or another which were well understood in their day and therefore used the more freely by the writer. We seem to lack the material for an inerrant interpretation of the allusions involved.

Though most writers brush the claim of Davidic authorship aside lightly though it is clearly stated in the heading, there are still those who find no other theory more plausible. Among more recent writers, *Koenig* stands almost alone in allowing for the possibility of authorship by David. Of the two possible situations in the life of this king that might be involved the Ammonite war (II Sam. 11) seems to deserve the preference rather than the occasion of the bringing up of the ark into the holy city (II Sam. 6), and allusions to the rebellion of Absalom may, perhaps, be detected here or there. The possibilities suggested for later dates are too numerous to mention.

A most varied assortment of corrections of the received text might be offered (as the apparatus of the *Kittel* edition so amply demonstrates), but these emendations too often grow out of a measure of impatience in determining what the author could reasonably be thought to say or else out of an unduly critical attitude. Some few slight emendations, which our Notes will explain, will be resorted to in the following pages.

We suggest the following outline of this beautiful psalm:
a) He who comes to overthrow enemies and to help His own (vv. 1–6)
b) He who guided Israel through the wilderness (vv. 7–10)
c) He who gave them the land of Canaan (vv. 11–14)
d) He who chose Zion for His habitation (vv. 15–18)
e) He who subdues all His enemies (vv. 19–23)
f) He who is honored by the solemn worship at His sanctuary (vv. 24–27)
g) He who brings the mighty at His feet in adoration (vv. 28–31)
h) He who is so great and mighty as to deserve the praise of all the earth (vv. 32–35)

Heading: *To the Choir Director. Of David. A psalm. A song*

The two titles that designate the type of psalm that is involved read the same as they did in Ps. 67. This psalm, like Ps. 67, ends on the note of universal praise that is due to the Lord.

a) **He who comes to overthrow enemies and to help His own (vv. 1–6)**

1. *God arises, His enemies scatter;*
   Those who hate Him flee before Him.
2. *As smoke is driven away, so Thou drivest them away;*
   As wax melts before the fire, the wicked perish before God.

3. *But the righteous are joyful; they exult before God;*
   And they are jubilant with joy.
4. *Sing unto the Lord, make music to His name;*
   Cast up a highway for Him that rideth in the deserts—
   His name is Yah—and exult before Him.
5. *A father of the fatherless and a judge of widows*
   Is God in His holy dwelling,
6. *A God who gives desolate ones a home to dwell in;*
   He brings forth the prisoners into a happy existence;
   But the rebellious dwelt in a parched land.

1. The theme that the God who marches on to victory deserves to be blessed is developed in the first half of the psalm (vv. 1–18) with a reference to the works He performed in days of old. A historical sequence is quite naturally followed as the outline indicates: the wilderness wanderings, the conquest, the occupation of Jerusalem. Through it all runs the basic theme: God is on the march. It is only in v. 4b that this thought finds vocal expression. V. 1 already begins to move in this direction, for God is represented as arising and about to go into action. This thought is worded in terms of the old victory cry that was raised whenever the signal for the march was given by the guiding cloud as Num. 10:35 shows. Whereas in days of old the hortatory note predominated, the form used in the present quotation states an ever-valid truth which is practically the equivalent of the statement: When God arises, His enemies scatter, and those who hate Him flee before Him. On this high plane of confidence the whole psalm moves. There are enemies. They are strong. But over against God they avail nothing. The lucid figures used in v. 2 make the issue still more emphatic. With what ease the wind whisks smoke away! How readily wax melts before the heat of the fire! So the opposition is driven away and perishes.

3. The righteous know this, and it gives them confidence in the life-and-death struggle in which they are continually engaged. They "are joyful," and "they exult before God, and they are jubilant with joy." This is certainly their feeling, not so much because of the discomfiture of the wicked as because of the victory of God's cause.

4. With this as the obvious groundwork on which the psalmist stands he begins blessing the Almighty Victor in the words of the summons here given. His thoughts seem quite naturally to revert to the ancient days when the Israelites went through the wildernesses or "deserts," and God rode on before them, He whose "name is Yah" (abbreviated form of Yahweh). In retrospect his own are called upon to join the jubilant throng on the march by preparing a way before him (a thought that is often found in Is. 40:3; 57:14; 62:10) and exulting

before Him. With a genial turn of thought which is indicative of the kindly attitude of the writer's theology the mighty Lord is represented, not as using what power He has in utterly destroying His foes so much as in helping the poor and needy. A worthy title for Him is "Father of the fatherless" and another, "Judge of the widows." This He is, for He does not remain immured in His "holy dwelling." He is a God who acts for those who are in need of divine action. Besides, He delights in kindly works such as "giving desolate ones a home to dwell in," which can also mean that He "gives the lonely woman a house full of children" as *Luther* translates. He also brings forth those who are innocently imprisoned by placing them into a happy existence.

But there was and had to be another aspect of His activity: that He made it come to pass that "the rebellious dwelt in a parched land," that is to say, that rebellious and wicked generation who saw all the mighty works the Lord performed in those days and hardened their hearts by continually murmuring against Him. In all justice, what other lot could be theirs than that they had to remain in the wilderness as this euphemistic statement says, which means of course: die there? With a brilliant sweep of thought the poet has led us through the first major period of Israel's history by showing us God's triumphant march and by blessing His holy name for it.

b) **He who guided Israel through the wilderness (vv. 7–10)**

7. *O God, when Thou didst go forth before Thy people,*
   When Thou didst march through the desert; (Selah).
8. *The earth did quake, the heavens also dropped rain at the presence of God—*
   There at Sinai—at the presence of God, the God of Israel.
9. *A rain of gifts freely given Thou didst sprinkle upon Thy inheritance, O God;*
   And that which was wearied Thou didst restore.
10. *The flock settled there;*
    By Thy goodness Thou, O God, didst make provision for the needy.

7. We find ourselves in the midst of the events of the wilderness wanderings. God is still thought of as being on His victorious march— "Thou didst go forth." He is leading His people on their perilous journey "through the desert." More particularly it is for the moment the glorious experience at Sinai as the parenthetical statement ("there at Sinai") indicates. The quaking of the earth at God's presence is noted in the original account (Exod. 19:18). No mention is made there of the falling of rain even as the presence of a great multitude of

the heavenly hosts is not referred to (Deut. 33:2). The earthquake seems to be considered an indication of God's majesty (Ps. 104:32).

9. The thought turns to the gracious gifts that were rained upon God's people: manna, quails, and water; and it reflects upon the strength that He imparted to the wearied ones on their long journeyings. After the somewhat harassing period of the first two months with all its strain and excitement God settled His flock (v. 10) there and gave it better than a year of rest to become reassured and to collect its thoughts. This experience is quite aptly summed up in the words, "By Thy goodness Thou, O God, didst make provision for the needy." All this, too, constitutes a series of mighty acts for which God, the victorious Leader, is to be richly blessed.

c) He who gave them the land of Canaan (vv. 11–14)

11. *The Lord uttered a word;*
Great was the company of women who spread the good tidings.
12. *Kings with their armies fled, yea, they fled;*
But the mistress of the house divided the spoil.—
13. *"Will you lie among the sheepfolds?"—*
Wings of a dove covered with silver and its pinions with yellow gold.
14. *When the Almighty scattered kings there,*
Snow fell on the Black Mountain.

11. The first brief statement seems to be intended to be sententious. When "the Lord uttered a word," this may be described as "one mighty word hurled from heaven like a thunder-clap" (*Maclaren*), implying that this utterance alone sufficed to take care of the opposition that was involved. For the section before us moves on in point of time to the occupation of the land by the Israelites. "Kings with their armies" stood ready to oppose Israel (v. 12). But when the Almighty One's word of victory had been spoken, the battle was ended, and the time had come to spread the news of the victory: "Great was the company of women who spread the good tidings." The women, left behind when their husbands went to battle, are the ones who spread the report like wildfire throughout the villages and from town to town. The substance of the news was: "They fled, yea, they fled." In each of the campaigns waged by Joshua the result was the same. In each case the next step could be taken: "The mistress of the house divides the spoil." Strictly speaking, she is "the beauty of the house." Cf., Judg. 5:30, to which event our passage seems to be an allusion.

13. We need not deny the fact that this verse has caused untold difficulty. We shall offer a possible and, we believe, plausible interpretation. The first half of the verse, obviously based on Judg. 5:16,

rebukes those who, like Reuben, refused to take their part in the exploit and seems here to be spoken as a kind of parenthesis to all such. The second half of the verse seems to be a description of some of the spoil, which the preceding verse speaks of as being in process of distribution. Only one of the costly items involved is mentioned by way of illustration.

14. A sort of summary description of the entire period is offered in v. 14. Again the verse has its difficulties. We offer a possible and reasonable explanation. The figure aims to show the effectiveness of the power of the "Almighty" who engaged in conflict in behalf of His people. He, indeed, scattered kings with their armies in such a fashion that at a later date their bleached bones lay white amid the dark trees of the forests that covered the mountainsides. There may have been areas in Canaan where such a sight was actually to be seen. Cf. also *Iwry,* JBL, 1952, III, p. 161ff., and *Schroeder,* ZAW. 1914, I, 70–72.

The victorious King is on the march!

d) He who chose Zion for His habitation (vv. 15–18)

15. *O mount of God, O mount of Bashan,*
    O mount of many peaks, O mount of Bashan,
16. *Why do you look askance, O mount of many peaks, at the mount*
    which God desired for His abode?
    Yea, the Lord will dwell there forever.
17. *The chariots of God are ten thousand times thousand twice told;*
    The Lord came from Sinai into His sanctuary.
18. *Thou didst ascend on high; Thou didst lead away captives;*
    Thou didst receive gifts among men;
    Yea, the rebellious who are destined to dwell with the Lord God.

15. The thoughts now center on the appointment of Mt. Zion as the place of God's sanctuary. For that selection involved more than the choice of an expedient place for the location of the ark of the covenant. At that time God came and took up His dwelling in that holy mountain. The comparative insignificance of the mountain which stands but a few hundred feet above the adjacent valley does not militate against this spiritual prominence of Zion. The mountains with which Zion is contrasted are the peaks of Hermon, which lie on the northern fringe of Bashan and tower more than 9,000 feet above sea level. By a bold figure these snow-capped peaks are described as "looking askance" at the holy mount. True, Mt. Hermon is impressive; it deserves to be called "a mount of God," for it is God who gave the mountains their height and their dignity. But by His own choice God, who delights in using the lowly and insignificant, "desired" Zion "for

His abode" and has promised His own that He will not forsake His sanctuary. This choice of His, like the exodus and the occupation of the land, is a mighty act of God, the Victor, which is written large in Israel's history.

17. The past—Sinai—and the present—occupation of Zion—are combined as two consecutive acts of major importance as though the things that lay between them were relatively secondary. For this reason it is said: "The Lord came from Sinai into His sanctuary." But that men may not get the impression that the choice of so lowly a hill means some kind of abdication or relinquishing of His might and dignity, the Lord is in this connection described as being attended by "the chariots of God, ten thousand twice told." Who can number the heavenly hosts that attend the almighty King?

18. In a connection as clear as that in which this verse appears God's "ascending on high" cannot refer to anything other than His taking up abode on His holy mount of Zion. Jer. 31:12 uses the same word for the "heights of Zion" that our writer uses for "on high." The days intervening between the days of Joshua and those of David are passed by as a mere moment of time. God is pictured as coming from the conquest of the land to occupy the mountain at Jerusalem. He is bringing captives won in war with Him—the customary picture of the victor. Many gifts that were presented in token of submission are in His hands. "Yea, the rebellious who are destined to dwell with the Lord God" are pictured as being subdued, whether they willingly accept the Lord's gracious rule or not. All this is highly figurative language that is designed to portray how complete the victory of the Lord was.

Again the note has been sounded: Blessed be the God who marches on to victory!

Paul's use of this verse in Eph. 4:8 is somewhat free ("to men" for "among men") but entirely in the spirit of the passage. He apparently regards the Lord's victorious entrance into Jerusalem as a type or figure of Christ's triumphant entry into the heavens, laden with the fruits of His encounter, fruits which He is ready to bestow on His own.

We come to the second half of the psalm which develops the theme in reference to the present and the future. The first emphasis is the same as that which was first in part one: He is the one who subdues His enemies. This aspect of the case is developed more fully.

e) **He who subdues all His enemies (vv. 19-23)**

19. *Blessed be the Lord day for day,*
   Who bears us up, the God of our salvation. Selah.

20. *The true God is for us a God of salvation;*
    Unto God the Lord belongs deliverance from death.
21. *Surely God crushes the head of His enemies,*
    The hairy crown of him who walks on in his guilt.
22. *The Lord has spoken: "I will bring them back from Bashan;*
    I will bring them back from the depths of the sea;
23. *That you may bathe your foot in blood;*
    That the tongue of your dogs may have its portion from the enemy."

19. As the close of the psalm draws nearer, the exhortations to bless and praise the Lord become more frequent. The mercies of God are here thought of as being sufficient in number to make it proper for us to bless him "day for day." The reason assigned for such blessings is that He who is so mighty stoops so far down as to "bear us up," and thus He well merits the description "the God of our salvation."

20. The individual and the nation can well make this confession their own: "The true God is for us a God of salvation." As the psalmist reflects upon the works He can achieve, he mentions no less a one than that He can also work "deliverance from death." He can help when deathly sickness has befallen one. But He can also help when death has snuffed out life. For we "shall not die but live."

21. In contrast with such deliverance is the treatment that God will give the enemies who defy and oppose Him. Their overthrow will be total. God is represented as "crushing the head of such." The figure may be drastic, but the point is clear. When the parallel passage dwells upon "the hairy crown" of certain ones it seems to refer to the custom of having men of distinction wear their hair exceptionally long (Deut. 32:42). But it is never the mere lust of revenge that is to be gratified. These persons are thought of as deserving the destruction they receive because they "walk on in their guilt." The verse might contain a veiled allusion to Absalom, were it not for the fact that it would seem almost impossible that such a statement could come from the pen of David.

22. The statement here attributed to God is like certain others (cf., II Sam. 15:25) that are to be thought of as a deduction that is made on the basis of certain things that the Lord did: through His acts He spoke. The substance of His pronouncement is that, though His enemies might have taken refuge in the far eastern fringes of Bashan, or might have fled to "the depths of the sea," He will, nevertheless, bring them back and inflict a drastic vengeance upon them so that the feet of the executioner step into their blood, or the very scavenger dogs feed upon them as they did on Jezebel of old (I Kings 21:23).

f) He who is honored by the solemn worship at His sanctuary (vv. 24–27)

24. Men have seen the processions in Thy honor, O God,
    The processions for my God, my King in the sanctuary.
25. First came the singers, then the players on instruments,
    Between them maidens playing timbrels.
26. Bless God in the assemblies,
    The Lord, you who are of the fountain of Israel.
27. There is Benjamin, the youngest, yet having dominion over them,
    The princes of Judah in their throng,
    The princes of Zebulon, the princes of Naphthali.

Further to picture what manner of God the Lord is, the poet takes us into the sanctuary to witness the solemn type of worship that may be observed there, more particularly the processions that might be held on any great festival or on lesser occasions. There may be nothing startling about the scene described. Other processions that were held at other temples might be equally impressive. The point at issue is that the greatness for which the Lord is being blessed is of such a nature that it distinctly calls for some kind of visible demonstration such as the processions that Israel was wont to have. It fact, the psalm may even have been designed to be used primarily on the occasion of solemn processions. Such ceremonies in honor of the true God could not but impress all who had shared in them. They would recall how (v. 25) the singers led the way; how the players upon instruments followed; how maidens playing timbrels moved about here and there. Such public confession and adoration God deserves "in the assemblies" (v. 26), and all who derive their life in faith from Him, "the Fountain of Israel," should offer them. By way of example for the rest four tribes are mentioned, two of the south, two of the north, implying that all between have been seen participating in such demonstrations.

With the widely varied history of the various tribes a matter of record, a thoughtful observer could not avoid having details of the memorable past of the tribes come to mind such as the fact that Benjamin, though he was the least in point of numbers and the youngest, yet had in the days of Saul held "dominion over them" all. Another heartening thing is the fact that the "princes" from all tribes vied in giving due honor to the Lord.

g) He who brings the mighty at His feet in adoration (vv. 28–31)

28. Command Thy might, O God;
    Display Thy strength, O God, in regard to that which Thou hast wrought for us

29. *From Thy Temple towering over Jerusalem.*
    Kings shall bear gifts to Thee.
30. *Rebuke the beast among the reeds, the herd of bulls with the*
    calves of the people,
    That cast themselves down with pieces of silver;
    He has scattered the people who delight in war.
31. *Princes shall come out of Egypt;*
    Ethiopia shall eagerly bring its full hands to God.

28. An added reason is given for blessing the great God who marches on to victory: It is He who causes the mighty in adoration to fall at His feet. Instead of making the simple statement that God does such things, the stronger form is used, the imperative of the verb which summons God to give evidence of His strength. That is what the figure means, "command Thy strength." All that God has ever wrought for His people is at stake and must be upheld. Quite appropriately the writer asks that the demonstration of God's power emanate from the Temple which towers over Jerusalem, for that is the place of His residence among His people. In brief, the result of such acts on His part will be that "kings shall bear gifts to Him."

30. It is more than likely that "the beast among the reeds" is nothing other than a figurative description of Egypt under the figure of either an alligator or a hippopotamus. In any case, it is less the individual nation that is referred to since Egypt represents all nations that are hostilely minded. Then "the herd of bulls with the calves of the people" would represent the lesser nationalities. As a result of such rebuke they are pictured as prostrating themselves with gifts in token of submission, and those that delight in war are thought of as being rendered impotent by being scattered. Thus the Lord maketh the devices of the heathen of none effect. The picture is completed (v. 31) by a description of delegates in the person of princes from distant nations coming to offer their submission in the spirit of Is. 2:1ff.; 60:1ff.

h) **He who is so great and mighty as to deserve the praise of all the earth (vv. 32–35)**

32. *Sing unto God, you kingdoms of the earth;*
    Make music to the Lord. Selah.
33. *To Him that rideth upon the heaven of heavens, which are from*
    of old;
    Lo, He utters His voice, a mighty voice.
34. *Ascribe power unto God; His majesty is over Israel*
    And His power in the clouds.

35. *Awe-inspiring is God in His sanctuary;*
    The God of Israel is He that giveth strength and power to His
      people;
    Blessed be God!

32. Since the theme is, "Blessed be God," it appears that the writer would end his psalm on a deep and strong note of praise, a token of praise in which all the earth has its part. So "the kingdoms of the earth" are bidden to sing and make music. What follows is designed to impress upon them that He whose praise they hymn is most eminently deserving of whatever praise they may tender, for He is the one (v. 33) who rideth on to victory—again the note of God's triumphal march —across the heaven of heavens which are from of old; He is the one who thunder with a mighty voice in the storm. For that is the force of the words, "Lo, He utters His voice, a mighty voice."

34. The kingdoms of the earth are summoned freely to confess the Lord's omnipotence, for that is the meaning of "ascribe power unto God." As proof of this divine power of His the writer cites the fact that "His majesty is over Israel," reminding men that Israel's history is an accumulation of historical incidents which have displayed the majesty of Israel's God in such a manner that all the nations have seen tokens of it and must be led to confess that His mighty acts tower as mighty memorials even into the very clouds. So the psalm closes on the strong note of victory: "Awe-inspiring is God in His sanctuary; the God of Israel is He that giveth strength and power unto His people; blessed be God."

NOTES

2. It seems best to point the first word as a niphal, *kehinnadeph*.

4. "Yah" is the short form of the proper name Yahweh, which appears practically only in poetic passages. Every prominent divine name is used in the exuberance of the thought voiced by this psalm.

6. "Happy existence" is one way of translating the word *cosharoth*, which appears only here. It could be rendered "prosperity" (*RSV*) or *glueckliche Verhaeltnisse* (*KW*). "Chains" (*AV*) is a poor guess.

7. The "Selah" appears in unusual positions (vv. 7, 19, 32) but not inappropriately for it always marks an interlude of music at an important juncture of the thought.

8. The demonstrative *zeh* is used adverbially. This furnishes a better sense than "even Sinai itself" (*KJ*) or "yon Sinai" (*RSV*). Cf. *KS* 43.

9. A smoother sequence is obtained throughout if "Thy inheritance" is joined to the first clause, contrary to the accents.

14. The conclusions reads literally: "Snow fell on Salmon." But since this root appears to mean "black mountain" (cf. the German *Schwartzwald*), we have ventured to translate the word in order to clarify the figure involved even though the reference may be to Mt. Salmon that lies near Shechem (Judg. 9:48).

18. *Ba'adham* can scarcely mean "for men" (*AV*) or "in the man" (*AVm*). It must be rendered "among men," being merely one feature in a larger picture of the conqueror.

20. The article in *ha'el* has about the force of "the *true* God."

24. "Thy processions" would quite obviously mean "processions in Thy honor."

28. Without changing more than the vowel points we arrive at the imperative "command," which far more readily fits into the whole picture.

30. Unless one adds "from Thy temple," etc., to the preceding sentence, an impossible thought develops which defies exposition.

Psalm 69

THE PRAYER OF A MAN SUFFERING BECAUSE OF HIS ZEAL FOR THE LORD'S HOUSE

BECAUSE OF THE obvious difficulties of determining the author and the circumstances under which this psalm was written some commentators have despaired of answering the question, Who wrote it? *Kirkpatrick* makes a sturdy defense of authorship by Jeremiah by referring especially to passages like Jer. 9:18ff.; 12:1ff., 15:10ff.; 17:12ff.; 18:18ff.; 20:7ff.; and adding that 15:15 might be taken as a motto for the psalm. Despite many other possibilities that have been suggested we still feel that the suggestion offered by the Hebrew text has the most to commend it—"of David." We shall attempt to remove some of the major objections at those points where they are suggested by the text. The claim that the psalmist speaks for the congregation and not as an individual, a view that is advocated also by *Hengstenberg,* strikes us as being too artificial. There is too much of vivid experience involved to allow for the colorless abstraction of the "collective I" in this psalm.

Psalm 69

The Messianic character of the psalm must come in for its share of attention. Next to Ps. 22 and 110, this psalm is the one that is most frequently cited in the New Testament. To attempt to make it a direct prophecy of the Christ is rendered impossible by the confession of wrong done, found in v. 5. The New Testament refers to this psalm in John 15:25; Rom. 15:3; 11:9, 10; Acts 1:20; Matt. 23:38. Each passage is so adequate, barring Matt. 23 and Rom. 11, which refer to matters that are more or less remotely connected with the life of Christ, that the issue must be faced. The simplest explanation seems to be that the writer, (we believe him to be David) becomes a typical example of the things that are experienced by all who are truly zealous for the Lord's house, and so what David experienced Christ may have experienced in certain obvious instances, for he is David's greater counterpart. The aptness of the language used, which is striking in each case, is due to the guiding influence of the Spirit of inspiration, who enlightened the writer in ways that were beyond his ability to appreciate at the time. The psalm may be classed as a lament. But these are hardly the words of a "frustrated reformer" (*Poteat*).

The distinctive feature of the psalm is, as our heading indicates, that it is the prayer of a man who is in great distress because he has boldly and openly championed the cause of the Lord and His house and has thus incurred the ill will of those who were inimical to such interests. True, the so-called "imprecatory" note comes to the fore very strongly in vv. 22–28—an issue with which we shall deal when we interpret that section.

The line of thought running through the psalm may be outlined as follows:
a) The psalmist's situation described (vv. 1–4)
b) A prayer for deliverance (vv. 5, 6)
c) The cause of his suffering (vv. 7–12)
d) An intensified plea (vv. 13–18)
e) A sad complaint (vv. 19–21)
f) A prayer for the overthrow of the ungodly enemies (vv. 22–28)
g) A sigh for help (v. 29)
h) Assurance of being answered (vv. 30–33)
i) A hopeful outlook for the future (vv. 34–36)

This outline does not indicate any particularly sharp logic in the matter of the sequence of thoughts, but in each division there is no painful break of the continuity.

The heading reads thus: *To the Choir Director. According to "Lilies." Of David.*

On "Lilies" Ps. 45 may be compared.

a) The psalmist's situation described (vv. 1–4)
1. *Save me, O God,*
   For the waters have threatened my very life.
2. *I have sunk into the mire of the deep where there is no foothold;*
   I have come into deep waters, and the wave has swept me away.
3. *I am worn out with my crying; my throat is hoarse;*
   My eye failed as I cried for my God.
4. *They that hate me without cause are more numerous than the hairs of my head;*
   They that would destroy me, being enemies of mine wrongfully, are powerful;
   Where I have not robbed, there I am expected to make restitution.

1. This is a partly figurative, partly literal description of the writer's lot. It is obvious from the opening statements that his case is very precarious. It's a matter of life and death for him. The figure of a man who has fallen or has been tossed into the waters is used to the full: the man's very life is in danger; the mire at the bottom of the waters holds him fast; the waters are deep; the waves are sweeping over him. The exact nature of the danger is not indicated. The grief caused by his anguish has worn him out (v. 3); he has cried himself hoarse in laying his needs before his God; his sight is impaired by much weeping.

4. Enemies are involved (v. 4), these mysterious enemies whose nature and character are not clearly defined in the psalm. They are very numerous. They are enemies without justification for enmity. They are bent on destruction. They make false accusations and demand restitution where no wrong has been done. Such charges are painful in the extreme.

b) A prayer for deliverance (vv. 5, 6)
5. *O God, Thou knowest my folly;*
   And my guilt is not hidden from Thee.
6. *Let not those be made ashamed through me who trust in Thee, O Lord God of hosts;*
   Let not those be disgraced through me who seek Thee, O God of Israel.

This prayer for deliverance is of an unusual character. Having just repudiated a false charge of wrong done, the writer freely confesses that he is not without guilt or folly. This is the obvious mark of frankness and uprightness. He has made his mistakes, which are in the nature of sins committed against God. He is well aware of the fact that God knows where he has erred. The precise substance of his prayer is that these sins of his may not in one way or another be allowed to do harm to those who trust in the Lord and seek Him. He knows well how damaging the unexpected effects of sin may be upon others, how those who, like him, love the Lord might have his mistakes cast into their teeth and thus be put to shame. Rare humility and insight are to be felt in this petition. Men pray thus when they have the burden of the welfare of souls on their heart.

c) **The cause of his suffering (vv. 7–12)**

7. *Because for Thy sake I have borne reproach;*
   Shame has covered my face.
8. *I have become estranged from my brethren,*
   An alien from my mother's sons.
9. *For zeal for Thy house has consumed me;*
   The reproaches of those who reproach Thee have fallen upon me.
10. *When I wept bitterly and fasted,*
    That became my reproach.
11. *When I made sackcloth my garment,*
    Then I became a byword to them.
12. *They that sit in the gate talk about me,*
    Also the ditties of the drunkards.

7. The writer explains what the cause of his suffering was. In a word it is "for Thy sake." He has identified himself with the Lord's cause; his opponents were antagonists of that cause. It could not but follow that the more vigorously he championed the cause of the godly, the more the opposition rose so that time and again they did things that brought it about that "shame covered his face." Even those of his intimate family turned against him by the unwarranted opposition of his foes (cf., Ps. 31:11; 27:10). "Mother's sons" are especially mentioned because as children of the same mother they would have been regarded as the closest of relatives in a day when bigamous marriages were a bit more common.

9. The "for Thy sake" is now elucidated a bit more fully: it is "zeal for Thy house." This may be thought of as zeal for all that the covenant religion stood for or as zeal for the very sanctuary itself. It is most likely that both factors were involved. This zeal was so strong that he could claim that it had consumed him, a feature which was never more perfectly exemplified than in the life and the ministry of Jesus (John 2:17). All who were in one way or another against the Lord of Israel would reproach this champion of the Lord's cause even as they expressed all their opposition to Him.

10. In the next three verses there are specific instances of the kind of taunts and reproaches that had to be borne (vv. 10–12). When the whole situation grieved the writer deeply, and he felt that it called

for some personal spiritual discipline such as fasting, which could be conducive to more effective prayer, immediately "that became [his] reproach." Whether his enemies used ridicule, or whether they made of his attitude an accusation that he was admitting himself to be in the wrong, is not indicated. Or when, on the other hand, he felt that this was an occasion that called for typical tokens of repentance on his part and theirs ("sackcloth"), then he "became a byword to them" because of this activity. Whatever course he followed, the opposition found some way of sharply criticizing him.

Matters had even gone so far that in the gate, where men congregated for the serious business of court trials and the like and for idle gossip when more serious matters had been disposed of—even there his case was being continually discussed. He was the talk of the town. To cap the climax, even in the taverns tipsy fellows composed "ditties" about him. It is not difficult to imagine how an upright and sincere soul would be deeply wounded by all such flippant treatment.

d) An intensified plea (vv. 13–18)

13. *But as for me, my prayer is unto Thee, O Lord, in an acceptable time;*
    O God, in the abundance of Thy steadfast love answer me in Thy saving faithfulness.
14. *Rescue me out of the mire lest I sink*
    That I may be delivered from them that hate me and out of the deep waters.
15. *Let not the flood of waters sweep me away;*
    Let not the deep swallow me up;
    Let not the pit shut its mouth over me.
16. *Answer me, O Lord, for Thy steadfast love is good;*
    According to Thy abundant mercy turn to me.
17. *And hide not Thy face from Thy servant,*
    For I am in distress;
    Make haste to answer me.
18. *Draw near and save my life;*
    Because of my enemies release me.

All this opposition drives the psalmist to more earnest prayers, for he somehow realizes that, though he has not yet been heard, it is still an "acceptable time." And thus an intensified pleading follows. One petition after the other wells forth from his lips. Occasional pleas are intermingled, pleas that refer to some attribute of the Living God such as His steadfast love, His saving faithfulness, His abundant mercy. Or the plea may take the form of some description of the distress that is

Psalm 69

upon him: he is still in danger of sinking into the mire; he is in deep waters; his enemies still hate him; the waters are deep, and they threaten to sweep him away; the deep might swallow him up; the pit might shut its mouth over him; he is in distress. These are the major issues. One may well feel that from the point of view of divine mercy as God's saints know it would be well-nigh impossible for God to refuse such strong petitions.

e) A sad complaint (vv. 19-21)

19. *Thou knowest my reproach and my shame and my disgrace;*
    My foes are all known to Thee.
20. *Reproach has broken my heart, and I have trembled;*
    And I hoped for sympathy, but there was none, and for comforters, but I found none.
21. *Rather men put poison in my food;*
    And for my thirst they gave me vinegar to drink.

19. These three verses could be regarded as being a part of the intensified plea that immediately preceded, for they are in the nature of a sad complaint which appeals strongly to God's sympathetic interest which He has in His saints. All the misery of the distressing situation that is upon him he well knows is not unknown to God. A good name is a great treasure, and to be compelled to suffer dishonor instead is gallingly painful. So God also knows all the psalmist's foes without having them enumerated to bring them to His attention. The Hebrew is a bit stronger than our translation in that it says: "Before Thee are all my foes." Even if the foes take the attitude that the Almighty cannot know what they are perpetrating they are continually in His very sight. There is comfort in that fact, too.

20. The suffering that the disgrace entailed is stated forcefully in the words: "Reproach has broken my heart." When he adds, "And I trembled," it may well seem that this implies a trembling in anticipation of further insults and reproaches. How often have good men in their suffering experienced the truth of the next statement: "And I hoped for sympathy, but there was none, and for comforters, but I found none"! In fact, the very opposite took place to intensify his grief (v. 21). The initial statement of this verse is quite likely not to be taken literally when he says: "Men put poison in my food," or as it may also be translated: "They gave me poison for food" (*RSV*). This indicates that they continued their cruel attitude by deadly plots and schemes that stopped short at nothing. The parallel statement ("And for my thirst they gave me vinegar to drink") may also be figurative. When I hoped for refreshment or some relaxation, they intensified their

cruel treatment. Strangely, this part of the verse met with literal fulfilment in the agony of Jesus on the cross (Matt. 27:34, 48 and the parallels).

f) A prayer for the overthrow of the ungodly enemies (vv. 22–28)

22. *Let their table become a snare before them*
    And for those that are secure a trap.
23. *Let their eyes become darkened so that they cannot see*
    And make their loins to tremble continually.
24. *Pour out Thy indignation upon them*
    And let Thy hot anger overtake them.
25. *Let their camp be desolate*
    And let there be no inhabitant in their tents.
26. *For him whom Thou Thyself hast smitten they persecute;*
    And they chat about the grief of him whom Thou hast wounded.
27. *Add guilt to their guilt*
    And let them not have part in Thy righteousness.
28. *Let them be blotted out of the book of the living*
    And let them not be listed among the righteous.

We have entitled this section, "A prayer for the total overthrow of ungodly enemies." We believe this statement follows a middle course between the two possible extremes to be met in the treatment of these verses. Some Christians would subscribe to them as a model that is still to be followed. They even go so far as in some instances to use these words against their own enemies. Against such abuse the warning *Hengstenberg* is still much in place: "Such utterances coming from impious lips may become very impious." On the other hand, what is here spoken may be condemned with such harshness as utterly to fail to recognize what true merit lies in such utterances, as when men speak of "incandescent lust for revenge" (*gluehende Rachelust*) or of "being overwhelmed by the blind rage of cruel feelings of revenge." *Leslie* comes much nearer the truth of the matter when he remarks: "Here is hot emotion fired by the strong Semitic feeling that evil is self-destructive, that injustice comes back in retribution upon its perpetrator." *Maclaren's* sane remark may be added: "It is impossible to bring such utterances into harmony with the teachings of Jesus, and the attempt to vindicate them ignores plain facts and does violence to plain words. Better far to let them stand as a monument of the earlier stage of God's progressive revelation, and discern clearly the advance which Christian ethics has made on them."

To this must be added a few further considerations. It may well be presupposed that the writer had absolutely no hope of the conversion of these obdurate sinners. It is certain that he was also motivated very strongly by the desire to see them made utterly incapable of doing God's people any further harm. To charge him with unbridled revenge may be doing him a grievous injustice. With these cautions in mind, we may seek to understand the various statements offered by recalling that the New Testament cites with approval v. 25 as having some element of the prophetic in it and as having been fulfilled in the fate of Judas.

22. The figure involved in the expression, "Let their table become a snare before them," becomes clearer when it is recalled that tables were originally that which was spread on the ground to have food placed upon it. A man might well stumble over such an object or become entangled in it and so be snared by it. Aside from that, the table, which represents blessing and a source of strength and delight, is thought of as becoming the very opposite under the impact of God's displeasure. The second half of the verse adds the reminder that these wicked men have been living on in their security but will be caught as in a trap when God's judgment strikes them.

The remaining items may be summed up briefly. They represent various means by which God may make inveterate enemies harmless. The implication is not that every one of these disasters may befall every man among them. There is first total blindness or palsy (v. 23). Then there is the full measure of God's holy and righteous wrath which may descend upon them in whatever form it may please God to afflict them (v. 24). Or it may be that their very habitations will become desolate (*Luther, Behausung;* and *KJ* generalizes in like manner and renders, "habitation"; but *RSV* is more literal when it translates "camp"), and that their tents are without inhabitant, for the tribe has either become extinct or else all have been scattered by some calamity (v. 25). As a motivation for such dealings with them there is added a reminder as to how heartless they themselves have been in persecuting individuals whom God had afflicted or making such persons the object of idle chatter (there is no indication here that the psalmist was sick). Having been unfeeling themselves, there is no impropriety about having them dealt with without mercy (v. 26).

The next verse might be paraphrased so as to yield the sense that these guilty ones may be allowed to add guilt to their guilt—for what else can befall them if they do not repent?—until it becomes apparent that their ultimate fate is fully deserved (v. 27a). Such being the case, justification of the guilty is impossible (v. 27b). The last of these petitions is not as cruel as some interpreters would make it, for it asks only that the evildoers "be blotted out of the book of the living," that is to say, that their life may be brought to an end; and assuredly, if they continue to abound in evil deeds, no one would want them to be listed among the righteous so that they may be able to enjoy such blessings as those enjoy who have done well and good.

g) A sigh for help (v. 29)

29. *But as for me, who am afflicted and in pain,*
    Let Thy help safeguard me, O God.

This brief sigh is spoken in the spirit of the statement made in Ps. 130, "If Thou, Lord, shouldest mark iniquities, O Lord, who shall stand?" Having invoked the just judgment of God, the writer feels that, unless God's help safeguards him, there is much because of which he himself would have to suffer, and so he casts himself upon God's mercy. This is scarcely an attitude of self-righteousness!

h) Assurance of being answered (vv. 30–33)

30. *I will praise the name of God with a song*
    And will magnify Him with thanksgiving.
31. *And that will please the Lord more than an ox*
    Or a bullock with horns and hoofs.
32. *When the meek see this they will be glad;*
    You that seek God, let your hearts revive.
33. *For the Lord hears the poor;*
    And He has never ignored His prisoners.

As happens so often in the psalms, toward the end of their effort the assurance of being answered steals quietly upon the mind of God's humble servants, and the note of praise begins to predominate. This usually takes the form of a sort of vow which will, no doubt, usually have been kept in public praises offered in the sanctuary. The psalmist knows well that such true praise is the essence of worship, and, though sacrifices of prescribed victims was still the order of the day, such sacrificing itself gave no pleasure to God unless the true sentiments of the heart were also in evidence. What the saints of all times have felt keenly on this subject this writer expresses a bit more graphically by reminding his readers of the "bullock with horns and hoofs."

One effect of God's deliverance will be that which is in evidence in the case of the meek, men who were, perhaps, troubled by afflictions that were similar to those of the psalmist but could do nothing more than commit their cause into God's hands. They will take note of what has happened and will be glad and let their hearts revive after the dismal death that seemed to hang over them. Reduced to a general principle, it amounts to this: "The Lord hears the poor; and He has never ignored His prisoners." The latter term appears to be used figuratively and would scarcely warrant the conclusion that the writer had suffered incarceration.

i) A hopeful outlook for the future (vv. 34–36)
34. *Let heaven and earth praise Him,*
    The seas and everything that moves in them.
35. *For God will save Zion and will build the cities of Judah;*
    And men shall dwell there and possess it.
36. *And the descendants of His servants shall inherit it;*
    And they that love His name shall dwell there.

The writer's thoughts rise to a still higher level, and in addition to hope for himself he has a more hopeful outlook for others. He recognizes that he himself is in all his life and thinking closely united with all the rest of the people of God. What had happened, let us say in the uprising of Absalom and the subsequent disorders, had apparently done great harm to the nation; figuratively speaking, "the cities of Judah" had been devastated (v. 35), and Zion's safety had been endangered. In the deliverance that he himself had experienced he finds a token of the restoration of all that Zion had lost during this tragic period and expresses the hope that men shall again "dwell there and possess it."

One need not be completely literalistic at this point and insist that statements such as these may be understood only in connection with the experiences of the Babylonian Captivity. So also shall succeeding generations dwell in the great city of God and contribute to its prosperity (v. 36). All of these things are achievements of the God of Israel which are of such magnitude that "heaven and earth" may well praise Him, "the seas and everything that moves in them." For only a mighty chorus of praise will do justice to so magnificent a deliverance.

NOTES

3. The subject of *meyachel* is not identical with the subject of the preceding verb but is derived from the suffix of the previous subject. *KS* 421g.

4. "Being enemies of mine wrongfully" is literally, "enemies of mine without cause," and could also be translated "lying enemies of mine" as *Weiser* renders it. Because the concluding clause has *'az*, ("there") the preceding *'asher* should be translated "where" to establish the correlation (*KS* 387g).

6. "My folly" has *le* to mark the direct object (*KS* 289i).

10. Though the construction of the clauses is "and . . . and," the first *waw* may well be regarded as introducing a conditional clause. "That became," neuter, as *KS* 323f explains.

13. In vv. 13 and 14 the modifying phrases might be rearranged as the *Kittel* text suggests, although this is not necessary.

15. Though *be'er* usually means "well," it is permissible here to regard it as merely another pointing for *bo'r,* the usual word for "pit."

21. *AV,* generalizing a bit on a term about which we are not yet too certain and following the lead of the *Septuagint,* translated: "They gave me also gall for my meat," as did also *Luther.* "Poison" appears to be the meaning of *ro'sh.* "They gave me to drink" is one of those instances where the *waw* consecutive and the imperfect are separated by another word. (*KS* 368i).

26. "They chat" is an imperfect like the one just referred to in v. 21.

28. In justification of the translation "book of the living" rather than "book of life" it should be noted that *chayyim* and *tsaddiqim* are parallel, both are nouns.

32. Though *ra'u* is the perfect, it may still be used conditionally (*KS* 390q).

Psalm 70

For Psalm 70 see Ps. 40:13–17.

Psalm 71

"DO NOT CAST ME OFF IN OLD AGE"

AS THE READER moves along into the body of this psalm, it becomes apparent to him that the writer is in some form of trouble, for he keeps crying out for deliverance in this lament of his. In fact, such pleas alternate with statements that breathe trust and confidence in God as a deliverer. There is a group of evildoers who lie in wait for him to destroy him, and it also becomes clear that he is an old man who has long enjoyed God's favor and anticipates still enjoying it. This last feature may be said to be distinctive of the psalm as our heading also indicates.

We shall not be unduly disturbed by the fact that the little poem is said to be defective in literary composition: somewhat unclear arrangement of thoughts, lack of originality, lack of distinctive excellence.

Psalm 71

The psalm is designed to portray a life situation which may have been of such a nature as to make logical arrangement of thoughts according to some outline a bit difficult. But no one denies the psalm its religious value. It is commended for its warmth and devoutness of godly feeling, and rightly so. Here is a man who clings to God with every fibre of his being; as he has done from his youth, so he does now.

The fact that this is a psalm which is composed of many little fragments taken from other psalms is also rather obvious. To be more precise, vv. 1–3 are but a modification of Ps. 31:1–3; vv. 5, 6 bear a close resemblance to Ps. 22:9, 10; and vv. 12, 13 involve echoes of Ps. 35:22; 40:13, 14; 22:11; 38:21, 22; 35:4, 26; 109:29. But the piecing together of these sections is done so naturally that one cannot but feel that the originals that were borrowed had become so thoroughly a part of the man writing this psalm that the use of these elements came naturally to him. The combination of them is most skillfully done.

It is not very likely that physical illness was a major factor among the issues that troubled the writer as those commentators contend who find "sickness-psalms" at every turn. Nor is it very likely that the psalm refers to the congregation rather than to an individual. Its tone is too intimately personal.

Since it appears without an indication of authorship, quite an array of candidates has been suggested, among whom Jeremiah might deserve the preference if anyone does. For there are numerous points of contact between his life and the situation here described. But even this guess at authorship is precarious.

It is to be freely admitted that the psalm defies division according to a sharply defined pattern. No two commentators divide the psalm in the same way. It seems to burden the psalm with the least encumbrance if it is thought of as consisting of two equal parts.

a) The plea of an aged saint of God (vv. 1–12)

1. *In Thee, O Lord, have I taken refuge;*
   Let me never be put to shame!
2. *In Thy righteousnes deliver me and rescue me;*
   Incline Thy ear unto me and save me.
3. *Be unto me a strong dwelling To which I may always resort.*
   Thou hast given commandment to save me, for Thou art my rock
      and my fortress.
4. *O my God, deliver me from the hand of the wicked,*
   From the power of the evildoer and the violent man.
5. *For Thou art my hope, O Lord,*
   My confidence, O Lord, from my youth.

6. *Upon Thee have I braced myself from birth;*
   Since I was born Thou art my deliverer;
   My praise is continually of Thee.
7. *I have become as a wonder to many;*
   But Thou art my strong refuge.
8. *My mouth is filled with Thy praise*
   And with Thy glory all the day.
9. *Do not cast me off in the time of old age;*
   When my strength fails, do not forsake me.
10. *For my enemies have spoken against me;*
    They that seek my life have consulted together,
11. *Saying: "God has forsaken him, pursue and seize him,*
    For there is no deliverer."
12. *O God, be not far from me;*
    O my God, make haste to help me!

1. In the first six verses pleas and assertions of confidence in God's help keep alternating. It is only when we come to v. 5 that a reference is made to the fact that this man has held close to his God from the days of youth, a thought that is at once developed more fully: since he was born he has had confidence in his God. That is to say, he cannot remember a time when he strayed away from this confidence in his God. V. 6b expresses this more vividly in the original as most versions indicate: "Thou art He who took me from my mother's womb" (*RSV*). Though praise had previously been implied here or there it does not become vocal prior to this point (v. 6c): "My praise is continually of Thee."

7. Having begun to reflect upon his previous life, the writer sums it up from another point of view: "I have become a wonder to many." "Wonder" could be understood in either the good or the bad sense, that is to say, it could be applied to a man in whose life the marvelous guidance of God has been plainly in evidence; or to a man whose heavy crosses and strange burdens made him stand out in an unusual way as a victim of God's judgment. Though the latter may be preferred because of the seeming contrast with the second half of the verse ("but Thou art my strong refuge") it is, perhaps, best to retain both possibilities. No matter how you view this man's life, the wonder of God's dealings with him is in evidence.

8. Since God's powerful and gracious guidance, even when He seemed to be leading the psalmist along a very difficult road, is much in evidence, it is but natural that the writer stresses the fact that he has themes for God's continual praise and cannot exhaust them. Viewed thus, the declarative form of the verse is to be preferred to the form that makes it a prayer: "Let my mouth be filled," etc.

Psalm 71

9. There follows a prayer (v. 9), which has been well prepared for by what preceded, that God might sustain this petitioner also throughout his old age. When his strength fails, may God not fail him. The immediate motivation of this prayer is the fact that enemies are lurking in the background who have prepared plans to close in on him, should an opportunity present itself. To them it seems that God has forsaken him, and thus there is no deliverer. God, the writer is sure, cannot let his enemies succeed. Therefore, we note his closing petition: "Be not far from me; make haste to help me." God will surely stand by him who had all his life stood by the side of God.

h) His plea repeated with greater confidence (vv. 13–24)
13. *My adversaries shall be put to shame and consumed;*
    They that seek my hurt shall be covered with reproach and dishonor.
14. *But I will hope continually*
    And will add more and more to all Thy praise.
15. *My mouth shall declare Thy righteousness, Thy salvation*
        all day long;
    For they are more than I can count.
16. *I will go my way in the strength of the Lord God;*
    I will make mention of Thy righteousness, Thine alone.
17. *O God, Thou hast taught me from my youth;*
    And I still declare Thy wonderful works.
18. *Now also when I am old and gray-headed, O God, forsake me not*
    Till I proclaim Thy power to this generation, Thy strength to
        all who shall come, and Thy righteousness.
19. *O God, the great works Thou hast done reach to the heavens;*
    O God, who is like unto Thee?
20. *Thou, who hast made us to see many and sore troubles, wilt revive us again;*
    From the depths of the earth Thou wilt bring us up again.
21. *Do Thou increase my greatness*
    And comfort me again.
22. *I will also praise Thee with the harp, namely, Thy faithfulness,*
        my God;
    I will sing praise to Thee with the lyre, O Holy One of Israel.
23. *My lips shall exult when I sing praise to Thee,*
    Also my soul which Thou hast rescued.
24. *My tongue shall talk of Thy righteousness all the day long;*
    For they have been put to shame and confounded who seek to do
        me harm.

13. These are practically the same thoughts that were expressed in the first half of the psalm. One new thought appears at the beginning of this section, that of the confusion of his enemies. The writer does not wish it; he predicts it. But he on his part anticipates living on after they have been overthrown and adding more and more to the praises of the Lord. And surely, in the course of a long lifetime in which God's praise was often on his lips much praise must have been uttered by him. This praise will become vocal in two areas (15): it concerns itself with God's always dependable fairness or righteousness, and with the many instances in which he has brought about one form or another of salvation for body and for soul.

16. The opening statement of this verse, despite its seeming clearness, poses a problem in its wording: "I will go my way." This could mean that the psalmist proposes to come to the sanctuary bearing offerings for the righteous deeds of God which he purposes to commemorate. Those interpreters that find a liturgical suggestion wherever they can would favor this view. In view of the fact that an old man is speaking, who has all but run his course, some writers interpret the verb to mean, "I shall come home," i.e., to my eternal home. It seems most suitable to translate the Hebrew verb "go my way" which implies that from here on he shall follow his prescribed course as long as God gives him days to live. In the rich strength which God supplies he will carry on.

17. The portion of the prayer that follows, which asks for support in old age, now (vv. 17, 18) sounds the special note of spending whatever time God may yet grant him in making Him and His works known to the present and the coming generations. When he says that God has taught him from his youth he appears to have in mind all the godly instruction in the Word of God that he was privileged to receive. For when that Word is taught, God teaches man through it. The psalmist is a man of keen theological insight.

19. As he thus moves along in his prayer the psalmist is inclined more and more in the direction of praise of God as v. 19 testifies. He sees God's mighty works that were manifest in his life towering high into the heavens. These are the works that he will teach to the younger generation. As this assurance grows upon him, he also becomes more confident that God will revive all those of the people of God who, like him, have suffered affliction. He is a man whose thinking and fortunes are tied up with the rest of God's people. So the plural seems quite natural: "Thou wilt revive *us* again," even as it was He who let the nation gravitate into affliction. When he describes this revival as bringing them up again from "the depths of the earth," that expression may

well refer to Sheol, into which they had as good as descended, which is merely a figurative way of saying: We were as good as dead.

When the writer prays: "Do Thou increase my greatness," this might, indeed, appear to be a selfish prayer; but it dare not be divorced from its connection. Since he himself and the nation are being restored, it might well be possible that the writer asks that he may be granted such strength as he needs under the new circumstances to fill his role well.

From this point onward resolution to praise the Lord occupies all the singer's thoughts: the different types of it that he proposes to offer; the musical accompaniment that he shall employ; what his lips shall say and his soul express. He is resolved: it shall be exuberant praise, for only such praise is worthy of "the Holy One of Israel" (cf., Is. 6:3).

NOTES

8. The fact that the psalm "does not adhere strictly to the classical form of a lament" is by some interpreters regarded as proof of literary inferiority. It is equally logical to conclude that this is a mark of originality.

Psalm 72

THE RIGHTEOUS KING

THIS PSALM bears the superscription, "of Solomon." After the analogy of other superscriptions this can mean only that its authorship is being attributed to Solomon. This possibility is usually rejected on the presupposition that Solomon would, if he had written this psalm, be expecting the people to use this prayer, prepared by himself, in behalf of himself. This is judged to be most improper. Yet if there is a reason for believing that Solomon knew of the unique destiny of the house of David, as II Sam. 12:7ff. abundantly indicates, such a prayer could well be interpreted to imply that he was teaching the nation to pray for the realization of the divinely appointed destiny of his father's house. Aside from this consideration, a king might devise prayers for the success of his reign if these prayers did not overstep the bounds of propriety as these certainly do not.

More important is the question, Is this psalm Messianic? Some commentators brush this question aside as if it scarcely deserved mention.

Others dispose of it with a gesture of impatience as though it had now been finally established that this can be only a psalm of petition for the success of some monarch's reign in Israel. However, there is much to be said for the Messianic interpretation. There is, first of all, the consistent tradition stemming from the ancient Jewish interpretation. For the *Targum* renders the opening line: "O God, give the precepts of judgment to King Messiah." Throughout the centuries the Christian Church held unwaveringly to the same conviction. Then there is the prominent fact that the nation of Israel was aware of the unique destiny of the house of David from the time of this monarch onward as II Sam. 7, above alluded to, indicates. Nor is there a reason for questioning the historicity of the event and the passage alluded to. If Solomon also knew of the divine promises with regard to the future of the line from which he stemmed, a prayer such as this is most reasonably attributed to him.

There is a grammatical factor that dare not be ignored, and that is the fact that in the Hebrew there is a basic difference between forms that are to be rendered by the optative and those that are to be thought of as presents or futures (although in both instances imperfect verb forms are involved). Although this distinction is frequently blurred, it is still true that the difference dare not be ignored. We have, therefore, rendered regular imperfect forms as futures when nothing in the context appeared to indicate that they should be regarded as optatives; and clear instances of jussives we have translated as optatives. Though even thus the decision is somewhat difficult to make, it may be noted that a kind of rhythmic pattern appears: first a description of what kind of king this divinely instructed ruler will be (vv. 1–7), followed by a prayer that his rule may be effective the world over (vv. 8–11); then again a description of how he shall deal with the lowliest and the helpless (vv. 12–14), followed again by a prayer for success (vv. 15–17). Prediction, prayer; prediction, prayer—that is the rhythmical pattern.

Yet we do not believe that the Messianic element is of such a nature that the psalm is pure prediction. The reigning monarch of Israel stands in the forefront, the Messianic King stands in the background. Both are in the picture by design. The psalm was to be used as a prayer for Israel's king: Solomon at first and others of the house of David as time went on. But the higher levels indicated in the psalm pointed beyond the temporal ruler to the ideal one who was to come even as a similar blend of the two concepts appears in the original passage, II Sam. 7: 12ff.

Lastly there is the obvious correspondence between the thought suggested by v. 10 about gifts being offered to this king and the coming of the Wise Men (Matt. 2). Though the New Testament nowhere makes

Psalm 72

allusion to this psalm, is it a requirement of Messianic characterization that the New Testament pedantically label each passage as referring to the Christ before we may allow for deeper implications? Least of all are we impressed by the remarks that there are many other and greater attributes of the Messianic King known from prophecy which the writer fails to refer to in this psalm. Cannot one prominent attribute of the Messiah be chosen and elaborated at length, just to show its tremendous possibilities?

1. *O God, give the king Thy principles of judgment*
   And Thy righteousness to the king's son.
2. *He shall govern Thy people with righteousness*
   And Thy poor with justice.
3. *The mountains shall produce prosperity for the people*
   And also the hills, by means of righteousness.
4. *He shall defend the rights of the afflicted among the people;*
   He shall deliver the children of the poor;
   And he shall crush the oppressor.
5. *Men shall fear Thee as long as the sun endures*
   And as long as the moon throughout all generations.
6. *He shall come down like rain upon mown fields,*
   As showers richly watering the land.
7. *In his days the righteous shall flourish*
   And abundance of prosperity until the moon be no more.

1. The pattern followed in the thought expressed is instructive. The first verse is a prayer for the king; the remaining verses of the section tell what shall be the result of having the king endowed with the attributes that the prayer specifies. In vv. 2–7 we might have used simple futures ("he *will* govern," etc.). We have used instead the stronger form (*"shall"*) in order to make the predictive character of the section clearer.

The gift sought for the king is "principles of judgment," which is most likely a reference to the laws and ordinances which God gave to Israel. For if the king knows what God expects of His people he will on his part be able to determine wisely how he should order and direct his government. These principles of judgment are at the same time an expression of divine "justice." And thus, if the king is endowed with these qualities, he will rule as God's effective and true representative. For all rule and justice, in the last analysis, stems from God. Cf., Deut. 1:17; Exod. 21:6; 22:7, 8; Prov. 8:15; II Chron. 19:6.

Such just rule will never be harsh; it will never be lax. *Mowinckel* translates: "Give the king Thy gift of judgeship (*Richtergabe*)." It is the ideal to which every king should aspire. It is, therefore, not to be wondered at that there follows a description as to how men will fare under such a rule. True, no king in Israel or Judah ever realized the high ideal here indicated. Consequently the passage may well be thought of as pointing beyond itself to the ideal fulfillment and the Fulfiller. The "king's son" is in this instance identical with the "king" of the first member of the verse. It merely adds the thought that the king is of royal extraction, not an upstart. To emphasize the royal descent is quite natural in the case of the unique line of David.

2. The first result noted in the description that follows is that the rule over the entire nation will be marked by "righteousness." Since the term "judge" is synonymous with the term "ruler" or "governor," we have preferred to use one of the latter. "Righteousness" always involves the reward of the good as well as the punishment of the wicked. In the second member the poor, or the meek, or the defenceless are mentioned in particular as being those who benefit from the judicious rule of the king. That is done to demonstrate the perfection of this rule the more drastically. For the poor and defenceless are under average circumstances, the ones who for the most part secure their rights last, if at all.

3. When mountains and hills are mentioned they are selected as the most prominent feature of the Holy Land, and thus by synecdoche they stand for the land as a whole. Furthermore, since "prosperity" (Hebrew: "peace") is frequently mentioned as a characteristic feature of the Messianic age, it may well be thought of as the sum total of all that that age or any age that remotely reflects the ideal would produce. When the land is said to bring forth these products, that is equivalent to saying that such prosperity shall be evident in abundance on every hand. A further exemplification of what this involves is added in the spirit of the preceding verse: the rights of the weak and helpless will be safeguarded in a special way. Here will be perfect rule; none will sigh and languish over rights violated or injustices to be borne.

5. The higher aspect of such perfect rule enters into the picture. Men, knowing that God alone can make such blessed results possible, will look up to God and as a result reverence Him as they never reverenced Him before. In fact, the perfect rule just described will be annulled no more, neither will there be anything to interfere with that perfect reverence which is characteristic of God's true people. The two expressions "as long as the sun endures" and "as long as the moon throughout all generations" signify uninterrupted continuance. For though a prosy interpretation of the letter might point to the fact that sun and moon will not continue forever, the Biblical use of such statements indicates that they were thought of as synonymous with eternity as Jer. 33:20 and Ps. 89:29 clearly indicate. We are here not dealing

Psalm 72

with terms that mark time with mathematical precision but rather with the equivalent of eternity.

6. The description returns to the visible manifestations of blessing that will be seen on earth. In a figure that gives an over-all evaluation such a reign is thought of as being like unto the blessed rain that descends upon the fields from which the crops or grains have been removed in the harvest and are now being prepared by heaven's gift for further fertility. Summing it all up, it will be the "righteous" in particular who shall flourish under such beneficent rule (v. 7), and "peace" or prosperity shall always be in evidence.

To draw the line sharply between the references to Israel's king and the Messiah is, of course, impossible. One figure blends into the other. One suggests the other.

8. *And may he have dominion from sea to sea*
   And from the River to the ends of the earth.
9. *Before him may those that dwell in the wilderness bow down;*
   And may his enemies lick the dust.
10. *May the kings of Tarshish and of the coastlands pay tribute;*
    May the kings of Sheba and Seba offer gifts.
11. *And let all kings fall down before him;*
    Let all nations serve him.

8. In the case of an individual that longs for righteous rule the enjoyment of it will quite naturally result in the desire that others, in fact, as many as possible may share it. Or looked at from another point of view, such a ruler deserves that his kingdom be extended endlessly. These prayers are not nationalistic or chauvinistic; they are wholesome and unselfish.

Though many attempts have been made to prove that "from sea to sea" must mean from the Mediterranean to the Dead Sea or, at best, to the Persian Gulf, yet the analogy of passages like Mic. 7:12 and Amos 8:12 indicates that the terms are used vaguely in the sense: from any sea to any other sea, and so are coterminous with universal rule. Though the expression "the River" usually refers to the Euphrates and is, therefore, capitalized it here means: begin at the outermost fringes of the territory promised to the children of Israel (Gen. 15:18) and go to the ends of the earth. So far may his reign extend. In order to make the description of what is asked for more colorful (v. 9), the untamed tribes that "dwell in the wilderness" as well as his enemies are represented as offering tokens of submission and thus coming into his blessed kingdom.

10. Or to use other colorful descriptions, far off to the westernmost

limits of the then-known world lies the famous old city of Tartessus in Spain, commonly known as Tarshish. Also along the shoreline of the Mediterranean lie many kingdoms that were vaguely known to the children of Israel. To the east in southern Arabia lies the ancient Sheba, to the south in old Cush or Ethiopia lies the realm known as Seba. May all these remote lands plus all that lie between them, of course, pay tribute for favors received or offer their gifts in token of submission—all kings and all nations (v. 11). He deserves nothing less. The writer prays for nothing less. On general principles the desirability of praying for the coming Messianic king as well as for Israel's ruler at any given time is important if prayer is to be effective as the psalmist without a doubt believed it was.

12. *For he will deliver the poor when he cries out,*
    The afflicted one and him that has no helper.
13. *He will have mercy on the lowly and the poor;*
    And he will save the life of the poor.
14. *From oppression and violence he will deliver their life;*
    And precious will their blood be in his sight.

As the ruler's attitude toward the lowly and helpless is being described, the same type of verb is used that predominated in the first section (vv. 8–11)—a good argument that in both sections "will" or "shall" should be used. The psalm has quite a bit to say about what the king for whom prayer is offered will do for the lowly and afflicted in particular. The little man was but lightly regarded in days of old. It is quite obvious as already stated above that, if the lowly get their rights, no one will be neglected.

Some interpreters have stated that, if Solomon should be thought of as lightening the burden of the afflicted, the very thought is sheer mockery, seeing that he was notorious for the heavy burdens of taxes and revenues that he laid upon subjects. However, it must also be considered that his early reign and attitude differed from the later as does day from night, and that many of the burdens resulting from major building projects may have at first been borne quite cheerfully by the people. So there is no impropriety involved in this prayer.

15. *So may he live, and may men give to him of the gold of Sheba;*
    And may prayer be made for him continually;
    May blessings be invoked upon him continually.
16. *May there be an abundance of grain in the land even on the tops*
    of the mountains;
    May its fruit rustle like Lebanon;

> *And may men blossom forth from the cities like the grass of the field.*
> 17. *May his name endure forever;*
> *May his name flourish as long as the sun;*
> *May men bless themselves by him, all nations call him blessed.*

15. A summary prayer for the blessings and success of the king's rule concludes the psalm. In this prayer he himself, the land, and his name are remembered. The opening statement of v. 15 is, no doubt, to be understood in the sense, "Long may he live!" an acclamation by which kings have often been hailed. And as his life continues, may he have the experience of seeing men give him of their best, even "gold of Sheba." May they also remember him in their prayers and invoke God's blessings upon all that he does. This last feature is by some interpreters regarded as being out of keeping with a Messianic interpretation, chiefly because this feature appears nowhere else in Messianic prophecy. To conclude that it dare not appear amounts to claiming that a man dare not arrive at any original thought.

16. When the tops of the mountains are brought into the picture, fertile cornfields are thought of as extending to the very peak, that is to say, no sterile areas will be left. When the fruit of the field is spoken of as rustling like Lebanon, this is, indeed, somewhat of a hyperbole, for grain can scarcely rustle like a forest. But, surely, grain in greatest abundance is being thought of. Also the cities are thought of as being the very acme of prosperity and success, men thriving in them and growing in thick profusion as does the grass of the field.

17. Since "name" is synonymous with fame and reputation, the prayer here expressed is obviously to the effect that lasting fame may be attained by this great king, and that men may wish for themselves the blessing wherewith he was blessed, for there is no higher blessing known.

The ease and naturalness with which one's thoughts continually turn from the imperfect earthly exponent of all the things envisioned to the perfect heavenly counterpart confirm the conviction that the Messianic features were clearly in the mind of the author. Thus the church did well to appoint this psalm for use in the season of Epiphany.

> 18. *Blessed be the Lord God, the God of Israel,*
> *Who alone does wondrous things;*
> 19. *And blessed be His glorious name forever;*
> *And let all the earth be filled with His glory. Amen and Amen!*

It seems best to us to regard these two verses as being a doxology that was added to the second book of the Psalms and concluded it. (cf., Ps. 41:3; 89:52; 106:48).

A further remark closes the book: *"The prayers of David, the son of Jesse, have an end."* This statement reflects editorial effort. There must have been a time when the entire psalter closed at this point, and for the time being at least no further psalms known to have been written by David were available.

NOTES

4. The expression "children of the poor" can signify that among the poor, even the more helpless ones, that is to say, their children, shall be the objects of his deliverance. But the word "children" may also be understood as designating the class of individuals, that is to say, "*all the poor.*" On this latter construction see *KS* 306 1.

5. For the word "men will fear thee" (*yira'ukha*) most present-day writers feel compelled to substitute *weya'arikh,* i.e., "and may he live long." The change is motivated largely by the dropping of the Messianic interpretation. It happens to be one of the strong supports of the Messianic thought in the passage and should be retained.

15. The second verb is *weyitten,* which is apparently used impersonally (*man wird ihm geben*), which we would render, "and may men give him." When the statement is rendered thus, everything falls into place, and there is no warrant for the somewhat trivial interpretation which makes this a gentle hint that the writer of the poem drops to the low level of asking that a bit of gold may be his reward for his nice poem honoring the king.

BOOK THREE

Psalm 73

THE SOLUTION OF THE PROBLEM OF THE PROSPERITY OF THE WICKED

FROM THIS TITLE it appears that we have another problem psalm before us, reminding us to some extent of Ps. 37 and 49. Its thought is not too far removed from the problem that is discussed in the book of Job. Mankind has always been more or less plagued by problems. In the Psalter these difficulties are taken into the presence of God and discussed with Him or they are illuminated by the light that emanates from Him.

To be more precise about the problem, it centers in the difficulty posed by the seeming prosperity of the wicked man. Why does he have more success and less troubles than do godly men who have been sincere about their godliness? Or restated, Does sincere piety affect the fortunes of man for good? Or, Can earthly happiness be obtained with a total disregard for God and His will? or in whatever other way men may care to formulate the issue.

We may indicate the distinctive nature of the solution offered in this psalm by noting that it penetrates deeper than does any other that has ever been attempted on the Old Testament level. It mounts to the very presence of God, holds close to Him, and then views the situation from that vantage point. This amounts to looking at things in the way that God sees them; and any man will readily concede that, viewed thus, things must come into far clearer focus, and the real issues must appear as what they are.

What can be said about the author? If the heading is not valueless— and we do not believe that it is—he was Asaph, the man who in David's day was prominent in connection with furthering the cause of Temple music under David's direction. Suppositions to the effect that he must have been a plain, humble fellow, who experienced his share of adversity in his day, are not too probable. Aspah would appear to have been a man of some distinction in his day, and thus such an approach had better be ruled out. To draw sickness that has just been overcome into the picture is quite unwarranted. To assume that David's day would not have given rise to such problems means to misunderstand human life and human nature. To arrive at conclusions on the basis of some forms that have an Aramaic cast (*Kessler*) overlooks the fact that the text of the Scriptures, especially, of course, in the versions, has often undergone a conscious or unconscious adaptation to the language of the day of the copyist, who in such a case did not feel that he was altering the facts of the text but merely the style of writing; and so such fluctuations of forms are to be attributed to copyists rather than to the author.

Not inappropriately *Weiser* says of the psalm: (it belongs) "among the ripest fruits that grew from the wrestling of faith in the Old Testament." And *Oesterley:* "This poem offers one of the few Old Testament adumbrations of a genuine doctrine of immortality."

The thought of the psalm may be outlined as follows:

1. An introductory summary (vv. 1, 2)
2. the prosperity of the wicked (vv. 3–14)
3. the solution of the difficulty (vv. 15–26)
4. the summarizing conclusion (vv. 27, 28).

a) **An introductory summary (vv. 1, 2)**

   A psalm of Asaph.
   1. *Surely God is good to Israel,*
      To those who are pure in heart.
   2. *But as for me, my feet had almost faltered;*
      My steps had well-nigh slipped.

1. One may very properly conclude that these words were written after the problem had been solved and the difficulty had been overcome. The conclusion at which the writer arrived is briefly and aptly stated. If he ever entertained any doubt as to whether God's goodness was manifest in Israel, those misgivings were overcome, and the doubts were resolved. With an initial "surely" the writer underscores the basic truth that God's entire attitude toward His people can be summed up in the statement: He is good to them in the richest, deepest, fullest sense of the word. That means, of course, to those who are truly what is implied in the name "Israel." A brief definition of who those that deserve this name are is given in the words: "to those who are pure in heart." This could be regarded as another way of saying, those who are sincere, or those who honestly strive to live the godly life, who strive after purity of heart and life.

2. But, as this verse indicates, the basic truth about God's goodness had grown uncertain in the writer's thinking. For doubt, in the last analysis, reaches as far as the truth concerning God, in fact, some form or aspect of divine truth is always involved when one looks at the root of the matter. This uncertainty is described by a double figure. When solid truth grows doubtful, a man has nothing but slippery ground under his feet, and his feet feel very insecure. Looking at the two verses together in the contrast that they express, they show us the steadfast, unmovable God in His unwavering goodness toward His people over against a poor individual who is struggling for a footing and is on the verge of a severe fall. One feels at once that there is something personal about the whole experience, and certainly that not some kind of collective personality is involved.

b) **The prosperity of the wicked (vv. 3–14)**

   3. *For I was envious of the arrogant;*
      Continually I saw the prosperity of the wicked.
   4. *For there are no pangs in their death;*
      Their bodies are well-fed.
   5. *They are not in trouble like other mortals;*
      Nor are they plagued like others.

6. *Therefore pride has hung itself on them like a necklace;*
   Violence covers them as a garment.
7. *Their eyes stand out with fatness;*
   The imaginations of their mind are overweening.
8. *They scoff and speak wickedly;*
   Loftily they threaten oppression.
9. *They set their mouth against the heavens;*
   And their tongue struts about on earth.
10. *Therefore the people turn to them;*
    And water in abundance is drained by them.
11. *And they say: "How can God know?"*
    And: "Is there knowledge in the Most High?"
12. *Behold, such are the wicked;*
    And living always at ease, they amass a fortune.
13. *Quite in vain I have kept my heart clean*
    And washed my hands in innocence.
14. *I have suffered affliction continually*
    And have been chastened every morning.

Job 21:7–15 is a close parallel to this section.

3. First of all, a longer statement is presented which makes clear what it was that had almost brought this writer to fall. It was really "the prosperity of the wicked." For all men have a more or less instinctive feeling that God should and does, as a general rule, reward the godly with tokens of His favor and punishes the wicked by withholding good or bringing down trouble on their heads. Generally speaking, that is a reasonable approach if it is not regarded as a broad rule that permits no exceptions. For the exceptions may be far more numerous than we think they ought to be. The final effect of seeing wicked or arrogant men thrive was that the writer became envious of them. *Luther* scales this on a slightly higher level when he lets the effect be merely a kind of righteous indignation (*es verdross mich,* i.e., "I became indignant at them."). But the word seems to imply actual envy as the reaction that set in.

4. There now follow several items that are descriptive of their prosperity. They are not necessarily intended as factors that were invariably in evidence in the lives of ungodly men; but they could at least be noted often enough. The wicked often seemed to have an easy, almost painless death. In general they gave every evidence of being sleek and well-fed. They seemed to be spared the troubles that other men have in much greater abundance (v. 5), or for that matter, the more grievous troubles that "plague" men. Besides, as a result of the promi-

nence that their wealth and prosperity gave them a certain pride took possession of them, and they wore it as though it were an ornament, not a character defect. In addition they grew heartless about others, who had often to be oppressed in order that the wealth that became the possession of the wicked might be extorted from them. This violence they also wore, if not as an ornament to boast of, at least as a garment of which they could well be proud. They certainly were not ashamed of either their pride or their violence. They boasted of both.

7. The description continues. The picture is not an attractive one. One feature of their appearance is well-defind: "Their eyes stand out with fatness." True as it is that there are some individuals who in growing fat develop a facial pattern that makes the eyes sink back into the layers of adipose tissue; it is equally a matter of observation that in some instances the growth of fatty tissue seems to push the eyes out and give a peculiarly bold expression to the countenance of the individual. It is this latter class that the writer reflects on.

What this physical characteristic seems to illustrate is the next feature mentioned: "The imaginations of their mind are overweening." As they look, so they think, in a proud and overbearing attitude. Their words are in agreement with their attitude and appearance, for "they scoff and speak wickedly" on the one hand, displaying their attitude toward God and holy things. Whereas down on earth "loftily they threaten oppression." This contrast as to how they are minded over against God as well as over against men is rephrased in v. 9: "They set their mouth against the heavens [and Him that sits enthroned there] and their tongue struts about on earth." Success had made them self-assertive, proud, without regard to the rights of God and of man. Indeed a repulsive spectacle!

10. A further indication of their seemingly unquestionable outward success is that they build up a following, men who acclaim them, approve of them, flatter and follow them. "The people turn to them" is a concise way of stating all this. A figure is introduced at this point, perhaps, as *Koenig* suggests, derived from a scene that might have been observed in an oasis, where a thirsty camel gulps down water in endless amounts. So these proud fellows "drain water in abundance."

11. God may have been ignored by them, but He is not entirely forgotten, and thus, since they do from time to time reflect on the fact that He has not interfered with their successful career, they express their sentiments in words such as these: "How can God know?" They just do not believe that He is even aware of what happens down here on earth. So blind they are. Or, to state the case a bit more sarcastically they say: "Is there knowledge in the Most High?"

12. Now to sum it up. The writer notes things down with fine care

Psalm 73

and in good order: "Behold, such are the wicked." We must admit that he has furnished us a rather telling description of this class. He then adds another summary, perhaps the one that strikes the eye of the multitudes more than does anything else: "Living always at ease, they amass a fortune." We can readily understand how contact with such people and their seemingly invincible prosperity could have aroused some envy in the heart of this godly psalmist.

13. He briefly contrasts his own life, attitude, and success with men of this class (vv. 13, 14). Whereas they had forgotten God and stained their hands with all manner of sins, he had kept both "his heart clean" and his hands, too, having "washed them in innocence." Other instances of the occurrence of the latter expression are Deut. 21:6–9; Ps. 26:6; Job 9:30, and the very famous Matt. 27:24. Whereas in some of the instances cited washing the hands was a symbolic act typifying innocence, it is here a figurative and colorful statement. In addition the writer can look back upon a life that was marked by many a grievous experience: "I have suffered affliction continuously and have been chastened every morning." God had seemingly not rewarded His faithful servant by granting him immunity from evil but, it seems, had let sufferings multiply. On this note of a conduct that was blameless but "quite in vain" the description closes, showing how acute the soul distress actually was.

c) The solution of the difficulty (vv. 15–26)

15. *If I had said, "I will speak thus,"*
    I would have dealt treacherously with the generation of Thy children.
16. *And so I pondered to know this,*
    Which was a grievous problem in my sight,
17. *Until I went into the sanctuary of God,*
    Took note of their latter end.
18. *Surely, Thou dost set them in slippery places;*
    Thou hast made them to fall down in ruins.
19. *How have they become a desolation in a moment!*
    They are done for, they are consumed with terrors.
20. *As a dream dissolves when a man awakes,*
    So when Thou, O Lord, awakest Thou wilt despise their shadow.
21. *Whenever my thinking was embittered,*
    And my inmost feelings were aroused,
22. *Then I was a dullard and knew nothing;*
    I was like a dumb beast toward Thee.
23. *Nevertheless I am continually with Thee;*
    Thou hast grasped my right hand.

24. *Thou guidest me by Thy counsel;*
    And finally Thou wilt take me hence in glory.
25. *Whom have I in heaven but Thee;*
    And being with Thee, I do not delight in the earth.
26. *Should my heart and my flesh fail,*
    Nevertheless, God is the strength of my heart and my portion forever.

Having described the preceding section as the author's story of his spiritual illness (*Krankheitsgeschichte*), Kessler rather aptly calls the section now before us the record of his recovery (*Genesungsgeschichte*). The section can be divided into two parts, the first, which describes the outcome of such a seemingly successful life, and the second, which states what the writer recognizes himself as possessing when he holds close to God.

15. With regard to all the thoughts that tumultuously surged through his mind the writer first remarks (v. 15): "If I had said, 'I will speak thus,' I would have dealt treacherously with the generation of Thy children." At this point some interpreters try to involve the writer in self-contradiction by observing that he had actually just said these things. But the truth of the matter is that he had voiced his misgivings before his God; he had not publicized them. The damage that unresolved doubts might do to others if they are rashly broadcast serves as a wholesome bit of restraint on the psalmist. What can harm others of God's children cannot be the right thing to utter. And so he kept on pondering over this grievous problem until he "went into the sanctuary of God" (v. 17).

It is not easy to determine whether this statement refers to the visible Temple as such and the attendance of public worship in it, or whether it refers to an entering into the truth that God knows and imparts to others concerning His strange dealings with the children of men. Perhaps one had better allow for both possibilities. All commentators are agreed that a mere physical entering into the sanctuary gives no deeper insight. One must either hear something of God's truth uttered in the sanctuary, or one must at least while worshiping there and pondering upon divine truth have been led by the guidance of the Spirit of God into new insights that resolve the troublesome problem. It is true that the latter may occur without the former. Both might have occurred in sequence. *Schmidt* proposes a solution which is a bit too literal and naive in that he assumes that the second half of v. 17 means that the writer, perhaps, saw one of these prosperous, wicked men suddenly fall dead as a result of a stroke in the very Temple. But "sanctuary" (a plural noun) can involve more than the visible Temple buildings. It can refer to the mysterious leadings of the Almighty and the understanding of them.

What item of God's providence it was that the psalmist learned to understand particularly is clearly stated when he says: (I) "took note of their latter end." The death of these men must be considered, and that does not mean merely to observe how they breathed their last—which may sometimes convey a striking lesson—but chiefly: What does the dying of such a person involve? This is now probed into at some length (vv. 18–20). It involves that some kind of catastrophic overthrow occurs which strikes the beholders as being the judgment of God upon these men. This does not necessarily mean that all the ungodly come to some disastrous end; but it does imply that such an overthrow, which suggests divine intervention, is common enough.

18. To begin with, such persons, though they themselves may not be aware of it, have been set by God in "slippery places." Whereas they assumed that they had chosen an impregnable position, God had let them choose, as it were, a very insecure footing. The result of this sooner or later was a sudden and catastrophic overthrow—"Thou hast made them to fall down in ruins." The ejaculation which follows aims to present the impression that this overthrow made on the beholder: "How are they become a desolation in a moment!" Because God let it happen suddenly, it was made all the more impressive. The parallel statements, added without connectives, make the effect a certainly breathless remark of the startled observer: "They are done for, they are consumed with terrors." Pertinent examples of such judgments of God on evildoers would be: the destruction of the hosts of Pharaoh in the Red Sea; the death of Korah, Dathan, and Abiram; the latter end of Saul, of Absalom, of Shimei, of Ahithophel, of Sennacherib, and of Judas.

20. One verse is added to show how utterly inconsequential the lives of such men really are. The comparison used implies that, as a dream is utterly without substance and very often, after a man awakes, is despised as the height of emptiness and futility, so when God, after what seems to us a long delay, goes into action He will despise and count as nought the shadow of such persons. For all they amounted to in their puffed-up importance was, in the last analysis, nothing more than an empty shadow. Those who deemed themselves so mighty were in God's eyes not even a substance.

21. The two verses that follow (21, 22) sum up very properly the evaluation that the writer feels he ought to put upon his whole attitude during the time when he was disturbed by the seeming success of evil men. He says: "Whenever my thinking was embittered, and my inmost feelings were aroused, then I was a dullard and knew nothing; I

was like a dumb beast toward Thee." It was not that at such times I saw the truth more keenly but rather the opposite: I was not even doing straight thinking; I belonged in the category of dunces and dumb brutes.

23. The beginning of this man's recovery has been narrated up to this point. The full truth of what he realized regarding what he possessed when he had God is now set forth with a fresh evaluation that shows that for him the whole experience had resulted in a much-deepened insight. To begin with, no matter what had happened, no matter what he might have passed through, "nevertheless" he was continually with God. That nearness was, however, not due to the fact that he had tenaciously clung to God but rather to the fact that God had not let *him* go, as is at once stated: "Thou hast grasped, or didst grasp, my right hand." I may have been in danger of slipping. Left to myself, I might even have left Thee. But with infinite patience God clung to His weak and sometimes almost wayward child (v. 23).

24. With that basic situation in mind, the writer now developes the potentialities that lie in being upheld by God. That means that in the future God will guide His child well and wisely through the tortuous paths of life, according to good plans that He has devised for His own. And after a life of divine guidance there will come an acceptance into His immediate presence "in glory." True, this glory is not defined more fully for the present, but it is, nevertheless, a marvelous and wonderful prospect. The same verb ("take") is used that was employed by the holy writer with regard to Enoch (Gen. 5:24) as well as with regard to Elijah (II Kings 2:3, 5, 9, 10). But in the last analysis his treasure and ultimate source of confidence are nothing less than God Himself (v. 25). For heaven is not in itself a joy. God presence and fellowship with Him make it a joy.

Furthermore, if he can maintain his closeness to God, then all earth's treasures and delights seem so very secondary and trivial by comparison. Nothing can really be said to delight a man who has tasted the supremest satisfaction. *Luther* gave a unique turn to the thought but certainly caught the essence of it in his memorable translation: "If I may but hold fast to Thee, heaven and earth become a matter of but slight concern to me" (*Wenn ich nur dich habe, so frage ich nichts nach Himmel und Erde*).

26. Lastly the issue of dying is thought through from this point of view, for that is what lies in the clause, "Should my flesh and my heart fail." The conviction arrived at is that even in that last and bitterest extremity "God is the strength of (his) heart and (his) portion forever." God remains a treasure that death cannot rob us of, and even

in the very experience of dying God supports His own and is more than ever their best possession. A fulness of faith and conviction speaks in these utterances that scarcely ever mounts to higher levels in the whole of the Old Testament. Like the conclusion of Ps. 16, this is a supreme example of what godly logic at its best can do.

d) The summarizing conclusion (vv. 27, 28)

27. *For, lo, those who are far from Thee shall perish;*
    Thou hast put an end to all who deny Thee.
28. *But as for me, it is good for me to keep close to God;*
    I have made the Lord God my refuge
    That I may make known all Thy works.

27. This conclusion summarizes all that has been offered in the psalm, and does so very effectively. The negative side of the matter is presented first. There is nothing more disastrous for man than to let distance intervene between him and his God. Being separated from the source of life, all such "shall perish." That we may, however, realize that such separation is more than a harmless and pardonable drifting, the writer uses a very strong term that is descriptive of the attitude of the drifter. He is also called one who "denies" God. To express this thought the original uses the strongest term imaginable, "to go awhoring," which likens the act to marital infidelity. Since such men seal their doom, the writer adds that of all such it must be said that God "has already put an end" to them. One notices that, whereas he once envied them, with his better insight the psalmist can now only pity them.

28. The positive side of the matter is the one that the author is resolved to follow. He will "keep close to God." This closeness won for him the better insight. There is nothing better than to stay with God after one has found Him. But it must be a matter of conscious resolve; therefore: "I have made the Lord God my refuge." Nor is what he has experienced going to be kept by him as a secret of which others shall never learn. What God has done for him and what God means to him are matters that he purposes to declare openly so that men may learn to know God and make Him their refuge. One feels at this point that the problem which gave occasion for the psalm has been successfully solved, and that the psalmist stands on firm and sure ground.

NOTES

1. The very first word allows for two possibilities of interpretation. Most of the commentators who follow the English tradition translate the *'akh* as "surely." The German tradition for the most part (ex-

cept *Luther*) follows the equally acceptable meaning "only," i.e., God has been only good to Israel. The choice is difficult since both usages are fully warranted.

2. One may follow the *Keri* or the *Kethib* in the two instances involved. As the text stands, "faltered" is a passive participle Kal, and "slipped" is third person, feminine, singular as though the word "steps" had been a singular. Both may be accepted as being correct.

6. The verb *ya'atoph* is an imperfect. It follows the main verb which was a perfect. The imperfect is in place because supplementary facts are added by imperfects. *KS* 154.

7. As our explanation shows, the verb used agrees very well with the subject "eye," and there is no need of changing the noun to "their guilt." *RSV* has translated the expression very well: "Their eyes swell out with fatness."

8. The first two verbs are not in the customary relation of the *waw* consecutive construction because they are parallel acts, almost synonymns. Cf., *KS* 370d.

11. It will be noted that we have translated the perfect *yada'* as a modal verb, "How *can* God know?" The perfect allows for this as *KS* 171c shows.

15. In this case the *'im* with the perfect introduces a condition that is contrary to fact.

16. It is better not to regard the first verb as suggesting a conditional sentence (e. g., *RSV*). *Waw* consecutive merely carries on the progression of thought.

19. The situation is somewhat like that in v. 8—synonymns but no connective. See *KS* 370h.

22. The plural for "dumb beast" is the categorical plural, *KS* 264d.

23. It is quite obvious that in the Hebrew the adversative is in this case a simple "and," but it is clearly of adversative character. *Luther's* very effective *dennoch* ("nevertheless") has found many imitators from the *KJ* translators down to our own time. *Kittel* even felt impelled to entitle the psalm, *Das grosse "Dennoch."*

24. The preposition "in" must be thought of as being in force in both clauses and, therefore, also before "glory." It will be noted that we have understood "glory" as a reference to future, eternal glory, not to honors here on earth. The fact that the verb is an obvious reference to the Enoch story demands this.

26. The initial verb is used in a concessive sense as is now quite generally accepted. See *KS* 373q.

Birkeland (ZATW 1955, I-II, p. 99ff.) has a few suggestive items that can scarcely be ignored. Among other things, in regard to v. 17 he has a significant comment in reference to the term *miqdeschey-'el.* He considers this as a regular plural and thinks it refers to the illigitimate places of worship, the sanctuaries that had been destroyed. When the author looked at them, they became to him a demonstration of the fate of paganism and pagans, i.e., of gentile idolatry. We prefer our interpretation.

Then regarding v. 24 he suggests that the statement may be translated: "Thou takest me after *kabodh,* i.e., glory, in the sense that glory is "a most attractive value both for the evildoer and the pious."

Psalm 74

A COMPLAINT OVER THE DEVASTATION WROUGHT BY THE ENEMY

WHAT SITUATION in Israel gave occasion for the composition of this psalm? Two answers are under consideration. It was either the Chaldean invasion which resulted in the destruction of the city and the Temple in 587 B.C., or it was the pitiful situation which developed in the days when Antiochus Epiphanes raged against the holy people and the holy city in the days of the Maccabees (168–165 B.C.). The latter view was particularly popular when the theory that many psalms belonged to the Maccabean period was more or less dominant. A change of opinion is now in evidence, at least in so far as the likelihood of the Maccabean origin is strongly questioned. Yet the possibility of the Chaldean invasion is not favored by some interpreters. These writers favor a period that is somewhere between the two extremes but find it difficult to point to a historical occasion like the one needed for this psalm, around the date of 351 B.C.

However, we believe that the situation that prevailed at the time of the destruction of Jerusalem under Nebuchadnezzar meets all the needs reflected by the psalm. One need only assume, as also *Kirkpatrick* does, that the psalm was "written some fifteen or twenty years after the destruction of Jerusalem." By that time terms such as "the perpetual ruins" (v. 3) and "cast off forever" (v. 1) or "how long" (v. 9) could well have been used. Furthermore v. 9b would be quite in order ("There is no longer any prophet"), for Jeremiah would have been the last of the prophets sent to guide the people in the land, and

Ezekiel would have been removed from the scene among the captives for quite a number of years. Besides, the destruction of the sanctuary would have been sufficiently fresh in the mind of survivors who saw it or heard of it on the spot to allow for the telling description in vv. 5–7.

When the psalm is ascribed to Asaph in the superscription, this must be a later Asaph than the one who was prominent in David's day. For the fact that "the sons of Asaph" were functioning as late as Josiah's time appears from II Chron. 35:15. Because these men had a famous name of long standing they would by preference be referred to by the family name rather than by their own personal name. The name appearing in the superscription agrees well with the known interest that the Asaphites always had in the sanctuary, of which vv. 4–7 again give clear evidence.

In addition to what has been indicated regarding the general character of the psalm, it may yet be noted that the word "forever" or "perpetual" keeps recurring (*netsach,* in vv. 1, 3, 10, 19), an indication that the distress had seemingly lasted interminably. It may be repeated that the congregation was also only too keenly aware of the fact that prophecy had ceased to offer guidance in a season of great need of it. But it should not be overlooked that the people of God have a strong conviction that God cares for the people of His pasture and cannot cast them off forever.

The psalm is further described in the heading as a *maskil,* "a didactic poem."

1. *O God, why hast Thou cast us off forever?*
   Why does Thy anger smoke against the sheep of Thy pasture?
2. *Remember Thy congregation which Thou hast acquired of old,*
   Which Thou hast redeemed to be the nation of Thy inheritance,
   Mount Zion where Thou hast made Thy dwelling.
3. *Direct Thy footsteps toward the perpetual ruins;*
   The enemy has destroyed everything in the sanctuary.

1. If the psalm must be put into category, it obviously belongs in the class of congregational complaints, which, being addressed to God and giving evidence of seeking help from Him in a humble spirit, are very proper in every way. For the writer does not give evidence of unseemly impatience or of bitterness. The hyperbole involved in the statement "cast us off forever" is but natural when a form of affliction has weighed heavily on the one afflicted, and the end is not yet. But the writer very properly teaches the congregation to evaluate its lot as being first of all the result of a casting off by God. Strong as the covenant that was given to Israel was, it was not beyond abrogation. Because of

protracted and stubborn guilt Israel could come into a situation of great grief and distress.

The parallel statement makes this plainer: God's anger is actually smoking against the sheep of His pasture. Enlightened insight speaks in terms of God's anger on an occasion such as this. Though the affectionate term "sheep of Thy pasture" is used (a phrase that occurs in psalms after the Exile, 79:13; 95:7; 100:3) the obvious possibility is reckoned with that the flock may behave in a manner that is quite unworthy of the title used. If the question is raised, Why does Thy anger smoke? there must have been some evidences of repentance on the part of the nation, otherwise the question would have been without justification.

2. The prayer calls to mind the significant circumstances under which God's more intimate relationship to His people came into being: He had "acquired them of old." The reference is no doubt to the Mosaic times and the establishment of the covenant. Still thinking in terms of the deliverance from Egyptian bondage, the author describes what God did as an act whereby He redeemed them "to be the nation of (His) inheritance," that is to say, the one nation with whom He entered into most intimate relationship as well as the nation that was precious to Him like an inheritance. For had He not even gone so far as to take up His dwelling among them on Mount Zion? It will be observed that the facts cited are works of God, not achievements of men. On such solid ground is this plea based.

3. Now comes the plea itself. May the Lord, who has long kept His distance, now "direct His footsteps to the perpetual ruins." The term "perpetual" would scarcely have been used if the ruins were not of many years, standing, and if it did not seem as though they would not soon be rebuilt (*Kessler*). The prayer is obviously more than a petition for the rebuilding of a material structure. But such a structure is a pledge of a greater interest and a promise of still better things. The ruin of the Temple cannot be a matter of indifference to Him whose it is. Therefore the added plea contained in the factual statement: "The enemy has destroyed everything in the sanctuary" (*J. M. P. Smith*).

4. *Thy foes have roared in the midst of Thy places of meeting;*
   They have set up their ensigns for signs.
5. *It was perceived to be as when a man*
   Lifts up an ax upon a thicket of trees.
6. *And now they have demolished all its carved work*
   With axes and hatches.
7. *They have set fire to Thy sanctuaries;*

They have profaned the dwelling place of Thy name down to the ground.
8. *They have said in their hearts, "We will utterly suppress them";*
They have burned all the meeting places of God in the land.

After the initial complaint and plea (vv. 1–3) there follows a description of the devastation wrought by the enemy (vv. 4–8). The scene is an amplification of that described in II Kings 25:9ff. The unseemliness of the wanton destruction of the house of the Lord still rests heavily upon the mind of the writer. There had been the enemy roaring like brutal wild beasts, stomping into the holy place where sacred silence or glad shouts of praise were wont to be in evidence. Where the banners of God's people had hung, there were now to be seen the "ensigns" of the enemy as the official banners of those in power. The emphasis is on the pronoun in the statement, "They have set up *their* ensigns for signs."

Another indication of the coarseness manifested was the fact that the marauders were noted to have behaved as a man might who comes into a thicket and lifts up his ax to cut down trees ruthlessly (v. 5). All the fine "carved work" (v. 6), of which I Kings 6:29ff. gives some indication, was demolished with axes and hatches by the destroyers. And then, when they had wreaked their vengeance on the structure and its contents, they set fire to what was left, and so they "profaned the dwelling place of (His) name down to the ground."

They raged with such fury that it was easy to detect what sentiments governed their hearts. They were saying to themselves: "We will utterly suppress them." Whenever the heathen raged against God's people, it was more than ordinary hostility that controlled their thinking; it was the inveterate hatred that the world always manifests toward those who are God's people. So the enemy would not stop with the single sanctuary which was at Jerusalem; it would include every place that had become sacred by past associations, places where the people had loved to assemble even though they had no sacrifices, which could be offered only in the Temple at the holy city. In other words, "They have burned all the meeting places of God in the land."

At this point the *AV* has the only instance of the use of the word "synagogues" in the Old Testament. Since the origin of the synagogue is still veiled in mystery, and since the Hebrew word used at this point must not be translated thus, *RSV* does not adopt this translation. The description as a whole is set forth before the Lord as an indirect plea for help: what is done to His sanctuary is not a matter of indifference to Him.

9. *We have not seen the signs we looked for;*
   There are no longer any prophets;
   There is nobody among us who knows how long this will last.
10. *How long, O God, shall the adversary utter reproaches?*
    Shall the enemy blaspheme Thy name forever?
11. *Why dost Thou withdraw Thy hand, even Thy right hand?*
    Take it from Thy bosom and destroy!

9. The writer utters a further complaint, this time because of the delay of help. Certain things that Israel had been wont to enjoy are no longer in existence. They had hoped that the Lord would sooner or later interpose in behalf of His house as He had done in the days of Hezekiah (II Kings 19:35ff.) and perform some remarkable sign. But nothing happened, nothing at all. They were bewildered. In their bewilderment in times past they had often had recourse for guidance to the prophets that were among them. They now discovered to their dismay: "There are no longer any prophets." For the first time in an emergency prophetic guidance was not available. No one had the slightest notion as to how long the present emergency would last. True, Jeremiah had made a statement that answered this question (Jer. 25: 11), but that prophet had been heeded so little that the statement in question somehow lay buried in oblivion.

10. Since these issues weighed so heavily upon the minds of the godly, they make an attempt to roll their burden onto the Lord. They re-enforce their plea by reference to the fact that reproaches against His name and blasphemies had been uttered. Dare God let this go on forever? What is the reason for His inaction these many years? The hand of the Lord that had on so many occasions done valiantly (Ps. 118:16) had now obviously been withdrawn. The prayer becomes almost impetuous at this point: "Take it from Thy bosom and destroy!" It need not be pointed out who or what needs to be destroyed. The prevailing circumstances make that plain enough.

12. *Yet God is my king from of old,*
    Working great deeds of salvation in the midst of the land.
13. *Thou didst divide the sea by Thy strength;*
    Thou didst break the heads of the great sea monsters by the waters.
14. *Thou didst crush the heads of Leviathan*
    And didst give him for food to the creatures of the wilderness.
15. *Thou didst cleave the rock to give fountain and stream;*
    Thou didst dry up the ever-flowing rivers.

16. The day is Thine, the night also is Thine;
    Thou hast established luminaries and the sun.
17. Thou hast set the boundaries of the earth;
    Thou hast formed summer and winter.

12. We may label this section a recital of the mighty acts of God in history and in creation. By the enumeration of great works that God has done the writer encourages himself and others to think of God in terms of being still able to achieve such works. The preceding section, which may be thought of as describing God as being impotent or at least as being inactive, is balanced by the one before us, which is in strong contrast with it, and, therefore, the initial conjunction had best be rendered as the adversative "yet."

There is a special propriety about having God described as the "king" of the nation, for the special hopes that had been attached to the Davidic line as a result of God's special promises in II Sam. 7 now seemed to have been erased, and the royal line seemed to be without hope. But God was still king as He had ever been "from of old." The reins had not slipped from His hands, and He still had that characteristic which history had so clearly established of being a God "working great deeds of salvation in the midst of the land." The latter phrase could also have been translated, "in the midst of the earth," indicating any and everywhere in the earth wherever He pleases. For the works that are immediately enumerated were done in different parts of the earth: some in Egypt, some near Sinai, some in Palestine. The emphasis seems still to be chiefly on the fact that He is capable of doing mighty things in the land where at the present moment there is no indication of His presence and activity.

13. Note the imposing array of works of the Lord listed. Back in the days of the Exodus He divided the Red Sea when His people also seemed to be hopelessly trapped. At the same time He broke the power of the mighty nation of Egypt. For she is the one referred to as "the great sea monsters by the waters" since she is stretched out along the winding course of the Nile. This powerful nation, fierce as a many-headed dragon, had its heads crushed in this encounter. This is what the figure used suggests; it is not necessarily a reference to Babylonian mythology as is currently claimed.

Similar is the next picture used (v. 14). Since the "Leviathan" is merely another name for the crocodile, and the crocodile is native to Egypt, that nation is in this instance likened to another powerful and dangerous beast which the Lord, as it were, encountered when He was delivering His people. Its head, too, was crushed and the body, as it were, scattered after having been hewn into pieces and thus given for food to any wild beasts that might happen to dwell there. Two powerful and colorful figures are used to describe one event because that event so signally illustrates what God can do to the mighty when they seek to crush His people.

15. We next have a reference to mighty deeds of help that were done while the children of Israel were on the way toward the land of promise. It was certainly a marvelous deed when God had Moses smite the rock and bring forth "fountain and stream," that is to say, a fountain that gushed in such abundance that a runlet of water was formed in the wilderness like a brook. On the other hand, He opened a passage for them when the Jordan River seemed to interpose an insuperable obstacle to entering into the land. Poetically speaking, He "dried up the ever-flowing rivers" (plural of the category, viz., such as the Jordan).

16. However, mighty deeds of His in the realm of nature may also be profitably considered. Even day and night which go on in continual alternation are wholly under His control. Both are His. So, too, are the luminaries, all of them, and the sun, the greatest of them. Could there be any question about His *ability* to help?

17. To this may well be added the thought that powers of restraint are His also when forces need to be restrained. This seems to be the motivation for the statement, "Thou hast set the boundaries of the earth." Though this statement may be understood in its broadest scope, it is apparently to be construed especially in the light of the second member of the verse, which indicates the type of boundaries that are referred to: he sets the limits that mark off the seasons like "summer and winter." One feels that the strain has gone out of the psalm at this point while the writer was dwelling upon the mighty works of which God is capable. Besides, this section has laid the groundwork for the last concluding plea, in which the note of petition is much intensified.

18. *Remember this, O Lord, that the enemy has uttered reproaches;*
    And a foolish people have blasphemed Thy name.
19. *Do not deliver the soul of Thy turtledove to the wild beasts;*
    Do not forget the life of Thy poor ones forever.
20. *Have regard for the covenant;*
    For the hiding places of the earth are full;
    They are habitations of violence.
21. *Let not the oppressed turn aside ashamed;*
    Let the poor and the needy praise Thy name.

540   *Exposition of the Psalms*

22. *Arise, O God, plead Thy cause;*
    Remember the reproaches which the fools utter all the day.
23. *Forget not the outcry of Thy enemies,*
    The clamor of Thy adversaries which goes up continually.

18. In the preceding section the personal pronoun "Thou" was expressed seven times, a unique emphasis in the Hebrew which stresses what mighty things God, and God alone, is able to do. This God is now summoned into action as plea after plea is directed to Him.

He is first asked to remember what reproaches the enemy has uttered in blaspheming His holy name. Remarks like those of Rabshakeh (II Kings 18:33ff.) were, no doubt, the order of the day when one nation made war upon another. It mattered little if heathen idols were reproached thus, for they were nothing. But when God is thus referred to, then blasphemy has been uttered. It may well be possible that "foolish people" spoke thus in their ignorance, but the holy name of the Lord has still been profaned.

19. Or, looking at the matter from an entirely different point of view, to surrender His people like a gentle and harmless dove into the power of "the wild beast" would be a heartless act that God could not become guilty of. Or again, there are the Lord's "poor" or the afflicted ones who have suffered for His name's sake—could God forget them and still be true to His name? These are not pleas that weigh lightly with God or man.

20. Or there was the "covenant" which the Lord had solemnly inaugurated in behalf of His people, the importance of which He had so often stressed in the hearing of His people. Could this nation be dealt with as though no such covenant existed? Under all circumstances the plea is warranted, "Have regard for the covenant." Dark "hiding places" throughout the land, the places of refuge of the mistreated, were full of people who had been compelled to flee to them; and time and again when men were apprehended by the cruel victors, these caves and dens in the rocks had been scenes or "habitations of violence." Could the covenant God let these things go on? Pleas like this were strongly motivated.

21. Or there were the many prayers of the oppressed and needy which had ascended to God throughout the land. Could God forever go on refusing to give ear to their prayer and so compel them "to turn aside ashamed" because they were not being heard? How much better it would be if, after receiving help from Him, all these poor and needy folk were to be enabled "to praise (His) name"!

22. One vigorous petition has followed hard upon the heels of the

Psalm 74

other and they have reached a climax so that the writer now utters the strongest of them all: "Arise, O God, plead Thy cause." This calls for an end to the period of inaction, for God has for a long time done nothing in the interest of His cause, and this cause has suffered. Quite apart from all that God's own people might be led to say, there were the ugly "reproaches, which the fools utter (ed) all the day," and they were reproaches of the name of the Holy One of Israel.

23. On this note the psalm closes by reminding God with all due respect and humility but also with the freedom of utterance that is characteristic of those that believed on Him not to forget "the outcry of the enemies, the clamor of the adversaries which goes up continually."

NOTES

2. The word for "nation" is in this case really "tribe." But it is quite obviously used in an unusual sense in this verse and refers, not one tribe of the nation, but to the whole nation.

After "Mount Zion" the regular form of the demonstrative pronoun (*zeh*) is used, which here functions as the relative and was translated "where."

3. The second member of the verse is difficult. *Koenig* translates: *Ganz schlimm hat der Feind es im Heiligtum getrieben,* that is to say: Quite badly has the enemy behaved in the sanctuary. Note: this gives *kol* a meaning something like "quite."

6. In the expression "its carved work" the possessive "its" must refer rather far back, namely, to the "places of assembly" in v. 4, which is not too remote an antecedent (*KS* 1).

7. It is a question as to whether the singular or the plural is found in the form *miqdashékha,* for the *seghol* with the *athnach* may be pausal or may be the plural suffix with *yodh* omitted. Much may be said for as well as against either claim.

9. The initial word actually means "our signs," which is a rather concise way of saying "the signs we looked for."

11. The second member of the verse is even a bit more abrupt than our translation has indicated. It says: "From the midst of Thy bosom destroy." The *Septuagint* must have had something like this in mind with the use of *eis telos,* which would mean something like, "to a finish."

12. *Yeshu'oth* can be translated "salvation," but since it is plural it refers either to the fulness of salvation that was wrought or to the "great deeds of salvation" as we have preferred to render it.

14. The form *titténu,* though it is an imperfect, is the usual way of

expressing subordinate circumstances after the perfect of the preceding clause had begun the narrative in the past. Therefore this *yaktul concomitans* must be translated as a past (*KS* 154).

In the expression *le'am letsiyim* the word '*am*, "people," is apparently used in reference to animals as is done in Prov. 30:25, 26, where it is used in reference to both "ants" and "badgers." Both are a people in a certain sense. We should prefer to say "creatures." The form *letsiyim*, though it is introduced by *le*, is in apposition to the preceding word and means "dwellers in the wilderness," whether man or beast; here it refers to beasts.

Psalm 75

GOD IS JUDGE

THE FACT that this psalm follows Ps. 74 is in this case particularly meaningful, for the latter psalm had ended on the note of "Plead Thy cause" and "Forget not the outcry of Thy enemies." This psalm is, as it were, the answer to these two challenges. God shows how He takes issue with those that presume to rise up against Him. The note of positive victory is strong throughout the psalm. But the impression that this psalm could have made has, perhaps, been dimmed by the traditional translation of the *KJ*, two verses of which can scarcely be clear to the ordinary reader. One of these is v. 1b, "for that Thy name is near Thy wondrous works declare"; and the second, v. 2: "When I shall receive the congregation I will judge uprightly." Under the handicap of two such perplexing statements no reader will discern what the psalm treats of.

Though it would be presumptuous to attempt to prove out of what historical situation this psalm grew, it yet appears to be eminently reasonable to think in terms of such an occasion as the Assyrian invasion in the days of Hezekiah (Is. 36, 37). For then it certainly appeared as if the very foundations on which the earth rested were shaken (v. 3), and the boastful (vv. 4, 5) were speaking very arrogantly. But God, on the other hand, spoke very reassuringly to His people, and He gave nations to drink of the cup of His wrath (v. 8); and so God's people were very much reassured (vv. 9, 10). Other points of possible contact will be indicated as the exposition progresses.

Psalm 75

The heading reads thus: *To the Choir Director. "Destroy not." A psalm of Asaph. A song.* "Destroy not" appears also in the heading of Ps. 57, 58, and 59, and seems to suggest a melody after which the present psalm is to be sung. On "Asaph" see the preceding psalm.

a) **God is always to be praised (v. 1)**

1. *We have always given thanks to Thee, O God, we have given thanks;*
   For Thy name is near; men have always declared Thy wondrous works.

On this positive note of assurance the psalm begins. Whereas the versions down to the *RSV* use the present tense (or the future: *Septuagint* and *Vulgate*) to render the first verb, it is a Hebrew perfect, which in this case should apparently be translated as a gnomic aorist, that is, a past expressing a constant truth such as, "We have always given thanks." For the truth to be emphasized is the fact that thanksgiving to God for His never-ending benefits and constant protection is characteristic of the church of God. God's people are always a grateful people. Reassurance in reference to God and His providence never dies out.

In line with this thought is the second: "Thy name is near." By a peculiar Hebrew idiom God's name often stands for Himself. So this to us strange assertion reasserts God's continual presence with His people in every eventuality. That is why continual praise of God rings out: He is always at hand to help. So effective is this presence of God that many "wondrous deeds" on the part of God have been effected in the course of time, and men have always been declaring them and, for that matter, still declare them. This basic approach is a kind of solid platform on which the rest of the psalm is built up. For this fundamental statement is at once abandoned and a pronouncement of God of a seemingly entirely different character is added, a transition of thought that is so abrupt that some interpreters feel that the text is corrupt at this point. But as the statement from the Almighty is fully developed, it becomes apparent as to how this initial verse fits into the picture.

b) **God declares that He has all issues of judgment wholly in His power (vv. 2–8)**

2. *When I shall reach the appointed time*
   I am He that judges with equity.
3. *The earth and all its inhabitants totter;*
   I am He that supports its pillars.

4. *I have always said to the boastful, "Do not boast,"
And to the wicked: "Do not lift the horn."*
5. *Do not lift up your horn on high;
Do not speak with proudly lifted neck."*
6. *For neither from the east nor from the west,
Nor from the wilderness comes lifting up.*
7. *But God is judge;
He humbles the one and lifts up the other.*
8. *For there is a cup in the hand of the Lord;
The wine foams, it is well mixed;
He pours out from it, and all the wicked of the earth must drain and drink its very dregs.*

2. The very first statement plunges us into the midst of a tense situation: men have been hoping and longing for the intervention of God. Things have been transpiring upon the earth that seemed to demand action on His part, but nothing happened. The reason for this is that God times His acts so that they may come at the time that is best suited for the results He desires to attain. In other words, He waits till He reaches "the appointed time." When that period has arrived, then it is He and none other that acts with decision and sometimes startling effectiveness. In doing this He may often let an issue develop into a certain crisis that is far beyond what man would have allowed to develop. But man cannot foresee outcomes as God can. Man's action would often be very premature. This is one of the basic laws of history and one of the fundamental rules in the kingdom of God. To this thought must be added what the adverbial phrase stresses: God's judgment is carried out "with equity." He does what divine justice demands should be done. Biblical instances of the use of the term "appointed time" would be Ps. 102:13; Dan. 8:19.

3. After the basic rule according to which God acts has been clearly set forth, the psalm describes the present emergency during which that rule seemed to have been held in abeyance. It is this: "The earth and all its inhabitants totter." This may refer to an emergency in the Holy Land, among God's people. But the movement that is involved, let us say, the Assyrian conquest of the time, seems to spell the ruin of the culture and civilization of that time. So men felt then and frequently feel now in times of crisis. But man cannot so disrupt a world which is still God's, and one whose order is upheld by Him. So He goes on to give the reassurance: "I am He that supports its pillars." This does not assert that the earth must according to plain Biblical doctrine actually rest on pillars but is a figurative mode of expressing the thought that there is some stability to this present world order.

4. Regard is now had for those who seem to be threatening the stability of things, and it is indicated how God feels toward such individuals. They are the "boastful" and the "wicked." The attitude of both is practically the same: the one boasts, the other arrogantly displays his bold strength or, to use a figure, he lifts the horn like a bull who is conscious of his strength and ready to use it. To all such individuals God has always said: "Do not boast," and, "Do not lift up the horn." Though He may have set forth His counsel to them in words of the prophets, which they will very rarely have heard, He has also spoken to all the mighty and wicked upon the face of the earth through the admonitions of their inmost conscience or the lessons that history teaches. They know that they are not to behave arrogantly. The truth that God in some way or other keeps impressing on the hearts of all such individuals is reiterated in v. 5 with additional emphasis and clarity. A very good example of the type of pride here condemned is recorded in Is. 36:4ff. Other instances of the use of the idiom of lifting up the horn can be found in Deut. 33:17 and I Sam. 2:1, 10.

6. This verse gains in meaning and its propriety becomes quite apparent when one reflects on what nations are wont to do first when another strong nation threatens the national security. Men cast about for alliances, for sources from which help might come. They look with alarm to every quarter of the globe. The fact that such a situation is reflected would become quite apparent if in the translation used above we had substituted the word "help" for the Hebraic mode of speech "lifting up." For the Hebrew figure is based on the simple fact that, when a man is down and helpless, he looks for someone to "lift him up."

In addition to the two points of the compass mentioned (east and west) the term "wilderness" would seem to refer to the area south of the Holy Land, the Negeb. One point of the compass would then have been significantly omitted—the north. This fact seems to offer an additional argument for the Assyrian calamity. For the north would represent the region from which Assyria would naturally channel her invasion. No one was looking to the north for anything other than the invader. Yet the statement is in the nature of a generalization: In emergencies do not cast about in futile fashion for deliverance through the agency of the power of man, for vain is the help of man. The next verse indicates where help is to be sought, no matter what the difficulty may be.

7. The truth that the psalm wants to set forth with emphasis is given a very effective formulation by its very brevity. It rings forth like a kind of motto: "God is judge." This implies that God finally decides all issues with reference to the welfare of the people of God as

well as the fact that God keeps all situations well under control while the outcome is still pending. For "judge" means "rule effectively." One aspect of God's effective judging is submitted: "He humbles the one and lifts up the other." For that matter, practically all judgment consists, perhaps, in bringing low and in raising up, depending on the nature of the individual involved. The proud are abased, and the lowly are exalted as I Sam. 2:7 had already clearly formulated the rule.

8. This principle is both illustrated and emphatically summarized in this verse, which has parallels in Jer. 25:15ff.; 49:12; 51:7; Is. 51: 17ff., some of which develop the figure in greater detail. In every instance of this kind the point of comparison is that an obnoxious and inebriating drink is administered which intoxicates the person that takes it with the judgment of God and compels him to stagger about, a victim of God's anger. Never for a moment does this imply that individuals are helpless victims of an arbitrary fate, but rather that they are reaping the just reward of their deeds.

God is the one who administers the drink ("a cup is in the hand of the Lord"). The content of the cup is a potent mixture; it "foams" and is "well mixed." He tilts the cup as He holds it to the lips of those whom His justice and wrath have singled out. In that sense "He pours out a potion from it," and then the "wicked of the earth," all of them, "must drain and drink" (the figure of speech called *hysteron proteron*) "its very dregs," no matter how repulsive it tasted, and how unwilling they may be to bring the judgment on themselves. In our day men do not seem to like this figure. It seems too vigorous and expressive, but no man dare declare that it lacks color and effectiveness.

It seems most appropriate to regard vv. 2–5 as being the pronouncement of God Himself, whereas vv. 6–8 appear to be more correctly understood as being statements of the writer himself or of the group in whose name he speaks when he begins the psalm with the statement, "We have always given thanks." Thus these last three verses are the confession of the godly congregation of Israel.

The two remaining verses of the psalm may then be thought of as expressing the thoughts and resolutions of this same group though they are cast in the form of the singular.

c) **This truth gives great confidence to God's people (vv. 9, 10)**

9. *As for me, I will declare this forever;*
   I will sing praise to the God of Jacob.
10. *And all the horns of the wicked I will cut off;*
    But the horns of the righteous shall be exalted.

9. That which is to be declared forever is the truth just enunciated, that God judges when the proper time has come, humbles the proud,

Psalm 75

and exalts the lowly. This is a truth that is worthy of perpetual proclamation. It is also a truth for which the "God of Jacob" is to be praised. For it is a part of the over-all truth that He does all things well.

10. It is very proper to go one step farther, and that this psalm does when the psalmist makes the pronouncement that he on his part (he speaks in the name of the congregation) will do what he can to check the influence of the wicked and to promote the success of the righteous. This is not to be thought of as a presumptuous venture on his part. He believes so wholeheartedly in what God will achieve that he also believes that man should do his utmost to support such a blessed work of God. Some interpreters are inclined to ascribe v. 10 to the Lord Himself though such a sudden, unmotivated shift of person is scarcely feasible. They also disregard emphases such as those which *Maclaren* voices so effectively: "God's servants are His instruments in carrying out His judgments; and there is a very real sense in which all of them should seek to fight against dominant evil and to cripple the power of tyrannous godlessness." Or his other statement: "This psalmist not only praised, but in his degree vowed to imitate." It is quite obvious that participation in such holy work requires much sanctified understanding.

NOTES

1. In the statement, "Men have always declared," the simple verb *sipperu* is the impersonal third person plural whereas the English idiom demands the substitution of the subject "men," for the vague "they."

A rather suggestive emendation of a permissible sort may be noted in regard to this verse. By a rearrangement of the consonants in the words, "For Thy name is near," one could arrive at the translation: "Calling upon Thy name, men recount Thy wondrous works." This would demand the insertion of an *aleph*. Since the expression, though unusual, makes good sense, one should not needlessly resort to textual changes.

2. *Luther* greatly simplified the problem found in the first half of this verse by translating as though it were a mere temporal phrase, *zu seiner Zeit,* i. e., "at the proper time." That conveys the thought of the statement excellently.

3. "Totter," Hebrew, *nemoghim,* is the plural of the niphal participle which agrees with the second of the two subjects rather than with the nearer subject. *KS* 349p.

Other passages where the figurative and illustrative use of "pillars" or "foundations" occurs are: Job 9:6; Ps. 18:15; 82:5; 104:5; I Sam. 2:8; Is. 24:18; Mic. 6:2; Jer. 31:39; Job 38:4–6; Prov. 8:29.

6. In support of the translation "lifting up" for *harim* it may also be said that, since the same verb occurs in v. 5 in the same stem though in reference to the lifting up of the horn and again in v. 7, such a use of

the infinitive is far from out of place or unusual. Though the form as such could be the word "hills," to translate it thus would make what is almost the key verse of the psalm a very difficult ellipsis, with the key thought to be guessed at.

Some interpreters assign the sections of the psalm to different individuals or to groups for liturgical rendition, but such a procedure has its difficulties. The psalm is then faulted because it will not readily fall into the pattern they have made for it. Our exposition indicates that the sections make a consistent composite whole.

Psalm 76

THE VICTORIOUS POWER OF THE GOD OF ISRAEL

IT HAS BEEN pointed out that this psalm is a fine sequel to the one that precedes, for after God has been described as a judge in Ps. 75 this psalm shows Him exercising this prerogative effectually.

Attempts to establish the historical situation out of which this psalm may have grown have quite frequently pointed to the Assyrian invasion under Sennacherib (701 B.C.) as it is recorded in Is. 36 and 37. Though such a connection can seldom be proved with utter finality, there is not one point in the psalm that offers any insurmountable difficulty to such an assumption. In fact, that event and the content of the psalm agree rather strikingly as we shall later point out. Other approaches such as referring the psalm to some type of dramatic pantomime that was staged in connection with the highly dubious festival of the enthronement of Yahweh lack sound evidence. Or again, the reference to the double campaign waged by David against Syria and Edom (II Sam. 8) can be supported only by rather bold changes in the Hebrew text.

The reference to the "stringed instruments" in the heading may be noted as appearing in connection with Ps. 4:1; 6:1; 54:1; 61:1; 67:1. On "Asaph" Ps. 75 may be consulted.

1. *In Judah God is known;*
 In Israel His name is great.
2. *His abode has been established in Salem*
 And His dwelling place in Zion.

3. *There He broke the fiery arrows of the bow,*
   The shield, and the sword, yea, even war itself. Selah.

1. This is a description of a recent mighty deliverance that has led to a new understanding of the Lord's greatness. "In Judah God is known" is in the nature of a general statement, but it may be understood to mean that as a result of what has just transpired God "has become known," His mighty act made Him known. Israel thought that she knew God rather well ("Judah" and "Israel" are synonymous here—*Mc-Cullough*); she has discovered new potentialities in Him that she had not been aware of. His "name," that is to say, His character has at the same time been more fully disclosed. It is largely through the acts of God that we learn to know and understand Him.

2. This verse indicates that a situation which was previously known has now become more vital. He who had His dwelling place in Zion has given a new emphasis to the truth that He desires that His name is to dwell there. In this sense "His abode has been established in Salem"—abbreviated form of Jerusalem. It is as though this verse were connected with the one that follows by a "for." For the event referred to in v. 3 was the occurrence that made the ancient truth become alive as it never had before. "There" should not be pressed too strongly. A careful reading of the Biblical record indicates that the overthrow of the Assyrian host took place at some distance from Jerusalem, perhaps, in the vicinity of the southern border of Judah. The Lord had apparently done something that had made the effectiveness of the ordinary armaments seem unusually futile. We may well think of similar statements in Ps. 46:9. An army may have suffered a unique defeat, and the implements of war may have been left scattered in profusion over the landscape as though the Lord had scattered them in confusion, "the fiery arrows of the bow, the shield, and the sword." In fact, to use the very broadest expression possible, the Lord might thus have broken "even war itself."

It must be admitted that no event could be conceived of that agrees more completely with what is here described than that which occurred on that great day when "the angel of the Lord went forth and slew a hundred and eighty-five thousand in the camp of the Assyrians," Is. 37:36. Reflect again on the unusual effectiveness of the summary: Now "in Judah God is known; in Israel His name is great." In this way the psalm writers served as interpreters of the great events of their day.

4. *Effulgent with light art Thou,*
   Glorious from the mountains of prey.
5. *The stouthearted were despoiled; they slept their last sleep;*
   And none of the mighty men have found their hands.

6. At Thy rebuke, O God of Jacob,
Both the chariot and the horse have sunk into deep sleep.

4. This section might be summarized as showing that also God's *glory* has been exalted, not only His greatness in general. It is as though the Lord had appeared to the spiritual eyes of His people in a brilliance of light never before observed. Though the second member of the verse is variously interpreted, we shall set forth briefly the one that seems both clearest and most effective to us and offer other possibilities in the Notes. "Glorious from the mountains of prey" is not only a simple literal translation, it also has the obvious meaning that God is coming back from some mountainous area where He engaged in battle and won much prey, which He now brings with Him as a token of victory and as proof of the new glory that He has attained.

5. This verse names those who were despoiled—"the stouthearted." If we recall the historical situation that we have referred to we may remember that the Assyrians were the finest men of war of their day. He that overcame them attained special glory. To indicate the completeness of their defeat, they are represented as men who have "slept their (last) sleep," all of which agrees very well with the notation in Is. 37:36: "There were all dead bodies" when men arose early and surveyed the camp. We have left the last clause of the verse in its unique Hebrew idiom: "And none of the mighty men have found their hands." We might have said that they were paralyzed with fright or were utterly incapable of action. The original has an implied helplessness that it is difficult to put into words.

6. Clarifying the matter still further, this verse attributes the whole of this unusual result to a rebuke that was uttered by the God of Jacob. He spoke, and mighty chariot forces sank into a deep sleep, and the much-vaunted Assyrian host became useless.

7. But Thou, O Thou art to be feared;
And who can stand in Thy sight when once Thy anger is aroused?
8. From heaven Thou hast uttered Thy verdict;
The earth feared and was still
9. When God arose to judgment,
To save all the meek of the earth. Selah.

7. These verses indicate how God's judgment caused all men to stand in awe of Him. In the most wholesome sense imaginable the event that occurred promoted the true fear of God in the hearts of the beholders. Thus the poet rightly defines the effect produced when God's just anger was aroused. It goes without saying that we are not to think of some uncontrolled passion that gets the better of an individual who is

unable to keep his feelings in check. It is simply true that God's anger is right and just, and that, when it is aroused, no mortal can stand in His sight. Or to set the whole issue into one effective picture: "From heaven Thou hast uttered Thy verdict, the earth feared and was still." His voice silences all words of men and produces a wholesome awe. Though no actual voice was heard speaking from on high, in this instance His deeds spoke louder than words.

9. Though one aspect of the matter is "judgment" and "verdict" and fear on the part of man, there is another gracious side to the judgments of God that dare not be overlooked. "When God arose to judgment," it was done for the purpose that He might "save all the meek of the earth." These "meek" ones were in this instance the people of God, whom fear and apprehension had rendered small and unavailing in their own sight, and who had wisely submitted their case into the hands of the Lord Himself. For God delights "to save all the meek of the earth." This little touch is particularly precious in this psalm and manifests the deep insight that is characteristic of the psalm writers.

10. *Surely, the wrath of man must praise Thee;*
    The residue of wrath Thou wilt gird upon Thee.
11. *Make vows and pay them unto the Lord, your God;*
    Let all that are round about Him bring gifts to Him who ought to be feared.
12. *He cuts off the courage of princes;*
    He is terrible to the kings of the earth.

This section shows how God's praise is established in every way.

10. The question is debated at length as to whether this verse refers to voluntary or involuntary praise on the part of men when it is said: "Surely, the wrath of man must praise Thee." It would seem to us that we must allow for both possibilities. That is to say, on the one hand, those who are God's avowed enemies or the enemies of His people, do what they will, must ultimately submit to God and admit that "the Galilean has conquered." Besides, though what they did was intended to defeat His cause and purposes, it had ultimately to help in promoting the very thing that was being opposed. On the other hand, it does not seem unlikely or impossible that certain of those who once raged against Him shall be so completely vanquished by His Spirit that they will willingly offer tokens of submission and sincere praise to His name.

Nor is this approach nullified by the much-debated second half of the verse: "The residue of wrath Thou wilt gird upon Thee." For this speaks of the case of those who, having been taken in hand by God, continue in their wrathful opposition, daring the Almighty, as it were, to do more to them than He has already done. There are still some such

Pharaohs. But whatever wrath still smolders after a severe check by God, God Himself will gird upon Himself as a warrior would a sword and will use as a destructive weapon against him who first wore it; and thus that "residue of wrath" shall ultimately contribute to the praise of God as did Pharaoh's drastic overthrow in the Red Sea. Though *Luther* departed quite a bit from the letter of the original, his translation is clear and very much in the spirit of the passage, so much so as to be regarded as classic: *Wenn Menschen wider dich wueten, so legest du Ehre ein; und wenn sie noch mehr wueten, bist du auch noch geruestet* (When men rage against Thee, Thou acquirest renown; and when they rage still more, Thou art still well armed).

11. For a brief moment the psalm reverts to exhortation by asking those that have been blessed by God's signal deliverance to make solemn vows of gratitude to Him and to be sure to pay their vows. For that matter, the work done by God is so great that those who are not His people but live round about and hear of what transpired should also feel impelled to "bring gifts to Him who ought to be feared." Perhaps more than we realize, men of the Old Testament sensed that God sought to bring all nations to Himself, and not Israel only.

12. The last verse cannot get away from the thought that the mighty of this earth, kings and princes, (cf. Ps. 48:4–6) if they are of this earth and against the Lord, must be cut off by Him as useless shoots that cumber the vine, cf. Is. 25:4; also Rev. 14:17–20, and must experience that He is terrible to hostile earthly potentates. All of this agrees so obviously with the situation that prevailed when Assyria was brought low that we cannot help but be impressed by the possibility that Sennacherib's defeat furnished the theme for this fine interpretation of the event.

NOTES

3. *Shammah* apparently has the same meaning as a simple *sham* as is the case in II Kings 23:8; Is. 22:18; 65:9, etc. The translation "fiery arrows" is far more prosy than is the original. For the Hebrew says: "flames or lightnings of the bow." Arrows are meant, of course. For *milchamah* it seems best to use the literal translation "war." Letting the terms stand for weapons of war by metonymy is not impossible but scarcely necessary.

4. To translate *na'or* "glorious" (*RSV*) is not inappropriate, but since the root meaning of this *niphal* form is "light," it would be more in keeping with this fact to render as we have done, "effulgent with light." "Mountains of prey" is a phrase that it is not easy to explain. But it is not so difficult as to demand such alterations of the text as have been current since the time of the *Septuagint,* such as "everlasting mountains," which *RSV* prefers to follow.

5. The first word of the verse is an *'ethpolel,* a variation of the *hithpolel,* and is used in a passive sense after the pattern of the Aramaic. Into the literal "they slept their sleep" we have ventured to insert the adjective "last" to make the sense more apparent. A sort of cognate object is involved, in which a word of the same meaning but not of the same root reinforces the verb. Cf. *KS* 329h.

8. In the case of the two verbs "feared and was still" we do not have verbs that are joined by the customary *waw* consecutive with the imperfect because the two acts involved are parallel, not consecutive. See *KS* 370k.

10. In interpreting this verse one is almost tempted to follow those writers who (like *Koenig*) let the consonants of the text stand and supply new vowels, thus: "For the wrath of (conquered) Edom will praise Thee; the remnant of Chamath shall celebrate festivals to Thee." The event referred to would then be David's campaign against Syria and Edom. But it does seem strange that none of the old versions discovered this possibility. Our approach avoids the difficulty of making the first "wrath" the wrath of man, the second the wrath of God, which is a somewhat arbitrary procedure.

Psalm 77

FAITH WANING AND FAITH PARTIALLY RESTORED

IT IS NOT an easy matter to associate this psalm with any known historical situation. The fact that this psalm has some relation with Habakkuk 3 has a bearing upon the case. But it will not be an easy matter to assign priority in point of time to the one or the other. One possibility which is strongly defended by *Delitzsch* is that this psalm was written first, perhaps in the days of Josiah, before the Chaldean invasion had materialized, and that Habakkuk was influenced by the approach that the psalm makes to his problem. We shall let that stand as a possibility; it is as reasonable as any.

Although historical references to a contemporary situation are wanting, we can at least discern what the personal problem of the writer is. It seems as though the Lord had cast off His own to the point where there seemed no likelihood of restoration, in fact, it seemed as though the very attributes of God which had been the sure refuge of His people were no longer being manifested. However, that is not only the writer's personal problem; it is also the problem that plagues all of God's saints. We can scarcely go so far as to claim that the psalm is to be regarded as a complaint on the part of the nation. It has just a little too much of the personal note in it to support such a view. The nation's trouble agitates the heart and mind of this writer so much that he feels it as keenly as does anyone. Or to restate the problem as such: Why does God let things go on as long and as tragically as they do without giving any tokens of His interest and concern?

The solution that the writer attempts to arrive at is instructive. It is less a solution than an attempt to cope with the situation or a method of arriving at a solution. His method is this: Learn the lessons of the past; how has the Lord in former times dealt with His people?

Two extremes are to be avoided as we delve deeper into the lesson that is presented. One is to regard the material offered in the psalm as though it presented a complete solution, ready and final in all its parts, as though before the end of the psalm is reached the poet had fully recovered his balance. Such an approach is scarcely warranted.

The other extreme is to insist that the tension described in the first half of the psalm is still present in unmitigated force by the time the end of the psalm is reached. We have indicated our position by the wording that we gave to the title of the psalm: "Faith Waning and Faith Partially Restored." That is another way of saying that we regard the writer as being well along on the road to recovery by the time the end of the psalm is reached. He has discovered a remedy; he has applied it; it has begun to work; a sure bit of solid ground has been recovered; from this vantage point the writer will be able presently to rehabilitate himself spiritually.

We have no sympathy with that type of interpretation which attributes to the psalmist such unwholesome views of God as to lead him to think of the Almighty as being "of a whimsical and uncertain temper." It is true, his own impression is that God has changed. But as soon as he has this thought clearly formulated he begins to take steps to remedy what he regards as an impossible and untenable conclusion.

More helpful is the suggestion that the problem lies rather in man and his wrong attitude than in God and what He does.

The heading of the psalm reads thus: *For the Choir Director. According to Jerusalem. Of Asaph. A Psalm.* Asaph is, therefore, the writer. However, the phrase "according to Jeduthun" is not of the same type as it was in Ps. 39:1 but rather like it was in Ps. 62:1. For Jeduthun is not the author, but the psalm is, perhaps, to be rendered as Jeduthun was wont to render psalms.

a) The psalmist is in perplexity about God (vv. 1–10)
1. *I will raise my voice unto God and cry out;*
   I will raise my voice unto God, and He will hear me.
2. *In the day of my trouble I have always sought the Lord;*
   My hand was stretched out by night and wearied not;
   My soul refused to be comforted.
3. *When I think of God I moan;*
   When I lament, my spirit is faint. Selah.
4. *Thou hast held my eyelids open;*
   I was restless and did not speak.
5. *I have considered the days of old,*
   The years of long ago.
6. *And by night I remembered my song;*
   I lamented in my heart, and my spirit searched.
7. *Will the Lord cast off forever*
   And never again be favorable?
8. *Is His steadfast love clean gone forever?*
   Are His promises at an end forevermore?
9. *Has God forgotten to be gracious?*
   Has He in anger shut up His compassions? Selah.
10. *Then I said: "This is my grief,*
    That the right hand of the Most High has changed."

The thought expressed in this section may be summed up thus: The psalmist is in perplexity regarding God. In a general way two things may be further noted about these verses. First, they do begin with the thought of turning to God in prayer, but this attitude becomes submerged and does not rise to the surface again until v. 11 is reached. The second is like unto the first: The writer begins by talking quite at length *about* God till finally he begins to talk *to* God (v. 13)—and the latter certainly marks a distinct advance in his attitude and is far more wholesome.

1. We are suddenly transported right into the midst of a given situation, at the point, namely, where the author decides to make his grief heard before God. This utterance is rather abrupt because in the Hebrew the verb is missing, and thus the opening words read: "My voice to God." That may be one of those ellipses in which the verb is quite naturally supplied from the context and would then read something like, "I will raise my voice." Or it can be interpreted as expressing the volume of the sound made: "I cry aloud to God" (*RSV*) although this approach disregards the "and" before the verb "cry out." The point of the outcry is that the psalmist has arrived at the point where the pain within

can no longer be held back, and he, therefore, resolves to give it free course. Nor does he regard what he says as merely giving vent to pent-up emotions, for the verse concludes, "and He will hear me." Faith is not dead but is simply perplexed.

2. The manner in which we have rendered this verse indicates that the connection of thought as we see it is that by thus raising his voice the writer is merely doing what he has always done "in the day of (his) trouble." He has made a practice of seeking the Lord and stretching out his hand and persisting in his supplications and refusing to be content until God had heard him. But in this case, as v. 3 begins to indicate, the answer is slow in coming. His thought about God is not fraught with comfort. His seeming failure to respond to the cry for help that is made leads the writer to "moan." He may attempt a lament, but it affords him no relief, no relaxation; for still his "spirit is faint." He may be described as having arrived at a spiritual impasse. *McCullough* remarks at this point that the emotional disturbance involved gives evidence of the same symptoms that are found in our day: "they are called depression, nervous fatigue, insomnia, aphasia."

4. The fact that the sleeplessness here spoken of is attributed to God is to be understood in the sense that He has permitted a state of affairs to develop which disturbs the poet so much that sleep is banished from his eyes. The second half of the verse could very properly be translated: "I was restless and *could* not speak." Distress weighs so heavily upon the writer that he cannot find utterance; his words choke him when he tries to speak.

5. What has made the situation worse is the fact that he has tried a remedy that has often been recommended for relieving a state of spiritual perplexity: he has "considered the days of old, the years of long ago." He knows about them; the lessons involved have been brought to his attention. Such reflections, however, do nothing constructive for him. Equally ineffectual was the effort made by night when he remembered his "song," literally his "music" that he made on stringed instruments (*Luther: Saitenspiel*). Many may have been the songs that he either composed or sang; and he had derived much spiritual refreshment from them. But that gave him no help now, it roused no responsive chord of faith. What probing and searching he did to find an answer to his present state of spiritual dearth is indicated by the words: "I lamented in my heart, and my spirit searched." Thus far only v. 3 had remotely indicated that all this had something to do with God when it stated, "When I think of God I moan." The real issue has not yet been formulated. However, the formulation or something akin to it now follows.

7. The problem is this: "Will the Lord cast off forever and never again be favorable?" Something has befallen His people which makes it

very plain to them that He is not favorably disposed toward them. This attitude of His has continued for some time without an indication of letting up. God was never wont to take such an attitude toward His people when they were in distress, not as far as those who are now involved can remember. They are becoming unsure about God. The immutable qualities that were characteristic of Him seem to have failed. One feels the deep pain of heart in the recital that follows in vv. 8, 9, where "steadfast love" and "His promises" and His graciousness are thought of as not being discernible. His "compassions" are shut up, and all that can for the moment be discovered is "anger." It is no light matter to be so troubled about God that the very thought of Him and what He does results merely in perplexity. V. 9 has a resemblance to Hab. 3:2.

10. The writer then rather aptly sums up his perplexity in the words: "This is my grief, that the right hand of the Most High has changed." God is not what He used to be. What was true with regard to Him in the past certainly does not seem to be so now. More particularly, it appears that God either has not the strength that is able to help, or else He does not care to use it if He has it. To be in such a situation brings with it a most anguishing dilemma. The very ground is gone from under a man's feet.

In the next section the psalmist recalls God's works of the past. This is apparently a more effective approach than was the one in which the "days of old" were considered (v. 5). He that gives meaning to the days of old or, for that matter, to any age is being brought into the picture.

b) He recalls Gods work of the past (vv. 11–15)

11. *I will call to mind the deeds of the Lord;*
    Yea, I will remember Thy wonders from of old.
12. *And I will meditate on all Thy works;*
    And I will reflect on Thy mighty deeds.
13. *O God, Thy way is holy.*
    Who is so great a God as our God?
14. *Thou art the God that doest wonders;*
    Thou hast displayed Thy strength among the peoples.
15. *Thou hast mightily redeemed Thy people,*
    The sons of Jacob and Joseph. Selah.

11. Some measure of purpose and resolution is expressed in the words, "I will call to mind," such as conscious immersion in the facts involved. This is more than a dreamy dwelling upon what once happened. If in addition the "wonders from of old" are in the picture, that implies that the magnitude of God's works and their effectiveness are under consideration. How intently the writer purposes to busy himself with this theme and draw the needed inferences from it appears also in

v. 12, where both meditation and reflection are also to be employed, and the objects of these verbs indicate that substantial and effective works of God are being studied as to their full import.

13. Almost at once, as a result of such intensive scrutiny of God's deeds of the past, certain old, established truths come prominently to light again such as: "Thy way is holy," that is to say, far removed from those defective and imperfect doings of the children of men. The course He follows is always above reproach. The fact that this truth is addressed to God shows that the writer again has God actively in the picture and is relating himself consciously to the Lord. Another way of stating this truth is by contrast with those that are called gods: "Who is so great a God as our God?" Such statements commonly mean no more than that God in every respect far exceeds those that are commonly designated as gods, without admitting that they have actual existence. This statement is practically a restating of an old confession that Israel had made in Moses' days (cf., Exod. 15:11).

Certain other broad truths of the same caliber are also recaptured by the author, all of them being corollaries of those just expressed, such as: "Thou art the God that doest wonders." For there are startling and marvelous acheivements of His on record. In fact, His deeds have often been of such a nature that surrounding nations were compelled to admit their magnitude, or as it is here stated: "Thou hast displayed Thy strength among the peoples." In fact, bringing the truth involved still more sharply into focus, just that which seemed to be lacking at the present is abundantly testified to by the past: "Thou hast mightily redeemed Thy people." Why God's people are specifically referred to as "the sons of Jacob and Joseph" is more than we can at present definitely determine, especially as to why Joseph should be injected into the picture. It could be an indication of a north-Israelite origin of the psalm.

The psalmist now centers his attention on one specific event of the past and recalls particularly the passage of the Israelites through the Red Sea.

c) **The passage through the Red Sea recalled (vv. 16-19)**

16. *The waters saw Thee, O God;*
    The waters saw Thee, they writhed with fear;
    Yea, the deep trembled.
17. *The clouds poured out water;*
    The skies gave forth thunder;
    Yea, Thy arrows went hither and thither.
18. *The roll of Thy thunder was like that of wheels;*
    Thy lightnings lighted up the earth;
    The earth trembled and shook.

19. *Thy way was through the sea
And Thy path through the great waters;
Yet Thy footprints were not noted.*

16. As is indicated in v. 19 and even more distinctly in v. 20, the scene described is the crossing of the Red Sea on the part of the children of Israel. The overpowering glory of that deed is sketched in vivid colors. In fact, there is a measure of poetic embellishment involved which is rather surprising. Apart from the poetry of the description, the mention of rain and thunder and the quaking of the earth rather surprises us. It may well be possible that all these factors were involved in what the prose account of Exod. 14:24, 25 describes as to its effects upon the Egyptians. There is the further possibility that rememberance of the details reported by the psalmist was kept alive in the traditions of Israel. In any case, it is very likely that this is more than purely rhetorical embellishment. It cannot be denied that to describe the receding waters as writhing and trembling (v. 16) at the sight of the Lord is unique and colorful poetry.

17. This verse indicates that a terrific storm was involved. The "arrows" that "went hither and thither" are the lightnings. The meaning of the first line of v. 18 seems to be, as we have rendered it, that the thunder may have been like unto the echoing sound that is produced by the chariot of God as it sweeps across the skies or, for that matter, by any chariot. What v. 19 seems to stress is the thought that the passage that was opened for the children of Israel by the Lord was His "way" for them, a secret and unknown path by which He was able to lead them safely from seemingly inescapable perils.

We might have added v. 20 as the conclusion of the last section of the psalm, which it quite obviously is. But we preferred to suggest that it may be considered a separate section which is the one basic conclusion that the writer arrives at as a result of his contemplation of God's mighty works in times past, for it is just that.

e) **He arrives at one basic conclusion (v. 20)**

20. *Thou didst lead Thy people like a flock
By the hand of Moses and Aaron.*

This is a thought or figure that the Asaphic psalms like to dwell upon (cf., 74:1; 78:52, 70–72; 79:13; 80:2). It is furthermore a basic and well-validated truth that augurs well for the future. It is like unto a foundation on which the writer has taken his stand, and which he finds important enough to have it represent the sum of his findings or at least the temporary and provisional solution that he has arrived at. That may well be regarded as representing the point of belief which he had reached at the time he wrote the psalm. It is not enough nor final enough in the long run. But when God's guidance is viewed as a valid factor in the history of the past, other issues will soon clear up.

The assumption that some verses which followed this verse may have been lost and to regard the conclusion as ineffective overlooks the distinctive character of the experience involved in this psalm. A man is well on the road to recovery from uncertainty and doubts if he is aware of the fact that the past records God's faithful guidance of His people and also records that God always provided adequate leadership.

The fact that at v. 16 the psalm changes from the 3:3 meter to the 3:3:3 pattern dare not be pressed to the point where the section vv. 16–20 is made a part of another psalm which someone attached to make our present Ps. 77. To believe that our writer is incapable of such modification of his metrical pattern involves having very low conceptions of his literary gifts.

Mention should be made of the rather striking fact that there is nothing in the psalm which suggests a sense of sinfulness on the part of the writer or the nation. This fact cannot be removed by any attempted explanation. In some ages such a conviction of sin is more apt to stand out prominently; in other ages it may be submerged. It is possible that the matter was inadvertently overlooked. It dare not be stated that, to be acceptable, prayer must grow out of a deep sense of guilt. Let us be content with the statement that in this psalm the subject of sin and guilt did not happen to be touched upon.

NOTES

2. We regard *darashti* as one of the perfects that functions as a sort of gnomic aorist and expresses the habitual.

3. It is true that the first three verbs have the familiar *qamets he* hortative appended to them. This could be expressed by the rendering that *Oesterley* offers: "I must recall God and must moan; I must meditate and let my spirit faint away." On the other hand, it is true enough that in many instances such an ending becomes more or less otiose. We have regarded it as such.

6. Though the imperfects might seem to call for a rendering that places the whole verse into the present tense, there is a likelihood, as *Koenig* (*KS* 200b) has suggested, that after the final *mem* of the preceding verse a *waw* has been dropped as happens quite frequently. The imperfect found in the next verb merely marks a subordinate item, and the last verb is a typical imperfect with *waw* consecutive.

10. The form *shenoth* can, of course, be translated "years," which gives rise to the *KJ* rendering: "I will remember the years of the right

hand of the most High." But then an unsuspected "but I will remember" has to be supplied, an omission that is altogether too harsh. We have regarded the word as the infinitive construct of the verb *shanah* which is used as a noun in apposition with "grief."

17. The whole verse is to be rendered in the past tense. *Yachílu* lost its *waw* consecutive after *mem* as it did in v. 6, and in connection with the last verb *'aph* serves the same purpose as such a *waw* would serve (*KS* 368e).

18. When we translated "like that of wheels," we took note of the possibility that the final *kaph* may have been written but once before *baggalgal* (haplography).

Psalm 78

THE LESSONS OF HISTORY THAT FAITHFUL PARENTS SHOULD TEACH THEIR CHILDREN

THE HEADING calls this "a didactic poem." In this case we can clearly discern the propriety of this designation. In its own way the psalm develops a kind of philosophy of history in a plain and practical form of instruction that can be passed on by parents to children.

If the heading further ascribes the psalm to Asaph, there is surely no valid reason for doubting the correctness of this statement. As I Chron. 25:1 and II Chron. 29:30 indicate, there is reason for believing that a man of this name was a contemporary of David. To think of him as the author of this psalm has as much to support it as has any rival claim.

There is at least one obvious point of contact between this psalm and Ps. 77. Whereas the latter closes with the thought of Israel's being under the leadership of Moses and Aaron, this psalm points to David's serving in a similar capacity. Aside from that there is also the point of view which loves to draw instructive and helpful lessons from the history of God's people. In this respect our psalm is also closely akin to Ps. 105-107, especially in its more extended treatment of records of the past.

Though it is didactic the psalm is far from pedantic. It manifests a free and genial treatment of history. Strict historical sequence is not so important as are the lessons taught by history. So, for example, the sequence of events happens to be: the exodus, the plagues, the occupation. But such a sequence does not impair the logic or the effectiveness of treatment. Surely, so much latitude may be allowed any writer who is not strictly a historian.

Though in many instances terms are used that are obviously to be found also in the earlier narratives of the Pentateuch, it would be a bit extreme to regard the material as being borrowed directly from this or that book. It would rather appear that the events referred to are presented as part and parcel of a living tradition that had developed in Israel, of course, with constant reference to the written sources that were also known from Mosaic days. The attempt that was made sometime ago to trace the material presented as obviously coming from some one of the so-called sources of the Pentateuch (J or E or D) is now generally abandoned as being untenable though it is still claimed that a so-called Deuteronomic touch is evident.

It would be unfair to the writer of the psalm to attribute to him an unwholesome bias in his attitude toward Ephraim or to advance the claim that he had "an ax to grind" in the interest of the house of David. His is the same approach as that of the historical books, which regard the rejection of the Ephraim group as well as the choice of the house of David as emanating from the wise providence of God, who is free to bestow His favors as His grace prompts Him to do.

Though we favor the supposition that the Asaph who lived in David's days wrote this psalm we recognize that there are no convincing arguments which make this approach necessary. Nor are there convincing arguments that compel the assumption of a late date of composition.

The current trend that makes it imperative to find a place in the cultus for every psalm gets its advocates into certain difficulties in the case of this psalm. For this psalm does not readily fit into such a scheme. *Schmidt* claims that the festival of the enthronement of the king would be the proper time for expressing the thoughts of the psalm. *Leslie* would have it read at the Passover festival. *McCullough* cautiously suggests the same possibility. *Oesterley* despairs of finding any suitable place in the cultus. It would appear that the cultus approach is a little too rigid to be applied to the whole Psalter.

Stier summarizes the practical purpose of the psalm by having the author say in effect: "Therefore serve this king whom God has faithfully given you (David); gather under the staff of this shepherd at the sanctuary of Zion, and do not again become unfaithful as your fathers did. This is the fundamental and final note of the whole psalm."

An outline will give a rapid insight into the plan and structure of the psalm:
a) The purpose of this didactic psalm: to instruct the coming generation against infidelity by the clear lessons of history (vv. 1–8)

b) Ephraim, a typical example of infidelity (vv. 9–11)
c) Instances of God's gracious dealings at the time of the exodus and the wilderness wanderings which were matched by Israel's unfaithfulness (vv. 12–31)
d) A summary of God's judgments and Israel's shallow repentance (vv. 32–39)
e) Israel's rebellion in the wilderness against the background of the mighty works of God done shortly before in Egypt (vv. 40–55)
f) Israel's infidelity after the occupation of the land and God's subsequent judgments (vv. 56–64)
g) Evidences of God's faithful care in the establishment of the kingdom under David (vv. 65–72)

1. *Give ear, O my people, to my instruction;*
   Incline your ear to the words of my mouth.
2. *I will open my mouth in a parable;*
   I will freely discuss perplexing issues from days of old.
3. *What we have heard and known,*
   And what our fathers have told us,
4. *We shall not hide from their sons,*
   Telling the coming generation the praiseworthy acts of the Lord
   And His might and His wonders which He has done.
5. *How He established a testimony in Jacob and appointed a law in Israel,*
   Which He commanded our fathers to make them known to their children;
6. *That the coming generation might know them, the children yet to be born,*
   That they might arise and declare them to their children,
7. *That they would set their hope in God*
   And not forget the works of God but keep His commandments;
8. *And that they would not become like their fathers, a stubborn and rebellious generation,*
   A generation that did not set its heart aright, and whose spirit was not faithful to God.

1. This introduction is quite similar in tone to the wisdom literature of Israel, especially the opening chapters of the book of Proverbs. After solemnly admonishing his people to give heed to what he is about to say the author describes what he has to offer as a "parable," or proverb, or as a discussion of "perplexing issues from days of old." From the sequel it appears that these "riddles"—as some interpreters translate this word—are those matters in history which are so hard to understand: the unyielding stubbornness of God's people over against

His unwavering faithfulness. How can a people spurn such grace? How can God continue to manifest such longsuffering? These are the great enigmas of history. When v. 2 is quoted in the New Testament (Matt. 13:34, 35) it is rather by way of practical application than of fulfilment of prophecy.

3. The writer goes on to develop the practical purpose that he has in mind in treating the problems of history (vv. 3–8). He lays stress chiefly on the fact that the basic lessons involved are to be taught diligently to their children by the fathers lest coming generations continue to make the same mistakes in a wearying and endless round. He admits that the true knowledge of these matters is abroad in the land. What he is indirectly exhorting his generation to do in regard to such important and saving knowledge is to point up the fact that in days of old God "established a testimony in Jacob and appointed a law in Israel." For him the whole life of the nation is built up on the Mosaic law. Possession of that law puts the fathers under obligation to make these blessed statutes well and thoroughly known to the generations that follow as the Lord Himself had so explicitly commanded Israel to do in the days when He gave His law (Exod. 10:2; 12:26, 27; 13: 8, 14; Deut. 4:9; 6:20–25). In fact, a solid tradition of continuous transmission of God's Word is thus to be established (v. 6) from generation to generation.

7. In order also to point up sharply the fact that all this did not involve merely a type of mechanical memorization of a stated number of words, the psalmist shows (v. 7) to what attitude toward God all this should lead—"That they would set their hope in God and not forget the works of God but keep His commandments." He appends to this a solemn reminder of the consistent attitude that the fathers of the nation had taken through well-nigh four hundred years (v. 8). It must be admitted that all this constitutes an effective practical introduction to the psalm.

Having just alluded to the unsatisfactory attitude of the fathers, he points up this subject by reference to a specific instance from history: Ephraim, which tribe was a typical example of the infidelity just referred to (vv. 9–11). The initial statement is not a historical allusion to a particular event but a general statement in figurative language, as much as to say: Ephraim furnishes us with such an example of failure when an actual test was imposed upon the tribe. It is in this sense that the expression "day of battle" is used.

It would appear that this is a reference to the over-all leadership of the tribe of Ephraim among the Twelve Tribes in the days of the judges, which had just concluded one major episode in Israel's history. Judah had not yet come into its own or manifested any particular capacity for leadership as she was to manifest after the days of David. So Ephraim had held the dominant position, at least in so far as such a position was held by any tribe. But her leadership was disastrous though she had all the qualifications and equipment that would have been required for success in shaping the destiny of the nation. This seems to be the force of the statement "though fully equipped with bows."

As v. 10 immediately shows, the failure involved was one of "not keeping the covenant of God and refusing to walk in His law." And that failure was again rooted, as v. 10 indicates, in the forgetting cf His works and wonders which He had showed them. There is nothing spiteful about these statements. They are a correct evaluation of the leadership of Ephraim during these days of the theocracy. The verses that constitute this second section read as follows:

9. *The children of Ephraim, though fully equipped with bows,*
   Turned back in the day of battle.
10. *They did not keep the covenant of God*
    And refused to walk in His law.
11. *And they forgot His works*
    And His wonders which He showed them.

Quite apart from the sort of leadership that Ephraim exercised, the great fault of the entire past history of the nation was the fact that all the instances of God's gracious dealings at the time of the exodus and the wilderness wanderings were consistently matched by Israel's unfaithfulness (vv. 12–31). Each kindness of God evoked a reaction that was just the opposite of what it should have been.

12. *In the sight of their fathers He had wrought marvelous things*
    In the land of Egypt, in the field of Zoan.
13. *He divided the sea and made them pass through it;*
    And He made the waters to stand like a heap.
14. *He led them with a cloud by day*
    And all the night by a fiery light.
15. *He cleft rocks in the wilderness;*
    He gave them to drink abundantly as from deep waters.
16. *And He brought forth streams from the rock*
    And caused waters to run down like rivers.
17. *Yet they kept on sinning against Him*
    By provoking the Most High in the wilderness.
18. *And they put God to the test in their hearts*
    By asking meat to satisfy their hunger.
19. *And they spoke against God;*
    They said: "Can God spread a table in the wilderness?"

20. "Behold, He smote the rock, and waters gushed forth, and streams overflowed;
    Can He also give bread, or can He provide meat for His people?"
21. Therefore the Lord heard and became angry;
    Fire was kindled against Jacob, and wrath mounted against Israel.
22. Because they believed not in God
    And trusted not in His salvation,
23. So He commanded the skies above
    And opened the doors of heaven.
24. And He rained down manna upon them to eat
    And gave them the grain of heaven.
25. Man ate the bread of angels.
    He furnished provisions in abundance.
26. He caused the east wind to blow in the heavens;
    And by His might He led forth the south wind.
27. And He rained flesh upon them like dust
    And winged birds like the sand of the sea.
28. And He let them fall in the midst of their camp
    All around their habitation.
29. And they did eat and were well filled;
    And so He brought them that which they craved.
30. They did not desist from their craving.
    While their food was still in their mouth,
31. The wrath of God came up against them;
    And He slew of the stoutest of them;
    And He laid low the choicest of Israel.

A few brief comments will suffice for the treatment of this section. Zoan (v. 12) lies on the second from the last of the east arms of the Nile delta and must thus have been located near Goshen. It was a very ancient city (Num. 13:22) and achieved prominence in the Twenty-first Dynasty (1090–945 B.C.) according to *Oesterley*. The poetic expression "like a heap" (v. 13) is found also in Exod. 14:22.

From v. 15 onward the two instances of the giving of water from the rock are considered jointly (Exod. 17:6; Num. 20:8ff), and the giving of the quail as narrated in Num. 11:31ff. is also brought into the picture. The point of view and the manner of treatment of all these incidents are practically the same as is that of the historic account in the Pentateuch. V. 22, like v. 7, points to the deeper issues involved in the various rebellions in the wilderness. They were in the last analysis a question of faith and of trusting in God's salvation.

In reference to the manna, one of the obviously great miracles of that period which is recorded chiefly in Exod. 16:14ff., the reference in

v. 25 to the "bread of angels" again lies in the area of rich figurative expression. To seek from this expression to establish the doctrine that angels literally ate manna would be stretching the point beyond what was intended. It is rather: food good enough for angels.

The total impact of the section is quite clear: God was very kind; Israel was most ungrateful. This is certainly one of the difficult riddles of history. It is not the deeds of the Almighty which are so perplexing. It is the attitude and behavior of man that are hard to explain.

In the next section (vv. 32–39) the writer summarizes God's judgments and Israel's reactions to them by showing in particular how even the repentance of Israel was but shallow and unsatisfactory and, therefore, not a cure of the traditional attitude. Consequently the same procedure was followed time and again.

32. *In spite of all this they sinned yet more;*
    And they believed not His wondrous works.
33. *And so He let their days vanish away as a breath*
    And their years in terror.
34. *Whenever He slew them, then they sought Him*
    And repented and sought after Him.
35. *And they remembered that God was their rock*
    And God Most High their redeemer.
36. *But they flattered Him only with their mouth;*
    And they lied to Him with their tongue,
37. *Whereas their heart was not steadfast toward Him;*
    They were not faithful to His covenant.
38. *But He, being merciful, pardons iniquity and does not destroy;*
    Yea, many a time He turns His anger away and does not stir up
    His wrath.
39. *And He remembered that they were but flesh,*
    A wind that passes and does not come again.

32. The first verses of this section dwell on the judgment of God that made the rebellious generation spend thirty-eight years in the wilderness until all of the original group that had taken part in the exodus had passed away: "He let their days vanish away as a breath." Whatever seemingly favorable reactions were shown by them were only temporary. When they seemingly made a good confession, it amounted to no more than "flattering with their mouth." As he has done in each preceding section, the author also here probes till he comes to the root of Israel's weakness, which is always the same—a lack of true faith: "Their heart was not steadfast toward Him; they were not faithful to His covenant" (v. 37).

38. This verse sets forth a general principle which holds good for

all times and should be translated in the present tense: "But He, being merciful, pardons iniquity." Echoes of Exod. 34:6, 7 are heard here (cf. also Ps. 130:14). This, too, is one of the deep enigmas of history, that the Almighty can be as compassionate as He is, man being so utterly undeserving of His mercy. Dropping back into the historical account, v. 39 indicates what motivates such gracious action on God's part: "He remembered that they were but flesh, a wind that passes and does not come again."

In the next section Israel's various acts of rebellion in the wilderness are sketched against the background of the signs and wonders God had wrought in the land of Egypt, especially of the plagues that had so grievously afflicted Egypt and spared Israel, all of which had happened but shortly before they went into the wilderness (vv. 40–55).

40. *How often they rebelled against Him in the wilderness,*
    They grieved Him in the desert!
41. *They kept on putting God to the test*
    And deeply grieved the Holy One of Israel.
42. *They remembered not His hand,*
    Nor the day when He redeemed them from the enemy,
43. *When He wrought His signs in Egypt,*
    His wonders in the field of Zoan,
44. *And turned their rivers into blood*
    So that they could not drink of their streams.
45. *He sent swarms of insects among them which devoured them*
    And frogs which destroyed them.
46. *He gave their crops to the grasshoppers*
    And the fruit of their labor to the locust.
47. *He destroyed their vines with hail*
    And their sycamores with hailstones.
48. *He gave over their cattle to the hail*
    And their flocks to lightnings.
49. *And He let loose upon them the fierceness of His anger—wrath,*
    indignation, and distress,
    An embassy of angels of woe.
50. *He made smooth a path for His anger;*
    He did not spare them from death but gave their lives over to
    the pestilence
51. *And smote all the firstborn in Egypt,*
    The first fruits of their strength in the tents of Ham.
52. *But He made His own people to depart like sheep*
    And guided them in the wilderness like a flock.

Psalm 78

53. *And He led them on safely so that they were not afraid.
    But the sea overwhelmed their enemies.*
54. *And He brought them to His holy land,
    The mountain which His right hand had gotten.*
55. *And He drove out nations before them
    And divided them as an inheritance by lot
    And gave the tribes of Israel dwellings in their tents.*

The attitude of Israel is quite correctly described as a putting to the test of the Most High. These were not trifling peccadillos; they were disastrous and devastating instances of deep iniquity. When it is said (v. 42) that "they remembered not His hand," the reference is to the mighty works which His hand had wrought. The passage which gives the record of the plagues referred to is, of course, Exod. 7–12. The plagues enumerated are the first, the fourth, the second, the eighth, the seventh, and the tenth— a fairly broad sampling of the type of deed done by God. When in v. 50 "the pestilence" is referred to, that is in part the language of the Exodus account (see Exod. 9:15) but offers another interpretation as to how the slaying of the firstborn may have taken place. The section concludes with the arrival of the people in the land of Canaan and the occupation. The "mountain" referred to in v. 54 is merely another term for the mountainous land of Israel as a whole. That last kindness of freely giving them the land with all that it offered prepares the way for the next section which by way of contrast cites further instances of Israel's infidelity (vv. 56–64).

It would appear at first glance that in v. 41 the name "the Holy One of Israel" must point to a later date than Isaiah because that term was seemingly first used when Isaiah began to employ it. But the development of such names and terms does not always proceed strictly according to the pattern that we might devise. By a flash of insight Asaph could have glimpsed possibilities in a new name, which he used but once, and which someone who wrote later than he did brought into prominence.

Having come to the time of the establishment of the nation in the land of promise, the psalmist goes on to dwell on this period of the history of his people and to show how many instances of infidelity they were guilty of in those years, and what sharp judgments God had to bring crashing upon their heads (vv. 56–64).

56. *But they put to the test and provoked the Most High God
    And did not keep His testimonies.*
57. *But they fell away and dealt treacherously like their fathers;
    They turned like an unreliable bow.*

58. *And provoked Him to anger with their high places*
    And moved Him to jealousy with their graven images.
59. *When God heard this He became furious*
    And greatly abhorred Israel.
60. *And He spurned His dwelling at Shilo,*
    The tent which He had established among men.
61. *And He delivered* (the symbol of) *His power into captivity;*
    His glory into the hand of the enemy.
62. *And He gave His people over to the sword;*
    He was furious at His inheritance.
63. *Their young men the fire devoured;*
    And their young maidens had no marriage song.
64. *Their priests fell by the sword;*
    And their widows chanted no funeral dirge.

56. The obvious sin of the age of the judges was (v. 58) the cult of graven images and the high places. But behind this outward wickedness lay the root fault of not "keeping the testimonies" of the Lord (v. 56). God's Word is always sinned against first; then follow the outward evidences of departure from Him. In taking this attitude the people of that age merely perpetuated the treachery of their fathers (v. 57) and so again proved themselves to be like an "unreliable bow" in the hands of a warrior. For with such a bow the bowman shoots at his target but is disappointed by his continual failure to shoot straight. Such disappointment continually came to the Lord from His people. His reaction to such behavior of theirs is described in unusually strong terms: He was provoked to anger and moved to jealousy; He became furious and greatly abhorred His own. Passive placidity on the part of God over against the sin of His children is an utter misconception of the divine nature.

60. So God did a number of things by way of chastising his people. "He spurned His dwelling at Shilo" (v. 60). Though the record in I Sam. 4 fails to mention what happened to Shilo, a later writer indicates what occurred (Jer. 7:12). Though He had established His name there He utterly overthrew the place. He at the same time delivered the peculiar symbol of His grace, the ark, into captivity, the ark being here called "His power" and "His glory," signifying, of course, the symbol of His power and glory. The whole nation was delivered over to death on the field of battle and in the cruelties of war. The fact that their young men were devoured by the fire, that is, by the relentless fury of war, may well be an allusion to the tragic death of Hophni and Phinehas (I Sam. 4:11). And thus because of a dearth of young men through-

Psalm 78 571

out the land the young maidens could not "have a marriage song," referring to the ancient custom of celebrating the bride in poetic odes on the occasion of her marriage. Priests (v. 64) also fell and could not be given a decent lament because of the stress of the times. A sad picture and an impressive lesson of history, to say the least.

The psalm closes with a section that gives emphasis only to the good and mighty works of the Lord that were done for His people and ends on a very positive note. That, too, is very instructive. Israel's many instances of waywardness and stubbornness do not change the basic attitude of Israel's God; their faithlessness does not cancel His steadfast love.

65. *Then the Lord awoke as one asleep,*
    Like a strong man shouting because of wine.
66. *And He beat His enemies back;*
    Everlasting shame He inflicted upon them.
67. *He rejected the house of Joseph;*
    And the tribe of Ephraim He did not choose.
68. *But He chose the tribe of Judah,*
    Mount Zion which He loved.
69. *And He built His sanctuary exalted;*
    Like the earth which He has established forever.
70. *He chose David, His servant,*
    And took him from the sheepfolds.
71. *From tending the ewes He brought him*
    To tend Jacob, His people, and Israel, His inheritance.
72. *He tended them with integrity of purpose;*
    And with skilful hand He guided them.

65. This passage sets in at a point in history when the enemies of Israel had been definitely and soundly defeated, let us say at the time when David had subdued all his enemies on every side. This complete victory is, however, to be attributed to the Lord Himself, who may be said to have aroused Himself and gone to battle like a hero who is exhilarated by wine. Though the last figure is bold, there is no need of resorting to the extravagant and somewhat irreverent translation offered by the *Septuagint,* "like a giant who had been overcome by wine." He it was (v. 66) "who beat His enemies back" and "inflicted everlasting shame upon them."

67. From that point the writer moves on to another very significant development in the history of the covenant people: the choice of David and his house to guide the destinies of the future. Naturally, as one views the course of history, that involved the rejection of another tribe

which had long aspired to leadership among the twelve. There is nothing spiteful about the writer's statements; he offers nothing more than a sober evaluation of facts as other Scripture passages plainly interpret them (cf. especially II Sam. 7). Involved in the choice of a tribe that was to be headed by a chosen individual was the selection of a place of habitation for that leader and for God's own sanctuary—Mount Zion. Though at the time of the writing of the psalm the beautiful and impressive Temple of Solomon may not yet have stood in Jerusalem as a "sanctuary exalted," yet the house of the Lord as such, apart from the structure that housed it, was by God's choice and preference exalted above all earthly sanctuaries and destined to a history that was to run far into the now hidden future (this being the basic meaning of the word "forever" here used).

70. Particular mention is made of David in this verse, and he is given an honorable epithet that is granted to but few in Sacred Writ, "His servant" (used also in reference to Moses, Joshua, Caleb, Job, etc.). The writer sees a striking analogy between the work David had engaged in previously and that which he was to do after God's choice of him as ruler of Israel: he first shepherded lambs, he now shepherds the people of God. As he had tended the one, so he tends the other "with integrity of purpose and with skilful hand," that is to say, sincere in his intentions and adept at carrying them out. Since, as our earlier quotation from *Stier* indicated, it was the writer's purpose to show God's people their proper attitude toward their God-given leader by accepting him as such and obeying him with sincere loyalty, the writer closes on this note.

NOTES

9. The literal translation of the two participles in the construct state is: "seizing, yea, shooting the bow." The plausibility of such a construction is demonstrated by *KS* 337m. The fact that we may not like it or think it according to the genius of the languages we are most familiar with does not make these words an error that calls for emendations. We believe that the force of the expression is given with a fair measure of accuracy by our translation: "though fully equipped with bows."

15. We consider the imperfect *yebhaqqa'* the imperfect of concomitant circumstances and so marking subordinate features of the account at this point.

18. The use of the infinitive *lish'ol* is rather familiar. It expresses manner, not purpose; cf. *KS* 402d.

31. The *be* after *yaharog* is the equivalent of a *min* partitive as *KS* has demonstrated (84).

45. The initial verb in the imperfect seems to express the iterative. Still the whole context suggests past time.

49. The last word of the verse is in the plural. It is apparently attracted into the plural by *mal'akhey,* which appears in the plural (*KS* 267e).

Psalm 79

LAMENT OVER THE DESTRUCTION
OF JERUSALEM AND PRAYER FOR HELP

THIS DOUBLE title, borrowed from *ARV,* indicates both the subject matter and the division into parts. The lament involved is stated in vv. 1–4, and the prayer for help constitutes the rest of the psalm. By way of further analysis we shall break down the second half (vv. 5-13) into four subdivisions.

It should be noted that this psalm has a very close kinship, even in the individual expressions used, with Ps. 74, and that, like this psalm, it seems best to assign it in point of time to the period of the destruction of Jerusalem under the Chaldeans although it would be rash to claim that we can either prove or disprove that the Temple still stood or was already in ruins; or whether the destruction of the city was total or partial.

Another feature of the psalm that calls for attention is its mosaic character. It has so many obvious points of contact with other parts of Scripture that it must be freely admitted that its author made copious use of what others had written. In some instances it becomes quite difficult to determine to whom the original statement must be ascribed, that is to say, whether our author borrowed from others or they from him. For a full analysis of all the features involved one may consult Oesterley. *Poteat* remarks that fifteen phrases are to be found.

It would scarcely be fair to the psalm to make the claim that it starts from a false premise, namely, the mistaken notion that God was to be charged with favoritism in that He regards Israel differently from other nations and treats her with unwarranted kindness (*Poteat*). Such an approach confuses two issues that lie in closely adjacent fields. It confuses the fact that God may choose a nation as His own in a particular sense, as He did in the case of Israel, with the supposition that as a result of this unusual relationship God applied a different norm of judgment in dealing with His favored people. The first thought may be clearly present because it can be based on historical experience (for Israel was the covenant nation) without necessitating the suggestion that the nation or its legitimate religion contended that Israel might lay claim to preferential treatment. Mercy on the basis of the covenant dare not be confused with the hope of favoritism, though it certainly cannot be denied that individuals did from time to time confuse the two. Yet such a charge may not be made against the writer of this psalm.

We must also absolve the writer of the psalm from the charge that his utterances are marked by "wild passion" (*Kittel*). For though here or there some strong statements may be used by him, two things should be borne in mind. One, that arm-chair criticism of a person who is in the midst of most trying distress is cheap. As *Weiser* points out, only one who has been in situations analogous to those of the writer can find the deeper understanding of the psalm opening up to him. The other matter is this: when God's saints are in exceedingly painful distress, not every remark that they may happen to make is to be regarded as necessarily being normative and exemplary; or if it is extreme in one way or another is not to be criticized for its want of balance. Extreme difficulties beget extreme statements, which the writer himself may deplore in calmer moments, and which we should neither defend nor harshly criticize.

A somewhat unusual quotation should yet be noted. V. 3 happens to be quoted in the apocryphal book I Maccabees (7:17). The fact that v. 3 appears in that book scarcely allows for the conclusion that I Maccabees was composed before this psalm. For then a historical situation prior to the date of the coming of Christ would have to be discovered when this psalm could have been written; and no such event is known. Therefore priority in point of time obviously belongs to this psalm.

> *A Psalm. Of Asaph.*
> 1. *O God, the heathen have come into Thy inheritance;*
>   *They have defiled Thy holy Temple;*
>   *They have laid Jerusalem in ruins.*
> 2. *They have given the bodies of Thy servants as food to the birds of the heavens,*
>   *The flesh of Thy saints to the beasts of the earth.*
> 3. *They have poured out their blood like water round about Jerusalem;*
>   *And there was no one to bury them.*

4. We have become a taunt to our neighbors,
   An object of scorn and derision to those round about us.

On "Asaph" see the introductory remarks on Ps. 74.

In this description the whole matter is laid before God, not with the intention of informing him, but with the manifest purpose of unburdening the heart of the writer of the grief that weighs him down. At the same time the thought is implied that such suffering of His covenant people is not a matter of indifference to God.

An invasion has occurred. The heathen have penetrated into the holy city. The Temple has been defiled—apparently not yet utterly destroyed. Ruins mark the city—whether total or partial is not stated. Dead bodies lie about in the streets; birds feed on them or wild scavenger dogs even though these persons are God's saints. No one is left to give these bodies a decent burial. The neighbors and the enemies have done the customary things under such circumstances: they have taunted the poor sufferers. Nothing more need be said. The situation is extreme to the utmost degree.

b) **The prayer that God may punish those who afflicted Israel (vv. 5–7)**

5. How long, O Lord, wilt Thou be angry? Forever?
   Will Thy jealous wrath burn like fire?
6. Pour out Thy wrath upon the heathen who do not know Thee
   And upon the kingdoms who have not called upon Thy name.
7. For they have devoured Jacob
   And have laid waste his habitation.

The chief thought of this prayer is that God may punish those who have afflicted Israel. Though we well know that the feeling of revenge could dominate such a prayer, there are other possibilities, objectives that are not unworthy of God's people. One such may be that the evildoer might be checked; another that he might receive his due reward. To adopt the least charitable view is scarcely warranted when one is charging others with lack of charity.

That we here have a prayer that was uttered by a person who has some depth of insight appears from the fact that Israel's sufferings are traced, not to some accident, but to the sovereign Ruler of the affairs of men, whose anger has been roused by the misdeeds of His people (v. 5). This anger has burned long and has had much pain inflicted upon the people. In the Old and the New Testament God's anger is very real and terrible and just. Its long continuance presses the cry from the psalmist's lips: "How long, O Lord, wilt Thou be angry? Forever?" This prayer, analogous to 13:1; 74:1, 10, seems to be self-contradictory: "how long" vs. "forever." Though it may thus be a kind of hyperbole, there are three possibilities of translation. The more common is: "How long wilt Thou be angry forever?" The second: "How long, O Lord? Wilt Thou be angry forever?" (*RSV*). Third, the one we have offered above. It is almost impossible to determine which deserves the preference. Our rendering makes the difficulty less acute.

6. When the writer prays that God may pour out His wrath upon the heathen that know Him not, the thought certainly cannot be that they are to be penalized because of their ignorance. Rather, since, positively, to "know" God involves man's deepest emotions according to the Hebrew verb involved, so, negatively, "not to know" Him implies the guilty rejection of the Almighty. So it is not a case of asking punishment upon the innocent but upon the guilty, and that in proportion to the wrong that they have done. Jeremiah quotes this statement (10:25), for we believe that the priority in point of time belongs to the psalm. Thus a very godly prophet utters the same sentiment without reservation. The fact that the persons involved have been guilty appears from what they are charged with in v. 7. As God desires the guilty to be punished, so does the psalmist. Must such a desire on man's part be wicked? Can it not rise to the level of God's thinking?

c) **The prayer seeking both aid and pardon (vv. 8, 9)**

8. *Remember not against us our past iniquities;*
Let Thy mercies quickly come to meet us,
For we are brought very low.

9. *Help us, O God, who art the source of our deliverance, for the glory of Thy name*
And deliver us and cover our sins for Thy name's sake.

The plea here presented centers in the thought of pardon or of a covering over of sin. After the forgiveness has been obtained help becomes possible. The greater evil is first to be removed.

It is not uncommon to read in commentaries in connection with this psalm that it bears no mark of consciousness of guilt. It is true that the first indication to the contrary could be obscured by the translation: "Do not remember against us the iniquities of our forefathers" (*RSV*). It is true that this translation is entirely feasible. Though it is accepted, surely the writer, like other men in the Scriptures, refers to the fathers' guilt, not as something foreign, not as blaming the fathers for the present difficulties, but rather in the sense of admitting that the present generation has shared in the sins of the fathers (cf., Dan. 9:16, etc.). This interpretation alone is feasible in the light of v. 9b. For the same reason we believe that it is preferable to translate v. 8a: "Remember not against us our past iniquities." God's mercy

Psalm 79

(v. 8b) is the only help or the reputation ("name") that He has achieved with His people in times past.

d) **The prayer that the guilty may be punished (vv. 10-12)**

10. *Why should the heathen say, "Where is their God?"*
    Let the avenging of the shed blood of Thy servants be made known among the heathen.
11. *Let the groaning of the prisoners come before Thee,*
    According to the greatness of Thy power spare those doomed to die.
12. *Requite our neighbors sevenfold into their bosom*
    Their taunts wherewith they have taunted Thee, O Lord.

10. This prayer that the guilty might be punished could be paraphrased: Let justice, which has so long been delayed, prevail. Such desires are not unholy, not as long as God is a just God who upholds the moral order of His earth. The taunt, "Where is their God?" was common enough in days of old. Cf., Ps. 42:3; 115:2. Wherever the heathen had often sinned ruthlessly against the people of God, it would serve as a wholesome reminder to them if "the avenging of the shed blood of (God's) servants be made known among" them.

11. We agree with those interpreters who think the term "prisoner" refers to those who are the victims of the present calamity, not necessarily persons who are actually confined in prisons. The pity of God for poor sufferers is invoked. When this is expressed by the words: "Requite our neighbors sevenfold," the meaning that we are inclined to associate with the numeral is absolutely wrong. The expression does not mean seven times as much as they have done. Seven is the number that from days of old (Gen. 4:15) was used to designate completeness of retaliation. And the phrase "into their bosom" implies no more than "well directed, so that it strikes to the very center, to their heart" (*Briggs*). We believe that the author means exactly what he says when he states that his concern is for the honor of God's holy name. Those interpreters who would ascribe lower motives to him overlook the total absence of selfish interest on his part.

e) **A vow to praise God for His help (v. 13)**

13. *Then we, who are Thy people and the flock of Thy pasture, will thank Thee forever;*
    And from generation to generation we shall recount Thy praise.

This concluding verse is, perhaps, to be regarded less as a motive that is calculated to induce God to help than as a natural promise to return thanks, which His deliverance will so strongly merit. The writer arrives at some measure of assurance and sees himself and the rest of God's people already pouring out their hearts in thanksgiving.

There is some likelihood in the claim that, after the congregational complaint and prayer for help have been voiced this verse could be a reassurance that was, perhaps, uttered by the priest if the psalm was rendered liturgically in public worship. However, certainty is impossible.

NOTES

7. "They have devoured," *'akhal,* is really a singular used impersonally, "one has devoured." Such a form is usually most conveniently rendered as a plural in connections such as this.

8. In further support of what has been said above it may be noted that *'awonoth* is more commonly masculine, therefore *ri'shonim* quite naturally agrees with it.

11. "Doomed to die" is literally "sons of death," that unique use of "sons" which makes it a relation word.

Psalm 80

THE ANGUISHED CRY OF A DESOLATE NATION

THE SITUATION which gave rise to this psalm may have been any one of those instances which are recorded as cases of nearly total desolation of the land of Israel (II Kings 6:24, 25; 10:32, 33; 13:22; 15:17–22; 15:27–31; 17:1–6). Judah was also involved in the affliction, for v. 2 seems to indicate this. Samaria was still existing, for v. 17 implies that her king is still upon his throne. Since we believe that practically all the psalms originated in Judah we accept the approach which takes the same position with regard to this psalm.[1]

It is heartening to note that there is a breadth of sympathy on the part of the Southern Kingdom with the affliction of the Northern, a feeling that may have been more or less prevalent throughout the history of the divided kingdom.

It would further appear that the calamity involved had been of longer duration, for the "how long" (v. 4) points in this direction as does

---

[1] The strongest statement of the idea of Northern authorship is offered by Otto Eissfeldt in *Geschichte und Altes Testament,* Mohr (Paul Siebeck) Tübingen, 1953, pp. 65-78.

Psalm 80

the description that pictures the vine as being badly damaged by creatures that did harm to it (vv. 13, 16).

Somewhat unique in this psalm is the rather full development of the figure of Israel as a vine of God's planting, which thought is so prominent as to have led some commentators to give this psalm the title "Yahwe's Vine" (*Kessler*). The whole development of this thought gives beautiful emphasis to the thought of God's providence exercised in behalf of His people.

Several critical approaches that are not too tenable may be touched upon at this point. Though it is possible that an individual may have voiced the prayer herein contained with the exception of the refrain (found in vv. 3, 7, 19), when liturgical use was made of the psalm, such an approach must remain entirely in the field of mere possibility. Again to believe that a distinct gain has been made by inserting the refrain at v. 14 in order to gain a somewhat more regular partition of the psalm is in the realm of pure conjecture.

The heading reads thus: *To the Choir Director. According to Lilies. A testimony. Of Asaph. A psalm.* It offers no particular problem, except that the two words "lilies" and "testimony" may be combined into a statement, which could be the title of a hymn or tune after the pattern of which this psalm is to be sung, thus: "Pure as lilies is the testimony" (*Koenig*).

a) A prayer for help (vv. 1–3)

1. *O Shepherd of Israel, give ear, Thou who leadest Joseph like a flock,*
   Thou who sittest enthroned above the cherubim, shine forth.
2. *As leader of Ephraim and Benjamin and Manasseh stir up Thy might*
   And come for our deliverance.
3. *O God, restore us;*
   Make Thy face to shine, and we shall be delivered.

1. It is true that the title "Shepherd of Israel" as applied to God appears only here in the Scriptures although similar titles were known from the days of the patriarchs (see Gen. 28:15; 49:24). The intimate relationship between shepherd and sheep, which is characteristic of the Orient, is at the bottom of this figure. Since in the parallel member of this verse "Joseph" is mentioned as being led after it had been "Israel," and since in the second verse three prominent tribes of the Northern Kingdom are mentioned, from the beginning of v. 1 onward the prayer is apparently to be thought of as being uttered specifically for the afflicted people to the north. In the expression, "Thou who leadest Joseph like a flock," the thought is also contained that it is as

easy for the Lord to take proper care of His people as it is for a shepherd to have the oversight over his flock.

In the further title used for God, "Thou who sittest enthroned above the cherubim," we find a predicate of divine majesty. Time and again this expression occurs (cf., I Sam. 4:4; II Sam. 6:2; II Kings 19:15) and it may well reflect the symbolism that was embodied in the arrangement of the Tabernacle, where God was thought of as being enthroned above the cherubim that stood over the mercy seat (see Exod. 25:22). Yet since in the Old as well as in the New Testament the cherubim uphold, as it were, the heavenly throne (cf., Rev. 4:6–8, etc.), it might seem best to think that in this verse there is a reference to the throne of God in heaven itself.

As to the cherubim themselves, apart from the description given in Ezekiel 1 and Rev. 4, it seems difficult to arrive at any finality as to what they actually looked like. *McCullough's* description reflects the currently most popular opinion when he says: "A cherub was seemingly a winged lion with a human head: the notion came into Hebrew thought through sculptural practices in Canaan and Phoenicia, and these in turn were dependant on both Egyptia and Mesopotamia." This may be true but is too much in the nature of an apodictic judgment. The fact that, when cherubim are first mentioned in Scripture, Gen. 3:24, they are not described, argues for a clear tradition as to their appearance, which made description of them unnecessary, and which may have reached back to earliest times and thus have been original with Israel by a direct line of transmission. In any case, this glorious Lord, who is served by such great and glorious creatures as the cherubim, is implored to stir up His power and come. When the verb "shine forth" is used, this implies that He has veiled Himself in darkness and momentarily restrained His omnipotent might. May it now flash forth into action.

2. We regard the translation "as leader of Ephraim" as being much clearer than the statement "before Ephraim." These three tribes were grouped together on the march and in the camp of Israel in the wanderings in the wilderness, see Num. 2:18ff. When they advanced for the conquest of Canaan, God went before them. What was true then is thought of as being again capable of realization. All He needs to do is to "stir up His might," an idiom we still have in "bestir yourself." He has been inactive in the matter of intervening in behalf of His people. The turn of the thought in the expression "and come for our deliverance" implies that the speakers are others than the ones prayed for; and no explanation seems more appropriate than that those who are praying are the people of the Southern Kingdom. Though Benjamin

Psalm 80

is often grouped with Judah, it is here thought of as being allied with the Northern Kingdom as it is in I Kings 11:13, 32, 36.

3. Thus far God's relation to His people, His might, and the plea for the three most prominent tribes have been brought into the picture. The essence of the plea is now succinctly set forth in the petition, "O God, restore us." This plea is very broad. Its primary thought is: Deliver us from the evils that beset us. The expression "deliverance" may well include physical as well as spiritual restoration but does not call for any thoughts about restoration from exile. Till now God's disfavor has apparently rested upon them: His face was clouded with displeasure as it were. The prayer now asks for the removal of this displeasure: "Make Thy face to shine" (cf. Num. 6:25), that is, Let Thy gracious attitude be reflected in a countenance that reflects Thy good will. So potent is God's good pleasure that, as soon as it becomes operative, deliverance sets in. Thus a nation, sadly beset by adversity, is taught to pray by this psalm.

b) A motivation for being heard (vv. 4–7)

4. *O Lord God of hosts,*
   How long wilt Thou be angry in spite of the prayers of Thy people!
5. *Thou hast fed them with the bread of tears,*
   And hast given them tears to drink in full measure.
6. *Thou hast made us an object of strife to our neighbors;*
   And our enemies mock among themselves.
7. *O God of hosts, restore us;*
   Make Thy face to shine, and we shall be delivered.

This section presents a motivation as to why the petition that is being made should be heard. Manifold are the approaches to such motivations. Here it is primarily the thought of the sad state of the afflicted nation.

4. God is first of all appealed to as the one who has all the forces of the universe in His control—"Lord God of hosts." It does seem strange and may well be stated in God's presence as being disturbing that His people should have been praying long and not have been heard. There is some measure of anguish in the "how long," which is not so much a question as it is an exclamation. The complaint goes on (v. 5), "Thou hast fed them with the bread of tears," a statement that is well paraphrased by *Kirkpatrick:* "Thou hast made tears their daily portion." The original is more poetical. The second half of the verse changes the figure to that of an unwelcome drink which is forced upon a man with the demand that he drink it all. We could reproduce the thought in prose: They have had their fill of tears.

6. If tears are their lot at home, ridicule is their lot among their foes. There enemies are already quarrelling as to how they shall partition the soon-to-be-vanquished foe. In that sense they (the Israelites) are "an object of strife." At the same time taunts of every sort and mocking statements are the order of the day when Israel is referred to, for her case seems hopeless. Such an attitude on the part of the enemy is always painful to bear. The refrain (v. 7), cf. v. 3, again gives relief to the troubled heart of the nation.

c) Prayer for Israel as a choice view of God's planting (vv. 8–19)
  His protective care in days of old (vv. 8–11)
  Israel's present ravaged state (vv. 12–16)
  The concluding petition (vv. 17–19)

8. Thou didst remove a vine out of Egypt;
   Thou didst drive out nations and plant it.
9. Thou didst make room for it;
   And it took deep root and filled the land.
10. The mountains were covered with its shade;
    And its branches were cedars of God.
11. It sent out its shoots to the sea
    And its offshoots to the river.
12. Why hast Thou torn down its walls
    So that all who passed by the way kept plucking it?
13. The boar of the forest kept ravaging it;
    And the creatures of the field kept feeding upon it.
14. O God of hosts, turn back;
    Look down from heaven and see and have regard for this vine,
15. The stock which Thy right hand has planted,
    And the shoot which Thou didst raise up for Thyself.
16. It is burned with fire like rubbish;
    They shall perish at the rebuke of Thy countenance.
17. Let Thy hand be upon the man who sits at Thy right hand,
    Upon the son of man whom Thou hast made strong for Thyself.
18. And we will not turn back from Thee;
    Let us live, and we will call upon Thy name.
19. O Lord God of hosts, restore us;
    Make Thy face to shine, and we shall be delivered.

This whole section is dominated by the thought that Israel is a choice vine of God's planting. The point of the comparison appears to be that, as the vine is a choice plant that requires much attention, so Israel is choice among the nations and is continually in need of God's providential care if she is to survive and bear fruit.

8. As the first phase of this development God's protecting care in

days of old is reflected upon. In fact, Israel's history up to the point of the present situation can be adequately described under the figure of a transplanted and well-nurtured vine. God takes this vine from the land of Egypt where it is growing. He removes what lies in the way (the Amorite nations dwelling in Canaan) and plants it in this new soil. Since room had been made for it, it could take deep root, which is necessary for sound growth, and it filled the land. The children of Israel did increase in great numbers.

10. Since this is a mountainous land, the description may well continue by stating that the mountainsides became, as it were, covered with terraced vineyards; and the lusty growth of the vine produced branches that could be likened to the sturdy limbs of the cedars, which are here by something stronger than a grammatical superlative described as thriving under the special providence of God. Down to the very sea on the west as well as down to the Jordan on the east the vine filled the land. There is much poetry as well as fine propriety about the extended use of the figure of the vine as it appears here. The figure as such is common enough in Biblical usage; see Gen. 49:22; Hos. 10:1; Is. 5:1–7; 27:2–6; Jer. 2:21; 12:10ff.

12. In contrast with the flourishing vine that Israel once was its present ravaged state is described in vv. 12–16. This description is partly cast into the form of a complaint (v. 12). Since God permitted the protecting wall, as it were, to be plucked down, this event is ascribed directly to Him: "Why hast Thou torn down its walls?" This is merely a strong statement of God's sovereign dispensation of all things, which is found so often in the Scriptures. The protective wall having been removed, passers-by pluck at the vine, boars of the forest can ravage it and do so; creatures of the field keep feeding upon it. All this has been going on for a long time as the Hebrew tenses indicate by a subtle construction.

14. This verse is a prayer that is somewhat in the nature of the refrain which is characteristic of this psalm but is adapted to the picture of the vine which dominates this section. The vine as such is regarded as being of such importance in God's sight that its plight should stir Him to action. It is (v. 15) "the stock which (His) right hand has planted, and the shoot which (He) did raise up for (Himself)." This object of His care is now a thing that is being "burned with fire like rubbish." For the moment the writer cannot contain himself. He reflects upon the fate of those who have dealt so ruthlessly with God's prized possession, and he asserts that those who have done this dastardly thing shall perish at the rebuke of His countenance. Thus closes this turn of the thought.

17. What is more natural than that the psalm should conclude as a

prayer that is permeated with holy resolves to return to the Lord and earnestly to follow Him? There seems to be no other feasible way of interpreting v. 17 than to think of it as being a prayer for the king that sits upon the throne of Israel. For though from one point of view Israel was in rebellion against the dynasty of God's choice, the house of David, yet from the angle of being oppressed by the godless heathen Israel's kings were frequently advanced to the throne by sufferance of Yahweh (cf., II Kings 9). That allows us to regard the king of Israel as the "man who sits at (God's) right hand" and as the one whom God "made strong for Himself." Israel was just not down on the level of the heathen round about her.

If it should please the Lord thus to strengthen and deliver the king and the people, the people of Judah on their part feel the need of returning to the ways of the Lord. They pray, in fact, that they may live and vow that they will make prayer to the name of the Lord their continual endeavor. The refrain, now heard for the third time, is a sturdy climax of prayer for deliverance and closes the psalm on a strong note.

NOTES

3. "And we shall be delivered" is an obvious case of coordination of clauses instead of making one of them a purpose clause: That we may be delivered. The sequence of clauses is also imperative and hortative. *KS* 364n.

4. The unusual genitive of the word "God" without the genitive ending may be explained on the score that in this book of the Psalter *'elohim* has often been substituted for *Yahweh*, see *KS* 285b. In *bithphillath* the preposition *be* has concessive force; *KS* 405b.

5. "Full measure" is an adverbial accusative without a preposition, see *KS* 332p.

8. The imperfect *tassia'* is to be explained as a historical present, see *KS* 158.

10. "Cedars of God" implies that even in the judgment of God these trees are impressive, or they owe their growth specifically to Him. See *KS* 309 1.

12. When the *waw* consecutive in *we'aruha* reduces the verb to an imperfect, the object seems to be to express the iterative character of the following acts, plucking, ravaging, etc., as the following imperfects indicate. *KS* 367g.

Psalm 81

A PLEA FOR FIDELITY TO GOD

Commentators seem about equally divided in their views as to whether the Passover festival or that of Tabernacles was the original setting for this psalm. In favor of the Passover the argument may be advanced that vv. 5–7 think in terms of the time of the Exodus. In favor of the festival of Tabernacles the strongest support is found in the later Jewish tradition. For the Targum inserts the name of the month Tishri into v. 3, which was the month of the observance of this festival. The truth of the matter may well be that textual evidence points to the one festival, tradition to the other. Yet the psalm is of so general a character that it could with little difficulty be used at the celebration of either festival. Nor does the main emphasis rest on the observance of a particular festival but on an admonition which is appropriate in connection with any observance, namely, a plea to be faithful to the Lord. That spirit would give validity to any festival.

It may at first appear as if the halves of the psalm (vv. 1–5 and vv. 6–16) do not have much in common. But as *Poteat* has perhaps pointed out most successfully, the inner bond of unity is the fact that the observance of any festival in public worship may degenerate into futility unless the deeper motive of true allegiance to God is vitally involved. Or, as could be said with equal propriety, a timely exhortation that the needs of the times suggested was felt to be the most urgent matter clamoring for attention on the part of a people that was far from being as true to its God as it should have been.

As to the time and the circumstances of the composition of the psalm it must be admitted that we have too little concrete data within the psalm to allow for any far-reaching conclusions. Since the Northern Kingdom may be addressed (v. 5), it appears to be a pre-exilic production. The whole tenor of the admonition (vv. 6ff.) points to the problem that vexed Israel before the Captivity. There seems to be some measure of difficulty with enemies according to v. 14. So Israel may have been under affliction by some external foe. But these are only possibilities.

The psalm is a plea for loyalty and fidelity in view of all that God has done for His people. To this there is added an indication that rich rewards would come on the heels of faithful attachment to Him.

Some interpreters have felt that the conclusion is far too abrupt. This abruptness may be due to the fact that originally the psalm may have been much longer, or that the writer suddenly ran out of material. But though, as some commentators state it, this conclusion ends on a somewhat "mundane note of abundant wheat and honey," it should not be forgotten that because of Israel's view that the Lord was the powerful Creator of all that exists earthly blessings were clear tokens of His grace and to be valued as such.

The heading: *To the Choir Director. According to Gittith. Of Asaph.* Though "Gittith" could mean after the Gathian manner, it can also mean according to the tune that is used when the winepress (*gath*) is trodden. We prefer the latter. On "Asaph" see Ps. 50. The idea that the writer may have lived in David's time seems less appropriate.

a) A summons to observe a festival (vv. 1–5b)

1. *Sing jubilantly unto God, our strength;*
   Shout for joy to the God of Jacob.
2. *Take a psalm, employ the timbrel,*
   The sweet lute with the harp.
3. *Blow the trumpet at the new moon,*
   At the full moon, for the feast day.
4. *For this is a statute for Israel,*
   An ordinance for the God of Jacob.
5. *Thus He has appointed as a witness in Joseph;*
   When He went forth against the land of Egypt.

1. When we labelled this psalm "a summons to observe a festival" we did not imply that it was not originally designed for a special occasion. It just so happened that there was no reason for being more specific at the time the psalm was written. Because of that breadth of purpose that frequently marks the psalms, we find that this one, too, is not intended exclusively for only one purpose. The specific objective is to remind the congregation of the need of sincere praise and thanksgiving unto the Lord God in order to make any festival worth while. Tame sentiments, shallow interests kill the spirit of devotion. Jubilant song, vociferous shouts of joy would be indicative of deep appreciation of what God, who is the "strength" of His people, has done for them. When He is termed the "God of Jacob," that may be merely a poetic variation of the "God of Israel." This initial summons would apply to the people at large.

2. This verse may be regarded as being addressed to the Levites, whose peculiar duty it was to supply the musical embellishment in public worship, especially by the use of psalms (cf., I Chron. 16:4ff.; 25).

The praises of God's deeds are to be made as beautiful and attractive as possible.

3. This verse must, however, be regarded as being addressed chiefly to the priests, whose specific prerogative it was to blow the trumpets in connection with sacred rites (see Num. 10:8, 10; Josh. 6:4ff.; II Chron. 5:12ff.; Ezra 3:10). The unique feature of this summons is that it calls for a double blowing of trumpets, one at the time of the new moon, the other at the time of the full moon, in connection with some type or other of "feast day," that is to say, when the month began (the lunar month), and when the full moon appeared. The time of the new moon was regularly ushered in with the blowing of metal trumpets. On this occasion the ram's horn (*shophar*) is also to usher in the festival and be blown at the time of the full moon, when both the Passover and the feast of Tabernacles were celebrated. On the basis of this double summons to blow the trumpet it would almost seem that the writer is thinking in terms of any and every festival that may be observed, for the general term "for the feast day" could mean just that. So the debate about the festival for whose celebration the psalm is intended is rather futile.

4. This type of ceremonial was divinely appointed to give a particular character to Israel's high festivals. It is, therefore, no trifle. In fact, it is classified as a fixed "statute," as a divinely ordained "ordinance," and as a solemn "witness." This appointment was made in those great eventful days "when He went forth against the land of Egypt." The festivals commemorated stirring events of days of old, and Israel was not to regard them lightly. It must be admitted that because of the general character of this summons to observe a feast day this psalm could be used for the celebration of practically any public festival on Israel's calendar.

b) An admonition: God's one demand—no strange gods (vv. 5c–10)

5c. *I heard a message I had not known:*
6. *"I took the burden off his shoulder;*
   His hands were freed from the basket.
7. *In distress you called, and I delivered you;*
   I answered you in the thundercloud;
   I put you to the test at the waters of Meribah. Selah.
8. *Hear, O my people, that I may admonish you;*
   O Israel, if you would but give heed to me.
9. *There shall not be among you any strange god;*
   You shall not worship any foreign god.
10. *I the Lord am your God, who brought you up out of the land of Egypt;*
    Open your mouth wide that I may fill it."

5c. This admonition states God's one demand upon His people—you shall have no foreign god. It is introduced as a "message" (literally: lip or speech) which was heard. There are two equally valid possibilities of interpretation of the introductory "I heard." It could refer to a single speaker in public worship, a priest or a prophet, who functions in a cultic capacity at the place of public worship and renders this admonition in a solo voice. It would surely be equally feasible to regard the verb "I heard" as being spoken by the congregation collectively. What follows would then be a new insight that was born in on the people at this time as an outgrowth of their reflection upon what God did for His people in the days of the Exodus, when He spoke words, whose import is now more clearly understood as being in force for all times. In both cases the object of "I heard" is not a direct message but a message that is mediated by reflection and is recognized as being granted by the Spirit of the living God. God is represented as speaking these words. Surely, these are thoughts that He would have His people heed. They are godly instructions that are being offered by enlightened servants of God.

6. The Exodus experience is summarized (vv. 6, 7) in brief. It amounted to this: God found His people with a heavy burden on their backs, the service into which they had been impressed in Egypt or with their hands carrying heavy loads in baskets as they produced their daily levy of bricks (Exod. 1:13; 5:10ff., etc.). He took this burden from them and freed their hands. Or again (v. 7) it was a period of great distress when they cried to the Lord, and He delivered them. His answer came in a "thundercloud" (literally: "a secret place of thunder"), an expression which could refer to the guiding cloud which guarded and guided Israel but wrought consternation among the enemy (Exod. 14:24); or it might have reference to the cloud from which He spoke on Mt. Sinai (Exod. 19:16) and pronounced the words of His holy law and made a covenant with His people. The second of these seems to be the more likely reference. As a third item the testing at Meribah is mentioned, which could refer to the two events recorded in Exod. 17:6f. and Num. 20:11f. This item was added after two blessings had been alluded to, to suggest that these testings were for the good of Israel and an occasion that helped Israel to find itself when it was in danger of going astray.

8. In all the events just enumerated God was in effect saying to His people what He Himself put into words in the first commandment of Sinai, and what is here presented as an admonition to which Israel should give diligent heed. It is a slight paraphrase of the First Commandment with new emphasis on the "strange" or "foreign" god that had previously been referred to only as "other" than the true God. Ex-

perience had by this time taught the people that all gods that were offered as substitutes were regularly taken over from the neighboring nations and were in that sense strange or foreign. Though the form of the commandment is negative, it aims at a definite positive, at a right relation to the living God who redeemed His people for the free service of Himself.

10. The motivation for allegiance to Him is now offered. It appears in the classic terminology of the introduction to the Decalogue, which because of the contrast which is here involved calls for a slightly different translation. It should not be translated: "I am the Lord thy God," but: "I the Lord am thy God." Over against the strange gods a statement is in order which says: I Yahweh am your God. The one great deed that He performed in behalf of His people is closely identified with Him: "who brought you up out of the land of Egypt." The obligation created by this phenomenal deliverance is of an enduring character and calls for nothing less than total and wholehearted commitment unto God. That, so to speak, is the one lesson that Israel's history thundered unceasingly into the nation's ears.

One is a bit startled at the turn that the thought takes in the second member of the verse: "Open your mouth wide that I may fill it." The subtle misunderstanding that the nation might harbor in its relation to its God is here reflected. Men might think that all of God's deeds were done for promoting His selfish purposes, that He might have a people who unfailingly offer their devotion to Him. He rather seeks their constant and unwavering attachment so that He might not be prevented from bestowing on them the countless blessings that His mercy has devised for them from days of old. Thus unfailing allegiance is the same as if they had trusted Him, expected many blessings from Him, and had not been disappointed in their hope. In that sense trusting is the opening of the mouth in anticipation of His tokens of good pleasure.

The liturgical interpretation finds in this last clause an indication that Israel is to expect a rich experience in this liturgcal service, a striking theophany of God, which He is most ready to grant. The context scarcely warrants such conclusions.

c) **A motivation for this admonition: God's punishment of Israel's waywardness (vv. 11–16)**

11. *But My people did not listen to My voice;*
    Israel would have nothing to do with Me.
12. *So I gave them up because of the stubbornness of their heart*
    That they might follow their own counsels.
13. *If only My people would listen to Me!*
    That Israel would walk in My ways!

14. *How easily I could have subdued their enemies
    And turned My hands against their foes!*
15. *They that hate the Lord would have cringed before Him;
    But their time would endure forever.*
16. *I would feed them with the finest of wheat;
    With honey out of the rock I would satisfy you.*

11. In this section a motivation for the preceding admonition is offered. This is twofold: on the one hand, it offers a resumé of the blessings that God would have been so ready to bestow; on the other, a record of the punishments that He was obliged to inflict. Israel's reaction to God's summons is set forth in a summary form. Particularly at that time His "people did not listen to (His) voice." The right relation to God is always a matter of obedience to His Word. But such obedience always goes down to deeper roots which lie imbedded in the inmost will of man. This is indicated in the explanatory statement, "Israel would have nothing to do with Me." We have rendered the thought in the English idiom. The Hebrew really says: "Israel was not willing to Me."

12. At this point Israel's history shifts from the events of the wilderness wanderings to the far more recent time of the psalmist's present, when it was again true that God "gave them up because of the stubbornness of their heart." Such a break in point of time which ignores centuries is, nevertheless, completely warranted. For history is pretty much of one piece and keeps repeating itself in many features. This giving up of His people is further specified as to its purpose. It was "that they might follow their own counsels." They were minded to do their own will; God gave them free reign. For only thus could they learn the harmfulness of man's self-indulgence.

13. There follows a touching word concerning the yearning of God for His people which is paralleled by such statements as Deut. 5:29; 32:29; Is. 48:18; Matt. 23:37. Again the form of the statement indicates depth of insight. One's whole relation to God is always a matter of listening to Him; and that again is a matter of walking in the ways which He has so clearly defined for His people.

14. The rest of the psalm is a brief indication of the blessings Israel forfeited by not walking in the ways of the Lord. They are first that God would have given them perpetual victory over all their enemies. As it was, Israel's history was dotted by defeats and tragedies. The fact that the almighty power of God could readily cope with the greatest force that man could muster is clearly indicated. One further statement of the case is given in 15a: The enemies would have been made to cringe before Him. But these enemies are described as "they that hate the Lord."

Men of our day are apt to find fault with the severity of the judgment

Psalm 81

involved in this description. But in the last analysis, the natural attitudes of fallen man against His Maker is one of hatred. So generally speaking, when Israel encountered much opposition among the nations, this opposition was an attitude that was grounded in an innate hatred of God. The psalmist is not giving evidence of a spiteful attitude but rather of deep insight into basic spiritual values. In contrast with the submission of the enemies is the happy lot of Israel that would have been realized under favorable circumstances: "But their (Israel's) time would endure forever," "time" being used in the sense of time of good fortune even as the word may mean time of judgment (see dictionaries).

16. One last forceful illustration is given of the type of blessing God loves to bestow on His people. He would have provided rich, satisfying food of the finest sort and goodly delicacies such as the wild honey which bees might deposit in the hollow of rocks. Many more could have been enumerated. But what has been stated indicates sufficiently that God has many rich stores in reserve for those whom He loves, and who walk in His paths.

NOTES

5. Though the form of the verb is *'eshma'*, an imperfect, the context suggests that it may be a case of the use of the historical present (*KS* 158).

The word for "speech" (*sephath*) appears in the construct. It is not followed by another noun but by an entire clause (*KS* 337y; also *GK* 130d).

6. The verb *ta'abhórnah* is apparently a case of the use of the imperfect consecutive form without having the *waw* immediately attached to it; in fact, the final *waw* of the preceding clause was apparently written but once and is to be read twice (*KS* 368i).

7. The same seems to be the case with regard to the verb *'ebhchanekha,* in which the *waw* after *mem* has been dropped, as happens frequently enough in the Hebrew (*KS* 194f and 330p).

8. "If you would but give heed" is an instance when verbs with a simple *'im* take on an optative meaning (*KS* 355x).

10. This is obviously direct discourse without direct introduction (*KS* 374b).

16. The Lord may very properly still be regarded as speaking if it is observed that the proper name (*Yahweh*) is substituted for the pronoun to emphasize the dignity of the speaker (*KS* 5).

The first word seems to be a form such as is found in II Sam. 1:8 where, in spite of the initial *yodh,* the form is still to be regarded as first person rather than third. Otherwise the change from third person ("feed them") to second ("satisfy you") is an instance of Hebrew flexibility.

Psalm 82

THE JUDGMENT OF UNJUST JUDGES OR RULERS

THIS TITLE indicates very clearly what, in our judgment, is the subject covered by this psalm. It presents a judgment pronounced by the Lord on the judges or rulers of Israel. For in Israel the term judges had practically the same meaning as the term rulers, the Israelite usage being derived from the chief function of rulers.

Up to about seventy years ago there was a practical unanimity in the church as to the interpretation of this psalm, commentators being agreed that it treated the subject we have just indicated. Or if there was a slight deviation, it was at least contended that the ones being judged were rulers outside of Israel. However, since that time a new approach has gained in popularity which insists that the judgment of the minor gods is the subject under consideration. What seems to have given credence to this approach is the concession, made rather too sweepingly by some, that there is in the Old Testament a major element of mythological terminology, and this is thought of as manifesting itself particularly in this psalm. For the ones to be judged are, according to v. 1, designated as "gods" (*'elohim*). It is claimed that this word allows for only one possibility, namely, the one just mentioned.

The value of this approach is said to be that it served to solve a problem, the problem of the unfair administration of justice on the earth, especially in the area of nation over against nation. The approach is this: The Lord, Yahweh, assigned the heathen gods to rule over the nations of the earth, each god over a nation. These failed to uphold justice, they allowed earthly rulers to practice injustice. So they became unworthy of the trust reposed in them. Now in a grand judgment scene, —highly poetic, of course—Yahweh assembles them for judgment, pronounces sentence, and removes them. This is supposed to be a very helpful approach.

Apart from having no foundation in the Old Testament or, of course, in the New, except a dubious passage in the *Septuagint* (Deut. 32:8) this approach creates far more problems than it solves as is usually indirectly admitted by the proponents of this view when they state, like *Weiser,* that the solution offered is actually no solution. On the face of it it must appear to be very dubious to have the Lord assign places of authority over nations to the heathen deities, who are according to the consistent approach of the Old Testament evil and wicked in what they stand for. Their very existence may be doubted. For the Lord to grant them authority and rule would be more than strange, yes, even quite questionable from the moral point of view. Such an approach makes a psalm like this a fumbling attempt to explain why justice miscarries, an attempt which helps no one. The somewhat grandiose adjectives used about the highly original thinking and very colorful and dramatic presentation of the thoughts of this psalm do not redeem this approach from the severe criticism that it merits if such are its basic thoughts.

One further approach regards those who are addressed as "gods" as the heathen rulers of the nation of Israel who since the Captivity are holding her in subjection. V. 8 does not in any sense demand this interpretation.

But what basis is there for the unusual use of the word *'elohim* which equates it with judges in the land of Israel or all judges? Here we must go somewhat afield after the manner of *Hengstenberg*. To begin with, man is made in the image of God. Furthermore, there are persons who take God's place on earth regarding certain others. Parents are in the place of God over their children. For this reason the Fourth Commandment may be put on the first table of the law according to the proper division of the commandments found on the two tables. Governments in general occupy the same position, more particularly judges. For this reason, for example, Solomon is said to have "sat on the throne of the Lord" (I Chron. 29:23). For the same reason God and the rulers are mentioned in the same breath in Exod. 22:28: "You shall not revile God, nor curse the rulers of your people." Along the same line of thought is the statement that asserts that men are not to be "partial in judgment . . . for the judgment is God's" (Deut. 1:17).

This brings us to the two verses in which it is at least possible that the word Elohim refers to judges although it appears to us that another interpretation should have the preference. We refer to the statements found in Exod. 21:6 and 22:8, 9, where it is said concerning a slave, "Then his master shall bring him to God." This apparently means to the sanctuary. But it at the same time implies as does the second passage that there will be certain persons present at the sanctuary who will act as both witnesses and authorities in the case in hand and render a verdict. For in the second instance, that of a breach of trust, "both parties shall come before God; he whom God shall condemn shall pay double to his neighbor." It is entirely too fantastic to suppose that in all such trivial matters of lawsuits the Lord Himself would pronounce a verdict. Consequently the expression "whom God shall condemn" must mean: he whom the appointed *judge* or *priest* functioning at the sanctuary shall condemn, and so either God is mentioned as the One in whose sight the whole transaction takes place, or (and this is not impossible) the judge who speaks in God's stead is called God in view of his solemn responsibility. This approach is in agreement with the statement made in II Chron. 19:6, 7, where Jehoshaphat after appointing judges throughout all the land instructs them about the impartiality they should exercise when he tells them: "For you judge not for man but for the Lord. . . . Now then let the fear of the Lord be upon you."

In view of all this it is most proper that the term Elohim be used in place of those who represent Him in courts of law. In John 10:34, 35 Jesus Himself apparently accepts an interpretation which is basically the same as this even though it does reflect current Jewish thought. It is no trivial matter, however, to dismiss His interpretation as though it reflected the prejudices of His times—a very dangerous view to take of the Savior's person and work.

Lastly, there is not sufficient reason for regarding v. 5 or v. 8 as interpolations. They fit excellently into the line of thought of the psalm. The psalm is a well-balanced unit. As to the time of its composition it is not unreasonable to assume that Asaph may have written it in the days of David, but the evidence is too meager.

a) **God's appearance for judgment and His indictment of the judges (vv. 1–5)**

A psalm of Asaph.
1. *God has taken His stand in the assembly of God;*
   In the midst of the rulers He pronounces judgment.
2. *"How long will you judge unjustly*
   And show partiality for the person of the wicked? Selah.
3. *Judge justly the case of the weak and fatherless;*
   Maintain the rights of the afflicted and the needy.
4. *Deliver the weak and the poor;*
   Rescue them from the hand of the wicked."
5. *They have neither knowledge nor insight;*
   They walk on in darkness;
   All the foundations of the earth are shaken.

1. It is characteristic of certain of the psalms of Asaph to depict judgment scenes; cf., 50, 75, 81. In some unusual setting or other God is envisioned as calling an assembly for judgment. The scene is "the assembly of God." The word 'edhah is frequently applied to the congregation of Israel as such. Since "judges" (Elohim) are members of that congregation and responsible to it also, it is fitting that it be the scene of the judgment. To translate the phrase involved as "the assembly of the gods" (*Leslie,* e.g.) is inaccurate, for the plural does not appear at

this point. Also "divine council" (*RSV*) is inaccurate. The added phrase reads literally: "in the midst of the gods." We have ventured to translate this interpretatively because the literal "in the midst of the gods" is not understood by the present-day reader. The expression merely makes it plain that in this scene the judges are present in the congregation. The fact that God "has taken His stand" implies that He has come for a particular purpose and is about to act.

2. Without a formal introduction the direct discourse represents the Lord as speaking and saying to the judges: "How long will you judge unjustly and show partiality for the person of the wicked?" This statement is analogous to the other statements of Scripture that deal with this subject, cf., Is. 3:13–15; Mic. 3:1–4; Jer. 22:1ff. God is the guardian of justice, He watches over the administration of it. This rebuke indicates that His patience is being sorely tried by such iniquity. The summary in vv. 3, 4 indicates that all classes of the lowly, weak, and afflicted that suffer wrong are the special objects of His care. There is something cowardly about taking advantage of the weak. There is something noble about championing their cause. God is elsewhere also represented as having particular care for all those that cannot help themselves; see Ps. 72:12ff.; Is. 11:3, 4.

5. This verse may be called a divine soliloquy. The Lord observes that His rebukes are going unheeded. The public rebuke of the unjust judges in the assembly of God leaves them untouched. Departing from the poetic representation of the highly idealized picture, we should say that all warnings that God in one way or another placed in the path of unjust judges simply went unheeded. Unaware of the gross iniquity they are committing and not giving heed to such cautions as have been directed to them, they may be said to "walk on in darkness." However, such miscarriage of justice always grievously disturbs those involved and undermines the very foundations of law and order in a land. No one knows this better than does the Lord. Therefore He is further represented as saying: "All the foundations of the earth are shaken."

b) **After the indictment comes the verdict (vv. 6, 7)**

6. *I did indeed say: "You are rulers*
   And all of you sons of the Most High.
7. *But you shall all die like men*
   And fall like any of the princes."

6. This is the last statement God is represented as saying in the assembly of God. What he had said to the judges or rulers was in effect that they were "gods." The same word is used which was employed in v. 1. That is, He had given them a position that was analogous to His in that He had made them administrators of justice, His justice. If in

addition He called them "sons of the Most High," that indicates that they stood in a relation of personal love to Him: He had treated them as being dear to Him.

But whatever honor and dignity they enjoyed was to be revoked. Their end shall be such that not a man will be able to discern the least trace of any favor that God holds toward them. Or we might paraphrase the statement: You shall all die ignominiously or at least in the common lot of men in its drabbest form.

7. This verse has been pointed to as being the chief obstacle to the traditional interpretation. For, it is argued, if it is said that beings shall die as men, they must belong to a class that is other than men. This does not at all follow. For the same expression if used by Samson, Judg. 16:7, 17, with only trifling verbal differences, and he obviously means: Just like any other man and not like the one who I should seem to be by virtue of my special endowments. The same turn of thought applies to the judges. They are merely being *reminded* of their lot of death; it is not a new lot that is unexpectedly inflicted (see *Kittel*).

c) **An added plea for universal judgment (v. 8)**

8. *Arise, O God, judge the earth,*
For Thou wilt take possession of all the nations.

This last verse could well be a suitable ejaculation on the part of the writer of the psalm. Seeing that God's judgment will in this instance correct such grievous evils, and seeing furthermore that all of God's judgments right wrongs, why should not a devout soul long for the consummation of God's judgment upon the earth? It is known that this will be God's last work on the last day. His saints have long waited for that day. They are here taught to pray for it. The motivation for this act of His is that, as His saints know, He will in any case take over all the earth and right all its wrongs. It behooves men to pray that this glorious day may come.

Psalm 83

AN EAGER PLEA
THAT GOD MAY CONFOUND HIS ENEMIES

WE CANNOT BE absolutely certain about the historical situation into which this psalm fits, but there is a large measure of probability that the circumstances described in II Chron. 20 fit the case well enough to be accepted as being the most likely. The king was Jehoshaphat; the enemies mentioned are Moabites, Ammonites, and Meunites, and Edom, too, is in the picture. The danger was great as the earnest prayer that was uttered indicates. Some guidance came from the utterances of Jahaziel, "a Levite of the sone of Asaph," who, for that matter, could have been the author of this psalm. It is true that our psalm mentions a total of ten nationalities that were allied against God's people. The historical account may have mentioned only the most prominent among them. The times of Nehemiah, claimed by some interpreters as being more suitable, fit the case in hand less acceptably ("Assyria" is by some writers changed to "Samaria" in order to get a greater measure of agreement). And in I Macc. 5 the historical situation is far different from the one mentioned in this psalm.

As to the character of this psalm, it is not one that may be classified as dubious and highly questionable, or as an "unedifying and tedious catalogue of bloody violence," nor as "spiritually valueless, being a hymn of hate." On closer inspection it will be recognized that we have here a normal prayer of an endangered people, for which no apologies need be made. Whereas v. 16 contains what may well be regarded as a redeeming feature that would prevent us from misconstruing the spirit of what preceded, the suggestion that this should be regarded as a gloss is all too harsh and unsympathetic. We hope to demonstrate that this verse fits into the picture very naturally.

The psalm has a close kinship with psalms like 46, 47, 48, and 76.

The heading offered in the text is: *"A song. A psalm of Asaph."* This author has been in the picture repeatedly since 50:1.

a) A dangerous emergency (vv. 1–8)

1. *O God, do not keep silence;*
   Do not be still and merely look on, O God.

2. *For, lo, Thy enemies are in an uproar;*
And they that hate Thee carry their head high.
3. *Against Thy people they have craftily devised a plot;*
And they consult together against those whom Thou hast sheltered.
4. *They say: "Come, let us annihilate them that they be a nation no longer;*
And that the name of Israel be remembered no more."
5. *Yea, they have agreed together unanimously;*
Against Thee they have contrived a covenant—
6. *The tents of Edom and the Ishmaelites;*
Moab and the Hagrites;
7. *Gebal and Ammon and Amalek;*
The Philistines together with the inhabitants of Tyre.
8. *Also Assyria has joined with them;*
They have become the strong arm of the descendants of Lot. Selah.

1. An address such as we find in this verse is spoken in the boldness of faith, which knows that it may speak freely to the Almighty. He seems so utterly unresponsive! Not a trace of interest and compassion has been noted. God often bides His time, and the children of men grow impatient until they cannot bear to keep silent any longer. We have ventured to insert the adverb "merely" before the last verb in an effort to catch the tone of impatience, which *Luther* also does by inserting several such adverbs. But the point is that God's people can bear His silence and inaction no longer.

2. The situation that calls imperatively for action is described. There are men who are the enemies of the people of God. He who hates God's people must hate Him. Thus faith treats issues of this sort in a kind of oversimplification. Therefore the persons in question are described as "Thy enemies." Their activity is described as "being in an uproar." They are apparently raging mightily and carrying on a tremendous activity of preparation or of attack. They appear to be proud and sure of success as the statement indicates, they "carry their head high," the expression being the same as that used in Judg. 8:28. In language that is borrowed from Exod. 20:5 they are further characterized as hating the Lord. When one considers all such statements about enemies of the people of God it should be remembered that in the characterization of His adversaries Christ sometimes used sharp terms of condemnation. Our pointing this out does not imply that in all controversies we in our day are permitted to speak thus of those that oppose us. But the evi-

Psalm 83

dence produced in v. 3 clearly shows that this description is not overdrawn.

3. Evidence must have been available and must have come clearly to light to the effect that a dastardly plot of the combined enemies had been projected as a result of careful planning together. The plot is aimed at those who are the special objects of His benevolent care, His people whom He loves. If He loves certain ones and the enemy seeks to destroy them, is that not evidence of a base and utterly ungodly attitude? The avowed purpose of the coalition is clearly formulated in words (v. 4) that indicate that total destruction of the nation—nothing less—is the present goal of the confederates. They would even go so far as to stop at nothing short of total extermination of the very name of Israel.

5. Strong emphasis is placed upon the total unanimity of the conspirators. Evil as well as good purposes may on occasion bind men together very firmly. But it must have been obvious to those who were well informed on the situation that in the last analysis all efforts of the plotters were aimed at the God of Israel—"against Thee they have contrived a covenant." The fact that enmity of ungodly men may be directed against God Himself and, in fact, is so directed is only too clearly revealed in the Scriptures and should not be spoken of as if some cheap slander had been uttered. Christ often spoke thus to and about His enemies.

6. There follows an enumeration of the confederates. Edom must have occupied a prominent place in the plot to be mentioned first. As the Edomites dwelt toward the south of the Dead Sea so the Ishmaelites were for the most part found east of the land of Israel. The Moabites, however, were directly east of the Dead Sea. The Hagrites (see I Chron. 5:10, 19f.) appear to have been located northeast of the land of Israel. According to the dictionaries Gebal lay to the north of Edom. Ammon is found to the east in a territory that was in part occupied by Midianites in days of old whereas Amalek was to the southwest. Philistines are to be sought along the coast to the west of Judah, and Tyre represents the Phoenicians to the north. Adding all these together, we get a practically total encirclement of the land of Israel by its enemies.

8. Finally Assyria is brought into the picture as backing those who seem to be the ringleaders of the movement—the descendants of Lot, that is, Moab and Ammon (see Gen. 19).

It is very true that the evidence that we have concerning Israel's history never once represents these ten nations as having simultaneously attacked Israel. This has led to the conclusion that we here have a situation that is poetically idealized. All nations that have at one time or another attacked Israel are combined into a single conspiracy without trying to claim that this ever took place historically. We believe this to be less likely than the possibility that the sum total of the enemies that were encountered in Jehoshaphat's time really included all the groups here enumerated. The author of II Chron. 20 simply did not list the total number of those involved, or he may have possessed historical documents which were not complete on this score.

Silence on the part of the Biblical record does not argue for error; many Biblical tales are much foreshortened. We further admit that we have no evidence that Assyria became a prominent factor in Near Eastern history in the days of Jehoshaphat (873–849 B.C.). That fact also may merely indicate that in this area, too, our records have manifest gaps and cannot of itself stamp this enumeration as being wrong. If the Biblical account of the event given in a historical book is incomplete, what should hinder a fuller statement of the case in the psalms from supplementing the historical record? In any event, the conspiracy was a formidable one and the danger so great that, if God did not intervene, the situation might soon become hopeless.

b) **A prayer for just retribution upon the assailants (vv. 9–18)**

9. *Deal with them as with Midian,*
   As with Sisera and Jabin at the brook Kishon,
10. *Who were destroyed at Endor,*
    Who became as dung for the ground.
11. *Make their nobles like Oreb and Zeeb*
    And all their princes like Zebah and Zalmunah,
12. *Who had said, "Let us take to our possession*
    The pastures of God."
13. *O my God, make them like the tumbleweed,*
    Like the chaff before the wind.
14. *As the fire consumes the forest,*
    And as the flame burns up the mountainside,
15. *So do Thou pursue them with Thy tempest*
    And terrify them with Thy storm.
16. *Fill their faces with disgrace*
    That they may seek Thy name, O Lord.
17. *Let them be put to shame and confounded forever;*
    Let them be disgraced and let them perish.
18. *Then they shall know that Thou, whose name is Lord,*
    Alone art Most High over all the earth.

9. In this prayer for just retribution upon the enemies individuals are, first of all, thought of who may be regarded as outstanding examples of cruel enmity in the past, who were also most calamitously overthrown; and prayer is made that the present enemies may meet the same

Psalm 83

fate as did those of old. The examples referred to are culled from the book of Judges, the first two from chapters 4 and 5, the second two from chapters 7 and 8. The total defeat of the former is covered by the terms that they were "destroyed" and "became as dung of the ground." A minor detail, not previously recorded, is that this event centered around Endor whereas the record brought only Mt. Tabor into the picture (Judg. 4:6) at whose foot Endor lay. The defeat of Jabin and Sisera was certainly a striking example of divine retribution which with its colorful details was deeply imbedded in Israel's thinking.

The second illustration of drastic overthrow has to do with two notable princes of the Midianites who lived in the days of Gideon. Therefore the application is made that a similar fate is to befall the nobles and princes of the present conspiracy. For these persons had manifested a cruel selfishness in that they wanted to dispossess Israel completely and take over her land, here called "the pastures of God."

13. It is true that from this point onward the psalm abounds in forceful terms that are indicative of total overthrow and disastrous defeat upon the head of the enemies—"make them like the tumbleweed, like chaff before the wind," "as fire consumes the forest and as the flame burns up the mountainside," also, "pursue them with Thy tempest and terrify them with Thy storm," also "fill their faces with disgrace." This is clearly recognized for what it is—energetic prayer against enemies.

What disturbs men in our day is the fact that the terminology used is so strong. This is thought of as being indicative of a vindictive and utterly unrelenting spirit, a conclusion that is not necessarily valid. For the ultimate purpose that the writer has in mind is clearly set forth in v. 16b.: "that they may seek Thy name, O Lord." This is obviously another way of saying: that they may be turned from their evil ways to Thee, whose mighty hand they have seen at work in what befell them. The same purpose is expressed more fully in v. 18, which seems to allow for the interpretation that, if total conversion to the Lord does not result, at least the supremacy of Israel's God will be acknowledged, which will in itself be a very wholesome thing.

16. We believe that the suggestion that these redeeming features (vv. 16b and 18) are later insertions that were intended to redeem the psalm from manifesting an utterly bloodthirsty and vindictive character may safely be rejected as being quite untenable. Thus, for example, when it is said that "there is a clear contradiction between v. 16 and v. 17." Such a conclusion overlooks a matter of simple sentence structure. For the arrangement of vv. 16–18 appears to be: first a summary statement in v. 16, which dwells first on God's treatment of Israel's enemies and then on the desired result. This same pattern is then expanded in vv. 17

and 18, this time God's treatment of the enemies includes both parts of v. 17, and the desired result is restated more fully in the whole of v. 18. This pattern is common in Hebrew writing: first the summary statement, then the amplified statement.

It may not be out of place to add that the Old Testament approach to the whole problem of imprecation may well be thought of as being quite realistic. Israel did not pray often for the enemies' conversion, chiefly because there were no instances on record when such a conversion had taken place, barring, perhaps, the unique case of Naaman (II Kings 5), who, to begin with, was not hostile to Israel as most Gentiles were. True, the nobler thoughts of Christ about praying for one's enemies had not yet been uttered, and they involved a possibility that men had had little occasion even to think about. In the face of such a situation there is something commendable about looking to God for the total overthrow of an enemy that threatens the very existence of God's people and trusting that He alone has the power to effect such a result. Should Israel have prayed for the *success* of the enemy? Is it not correct to assume that also God desires to bring about the defeat of Israel's foes? Why not pray intensely for that which you well know God also wants?

NOTES

11. The beginning of the verse reads literally: "Make them, that is, their nobles"—a construction that involves a kind of self-correction or a more precise formulation of a statement just made (*KS* 340o).

13. What we have translated as "tumbleweed" is really the wild artichoke, which presents a light ball which is as readily whisked along by the wind as is our tumbleweed.

14. The point of comparison is the utter swiftness with which the flames of a forest fire sweep along. So may the enemy's overthrow be swift and sudden.

18. We have followed the lead of more recent writers, who have divided the verse differently than the Hebrew text has it and have construed the word "alone" with the second clause (*KS* 344c).

Psalm 84

LOVE FOR THE SANCTUARY

It appears that almost all the more recent intrepretations of this psalm are swept along by the popular current of opinion which makes this a psalm of pilgrimage. This entire approach hinges upon one word that occurs in v. 5 which never means "pilgrimage" but is consistently treated as though it did. This is the word translated "ways" (*KJ*) and "the highways to Zion" (*RSV*), though in the latter instance the phrase "to Zion" is lacking in the Hebrew text. For further details on this issue see the Notes after the conclusion of the exposition. As long as this unwarranted approach is insisted upon, no interpretation can do justice to this choice psalm.

What this misleading approach introduces as incidental is the major factor—the love for the sanctuary. Seldom has that love found such touching and eloquent expression. As a result this is one of the best-loved psalms in the entire Psalter.

Little can be said about the author or the time of composition. Since the "sons of Korah" are named as the authors, there is the possibility that one of their number had an experience that gave rise to this psalm. This experience may have been (note the proper interpretation of v. 2) a temporary banishment from the sanctuary like that mentioned in Ps. 42. After the period of banishment is ended, and the writer is again able freely to visit the house of the Lord, he has an appreciation of such a privilege as he never had before. Besides, the fact that the king is remembered in prayer (v. 9) indicates that the psalm was written at the time of the existence of monarchy in the Southern Kingdom. Aside from this the personal situation of the writer is quite unknown to us.

On "choir director" see 5:1. On "Gittith" see Ps. 8. On the "sons of Korah" see 42:1.

The heading reads thus:

For the Choir Director. According to Gittith.
By the sons of Korah. A psalm.

a) **The blessedness of having access to the house of the Lord (vv. 1–4)**

1. *How lovely is Thy habitation,*
   O Lord of hosts!

2. My soul has longed and even pined for the courts of the Lord;
   My heart and my flesh sing aloud for joy to the living God.
3. Even the sparrow has found a house and the swallow a nest for herself,
   Where she may put her young, even Thy altars, O Lord of hosts, my king and my God.
4. How very happy are those who dwell in Thy house!
   They shall praise Thee forever. Selah.

1. This verse strikes the keynote. The fact that it is in the form of an exclamation testifies to the deeper feeling that it expresses. It so happens that the adjective used may be translated either "loved" or "lovely." The latter seems to deserve the preference here though no one would venture to rule out the thought of the love of God's house. The divine name used, "Lord of hosts," suggests that He who is the Lord of the whole host of things that fill God's creation in the heavens and on the earth deigns to dwell in a particular earthly habitation, which indwelling is the chief glory of the otherwise already beautiful sanctuary. Quite obviously the writer actually has the visible structure of the Temple at Jerusalem in mind though elsewhere in the Scriptures the equivalent terms like "house of the Lord" and dwelling in it may refer more to living in true fellowship with God and not so much to a journey to the physical Temple as such (thus apparently Ps. 23:6; 15:1; 24:3, etc.).

2. This verse indicates that the writer was apparently barred from access to the sanctuary. The past tense of the two verbs is most simply explained on that score: there was a time when I was longing and pining for the courts of the Lord. But that past gives way to a present tense that describes the present situation: "My heart and my flesh sing aloud for joy." What kept him from the holy place we shall never know—sickness, banishment, misfortune, or some particular turn of circumstance. But strong, even to the point of physical involvement, as the longing and pining were, so exultant is the jubilation that has replaced them. Some interpreters venture to introduce the second member of the verse by a "now." In any event, in this man's life the sanctuary played a large role.

3. The simplest explanation of this verse is to regard it as a pure observation: these birds were continually to be seen in the Temple area; they felt at home there. The point that is being made is not expressed; each man may formulate it to suit himself. It amounts to this: so do we feel at home in the Lord's house when we have free access to it; and with that being-at-home feeling there goes a sense of security, of belonging. The statement is not to be thought of as being a kind of allegory in which the bird represents the writer or any worshiper. Nor do the "young" in this case symbolize the children of the writer. Nor is the

term "altars" to be understood in absolute literalness as though the writer were trying to indicate that birds actually built their nests upon the altars which were in use every day, and on which daily fire was kindled or even a perpetual fire was found. By metonomy "altars" signify the sanctuary, its central activity being named for the place as such.

4. Thus this verse becomes, first of all, an application of the idea expressed in v. 3. There are birds that find sanctuary in the holy place; even so there are persons who have the privilege of dwelling there officially, priests, Levites, attendants, and the like. What a happy lot theirs is to have the privilege of a continual presence in the physical structure! Such would customarily and traditionally give expression to a sense of privilege by repeatedly singing the praises of the Lord.

One can scarcely eliminate a subtle second thought at this point. There was without a doubt in the writer's mind the thought of all those who dwell with the Lord in spiritual fellowship; they, too, will be much given to the singing of the praises of the Lord. But the obvious first thought is the one suggested by v. 3—that of physical presence. A break in the thought is appropriately suggested by the "Selah."

b) The blessings going forth from a life lived in fellowship with God (vv. 5–7)

5. *How very happy are the persons, the source of whose strength is in Thee*
When ways (courses of action) *are being pondered in their hearts,*
6. *Who, as they pass through the parched valley, make it a place of springs;*
The early rain also covers it with blessings.
7. *They go from strength to strength;*
The God of gods will appear in Zion.

5. By a natural transition of thought the author advances from those who love and frequent the sanctuary to the blessings that flow from such a properly centered life. He indicates, first of all, that it is not the sanctuary as such which is the chief object of their love but the Lord Himself, who is wont to meet His worshipers there. Another way of stating that is to say that the strength (that is to say, the source of strength) of such lies in the Lord. Close fellowship with Him makes them strong. Furthermore, the realization that this is so fills their bosom with happiness.

As the thought is further developed, this happy situation is merely regarded as the prelude to another fact, namely, that as they ponder what course they are to take in the various situations that arise in life, the fact that their whole life is rooted in God controls all the thoughts of their heart. That is what is meant when it is said: "When ways are being pondered," ways being the direction or course of action that is to be followed in a specific situation.

The currently popular interpretation that is usually offered here equates "ways" with "the highways to Zion" and dwells long and quite unnaturally on the idea that pilgrims are especially addicted to thinking of these pilgrim paths as such, which, though they lead to Zion, may have been given very little thought by the pilgrims. The route taken was certainly not as such the object of fond remembrance. Sometimes or even for the most part those pilgrimages were long, dusty, and tiresome. They were not from this point of view idealized. But the other thought that it is a blessed thing to lean on the Lord when making plans for life's situations as they arise is a very worth while and helpful thought. By a brilliant stroke *Luther* arrives at about the same result when he translates, *und von Herzen dir nachwandeln* (i.e., wholeheartedly they follow after Thee). This is, of course, a blessing which such persons have in their own life.

6. There are further blessings by which these same persons enrich the lives of others. The case is stated figuratively. Life, as they pass through it, is likened to a "parched valley," a thought that is not too far removed from Luther's translation *Jammertal* (vale of sorrow). As the persons in question pass through it they bestow by the life they live and by the works they do, so much blessing upon others that they may be said to make the parched valley "a place of springs." Or to use a somewhat parallel figure, as a result of their having lived in their place in this world the helpful "early rains" of fall may be said to have come upon it and "covered it with blessings." It is not so much literal rain that is being thought of but rain as a symbol of many basic and essential blessings. The thought is expressed too ineptly when in a strongly literalistic sense it is said: "He passes through the valley . . . the face of the land changes. Rain falls, and springs rise from the ground." Are we supposed to be dealing with rain makers who exercise some potent magic?

7. Coming back to the blessings that the devout soul reaps for itself as it lives the God-devoted life, the psalm indicates that there is a continual growth and increase of strength: "They go from strength to strength." At this point the line of thought turns back to the point from which is went forth: as God is the *source,* so ever-increasing fellowship with God is the *outcome* of such a fruitful life. Again and again worshipers experience how "the God of gods will appear in Zion." Visible appearance of the Almighty is not the issue but a real contact and real fellowship with Him, as real as His actual appearance would be, is the subject under consideration. Thus it appears that this verse does not speak of two unrelated subjects in the two statements of the verse.

c) A prayer for a blessing upon the king (vv. 8, 9)

8. O Lord God of hosts, do hear my prayer;
   Give ear, O God of Jacob. Selah.
9. O God, our shield, behold
   And look upon the face of Thy anointed one.

From the tone of godly reflection the psalm turns to prayer. At first thought there would seem to be no motivation for the insertion of a prayer for the king who is, without a doubt, the "anointed one" spoken of—not the people, nor the priest. *Delitzsch* seems to indicate best what the connection in thought is. He says: "Loving Jehovah of hosts, the heavenly King, he loves also His inviolable, chosen one." In the life of the true Israelite, who was acquainted with the promises that God had given to the house of David, prayer for the royal house would occupy a place of unusual prominence. One might add that the author of the psalm, perhaps, recalled that the house of David had in many instances been particularly active as men who supported and developed true worship as well as the central sanctuary in Israel. This thought may have further induced the writer to include this brief prayer. But almost at once after this brief interlude the psalm returns to its main theme and stresses as its last major thought the blessedness of trusting in the Lord of the sanctuary.

d) The blessedness of trusting in the Lord of the sanctuary (vv. 10–12)

10. For a day in Thy courts is better than a thousand elsewhere;
    I had rather stand at the door of the house of my God than to
    dwell in the tents of wickedness.
11. For the Lord God is a sun and shield;
    The Lord bestows favor and honor;
    No good thing will He withhold from those who walk uprightly.
12. O Lord God of hosts,
    Blessed is the man who trusts in Thee!

10. The initial "for" apparently reaches back to v. 7, passing over the intervening prayer. The fruitfulness of godly lives is now traced to love for the sanctuary. There the true roots of godliness lie. It cannot be sound without the help that is afforded by regular worship in public. What the writer would especially stress over against those who regard such worship as a hard demand or an unwelcome chore is that it is a matter of rare joy. Thus, for example, one day in the Lord's courts outweighs in solid satisfaction any thousand others that might be spent elsewhere. Or to state the case differently, even getting near to the sanctuary outweighs comfortable dwelling in "the tents of wickedness," that is to say, the places where the Lord and His worship are lightly

esteemed. It may seem to be a strong statement to describe those who are disinclined to worship the Lord as being guilty of wickedness. But that is where the root of all wickedness lies, shunning fellowship with God.

11. The writer then goes on to show why this must be as he has just said. God means so much to those that know Him: He is their "sun and shield." He gives so much to those who keep coming into His presence, blessings such as "favor and honor," both in His own sight and in the sight of men. In fact, a very strong statement dare be made regarding how much He does bestow: "No good thing will He withhold from those who walk uprightly." The assumption is, of course, that only those good things which are good for the individual will be bestowed.

12. With a thought-provoking conclusion and summary the psalm draws attention to what must needs be the chief ingredient in all worship and in every relation to the Lord, and that is that one *trust* in Him. He who has learned that lesson is among the most fortunate of the children of men.

NOTES

1. "Dwellings" is a plural form (amplificative) but scarcely refers to the various dwellings that were found at the sanctuary but rather to the dignity of the one Temple. The adjective agrees in number with this plural noun.

2. By writing the first verbs as perfects (which may also be "gnomic aorist") and the verb of the second member as an imperfect the Hebrew attempts to cover the whole area of time (so *Koenig*). Our explanation offered above regards the perfect as historical and has the imperfect reflect the present situation at the time the psalmist wrote.

3. The meaning "sparrow" for *zippor* is not fully established.

6. The word rendered "Baca" (*KJ*) is the difficult word in the first member. The word appears to be used in the plural in II Sam. 5: 23f. and I Chron. 14:14f., where it may mean balsam trees or mulberry trees. But the plural used in that instance does not explain the use of the singular here. *KW* seems to offer the best lead for a meaning of *bakha'*. According to an Arabic parallel it means "lack of springs" or "dryness." We sought to express this thought by the use of the adjective "parched." By elaborate combinations some interpreters conjure up a valley of balsam trees near Jerusalem, through which travellers were supposed to approach the city. If *bakhah* (final *h*) had been written it could mean "vale of tears" (versions and *Luther*).

In the second member of the verse the difficult word is *moreh,* which can mean "teacher" (*Luther*); but in this connection the other meaning "early rain" fits far more readily.

8. The "Selah" seems to us to be misplaced and does not aptly mark a division.

9. It is true that according to the parallelism, if it is taken strictly, "shield" could refer to the king: O God, behold our shield and look upon the face of Thy anointed. Though *maghen* is a few times used with reference to warriors, it is more often used with reference to God. We have, therefore, kept the traditional rendering.

10. The "elsewhere" is not in the text but seems quite obviously to be demanded by the connection. So also *Luther* and *RSV*. "Stand at the door" is a verb that allows for several possibilities of interpretation. "Be a doorkeeper" (*AV*) is not directly suggested by the root of the verb. Most suitable seems to be the idea that, even if no more is granted than the privilege of advancing as far as the threshold, that is to be preferred to all that the best contacts with the wicked can offer. Though *dur* may be a verb that is used in the Aramaic, that does not give sufficient warrant for dating the psalm late, at a time when the Aramaic was generally used.

Psalm 85

A PRAYER FOR RESTORATION

EVEN IF WE cannot determine when this psalm was composed or under what circumstances, there is one situation into which it could fit with more than average propriety. That is the time shortly after the return from the Babylonian Captivity. For that was a time when ample evidences of divine favor were still remembered as having been bestowed but a short time before. For it was, indeed, a remarkable instance of restoration when God suffered His people to return after having been completely unrooted. No nation had had such an experience. He had at that time also obviously forgiven their sins and pardoned their iniquities. His wrath which had once burned so fiercely against His people had also ceased to manifest itself. Because of these manifest tokens of divine goodness shown them the people were extremely happy, and exuberant shouts of joy were commonly heard among them.

But this joy was short-lived. All the excellent beginnings and all the high and holy aspirations soon deteriorated, and the forward movement of restoration was completely stalled. In other words, there had been a season of very great joy over great favors received, and there had been a noteworthy beginning of re-establishment. But in a surprisingly short time all this had been stopped, and the situation regarding Israel had looked quite hopeless. At least to think of the time some twenty years after the return would give us a situation out of which a psalm like this one could easily have been written. In other words, we have a psalm before us in which a very hopeful situation failed, and the people were driven to prayer that God might, nevertheless, bring their hopes to pass.

Also in the interpretation of this psalm the cultic approach has been attempted, and one might be inclined to see some justification for it. That would mean that the first three verses are, perhaps, ascribed to a choir; the next four would be a common prayer spoken by the nation; the rest of the psalm would be a prophetic voice of some individual. There is no doubt that the psalm could have been rendered thus in public worship, but there is nothing to indicate that that was actually done. In fact, how much lively imagination is allowed to play into the interpretation becomes evident when some commentators write as though the psalm described the assembled congregation as appearing "in the garb of penitents, lying on their knees, men and women" (*Schmidt*). It must be admitted that without thinking in terms of formal public worship this psalm may have served its purpose just as well if it is thought of as being written for the private use of individuals in the distressing times described above or for groups here and there.

The heading: *To the Choir Director. By the sons of Korah. A psalm.*

On the meaning of the terms employed previous psalms may be consulted.

a) **An acknowledgement of divine favors in the past (vv. 1–3)**

1. *O Lord, Thou wast gracious to Thy land;*
   Thou didst restore the fortunes of Jacob.
2. *Thou didst forgive the iniquity of Thy people;*
   Thou didst cover all their sin. Selah.
3. *Thou didst remove all Thy wrath;*
   Thou didst turn away from the heat of Thy anger.

1. In addition to what was said in the opening remarks on this psalm, which were in brief an interpretation of this section, let us state the following. The return of Israel could well be termed a being "gracious" on God's part. He had let an enemy-infested land, full of ruins and devastation, receive a substantial contingent of inhabitants. He had furthermore worked a complete change in the situation in which His beloved Jacob found himself.

2. But all this would surely have never happened unless the nation

had penitently sought the face of the Lord and been granted divine pardon and a covering of all its sin.

The Selah that stands at this point does not so much mark a significant division in the psalm but would rather suggest that a vital thing like forgiveness may well be meditated upon, of course, during the time of the musical interlude which the Selah suggests.

3. Another serious burden that had not been regarded lightly by the guilty people was the burden of the "wrath" of God, which He had taken from them; or to phrase it still more vigorously, He did "turn away from the heat of (His) anger." No Old Testament writer is known who thought of God's anger as a matter that was to be regarded lightly. Even as the burning of God's anger is bitter, so when He turns away from it, His people may breathe more easily.

All these blessings are recalled as having been keenly enjoyed at the time when Israel first returned. Each blessing was a distinct reality. They are all acknowledged as tokens of great divine favor. They are at the same time being practically used as a foundation on which the petition that follows is built.

Oesterley is one commentator who most vigorously rejects our approach. He cites (especially in connection with Ps. 126, which is supposed to reflect the same situation) numerous passages from Nehemiah and from the latter part of Ezra to prove his contention that Israel's lot was unhappy when it first returned; but he completely ignores the significance of Ezra 3, which pictures the early flush of victory and joy, and which describes a situation which for the time being was very encouraging and called for much thanksgiving.

b) **A prayer for manifestation of God's mercy in the present (vv. 4–7)**

4. *Restore us again, O God of our salvation;*
   Cancel Thy indignation which is against us.
5. *Wilt Thou be angry with us forever?*
   Wilt Thou draw out Thy anger to all generations?
6. *Wilt not THOU revive us again*
   That Thy people may rejoice in Thee?
7. *Display to us Thy steadfast love, O Lord,*
   And grant us Thy salvation.

4. Two thoughts are prominent. One is the prayer for a restoration shortly after a previous restoration had taken place. Some restorations may be long and lasting; others, due to the weight of adverse circumstances, may soon collapse. That seems to have been the case here, so that there is no incongruity between acknowledging that there was a restoration in the earlier part of the psalm and yet praying for another one shortly thereafter. And to tell the truth, according to the book of

Haggai and that of Zechariah such a second restoration actually came to pass about twenty years after the first.

The second thought that is prominent is that there is a just indignation on the part of God to be admitted under the circumstances. Israel had brought its misfortunes down upon its own head but might yet venture to pray that God would cancel His indignation in answer to its penitent request.

5. This last phase of the thought is dwelt on at some length. Even if there had been some ten or fifteen lean years, during which the nation languished under God's anger, it may well have seemed like a "forever" to the afflicted ones, or as though it had been "drawn out to all generations." Such pleas do not so much reflect impatience as they do an honest expression of how painful it has all been. And thus (v. 6) the prayer at once takes on the note of a more hopeful and positive request: "Wilt Thou not revive us again?" The motive that is added goes on the supposition that the Lord Himself takes much more delight in seeing His people rejoice in Him than in suffering under His wrath.

7. So the petitions grow bolder and pray for that which is the epitome of God's gracious attitude toward His people—His "steadfast love" or, what is a good paraphrase of this covenant steadfastness, His "salvation," which here implies nothing less than the removal of the entire burden under which the people groan.

To restrict such prayers to public worship as such and thus to make them purely cultic, limits their range of application altogether too much. The psalm gives the nation a suitable prayer amid the needs of the present which can be used in all possible situations.

It is quite natural to expect that the remainder of the psalm will give some encouragement to the people of their prayer being heard. But here again to build up an elaborate cultic situation burdens the psalm with much extraneous material. In other words, to assume that because of the "I" at the beginning of the next section it is necessary to assume that some prophetic personage, even for that matter, perhaps, a professional prophet who was kept at the sanctuary for cases of this sort to give a divine oracle in the midst of the cultic prayer was available, and that it was he who speaks the words that follow, is surely a case of letting the imagination invent interpretations of which the text gives no evidence. By a natural turn of thought such as we all may take under such circumstances those who before referred to themselves in the plural ("us" in each of the preceding four verses) now could think of themselves as a unit group and speak in the collective "I," and thus the speakers in parts two and three of the psalm could quite easily be the same.

c) A divine promise of mercies for the future (vv. 8–13)
8. *I will hear what God the Lord will speak;*
   Surely He will speak peace to His people and to His saints;
   And "may they not return to folly!"
9. *Truly His salvation is close to them that fear Him*
   That glory may dwell in our land;
10. *That steadfast love and faithfulness may meet;*
    That righteousness and peace may kiss each other.
11. *Faithfulness will spring out of the earth;*
    And righteousness will look down from heaven.
12. *The Lord will also give that which is good;*
    And our land will yield its increase.
13. *Righteousness shall march before Him;*
    And it shall make His footsteps a way (to walk in).

8. We quite naturally raise the question, In what way does the speaker expect to hear "what God the Lord will speak"? The Greek translators of the *Septuagint* felt the need of a bit of interpretative translation at this point so strongly that they added a phrase—"within me." No special revelation or act of inspiration is thought of. This is merely a poetic way of giving expression to an inner assurance that dawns afresh upon the speaker's heart and mind. Nor is the substance of what God gives to those that speak anything that had not been previously known. Old convictions come alive in the heart in answer to earnest prayer.

The substance of that renewed conviction is twofold. It is, first of all, that God's word is one of blessing and fatherly reassurance. For His people, who have dedicated themselves to Him, have just prayed, and He is answering them. To that is joined a most suitable admonition that is also spoken by the Lord—and here the verse suddenly becomes unannounced direct discourse—"May they not return to folly!" They had on many an occasion in the past soon turned to folly. Even quite recently, after a good beginning after the return of 538 B.C., they had turned to the folly of doubt and misgivings and had thus turned a good beginning into defeat. There is nothing out of the way about this injected admonition.

9. The preceding verse was introductory to the answer which God gives to the prayer of His people; the answer itself begins in this verse. It indicates, first of all, that the needed help is never far away if only men "fear Him." It may be just around the corner but does not as yet happen to be seen; it is "close." In summary, when the help is granted it will again restore "glory" to the land which is sadly afflicted and devoid of all brighter and encouraging things.

We venture at this point to suggest a fresh approach to the question as to the qualities that are mentioned from here on (glory, steadfast love, faithfulness, righteousness, and peace), as to whether they are to be thought of as divine attributes or as qualities and virtues that are manifested by man. We feel that all of them may be understood in the broadest sense quite apart from the question as to whether God or man manifests them. It is true that the emphasis is sometimes more on the *divine* manifestation of the virtue spoken of as when (v. 11) righteousness is thought of as looking down from heaven; but that should not prevent us from admitting that in v. 10 man's righteous conduct may be thought of as being in the forefront. So also in v. 11 faithfulness must be considered primarily as a *human* attribute because it springs out of the earth; but that again does not rule out the possibility that in v. 10 it was primarily the divine faithfulness that came into the picture.

So, then, in this highly figurative and beautiful scene that is painted many charming angelic figures, as it were, dot the landscape. Some go along hand in hand as charming companions who are strongly attached to one another. Such are steadfast love and faithfulness. Others bestow a loving kiss of friendship on one another as, for example, righteousness and peace. Some seem to spring from a fertile earth that is blessed by God (again faithfulness); others, like attendant angels, glance down upon the blessed scene from high heaven as righteousness. Blessed virtues all over the picture!

12. Generalizing for a moment and dropping this set of figures, the author represents the Lord as bestowing everything that goes under the name of "good," and the land as yielding its normal increase under His beneficent blessing. A closing verse rounds out the scene in terms of the blessed figures that again walk about freely among God's people and introduces "righteousness" as marching on before the Lord Himself, who again deigns to walk freely among His pardoned people.

To us it seems like wasted effort in this case to limit righteousness to either the divine or the human manifestation of that virtue. Why not both? As kings and potentates have their forerunners and heralds, so does He; and His forerunner is righteousness. The particular function of this herald is "to make His footsteps a way" (to walk in) for the children of God. This interpretation, which calls for the brief parenthesis that we have supplied, seems to us the simplest of the many which could be offered for this difficult verse. Righteousness is then conceived of as doing man the service of showing him what path the Lord walks in in order that man may follow in that way after having been duly instructed as to what the way was. The writer of the psalm is certain that the Lord will surely give all these blessings in answer to the earnest prayers of His people. On this positive and somewhat victorious note the psalm comes to a close.

NOTES

1. The perfect tense of the verbs used in the first three verses fits so well into the historical situation that one would have been justified to make this fact overly prominent as *Luther* does by inserting the adversative *vormals* (previously) several times in order to design these three verses from the next four. To make this perfect a *perfectum propheticum* is forced and unnatural.

The expression "restore the fortunes," *shubh shebuth,* was formerly rendered "bring back the captivity" (*KJ*) on the assumption that the second word came from the root *shabhah,* "take captive." This is still the view of *BDB*. Many interpreters now prefer to derive the second word from the root of the first, "to turn back, return," and so make it a cognate object in the sense of causing a complete change or, as we have translated, "restore the fortunes." This seems much to be preferred, especially in the light of Job 42:10, where no other rendering would fit. The uncertainty regarding this problem is indicated by the fact that the second word occurs in two forms: some passages have *shebuth,* others *shebith,* and some have what would in the Hebrew be called a mixed form.

6. The "Thou" of this verse is emphatic, an emphasis which we sought to convey by printing the word in capitals.

Psalm 86

A PRAYER FOR DELIVERANCE FROM ENEMIES

THE GENERAL reader is not likely to notice that this psalm is pieced together by adapting sections of a number of other psalms, not by way of many direct quotations, but rather by the use of materials found in almost the same form elsewhere. In other words, it is a mosaic.

That fact does not, however, lessen the value of the psalm. As *Maclaren* rightly suggests: "God does not give originality to every devout man." The writer was adept in the use of familiar materials by piecing them together with rare skill and producing the equivalent of a new production. Although it is not original the psalm is still very effective.

This raises the question of authorship. The heading attributes the psalm to David. This suggestion is almost universally brushed aside as being unacceptable. The psalms from which our psalm draws materials are 25–28 and 54–57, all of which are Davidic according to the headings, which we believe to be reliable. This reduces the question to approximately this form: Would David have used secondhand material that had previously been written by him in other psalms? Why not? Why should that be impossible or preposterous? Even musicians occasionally write scores by using phrases and combinations that they have been known to use in other works of theirs. Even Christ Himself frequently quoted or re-employed materials that had been used by Him in other connections. We for our part are ready to admit the possibility of authorship by David though no man can point to a particular historical situation out of which the psalm grew. There is another possibility that Davidic materials which were assembled by another man may still yield a Davidic psalm.

Two features of the psalm are distinctive in spite of its lack of originality. It stresses the universal extent of the kingdom of the Lord (v. 9) as do a few other Scripture passages of the Old Testament (cf., Zeph. 2:11; Zech. 14:9, 16; Ps. 22:29). This may well be regarded as a Messianic note, for it touches upon a fact that is to be realized in the kingdom of the Messiah. Then in v. 11 it dwells in a unique fashion upon the unity of purpose which should characterize a man's relation to his God.

There are some interpreters who discover a note of self-righteousness in the psalm, especially in v. 2 and, perhaps, in v. 4. However, isolated statements may create a wrong impression. Vv. 5 and 15 distinctly establish the fact that the writer is dependent on the mercy of God rather than upon his own achievements.

We do not believe that those commentators who rearrange the material of the psalm because they regard it as being in a state of disorder have sufficient warrant for what they do. *Schmidt* has sought to blaze a trail by claiming that the sequence of parts should be and originally was vv. 1–7; 14–17; 8–13. The presupposition is that we have now definitely determined in what order various elements should follow, such as petitions, reason for petition, thanksgiving, praise. Such patterns can become highly artificial when exclusiveness is claimed for them. According to the mood of the writer thoughts may flow in all manner of possible sequence, all of which may be perfectly natural and normal.

It appears to be quite obvious that the author of the psalm is writing

Psalm 86

in his own person and not for the congregation of Israel, whose mouthpiece he is. The tone of the psalm is quite personal.

Always granting that any one of the psalms may on occasion have been used in public worship, there is still scarcely enough material in the psalm that allows for its being regarded as a liturgical piece to be used when, for example, a kind of ordeal is to be undergone in the hope of securing a divine verdict (e.g., the "sign" mentioned in v. 17).

It is, indeed, somewhat unusual but far from unnatural that the issue that causes grief to the psalmist is not divulged until v. 14 is reached. There it becomes clear that "insolent men" and a "crowd of ruthless men" seek the life of the writer. But if that fact is not related in the opening sentences, can it not easily be understood on the score that the writer was well aware of the fact that God knew what his chief difficulty was?

The quotations or half-quotations that appear in the psalm may be conveniently grouped together. On v. 2 see 25:20; on v. 3 cf. 57:1, 2; on v. 4b cf. 25:1; in connection with v. 6, 55:1, 2 may be compared; and with v. 7, 77:2. V. 9 certainly reminds one of 22:27; with v. 10, 77:13, 14; 72:18. V. 11 is taken word for word from 27:11, and v. 14 is taken almost word for word from 54:3. With v. 12, however, 57:9, 10 may be compared. With v. 15, Exod. 34:6; with v. 16, 25:16; and with v. 17, 40:3; 35:4.

a) A cry for help (vv. 1–7)

A Prayer of David.

1. *Incline Thy ear, O Lord, and answer me,*
   For I am needy and poor.
2. *Preserve my life, for I am a godly man;*
   O Thou my God, save Thy servant that trusts in Thee.
3. *Be gracious unto me, O Lord,*
   For unto Thee do I cry all the day.
4. *Make glad the soul of Thy servant,*
   For unto Thee, O Lord, do I lift up my soul.
5. *For Thou, O Lord, art good and ready to forgive*
   And abounding in steadfast love to all who call upon Thee.
6. *Hear my prayer, O Lord,*
   And be attentive to my loud supplications.
7. *In the day of my distress I will call upon Thee,*
   For Thou wilt answer me.

1. The psalm begins on a somewhat plaintive note, a cry for help. Almost each one of the petitions offered is backed by a particular

reason for being heard. These reasons are: "I am poor and needy"; "I am a godly man"; "unto Thee do I cry all the day"; "Thou, O Lord, art good and ready to forgive"; and "Thou wilt answer me." To these could be added the modifying clause found in v. 2, "that trusts in Thee." Considered together, these reasons stress the petitioner's need and distress on the one hand and God's goodness on the other. They are all of the kind that God's children are wont to use when they are in distress. The one listed in v. 4 was not mentioned, for it is a bit unique: "for unto Thee do I lift up my soul." That is as much as to say: Those who are in the habit of appealing to Thee cannot be disappointed.

The petitions offered may also be grouped together so as to enable us to get a total picture of the need of the author. They are: "incline Thy ear and answer me"; "preserve my life"; "save Thy servant"; "be gracious unto me"; "make glad the soul of Thy servant"; "hear my prayer"; "be attentive to my loud supplication"; "in the day of my distress I will call upon Thee."

5. It is quite obvious that the chief basis for being heard is God's known goodness and faithfulness. It is also rather clear that both the petitions and the motivations are such as to allow for their being used in any number of cases by men in the widest variety of circumstances.

Two additional matters call for comment. In v. 2 the writer describes himself as a "godly man"—"holy" (*KJ*). What smacks somewhat of self-praise in either form is not likely to be regarded thus in German, *fromm*. The term itself implies that the speaker is a loyal follower of the Lord. If a man is such a follower, dare he not make mention of the fact without becoming guilty of self-righteousness? Then in v. 4, where the writer prays that God may make glad his soul, that common point of view of the Old Testament becomes an issue, namely, that the life of God's people is marked by joy more than is the life of the rest of mankind.

b) **God's singular greatness (vv. 8–10)**

8. *There is none like unto Thee among the gods, O Lord;*
   Neither are there any works like Thy works.
9. *All the nations whom Thou hast made shall come and worship before Thee, O Lord;*
   And they shall glorify Thy name.
10. *For Thou art great and doest wondrous things;*
    Thou alone art God.

These words are spoken in praise of God's singular greatness. It is certainly a healthy sign when in the midst of distress a soul can reflect at length on the incomparable greatness of God and not be immersed

Psalm 86

in its own troubles. One feature of such praise is to recall that no one of those called gods can in any wise be matched with God or do any works like those with which He is credited. Besides, there is no God whose worshipers believe and know that ultimately all the nations which He has made "shall come and worship before Him." The good reason that they shall engage in such blessed devotion is that the Lord is truly great (v. 10) and does wondrous things, yea, in fact, alone is God.

c) **Praise of God for the help anticipated (vv. 11–13)**

11. *Teach me the way pleasing to Thee*
    That I may walk in faithfulness toward Thee;
    Grant me to have only the one purpose to fear Thy name.
12. *I will praise Thee, O Lord my God, with all my heart;*
    And I will glorify Thy name forever.
13. *For great is Thy steadfast love toward me;*
    And Thou wilt save my life from the very brink of death.

11. Though he is still in the midst of trouble, the writer thinks in terms of praise of God for the help which he is sure will come to him. The thoughts take the following course: A petition to understand the way that is pleasing to God, coupled with the firm resolve that, as soon as this way is known, it will be followed. Or what amounts to the same thing, he prays that he may have only one purpose in life, and that, to fear God's name.

12. When this comes to pass, and the psalmist seems to think of it as being the same as being delivered from his present troubles, he on his part will engage in the praises of God and will glorify His holy name forever. Besides, a new revelation of the greatness of God's steadfast love has dawned upon him through this whole experience, an insight which enables him to say that, if he were on the very brink of death, the Lord could and would save his life. Being sure that God is capable of such a deliverance, the writer implies that all his present needs are included, and deliverance from them will also follow in due time.

There is something of deep insight in the manner in which v. 11 prays to have only one purpose. For, as has just been indicated, the Lord is God alone—He is one. The total affection of the heart should concentrate on this one whose position is so unique. Though the last petition of the verse is in the Hebrew expressed in one concise verb, which we have translated, "Grant me to have this one purpose," we feel that the *KJ,* correct as it is in rendering this one verb "unite," does not enlighten the reader very much by this translation. We felt constrained, therefore, to follow Luther who translates: *Erhalte mein*

Herz bei dem Einigen, dass ich deinen Namen fürchte (practically the same as our translation).

d) A renewed cry for help by describing the present situation (vv. 14-17)

14. O God, insolent men have arisen against me;
    A crowd of ruthless men seek my life;
    And they have not set Thee before them.
15. But Thou, O Lord, art a God, merciful and gracious,
    Patient and abounding in steadfast love and faithfulness.
16. Turn to me and pity me;
    Impart Thy strength to Thy servant and save the son of Thy handmaid.
17. Show me a sign for good
    That they who hate me may see and be put to shame,
    For Thou, O Lord, hast helped me and comforted me.

14. Quite obviously the note of appeal for help predominates in these words, dominating particularly the last two verses. But, as was already indicated, it is only in this section (v. 14) that the specific nature of the difficulty that besets the writer becomes clear. Men have arisen against him, proud and insolent, bent upon his destruction, with never a thought of God in all their wicked plottings. It seems sufficient to the writer without further comment to lay the case as such before the Lord, who will know what action is appropriate under the circumstances.

15. Rather fittingly after the manner of men who put their trust in the Lord the psalmist merely pits what God is over against what confronts and threatens him by putting the emphasis on the manifold gracious attributes that are known to be marks of God's holy being. The statement is built primarily on Exod. 34:6 or is echoed in Ps. 103:8. Out of the rich measure of God's goodness such help as is needed will fall to the lot of this devout soul that trusts in Him.

16. This verse utters a strong petition that this may come to pass. The plea is reinforced by the indication that the speaker needs strength badly as well as by an indication of the fact that he stands in the relationship of a "servant" (really "slave") as well as that of a son of a godly woman who was wont to put her trust in the Lord and had with good reason taught her son to do the same. The use of terms like "servant" in this connection is due to modesty on the part of the petitioner over against the exalted Lord.

17. The psalmist gives particular point to his petition when he indicates that the thing he particularly desires is that God may "show (him) a sign for good," which means, to grant him some favorable and

encouraging experience that can make him feel that God has taken note of his petition. ("Sign" is here scarcely used in the sense of an outstanding, miraculous occurrence). For by doing this those who unjustly hate the speaker will be put in their place when they see that God is on the side of this man who receives both God's help and comfort. The perfect tense of these last two verbs conveys a note of strong assurance before the actual answer to prayer is received.

NOTES

6. Many interpreters prefer to translate an expression like "the voice of my supplications" as "my loud supplications" as we have done. There is some justification for this rendering.

9. A number of commentators transpose the words "whom Thou hast made" to the beginning of the next verse on the ground that *Israel* is the nation whom God has made. But such a transpositions is not warranted because it is taught with equal clarity in the Old Testament that all the nations on the face of the earth owe their existence to the Lord.

13. The Hebrew equivalent for what we have rendered "the very brink of death" is "deepest Sheol." But since the latter expression means little to the average reader; and furthermore, since it appears to be a figurative expression, it can scarcely be said to mean more than we have indicated by our translation. It is an obvious hyperbole for some mishap that might have ended fatally.

Psalm 87

THE GLORIFICATION OF ZION
BY THE ADOPTION OF THE GENTILES

IN THIS PSALM, as is so often the case, a particular thought of the preceding psalm is developed more fully, namely, the thought expressed in Ps. 86:9: "All the nations Thou hast made shall come and bow down before Thee." The form that this new approach takes is exuberant praise on the part of Zion herself over the prospect of adding these many outside nations to her citizenship rolls. Therefore this psalm is eloquent testimony to the high hope of its world-wide mission that Zion had in days of old. Seldom does that hope find more eloquent expression than it does in this brief psalm.

It is true that the average reader is apt to be more perplexed than edified and impressed by what he reads here. This is partly due to the unusual conciseness of the psalm, a conciseness which borders almost on obscurity at times. On the other hand, it may be due to the inadequacy of the translations current although the chief of these have now been corrected by *RSV*, which in the opening statement uses an approach that is quite similar to that of *Luther*.

We feel inclined to take our place by the side of those who would suggest the days of Hezekiah as the time that is most suitable for the writing of the psalm though no writer dare speak on this subject with finality. In support of this approach let the following be noted. Isaiah himself, the chief prophet of Hezekiah's time, calls Egypt Rahab (Is. 30:7). Contacts with Babylon had been established as appears from Is. 39. Assyria, therefore, seems to have passed out of the picture, for no mention was made of her; and this was actually the case in Hezekiah's time. The rather confident tone that prevails in the psalm would be characteristic of the time of Hezekiah when God's remarkable deliverance had greatly inspired the hopes of the nation in regard to the security of the holy city. A broadening of viewpoint would be indicated also by the fact recorded in II Chron. 32:23, that after the deliverance of Jerusalem from the power of Sennacherib "many brought gifts to the Lord to Jerusalem." To this we would add that nothing suggests the times and the experiences of the Exile.

Because of the fact that the meaning of the psalm is not immediately apparent, some interpreters have resorted to the always precarious device of rearranging the verses or parts of verses so that scarcely a modern commentary leaves the psalm untouched from this point of view. The *RSV* fortunately does not tamper with the text of the psalm. Whether one line is shifted such as placing 5c after 1b, or whether many relocations are attempted, all such attempts put the psalm utterly at the mercy of the ingenuity of the commentator and are liable to produce almost any new or novel possibilities.

The assumption that the psalm reflects a time when proselytes were rather commonly to be seen in the Temple courts at Jerusalem, and that the sight of them inspired the writer to the utterances here recorded has nothing substantial to recommend it.

The psalm may be outlined as follows:

1. Praise of Zion (vv. 1–3)
2. The incorporation of Zion's ancient enemies among her citizens (vv. 4–6)
3. The spirit that shall animate Zion's festive gatherings (v. 7)

The heading: *By the sons of Korah. A psalm, a song.* On the sons of

Korah see Ps. 42:1. The word "psalm" is the most distinctive word for psalms as such; "song" is the most general. What special connotation "song" had in a heading such as this we are quite unable to determine.

a) **Praise of Zion** (vv. 1–3)

  1b. *His foundation in the holy mountains,*
  2. *The gates of Zion, the Lord loves*
     More than all the other dwellings in Jacob.
  3. *Glorious things are spoken of you,*
     O city of God. Selah.

1. The interpreter has his choice of two major possibilities in regard to this verse. He either considers it complete in itself and supplies some verb like "is" or "stands" and thus arrives at some translation like *RSV:* "On the holy mount stands the city He founded" ("city" also being supplied); or he regards the material offered in v. 1 as the object of the verb "loves" in v. 2, to which "the gates of Zion" are in apposition. We have construed the matter in this way. It is true that the reader is then plunged into the very midst of things by having a double object at the very beginning of a sentence. This may have been the very purpose of the author. In fact, the initial "his" without an antecedent immediately discernible constitutes a sort of challenge in itself. But this somewhat proleptic use of possessive pronouns is not unheard of.

The thought is this: That which the Lord has founded in the holy mountains of Jerusalem, which is pre-eminently, of course, the very central sanctuary itself, is in a very special sense the object of His affection as are the large and beautiful "gates of Zion" which typify the strength and beauty of the entire sanctuary (a synecdoche). In fact, there is not one of the many dwellings in the whole land, including all its palaces, that has the same claim on the Lord's interest and affection as does this sanctuary, the site of which He Himself chose (II Sam. 24), and where He in a very special way gave a token of His divine approval by the appearance of the cloud of His presence on the day of dedication (I Kings 8:10f.).

3. Furthermore, there are many glorious things that the holy prophets have at one time or another spoken regarding this divinely appointed sanctuary. *McCullough* lists typical utterances that might be thought of in this connection such as that "the Lord has chosen Zion for His habitation" (Ps. 132:13); or that His holy mountain "is the joy of all the earth" (48:2); or, "out of Zion shall go forth the law" (Is. 2:3); or that it is "a habitation of justice" (Jer. 31:23). All these may very properly be summed up in the most appropriate title that the writer applies to the object of his special praise, "O city of God." Brief and con-

cise but eloquent are these words spoken in praise of Zion. But her outstanding beauty consists in the fact that the Lord loves her.

b) **The incorporation of Zion's ancient enemies among her citizens (vv. 4–6)**

4. *"I mention Rahab (Egypt) and Babylon among those who acknowledge Me;*
Behold, Philistia and Tyre together with Ethiopa—each of these was born there."
5. *And of Zion it shall be said: "Every single one was born in her; And the Most High, He Himself shall establish her."*
6. *The Lord will enumerate as He records the peoples: "This one was born there." Selah.*

4. In this section in which the inclusion of Zion's ancient enemies and neighbors among her citizens is recorded a rather unusual device is resorted to to give dramatic liveliness to the account: direct discourse is employed without being directly introduced. Thus in v. 4 the Lord is to be thought of as uttering the sentiments recorded. In v. 5 the sentiments of men generally are voiced. V. 6 does place the thought expressed in b. into the mouth of the Lord. Unless these facts are noted, interpretation is hopelessly at sea. Ps. 2 has a number of instances of similar direct discourse which is not introduced as such.

"Rahab," as already indicated, is Egypt, the "arrogant" one, as the root of the word signifies—an appropriate name ever since the arrogance of Pharaoh in the days of the Exodus manifested the basic attitude of this nation toward Israel. But if both she and proud and imperial Babylon are ready to acknowledge (literally: "know" in the sense of loving, interested acceptance) the Lord, then an almost unthinkable transformation of the entire attitude of these once so very superior nations must have taken place. That is the very point that the verse is making.

In this catalogue of nations who thus openly come over to the Lord's side is to be found also the inveterate foe, Philistia, so long a thorn in Israel's side. Then there will be Tyre, the worldly commercial city, in a sense a symbol of sophistication; and lastly Ethiopia, which lay to the south of Egypt and is a representative of the nations that lie remotely on Israel's horizon, who, however, at times even ventured to assail Israel (II Chron. 14:9).

The expression used with reference to this latter group of three nations is to be noted: "each of these was born there." Suddenly a new standard of judgment appears. More than submission is involved. Though the New Testament doctrine of the new birth does not appear clearly in the Old Testament, the expression here used surely implies some deeper kind of transformation that is to take place. These people will be natives in the sense of native-born. Thus ends the pronouncement of the Almighty. Unusually deep insight is manifested in this statement concerning the nature of the new relation that shall be evidenced in the age of the Messiah on the part of once hostile groups toward Israel and what she stands for.

5. A second time this significant statement about men being born in her appears, this time as the outstanding pronouncement about Zion herself. In other words, when men shall try to put into words what the unique feature about her new citizenship is they shall offer the suggestion that her new people are as truly her own children's as though they had actually seen the light of this world within her walls. But more should be noted. Since such a unique relationship is possible only through the working of the Almighty Himself, He will not only create such a situation, but He will also maintain it: "the Most High Himself shall establish her." In other words, Israel's new achievements shall not be something ephemeral, they shall not soon pass off the scene as a momentary phenomenon. This new state of affairs shall continue. It will be that for which Israel is chiefly noted.

6. From another point of view this same thought is driven home to our thinking. A scene is envisioned in which the Lord, deeply concerned about the weal and woe of His people, Himself keeps book on the nations that are affiliated with His people—an attractive anthropomorphism. As *Gunkel* rather aptly remarks in this connection, it is as though "the writer in a sense were looking over the Lord's shoulder as He keeps these books and overhears what He says to Himself as He writes." At each new entry the now familiar words are heard: "This one was born there." Even to the Lord Himself it is a matter of concern and interest that the new affiliates are born and transformed to their new situation. All of which reminds one of the Savior's formulation of the truth involved: "Except a man be born again he cannot enter the kingdom of God." Here as above (v. 3) the Selah marks an appropriate division in the sequence of thought.

The thought of keeping a register of the inhabitants of a land in appropriate records appears frequently enough in the Old Testament (Jer. 22:30; Ezek. 13:9; Ezra 2:62; Neh. 7:5; II Chron. 2:17).

c) **The spirit that shall animate Zion's festive gatherings (v. 7)**

7. *Singers and dancers alike say:*
   "All my springs arise in you."

The spirit that animates the worshipers in Zion is apparently described in this verse. Admittedly the verse presents difficulties as the earliest versions already indicate. The first clause lacks a verb. "Say" is the simplest one to supply. We may then regard the verse as depicting what happens or, perhaps, will happen at the sanctuary in Zion when this multifarious and polyglot group which is to make up the citizenry of the holy city comes together for the solemn festivities that it desires to observe. There will be present "singers" who in trained chorus or freely on their own initiative offer their praises to the Lord. There will be those who, like David of old, desire to give more exuberant expression to their deep joy in the sacred dance (II Sam. 6:14). But the sentiment that wells deep from the heart of these two groups as well as from all others will be: "All my springs arise in you" (again a suitable verb has to be supplied in making the translation). The "springs" are apparently the deep sources or roots of one's being. Passages like Is. 12:3; Hos. 13:15; Ps. 36:9 may be compared.

So this psalm is a psalm that is full of Messianic anticipation, rich in evangelistic hopes, and deeply grounded in the insight that the inner sources of a man's life are transformed when he becomes a true citizen of Zion.

NOTES.

Most of the critical and textual issues that the psalm presents were in this instance more conveniently dealt with in the exposition of the text.

1. One item in connection with the opening word of the text of the psalm may yet be touched upon. The suffix of *yesudhatho* is masculine, thus eliminating the possibility of a reference to the city—"*her* foundation." It must refer to the *Yahweh* of the next verse. Such anticipatory use of a pronoun is common enough in all languages and in the present instance stimulates interest in who it is that the suffix refers to, though the answer is almost at once anticipated correctly.

Psalm 88

AN AGONIZED OUTCRY

ON ONE MATTER at least all commentators who deal with this psalm are fully agreed: it is the gloomiest psalm found in the Scriptures. Expressed a bit more accurately, there appears to be no relief from the dark hopelessness that marks the psalm though the writer may have earnestly prayed to God. It does seem strange that a man would begin his prayer, "O Lord, God of my salvation," and then continue to the point where the last word is still "darkness." The psalmist is as deeply in trouble when he has concluded his prayer as he was when he began it.

A number of writers point out that it is a good thing that this psalm has found a place in the book because otherwise one experience that men who fear God may have would not be reflected in a book which seems to reckon with all the possibilities that may be met with in life's stormy voyage. Prayer usually brings relief to the afflicted soul sooner or later. Here this is apparently not the case.

We dare not be too positive about identifying the type of physical ailment from which the writer suffers as *Kittel* does when he entitles the psalm, "The Cry of a Leper." We may be inclined to admit that the ailment could have been leprosy. It could have been one of any number of other diseases. Present-day writers are for the most part agreed that the whole psalm is too personal to allow for a collective I as its subject. It is not the nation which is in some form of distress such as the Babylonian Captivity. It would be straining the words of the psalm too greatly to make its various descriptive terms figurative in character.

It could be argued that the writer had some acquaintance with the book of Job and understood its message well. Rather than to try to trace this possibility piecemeal as we proceed, let us at once submit all the material in brief. Regarding v. 6 one may compare Job 10:21, 22. Regarding v. 8, Job 19:13-19; 20:10; 3:23; 13:27 would be relevant. Regarding v. 10 one could compare Job 10:20-22, etc. But even then a positive conclusion cannot be reached. One could at most say that the writer of this psalm may have seen and used the book of Job.

There are, of course, points of similarity with other psalms. Sickness seems to have been an issue in Ps. 38, 22, and 41, and without a doubt Is. 38:10-20, the prayer of Hezekiah, is somewhat analogous.

To discover an outline of thought for the psalm is difficult. When the heart and the mind are greatly disturbed, a man is not apt to be particularly careful about the logical arrangement of the thoughts that he records. Yet it cannot be said that the psalm utterly lacks plan and purpose of arrangement. Perhaps as helpful an approach as any is to follow *Maclaren,* who suggests that the three instances when the psalm directly addresses God mark a division of material with sufficient clearness to serve as helpful guides.

The heading reads thus: *"A song. A psalm of the sons of Korah. To the Choir Director. According to Mahalath Leannoth. A maskil of Heman, the E   ite."*

a) **A cry for help based on the wretchedness of the writer's situation (vv. 1–9a)**

Much of this heading is obscure. We are unable to determine how a psalm may be a "song" and a "maskil" as well, the latter term signifying a didactic poem. *Schmidt* solves the problem of having the psalm ascribed to both the sons of Korah and Heman by the suggesting that Heman was the author, and that he belonged to the guild of singers called the sons of Korah. *Mahalath Leannoth,* which most likely refers to the tune to which the psalm is to be sung, could mean: "the sickness of a certain one; to make humble" (*Koenig*) and might thus contain a subtle suggestion that the sickness of the writer was to teach him humility. Heman, a wise man, is mentioned in I Kings 4:31; Heman, a singer, in I Chron. 6:33; 15:17; 25:4–6. It is most likely the latter who is here referred to.

1. *O Lord, God of my salvation, by day have I cried out;*
   At night I lie before Thee.
2. *Let my prayer come before Thee;*
   Incline Thy ear to my cry.
3. *For my soul has had its fill of troubles;*
   And my life draws near to the grave.
4. *I am reckoned with those that go down to the pit;*
   I have become like a man who has no more strength.
5. *Free among the dead? Rather, I am like the slain that lie in the grave;*
   Whom Thou rememberest no more, and they are cut off from Thy hand.
6. *Thou hast laid me in the lowest pit,*
   In deep darkness under the waves.
7. *Thy wrath presses down upon me;*
   Thou hast made all Thy billows to roar over me. Selah.
8. *Thou hast made my acquaintances to keep at a distance from me;*
   Thou hast made me utterly abhorred to them;
   I am shut in and cannot go out.
9a. *My eyes grow dim because of sorrow.*

In this plea, which is motivated by the wretchedness of the writer's situation, it is not as though he were trying to move God to pity, or as if he were trying to persuade a reluctant deity to do what He is disinclined to do. The psalmist rather feels the need of unburdening himself to the One to whom he feels he may freely tell his troubles.

1. There is some measure of confession of faith in the first two

Psalm 88

verses. The Lord is the "God of his salvation." God is further regarded as the One to whom prayer is to be made, and who is wont to incline His ear to the cry of those who lay their petitions before Him. His plea may have been ineffective thus far, but by day he has cried, and at night he lies before Him.

3. Among the things to be mentioned in this motivation (note that it begins with a "for") is the fact that his soul has had its fill of troubles —it cannot swallow any more—and his life has drawn near to the grave, or as we are wont to say, there is but a step between him and death. In his weakness (v. 4) he is as far gone as are those that go down to the pit, utterly lacking strength. Utter exhaustion has overtaken him. Not a pleasant feeling, to say the least.

5. It may be possible that he is at this point half quoting a remark that some, who sought to comfort him, may have made to the effect that it won't be long, and he will be rid of all his troubles or "free." Half-bitterly he ejaculates: "Free among the dead?" as much as to say, What kind of freedom do you call that? The facts of the case are that he had better be likened to men who were slain, let us say, on the field of battle and then tossed into their grave, to be forgotten, or what seems worse, to be cut off from God's hand, that is, beyond the point where even God can do anything for them.

6. Several other features of his unhappy lot are now set forth. The writer has gotten as low as a man can get, "in the lowest pit." Darkness, the concomitant of despair, completely enshrouds him wherever he turns. He is like a man who has been washed down under the deepest billows. Again and again the thought has come to him that he must in some special way be the object of God's "wrath," which presses down hard upon him. Whether he implies that he justly merits God's wrath is extremely difficult to determine; he says nothing one way or another.

To all this must be added the rather painful attitude of his "acquaintances" who for some reason or other stay away from him. In what way he is to be thought of as being "utterly abhorred" by them is a matter of surmise. It could have been due to repulsive sickness; it could have been because his suffering had continued for so long a time. Who likes to be a witness to any man's agony? To all this must be added the fact that he is not free to go out among men (8c), and that either his sickness or his tears have made his sight become dim. All in all, a picture of abject misery long drawn out!

But the psalmist bestirs himself. He may not have received an answer, but he will keep on crying out. The name of God as the "God of (his) salvation" is real to him. As the hymn states it: *Von Gott will ich nicht lassen* ("I refuse to let go of God").

b) **The cry repeated, now urging help before it is too late (vv. 9b–12)**
  9b. *I call upon Thee, O Lord, every day;*
     I spread out my hands to Thee.
  10. *Canst Thou do wonders for the dead?*
     Or will the shades rise up to praise Thee? Selah.
  11. *Will Thy steadfast love be declared in the grave,*
     Or Thy faithfulness in destruction?
  12. *Will Thy wonders be known in darkness*
     And Thy righteousness in the land of oblivion?

This second plea for help seems to be motivated by the idea that, if God does not help soon, it will be too late. It is quite obvious that the Old Testament saints had for the most part but a dim knowledge of the hereafter and consequently little faith in it. Thus, for example, whatever God might do for him after he is dead and gone, even though it is a wonder (v. 10), he could not appreciate. He is dead. Or again (a rather unique way of looking at the situation) praise of the Creator was an important part of the life of God's people, but once they are dead they can praise no more. To tell the truth, v. 11, too, speaks according to what the eye sees. And who has ever seen a corpse in the grave speak up to declare God's steadfast love or His faithfulness after the body had begun to decompose? The writer speaks realistically; he could not use the New Testament language of faith because he did not yet have this faith. The same applies to v. 12: in the darkness of death and in the land of oblivion those things which the Jews regarded as so important, God's wonders and His righteousness, just could not be experienced any more.

It might be possible that here as often elsewhere in the Old Testament extreme suffering had brought the light of faith to a very low point in the heart of the afflicted person, and that such afflicted persons often spoke out of this low ebbing of faith. Ps. 16:10, 11 indicated a far different approach. But affliction can dim faith.

c) **The cry again repeated, urging further details of his unhappy lot (vv. 13–18)**
  13. *But as for me, unto Thee, O Lord, have I cried;*
     And in the morning my prayer comes before Thee.
  14. *Why, O Lord, dost Thou cast me off?*
     Why dost Thou hide Thy face from me?
  15. *Wretched am I and close to death from youth up;*
     I have suffered Thy terrors; I am beside myself.
  16. *Thy wrath has passed over me;*
     Thy terrors have silenced me;

17. *They enclose me like waters all day long;*
    They encircle me altogether.
18. *Thou hast put lover and friend at a distance from me;*
    And my acquaintances are—darkness.

We shall outline briefly only the new features which are added as a motivation for the last plea. One is the expostulation concerning the Why of it all (v. 14). Another, that affliction, which has kept him close to death, has been his lot "from youth up" (v. 15). All this has not left him cold and calm: he has "suffered terrors" because of it. He is virtually "beside himself." For a second time he makes mention of God's "wrath" that has passed over him. This was not a misapprehension of what was actually transpiring. God's wrath was real to God's saints, and they knew when it had hit them. In addition, God's terrors (v. 16) have silenced him. He is intimidated; he does not dare to speak for fear of stirring up more of God's wrath.

The last part of the last verse is acknowledged on every hand to be extremely difficult. By inserting an "are" we arrive at a thought that may be stated thus: Far from being able to afford him any relief or joy or cheerfulness, his friends, having completely neglected him, are about as much help to a soul under the clouds of affliction as is darkness—a rather gloomy prospect.

NOTES

1. The second half of the verse reads: "at night before Thee." The simplest way to render the meaning of this elliptical statement is to insert a verb like "I lie." This expedient also preserves the parallelism.

3. The word *Sheol,* which we translated "the grave," will forever be a problem for translators. Sheol means the afterlife but is used for a number of other terms that we employ to make further distinctions. It sometimes seems to mean simply the grave; it may then seem to mean hell; quite often, it in some vague manner signifies merely the hereafter. In this instance we used "the grave" as its equivalent, for that is apparently the expression we should have used.

4. "The pit" (*bor*) is approximately another synonym for Sheol. So also in v. 6, where the same word appears. But in v. 11, though the thought seems to be about the same, the word *'abhaddon* is used, which means "destruction." In the New Testament (Rev. 9:11) the angel of the abyss bears this name.

5. The words "among the dead free" have long constituted a crux for interpreters. As our explanation above indicates, we have felt that to regard this as a half-ironic question is the most acceptable approach.

8. For "utterly abhorred" the Hebrew has a plural—"abominations." For "shut in" a pronoun subject has to be supplied, which is readily suggested by the context as "I." *Kalu'* is a Kal passive participle.

10. As a translation of *ta'aseh* the potential "canst Thou" seems best.

Psalm 89

THE LORD'S COVENANT WITH DAVID
AND ISRAEL'S SAD AFFLICTION

THIS IS A PSALM that informs us indirectly as to how deeply the Messianic hope was imbedded in the thinking of at least the faithful in Israel. For in a time of affliction it is keenly felt how sadly Israel's desolate state is at odds with the glorious hopes that God had kindled in the heart of the nation by the promises of the future greatness of the nation and its great king.

To question the unity of the psalm as some interpreters do and to make of it two psalms that are to be treated separately is quite ungrounded. To claim to be able to detect several sources, that is to say, earlier poems which were welded together to produce the present psalm, is quite artificial and an evidence of an obsession which has momentarily blinded men by thoughts of man's unique gifts of discernment.

So, too, the question of a possible liturgical use of the psalm on some special festival still remains and very likely will continue to remain speculation. Neither does it seem possible to arrive at a satisfactory conclusion regarding the question of the possible time of the composition of the psalm. The fact that the kingdom had been brought low and the king made ineffective and greatly humbled is quite evident. It seems less likely that so early a time as that of Rehoboam should be thought of. The days of Josiah or even of Zedekiah just before the fall of Jerusalem would seem to fit the situation better.

Ethan, the Ezrahite, is credited with the composition of this one psalm only. It is a *maskil,* a didactic poem, as nearly as we can ascertain.

The content of this psalm may be outlined as follows:

Psalm 89

1. the praise of God for His manifold mercies (vv. 1–18)
2. a rehearsal of the Messianic promise given to David (vv. 19–27)
3. the sad contrast with the present situation (vv. 38–45)
4. a plea for divine intervention (vv. 46–51)

a) **The praise of God for His manifold mercies (vv. 1–18)**

1. *Of the mercies of the Lord will I sing forever;*
   From generation to generation will I make known Thy faithfulness with my mouth.
2. *For Thou didst say, O Lord: "Forever shall steadfast love be built up"—*
   In the very heavens Thou hast established the sign of Thy faithfulness—
3. *"I have made My covenant for My chosen one;*
   I have sworn to David, My servant:
4. *'Forever will I establish your posterity*
   And build up your throne for all generations.'" Selah.
5. *And the heavens shall praise the wondrous thing Thou hast done*
   And Thy faithfulness in the assembly of the holy ones.
6. *For who in high heavens can be compared with the Lord?*
   Who among the heavenly beings is like the Lord,
7. *A God greatly to be feared in the council of the holy ones*
   And to be had in reverence by all that are round about Him?
8. *O Lord God of hosts, who is like Thee?*
   Strong art Thou, O Lord, and Thy faithfulness is round about Thee.
9. *Thou rulest the raging of the sea;*
   When its waves rise, Thou stillest them.
10. *Thou hast crushed Rahab* (Egypt) *like one that is slain;*
    Thou hast scattered Thy enemies with Thy strong arm;
11. *Thine are the heavens, and Thine is the earth;*
    The world and all that is in it Thou hast founded.
12. *The north and the south Thou hast created;*
    Tabor and Hermon are jubilant over Thy name.
13. *Thou hast a mighty arm;*
    Strong is Thy hand, and Thy right hand is exalted.
14. *Righteousness and justice are the foundation of Thy throne;*
    Steadfast love and faithfulness go before Thee.
15. *Oh, how very happy are the people that know the jubilant shout!*
    O Lord, in the light of Thy countenance they shall walk!
16. *In Thy name shall they rejoice continually;*
    And in Thy righteousness shall they be exalted.

17. *For Thou art the glory of their strength;*
    And by Thy favor our horn is exalted.
18. *For our shield belongs to the Lord*
    And our king to the Holy One of Israel.

1. The first four verses serve as a sort of introduction to this first section of the psalm, which sings the praises of God's manifold mercies, and v. 1 in particular may be regarded as the theme sentence. Instead of the caption that we gave to the psalm, it might also be entitled, "I will sing of the mercies of the Lord," on the assumption that the chief of these mercies are the "sure mercies of David" (Is. 55:3). The word for "mercies" is the one whose singular is quite regularly translated "steadfast love" in *RSV*. It seemed impossible to capture the force of the Hebrew plural without resorting to a form like "mercies," which can also mean "instances of merciful dealing." This theme is so great that it deserves to be reiterated "forever." The psalmist expects never to exhaust the theme of God's covenant faithfulness, especially in so far as this has been manifested toward David. "With my mouth" is the equivalent of our "with a loud voice."

Vv. 2–4 are the rest of the introduction. They are a brief recapitulation of the substance of what God promised to David in days of old. This again, stated more briefly, is: "Forever shall steadfast love be built up." If the verb "build" seems somewhat unusual, the figure involved says in effect that this is a structure at which the Lord will keep building perpetually. This is, of course, not a literal quotation but rather a free paraphrase of the promise given in II Sam. 7. Before the writer proceeds, however, further to summarize this promise he inserts a sort of parenthesis (which we have enclosed in dashes) which reminds his readers of the well-known faithfulness of the Lord with regard to promises which He makes. One of the most ancient is the promise made after the Flood that there would never be a recurrence of this great disaster, in token of which He established "in the very heavens the sign of His faithfulness," the justly famous rainbow, of which we read in Gen. 9:13.

There follows in vv. 3, 4 an effective summary of what is chiefly under consideration as a proof of God's mercies. God made a covenant with this His servant David: his posterity shall not fail, and the throne of his kingdom shall in some mysterious way be established forever. Though in the original record in II Sam. 7 no statement appears to the effect that God "swore" to do this, nevertheless, all of God's pronouncements are so firm that they may be regarded as having been given under oath. The hope of the nation and the very faith of Israel were to a very large extent based on this promise of God.

Psalm 89

When from this point onward in this section the details of the marvelous mercies of God are recounted by way of praise, it may be noted that this is the equivalent of presenting a review of the character and being of God, which review is very appropriate. For if God's promise is rehearsed, it is very much in order to show how God's attributes underwrite the keeping of this promise.

5. First (vv. 5–13) those attributes of the Lord are reviewed which manifest themselves chiefly in the control of the physical world. In v. 14 His attributes chiefly in the realm of moral character are considered, and in the verses following (15–18) how the nation naturally reacts to such a Lord and the promises He has made to it.

So grand are these promises of God that, when He gave them, the very heavens praised and shall continue to praise what He did, and the "assembly of the holy ones," i.e., the holy angels themselves, (see Job 5:1; 15:15; Deut. 33:2) took note of what God had promised to do on earth in Israel. For the Lord is a being that is in a class peculiarly His own; not even the "heavenly beings" (again the angels) could one venture to compare with Him (cf., Ps. 29:1). But not only greatness is characteristic of Him, but a greatness that begets deep reverence in the hearts of all who consider who He is, a reverence which is most in evidence on the part of the heavenly beings that surround His throne (v. 7). All of this appears like an echo of Exod. 15:11. Attention is furthermore given in eloquent praise to God's great strength and faithfulness (v. 8).

9. A historic instance of this strength is given by a reference to what God once did in controlling the waters of the sea in days of old when the sea would have proved the destruction of His people at the time of the Exodus at the Red Sea. There God wonderfully ruled "the raging of the sea" and stilled the waves even to the point where the children of Israel could cross dry shod. Egypt (here again designated *Rahab* as in Ps. 87:4) was at that time crushed "like one that is slain," that is to say, it lay prostrate like a corpse. So the enemies that had raged against Him (cf., Exod. 5:2) were scattered by the strong arm of the Lord (v.10).

11. But the Lord's power extends much farther than over merely one of the mighty kingdoms of the earth. The very heavens and the earth and all that it contains are His very own, with which He can do as He sees fit (v. 11). Coming down to the area that lies around God's people, there the north and the south are His; also the mighty mountains that tower above the land, like Tabor and Hermon, which could properly represent the east and the west; for they are situated on either side of the Jordan. In summary, strength belongs to Him in a singular sense

(v. 13): "Strong is Thy hand, and Thy right hand is exalted." Could anyone on the basis of these facts doubt the ability of the Lord to make good His promise?

14. More marvelous are God's moral attributes (v. 14). Two of these may in a beautiful figure be compared to the bases on which His regal throne is erected—"righteousness and justice"—the one of these being "the principle of justice" and the other "the application of it" (*Kirkpatrick*). In addition to the fact that all His doings are built out of that which is absolutely right and just and thus can never become weak, there is that other pair of attributes that has so frequently cheered the saints of God—"steadfast love and faithfulness." For these continually march on before Him through history wherever He goes. This truth is so important as to be reiterated in Ps. 97:2.

15. Israel's happy lot is now reflected upon, for in Israel, at least by the faithful ones among the nation, these things were grasped in faith and made the hearts of men extremely glad. This statement goes to show how thoroughly the spiritual element in Israel had grasped the import of the significant promise given to David. When Israel remembered God's reassuring words it burst forth into a "jubilant shout" (v. 15); the nation virtually walked in the bright light that this great word shed on its path. It was hope like this that gave a deep groundnote of joy to the life of the children of Israel. They did not feel strong in themselves, but He was "the glory of their strength" (v. 17).

18. But in a sense that no other nation of days of old knew this joy centered in the future that God had in store for Israel's king. And so the people regarded their king as "belonging to the Lord"—for "shield" manifestly refers to the Israelite king of the line of David as the parallel member of the verse (v. 18) clearly shows: "king" and "shield" are synonymous. Thus ends the section which sings the praises of the Lord.

b) A rehearsal of the Messianic promise given to David (vv. 19-37)

19. *In days of old Thou didst speak in a vision to Thy faithful ones, saying:*
"I have appointed help for one that is mighty;
I have exalted a chosen one above the people.
20. *I have found David, My servant;*
With My holy oil have I anointed him,
21. *So that My hand may support him;*
And My arm shall strengthen him.
22. *The enemy shall not deceive him;*
Nor wicked fellows afflict him.
23. *But I will dash in pieces his enemies before him;*
And those that hate him I will smite.

24. *My faithfulness and My steadfast love will be with him;*
    And in My name his horn shall be exalted.
25. *And I will set his hand on the sea*
    And his right hand on the rivers.
26. *He then shall call to Me: 'Thou art my father,*
    My Mighty God and the Rock of my salvation.'
27. *Yea, I shall make him My firstborn,*
    The highest among the kings of the earth.
28. *For evermore will I keep My steadfast love for him;*
    And My covenant shall remain secure for him.
29. *And I will establish his posterity forever;*
    And make his throne endure as long as the heavens.
30. *If his children forsake My law*
    And do not walk according to My ordinances;
31. *If they profane My statutes*
    And do not keep My commandments,
32. *Then will I punish their rebellion with the rod*
    And their iniquity with blows.
33. *But My steadfast love will I not withdraw from him;*
    Nor deny My faithfulness.
34. *I will not desecrate My covenant;*
    Nor alter that which My lips uttered.
35. *One thing have I sworn by My holiness:*
    I will not lie to David.
36. *His posterity shall continue forever*
    And his throne as long as the sun before Me.
37. *And like the moon which is established forever,*
    And the witness in the skies is faithful." Selah.

Very few comments on this section are necessary. It is a free paraphrase of II Sam. 7:8–16 and underscores a few points for special emphasis. We shall retrace briefly the line of thought that this version of the promise gives. God is represented as speaking throughout. He says that David is in a special sense the man of His choice. The expression, "I have found David," (v. 20) is to be understood in the sense of: I have "sought out and provided" this man (*Kirkpatrick*). God vows that He will support him (v. 21). In the conflict with his enemies that will undoubtedly ensue God will give him success (vv. 22,23) so that he becomes famous (v. 24). The limits of his kingdom shall be extended (v. 25). But he on his part will freely acknowledge that it is God who has granted him all this (v. 26). God will go so far as to grant to his chosen one a position of pre-eminence above all the monarchs on earth (v. 27).

But the basic reason for allowing him to have such success is that God's covenant with the man cannot be invalidated (v. 28). This covenant applies to David's descendants as well (v. 29). If they, however, fail to walk faithfully in the ways of the Lord they will be duly punished by Him (vv. 30–32). But He will remain faithful to His covenant obligations (vv. 33–35). For His covenant is an eternal covenant, lasting as long as this created world lasts (vv. 36, 37). God who speaks these things is faithful and cannot lie (v. 37b). This is, therefore, an enduring covenant upon which the whole future of this nation is based. So clearly did enlightened men in Israel recognize how important this pronouncement of God was. Regarding v. 37b, Job 16:19 and Jer. 42:5 may be compared.

If one would in a more detailed fashion note how this whole section is built on II Sam. 7, the following passages may be compared. Regarding v. 22 see II Sam. 7:10b. Regarding v. 25, II Sam. 8:3 and 13 may be compared—the only reference outside chapter 7. Regarding v. 26, II Sam. 7:14a. Regarding v. 30 see 14b; and regarding v. 33, 15a and 16.

c) **The sad contrast with the present situation (vv. 38–45)**

38. *But it is Thou who hast cast off and rejected*
    And hast let Thy anger rage against Thy anointed.
39. *Thou hast spurned the covenant with Thy servant*
    And hast defiled his crown down into the dust.
40. *Thou hast torn down all his fences*
    And hast made his strongholds ruins.
41. *All that pass along the way plunder him;*
    He has become an object of scorn to his neighbors.
42. *Thou hast raised up the right hand of his opponents;*
    Thou hast made all his enemies glad.
43. *Yea, Thou hast turned the edge of his sword*
    And dost not allow him to prevail in battle.
44. *Thou hast made every trace of his glory to cease;*
    His throne hast Thou cast down to the ground.
45. *Thou hast cut short the days of his youth;*
    Thou hast covered him with shame. Selah.

This section contrasts the sad present with the glorious future that had been promised. The king and the nation are throughout practically identified—sometimes the king is spoken of as an individual, sometimes it is quite obviously the nation as a whole that is under consideration though the king still seems to be referred to. All the disasters that have befallen the nation are attributed directly to the Lord Himself, for v. 38 begins with an emphatic "Thou" to convey this thought. Even the cove-

Psalm 89

nant, whose permanence was so highly lauded in the preceding section, has been "spurned" by the Lord (v. 39). In vv. 40, 41 there is an obvious allusion to Is. 5:5 and at least a similarity with Ps. 80:13. Not only does the enemy scorn Israel and its humbled king (v. 41b), but it would appear that the Lord Himself had given it success and made it glad with victories over His own people. When the nation attempts to deliver itself, the very edge of its sword seems to be turned back, and so it cannot have success in battle (v. 43). We cannot tell whether it is the king or the nation that is referred to in vv. 44, 45, or whether both ideas blend into one another. Premature aging has come upon both; they stand there covered with shame.

The psalmist may have felt that all this could have taken place because of the infidelity of his people. But it seems that there must also have been a sizable remnant of the godly, for whose sake the Lord might have had mercy. In any case, the situation is very painful and the disappointment grievous.

d) A plea for divine intervention (vv. 46–51)

46. *How long, O Lord? Wilt Thou hide Thyself forever?*
    Shall Thy wrath burn like fire?
47. *Remember how short my life is,*
    For what frailty Thou hast created all mankind.
48. *What man shall live and not see death?*
    Will he deliver his soul from the power of the grave? Selah.
49. *O Lord, where are Thy former tokens of love,*
    Which in Thy truth Thou didst swear to David?
50. *Remember, O Lord, the disgrace of Thy servants;*
    I must bear in my bosom the disgrace of all the many peoples,
51. *Wherewith Thy enemies have reproached Thee, O Lord,*
    Wherewith they have reproached the ways of Thy anointed.
52. *Blessed be the Lord forever. Amen and Amen.*

This 52nd verse is a doxology which closes the third book of the Psalter and has no direct connection with the rest of Ps. 89.

Vv. 46–51 are a plea for divine intervention. One evidence offered for this plea is the fact that the current afflictions have gone on for a long time—too long to endure, in fact. At this point the psalm appears to take on a personal touch in that the writer reflects on his own grievous pain that he endures. For himself he pleads the brevity of human existence: it is short enough as it is; why should it be burdened with many griefs besides (v. 47)? All are going down to the grave from which they cannot deliver themselves. Death comes soon enough. A number of other inducements are urged as facts that could move God to give some consideration to the oppressed people: the oath which God swore to David in days of old; the disgrace which is to be borne by God's own in the sight of and at the hands of many peoples; the reproaches wherewith God has been reproached and in particular His anointed one, the present descendant of David that sits upon the throne.

At this point the psalm comes to a close. Man's need has been urgently set before the Lord. The close of the psalm seems to imply that these issues must be left with the Lord: He will act in due time.

NOTES

2. In the translation, "Thou didst say, O Lord," we have followed the suggestion of *Koenig,* who arrives at the second person rather than the first, as the pointing of the text would suggest, by regarding the final *yod* of *'amarti* as an abbreviation of *Yahweh,* an abbreviation which was certainly at a later date common in Hebrew writings. The consonants of the verb are then pointed as the second person. *Koenig* cites as other possible instances of the occurrence of this abbreviation in the Psalms, Ps. 31:7; 2:12.

5. Regarding "shall praise" there is another possibility: keeping the consonants as they stand, point the *waw* with *pathach,* and the result is, "and they praised." The meaning is that the very angels in heaven at the time when God gave His promise to David praised Him for His grace and have been praising Him ever since.

9. The "Thou" in each member of the verse is emphatic. Our translation can scarcely attain that result without some cumbersomeness.

18. It will be noted that we have regarded the two *le*'s as datives of possession.

22. "Wicked fellow" would be literally "son of wickedness" (*AV*). Since this is obviously a case when *ben* is a relation word, and this word is clearly used in a collective sense, we have rendered as we have.

44. The words "every trace of" are not in the text but result from the fact that a *min* partitive follows a negative verb, as *Koenig* indicates.

47. The construction is harsh, but not so harsh as to require a reconstruction of the text. It literally reads thus: "Remember—as far as I am concerned (nominative absolute) what measure of life."

50. The simplest solution and one that is quite commonly accepted with reference to the latter part of the verse is to supply a second "disgrace" for the second member of the verse. Otherwise one would have the almost impossible translation: "I must bear in my bosom all the many peoples."

51. It is most interesting to observe how the *Targum* has viewed this verse with reference to the delay of the advent of the Messianic kingdom: "For Thine enemies reproach, O Lord, they reproach the slowness of the footsteps of Thine Anointed."

BOOK FOUR

Psalm 90

MAN'S TRANSITORINESS

BOOK IV of the Psalter begins with this ancient psalm, which has a character all its own. No interpreter it seems, has more successfully caught the spirit of this psalm than *Maclaren,* who says: "The sad and stately music of this great psalm befits the dirge of a world. How artificial and poor, beside its restrained emotion and majestic simplicity, do even the most deeply felt strains of other poets on the same theme sound! It preaches man's mortality in immortal words." To this remark may be added the observation that a certain originality characterizes this psalm, especially as to its language. In no statement does it borrow from other psalms or have any affinity with them.

The heading labels it, "A Prayer of Moses, the man of God." There is ample reason for accepting this as a valid editorial heading. There are points of contact in it with the other poems that are to be ascribed to Moses. We shall list the more important of these. V. 1 may well be compared with Deut. 33:27. V. 2 has points of contact with Deut. 33:15 and 32:18. Apart from poetic portions, v. 3 suggests Gen. 3:19; and on the whole of the section vv. 7–12, Gen. 3 as a whole may be compared. It may also be noted that *'adhonay* as addressed to God is used by Moses in Exod. 15:7 and Deut. 3:24.

The objections to Mosaic authorship seem weak and ineffective. When v. 10 ascribes a length of life of from seventy to eighty years to man, that is said to conflict with the known age of Moses himself (Deut. 34:7). However, it is clearly understood from the whole of the Pentateuch that Moses' longevity was an exception. The generation of his contemporaries must have died comparatively young if it had been removed from the scene by the time the forty years of wandering in the wilderness were at an end.

More importance is to be attached to the second argument against Mosaic authorship. In v. 1 Moses speaks of the generations of worshipers of Yahweh who have preceded him whereas he and those who emigrated with him constituted the first generation of the nation of

Israel. How can one, however, overlook those generations of faithful believers in the developing nation since Abraham's time, all of whom made the Lord their dwelling place? Note besides that the psalm does not speak of "Yahweh worshipers" (v. 1) but addresses God as *Adonai*. Without a doubt there were many generations from the time of God's covenant with Abraham who made up the roll call of the faithful among the chosen nation.

Some interpreters would make an issue of the fact that the psalm seems to appear so late in the Psalter—at the beginning of the Fourth Book. We know too little about the manner of the compilation of the Psalter to try to make such an argument convincing. For that matter, even the fact that this is a *tephillah* ("a prayer") and not a *mizmor* ("a psalm") may have for centuries kept it out of the growing Psalter.

Coming down to more important issues, we freely admit that the title we have affixed to the psalm fails to do justice to the subject under consideration. "Transitoriness" is largely a negative concept which does, indeed, sound a groundnote that runs through the psalm; but though it rings through the whole piece as our outline will show with particular emphasis, the very first verse has a far more positive approach. No one has yet found a theme that is big enough for this prayer.

Nor should we overlook the depth of theological insight manifested by the psalm, especially the fact that sin is the cause of God's wrath, and that God's wrath and not some mischance is the cause of man's wasting away. Yet the depth of this somewhat pessimistic outlook does not mar the hopeful outlook which the psalm takes throughout. The courage with which these discouraging factors are viewed far outweighs the hopelessness that they might have engendered.

It has struck some commentators as being strange that over against the vanity of human existence and its acknowledged brevity there is no reference to the hope of immortality. Some have sought to redeem the good name of this poem from this charge directed against it by seeking to find some hidden allusions to this important doctrine. However, it should be readily admitted that this hope burned very dimly in Mosaic times and obviously finds no expression in this psalm.

The presently popular liturgical approach, which would cast all psalms into one sort of liturgical mold or another, has done its part in regard to this prayer also, but without convincing proof of any sort. To claim that this is "a prayer of penitence for a regularly recurring service of penitence of the Jewish congregation" (*Leslie*) is an assertion that lacks substantiating proof. To state the case more elaborately (*Schmidt*) with colorful detail is still not proof, as when, for example, the congregation of worshipers is said to be clad in penitential garments, and the service in the Temple is set for the night, and an old priest stands up

Psalm 90

and utters this prayer in the name of the congregation; and all this as a result of successive years of drought which have brought the land and the people very low. Such remarks are rather to be described as being a prolific exuberance of imaginative details.

The title for Moses—"the man of God"—is most appropriate in its simplicity. If Moses was anything he was certainly that. Compare the other instances of the use of this title for him: Deut. 33:1 and Josh. 14:6.

a) **God is the true abode of man in his transitoriness (vv. 1–6)**
1. *O Lord, Thou hast been our dwelling in all generations.*
2. *Before the mountains were brought forth;*
   Or ever Thou hadst produced the earth and the world;
   From everlasting to everlasting Thou art, O Mighty God.
3. *Thou didst turn man back to the dust*
   And didst say: "Turn back, O children of men!"
4. *For a thousand years in Thy sight are as yesterday when it is past*
   And as a watch in the night.
5. *Thou hast swept men away as with a flood;*
   They became like a sleep;
   They were like grass which sprouts again in the morning.
6. *In the morning it shoots up and sprouts again;*
   In the evening it is cut down and withers.

1. The theme that is soon to be stressed is drab and uninspiring enough, but it has not put out the light of hope in the writer's heart, and thus, speaking in the name of his people, who are to be persuaded to hold fast this unwavering hope, he lays down the basic assertion that God is still "the dwelling" of His people, sad as the lot of men may appear otherwise. "Dwelling" is the meaning of the Hebrew word here used. When in the German tradition *Luther* has emphasized the other thought that God is "our refuge" (*Zuflucht*), that is certainly validly included in the idea of dwelling as the Greek translators already knew. But the broader concept is and remains "dwelling." For in a dwelling we stay even when we are not taking refuge from dangers or the elements.

The thought implied is that we should always be found in Him. He permits us to make such use of His gracious being. Other psalms use the same word such as 27:1; 31:4; 37:39, etc., where *RSV*, departing from its use in this instance, translates the word "refuge." It should not be overlooked that the writer is reminding the people of God that, as the weary generations follow one after the other, God's people have found it a proved and tried course of action that it is good to abide in the Lord.

2. In order that man may feel still more inclined to keep making the Lord his dwelling the writer now stresses the thought as to how sure

such a dwelling is by contrasting God's eternity with man's transitoriness. In the Scriptures the mountains are frequently regarded as being among the very first elements of God's creation (cf., Deut. 33:15; Ps. 65:6; 104:8; Prov. 8:25; Job 15:7). Their origin is figuratively described as a being born. By use of the same figure God is said to bring forth "the earth and the world." If the simple, expressive figure is rightly understood, there is no need of resorting to a textual change as though the statement that God had "produced" (or "brought forth," *KJ*) the earth and the world were in conflict with the rest of Scriptural truth. In any event, from the most ancient times thinkable (i.e., "from everlasting") to the most remote future time imaginable (i.e., "to everlasting") God has existed, the "Mighty God" (Hebrew *'el*), whose might and dependability have been the same throughout the ages. What more certain ground could faith conceive of than this? The translation, "Thou art God" (*KJ*) is less appropriate, for the issue has not been whether God exists or not.

3. Another feature was in the picture for Moses and the people of God, a fact that had been underscored with unusually heavy lines by the Almighty Himself, and that was the transitoriness of man as a generation was wasting away prematurely in the wilderness of Sinai by virtue of an inescapable divine edict. All above the age of twenty were doomed to die. There the ancient experience of man's mortality came home to Israel's mind with fresh force. The God who had decreed: "Dust thou art, and unto dust shalt thou return" (Gen. 3:19) was now and throughout the history of mankind turning man back to the dust. His divine summons to return to the element from which man was taken was, as it were, continually sounding from heaven as a command: "Turn back, O children of men," a statement which, of course, meant Turn back to your native element. By this means the dying of men is tied up with man's fall, and God is seen effectually carrying out the first threat heard by human ears: "Thou shalt surely die." The contrast between v. 2 and v. 3 is indescribably profound. For "return" *Weiser* translates rather appropriately, *Kehrt heim*—return home.

4. Thinking in terms of God's eternity, which was stressed in v. 2, the writer continues to expound it more fully in v. 4, so that the initial "for" reaches back over v. 3 to v. 2. What comparisons will suffice to demonstrate to mortal man what God's eternity is like? Several are used quite effectively. One is that a thousand years, a millennium, are in the sight of the Lord no more than a brief "yesterday when it is past." A flash of thought, and we have reviewed the whole of it. Or again, the same thousand years are like one of the watches of the night, a space of four hours, through which a man may have slept normally without being aware of their passing (the night was divided into three watches

Psalm 90

by the Hebrews; cf., Judg. 7:19). This thought provides a background for an attempt to sketch the brevity of human existence.

5. The whole picture of what has been going on is cast in the past tense. The writer records what has been observed by him and by all men. Summing up the entire work of God from another point of view, God may be said to "have swept men away as with a flood." Death is not a matter of man's paying his debt to nature. God has a hand in it even as man has brought it upon himself.

Or to vary the figure, Men have become like a sleep. For when one awakens, whether it be the whole of life that one thinks back upon or merely the night just passed, both seem to be of about the same duration. Or to employ a third figure, there is the grass, that is, all the fresh vegetation that covers the dust of the earth. After a night's rain it grows luxuriantly in the morning. Whether it is the same evening or one not so long thereafter matters little, by evening it is often cut down and withers. Such an evanescent thing is our life!

It was thoughts such as these that Moses and his generation, dying in the Wilderness of Paran, were led to ponder. Life flees away; God endures. There does not appear to be any trace of bitterness or of undue pessimism. Just plain, realistic thinking marks these words.

b) **Man's sin and God's wrath explain the transitoriness of life (vv. 7–12)**

7. *For we are consumed by Thy anger;*
   And by Thy wrath we are terrified.
8. *For Thou hast set our iniquities before Thee,*
   Our secret sins in the light of Thy countenance.
9. *For our days have passed away because of Thy indignation;*
   We spend our years as a whisper.
10. *Our life lasts seventy years;*
    And if by reason of sturdy health it reaches eighty years;
    Yet what we take pride in is but toil and vanity;
    For it quickly passes by, and we fly away.
11. *Who regards the power of Thy anger*
    And Thy wrath according to the fear that is due Thee?
12. *So teach us to count our days*
    That we may obtain a wise heart.

7. The profound cause of the brevity of mortal life is revealed. Two factors are intertwined. The final cause is man's sin. The operative cause is the wrath of God which is called forth by man's sin. Both these factors are stern realities. Moses had apparently learned the lesson taught in Gen. 3 well. He had caught its full import. What must have struck the men of his generation most sharply in probing back to the

cause of what was befalling all men in general and Israel in particular in a most distressing way? It appears to have been nothing other than God's wrath. For Israel had heard God's verdict upon its stubborn and self-willed way. That verdict was anger. That anger burned hot and real. The Israelites were still "terrified" by the thought of it as well they might have been.

8. From this anger as such the writer moves back to that which was its direct cause: "iniquities" and "sins." These misdeeds of Israel, God did not and could not ignore. There were no extenuating circumstances. His grace had borne with the nation for a long while, giving warning after warning. The nation had made the measure of its iniquity full. The sin was, as it were, brought out into the open and set before God to be evaluated as what it really was. Result: it clamored for punishment. Israel knew that well. In fact, since the bright light, which God Himself is, falls like a glaring beam upon the whole of our life, especially in such hours of judgment, Israel felt that even its inmost thoughts were being brought forth into the open and revealed for what they were. Moses and the nation must have felt that the verdict pronounced had been entirely just, for there is no complaint as though God had dealt with them too severely.

9. The initial "for" introduces a clause of evidence, not of cause. Since the life of the nation since the doom was imposed has passed away under the cloud of God's "indignation," this makes it very clear that the Israelites' sin was being treated as it deserved, and that God's wrath rested upon the sinful ones. The parallel statement of their sad lot words it thus: "We spend our years as a whisper." A whisper that is softly breathed and is gone, that is the new comparison to make clear to what level life has been reduced by Israel's sinful ways.

10. The writer now sums up life in terms that have become classic in that they try to express the utmost of what life may be said to amount to. The average span of it was seventy years at that time and, perhaps, already for some generations prior to that time. A few are more sturdy than the rest; they reach eighty years. But that part of life and its natural endowments that mankind generally prizes highest was not gotten without much "toil" and in itself amounted to nothing but "vanity." None of life's natural achievements are really worth the struggle of acquiring them. And this is again due chiefly to the fact that the things or "what we take pride in" quickly pass and are held in hand but a brief moment. And we ourselves "fly away" quickly like a bird that is frightened from its roost. The brevity of it all makes for its vanity.

11. If there is in the face of all this one truth that man should have discerned this long while it is "the power of (God's) anger." But that just happens to be the one truth that men do not regard. Life could not

Psalm 90

be the futile thing that it is if God were not thoroughly displeased with men. No other force could reduce life to the level on which it is lived. This failure to appreciate these ultimate causes that shape man's life is in its last analysis due to the fact that man does not have toward God "the fear that is due (Him)." The measure of our true reverence for God determines the degree to which we learn to grasp what God's wrath truly is. To make light of God's wrath is due to irreverent thinking.

12. This aspect of the subject is brought to a very practical conclusion by reducing the issue to a brief prayer to the effect that God may help us so to take note of the brevity of human life and of the few days that are ours that we may consider what the deep causes are and so get a "wise heart." According to this statement wisdom seems to consist in a full awareness of what is wrong with mankind and a full retreat to God as the only dwelling in this stormy existence where man can be safe. This conclusion is based upon all that the psalm has thus far stressed.

c) **A prayer that God may redeem our life from its transitoriness (vv. 13–17)**

13. *Turn back, O Lord!—How long wilt Thou delay?*
    And take pity upon Thy servants.
14. *Satisfy us early with Thy steadfast love,*
    Then we shall exult and be glad all our days.
15. *Make us glad in proportion to the days wherein Thou hast afflicted us*
    And to the years wherein we have seen evil.
16. *Let Thy work become apparent to Thy servants*
    And Thy glory to their children.
17. *And let the favor of the Lord our God be upon us;*
    And establish Thou the work of our hands upon us;
    Yea, the work of our hands establish Thou it.

13. Because of this section of the psalm the whole of it may very appropriately be termed "a prayer," for down to the very conclusion petitions prevail. True, as already noted, the preceding verse contained a petition, but that was rather by way of concluding the preceding section. God is thought of as having turned His back upon His people. Therefore the cry, "Turn back!" is appropriate. Nothing is more disastrous than to have Him continue to remain turned away from His own. The "how long?" that follows is an aposiopesis; the statement would be concluded either with the words, "wilt Thou be angry" or as we have suggested above, "wilt Thou delay?" In the psalms God's saints have often cried out thus when God's help seemed slow in coming. A plea

that may well carry weight is the rest of the statement, which reminds God (anthropomorphically speaking) that those who cry out are His "servants," a relationship which He, because of His covenant, cannot ignore.

14. Whether Israel always thought specifically of the covenant when the word "steadfast love" (*chesedh*) was heard or not, the word connotes His covenant faithfulness. To know that the nation dwells under the shadow of that love is sufficient to lay the basis for an enduring gladness over against the oppressive grief that had now for some time brooded over the people. If one can only be sure of that love, then there is reason enough for exulting and being glad all the days of one's life. So well was the love of God understood already in earliest times.

15. In fact, that new happiness, which consists in the certainty of being loved by God, is also thought of as the only factor that can outweigh or counterbalance the days of affliction or the years wherein evil has been the order of the day. This is a rather appropriate way of evaluating the proportionate amount of gladness that may rightly be expected by a nation that has previously been under affliction. God sent the grief. May He not be trusted for that which outweighs and neutralizes the grief borne?

16. How any commentator can regard the last two verses of the psalm as a gloss (*Briggs*) is beyond our comprehension. No more suitable conclusion can be conceived. The tenor of this section agrees most beautifully with the positive approach of the opening of the psalm. In the last analysis theses verses offer the potent and effective antidote against hopelessness and discouragement. They raise the eyes of him who prays thus from the puny and ineffective work that man toils over down here on earth to the great and successful work that God does both here and in heaven. The trouble with man all too frequently is that he sees nothing of the work God is doing. We refer to that work which from the point of view of our most urgent concern is the work of the salvation of mankind. Stated in terms of the great over-all purpose of God in so far as it affects men, it had, perhaps, better be described as the work of the kingdom of God and all that is involved in that broad concept.

But for a servant of God to be unaware of what God is doing and not to see at least some dim glimpses of the success of God's work can well be the cause of utter hopelessness. Then the prayer is so appropriate and necessary: "Let Thy work become apparent" (literally, "let it be seen"). The second member of the verse beautifully supplements the first by suggesting that this work is for man the "glory" of God. One really sees His glory in a most effective way when one sees how marvelously He does His work. And all this is a realization that old and young need to reach. Only when one has been conditioned from youth to become aware of the evidences of God's glorious work going on continually and uninterruptedly can one live the hopeful life that such an awareness begets.

17. Many writers feel that "favor" catches the import of the Hebrew word here used far better than does "beauty" (*KJ*). In other words, the term used is apparently a synonymn for "steadfast love." To be sheltered by God's favor as the nation was visibly sheltered by the guiding cloud in the days of Moses is the sum of all blessings that God's people may aspire ever to enjoy. Man has his assignment from his divine taskmaster: man has a work to do under God in and among the rest of God's people. He himself cannot give stability and success to the task thus assigned to him, for success comes only from God. Therefore the prayer turns to the other side of the matter: "Establish Thou the work of our hands upon us." Unless this is done, all human endeavor proves futile as the first member of the verse had clearly suggested. The phrase "upon us" in the above statement strikes us as being a bit unusual. It seems to suggest the thought "in our midst," namely, that we may see it and enjoy it as we behold it. The repetition of the last prayer has a certain solemn effectiveness; it lends weight to the petition.

Thus ends the psalm, a prayer from which the most profound lessons on human need and divine grace can be learned, a prayer which in one form or another mankind needs to pray continually, a prayer which has been of great help and consolation to countless generations of God's servants.

NOTES

1. To arrive at the result of making the first word have the equivalent of an indefinite article the Hebrew does not use the usual construct relationship for *tephillah* but lets it be followed by a dative. Cf. *KS* 280n.

3. For "man" the appropriate word *'enosh* is used, signifying the "frail one."

9. We have rendered *hégheh* "whisper." Many other possibilities may be considered. *Luther: Geschwaetz,* "idle talk." *KJ:* "a tale that is told"—which is rather a paraphrase. Some interpreters suggest: "a thought" with the emphasis on how soon a thought passes. In other connections the word has meanings such as "moaning, grumbling, sigh." In any case, something light and swift is under consideration.

Psalm 91

THE LORD IS MY REFUGE

THIS IS a noble psalm of trust which can rightly be compared with Ps. 46. It has been the comfort and source of strength of believers in all sorts of situations. It has been committed to memory by many and used faithfully by generation after generation. However, it is in striking contrast with Ps. 90. The latter is somber and stately; this is bright and simple. The one breathes deep insight; the other cheerful trust.

The unusual grammatical problem involved is the peculiar change of pronouns, particularly the frequent use of those of the second person. To dispose of this problem at once, it is to be noted that the type of second person pronoun used is that which is sometimes called the "ideal second person," which is the equivalent of the second person used impersonally, almost like the German *man* or like the impersonal "one." Thus, though it would be poor English, one could translate v. 3: "For He will deliver one from the snare of the hunter," and v. 4: "With His feathers He will cover one," etc. One exception to this use of the second person seems to be v. 9b, where, as we shall indicate, the one addressed appears to be the same person who in 9a made a strong confession of faith in the Lord. It is, of course, equally feasible from this point onward (i.e., from vv. 10–13) to think of this same person as still being addressed. On the other hand, this same section could be in the ideal second person as it was in the first section of the psalm.

The understanding of the psalm is not helped by assuming that reference is being made to Babylonian superstitions about various types of demons that the Babylonians were supposed to be afraid of and going on the assumption that the selfsame superstitions would naturally be current in Israel, for that matter, even among the godly in Israel. Unless some type of proof for the prevalence of such queer beliefs among Israelites can be adduced—and that has not hitherto been done—it is very unsafe to use such an approach, popular as it may be at the present.

The cultic character and use of the psalm have also been but poorly substantiated. It does not belong in the category of psalms which is described by some interpreters as *Pfortengespraeche* (a dialogue conducted at the Temple gate), nor does logic require that, because the verb "abide" is used, which could also mean "spend the night," the

Psalm 91

night would obviously be spent in the Temple in devotional thoughts such as the psalm suggests. Equally precarious is the attempt to assign the various parts of the psalm to different voices and to have it rendered responsively. That vv. 14–16 are obviously to be ascribed to God no man would deny. That v. 2 was spoken by the writer is equally clear (unless textual alterations are resorted to). Nor can we be expected readily to assume that the psalm is a ritual piece to be used against diseases that are occasioned by attacks of evil spirits. *Gunkel* very properly rejects the idea that the psalm should have been used when amulets were distributed (*Einleitung,* etc., p. 394). We might also indicate briefly that we are not of the opinion that the state of the text of the psalm is such as to warrant numerous alterations, especially in vv. 1 and 2. The text as it is written makes very good sense.

The tone of the psalm is so general that we cannot detect any occasion that may have given rise to the writing of it. To single out some "pestilence" merely because the word occurs twice involves drawing a conclusion on the basis of too meager evidence. Quite a number of other possible occasions could with equal facility be adduced from the psalm. Thus it must be equally obvious that we can offer practically nothing that could help us determine the time of its composition.

a) Summary statement of the theme (vv. 1, 2)

1. *Dwelling in the shelter of the Most High*
   And abiding under the protection of the Almighty,
2. *I say to the Lord: "My refuge and my fortress,*
   My God, in Him will I trust."

1. We reserve the discussion of the problems of the text as it is written for the *Notes*. As to the substance of what is said by these verses, two parallel statements introduce it, each saying practically the same thing though with a change in figure. It might not be inept to let the first statement be interpreted in terms of seeking refuge from a threatening attack in a bomb shelter although the writer had no more in mind than a place where one could be sheltered against the elements or against wild beasts that might be roaming in a given place. The "protection of the Almighty" seems to suggest the figure of a host who, following Oriental custom, offers protection to his guest at the cost, if need be, of even his own life. Reduced to nonfigurative language, this verse says: Since I am in every way safeguarded by the protection that the Almighty provides for me, therefore . . .

2. What he does say is addressed to the Lord, for the writer would honor God by ascribing to Him whatever advantages he enjoys. Countless saints of God have experienced the fact that in God they have both a place of refuge from danger and a strong fortress that shields them

against everything that would work their harm. Thus the resolve is nurtured in the heart: Let come what will, "in Him will I trust." I shall never cast away my confidence in Him. The writer is safe and knows how safe he is. He goes on to unfold the many separate kinds of safety this involves.

b) **The evils from which God delivers those who trust in Him** (vv. 3–8)

3. *For He will deliver you from the snare of the hunter,*
   From the dangerous pestilence.
4. *With His feathers He will cover you;*
   And under His wings you will find refuge;
   His faithfulness is a shield and a buckler.
5. *You need not be afraid of the terror of the night,*
   Nor of the arrow that flies by day;
6. *Nor of the pestilence that stalks in darkness;*
   Nor of the plague that devastates at noonday.
7. *Though a thousand fall at your side*
   And ten thousand at your right hand,
   It will not come near you.
8. *You will merely look on with your eyes*
   And observe how the wicked are recompensed.

3. This recital of the various evils from which God can and will deliver those who trust in Him is rather detailed. Figurative language seems to be employed for the most part. The "snare of the hunter" may well represent those hidden dangers that unexpectedly catch us and bring us to fall. The "dangerous pestilence" may not be a figurative expression but may represent that one danger which in days of old so frequently took its toll in countless lives and was so very much dreaded.

4. In this and in every similar danger you can rest assured that God shelters His own as carefully as does the mother bird her young (cf., Exod. 19:4; Deut. 32:11; Matt. 23:27). Or to vary the comparison, it is as though the faithfulness of the Lord were a trusty shield that He Himself holds before those that seek refuge with Him, or it may even be a shield which they can hold up before themselves to ward off danger. Some interpreters prefer to regard the word rendered "buckler" as "armor" since we are not entirely sure as to its meaning. It seems to signify that which encloses a man. Either term seems appropriate.

5. There follows an enumeration of four misfortunes which are usually regarded as being extremely dangerous but are here thought of as being utterly unable to harm him who takes refuge in God. The "terror by night" would seem to include everything that could threaten our

safety during the course of the night, and it is called "terror" because in the dark of the night the unseen dangers are apt to be more terrifying. No single specific evil is under consideration, least of all some kind of night spirit or night hag. The "arrow that flies by day" is every deadly force that might strike us during the course of a day. In regard to the former we may involuntarily think of Biblical incidents like those recorded in Exod. 11:4f. and Judg. 7:13ff. To use the plainest prose, we could say: No danger can harm you by night or by day.

6. Again the same pattern of day and night is used with the same purpose of covering all time. Pestilence is mentioned again because of its extreme deadliness in the case of epidemics, a scourge which the present-day reader may fail properly to evaluate. "Pestilence" and "plague" are quite likely one and the same evil. It sometimes seems to run its deadly course in the darkness of the night; then again it marches abroad boldly in the very heat of the day, perhaps even being aided by a muggy heat that prevails. Yet we admit that "plague," which means literally "stroke," can describe any major calamity that suddenly smites a man.

7. Faith grows a bit exuberant at this point; it becomes eloquent. A very extreme situation is depicted: men falling by the thousands and ten thousands on every side, but the man of faith, exposed to the same dangers, comes through them all unscathed. The danger, whatever it is, "will not even come near" such a one. We may remark that the faith of the children of God does not necessarily anticipate that harm will never come to them. What extreme statements like this one mean is that it is possible for God to defend His own in cases of seemingly inescapable dangers, and He will frequently do so. But they also know full well that there will be occasions when it does not please God to work miraculous deliverance. In such an event they will cheerfully submit to whatever is the will of their Lord. Many who have been exposed to the dangers of the field of battle where many lost their lives could not help but apply these words to themselves when their life was spared. The verse states, not what must necessarily happen, but what God can bring to pass.

8. This verse is misconstrued when it is intimately tied up with v. 7 in the sense that, when men perish in danger, the godly man at once concludes that this is due to their wickedness (*Kittel*). *Weiser* rightly labels such a judgment "peculiar, senseless, stubborn, hard, and unjust." Such an interpretation would make those who speak out of the fulness of faith as the writer does singularly uncharitable in their judgment of others. What v. 8 does say is that, when the godly are delivered, they will at the same time often witness how the wicked are paid back

in full for their wickedness. For God's faithfulness reckons with both the godly and the ungodly. In the course of one's lifetime one can witness many instances when the wicked receive their due reward.

c) **The complete security enjoyed by those who trust in the Lord (vv. 9–13)**

9. *Surely, Thou, O Lord, art my refuge.—*
   You (O man) have made the Most High your dwelling.
10. *No evil shall befall you;*
    And no plague shall come near your dwelling.
11. *For He will give His angels charge over you*
    To guard you in all your ways.
12. *On their hands they will bear you up*
    Lest you dash your foot against a stone.
13. *On the lion and adder you shall tread;*
    You shall trample upon the young lion and serpent.

The pattern used in the first two sections of the psalm in a sense repeats itself. Vv. 1 and 2 were a thematic statement; the results of the position described in these two verses were then given at length in vv. 2–8. The thematic statement, in substance practically the same as it was in vv. 1 and 2, is again given, though this time more briefly. The results of the position taken follow in vv. 9–13, although we above described the ground covered by these verses as "the complete security enjoyed by those who trust in the Lord."

9. An unusual turn takes place within this verse. In 9a God is addressed in the words by which the writer expresses his confidence in Him. In response to this basic statement, in a kind of dialogue, anyone of like mind who hears him is thought of as replying to this position taken and restating it thus: "You have made the Most High your dwelling." By some means or other to indicate this change of person within the verse we inserted an explanatory "O man" in the second member, a term which does not occur in the Hebrew, of course.

10. We prefer the second of the possibilities described above in reference to the second person here used and shall interpret these verses from this point of view. That means that the words, "No evil shall befall you," are to be understood in the sense: "No evil can befall a man who takes the position you do." The "ideal second person" may be construed thus. In a sense the immunity of such a person from danger is being described at length. Not only shall no evil light upon him; it shall not even approach his dwelling place ("tent" for "dwelling" in a poetic mode of speech).

11. This immunity is again explained as being due to the protection afforded by holy angels who watch over God's children and serve as

their protectors. This does not say, as was sometimes thought in times past, that a special angel is assigned to each individual. It merely guarantees angelic protection as it may be needed.

12. In colorful poetic fancy these angels are portrayed as actually lifting the individual over every stone over which he might stumble and fall and come to hurt. And with still greater exuberance of faith as in v. 7 of the kindred earlier section the believer is thought of as being in a position where he could without harm to himself tread upon the fiercest and most poisonous of animals without suffering harm; in fact, even as cheerfully and fearlessly "trampling" upon them without suffering the least ill. One cannot help but think of New Testament instances where the Lord, all but quoting this verse, promises similar protection to those that go out to serve Him (see Mark 16:18 and Luke 10:19). Acts 28:1–6 gives at least one instance when this promise was literally fulfilled. We should, perhaps, have substituted "cobra" for "adder" although the former does not appear in Palestine.

d) God's rich promise to those who trust Him (vv. 14–16)

14. *"Because he clings to Me I will deliver him;*
    I will protect him because he knows my name.
15. *When he calls upon Me, I will answer him;*
    I will be with him in trouble;
    I will deliver him and honor him.
16. *With long life will I satisfy him*
    And show him My salvation."

14. This rich promise of God, given to all those who are His own, is not introduced by any form of statement that indicates that from this point onward to the end of the psalm the Lord Himself is speaking. It is apparently sufficiently obvious that God is the speaker from the first moment that He speaks. This abruptness of presentation makes this section more dramatic. There is nothing difficult in this address of divine reassurance. Every statement is full of satisfying comfort. The various gifts that are promised by the Lord are stated in a sort of ascending climax: deliverance, protection, the answer to prayer, God's presence in trouble, deliverance of a kind that confers honor on the one that is delivered, length of days in this life, and a full and comprehensive understanding as to how rich and many-sided the salvation of God actually is.

A few of the reasons that moved God to act are added. They are those that are frequently found in the psalms. However, the first of these reasons is comparatively new: "because he clings to Me." Even as the fact that a child clutches the parent's arm in fear and need of protection puts a stronger urge into the love which is of itself already willing to help, so does the fact that God's child holds fast to Him not leave Him untouched. The second reason is, "he knows My name." Since "name" equals "character," this statement means: he knows what kind of being I am, and such true knowledge is not to be answered with disappointment. The other reasons are briefly: "he calls upon Me"; he is "in trouble." The matter is as simple as that. All our customary needs and anxieties serve as motives that move God to action.

16. The last promise calls for special comment. Long life is elsewhere in Scripture stressed as a blessing with which God loves to reward His own (see Ps. 21:4; 23:6; Deut. 30:20; Prov. 3:2, 16; and the conclusion of the Fourth Commandment). A general rule is laid down. There will, of course, be occasional exceptions to this rule. Length of days is a good gift of God. It comes from the same Father who gives many other gifts richly and abundantly. But the summarizing statement—"and show him My salvation"—makes this one gift stand out with particular clarity. Since "salvation" is a term of such breadth as to include every possible form of deliverance, physical and spiritual, the statement amounts to this: I will give my own true followers so many proofs of the help that I bestow upon them that the one fact that will impress them above all others is: how wonderfully God can deliver in all needs of body and soul! V. 15 has a very close affinity with Ps. 50:15.

NOTES

1. The fact that the first two verses have always offered a problem appears in current versions. The *KJ* renders: "He that dwelleth in the secret place of the Most High shall abide under the shadow of the Almighty." Many interpreters have felt that this translation states a result in the second half which borders on the obvious and is a far weaker conclusion than one would have expected. *Luther* resorted to a textual change by making the first word in v. 2 third person rather than first, and he also made the two clauses of v. 1 strictly parallel: *Wer unter dem Schirm des Hoechsten sitzt und unter dem Schatten des Allmaechtigen bleibt, der spricht zu dem Herrn.* That seems more satisfying and is still adopted by some translators, but it involves changing the text. As indicated above, we believe the text should be left as it is. It makes good sense.

The first verse offers two parallel statements that describe this attitude of a believer. The first clause has the verb in the form of a participle (as our translation also shows). In the Hebrew there may be a change from the participle to an imperfect (cf. *GK* 116x and *KS* 413k) without interrupting the natural sequence of thought. Since we cannot do this in English, I have retained the participial form for the second verb. I have done so because this construction makes it apparent as to how strictly parallel the first two statements are. Both these participles modify the subject of the first verb in v. 2, "*I* say," and thus the construction amounts to this: "I who sit . . . and who abide . . . say."

Among the various other attempts to solve the problem the most common is, perhaps, the one which supplies an *'ashrey* ("blessed") before the first word of v. 1. Quite apart from the fact that grammatically the text makes good sense just as it stands, it would seem very strange that the initial word of the psalm should by some accident have been lost.

2. In the second half of the verse there is a change of person from the second ("my God") to the third (" in Him"). The Hebrew does this sort of thing so frequently by moving in either direction: from the second to the third, or from the third to the second with a facility which we are inclined to regard as utter license.

9. This verse remains difficult, no matter how it is explained. We believe the explanation offered above squares best with the text. *Luther* again changed the text to: "For the Lord is *Thy* (instead of "my") refuge." That involves the loss of the responsive element in the verse. *KJ* has a highly involved statement, which cannot help but puzzle the unitiated: "Because thou hast made the Lord, which is my refuge, even the Most High thy habitation."

Psalm 92

"IT IS A GOOD THING TO GIVE THANKS TO THE LORD"

THE OPENING WORDS of the psalm, which we would designate as the theme, would almost lead one to believe that the psalmist is about to demonstrate what a good thing it is to sing the praises of the Lord. But presently he limits his thinking to those instances of what the Lord has done, when the overthrow of the wicked and the sustaining of godly men are considered. Because of this fact the possibility enters into the picture that the psalm could have been written at a time when some significant overthrow of the wicked had occurred, which was, perhaps, associated with some special instance of the deliverance of the righteous. It is this possibility which has induced some interpreters to believe that the psalm would fit best into the time when Babylon fell into the hands of the Persians, and the captives of Israel were restored to their land. This is as near as we can come to determining some definite occasion that could have given rise to this psalm V. 4a could be a reference to this great work of the Lord. But let no man venture to go farther than to claim a mere possibility for this approach. Otherwise this psalm has an obvious kinship with Ps. 37, 49, and 73 in that it in its own way deals with the ultimate overthrow of the ungodly and the ultimate victory of the righteous.

An ancient Jewish tradition, reflected in the *Septuagint,* is part of the heading of the psalm, namely, the words, "a song for the Sabbath Day." The *Mishna* reports (see *Koenig,* Kommentar) which psalms were appointed for the weekdays: For Sunday, 24; for Monday, 48; for Tuesday, 82; for Wednesday, 94; for Thursday, 81; for Friday, 93. At least this much will have to be conceded regarding this schedule, that praise was particularly well suited to the Sabbath Day, the day on which God originally rested from His creative work.

The psalm is equally well adapted to congregational and to individual use, and because of the closing verses, may also, be classified as a psalm of love for the sanctuary. But it is more of a psalm of praise. To regard the occasion of its composition a case of recovery from severe illness (*Krankheitspsalm*) is farfetched.

a) The propriety of praise of God (vv. 1–3)

1. *It is a good thing to give thanks to the Lord*
   And to sing praises to Thy name, O Most High;
2. *To declare Thy steadfast love in the morning*
   And Thy faithfulness at night
3. *Upon the ten-stringed instrument and lute,*
   To meditative music upon the harp.

1. "Good" seems to be a rather colorless word for describing how "salutary" and "delightful" (*Kirkpatrick*) it is to praise the Lord. *Luther* interprets well when he renders the word *koestlich* (precious). For to tell the truth, one of the finest undertakings that can occupy any man at any time is to praise the Lord. It is not inappropriate to assert that man was essentially created for this purpose. The angels appear to fulfill this purpose much more perfectly than does man. To have the day that is to be "sanctified" set apart for this holy occupation is most fitting though it may never have been the original purpose of the author of the psalm to set it apart for use on the Sabbath. The verb for "singing praises" in the second member of the verse comes

from the root from which the distinctive Hebrew word for "psalm" is derived.

2. To indicate in a summary way what it is that should particularly engage one's attention when the praises of the Lord are sung, the psalmist suggests two broad themes: "steadfast love" and "faithfulness" such as God has manifested toward His children. Though these two divine attributes could be exchanged for mention in the morning and the evening, there is a certain propriety about their being assigned to the part of day for which they are fitting. In the morning one may attribute the protection enjoyed during the night just passed to God's steadfast love; and in the evening God's faithfulness is to be considered as the force which above all others carried us through the manifold situations that were met with in a busy day.

3. Special musical instruments are mentioned as being suitable for use in the praise of God, but we know too little about their distinguishing nature to be able to tell just why these and not others should have been singled out. Had these recently come on the scene, and was a "new song" to be sung on them? Do they signify the larger ("ten-stringed") and the smaller instruments ("the lute")? The ones mentioned are, perhaps, the ones which the writer himself was qualified to play.

b) The reason for praise: What God has done (vv. 4–6)

4. *For Thou, Lord, hast made me glad by Thy work;*
   I will exult in the works of Thy hands.
5. *O Lord, how great are Thy works!*
   Thy thoughts are so very deep.
6. *A brutish man does not know this;*
   Nor does a fool understand it.

4. When we state that the reason for praise is the contemplation of "the works of God's hands," that thought immediately takes us from the marvelour being of God Himself into the area of what He has done. There is a sort of general character about the things that are mentioned as is so often the case in the psalms so that manifold use of them may be made in all manner of situations. But it scarcely seems improper to let the first reason for praise mentioned—"Thy work"—refer to something that had recently taken place and was still fresh in the mind of the writer and, perhaps, even of the first readers of his psalm. The possibility that this could have been deliverance from Babylonian captivity has been indicated above. Thus the word "work" could refer to divine providence, and it is at least possible that "the works of Thy hands" could refer to the works of creation, which make up this world in which we live and move. Yet the distinction of usage does not seem

to be too sharply drawn in regard to these two nouns. For our purpose the important thought is that God's deeds, whatever they may be, have brought gladness into the heart of the man who has reflected upon them—as they always do—and has made him "exult."

5. The more one reflects on what God has done, the more do His works grow on one. Thus the exclamation, "How great are Thy works!" comes very naturally and expresses a thought that is frequently voiced elsewhere in the Scriptures (cf., Ps. 36:6; 40:5; 139:17, 18; Is. 55:8, 9—a classic passage; and Rom. 11:33, 34—the greatest of them all). Behind the works of God lie His thoughts. They, too, are characterized by a depth which the human mind can never plumb; and so an exclamation is all that is left to us, a deep and reverent exclamation.

6. The evidence for the exalted nature of God's works and thoughts is so great that, if a man fails to acknowledge them, he must need be put into the category of the "brutish man" and the "fool." The author's major concern, however, is not to speak harsh things about man but to emphasize how overwhelmingly powerful the manifestation of God's works is. Ps. 73:22 expresses practically the same thought. In other words, there is something degrading and brutalizing about not joining in the praises of God, for which there is such abundant reason.

c) **The impending overthrow of the wicked (vv. 7-9)**

7. *Though the wicked flourish like grass, and all the evildoers spring up,*
It is that they may be destroyed forever.
8. *But Thou, O Lord, art most high forevermore.*
9. *For, lo, Thy enemies, O Lord,*
For, lo, Thy enemies always perish;
All evildoers are scattered.

7. The inevitable lot of the wicked is set forth: their overthrow is inescapable. As long as there are godly and wicked persons on the face of the earth, just so long will there be need for stressing what the ultimate outcome will be for both classes. By the final outcome that must inevitably come to pass God solves the problem. That this could be an allusion to Babylon's more or less recent overthrow must be granted as a possibility.

But the emphasis lies, first of all, on the fact that the prosperity of the wicked is frequently much in evidence for a while. Impatient man cannot understand why God should bear so long with those that fail to turn to Him and acknowledge Him. The springing up of the grass is a good comparison, for when it appears in the Holy Land in the spring, its growth is so surprisingly rapid. So often the success of

Psalm 92

the wicked may be phenomenal. On the other hand as the grass and all attendant vegetation soon perish with the coming of the hot weather, so the flourishing of the wicked has, so to speak, as its purpose, "that they may be destroyed forever." They flourish to die. What is desirable about a lot like theirs?

8. In contrast with the lot of the evildoers is the fact that God forever continues to have sovereign control over those things that befall men. In a brief unit statement this is made all the more emphatic by the absence of a parallel statement. For "most high" the Hebrew has a noun, "height." This may seem to be unusual, but it does not imply that the Hebrew text is obscure.

9. By pointing, perhaps, to some recent instance of the overthrow of God's enemies with a "lo" and then repeating the reference for emphasis the author states a general rule (using the Hebrew imperfect, which covers such matters): "Thy enemies always perish." The transition from "evildoers" to "enemies" grows out of the fact that wickedness and enmity against God are synonymous. The last member of the verse is also instructive. For though the enemies of God seem to be solidly banded together, in their overthrow they will be routed and scattered, no matter how apparently strong the bonds were that bound them together.

d) The blessings God bestows upon the righteous (vv. 10–12)

10. *But Thou hast exalted my horn like that of a wild ox;*
    I have been anointed with fresh oil.
11. *And my eyes have seen the fate of those that lie in wait for me;*
    My ears have heard (welcome news) *of those wicked ones who rose up against me.*
12. *The righteous shall flourish like a palm tree;*
    He shall grow like a cedar in Lebanon.

10. By the law of contrast the writer now turns to the opposite class of which he is a member and can thus speak of himself while he describes what is customarily their experience. He has experienced it to be the general rule that God increases for His own the strength that they need to meet emergencies, or to use a typical figure of that time, God has exalted his horn like that of a wild ox. The exuberance of strength is the thought conveyed by this comparison. There is nothing of wildness in it, for the Hebrew has but a single term for this creature. It may be possible that the anointing with fresh oil is to recall (as in 45:7) some joyous occasion for which men would in days of old anoint their face (cf. also Matt. 6:16–18). In other words, his experience tells him that God is in the habit of supplying gladness and strength to those that fear Him.

11. To this must be added another experience that they can recall: theirs has been the satisfaction of hearing about and seeing the overthrow of ungodly opponents who espoused a cause other than the Lord's. One should not claim to detect in this statement a note of gloating over the downfall of enemies. Nothing more is said than that those who attempted wicked things against me were prevented from achieving their evil purpose; and, quite naturally, at this I rejoiced.

12. This verse may be regarded as a sort of generalization as to what the lot of the righteous is: they flourish like sturdy palms and cedars of Lebanon. It may not always seem so; it may not always be immediately apparent, but it is true, and all godly men will cheerfully subscribe to the validity of the claim made.

d) **The vital place of the sanctuary in the lives of godly men (vv. 13–15)**

13. *They that are planted in the house of the Lord*
    Shall flourish in the courts of our God.
14. *They shall still bring forth fruit in old age;*
    Fresh and green shall they be,
15. *To declare that the Lord is upright;*
    He is my rock, and there is no unrighteousness in Him.

13. This last section shows what a vital role the very sanctuary of the Lord plays in the lives of the godly. The question has been frequently discussed as to whether in Old Testament days trees were actually planted and grew in the courts of the Temple at Jerusalem. No evidence to that effect is available. What happens to be the case in the Mohammedan mosque found on that site at the present time is no criterion for days of old. Nor do we need to assume that such was the case. To regard the first verse of this section as figurative language yields a good meaning. Those whose life is rooted in God's sanctuary flourish in their nearness to God which is a reality in their lives. To think of them as being a fine, flourishing tree yields a very suitable picture.

14. The continuation of that figure in this verse yields other suitable conclusions. The strong faith that a wholesome life in God supplies has in many cases made such lives productive of much good even after others of a similar age have long ceased to produce. Faith seems to impart a certain spiritual resiliency so that, still speaking in terms of the tree, such persons may be said to be fresh, i.e., full of sap, and green with the color of a healthy plant as it were.

15. The conclusion very appropriately returns to the theme set forth in the opening words of the psalm, the theme of the praise of God, which is such a good thing to engage in. So then a typical righteous

man, by his very age, fruitful as it is, as well as by many other things that his life shows, stands there as a living declaration of the uprightness of the Lord. Or to rephrase the testimony that such persons will give concerning their experience of God in their lives, God has been a solid rock upon which they could build a firm and unshaken life, and not one bit or trace of dealing on the part of God that disappoints His believers has ever been detected by any one of them.

NOTES

3. *Higgayon* presents some difficulty. Since it comes from a root that signifies to murmur or mutter it could mean "melody" (*RSV*) or "meditative music" as *Kirkpatrick* translates.

10. Though "unicorn" (*KJ*) is not what the Hebrew word *re'em* means, the translators of the *KJ* were scarcely referring to the fabulous beast of antiquity but merely to some one-horned creature like the rhinoceros. See English dictionaries on this word. *Koenig* prefers the translation "antelope." Most grammars prefer the "wild ox."

Ballothi, which we have rendered a bit freely, "I have been anointed," would really seem to mean, "I have been mingled or stirred in with" (*KW* suggests: "I have been stirred in with.") Such a translation would tend to perplex the uninformed, and so we have chosen the simpler rendering. The figure could be regarded as referring to freshening up dry batter. Though it is difficult to determine the precise meaning of this word, the general thought it conveys seems to be along the line of Ps. 23:5b.

15. The usual form of the noun for "unrighteousness" (*'awlah*) is not used here. The margin suggests *'olathah*. But there can scarcely be any doubt that the unusual form has the meaning we have indicated.

Psalm 93

THE LORD IS KING

THIS BRIEF PSALM is mighty in utterance, colorful in language, and a strong incentive to faith. Its opening sentence is its theme. It is, therefore, related to the group that follows with the exception of Ps. 94, which interrupts the train of thought. Psalms 95–100 reiterate the theme with various shadings of emphasis. The kinship between these related psalms is scarcely so close as to allow for combining them into one original unit psalm (*Briggs*). Our psalm is at the same time not unrelated to Ps. 92, for in v. 8 of that psalm there is a similar emphasis on the exalted position that the Lord occupies even as our entire psalm is controlled by this thought. The headings in the *Septuagint* and the *Vulgate,* which ascribe the psalm to David and appoint it for reading on the Sabbath Day, seem to be valueless.

Though no man could venture to be entirely positive about the time of composition of this psalm, there is at least one period of time into which the psalm would fit wonderfully well, and that is the time immediately after the Exile as we shall presently demonstrate.

All of the more recent commentators are impressed by the possibility that v. 3 in particular could be a reference to the old Babylonian creation myth, particularly to that part of it which represents the struggle between the god Marduk and Tiamat, the old sea-water goddess, a struggle which is painted in the richest colors in the Babylonian tale. We believe this reference to be of dubious value. Always admitting that the language of the Old Testament may have here and there retained some elements of the mythological inasmuch as it was the old Canaanitish language before the days of Abraham, we do not believe that the Israelites were, as a rule, conscious of the mythological connotation, chiefly because the mythological terminology does not seem to have affected their theological thinking. In other words, whereas the present-day archaeologist immediately thinks in terms of the possible Babylonian parallel, the ancient Israelite may seldom if ever have had such thoughts. Israel was in its theology not half as much influenced by Babylonian parallels as many commentators are inclined to believe. Though such an approach is possible, we are inclined to think that it has been much overplayed.

a) **The Lord's kingship is eternal (vv. 1, 2)**

1. *The Lord is king; He has put on majesty;*
   The Lord has put it on, He has girded Himself with strength;
   Yea, the world is established immovably.
2. *Thy throne is established from of old;*
   Thou art from everlasting.

1. Admitting that there are other situations into which this psalm might have originally fitted, let us put it into the setting of the time when Israel had just returned from exile. The effectiveness of God's kingly rule may well have become doubtful in the minds of some in Israel, but now a new demonstration of the fact that He is and has continually been in control has been provided, and so the old truth that the Lord really reigns (*KJ*) or "is king" has again been under-

Psalm 93

scored, or it may even be said: "The Lord has become king." Yet this latter statement is not to be understood to mean that He had abdicated or had momentarily been crowded from the throne. The sense is rather: His effective rule has again become apparent. That is what the *Septuagint* seems to mean with its aoristic translation of the verb: "He has again begun to rule," inceptive aorist. The words of the theme are, therefore, fitting whenever the old truth comes to the mind of men afresh after having been temporarily beclouded.

To describe more fully what this means, speaking in terms of an enthronement or a coronation: It is He who has vested Himself with the royal robes which are emblems of His dignity; but these robes are not made of ordinary texture; they are to be described as "majesty." With a solemn reiteration the writer says in effect, Yea, "He has put it on." Or since the boldest and most colorful human terms are weak in comparison with the divine reality involved, the psalmist attempts another rewording: "He has girded Himself with strength." Like Isaiah in his famous inaugural vision (Is. 6), the psalmist does not presume to describe the person of the king; it is a sufficient venture for him to describe His vestments.

Since He is such and thus vested, the conclusion to be drawn for man's understanding of the state of the world is that "the world is established immovably." That is to say, that one aspect of the Almighty's domain that at the moment requires new emphasis is that under the firm government of this King there can be no doubt about what the nature of His government of the world must be—firm and immovable as He is. With God things in this world never get out of hand.

2. Speaking of the Lord's entire rule, the psalm makes the assertion that there was never a time when the full control of His reign was in question. It may have seemed otherwise to man, but "Thy throne is established of old." At this point the psalm quite naturally moves from the area of objective consideration to that of subjective adoration in direct address of God. But even the truth just mentioned about God can be tied up with His total immutability and eternity. The groundwork of His unshaken rule is this: "Thou art from everlasting." God is and ever was the Eternal One.

Old truths, all of these, but newly acquired in the new insight that Israel could well have gained when she witnessed how God restored His ancient people to their ancestral land. Thus far the thoughts of the psalm have centered in God. For a moment the forces that were in opposition to Him are now examined (vv. 3, 4).

b) He maintains His rule effectively over against every power that would assail him (vv. 3, 4)

3. *Floods have lifted up, O Lord, floods have lifted up their voice; Floods will lift up their voice* (again).
4. *Above the sound of great majestic waters, yea, breakers of the sea,*
   Majestic on high is the Lord.

3. There is, perhaps, nothing more involved in the initial statement than that there have been times innumerable when floodwaters or roaring streams (the word can mean either) were on the loose and roared or lifted up their voice. It has happened and will happen again. This does not say that the floods signify or symbolize something. It is true, of course, that in the Scriptures swollen floodwaters have been used as a simile or metaphor for the agitation of powerful nations when they were rising in hostility against the people of God (cf., Ps. 46:3; 89:9; Is. 8:5-8; 17:12, 13). But it would scarcely seem that the psalmist is limiting himself to the idea that God can master floodwaters when they are on a rampage. Almost involuntarily one arrives at the application or draws the conclusion: Even as the Almighty controls raging waters of every sort, so He remains in full control of every other force that may arise and seem to challenge His authority. In one sense or another the sea is used "as an emblem of hostile powers," (*Kirkpatrick*). In a sense the history of the experiences of the people of God is here briefly told: hostility has raged against them; it will continue to rage periodically as long as this present world stands.

4. The other side of the matter is that, majestic though the roar of waters powerfully in motion may be, fierce though the breakers of the sea may roar, there is something that is more majestic by far—the Lord on high Himself. Never is His majesty appreciated and understood better by us than when the Lord asserts Himself and curbs the raging waters. The psalmist makes this incisive statement and lets the matter rest there. The brevity of these sharply chiseled phrases is what makes them doubly effective.

c) His testimonies and His house will endure forever (v. 5)

5. *Thy testimonies are utterly to be trusted;*
   Sanctity befits Thy house, O Lord, forevermore.

As many writers remark, at this point the psalm moves from the turbulence of the elements into the calm of eternal truth. The psalmist is, as it were, reducing what he is saying to general truths which have practical and lasting validity. The first of these is, that as a result of Israel's recent experience which was just described the nation has gained a new insight into the absolute trustworthiness of the words that God has spoken to His people. These words are of various sorts and kinds—instruction, warning, commandment, ordinance. Here a comprehensive word for all of these various sorts of words is used—"testimonies." The emphasis would seem to be chiefly on the promissory aspect of the divine words, that Israel now clearly understands again how reliable these promises as well as all other divine words are. Paraphrased more freely, Israel recognizes "that whatever the Lord says can be absolutely relied on in spite of appearances to the contrary."

The other truth that now shines forth with clearer lustre is the fact that "sanctity befits God's house forevermore." That means that its sacred and inviolate character cannot be successfully assailed by anyone. God's true sanctuary must endure forever even as He does. It may incidentally happen that the earthly Temple as such must be surrendered to the hands of the enemy and be destroyed. But no eternal value has been lost as a result. The visible building may from time to time be consigned to destruction. The eternal house of God stands on; He is still there to be met by His people, and He there consorts with them. Eternal values such as these just are not lost. This statement, therefore, does not tell man how he should behave in God's house; it rather tells what God guarantees regarding the endurance of His house. This is just another way of saying that the kingdom of the Lord endures forever. These two things are the inalienable heritage of God's people: God's absolutely reliable word or promises and the vital fellowship which God's children have with Him.

NOTES

1. We have translated the clause *bal-timmot* as an adverb ("immovably," instead of "it shall not be moved"), a construction which is explained in *GK* 156g.

3. The change from the two perfects in the first two clauses to the imperfect form of the same verb in the third clause is obviously designed to indicate that the situation extends over all time, past and present.

Psalm 94

AN APPEAL TO THE JUST JUDGE

THIS IS a psalm which prays to the Lord for relief in days when justice is miscarrying. The evil seems to have advanced to the point where it is beyond the power of man to rectify it.

The miscreants involved do not appear to be heathen oppressors who have been afflicting a victimized people, but rather men from within Israel as many writers are now beginning to maintain in conformity especially with v. 8, as also in his day *Luther* strongly insisted: "In my opinion this psalm does not lament about the heathen but about the kings, princes, priests, and prophets and calls them fools among the people."

It is very difficult to determine the time in which the psalm originated. Few interpreters assign it an early date. Others fluctuate, assigning it to the early Chaldean period, as to the time of the Exile, or to the time shortly after the Return, or even to the Greek or Maccabean periods. We prefer to remain neutral in regard to the question.

There will always be those commentators who will take serious exception to the propriety of the mode of address used in the psalm, "Thou God of vengeance," (*RSV*), which is even stronger in the Hebrew in that a plural ("vengeances") is used. They will venture the opinion that "there is a dangerous mood in the opening sentiment" (*Poteat*). This writer goes on to state that "such feelings, unchecked, will lead men on to the most forms of retribution." But a sympathetic approach is possible if we will but venture to put the best construction on what is said and consider that in the case of a godly man the much-needed restraint will be clearly in evidence. The words of *Maclaren* are very helpful: "There are times when no thought of God is so full of strength as that He is the 'God of recompenses' as Jeremiah calls him (51:56) and when the longing of good men is that He would flash forth and slay evil by the brightness of His coming." *Oesterley* says very properly: "It is necessary sometimes to insist on the truth that there is such a thing as divine retributive justice."

If one wonders how this psalm comes to be found in a group that lays special emphasis on the kingship of the Lord one need only reflect on the fact that "the theme of God the Judge is closely allied with that of God the king" (*Maclaren*).

Psalm 94

Certain approaches of our day that fail to impress us are among others the contention that we here have two distinct psalms. It is not hard to see the unity that lies behind the total thought pattern. Or that we here have a distinctly cultic piece about an individual who just barely escaped being compelled to stand before the congregation in a painful ordeal of some sort, the escape from which is reflected in this psalm. Or the supposition that the first half (vv. 1–15) is congregational in character, and the rest is the plea of an individual.

a) An appeal to God to take the wicked in hand (vv. 1, 2)

1. *O Lord God, to whom vengeance belongs,*
   God to whom vengeance belongs, shine forth!
2. *Arise, O Judge of the earth;*
   Render retribution to the proud!

1. In this appeal to the Lord to take the wicked in hand the Hebrew does, indeed, say, "O God of vengeance." But that form of statement sounds much harsher to our ears than the Scripture intends, for this expression is not the outgrowth of an unworthy conception of God but rather an appeal to a function that He will from time to time exercise. It seems to us that the expression we borrowed from the *KJ* comes closer to our way of stating the same truth: "God to whom vengeance belongs," implying that there are times when it must be exercised, and when such times come, the issue rests safely in the hands of Him who knows how to administer this difficult function. The fact that it is a distinctive work of Yahweh the repetition of the expression brings to our attention. The verb used—"shine forth"—implies that He has kept Himself together with His just judgment hidden. This call to action would have Him manifest this just attribute of His by the deliverance of the afflicted and the punishment of the evildoer.

2. The parallel statement shows the Lord's qualification for the proper exercise of this His divine function, for He is "the judge of the earth," a fact that is stressed also in Gen. 18:25; Ps. 58:11; 82:8. The writer asks for no more than should justly be rendered when he prays the Lord to "render retribution to the proud." The name by which the wicked are referred to indicates that they have asserted their own rights at the expense of the rights of others, including the Lord's. Nothing unseemly is being sought. If it is God's function to do such work, it surely cannot be improper to pray that He exercise this prerogative. Man, godly man, may be of one mind with God in this matter.

b) A description of their wickedness (vv. 3–7)

3. *How long shall the wicked, O Lord,*
   How long shall the wicked exult?

4. *How long shall they gush forth insolent words?*
   How long shall they exalt themselves, all the workers of iniquity?
5. *They have been crushing Thy people, O Lord;*
   They have been afflicting Thy heritage.
6. *They have slain the widow and the alien*
   And murdered the orphans.
7. *And they say: "The Lord does not see it;*
   The God of Jacob does not notice it."

It was deeds like these that moved the psalmist to cry out to the Lord to rectify what lay beyond the power of good men in the land to set right.

This tragic state of affairs had apparently continued for some time (v. 3). The repetition seems to express the feeling of frustration on the part of the godly. Besides, the situation had been rendered more painful by the fact that the wicked were gloating over the success of their misdeeds. The complaint that lies in the "how long?" continues through v. 4. The wicked seem to have cultivated the habit of speaking much and insolently about the seeming success of their wicked devices, and they have thus taken to exalting themselves as being the individuals to whom rule and authority belonged.

Aside from this attitude of theirs there is the long list of wicked deeds that they have perpetrated and as it were entrenched themselves behind. These misdeeds are apparent chiefly in the area of social injustice. The psalmist shows an interest like unto that which the prophets often stress (cf., Is. 1:23; Amos 5:10ff.; Jer. 22:3; Ezek. 22:7; Mic. 3:1–3; Zech. 7:10; Mal. 3:5). Those who have wealth and power prey on those who have none. The cowardliness of the attacks of the strong upon the weak makes their deeds all the more reprehensible. They may not have made a practice of regularly slaying these helpless victims, but instances of such extreme cruelty must have occurred. It was the widows and the orphans who suffered most.

The fact that these oppressors have at least some regard for what the Lord might do would point to their being members of the covenant people. A peculiar delusion has taken hold of them. Since they practiced oppression repeatedly, and the Lord did not strike them with swift vengeance, they concluded, "He does not see it" or "does not notice it." A sober second thought could well have told them how wrong they were in drawing this conclusion. A very cheap opinion about the Almighty must be theirs if they actually harbor such views about Him. But that is just one feature of the dangerous position into which they have maneuvered themselves.

c) Instruction addressed to the wicked (vv. 8–11)

8. *Note this, you brutes among the people*
   And you fools—when will you become wise?
9. *He that planted the ear, does He not hear?*
   He that formed the eye, does He not see?
10. *He that disciplines the nations, does He not correct?*
    And He that teaches man knowledge—.
11. *The Lord knows the thoughts of men,*
    That they are but a breath.

8. Dramatically the writer addresses these oppressors among the people and instructs them as to their folly. Firmly and positively he addresses them. He minces no words. By virtue of what they have done they are "brutes" (which connotes lack of intelligence rather than cruel behavior) and "fools." Impatience marks his words to some extent. These foolish men should have known better than to harbor such a silly thought as that the Lord was ignorant of what they were doing. By means of a series of questions he helps them recall that the Creator is the author of every ability that man has. How much more must He be capable of those very functions! Only He that hears superbly can impart hearing to others. Only He who has perfect sight such as man cannot even conceive of is capable of giving seeing eyes to men.

10. To remind men that the Lord's activities are not in any sense limited to His chosen people, an area of His activity that is not too frequently considered in the Old Testament is taken into consideration: He is in the habit of disciplining the nations by the course of history, for He is Lord of all. If He then at times sets them right by His sovereign control, is not that His prerogative? And lastly, He is the one "that teaches man knowledge." All knowledge emanates from Him. If He did not give man the ability to learn, man would be no better than the beast. By not drawing the conclusion from this last statement—an impressive aposiopesis—the writer invites the ones addressed to arrive at their own conclusions.

After these very suggestive rhetorical questions the psalmist by way of conclusion gives the *Lord's* estimate of the thinking of *man* after he had expressed man's estimate of the knowledge of God. This estimate is: "The Lord knows the thoughts of men, that they are but a breath." This last word is in the Scriptures frequently translated "vanity." Man's thinking is at its best not very substantial, especially when it is contrasted with the thoughts of God. There has, perhaps, never been a more devastating demonstration of the foolish thinking which men occasionally become guilty of when they imagine that the Lord is not aware of what they are doing.

d) Encouragement addressed to the godly (vv. 12–15)

12. *Blessed is the man whom Thou dost chasten, O Lord,*
    And whom Thou dost instruct out of Thy law,
13. *That he may have relief from the days of evil*
    While a pit is dug for the wicked.
14. *For the Lord will not reject His people;*
    Nor will He abandon His heritage.
15. *For judgment will again become just;*
    And all the upright in heart will follow it.

12. Though it is not explicitly stated, those who are now being addressed (singly or collectively) are the individuals who have suffered from or been disturbed by the arrogant dealings of the proud. Another way of evaluating their situation is to note that the Lord did allow them to be chastened. The affliction was for their betterment. This is one of the most beneficial forms of experience that the Lord lets men live through. For that reason the beatitude here expressed is in place. Cf., Prov. 3:11, 12. But at such a time of chastisement a man needs another guide to help him to understand what the purposes of the Lord are, and that guide is the law of God's revelation, whether it is specifically the Pentateuch as in this instance or any other good and helpful word of the Lord. That word gives instruction or, more accurately: God gives instruction through it, and thus a man becomes wise with a higher wisdom and understanding.

13. This instruction has as its direct purpose that the man who is thus instructed "may have relief from the days of evil." These are the days "when wrong and wrongdoers seem to have undisputed sway," as *Kirkpatrick* aptly states it. The instructed and enlightened man knows how to meet such trying situations. Whereas he on his part knows how to bear what is happening because he sees what purposes God has in and through it all, "a pit is dug for the wicked." The figure used implies that a means of entrapping the wrongdoer is in the making, and such a one will surely be caught in it, and that will be his end. Cruel injustice cannot flourish for any length of time. Such knowledge gives the informed and chastened man "relief."

14. Such brave claims as to what will be done for the godly call for some measure of substantiation, and the psalmist, therefore, refers to a truth that was well known among the people of God: "The Lord will not reject His people." Since He cannot forsake them when they are afflicted He must act and come to their relief. Or phrased in the language of old in terms of the original occupation of the land: "He will not abandon His heritage."

15. Another statement by way of comfort is appended, and this

deals with the net result that follows situations like the one just described. That result is: "Judgment will again become just." During the time described above (vv. 3–7) the administration of justice had often miscarried; judicial verdicts were often unfair. To permit such a state of affairs to continue for a long time would utterly confuse men. Therefore God will see to it that judges again render just decisions, and that justice is maintained in every way. When this result is obtained, "the upright" are found faithfully adhering to justice and following it, and thus truth marches on. *Luther* has a justly famous rendering of v. 15, which, though not literally exact, effectively sets forth the truth of the matter: *Recht muss doch Recht bleiben,* i.e., The right must in the end prevail as the right. The Hebrew says literally: "Judicial decision shall again turn to justice."

e) Past experience of God's faithfulness (vv. 16–19)

16. *Who will rise up for me against the wicked?*
    Who will stand by me against the evildoers?
17. *If the Lord had not been my help,*
    My soul had almost taken up its dwelling in the land of silence.
18. *When I said, "My foot has slipped,"*
    Thy steadfast love, O God, has always sustained me.
19. *When the thoughts of my heart were many,*
    Thy comforts made my soul glad.

At this point the psalmist records his own experience of God's faithfulness. He states that there was a time in his own life when he found the wicked and the evildoers previously described opposing him and forcing him to cry out: "Who will stand by me against them?" The answer to the question posed is given in the verse that follows. It says in effect, But for the Lord's strong help I should have perished: I all but perished and almost dropped off into the land where total silence prevails. He describes the realm of the dead from the point of view of what man can in this life actually observe with regard to the dead: no voice sounds across their realm to ours. The Old Testament writers usually spoke thus, for they did not have the lively hope of the resurrection that is ours.

Not only was his a close escape at the time; there was also a very encouraging feature involved, for it happened time and again that in his extremity the psalmist had to say: "My foot has slipped." He had all but succumbed to the attacks of the wicked men who were in power. But in each instance, when he thought he had lost out, he was upheld by the steadfast love of God. Or to describe the situation from another point of view, when troubled thoughts accumulated within him to the point where they might have seemed to submerge all things else, the comforts which the Lord grants those that trust in Him always made his heart glad. He could taste of the sweetness of the solace that his soul so sorely needed. Such experiences transpire in the hidden recesses of the soul and are the basis of the reassurance that makes God's people strong.

f) The certainty of the destruction of the wicked (vv. 20–23)

20. *Can the throne that is based on wickedness be allied with Thee,*
    Which frames mischief by statutes?
21. *They band together against the life of the righteous*
    And condemn innocent blood.
22. *But the Lord was a fortress for me,*
    And my God the rock of my refuge.
23. *And He repaid their iniquity upon them;*
    And He will destroy them because of their wickedness;
    The Lord our God will destroy them.

20. Not only will the godly be helped, but also the destruction of the wicked is entirely certain. This section, which develops this last thought, begins by showing how utterly antagonistic these two approaches are. It asks the question: "Can the throne that is based on wickedness be allied with Thee?" The figure of speech involved in the expression "throne of wickedness" briefly describes the situation that seemed to prevail: the wicked seemed to have rule and dominion, and to have it with the consent of the Almighty. He and they seemed to be in an alliance which let them continue in power. By posing the question whether this would ever be possible the writer answers it. He adds another factor that makes such a combination doubly impossible: These persons "frame mischief by statutes." This seems to mean: They attempt to legalize their wicked course by passing statutes that would regularize what they are doing. Can God allow that? Never!

21. Another feature is added which is in line with the description of these evil men that was given in vv. 3–7. "They band together against the life of the righteous." Ordinarily sensible men band together in order to gain mutual support in upholding what is right and good. Here the perversity involved made the very life of righteous men the object of assault, and thus innocent blood was being condemned.

22. The psalmist seems to imply that he was one of those who were thus victimized, and that his own life had been imperiled. But he had had the experience that the Lord protected him ("was a fortress for me"), and his God in whom he took refuge was his deliverer. He took the wicked in hand (v. 23), "and He repaid their iniquity upon them." From this as a broad and firm base upon which he stands the psalmist then notes what is to be expected in the future: "He will destroy them

because of their wickedness"—an assertion which is repeated to convey the thought that it is absolutely certain to occur. There is no unwholesome, vengeful gloating in these words. To the writer the overthrow of the evil is just as assured as is the deliverance of the godly. On this affirmative note this psalm ends.

NOTES

1. "Shine forth" (*hophia'*) looks like a form of the perfect but according to the parallelism should be regarded as an imperative. The initial "h" of the next word has to be read twice, thus making it an *ah* hortative which confirms the imperative (see *KS* 203b; *GK* 69v).

17. The *ah* ending on '*ezrathah* gives it a meaning like, "to my help" (*KS* 287b).

21. As a meaning of *yagoddu* most dictionaries give "attack" rather than "band together."

Psalm 95

THE TRUE PRAISE OF GOD

THERE CAN BE no question that Psalms 95 to 100 have a common theme in that they all begin with a summons to sing praises unto the Lord though each has its distinctive note of praise. This psalm may be regarded as striking the keynote.

Though there is not enough material within the psalm to warrant the dating of it with any measure of finality, it seems quite reasonable to set its time after the return from the Babylonian Captivity, in fact, there seems to be scarcely a plausible objection to the idea of its being sung at the time of the dedication of the Second Temple.

From days of old the church has always recognized that this psalm was an invitation to worship, witness its use in the Matins service, dating back even to the time of Athanasius and, for that matter, to the time of the ancient Jewish Church (see *Kirkpatrick*).

Those interpreters who insist that the psalm must have been intended for use in public worship have difficulty in agreeing as to how this liturgical rendition took place. Its possibilities along this line cannot be questioned, but a final verdict as to the original intention of the author lies outside the range of present possibility.

Why question the original unity of the psalm? If any later editor was ingenious enough to discern that the two thoughts which make up the psalm dare be set side by side to supplement one another, there seems little reason for doubting that an original writer will have had sufficient insight to discern this possibility and may himself have combined them into one psalm.

A twofold division of the psalm seems most natural:
a) A summons to praise (vv. 1–7)
b) A warning against disobedience (vv. 8–11)

Both added together may be said to state as the theme of the psalm: "The True Praise of God."

a) **A summons to praise (vv. 1–7)**

1. *O come, let us give a ringing cry to the Lord;*
   Let us raise joyful shouts to the Rock of our salvation!
2. *Let us come into His presence with thanksgiving;*
   Let us raise joyful shouts to Him with psalms!
3. *For the Lord is a great God*
   And a great King above all gods.
4. *In His hand are the unexplored regions of the earth,*
   The resources of the mountains are His also.
5. *The sea is His, and it is He who made it;*
   And His hands formed the dry land.
6. *O come, let us worship and bow down;*
   Let us kneel before the Lord, our Maker.
7. *For He is our God, and we are the people of His pasture*
   And the sheep of His hand;
   Oh, if today you would but hearken to His voice!

1. This is a great invitatory. It is general enough in tone to fit almost any situation. Any group at worship could exhort itself in terms of the psalm, or all could exhort one another to sing the praises of the Lord. It would be suitable for a procession going to the sanctuary or walking about in the sanctuary. One individual could fittingly address these words to others. The verbs that are employed urge men to use more than tame terms and methods of praise. The familiar, "O come, let us sing," is not forceful enough. The verb that is used involves the idea of a ringing cry. The second verb suggests loud shouts. Tepid praise defeats its own purpose. In the Old Testament Temple worship may often have been characterized by a vigor and forcefulness that we are strangers to. The Oriental nature is more inclined toward a certain demonstrativeness than we are.

2. This verse indicates what the best offering or sacrifice is that God's people can bring to Him—"thanksgiving." "Psalms" are spoken of as another familiar means of expressing praise.

3. Two major reasons for singing the Lord's praises are now advanced, the first includes vv. 3–5, the second vv. 6, 7. The first may be summed up as being the very greatness of the Lord Himself. He is to be praised for the fact that as God He is as great as He is, indeed for that matter, in a class that allows for no rivals. For when He is said to be "a great King above all gods," that could, indeed, be understood to mean that the actual existence of other gods is granted. But considering the enlightened state in which Israel lived and the clear utterances which the prophets had made, such an interpretation of the words would call for a lapse on the nation's part into a state of ignorance that had long been surpassed. Note what Jeremiah had said (10:3ff.) and Isaiah in his sharp tirades against the futility of all idols (40:18ff.; 44:9ff.). Thus for all practical purposes the term "all gods" might be understood to mean: "those that the nations round about are wont to describe as gods."

4. Several examples of the Lord's greatness are offered in terms of the areas that are under His control. Even those vast unknown and "unexplored regions" of the earth that seem to lie there forgotten and purposeless remain entirely within His control. Also, for that matter, everything that lies buried and hid in the mountains, of whose vast mineral wealth we are now more than ever aware—what we might call "the resources of the mountains"—these are His also. He controls the areas which the hand and the power of man cannot reach.

5. Furthermore, the sea is a part of His domain in all its vastness and mystery, for "it is He who made it" to be what it is. Then, too, the area that we, the children of men, are more familiar with—"the dry land"—was formed by His hands. The thought is that He who made it has never lost control over that which He brought into being. Weigh these things well, and a new conception of the greatness of God will be the result.

6. A second more intimate reason for praising the God of Israel is now advanced (vv. 6, 7), and it is prefaced by a new summons to praise. In this summons a new feature of praise is stressed, namely, the humility with which it should be offered: "Let us bow down; let us kneel." The reason for the praise to be offered is: "We are His people." But the people that confess this, be it Israel of old or His New Testament church, are always unworthy and undeserving of so high an honor. The situation in which Israel finds itself is described in a more colorful way by likening the nation to flock which the Lord tends and leads out to pasture. What people deserves such favors? The shepherd practically makes himself the servant of the flock that he tends. Who dare lay claim upon the Lord for such services? Yet He has thus watched over His chosen ones.

7. It is at this point of reflection that the thought of the many instances of the nation's faithlessness and disobedience come forcibly to the writer's mind, and he involuntarily breaks forth into a plea that his generation may not duplicate the sins of the fathers, who in spite of their many advantages time and again turned their backs upon Him and refused the obedience that their fortunate position made incumbent upon them. The note of warning is all the more effective by being introduced so unexpectedly and sharply.

The note just sounded is now developed into an extended plea, which is in substance a warning against disobedience. It is spoken by the Lord Himself. It must be admitted that the clash between the rather joyful character of the first half of the psalm and this sharp note of warning of the second half is rather jarring. But that by no means finds fault with having the two side by side, nor do we find anything in this sharp juxtaposition of these two elements that merits criticism. Praise must be kept wholesome, and praise from a disobedient heart is dangerous. True praise and submissive obedience go hand in hand.

b) A warning against disobedience (vv. 8–11)

8. "Harden not your hearts as at Meribah!
    As on the day of Massah in the wilderness!
9. When your fathers put Me to the test they made trial of Me,
    Even though they had seen My work.
10. Forty years I felt loathing for a generation;
    And I said: 'They are a people who err in their hearts,
    And they have not known My ways.'
11. So that I swore in My wrath
    That they should not enter into My rest."

8. Though God never spoke the words that are here attributed to Him in exactly this form, it must readily be admitted that they effectively embody the substance of what He said again and again, either by the mouth of His holy prophets or by the very works that He did among the children of men. To be a witness of the mighty acts of God and not to be drawn into closer allegiance to Him must result in an experience of hardening which progressively dulls all finer spiritual perception. Against this carelessness the Lord is represented as warning His people at all times. Classic examples of what should not be imitated are the events which took place at Meribah or Massah (cf., Exod. 17:1–7) where shortly after the deliverance from Egypt Israel both strove with God ("Meribah" means "strife") and put Him to the test ("Massah"—"testing"). Num. 20:1–13 furnishes a parallel to the original Meribah.

God's "work" here referred to as having been witnessed by Israel seems to refer to more than the giving of water from the rock. It could well include that whole complex of mighty deeds of the Lord that culminated in the great exodus. The more the nation was privileged to witness the greatness of God's power, the greater became its responsibility. The careless heart can become amazingly callous to the Lord and to what He does. There is no parallel on record when God decreed the death of a whole generation as He did in connection with the stubborn sin of Israel.

10. How repulsive such an attitude on the part of even His own people can be in the sight of God is reflected in the words: "Forty years I felt a loathing for a generation." The absence of the article before generation focuses attention on the wide compass of the word as though He had said: "a *whole* generation" was given over to a slow death by Me because of this unwholesome spiritual attitude. There is an unusual force in the verb "I felt a loathing." Patiently as He bore with Israel, He, nevertheless, continually felt this repugnance for them during the whole of the forty years. Strong words to brand a repulsive sin!

By way of further explanation of what their sin amounted to God is represented as evaluating them as a people who wilfully stray in their innermost thoughts: they persist in going the wrong way in spite of the strong compulsion that the Lord brings to bear upon them. He also charges them with "not knowing His ways." Because of the unique force that the Hebrew verb "know" has, this means about as much as being utterly deficient in sympathetic understanding and appreciation of the kindly ways in which God led His people. This divine diagnosis of Israel's state of heart proves that self-induced stubbornness is possible in a person's or nation's dealings with God.

11. The final result of that unwholesome attitude, so familiar to every Israelite, is once again emphatically set forth in all its terribleness: "I swore in My wrath that they should not enter into My rest." The fact that the decision is irrevocable is indicated by the oath by which the Lord bound Himself. How strong His reactions to their ingratitude was is indicated by the fact that the oath was taken "in wrath." "Rest" would seem to mean the Promised Land itself, in which they would have enjoyed rest after years of wandering. Cf. Deut. 12:9. Because of the very abruptness of its ending the final warning is made all the more impressive.

NOTES

4. It is true that *mechqerey* is difficult. Since the root from which it comes means "to search," the word could well mean: areas that are to be searched out or explored. We, therefore, translated: "the unexplored regions." In like manner *to'aphoth* which means "to be weary" is also difficult. The feminine plural could refer to things that men have

to toil over in order to acquire them. We venture the translation, "the resources." There is no need for textual emendations.

7. To be prosily literalistic one might feel inclined to correct the text to read as many interpreters do: "people of His hand and sheep of His pasture." But there is nothing wrong with the uniquely different form of statement as it appears in the text.

8. For "as at Meribah" the Hebrew has a contracted comparison: "as Meribah."

10. The imperfect *'aqut* is a durative imperfect, which might have been rendered: "I kept feeling a loathing."

The expression "who err in their hearts" is the construct of the participle plural followed by "heart," a construction that must be translated as we rendered it.

THE MESSIANIC INTERPRETATION

To the way of thinking of our generation it seems somewhat peculiar to have vv. 7b–11 cited in part in Hebrews 4:1–10 as being fulfilled in the days of the New Testament. Consequently interpreters speak of the reference the passage makes to the age of the Messiah. That should not be understood as meaning that an intentional and exclusive portrayal of Messianic times is intended. The point of approach seems rather to be this: The true entering into God's rest (v. 11) does not occur until the Christ comes; at the same time the summons to refrain from hardening the hearts sounds through all the ages and should be noted particularly in the time after Christ lest those of the new generation sin after the manner of the generation that perished in the wilderness.

Psalm 96

PRAISE THE LORD, THE KING

IT IS INTERESTING to observe that this psalm appears with slight variations in I Chron. 16:23–34 as having been rendered at the time when David first moved the ark of the Lord to its place of honor in the city of Jerusalem. The differences between that version and the one that is before us may be further studied by anyone who is interested.

This use of the psalm as recorded in I Chron. 16 may have some bearing on the authorship and the date of composition of the psalm. It cannot be denied that the writer of Chronicles may have inserted this

Psalm 96

psalm into his account as aptly expressing the sentiments that were voiced in the praises of Israel on this important occasion without necessarily indicating that this psalm was actually sung. On the other hand, it cannot be denied that David possibly composed the psalm as a half-contradictory heading in the *Septuagint* indicates. In that case, perhaps before Chronicles was written, the psalm was taken from the same source in which the author of Chronicles found it and was with perhaps slight modifications added to the collection of psalms. Yet it must be admitted that the similarities between this psalm and the second half of Isaiah are rather striking and seem to call for a date of composition that was later than the time of Isaiah. As is usually the case, the psalm is cast into so general a form as to have lost almost all specific references to the occasion that gave rise to its composition.

No writer would venture to contradict the assertion that the psalm must originally have been composed for some use in public worship, and that this worship was most likely to be thought of as taking place in the Temple. To be more precise than this about the exact liturgical use for which it may have been designed is bound to lead to questionable results. Among such efforts we class the attempts to assign to it some use in public processions to or in the Temple. More particularly, to claim that it must have been designed almost beyond a shadow of a doubt for the New Year festival in connection with the so-called enthronement festivities held in honor of Yahweh would, indeed, be in keeping with the almost universal claim to this effect on the part of present-day writers. But both the enthronement festival and the New Year's celebration have not yet been lifted out of the realm of vague conjecture.

Together with these approaches certain other interpretations must fall by the wayside, chiefly those attempts that are being made to reconstruct the details of the enthronement liturgy out of this psalm. The point at issue seems to be that the somewhat general tone of the psalm which we noticed in connection with almost all the psalms that we have referred to above allows men of every age to fit the psalm into a wide variety of uses. These are, however, practical adaptations of the psalm and not intrinsic features of its original use.

The broad eschatological outlook of this psalm is remarkable. It throbs with the hope of the Lord's coming, which it regards as having in a sense already taken place but also as certain to take place in times to come in a manner that should enlist our fondest anticipation. That coming involves the blessed event of judgment. The psalm is definitely of a Messianic cast and may as many interpreters have remarked have been of great service in keeping Messianic expectation alive. One issue is not touched upon, and that is what the relation of the Messiah may be to the Lord who is to come. Time was not ripe for the solution of this problem.

One further feature of the psalm that must frequently strike those that use it in every generation is the jubilant note that rings through it, and let it once again be remarked more explicitly that this note of joy is combined with the thought of the impending judgment of the Lord. We shall apparently have to revise our views of what judgment meant in the thinking of Israel.

In the light of all that has been written it would seem to be almost imperative that such a psalm be an entirely original composition. But it so happens that it is very much of a mosaic. It has obvious points of contact with many other psalms as well as with Isaiah. The following are the points of contact with other psalms, referred to by almost every commentator and here grouped according to *McCullough:* with v. 1 cf. Ps. 33:3; 40:3; 98:1; with v. 3, cf. Ps. 9:11; 105:1; with v. 4 cf. Ps. 48:1; 95:3; with vv. 7–9 cf. Ps. 29:1, 2; with v. 13, Ps. 9:8; 98:9. Besides this, on v. 2 cf. Is. 52:7; on v. 3, Is. 60:6; 66:18, 19; on v. 11, Is. 41:19; 44:23; 49:13, as well as Is. 35:1ff. Going back to v. 5, cf. Is. 40:19ff.; 41:23, 24; 46:5–7; 44:9ff. But the unique originality of the author consists in this, that he so effectively combines these various quotations and at the same time adapts them to his particular purpose that they yield a final result that has no trace of a painful combination of heterogeneous elements.

a) A summons to Israel in particular to praise the Lord (vv. 1–3)

1. *O sing unto the Lord a new song;*
   Sing unto the Lord, all the earth!
2. *Sing unto the Lord, bless His name;*
   Proclaim the good tidings of His salvation from day to day!
3. *Tell of His glory among the nations,*
   His wondrous works among all the peoples!

1. The persons to whom this admonition is addressed must be the Israelites, for they are the only ones who according to v. 3 could tell of His glory among the nations. The thought of a "new song" does not involve the idea of a new poetic or musical composition, but as we believe *Briggs* rightly claims, "a new outburst of song because of a new event that evokes it." The Lord is so great and His works so wonderful that it takes "all the earth" to do justice to such a theme. When the verb "sing" is used three times, this serves to make plain the compulsion to utter vocal musical praise when the thoughts of the Lord's greatness are entertained. The thought kindles the fires of devotion to the point where praise cannot be restrained.

2. The different form of our translation of 2b is due to the fact that

the Hebrew verb very distinctly means "to bring good tidings." That is much more than a colorless "tell." "Salvation" which is the object of praise is again so broad a term and so general in its scope that it allows for including any form of God's help and deliverance that anyone may have experienced at any time in soul or body. It is true, the exuberance of praise that God's salvation produced is such that nothing less than a very great deliverance must originally have been under consideration, a fact that leads *Briggs* to claim that it must have been "some worldwide transformation, some change that gave joy to the world, which was so extraordinary that it could only be ascribed to the divine intervention." He then suggests as the most likely occasion the overthrow of the Persian empire by Alexander the Great. We believe that many equally important events that occurred prior to this event could be pointed out that were sufficient in magnitude and more in keeping with the possible date of the psalm, perhaps somewhere in the late sixth century B.C.

The writer must have been deeply impressed by the greatness of the glory of the Lord and the greatness of "His wondrous works" to feel that this knowledge was something that the nations needed to hear and would gladly receive if they but heard it. The chief point at issue is that, if one truly grasps the greatness of our God, that makes him vocal in letting others know what great things the Lord has done for him and is ready to do for all men.

b) The reason for praise: God's incomparable greatness (vv. 4–6)

4. *For great is the Lord and highly to be praised;*
   He is to be feared above all gods.
5. *For all the gods of the nations are things of nought;*
   But the Lord made the heavens.
6. *Honor and majesty are before Him;*
   Strength and beauty are in His sanctuary.

4. The psalmist makes an issue of the Lord's incomparable greatness as being the chief factor that he wishes to stress in this psalm. We have a situation like that presented in Ps. 93:3, where God was also said to be great above all gods, which we would paraphrase to mean: greater than all those that men are wont to call gods. Note how in v. 4a God's greatness and His praise inevitably go together. One cannot consider the one without breaking forth into the other. If any of the beings commonly called gods called forth fear in the minds and hearts of their worshipers, so much more will the Lord do so. This naturally implies that the fear His knowledge evokes is wholesome and true: it is a godly reverence.

5. When the psalmist goes on to say that "all the gods of the nations

are things of nought," it will always be a question that arises at this point as to whether he meant that they had no existence or that they were utterly impotent beings. It must be remembered that already in the early Christian Church the view was commonly held that the heathen idols were fallen angels who had managed to get the heathen nations under their power, a view that is reflected also in Milton's *Paradise Lost*. In any case, their utter lack of power is being pointed out over against the Lord who can control them if they exist but surpasses them in any case, for He it is that "made the heavens." This great creative work of His keeps impressing us with the greatness of its Creator.

6. A further way of describing His greatness and one that is most beautiful and poetic is to point out what manner of beings are in attendance upon Him. The abstract qualities mentioned are regarded as so many angelic beings that grace His throne. They are "honor and majesty" as one pair, "strength and beauty" as a second. In the Hebrew the first two are an effective alliteration: *hodh—hadhar*. They indicate especially how everything in the presence of so great a King is of so high an order. The other two intimately condition one another as *Maclaren* has well pointed out: "strength and beauty are often separated in a disordered world, and each is maimed thereby, but in their perfection, they indissolubly blend." All this is a brief but a very effective sketch of the greatness of the Lord.

c) A summons to all people to praise Yahweh's kingship (vv. 7–10)

7. *Ascribe to the Lord, O families of the peoples,*
Ascribe to the Lord glory and strength.
8. *Ascribe to the Lord the glory due unto His name;*
Take an offering and come into His courts.
9. *Worship the Lord in holy array;*
Tremble before Him, all the earth.
10. *Say among the nations: "The Lord is king;*
Yea, the world is established, it shall not be moved;
He shall judge the peoples righteously."

Quite often vv. 7–9 are said to make up this section. It seems far better to us to include one additional verse in it. The whole piece then becomes a summons to praise Yahweh's kingship. The persons addressed are the "families of the peoples." These are to ascribe to the Lord "glory and strength" or more particularly "the glory due unto His name." Though the Hebrew says that these qualities are to be "given" to Him, that clearly signifies that His possession of them is to be openly confessed. Since in days of old every major act of worship found expression in a sacrifice, all these subjects of Yahweh are bidden to "take an offering and come into His courts." This whole approach of theirs is further described as worship of the Lord "in holy array," that is to say, in such outward garb and demeanor as befits those that recognize the nature of the God they adore. And lest their approach be purely perfunctory, they are to approach in the spirit of deepest awe, that is to say, "tremble before Him."

10. The approach of "all the earth" is for the purpose of making the confession that "the Lord is King." The magnitude of this assertion is to be grasped in its fullest scope, and it will then impel him that has grasped its meaning to seek to make full and strong confession and proclamation of it, for this is a startling fact and a truth of greatest import. Until one has appropriated this truth he stumbles about blindly. When it has been fully grasped, insight into the whole world and its government becomes absolutely clear. For if He reigns, then also "the world is established, it shall not be moved." For His government is effective and adequate in every detail. The knowledge of this truth is essential for that sense of security that man so badly needs. In this verse there throbs the very heart of the psalm. A paraphrase of the truth involved can be worded thus: "He shall judge the peoples righteously." What joy and satisfaction to know that the administration of the world and its affairs is in competent hands, and that there is no possibility of His failing in any respect in the work that is rightly His!

d) A call to all created things to praise the Lord (vv. 11-13)

11. *Let the heavens rejoice, and let the earth exult;*
    Let the sea roar and all that fills it.
12. *Let the field exult and all that is in it;*
    Then shall all the trees of the forest shout for joy
13. *Before the Lord, for He comes, He comes to judge the earth;*
    He will judge the world with righteousness and the peoples with
    His truth.

All created inanimate things are called upon to join in the praises of the Lord and His just government of the world: the heavens, the earth, the sea and all the beings that swarm in it, the field and all that it produces, plus all the trees of the forest. For very joy they are to rejoice, exult, and shout. But that particular aspect of His work that especially calls for vocal confession is the fact that He comes to judge, and that this judgment will be carried out in righteousness.

We associate the thoughts of God's judgment with all manner of dread expectations. In the days of the Old Testament this judgment was also thought of with most joyful anticipation, for judgment involved the fact that all things that are now in disarray and disharmony, suffering from injustice and violence, shall be set right and adjusted. That positive and constructive side of God's judgment was the broader aspect of the truth that the Old Testament saints believed and enjoyed. How near at hand this great day may be is immaterial. The mere fact that it will come to pass is what matters. Each time that thought arises, there is occasion for gratitude to God, for all created things are involved in that great divine restoration, and all should, therefore, contribute their portion of the vast chorus of praise that should continually rise to heaven because of this great prospect.

NOTES

4. In this verse and the next, in the interest of accuracy of expression, we should really say: He is to be feared above all *other* gods; and all the *other* gods of the nations are things of nought. The Hebrew assumes that what it says is to be thus understood.

10. In 10a the Old Latin version has the addition *a ligno* ("from a tree") obviously referring to the cross. From the Latin this went over into editions of the *Septuagint* (see *Rahlfs, Septuaginta*, vol. 1, p. vii). This uncritical reading was so commonly accepted in its day that Justin Martyr could charge the Jews with having maliciously removed it from the original text.

Psalm 97

THE NATURE OF THE LORD'S KINGSHIP

IT IS RATHER obvious that this psalm has much in common with the psalms of this group, beginning with Ps. 93, and especially Ps. 96–100, which present variations on the theme, "The Lord is King." The new features that are offered are these: there is a description of the Lord as He sits upon His throne; there is a distinctive emphasis on the truly spiritual character of His rule; there is a still clearer setting forth of the futility of the worship of those vain things called idols; and there is also a clear statement as to the manner in which God's saints react to this great divine truth.

It is a bit difficult to ascertain the time to which the psalm refers, especially in view of the claim so positively advanced that the psalm is distinctly eschatological in character. It would seem, however, that behind the statements of the psalm is a recent experience that Israel has had which has set forth the old truth of the Lord's sovereignty in much sharper outline, and this experience might well be the return from

Psalm 97

Babylonian Exile. Aside from this, it would appear that the verb forms used in the original solve the question of the time referred to in a rather simple fashion. The first three verses describe God as He always is and will always be. Then the change in tense to the past suggests what Israel has experienced under this head in the past. By a very natural progression of thought the psalm goes on to describe the two possible ways in which men may react to what the nation has witnessed under this head. Thus the conclusion seems well warranted that the psalm is largely historical in character. The slight measure of the prophetic that may be involved is stated especially in v. 7, where the ultimate victory of the Lord is clearly set forth. The attempt, quite popular at present, to correlate all psalms like the one before us with the so-called enthronement festival, that mysterious and elusive thing that nowhere appears openly but must be assumed to be lurking in the shadows almost everywhere, makes a helpful understanding of the psalm quite difficult.

The rather simple progression of thought set forth in the psalm is as follows:
a) What manner of king the Lord is (vv. 1–3)
b) Past evidence of His mighty rule (vv. 4–6)
c) The twofold reaction His kingship calls forth (vv. 7–9)
d) How the Lord's saints appropriate this truth (vv. 10–12)

It is the third section of the outline that would contain some measure of Messianic thought in that the ultimate victory over the idols, which is here ascribed to Yahweh, will frequently be thought of as belonging to the Christ. Thus the psalm is only indirectly Messianic.

1. *The Lord is King, let the earth rejoice;*
   Let the many coastlands be glad!
2. *Clouds and darkness are round about Him;*
   Righteousness and justice are the foundation of His throne.
3. *Fire goes before Him*
   And consumes His adversaries round about.

1. A visualization of this great King whom Israel acknowledges and adores is presented here. The writer based his picture on those descriptions of the Lord that have been presented elsewhere. The dark clouds that were wont to enshroud Him when He appeared to the children of men and the accompanying darkness are found also in passages like Exod. 19:9; 20:21; Deut. 4:11; 5:22; I Kings 8:12, even in Job 22:13, 14. The fire that flashed forth from these clouds, no doubt as lightning in most instances, is referred to in Ps. 50:3; but also already in Exod. 3:2; 13:21; 19:18; Deut. 1:33, etc.

The psalmist prefaces the description that he offers by a statement of the kingly rule of Yahweh, of which some recent proof had been witnessed by the nation. It was a rule which should above all at the very thought of it induce the earth as a whole to rejoice and the remote coastlands of the Mediterranean to join in jubilation. At this point the writer shows deep insight into the ultimate destiny of the heathen: they, too, shall have access to the saving truth of the God of Israel. But the Lord's kingly rule is a truth that is sufficiently great to make the heart of all mankind glad.

2. Though He had been wont to appear shrouded in clouds and accompanied by fiery lightnings flashing forth round about Him, and though He is, therefore, a God who is veiled in mystery, more outstanding than these physical manifestations of His glory is the spiritual aspect of His rule, which is reflected in the statement, "Righteousness and justice are the foundation of His throne." Strip off the poetic form of the statement, and you have the simple truth that God rules according to the principles of strict righteousness, and as a result every deed He does is completely just. On the other hand (v. 3), so strong is His reaction against all those who oppose His just rule that they shall be consumed by the fire that goes forth before Him. This brief description is blinding in its brilliance, but such a God is our Lord.

4. *His lightnings have lighted up the world;*
   The earth has seen it and trembled in awe.
5. *Mountains have melted like wax before the Lord,*
   Before the Lord of all the earth.
6. *The heavens have declared His righteousness;*
   And all the peoples shall see His glory.

4. In the Hebrew of this section the first five verbs are perfects. They point to things that have happened, which manifested the Lord's mighty rule. It is true, the items referred to are in the area of things physical. But these evidences of the manner in which He rules beautifully supplement the thoughts concerning the spiritual character of His government. Lightnings are not the mere operation of the laws of physics; they are *His* lightnings as with one flash they light up all of the visible world that we are able to behold at the moment. Whenever the earth and its inhabitants witness such flashes of brilliance on the part of the Lord, they tremble in awe. Still more awe-inspiring is the eruption of volcanoes (for that is what v. 5 seems to be describing). But this is again not a mechanical operation of physical laws but, in the last analysis, something like the Lord's touching of the hills; that is why they melt in the process of eruption. Such a view properly sets forth the higher causality.

6. May we not say that the very heavens have re-echoed with testimony as to how righteously the Lord does all the things that He does? And that they have again and again borne such witness? At this point the tense changes—a fact that is seemingly ignored by many commentators—and the truth stated looks forward to the future for a brief moment, as much as to say that this clear manifestation of God's all-sufficient glory shall presently advance to the point where all the peoples shall see it openly displayed. This suggests, it would seem, the final fulfilment that is to come in the age of the Christ. The section as a whole reflects evidence of the effective rule that God's saints have seen and understood.

7. *They that worship graven images shall be put to shame, they*
   that boast of things of nought;
   All gods have already bowed before Him.
8. *Zion heard and was glad;*
   And the daughters of Judah rejoiced because of Thy judgments,
   O Lord.
9. *For thou, O Lord, art the Most High over all the earth;*
   Thou art exalted far above all gods.

7. Not all men will be alike affected by the truth concerning the all-powerful rule of Yahweh, the God of Israel. The worship of graven images is such folly that those who engage in it must of necessity sooner or later suffer the consequences of their folly and be put to shame. For that matter, in the eyes of enlightened men the idols have already bowed before Him. Their utter futility is becoming more and more apparent. This emptiness of idolatry was one of the insights that came home to Israel with renewed emphasis during the time of the Captivity. This psalm endorses that sentiment.

8. On the other hand, the city of God, Zion, and the villages that lie round about her ("the daughters of Judah") are glad when the kingship of the Lord is proclaimed, for it means much to all those who know the Lord and fear Him. All these continually take note of the "judgments" of the Lord, that is to say, the mighty acts that He does in the course of history, whereby He gives evidence of His sovereign control. For the fact that God's people grasp clearly is that the Lord's rule is world wide and effective, and that there is simply no comparison between Him and all those who are called gods but are not.

10. *They that love the Lord, let them hate all evil;*
    He that preserves the lives of His saints will deliver them out of
    the hand of the wicked.

11. *Light is sown for the righteous
    And gladness for the upright in heart.*
12. *Rejoice in the Lord, O ye righteous,
    And give thanks to His holy name.*

To the saints of God such a truth as this psalm dwells upon is more than a matter of intellectual approval. Truth affects life in various ways if all is right. For one thing, to love such a Lord leads men to depart from evil and hate it. This is what the psalm, therefore, encourages all such to do. More than that. They are reassured that the Lord that rules so effectively also makes His control felt for good in their own lives by guarding them against all danger and delivering them from the power of the wicked. The blessings they enjoy may, therefore, be summed up thus: "light," that is, fortunate and blessed experiences, is continually prepared for them so that it springs up and becomes fruitful in their lives. This is expressed in a rather bold figure which asserts that "light is sown for the upright." The "gladness" that is mentioned as the second thing that is sown for them signifies all manner of pleasant and joyful evidences of divine providence.

Having such a God as their God, the righteous are, therefore, bidden to rejoice in the Lord and to give thanks to His holy name. Such thanks will be an ample token that they have rightly grasped the truth involved.

NOTES

The fact that this psalm, too, is a mosaic, being made up of one quotation after the other, becomes apparent if we but note the following: on v. 2 cf. Deut. 5:19; on v. 3, Ps. 50:3; v. 4 is taken from Ps. 77:18; with v. 5, Mic. 1:4 and 4:13 may be compared; v. 6 is taken from Ps. 50:6; v. 7 is related to Is. 42:17; in v. 9 both Ps. 83:18 and 47:10 are involved; on v. 11 cf. Ps. 112:4, and on v. 12, Ps. 32:11 and 30:5. Despite the high ratio of quotations the work of weaving them together into a homogeneous whole is so skillfully done that the whole psalm makes the impression of being an original composition. So thoroughly were some of the Old Testament psalmists familiar with earlier psalms, and so completely had they assimilated what they knew.

3. There is no good reason for changing "His adversaries" to "His steps" in the Hebrew text and giving another meaning to the verb. It would appear to be a part of the trend of modern thinking to remove every possible trace of divine wrath from the concept of the deity.

4. We translated the last verb "trembled in awe" to avoid the connotation of a mere physical shaking of the ground.

7. By inserting an "already" before the verb ("bowed") we feel

we have captured the force of the Hebrew perfect a bit more adequately.

8. "Daughters of Judah" in the sense of her villages appears, e.g., in Josh. 15:45 and Jer. 49:2.

10. Those interpreters who believe that an exhortation to hate all evil is out of place at this point will alter the text to arrive at the result: "The Lord loves those who hate evil" (*RSV*). In place of the forceful statement of the Hebrew text a mild platitude is obtained by such a change.

12. The familiar "at the remembrance of His holiness" (*KJ*) does not catch the force of the Hebrew. As *BDB* well remarks, the second meaning of *zékher* nearly equals the word "name," and he cites as examples Prov. 10:7; cf., Eccl. 9:5. We have, therefore, translated: "And give thanks to His holy name." The *Targum* also points in this direction with its rendering: "Give thanks at the remembrance of His holy name."

Psalm 98

PRAISE THE LORD, THE JUDGE

THIS PSALM is characterized by a tone of exuberant praise. The occasion for its composition is apparently the deliverance of Israel from Babylonian Captivity. The reason for regarding this event as the event that gave rise to this psalm of praise is the fact that quite a few statements in the psalm are obviously quoted from Is. 40–66, where the constant theme is this very deliverance. Though this event is not referred to in plain terms it may yet be said continually to be in the background of the psalm. In substantiation of the claim that Isaiah the prophet is being quoted it would suffice to note the following: 1b is to be compared with Is. 59:16 and 63:5; v. 2 rests on Is. 52:10; v. 3 on Is. 63:7; v. 6 is reminiscent of Is. 6:5, and v. 8 appears to have Is. 55:12 in mind.

There is one feature which is quite unique as far as the structure of this psalm is concerned: the specific occasion for praise that the psalm mentions is held in reserve until the very last verse. But even in that verse it is not a specific historical event that is mentioned but a general work, the work of judgment. Thus far the point involved is this: if we are correct in our initial claim that deliverance from Babylonian Captivity directly occasioned the psalm, this deliverance is viewed from the broader point of view of being a notable act of judgment. In the event God has come for judgment, which judgment, however, appears under a double aspect: first as the judgment that humbled Babylon, then as the judgment that raised Israel out of the dust. Judgment has these two aspects. But the writer does not stop short with this thought but sees in the one significant act of judgment a prelude and guaranty of future judgments in which God will act righteously and ultimately the very last judgment itself as the climax.

Almost equally unique is the further thought that such judgment is a matter for which God is greatly to be praised, in other words, Judgment has something constructive about it. It accomplishes so much of lasting good that men should rejoice exceedingly that the Lord does judge. The servile fear of the unregenerate and the typical approach of our day to the very idea of judgment are quite foreign to the thinking of this psalm.

A few additional comments are in place. We regard the rather popular approach of our day in reference to this psalm quite unfortunate, the approach, namely, that regards it as a psalm that reflects the enthronement of Yahweh festival, of which Israel's sacred writings give no evidence in spite of the many dozens of passages that are currently cited as evidence.

We mention it chiefly as a matter of curiosity that this is the only psalm which has as a heading merely the word "a psalm."

a) **A summons to praise God for a mighty work done for Israel (vv. 1–3)**

1. *O sing unto the Lord a new song, for He has done marvelous things;*
   His right hand and His holy arm have gotten Him the victory.
2. *The Lord has made known His victory;*
   In the sight of the heathen He has displayed His righteousness.
3. *He has remembered His loyalty and His faithfulness to the house of Israel;*
   All the ends of the earth have seen the victory of our God.

This psalm begins and ends like Ps. 96. The marvelous thing that the Lord has done for Israel is a remarkable display of His omnipotent power or of the strength of His holy arm. Not without reason this restoration of Israel is said to have taken place in the sight of the heathen, for the heathen nations had never witnessed an instance when a displaced nation came back to its own land and was restored to national unity. As a result the nations were compelled to admit that Israel's God could do marvelous things. When this work is described as being a display of righteousness, that merely suggests that righteousness is apparently something like the energy with which God upholds His promises to His people Israel. This gracious work of deliverance is rightly traced back to promises and pledges given by God to His own in days of old.

b) **How this praise is to be rendered (vv. 4–6)**
4. Shout aloud to the Lord, all the earth;
   Rejoice, exult, and sing praises.
5. Sing praises to the Lord with the lyre;
   With the lyre and the sound of a song,
6. With trumpets and the sound of a horn
   Make a joyful noise before the King, the Lord.

It is a rather universalistic approach when this psalm suggests that what happened to Israel is of sufficient importance to all the earth to induce it to share in the praises that are due to the Lord. Every type of musical instrument is to be employed in giving expression to proper praise. In terms of our day, it would take a symphony orchestra to do justice to the exuberance of the praise that should be offered on this occasion. In fact, as the next section suggests, only a symphony orchestra of stupendous proportions could do justice to this task, for all the forces of nature (vv. 7, 8) are to be drafted to take part in the paean of praise. Rare and very proper poetry finds expression in v. 8 when the rivers are said to clap their hands (the lapping of the waves), and the very mountains are bidden to exult together in their towering majesty.

c) **A summons to all nature to participate in this praise (vv. 7, 8)**
7. Let the sea thunder and that which fills it,
   The world and those that live in it.
8. Let the rivers clap their hands;
   Let the mountains exult together.

d) **The specific occasion for all this thanksgiving is finally stated (v. 9)**
9. Before the Lord, for He comes to judge the earth;
   He will judge the world with righteousness and the peoples with equity.

Let the thought of this last verse be added to what was said above: righteousness obviously implies setting all things right. Let it also be pointed out that no more fitting interpretation could be given of the words, "He comes to judge the earth," than to refer them to the very event just witnessed in so impressive a fashion by Israel when the Lord redeemed His people from Babylon. In that event the writer sees a judging of the earth even though only that part of the earth was involved that had a bearing upon Israel's future. He also expresses the conviction that a final and great judgment will come upon the earth when those things that were adjusted but in part will meet a final and complete adjustment—a hope that is surely to be held fast in the fear of the Lord.

NOTES

1. When we translate *hoshi 'ah-lo,* "have gotten Him the victory," we are well aware of the fact that the verb really means "has wrought deliverance" or the like. But in this case the emphasis seems to rest more on what was achieved than on the evil from which deliverance was secured. *Luther* seems to have blazed the trail for the "victory" idea (*Er sieget mit seiner Rechten*); he was followed by *KJ; RSV* did well to remain in the line of this tradition.

3. It seems a bit artificial always to translate the *chesedh* of God for His people as "steadfast love" as *RSV* usually prefers. We felt that in this connection "loyalty" helped catch some of the other rich implications of this term.

6. Though it is a minor matter, the Hebrew has "before the King, the Lord," not as *Luther* and *KJ* translate: "the Lord, The King." What the original order of the words makes more emphatic is God's effective governance of the affairs of this world, a thought that is expressed by putting the "king" first.

Psalm 99

LET MEN PRAISE THE HOLY ONE OF ISRAEL

IT IS QUITE OBVIOUS that this psalm has points of contact with the other psalms that are found in this part of the Psalter: it emphasizes the thought that the Lord is King in the same manner as do Ps. 93, Ps. 97, and Ps. 98:6. But it has a distinctive character all its own. For first of all, the reaction of the "peoples" to God's kingship is thought of as being one more of awe than of joy. Then as to structure, this psalm loves to repeat the refrain, "Holy is He"—which helps to determine the caption of the psalm. This refrain is threefold (vv. 3, 5, 9). It then has some allusions to three prominent historical characters (vv. 6, 7). In addition, the psalm indicates that the reaction of the Lord to the deeds of men may be twofold, depending on men's attitude toward the Holy God (v. 8).

As to the time of the composition of the psalm we must exercise a measure of restraint because no man can arrive at any conclusion that may be demonstrated as being correct. Some possibilities may be slightly more plausible than are others. The thought that the Lord must have done something to demonstrate the effectiveness of His rule gave rise to the suggestion that the psalm should be dated after the deliverance from Sennacherib's invasion. One equally vague point of contact is the question whether the psalm indicates that the ark of the covenant no longer existed, for it is known to have been lost in the destruction of Jerusalem in the days of Nebuchadnezzar. It will, perhaps, suffice to assume that, since all the psalms from 93–100 seem to fit into the time of the Restoration, this psalm, too, may well be thought of as belonging to this period.

1. *The Lord is king; let the peoples tremble;*
   He is seated above the cherubim; let the earth shake.
2. *The Lord is great in Zion;*
   And high is He above all the peoples.
3. *Let them praise Thy great and terrible name:*
   "Holy is He!"

These words appear especially to stress the thought of the majestic greatness of Israel's holy God. He is king and has, it would seem, but recently again given a clear indication as to how effectually He reigns. In the mind of His worshipers He sits enthroned above the cherubim. It will be difficult for us to determine whether the poet has the sanctuary in Jerusalem in mind or the heavenly sanctuary where these symbolic beings are especially real. Exegetically it will be almost impossible to determine whether we should translate, "let the peoples tremble," or, "the peoples tremble." Both translations make such very good sense. The nations do and should tremble.

A solemn awe governs this approach of the psalm. His greatness has been manifested in unusual ways in Zion, the place of His own choice, and there His unique exaltation has been felt most keenly. We have the same problem here that we had in v. 1: Are the people being exhorted or is their natural reaction being recorded? As our translation shows, we are still inclined mildly in the direction of the exhortation. It seems a bit more effective to regard the last words, "Holy is He," as the acclaim that the peoples utter rather than as a reflection of the psalmist. It is direct discourse without the formal introduction that usually accompanies it. In this brief statement there is summed up that aspect of the divine majesty which is to be especially stressed: He is "holy." That does not signify that He is sinless, but that He is removed from and far above all those limitations and imperfections that mark man.

b) **His just rule merits high praise (vv. 4, 5)**

   4. *And the strength of the king is that he loves justice;*
      Thou indeed hast established equity;
      Thou hast executed justice and righteousness in Jacob.
   5. *Exalt the Lord, our God; and worship at His footstool;*
      "Holy is He."

Another divine attribute is referred to which also merits notice and high praise—God's justice. For a king He is, and this is a most notable quality of any king or, as the thought is here phrased in the form of a general principle: "The strength of the king is that he loves justice." We understand "the king" to mean "any king." But what applies to all applies specifically to the greatest of all. Whereas justice is a splendid attribute, its companion, "equity"— fair, straightforward dealing —is also to be noted. Manifestations of these attributes of the Lord God of Israel have been abundantly in evidence "in Jacob" as her history so richly declares.

Thus Israel is urged to make this aspect of the divine being the theme of its worshipful adoration at God's footstool. It might be debated as to whether the "footstool" of God refers to the earth (as it does in Is. 66:1), or to Zion (as it apparently does in Is. 60:13), or even specifically to the ark itself (as in I Chron. 28:2). It seems to be most fitting to regard this as a reference to the very throne of God in heaven before which the devout worshiper feels that he steps when he rightly worships the Lord. In any case, our lowly posture at the footstool reflects the humility which marks all true worshipers. We again believe that the refrain is to be thought of as the very praise by which the Lord is to be exalted.

c) **His readiness to hear, to forgive, and to punish (vv. 6–9)**

   6. *Moses and Aaron among His priests and Samuel among those*
         that called upon His name—
      These men cried unto the Lord, and He Himself answered them.
   7. *In the pillar of the cloud He spoke to them;*
      They kept His testimonies and the ordinance that He gave them.
   8. *O Lord, our God, Thou didst answer them;*
      Thou wast a God that forgavest them
      Though Thou didst take vengeance on their evil deeds.
   9. *Exalt the Lord, our God, and worship at His holy mountain,*
      For holy is the Lord, our God.

6. The heart of this section appears to be v. 8, which stresses certain further qualities of the Lord that should induce men to praise Him. They are: He answers prayer, He forgives, and He punishes wickedness. All of these are remarkable and wonderful attributes of the divine being. The first of these is set forth in greater detail by reference to three notable examples of men who excelled in prayer. Why just these three should be grouped together we can scarcely determine. Moses was obviously exceptionally great as a man of prayer (cf., Exod. 33:12ff.; 17:10ff.; Ps. 90). In regard to Samuel we may compare I Sam. 7:5ff.; 12:18ff. For Aaron we can cite only Num. 16: 44–48. The response of God was particularly striking in that He actually spoke from the cloud in dealing with Moses and Aaron (to Samuel this does not seem to apply directly). Who would deny that those noteworthy instances of God's answers to prayer deserve particular mention and special praise? The psalmist deems it worthy of note that these men whom God heard did not render themselves unworthy of being answered but "kept His testimonies and the ordinance that He gave them." Sanctity of life has also been a mark of great men of prayer.

8. With wonder the writer again exclaims over the fact that God did consider them worthy of an answer (v. 8), and he then adds a fact that is even greater: He forgave them. In fact, holy as their life may have been, it had many a weakness and fault in it, for which they had to be forgiven if God was to hear them. For a full statement of the case it should also be noted that He is not a God who shows partiality. He, therefore, also took vengeance on their evil deeds. A number of references indicate what sins of these men of God are under consideration (cf., Exod. 32:35; Num. 20:12; Deut. 3:23–27; 9:20). Rightly viewed, His punitive justice redounds to His honor also, and for it He is to be praised.

9. So then, since praise is the keynote of the psalm, and God's holiness is its theme, the last verse brings all this into clear focus: "Exalt the Lord, our God, and worship at His holy mountain, for holy is the Lord, our God."

NOTES

4. Almost all modern commentators feel compelled to resort to some emendation of the text at the beginning of this verse. Two possibilities of retaining the text intact deserve consideration. *Hengstenberg* construed the words as follows (assuming that the relative had been dropped as is often the case in the Hebrew): "And the strength of the king, who loves justice: Thou hast established equity." In other words, in place of the colon we might have inserted an "is." But even

better than this is the suggestion of *Koenig,* who translates much as we do: "And the strength of the king is that he loves justice." To account for the "that" in his translation *Koenig* suggests that there may have been haplography (a single writing) of the letter *k* which concludes the word for king (*melek*)—a manner of writing that is occasionally found in the Hebrew text. That *k* would represent the *ki* in the defective style of writing which was employed before the vowels came to be used. We believe this translation is to be preferred to all other attempts to solve the difficulty of the passage. Luther's: *Im Reiche dieses Koenigs hat man das Recht lieb* (In the realm of this king men love justice) is altogether too free. *KJ:* "The king's strength also loveth justice" is quite obscure.

Psalm 100

AN EXHORTATION TO WORSHIP

IN THE INTERPRETATION of this psalm much depends on determining to whom the initial summons of v. 1 is addressed. We have our choice of one of two possibilities: we either follow *KJ* (et al.), "Make a joyful noice unto the Lord, all ye lands," or we follow those who translate, "Shout aloud to the Lord, all ye inhabitants of the land." All the earth is exhorted or only those who dwell in all the land of Israel. As far as the Hebrew word that is used is concerned, one possibility is as feasible as the other; it can mean "earth" or "land." Since in the rest of the psalm Israel is specifically addressed, and the inhabitants of all the earth are totally ignored, we feel compelled to follow the second school of thought and to regard the psalm as being addressed to the chosen people. The more universalistic note that addresses all the inhabitants of the earth is found, for example, in the two preceding psalms and in many other instances in the Scriptures. Our psalm prefers to address a narrower circle.

The liturgical interpretation is quite generally again insisted upon. Whereas we cannot deny that the psalm could lend itself to a variety of liturgical uses, we also draw attention to the fact that scarcely any two interpreters who follow the liturgical approach see eye to eye as to the number of choruses involved, the place where the psalm is to be rendered, the specific purpose to be thought of. In fact, quite a bewildering array of differences is encountered in this area. Under those

Psalm 100

circumstances it will scarcely do to insist on this type of interpretation.

When the psalm is viewed as an exhortation to worship in a more or less general sense, this does justice to all the facts of the case. In fact, we may discern two separate summons, the first of which might be described as a summons to glad worship of Him who is Israel's Maker, the second as a summons to bless Him for His goodness. It will at once be noted that there are many other possibilities in the area of worship. Our psalm has concern for only these two points of view.

This psalm concludes the group which began with Ps. 91. An interesting study could be made as to what these psalms have in common and in what respects they differ. Each interpreter who is interested in making such a study can easily assemble the requisite material. We feel that such an effort lies outside the scope of our present study.

The heading given in the text is: *A Psalm of Thanksgiving*. The last word can mean "a thankoffering" that is brought as a sacrifice upon the altar. If that were the intended meaning of the term, we feel that there would be some statement in the rest of the psalm that would point in this direction. The parallelism of v. 4 points rather in the direction of plain "thanksgiving," and to this meaning we shall adhere.

1. *Shout aloud to the Lord, all ye inhabitants of the land.*
2. *Serve the Lord with gladness;*
   Come into His presence with jubilation.
3. *Know that the Lord is God;*
   It is He that has made us and not we ourselves;
   We are His people and the sheep of His pasture.
4. *Enter into His gates with thanksgiving and into His courts with praise;*
   Give thanks unto Him and bless His name!
5. *For the Lord is good, His steadfast love endures forever*
   And His faithfulness to all generations.

1. The initial verse has been likened to a single trumpet blast (*Delitzsch*) that calls the worshipers of the Lord together from all the corners of the land. The word "serve" that introduces v. 2 is a reference to the service that is offered in public worship. The distinctive feature about this summons is the fact that it exhorts that such service be marked by joy and gladness, for it is in reality a happy matter. Solemn though it may be, when God's own come into His presence, joy should never be absent.

3. As is usually the case when the verb "know" is used, it involves a deeper knowledge which includes complete inner acceptance of the truth which is acknowledged. In that spirit the fact that the Lord is God and none other is here set forth. But if He is the only one to whom

the concept God may be applied, then to Him must be attributed the fact that Israel has become God's people: He made it such, and He alone, not they or any achievement that they were able to present. (On this interpretation of the last words see the Notes).

What He made them to be was "His people and the sheep of His pasture." This statement is meaningful even if one does not resort to the idea that it was sung by the national group of worshipers as they came streaming through the Temple doors and into the sanctuary, giving the impression that they were like a flock which was following the shepherd's call. What a rare privilege that was to be singled out from among all the nations on the face of the earth to be in a very special sense God's people and His only people! No man who weighs this fact aright can remain cold and unresponsive.

4. Entirely parallel with the first summons is the second (vv. 4, 5); for "entering His gates" is obviously to be thought of as being done for the purpose of "serving Him." Whereas joy had been stressed in the first call to worship, it is now thanksgiving, which is just as important and may also be included in the idea of "blessing His name."

5. The particular qualities of God that are especially stressed in this verse center around the idea that Israel is God's people, and that this is a lasting relationship even as His faithfulness cannot change. It is for gifts that endure into the eternities that praise and thanksgiving in a special sense should be offered.

Strangely, all the aspects of worship that this psalm stresses are constant factors that deserve to be noted wherever and whenever God's people come together. That is the timeless feature of this psalm.

NOTES

3. The words *welo' 'anachnu* are one of the fifteen instances noted by the Jewish grammarians (see *GK* 103g) when two like-sounding words may have been confused— *lo* and *lo'*. The text reads: "and not we ourselves." The suggested correction reads: "and to Him we (belong)," or: "and His we are." This latter reading is quite commonly accepted, and it is usually claimed that it fits the situation much better. We do not believe that to be the case. Since the pronoun subject of the preceding clause is expressed, there is nothing that quite catches that emphasis as well as does the contrast between: *He* made us and not *we* ourselves, which is the traditional text.

Psalm 101

THE IDEAL RULER

It must still be maintained that "the contents of this psalm go far toward confirming the correctness of the superscription in ascribing it to David" (*Maclaren*). If we attempt to select some particular time in the reign of David, the evidence available does not point toward the beginning of his reign, when on general principles a pronouncement such as this could be very appropriate. Since the psalm seems to contain a direct allusion to a particular episode in David's life, the time when David was well established on the throne might be most suitable. When the psalm asks. "O when wilt Thou come to me?" (v. 2), this statement says in effect what David uttered at the time when he almost despaired of ever having the ark of the Lord, the very symbol of His presence among His people, come to Jerusalem. For he exclaimed after the Uzzah incident, which had so shocked the whole nation: "How can the ark of the Lord come to me?" (II Sam. 6:9). To David the presence of the ark and the presence of the Lord were synonymous.

We may mention further points that agree with the life and conduct of David as we know it. When v. 2 speaks of the discreet attention that David purposes to give to blameless conduct, the very same verb is used in I Sam. 18:14, 15, where David is said to have "behaved himself wisely in all his ways." Long before he ever became king, blameless conduct was his idea and a pattern of life that was consistently followed. Furthermore, a similar description of a man whom the Lord will allow to come into His presence in the sanctuary as it is given in Ps. 15 agrees so obviously with our psalm that it may well be claimed that consistent objectives of the life of David are here being set forth. To all this must be added the fact that the earlier years of David's reign were well known to have been irreproachable: David practiced what he preached.

We are, therefore, justified in arriving at the conclusion that we have in this psalm "a mirror for magistrates" (*ein Regentenspiegel*) as *Luther* already maintained. There is not enough evidence to warrant the conclusion that this psalm was, so to speak, a liturgical piece, "a part of the annually recurring festal liturgy of the autumnal New Year"

(*Leslie*). For this can be claimed only on the basis of a number of unproven conjectures which mount high at this point when the claim is made that the following three Biblically unmentioned festivals coincided: the New Year's celebration, the enthronement of Yahweh festival, and the enthronement of Israel's (or Judah's) king. *Taylor* comes much closer to the point at issue when he suggests the title, "Moral Ideals of a King."

As we present the following outline for the psalm we suggest that the first subhead is formulated as it is, not on the basis of the first verse alone, but on the trend of thought of the entire psalm.

a) Kindness and justice are the objectives of a good ruler (v. 1).
b) This must be in evidence in his own personal behavior (vv. 2–4).
c) It must be true in what he requires of those about him (vv. 5–8).

The psalm has the heading: *Of David. A psalm.* As already indicated, there is no reason for doubting the correctness of this superscription.

1. *Kindness and justice are the theme of my song;*
   To Thee, O Lord, will I (thus) tender praise.

As one looks at the first line of the psalm only one might be inclined to raise the question: Are God's "kindness and justice" under consideration or man's? For on other occasions these two attributes are ascribed specifically to God, cf. Ps. 89:14. But it is equally true that in Is. 16:5 the same qualities are set forth as being distinctive of good human rule. Besides, the rest of the psalm makes it entirely clear that these qualities in so far as they are in evidence in a worthy ruler's life are under consideration. In fact, by describing what he himself intends to practice David sets down a pattern of godly conduct for all rulers.

It must be immediately apparent that these two traits in the conduct of a man reciprocally check one another. Kindness prevents justice from becoming too harsh; justice saves kindness from becoming flabby. Thus it becomes apparent in what sense the poet makes these two qualities "the theme of his song." All that follows is a detailed description of what belongs under this head.

It will be noted that in the second half of the verse we have inserted a "thus" in parenthesis because we are in this way able to indicate the relation of the two halves of the verse to one another. For 1b is not a separate announcement that the psalmist aims to write a psalm that is expressly a psalm of praise, but he does have the intention of letting his description of the ideal ruler be sung to the honor of God. For the verb that we have rendered "tender praise" is the one that usually means "sing a psalm" but may also be rendered "magnify God through song and music" (*Gott durch Gesang und Spiel verherrlichen—Buhl*). So the Mirror for Magistrates indirectly redounds to the praise of God, who inspires such ideals and gives such enlightened insight.

> 2. *I will give discreet attention to blameless conduct.*
> *Oh, when wilt Thou come to me?*
> *I will walk in the integrity of my heart within my own house.*
> 3. *I will not consider any worthless undertaking;*
> *I hate the doings of those who fall away;*
> *Such things shall not cling to me.*
> 4. *A perverted heart shall depart from me;*
> *I will not acknowledge a wicked person.*

2. The royal singer begins very properly by outlining what his personal conduct ought to be. We translated, "give discreet attention to" because the verb means to behave oneself wisely. As pointed out above, this resolution may have reached a climax as the result of the previous attempt to bring the ark of the Lord up to the capital city, when Uzzah was struck dead, and the whole nation was warned that the Lord and His worship were to be taken seriously (II Sam. 6:1–11). This experience caused David seriously to wonder if his goal of finding a house for the ark in the new capital (v. 2b) would ever be achieved.

He realizes that blameless conduct on his part and that of the nation is a prerequisite for the fulfilment of his ambition. For this reason, it appears, this brief question is injected into the middle of the verse. The former train of thought is then resumed, in which the author expresses his resolution that, as far as he is concerned, he shall study to show himself above reproach in his personal family life. For all outward manifestations of irreproachable conduct are hollow if they are not accompanied by the same irreproachableness in the immediate family circle. But even there it must be more than the observance of certain outward conventions; the situation demands "integrity of heart."

3. Unfolding this pattern of personal conduct more fully, the psalmist indicates what type of projects are to engage his attention: never "any worthless undertaking." In this general category belongs the question of the writer's attitude toward apostates, "those who fall away," for such unreliable conduct should be abhorred by any right-thinking man. Speaking still more strongly, he will not allow such an attitude to cling to him. That is to say, he intends to make it quite plain that he will have no association with those who become untrue to the Lord. There must have been many worthless men in Jerusalem and elsewhere in David's day, and it was his duty to let men know how he felt about this class of evildoers.

4. At first glance it might appear as if this verse began to consider

others more than the psalmist himself. On second thought, however, the claim that "a wicked heart shall depart" from him does seem to imply that he on his part will not let a wicked heart be his. In a similar manner the second half of the verse may then be considered as presenting a further attitude on his part toward wicked persons: he "will not acknowledge" them. This statement means that he will not concede that such people are friends or intimates of his. Disavowal of evil men is as important as are the acceptance and acknowledgment of those who are true and upright.

Thus the holy writer has sketched briefly what belongs to true integrity and blamelessness of conduct. This is his ideal, and the major part of his reign furnished the proof as to how sincerely he meant what he said here.

5. Him that secretely slanders his neighbor I will destroy;
   Him that has a proud look and an arrogant mind I cannot tolerate.
6. My eyes are upon the faithful in the land that they may dwell with me;
   He that walks in a perfect way, he shall serve me.
7. A man that practices treachery shall not dwell in my house;
   A man that tells lies shall not stay in my presence.
8. Every morning I will destroy all the wicked in the land
   In order to cut off all evildoers out of the city of the Lord.

5. Even as a man should be meticulous about his own conduct, so, if he occupies a prominent public office, he should exercise extreme caution in the choice of his associates and, for that matter, in the whole issue of the individuals whom he tolerates at court. To express high ideals in this respect is not vainglorious or self-righteous but is the equivalent of a proclamation of public policy to be followed by a man while he is in office. If wicked men have played an important part in governmental affairs they must be publicly disavowed. That is what the psalmist does here.

If he seems particularly severe in his attitude toward slanderers, it must be remembered that they are character assassins, and that slanders spoken about men in high places often led to the execution of those who were slandered. David, therefore, apparently threatens to do nothing worse than the persons in question themselves have been quilty of. For that matter, royal courts have almost universally been hotbeds of intrigue. To the slanderer are added two classes of men at court with whom the king is utterly out of sympathy : the proud and the arrogant. The one betrays his attitude by his manner of looking ("proud look") and the other by his thinking ("arrogant mind"—Hebrew: heart).

6. After the negative side of this issue has been stated, the positive

follows almost of necessity. Whom does the king favor? Who are the men whom he loves to have about him? First of all, "the faithful in the land" whom he loves to have dwell with him or to be found in his immediate presence. In the Hebrew the idea of "faithful" is linked with the concept of "faith" just as it is in the corresponding English words. The parallel statement brings into the picture the man "that walks in a perfect way." In this expression the emphasis is not so much on absolute perfection as it is on well-rounded character. Such men the king will choose to "serve" him in various public offices and in manifold duties great and small.

7. The last two verses revert to what the king purposes to do with wicked men whom he finds at court. When one considers the fact that the psalms so frequently make an issue of various kinds of evildoers that seem to have caused godly kings difficulty one can well understand that this must have been one of the foremost problems that engaged the attention of good men. So, then, a treacherous man, once his character becomes apparent, shall have no place in the king's company; and similarly the liar shall also be put aside.

8. On the face of it the next statement could create the impression that the good writer is for the moment being carried away by his own eloquence on the subject when he promises to destroy all the wicked every morning. But a careful consideration of the customs that prevailed in days of old will reveal that Oriental tradition made the king also a judge who disposed of cases daily, beginning the sessions of his court for this purpose early in the morning (cf., II Sam. 15:2). An equivalent expression for "every morning" would, therefore, be: "each time the king conducts court trials." To cherish the purpose of disposing effectively of all the wicked, whom the proper trials reveal to be such, is, therefore, nothing less than a wholesome ambition. The writer himself, however, discloses what goal he has in mind as he thus vigorously upholds the cause of justice in the land. His aim is "to cut off all evildoers out of the city of the Lord." More and more, as time went on, it became customary to call the new capital, Jerusalem, "the city of the Lord" (cf., Ps. 46:4; 48:1, 8; Is. 1:26). Life and conduct in the holy city should do honor to Him to whom the city is dedicated and after whom it is named.

All in all it must be admitted that the king set a praiseworthy goal for himself as he went about carrying out the duties of his office. What this good goal is he has here described.

NOTES

3. "The doings" is a construct infinitive for *'asoth. Setim* is a noun that is dependent on the infinitive, the infinitive being regarded as a noun in the construct state. The subject of *yidhbaq* would be an "it"

whose antecedent is this same infinitive. To avoid misunderstanding we substituted "such things" for "it."

5. *Melawshni* is a sort of poel participle derived from the root *lashan,* cf., the noun *lashown* (tongue) Thus the verb refers to the improper use of the tongue. The final *i* is an old case ending, and the participle is in the construct state which is followed by a phrase.

8. In *labbeqarim* the article is the article of totality, which imparts to the phrase the meaning "*every* morning." *KS* 301b.

Psalm 102

A PLEA FOR HELP
ADDRESSED TO THE ETERNAL GOD

THERE IS an obvious unity of parts in this psalm which makes it appear as a well-integrated whole. This will become clearer when we examine a brief outline.
a) The psalmist's plea for help (vv. 1, 2)
b) His wretched lot, which forced this plea from him (vv. 3–11)
c) God's readiness to help both him and Zion as the reason that the psalmist approaches God (vv. 12–22)
d) A renewed complaint addressed to the Eternal One (vv. 23–28)

It would appear to be quite natural, after having uttered a plea for help, to indicate what it is that disturbs the one who prays. When God's readiness to help is then reflected on at greater length, that is the natural thing to do when a man attempts to regain his assurance. Such assurance is built on the very strength of the living God. Thus far the psalmist has presented both direct and indirect reasons for his prayer. When after such an approach the writer reverts to the matter that afflicts him, that is but natural, for a single effort at prayer does not always produce the desired results. When in that last appeal to God the chief point of view kept in mind regarding the Lord is the fact of His eternity, that shows what kind of foundation the writer is seeking for his weak faith.

Though the personal note is very much in evidence throughout this psalm, this is not the only note that may be observed. It appears that the writer is also deeply concerned about the welfare of Zion. In fact, it may even be possible that the wretched state of Zion is part of the affliction that bears the psalmist down. That, however, need not at all mar the unity of the psalm. For surely, the writer would not be the first man who had his private affliction made heavier by the lowly estate of the church at a given time. Both afflictions grieve him.

The heading of the psalm centers attention on the personal side of the writer's difficulty when it reads: *"A prayer of an afflicted man when he is overwhelmed and pours out his complaint before the Lord."* An almost apologetic note appears here, as much as to say: If all that is said in the following is not all that might be hoped for, let it be remembered that the writer was weak and borne down to earth by adversity. There is not enough evidence in the psalm to warrant the conclusion that its author was suffering from an intestinal ailment (*Ehrlich*).

We note in the case of this psalmist also that he had apparently nurtured his piety by the use of earlier psalms which he quotes with indications that he had absorbed the spirit of what had been offered by those that preceded him. We shall assemble the evidence briefly: v. 2 strikes a similar note to Ps. 27:9 and 69:17; v. 2b reminds one of 31:2; v. 3 rather clearly resembles 37:20; v. 12 is like Lam. 5:19; v. 19 recalls 14:2 and 33:13; cf. also Is. 63:15; v. 20 alludes to 79:11; and v. 28 is akin to 69:35f. That does not make the writer "a cold-blooded compiler," as *Maclaren* says, "weaving a web from old threads, but a suffering man." Why should the later psalm writers not use what their predecessors had written?

The church has through the centuries listed our psalm among the penitential psalms. This classification should not be abandoned. For, as *Weiser* has pointed out, though lament and petition predominate over against the note of repentance, the thought of humbly bowing down under the judgment of God is clearly set forth in vv. 10 and 24. To this *Vilmar* adds the suggestion that this is the only penitential psalm which sounds the distinctive note that death is the wages of sin (see again v. 20).

It has become quite the order of the day to question the unity of this psalm and to point to the section vv. 12–22 as being a heterogeneous element that was presumably borrowed from another source or was at least composed at some earlier time by the same writer. But the weight of evidence pointing in this direction is not very substantial.

As one reflects on another commonly accepted possibility, namely, that this psalm dates from the time of the Exile and, perhaps, shortly before the time when the rebuilding of Jerusalem and the Temple began one may feel attracted to a possibility that grows out of *Koenig's* approach, that the words, "He has weakened my strength in the way," point to a sickness that befell one of the returnees on the way back from Babylon. This was what occasioned the prayer, it is claimed. However, this possibility is scarcely more than a mere likelihood.

One further remark about the heading. Some commentators would translate, "for an afflicted man," and thus arrive at the conclusion that the heading indicates the devotional use to which the psalm is to be put rather than the situation out of which it grew. This is, however, scarcely the case as we shall show in the *Notes*.

a) The psalmist's plea for help (vv. 1, 2)
1. Lord, hear my prayer;
   Let my plea for help come unto Thee!
2. Hide not Thy face from me in the day of my distress;
   Incline Thy ear unto me;
   In the day when I cry unto Thee answer me speedily.

This plea for help begins the psalm, a common beginning in the very nature of the case. The first utterances are very brief. Asking to be heard is not the outgrowth of expecting not to be heard but rather an effective way of recalling that God is ready to hear. The five separate petitions are practically the same request. They reflect nothing more than an attempt to acquire certainty about being heard. The fact that some doubts may have assailed the writer is also quite likely. The fact that he quotes more or less from other psalms shows how very useful the knowledge of good devotional helps may be in a day when it is doubly difficult to pray original prayers.

b) His wretched lot, which forced this plea from him (vv. 3–11)
3. For my days have wasted away like smoke;
   And as for my bones, they are charred as on a hearth.
4. My heart is smitten and withered like grass,
   For I have even forgotten to eat my food.
5. Because of my loud groans
   My bones cleave to my flesh.
6. I have become like a pelican in the wilderness;
   I have become as an owl in the ruins.
7. I cannot sleep
   And am become like a lone bird on the housetop.
8. My enemies continually taunt me;
   Those mad against me curse by me.
9. For I eat ashes like bread
   And mingle tears with my drink
10. Because of Thy indignation and anger,
    For Thou hast picked me up and flung me away.
11. My days are like a lengthening shadow;
    And I wither away like grass.

When the psalmists, as is so often the case, present a rather detailed account of their sufferings and wretchedness, this is not done because they were of the opinion that the Lord was not aware of their situation. Since they knew that they had permission to pray to the Lord they felt that they could with full freedom, approach the Lord and tell Him all that burdened them. For they must have known, as we do, that to get a burden off one's heart and mind provides a good measure of relief. Besides, they may well have known that they were writing for generations of God's children yet to be born, and that it would be a comfort to such readers if many years afterward they found that the sufferers of old had the same difficulties that men now have.

3. In Ps. 37:20 the writer describes one's wasting away as smoke as being the lot of the wicked. The writer of this psalm is thinking that at the present time his situation is no better. His physical affliction must have been great if his bones feel as though they had been "charred as on a hearth." The heart (v. 4) seems to be regarded as the seat of the deepest thoughts and emotions. All these seem to be utterly withered as grass that is burned by the heat of the sun. As evidence of this the psalmist points to the fact that for some time food has had no appeal for him.

5. Like a typical Oriental, the writer did not hestitate to give vent to his feelings by "loud groans" ("the sound of my groan" as the expression reads literally). To these loud groans he ascribes the feeling of utter weakness that weighs him down, though it was, no doubt, his ailment as such that did it, whatever that may have been. When bones "cleave to the flesh," that seems to mean that strength has so completely left him that the bones cannot drag the rest of the body along. To this must be added the great loneliness (v. 6) that affliction often brings with it. The point of the comparison with the pelican and the owl is that these are birds that seek lonely haunts even though it is not possible to identify the bird we have called the pelican with absolute certainty.

7. When insomnia is added to a long list of other afflictions it becomes very burdensome. After mentioning it, however, the writer reverts to his loneliness with an expression that has become more or less proverbial—"like a lone bird on the housetop," where especially the sparrow may be found in the Holy Land. A far more painful trouble is the mockery of heartless enemies who pour out a continual stream of taunts. In fact, some of them go so far as to make his name a term to curse by, for he appears like a man who has been cursed above all other men. So heavy is his burden. The writer's sufferings do not evoke the pity of those who have worked themselves into a very dither of madness.

9. One thing that seems to lend color to the charge that the psalmist is, indeed, a cursed man is the fact that he sits on an ash heap, as men in their affliction often did. It seemed to him that the very ashes became mingled with his food while his tears dropped into the cup from which

he drank. One who was thus afflicted might well have appeared to be a singular example that demonstrated how God may curse guilty men.

10. There follows the most painful complaint of all when, on the one hand, the writer describes his lot as being that of a man whom God had picked up and thrown away and, on the other hand, says that such an action on God's part was done in "indignation and anger." This last phrase implies that, if God is angered, man has done that which has provoked His anger. There is an admission of sinfulness and guilt at this point. This thought had kept the writer from charging God too bitterly. His suffering was merited.

11. Largely because of this anger on the part of God the writer sees his life gradually fading out like "a lengthening shadow" which, when the sun has completely sunk, will have vanished entirely. The note of complaint has been rather subdued throughout. There is no bitterness; no wild accusations are hurled at high heaven. Still the writer's lot is one that clearly requires divine help.

c) **God's readiness to help both the psalmist and Zion as the reason that he approaches God (vv. 13-22)**

12. But Thou, O Lord, wilt sit enthroned forever;
    And Thy remembrance shall endure from generation to generation.
13. Thou wilt arise and have mercy upon Zion,
    For the time to show mercy, yea, the set time has come.
14. For Thy servants delight in her very stones
    And have pity on her dust.
15. So the heathen shall fear the name of the Lord
    And all the kings of the earth Thy glory.
16. For the Lord builds Zion;
    He appears in His glory.
17. He turns Himself to the prayer of the destitute
    And does not despise their prayer.
18. This shall be written for the generation to come;
    And the people who shall yet be created shall praise the Lord.
19. For He has looked down from His holy height;
    Out of heaven did the Lord regard the earth;
20. To hear the groans of the prisoner,
    To set free those that are doomed to die,
21. That men may declare in Zion the name of the Lord
    And His praise in Jerusalem
22. When the people gather together
    And the kingdoms, to serve the Lord.

Psalm 102

12. As the writer turns to the subject of God's readiness to help, his first statement reflects on the eternity of God and thus makes a striking contrast to the close of the preceding section in which man's brevity of life had been set forth in a colorful way—he is like a lengthening shadow which is soon to be lost in the shades of night. God not only endure forever, but He "will sit enthroned forever," having all things perpetually under control, and as such He will be remembered from generation to generation. This aspect of His being shall never fade from the minds of men.

13. Having once been appealed to, this unchanging God will in due time act as He has been known to act: He will "arise and have mercy upon Zion." When the writer asserts in a somewhat positive way that the time to "show mercy" has come—for that matter, even "the set time"—he is not at this point trying to impose his wishes on God. He must, however, have had adequate reasons for such an assertion. The one statement of Scripture that would allow for such a claim as this without involving human presumption could well be Jer. 29:10, which indicates how long God will let the Babylonian Captivity continue before He will restore Israel to its own land. God Himself had set the time when His judgment would have run its full course.

14. An added motive for granting this request lies in the fact that the psalmist himself as well as all those who were of like mind with him loved even the very rubble of the ruined site of the holy city, "her very stones" and "her dust." Such love for God's ancient city is touching, and seeing that He Himself loves it, He cannot refuse their petition.

15. The writer goes on to unfold those results that the restoration will bring about (vv. 15–17). It will bring about a fear of the name of the Lord on the part of the heathen, for they will become aware of the fact that the Lord's power is far above what any other god, so-called, was able to accomplish. The same conviction shall come home to those who stand in high positions in this world, kings, men who are in a position to judge and evaluate unusual occurrences when they encounter them. The rebuilding of the holy city, when it occurs, will seem as if the Lord Himself had done the work. It will be such a manifestation of what the Lord can do that men may well exclaim that "He appears in His glory" when this restoration takes place. We cannot help but take note of the fact that the love for God's city is strong in the writer. Among those servants that may be said to love the stones and the dust of Zion (v. 14) he himself is, no doubt, to be found.

17. Another way of describing the restoration of Jerusalem is to say that the Lord hears the prayers of His children: "He turns Himself to the prayer of the destitute and does not despise their prayer." When

such blessings as restoration fall to the lot of the church, the prayers of God's children had a notable part to play in the process. The word "prayer" appears twice in this verse and puts an emphasis on just plain prayer as such, a fact which is obscured by the translation of the *RSV*.

18. At this point the writer turns to an evaluation of the restoration, which he is sure will take place soon, and indicates that it will become a matter of perpetual record, reduced to writing, for that matter, "for the generation to come." Those who witness it shall deem it so precious that they shall be at pains to see to it that proper records of this marvelous act are made and transmitted. He also believes that for many a generation to come there will always be those among God's people who will keep praising the Lord for what He did. With the passing of time other events may become dwarfed in the minds of men. Not so this restoration.

19. He then goes on to present a further appreciation of this act. It is as though God, who is greatly exalted and dwells in high heaven, had looked down from His dwelling place and taken note of what transpires on earth; He had more particularly noted how the prisoner among the captives of Israel had groaned under his burden of captivity; and God had noted how miserable he was and had stooped to set him free though, humanly speaking, he would have appeared as one who was doomed to die.

21. All this He had done with the very intent and purpose that in Zion itself men might declare in their praises how great the name or character of God actually is and might praise Him in His holy city. At this point an exceptional broadening of the writer's vision takes place, and the oft-revealed truth of the prophetic writers comes home to him with new force.

22. He sees how all manner of people and kingdoms assemble at Jerusalem to join in the worship of the true and living God. When they utter their praises they will include among them a commemoration of this restoration for which he so earnestly longs, and for which he so confidently hopes. Though this statement seems to make the worship of God on the part of many nations in days to come center in the physical Jerusalem, this is only an incidental feature of the picture that need not be stressed as being essential.

It will again be noted throughout this section that private grief has merged with the grief over the lot of the holy city, and relief from the one is thought of as being combined with relief from the other.

d) A renewed complaint addressed to the Eternal One (vv. 23–28)

23. *He has weakened my strength in the way;*
He has cut short my days.

Psalm 102 713

24. *I said: "O my God, take me not away in the midst of my days;*
    Thy years are throughout all generations!"
25. *Of old Thou hast laid the foundations of the earth;*
    And the heavens are the work of Thy hands.
26. *They shall perish, but Thou shalt endure;*
    All of them will wear out like a garment.
    As a raiment Thou shalt change them, and they shall be changed.
27. *But Thou art the same;*
    And Thy years have no end.
28. *The children of Thy servants shall abide;*
    And their descendants shall be established before Thee.

23. Moods fluctuate, and assurance may often fade and merge into complaint. From the higher level of the preceding section the psalmist drops to the point of voicing his griefs and sorrows, which have not yet been completely overcome. To begin with, it still seems as though the nature of his affliction is such that his life will be shortened by whatever now burdens him. As he goes along life's "way" he finds himself much weakened. He even faces the prospect that his days will not reach the hoped-for number; in fact, that his life may be considerably shortened.

24. This leads to the prayer that such may not prove to be the case. We can well understand this Old Testament prayer when we remember that in days of old men did not have a clear light of revelation as to the nature of the life of God's children with Him after they depart this earthly life. Besides, it must be remembered that life itself was regarded as a great blessing from God, and a normal span of days was a grace bestowed by God. To this may be added the thought that an early death may prevent a man from achieving in the course of his lifetime those things that he might normally be expected to accomplish. Therefore he prays for the gift of the full measure of his days. After this prayer has been voiced, the psalmist finds himself carried away by the thought of God's eternity which alone can make something of man's finiteness. In fact, he breaks forth in eloquent praise of both God's eternity and His changelessness (24b–27).

25. The basic assertion is: "Thy years are throughout all generations." God outlasts all of mankind, to put it very prosily. This statement ends the exclamation that came from his lips when the feeling of his wretchedness again overwhelmed him. He now adds (vv. 25–28) some further observations which develop at some length the thought of God's eternity as it stands forth all the more clearly in the light of the impermanence and frailty of the whole framework of this old earth. In doing this he stresses the fact that the earth and the heavens owe

their very existence to God from the very moment they came into being. He laid the foundations of the earth; the heavens are the work of His hands. This visible earth is much inferior to Him who is its Creator. But more than that: all of this physical universe is destined to pass away whereas He cannot do otherwise than continue forever and ever. Speaking figuratively, as a garment gradually wears thinner and thinner with use and must ultimately be discarded and replaced by another, so the visible heavens and earth will also in due time wear out, perish, and be changed. All this seems to point to the conviction of Old Testament and New Testament writers that the old earth must perish before the new one can come into being. Cf. Is. 54:10; Matt. 24:35; Luke 21:33; II Pet. 3:7, 10, 11.

27. As for God Himself, He remains immutable and eternal. "But Thou art the same; and Thy years have no end." Yet it is not this doctrine itself that especially interests the psalmist but rather its practical implications. Chief of these is the implication (v. 28) that the race of the godly goes on and on. It is not exterminated nor overcome but is rather endlessly established before the Lord. This conclusion is rather remarkable in that the writer seems far less concerned as to whether he himself shall be rescued and survive or not. The fact that the generations of God's children continue, that is important. In other words, if he must perish, well and good, as long as God's people or His holy church continues to exist. How early or how late God's help will come is far less important than is the fact that it will come. On this note of confidence the psalm closes.

NOTES

Coming back to the heading, the chief reason that the translation should read, "the prayer of an afflicted man" and not "for an afflicted man" is that, when the preposition *le* is used in headings, it regularly indicates authorship. In this case the author refers to himself in a somewhat impersonal fashion, for he is the representative of a class, all of whom may have the same experience.

3. The Hebrew says "as a hearth," omitting the preposition after the "as." We say: "as *on* a hearth."

4. The "for" of the second clause is not causal but helps to introduce an adverbial clause of evidence.

8. For "those mad against me" the Hebrew uses a unique conciseness of expression by attaching a suffix to the participle to take the place of a preposition. *KS* 23.

18. The passive participle *nibhra'* is practically the equivalent of a future perfect. Cf. *GK* 116e and *KS* 237d.

20. For "doomed to die" the Hebrew has an idiom all its own, "sons of dying," which has passed over into the German *Kinder des Todes.*

27. For "Thou art the same" the Hebrew has, "Thou art He." Luther made this expression more idiomatic by translating, "Thou abidest as Thou art," *Du aber bleibest wie du bist.* The *KJ* and the *RSV* are very good.

Psalm 103

PRAISE FOR THE MERCIES OF THE LORD

THIS PSALM may well be called a pure note of praise. It has an undercurrent of soberness at one point, but that does not cancel the correctness of *Maclaren's* remark: "There are no clouds in the horizon, nor notes of sadness in the music, of this psalm. No purer outburst of thankfulness enriches the church." As it progresses this psalm swells into ever fuller chords of the praise of the Almighty.

Though it has long been quite fashionable to deny the possibility of Davidic authorship to this psalm, there is still sufficient reason for holding the old Jewish tradition, indicated in the heading. The so-called Aramaisms are never a sure index of date. Because of similarities with words of Job or of the second half of Isaiah it does not follow that our psalm was written later than these. It may be the original from which the other two borrowed. To tell the truth, little is gained by assigning it an earlier or a later date.

The personal note is in evidence, especially in the opening verses of the psalm; but the words do not confine themselves to that aspect of the case. The writer takes the attitude that what he has experienced is the personal experience of the nation in another form.

Nor is there any particular gain to be derived from the claim that this is a piece that was designed for liturgical use. Such a claim is assumption though it cannot be denied that liturgical use of the psalm could have been made. But equally correct is the claim that the psalm is beautifully adapted to personal use.

For once the claim that most psalms were designed for use on the fictitious festival of the enthronement of Yahweh is almost completely silent. Only by a *tour de force* can this song be thrust into such channels.

a) A self-exhortation to bless the Lord for all His benefits (vv. 1-5)

1. Bless the Lord, O my soul;
   And all that is within me bless His holy name.
2. Bless the Lord, O my soul,
   And forget not all His benefits;
3. Who forgives all your iniquity;
   Who heals all your diseases;
4. Who rescues your life from destruction;
   Who crowns you with steadfast love and mercies;
5. Who satisfies your mouth with good
   So that your mouth is renewed like the eagle's.

1. From time to time a man must bestir himself to offer praise to the Lord for the manifold blessings received. The writer feels the impulse to do this without apparently having been moved to do so by any one particular experience. The multitude of the Lord's mercies impresses him. In addressing himself to the task he seeks to enlist the help of his whole personality ("soul") and of his entire inner being ("all that is within me"). Both terms seem designed to avoid praise that is merely external in character. God's "name" is His character as He has revealed it to man in His dealings with him. This name is to be blessed.

2. The second summons to engage in this task grows out of the common experience that we are so very prone to forget especially those mercies that come to us often. Forgetfulness in this respect is a danger that is especially to be guarded against.

3. Among the separate blessings that especially call forth the praises of the Lord, forgiveness of our iniquities very properly stands first. There is no blessing that is greater in scope for poor sinners, nor any that is so entirely undeserved. This approach is an indication of deeper spiritual insight on the part of the writer. When diseases are mentioned next in order, it is only too true that recovery from grievous or ordinary diseases in always one of God's major blessings as we recognize especially at the time of recovery. To this must be added another evil from which deliverance has been experimental, namely, that He has rescued the man's life from "destruction," which refers to anything that might have destroyed his life and the things that are important to him, that is to say, any threatening calamity and not only the pit or the grave.

4. There follows an enumeration of certain major benefits that the Lord has bestowed in His mercy, for there is always abundant cause for praise both in the case of the evils from which we have been delivered as well as in the case of blessings that we have enjoyed. First among the latter is the great number of instances of steadfast love and

of mercies that the Lord uses to adorn His children with as with a crown of beauty upon their heads.

5. In addition He has again and again satisfied the longing of His children for good things of many a sort even as man's hunger is stilled by good food; and thus in consequence of the many wholesome things with which He feeds His children are enabled to go on with continually fresh strength even unto a great number of years as is the case with the sturdy eagle, whose life goes on for many a long year (Is. 40:31). This is a beautiful summary of all the good things that the psalmist was conscious of having received from God, and almost without exception God's children will always be able to find the same catalogue of blessings to be their own lot.

b) An exhortation to Israel to bless the Lord (vv. 6–13)

6. *The Lord executes righteousness*
   And justice for all that are oppressed.
7. *He made known His ways to Moses,*
   His acts to the children of Israel.
8. *The Lord is merciful and gracious,*
   Slow to anger and abounding in steadfast love.
9. *He will not always chide,*
   Nor will He keep His anger forever.
10. *He has not dealt with us according to our sins,*
    Nor rewarded us according to our iniquities.
11. *For as the heavens are high above the earth,*
    So great is His steadfast love to those who fear Him.
12. *As far as the east is from the west,*
    So far has He removed our transgressions from us.
13. *As a father pities his children,*
    The Lord has always pitied those who fear Him.

6. This section of the psalm is a broad background for the first section. The blessings that he personally enjoyed the writer sees against the background of his life in a nation that has also been the recipient of an unusual number of corporate blessings. These latter are also his because he belongs to this people. In addition, it should be noted that what the nation enjoyed is listed in a record of historical events that are the venerable tradition of this nation's past. A general statement opens the catalogue of the national blessings for which the Lord is to be praised: God is the Deliverer of "all who are oppressed." This is not based merely on an experience that was shared by a few. The *nation* was once in bondage—for it is back into the Mosaic days to which this word of retrospect goes—and the Lord manifested both His *righteousness,* that is, the vigor with which He maintains His covenant

obligations, and His *justice,* that is, the fairness with which He upholds the rights of those who have been wronged. The specific action referred to is the deliverance from Egyptian bondage.

7. A further blessing for which the nation should never fail to be thankful is that "He made known His ways to Moses," which statement should apparently be judged in the light of the prayer made by Moses in Exod. 33:13, where "ways" must mean "His methods of dealing with men" (*Kirkpatrick*) and not the ways that He would have them go. For this latter interpretation is scarcely in line with the second half of the verse, where "His acts to the children of Israel" must refer to the things that He had done for His people in leading and guiding them. These gracious ways in which the nation has been led are blessings for which God should be thanked.

8. From thsee more individual considerations the writer broadens his thinking to the point where he reflects on the whole nature and being of God, the chief attribute of which must for poor sinners always be the fact that "He is merciful and gracious" a statement which appears to be an obvious quotation from Exod. 34:6. For it must be remembered that the sentence which is being quoted is God's own statement in which He conveyed to man a revelation of His inmost being. A significant negative concept is injected at this point, the thought, namely, that this God is "slow to anger." Of that quality of His the nation also has had abundant proofs. To state it positively, He is "abounding in steadfast love." This, then, is the broad, comprehensive picture of the Lord that the psalmist is drawing, and which he regards as living in the consciousness and experience of the children of Israel.

9. The psalmist proceeds to make a fuller statement of this glorious truth about the Lord that dwells in Israel. This means, among other things, that the Lord "will not always chide," (cf. Is. 57:16). According to the peculiar flavor of the verb used, this means that, whereas the Lord would have a legitimate cause for striving with Israel, He does not carry this through to the bitter end. Another way of stating the case would be: He does "not keep His anger forever."

10. Many a time Israel has seen Him not exercise the measure of anger that a given case in her history would have warranted. Wording the case somewhat more specifically in terms of sin and what it merits, the writer arrives at the classic formulation: "He has not dealt with us according to our sin, nor rewarded us according to our iniquities." What more could be said by way of grateful acknowledgment of the Lord's steadfast love?

11. Ah, yes! one might attempt to extol the vastness of this love more fully by several comparisons that have a tremendous sweep. One such comparison would reflect on the incalculable distance between

Psalm 103

the heavens above and the earth. To our limited human sight that distance spells infinitude. But that, as a very proper phrase interjected at this point reminds all readers, is an aspect of the character of the Lord with which only "those who fear Him" may comfort themselves. The psalmist would not carelessly give unwarranted comfort to persons who are careless about sin.

12. A second comparison follows. Its sweep is as vast as that of the first— "as far as the east is from the west." That marks the distance at which He has put our sins away from us.

13. But the third comparison is the most effective of all: "as a father pities his children." That brings a touch into the picture that almost all of mankind immediately appreciates. The force of the application of this comparison gains a special emphasis in the Hebrew in that a tense form is used that stresses the fact that the Lord "has *always* pitied those who fear Him." The Lord has a long record among His own of pardons freely bestowed. But again, as in v. 11, only those who have becoming reverence for God (i.e., "fear" Him) dare hope to share in this rich mercy of God.

c) **God's consideration shown for man's frailty (vv. 14–18)**

14. *For He knows our frame;*
    He remembers that we are dust.
15. *As for man—his days are like grass;*
    As the flower of the field, so he flourishes.
16. *When the wind passes over it, it is gone;*
    And its place knows it no more.
17. *But the steadfast love of the Lord is from everlasting to everlasting upon those who fear Him;*
    And His righteousness to children's children
18. *Of those who keep His covenant*
    And of those who remember His precepts to do them.

The Lord is being thanked because He shows so great consideration for man's frailty. The contrast is this: just as frail as man on his part is, so exceedingly great in compassion with this frail being is the Lord on His part. The one is so very frail; the Other is so amazingly great.

God must know how weak man is, for He made this feeble frame of ours (v. 14). He who made us will scarcely forget that He made us of dust, and that the mark of our origin will ever be upon us. Being made of such constituent parts, the span of man's life or "his days" (v. 15) are aptly compared to that very perishable substance called "grass," which in the dry Orient is so often of such short duration. It flourishes a short time, and so does he. It takes no more than the passing of the hot wind of the desert over it on certain hot days, and the grass (i.e., all vegetation above ground) is gone, and its place knows it no more (cf. Is. 40:6–8).

This bit of sober reflection helps to set into more powerful contrast the emphasis on God's "steadfast love" that is to follow. Quite appropriately the sentence that conveys this emphasis is the longest line in the psalm as though the magnitude of his subject swept the writer away into a richer and fuller statement of the grand subject that engages his thinking. But again, and now for the third time, there is that careful reminder that only those who have the true fear of God in their hearts dare comfort themselves with God's forgiving mercy. In terms that are reminiscent of Exod. 20:6 the writer is pleased to recall that the abundant mercy of God overlaps from one generation to the other. We substituted "mercy" for "righteousness" only because the idiom of our day still associates too much of stern justice with righteousness and not so much of the gracious dealings that are also included in righteousness.

The eighteenth verse is a further strong reminder to all who read the psalm that the person who is grateful for the steadfast love of which the psalm sings produces the fruit of godliness by keeping the Lord's covenant and His commandments. But the basic thought was to show how beautifully the loving-kindness of God is made to stand out by virtue of the fact that it is bestowed upon the weak creature that seems to have so little claim upon such kindly treatment.

d) An exhortation for all that is in God's kingdom to bless Him (vv. 19–22)

19. *The Lord has established His throne in the heavens;*
    And His kingdom rules over all.
20. *Bless the Lord, O you His angels,*
    You mighty heroes who do His commandments, obeying the voice of His word.
21. *Bless the Lord, all His hosts,*
    You servants of His who carry out His will.
22. *Bless the Lord, all His works, in all places of His dominion;*
    Bless the Lord, O my soul!

In traversing the ground that the psalmist has covered by recalling those things that call for praise he seems to be so deeply impressed by the magnitude of praise that the goodness of the Lord merits that he feels inclined to call upon all who could in one way or another contribute to produce adequate praise. He begins by reminding himself how wide the sweep of the Lord's kingdom is. His kingdom rules over all, and His throne is established in the high heavens. No praise can be too great for such a king.

The summons that are now addressed to one group after the other to contribute to the Lord's praise grow out of the consciousness that all of those things and beings that God has created constitute one vast harmonious order, where all are minded as he is to sing the praises of the Almighty. The consciousness of the unity of the church above and the church below is in the background of his approach. There are first the great and holy angels themselves (v. 20), these mighty heroes, whose business it is to "do His commandments, obeying the voice of His word." It is not presumption on the psalmist's part thus to address these superior beings. The consciousness of being part of the same great church makes him feel that they are of one mind with him in this matter. Since they have been privileged to serve Him and to know the wonders of His gracious will as a result of such service, the psalmist knows that they will readily follow his suggestion.

God's "hosts" are then summoned to do their part. We are inclined toward the opinion that this term refers to the celestial bodies as this usage is reflected in Deut. 4:19 and many other passages rather than to have it refer, as the term well could, to the holy angels who have already been addressed. In the functions that they perform these heavenly bodies are in manifold ways "servants of His who carry out His will" as Gen. 1:16ff. indicates. In what way they are to bless the Lord need not be more fully defined in a poetic passage such as this. And should anything that God has created have been passed by, a summary exhortation to "all His works" rounds out the possibilities for "all places of His dominion." But the psalmist is intent on fulfilling his own great obligation over against his gracious Lord and so concludes: "Bless the Lord, O my soul."

NOTES

4. Though many interpreters prefer to render *shachath* as "the pit" and think of death and Sheol, "destruction" seems to be the broader and preferred meaning of the term. See *KW* p. 495.

8. In "slow to anger" the Hebrew uses the construct relationship instead of an accusative of specification. See *KS* 336h.

13. We have rendered *rich(ch)am* as a perfect of experience and therefore, "has always pitied." *KS* 126.

16. It is possible, of course, to understand *bo,* a masculine, in the sense of "over him" and thus refer it to man. We prefer to refer it to the grass last mentioned in the preceding verse.

Psalm 104

THE CREATOR'S MARVELOUS GREATNESS

THIS STRIKINGLY beautiful psalm is a fine companion piece to the one that precedes it; both are exuberant in the praise of God.

Shall we accept what the Greek and the Latin versions give as the heading—"a psalm of David"? There seems to be no internal evidence whatever that points in this direction, and so we shall have to classify our psalm among the "orphans."

What is its relation to the creation account found in Gen. 1? This psalm is not based directly on this Scripture passage, but it does show familiarity with it and may well be regarded as a free treatment of the known facts of creation with particular attention to various other factors that the concise account of Gen. 1 could not have brought into the picture. The poet is writing this psalm, not the writer who records strictly factual material. Yet he does not consider the beauty of the various aspects of creation from the purely esthetic point of view. Nor, for that matter, do we have what might be called a "nature hymn." For nature regarded as an independent entity that operates on its own, and is governed solely by some omnipotent laws is quite foreign to the Biblical way of thinking, which sees God's hand in all the processes that we call natural.

As to the question, How much of the mythological is to be found in this psalm? the statement of *Weiser* may be referred to as being a fairly adequate statement of the case: "From the palette of nature mythology, which maintains itself longest in the language of the cultus, the author has taken his colors, and using them, has painted his picture that completely overcomes every feature that could be labelled 'heathen-mythology' and serves the purpose of representing one thought only: This world of ours was created for one purpose, and that is that God made it exclusively for His own sake."

A question that cannot be ignored is the one that seeks to determine the relation of this psalm to "The Hymn to the Aton" (see *Ancient Near Eastern Texts,* ed. *Pritchard,* p. 370–371). The fact that is most commonly referred to in this connection is the manner in which these two hymns correspond with each other. Though some measure of similarity cannot be denied, and though these similarities may even be regarded as being somewhat striking, it is equally true upon closer inspection that the dissimilarities between the two poems are more striking. Chief of these is the fact that the Egyptian hymn regards the sun as a god who seems to control almost all vital functions. There is always the possibility that either author may have known the other's production and may have in a measure been influenced by it. But the main emphasis set forth by the two is radically different, and so to think in terms of dependence of the Psalm on the Hymn becomes almost absurd.

It will be almost impossible to determine whether the psalm was designed primarily for cultic or for individual use. The fact that it contains some obvious traits that point to a Palestinian background is almost unavoidable (*Schmidt*).

Whether the whole is a kind of allegory, which sets forth the basic thought that, as God is well able to control the forces of nature, so He is also quite able to control all human agencies that are hostile to His oppressed church (*Hengstenberg*)—this may well be questioned, for there is nothing in the psalm that would indicate this as its purpose. Anyone who desires to make a practical application of this sort will be free to do so without being in a position to claim that such a conclusion lay within the original purpose of the psalm.

a) God's marvelous greatness (v. 1)

1. *Bless the Lord, O my soul!*
   O Lord, my God, Thou art very great;
   Thou art clothed with honor and majesty.

The opening line, which is almost identical with the closing line of the psalm, is not strictly of one piece with the psalm and could be regarded as a kind of afterthought. However, it is just as reasonable to suppose that the original writer himself added both as a personal reminder that so great a God should be blessed by himself personally. Claims about later additions to the psalm here and elsewhere are based on subjective opinions. The theme itself is very clearly set forth, God's superlative greatness. As the psalm advances, it becomes apparent that God the Creator is referred to. A paraphrase of the same thought is the statement: "Thou art clothed with honor and majesty." From this point onward a rather natural pattern of thought is followed. Since God is a mighty monarch, those things that are commonly observed about monarchs will be found about Him, too: His robe, palace, chariot, court attendants, and the like.

b) His relation to the light (v. 2a)

2a. *Who didst deck Thyself with light as with a garment.*

This brief verse parallels the work of the first day of creation. This is all that is to be said as to how light is related to God. That is quite enough. One brilliant thought is offered. The ethereal substance called light alone is to be considered worthy to clothe God, who is a spirit. *Maclaren* says very aptly: "The Uncreated Light, who is darkness to our eyes, arrays Himself in created light, which reveals while it veils Him." *Luther* simplifies the thought but retains its full beauty: *Licht ist dein Kleid, das du anhast* (The vestment that You are wearing is light).

c) His relation to the heavens (vv. 2b–4)

2b. *Who didst spread out the heavens as a tent curtain;*
3. *Who did build His roof chambers upon the waters;*
Who made the thick clouds His chariot;
Who marched along on the wings of the wind;
4. *Who made the winds His messengers,*
Flaming fire His ministers.

2. Since God's relation to the heavens is being considered in its various aspects, this is a reference to the work of the second day of creation. Note the change in person in passing from vv. 2b to 3ff. The reason for this is that the Hebrew uses participles, which continue the person of the preceding finite verb. Presently the use of the second person goes over into the third, a change which the Hebrew does not consider irregular. Some translators prefer to change all forms to the second person (*RSV*). The Hebrew construction is unobjectionable.

3. The initial statement indicates the ease with which the Lord created the heavens. As a man erects his tent, so the Lord by a few simple movements erected the heavens. But from the third verse onward the writer does not seem to restrict himself to the works of creation. V. 3a still thinks in terms of what was done on that great second day: God built His heavenly habitation, here called "roof chambers" because it is an elevated structure like those rooms which Orientals built on the top of the flat roof for greater coolness. God's high palace, or rooms, extends over the entire heavens, and so the beams on which it rests must be laid on the waters that lie out on the horizon—the seven seas. This is a rather bold thought.

This royal monarch also has his royal equipage, His chariots on which He seems to ride from place to place, to speak humanly of the Omnipotent One; and these are the clouds. But this seems rather to be a reference to some historical event, that, namely, mentioned in Exod.

14:19, when from His "thick cloud" He guarded Israel against the Egyptians by interposing the cloud of His presence between His people and the enemy. Exod. 19:9 could serve as another illustration as to how the Almighty comes to men. For all that, the thought might still be that at the time of the creation of all things God formed the "thick clouds" also for this purpose. Another force that might serve as a means of transportation for Him may be "the wings of the wind." Whatever other purpose the wind may serve, this is its purpose in the direct service of the Creator.

4. Another aspect of these forces of nature is to be considered. The winds may also be said to have been created for the purpose of serving as God's messengers, whom He dispatches swiftly here and there to do His work (Ps. 148:8). And "flaming fire," that marvelous form of energy that Gen. 1 does not mention, belongs in this same category. The Lord makes it, too, His "minister" as Exod. 3:2 testifies concerning a later incident. Since all these forces move through the skies (clouds, winds, fire) they may well be listed in connection with the work of the second day.

d) His work of establishing land and sea (vv. 5-12)

5. *He based the earth on its foundations*
   That it should not be shaken forever and ever.
6. *As for the great deep—Thou didst spread it out as a garment;*
   The waters stood above the mountains.
7. *At Thy rebuke they fled;*
   At the sound of Thy thunder they hurried away in alarm.
8. *The mountains rose, the valleys sank down*
   To the place which Thou hadst founded for them.
9. *Thou didst set a boundary that they could not pass*
   That they might not return to cover the earth.
10. *He makes fountains to flow down as rivulets;*
    Between the hills they run along.
11. *They give drink to all the beasts of the field;*
    There the wild asses quench their thirst.
12. *Beside them dwell the birds of the heavens;*
    They sing among the branches.

5. On the third day of God's great creative work dry land and water were separated. This aspect of creation is now under consideration (vv. 5-9). The dry land is considered first. It is spoken of as "the earth," which seems in this case to be the equivalent of plain *terra firma*. On that day matter coagulated, so to speak, and the continents were formed and "based on (their) foundations that (they) should not be shaken forever." So efficiently was that part of the work done.

What sort of world picture the Scriptures seek to convey is a bit difficult to determine. No fixed doctrine is presented in any case. Two points of view seem to be regarded as being reasonable. Beyond these, God had no distinct revelation in days of old. One is that expressed in Job 26:7, where God is represented as hanging the earth upon nothing. The other is that reflected in the same book (38:6) where the earth rests on solidly established bases. Both points of view present some aspect of the truth. We still employ them. Our passage reflects the second point of view.

6. This verse describes how God dealt with the waters. The "great deep" (*tehom*) appears to represent the seven seas. They were spread out upon the surface of the earth "as a garment." That is a summary way of stating that aspect of the task. There follow certain colorful and poetic details as if the author had said: "This work could be visualized as follows," and then began to describe how, when the dry land had gathered together into one place, the waters at first still stood above the mountains. Or shall we say that all the acts described here took place simultaneously?

7. God then spoke a word of sharp rebuke that the waters might give way to the land, and as a result the waters "fled." Or since that rebuke was uttered with a voice of thunder, they are represented as "hurrying away in alarm" at the moment the word was spoken.

8. Simultaneously "the mountains rose," and "the valleys sank down." We can scarcely conceive the stupendous upheavals and readjustments that took place at that time and on so vast a scale. But none of this movement was left to blind chance: both mountains and valleys sought out the place that God had founded for them. Everything was continually under perfect divine control. Another possibility deserves mention here. V. 8a should, perhaps, be regarded as a parenthesis. Then the waters that hurried away (v. 7) go (v. 8) to the place founded for them. That seems to make things work out more smoothly.

9. An added thought is offered in this verse, a thought that is often presented in the Scriptures in one form or another. A boundary is set for the waters so that they never quite succeed in getting totally out of hand. Never again shall they cover the earth as they once did (Gen. 1:2). Cf., Gen. 8:21; 9:11; Is. 54:9; Jer. 5:22; Prov. 8:27–29; Job 38:8–11.

10. From this point to the end of the section the writer seems to depart from his contemplation of the work of creation and to busy himself with God's control of the waters on the face of the earth, for the many types of animal life that they may have a sufficiency of water to drink from the streams great and small that are fed by the fountains and

Psalm 104

regularly flow down the hillsides to the valleys, at least in the Holy Land with its many mountains. Two forms of animal life are mentioned in particular: the wild asses, which keep far from man; and the birds that sing in the branches and need water, too, though we may seldom see them drink. The passage has a gentle touch of poetry without dwelling on that which is beautiful only because it is beautiful. In all that transpires under this head the controlling divine activity is being underscored.

e) His work of providing vegetation (vv. 13–18)

13. *He waters the mountains from His upper chambers;*
    The earth is satisfied with the fruit of Thy work.
14. *He causes grass to grow for the cattle*
    And vegetation to be tended by man, to bring forth bread from the earth
15. *And wine which is to make glad the heart of man,*
    And oil which is to make his face to shine,
    And bread which is to strengthen the heart of man.
16. *The trees of the Lord have their fill of water,*
    The cedars of Lebanon which He planted.
17. *There the birds have their nests;*
    The stork has its dwelling in the cypress.
18. *The high mountains are for the mountain goats;*
    The rocks furnish a refuge for the badgers.

The work of the second half of the third day of creation interests the writer chiefly in this section, except that he combines with it the thought of the living beings that come into existence on the sixth day inasmuch as vegetation is the primary article of diet of these beings. So the sixth day gets only incidental attention.

13. This verse must be regarded as a sort of transitional verse. It leads over from the water to vegetation. Thus "the mountains" are here apparently the uplands where grain grows. There "the earth is satisfied with the fruit of God's work," this "work" being God's activity in providing water. When it is construed thus this verse leads over into v. 14 by a very natural progression of thought. Two classes of things that grow are considered: the "grass" which feeds the cattle and "the vegetation to be tended by man," which includes all that man raises for his own sustenance, "bread" being the equivalent of food.

15. Under the head of the food that is essential for man's well-being three items are mentioned which the ancients regarded as the most important: wine, oil, and bread. In a land where good drinking water did not abound, wine had to supplement to quench man's thirst When wine is thus moderately and regularly used, it is quite in order to de-

scribe one of the effects of its use as being "to make glad the heart of man," which is the most common Biblical approach to the evaluation of this gift of God.

17. Though the mightiest trees do not provide food for man they still have a particular use that was intended by Him that makes them grow. They provide a place where the birds of the heavens may have their nests. Since because of their size such trees display the power of the Lord, and also since they grow without being planted by man, they are aptly called "trees of the Lord"—a kind of superlative. That the need of water is again stressed, as it is repeatedly from v. 6 onward, is due to the fact that the Orientals appreciate especially the important function that water serves. In v. 17b the thought that it is the Lord who provides nesting places for the birds like the stork gives further emphasis to the all-inclusiveness of His providence. That thought is followed, not inaptly, by the further one that the mountains also furnish habitation for certain other creatures which, though they are remote from the habitations of man, are not forgotten by their Creator (v. 18).

f) The luminaries He made (vv. 19–23)

19. *He made the moon to mark certain seasons;*
    The sun, which knows its time for setting.
20. *When Thou makest darkness, and it is night,*
    Then all the beasts of the forest creep forth,
21. *Such as the young lions that roar after their prey,*
    And who are intent upon seeking their food from God.
22. *The sun rises;*
    They withdraw and lie down in their dens.
23. *Then man goes forth to his work*
    And to his labor until the evening.

19. In the pattern that the writer is following we have arrived at the fourth day's work of creation, the work of providing the heavenly bodies in their various functions. The beginning is made with the moon, perhaps because the Hebrew day began with the evening. This luminary shares in the work of marking "certain seasons" for the convenience and guidance of men (Eccles. 43:7), the sun being the sister luminary. When the setting of the latter is especially mentioned, that may in part be due to the fact that its setting prepares for the next verse, and partly because there is something noteworthy about the sun's regularity in setting.

20. A fact that is not too frequently noted by men but one that is worthy of consideration is to observe how particularly the beasts of the forest creep forth after darkness settles. Then creatures like the strong young lions go forth and roar after their prey. The more en-

Psalm 104

lightened way of stating the case is that they "are intent upon seeking their food from God." For in its own dumb way such a creature anticipates that He who made it will have provided for it. The very brevity of the description makes it the more impressive.

With the rising of the new sun all these creatures "withdraw and lie down in their dens." The rising of the sun serves as a signal for them to get off the scene. "Then man goes forth to his work and to his labor until the evening" (v. 23). The function of these heavenly bodies to mark time for man in his daily routine and also for the beasts is, perhaps, the most usual one and yet one that is not too often thought of as being regulated by the luminaries. This part of the account somehow always seems to strike a responsive chord in man's mind. But God's ordering of man's affairs is the chief issue. To make this impressive the psalm for a moment passes over into the second person (v. 20).

g) Praiseful reflection on the sea (vv. 24–36)

24. *O Lord, how manifold are Thy works!*
    In wisdom hast Thou made them all;
    The earth is full of Thy riches.
25. *There is the sea, great and wide in every direction, teeming with creatures without number,*
    Living things both great and small.
26. *There go the ships;*
    There is the whale whom Thou hast formed to frolic therein.

24. As was the case in the preceding section, when the sea is now thought of it is in relation to Him who made it so vast; and thus this section begins with an exclamation of thanksgiving. All this is, of course, a part of the work of the fifth day when the birds of the heaven and the fish of the sea were brought into being. The birds having been already discussed (v. 17), there are left the fish of the sea. But since God's work is being reflected on throughout, the writer cannot but inject the very proper observation, which is borne out by all that he has thus far set forth, that all of God's works have been made in wisdom (cf., Prov. 3:19), and that the earth is full of the manifold things that God has created. One is somewhat at a loss as to whether the Hebrew word involved should be translated "riches" or "creatures." Both meanings are well established.

26. But one cannot think only of the fact that the sea teems with all manner of life both great and small. The vastness of the sea keeps impressing the beholder each time he sees it. Two things particularly impressed this writer: the ships and the whales. Since the writer embellishes his description freely with many a unique detail, who is to pass judgment upon what he may introduce and what not? The word "ships"

need not be changed into "sea monsters" or the like even though this is the only man-made feature that has been introduced into this description. The whale is without a doubt the most impressive of the creatures of the sea. Quite aptly the psalmist states that God made him in the sea "to frolic therein." The whale gambols and disports himself in the deep and seems in his own way to have a remarkably good time.

h) God's relation to all living creatures (vv. 27-30)

27. *These all look to Thee*
    To give them their food in due season.
28. *Thou givest them; they gather it up;*
    Thou openest Thy hand; they are satisfied with good things.
29. *Thou hidest Thy face, they are terrified;*
    Thou takest away their breath, they die and return to their dust.
30. *Thou sendest forth Thy Spirit, they are created;*
    And Thou renewest the face of the ground.

27. In this description the emphasis is on the absolute dependence of all these creatures on God. The thought expressed in v. 21b is amplified so as to apply to all forms of wild life that have been mentioned. The world over living creatures are continually looking to heaven for food "in due season," that is, whenever these creatures need it. In a measure that surpasses our comprehension God gives them what they needs. *Luther* once remarked that the Lord must have a large kitchen. One aspect of the process is that these animals gather up what God gives them, some with more sense of good husbandry, some with less. Another aspect is that God opens His mighty hand into which He has snatched an amount of food from His rich storehouses. He drops before them what they need, and they are satisfied with good things. This is a picture that is drawn on so vast a scale that one scarcely knows whether one should be more amazed at the prolific imagination of the writer or at the abounding gifts of God.

29. There is another aspect of animal life: the dying of the old and the coming of the young and the new. That, too, is controlled by the working of the Almighty. All these live by the favor of His countenance. If He hides that countenance, they are terrified, their breath is taken away, they die, and return to their dust. On the other hand, the power of His Spirit goes forth to re-create animal life, and thus a new generation of beings appears on the face of the earth, and its whole appearance is renewed. These are not natural processes that go on endlessly and in their own strength. God the Creator still creates, and nothing even on this level comes into being except by the work of His life-giving Spirit—and here the Spirit is no doubt the personal Spirit of God Himself.

Psalm 104

i) Praiseful reflection on other forces imbedded in God's creation (vv. 31, 32)

31. May the glory of the Lord endure forever;
    May the Lord rejoice in His works,
32. He who looks upon the earth, and it trembles;
    He touches the mountains, and they smoke.

31. One cannot consider such mighty works of God for long without being moved to praise. It is as though the praise began at this point but is interrupted by a kind of afterthought concerning other impressive works that God brings to pass. The word of praise is in the nature of an earnest plea that such manifestations of God's glory as have been considered may never cease, and that the Almighty Himself may never cease to take pleasure in what He thus creates for the good of man, a thought that is analogous to Gen. 1:31.

32. The afterthought involves both earthquakes and volcanic eruptions. These are again not merely the operation of certain natural potencies that are imbedded in nature and are bound to appear by way of automatic reactions, though there is an element of this involved, too. The major thought is that even such powers operate only at the bidding of the Lord. A glance of His at the earth in displeasure, and there is an earthquake. So simple is the matter for Him. One Scriptural example is available, Exod. 14:24. As for the eruption of volcanoes, merely a touching of these mountains is required, and they burst forth with destructive force.

j) Resolution to praise the Creator (vv. 33, 34)

33. I will sing to the Lord as long as I live;
    I will praise my God while I have my being.
34. May my meditation be pleasing to Him;
    I will be glad in the Lord.

As the psalm draws to a close, the resolution to praise the Mighty Monarch of this earth finds strong expression. A lifetime of praise is necessary to do justice to such great works. Only those individuals will be minded thus who, having referred to "the Lord," can also speak of Him as: "my God." Even down to one's dying breath praise is fitting for creatures that are brought into being by such a Lord. Feeling for a moment how unworthy of so high and holy a purpose all our endeavors are, the psalmist adds the thought, "May my imperfect efforts find favor in His sight." Being sure also that they will be accepted, he reasserts that he for his part will be glad in the Lord, and that includes the fact that his joy will become vocal.

k) The one jarring note in God's creation—prayer for its removal (v. 35)

35. Let sinners vanish from the earth;
And let the wicked be no more.
Bless the Lord, O my soul! Praise the Lord.

A unique closing note, that is indicative of a clear sense of moral values, marks this psalm. There is a jarring note in God's creation. The writer seems to assume that all who read his psalm know about the fall. Since that time there have been sinners on God's good earth. To remove them will restore the harmony that all right-minded men long for. Though the psalmist prays thus in a somewhat sharp tone, we might do him an injustice if we went on the assumption that he has no interest in the conversion of sinners. This happier solution, we believe, is much to be preferred; but before Christ's redemption conversion was not too common. That left only the other alternative of the extinction of the wicked. Other psalms think in the same terms; cf., 1: 4–6; 5:5, 6; 37:38. In this psalm there is certainly no gloating over the final lot of the wicked.

The psalm rings out on a note of personal praise.

NOTES

4. Grammatically the translation offered by the *Septuagint* is as feasible as is the one we present. It is also followed by *KJ:* "Who maketh His angels spirits, His ministers a flaming fire." The fact that the New Testament seems to sanction this translation (Heb. 1:7) may have led to the perpetuation of this rendering. *Luther* also renders thus. However, to place the inanimate object first and the animate one as the factitive object agrees best with the context.

6. *Tehom* appears to be used as an independent nominative.

8. In the phrase "place which" *zeh* serves as the relative. Cf. *GK* 130c.

12. The final *qol* could well be read *qolam* by reading the initial letter of v. 13 twice. This would complete the Hebrew idiom involved.

14. The word *'abhodhath* could mean "for the service of man" (*KJ*). It can also mean "to be served by man." Our translation favors the latter.

15. We prefer to insert the relative pronoun after the nouns used and to make the nouns the object of the verb *matsmi(a)ch* (v. 14).

20. The initial verb in its jussive form is conditional. *GK* 159d; *KS* 193bc.

29. *Toseph,* sounding like *t'oseph,* is contracted from the latter form.

Psalm 105

THE LORD'S WONDERFUL WORKS
IN ISRAEL'S EARLY HISTORY

WHAT GOD DID for Israel in the early years of its history is related from the point of view of being a series of praiseworthy acts. This is quite obviously a psalm of thanksgiving as the keynote sounded in v. 1 immediately shows: "O give thanks unto the Lord." It is closely related to Ps. 106 and Ps. 78. The difference between this psalm and Ps. 106 is that in this psalm the note of praise predominates, and the eyes are continually fixed on the magnificence of the works of the Lord. In Ps. 106 there is more of the negative note; Israel's ingratitude and impenitence are strongly stressed. Thus these two psalms complement one another. Alone each one would present but a one-sided picture of what transpired in days of old. In Ps. 78 both these approaches are blended into one with special emphasis on the fact that God's mighty works are to be taught to the younger generation.

A psalm such as this could appropriately also be classified as being historical in character. It is noteworthy, however, that the author is quite free in his treatment of history. He does not bind himself to the letter of the record as this is found in the historical books of the canon. He inserts items that are either the product of a legitimate free play of the imagination or the outgrowth of a living tradition that survived in Israel.

Only those commentators who are committed to the idea that everything in the Psalter is designed for liturgical use will insist that this psalm was designed with such an objective in mind. That it may well lend itself to such use cannot be questioned. Equally dubious is the contention that it was designed for the Covenant Festival, which some interpreters feel they have discovered as being a major festival in Israel.

Many interpreters are of the opinion that the psalm was designed to offer encouragement to a discouraged people in the days after the Return from Exile, when nothing seemed to thrive in Israel. By glancing back at the manner in which God dealt with His people in days of old, the psalm would remind them that God never fails His own and is able to save to the uttermost all those that put their trust in Him. Though there is nothing in the psalm that would directly indicate that this is its purpose, it certainly cannot be questioned that the psalm would also have lent itself to such a use. Most writers are agreed that an exilic or postexilic date is quite likely, which view is supported by quotations from portions of the book of Isaiah.

There seems to be some reason for following the suggestion of those commentators who would detach the concluding "Hallelujah" from the preceding psalm and prefix it to this one and thus obtain the same type of opening that Ps. 106 has.

Vv. 1–15 are almost indentical with I Chron. 16:8–22. This psalm appears to be the original.

a) A summons to praise (vv. 1–5)

1. *O give thanks unto the Lord, proclaim His name;*
   Make known His deeds among the peoples.
2. *Sing unto Him, sing praises unto Him;*
   Tell of all His wonderful works.
3. *Make your boast of His holy name;*
   Let the heart of those that seek the Lord rejoice!
4. *Seek the Lord and His strength;*
   Seek His presence continually.
5. *Remember the wonderful works that He has done,*
   His signs and the verdicts of His mouth.

1. One cannot help but feel that the summons to praise is somewhat eloquent and exuberant. The writer has mighty works of God in mind, for which He is to be roundly praised. Tame, lukewarm praises are insufficient. The various possible shadings of praise are stressed as these are called for by what God has done for Israel. First of all, there is the giving of thanks itself, which always has some element of praise in it. Then there is the setting forth of God's remarkable character ("name") which He has manifested by His works. Then there is the giving of expression to the thought that God's deeds are too great to be kept silently in our mind (cf., Ps. 9:11). For that matter, they even deserve to be published abroad among "the peoples" all over the face of the earth, not "people" (*KJ*), which would be Israel. Besides, praise always seeks utterance to the accompaniment of melody and song, of which the unending theme is "His wonderful works." Cf., Is. 12:4; also the beginning of Ps. 106, 107, 136.

3. Among the forms of expression that deeply felt praise will find is also the making one's "boast of His holy name," that is, being in a wholesome sense proud and happy of knowing what manner of reputation the Lord has attained among His saints. Since such experiences are the lot only of those "that seek the Lord," they are bidden in a

particular sense to rejoice in their inmost thoughts and heart, for praise is always a happy exercise.

4. Two other features belong to thanksgiving that is fully rounded out: they are the unwavering seeking of God (v. 4) and the faithful remembrance of what He has done (v. 5). For such seeking of God is nothing other than maintaining continual and fresh fellowship with Him, the unfailing source of all our strength, and so this means drawing ever closer to Him ("seek His presence"). Though in the case of Israel God's great works included a large measure of very obvious "signs," a similar factor will always be involved in all of God's dealings with His children. This may, perhaps, be less obvious to the outsider, but it is nonetheless very real to the person involved. In Israel's case in particular there were "the verdicts or judgments of His mouth," which were, in the last analysis, the Ten Plagues, whereby His judgments were inflicted upon a stubborn nation and king: By this last turn of the thought the way is prepared for the recital of the history of the time of the patriarchs.

b) God's goodness to the patriarchs (vv. 6–15)

6. *O descendants of Abraham, His servant,*
   O children of Jacob, His chosen ones,
7. *He is the Lord, our God;*
   He judges over all the earth.
8. *He remembers His covenant forever,*
   The word that He commanded, for a thousand generations,
9. *The covenant which He made with Abraham*
   And His oath to Isaac.
10. *And He confirmed the same to Jacob for a statute,*
    To Israel for an everlasting covenant,
11. *Saying: "To you will I give the land of Canaan,*
    The portion which is your inheritance."
12. *When they were but few in number,*
    Of little importance and strangers in it;
13. *When they wandered about from one nation to another,*
    From one kingdom to another people,
14. *He allowed no one to oppress them;*
    He rebuked kings on their account:
15. *"Touch not My anointed ones*
    And do My prophets no harm."

6. The dominant thought in this summary of God's goodness in dealing with the patriarchs is that God made a covenant and adhered faithfully to it though the people involved could not always see that

such was the case. In v. 6 the parallelism might seem to suggest that "His chosen ones" should be corrected to read as a singular or else that "His servant" should be made an apposition to "descendants." But the text makes good sense as it stands. Special emphasis is to be given to the fact that Abraham was in a special sense to be described as God's servant; yet at the same time the whole nation was God's "chosen ones." Though He thus stands in a special relationship to Israel the true representatives of the nation never thought of Him as being merely a tribal God but rather one who "judges over all the earth" (to follow *Luther's* simpler version).

8. It would seem to be best to understand the phrase "for a thousand generations" as describing the length of time that God remembers: He was always mindful of the covenant. Cf., Lev. 26:42–45. That covenant was a marvelous and striking factor in the lives of the patriarchs; with no other person had God even entered into such an agreement, a divine promise that was solemnly supported by an oath. Abraham was the first to receive. It was then solemnly renewed to Isaac (Gen. 26:3). For Jacob it was re-established as an unalterable "statute" (Gen. 28:13; 35:12), and in Jacob, who also bore the name Israel, it became valid for the whole nation which bore the same name.

11. This verse would seem to indicate that the promise of the "land of Canaan" was an effective summary of all that God's covenant embodied. To show the effectiveness of the covenant, it is pointed out that the promises that it included might well have seemed impossible of realization, seeing that at the time of the giving of the promises, the children of Israel were so "few in number" and of seemingly "little importance" and only "strangers" in a land which was ultimately to become theirs. Furthermore, the fact that they seemed to be continually on the march, wandering from kingdom to kingdom and from nation to nation, seemed to indicate anything but fixed possession of the land. They seemed to be doomed to perpetual nomadism.

14. The fact that unusual good things were in prospect was already then being indicated by the gracious and quite undeserved manner in which God's protecting hand was held over these men of His choice (vv. 14, 15). On the one hand, He allowed none of the mighty and absolute monarchs of that time "to oppress them" (cf., Gen. 12:17; 20:3ff.) and on the other hand, He administered effective rebukes even to kings when they would have interfered with the life and safety of His chosen ones. At this point a free paraphrase of what God said in effect to the kings of that time is given: "Touch not My anointed ones." It is quite obvious that the patriarchs were not actually anointed as were kings, priests, and prophets of a later date. Yet there is evidence that they did have some measure of God's Holy Spirit, a fact which

Psalm 105

even a king like Pharaoh was able to detect (cf., Gen. 41:38). It was that gift which was in a special sense the essence of anointing (I Sam. 10:1–6). It is therefore, quite proper to designate these men as "anointed."

God also said in effect with reference to them: "Do my prophets no harm." Though they were not prophets in the later sense as being God's special mouthpieces to His people, they were the ones to whom the word of the Lord had been committed, and God Himself was pleased to describe one of them by this title to a heathen king (Gen. 20:7). Surely, this brief but effective summary of what God did for His own in patriarchal times is of such a nature as even now to stir our hearts to praise for His "wonderful works."

c) **His providential care of Joseph (vv. 16–22)**

16. *Moreover, He called a famine against the land,*
    And He destroyed the entire supply of bread.
17. *He sent a man on before them;*
    Joseph was sold as a slave.
18. *They forced his feet into fetters;*
    He was put into irons
19. *Until his word came true;*
    And the word of the Lord proved him to be right.
20. *The king sent and released him;*
    The ruler of the peoples set him free.
21. *He made him lord of his house*
    And ruler over all his possessions,
22. *To bind his princes to his person*
    And to teach his elders wisdom.

16. In dealing with the story of Joseph the writer makes the providential factor stand out more prominently even than the Genesis account does, by ascribing everything that took place to divine guidance. First of all, God let the famine come upon (better "against") the land, which resulted in the loss of the entire "supply of bread." Quite appropriately the Hebrew calls this "the staff of bread" (cf., Lev. 26:26; Is. 3:1), for mankind leans heavily on the bread supply for its very existence.

17. But that divine act was merely preliminary to the second which resulted in the selling of Joseph into slavery in Egypt that he might be at hand when the famine became a reality. Though the sacred record says nothing of Joseph's being shackled in the days when he was in prison, there is always the possibility that such treatment of prisoners was so commonly the case that it must have happened also to Joseph.

19. This unhappy situation in which Joseph found himself contin-

ued until the day came which vindicated in an unusual way the truth of what he had said about the meaning of Pharaoh's dreams. What God inspired him to say at that time "proved him to be right"—which form of statement stresses the fact that there must have been some measure of unbelief on the part of those at court when Joseph offered his interpretations about the seven years of plenty and the seven years of famine. Though this verse gave the result of this first episode, the author retraces his steps a bit when he especially stresses the fact that it was upon the commandment of the king, the ruler of peoples, that Joseph was liberated. Thus God bent the will of the mightiest on earth to His purpose when He was minded to liberate Israel or, for the present at least, was minded to provide for His own during the season of famine. With this in mind, Joseph's work as food administrator is not dwelt upon directly but rather the eminence of his position over against Egypt's mighty men. For Joseph ruled not only over the king's household but in effect also "over all his possessions."

Two unusual aspects of this phase of Joseph's work are stressed that might not have occurred to us, but the knowledge of which might well have lived in the valid traditions of Israel. The first is that the king himself bound "his princes to his (Joseph's) person." This possibility is surely included in Gen. 41:44. Next to the king's authority Joseph's was absolute in the land. The second aspect of it is that he was "to teach his elders wisdom" (*KJ* calls them "senators"). Certainly the wise administration of the food resources of the land may fall into the category of "wisdom." In reflecting upon the episode of Joseph in her history Israel might well feel its heart beat higher at the thought of the great things God did in those days.

d) His providential care during the sojourn in Egypt (vv. 23–25)

23. *Then Israel came to Egypt;*
    And Jacob sojourned in the land of Ham.
24. *And God made His people very fruitful;*
    He even made them stronger than their foes.
25. *He turned their hearts to hate His people,*
    To deal treacherously with His servants.

The long stay in Egypt is described in a very concise fashion. Israel's exceptionally prolific growth in numbers is, as in the book of Exodus, ascribed to the providence of God (Exod. 1:7, 9). The net result is stated in rather strong terms: "He made them even stronger than their foes." That can scarcely be intended to be understood in the most literal sense. Yet in the contest that ensued Israel, under divine protection, proved stronger than its rival. So we need not take exception to the statement. When the writer ascribes to God the hatred that the governing nation had for the sojourners, that is a strong statement of the overruling governance of God. Their treachery is traced to the same source. Perhaps the safest statement of the case is that of *Kirkpatrick* who words it thus: "The psalmist does not shrink from attributing the hostility of the Egyptians to God's agency, because it was due to the blessings which He bestowed upon Israel; and inasmuch as it led to the Exodus, it was the link in the chain of God's action." It was certainly far removed from the thinking of the psalmist to make God the author and source of the wrong that men did.

e) God's mighty works wrought through Moses (vv. 26–36)

26. *He sent Moses, His servant,*
    And Aaron, whom He had chosen.
27. *They wrought (the matters of) His wondrous signs among them*
    And wonders in the land of Ham.
28. *He sent darkness and made it very dark;*
    And they did not rebel against His words.
29. *He turned their waters into blood*
    And made their fish die.
30. *Their land swarmed with frogs*
    Even in the chambers of their kings.
31. *He spoke, and swarms of flies came,*
    Gnats throughout their country.
32. *He made their showers of rain to be hailstorms,*
    Flashes of lightning throughout their land.
33. *He smote their vines and their fig trees*
    And shattered the trees of the country.
34. *He spoke, and the locusts came,*
    Yea, locusts innumerable.
35. *And they devoured all the vegetation in the land;*
    Yea, they devoured the fruit of their fields.
36. *And He smote all the first-born in their land,*
    The choice of their strength.

In this section the interest centers quite naturally on the plagues of Egypt, which are appropriately called "signs" and "wonders." The fact that they were all mediated through Moses and Aaron as being men who were in a particular sense commissioned by God has the first emphasis. The second reference to the "land of Ham" (cf. v. 27) indicates that the ancestry of the Egyptians was well known to the Israelites.

In the enumeration of the various plagues there are to be found certain embellishments that were not transmitted in Exodus. Besides, the treatment of the whole subject is marked by great freedom. Two plagues are not mentioned at all. The ninth is mentioned first; and the sequence followed by the psalmist is briefly 9, 1, 2, 4, 3, -, -, 7, 8, 10. Some of the considerations that compelled him to follow his particular form of treatment of the subject will forever elude us. Darkness may have been put first because it may have struck an unusual fear into the hearts of the Egyptians. In fact, the second half of this verse (v. 28) must be kept strictly in its context. It would appear that the overwhelming impact of this fear was such that it did more to break the resistance to God's demand of release than did anything that preceded; and in this sense it is said that they "did not rebel against His words" any further, the reference being to the Egyptians (cf. Exod. 11:3).

Aside from this, almost every reference is immediately plain. The climax was the smiting of the first-born, who are here called "the choice of their strength" even as Gen. 49:3 indicates. The expression could also be aptly rendered "the first issue of all their strength" as *RSV* words it. But in practically every verse the miracle is ascribed directly to God's agency by leaving out of consideration the intermediate agency of Moses and Aaron, on which Exodus dwells somewhat more at length.

f) **God's mighty works in the exodus and until the time of occupation of Canaan (vv. 37–45)**

37. *Moreover, He brought them forth with silver and gold;*
    And among his tribes there was not one who stumbled.
38. *Egypt was glad when they departed,*
    For the dread of them had fallen upon it.
39. *He spread a cloud for a covering*
    And fire to give light by night.
40. *He* (Moses) *asked, and God brought quails;*
    And He satisfied them with bread from heaven.
41. *He opened the rock, and waters gushed forth*
    And flowed through the dry desert like a stream.
42. *For He remembered His holy word*
    Given to Abraham, His servant.
43. *And He brought forth His people with joy,*
    His chosen ones with gladness.
44. *And He gave them the lands of the nations;*
    And they took possession of the goods of the peoples
45. *In order that they might observe His statutes*
    And keep His laws. Praise the Lord!

37. A few striking facts concerning the Exodus are made to pass in swift review. There is the noteworthy fact that these people who were practically slaves did not go out of Egypt in extreme poverty but were

in a unique way enriched with a substantial amount of silver and gold (cf., Exod. 12:35ff.). To this is to be added the fact that the Lord bestowed upon His people an exceptional measure of good health and strength so that it could be said of them: "Among his (Israel's) tribes there was not one who stumbled." Deut. 25:17, 18 presents the other side of the matter, and thus our passage will be regarded in the nature of an idealization of the case but still an indication of exceptional blessing from God.

38. Egypt's reaction serves as an effective backdrop for Israel's joyous exodus: the oppressor was more than glad to see the oppressed depart. The cloud of the divine presence is then briefly recalled (see Exod. 13:21, 22) and its shielding effect by day and by night. Quail and manna are added (v. 40). The water from the rock that flowed freely in the wilderness is mentioned (see Exod. 17:1; Num. 20:11); and thus a substantial array of mighty works performed during this period is assembled.

42. In vv. 42, 43 one aspect of the deliverance that is not so frequently noted is dwelt upon, the fact, namely, that the deliverance from Egyptian bondage was the fulfilment of a promise that had been given already to Abraham (Gen. 15:16) that after sojourning for a specified time in a land in which they were strangers the Israelites would ultimately be delivered. Quite appropriately this summary dwells in closing upon the joy that pervaded the nation on the occasion of the Exodus (v. 43). It is here especially that echoes from Isaiah become evident (Is. 35:10; 51:11; 55:12). And lastly, so as not to leave the liberated nation stranded in the desert as it were, the writer sums up the occupation of Canaan by specifying that both the land and its good things fell to Israel's lot.

When one definite divine purpose that lay behind all these gracious favors is now brought to the fore, namely, that "they might observe His statutes and keep His laws," this is not to be faulted as involving an unwholesome emphasis on the use of the law of the Lord but is rather to be approved as being an indication of deeper insight into God's purposes. True gratitude will always express itself by more faithful adherence to the divinely revealed will. With an appropriate shout of praise ("Hallelujah") this summary of divine grace that was manifested in Israel's past comes to a fitting conclusion.

NOTES

4. The difference between the two verbs used to express the idea of "seek" is that the first implies search, the second, looking up. Furthermore, the Hebrew word for "presence" is usually "face."

6. This verse opens the statement that finds its conclusion in v. 7, where the initial word has distinctive emphasis: "He (the one whom we have just so roundly praised) is the Lord, our God."

11. The direct address of this verse merges imperceptibly into discussion of the situation in hand. Vv. 12 and 13 are then the protasis to v. 14.

18b. The Hebrew is difficult at this point, reading literally: "His soul came into iron." As in v. 22, the word *nephesh* here apparently means the person involved, not his inner personality as such. The statement, therefore, says nothing more than our idiomatic translation (from *Kirkpatrick*) attempts to convey: "He was put into irons" or fetters. The old Prayer Book Version, "The iron entered into his soul," though oft quoted and enjoying some measure of popularity, scarcely covers the case. *Brinktrine* (ZATW, 1952, ¾, p. 251ff.) revives it. "His neck was put in a collar of iron" (*RSV*) has nephesh mean "neck."

26. Between the halves of the verse the final *waw* in 'abhdo was apparently intended to be read twice to yield the needed "and."

40. The form *yasbi'em* seems to be one of those imperfects which has become separated from the *waw* consecutive (*KS* 368r) and is, therefore, to be translated as a simple past tense.

Psalm 106

A NATIONAL CONFESSION OF SINS

IT SEEMS most appropriate to recall two remarks of *Maclaren's* as one approaches this psalm. He says: "Surely never but in Israel has patriotism chosen a nation's sins for the theme of song, or, in celebrating its victories, written but one name, the name of Jehovah on its trophies." He says also: "The history of God's past is a record of continuous mercies, the history of man's one as of continuous sin."

As to the date of its composition this psalm offers practically only one clue, and that is v. 47, which indicates that there are some who are to be gathered from among the nations. Though it is true, as some interpreters point out, that there were often those who were scattered among the nations through the centuries, yet the manner in which this is stated in this psalm would seem to imply that the whole body of the

Psalm 106

nation or at least as much of it as is left is involved in this disaster. Such a state of affairs prevailed only after the Exile or during it. So an exilic or postexilic date may well be claimed for the psalm. To this conclusion must be added the fact, discussed later, that three verses of this psalm are quoted in I Chron. 16, and Chronicles is one of the last books to be added to the canon.

This psalm represents another way of looking at the past. In the preceding psalm the emphasis rested on what God had done for His people; the atmosphere was cheerful and sunny. In this psalm the emphasis is placed on the manner in which Israel requited the Lord. In the very nature of the case the tone is somber and sad. There is obviously as much justification for this manner of reviewing the facts of the past as there is for the other.

The pattern of thought that runs through this psalm may be outlined somewhat as follows:
a) The background against which the confession is to be evaluated (vv. 1–5)
b) The confession itself (vv. 6–42)
c) The mercy of God which was in evidence in spite of Israel's sin (vv. 43–46)
d) The final plea for restoration of the captives (v. 47)
e) A song of thanksgiving (v. 48)

The fact that the first five verses are not in the nature of a confession but obviously begin on the note of praise is no reason for the criticism that they should not have a place in this psalm. It will be seen as we progress that they quite logically lead up to the confession proper.

When the question is raised as to whether this psalm was originally designed for liturgical use, the utmost that may be claimed on the basis of the statements of the psalm itself is that it does lend itself to such use. Equally in place is private use by the individual as the fourth verse indicates. Just as proper is the didactic purpose which the psalm may serve for the nation as a whole when it was read by groups or to groups and individuals. By these suggestions we indicate that we scarcely see any reason for dividing the psalm into sections that were to be assigned to solo voices or choirs. Such allocation of parts is too highly subjective. Many approaches may be suggested; none can be proved.

I Chron. 16:34–36, which in our discussion of the preceding psalm had been pointed out as incorporating a portion of Ps. 105, also embodies vv. 1, 47, and 48 of this psalm. The commonly accepted position on the question of priority is that the book of Chronicles is the borrower.

a) **The background against which the confession is to be evaluated (vv. 1–5)**

1. *Praise the Lord!*
   O give thanks unto the Lord, for He is good;
   For His steadfast love endures forever.
2. *Who can fully describe the mighty acts of the Lord?*
   Who can show forth all His praise?
3. *Blessed are they who practice justice,*
   Every one that does righteousness at all times.
4. *Remember me, O Lord, with the favor that Thou showest to Thy people;*
   O visit me with Thy help!
5. *That I may see the welfare of Thy chosen ones;*
   That I may share in the joy of Thy nation;
   That I may glory with Thy heritage.

1. Even though a godly man sets out to make a full confession of sin in the name of his people, does it not serve as a good approach when even in such a psalm God is first of all praised for the mighty works that He has again and again done for His people? When it is furthermore emphasized that man can never adequately praise the Lord for His mighty acts (v. 2), is such a reminder not continually in place? It would appear that v. 3 fits very well into this connection. After two verses that show the continual propriety of praise of God there follows one verse that stresses the fact that being the recipients of God's favor puts men under obligation to be extremely careful of leading a life that is worthy of those who bear the name of children of the heavenly Father. When, however, this thought is cast into the form of a beatitude, that manner of writing intends to serve as a reminder that godly living is in itself a joyous and happy thing.

4. When the note of instruction turns to one of petition, and this petition pleads for God's favor, this prayer is already motivated by the thought that the nation is not at the moment under God's favor and sees how utterly necessary it is to receive God's mercy. This thought is continued in v. 5, where all those things that make for peace and blessedness are pointed out as being the outgrowth of God's goodwill, which rests upon those who do His bidding. From this point of view it would appear that the introductory verses of this psalm are well motivated and lead directly to the confession which now follows.

b) **The confession itself (vv. 6–42)**

6. *We have sinned together with our fathers;*
   We have transgressed; we have done wickedly.

Psalm 106

7. *Our fathers in Egypt did not give due regard to Thy wonders;*
   They did not remember the multitude of proofs of Thy steadfast love.

6. We must pause at the sixth verse. It is the confession in brief form. In it the writer considers his own generation together with the fathers of old and regards the sin done as being of one piece. So deeply is each generation involved in the sins of its time and of the past. We may think ourselves free of the general failings that mark our age but are in reality continually involved in them without even seeing our involvement. Our fathers' sins and our own are one. For this reason other men of God of deep insight made the same type of confession (see Dan. 9:3-6; Ezra 9:6, 7). As a rule we follow the pattern set by our fathers whether it is for good or for ill.

The writer's thought is, of course, not for a moment that the fact that his generation is caught in the sins of the fathers would excuse him and his contemporaries. He, therefore, writes in the first person from this point onward: "*We* have transgressed; *we* have done wickedly." By designating sin by different terms the psalmist indicates how many-headed a monster it really is. It involves going astray, perverting what is right, and commiting iniquity. By the use of such terms the writer would depict the evil as grievous as it actually is. Rather notable is the fact that the writer knows his Bible well, for the terms used are quoted from the prayer of Solomon at the time of the dedication of the first Temple (I Kings 8:47).

7. There follows a statement as to the particular form that the sin of the fathers took in days of old. In their case it was a matter of not giving due regard to the mighty wonders that He did in their behalf in the land of Egypt. Or to state the case differently, they did not take sufficient note of the "multitude of proofs of (His) steadfast love." But even this involved the present generation. For these proofs of steadfast love were given to the same nation of which this generation is a part. (We break v. 7 at this point because the last member leads over to a consideration of what happened at the Red Sea, which situation is under discussion to the end of v. 12).

7c. *They showed rebelliousness by the sea, by the Red Sea.*
8. *Yet He saved them for His name's sake*
   That He might display His mighty power.
9. *So He rebuked the Red Sea, and it became dry;*
   And He led them through the deep waters as in a plain.
10. *And He saved them from the hand of the enemy*
    And delivered them from the hand of the foe.

11. *And the waters covered their adversaries;*
    Not one of them was left.
12. *Then they believed His words;*
    They sang His praises.

This instance of sin as confessed by the psalmist may be called "rebelliousness." For the first reaction of the nation when danger began to threaten at the shores of the Red Sea was to raise the cry that God had brought the Israelites out of Egypt in order to slay them. That can scarcely be classed as gratitude for the mighty works that He had done in their behalf. See Exod. 14:10–12.

In his treatment of this instance of disobedience the writer dwells particularly on the remarkable goodness that God manifested toward His unworthy people. When He did save them in spite of their rebellion, it was "for His name's sake," and "that He might display His mighty power." Then follows a summary account of the passage through the Red Sea. Though from one point of view the account very correctly ascribes the receding of the waters to a powerful east wind that the Lord caused to blow, it may also be attributed to the direct agency of the Lord, who is here said to have "rebuked the Red Sea, and it became dry." With equal propriety it is claimed that He "led them through the deep waters," that is to say, through the place where there had been deep waters. Their passage was as unimpeded as though they had marched along "a plain." Thus they were saved while their adversaries were covered in a noteworthy overthrow so that "not one of them was left." There was nothing doubtful about the effectiveness of their overthrow. When the concluding statement remarks that "then they believed His words," the emphasis does not lie on Israel's faith but on the fact that even this recalcitrant nation was compelled in faith to yield to God's faithfulness, and their praise is practically regarded as something that was forced from their reluctant lips.

13. *But they quickly forgot His works;*
    They waited not for His counsel.
14. *They abandoned themselves to their cravings in the wilderness;*
    They put God to the test in the wilderness.
15. *And He gave them their request,*
    But sent a wasting disease among them.

This incident took place in the wilderness. It involved the sin of lusting after what they could apparently not have at that time. It is quite correctly described as being the result of their forgetting God's works as well as being unwilling to "wait for His counsel," which is another way of saying that they were not ready to go as God in His wise providence led them. The incident was a case when "they abandoned themselves to their cravings," and by so doing they put God to the test in an unwholesome way by issuing a kind of challenge as to whether God could actually perform a deed of the magnitude which they specified. The account in Exod. 16 does not put the matter in quite this light, but this aspect of it was no doubt involved. When He granted them their request, it is said that He also "sent a wasting disease among them." Here the second episode of this sort is apparently chiefly under consideration (Num. 11:33). The thought seems to be that, though they gorged themselves with meat, it availed them nothing, but they wasted away in sickness ("a very great plague"). *Koenig* prefers to call this "wasting disease" *Fresskrankheit* (a morbid appetite that failed to appease their hunger).

16. *Then men became enemies of Moses in the camp,*
    Also of Aaron, the consecrated of the Lord.
17. *The earth opened its mouth and swallowed Dathan;*
    And it covered the rabble of Abiram.
18. *And fire kindled in their rabble;*
    And flame devoured the wicked.

Num. 16 relates this incident. We have a new scene—the camp. The time is shortly after the spies had been sent out. The sin involved is envy on the part of a select group of the chosen leaders of Israel, Moses and Aaron. The matter is disposed of briefly, and the startling outcome is especially dwelt upon: how the earth opened up and swallowed some, and how fire devoured others. Rather than follow those translations which give a dignified or half-dignified title ("company") to the ringleaders, we have sought to capture the force of *Luther's* translation, which called them *eine Rotte,* by using the term "rabble," not a "congregation" or a "company." When such marvelous leaders as Moses and Aaron are sent to a nation by God, opposition to them is doubly wicked. The fact that Korah, the prime agitator, is not mentioned is purely incidental.

19. *They made a calf in Horeb*
    And worshiped a molten image
20. *And so changed their glorious God*
    For the image of an ox that eats grass.
21. *They forgot the Mighty God, their Savior,*
    Who had done great things in Egypt,
22. *Wondrous works in the land of Ham*
    And awe-inspiring works by the Red Sea.

23. *Therefore He said He would destroy them,*
Had not Moses, His chosen one, stood in the breach before Him,
To turn back His wrath from destroying them.

We go back in point of time to the days after the giving of the law at Mt. Sinai, also called Horeb. The sin involved may strike us as being the most heinous of all—God Himself was rejected. The essence of the unholy deed is well caught in the sarcastic statement of the enormity of the sin in which they "so changed their glorious God for the image of an ox that eats grass." This again involved forgetting all the gracious deeds that God had wrought in their behalf—"great things, wondrous works, awe-inspiring works." At this point they were in greater peril of destruction than at any other during the course of their wanderings in the wilderness; and it was only through the valiant intercession of God's chosen servant, Moses, (Exod. 34) who, like a sturdy hero of days of old, stood in the breach made by the enemy in the city walls and succeeded in warding of the disaster, in this case the wrath of God that would have destroyed them.

As the instances of sinning multiply, one cannot help but feel, that in its past Israel had heaped up guilt upon guilt. But the writer who composed this prayer felt that the nation's attitude had not changed by the time his generation appeared on the scene.

24. *They also despised the pleasant land;*
They did not believe His word.
25. *But they murmered in their tents;*
They did not give heed to the voice of the Lord.
26. *Therefore He raised His hand in an oath against them*
To make them fall in the wilderness;
27. *And to make their descendants to fall among the nations*
And to scatter them in the lands.

We are at the point in history when the spies had brought back their report about the pleasant land (for this title cf. Jer. 3:19; Zech. 7:14). The sin involved is described as being both disobedience (v. 25) and unbelief (v. 24). The nation was poised on the borders of Canaan. When the spies reported, it was God who spoke through the encouraging words of Joshua and Caleb. Although they were within reach of their goal they refused to go in and take possession of the land. Little wonder that the sin is regarded as being so grievous as to induce God to raise His hand in an oath against them (raising the hand, the typical gesture that accompanied the taking of an oath). The justice of the punishment that destined them to die or fall in the wilderness is very apparent: they would not go into the land, let them die outside of it.

V. 27 carries the consequences of this kind of spirit in Israel down to the author's present when it indicates that whenever this same spirit prevailed, that was the cause of their being scattered "in the lands" as they now were.

28. They attached themselves to Baal Peor
    And ate sacrifices offered to the dead.
29. Thus they provoked Him by their doings;
    And the plague broke in upon them.
30. Then stood up Phinehas and interposed;
    And the plague was checked.
31. And that was counted to him as righteousness
    To all generations forevermore.

The episode referred to is related in Num. 25. Baal Peor is the idol of the Moabites that was kept at Peor. They "attached themselves," or as Num. 25:3 *RSV* translates the same verb, "yoked themselves" to this idol. Of the abominations involved the text mentions only the offering of sacrifices, describing these as being offered "to the dead." This statement is interpreted best as referring to the idol itself as the dead thing rather than as a reference to some kind of cult of departed persons. The other unwholesome aspect of the deed, the cult prostitution, is passed by as being understood to be involved.

When the punishment of a plague came upon the nation, it was Phinehas who interposed energetically by killing the leaders among the participants in drastic and fearless action. "And the plague was checked." What is added by way of commendation that this "was counted to him as righteousness" can mean nothing more than that he, a man who stood right with God, was deemed worthy of deserving the reward of a right deed. As some commentators have stated it, this is the *second* righteousness which God is pleased to reward, not the *first*, which justifies.

32. And they provoked Him to anger by the waters of Meribah
    So that it went ill with Moses on their account.
33. For they had provoked his spirit
    So that he spoke rashly with his lips.

This incident is reported in Num. 20. The location of Meribah must be sought near Kadesh, near the territory of Edom. This incident occurred near the end of the period of wandering in the wilderness. It shows how Israel's sin was of so infectious a character that it caused even Moses to sin grievously. He was swept along by the current of unholy passions that Israel manifested. To tell the truth, Moses' sin, is not defined too precisely. But the fact that some form of rash utterance was involved is clear enough. It is difficult to decide whether "his spirit" in v. 33 is to be understood as referring to God as the parallel remark in v. 32 might indicate, or as referring to Moses as the conclusion of v. 33 seems to suggest. Is. 63:10 supports the former approach. We prefer the latter.

34. They did not destroy the nations
    As the Lord had commanded them.
35. But they mingled themselves with the peoples
    And learned their works.
36. They served their idols,
    Which became a snare unto them.

The sin confessed here takes us to the time after the occupation of the land of Canaan. In Exod. 34:11–13 God had plainly indicated to the Israelites that nations were to be destroyed, which God listed by name. To ignore such a behest was sinful and in the nature of the case very harmful to Israel. For it led to a mingling of themselves in marriage with these idolaters; it meant imitating their works; it meant serving their idols and thus being ensnared by the worst of the sins of the nations that had contaminated Canaan. We could have continued this section of the psalm down to v. 42, but we preferred to have the sin of sacrifice of children stand out separately as the horrible thing that it was.

37. They sacrificed their sons and their daughters
    To the demons
38. And shed innocent blood, the blood of their sons and their daughters,
    Whom they sacrificed to the idols of Canaan;
    And the land was polluted with blood.
39. Thus they became unclean by their works
    And played the harlot with their doings.
40. Then the anger of the Lord was kindled against His people;
    And He abhorred His heritage.
41. And He gave them into the hand of the nations
    So that they that hated them ruled over them.
42. And their enemies oppressed them;
    And they were subdued under their hand.

That horrible sin that marked the Canaanite religion as a debased and debasing thing is referred to at greater length because it shows how evil the deeds of the nation became in the course of time. When it is specifically asserted that the anger of the Lord was kindled because of this sin, one feels quite keenly that such anger was totally justified. On the

Psalm 106

other hand, the point of view of the psalm is that in this confession past misdeeds are to be set forth without minimizing their enormity. The whole unwholesome mess must be confessed without reservation.

It is interesting to note the comment that such sacrifices of children were in the last analysis performed "to the demons." In some subtle way demons had insinuated themselves into these religions and were the deceiving force behind them. The fact that sacrifices that were thought to be acts of devotion should have been offered to the evil spirits shows how depraved these expressions of religion must have been.

It was sins like these that led to the captivity in Babylon. We might have preferred another form of statement of the case, but in harmony with the whole of the Scriptures, this psalm attributes calamities like the captivity to God's anger (v. 40), or to use another form of statement, "He abhorred His heritage." What should have been dear to Him became an object of disgust. Men should not make light of the reality of God's wrath and its serious character. As a result of this His aversion to His people God then gave His people into the hand of the nations round about (v. 41) and let their enemies rule over them and oppress them. Such basic explanations of the captivity had to be presented to the nation again and again when it experienced this misfortune so that it might see clearly what it was that had befallen it, and why it had to happen.

c) The mercy of God which was in evidence in spite of Israel's sin (vv. 43–46)

43. *Many times He delivered them;*
    But they rebelled against His counsel;
    And they were brought low by their transgression.
44. *Nevertheless, He regarded their affliction*
    When He heard their cry.
45. *He remembered His covenant for them;*
    And He felt pity for them according to the greatness of His steadfast love.
46. *He made them objects of compassion*
    Before all those that held them captive.

The other side of the matter must also be brought into the picture lest the statements concerning God's wrath leave a one-sided impression. God's mercy is a more important factor and is for that reason given attention at greater length. The record of the past of this nation may be summed up thus: "Many times He delivered them." Their is a history of deliverances even though they had rebelled and had been brought low by their transgressions. There follow certain statements, each of which presents God's kindly love from a different point of view.

For one thing: "He regarded their affliction." He could not shut His heart to their cry, sympathetic Father that He was. Then there was His "covenant" which He had made with the fathers. Then there was His marvelous "pity" which has as its synonym that other stupendous factor, His "steadfast love." So that He finally wrought for them that great and mighty miracle that their very captors bestowed their compassion on them and set them free. Some token of good will on the part of those that took Israel captive must have been in evidence at the time when this psalm was written. How far it would actually reach was not yet clear. But by this statement the way is prepared for the petition that follows.

d) The final plea for restoration of the captives (v. 47)

47. *Save us, O Lord, our God, and gather us from the nations*
That we may give thanks to Thy holy name
And glory in Thy praise.

The whole psalm reaches a climax in this goal and objective—a prayer for Israel's liberation from captivity. Nations cannot gather themselves after having been scattered abroad as Israel was. God is, therefore, asked to do the gathering. Two further objectives will be attained if He hears this prayer. One, they will be enabled to give thanks to His holy name; the other, they will glory in His praise. The question as to whether this indicates an exilic or a preexilic situation was discussed above.

e) A song of thanksgiving

48. *Blessed be the Lord God of Israel from everlasting to everlasting;*
And let all the people say, Amen.
Praise the Lord!

It seems best to regard this verse as serving a double purpose. It may rightly be considered the concluding doxology of the fourth Book of the Psalter, each book closing with some sort of doxology. At the same time it is so appropriate a conclusion of the psalm itself that this fact could scarcely be a matter of accident. Having just said that Israel's liberation will result in thanks and praise, the writer may well have penned a brief summary of the praise due to the Lord for a favor that he knew would be granted. Thus the psalm ends in a paean of thanksgiving.

NOTES

2. The imperfects used in this verse are to be regarded as expressing what is potential. See *GK* 107r.

3. With that mobility of point of view that is characteristic of the

Hebrew a change occurs from the plural to the singular *'oseh,* a thought that we have sought to reproduce by rendering: "every one that does," etc.

5. "Nation" happens to be the word that is usually employed in reference to the Gentiles. But Zeph. 2:9 offers a parallel.

7. The expression "by the sea," *'al-yam,* though supported by the *Septuagint* and the *Vulgate,* is popularly rendered (even *RSV*) as though it read *'elyon,* "the Most High." We see no reason for the suggested emendation.

9. "As in a plain" in the Hebrew leaves out the "in" which is readily supplied. See *KS* 319g. Is. 63:13 has the same expression.

13. The Hebrew says, "they hasted, they forgot" for, "They quickly forgot." A common construction; see *GK* 120g.

14. An example of a cognate object. *GK* 117p.

23. A negative clause of purpose introduced by *min; KS* 406o.

BOOK FIVE

Psalm 107

PRAISE FOR THE RESTORATION

THOUGH THIS PSALM marks the beginning of the fifth book of the Psalter it is, nevertheless, closely related to the two psalms that precede it. Let just a few indications of this be given. Ps. 105, of a character all its own, leads the reader through Israel's history to the time of the Exodus. Ps. 106 carries him along to the time of the going into the Babylonian Captivity. Ps. 107 takes up the sequence referring to the Restoration from this exile. Thus it might also be noted that Ps. 106:47 prays for the Restoration; Ps. 107 thanks for the Restoration.

The main point at issue in interpretation is whether the psalm is to be regarded as thinking in terms of the Restoration throughout, or whether after reflecting on this event the writer branches out into various areas of life where God's providential care has been noted and thus may be said to meditate on the manifold expressions of God's providence. Though the former of these approaches has now been largely abandoned, it cannot be dismissed as being of no consequence. For the reader cannot help but feel that the opening three verses announce this very Restoration as a theme of thanksgiving. It would seem more than strange to summon those that have been restored to make their praises vocal and then to begin to thank for all manner of *other* instances of God's divine providence. The Restoration was not only one of a great number of instances of the steadfast love of the Lord, it was *the* outstanding example, for which much and strong praise was to be offered. It presented a theme that was inexhaustibly rich. It was not to be noted merely in passing.

What follows in a series of four successive life situations merely presents the Restoration figuratively from the point of view of each of these. For the Exile was much like having a caravan lost in the wilderness and straying about aimlessly (vv. 4–9). It was also like an imprisonment (vv. 10–16). Again the Restoration was very much like a recovery from severe illness (vv. 17–22). And it surely cannot be denied that the deliverance had many points of similarity with the deliverance of a ship at sea from the dangers of a great storm which threatened the life of all aboard (vv. 23–32). These are not farfetched comparisons but are apt in every sense.

It is true that, if the points involved in these figures are not caught by the reader, he would naturally regard the psalm as, for example, even *Luther* does as "a psalm of thanksgiving for all sorts of help which God shows to men in their extremities," and the writer may have sensed that possibility and seen that the psalm could still serve a good purpose even though its original purpose had been lost sight of. In the last analysis the difference seems to lie between the original purpose of the psalm, which we believe to have been extended and eloquent praise for the Restoration from Babylonian Captivity, on the one hand, and the use that men in our day may be inclined to make of the psalm, which is to regard it as giving examples as to how God may be praised for the manifold instances of His care of the children of men.

These four figurative representations of the Exile and deliverance therefrom fall into a certain pattern: a trying and dangerous situation is described; then God's help in answer to the cry of men; then the summons to praise Him for what he has done in a refrain that recurs in vv. 8, 15, 21, and 31; and finally a special concluding summons to praise adapted to the individual case. But in the section vv. 33–43 this pattern is abandoned, and a summary presentation of God's providential government of men in all manner of situations is set forth. This latter section could be regarded as a congregational hymn. The preceding separate parts could be thought of as being examples of great dangers from which God delivered His own.

This leads quite naturally to the question of the possible liturgical use for which the psalm may have been designed, if any such use was intended. Far be it from us even to suggest that this or other psalms could not be adapted to various liturgical uses. The point at issue is rather whether such use was originally designed and can at this late date be detected and shown to be native to the psalm. We examine one of the various liturgical scenes that are envisioned in this psalm. A huge throng of worshipers fills the Temple court. In the forefront of this throng are groups of individuals, each with the victim that he intends to offer as a thankoffering. One of these groups consists of leaders of caravans, who had been stranded in the wilderness on their way to the holy city; another group is made up of prisoners who have been set free; another, each man still pale from the bed of sickness from which he has but recently recovered, consists of men who were dangerously ill; then a group of sailors. They have been arranged in groups and carefully coached beforehand by a priest, who has experience along such lines. The priest appears on the steps overlooking the groups and exhorts them to praise the Lord. He addresses the various groups by recalling their experiences and exhorting them separately to pay their vows and sacrifices of gratitude. The second half of the psalm (vv. 33–43) is a congregational hymn that generalizes and summarizes the thoughts involved in this approach of the psalm. This approach seems so attractive and so fitting that one may well be inclined to consider it the very essence of a correct interpretation of the psalm.

But note the following inconsistencies. What a strange selection of what are, no doubt, supposed to be typical cases of persons who have been delivered from great distress! As far as the first group is concerned, the presupposition has to be that a certain percentage of festival caravans regularly got lost, regularly found their way again, and expected after having arrived at the sanctuary to have a special ritual procedure ready for their use. Similarly there is the expectation that there are to be regular groups of released prisoners who expect to pay their sacrifices of thanksgiving for release from prison, thieves or crooks, it is true, but, nevertheless, devout men, for whom annual provision is made in a liturgy especially provided for the purpose. This taxes our credulity. Then a group of sailors who are grateful for deliverance from severe storms, and that in view of the fact that during the times when canonical Scriptures were written the Hebrews had practically no contact with life on the seas. If these episodes are regarded as figurative illustrations of Israel's experience in the Exile, all these difficulties are removed.

A possible occasion for the liturgical rendition of a psalm like this might be that described in Ezra 3:1–7, where the first Feast of Tabernacles was kept after return from the Exile.

Traditionally, as the *Kittel* text indicates, the Hebrew manuscripts printed a series of inverted *n*'s (the Hebrew letter *nun*) at the side of vv. 21–26 (some say vv. 23–28). Many shrewd suggestions as to the significance of this device have been suggested, each of which is highly conjectural.

1. *O give thanks unto the Lord, for He is good;*
   For His steadfast love endures forever.
2. *Let the redeemed of the Lord say so,*
   Whom He has redeemed from the hand of the enemy
3. *And gathered them in from the lands,*
   From the east and from the west, from the north and from the sea.

This is obviously a summons to praise the Lord for having gathered the scattered members of Israel from all lands. The first line, "O give thanks unto the Lord, for He is good," seems to have been a favorite just after the Exile and may have originated at that time. Since thanksgiving for even the greatest favors of the Lord is so frequently postponed and then finally completely forgotten, it is most proper to exhort men: "Let the redeemed of the Lord say so." In the enumeration of the areas from which the captives have been brought back the south is missing, for the very good reason, perhaps, that none were brought back from areas like Egypt. The demand that in enumerations like these all four cardinal points of the compass must be represented is quite artificial, and textual changes made to produce this result are quite questionable. Since the occasional points of contact between this psalm and the second half of Isaiah are rather obvious, it will be in order to indicate at least some of them. The expression "the redeemed (of the Lord)" is found also in Is. 62:12; 63:4. V. 3 reads much like Is. 43:5, 6.

4. *They wandered in the wilderness, in a waste place;*
   The way to an inhabited city they could not find.
5. *Hungry and thirsty,*
   Their soul fainted within them.
6. *Then they cried to the Lord in their trouble;*
   And He delivered them out of their great distress.
7. *And He led them in the right way*
   That they might go to an inhabited city.
8. *Let them thank the Lord for His steadfast love*
   And for His wonderful works for the children of men.
9. *For He satisfies the thirsty soul*
   And fills the hungry soul with that which is good.

According to the approach which we have suggested above this description of a caravan which had lost its way and was by God's grace enabled to find it again and come to an inhabited city and find meat and drink is a good illustration of what had befallen Israel in the Babylonian Captivity. It was lost and at the point of perishing. The Israelites then cried to the Lord, and He heard them, and when all hope seemed at an end, they were restored. If any individuals now use this passage after an experience of being lost in the wilderness and find it in an apt summary of their experience and follow the summons to praise God for what He did for them, that is certainly not an abuse of the passage. We feel sure that many an Israelite who may have read this psalm especially after the Return had just taken place could not help but see how aptly his experience was here described.

10. *Those that sat in darkness and deepest gloom,*
    Bound in affliction and iron
11. *Because they had rebelled against the words of God*
    And had despised the counsel of the Most High;
12. *Therefore He humbled their hearts with labor;*
    They stumbled, and there was no one to help them.
13. *Then they cried to the Lord in their trouble;*
    And He helped them out of their great distress.
14. *And He brought them forth out of darkness and deep gloom*
    And broke their bonds asunder.
15. *Let them thank the Lord for His steadfast love*
    And for His wonderful works for the children of men.
16. *For He shattered bronze doors*
    And hewed asunder bars of iron.

When Israel was in Babylon, its sojourn there was like the experience of a man shut up in prison, wrapped in darkness and gloom, unable to free himself. In this case the reason assigned for imprisonment (this is usually overlooked) is not at all such a one as civil courts take note of, for v. 11 says: "They had rebelled against the words of God." That was Israel's root sin which led directly to the Captivity. The words of the prophets that God had sent them were not heeded (cf., Zech. 1:4). The good counsel that the Most High gave them was thus actually despised. Verse 12 is then a good description of Israel's lot, figuratively speaking, when many a heavy burden of work was laid upon the captives, when they stumbled, and there was no one to help them. But when they humbled themselves and cried to the Lord, then deliverance dawned. For when He freed them, it was like having a mighty man come and shatter the bronze prison doors and hew asunder the bars of iron (v. 16). Here again v. 10 appears to refer to Is. 42:7 and 49:9; v. 16 draws on Is. 45:2; vv. 13 and 15 are in the nature of refrains, which by the repetition of the summons to cry to the Lord and also to thank Him for what He does make their point very effectively.

17. *Fools, because of their wicked ways*
    And because of their iniquities, were afflicted.
18. *They loathed every kind of food;*
    And they drew near to the gates of death.
19. *And they cried unto the Lord in their trouble;*
    And He delivered them out of their great distress.
20. *And He sent forth His word and healed them*
    And delivered them from their destruction.
21. *Let them thank the Lord for His steadfast love*
    And for His wonderful works for the children of men.
22. *And let them offer the sacrifices of thanksgiving*
    And tell of His works with rejoicing.

The Restoration could also be likened to the recovery of health after a severe illness. The propriety of this comparison can scarcely be questioned. The basic assumption is that sickness is oftentimes punishment for sin. The truth of that claim should be admitted freely. The Old Testament stresses this truth to the point where it seems to regard it as a general rule. But such sinfulness that displeases the Lord is basically "folly" in the language of the Old Testament. Therefore the address "fools" has a profound propriety and should not be corrected away as is almost generally done. (Note the exception of *J.M.P.Smith, Am. Trans.*) A few symptoms of illness are mentioned to lend color to the description: the loss of appetite and being close to death. For the nation Israel was near to extinction as a nation as so many other nations had found exile to be the end of their very existence. The *Prayer Book Version* has a very apt rendering for 18b: "hard at death's door."

The recovery described has a unique point: it is attributed to a special messenger from God who heals the sick man, and this messenger is God's word. The word is regarded almost as a personal agent (cf., Ps. 147:15, 18; Is. 55:11). In this instance the exhortation to praise the Lord adds the suggestion not to forget the sacrifices of thanksgiving, which were the traditional expression of thanks in public worship. This most wholesome suggestion does not yet stamp the psalm as being of liturgical design as some modern interpreters claim all too positively.

23. *Those who go down to the sea in ships*
    And do business on the great waters,
24. *They indeed have seen the works of the Lord*
    And His wonders in the deep.

25. *For He spoke and raised up a stormy wind;
    And its billows lifted themselves up.*
26. *They mounted up to heaven, they went down again to the depths.
    Their soul melted away in such an evil plight.*
27. *They reeled and staggered like a drunken man;
    And all their wisdom was at an end.*
28. *And they cried to the Lord in their trouble;
    And He delivered them out of their great distress.*
29. *He settled the storm to a whisper;
    And the waves were hushed.*
30. *Then they were glad that they had quiet;
    So He brought them to their desired haven.*
31. *Let them thank the Lord for His steadfast love
    And for His wonderful works for the children of men.*
32. *And let them exalt Him in the assembly of the people
    And praise Him in the council of the elders.*

Why should it be difficult to regard this description of a deliverance from a great storm at sea as being another figure of the deliverance of the nation of Israel from a grave danger that might well with its threatening billows have destroyed the nation forever? For that matter, nations often use this very figure when they say that the ship of state is threatened. The storm of the Captivity had swept over the nation; all seemed lost. It is true that not every little detail of this allegory, if such it may be called, calls for a special interpretation. Several details are inserted merely to make a complete picture: the ship mounting up to the heavens and dropping down again into the depths; the sailors staggering on deck; the utter helplessness of the crew. These features show how grave the danger was. Of all who have had such experiences it can be said in a special sense that "they indeed have seen the works of the Lord," both when He raised the storm and also when He quieted it. Those who lived through the recovery of a nation from a captivity can in a very real sense claim to have seen His works.

A few matters call for special comment. The opening line, "those who go down to the sea in ships," represents a peculiarly Hebrew point of view. Since Israel was mountainous country, the only way to get to the sea was to "go down." The phrase really means nothing more than *Luther* puts into it when he translates: *Die mit Shiffen auf dem Meer fuhren* (those who sailed the sea in ships). We have also retained the Hebraism of 27b: "And all their wisdom was at an end." Both the English ("They were at their wits' end") and the German (*Und wussten keinen Rat mehr*) translated idiomatically and effectively.

In v. 32 the two places where the Lord's praises are to be spoken seem to differ in this way: "the assembly of the people" is any gathering of an informal sort whereas "the council of the elders" is any official and formal gathering of representatives of Israel.

By means of four different approaches the same idea has been developed by the use of one and the same pattern. Must a pattern that has once or repeatedly been used by a writer be followed to the end of what he writes? Some interpreters make this claim but have nothing to substantiate it. Quite a different pattern is followed from this point onward when God's providential guidance of men in all manner of situations is presented.

33. *And He also made streams into a wilderness*
    And springs of water into dry ground.
34. *Fruitful land He made into a salt waste*
    Because of the wickedness of its inhabitants.
35. *Again He turned the dry wilderness into a pool of water*
    And barren land into springs of water.
36. *And there He let hungry people dwell;*
    And they established a city to dwell in.
37. *And they sowed fields and planted vineyards,*
    Which yielded fruit for harvest.
38. *And He blessed them and multiplied them greatly;*
    And He did not let their cattle decrease.
39. *On the other hand, they decreased and were brought low*
    Because of oppression, calamity, and grief.
40. *"He pours contempt upon princes . . .*
    And makes them wander in pathless wastes."
41. *Or He raises the poor out of misery*
    And makes their families like flocks.
42. *The upright shall see it and rejoice;*
    And all wickedness must shut its mouth.
43. *Whoever is wise, let him heed these things;*
    And let men consider the gracious deeds of the Lord.

Far from marring the unity of the psalm, this last section puts the capstone upon the truths the psalm sets forth. Up till this point the issue was that it was the Lord who brought about this marvelous turn in the fortunes of Israel. There follows a section that turns from specific instances to a general truth: the up's and down's, the success and the failure, the prosperity and calamity in the lives of individuals and nations are entirely in the control of and brought about by the will of the Almighty. None are brought low or raised on high unless He wills it.

Quite a number of separate illustrations as to how this rule works are offered. A land that was fruitful and well watered may become dry ground, a "dust bowl" or a "salt waste." It seems most likely that at this point the writer had Sodom and Gomorrah in mind (Gen. 19:25, 26). The reverse can also happen. Arid, desiccated land becomes well watered and fruitful, and then He allows hungry people to dwell there and prosper, sow fields and plant vineyards, and increase greatly under the blessing of the Almighty. It seems that in these words there is a description of the completion of an irrigation project which succeeded because the Lord gave His benediction. The reverse may also be the case (v. 39).

Or moving to another group—princes may be humiliated and become dispossessed whereas the poor may be raised from their misery and become prosperous. Things like this do not just happen of themselves; they are proofs of the sovereign and wise providence of God. The righteous observe that such is the case and are glad over it and rejoice. In the face of this well-established truth wickedness must lapse into silence, for God governs this world effectively and well. With a precise proverb the psalm concludes by bidding men to learn this truth well if they would be wise and exhorting them to see how gracious the deeds of the Lord are.

NOTES

5. *J. M. P. Smith* translates v. 5b, "Their courage collapsed within them." That is a good idiomatic translation.

7. The Hebrew really says "straight way." That obviously means the one that leads right to the goal; therefore, "right way."

17b has a clever little play on words in the original.

20. Between vv. 19 and 20 after the *m* a *waw* consecutive may have been lost.

26. For "their soul melted away" we could substitute, "They were dissolved in their distress" (*J. M. P. Smith*).

40. We put this sentence into quotation marks, for *a* is quoted from Job 12:21a and *b* from v. 24b.

One somewhat unique approach to the entire problem of the psalm may yet be indicated. Eerdmans regards these several groups mentioned as groups of exiles who either became sick, or were imprisoned, or were scattered widely as a result of the Exile. This approach has possibilities.

Psalm 108

GOD IS PRAISED
AND ASKED TO GIVE VICTORY

THIS PSALM is composed of two parts which are taken from Ps. 57 and 60, respectively, in the following manner: vv. 1–5 of this psalm come from 57:7–11, and vv. 6–13 are taken from 60:5–12 (according to the numbering of the verses as found in the English text).

The resultant psalm would then offer the following outline:

a. A resolution to praise God for deliverance (vv. 1–6)
b. The recalling of God's ancient promises (vv. 7–9)
c. Confidence of achieving the conquest of Edom (vv. 10–13)

For details of exposition the two psalms involved may be consulted.

The minor changes in the text between those two psalms and this one are here listed: the present version of v. 1 omits the second "my heart is resolute." The verse closes with "also my soul," not "awake my soul." The Ps. 108 version also substitutes *Yahweh* for *'adhonay* in v. 3.

In the second portion of the Ps. 108 version v. 6 has answer "me" for "us." In v. 6 in the verb "I will exult" there is a simple *schwa* under the *'ayin* for the compound *schwa*. In v. 7 "Manasseh" for "and Manasseh." In v. 8 we have "over Philistia *I* shout in triumph" for "Philistia, tender *me* your shouts." In v. 9 the expression *'ir mibhtsar* occurs for *'ir matsor,* both to be translated "fortified city" with a mild difference in the original. In v. 10 the "Thou" as a separate pronoun is omitted, being found only in the verb form as such. In the word "armies" the defective style of writing the form is used in Ps. 108.

It will be obvious that these textual differences are of a very minor character. It will be difficult to prove that they were designed for they scarcely affect the meaning. Whether Ps. 108 drew on the preceding two psalms or whether all three drew on a common source is obviously one of those textual issues that can never be resolved.

The fact that portions of psalms are here pieced together is scarcely sufficient reason for assumptions that such a procedure was commonly practiced, or for drawing conclusions of a sweeping sort about existing psalms which are assumed to consist of portions thus pieced together.

From the manner in which Ps. 60 is developed it might appear that the national crisis involved in the situation there pictured was of a very serious sort. Perhaps the writer who gave us Ps. 108 pieced the elements together as he did with the purpose of producing a psalm for the same emergency that would begin with a more confident note. Two good hymns for an emergency are better than one.

Psalm 109

PRAYER FOR HELP AND FOR JUDGMENT OF UNGODLY ADVERSARIES

THE HEADING ascribes the psalm to David. Impossible as it is to furnish complete proof for this claim on the basis of the material contained in the psalm, it is equally impossible to disprove the claim. *Koenig* seeks to invalidate it by pointing to v. 22, "I am poor and needy." Yet even a rich king may speak thus figuratively when he is in affliction. More particularly, in the days when Saul persecuted him, David had occasion to make a statement like that even in a literal sense. In view of the reliability of the headings generally we feel prompted to accept this claim of Davidic authorship as being correct.

The distinctive problem involved in this psalm begins to appear after one has read past v. 5. It is an imprecatory psalm which presents some of the strongest imprecations to be found anywhere in the Psalter.

There are two major types of interpretation to escape the difficulty that these imprecations seem to offer. We refuse to be moved by the extreme statements of the case made, for example, by *Kittel* when he speaks of the "utterly repulsive maledictions inspired by the wildest form of vengeance, which make this one of the most questionable hymns of cursing," and ascribes all to "carnal passion that is utterly inexcusable." Certain basic considerations have been overlooked in such an approach.

One of the ways in which to escape the difficulty is to regard vv. 6–20 as a quotation that is not formally introduced. These would then be the words that were used against the psalmist by the enemy. In this connection it has become quite common to regard these words as a parallel to Baylonian curses and execrations and thus to claim to have them clearly and correctly catalogued. However, quite apart from the fact that this interpretation is anything but clearly apparent to the casual or even the careful reader, it is very doubtful that v. 18 would have been true in regard to the psalmist. More particularly, after the record of the psalmist seems to have been cleared by the claim that these objectionable words are words that were spoken by others against him, the advantage gained by this claim is completely invalidated by v. 20, in which the writer in one fell swoop turns the whole list of imprecations back on the head of those who wished him ill.

The second attempt is this, that all verb forms in the Hebrew that are not strictly to be construed as optatives (jussives) are regarded as futures (an interpretation which is grammatically quite possible). Thus the sting seems to be taken out of them. The writer does not wish these things to befall others; he merely predicts them as likely to befall them. However, since these predictions continue at such length and with such detail, it is all but impossible to keep the wish that they might occur from becoming a reality. This distinction is too finely drawn to be of any consequence.

Several statements may be made by way of explanation. In the first place, there is nothing in the rest of the psalm that would raise a question about the sincere piety and godliness of the writer. If he is not an utter hypocrite (and who has ventured to claim that?) then he puts his hope sincerely in God, pleads humbly for His help, insists strongly on his innocence of all that may have aroused antagonism, and gives assurance of earnest praise of God when the Lord shall have delivered him. It is as *Maclaren* notes: "The combination of devout meekness and trust with the fiery imprecations in the core of the psalm is startling to Christian consciousness." But the wholesome factor is there.

We believe that there is also an unspoken presupposition in all cases of this sort, namely, should the wicked opponent turn from his ungodliness and seek the Lord, no one would be happier than the writer of the psalm. But these opponents of his were apparently not very likely to give any evidence of repentance. Since these were men whose wickedness was deeply ingrained, it was but natural to wish for the total overthrow of these men and what they stood for. A godly man could certainly not pray for their success.

To this must be added the observation that "divine retribution for evil was the truth of the Old Testament as forgiveness is that of the New." This was a valid and important truth, the upholding of which was very important, and the success of which we must to this day earnestly desire. That there was room for the maintaining of such a principle cannot be questioned.

As long as men were on the Old Testament stage of revelation, and the example of the blessed Savior had not yet been given and His

Psalm 109

blessed words were not yet known, it would be unreasonable to expect these saints to rise to levels that do justice to New Testament thinking. *Luther,* too, could blast away at Tetzel unmercifully but in the spirit of Christ could write him a consolatory epistle at the time when he lay sick and was in need of comfort. Such a spirit presents a blend of what is good and wholesome about psalms like this one but adds the teachings of the Savior in all their excellence to the Old Testament approach.

a) **A plea for help, reinforced by a statement of the wrong that has been suffered at the hand of the enemies (vv. 1-5)**

> *To the Choir Director. Of David. A psalm.*
> 1. *O God of my praise, be not silent.*
> 2. *For the mouth of the wicked and the mouth of deceit have been opened against me;*
>   *Men have spoken against me with a lying tongue.*
> 3. *Words of hate have been all around me*
>   *And have warred against me without cause.*
> 4. *In return for my love they have antagonized me;*
>   *But I have resorted to prayer.*
> 5. *But they have rewarded me with evil for good*
>   *And with hatred for my love.*

When God is appealed to not to be silent, that is another way of asking that He may act in behalf of His afflicted servant. When God is called "God of my praise," this compact expression implies that God is One who has always merited the psalmist's praise by what He has done for him. (Cf. also Deut. 10:21; Jer. 17:14). In the verses that follow, the utter wrong of his attackers and the utter groundlessness of their attacks are maintained. Not only that, the writer's opponents have even gone to the extreme of repaying good with evil, love with hate. In other words, the writer maintains his absolute innocence. It is true enough that in cases of controversy both parties have been known to make claims of complete innocence. But in instances like the one before us, where the writer humbly and devoutly bares his very soul before his God, we can accept his statements as being unbiased. Godly men would not have regarded questionable psalms as worthy of having a place in the Psalter. The expression used in v. 4b is even stronger than our translation would seem to indicate. The force of it can be felt but scarcely caught by any form of rendering, for the Hebrew says, "But I, prayer." While his enemies engage in slander and malicious attacks, he is busy with devout prayer. A similar construction occurs in Ps. 110:3 and 120:7.

b) A prayer that God may requite these evil doers (vv. 6–20)
  6. *Appoint a wicked man over him*
     And let an accuser stand at his right hand.
  7. *When he is tried, let him come forth guilty;*
     And let his prayer become sin.
  8. *May his days be few;*
     And may another take his office.
  9. *May his children be fatherless*
     And his wife a widow.
 10. *May his children continually stray about and beg;*
     And may they be expelled from their hovels.
 11. *May the creditor seek to possess all that he has;*
     And may strangers plunder his earnings.
 12. *Let there be none to show him any consideration;*
     Neither let anyone show mercy to his fatherless children.
 13. *Let his posterity be destined to be cut off;*
     And in the next generation may his name be blotted out.
 14. *Let the iniquity of his fathers be remembered before the Lord;*
     And may the sin of his mother not be blotted out.
 15. *Let them be before the Lord continually;*
     And may He cut off the remembrance of his ancestors from the earth.
 16. *Because he so utterly failed to show mercy*
     But persecuted the poor and needy
     And hounded the timid-hearted to death.
 17. *He loved the curse, so let it come upon him;*
     And he took no pleasure in blessing, so let it stay far from him.
 18. *He clothed himself with cursing as with a garment;*
     May it come like water into his body and like oil into his bones.
 19. *May it be to him like a garment that he wraps around him*
     And like a girdle that he always wears.
 20. *May this be the reward of my opponents from the Lord*
     And of those that speak evil against my soul.

6. It should be noted that everything in this section is committed into God's hands, and it must thus ultimately rest with the Almighty whether or not these requests are granted. The first five verses concentrate on the person of the chief opponent and his family. There is an obvious turn from the plural used in the first section (vv. 1–5) to the singular employed throughout this section (vv. 6–20). This is, perhaps, best explained on the assumption that there was one outstanding leader of the opposition against the psalmist, in whom the whole movement centered. He is particularly thought of, the rest are indirectly in-

cluded. The first wish made with regard to this one is that he may be brought to trial under a "wicked man," where he will experience the same kind of injustice that he has dispensed. If he is to come forth with the sentence of guilty, that is obviously what he merited by his conduct.

7. When the second half of v. 7 expresses the desire that "his prayer may become sin," that is, first of all, quite in line with other statements of holy writers in analogous situations, cf., Is. 1:15, 16; Prov. 28:9. The prayers of such an impenitent, guilty man can scarcely be anything other than sin, for the first requirement of acceptable prayer is a truly penitent heart.

8. Since the blessing of God upon those that walk in the ways of His commandments is length of days, a further result to be anticipated is the shortening of such a person's life, as a result of which whatever office he held must fall to another man's lot. As is well known, this statement is quoted in Acts 1:20 in reference to Judas Iscariot. The reason for this quotation is that Judas was a character of the same sort as David's opponents. The quotation is apt because nothing more is intended than to show that such a change of fortune would befall thoroughly evil men. Note two things. First, that the writer of Acts is not hostile to the spirit and letter of this psalm. Note also that this quotation does not make the whole psalm Messianic. In fact, in the Christian Church it has become known as the *psalmus Ischarioticus*.

10. It is not very likely that the prayer would single out the children of the man involved if they had not given evidence of having the same spirit that controlled their father. The same applies to the wife. For only when the children, like their fathers, hate God (Exod. 20:5) do they come under the condemnation of the same judgment. God said that He would visit the iniquities of such upon them; the psalmist prays that He would do so. Without advocating that men of our day do the same, I trust we can at least understand some of the motivation that lay behind this prayer.

11. The psalm goes on to consider the personal possessions of this wicked man with the thought that he may be dealt with as he has dealt with others (v. 12), with his posterity, whose lot was partly explained by our remarks above, and with his ancestors, who are apparently referred to as they are because they manifested the same heartless and wicked spirit that their son did over against the psalmist, vv. 14, 15.

16. This verse serves as a strong reminder as to how utterly cruel this evildoer must have been: there was no mercy or pity in his dealings with others. To this is added a further imperfection in the character of this man. He seems to have been habitually addicted to cursing in its most violent and obnoxious form. If he was forever invoking curses

upon others, the propriety of making him the recipient of the same treatment is at least obvious (vv. 17, 18). The figure of "coming like water into his body and like oil into his bones" implies nothing other than that the curse may enter wholly into this man and become part of him. V. 19 implies that the curse is always to be present with him who so much loved to curse others.

20. The closing verse of the imprecatory section of the psalm still leaves the issue entirely with the Lord (". . . reward . . . from the Lord") and thus is in conformity with the principle: "Vengeance is Mine, I will repay, saith the Lord." When the last remark describes the opponents as speaking evil against his "soul," "soul" is apparently to be understood in the sense of "life." They are bent on nothing less than the murder of him whom they oppose. This shows how foul their plots were. At this point the description has swerved back from the singular to the plural, showing that the one outstanding opponent was being discussed as being typical of the rest and their leader.

c) **A further plea for help stressing the psalmist's affliction (vv. 21–29)**

21. *But Thou, O Lord, do something together with me for Thy name's sake;*
Because Thy steadfast love is good, deliver me.
22. *For I am poor and needy;*
And my heart is pierced within me.
23. *I am gone like a declining shadow;*
I am shaken off like a locust.
24. *My knees give way through fasting;*
And my flesh wastes away lacking oil.
25. *And I myself have become an object of mockery to them;*
When they see me they shake their heads.
26. *Help me, O Lord, my God;*
O save me accodring to Thy steadfast love.
27. *That they may know that this is Thy hand;*
That Thou, O Lord, hast done it.
28. *Let them curse, but bless Thou;*
When they arise, let them be put to shame;
But let Thy servant rejoice.
29. *Let my accusers be clothed with shame;*
Let them wrap themselves in their own disgrace as in a mantle.

The writer is doing all he can under the circumstances to avert the evils that have been plotted against him. He now prays that God may "do something together with (him)," that is to say, that He may lend

His great and mighty aid. The expression is unusual but quite clear and obvious.

Several motives for action are laid before the Lord. The first is, "for Thy name's sake," that is to say, in line with that reputation that God has established among His people for help in time of trouble. The second motive is, "because Thy steadfast love is good." An unwavering fidelity rooted in love is another mark of the God of Israel.

Then there follows in vv. 22–24 a description of the sorry physical state in which the writer finds himself, which is summed up in the familiar sentence, "I am poor and needy." The various figures employed stress the extremity of his need: the pierced heart, the declining shadow, being shaken off like a repulsive locust, the weakness brought on by fasting, the wasting away of his body. God is not unaware of the physical sufferings of His children; they touch Him deeply. The whole picture may be summed up in the terms that describe the psalmist as an object of the mockery of men, a poor spectacle of a fellow at whom all men shake their heads.

As the plea for help is renewed (v. 26), the new motivation is added that the delivery experienced will be a clear indication that God Himself has taken a hand in a matter that was getting out of control, and that He Himself deemed His servant's cause worthy of His intervention. The psalmist is reconciled even to the painful curses that have been hurled at him, if only God will bless. So as a summary it is for this that he prays. He prays that the opportunity may be given him of rejoicing when God's day of deliverance comes. The whole issue will then appear as it really should, that his own conduct was above reproach, and that his foes deserved to be clothed with shame and disgrace (v. 29), an outcome for which he earnestly prays.

d) A resolve to praise God (vv. 30, 31)

30. *I will thank the Lord greatly with my mouth;*
    Yea, in the midst of many people will I praise Him.
31. *For He will stand at the right hand of the poor,*
    To save him from those who would condemn him to death.

The psalmist confidently looks forward to the deliverance that he has prayed God to send by expressing his readiness to praise and thank in the form of a promise to the Lord. It is praise that will be offered in the presence of others with the mouth, even in sight of many people, no doubt, in the sanctuary. For one conviction controls the good man's thinking mightily, and that is that the Lord takes the part of the poor by standing at his right hand to defend him and to save him from those who wickedly plot his death.

NOTES

2. There is not sufficient reason for repointing *rashaʻ* to make it read wickedness, all the more so since in v. 6 there seems to be an obvious reference to this verse in the second use of *rashaʻ*.

8. *Pequdah* could mean "goods" (*RSV*), but that aspect of the case appears in the verses that follow. Therefore the accepted meaning of "office" deserves the preference.

10. Though we have translated *dorshu* "expelled," this was not done because we favored changing the verb to *yeghoreshu* but in an attempt to catch the poel meaning involved, which is something like: "May they be summoned forth," *herausgefordert werden* (Koenig).

17. Also in v. 18 the verbs are better pointed with *waw copulativum* than with *waw consecutivum,* i.e., *we* rather than *wa* with a following daghesh forte. The context suggests the optative rather than a historical narrative of what took place.

21. *'itti* does mean "with me," so that all renderings like "on my behalf" are inaccurate.

28. *Qamu* is like a future perfect used in a clause of condition.

May we add that the interpretation that is farthest removed from the truth of the matter appears to us to be *Mowinckel's* who regards the psalm as an "effective curse" (*ein brauchbarer Fluch*) against a sorcerer, known or unknown, who had sought to harm the author.

Psalm 110

THE MESSIANIC PRIEST-KING

IT IS NOT MERELY a coincidence that this psalm is quoted more often in the New Testament than is any other. This fact is a testimony to its importance.

To summarize the contents of the psalm briefly, it is to be noted that the first four verses describe the dual office of the Messiah: He is both king and priest (vv. 1–4). His successful warfare is then briefly but effectively described (vv. 5–7). From this outline it is immediately apparent that we do not here have a description of the total work of the Messiah but primarily that of His conflict with His enemies. There are possibilities of atonement hinted at in the reference to the fact that

He is also to be a priest. But that side of His activity is not developed at all.

Let us indicate the line of thought that is followed by the psalm with a somewhat greater measure of detail. We cannot but accept the claim presented in the heading of the psalm that its author is David. Nothing in the psalm or in the nature of the case conflicts with or invalidates this claim. Already at this point a guiding observation must be made. If one approaches the poem with the assumption that men like David cannot have had a very clear understanding of the words that God gave them in their day and thus denies these men a deeper grasp of the revealed truth they possessed, then the interpretation of this psalm would have to use an entirely different approach than we are about to make. But we believe with men like *Luther* that these saints of God were not deficient in faith nor in a relatively clear and full understanding of the truth involved.

The writer begins by quoting a divine "oracle" ("The Lord said in reference to my Lord") which has a bearing upon Him who is at the same time David's Lord, the Messiah. When and how this oracle was pronounced we cannot determine. It might have come from Nathan even as the words recorded in II Sam. 7:4ff. stemmed from this prophet. This "oracle" might even be a free paraphrase of II Sam. 7 which was spoken by David himself. It is sufficient to note that David regards it as being an entirely authoritative statement. It revealed to David that no one less than the Lord God of Israel Himself ("Yahweh") had designated for the Messiah a position at His own right hand, making Him coequal in rank and authority with Himself and so virtually declaring His divine character.

This could well have been a conclusion that David drew from the fact that II Sam. 7 had stressed the eternal character of the throne and kingdom of Him who was to be his greater son. That the occupation of this place at the right hand of the enthroned majesty on high was no idle honor appears from the words that follow, which guaranty that God shall exercise His power in behalf of Him who sits at His right hand and take up battle with His enemies until He has them all reduced to the position of abject servility where the conqueror sets His foot on their necks (cf., Josh. 10:24). Thus the initial statement of the psalm guaranties unequalled position and victory to the Messiah, in reference to whom David here speaks.

David (v. 2) addresses himself directly to Him about whom he spoke in the first verse by indicating more fully what the Lord on high will do for the Messiah. The Lord will make the Messiah's influence and authority extend from Zion, the center where He has allowed the kingdom of Israel to concentrate. From Zion as a starting point Messiah's influence will extend ever and ever farther outward, and He will exercise rule and authority though He is continually surrounded by His enemies. It shall be characteristic of His kingdom that enemies shall be in evidence continually. But it is not *they* that shall have dominion but *He*.

Nor shall He be alone in this warfare (v. 3). When He sets forth to give evidence of His power and control, there will be a great army of men in the prime of their youth who shall cheerfully volunteer their services and shall come fittingly equipped for holy warfare in holy garments, that is, arrayed in true righteousness and holiness. As dew in unnumbered gleaming globules is born at each new dawn, so shall these warriors be, numberless and continually fresh.

It would almost seem as though the next verse (4) indicates that the deeper source of the holy consecration that these soldiers of the Messiah manifest lies in the priesthood which is also a basic office that the Lord's Christ holds. But whether there is this deeper connection between vv. 3 and 4 or not, there is still this remarkable pronouncement in v. 4, that David's Lord holds a second major office. He is not restricted in this respect (cf. II Chron. 26:16ff.) as the kings of Israel were in that they were kings only and could at best merely second the priesthood in the performance of some of its duties. When this One comes He shall be One who has an unending priesthood; and since no such priest had ever been on the royal throne, this One is described as being of an order that is different from the Levitical priesthood, namely, the order of Melchizedek, who in days of old was both king and priest (Gen. 14:18ff.). This new feature of his dual office is said to be founded on nothing less than an immutable oath of the Lord Himself. More is not said at this point about the duties and functions of this great Priest.

The successful warfare that this unique personage wages is now described in brief but powerful figures, each of which is strikingly brief but extremely suggestive. It is not always easy to determine whether the One spoken about is Yahweh, the Lord Himself, of whether it is the sublime personage who fills the dual office just described. It may be more satisfactory to regard the One addressed as being the Messiah even as this was the case in v. 2. Then the One who shatters kings in the days of His wrath is the Lord, Yahweh Himself.

That He should now be at the right hand of David's Lord, where He gave to the latter a position of honor at His own right hand (v. 1) is due simply to the fact that the bestowal of the seat of honor is not to be understood in the sense of involving a particular spatial limitation as though from that moment onward He could be only in this one place. To convey the impression that the Lord Yahweh engages in

Psalm 110

conflict with a great display of power (for in many passages the right hand is the symbol of *power*) He Himself is spoken of as being at the right hand of His Anointed One.

By way of a colorful example of what He can do the most powerful adversaries are singled out—kings. They are shattered by Him in the encounter. But the range of His judgment goes farther than only the kings; it includes the nations, whose dead bodies shall lie scattered all around after the Lord's judgments are concluded (speaking in bold figures, of course), and the chief rulers over the wide earth will also be shattered by Him. This indicates merely that all judgment lies within His province, and that the conflict between the two kingdoms cannot continue as a stalemate forever. A definite victory will be on the Lord's side of the struggle.

It is in keeping with this thought that the last verse throws a bit of colorful detail on the screen, which makes the psalm end on a significantly triumphant note. It could well be possible that at this point the Messiah again moves into the forefront of the picture, for He cannot be thought of as being idle while the mighty contest is being waged. The description does nothing more than to depict Him as He for a moment with a swift movement refreshes His strength as Gideon's 300 men did at the spring of Harod (Judg. 7:6, losing not a bit of the precious time that is to be devoted to battle; or as Samson did in days of old after a great victory (Judg. 15:19), although there is this significant difference: Samson drank in utter exhaustion; this One experiences no such exhaustion and is never weary. Therefore, as He goes on He not only lifts up His head and recovers from weariness but continues with a wholesome self-consciousness by carrying His head high. Thus the Victorious One marches off the scene in further pursuit of the enemies. On this bold note the psalm closes.

Did these insights lie so far beyond David and his times as to make them impossible in that day and age? We believe not; and we are strongly of the conviction that this type of interpretation agrees best with the words: "David in Spirit called Him Lord," Matt. 22:41–46; Mark 12:35–37, as Jesus Himself told His generation.

It seems necessary to take issue with the many other approaches that have been offered in connection with the interpretation of this psalm. Much new material has been brought into the picture, but in connection with this psalm it has contributed little to a helpful interpretation. Men do see far more clearly nowadays than was once the case that the Orientals in particular regarded their kings as divine. Thus our psalm is regarded as such a pronouncement with regard to Israel's king, David, Solomon, or other rulers down to the time of the Maccabees. But Israel's views of its kings were not of this character.

Equally valueless is it to tie up the psalm with the never-mentioned festival of the enthronement of Yahweh, a part of which was the divine enthronement of Israel's king. Such a view does not give the importance to this psalm that our good Lord attached to it. The contention that Israel's kings were normally priests and shared in priestly functions and thus to explain the dual capacity of the ruler here stressed misconstrues most of the passages involved (II Sam. 6:12–19; 8:18; I Kings 8:14, 55, 56, 62, 63; 9:25; II Kings 16:12–15). In some instances the offering of sacrifices surely involved no more than having them properly sacrificed by the priests. The quotations from the Tell el Amarna letters or from Ugaritic texts do no more than to illustrate that certain of the phrases used were ancient Semitic material.

We do not believe that those interpreters do well who leave out of account or brush aside the testimony given in regard to this psalm in Matt. 22:41ff. and the parallel passages. When it is said in one form or another that the issue in Christ's debate with the Pharisees was not whether the psalm was or was not of Davidic authorship, but that He merely used their own arguments against them, that view of the case would have Jesus operate with dubious methods as long as He could only win the argument. Or to use the more careful statement that one of Jesus' methods of teaching was " ' to ask men questions such as would lead them to cross-examine themselves closely in the light of their own principles' " (*Gore*) as quoted by *Kirkpatrick*. We fail to see that this motive attributed to Jesus is in evidence in this case. Again, when it is asserted that, when the psalm is construed as above, namely, David's addressing the Christ before His birth, this is absolutely without parallel in the Psalter, we freely admit that. Do there have to be parallels before a thought dare be accepted as being true?

We would briefly take issue with the various possibilities that have been suggested as to the one whom the writer addresses. *Koenig* offers the shrewd suggestion that David could have spoken thus to Solomon in that last brief period of his own life after Solomon had been anointed king. For the aged David to call Solomon "lord" seems rather unnatural. Or then, what king was there in the ninth or eighth century that would have seemed to be a fitting personage for such flattering description? To bring the bombastic court style of court poets into the picture cheapens the psalter and its writers. To find Simon the Maccabee in a fictitious acrostic of the first four verses, impressive as it seems at first reading, requires too much manipulation of the text to make it reliable and is now accepted by very few interpreters. Or even to have David addressed by a court prophet who was also a priest comes too close to making light of the divine majesty, in that a man is elevated to a position of honor next to the Lord Himself. There is an unacceptable incongruity about such an approach unless we again have Israel's prophets engage in fulsome flattery when they spoke the language of sycophant courtiers.

It appears desirable that we go into further detail in the exposition of this psalm.

a) The dual office of the Messiah-He is both king and priest (vv. 1–4)

Of David. A psalm.
1. *The Lord said in reference to my Lord: "Sit at my right hand Until I make your enemies your footstool."*
2. *The Lord will extend Thy mighty sceptre from Zion; Rule in the midst of Thy enemies.*
3. *Thy people will offer themselves freely on the day of Thy power in holy array; Like dew from the womb of the morning Thy young men will come to Thee.*
4. *The Lord has sworn, and He will not retract it: "Thou shalt be a priest forever after the order of Melchizedek."*

1. Two different words are used for the terms which we have translated "Lord." In the first instance it is the word *Yahweh* (often written as "Jehovah"), and in the second it is *'Adhoni* which means "lord" or "Lord," being either merely a respectful form of address between man and man, or a word that may refer to the Lord in the highest sense of the term. In Gen. 23:6 it is used when Abraham is addressed. It could be applied to kings (see I Sam. 22:12; II Sam. 13:32). In what sense it is to be understood must be determined from the connection. Here the whole context suggests the divine implication. For this reason we have capitalized the pronouns in the translation whenever this personage is referred to. A unique word is also used for what we have translated "the Lord said." It is the word *ne'um,* which means "prophetic oracle," strictly: that which is whispered into the ear. But the word is used only with reference to communications that prophets received from the Lord. As a general rule, the word is then used at the close of some prophetic communication. Here it appears at the beginning.

The expression to sit at one's "right hand" involves only distinctive honor (cf., Ps. 45:9; I Kings 2:19). But in this instance the honor is of so unusual a nature that the one addressed as *'Adhoni* ranks on a par with the Lord and must, therefore, be regarded as divine, which happens to be the point of the argument which Christ directed at the Pharisees. The last clause might seem to weaken this claim in that the sitting at the right hand seems to be limited until the enemies are reduced to subjection. But also in the Hebrew the word "until" leads up to a certain point and no farther, saying neither that the action will continue, nor saying that it will not. For that reason the thought of the verse is well caught when the other translation "while" is used in this case. *McCullough* cites an appropriate parallel from a Ugaritic text: "And he caused [him] to sit at the right hand of Aleyn Baal" although this parallel merely confirms the idea of the place of honor involved.

2. When it is claimed in this verse that the Lord will extend this One's sceptre "from Zion," this merely states the fact that Christ's kingdom did take its beginning from among the Jews and in the congregation established at Jerusalem, for "salvation is of the Jews," John 4:22. The historical starting point of the kingdom of the Christ is here correctly designated.

3. This Lord is not without people. These people are not, however, pressed into service against their will. They are volunteers, whose wills He has strongly influenced so that they have cast their lot with His and live for Him in the finest freedom. For "offer themselves freely" the original has a noun, "freewell offerings." The term was applied to any sacrifices or offerings that were entirely voluntary. Here the term is used figuratively.

The day of the "power" of the Lord means, of course, the day when He displays His power. The word could be translated "the day of your campaign" (*Heereszug*). But our translation seems to capture the more important thought. The phrase "in holy array" (not so good: "In the beauties of holiness," *KJ*) implies that for such higher warfare as that which is here involved certain moral qualifications must mark those who participate. The Hebrew text joins this phrase to the second half of the verse, which seems to overload that half.

The highly poetic phrase, "from the womb of the morning," says rather uniquely that dew is born afresh with each dawning of the day. Like this dew, which is especially copious in parts of the Holy Land, are those who volunteer for the Lord's service: numerous and fresh. Itseems to be well justified to find these two points in the comparison. Some would add the idea that, as there is something mysterious about the origin of the dew, so, too, is there about the holy birth that makes men God's children. This seems like laying a bit more into the phrase than it can legitimately carry. "Youth" (*KJ*) for "young men" seems a bit ambiguous. We cannot help but present a free translation of *Luther's* version of this difficult verse, which, though it permits itself some liberties, is remarkably fresh and helpful: "After Thy victory Thy people will willingly offer sacrifice in holy array; Thy children are born unto Thee like dew out of the dawn."

4. The idea of God's swearing is like that of His making a covenant

with Abraham (Gen. 15:18). It is a human way of saying that God's pronouncement on such vital matters are irrevocable. The truth involved must be an exceedingly important one. It cannot be denied that Chirst's eternal priesthood be thought of too highly.

The untenability of the views that would make Maccabean rulers the ones under consideration here may yet be touched upon in connection with this matter of the priesthood. They were priests to begin with as we read in I Macc. 2:1. A solemn oath that they are to receive what they already have is a bit on the incongruous side. However, since the oath refers to what will occur in future, it is far better to translate, "Thou wilt be" than, "Thou art."

This is the first clear indication in Messianic prophecy that the Messiah shall have a twofold office, and what his second office is. For practical reasons there seemed to be a strong ground until this time for stressing the fact that the Messiah would encounter many foes and always be victorious in the encounter. Exclusive emphasis on this aspect of the case could lead to distortion of the truth. That it is granted to David to see more than others had seen must here also be attributed to the fact that David was "in the Spirit." Truth of this sort is revealed by divine inspiration. It might well have been possible that, as *Hengstenberg* points out, David wrote this psalm after his grievous fall into sin, when he was made to feel acutely the need of priestly mediation in behalf of poor sinners; and thus his mind may have been prepared for the insight that also such work would be done by the coming Deliverer. The best commentary on the words "after the order of Melchizedek" is, of course, to be found in Hebrews, 5 and 7.

b) **His successful warfare is then briefly but effectively described (vv. 5–7)**

5. *The Lord at Thy right hand*
   Will shatter kings in the day of His wrath.
6. *He will execute judgment among the nations, dead bodies will lie around everywhere;*
   He will shatter the chief rulers over the wide earth.
7. *Along the way he shall drink of the brook;*
   Therefore he shall carry His head high.

5. When we emphasized above that the "right hand" may also designate power or action, we find this to be in line with a goodly number of passages where this aspect stands out, as it apparently does here. Cf. Ps. 16:8; 18:35; 20:6; 73:23; 118:15; 139:10. There are other passages that also use vivid colors in portraying what God will do in the day of His wrath such as Joel 3:9ff.; Nah. 1:8ff.; Zeph. 3:6ff.

6. Strictly speaking, the Hebrew uses the verb "fill" or "be full"

without indicating whether it is to be understood transitively or intransitively. We sought to capture the force of the statement without using the verb "fill" by the idiomatic expression, "Dead bodies will lie about everywhere." For "chief rulers" the original has "head," which we believe is used collectively. The "heads" of the nations are their "chief rulers" or "chiefs" (*RSV*). Especially here it becomes apparent that only one side of the activity of the Messiah is being portrayed, the victor role. But even to this day that facet of His work has not been fully grasped.

7. In order to stress the fact that the first phrase, "along the way," does not modify "brook" we have separated the two and attached the phrase to the verb. Many commentators cannot extract any fitting sense from the verse and set about changing it till it agrees with what they feel should have been said. Results such as these are to be noted: "He waters the brooks with their blood" (*Oesterley*); "(An inheritance) on the way he maketh it, therefore he is exalted" (*Briggs*); or this is regarded as a rubric which directs the king in the course of the ceremonies of the day to drink at the fountain Gihon before the procession to the holy hill starts (*Weiser*). How much more satisfactory is the simple original in its natural sense!

Thus the psalm ends on a positive note of victory. Few psalms pack away so much depth of truth and insight as does this little gem of seven verses.

NOTES

3. Many commentators would change "in holy array" to "in holy mountains" by changing the *d* of the noun to *r* as is done in some manuscripts and by *Symmachus* and *Jerome*. The text as it stands seems far more appropriate. *Mishchar* could have resulted from a dittography of the *m,* and *shachar,* the usual form, could have been intended. Little is gained either way.

Helen Jefferson (JBL, 1954, III, p. 152ff.) shows that this psalm has a Hebrew vocabulary that has many parallels with the Ugaritic. There is always the possibility that the psalm may have some analogy with an old Ugaritic original, which it largely recasts, even as is the case with Ps. 29. The acknowledgment of this possibility does not in any way modify our interpretation.

Psalm 111

GREAT IS THE LORD
AND GREATLY TO BE PRAISED

THIS PSALM and the one that follows are a pair: both are acrostic, each verse beginning with a different letter of the alphabet; both have the same number of verses and the same length of verses. Further points of similarity will be discussed in connection with Ps. 112.

We clearly have a psalm of praise before us as our caption indicates. In the course of it God is praised both for what He is and for what He does. Strictly speaking we should not say "for what He is" because it is not His being in the abstract that is being discussed but His acts. For, as is well known, in the Old Testament God is always the God of action.

By almost common consent the postexilic date of the psalm is accepted. Since the era after the return from the Babylonian Captivity was one of discouragement and littleness of faith, one cannot help but feel that the psalm was written to hearten the faith of that generation by showing the nature of God's works throughout the history of His chosen people and then concluding with the pertinent observation that the fear of the Lord and the doing of His commandments were still basic for God's people as they had always been.

Whether, on the basis of v. 4, the psalm is to be thought of as being originally designed for the observance of the Passover festival may well be questioned, for v. 5 could with equal propriety point to the festival of Tabernacles, and v. 7 might point to the festival of Weeks, which was commonly associated with the giving of the law. In like manner, though a long tradition supports the contrary opinion, v. 4 does not point forward to Holy Communion, though this view is still held in certain areas.

The text of the Hebrew, though no better than customarily, is admitted to be exceptionally good. The acrostic form is also found in the following psalms: 9; 10; 25; 34; 37; 112; 119; 145.

It is true that this somewhat artificial mold into which the psalm is cast does put some restraint on the free flow of thought and upon the logical sequence of development. This is but a minor difficulty. For an obvious unity and progression are quite readily to be detected.

a) The Lord is to be praised for His works (vv. 1–4)
1. *Praise the Lord!*
   I will give praise to the Lord with my whole heart
   In the assembly of the upright and in the congregation.
2. *Great are the works of the Lord,*
   Deserving to be studied by all who have pleasure in them.
3. *Majestic and honorable is His work;*
   And His righteousness endures forever.
4. *He made His wonderful works to be remembered.*
   The Lord is gracious and compassionate.

1. The holy writer begins with a general summons to praise the Lord. Because this "Hallelujah" stands outside the acrostic does not stamp it as a later addition or as an extraneous element of the psalm. The writer would have all men praise the Lord. Since the proof of sincerity is yourself to do what you would exhort others to do, he indicates his readiness to engage in such prayer and praise, and that publicly in the sight of others, not that he might display his piety but that he might give proof of it.

A further indication of the sincerity of his purpose is the fact that his praise shall issue forth from his "whole heart." Obviously the reason the "assembly of the upright and the congregation" is mentioned is that it is so much more natural and easy to praise the Lord in the company of the like-minded. These persons are here described by two terms. The first of these indicates that the true servants of God are motivated to praise by uprightness as they are in all other things that they do whereas the term "congregation" points up the fact that these same persons have such a community of interests that they are quite naturally drawn together and form a unity.

2. If praise seeks a theme it has not far to go, for the "works of the Lord" are always in evidence, and the obvious thing to be said about them is they are always "great." Their many-sidedness constitutes a challenge to those who have pleasure in such things to give careful thought to the magnitude of that which the Lord has done. God's works should be reflected upon frequently and earnestly. Such reflection will always stir the thoughtful soul to praise.

3. Aside from the general descriptive term "great," there are other more specific designations that should be employed. There are terms such as "majestic and honorable" that aptly describe the works of the Lord. When God acts, His deeds are always done on a high level and worthy of the great Lord who performs them. Equally in evidence in works that He performs is the attribute of righteousness, which may be defined as the intensity with which He carries through His covenant

obligations to His people. This is always in the picture, and, therefore, it "endures forever." This immutability of God is prominent in this verse as well as in vv. 5, 8, 9, 10.

4. Another characteristic of the Lord's works is that He does them in such a way that they are not soon forgotten: they stick in the memory of His people, and the wonder of them engages their fancy from generation to generation. That leads the poet to list as a climax of the adjectives that have been employed to characterize what the Lord has done the fact that He is "gracious and compassionate." The very phrase would appear to be borrowed from Exod. 34:6. On the whole, a rather comprehensive array of divine attributes has been enumerated as being worthy of man's finest praise, both in his own heart and publicly with his lips.

b) He is to be praised for the mercies bestowed upon Israel (vv. 5–9)

5. *He gave food to those who feared Him;*
   And He was ever mindful of His covenant.
6. *He displayed the power of His works to His people*
   By giving them the heritage of the heathen.
7. *The works of His hands are true and just;*
   Utterly reliable are all His precepts.
8. *They are established forever and ever*
   And are appointed in truth and uprightness.
9. *He sent redemption to His people;*
   He commanded His covenant forever;
   Holy and awe-inspiring is His name.

5. We fear that the distinctive nature of this section is lost when the tense of the verbs used is ignored. They are plain past tenses, not presents as *KJ* and *RSV* and also *Luther* render them. We have in these verses a reference to certain historical incidents, some of which are unmistakably clear, others of which have to be interpreted in the light of their connection.

Though a somewhat unusual word is used, due to the restrictive nature of the acrostic arrangement, the "food" referred to would most naturally be the manna, which was furnished from heaven throughout forty years—a miracle that is too great to be lightly passed by. This miracle He wrought for those that fear Him—an apt description of the people of God for all times. In thus providing for them He gave a striking instance of "how He was ever mindful of His covenant." It was not their worthiness that brought them this great boon but God's fidelity to what He had promised.

6. Perhaps next in point of downright greatness of the act done is the possession of the land of Canaan which He bestowed upon Israel,

giving a land to a nation, complete and entire, when it was without a country of its own. Of this act the writer significantly remarks that it was an instance of "displaying the power of His works to His people."

7. The writer must pause for a moment and engage in a summary reflection. Such works of the Lord's hands "are true and just," a new set of attributes that he has not had occasion to make mention of before. But quite in line with this thought is the next that has reference to that other marvelous gift which the Lord gave to Israel—His law or His precepts. In a list of mighty works such as these who will say positively which is absolutely the greater and which exactly next in order, works such as giving of manna, giving of Canaan, giving of the law? In any case, these marvelous precepts deserve to be described as being "utterly reliable." To this must be added the thought (v. 8) that these precepts have a validity that endures and are not like the uncertain ordinances expressed by the law of man. In other words, "They are established forever and ever; they are appointed in truth and uprightness."

9. Two notable works of that general period of Israel's history should with all propriety be mentioned. They are the exodus from Egypt as such ("He sent redemption to His people") and the establishment of the covenant with Israel at Mt. Sinai, described in Exodus, 19–24 ("He commanded His covenant forever"). The word "redemption" is of so general a character that it could very rightly be referred to the restoration from the Babylonian Captivity. But the general context of all the other works mentioned directs our thinking to a much earlier work of God. As in v. 7 the need was felt of summarizing the works of God by a more general statement, so here there is a need of making a comprehensive statement of the character or "name" of God. For this is the force of the remark: "Holy and awe-inspiring is His name." "Terrible" (*RSV*) is a less appropriate translation of the last adjective, for the feeling involved is an entirely wholesome one since the root of the verb connotes some measure of wholesome fear. Besides, it is this root that serves as the connecting link between v. 9 and 10. For the word "reverence" mentioned in v. 10 stems from this root.

c) **Reverent awe of Him and the keeping of His commandments is still the better part of wisdom (v. 10)**

10. *The chief thing in wisdom is reverence for the Lord;*
    Good understanding have all who keep them;
    His praise endures forever.

Some interpreters resent somewhat the thought that the psalm closes with a statement that is so strongly reminiscent of the utterances of wisdom literature. Others draw from this verse the conclusion that the

Psalm 111

psalm must be late because they date books like Proverbs as being exilic or postexilic in spite of its professed authorship, for the most part, by Solomon himself. Neither of these views deserves special consideration. What if for just one verse a writer departs from the hymnic strain to the more didactic? Must types of style be adhered to with such rigidity?

As already indicated above, this concluding remark may well present by way of summary the chief objective that the writer had in mind aside from the praise of the Lord. To an age when Israel, due to its depressed state, was inclined to give up the fear of the Lord and the faithful adherence to His commandments the author virtually says: Now as always in the past the due "reverence for the Lord" is not only important, it is the very "chief thing," the "essence," the "foundation," "the zenith" (*Oesterley*) of wisdom. To abandon it is the part of folly. So likewise all those who faithfully keep God's precepts give proof of "good understanding."

Praise was the psalmist's initial goal, and instruction was merely incidental. Thus the author returns to his first objective and closes on that note: "His praise endures forever." There is a connection between that claim and the remarks that immediately preceded. It is this: Those who are firm in their reverence for the Lord and in their keeping of His commandments will have such experiences of the faithfulness of God as will give them ample occasion to utter the praises of the Lord forever. By this last remark the writer begins to venture over into the domain of the next psalm.

NOTES

2b. This verse has been variously translated. The passive participle *derushim* may be regarded as a plain passive, "sought out" (*KJ*). But with equal propriety it may by a natural transition in thought express that which *should* be done. It is like the German *erforschenswert*. This suggested our translation "deserving to be studied." The question then arises whether *chephtsehem* is to be derived from *chéphets,* "delight," or from *chaphets,* "delighting in." As to form, both are possible as *KW* also amply demonstrates. Consequently our translation may be upheld.

4. This verse begins literally: "A remembrance He made for His wonderful works." This could be a direct reference to the Passover, which was definitely instituted for the purpose of keeping the remembrance of this deliverance alive (Exod. 13:9, 10). But up to this point in the psalm nothing as yet indicates that this era of Israel's history is under consideration. Therefore a more general meaning is to be preferred, which the *KJ* translators caught beautifully with the words:

"He hath made His wonderful works to be remembered." That statement holds good with regard to all the works of the Lord. We can understand how the ancient church could interpret the verse as a sort of prophecy of the Holy Supper, especially in view of the somewhat literal rendering of the Latin: *Memoriam fecit mirabilium suorum,* which Luther, following this same tradition, translated: *Er hat ein Gedaechtnis gestiftet seiner Wunder.*

10. In the clause "who keep them" the word "them" appears to be without a proper antecedent, which fact led the *KJ* to translate more grammatically from the point of view of good English: "that do His commandments." However, the thought is apparently that those have good understanding who keep the fear of the Lord referred to in v. 10a. At the same time there seems to be a remembrance of the "precepts" referred to in v. 7. That plural noun could have produced the plural suffix "them." In any case, the thought is clear though many interpreters would after the lead of the *Septuagint* change slightly the suffix of the feminine singular.

Psalm 112

THE PRAISE OF GOD AS SEEN IN WHAT HE DOES FOR THOSE WHO FEAR HIM

THIS PSALM has been approached from various angles with a great variety of different results. One writer regards it as glorifying the law; another calls it a psalm of comfort; another says that it exalts the steadying power of trust in God. To tell the truth, each of these items comes in for consideration. But it is still true that the opening note is, "Praise the Lord." It is equally true that, whereas the preceding psalm showed how greatly deserving of praise the Lord Himself is, in this psalm the emphasis is on the praise that He deserves because of what He does for those who truly fear Him.

It can now be pointed out what a strange parallelism exists between these twin psalms (111, 112). Not only do both have the same number of verses with the same length of each verse in acrostic order, but phrases and groups of words are in the one psalm used with reference to the believer whereas the same words were used with reference to God in the preceding psalm. The third verse in each psalm is a striking parallel.

Also vv. 4 and 8. The fact that the second says about man what was previously said about God leads some interpreters to suggest that for this psalm the superscription might be used: "Be ye perfect as your Father in heaven is perfect." From another point of view it might even seem irreverent to say of the godly man that he is "gracious and full of compassion, and righteous," exalted adjectives which seem to be reserved exclusively for the Lord (cf. Exod. 34:6).

The author is unknown. Some manuscripts of the *Septuagint* have as a superscription "at the time of Haggai and Zechariah." The psalm may be even later than that, for the occupation of the man described seems to move in the area of business and commerce rather than in agriculture. The psalm bears some resemblance to Ps. 15 and even to Ps. 24. The emphasis on the importance of the law does not date from the recent appearance of books like Leviticus but could have been in the picture as early as the days of David and Solomon.

The outline may not be as distinctly marked as it is in some other psalms, but there is still an orderly and noticeable progression of thought.

a) The happy state of man who fears the Lord (v. 1)

> 1. *Praise the Lord!*
> *O how very happy is the man who fears the Lord,*
> *Who delights greatly in His commandments!*

We repeat: the praise of God is to be discovered also in what He does for the man who fears Him and keeps His commandments. These two items belong together. The deep taproot of godly living is the fear of the Lord, which, as has often been remarked, is almost the equivalent of faith and trust in God. Whenever such fear is sincere it expresses itself in the keeping of God's commandments (cf. also Luther's explanation of the Ten Commandments). But it is not the *keeping* of the commandments that is stressed but the *delight* that such a one has in them. Ps. 1:2 immediately comes to mind. He studies them, reflects on them; and such deep interest in them, if it is sincere, must eventuate in the ready obedience to them all.

b) The details of the happy state of the man who fears the Lord (vv. 2, 3)

> 2. *His descendants shall be outstanding in the earth;*
> *As a generation of upright men they shall be blessed.*
> 3. *Abundance and riches will be in his house;*
> *And his righteousness will endure forever.*

2. One is at a loss as to whether the tense in which these statements are worded is the present or the future (in v. 4, for example, a gnomic

aorist appears to be used, which is usually best translated as a present). The tenses used allow for either interpretation, and one is as good as the other. Both what a truly godly man enjoys and what he will enjoy are in the picture. Since a man usually thinks in terms of himself and his children that come after him, it is much in order to describe the first feature of the happy lot of the one who fears God as being that his descendants fill their place well on earth. Here it is said: "They shall be outstanding" (in the original: "heroes") wherever they may be on earth. Because the natural assumption is that they will follow in their parents' footsteps they, too, shall be upright men and shall enjoy the same blessing that their elders enjoyed. That is one major blessing.

3. Another notable one is that "abundance and riches will be in such a one's house," for the Lord delights to reward also with earthly blessings all those that are true to His law. This is a common emphasis in the Old Testament and is not so much an indication of a some narrow point of view but rather of a depth of insight inasmuch as earthly blessings are good gifts of the good God who made them and are not to be esteemed lightly.

The third of the notable blessings enumerated is: "And his righteousness will endure forever." As to form, this statement was motivated by 111:3, which concludes in the same way, but in reference to God. In a certain sense the same dare be predicated of the Lord's children. But as many interpreters have already pointed out, the thought really states as *Weiser* has worded it: Righteousness "is not in this instance a moral quality but a gift of God, the gift of salvation in the inner and in the outward aspects of life." This man's righteousness is not the good record that he has compiled but the salvation that God has bestowed upon him. This comes very close to the New Testament justification by faith. Note the emphasis on the enduring nature of the things God's grace has produced in the lives of such men: "forever" appears here and in v. 6 and in v. 9. God builds solidly in the lives of His saints.

c) The attitude of helpfulness toward the needy (vv. 4, 5)

4. *He arises like light in the darkness for the upright;*
   He is gracious and full of compassion and righteous.
5. *Happy is the man who is gracious and ready to lend;*
   Who manages his affairs with justice.

4. It is to be expected that in the picture of so happy a man some traits of unselfishness will appear. He is here portrayed as taking pleasure in helping others. Several other statements in the psalm are of a rather challenging nature, for they use terms with reference to the righteous man that are almost too bold. The verse can be translated: "Light rises in the darkness for the upright." But such a rendering is out of

Psalm 112

line with the second member of the verse, which is then usually changed so as to make it apply to God. That is the daring feature of this psalm, that its vigorous statements move to the very border line of what dare properly be asserted about God's children. If the man who is being described loves to help his needy fellow men, it must be admitted that in every instance of such help he can be thought of as arising like "a light in the darkness for the upright." Since he acts in the spirit of his heavenly Father, there is a propriety about describing him as being "gracious and full of compassion and upright." With this approach v. 5 falls so naturally into place that the merit of such an interpretation is strongly underscored.

5. Doing what was just described brings with it its own rewards: such a man is "happy," which is a term that is not quite as strong as is the "O how very happy" of v. 1. It stands about on the level of "O what a fine thing it is" to find a mind so charitably disposed to others; and how rewarding it is for him himself! Another direction in which his attitude may express itself is that he is "ready to lend." Many further examples of this type of mind could be added, but enough for the present. A well-balanced situation is usually found in the case of those who are unselfish in the help they are ready to grant to others: they usually manage their own affairs judiciously. Wholesome concern for another's welfare makes a man more adept at handling his own affairs well.

There follows an attractive emphasis on another fruit that such a life produces, or, if you will, on another grace that God in His mercy bestows on this type of man. He is apt to be marked by a certain type of stability in all his works and doings.

d) The stability of a man thus blessed by God (vv. 6–8)

6. *For he will never be shaken;*
   A righteous man will be remembered forever.
7. *He will not be afraid of bad tidings;*
   His heart is firm, confidently relying on the Lord.
8. *His heart is sustained, he will not be afraid*
   Until he sees his desire upon his enemies.

Since the foundation on which he rests is his God, and since the eminent blessings of God are showered upon him, the righteous man does not soon topple from his position, is not soon moved, has about him a certain steadfastness that all men yearn for. When the second member of the verse says that such a one "will be remembered forever," that is largely due to the fact that the man was not minded one way on one day and differently the next. By his very solidity and firmness he made a definite impression on his generation, always remembering that in the view of this psalm such stability was the result of God's gifts to him.

Another storm that such a one was able to weather was that of receiving "bad tidings." That does not say that bad tidings never came to him. In many cases they may have been reduced to a minimum, but he did not live in continual apprehension of them because his heart was fixed in the Lord, the ever-present helper, as the rest of the verse asserts: "His heart is firm, confidently relying on the Lord," and as the beginning of v. 8 carefully reiterates: "His heart is sustained, he will not be afraid." The opposite, however, is the case regarding his enemies. The assumption is not that personal enemies are here thought of, with regard to whom one selfishly expects that, just because they antagonize *us,* they must be worsted. The writer rather knows his own cause to be the Lord's and that of his foes to frustrate the work of the Lord. By thus bringing the enemies into the picture the writer prepares the way for the contrast that appears in the last two verses.

e) **A summary description of the happy man in contrast with the disappointment of the wicked (vv. 9, 10)**

9. *He gives freely to the poor;*
His righteousness endures forever;
His horn is exalted in honor.
10. *The wicked will see it and be displeased;*
He shall gnash with his teeth and consume away;
The desire of the wicked will not be realized.

9. In this summarizing statement, which is still in the nature of praise of God for the things that He does for those that fear Him, two classes of men are contrasted: the righteous and the wicked, as indicated above. The following fine points of the life of the righteous are stressed: a) "he gives freely to the poor" (Hebrew: "He scatters and gives"); this kind of charity is especially stressed in the psalm; b) "his righteousness endures forever" (cf. the remarks on this same statement above, v. 3b; c) "his horn is exalted in honor" (since "horn" signifies strength, his sturdy attitude on all of life's issues is thought of as contributing to his good report and the fine opinion that good man have of this person everywhere).

10. In obvious contrast with this man who pleases God is the wicked man, who displeases Him. He will see the manifest prosperity of the righteous, and it will irk him strongly. It will even arouse his indignation to the point of utter frustration, when he gnashes his teeth over the man and "consumes away" (*PBV*), literally, "melts away." As a further description of the disappointment he will experience it is said of the wicked that "the desire of the wicked is not realized."

The goals he has set for himself are not attained. His ambitions are not realized. One is reminded of the parallel description in Ps. 1:6: "But the way of the ungodly shall perish." This is not vengeful and unkind thinking in regard to the wicked. It is insight into how the Lord rewards those that truly fear him and prevents the enemies of His people from seeing their evil purposes come to fruition. That is something for which God may be truly praised. True, there are some exceptions to this rule. But it is still a rule, the validity of which is commonly to be observed.

NOTES

5. "A good man showeth favor" (*KJ*) is a rendering which slightly misses the point and is not in keeping with the Hebrew original.

Psalm 113

THE UNIQUE GREATNESS OF THE LORD

SUCH A SUBJECT as the caption indicates must stimulate the praise of God's people. Therefore this is properly classified as a psalm of praise. The outline of its contents would indicate this a bit more clearly.
a) A summons to praise God (vv. 1–3).
b) His incomparable greatness (vv. 4–6).
c) Two striking instances of such greatness (vv. 7–9).

The opening and the closing Hallelujah ("Praise the Lord") serve to mark this still more clearly as a song of praise.

All commentators agree that the psalm is postexilic as to date. Most writers are at the same time ready to concede that an unexpressed purpose may lie behind its words. For it is generally understood that after the return from the Exile Israel's state was a rather discouraging one. She might be likened to the poor man sitting on the ash heap (v. 7) or to the childless mother of the household (v. 9). The psalm stresses the thought that the Lord helps such unfortunate people; and thus the psalm is to be thought of as being a word of comfort in evil and depressing times, that it was written for the "worm Jacob" (Is. 41: 14) and for the "afflicted and stormtossed one" (Is. 54:11) as *Hengstenberg* so aptly states it.

In Hebrew lore this psalm is the first of the group of psalms (113–

118) called the *Hallel* (which means "praise"). These, as *Delitzsch* so well describes them, were reserved for use on the three great festivals —Passover, Weeks, and Tabernacles—for the new moon celebrations (except New Year) and for Dedication. The first two psalms of this group would be sung before the meal and the rest after the meal and the filling of the fourth cup. What gives a certain poignancy to this practice is that the Gospels refer to our Savior's observance of this practice on the occasion of the last supper (Matt. 26:30; Mark 14:26).

It is rather doubtful whether we dare put a particular liturgical construction upon the psalm and regard it as containing in v. 1 a rubrical direction that praise is to be chanted, which is followed by two separate choruses, the first comprising vv. 2–4, the second vv. 5–9. Though such a use could be made of the psalm, there is too little of clear-cut evidence in the psalm that indicates that such use was designed by the writer.

1. *Praise the Lord!*
   Praise, O servants of the Lord,
   Praise the name of the Lord.
2. *Blessed be the name of the Lord*
   From this time forth and for evermore.
3. *From the rising of the sun to its setting*
   Let the name of the Lord be blessed.

1. This threefold summons to praise the Lord is addressed to those who are called His "servants." This may well refer to the whole nation, which is called the "servants of the Lord" (see 136:22; Is. 41:8, 9) or to the individuals of that nation who are similarly designated (see Ps. 34:22; 69:36). In the absence of any reference that would limit the term to priests or Levites in the Temple, it is best to understand the term as referring to individual Israelites. Therefore all who call upon the name of the Lord are addressed in this summons. When in a parallel expression they are asked to praise "the name of the Lord," that name is the comprehensive summary of all that God has revealed about Himself in word and deed, in other words, it is the Lord Himself in the fulness of His divine character.

2. Since His deeds are so manifold, His praise should be continuous and unending. The phrase "from this time forth and for evermore" appears repeatedly in later psalms as a favorite expression (see Ps. 115:18; 121:8; 125:2; 131:3).

3. As all time is to be marked by praise, so there is to be no place in the wide expanse of the earth where these praises are not chanted. They are to be heard from "the rising of the sun"—an expression that

practically always refers to the place where it rises—to its setting. With a breadth of vision all nations are thought of as participating in this praise, for even those that do not know Him as Israel does are the recipients of unnumbered blessings of His. These words remind one of Ps. 50:1 and Mal. 1:11.

4. *The Lord is high above all nations,*
   And His glory above the heavens.
5. *Who is like the Lord, our God,*
   Who has seated Himself so high;
6. *Who looks so far down*
   Upon the heavens and the earth?

Imbedded in the heart of the psalm is the description of the incomparable greatness of the Lord. It consists of two factors which reciprocally condition one another. The one cannot be evaluated without the other. The one is His unspeakable exaltation, which is "above all nations," no matter how great and powerful they may seem to be, and even "above the heavens" themselves, which physically are the highest of the high. In fact, there is no one that can be compared with Him. This echoes the thought expressed in Exod. 15:11.

He has done two things, each of which seems to make the other impossible. He has first taken His seat so high that no one can match Him, yet He has regard for the lowliest of the low in that He "looks down so far." Though the heavens seem high, when He looks at them He looks down even as He does upon the earth. More than physical height and depth are certainly referred to here although the figure moves in the area of the physical. Isaiah also expressed this thought in 57:15. His greatness, therefore, does not consist in a proud overlooking and ignoring of the lowly but in having regard for it and noting its need of help. For it is on that level where help is usually most sadly needed.

7. *He raises up the poor from the dust*
   And lifts the needy from the ash heap
8. *To make him sit with princes,*
   With the princes of the people.
9. *He makes the barren woman abide in the household*
   As a happy mother of her children.

7. From this point onward the echoes of I Sam. 2, the Song of Hannah, ring through the psalm, especially vv. 8 and 5 of that poem, even as the echoes of the Magnificat are to be discerned. The poor man or the lowly one as the Hebrew words it is the insignificant personage, whom affliction or disease (cf. Job) may have made almost an out-

cast of society so that in his despair he takes his place on the refuse heap of a town together with all the rest of that which men have cast off. Such gestures are typically Oriental. But he that has humbled himself because the Almighty has humbled him finds that no one less than the great Lord of heaven and earth Himself raises him up and lifts him out of his distress.

8. This verse implies that the Lord can for that matter raise these lowly ones even to the point where the highest seats of honor come to be theirs, "with princes, with the princes of the people." The writer would scarcely claim that every case of exaltation involved such a measure of dignity. Joseph and Job would be classical examples, also David and Saul.

9. The second illustration of the Lord's mode of dealing with the lowly is that of the frustrated Oriental woman who has been childless. I Sam. 1 shows clearly how great such disgrace was thought to be in days of old. The great Lord can and often does effectually change the situation of such a one. When her changed lot is described as being an abiding in the household, that involves that her position as a wife was often dubious until she had borne children to her husband. In reading both these illustrations Israel could well reflect upon her own lot. She was the one who was humbled to the dust. She was barren and destined to extermination. The Lord had put an end to her despair and made plain His greatness in doing thus. Those who understand that the Lord loves to work after this pattern have deep insight into the ways of the Lord.

NOTES

5. The Hebrew uses a somewhat strange construction at this point. For "seated Himself so high" it reads: "He that maketh high the sitting" and then: "He that maketh low the sitting" for the next expression. The auxiliary infinitive expresses the chief feature of the thought. Cf. *GK* 90, 3 and 114n.

Psalm 114

THE DELIVERANCE FROM EGYPT RECALLED

It seems quite likely that this psalm dates from the time after the return from the Babylonian Captivity. Most of the psalms in this section of the Psalter do. Judah and Israel do not refer to the two parts of the divided kingdom (v. 2), for even after the return Judah was regarded as the outstanding tribe, and Israel was still the common name for the nation.

If this date for the psalm is assumed, it is quite likely that the immediate purpose of the psalm was to encourage the downhearted people in those gloomy days that followed for quite a while after the captives had come back home and were encountering nothing but difficulties and disappointments. By recalling the mighty deeds God wrought in the past the writer is bolstering the courage of his generation to believe that the same God is mighty still. The propriety of the use of the psalm in the "Hallel" must at the same time be noted. For in the Passover season the various aspects of that great deliverance would be considered, though that fact does not necessitate that the psalm was composed for this festival.

Brief though the psalm is, its poetic beauty and vividness of style are conceded on every hand. It has something of the dramatic element in it, with questions and answers, with personifications and bold imagery.

In the Christian Church it came to be associated with the burial service because the psalm spoke of a departure, which could also be regarded, as far as the words themselves were concerned, as the departure from this life. It is also readily understood how the psalm became a proper psalm for Easter Day, which is our New Testament Passover.

The psalm may further be thought of as a companion piece to Ps. 113. Whereas the latter dwells on God's condescension to the lowly and helpless, this psalm gives striking examples of such condescension in action. Various writers have dwelt on the fact that, whereas Egyptian and Babylonian writers also extol the mighty works of their gods, the works reflected on lie in the area of mythical deeds of the past, not in the realm of actual historical events in the nation's history. Attempts to associate the psalm with the mythical enthronement festival, no trace of which appears anywhere in the sacred records of Israel, is quite futile and misleading.

The psalm quite naturally falls into four sections of two verses each.

a) **What the exodus meant for Israel (vv. 1, 2)**

1. *When Israel went out of Egypt,*
The house of Jacob from a people of unintelligible language,
2. *Judah became His sanctuary,*
Israel His mighty dominion.

We are immediately in thought transferred to the time of the Exodus by the opening clause. The parallel statement reminds us that one of the oppressive features experienced by the Israelites was the fact that the people of the land in which they were strangers spoke a language that was quite unintelligible to the Israelities, a fact which made them feel still more strange in the land (cf., Deut. 28:49). At that time Israel was given a certain status by God, so that, on the one hand, the nation came to be God's sacred possession ("His sanctuary") and, on the other hand, she became "His mighty dominion," the realm on earth over which He Himself assumed rule and authority in a special sense. We are reminded of the statement in which God defined Israel's peculiar status (Exod. 19:6): "Ye shall be to Me a kingdom of priests and a holy nation." That the time thought of is not to be limited to the precise day when the Exodus as such occurred appears from the fact that the events referred to run from the beginning of the Exodus through to the occupation of the land after the crossing of the Jordan.

b) **Striking events that occurred in nature at this time (vv. 3, 4)**

3. *The sea looked and fled;*
The Jordan turned back.
4. *The mountains skipped like rams*
And the hills like young lambs.

The poetic imagery now becomes rather vivid. Exactly what it was that the sea and the Jordan, the mountains and the hills saw and thus became filled with fright and consternation is not stated. Was it the event as such, a nation on the march from bondage to a land of freedom? Was the sight of a nation liberated? Or was it, as some interpreters claim, the Lord Himself? The last approach would seem to requite a definite statement if the Lord Himself had been referred to. In any case, the events referred to were immediately plain to the well-informed Israelite. The sea looked and fled at the time when the children of Israel crossed the so-called Red Sea (Exod. 14:21), and the

Psalm 114

Jordan turned back at the time when Israel entered Canaan (Josh. 3: 14–16). The mountains and the hills skipped when the law was given on Mt. Sinai (Exod. 19:18; Judg. 5:4): the earth did quake greatly.

Each figure is bold. The thought of mountains skipping like rams is almost fantastic. But exuberance is also a good quality in poetic descriptions. In any case, by personifying the elements in nature that were affected, the writer makes it plain that the forces of nature were in great awe of the Lord of all, and that that is why they behaved as they did. Nature and its forces do not according to the Old Testament conception operate independently of the Creator; they are not controlled by fixed laws, which work by their own power. They are under the Lord's sovereign rule and can in manifold ways contribute to the welfare of His kingdom.

c) **An inquiry into the cause of these natural manifestations (vv. 5, 6)**

5. *What ailed you, O sea, that you fled?*
   You, Jordan, that you turned back?
6. *You mountains, that you skipped like rams?*
   You hills, like young lambs?

Four rhetorical questions which are to stimulate thought as to the great controlling force that brought about these manifestations of uneasiness in the case of the four creatures mentioned. At loss for a better rendering, we can scarcely do without the verb "ailed" though this might seem to imply that something was wrong with the sea, the Jordan, the mountains, and the hills so that they reacted as they did. This is certainly the last thought that the writer would have sought to convey. The more familiar versions avoid this difficulty by translating a bit more literally, like *Luther, Was war dir, du Meer?* The cause of this alarm on the part of the forces of nature is being inquired into.

Strictly speaking, the author leaves his fourfold question unanswered. His readers know the answer. Nor is the last section (vv. 7, 8) an answer. It is rather an inference that goes on the assumption that all readers know well that it was God's mighty presence among His people that made the earth and its strong forces tremble. In fact, that is the very reaction that, poetically speaking, the author would encourage on the part of the seemingly dull and insensitive earth.

d) **A summons to the earth to tremble at God's mighty presence (vv. 7, 8)**

7. *Tremble, O earth, at the presence of the Lord,*
   At the presence of the God of Jacob,
8. *Who turns the rock into a pool of water*
   And the flint into springs of water.

Some interpreters find the theme of the psalm in v. 7. One may regard the verse as the practical application that the writer makes in view of the mighty works of the Exodus. Some of the forces of this old world had been shown to have reacted strongly to God's mighty works for Israel. It is now concluded that the very old earth itself should show a similar sense of reverence in God's presence, who, in the parallel statement, is called "the God of Jacob," reminding the nation that so great a God stands in a relation of unusual intimacy with this ancient people.

To reinforce the argument, a few additional works of the Lord are briefly alluded to in the last verse, instances when the Lord displayed His power by providing water in the wilderness at a time when the nation might well have died of thirst. One of these instances occurred shortly after the land of Egypt had been left (Exod. 17:6), the other when the land of promise was almost in sight (Num. 20:11). Again the statements are highly poetic in character, for rocks were not transmuted into water nor flint into springs. But all except those who use a very prosy approach like such sturdy and expressive figures.

Though we reject all allegory we cannot refrain from quoting *Luther's* statement as to what thoughts Christian people associate with a psalm like this when they read it. He says: "We on our part sing this psalm daily to praise Christ, who leads us out of death and sin, through the midst of the ragings of the world, the flesh, and the devil into life eternal."

NOTES

2. The expression "His sanctuary" uses a personal pronoun without indicating its antecedent, a usage that is rather common in the Old Testament in reference to Him who is the common subject in religious texts. We tried to catch the force of the plural of *mamshelothaw* by adding the adjective "mighty" to "dominion." Cf. *KS* 319 1.

5. We render the verb "ailed" as a past tense because the whole setting of the events described lies in the past.

6. The article is used with the vocative (*KS* 290e). We felt this could be caught in part by using "you" with "mountains."

7. Scholars point out that this is the only place where '*adhon* ("Lord") appears without an article.

8. The participle has the old case ending *i* like a number of forms in the preceding psalm. This is perhaps simply an intentional archaism on the part of the poet. Similarly an old case ending appears on the word for "springs." Cf. *GK* 90n.

Psalm 115

MAY THE ALMIGHTY VINDICATE
THE HONOR OF HIS NAME

IN THIS PSALM a pattern of a liturgical sort appears rather prominently so that the responsive character of the psalm must freely be admitted. Yet expositors encounter no end of difficulty in determining exactly what the responsive pattern is, as they all admit. *Kittel's* arrangement is as nearly acceptable as any. He assigns vv. 1, 2 to the congregation; vv. 3–8 to a choir; vv. 9–11 to Levites; vv. 12, 13 to priests; vv. 14, 15 again to the choir; and vv. 16–18 to the congregation. This would have to be supplemented by the suggestion that vv. 9–11 demand that in each case the second member of the verse be assigned to some group to offer the response. Construed thus or similarly, it must be admitted that the psalm has a lively liturgical pattern of rendition.

Aside from this more or less formal feature, as to contents the psalm is unique in that for the first time it presents a strong polemic against idols. The section involved (vv. 3–8) appears again in Ps. 135:15–18 and is not entirely unique in the Old Testament Scriptures. Compare similar briefer utterances in Deut. 4:28; 28:36; Hab. 2:18; Jer. 2:8; 16:19; Is. 42:17; 57:13; Ps. 96:5. The obvious note of sarcasm, here legitimately introduced, appears also in the lengthier accounts of the manufacture of idols that Isaiah offers in 40:19f.; 44:9–17. The apocryphal book of the Wisdom of Solomon has some similar passages: 13:10–19; 14:12–21; 15:7–17.

If we set the time of the composition of this psalm shortly after the return from the Babylonian Captivity, this feature of the psalm is most readily understood. For during their residence in Babylon the captives had had ample opportunity to observe both the prevalence and the futility of idol worship and to reflect thankfully on the enlightened position that Israel held on this question. For that matter, the folly of idolatry must have become strikingly apparent.

At this point some interpreters object to the fact that the writer of this psalm identifies the idols with their images, an identification that the more enlightened among the heathen repudiated. But in actual practice this distinction was without a doubt scarcely made, and the heathen worshiper usually identified the image with the god. The writer must have observed this and knew whereof he spoke.

In this connection it may also be stressed that as a result of this polemic on idolatry the psalm becomes an exponent of monotheism, clearly expressed. In this respect the psalm agrees with Ps. 86:9, 10 as well as with Ps. 135:17, 18 where our passage recurs.

The tone of the psalm is fresh and bold and its literary structure vivid and original.

a) **A basic plea for help on the part of the nation (vv. 1, 2)**

1. *Not unto us, O Lord, not unto us, but unto Thy name give glory*
   On the basis of Thy steadfast love, on the basis of Thy faithfulness.
2. *Why should the nations say:*
   Where now is their God?

1. It might be suggested that the order of the thoughts of this petition should proceed in about the following fashion: Deliver us, O Lord, for the nations are dishonoring Thy name because of our helpless state and are taunting us and saying, "Where is their God?" Help us on the basis of Thy steadfast love and faithfulness. The glory will then be Thine, not ours, for we cannot save ourselves. But the psalmist is concerned about the honor of his God and, therefore, puts the last thought first, leaves the plea for help unstated though implied, and reveals the basis on which such help may be anticipated from God: His steadfast love and His faithfulness. The result is that the first verse has become a classic expression of how to give God all honor and glory and disavow man's achievements in God's sight. Furthermore, as a result of this order of thought careless reading of the psalm has overlooked the fact that this is really a plea for help which is rather uniquely stated.

2. The fact that the nations are represented as saying, "Where is their God?" shows how desperate Israel's lot must have been at the time. Outsiders could not detect that the Lord was with His people or doing anything for them. Observe the same taunt in Ps. 79:10 and 42:3. But whenever such disparaging remarks are being made, the glory of God is being indicted. For, in the last analysis, He it is alone who can help and has valiantly supported His people at all times. This complete brushing aside of the glory of man in favor of the glory of God finds expression elsewhere in the Scriptures: see Dan. 9:18, 19; Is. 48:9, 11; Ezek. 20:9, 14; 36:21–23.

b) **God's power highlighted by the impotence of the idols (vv. 3–8)**

3. *But our God is in the heavens;*
   He does whatever He pleases.

4. *Their idols are silver and gold,*
   The work of men's hands.
5. *They have a mouth but do not speak;*
   They have eyes but do not see.
6. *They have ears but do not hear;*
   They have a nose but do not smell.
7. *They have hands but do not touch;*
   They have feet but do not walk.
   Nor do they make a sound in their throat.
8. *Those that make them are actually like them;*
   So are all who trust in them.

3. The God who has not been acting but has been appealed to to do something fills His devout children with great confidence, a confidence which is all the stronger when the utter impotence of the idols is considered. Thus in this section the first verse is a fine statement of the undoubted and boundless power of God. To provide a dark background against which the brightness of this truth stands out the more strikingly, the remaining verses sketch at length and almost tauntingly the total incapacity of the idols till in the last verse both idols and their worshipers are lumped together as being of one kind.

By the statement: "But our God is in the heavens," the writer does not create a deistic being who is removed from the earth as a scene of activity. The opposite is rather the case. Even as Christ has ascended far above all heavens that He might fill all things, so this claim is the equivalent of saying: He sits enthroned on high, where only He may sit who rules all things in heaven and on earth. The second member of the verse requires such an interpretation. For "He does whatever He pleases" does not connote caprice or unpredictability. It assumes that what He pleases is always good and perfect and asserts that He infallibly carries out His desires. "He hath done whatsoever He hath pleased" (*KJ*) does not make this statement say enough. It removes the situation into the past and predicates nothing about the future. The Hebrew perfect presents a case of general validity (a gnomic aorist). The contrast between this unlimited capacity of God and the total incapacity of the idols could scarcely be stated more strongly.

5. Not a whisper, not a movement, not a sound, not a single token of life ever issues from these fabricated gods. To list the separate deficiencies one by one gives the account a particular cast, as though the writer had taken the hand, the foot, the eye, the ear; had examined and touched and re-examined each one; had valiantly tried to elicit a response. All to no purpose. They could not produce even the least sign of life—not even a slight "sound in their throat." This approach, as

previously indicated, is rather common in the Scriptures; but nowhere is it carried through so thoroughly as is done here.

The last verse is the climax: futility is the mark of the idols; futility marks their worshipers. The expression "those that make them" does not apply so much to the craftsmen as to those who hire them to produce the idols. Some interpreters have regarded this examination of the idols as trivial and repetitious. Most readers are impressed with the effectiveness and the thoroughness of the treatment.

c) **An exhortation to trust in the Lord (vv. 9–11)**

9. *O Israel, trust in the Lord!*
   He is their help and their shield.
10. *O house of Aaron, trust in the Lord!*
    He is their help and their shield.
11. *You that fear the Lord, trust in the Lord!*
    He is their help and their shield.

At this point the assumption that successive lines were appointed to be sung by different groups becomes almost imperative otherwise the change of person from the second to the third cannot be accounted for. Whether the ones entrusted with the first line of each verse were the Levites might be questioned. In any case, the Levites were qualified instructors of the nation, and these lines are instruction. The lesson to be impressed, as the threefold repetition indicates, is the lesson: "Trust in the Lord." This comes with fine propriety after the untrustworthiness of the idols has set the trustworthiness of God into clear light. The reason the response is not worded in the same person as is the summons may, as some interpreters have suggested, be due to the fact that "there is a note of humility, a feeling of being far removed" (*Abstandsgefuehl*) that prompts men to speak thus. On this assumption we could, however, dispense with supposition that a separate choir is necessary to render the second half of the verse.

This exhortation to trust is addressed to three separate groups: Israel; the house of Aaron, i.e., the priests; and those "that fear the Lord." Addressing such groups separately makes the procedure more impressive. The summons is being particularized. The individual is not lost in the crowd. First comes the nation as a whole, then the priests, then, it would seem, those who would in a particular sense be inclined to respond because they belong to that group, the *élite*, who actually fear the Lord. Some interpreters consider the third term as merely embracing the first two mentioned. But such an approach is a little too idealistic inasmuch as it is too much to hope that the whole nation and all its priests actually stand in a living relation to the Lord.

The majority of writers of the present time refer the expression they "that fear the Lord" to the proselytes, as *Rashi* stated. True as it is that proselytes are referred to as early as I Kings 8:41 and again in Is. 56:6; and true as it is that they are to be found in the New Testament, practically under the same name (Acts 13:16; 16:14; 18:7, 13), yet, though the debate still rages hotly, *McCullough* has effectively disposed of this supposition by pointing out that "it is improbable . . . that proselytes were present in the temple in sufficient numbers to form a special group of worshippers."

Those who have appealed for the Lord's help have now been admonished to believe that He will grant it.

d) Assurance of God's blessing (vv. 12, 13)

12. *The Lord has been mindful of us, He will bless us;*
    He will bless the house of Israel, He will bless the house of Aaron.
13. *He will bless those that fear the Lord,*
    Both small and great.

The attitude of the speakers in the psalm changes. Until this point it was suppliants that spoke. The note of assurance now becomes strong. The writer does not think in terms of God's neglect of His people but in terms of the help He gave—"The Lord has been mindful." This change of mood has led some interpreters to assume that between the words of vv. 11 and 12 the sacrifice was offered, and because of this sacrifice new hope now fills the singer or the worshiping congregation. Others assume that some kind of theophany intervened, as though such occurrences were common and could easily be obtained in the sanctuary. Neither assumption is necessary. Moods fluctuate. The former mood of pleading for help has passed. The assurance of help has stolen into the heart. The fact that the Lord has helped in the past begets the assurance that He will not fail to bless His people.

The recipients of this blessing are now listed. They are the same three groups that were mentioned in vv. 9–11. The concluding phrase "both small and great" seems to refer to young people and old people. Since the bestowal of the blessing was reserved for priests, the assumption is not unwarranted that in public worship the *priests* may have chanted these verses. Yet the claim that He will bless is not quite the same as imparting a blessing. The actual blessing is contained in vv. 14, 15, which was above assigned to the choir. We see good reason, therefore, for ascribing these verses to the priests rather than to the preceding two classes. We have inserted this in order to indicate the difficulties involved in seeking to determine to whom the various parts of the psalm should be assigned.

e) **Prayer for blessing (vv. 14, 15)**

14. *May the Lord add to your numbers,*
    Both your and your children's.
15. *Blessed be you of the Lord,*
    Who made heaven and earth.

These two verses are not as far removed from the general purpose of the psalm as it may seem at first glance. For one major disadvantage of the nation of Israel after its re-establishment was that it was few in number. Healthy growth in numbers was in Old Testament times always regarded as a signal blessing from God. This marked a basic need of the nation. It could never be strong if it were not sufficiently strong in numbers. Here the word of blessing includes the present generation and those to come. On the whole the statement is reminiscent of Deut. 1:11. To this initial blessing is added a more comprehensive one which, by specifying nothing, includes everything needful and leaves it to the wisdom of the almighty God "who made heaven and earth" what He would be pleased to bestow. This statement seems to be reminiscent of Gen. 14:19.

f) **Resolve to bless the Lord (vv. 16–18)**

16. *The heavens are heavens of the Lord;*
    But the earth He has given to the sons of men.
17. *Not the dead will praise the Lord;*
    Nor any that go down into silence.
18. *But we will bless the Lord*
    From this time forth and forevermore.
    Praise the Lord!

When the psalm closes with a resolution to praise God, assurance has by that time mounted so high that those that pray are sure of God's help and promise to praise him for it. The Lord's omnipotence is best comprehended if He is understood to be the one who made the universe, heaven and earth. The various parts of this universe are now thought of in their relation to the praise of God. The heavens are "heavens of the Lord." There things are done more perfectly than they are done on earth because in that realm God's will is always done. Thus His praises are always sung there. The earth is the particular domain where *man* holds forth. There he must work out his life and destiny.

There is a third realm, that "of the dead," where those are found "that go down into silence." They are beyond the point where praise is possible. When this realm is called the place of silence, the writer apparently reflects on nothing more than the obvious fact that corpses do not praise the Lord. He himself, however, being one of those who are assigned to this earth, resolves that he will do his duty in this respect while he still may and vows that he will thank God now and forevermore. Man fulfills an essential part of his destiny when he engages in the praise of God. The certainty that there will be enough occasions to praise God is included in this statement. Thus the somewhat depressing note on which the psalm began has given way to a note of joy and assurance with the prospect of worthy praises of God to be sung by those on whom He has bestowed help.

NOTES

2. Questions may be the means of expressing a wish; see *KS* 354e.
8. The "actually" of our translation is not found in the text as a separate word. We have inserted it to try to catch the force of the copula *yihyu*, which is usually not expressed.
14. The verb *yoseph* says only, "may He add." Since that alone would be ambiguous, we have added the object implied: "To your numbers."

Psalm 116

THANKSGIVING FOR DELIVERANCE FROM DEATH

WE CAN SCARCELY escape the conclusion that this psalm is the thanksgiving of an individual. That it is placed in the midst of psalms that have to do largely with *Israel's* return from captivity may be due to the fact that it is not inapropos for the individual to think of the nation's deliverance as being analogous to his own.

Many passages of older Scripture are quoted in this piece, which clearly indicates that the writer was at home in the Scriptures in so far as they were available in his day.

Some commentators seem to feel that the logical development of thought is not as carefully carried through as it might be, a fact that may have contributed to the division of the psalm made by the Septuagint (followed by the *Vulgate*) into two separate psalms: vv. 1–9 and vv. 10–19. However, when the feeling of gratitude moves along as strongly as it does in this case, the stricter concerns of logic may momentarily be disregarded. It may still appear after careful examination that the psalm is pretty well unified.

We may be going a bit farther than the evidence warrants when we insist that the psalm was to be rendered in public worship as an accompaniment to the sacrifices that were to be offered when the psalmist pays the vows he had made. But all the writer actually says about what he will do "in the presence of all His people" is that he will pay his vows there, that means, offer the sacrifices that his vow prescribed. This is scarcely a liturgy for similar cases to be publicly used as here given though many a grateful soul has, no doubt, found these words an apt vehicle for his praise also in the sanctuary. The understanding of the psalm is not furthered by the introduction of the thought that a kind of ordeal took place in connection with the use of this psalm, part of which ordeal was the drinking of a cup (v. 13) to determine a man's guilt or innocence. Such an approach elevates factors that the Scriptures subordinate and is furthermore built on insufficient evidence.

a) A summary of the psalmist's experience (vv. 1–11)
1. *I love the Lord
    Because He has heard my voice, my supplication;*
2. *Because He inclined His ear to me;
    Therefore as long as I live will I call upon Him.*
3. *The bonds of death closed around me;
    The distress of Sheol found me;
    Trouble and sorrow I found.*
4. *Then I called on the name of the Lord:
    "O Lord, I beseech Thee, save my life!"*
5. *Gracious is the Lord and righteous;
    Besides, our God is merciful.*
6. *The Lord guards the simple;
    I was brought low, and He helped me.*
7. *Return to your rest, O my soul,
    For the Lord has dealt bountifully with you.*
8. *For Thou hast delivered my soul from death,
    My eyes from tears, and my feet from slipping.*
9. *I may walk before the Lord
    In the land of the living.*
10. *I kept the faith when I spoke;
    I was greatly afflicted.*
11. *I said in my agitation:
    "All men are utterly unreliable."*

1. In the first part of the statement of his experience the psalmist asserts that he loves God because He helped him (vv. 1–4). Readers who are familiar with the German version will in the English translation miss the genial warm touch of the first verse: *Das ist mir lieb, dass*

Psalm 116

der Herr meine Stimme und mein Flehen hoeret, which, no doubt, influenced the *Prayer Book* version: "I am well pleased that the Lord," etc. However, though one might venture to translate thus, that rendering scarcely does justice to the text, which asserts that the writer *loves the Lord,* not the fact that He heard him. True, the object is held in reserve till after the next verb. But that is not unnatural. In other words, the writer's love of God is based on a very vital experience of help which is restated in the second verse, where in a familiar figure, the Lord is represented as bending down from heaven to catch the plea from the lips of His child. The conclusion of the writer's resolve is that he will continue to call upon the Lord as long as he lives, implying quite likely, whether he is in trouble or out of it. What these two verses say emphatically is that the writer has grown to love God. All this is quite obviously based on the opening verses of Ps. 18, which must have been known to the psalmist.

3. How precarious the situation had been is now described in figurative language (vv. 3, 4). He was like a being who was entrapped and all but fully caught in the meshes of the hunter, who was death. The second figure likens the danger to narrow walls that are closing in on a man, for that is the root meaning of the term "distress." "Sheol" is here synonymous with death. Even as distress found *him,* so *he* found trouble and sorrow. Whether this suggests sickness unto death or some form of danger cannot be determined. The psalms often seem to be purposely vague regarding such situations so that any man might find his own situation reflected. When everything thus closed in on him, he "called on the name of the Lord," which is more than the bald statement of calling on the Lord. The name implies the fulness of revelation that the Lord has made concerning Himself. His cry is given in brief and seems rather poignant: "O Lord, I beseech Thee, save my life" or soul as the Hebrew states it, life often being the meaning of the word. Petition is not so much a matter of many words as it is the effective approach to the name of the Lord. The poet does not go on to say that the Lord then heard him. That has already been said at the very outset. V. 3 is again based on Ps. 18:4.

5. The next section (vv. 5–9) describes the new experience of the nature of the Lord that grew out of being delivered from such trouble. Two attributes are combined that do not usually appear in union. They are "gracious" and "righteous." The first stresses the undeserved character of the help given, the second the energy with which God maintains His honor according to His covenant obligation to His people. He is also marked by a deep sympathy for the one in need—"merciful." These qualities are intensified when one considers that the psalmist belonged to the class of those individuals who were called the "simple,"

which implies keeping the mind open to instruction though this word is not always used in the good sense. After this explanation as to why the Lord extended His help to His true follower the writer summarizes his experience from another point of view: "I was brought low, and He helped me," the implication being that He lifted him up.

7. Still elaborating on what befell him (vv. 7–9), the writer soliloquizes by exhorting himself to enter into the full enjoyment of the rich rest that God has created for him by delivering him and saying to his soul: "Return to your rest." Luther rendered this beautifully: *Sei nun wieder zufrieden, meine Seele* (Be content again, O my soul). As a motive for enjoying this newly won rest to the full the writer describes what has just transpired: "The Lord has dealt bountifully with you," which, by the way, is an inimitably beautiful touch of the *KJV*. It seems as though his experience was so rich that the psalmist can do nothing more than again and again to describe what he lived through. The effective summation of it all is classic in its beauty: "Thou hast delivered my soul from death, my eyes from tears, and my feet from slipping." He must have skirted very close to the edge of destruction. This statement was not original; it appears in Ps. 56:13, which with a slight variation includes also v. 9 of this psalm. This last verse seems to express, not so much a resolution ("I will walk," *KJV*) as the permissive idea: "Now I am permitted to walk again before the Lord," a feeling that is often very strong after deliverance and seems to imply that one's whole life is now actually being lived in the sight of the Lord.

10. The last two verses of this section (vv. 10, 11) are admittedly difficult, even to the point of the despair of some commentators. It would seem that the writer had said some things during the time of his great trouble, words that might have been construed as though he had been driven to the point of abandoning the faith. It appears that he here speaks in self-defense. With this approach in mind, let us paraphrase what he says: I did not cast away my faith at the time when I said what could be misconstrued; true, I was greatly afflicted and spoke under the stress of strong emotion; but what I said at the time was: "All men are utterly unreliable." That was, however, not so much a pessimistic reflection upon how evil other men are but rather a statement to the effect that, in the last analysis, help must be sought from Him who alone is absolutely dependable. Thus that statement led me back to seek help from God. It would seem that these two verses help to clear up a little issue that had arisen at a time when great distress was upon the psalmist. He disposes of the matter briefly, for it was not of great moment. The important truth was throughout that he had not at any time denied the faith.

When Paul quoted this statement (II Cor. 4:13) he followed the

Psalm 116

Septuagint version strictly, which was then commonly in use in the Greek-speaking world. This version does, indeed, render this passage: "I believed, therefore have I spoken." Though this may not be a defensible translation, it is not out of harmony with the spirit of the original utterance and, therefore, not a distortion of it.

b) The payment of his vows (vv. 12–19)

12. *What shall I render to the Lord*
    For all His benefits toward me?
13. *The cup of salvation I shall lift up*
    And call upon the name of the Lord.
14. *I will pay my vows unto the Lord,*
    Yea, in the presence of all His people.
15. *Precious in the sight of the Lord*
    Is the death of His saints.
16. *Ah, now, Lord, I am Thy servant,*
    I am Thy servant, the son of Thy handmaid;
    Thou hast loosed my bonds.
17. *To Thee will I offer the sacrifice of thanksgiving,*
    And upon the name of the Lord will I call.
18. *My vows will I pay to the Lord,*
    Yea, in the presence of all His people,
19. *In the courts of the Lord's house,*
    In the midst of thee, O Jerusalem.
    Praise the Lord!

Though the one subject of the payment of vows is under consideration, it is developed in two parts. The first of these thinks in terms of vows as such and the need or manner of the payment of them. Vows were never commanded in the old covenant. The point stressed was always that, when they were made, they had to be kept punctiliously. Here all this is considered under the head: "What shall I render unto the Lord for all His benefits toward me?" First of all he mentions what may well have been a kind of symbolic gesture: a man would take up a cup filled with good wine, and the drinking of it, perhaps publicly, would typify that, even as the pleasant draft is drunk, so does a one gratefully take to himself all that the Lord has granted him. For in that connection the person involved would "call upon the name of the Lord," which had, perhaps, better be translated, "proclaim the name" (*des Herrn Namen predigen*). This would then mean that a man would tell all that the Lord had done for him. This is the first step in proper thanksgiving.

He then vows (v. 14) that he will pay his vows, whatever they may have been—a matter that is too personal and need not be specified precisely. That is to be done publicly so that men may learn that some mercies of God are being acknowledged. To this the writer at this point appends a new bit of knowledge that he acquired as a result of his experience, namely, that the death of the Lord's saints is precious in His eyes (v. 15). That seems to involve at least two things. One is that He is manifestly watching over what takes place even when His saints are not rescued but seemingly perish. The other is that He frequently intervenes and will not allow them to perish. His saints can have assurance either way. This thought is closely analogous to Ps. 72:13, 14.

The psalmist then continues to dwell on the same thought of paying his debt of gratitude to Him who delivered him (vv. 16–19). What seems to have gained new meaning for him is that he stands in the relation of a servant to the Lord, that is, a member of His household even as his godly mother had been before him. He has been true to the family tradition (cf., Ps. 86:16). This was why the Lord set him free when bonds entangled him. Thus he again vows to pay those obligations that a grateful heart promised to the Lord when his great deliverance came, and pay them publicly and in the holy city, which was sacred with many associations for the people of God.

NOTES

1. It seems most in keeping with the rest of the statements of the opening verses to read the second verb, not as an imperfect, but as a perfect, going on the assumption that this is a case of dittography, *y* having been written twice by mistake (therefore *shama‘* rather than *yishma‘*).

7. "Rest" (*manoach*) is by some interpreters understood in the sense that God is the true rest of the soul. However, nothing seems to have the verse point in that direction. Neither must the word be understood in the sense of "resting place." "Condition of rest" (*BDB*) seems a well-established possible meaning. Cf., Ruth 3:1.

Psalm 117

ISRAEL'S BLESSINGS
ARE THE HOPE OF THE GENTILES

THIS PSALM is surprisingly brief. This does not, however, warrant the conclusion that it is a fragment, for it develops its thought in a manner that may be said to round it out all-sidedly though concisely. As a complete entity it lends itself to all manner of uses even as does its longer counterpart, Ps. 119. The attempt to add our psalm to Ps. 116 makes it dangle rather loosely. To prefix it to Ps. 118 makes it appear rather superfluous. To append it to Ps. 148 is farfetched. To maintain that it is a portion of a psalm, the rest of which has been completely lost is beyond proof. To claim independence and completeness for it makes good sense.

The one thought that is set forth is that God has done such great things for Israel that the nations, should they hear of them, cannot but feel impelled to add their praises to Israel's. Unfortunately, we cannot tell precisely how the writer envisioned this activity on the part of the Gentiles. It can scarcely be thought of as a direct summons that was in one way or another broadcast to the nations and brought to their direct attention. Without attempting to weaken the thought set forth, we must maintain that the psalm expresses an ideal in a somewhat figurative manner. The writer apostrophizes the Gentiles, implying that, if they were as they later will be enabled to see the marvelous things that the Lord did for His people, they would burst forth into songs of praise.

In this sense the psalm may rightly be called Messianic. For the time did come when the Gentile religions had collapsed because of their very emptiness. The coming of the Messiah was so timed as to coincide with the occurrence of this collapse. Therefore it was in the Messianic age when the thing here envisioned or prophesied began to be fulfilled. In this sense Paul quotes from this psalm, Rom. 15:11.

This psalm manifests a breadth of outlook and a depth of insight that is amazing. It seems that Israel never forgot its mission to be the mediator of saving truth to the other nations on the face of earth. At times this mission became submerged. Sometimes it was more clearly set forth. Our psalm is one of the outstanding instances of the latter type.

1. *Praise the Lord, all nations;*
   Laud Him, all peoples!
2. *For mighty is His steadfast love toward us;*
   And the faithfulness of the Lord endures forever.

Only that man can rightly sing as this psalm does who is deeply impressed with the magnitude of the things that God has done for His people. The things mentioned are "steadfast love" and "faithfulness." That sense of their magnitude can induce a sense of the magnitude of the scope and purpose that lay behind what God did for Israel.

The note here struck is not an isolated one. Other passages in the psalms indicate that others shared this breadth of outlook; among them are Ps. 47:1, 2; 66:4; 98:4. With these may also be compared Ps. 67; 22:27; 86:9. The terms used are interesting. The word for "nations" is the one frequently translated "Gentiles," which also usually connotes some measure of hostility toward the people of God. "Peoples" implies "nationalities" and thinks in terms of the wide diversity of types found in the national groups. The word happens to be a more Aramaic form.

2. The initial verb of this verse appears in Ps. 103:11. An exultant Alleluiah very appropriately closes the psalm.

Psalm 118

"O GIVE THANKS UNTO THE LORD"

A RESOUNDING HYMN of praise, which announces its theme in the first verse and closes by repeating this theme thought, thus leaving no doubt as to its purpose. That so commonplace a theme should have been chosen as a heading for a psalm which has such a distinct character happens to be the result of the fact that this psalm has given a classic treatment of this theme. There is enough of a general tone about the psalm to make it suitable for all manner of occasions when the Lord has manifested His steadfast love.

Without claiming that only one known Biblical situation would fit the contents of the psalm, we would claim that no occasion seems to fit better than does the event when the walls of Jerusalem had just been completed after almost a century of delay in the days of Nehemiah (444 B.C.) as recorded in Neh. 12:27ff., where special mention is

Psalm 118

made of the celebration with thanksgiving. This calls for an interpretation which has the "I" refer to the whole congregation of Israel at that time—a practice that is still quite common in hymnology.

The responsive character of the psalm is most obvious, so much so that the earliest Jewish tradition remarks about it as does almost every commentator. The only drawback is that it is difficult to agree on the details of the interpretation, i.e., fixing precisely to whom the different portions, smaller or greater, should be assigned. As to the general approach, it seems safe to say at least that the first 18 verses may be ascribed to the throng of worshipers, the festive multitude, who sang this section as they approached the sanctuary. Then vv. 19–28 would have been rendered after the immediate Temple precincts had been reached.

The references to other Scripture passages are frequent, a fact which points to the comparatively late date of the psalm and to the familiarity of its author with the Psalter as it was then in use.

The following outline may, perhaps, succeed in part in bringing the various rich elements of the psalm into clearer focus:
a) The thanksgiving of the assembly as it approaches the Temple (vv. 1–18).
b) The blessing that is bestowed upon the worshiping throng (vv. 19–28). The subdivisions of these sections will be indicated as the exposition progresses.

Among new and novel approaches that have been attempted in the interpretation we mention the following as being interesting but unsatisfactory. Attempts to make the psalm a part of the supposed cult of the king, which Israel is thought to have observed, lack Scriptural evidence. The supposition that three groups of persons who have been delivered from various dangers come together and successively present their story and are then joined in their thanksgiving by the rest of the assembled multitude is rather farfetched and requires too many changes of the text to make it plausible. The interpretation which has discovered an original psalm (vv. 5–19) by an individual, which psalm was later adapted to congregational use by various additions and interpolations, is an interpretation which requires too much ingenious manipulation. Lastly, the approach which makes the psalm the outgrowth of the experience of a victorious general who especially in v. 5ff. recounts his recent experiences and deliverances, explains some things but creates more problems than it solves.

Luther considered this psalm his favorite. Almost all commentators quote a part of his introduction: "This is my own psalm which I specially love. Though the entire Psalter and the Holy Scriptures are indeed very dear to me as my sole comfort and my very life, yet I have come to grips with this psalm in a special sense, so that I feel free to call it my very own. For it has done me great service on many an occasion and has stood by me in many a difficulty when the emperor, kings, wise men and clever, and even the saints were of no avail..."

As we shall see later, the Messianic character of this psalm is unique. For the present let this suffice: Israel, who is the speaker at various points in the psalm, prefigures Christ by the workings of the overshadowing providence of God, so that what is relatively true of Israel is found to be completely true of the Messiah of God. God so guided the destiny of His people that this result might be attained.

a) **The thanksgiving of the assembly as it approaches the Temple (vv. 1–18)**

1. *O give thanks unto the Lord, for He is good,*
   For His steadfast love endures forever!
2. *Let Israel now say:*
   "His steadfast love endures forever."
3. *Let the house of Aaron now say:*
   "His steadfast love endures forever."
4. *Let those who fear the Lord now say:*
   "His steadfast love endures forever."

As on this glad day of thanksgiving the festive throng begins to make its way to the sanctuary it gives voice first of all to a summons by which it encourages itself to give thanks. Briefly stated, the basis on which its thanksgiving rests is the fact that God is good, and that His steadfast love endures forever. These are basic divine characteristics which have been experienced by God's people. Various groups are addressed and summoned to do their part, as in Ps. 115:9–11: Israel, the house of Aaron, and those that fear the Lord. For further comments on these groups see Ps. 115. It is quite possible that at this point the antiphonal rendition of the psalm was begun. By letting the basic truth that the Lord's steadfast love has no end ring out strongly four times this truth is well underscored. Similarity with Ps. 100:4, 5; 106:1; 107:1 should be noted in passing. Before any details are presented, stress is laid on unwavering attributes of God which are the same yesterday, today, and forever. Thus the psalms go to the root of the matter.

5. *Out of my distress I called on the Lord;*
   The Lord answered me and set me at large.
6. *The Lord is on my side, I will not fear;*
   What can man do to me?
7. *The Lord is on my side as my helper;*
   I shall look victoriously on those that hate me.

8. *It is better to take refuge in the Lord*
   Than to put confidence in man.
9. *It is better to take refuge in the Lord*
   Than to put confidence in princes.

5. The occasion that gave rise to the praise that is being offered is now set forth (vv. 5–14). In the first half of the section the emphasis is on the fact that when he was in distress, the Lord was on the side of him who speaks (vv. 5–9). He who speaks is the nation Israel as the majority of commentators admit. The first verse of the section again summarizes what follows: The nation was in trouble; it called on the Lord; the Lord answered; He set the nation at large (or as *KJ* states it: "in a large place"). The figure is a simple one: a man is caught between forces that threaten to destroy him; liberation means the removal of those forces and providing ample room to move about. Israel's particular distress in which she was caught was the captivity in Babylon and after her return to her own land the hostile opposition of her neighbors, which Neh. 4:7, 8 records. The very next verse in the passage alluded to tells how the nation prayed in her distress. Her utter defenselessness, which had continued as long as the city had been without walls, was now at an end, and her defenses were strong. This brief reference to a historical situation shows how these words may have been meant.

6. This experience led to an insight into a broader truth, which is aptly phrased: "The Lord is on my side." On this basis a good conclusion is arrived at: "I will not fear." No doubt, as so often, the experience of deliverance at the hand of the Lord leads to the resolve never to let fear master one again. Especially when man is the opponent, we are justified in saying: "What can man do to me?" This sentiment appears to be carried over from Ps. 56:4, 11. The previous thought that the Lord was on his side strikes the psalmist as being of such importance as to merit repetition. His glad heart dwells on this happy discovery, save that the thought is amplified by the addition of "as my helper."

A second conclusion is drawn from this newly won insight: "I shall victoriously look on those that hate me." One need not assume that there is anything unwholesome in this thought as, for example, a bit of the spirit of revenge. The nation expects its good cause to be successful, and the evil cause of its opponents to come to naught. Even if the following translation is adopted: "I shall see my desire" (*KJ*), this construction could still be put upon it. Faith is wholesomely triumphant. Ps. 54:4, 7 expressed the same sentiments that are found in this verse.

8. In vv. 8, 9 the same experience of deliverance is being reflected

upon. It is brought into a new focus when what Israel did is described as "taking refuge in the Lord." At times men and nations have no other recourse. That course leads to ultimate satisfaction and achievement whereas taking refuge in man is often so totally disappointing. Some interpreters inject the thought that the reference to "princes" may involve a momentary glance at the Persian monarch Artaxerxes II who gave the Israelites permission to return and many assurances of protection and good will but, when the actual difficulties arose, was conspicuous by his absence and failure to help.

The entire experience of the nation is again recounted and evaluated (vv. 10–14).

10. *All nations surrounded me;*
    In the name of the Lord I cut them down.
11. *They surrounded me, yea, they surrounded me;*
    In the name of the Lord I cut them down.
12. *They surrounded me like bees;*
    They were quenched like a fire of thorns;
    In the name of the Lord I cut them down.
13. *I was pushed violently to make me fall;*
    But the Lord helped me.
14. *The Lord is my strength and my song;*
    And He has become my salvation.

10. The nation, as is also the case with individuals, seems strongly preoccupied with the grave danger from which it has just escaped: the captivity and the antagonism of the surrounding peoples after the return. We are made to feel how keenly the nation sensed the gravity of the crisis in which it found itself. Therefore in this section the emphasis lies upon these particular items of the experience. The refrain-lie statements make this section particularly well adapted to antiphonal rendering.

Thinking, perhaps, more particularly upon the more recent aspect of the trouble indicated, how Samaritans, Arabs, Ammonites, and Ashdodites (Neh. 4:7f.)—practically all the nations with whom they were having contact at the time banded together to exterminate the Jews, the nation first describes how it was hemmed in or surrounded on every side. Though the odds were strongly against the Israelites, they were able "in the name of the Lord to cut them down." Repetitions like those occurring in v. 11 can be very effective, especially in solemn assemblies. Their very reiteration shows the urgency of the danger. The figures employed (v. 12) are very colorful: "they surrounded me like bees," "They were quenched like a fire of thorns"—which type of fire burns hotly and with much crackling and suddenly dies down.

13. An entirely new description, yet one that is equally effective, presents the figure of a person who was strongly pushed about in an effort to bring him to fall but who still managed to stay on his feet. This is not vainglorious boasting, for the cause assigned for having success in overcoming the danger is: "The Lord helped me." This leads the nation to attempt something like a generalization or a more precise formulation of the conclusion arrived at, and that is the classic statement, coined by the song sung after the victory at the Red Sea in Moses' days (Exod. 15:2) and then again used effectively in Isaiah's days (Is. 12:2), "The Lord is my strength and my song and is become my salvation." The echoes of this song ring down to the New Testament (Rev. 15:3).

The sequence of terms in this quotation has been faulted: strength, song, salvation. The propriety of this sequence in the present setting can be easily demonstrated. The prime issue under discussion is: Where did the nation get its strength in the trying times just described? The Lord was her "strength." The fact that He made the weak strong put a "song" on their lips. But strength is oftentimes exerted to the uttermost without achieving the hoped-for result. It was not so in this case: deliverance (here called "salvation") resulted, but again it was granted through Him who came to mean much for His people. No quotation could have been a more apt summary of what was really involved.

15. *Hark, the sound of rejoicing over deliverance is in the tents of the righteous;*
    "The right hand of the Lord does valiantly."
16. *The right hand of the Lord is exalted;*
    The right hand of the Lord does valiantly.
17. *I shall not die but live*
    And tell of the deeds of the Lord.
18. *The Lord has chastened me sore;*
    But He has not given me over to death.

15. We seem to have a double metonomy in this verse. It reads thus in the original: 'Hark, rejoicing and deliverance,' which we think means: the sound of rejoicing and the experience of deliverance. These two expressions constitute a hendiadys, the second of the terms being a genitive that is dependent on the first. This yields our translation: "the sound of rejoicing over deliverance."

All this is, of course, only introductory to the substance of the song that is being sung by God's delivered children. We may regard this song as being summed up in v. 15b, or it may be thought of as extending through v. 15b–18. In any case, we have in these verses a jubilant description of what God's mighty work looks like to His people. Incidentally, when it is said that this song was heard in the "tents" of the righteous, this may be just a poetic way of returning to the form of speech that was used for "homes" in the wilderness-wandering days. Thus we have not only public worship for official thanks of God but also private praise in every home on the part of a grateful people. In those great days everyone without a doubt shared deeply in the nation's joy. If all that God did is ascribed to His "right hand," that is another way of saying that it was to be attributed to His omnipotent power.

16. When this verse reiterates the last thought expressed in v. 15, that may be another instance when the responsive rendering of the psalm was followed with particular effectiveness. One group makes a claim; the other group makes that claim its own with a slight modification of statement. A beautiful instance of solemn reiteration!

17. This verse tells the story as being one in which a life-and-death issue was involved. Israel is the one that makes this claim: I as a nation shall not die but live. Nations that were carried away into captivity in days of old regularly perished, lost their identity, and were merged with other racial groups. That was the fear that dogged Israel's steps. But she now clearly sees that her case was an exception: she shall live to declare what God has done for her.

18. It was, indeed, no light and easy experience. With emphasis the nation alludes to the severity of the chastening which she had to endure for her own good. But the Lord's aim was not death but correction and salvation. These many aspects of its experience that the nation is taught to express or does actually express in this psalm are tokens of how richly she benefited by her trying experience, and how well she learned her lesson.

It may further appear as highly appropriate that matters such as these should be reviewed as the nation marches in solemn procession up to the very gates of the inner sanctuary.

b) The blessing that is bestowed upon the worshipping throng (vv. 19–28)

19. *Open to me the gates of righteousness;*
    I will go into them; I will praise the Lord.
20. *This is the gate of the Lord;*
    Righteous men may go into it.
21. *I thank Thee that Thou hast heard me*
    And hast become my salvation.
22. *The stone which the builders rejected*
    Has become the cornerstone.

23. *This is the Lord's doing;*
    It is marvelous in our eyes.
24. *This is the day which the Lord has made;*
    Let us rejoice and be glad in it.

19. We might have stated the case thus: Till now the procession had moved through the outer courts; it now stands before the gates that lead into the inner court. Vv. 19 and 20 may be regarded as transitional. The place that marks the more immediate presence of the Lord has been reached. It is very proper to mark the passing of this particular point with due solemnity. Either the whole procession or a spokesman in a solo voice speaks the challenge to open the gates that an entrance may be effected, and that the still higher praises of the great Lord of the covenant people may be presented. These gates are very significantly described as "gates of righteousness" because they lead to the Lord who is righteous, and who imparts righteousness to those that reverently and humbly appear before Him, seeking the righteousness which only He can give. Something of the imputed righteousness of the New Testament shines through rather clearly at this point in the Old Testament.

20. In this verse the translation, "This is the gate of the Lord," blurs the issue somewhat. The Hebrew plainly reads: "This is the gate *to* the Lord," a statement that is most likely a response to the request that was voiced in v. 19, affirming that those who made the request were right in thinking in terms of a more intimate approach to the Lord. A kind of caution is given in the second half of the verse, or shall we call it a warranted conclusion that is drawn from the name that was just given to this gate. If it is the gate of righteousness, then only righteous persons may aspire to enter in at it, a note that is also struck in Ps. 15 and 24.

21. It would seem that with this verse the praise of which v. 19 spoke is actually being presented to the Lord, and in the course of it fresh evaluations of the experience that has just been concluded are offered. For this experience was rich and many-sided, calling forth ever fresh statements worthily to glorify the name of the Lord. First of all, the nation dare not forget that a prayer experience was involved. Many were the times when Israel had earnestly called upon the Lord. Such prayers are effective: the deliverance granted is an answer to these fervent petitions. Therefore: "I thank Thee that Thou hast heard me and hast become my salvation," gains meaning in this setting and especially if it is thought of as referring to the return from exile and to the new hopes after the city walls have taken shape.

22. It is particularly this verse which offers the most effective statement of what Israel's recent experiences mean. Here we have a breadth of outlook and a depth of insight that are amazing. When it is claimed that the stone which the builders rejected is become the head of the corner, the reference is to the nation of Israel, to God's holy people. The builders referred to are the empire builders of that day, who enjoyed prominence, and who seemed to have unusual success. The Persian empire was one of their mighty edifices. The fatal weaknesses of this structure had at this time not yet become apparent. But when they had the captive nation Israel on their hands, this stone did not, so to speak, seem to fit into the picture anywhere. It could not be a vital segment in the whole array. So they "rejected it," which in this case might mean nothing more than: They intentionally passed it by as being of little or no use in their over-all plans.

Not so the Lord. He had chosen this nation in Abraham. He had invested divine capital in it. His plans were concerned with the eternities. Man had momentarily interrupted the progress of His purposes. That interruption was now at an end. To those whose eyes the Spirit of God had enlightened the recent successes of Israel, meagre as they might seem, were tokens of the great future which God had unwaveringly kept before His mind's eye. The divine plan was now beginning to become apparent to those who knew the light. This small and underestimated nation was the one about whom the purposes of God were built. Just as the cornerstone determines the direction that the walls of the building take and is determinative from that point of view, so Israel is vital and central in God's plans with the nations. This thought was not entirely new and novel. Under a different approach Isaiah had dealt with the same matter (Is. 28:16). The fact that the divine initiative and God's wisdom alone had brought these things about and not the religious genius of Israel or the nation's mighty strivings is expressly asserted in v. 23: "This is the Lord's doing; it is marvelous in our eyes." When insights like these come to men, the marvel of it all strikes them with renewed impact.

24. To sum up this treatment of the subject this verse very aptly says: "This is the day which the Lord has made; let us rejoice and be glad in it." The new day that has dawned on Israel's horizon is of the Lord's making: "Hitherto hath the Lord helped us." The joy that such an insight begets is not of this earth, yet the expression of it should not be neglected.

It is well known that the Lord Jesus Christ publicly referred the statement about the rejected stone to Himself in His disputations with the scribes and the Pharisees (Matt. 21:42; Mark 12:10, 11; Luke

Psalm 118

20:17). The same approach is met with in Acts 4:11 and I Pet 2:7. Paul thinks similarly (Eph. 2:20). What shall we make of this?

As indicated above, Israel is a type of Christ. What the nation ought to have been, Christ was. He realized in His own life to perfection what the nation should have achieved. Therefore it is not inappropriate to have various matters in the life of the nation prefigure the Son of man. Israel is in a sense the servant of the Lord. Christ is the true Servant of the Lord in every sense of the word. Though it lies in the realm of detailed Messianic prophecy to show the fulness of the implications that this involves, we have said enough to indicate in what sense this passage may be called Messianic. The passage before us does not prophesy concerning the Christ apart from Israel. It is not directly Messianic. But to be Messianic by way of type is one of the legitimate and important aspects of this type of prophecy. Some writers describe cases of this sort as "homologies."

25. *Help, we beseech Thee, O Lord;*
    O Lord, we beseech Thee, give success.
26. *Blessed in the name of the Lord be he who enters;*
    We have blessed you from the house of the Lord.
27. *The Lord is a mighty God, and He has given us light;*
    Bind the festal sacrifice with cords even to the horns of the altar.
28. *Thou art my God, and I will thank Thee;*
    Thou art my God, I will exalt Thee.
29. *O give thanks unto the Lord, for He is good;*
    For His steadfast love endures forever.

25. In this last section of the psalm, which gathers up all the loose ends, the factor that stands out most prominently may be formulated thus: the blessing terminates in praise, knowing full well that it does not cover all items. There is first a prayer to the effect that the Lord might bring all these mighty ventures, which are in the making, to a full measure of success. That is what the plea of this verse involves, which contains four little words that give it a tone of a somewhat fervent and eager petition—a factor that cannot be reproduced in translation. God brought these promising results into the picture; He alone can bring them to a full realization. In the Hebrew the key word is Hosanna (*hoshi'ah-na'*), which became a prominent factor in the celebration of the festival of Tabernacles, where especially on the seventh day, which was called the "Great Hosanna," palm branches, called *lulab,* were waved, and these branches, too, were called Hosannas.

26. Though in our minds this verse has a kind of Messianic interpretation because of its use by the people of the Jews in Matt. 21:9,

in this psalm the meaning appears rather to be a benediction that was spoken, most likely by the priests of the sanctuary themselves, upon those who had entered the sacred precincts with the very purpose of receiving such a blessing. "He who enters" is then obviously the worshiper.

27. In the light of the blessing received as well as in view of the entire joyous experience that called forth this original celebration the congregation now sums up its feelings in the praiseful confession: "The Lord is a mighty God, and He has given us light." In the light of Exod. 13:21 this latter expression may be interpreted to mean: He has granted us a joyful deliverance. It could also be viewed in the light of Num. 6:25.

The rest of the verse is unusually difficult. Many translations of these words have been attempted. Many emendations of the text have been suggested. We shall disregard the emendations as involving too much subjective thinking. Leaving the explanation and justification of our approach to the "Notes," we shall briefly interpret the statement in a manner that seems to fit, as nearly as we can judge, rather well into the context of the psalm. In Israel the expression of thanksgiving as well as other emotions and needs were usually associated with a sacrifice that was provided for by the law and gave corporate expression to the devout sentiments of the worshipers. In this case, too, sacrificial victims had been brought along. The offering of them had been delayed by the welling-up of strong feelings of gratitude. But that their purpose might not be overlooked, and that they might receive due attention, a reference to them is injected which suggests that they be firmly hitched to the horns of the altar till the situation in the progress of public worship allows for their being offered on the altar in the accustomed manner.

28. After the parenthetical reference to the sacrifice the note of praise is once again sounded forth and concluded by the use of the opening verse of the psalm. One gets the feeling that on this particular occasion praise flowed very generously, wave after wave of it sweeping across the assembled throng. In a new sense Israel now claims God for her own: after this deliverance she knows Him as she never knew Him before. She vows to thank and exalt Him for what He has so graciously done.

NOTES

5. On the form *'anāni* with a long connecting vowel see *GK* 75 11.

10. The form *'amilam* is a hiphil from *mul*, which does mean to "circumcise." But it savors too much of a stiff literalism to give this word the meaning, "I shall cause them to be circumcised," as though this was going to be the particular form of vengeance that Israel would take

on the nations. In a connection such as this the meaning could well be, "I cut them off," (*RSV*) or, "I cut them down."

23. On the form *niphla'th* cf. *GK* 74g.

26. The participle "blessed" must be construed with "in the name of the Lord" as the following passages suggest: Deut. 21:5; Num. 6: 27; II Sam. 6:18; Ps. 129:8. The Hebrew accents suggest the same construction.

27. The noun *chagh* usually means festival. Here, as in Mal. 2:3, it can mean "festal sacrifice." The chief difficulty involved in our interpretation is that "unto the horns of the altar," construed with "bind," does constitute a rather pregnant construction but not an impossible one. The fact that we hear nothing of the practice of binding sacrifices to the horns of the altar is simply another instance to show how many of the details of procedure in public worship in the sanctuary have not been revealed in the sacred record. To claim that the horns were too short for binding anything to them goes on the assumption that we know how large or small they were—which is not the case.

Psalm 119

THE GOLDEN ABC OF PRAISE
OF THE WORD OF GOD

PERHAPS THE MOST remarkable thing about this psalm is its unusual length, 176 verses. The theme, generally speaking, is the Word of God. The primary emphasis of such lengthy praises of the Word must then be that the man of God cannot weary in extolling the merits of the Word of the Lord.

The author—whoever he may have been—laid a threefold restriction upon himself. He apparently resolved to address God continually throughout his song, barring the first three verses. He further resolved to make mention of the law of God in one way or another so that synonyms for the law appear in all verses except vv. 122 and 132. Strictly speaking, to these exceptions must be added vv. 84, 90, 121, 149, 156, though the word *mishpat,* usually signifying "judgment" appears in them. Lastly he laid down a fixed pattern for himself in that he proposed to make this psalm an acrostic, in which eight successive verses were to begin with the first letter of the alphabet, eight with the second, etc. In spite of these artificial restrictions the psalm has an unusual warmth and devoutness of tone. We need scarcely expect lofty flights of thought under the circumstances. In fact, logical sequence of thought is practically dispensed with. Each group of eight verses is a disconnected series of more or less striking utterances about God's law. Some interpreters insist that a general theme may be discovered for the eight verses within each group. Though in some instances such a theme may be discovered, there are cases where the theme found seems a bit arbitrary. The English versions head each section with the name of the initial Hebrew letter—*Aleph* is the first, *Beth,* the second, etc.

Bible readers incline rather generally to the idea that wherever the word "law" or its synonymns appear in the Old Testament there is a reference to those portions of the Word of God that contain legislation of some sort or another. However, in cases like the present the term "law" is a much broader concept. It apparently includes the whole wide range of what God has revealed in His Word, words of instruction, of caution, of precept, and of comfort. To tell the truth, the things that the *prophets* offer do not receive special treatment in our psalm; but the word law dare not be understood in a narrow sense.

By way of achieving variety of treatment the writer uses ten synonymns for that which we have designated by the collective term "law." These ten synonymns are: law, word, saying, commandment, statute, ordinance, precept, testimony, way, and path. In each section of eight verses the majority of these appear; and though they are distinctive terms that convey the many-sidedness of the Word of God, the specific connotation of the root meaning of the Hebrew word dare not always be pressed too precisely. The use of the various terms is the author's way of securing variety of treatment of his subject.

The particular emphases that come to the fore again and again as the psalm progresses are thoughts such as these: thanksgiving for the law or the Word of God; prayer that it may be faithfully kept, or that one may experience the comfort of that Word in trying times; prayer for steadfastness, or that God may not forsake His servant; the overthrow of the ungodly; praise of the law in its various aspects; prayer for understanding of God's Word and for ability to keep it.

There seems to be good reason for believing that the psalm dates from the days of Ezra and Nehemiah, a time when the people of God had much affliction to endure from their enemies. Since the Word of God had been ignored in bygone days when the prophets preached in the name of the Lord, those that had returned from the Babylonian Captivity and their descendants did not want to make the same mistake and ignore that Word again. Thus a heavy emphasis on the importance of the Word was bound to come to the fore. Besides, since the cultus had suffered by the permanent loss of the ark of the covenant, the Word came strongly into the forefront as a means of worship.

We should also note that it is scarcely to be expected that this psalm would show a Pauline understanding of the law of God. That, however, is due chiefly to the fact that the term law is scarcely to be understood as Paul understood it: God's sharp demands which are far above the poor sinner's power to fulfill. As was shown above, the law in its exacting and demanding character was not the law as the psalmist understood it. This will help greatly in determining what our writer means by statements like, "I have kept Thy law." That means: not, I have fulfilled its sharp demands to the letter; but rather: I have faithfully adhered to Thy Word and prized it highly. There is, therefore, no complacency or shallowness reflected in the psalm, nor a lack of due sense of sin; nor does the writer take God's law lightly. The law is to him quite a different concept. Yet in a very definite sense the writer knows himself to be entirely dependent on God's mercy and is not deficient in spiritual insight.

Some interpreters complain about the tone of the psalm: it does not seem to breathe the fresh air of the out of doors—figures from nature are rare—but savors rather of the musty air of the study. That criticism need not be taken too seriously; not all minds run in the same channels.

Those interpreters misunderstand this psalm who claim that it paved the way for the unwholesome scribism that prevailed in Jesus' days on the part of the scribes and the Pharisees. Some seem to feel that it is precarious business to sing the manifold praises of the Word of the Lord. In its own way this psalm fills an important place in the Psalter by its emphasis upon the rich manifoldness of the Word of the Lord.

a) **The joy of walking in the precepts of the Lord (vv. 1–8)**

Aleph

1. *O how very happy are they whose conduct is blameless,*
   Who walk in the law of the Lord!
2. *O how very happy are they who keep His testimonies,*
   Who seek Him with their whole heart;
3. *Who also have done no wrong*
   And have walked in His ways!
4. *Thou hast appointed Thy precepts*
   To be kept diligently.
5. *O that my ways were firmly grounded*
   To keep Thy statutes!

6. Then shall I not be put to shame
   When I regard all Thy commandments.
7. I will praise Thee with an upright heart
   By learning Thy righteous judgments.
8. Thy statutes will I keep;
   O forsake me not utterly!

1. The opening verse plunges right into the midst of things. Though it seems to praise a certain class of people as being happy it intends in reality to praise the advantage that the law of God gives to those who walk in it. Only because these persons walk in the law of the Lord do they become the subjects of this beatitude. It is this law that brings about blamelessness of conduct.

2. The second verse has practically the same approach. The persons referred to in v. 1 are here described as both seeking the Lord with their whole heart and as keeping His testimonies as a consequence of such seeking. Where these prerequisites are found great happiness results.

3. Since this verse is a continuation of the thought, two further things are added to the picture, things that make the ultimate happiness referred to possible. These two factors are: they have done no wrong, and they have walked in His ways. Note throughout how the law is sought for the very purpose of being kept, not for the sake of attaining a theoretical knowledge of it.

4. The attitude just referred to is reflected particularly in this verse. God's precepts are given with the very idea in mind that they may be kept, and kept diligently (the Hebrew says: kept very much). To this thought the earnest wish or prayer is appended that the speaker's ways might be so firm in their whole nature that he might keep God's statutes. We might say by way of paraphrase: O that the bent of my mind were firmly set in the direction of always keeping what Thou hast commanded!

6. We might rearrange the clauses of this verse in order to clarify the thought: When I regard all Thy commandments, then shall I not be put to shame. The shame and embarrassment that come from having done the wrong thing will be avoided if one keeps looking in the direction of the suggestions that the commandments offer. This may sound like utilitarian advice, but it is meant in a wholesome sense. It is a valid reflection.

7. This verse is somewhat striking. Upright praise as being offered by the way of learning God's righteous judgments seems to be an incongruity. But not if "judgments" is thought of in the sense of those words of God that render a verdict for guiding a man's course of con-

duct, and if it is kept in mind that this word is one of the many synonymns of the Word of God. In practice you praise God by esteeming His Word so precious that you make it your business to learn it. Such learning is an act of praise.

8. The section ends with an expressed resolution. The spirit of it is: I cannot keep these statutes unless the Lord helps me. Therefore: "O forsake me not utterly!" No smug self-righteousness here!

b) The resolve to keep God's ordinances faithfully (vv. 9–16)

Beth

9. *How can a young man keep his conduct pure?*
   By watching it according to Thy word.
10. *With my whole heart have I sought Thee;*
    Let me not wander from Thy commandments!
11. *I have stored up Thy Word in my heart*
    That I might not sin against Thee.
12. *Blessed art Thou, O Lord;*
    Teach me Thy statutes!
13. *With my lips have I declared*
    All the pronouncements of Thy mouth.
14. *In the way of Thy testimonies I have always delighted*
    As much as in all riches.
15. *I will meditate on Thy precepts*
    And have regard unto Thy ways.
16. *I will seek my delight in Thy statutes;*
    I will not forget Thy Word.

9. The ninth verse suggests that the Word of the Lord is of distinct blessing also to the young in that it can, if it is faithfully appropriated, enable them to shun all the contamination of sin. The deduction made from this verse to the effect that the psalm is basic instruction for young people is not warranted by the evidence. The thought takes the turn that the writer asserts that he has with his whole heart sought the Lord, and with becoming humility he adds the petition to be guarded against straying from the commandments of his God. Certainly, no presumptuous attitude of self-sufficiency here! The further reflection is added that the very purpose that the psalmist had in mind in accumulating a store of divine precepts was that they might be within him a defense against sin.

12. An entirely new thought is injected: God is blessed and immediately implored to teach the writer His statutes, for he, the writer, does not deem himself competent to master God's statutes by his own unaided strength. To this v. 13 would seem to add the thought that the

psalmist was not hesitant about making the truth of the divine words known to others. He has publicly declared them.

14. In this verse the assertion is made that the writer delights in God's testimonies as much as he does in all riches. This is the treasure above all treasures. The very meditation upon these riches is a source of great delight, but the type of meditation involved is always such that faithful doing of the Word learned results. The same thought is stated in the form of a resolution in v. 16.

c) The faithful adherence to God's law affords strength in persecution (vv. 17–24)

Gimel

17. *Deal bountifully with Thy servant that I may live;*
    And I will keep Thy Word.
18. *Uncover my eyes*
    That I may behold wondrous things out of Thy law!
19. *I am but a sojourner on earth;*
    Hide not Thy commandments from me!
20. *My soul is consumed with longing*
    For Thy judgments at all times.
21. *Thou hast rebuked the proud, the accursed,*
    Who go astray from Thy commandments.
22. *Take away from me disgrace and scorn,*
    For I have kept Thy testimonies.
23. *Though princes hold sessions against me and discussions,*
    Thy servant meditates on Thy statutes.
24. *Thy testimonies are my delight,*
    Yea, my counselors.

Although each verse in this section is a separate unit many writers feel that there is a hidden connection and progression of thought that is a little more in evidence than usual.

17. Living is not mere physical existence for the psalmist. Living consists in receiving the bounties of God's mercies. And again life has as its objective to keep God's Word. That is not a narrow spirit of slavish reverence for the letter of the law but a drawing upon the deep resources of revealed truth for sustenance. Note how often this concept of living appears in this psalm: vv. 25, 37, 40, 50, 77, 88, etc.

18. This faithful use of the Word involves ever new insights into the richness of God's revelation. It is for these that prayer is made. Man is viewed as being afflicted by a natural blindness over against the Word, a shortcoming that God can remove by uncovering the eyes of a man. God's Spirit alone can lead into all truth. The things that are disclosed by the enlightening effort of the Spirit of God are described

as "wondrous things." This expression is apt to lead us to think of the deep and marvelous revelation that is disclosed in the divine Word. But in view of the practical slant of this psalm there is great likelihood that the psalmist has primarily in mind "simple practical truths of the law," which man does not naturally discern unless the Spirit of God assists him. A reference to additional revelations that are great and deep need not be excluded.

Maclaren has worked out with unusual clarity the possibility of the inner connection between verses in this section. He remarks that the point of contact between vv. 18 and 19 may be this, that in the former the psalmist "desires subjective illumination" while in the latter he seeks "objective revelation." In any case, v. 19 should be translated, "I am but a sojourner on earth," not, "a stranger in the land." For the writer is obviously a native Israelite. Besides, the burdensomeness of the human lot on earth is a common topic touched on by the Biblical writers as *Koenig* remarks (cf., v. 25; Ps. 39:12; 90:3; I Chron. 29: 15). The connection between the halves of the verse appears to be: Since mine is a temporary existence here on earth, grant me what can give some lasting value to this brief life of mine. Then v. 20 seems to go on portraying the intensity of longing that gave birth to the prayer of v. 19b. A very strong verb is used, it is even stronger than "consumed." It should be rendered "crushed." But that verb seems stronger to us than the case warrants. It may help to note that here and elsewhere in the psalm "judgments" mean "the authoritative declarations of God's will."

20. Here again there may be an unexpressed connection between vv. 20 and 21. The terrible fate of those who go astray from God's commandments leads the writer to pray all the more earnestly that God may keep him faithful to that Word which he so ardently desires. Under the head of God's rebukes the writer may think of all those instances of the past when God did as He is always wont to do and has visited His punishments on the proud that disregard His Word, like Pharaoh of old. To be rebuked means virtually to be accursed.

22. At this point the thought may be bridged over to the next verse in this way: The faithful adherence to God's Word may have been the factor that brought "disgrace and scorn" on the writer. Painful as the experience may be, God can deliver a man from this burden even as in days of old He took action in behalf of His people (cf., Josh. 5:9). For that matter, as v. 23 now goes on to point out, the disgrace that was experienced emanated chiefly from prominent personages, "princes," who deliberately sat down and held sessions to discuss this man's case. In spite of enmity in high places the psalmist is calm and of a peaceful frame of mind. It is almost touching to observe that, while

the adversaries plot wicked things, he calmly meditates on the statutes of the Lord. They are his life and his delight. In such meditation lies the source of his strength.

A note of caution may be inserted. We have spoken of the writer as though the things recorded were practically autobiographical in character. It may be more in keeping with the facts of the case if, instead of understanding these incidents as happenings in his own life, we were to regard them as experiences that the godly of that time had rather generally. That does not mean that the nation is speaking throughout the psalm. To interpret thus would mean to move too far in the other direction.

24. This verse appears to describe more fully how in the face of ungodly opposition a godly man maintains his peace and composure by meditating upon God's "testimonies." The verse "heightens the impression of the psalmist's rest."

NOTES

21. The second member of this verse may be begun with the passive participle "cursed." It seems less in keeping with the entire spirit of the psalm to pronounce a malediction such as this though grammatically such a translation is quite feasible and would express the psalmist's strong abhorrence of evildoers.

22. The first word could be pointed *gol*, imperative from *galal*. Yet some commentators find the meaning "remove" in this *piel* from *galah* (*BDB*).

23. The initial *gam* can be regarded as an abbreviated *gam ki*, which introduces concessive clauses (*GK* 106b; *KS* 394d).

24. In the Hebrew "counsellors" is "men of my counsel"; see *KS* 306n.

d) **In the midst of affliction the psalmist seeks deeper insight into God's word (vv. 25-32)**

Daleth

25. *My soul lies prostrate in the dust;*
    Revive me according to Thy Word.
26. *I have fully declared my ways, and Thou didst answer me;*
    Teach me Thy statutes!
27. *Make me to understand the way that Thy precepts prescribe;*
    And I will meditate on Thy wondrous works.
28. *I waste away with sorrow;*
    Raise me up according to Thy Word!
29. *Let the false way be far from me*
    And graciously grant me Thy law.

30. *The way of steadfastness have I chosen;*
    Thy ordinances have I found irreproachable.
31. *I have clung to Thy testimonies;*
    O Lord, let me not be put to shame!
32. *I will run the way of Thy commandments,*
    For Thou broadenest my understanding.

It may be a fair summary of this passage to say: In the midst of affliction the psalmist seeks deeper insight into God's Word. It is again difficult to determine whether the individual lot of the psalmist is being described, let us say in vv. 25 and 28. Perhaps the lot of the people generally induces the individual to speak thus. Many people can say the same thing. It is in this sense that our statement by way of summary was meant.

25. It is true that the Hebrew reads: "My soul cleaves to the dust" (*RSV*), but that is scarcely an English way of speaking. That is why we followed *Luther*—"lies prostrate in the dust." The additional reminder is in order as *Oesterly* states it: "As elsewhere in this psalm, *soul* is used for the personal self."

26. It is very difficult to determine what is meant by: "I have fully declared my ways." It is very likely that this does not refer to the crooked and wrong ways that the writer had followed but rather to the many difficulties that had befallen him (*Schicksale,* says *Koenig*). That view agrees best with the sequel, "and Thou didst answer me." The psalmist recounted what had befallen him and implied that God might deliver him; and He did. Such an experience drives the writer to seek to learn more about the divine "statutes" that instructed him to follow this course. In such and in all similar cases the writer clearly sees the desirability of always taking this way of approach to God (v. 27). For that is the way that God's "precepts prescribe." This type of deeper understanding is the object of frequent prayer in this psalm (cf., Ps. 34, 73, 123, 144, 169). For when one goes this way, new insight into the marvels of God's doings always grows upon a man and leads him "to meditate on [His] wondrous works."

28. The times must have been difficult for men of God. For in addition to v. 24 we have the description given in v. 28: "I waste away with sorrow." God has promises for such sufferers. They may pray that God would help them and "raise [them] up according to [His] Word." This seems to lead directly to v. 28. Not to follow the course that he has followed, the course that resorts to prayer that is based on God's promises, is apparently the "false way" (v. 29) whereas the course taken is the "way of steadfastness" (v. 30).

By deliberate choice the writer set his footsteps on this latter course.

As a result he has recaptured an old experience: The ordinances of the Lord have been "found irreproachable." Not all problems have been solved; the victory is not yet complete. But the writer's attitude is described quite effectively: "I have clung to Thy testimonies" (many readers will like the *Prayer Book* version: "I have stuck unto Thy testimonies"); "O Lord, let me not be put to shame!" No matter what the issue may be, the relation to the Word of God is what the author continually brings into the picture.

32. This matter of gaining deeper insight into the ways of the Lord as expressed in His "commandments" finds excellent expression: "I will run the way of Thy commandments." The vigorous "run" implies more than an apathetic following. It bespeaks eagerness in following the prescribed course. For the psalmist recognizes that, the more he goes onward on this path, the more does God "broaden the understanding" of the divine ways. Insight rather than comfort seems to be the issue here though some interpreters think that Is. 60:5 points in the latter direction, including *Luther: wenn du mein Herz troestest*.

e) **Prayer for understanding and guidance (vv. 33–40)**

He

33. *Teach me, O Lord, the way of Thy statutes;*
    And I will keep it unto the end.
34. *Give me understanding that I may keep Thy law,*
    And that I may observe it with my whole heart.
35. *Lead me in the path of Thy commandments;*
    For in it I delight.
36. *Incline my heart to Thy testimonies*
    And not toward profit.
37. *Turn my eyes away from looking at vanity*
    And give me life in Thy way.
38. *Establish Thy promise to Thy servant*
    That I may fear Thee.
39. *Turn away from me the reproach which I dread,*
    For Thy ordinances are good.
40. *Behold, I long for Thy precepts;*
    In Thy righteousness give me life.

We suggest as the key thought for this section: prayer for understanding and guidance. All guidance is, of course, on the way suggested by God's commandments. Understanding, too, is basically understanding of the Word of the Lord.

33. The attitude of the speaker reveals that he senses that there are hidden depths to God's revelation that cannot be searched out by man without divine aid. So he prays to be instructed and for the deeper in-

sight which goes hand in hand with the statutes of the Lord. In both instances (vv. 33 and 34) the practical result of doing what has been learned to be good is involved. Besides, he who prays is interested in wholehearted and effective keeping of the precepts of the Lord. The new thought that is added to such a prayer in v. 35 is that such keeping of the Lord's law is not burdensome but a true delight.

36. In the next two verses the approach is that the Word of God in its manifold aspects is to be sought rather than certain inferior values that are apt to beguile men. One of these lower values is financial profit, which has been known often to become the object of a man's pursuit. When the clause is added, "incline my heart," that means, let me bend all my thoughts in that one direction.

The other objective that could be substituted for these higher values is "vanity." This word implies all that is hollow, worthless, and trivial. The cheapest objectives for life may be selected by men and captivate a man's eye or fancy. So this prayer specifies that the eyes may be turned away from trivialities by the grace of Him who alone can shape the deeper destinies of our life.

38. In this verse the term "promise" is really "word." The whole tenor of the prayer seems to be to make a promised word come true. Only thus can a word be established. The result of such an experience would be an increase in the true fear of God, which is always a wholesome reverence.

39. Two possibilities must be reckoned with in determining what sort of "reproach" is referred to in this verse. It could be the reproach that comes from God when His good ordinances are not kept. Whether God speaks or not, the guilty conscience of the sinner would speak of that reproach. Or it could be the reproach that comes from unsympathetic men, which we "dread" or fear to encounter because of our timidity of faith. Because of the concluding statement ("for Thy ordinances are good") it would seem to be this second kind of reproach that is thought of. For God's ordinances should be confessed and upheld, and whatever reproach we may suffer in upholding them God is readily able to turn away from us. That is the import of this prayer.

40. This verse might seem to suggest that the author longs for one thing but prays for another. The two thoughts blend into one when we remember that the psalm is, no doubt, of the opinion that the knowledge of the precepts of the Lord and the keeping of them are the very path of life.

NOTES

33. The expression "unto the end" involves some difficulty because the word used (*'eqebh*) usually means "consequence." But v. 112 sug-

gests that the translation "unto the end" is defensible because the same expression is used as a parallel to "forever." *Koenig's, mit Erfolg* ("with success") is a not so happy rendering.

38. We have gone back to *Luther* for the last clause, which KS rendered, "who is devoted to Thy fear," whereas the outstanding word ("devoted") is not even in the text. Many have been the attempts to catch the force of the clause. They usually say in an involved way what "that I may fear Thee" says with the utmost simplicity. The *Prayer Book* version followed *Luther*.

46. *Oesterley* renders the thought of the latter part of this verse effectively, if not quite exactly, when he translates: "In the presence of kings without fear."

f) **The prayer for grace and courage (vv. 41–48)**
Waw (also spelled *Vau*)

41. *And let Thy tokens of steadfast love come upon me, O Lord, Thy help according to Thy promise.*
42. *Then shall I have an answer for him that derides me, For I have trusted in Thy Word.*
43. *And take not the Word of truth utterly out of my mouth, For I have set my hope on Thy ordinances.*
44. *And I shall observe Thy law continually, Forever and ever.*
45. *And I shall walk about unhampered, For I have always sought Thy precepts.*
46. *And I shall speak of Thy testimonies before kings And shall not be ashamed.*
47. *And my delight shall be in Thy commandments, Which I love.*
48. *And I longingly stretch out my hands for Thy commandments which I love; And I will meditate on Thy statutes.*

The emphasis is now directed toward the prayer for grace and courage to be enabled to make a good confession. The matter to be confessed is, however, the superlative truth of God's Word.

In the Hebrew the letter *waw* which opens each line is in each case the conjunction "and" because so very few words beginning with this letter appear in the language. We have sought to reproduce this factor in our translation, only in v. 42 departing from the pattern because there a "then" seemed more in place.

41. In this verse the psalmist prays for that rich variety of blessings that flow from God's steadfast love, blessings which guarantee us help when we need it. Thus equipped, a man shall know how to answer

Psalm 119

effectually him that derides him, for his wisdom is not his own ingenuity but the Word that God gave him. The verse that follows is related in thought, for the "word of truth" is nothing other than the wholesome precepts of the Lord. Not to have them taken out of one's mouth means not to be deprived of the opportunity of speaking to others the wholesome truths embodied in these words. The concluding motivation that is added involves the thought: I have myself set or built my hope on God's ordinances and would like to make the most of the opportunities to present this word of hope to others.

44. In line with such thinking is the expressed ambition to observe such a law continually because its precepts are so helpful. This is another way of saying: I shall pursue this ambition throughout my life. To this is attached the idea of the blessing that grows out of faithful observance of the law of the Lord. Our misdeeds, which are contrary to the law, entangle us in all manner of difficulties. Free, unhampered going (v. 45) is enjoyed only by the man who has always sought both to know and to do the Lord's precepts.

46. This verse is fitted into this connection rather loosely. It seems to express a hypothetical resolution. We cannot deduce from the form of statement that the writer would have opportunity to carry out his resolution in the presence of kings and thus must have had free access to the presence of the kings of his time. The case is hypothetical. He means: Should the opportunity ever present itself to testify to the excellency of God's Word and law, I shall by no means hesitate, and I refuse to be ashamed. Whether the opportunity ever came in his life we shall never know. Historically this verse has achieved fame in that it was often referred to by writers in describing Luther's heroic stand at Worms, and also because it appears as a heading or motto at the beginning of the Augsburg Confession, where it is quoted from the Vulgate version. The second half of the verse expresses a resolve rather than a result.

47. The last two verses of the section dwell on the joy that is experienced when a man busies himself with the Lord's commandments, which he loves. No occupation can be more delightful than this. Thus the section closes with an expressed longing for these commandments. We have sought to express the meaning of the gesture of stretching forth the hands by inserting the adverb "longingly." For a man does stretch forth his hands for that which he longs for. Thus he desires what he does not yet know and "meditates" on that which he has acquired.

61. The independent clause that opens the verse is, nevertheless, the equivalent of a subordinate clause of concession (*KS* 373q).

g) The Word of God sustains the psalmist in the midst of affliction and opposition (vv. 49–56)

Zayin

49. *Remember Thy Word unto Thy servant
Because that Thou hast made me hope.*
50. *This was my comfort in my affliction,
That Thy Word gave me life.*
51. *The proud have derided me very much;
Yet did I not turn aside from Thy law.*
52. *I remembered Thy judgments of olden times, O Lord;
And I was comforted.*
53. *Hot indignation has seized me because of the wicked,
Who have forsaken Thy law.*
54. *Thy statutes have been the theme of my songs
In the house of my pilgrimage.*
55. *Even at night I have remembered Thy name, O Lord,
And have kept Thy law.*
56. *This blessing has fallen to my lot,
That I have kept Thy precepts.*

49. It is true that the first verse is a petition. But in the rest of the section a somewhat autobiographical tone prevails which is in keeping with the theme announced. V. 49 conveys this thought: Because Thy Word kindled hope in my heart, let me not be disappointed in this hope. The "Word" that is to be remembered is practically every word of promise. Thus the prayer is for the fulfilment of all the things that God promises His own.

50. Practically the same thought is to be found in this verse: Thy Word revived me when affliction and trouble had brought me low. That experience was my chief comfort in the midst of my affliction. It seems that the expression "give life" does not refer to inner spiritual processes such as regeneration but to the revitalizing of the ebbing strength of body and soul.

51. Another of the afflictions that had to be borne was the derision of the proud, derision apparently because of his faithful adherence to God's Word. To be mocked for such loyalty did not drive the writer away from God's law: if others did not know how to value it, he did. One aspect of that Word or law is that it has been set forth by the Almighty in "olden times." It has been long known and tested, and those that have built their confidence on it have seen its absolute trustworthiness. Thus merely to recall that Word and its instruction and promises can afford a man great comfort.

Psalm 119

53. The attitude which is the opposite of this is reflected on in this verse. There are those who have forsaken God's law. If God is so gracious as to give so blessed a law, then it is the utmost irreverence for any man to turn away from it, a reprehensible act which may well arouse "hot indignation" on the part of him who knows how blessed that Word is.

54. There is another aspect of the use of divine Word that may be reflected upon: it may well rouse the grateful songs of him who knows it even as the whole of this psalm is, as it were, an elaboration of this theme. If these songs are said to have been sung "in the house of [his] pilgrimage," that means, during the course of this earthly and temporary existence, and, no doubt, many are the days that have been gladdened by such a song on the theme of the excellency of the divine statutes. God's Word deserves high praise.

55. That thought is dwelt upon in this verse, a fact which we have tried to indicate by inserting an "even" in the translation, which does not appear in the original. If the mere reflecting on God's faithful words makes the tongue eloquent with songs of praise, then it is not to be wondered at that even in the silence of the night his thoughts should have busied themselves with the law of God. To that consideration the last verse seems to attach itself. The writer has kept the Lord's precepts. These precepts were not burdensome or hard but rather a blessing that has fallen to his lot.

h) **The psalmist busies himself with God's Word in the fellowship of God's saints (vv. 57–64)**

Cheth

57. I have said, O Lord, that this is my portion,
That I have kept Thy words.
58. I have entreated Thy favor with my whole heart;
Be merciful to me according to Thy Word!
59. I have considered my ways
And turned my feet unto Thy testimonies.
60. I made haste and delayed not
To keep Thy commandments.
61. Though the snares of the wicked enmeshed me,
Yet have I not forgotten Thy law.
62. At midnight I arise to give Thee thanks
Because of Thy righteous ordinances.
63. I am a companion of all that fear Thee
And of them that keep Thy precepts.
64. The earth is full of Thy steadfast love;
Teach me Thy statutes!

The dominant thought of this section is that the psalmist busies himself with God's Word in the fellowship of God's saints. Others are of the same mind as he is. They all have a common pursuit that welds them into one great body.

57. Far from finding the words of the Lord a heavy burden, the writer has had the experience that the keeping of God's Word was a rare privilege, his "portion," in fact, a word that is used to express the idea of a worth-while inheritance that falls to a man's lot. When he refers to the fact that he once said that this was his attitude he implies that he has not changed his conviction in the matter but would still maintain it.

58. In catching the spirit of this verse it may be best to regard the two members of the verse as expressing the same thought. The petition involved according to the second member is that, since God has promised mercy in His Word, the psalmist makes bold to implore such mercy. The thought of the first member of the verse covers the same ground by emphasizing the earnestness with which this petition has been made.

59. As *Maclaren* has indicated, the next five verses turn from the thought of petition to that of "profession of obedience." The thought is first stressed that the way to be followed has been carefully considered and then deliberately pursued. In fact, a certain eagerness marked this course of procedure. It was not a case of languid and halfhearted following the goal the Lord has prescribed.

61. This was not an easy matter. The wicked had created certain situations for him that might well have brought about his overthrow. But he did not allow himself to become so disturbed over the snares that had all but enmeshed him as to let that difficulty drive from his mind the law of his God. That was still his treasure and his delight. So deeply was he engrossed in it and its wisdom that at the thought of the rich treasure that this Word was to him he would arise at midnight (v. 62) to give thanks for these righteous ordinances that the Lord had taught him to know and to prize. One cannot but be moved by the utter devotion that this procedure testifies to. The close of this section that testifies to his devotion to the law is made by indicating the fact that his attitude puts him into that select company of men who both fear the Lord and keep His precepts. In the last analysis this is the procedure followed by all true children of God.

64. The thought expressed in this verse is also a rare gem. Because wherever one looks, evidences of God's steadfast love are discernible, such a loving Lord must have given statutes to the children of men that are in every sense most valuable and delightful. The psalmist begs the

Lord to grant him the true understanding of what He has revealed in manifold ways. Such revelation is a precious treasure.

i) God's goodness drives the psalmist closer to the Word (vv. 65-72)

Teth
65. Thou hast treated Thy servant well, O Lord,
    According to Thy Word.
66. Teach me good judgment and knowledge,
    For I have believed in Thy commandments.
67. Before I was afflicted I went astray;
    But now I keep Thy Word.
68. Thou art good and doest good;
    Teach me Thy statutes.
69. The insolent besmear me with lies;
    But as for me, with my whole heart I keep Thy precepts.
70. Their heart is gross like fat;
    But as for me, I delight in Thy law.
71. It is good for me that I was afflicted,
    That I might learn Thy statutes.
72. The law of Thy mouth is better to me
    Than thousands of gold and silver.

It seems to us that this section follows this basic line of thought: God's goodness, manifested also in the affliction which He permits His servant to suffer, drives him closer to the Word. Other subsidiary thoughts are woven into the picture.

65. The section begins with a confession of the Lord's goodness toward the writer. Our translation lacks the more elegant touch of the *Authorized Version:* "Thou hast dealt well," but avoids the archaism. The point, however, is that, when the Lord deals thus with His servants, that is in conformity with what His Word or promises toward them had led them to anticipate.

66. The progression of thought marked by this verse could apparently be this: Even as a good bit of insight was revealed in the sentiment just expressed, so the writer prays for further insights, here designated "good judgment and knowledge." He motivates his plea by pointing to the source from which most of these insights come, the "commandments" in which he has had much confidence.

67. This, however, seems to suggest another source of deep insight, affliction. Affliction furnishes not only deeper understanding but other safeguards such as making a man more reliable in his ways. For the writer confesses that before he was afflicted he was inclined to go astray

from the Lord's ways. He now keeps the Word, which teaches the ways of the Lord, with greater fidelity. V. 67 is one of the instances when one might be inclined to adopt the interpretation that the speaker is the collective "I," the congregation of Israel, which experienced a helpful correction in the Exile. The evidence, however, is not quite sufficient to warrant such an assumption.

68. As the plea for greater insight of this sort continues, the author appeals particularly to the fact that God is good and loves to do good to His faithful ones. An experience seems to occur to him that has made this course difficult (v. 69): the wicked have defamed him (very graphically described as a "besmearing with lies"). Far from being deterred by that experience, the psalmist abides by the keeping of God's precepts with greater fidelity. The contrast between his own ideals and those of the opposition strikes him so powerfully that he cannot help but set down what this contrast is: "Their heart is gross like fat," a description of men who are devoid of spiritual capacity (Ps. 73:7). He on his part cannot but find great delight in that law which is meaningless to these contemptuous souls.

71. Even as in v. 67 the writer pointed out how affliction had been beneficial, he feels impelled again to stress this thought, for this experience, rightly met, gives a man deeper insight into God's statutes.

72. This leads him to offer a strong statement by way of a summary as to how precious the words of the Lord's mouth have become to him, they are more to him "than thousands of gold and silver." Involved is the helpful thought that God has in the course of time in one way or another spoken to men, and thus this is the "law of [His] mouth."

NOTES

66. The expression involved is a bit stronger than "good judgment." For "good" the Hebrew has a noun, somewhat to this effect: Teach me excellence of judgment and knowledge. We have not translated thus because the expression becomes a bit cumbersome in English.

67. The term "afflicted" could be translated "humbled" as *Luther* rendered it. He thus stresses a result (dictionaries allow for this translation) whereas our versions stress the process.

72. After "thousands" a noun like "shekels" is omitted. It seems that in passages like these the Hebrew usage has affected the English idiom. Cf. *KS* 314h.

j) **The deliverance of God to His servant is a mighty comfort to other saints (vv. 73–80)**

Yod

73. *Thy hands have made me and fashioned me;*
Give me understanding that I may learn Thy commandments.

74. They that fear Thee shall see me and be glad,
    For I have hoped in Thy Word.
75. I know, O Lord, that Thy judgments are right,
    And that in faithfulness Thou hast afflicted me.
76. Let Thy steadfast love be for my comfort
    As Thou hast promised Thy servant.
77. Let Thy great mercy come upon me that I may live,
    For Thy law is my delight.
78. Let the insolent be put to shame, for they have oppressed me deceitfully;
    As for me, I will meditate on Thy precepts.
79. May they that fear Thee turn back to me
    That they may know Thy testimonies.
80. May all my thinking be wholly on Thy statutes
    That I may not be put to shame.

One might summarize the unique emphasis of this section as follows: When God delivers His servant who has kept His Word, such deliverance will mightily comfort others of God's saints. There is, of course, a slight reference also to the advantage that comes from having been afflicted (v. 75), with the additional emphasis on the fact that the writer is willing to accept whatever the Lord may send him in this respect.

73. The opening thought is the familiar note of prayer for better understanding of the Lord's commandments. The particular shade of thought is in this case that the Lord has given him his physical being; may He add spiritual understanding. The advance in thought in v. 74 may be this: When Thy children, O God, see how I grow in the knowledge of Thy revealed truth they will rejoice with me that Thou hast helped me. The reason my prayer for light was not in vain was that "I have hoped in Thy Word," which, in turn, promises enlightenment to those that seek it there.

76. This verse seems to grow out of v. 75 and the reference to affliction. The one important fact that can always serve as a substantial comfort to those who suffer affliction is that God's "steadfast love" is the supreme comfort as God has promised that it will be. Analogous is the prayer uttered in v. 77, for God's "great mercy" is ready to be shed on those that need it and will ask for it. And strange as the definition may seem, to be the recipient of God's mercy is to "live." That the one who prays will not receive such a great gift idly or foolishly is guaranteed by the fact that God's "law is [his] delight."

It was, perhaps, by way of contrast that the writer was reminded of the "insolent," who so often make the lot of the righteous heavy and burdensome in that they try to bring men like the psalmist to fall. He, therefore, prays that they may be foiled in attaining their purpose or be "put to shame." Let them persecute him as much as they please for his fidelity to God's precepts, he will not cease meditating upon them.

79. This verse is paraphrased thus by *Kirkpatrick:* "Let my experience of Thy mercy show the godly the blessedness of keeping Thy testimonies." With the importance of the Word of God thus again emphasized, the writer may well close the section with the petition offered in v. 80: "May all my thinking be wholly on Thy statutes." Wholesome meditation on the divine Word should be our continual occupation. To those that follow this rule there shall never be disappointment.

NOTES

77. The Hebrew has an intensive plural, which we have rendered by the insertion of the adjective "great" before "mercy."

79. The form behind "that they may know" (literally: "and they shall know") allows for the other rendering: "and those that have known" (*KJ*). It does not matter which rendering is followed. We feel that the finite verb suits the context best rather than the participial construction.

80. Though the Hebrew says: "May my *heart* be blameless" (*RSV*), it should not be forgotten that the heart is the center of all thinking activity (*Denkwerkstaette*). The emphasis seems to be on being totally occupied with the Lord's statutes rather than on sinless thoughts.

k) In the midst of persecution, the psalmist hopes in God's Word (vv. 81–87)

Kaph

81. *My soul pines for deliverance;*
    I hope in Thy Word.
82. *My eyes look with longing for the fulfillment of Thy Word;*
    I say: "When wilt Thou comfort me?"
83. *For I was like a wineskin in the smoke;*
    Yet I have not forgotten Thy statutes.
84. *How long shall Thy servant live?*
    When wilt Thou execute judgment on those who persecute me?
85. *The insolent have dug pits for me,*
    Men who do not live according to Thy law.
86. *All Thy commandments are reliable;*
    Men persecute me treacherously; do Thou help me!
87. *Men had almost disposed of me in the earth;*
    But as for me, I did not forsake Thy precepts.
88. *Revive me according to Thy steadfast love*
    That I may keep the testimonies of Thy mouth.

The specific turn of the thought under consideration is: In the midst of persecution and affliction the psalmist hopes in God's Word. It has been rightly remarked that in this section the enemies are "more fully dealt with." (*Oesterley*).

81. The writer is in some form of trouble which makes him long eagerly for deliverance. Till the help comes, he fixes his hope on the Word in which God has promised to His children such help as may be needed by them. The same thought appears in v. 82a, with this slight change of figure, that the writer is represented as straining his eyes to see the longed-for deliverance come. He furthermore asks plaintively: "When wilt Thou comfort me?"

83. The figure employed in this verse has elicited a number of interpretations. A wineskin was obviously the Old Testament equivalent of a bottle (see *KJ*). Unused wineskins would be hung near the rafters of a room for storage. Hanging there for any length of time, they would become shrivelled and browned with smoke. If the point of the comparison were to describe the emaciated condition of the psalmist, the very point of the comparison would have been left unexpressed. The contrast with the second half of the verse suggests that this wineskin represents a forgotten object, the point being that, even though God seems to forget His servant, he on his part has not forgotten the statutes of the Lord to which he is obligated.

84. The literal rendering of 84a is: "How many are the days of Thy servant?" The thought is: They are too few. The brevity of human life appears to be used as a plea for early help when the poet asks: "When wilt Thou execute judgment on those who persecute me?" He longs to see justice done, but he leaves the matter in the hands of the Just Judge of mankind.

85. In this verse the opponents are still under consideration. It is obvious that these opponents are not good men. This has led some interpreters to translate the word involved "godless men." The root meaning of the term is "insolent." It is this delayed justice that apparently prompts the writer to remark that, though the words of the Lord are seemingly not being fulfilled immediately, yet "all [God's] commandments are reliable." To this is added a reminder that the persecutors are acting treacherously (literally: *in a lie*), therefore, the Lord should help His servant.

87. The issue was a serious one; it involved life and death. The psalmist could truthfully say: "Men had almost disposed of me in the earth." They would not stop short of murder if need seemed to require it. The phrase "in the earth" seems to be pointless unless one thinks of the verse that lies but a short distance back (v. 85): "The insolent have dug pits for me." That is the manner in which they had almost

disposed of him in the earth. We admit that in both verses the expression is figurative. But such machinations on their part did not deter this man from keeping the precepts of the Lord. He goes on to pray for the ability (v. 88) to continue along this path in the strength that God supplies.

l) **The psalmist praises the immutability of God's Word which has upheld him (89–96)**

Lamed

89. *Forever, O Lord,*
    The Word stands fast in the heavens.
90. *From generation to generation Thy faithfulness endures;*
    Thou didst establish the earth, and it stood.
91. *According to Thy ordinances they stand this day,*
    For all things are Thy servants.
92. *If Thy law had not been my delight,*
    Then I had perished in my affliction.
93. *I will never forget Thy precepts,*
    For by them Thou hast revived me.
94. *I am Thine, save me;*
    For I have sought out Thy precepts.
95. *The wicked lie in wait for me to destroy me;*
    But I consider diligently Thy testimonies.
96. *I have seen an end to all perfection;*
    But Thy commandment has a very broad scope.

89. The writer begins by considering the work of God's creation (vv. 89–91). The heavens themselves have an enduring quality. It is as though the author were saying that in those eternal heavens the Word, which proceeds from the eternal Lord of the heavens, has its abiding resting place and will, like them, endure forever.

90. To this is added the thought that, even as God's earth has been established by Him and stands fast as a result, so also from generation to generation the faithfulness of God is immutable, which faithfulness has found expression in His Word. We feel impelled to introduce the Word because the word "faithfulness" apparently contains a hidden reference to it; otherwise there would be no synonym for the Word in the verse.

91. The thought of the permanence of creation is continued in this verse. The "they" of the first clause must include the heavens and the earth, which are mentioned in the two preceding verses. The reason both continue to exist is that God's Word upholds them or as the psalm words it, "according to Thy ordinances." This claim is upheld by the deep and broad statement, "for all things are Thy servants," implying

that they continually obey His beck and call and, for that matter, also continue on the scene as long as He bids them do so.

92. This Word or law of the Lord is not something that is strange to the psalmist. It has always been his delight, and but for it he would have perished in his affliction. Therefore he can and will never forget God's precepts, for by them He has often revived him and given him a fresh lease on life. In the next two verses the writer returns to the subject that has caused him much distress: how wickedly his opponents have lain in wait for him to destroy him (v. 95), and it was this extremity that caused him to cry out, "Save me" (v. 94). He motivates his anxious plea by claiming to be God's own and by indicating that he has had a tremendous respect for the Lord's precepts. He knows that those that love the Lord so much that they regard His precepts earnestly are, in turn, also loved by God and safeguarded in the evil day. The contrast involved in v. 95 seems to be that, though the adherence to the Lord's testimonies involves him in danger, he will not fail to consider diligently the testimonies of the Lord.

96. This seems to be the thought that leads to the last verse which presents an entirely new thought but is at the same time a statement of resounding praise of a new aspect of revealed truth. There is a contrast in the verse. All things that are apart from the Word, no matter how excellent or nearly perfect they may be, are temporal and ephemeral. The contrast to that thought is not expressed but implied. It is the old familiar principle that the Word of the Lord endures forever. The contrast that is expressed is that God's "commandment has a very broad scope." We translate thus though the Hebrew idiom says only: "Thy commandment is exceedingly broad" (*RSV*). That idea of breadth must involve the thought that the scope of this divine Word is simply without parallel as far as other earthly things and values are concerned. *Kirkpatrick* adds this thought: "God's commandment is unlimited in extent and value."

m) The law of God, if it is truly loved, imparts wisdom (vv. 97–104)

Mem

97. *Oh, how I love Thy law!*
    It is my meditation all the day.
98. *Thy commandments make me wiser than my enemies,*
    For they are mine forever.
99. *I have more insight than all my teachers,*
    For Thy testimonies are my meditation.
100. *I have more understanding than the aged,*
     For I keep Thy precepts.

101. *I have held back my feet from every evil way
In order that I may keep Thy Word.*
102. *I have not turned aside from Thy ordinances,
For Thou hast taught me.*
103. *How sweet are Thy words to my taste,
Sweeter than honey to my mouth!*
104. *From Thy precepts I get understanding;
Therefore I hate every false way.*

The theme of this section could be stated thus: The law of God, if it is truly loved, imparts wisdom. It has also been observed that there is no petition involved here whereas most of the sections have some element of this sort included.

It might be remarked that if, on the one hand, the unusual form of the psalm prevents unusual heights of poetic fancy from finding expression, on the other hand, a tone of high and well-sustained fervor is in evidence throughout. In spite of its length the poem moves on a high plane.

97. The section begins with a protestation of sincere and unfaltering love for the law of the Lord. Evidence of this love is the fact that the writer meditates on this subject all the day. From this point onward the psalmist goes on to say how such meditation has rendered him wiser than three classes of persons, the last two of which are usually regarded as being wiser than most men. First, however, the enemies are mentioned, whom we have met previously, and who are not merely personal enemies of his but those proud disdainers of godly men who make themselves obnoxious by this superior attitude. Being by nature proud, they would not be inclined to submit to the discipline and instruction of God's commandments. The psalmist can claim that the divine law is his forever, meaning, of course, that he continually keeps it in use.

The second class whom he surpasses is "all [his] teachers." This can scarcely mean that he cultivates an attitude of more intense devotion to, and study of, the divine law than did the preceding generations, to which his teachers belonged. The teachers are rather to be thought of as those who have studied ordinary human wisdom. Such wisdom cannot impart what is gained from the testimonies of God. In the same way the psalmist is filled with a better understanding than the aged, who grew old in experience but not in the experience that the precepts of the Lord can impart.

101. This verse presents a searching test of true wisdom: Does it enable a man to shun evil? The psalmist claims for himself that he has been taught such restraint, and the connection between the halves of the verse would seem to suggest the thought that such avoidance of

Psalm 119

evil was practiced with the very intent that the instruction given by the Word might be heeded. One cannot be lax about evil and expect to profit in the use of the Word.

102. In this verse he adds another reason by way of explanation as to why he will not deviate from the divine ordinances: he knows that through the Word that God has taught him. Negatively, that was the very thing he was taught, namely, that he should shun evil.

103. Reflecting, it would seem, on this and all the other benefits that the divine words had conferred upon him, he breaks into the exclamation: "How sweet are Thy words to my taste!" Then, like the writer of Ps. 19:10, he claims that this sweetness excels the finest sweetness that he knows, even that of honey.

104. He concludes this section on the same note that had been so prominent in the opening verses: The divine precepts impart understanding, and part of that understanding always manifests itself as the hating of every false way.

NOTES

98. It appears that there is a certain incongruity (as *KS* also points out, 348h) between the singular verb and the plural subject, "commandments." This may be regarded as one of those many instances when the statement begins with a singular, but it later becomes apparent that the subject is plural, yet the incongruity is allowed to stand.

n) **The psalmist vows fidelity to the enlightening Word of God under all circumstances, let the cost be what it will (vv. 105–112)**

Nun

105. *Thy Word is a lamp to my foot*
     And a light to my path.
106. *I have sworn an oath and performed it,*
     To observe Thy righteous ordinances.
107. *I am afflicted very severely;*
     Revive me, O Lord, according to Thy Word.
108. *Accept, O Lord, the praise of my mouth, freely offered;*
     And teach me Thy ordinances.
109. *I carry my life in my hand continually;*
     But I do not forget Thy law.
110. *The wicked have laid a snare for me;*
     Yet I do not err from Thy precepts.
111. *Thy testimonies have I taken as a heritage forever,*
     For they are the joy of my heart.
112. *I have inclined my heart to do Thy statutes*
     Forever to the end.

105. One might regard this verse as offering the distinctive thought of the section were it not for the fact that the remaining verses never allude to this thought. Prov. 6:23 is a good parallel to this verse. It may be possible that the thought is this, that the lamp gives light by night, but light is there throughout the day. Thus by day and by night the Word exerts it light-giving influence. He that uses it faithfully learns where to set his foot as he walks along the slippery paths of this life. He need not stumble or fall.

106. How strongly the writer's mind is set on doing what the Word of God bids him do is well illustrated by this verse. He has put himself under oath to observe God's ordinances by calling to witness all that is high and holy, and he has also kept his oath. But his fidelity has not been without serious affliction.

107. The thought expressed in this verse may mean that men have made him suffer for being so faithful in the doing of God's will. But he has recourse to prayer that God might revive him, that is, increase his physical strength to bear what must be borne. Nor will he allow himself to be unduly depressed by that which weighs heavily upon him. He can tender praises for the many good things that he still enjoys. In great humility he feels that his poor praises are not acceptable to God unless God condescends to receive them. He would praise Him especially for the help that His Word afforded. Almost in the same breath, as he praises God for what that Word has done for him, he prays that he may learn still more of that priceless treasure.

109. It may be possible that this verse and the next verse are intended to show more fully what the affliction is of which v. 107 spoke. The somewhat unusual expression, "I carry my life in my hand continually," involves the meaning: I am "taking a grave risk," or, "I find myself in grave danger." Judg. 12:3; I Sam. 19:5; 28:21; Job 13:14 give us the needed light on the expression.

110. The exact nature of the danger involved is shown: "The wicked have laid a snare for me." Whether this is to be understood literally or to be regarded as merely expressing the thought that plans are afoot to bring him to fall, the danger is extreme. But such tactics do not induce him to make less use of the law of the Lord or to forget it or even to err from the divine precepts. Let happen what will, the Word of the Lord must reign supreme, and its behests must be followed.

111. This verse offers the thought that, even as a man may aspire to receive a heritage as a highly prized possession, so to the poet God's testimonies are such a heritage continually. He purposes never to depart from his allegiance to them. They have so often made his heart glad and are still "the joy of [his] heart." The last expression of sincere loyalty to the revealed truth appears in v. 112.

NOTES

105. Though the old versions have changed the word (the Hebrew reads: "lamp to my *foot*," singular), that singular may be retained. The singular often individualizes and means as much as to each foot.

106. The *KJ* does not translate as the text reads when it renders: "I have sworn and *I will perform it*." The form of this part of the thought is as we have rendered it: "I have sworn . . . and performed it." The psalmist speaks, not of intentions, but of results achieved.

108. The *KJ* translates very correctly, retaining the Hebrew idiom: "Accept . . . the freewill offerings of my mouth." The reader is perplexed as to whether this refers to all forms of prayer, petition, and praise that he might have offered. Our translation, following the lead of Heb. 13:15, interprets these fruits of the lips as being praises offered to God rather than, for example, the petition immediately preceding in v. 107b. For only praise seems to come under the category of that which is freely offered to God. Petitions and requests grow out of the compulsions that accompany dangers and difficulties.

o) Prayer for strength to remain loyal to the Word in the face of much opposition (vv. 113–120)

Samech

113. *I hate double-minded persons;*
    But Thy law do I love.
114. *My hiding place and my shield art Thou;*
    In Thy Word do I hope.
115. *Depart from me, you evildoers,*
    That I may keep the commandments of my God.
116. *Uphold me according to Thy Word that I may live,*
    And shame me not in my hope!
117. *Support me that I may be safe;*
    And I shall contemplate Thy statutes continually.
118. *Thou hast always cast off all who stray from Thy statutes,*
    For their deception is utterly false.
119. *Thou puttest aside all the wicked of the earth like dross;*
    Therefore I love Thy testimonies.
120. *My flesh creeps in awe of Thee;*
    And I am afraid because of Thy judgments.

This section appears to be a prayer for strength to remain loyal to the Word in the face of much opposition. In the Hebrew certain little-used words appear because the initial letter of each verse is one that is among those letters of the Hebrew alphabet that are least used.

113. One can readily understand the sentiment expressed when one

considers that what the writer upholds throughout is unswerving devotion to the law of the Lord. He who does not share this attitude is "double-minded" and is thus abhorred. The very thought of such persons drives the psalmist that much closer to the law.

114. Expressive of the same fidelity is this verse. What may at first glance seem to be incongruous is the fact that the writer takes his refuge as much in the Word of the Lord as he does in the Lord. This is not an attitude to be deplored. It is rather the normal procedure. Both loyalties always run parallel.

115. The summons addressed to the evildoers to depart may be understood to mean, You can do me no harm by your hostility; therefore get out so that I may pursue all the more undisturbed that which is my delight—the keeping of the commandments of my God.

116. This does not imply an attitude of self-sufficiency as this verse indicates. Unless God upholds him and gives him life, he will not succeed in adhering loyally to the doing of the Lord's will. The latter is apparently meant by: "Shame me not in my hope!"

117. This verse offers a prayer of the same intent. Only as God upholds him can he be safe from the dangers and the enemies that beset him. When that safety is obtained, the poet hopes to put it to use by contemplating the Lord's statutes continually.

118. Looking at the men of the opposition, who represent the very opposite of what his own life stands for, he expresses the thought that those who put the commandments aside are always cast off or "spurned" (*RSV*) by God. The concluding clause explains why God must do this. Their "deception," i.e., the hollow pretences and arguments by which they attempt to validate their position, is "utterly false," that is to say, based entirely on lies.

119. Analogous to the first thought of the verse is that of this verse, which states the thought with a bit more color: "Thou puttest aside all the wicked of the earth like dross." God aims at producing purified characters as the smelter of precious metals aims to secure pure metal. What comes out of the smelter as dross, the slag, must be removed and disposed of. That explains the ultimate fate of those who fall away from God's Word. This consideration makes the writer love the Lord's testimonies all the more.

120. The God who works so wonderfully and with such authority as the Judge of all mankind is one whom no man dare regard lightly. Reverent awe fills the psalmist's being at the thought of the unspeakable greatness of the God whom he knows, an awe that makes "his flesh creep." The judgments of the past that God has visited upon the wicked (cf. Sodom, Egypt, and Canaan) increase that feeling of reverent awe for Him. The deep love that God's saints had for Him and His Word

did not exclude humble reverence. The distance between the Creator and the creature just could not be ignored.

NOTES

118. The "always" found in the first member of the verse grows out of the approach which regards the verb as the equivalent of a gnomic aorist, therefore expressing what is always true. The "utterly" inserted in the second member is an attempt to catch the force of the *shéqer,* which is in a somewhat emphatic position and, therefore, means something like "wholly a lie" or "utterly false."

120. It must be conceded that, whereas we have understood *mishpat* in the sense of a punitive judgment, it may, especially in this psalm, also be understood in the sense of "the laws and ordinances according to which [men] are punished" (*Kirkpatrick*).

p) God's faithful servant commits his cause into God's hands and clings steadfastly to the Word of his God (vv. 121–128)
Ayin

121. *I have done what is just and right;*
Leave me not to my oppressors.
122. *Go surety for Thy servant for good;*
Let not the proud oppress me!
123. *My eyes pine for Thy deliverance*
And for Thy righteous promise.
124. *Deal with Thy servant according to Thy steadfast love*
And teach me Thy statutes.
125. *I am Thy servant; grant me insight*
That I may know Thy testimonies.
126. *It is time for God to act;*
They have broken Thy law.
127. *For that very reason I love Thy commandments*
More than gold and fine gold.
128. *For that very reason I have always esteemed each and every one*
of Thy precepts to be right;
I hate every false way.

We suggest the following thought for this section: God's faithful servant commits his cause into God's hands and clings steadfastly to the Word of his God. The term "servant" appears three times, and though it is obviously another way of saying "I," it breathes a fine humility—the writer knows his place over against God.

121. Opposition against good men is apparently strong; they are being oppressed. The first three verses sound this note. As a reason for deliverance from these evil men the psalmist urges that he has "done

what is just and right." Though he may not merit deliverance he has at least not done that which would make him unworthy of it. Some measure of peril must have been involved, otherwise he would scarcely have prayed to be delivered from his "oppressors."

122. The same plea is found in this verse. By the translation, "go surety for Thy servant," we mean nothing more than what is more popularly expressed as "to go good for a man," which is the meaning the *KW* gives for the verb: *fuer jemanden eintreten,* which, in turn, means "to stand up for someone." Though it may seem to be superfluous to add to the expression the phrase "for good," such an addition lends color: it will do him that prays so much good if God does this.

123. The eagerness with which the writer looks out for help is well caught in the words: "My eyes pine for Thy deliverance." So eagerly does he peer into the future that because of the intensity of his looking his eyes have wasted away. By the expression, "and for Thy righteous promise," he means, "For the fulfilment of Thy righteous promise." In the original the words read thus (literally): "for the word of Thy righteousness."

124. The next three verses apparently add pleas because of which the Lord should give heed to his prayer. The first is an appeal to the Lord's "steadfast love," that covenant faithfulness according to which God has been wont to act for His servants. When the psalmist adds: "And teach me Thy statutes," he would imply that deeper knowledge of God's truth enables a man to meet emergencies more effectively.

125. In this verse the special plea centers on the fact that the one who makes it is God's "servant." God should become active in behalf of His own. The added petition for insight and the knowledge of God's testimonies may well be a prayer for the insight that helps a man to meet difficult situations such as the one in which the psalmist now finds himself.

126. The third plea is that "it is time for the Lord to act." Though he could have said: "for they have afflicted Thy servant," he looks at that fact from another angle, that what was done to him involved a breaking of divine law, a deed toward which the Lord cannot remain indifferent.

127. In defending the correctness of the text in the use of the phrase "for that very reason" *Koenig* suggests that it means: "because the authority of the divine law is at this very moment endangered." Knowing this law's value leads the author of the psalm to love it all the more dearly. "More than gold and fine gold" is reminiscent of Ps. 19:10.

128. This verse continues the same approach. An analogy would be to see the flag of our nation, which we esteem highly, dishonored by some unpatriotic persons. That very act of theirs would call forth

a reaction on our part which would impel us then and there to express our esteem for it all the more emphatically. In this instance, when some have shown disrespect for God's holy law, the psalmist feels the need of stating that he has always "esteemed each and every one of [God's] precepts to be right." His aversion to what the opposition has done is expressed in the words: "I hate every false way."

NOTES

121. The Hebrew uses two nouns: "I have done justice and righteousness." We have given their equivalent in the English idiom.

128. It is commonly assumed that there must be some irregularity in the text, for it has the word *kol* ("all") three times. To us it seems that the first two stress rather aptly the utter rightness of the precepts and may well be the equivalent of our "each and every." The verb employed, *yishsharti,* again offers an example of a perfect serving as a gnomic aorist.

q) **God's wonderful testimonies confer many blessings; therefore they are to be faithfully kept (vv. 129–136)**

Pe

129. *Thy testimonies are wonderful;*
  Therefore has my soul kept them.
130. *The unfolding of Thy Word enlightens men;*
  It gives understanding to the simple.
131. *I have opened my mouth and panted,*
  For I long for Thy commandments.
132. *Turn to me and be merciful to me*
  As Thou art wont to do to those who love Thy name.
133. *Make my steps firm by means of Thy word;*
  And let not any iniquity have control over me.
134. *Deliver me from man's oppression*
  That I may keep Thy precepts.
135. *Make Thy face to shine upon Thy servant*
  And teach me Thy statutes.
136. *My eyes overflow with streams of water*
  Because men do not keep Thy law.

The major thought of this section may be summarized thus: God's wonderful testimonies confer many blessings, therefore they are to be faithfully kept.

129. When the writer states that God's testimonies are wonderful he does not specify in what particular respect they are to be thus described, chiefly, perhaps, because the wonders of God's law are so manifold. That characteristic surely offers another good reason for

keeping them. One of the wonders of the divine Word is that, when its truth is unfolded to men, it brings with it new and deeper insights to all men and particularly to the "simple" who are the ones who keep their heart open to its beneficent influences (v. 130). Of course, if that Word is all that the psalmist claims for it, it should be eagerly desired. That the psalmist has always done (v. 131): he has opened his mouth, as it were, in great thirst and panted for these commandments.

132. This verse does not contain a word about God's law. When, however, the prayer of the psalmist is that God might turn unto him and have mercy upon him, we know that God usually does such conferring of His help and mercy through His Word. What makes the psalmist bold to pray thus is the fact that God's gracious attitude toward men is His customary procedure in dealing with His own. The second half of the verse which claims this may, however, be translated: "as is the right of those who love Thy name," "right" being used in the sense of a right that is guaranteed by His promise and not something that man may presumptuously claim for himself, cf. Deut. 18:3.

133. A kindred prayer to that offered in v. 132 appears also in this verse, a prayer for firmness and constancy in walking in the godly way, which is the very antithesis to letting "any iniquity have control" over him. What he means by this statement is, perhaps, best conveyed by the next verse: "any iniquity," which would then be "man's oppression." For to be under such oppression makes it difficult to "keep [God's] precepts."

135. The last two verses present an antithesis. The first asks for God's gracious favor that the psalmist may be taught the divine statutes; the second shows his grief over the reckless way in which men disregard the law of the Lord. Such personal grief, so deeply felt, may well shame all those who feel far less keenly on the subject.

NOTES

130. *Péthach* may be read in one of two ways: with a short *e* it means "door," with a longer *e* it means "unfolding" or "revealing." Quite a bit can be said for either interpretation. The former explains why *KJ* translates: "the entrance of Thy words." Luther had the second meaning in mind when he translated: *Wenn dein Wort offenbar wird* (When Thy Word is revealed). We feel that the latter deserves the preference.

136. In the Hebrew it might almost appear as though "streams of water" should be regarded as the subject. A comparison with Lam. 3:48 indicates that "eyes" is the subject. Cf. *GK* 117z. The other potential subject serves as an adverbial accusative. On *'al* followed by a clause see *GK* 158c.

r) "The righteousness, purity, and truth of God's law command the psalmist's deepest love and reverence" (Kirkpatrick) (vv. 137–144)

Tsade

137. Righteous art Thou, O Lord;
And right are Thy judgments.
138. Thou hast appointed Thy testimonies in righteousness
And in great faithfulness.
139. My zeal has put an end to me,
For my enemies have forgotten Thy words.
140. Thy Word is thoroughly refined;
And Thy servant loves it.
141. I am small and despised;
Yet have I not forgotten Thy precepts.
142. Thy righteousness is righteous forever;
And Thy law is true.
143. Trouble and anguish have befallen me;
Thy commandments are my delight.
144. Thy testimonies are always righteous;
Help me to understand them that I may live.

137. Since "righteous" and "right" are closely related, the psalmist derives the attribute of rightness which he ascribes to God's judgments from that very attribute of God: both belong together. Continuing in the same strain: It was the righteousness of God which induced Him to appoint His testimonies for the children of men (v. 138). These fine attributes of the Word were the quality that engendered in the heart of the writer the zeal he refers to (v. 139), zeal for that Word and the knowledge of it.

Such an attitude will always irritate a certain class of men who refuse to be bound by that Word. These are the psalmist's enemies that may also be described as having forgotten the Lord's words. This attitude of theirs was, no doubt, the cause that brought about the result that the poet's zeal "had put an end [to him]." He was being persecuted for the Word's sake and is all but consumed.

140. Even though some men are hostile, that does not make the author think less of that Word. On the contrary, he praises it as a Word that is "thoroughly refined" and as a result very pure, like a precious metal smelted in the furnace. That is one of its attributes that makes him love it all the more.

141. He may, indeed, be personally unimportant, yet he can claim one thing for himself—that he has not forgotten God's precepts. So he goes on to sing the praises of that wonderful law: As the righteousness of God is always righteous, so is His law ever true.

143. In this verse he comes back to the subject so regularly touched on in the psalm, that the writer's position has involved him in "trouble and anguish." But that does not drive him away from the divine commandments but has moved him all the more to find his delight in them. They are a real solace at such times. A thought that has appeared twice before in this section (vv. 137 and 142) is stressed once more in this connection: these testimonies of the Lord are so absolutely right or righteous. No fault is to be found in them on any score. But this time he does not pledge his adherence to them but prays that he may understand them the better and thus may survive because of the higher life that they impart.

NOTES

137. In the second half of the verse the predicate that is to be construed with "judgments" is in the singular after the common Hebrew pattern of beginning with the singular verb as long as the number of the subject has not yet been disclosed. See *GK* 145r.

144. In the second member of the verse we have again added the object "them" after the verb "understand." To have the statement reflect merely a general desire for understanding is in this connection not so appropriate as to think of understanding the "testimonies" which have just been mentioned.

s) **With trouble on every side, the psalmist continually turns to God in prayer and guides his steps by the unfailing Word (vv. 147–152)**

Koph

145. *I have called with all my heart; answer me, O Lord;*
     Thy statutes will I keep.
146. *I have called upon Thee; save me;*
     And I will keep Thy testimonies.
147. *In the earliest dawn did I cry for help;*
     I hope in Thy words.
148. *I wake up early*
     That I may meditate in Thy word.
149. *Hear my voice according to Thy steadfast love, O Lord,*
     According to Thy judgment revive me.
150. *Men who follow after evil designs draw near against me;*
     But they are far from Thy law.
151. *Near art Thou, O Lord;*
     And all Thy commandments are true.
152. *I have long known from Thy testimonies*
     That Thou hast founded them forever.

Psalm 119

145. The first two verses go together. There is a certain urgency about a man's situation when he thus pleads that his prayer may not be ignored. Still he knows "what firm abides"—God's statements and testimonies. But it is not only urgent cries for help that he keeps presenting half-importunately before the throne of God; he also addresses himself earnestly to much meditation in God's Word, rising up early for this purpose, even as he often arose at an early hour to bring his needs to the Lord.

149. It is interesting to note on what the psalmist bases his petitions: on the one hand, on God's "steadfast love" and on the other, on His "judgment." That word does not connote what the familiar English idiom of our day may suggest—using one's best judgment. Nor does it here refer to acts of judgment whereby men are punished but to "the gracious rule of action that [God] has laid down for Himself" (*Kay* quoted by *Kirkpatrick*). In the particular situation in which the psalmist finds himself a large part of the difficulty seems to have been caused by "men who followed after evil designs," who in a spirit of fierce hostility were closing in on this poor man. He knows their character: they are not merely personal enemies; they are men who "are far from [God's] law." The distance that they kept from the divine Word had, no doubt, largely contributed to their being what they were. An obvious contrast is intended. These men may be far from the law of God, but God is near to His humble follower. This is the fact (v. 151) that gives the psalmist great comfort. This God who is so near has at the same time made known His will in His commandments which are absolutely reliable and a safe norm to steer a safe course by.

Closing on that note in a spirit of strong assurance, the psalmist says that what he knows about the value of the Lord's testimonies is a truth that has long been his conviction, that God's words are "founded forever." They are the immutable factors in the changing situations of life.

NOTES

147. The Hebrew idiom is almost impossible of translation in this and the next verse, where the chief verb is the equivalent of an adverb, and the complementary verb serves as the chief verb (see *GK* 120). Bible readers have had no end of difficulty with: "I prevented the dawning of the morning" (*AV*), and: "Mine eyes prevented the night watches." This was due in part to the Hebrew idiom as noted, and equally to the Latin usage that is inherent in "prevent," meaning "go before" or anticipate." Again we follow *Luther's* lead in translating these two statements: "In the earliest dawn did I cry for help," and: "I wake up early." For that is what is meant.

t) In the midst of wicked enemies the psalmist looks to God to "revive" him (vv. 153–160)

Resh

153. Behold my affliction and deliver me,
For I do not forget Thy law.
154. Plead my case and deliver me;
Revive me according to Thy promise.
155. Salvation is far from the wicked,
For they do not seek Thy statutes.
156. Many are Thy mercies, O Lord;
Revive me according to Thy judgments.
157. My persecutors and my enemies are many;
Yet I do not turn aside from Thy testimonies.
158. When I saw faithless men I loathed them
Because they do not keep Thy Word.
159. Consider, O Lord, how I love Thy precepts;
Revive me according to Thy steadfast love.
160. Thy Word is nothing but truth;
And every one of Thy righteous judgments endures forever.

The basic thought of the section is this: In the midst of wicked enemies the psalmist looks to God to "revive" him. This petition concerning reviving occurs three times. We should again draw attention to the fact that this verb, frequently used in this psalm, does not involve the idea of "spiritual quickening" but rather that the many burdensome things that weigh a man down may be taken away, and thus life becomes free and joyous again.

153. The first verse scarcely charges God with being indifferent. It voices rather the thought that, if the writer's needs are fully considered, God cannot but be moved to action. The writer knows that God is doubly eager to help the man that does not forget the law. If we consider the next verse, the affliction involved, appears to consist in sharp antagonism on the part of hostile men. God is asked to take the part of him that prays as a lawyer pleads the case of a man. This is regarded as being so effective that the result will be a reviving of the sort that God has promised to those that turn to Him. A contrast seems to occur to the psalmist at this point: The wicked (v. 155) dare not thus look for deliverance: Salvation is far from them, for they do not seek, i.e., study, God's statutes.

156. Again reflecting on the persecutors that are being encountered, the psalmist dwells on the great number of the mercies of God. According to the original, it is as appropriate to translate: "many" are Thy mercies, as it is to render: "great" is Thy mercy. In any case, the mercies are exceedingly rich. To appeal to such a Lord makes good

sense. The contrast suggested by the word "many" calls to mind that the persecutors and enemies are also many. Though it is always a temptation to a man who finds himself associated with a minority to change his allegiance, the writer insists that such a situation is not going to influence him to turn aside from God's testimonies. The value of the latter has been too fully tested to allow for basely abandoning them.

158. This verse seems to present what is a logical progression of thought from this point onward: Not only was he not envious of these evil men or desirous of changing his course one iota, but also, seeing them for what they were, he "loathed" them, viewed them with strong repulsion. They were guilty of that archtreachery of not keeping the divine Word, and that is the allegiance above all allegiances because a man's attitude to his God and his attitude toward the Word of his God have a certain identity.

159. A petition such as is offered in this verse could be presented in a spirit of the baldest work-righteousness. What we know of the psalmist shows us that such a spirit is out of the question in his case. Living his life as he does before the very eyes of God, it is but natural to suggest that God is noting how faithfully he loves His precepts. That may be a wholesome motivation for the renewed petition to be revived.

160. Again, as usual, the section closes with a sort of summary statement, which could be translated: "The sum of Thy Word is truth." However, that is still a mode of speech that is a bit foreign to our way of thinking; and so we have ventured to move over entirely into the idiom of our language by following *Luther:* "Thy Word is nothing but truth," *Dein Wort ist nichts denn Wahrheit.* The second member continues in the same vein: "And very one of Thy righteous judgments endures forever!" The Word is one of the few things that continue unshaken and immovable through the ages. Happy the man whose life is built on that foundation!

NOTES

155. In the Hebrew "far" has the masculine form though it agrees with "salvation," a feminine noun. On this lack of congruity see (*GK* 145r): the masculine predominates until the gender has been more nearly determined.

158. The meaning of the verse becomes clear when the first co-ordinate clause is made subordinate, a change that is often called for in Hebrew syntax.

u) **The psalmist has both loved and kept God's law (vv. 161–168)**
Shin

161. *Princes have persecuted me without cause;*
    But my heart stands in awe of Thy Word.

162. *I rejoice over Thy Word
As one that finds great spoil.*
163. *I have hated and loathed lies;
Thy law have I loved.*
164. *Seven times a day have I praised Thee
Because of Thy righteous judgments.*
165. *Great peace have they who love Thy law;
And they shall not stumble.*
166. *I have hoped for Thy deliverance, O Lord,
And have done Thy commandments.*
167. *My soul has kept Thy testimonies;
And I love them exceedingly.*
168. *I have kept Thy precepts and Thy testimonies,
For all my ways are before Thee.*

The author has both loved and kept God's law. That is the burden of this section. It has been remarked that with the exception of the first verse (v. 161), everything is bright and sunny.

161. The familiar note of persecution which the writer endured at the hands of some of his contemporaries is again struck. Who these princes are can scarcely be determined precisely. Were they ungodly men of Israel or heathen officials? What moved them to persecute seems to have been this man's fidelity to his God and His Word. Even though pressure was brought to bear upon him to deny that Word, the psalmist could not do so, for basically he stands in great awe of it and its rich values.

162. This thought is then expressed in a form that is frequently found in this psalm: "I rejoice over Thy Word." Awe-struck indeed; but it is a delightful state to be thus. In fact, here again the thought finds expression that the Word is the superlative treasure. It may well be possible that we here have a looser use of the word "find." It would seem to mean to come legitimately upon great spoil as would that man who has won his share of booty in a hard-fought conflict.

163. Such positive attitudes often involve strong antipathies. One thing that he is strongly opposed to is "lies," everything that savors of untruth; for that is the essence of all ungodliness. But that hatred is kept wholesome by a strong love for the Lord's law.

164. If the law of the Lord is so great a treasure that calls forth such strong affection, it is surely most fitting that God should be praised abundantly for it. This "abundantly" is expressed as being "seven times a day." Precise arithmetic is out of the question in such an ideal statement. Seven merely signifies a comparatively large number as Ps. 12:7 would also seem to indicate. The perfect tense of the verbs used here

and repeatedly throughout the rest of the section expresses the habitual. This frequent praising of the Word is what the writer regularly does, for the helpful ordinances of the Lord are "righteous," which we might define as meaning: Everything about them is right.

165. From praise the writer's thoughts turn to two great blessings which fall to the lot of those men who love God's law. The first of these is "great peace," a broad term which connotes that rich measure of well-being when nothing essential is lacking. One form in which that peace finds expression in a man's life is that such men "shall not stumble," which has been defined that they shall "walk firmly and safely in the clear path of duty." "Nothing shall offend them" (*KJ*) is not quite strong enough.

166. But it is quite obvious that all such glorious prospects as great peace are only partially attained in this present life. Those things that still burden and afflict us are committed into the hands of our gracious Lord, for whose help in all of them we continually do pray, using, perhaps, the words of Jacob of old: "I have longed for Thy deliverance, O Lord!" Gen. 49:18. In the meantime the sincerity of the longing of a godly man will always be marked by faithfully observing the Lord's commandments. When the psalmist says: "I have done Thy commandments," that is again not Pharisaical pride or self-righteousness. In fact, throughout this section all statements to the effect that certain things have been done and achieved are modestly laid before the Lord as tokens of sincerity of purpose and not by way of self-aggrandizement.

167. The last note that was struck—doing God's will—is now followed through to the end of the section. When the keeping of the testimonies is ascribed to the "soul," that is just a Hebrew way of saying more effectively that a man himself has kept them, "soul" often being the equivalent of the personal pronoun. But that such observance of the Lord's will is not mere formality in the case of this man is asserted by the statement, "And I love them exceedingly."

168. It is the second half of this verse that especially justifies our remarks to the effect that statements about what the writer has done and performed are not made in a spirit of pride or boastfulness. For the author lays the issues before God as the judge: "For all my ways are before Thee." He invites divine inspection and expects that God will readily discern the sincerity of purpose that has marked all his conduct.

NOTES

162. In the light of what was said above it will be obvious that there is no serious objection to the use of the verb "finds" in connection with "spoil." It will also appear that a change of text from "finds" to "brings forth"—a very slight change in the Hebrew text—is unnecessary.

167. In the Hebrew the verb "I love" is an imperfect form written with one *aleph*.

v) Prayers for insight (vv. 169–176)
Taw

169. Let my cry come before Thee, O Lord;
Give me insight according to Thy Word.
170. Let my plea come before Thee;
Deliver me according to Thy Word.
171. Let my lips pour forth praise,
For Thou wilt teach me Thy statutes.
172. May my tongue sing of Thy Word,
For all Thy commandments are right.
173. Let Thy hand be ready for my help,
For I have chosen Thy precepts.
174. I have longed for Thy deliverance, O Lord;
And Thy law is my delight.
175. Revive me that I may praise Thee;
And let Thy ordinances help me.
176. I have gone astray like a lost sheep;
Seek Thy servant, for I do not forget Thy commandments.

The psalm closes with what may be called a cluster of pleas for insight and help and for "the grace of thankfulness" for the divine Word. Almost every verse is a petition. Since this illustrates the fact that the writer is utterly dependent upon God's help, this fact must be added to the issue involved in the preceding section, which some interpreters regard as evidence of spiritual pride. Such a spirit of utter humility that seeks all it needs from God is the very antithesis of pride.

169. It is surprising how many times the prayer for insight has appeared in this psalm. Then as now the magnitude of the thoughts of God drove men to prayer for a better grasp of the depths of divine revelation.

170. Then as now men were dependent upon God's help in their manifold afflictions, and when they phrase their petition, "Let my plea come before Thee," the sovereignty of the Lord in even such matters is clearly set forth. God is under no obligation to hear us; His answer to our petitions must be thought of as being entirely within His good pleasure. Men do, indeed, have His word for it that He delights to help. But it still behooves us to approach Him in the spirit: "Let my plea come before Thee."

171. There is wisdom in the prayer which asks to be enabled to praise God. The object of praise is in this instance God's statutes, which the writer knows God will teach him, and for the increase in the knowl-

edge of which we can never be sufficiently grateful. Being on the subject, the author continues by praying that he may be permitted to use his tongue in singing of that blessed Word of God. Of the many things that he could have mentioned as praiseworthy in connection with the Word he in this instance singles out the fact that the Lord's commandments are "right."

173. The many pleas for help that have been noted in the psalm are again brought to our attention. Seldom is the exact nature of the trouble that calls forth these pleas made clear. This, as is often the case in the psalter, is, no doubt, due to the fact that the general use of the psalms by men in all manner of situations is thought of and made possible by a more general statement of the case. In this verse and the next the motive for help pleaded by the poet is that God's precepts and law have been chosen as the one great treasure and have been the object of sincerest delight. The psalmist knows well that such an attitude is well-pleasing in the Lord's sight. In this last verse, as in v. 166, Jacob's prayer seems again to have been in the writer's mind (cf., Gen. 49:18).

175. We think that "revive me" is more to the point in translating the Hebrew verb involved than, "let me live" (*RSV*) or, "let my soul live" (*KJ*). For the point at issue is that a man may be given fresh strength to carry on rather than that he may be permitted to go on living in a situation where he is in danger of death. For the purpose of the reviving is that he may the better praise God. In that connection a new thought appears: "Let Thy ordinances help me." This involves some conception of the means of grace; God's Word is the channel through which God's aid flows to man.

176. An equally new and original thought is the last verse, to which some interpreters have taken exception. When the writer asserts that he has gone astray like a lost sheep he can scarcely be using this expression in the familiar New Testament sense of spiritually departing from the Lord and the path of righteousness. If the latter were the case, all the professions of loyalty met with in the psalm would be a hollow mockery. These words must, therefore, refer to the outward situation in which the man finds himself, to his need of help and assistance. He indicates nothing more than that his present situation is perilous like that of a sheep that has gotten beyond the shepherd's care. In this sense the continuation of the prayer must be understood, "Seek Thy servant." The concluding profession of loyalty establishes our interpretation. For he that can claim: "I do not forget Thy commandments," has been true to his God and may well expect that God will not fail to hear him.

Psalm 120

A PRAYER FOR HELP AGAINST SLANDER

THIS PSALM and those that follow up to Ps. 134 have a heading which in the more familiar version is, "A Song of Ascents." We feel it would be far more appropriate to render this heading: A Pilgrimage Song. We must go into this subject a bit more at length.

The Hebrew word involved allows for four major interpretations, each of which has found adherents. Since this word could be translated "steps," it is by some interpreters referred to the internal structure of the psalms in question. It cannot be denied that a number of them show this steplike progression in a rather prominent form. Ps. 121:1b has the noun "help" and v. 2a takes up the word "help." Thus also in the same psalm in vv. 3, 4 and again in vv. 7, 8. Then also Ps. 126: 2, 3 and 128:4, 5, etc. But it is just as obvious that some of the psalms, like Ps. 120, show nothing of this type of progression. Consequently what is regarded as the chief requirement of this interpretation is a bit more conspicuous by its absence than by its presence. This purely literary device would scarcely have given rise to the use of this particular title.

The second interpretation of the term uses as a starting point the fact that the word involved means "steps." The actual steps of the sanctuary, those that lead up to the Court of the Men, are thought of. There were fifteen of these. A remark in the Talmud (*Middoth* ii. 5, *Succa* 51b, according to *Delitzsch*) to the effect that the fifteen "songs of ascents" correspond in number to these fifteen Temple steps does not, however, assert that these songs were sung on these steps as *Delitzsch* and others have pointed out. *Luther,* knowing this Jewish tradition, was by it led to translate this title of these psalms in this manner: *ein Lied im hoehern Chor* which could be translated, "a song from the choir loft."

The third interpretation uses as its point of departure the fact that the singular of the noun used in these titles means "ascent" in the sense of the going up of the children of Israel from captivity in Babylon to the Holy Land. That meaning appears in Ezra 7:9. This would, however, not serve to explain why the plural should be used here though the interpretation involved would suggest that these fifteen psalms were used by the Jews during the course of their long marches back from the land of Babylon. For the reason just indicated this interpretation should be rejected.

That brings us to the fourth interpretation: the title used means "a pilgrim song." A rather common usage of the verb root involved is that wherever the verb is used it means "to go up" to Jerusalem or to the holy place (cf., I Sam. 1:3). Such going up was characteristic of the three major festivals in Israel. In some instances a phrase of the pilgrimage experience is clearly reflected, as in Ps. 122:2; 125:2; in a number of these psalms nothing of the sort is in evidence. There is the possibility that these fifteen paslms once constituted a little book of devotions used by pilgrims which was helpful, whether it bore directly upon some aspects of pilgrim experience or not. Three of the psalms in this section are ascribed to David; one to Solomon.

It has been pointed out that these psalms do not reflect that vigor of faith that is met with in the book of psalms elsewhere. They rise to very moderate levels of faith and courage. They are marked by a kind of plaintive note, by a mild sadness. If this is true, they may be assigned to the postexilic period when there was faith but not in any sense a faith of the bold and heroic type. In point of style these psalms are characterized by a certain brevity as well as by a somewhat graphic mode of expression.

One may be tempted to follow the lead of *Hengstenberg* in this connection who strongly advocates the approach which would regard all of the psalms of this little booklet as having no individual character of their own, never referring to an individual, but always speaking with the collective "I," but the evidence is not quite strong enough to allow for such a conclusion.

Coming to Ps. 120 in particular, we must admit that it does not make the impression of having been written for use of pilgrims on their journey to the holy city. Assuming that a postexilic situation is reflected, and remembering that conditions were somewhat depressing, and that the Israelites were frequently plagued by enemies who resorted to slander to make difficulties for the Israelites, we can well understand how an individual has an experience like the one described here and may express his pain at being treated thus.

It is not easy to classify this psalm as belonging to one category in particular. Is it a lament? Shall we designate it as voicing a petition? It has elements of both. It also recounts a previous spiritual experience. It must be confessed that it has points of contact with Ps. 64, 140, 142.

a) Turning to God when distressed by slander (vv. 1, 2)
b) Suggesting the just punishment of the slanderers (vv. 3, 4)

c) A mild lament over an unhappy lot (vv. 5-7)
   A Pilgrim Song
   1. *To the Lord did I call in my distress;*
      And He answered me.
   2. *O Lord, deliver me from lying lips,*
      From a deceitful tongue.
   3. *What shall He give you,*
      And what shall He add more, O deceitful tongue?
   4. *Sharp arrows of a warrior*
      And glowing coals of the broom shrub.
   5. *Woe is me that I sojourn in Meshech,*
      That I dwell among the tents of Kedar!
   6. *Too long have I been dwelling*
      With those who hate peace.
   7. *I am a very peaceful man;*
      But when I speak, they are all for war.

1. That it is slander that has made the heart of the writer of this psalm heavy appears from the fact that someone has been using a "deceitful tongue" against him, so much so that the guilty person is addressed "deceitful tongue." In the face of such adversity the psalmist turns to God. His first act is to recall what has so often happened in the past when he was in distress. He always called to the Lord, and the Lord always answered him. Construed thus, the first verse records the experience of a lifetime. This is put into the picture as furnishing substantial ground to stand on.

2. By contrast this verse takes up the present situation: having been heard in the past, the writer makes bold to hope that he will not be ignored in the present extremity. He, therefore, beseeches the Lord to deliver him from "lying lips." Only when the slanderous charges referred to are entirely untrue dare such a designation be used. Lies have besmirched his fair name. To him personally the slanderer apparently used smooth blandishments, but in the hearing of others he resorted to distortion of the truth. For this reason the "deceitful" tongue is referred to.

Only he who has known how utterly painful and harmful such attacks made by the tongue may be will recognize that the burden of this prayer does not center about a trivial issue.

3. The second section of this psalm represents the psalmist as suggesting the just punishment of the slanderers, and we notice that in the background of this approach is the strong conviction that the wrong done to the writer is so great that it clamors for divine intervention in the form of punishment. In effect he says: Do you know what happens

to persons who engage in so malicious a practice as you are engaging in? Or another way of stating it is: God helps those who are thus wickedly attacked. This interpretation goes on the assumption that the "He" introduced without identification in v. 3 must refer to God. We believe it does so on the warrant of many instances in religious texts where the one not further described is assumed to be none other than God. That approach applies here because the wrong done is enough to call for divine intervention.

The unusual form of the statement used is based on a form of oath which appears several times in the Old Testament (I Sam. 3:17; I Kings 2:23; Ruth 1:17). It is the expression: "May God do so to me and more also." Because of its very vagueness it becomes all the more ominous. This implies that some great evil will befall the speaker and even a greater one, neither being precisely identified.

4. This verse is the answer to the question just posed. There is a weighty brevity about this answer. Two classes of objects are mentioned —arrows and coals—in an elliptical statement. The imagination must be employed to determine what is to be done with these objects. The deadly arrows of a warrior are apparently thought of as finding their target in the body of the slanderer; and the hot coals are thought of either as falling upon him and painfully burning him, or as being thrown into his tent and setting the tent or home and all that it contains on fire. Deadly and painful punishment is in other words represented by the arrows and the coals. It is claimed to this day that the Arabs of the Near East regard coals of the broom shrub as burning the hottest of all charcoals. Thus the case of the slanderer is dramatically disposed of.

5. The last three verses do, indeed, contain a mild lament of the writer over his unhappy lot. As the initial statement of faith does not rise to spectacular levels, so this lament is marked by a somewhat subdued note. The first statement likens the psalmist to one who has the misfortune to be obliged to dwell among barbarous people with whom he has nothing in common. One name for these is "Meschech." Most writers locate this tribe southeast of the Black Sea; therefore far removed from Israel, little known, and because of its remoteness, associated with the idea of the barbaric. See the references in Gen. 10:2; Ezek. 32:26, 27; 38:3; 39:1. "Kedar," on the other hand, is located in the desert of Syria south of Damascus. It is referred to in Gen. 25:13; Jer. 2:10; 49:28–30. A similar thought is associated with these tribesmen as was associated with Meschech. Since the two countries are so far removed from one another, the writer can scarcely be claiming that he is actually living in both. Thus these two terms become terms that figuratively describe the slanderers previously referred to as being utterly uncivilized and cruel people, men that it is not pleasant to live with.

6. The lament voiced in the preceding verse is continued with particular reference to the fact that the unpleasant associations with the unlovely people has gone on altogether too long. The writer can endure little more; he is at the end of his patience.

7. The concluding note is also one of mild complaint. He is scarcely speaking boastfully when he says that he is "a very peaceful man." He merely claims not to be the one who inaugurated the present difficulties. We trust our rendering of the statement has caught its essence. In the original the writer says: "I am peace," which means: all peace. Peaceful though he is, the moment he speaks the opposition is all "for war." The Hebrew again uses the same construction: "They are war." The words, "But when I speak," seem to be more properly referred to those instances when he brings up the subject of their unreasonable hostility. All that results is bitter strife and contention. They would scarcely be thought of as flaring up at every harmless remark. Thus as some interpreters have pointed out, with the harsh antithesis of "peace—war" the psalm closes in a clashing discord.

NOTES

1. Most writers of the present time translate the verbs involved as though they were present tenses. That is sometimes done when an attempt is made to capture the force of a perfect which is the equivalent of a gnomic aorist as *Koenig* also translates at this point: *Ich habe schon immer . . . gerufen*. But simpler and more appropriate is the translation with perfects which renders them as covering events that occurred in the past, as we have done.

Psalm 121

THE LORD, THE GUARDIAN

IT IS QUITE FUTILE to try to determine the circumstances under which this psalm was written. Many of the psalms that appear in this section of the Psalter are postexilic. That fact shows how much warrant there is for claiming that it must be assigned to this period. Whether it was composed for pilgrimage purposes remains an open question. It could have been written for use at the time when the hills of the Holy City first came into view. It might have been designed for use in the last camp for the night, before retiring for the night, when the distant hills

Psalm 121

of Jerusalem had already been discerned from afar. In any case, when the time and the circumstances of composition are uncertain, this could often be providential, allowing for the broadest possible use of the psalm under all manner of circumstances.

So much is clear, it is written across the face of the psalm—it is a psalm of trust. It counsels men to trust in the Lord in all situations of life. It does not rise to any supreme heights of faith. Like most of the psalms in this part of the collection, it breathes a somewhat subdued faith, but faith without a question. It exhorts indirectly to trust in the Lord in all conceivable situations of life. Its tone is very plain and practical. Many hearts have been strengthened for the pilgrimage of life by this song.

Commentators have been intrigued by the possibility that this psalm may originally have been designed to be rendered as a kind of dialogue (so also *Gunkel,* p. 409, *Einleitung in die Psalmen*), for questions are asked, and answers are given. But more likely than not the questions are rhetorical in nature, raised for the purpose of making the answer appear more vivid. Though it is rather common procedure to venture into the area of reconstructing the text in order to secure a dialogue arrangement, such efforts are highly questionable. We cannot but feel that the wish is largely father to the thought, and therefore needless and unwarrantd changes are made throughout. If the text as it is written were beyond the range of reasonable interpretation, conjectures as to the possible original form might be considered reasonable. But the difficulties are far from insuperable. The earliest versions have practically the same form of text as we now have, at least in the case of this psalm.

If we, then, accept the thesis that the questions are rhetorical we must eliminate such further attempts as to select one person as the interrogator and another as the one who answers. Thereby we also eliminate the attempt to make the psalm one that was intended for specifically antiphonal use. It is not some layman who asks, and some priest who answers. It is not a member of the caravan who poses questions, and the leader of the group who furnishes the answer.

In the light of what was said above the reason for our choice of a title for the psalm is partly indicated. But there is more that points in this direction. It so happens that the Hebrew root, which we have translated "guards" and the corresponding noun "guardian," appears six times in the psalm and so stamps that thought more prominently upon the whole.

The title given in the text, which may also be translated "a pilgrimage song," differs slightly from the form which this title usually has in these fifteen psalms in that it reads: "a psalm for pilgrimages." This difference is, however, too unimportant to allow for any further conclusions.

a) My help comes from the Lord (vv. 1, 2)

1. *I lift up my eyes to the mountains;*
   Whence does my help come?
2. *My help comes from the Lord,*
   Who made heaven and earth.

1. When a native Israelite said that he looked for help to the mountains, that expression had a very specific meaning. It is true enough that significant events in the life of the people or its forefathers took place on mountains (cf., Gen. 22:2ff.; Exod. 3:2; 19:3ff.; II Sam. 24:16ff.; I Kings 19:8). But these events were not always "help," and thus from that point of view would scarcely give warrant for the conclusion: "My help comes from the Lord."

Somewhat more to the point is the fact that it was commonly known in the later days of Israel's history that the place that had been appointed by Yahweh to be the central sanctuary of the nation was on the Temple hill at Jerusalem. There God had promised to dwell among His people. But that one hill in the complex of what made up the city of Jerusalem was one of a group of several others. Thus the "hills" became synonymous with the holy city, cf., I Kings 8:33, 35, 42, 44, 48. If anyone, therefore, lived in the tradition of his people, the normal, divinely appointed place of prayer, which would occur to all as being the place to which they should turn, was the Temple that stood on these hills. By a simple metonomy, rooted in the best insights of the nation, "hills" or "mountains" and the true sanctuary were one and the same thing.

By such a statement a godly writer was reminding himself and others that such a procedure had divine sanction, and the prayers made toward this holy place had the promise of being heard. It is in that spirit that the question is put: "Whence does my help come?" a question, which like many asked among us, is merely to highlight the answer. He who puts the question is not perplexed; he is not in search of information. For he at once answers in a way that is full of assurance.

2. According to the interpretation that we are following it is not even necessary to assume that a kind of dialogue with one's self in being offered here. Note also how concise and sure the answer is. This man has never been at a loss as to where help was to be sought, at least not in this psalm. When he says: "My help comes from the Lord," that particular name has the connotation of the faithful covenant-God of Israel who has always been true to His promises. The initial basic statement is at once re-enforced by a clause: "Who made

heaven and earth." This statement recalls the omnipotent power of the one that is being appealed to. Heaven and earth constitute the universe. If the Lord made the all, then the conclusion is very correct that all the parts of the whole are fully under His control and to help is an easy matter for Him. It seems almost as though this last clause had become the equivalent of a new name or title for the Lord, for it appears also in Ps. 115:15; 124:8; 134:3; 146:6.

b) **The theme unfolded at length for all possible eventualities (vv. 3–8)**

3. *Would He let your foot slip?*
   Would He that guards you slumber?
4. *Lo, He that guards Israel*
   Will neither slumber nor sleep.
5. *The Lord Himself is your guardian;*
   The Lord is your protection at your right hand.
6. *By day the sun shall not smite you,*
   Nor the moon by night.
7. *The Lord will guard you from all that is bad;*
   He will guard your life.
8. *The Lord will guard your going out and your coming in*
   Henceforth and forever.

3. After the theme to be developed has been briefly stated, the psalmist traces the rich possibilities involved in the theme through a variety of situations. He begins with two possibilities that may have been taken from the experiences of those who were on a pilgrimage to the festivals in the holy city. Roads were no more than trails. Slipping or stumbling could be dangerous with rocks and stones strewn in the path. Would God be guilty, not for the present to speak of great and weighty things, of allowing such slipping to occur? To ask the question is to answer it. He watches over every step that His faithful children take. Or is it thinkable that He could at any time, even for a moment, be off guard? It is possible that, as *Schmidt* suggests, there is an implied contrast here, namely, that of the fertility gods of Canaan, who, when vegetation died off, were thought of as having gone off duty or as being asleep for a period.

4. This verse suggests the utter impossibility of such an abdication on the Lord's part. The "lo" seems to make the obvious nature of the remark that is to follow prominent. Yahweh has the great task of being the guardian of all Israel. How could He fail in the comparatively simple task of guarding the individual member of the nation? Not momentary slumber, least of all actual sleep, dare be thought of in reference to Him.

5. From that angle of the thought a transition is made to the very nature of Him that is involved. The subject Yahweh stands prominently in the forefront, a fact which the *Prayer Book* version alone has ventured to capture by translating as we have: "The Lord Himself." Sentry duty is ordinarily assigned to the ordinary soldier. Here it is the Lord who has assumed this responsibility. Since in the Orient in particular the right hand indicates the position of honor, the Guardian who stands near to His true worshiper can be thought of as having no other position than that at one's "right hand." Whereas practically all the familiar versions render the word involved "shade," it is not immediately apparent to the average reader that that term means "protection." Where the sun shines with tropical heat a bit of shade is often a lifesaver; and thus the word "shade" quite frequently comes to mean protection.

6. A number of further reassurances are given throughout the rest of the psalm. First, all time is covered ("day" and "night"). Since the bright light of the sun appears throughout the day as well as that of the moon throughout the night, these two subjects represent all influences that might harm a man. How dangerous a sunstroke can be, especially in a hot climate, everyone knows. God wards off dangers of even that sort that may come on us unawares (see II Kings 4:19). When the statement goes on to say that a similar protection is to be assigned to Him in regard to possible harmful reaction from the moon, that does not authenticate the supposition that the moon does exert a pernicious influence and can cause what could be called a moonstroke. The expression does allow for the fact that such a notion was spread abroad in Israel. All that the psalm asserts is that such ill-defined dangers are also under the control of the Almighty.

7. From that vantage point the psalm broadens the list of dangers that are averted: He "guards from all that is bad." We suggest the word "bad" for the traditional "evil" because we feel that it captures more of the breadth of the original. "Evil" lies largely in the field of things moral. "Bad" takes in the whole realm of the physical as well. From this thought the author steps up to that which is always at stake when protection is needed—our very "life." "Soul" again leads Bible readers to think almost exclusively of spiritual values. But in the Hebrew "soul" often means life, a fact which *Luther* stressed at this point.

8. Two possible factors may yet be brought into the picture, and then the range of God's protecting care will have been fully spelled out. One of these is the whole sphere of man's activity. In the morning a man went out of the chamber in which he had slept and took his daily tasks in hand; in the evening he entered again into that same chamber. Therefore the expression "going out" and "coming in" was intended to

cover the totality of a man's activities together with all that lay between the two terminal points mentioned. Note the use of this same expression in Num. 27:17; Deut. 28:6; 31:2. The second of these factors is the whole category of time which is amply covered by "henceforth and forever." Generally speaking, there is nothing to which the providential care of God does not extend. One has the feeling that every sphere of influence to which this care extends has been touched. Such treatment of the subject carries with it sturdy reassurance.

NOTES

1. We prefer rendering the initial verb as a present tense with *Luther* and against *KJ,* which makes it a future. The psalm seems to demand an expression of what the present attitude of the speaker is, not what it would be in possible future cases. Though *RSV* translates "hills" whereas we have rendered "mountains," the point at issue is that the word can mean either. "Mountains" seems to conform better to the dignity of the city of Jerusalem that was located on these mountains. In the Hebrew "whence" always appears as an interrogative as any dictionary will show.

3. The needs of the case seem to be met best by taking the suggestion that *Koenig* offers (*KS* 353d) that *'al* with the imperfect introduces that suggest a negative answer. This is more to the point than to render the two members of the verse as expressing a wish: "May He not." Cf. *KS,* 353d.

Psalm 122

JERUSALEM—THE GREAT CAPITAL CITY

THE ESTABLISHMENT of authorship has much bearing on the interpretation of this psalm. The Hebrew text ascribes the psalm to David. The problem is complicated by the fact that most manuscripts of the *Septuagint* do not; nor does the *Vulgate.* But these omissions alone are not sufficient to discredit the claim of the Hebrew text. Yet commentators have, for the most part, discarded the possibility of authorship by David. We on our part feel that there is every reason to maintain it, not only because the Hebrew headings are generally reliable but also chiefly because of internal evidence.

The main argument that is usually advanced against the possibility of Davidic authorship is v. 9 with its reference to the "house of the Lord." The criticism is offered: The Temple had not as yet been built in David's day. However, the fact that is overlooked is that the tent sanctuary, the old Tabernacle, is repeatedly called the house of the Lord (cf., I Sam. 1:7, 24; II Sam. 12:20; Judg. 19:18) long before the Temple was built.

The objection is also offered that it would have been unnatural to have v. 4 refer to the tribes' having gone up to the Lord's house in David's day inasmuch as the ark of the covenant had been lost ever since its capture by the Philistines in Eli's day. However, it must be recalled that David restored the ark to its place of central importance almost as soon as he had established Jerusalem as his capital city. If the psalm had been written some twenty years later, the coming of the tribes to the sanctuary could easily be referred to as a traditional procedure. In the same manner after such a lapse of time a reference to law courts established and conducted by David and the princes of his family would be very much in order.

In other words, under this feasible approach David would be cataloguing briefly the excellencies of this comparatively new capital city of Jerusalem and instructing his people as to the blessings that grew out of having such a representative city as the center of the national and spiritual interests of the people of God. The psalm has a wholesome propaganda for the city, the value of which was not immediately apparent to every Israelite.

Is the psalm somewhat autobiographical in character? Is David, regarding himself, perhaps, as a typical Israelite, telling of his own experience in reference to this fine city? That is less likely to be the case. For the very first statement about the joy with which the speaker welcomed the suggestion about going on pilgrimage to the holy tent could never have been made in David's earlier life, before he became king; for that was the time when such pilgrimages were interrupted because of the removal of the ark from the scene.

In the second place, after the ark achieved the place of prominence that it deserved, David resided in the holy city, and v. 1 would again be an impossible statement for him to make. We are, therefore, driven to the conclusion that the psalm pictures a typical Israelite voicing his various sentiments on the subject of what the good city meant to those who were the more faithful of the children of Israel. Any one of that group would find his feelings suggested by the psalm and a few additional points offered for his further instruction. The psalm, therefore, expressed what an Israelite might or should feel in reference to the capital city. It is cast in the more precise form of a meditation upon

Psalm 122

the city and its importance, made at the point when the individual has arrived at the gates of the city and is waiting for the rest of the caravan from his home town and vicinity to gather and order its march.

The other approach which suggests that we have a meditation that is made after the festival stay at the city has been completed and the pilgrim is now on the way home has some measure of plausibility but does not quite so well agree with the simplest translation of v. 2. Besides, the tone of the psalm is too fresh and vivid for afterthoughts; it seems to grow out of a living experience of the present.

Another major difficulty which is created by the assumption of postexilic authorship or even, for that matter, of the time of the later monarchy is that no one could have spoken of the coming up of the various tribes of the nation to Jerusalem. For, as I Kings 12:27f. reminds us, after the division of the kingdom, Jeroboam, took immediate steps to wean the Ten Tribes away from Jerusalem by establishing a rival sanctuary or sanctuaries, Bethel and Dan. It should also be noted that the translation which offers the word "rebuilt" in v. 3 is not offering an actual meaning of the word involved but only a possibility that is allowed for when the circumstances actually prove that the building done was a rebuilding of an old site. *RSV* has wisely rendered the word "built." Cf. also *Hans Schmidt*.

a) **The situation (vv. 1, 2)**
   A pilgrimage song. Of David.
   On the first part of this superscription cf. 121:1.
   1. *I rejoiced over those who said to me:*
      "We are going to the house of the Lord."
   2. *Our feet have been standing within your gates,*
      O Jerusalem!

1. We regard the first verb as a plain historical past tense. The ideal Israelite of whom David here writes is stating what feelings always surged through his heart when his townspeople indicated that they were ready to make one of the usual pilgrimages to the capital city on the occasion of one of the great festivals. He was glad over those who informed him of their intention. He liked that kind of people who loved the house of the Lord sincerely enough to plan to go there three times a year as a true Israelite was in conscience bound to do (cf., Exod. 23:17; 34:23; Deut. 16:16). Something is implied in the statement which the friends of the speaker made. On the basis of their knowledge of him and of their past experience they feel that he will be one of their number and will be glad to go along with them. His participation is so obvious to them that a mere statement of their own purpose suffices as an invitation.

2. At the time, when he recalls how the subject of the pilgrimage to the Lord's city was broached, he himself is to be thought of as already standing at the city gates. His eagerness may have carried him a bit ahead of the rest of the group. Besides, it may have been understood that, if their group should have become disorganized, they would reassemble at the city gate. Thus, while the pilgrim pauses there, he engages in reflection. Such normal reflections as a typical Israelite could or should have made, are now offered. The fact that already at this point the speaker begins to apostrophize Jerusalem indicates that she is the object of his thoughts and reflections. Though she may have been the national capital for only a modest number of years, yet she has attained to such a stature in the minds of those that knew how much the holy city meant to the welfare of the entire nation that the mere privilege of having one's feet stand within her ancient gates was a fact that was worthy of note. The fact that the plural for "gates" is used implies that similar emotions are felt by any number of pilgrims who are in like manner entering any one of the several gates of the city.

b) **A concise summary of certain features of the holy city that constitute her glory (vv. 3–5)**

3. *Jerusalem is the one that is built,*
   A city which is compactly joined together for its own good.
4. *For thither the tribes have gone up, the tribes of the Lord—*
   It is an ordinance for Israel—
   To give thanks to the name of the Lord.
5. *For there tribunals were set for the trying of cases,*
   The tribunals of the house of David.

3. First of all, the imposing appearance that the city with its new and attractive buildings represents is dwelt upon. Building activities have been so intense that in a concise idiom that defies translation this fact is conveyed by a statement which reads literally: "Jerusalem, the built one" (participle). By this time the royal palace (cf., II Sam. 5:11), administrative buildings, sturdy homes of prominent citizens as well as the new and adequate walls of the enlarged city (cf., II Sam. 5:9) were very much in evidence. This gave the city a dignity that no other city in the land had, and one that could well be the pride and joy of the people.

The second half of the verse suggests that the city has profited immensely by all these building operations and now represents a composite whole that has no ugly gaps; it represents houses and structures in solid rows whereever the eye may look. The fact that it was "for its own good" that it was so solidly and compactly constructed is apparent. A

Psalm 122

concise reference to the point at issue is sufficient. The speaker goes on to another of the glories of the city of David.

4. For a number of years such a typical Israelite had witnessed another scene, which had tended to make his heart glad: the coming up of the various tribes and their mingling together at the sanctuary in worship and thus being built into a solid spiritual unity. Prior to this time, when there was no capital city to serve as a rallying point, almost the entire history of the people since Joshua's day had been one of internal strife and dissension: Ephraim against Judah, primarily; north against south; smaller unit against smaller unit. These old tensions were now becoming a thing of the past. To have representatives of all tribes rub shoulders together in the narrow streets, to have them pray and worship together, to make acquaintances with men of tribes other than your own—all these things built up better understanding and wiped out old prejudices.

These pilgrimages were apparently divinely appointed also for this purpose. Their primary purpose was, of course, "to give thanks to the name of the Lord." Worship must always have a large element of thanksgiving in it. Whether this emphasis points directly to the festival of Tabernacles as being the one that was in the writer's mind may well be questioned. Though that festival was eminently designed for a national thanksgiving for the fruits of the land, every festival must have incorporated more or less of the element of thanksgiving.

The thought is conveniently inserted that such coming on pilgrimage was "an ordinance for Israel." Though this part of the verse is merely a noun with a modifier, we have ventured to make a complete statement of it for clarity's sake. Under v. 1 we have indicated where the relevant passages are to be found that record this ordinance.

5. In addition to the extensive building operations and the pilgrimages of the various tribes there is another factor that may well make a patriotic Israelite proud of the city which the Lord has made to prosper so abundantly, and that is the efficient functioning of the law courts which David had established in his capital city. II Sam. 15:1–6, which records the defamatory remarks that Absalom made about the administration of justice under David cannot well cancel the claim that we have just made. Absalom was obviously distorting the truth. The episode just referred to rather substantiates our claim. Besides, Deut. 17:8, 9 show that sooner or later such steps as David had taken to provide for better courts were in order. Prior to David's time the administration of justice had been more or less haphazard and elementary David had set up effective tribunals. The fact he had set over them men of his own family whom he could trust and of whose fidelity he

knew was not a matter for criticism. Many in Israel may not have appreciated what a fine progressive move was involved. This psalm reminds all such Israelites to consider carefully what an achievement this was. It will be granted that nothing that David says is inappropriate, nor is there a single remark that David could not well have made.

c) A prayer for the welfare of the holy city (vv. 6–9)

6. *Pray for the peace of Jerusalem:*
   "May they prosper who love you!
7. *Peace be within your outworks*
   And prosperity within your citadels!"
8. *For the sake of my brothers and friends*
   I will say: "Peace be within you!"
9. *For the sake of the house of the Lord, our God,*
   I will seek your good.

6. In the spirit of the entire psalm up to this point the poet-king now encourages Israel, not only to admire the city and be proud of it, but also to pray for it. Without such prayer pride might degenerate into vainglory. Men need always to be encouraged to pray for the rest of the people of God. This prayer includes the welfare of the sanctuary as well. Though the latter had not been specifically mentioned, it must be quite obvious that it was in the picture in v. 4 as the place where the tribes had come for thanksgiving. Thus prayer for Jerusalem in this context means the city of God in its broadest sense. In a very practical spirit the psalmist not only exhorts to such prayer but also gives a form of words as the very petitions that could well be used by every man. This suggested prayer very likely extends from v. 6b through v. 7, which verses have for this reason been enclosed in quotation marks.

6b. The reason for stating the case thus is that the words seek to remind all who hear them that more is required than the repetition of a certain form of words or certain formulas. Those who "love" Zion are the ones for whom the prayer is made. That is another way of saying, all true believers in the Old Testament church. Their well-being is prayed for; "prosper" is meant in the broadest sense. May all that is needful be granted to such as love the Lord's holy city.

7. After the inhabitants have been prayed for, the city itself is prayed for. "Peace" is again far more than the absence of war. It involves having all that a well-rounded life needs. If this is to extend from the outermost tip of the fortifications of the city to the citadels or palaces that constitute the innermost strength of it, that, according to a colorful Hebrew idiom, aims to cover all by referring to the two outside limits.

8. The last two verses contain a gentle reminder to the effect that

all such prayer for the people of God dare not move on a selfish level, namely, that a man prays for God's people because he is among them and, in the last analysis, thinks of how such blessing may benefit him personally. It should be unselfish prayer offered wholeheartedly for the sake of "brothers and friends" and should think only of them and their prosperity. Such is the nature of a wholesome prayer for success.

9. A still higher interest should also be present. It must be prayer "for the sake of the house of the Lord." Concern for God's sanctuary should motivate the prayer for the city that houses that sanctuary. Such reminders are very much in place when one considers how subtly selfishness may worm its way into and pollute our seemingly noblest endeavors. Regarding the translation, "I will seek your good," it may be well to be reminded as to how Luther renders these words: *will ich dein Bestes suchen,* (I will seek what is best for you).

NOTES

1. Though we rendered the first part of this verse, "over those who said" because of the use of the participle, we do not question the possibility of rendering it, "when they said to me" (*KJ* and *RSV*). Koenig (*Kommentar* and *KS*) allows for both possibilities. To render it so as to make it a joy over a certain kind of persons seems in our opinion best to catch the distinctive form of the statement.

2. We prefer to render the verb "to be" plus a participle: "Our feet have been standing," expressing continued action in the past. To make it a plain past or a plain present misses the distinctive feature about the form (see *GK* 116r).

3. In the second part of this verse and also in v. 4a we have the short form of the relative (*she*). Cf. *GK* 36 also for the fact that this form does not represent an exclusively late usage. Therefore its presence dare not be used as an argument against authorship by David.

5. It is not inappropriate to render *yashabh* "were set," because intransitive verbs are sometimes used passively. See *KS* 98. The ^le before *beth* is to be regarded as an exponent of the genitive, not the dative. See *KS* 280w.

Psalm 123

LOOKING TO THE LORD

THE SPIRIT of this little, attractive psalm is caught rather well in a sentence written by *Maclaren:* "A sigh and an upward gaze and a sigh!"

Though nothing specific is indicated as to the time and the circumstances of its composition, we are in a position to draw conclusions from the portion of the Psalter in which the psalm appears and from its general tone. Almost all writers would place it in the Persian period, when the exiles of Israel had returned from captivity with high hopes but were soon bitterly disappointed because very few of these hopes were realized. What hurt was that the hopes of the nation were centered on the fact that the Lord would grant to His people a rich measure of success—did they not represent His cause on earth? Instead they were failing in all their efforts at rehabilitation. This elicited from their enemies many a scornful laugh as passages such as Neh. 2:19; 4:1–4, 7ff. amply indicate. Scorn is hard to bear, and Israel was too weak to do anything effective about it. So much for the situation in general.

Whether this psalm is to be thought of as being spoken by a typical group of Israelites anywhere in the land, or spoken particularly as they came on pilgrimage to the Holy City, or whether it is to be thought of as expressing more particularly the feelings of those who had come from more distant lands where they were also exposed to shame and ridicule because of the lot of their native land—seems to matter but little. One group could have given expression to its thoughts by the use of the psalm as well as the other. But it is quite proper to observe, as most commentators do, that this is not the voice of the individual expressing his personal feelings. The writer speaks for the congregation of Israel.

By penetrating more deeply into the spirit of the psalm we notice that it has a very distinctive character. There is nothing powerful, moving, or sublime that finds expression here. A quiet, submissive tone prevails throughout. It is subdued in character. There is no loud complaint. There is no impetuous plea. The outline that we offer makes this still more plain.

Psalm 123

a) An expression of complete submission to God till He be pleased to help (vv. 1, 2)

A pilgrimage song.
1. *To Thee do I raise my eyes,*
   O Thou who dwellest in the heavens!
2. *Lo, as the eyes of servants are turned to the hand of their masters,*
   As the eyes of a maid to the hand of her mistress,
   So our eyes are turned to the Lord our God till He have mercy upon us.

1. This psalm expresses, not words that were spoken so much as a gesture, a quiet hopeful look. All the writer does at first is to raise his eyes to the only One whom he will acknowledge as helper. He feels how greatly exalted this One is. He knows what resources of power and readiness to help are His. It is this latter fact that is reflected in the expression, "O Thou who dwellest in the heavens." He who has such a dwelling place is the Monarch of monarchs. *RSV* also renders this well by translating: "O Thou, who art enthroned in the heavens!" The exalted majesty of God gives ground for confidence.

2. The spirit of this attitude is reflected more accurately in the words that follow in this verse. The writer's looking to God is likened to the looking of servants or slaves and maids to the hand of their respective master or mistress. Since, however, the writer does not say precisely what the hand in question is to do, some confusion of understanding has resulted. One interpreter champions one possibility to the exclusion of all others. Another champions another with equal fervor. But may we not escape all this uncertainty by noting that this seemed to be an age when the helpful power of the hand of God was particularly thought of and frequently referred to. Note the following instances of the use of this expression: Ezra 7:6, 9, 28; 8:18, 22, 31; Neh. 2:8, 18. If the hand of God seemed to enter prominently into the thinking of that day, there can be no doubt that many activities of that hand could be thought of. His hand helps when a man is in need; it punishes when he has done wrong; it gives when man is in need. This amounts to the following: Whatever the need of God's people is, the hand of the Lord will be adequate for the occasion. Of course, that which is particularly expressed is the thought: "until He have mercy upon us." Whatever they need to be delivered from (what it is has not yet been expressed), God's mercy will take care of the situation in due time. Thus this first phase of the psalm ends on the note of patient and hopeful waiting. Submission is the proper attitude for faith.

b) An earnest plea for help from contemptuous treatment (vv. 3, 4)
3. Have mercy upon us, O Lord, have mercy upon us;
For we have been sated overmuch with contempt.
4. Overmuch have we been sated with contempt,
With the scorn of men who are at ease, with the contempt of the proud.

It will be noted that due to the modest tone of the first part of the psalm the psalmist did not even venture to pray for mercy. He merely expressed the hope that mercy would be shown. Now at least so much of feeling is manifested that the author twice over cries out, though we must imagine rather softly, "Have mercy upon us." What presses the cry from his lips are the wounds caused by the contemptuous treatment on the part of the enemies. Scorn and contempt almost always wound. In this case there has been "more than enough of contempt" as *RSV* translates not inaptly; "exceedingly filled with contempt" is the rendering of the *KJ*. The writer dwells on this a bit longer by first repeating the initial statement almost verbatim. He then describes the hateful thing as emanating from men "who are at ease" and "proud." Those who are without distress themselves but cause distress for others are men from whom this painful treatment comes. This makes the experience all the more galling. Besides, it is the attitude of the proud which makes the words spoken twice as cutting.

On this somewhat unattractive note the psalm comes to a close. It is for all that a fine example of restraint in prayer under adverse circumstances and breathes a fine attitude of submissive faith.

Psalm 124

THANKSGIVING FOR NATIONAL DELIVERANCE

THE FIRST IMPRESSION made by the reading of this psalm is that it opens like a kind of gasp that is uttered by one who has just escaped from grave, threatening danger, has just arrived in some safe place and in brief gasps out to those present what has happened. Equally clear and written over the face of the whole psalm is the emphasis on the one outstanding fact to be stressed—The *Lord* wrought the deliverance involved. Another impression is apt to record itself on one's consciousness—The *nation* was involved, not the individual only.

Psalm 124

As one begins to seek for a fitting historical situation into which this psalm might fit one can scarcely escape having the feeling that in this portion of the Psalter the Return from Babylonian Captivity seems to deserve preference. But there again further reflection drives one to the conclusion that this return was not in the nature of a hairbreadth escape. It came as the result of a long, drawn-out process. One might then decide upon the deliverance that came in the days of Nehemiah, when there was certainly plenty of hostility on the part of enemies who were ready to swallow up the nation of Israel but also a deliverance from the immediate danger as soon as the walls enclosed the city. Some interpreters think of the mighty work that God did in driving back the Assyrians in 701 B.C., (see Is. 36 and 37). Others feel that the totality of God's mighty works for Israel could be in the writer's mind although this would scarcely account for the freshness of the opening statements.

What about David's time? Is he not mentioned in the heading? There were without a doubt situations in David's life when escape from danger on the part of the nation was recent and striking, like the Syro-Ammonite campaign (II Sam. 10). But it must be admitted that there are Aramaisms in the language of the psalm (see Notes below), though not as many as some commentators would have us believe. Though it could well be claimed that some reminiscences of the style of David occur in the psalm (cf., vv. 6, 2i; Ps. 28:6; 31:22), yet the fact that the heading, which inserts the name of David, is wanting in three of the chief manuscripts of the *Septuagint* as well as in the *Vulgate,* shows that Davidic authorship is textually none too well supported. We could at least concede that this might be an open question.

To suggest some type of antiphonal arrangement of the subject matter of the psalm because of the clause, "Let Israel now say," is precarious. Nothing falls clearly into place. This does not, however, deny the possibility of liturgical use.

Is it a pilgrim psalm as the heading suggests? This part of the heading seems to be found in all manuscripts. It must be admitted that nothing that is distinctly of use on pilgrimages is involved. It may, however, be quite likely that the psalm may have been used on pilgrimages to help pilgrims recall the many instances in days of old when God mightily helped His people Israel. It may have come into use in the days of Nehemiah after the grave threat of the hostility of the neighbors had been removed. That may have been an event that was deemed worthy of commemoration.

A brief remark should yet be made regarding the abundance of illustrative figures that are used in the psalm, figures which are of so widely divergent a sort that they do not readily blend into one harmonious whole. But, as has often been remarked, the Hebrew mind was less impressed by the need of total logic than it was by the desirability of colorful and vivid impressions. The latter are surely not lacking in the description offered.

A pilgrimage song. (Of David).
1. *If it had not been the Lord who was on our side—*
   Let Israel now say—
2. *If it had not been the Lord who was on our side*
   When men rose up against us;
3. *Then they would have swallowed us up alive*
   When their anger burned against us;
4. *Then the waters would have swept us away;*
   A torrent would have gone over us.
5. *Then over us would have gone*
   The seething waters.

1. These verses describe the situation out of which the psalm grew. Their substance is in brief, this: But for the Lord's intervention there would have been utter destruction of the nation.

Amplifying what was noted above, we cannot help but feel that the first two verses represent a sort of gasp on the part of a refugee who has escaped into a safe haven of refuge, has slammed the door shut, slumps against it, and gasps out a statment like this. Twice over he puts into the forefront what *Yahweh* has done. But for Him, this poor wretch would have been hopelessly lost. The wretch involved is the nation as the expression "who was on our side" indicates as well as the exhortation, "Let Israel now say."

2. This verse makes clear what the danger was that was involved. Men had risen up against the nation. Is the term "men" to be regarded as distinctly implying something different than "nations?" Perhaps we lay too much into a possible contrast that may be involved. It is just as possible that the term is used in contradistinction to the Lord who had been referred to so prominently twice over.

3. Vv. 3 and 4 continue the sentence. They make it clear that the danger involved was a deadly one: the nation could have been swallowed up alive (cf., Num. 16:32, 33). So great was the enemies' anger at the moment. See Neh. 4:1 for such a situation. But the thought is further developed in v. 4 where, instead of enraged men, a raging flood is referred to, perhaps a flash flood in a typical wadi or dry mountain torrent of Palestine. Such floods come so suddenly and rise so swiftly that they may well be used to describe a major danger. The fact that this figure is a common one—raging waters representing grave dangers or calamities—appears from the following passages that may be cited

as parallels: Is. 8:7f.; 28:17; 43:2; Ps. 32:6; 66:12; 69:1f.; 144:7; Lam. 3:54.

5. This verse repeats the sentiment of the section in brief, somewhat as vv. 1 and 2 repeat the initial statement. The total description is effective, depicting how many-sided and grave the danger was, and how the Lord helped.

> 6. *Blessed be the Lord,*
> *Who has not delivered us as a prey to their teeth.*
> 7. *We are like a bird,*
> *Which has escaped from the snare of fowlers;*
> *The snare is broken and we, we are escaped.*
> 8. *Our help is in the name of the Lord,*
> *Who made heaven and earth.*

This section of the psalm offers thanksgiving for God's intervention.

6. To tell the truth of the matter, the first section did not state that God had delivered His people. It implied clearly, however, that such was the case. An explicit statement is now given, particularly in v. 7, but also indirectly in v. 6. The whole section is cast into the form of thanksgiving. For that is what "Blessed be the Lord" regularly means.

The escape is now thought of as involving deliverance from the sharp teeth of a wild beast. The emphasis again lies on the terrific danger involved. But the figure immediately changes to that of a bird that had already been caught in the meshes of the fowler's net, but some soul was kind enough to break the framework of the net, and the bird was enabled to wing its way to freedom. This figure suggests the utter lack of strength on the part of the one caught and the radical nature of the intervention of the One who proved to be the nation's Deliverer. This apt figure appears also in Ps. 91:3; Prov. 6:5; Hos. 7:12; Amos 3:5.

8. With fine practical skill the writer sums up the nation's experience and attitude in a statement that has become justly famous in the church to this day. When "name" of the Lord is used for the plain term "Lord," the aim is to include in one term all the marvelous revelation of His mighty power to help that the Lord has so amply demonstrated in the course of the history of His people. When the appositional statement reminds the reader that He "made heaven and earth," the suggestion is that in that area which His providence has brought into being He must indeed be able to control all situations that arise, and do that, by virtue of His omnipotent power. Cf. 121:2.

NOTES

The features that may be regarded as Aramaic in character or at least indicative of later origin of the psalm are: *She* (in vv. 1, 2) for the relative; *'azay* for *'az* (though **Koenig** considers the longer form the older); and lastly *zedhonim* (v. 5) for "seething," a term that appears in later Hebrew only as far as we know.

1. For the construction of the contrary to fact sentence see *GK* 159 1.

4. The use of the word "soul" for person is rather obvious: "The stream has gone over our soul" (*KJ*) is quite misleading in that it points to an inner soul struggle that is not implied in the Hebrew.

Psalm 125

THE LORD IS THE PROTECTOR OF HIS PEOPLE

THIS PSALM is a hymn of trust. Interpreters like to compare it with psalms such as 23, 123, 131.

Two factors in the psalm are somewhat difficult to determine. One is: to whom is reference being made when persons in positions of authority are rebuked as wielding the "sceptre of wickedness?" The other is: who are the evildoers who are so prominent at the time and so harmful in their doings that there is need for the prayer that their wicked devices may be brought to nought? When all the facts of the case are carefully weighed, it appears that no time is better suited to them than the days of Nehemiah. For then, as we read in Neh. 6, there were persons in positions of authority who were allied with influential persons from among the Jews themselves who were in danger of getting the upper hand over the righteous. Their deeds were far from upright, and thus they may well be described as persons "who turn aside to their crooked ways." That such a situation could cause those among the people of God who were right-minded to have serious misgivings about the final outcome is rather obvious.

Two colorful and helpful comparisons are used at the beginning of the psalm as is so often the case in the pilgrimage songs, comparisons that seem to give a particular character to the psalm in which they appear.

a) **The security of those who trust in the Lord (vv. 1–3)**

A pilgrimage song.

1. *They who trust in the Lord are like Mount Zion,*
   Which cannot be moved but abides forever.

Psalm 125

2. *As for Jerusalem—mountains are round about her;
So the Lord is round about His people henceforth and forever.*
3. *For the sceptre of wickedness shall not rest upon the lot of the righteous
Lest the righteous put forth their hand unto wrong.*

1. The two figures referred to as depicting the security of those who trust in the Lord are: first, the one that describes the solidity and immovability of Mount Zion itself. There can scarcely be a finer comparison to convey the thought of a completely unshaken solidity than that of a mountain rooted deep in the rock of the earth. Should the mountains tremble with the shock of an earthquake, it is still true that they "cannot be moved" from their place but abide forever. Something of that characteristic inheres in those who trust in the Lord, chiefly because the Lord Himself is immovable, not because man becomes so firm.

2. The second figure is taken from the peculiar situation in which the city of Jerusalem finds itself topographically. It is surrounded by and overtopped by hills as travellers have again and again reminded us. As a result he who approaches the city does not catch sight of it until he has come to the top of the hills that surround it. In a similar manner the Lord's protecting care encircles His people at all times. He is for them an impregnable wall of defense. So He has been and so He will always be. One is reminded of Zech. 2:4, 5, or of II Kings 6:17; even as in connection with v. 1 Is. 28:16 may aptly be considered.

3. The problems connected with this verse have in part been suggested above. Persons with influence and authority were apparently unscrupulous in the use of the power they had. The sphere in which they exercised undue pressure is described as being "the lot of the righteous." This expression refers to the Holy Land as such, which in the days of Joshua had been divided among the twelve tribes by the casting of lots. It may be possible that at this time the significant portion of the land that was particularly afflicted was the Jerusalem area. Power and influence were being used in an ungodly way, and the ones who suffered as a result were particularly the righteous. In fact, their unjust sufferings and the manifold ways in which they were being discriminated against irked them so thoroughly and disappointed them so bitterly that they were ready to abandon their righteousness and become careless about their conduct. To what particular form of ungodliness they may have been tempted we may never know. God did not seem to care. Wickedness was not being promptly punished. The confidence expressed in v. 3 is that this misbegotten situation will not continue. Before harm comes of it, the Lord, who so strongly defends His people,

will correct the evil. Thus the tone of the first three verses is one of confidence and assurance.

The dissonance that was felt in spite of this confidence prompts the writer to give utterance to a prayer for relief from the emergency that prevailed.

b) **A prayer for them and for the removal of the wicked (vv. 4, 5)**

4. Do good, O Lord, to those who are good
And to those who are upright in their hearts.
5. But they who turn aside to their crooked ways—
May the Lord drive them away with the evildoers.
Peace be upon Israel!

4. This prayer is two-sided. Blessing is asked for those who do good, but not as though by such doing they merited God's blessing. What they do is indicative of their basic thinking. That more than external goodness is thought of appears from the parallel statement, "to those who are upright in their hearts." Spurious godliness is repugnant to the Lord. A true heart piety is acceptable to Him and often leads to the bestowal of blessing upon such persons when they are in need of it. This prayer is to the effect that they may be strengthened in their godly endeavors.

5. The evildoers who are referred to will without doubt have been men whose wicked ways were entirely apparent to all who knew the situation. Their deeds are described as being "crooked," for the reason, no doubt, that they were obviously far from upright. Surely, the Lord could not be asked to support them in their evil ways! Since He is known as the just Judge of mankind, who will separate the sheep from the goats and deal with each group as is just, the psalmist rather prays that He may exercise His just judgment and so clear up a pending issue. Toward the people of God his thoughts are the kindliest. He prays that they may receive the total of all those blessings that God loves to bestow on His people, cf., Ps. 122:6–9; 128:6; 131:3; Gal. 6:16.

NOTES

5. The word *hammattim* is a hiphil participle plural from *natah*.

Psalm 126

A PRAYER FOR FULL RESTORATION

THIS PSALM has a warmth and a depth of confidence all its own. It begins with a reminiscent note by thinking back upon the happy days when Israel had apparently just returned from the land of its captivity, Babylon, and was jubilantly glad with a joy that beggared description. It begins thus, however, with the obvious intent of furnishing a background for the petition that this great work of rehabilitating a nation, which was begun in those days, might now after a grievous interruption be brought to full completion. With this approach we can see how the psalm seems to be able to say in one breath: "We were restored," and in the next: "Restore us."

Failure to understand this basic problem has led quite a few commentators to interpret the psalm with reference to the Messianic age or to the glorious eschatological conclusion. Let us remark briefly for the present only that the tense of the first verb is an obvious past. Since this yields a good sense which fits well into the total picture, we shall do well to accept this fact and not attempt artificial constructions. It will then appear that this psalm has much in common with Ps. 85, where some measure of restoration is in the picture, but a fuller measure is still earnestly to be desired.

Luther is the exponent of all who advocate a translation that looks to the future consummation. The *KJ* represents the other point of view, which we strongly advocate.

The psalm strikes a note of strong comfort and encouragement. It will always be treasured by those who have known adversity but have in the midst of it cast their burden upon the Lord. This psalm, like most of the psalms in this group, is chiefly a psalm in which the church speaks rather than the individual. It will scarcely have been composed for special use on pilgrimages but may have come to be used in this way in troubled times.

A pilgrimage song.
1. *When the Lord restored the captives of Zion,*
   We were like those who dream.

2. *Then was our mouth filled with laughter and our tongue with jubilant shouts;*
Then men were saying among the Gentiles: "The Lord did great things for them."
3. *The Lord did great things for us;*
We were glad.

1. This first half of the psalm is descriptive of the joy of deliverance. It very likely refers to the first few years or at least months after the return from Babylon (537 B.C.). It would not be inappropriate to think of the time a few years later when Ezra and Nehemiah did their great work (458–444 B.C.) as the time of the composition of the psalm, though most writers seems to prefer a time around 516 B.C. The happiness that the people of God experienced at that time was so exuberant that they were scarcely able to believe that all that had happened to them was real. Acts 12:9 may be compared.

2. At that time laughter came easily. That was true already in the land of Babylon, equally so on the march, and still more so in the first months after the return. More than that, the demonstrative Oriental temperament brought even "jubilant shouts" to their lips. This had been specifically prophesied by Isaiah as being characteristic of this experience; cf., 44:23; 48:20; 49:13; 51:11; 54:1; 55:12. This same word occurs three times in the psalm. So much for the joy that was manifested within Israel.

Something akin to this was to be observed on the part of the Gentile nations that heard of Israel's restoration. These outsiders were saying: "Yahweh [the One known to be the God of Israel] did great things for them." This remark was made with obvious wonder and surprise. No God of the ancients was ever known to have achieved the restoration of His people after their deportation. Cf. Is. 52:10.

3. What the heathen were compelled to say with a sort of grudging admiration, Israel could say with deep conviction by using the selfsame words: "The Lord did great things for us." But the Israelites could add in an obvious understatement, "We were glad." This was the gladness that marked the first few months and years. One is tempted to remark how often in the course of a lifetime or in the experiences of the church overpowering wonder at the magnitude of God's achievements in behalf of His own is the order of the day. But this joy was short-lived.

4. *Restore our fortunes, O Lord,*
Like the dry river beds of the Negeb.
5. *They who sow in tears*
Will reap with jubilant shouts.

Psalm 126

6. He that keeps going along and weeping as he bears his seed for sowing
Shall surely come back with jubilant shouts as he brings in his sheaves.

This section of the psalm is a prayer for the completion of the deliverance combined with strong hope.

4. Even as above whatever restoration had taken place was ascribed to the Lord, so here the continuation of that gracious work is thought of as being achievable by Him alone. "Restore our fortunes" is readily understood but is a bit unfortunate in that it brings the heathen goddess of good luck, Fortuna, into the picture. More to the point would be an expression like, "Work a total change in our situation," as a translation of the unique Hebrew expression, which in the *KJ* usually appears in the form, "Turn again the captivity."

The comparison used by way of illustration is very suggestive. In the South Land (nowadays again called, even in newspaper accounts, "Negeb") are many *wadis,* stream beds, that are dry eleven months out of twelve and apparently unable to produce even a trickle of water. When, however, the rainy season comes, they fill up quickly and often become raging torrents. So completely can the Lord change the status of His people. For such a total change the psalmist prays in Israel's name.

5. Immediately thereafter he begins to express his strong hope that this prayer will not be spoken in vain. The first form in which this hope finds expression is that of an obviously proverbial statement that is reminiscent of Jer. 31:9. In the Hebrew this statement is somewhat more epigrammatic than it is in English: "The sowers in tears will reap in joy." Again, however, the word for "jubilant shouts" is used rather than "joy." The statement as such is perfectly plain. The sowers of old will often have sown with little prospect of rains to make growth of the seed possible, and they may have bemoaned that fact. But unexpected rains came, and sadness was turned into gladness. References to a supposed Egyptian custom of regularly sowing to the accompaniment of tears because the god of vegetation was dead do not seem to help our understanding of this passage.

6. What was said in v. 5 obviously applied to all constructive endeavor and not to sowing only. Yet the figure, having been introduced, is carried out in more detail in this verse. By a unique device of Hebrew syntax the impression of a man patiently plodding along at his task is brought before our mind's eye, grieving over the apparent hopelessness of it all but still going on, bearing his seed for the sowing. By the same device the certainty of his coming back in the end after having gone

forth is indicated; but he now bears the sheaves that have grown from the seed sown. On the lips of such a one are again the "jubilant shouts" noted repeatedly in this psalm. With that happy outcome the psalm closes by admonishing Israel and all people of God at all times faithfully to perform their given tasks and to wait for the Lord's blessing which will surely not be wanting.

NOTES

1. The noun *shibhah* should be retained in the meaning that the root indicates, "the captives," and though the expression is a bit unusual, textual changes to make the expression conform to v. 4 are unnecessary. For a further discussion of the expression in v. 4 see Notes on Ps. 85 and *KS* 329i.

2. The verb following *'az* gains its time of action from the context in which it appears, *hayinu* (v. 1), an obvious perfect. See *KS* 137 and *GK* 107c.

3. The hiphil form *highdil* serves as an adverb, a common device in Hebrew; see *KS* 399m.

6. According to *Koehler* the noun *méshekh*, could mean "bag" for seed. That part of the verse could then read: "as he bears the bag for sowing the seed." We have been unable to determine why *Luther* put the adjective before seed, *edlen,* which was copied by the *KJ* "precious."

Psalm 127

MAN'S NEED OF THE BLESSING OF THE ALMIGHTY

LIKE THE NEXT PSALM, this is a psalm that is designed to give instruction and thus may be classed as belonging to the wisdom literature of the children of Israel. Other psalms in this class would be 1, 49, 73, 128.

In spite of strong disinclination on the part of many interpreters to accept the suggestion of the heading that this psalm was composed by Solomon, there are good reason for regarding it as being reliable as *Koenig does*. Solomon wrote many a wholesome piece of wisdom literature in the Proverbs. Prov. 10:22, for example, is much in keeping with the tenor of this psalm. When the psalm speaks of God's gifts being given to "His beloved" (v. 2), that would agree well with the very name that God Himself bestowed on Solomon according to II Sam. 12:25—Jedidiah, which means: "Beloved of Jehovah." Besides, it was in a unique sense true that great blessings were bestowed on Solomon himself as he slept at Gibeon, I Kings 3:5ff., and thus the expression "while he sleeps" could be a quiet allusion to this experience. Nothing in the psalm militates against Solomonic authorship. When Jewish scribes among others associate the idea of the building of a "house," v. 1, with Solomon's building of the house of the Lord, that does, indeed, seem trivial and may be dropped. But on the whole we have here good instruction such as Solomon might have offered to Israel in his earlier life.

It is immediately apparent that this brief psalm emphasizes the need of divine blessing for all undertakings. It conveys this lesson with unmistakable clearness and clear emphasis. It would appear that no proverb known to us conveys the sentiment of this psalm quite as well as does the German proverb: *An Gottes Segen ist alles gelegen.* (Everything depends of God's blessing).

In spite of the first impression to the contrary, the psalm has a deep inner unity. The break between v. 2 and 3 is more incidental than real. In the first section of the psalm (v. 1, 2) the theme indicated above is examined as to its application in the area of two common undertakings among men—building a house and guarding a city. Then without a formal transition a third major undertaking in the lives of men is touched upon—the establishing of a household. Instead of stating the case thus, the psalm at once turns to the chief purpose of establishing a home—children—and stresses the fact that the having of them is dependent on divine blessing. Such unity of the whole is not difficult to see.

There may be a distinct Palestinian flavor to this psalm, especially in its second section, as *Hans Schmidt* points out. For it may be observed that, when a son in particular is born to a Palestinian farmer, the neighbor women gather before the house where this happened and sing and dance, and compose little poems that seem appropriate to the occasion (cf., Ruth 4:14f). Note that v. 5 of this psalm could be regarded thus. Besides, the Oriental attitude on the question of having children is very much is evidence in the psalm. But the point of view that pervades the psalm as a whole is more than a local and provincial attitude.

It may also be said that for the purpose of keeping the instruction offered by the psalm within wholesome bounds it would be obviously unfair to the psalm to charge it with encouraging indolence. It addresses typical men of God who have the insight needed to keep them from falling into extremes of thinking and acting. In like manner it could scarcely be charged against this psalm that it teaches that the blessing of children must invariably come to men who fear the Lord and trust in His goodness. Certain reasonable limitations must be imposed upon this brief psalm and its teaching.

A pilgrimage psalm. Of Solomon.
1. *Unless the Lord builds the house, they who build it labor in vain;*
Unless the Lord guards the city, the guard watches in vain.
2. *It is all in vain for you who rise up early and sit down late,*
Eating your hard-earned bread—
He will give what is right to His beloved while he sleeps.

1. An excellent bit of instruction needed by all men! It teaches them that success depends on more than hard work and honest endeavor. The unseen but all-important factor is that God must bless what man does. Stated more drastically: He Himself must build the house and guard the city. Jesus, in His own way, taught this lesson in the Sermon on the Mount (Matt. 6:25ff.). Industrious and hard-working people, who enjoy good health and strength, especially need to be taught this lesson lest they fall into self-sufficiency.

2. The threefold "in vain!" which stands with double emphasis at the beginning of this verse comes to be a powerful refrain. We have sought to capture the force of its emphatic position at the beginning of the verse by the translation: "It is all in vain." Rising up early as such is obviously not condemned in this verse, nor is keeping tirelessly at one's task till late at night. But the point is that, if one does this and does not put his major emphasis on the need of divine blessing, such indications of wholesome industry become quite useless. There is much discussion of the word that we translated "sit down late." It is difficult to determine whether it means to sit down to rest, or to sit down to eat, or merely marks the "cessation" of work even as rising up early marks the beginning of work. We agree with those interpreters who maintain that in this case it matters little how the verb "to sit" is understood. To us it seems to be as general in character as when we say that a man scarcely takes time to sit down. Who cares, for what? The point is still: Long-continued and assiduous effort without a thought of the need of divine blessing is the height of futility. Those who have put their trust for success in what it may please God to give have found it to be true time and again as the psalm says: "He will give what is right to His beloved while he sleeps." That does not promise indiscriminate success to everyone that takes this attitude. The clause "what is right" leaves the time and the measure of what God bestows entirely in His

hands. The familiar: "So He giveth His beloved sleep," (*KJ*) introduces a wrong contrast. The point at issue was not, who gets sleep and who does not; but, how does success come? The answer is, God gives it at a time when man's participation is ruled out, so to speak, and thus the fact that it is purely a divine gift is made all the more apparent.

3. *Lo, children are a heritage from the Lord;*
   The fruit of the womb is a reward.
4. *Like arrows in the hand of a mighty man,*
   So are the children of one's youth.
5. *Happy is the man who has his quiver full of them;*
   They shall not be put to shame when they speak with their
      enemies in the gate.

3. The "house" referred to in v. 1, is to be thought of as being an actual house of wood, plaster, and stone, not as a household or family. In this verse "children," by way of synechdoche, represent the family though they are, of course, the only part of the family mentioned. Yet every reader recognizes that they are the chief part. If a man has any children, he is not to think that he is capable of producing them. Children are a free gift of God, a token of His grace. In the Hebrew way of thinking this is expressed by designating them as "a heritage from the Lord," an expression that is often used in the Old Testament with reference to the land of promise which came to Israel as unearned as is any inheritance. The parallel expression terms them "a reward." One caution should be observed in evaluating this term as *Kirkpatrick* has stated it: "If the thought of recompense is included at all in 'reward,' it is in accordance with the spirit of v. 1 and 2, as a recompense for the fear of the Lord . . . that children are given."

4. A rather unique but effective description of what children may mean to a man is given in this verse. In days of old, what was a warrior without weapons or a "mighty man" without "arrow"? So is a man without children. For there will be situations when he needs support, times when he cannot stand alone. To have children, begotten early in life, who are ready to stand by a father in all manner of situations is a happy state of affairs. As an example could be cited the case of the farmer who has sturdy sons to help him in his daily task. "The children of one's youth" are, of course, those which were born to a man comparatively early in life and thus have an opportunity to grow up earlier and be of help, cf., Gen. 49:3.

5. The particular situation that the psalmist uses as a comparison is the one offered in this verse. That man is described as being particularly fortunate who is supported by stalwart sons is the city gate. It must be born in mind that the city gate was the place where persons

most generally congregated. There business was transacted; there cases were tried in a kind of popular court. Whatever the situation was, when a man encounters opponents, happy is he to have some sons of his own as backers, stalwart young men who support him and prevent the opposition from taking advantage, as it sometimes well might, of a lone-standing individual. The verse blends in with the preceding one by likening this sort of man with a warrior who when in dangerous battle, has a quiver full of arrows. On that note, abruptly but effectively, the psalm comes to a conclusion. Wisdow literature is epigrammatic and aims at brevity.

NOTES

2. This verse has three participles, all in the vocative, agreeing with "you." The first two are hiphils used as substitutes for adverbs (*KS* 399o). For "hard-earned bread" (so *J.M.P. Smith*) the Hebrew has "bread of toil or sorrows." We have translated *ken* ("so" in *KJ* and omitted by *RSV*) as a noun, following *Koenig* and *Weiser*. Though the word can mean "so," one is at a loss as to how to construe it when it is translated thus. "His beloved" (*yedhidho*) is a singular used in the collective sense of "anyone whom He loves."

4. "One's" before "youth" is a happy turn of the phrase which contributes to clearness at a glance (*Smith* and *RSV*).

5. Some interpreters feel that they must change the plural of the verbs in the second half of the verse to singulars. This is quite unnecessary. The construction is according to the sense (*construction ad sensum*). The "man" mentioned in v. 5a is taken together with his sons, making a "they," for both together constitute a unit. Though, as indicated above, the activity referred to as taking place in the gate may be of various kinds, the following passages indicate that city gates served as courts: Gen. 19:1; Deut. 25:7; Ruth 4:11; Amos 5:10; Is. 29:21; Ps. 69:12.

This psalm and the next one have been traditionally used in the church from days of old. They are appointed to be read in the Order for Marriage.

Psalm 128

DOMESTIC BLISS AN OUTGROWTH OF THE FEAR OF THE LORD

WITHOUT A DOUBT the purpose of this psalm is didactic: it belongs in the class of wisdom literature. Other incidental applications are derived from the nature of the case rather than from the express purpose of the psalm. We can understand why Luther called it a psalm of comfort for those who have experienced the crosses that are incidental to married life. Looking at the first verse, we can see why some interpreters regard it as typifying the praises of the law of the Lord. Looking at the Order for Matrimony as our church has it, we see how aptly it fits into such a service. This psalm is a companion piece to the one that precedes. Whereas Ps. 127 showed how all blessings are attributable to God alone, this psalm shows what responsibility rests upon man if he would share in God's rich blessings.

Though there is nothing which directly indicates the situation out of which the psalm may have grown, some interpreters think of the scant population and the heavy taxes that were characteristic of the days of Nehemiah (see Neh. 5). The scarcity of population was contrary to all that the prophets had predicted (see Jer. 30:18ff.; 31; Zech. 8:1–17). The taxes were doubly hard on a people who had not yet begun to prosper. No other part of Israel's history seems to fit quite as well as does this period.

Shall we regard the psalm as being initially designed for liturgical use, let us say, on the occasion of the Festival of Booths (Tabernacles)? To claim this is to confuse possible use with original purpose. Shall the last verses be thought of as being most aptly spoken by a priest? The same criticism applies to this approach.

Briefly stated, the purpose of the psalm is to show that the basis of domestic bliss is true fear of the Lord. Incidentally the basis of national prosperity is at the same time indicated. For as the individuals go, so goes the nation. He who honestly fears the Lord, which implies walking in the ways of His commandments, will receive a blessing from the Lord which consists, generally speaking, in the success of all that he undertakes and in the happy state in which his family lives. If some interpreters regard this as a somewhat inadequate doctrine of retribution which is characteristic of Old Testament morality, such as approach is now being more clearly regarded as a failure to understand the true appreciation of earthly blessings which the covenant people had. Naturally, not every aspect of the case can be discussed within the brief compass of this psalm. Naturally, there will be exceptions to the general rule. But to harbor the expectation that the true fear of the Lord will result in manifest tokens of His blessing is a wholesome attitude of faith.

a) **The blessing viewed from the aspect of individual family life (vv. 1–4)**

A pilgrimage song.
1. *O how very happy is everyone who fears the Lord,*
   Who walks in His ways!
2. *That which your hands have toiled for you shall surely eat;*
   Happy are you, and it shall go well with you!
3. *Your wife shall be like a fruitful vine inside your house;*
   Your children shall be like olive shoots around your table.
4. *Lo, so indeed shall a man be blessed*
   Who fears the Lord!

1. The fact that the fear of the Lord is the important prerequisite to blessing is made obvious by stating it in the first verse and drawing attention to it again in the fourth. Aside from what was said above by way of interpretation of this verse, it may yet be noted that the initial word, which we have translated, "O how very happy," indicates a kind of superlative. Besides, in a very apt manner the two sides of the godly life are well defined as involving first the fear of the Lord, then as evidence of such an attitude the walking in His ways, which are quite obviously the ways He has defined for man in His commandments.

2. The first blessing pointed out as, as a rule, resulting from a godly attitude and godly conduct is daily bread regularly and abundantly provided by the mercy of God. To know that your own hands have toiled for it always adds to the satisfaction of enjoying the blessing. Since such daily gifts are sometimes thought commonplace because they keep coming continually, the author pauses to indicate that, where such a situation prevails, there is abundant case for classifying a man as having a supremely happy lot. How many god-fearing men can testify to the fact that they have enjoyed thousands of days of this sort, where it has gone well with them!

3. Aside from having basic wants satisfied by daily bread, there is the remarkably rich blessing of having wife and children. The description of the wife of such a man is both beautiful and to the point. A

fruitful vine is a pleasant plant. Beautiful is true motherhood. A sad thing is a family where the blessing of children has been providentially withheld. The little phrase "inside your house" merely draws attention in passing that the normal sphere of the mother is largely indoors, making the house a home. The children that come as a "reward" from the Lord (Ps. 127:3) are by another typically Palestinian comparison likened to "olive shoots around (a man's) table." Many are the descriptions that have been offered of the typical olive tree, how little shoots keep coming up all around the parent tree. So numerous, speaking hyperbolically, are the offspring of the richly blessed man of God, especially in evidence as they sit around the table at mealtimes. These are the true riches of a happy couple. Cf. at this point: Zech. 8:5; Ps. 52:8; Jer. 11:16.

4. To this aspect of the case this verse specifically draws attention: "Lo, so indeed shall a man be blessed who fears the Lord!" Material wealth aside from this is secondary. In the comparison used above the point at issue in the case of the vine is as expressly stated its fruitfulness; its beauty and its healthfulness are, perhaps, to be thought of, but only in passing. In the case of the olive tree its shoots convey only the unit picture of the many clustering around the one. Few instances could be cited from literature where so attractive and helpful a picture is drawn so effectively with so few strokes of the pen.

b) The blessing prayed for from the aspect of national prosperity (vv. 5, 6)

5. *The Lord bless you from Zion*
   That you may see the prosperity of Jerusalem all the days
   of your life;
6. *And that you may see your children's children!*
   Peace be upon Israel!

Having described the ideal Israelite and the basic blessings that he enjoys, the psalmist feels impelled to draw the circle a bit wider. For to be content with one's own family's happiness and live for no more than that could, indeed, become an ingrown tendency that promotes selfishness. When drawing attention to the fact that true family happiness involves and is dependent upon the broader prosperity of the nation and of the church the author does this by casting it into the form of a prayer to the effect that the smaller circle of happiness may stand in the setting of the broader prosperity. Since Zion has become synonymous with the Old Testament church, and since this church is the center from which blessings flow upon all its members, this is the thought of the first part of the prayer. The Holy City is intimately tied up with the sanctuary, also its prosperity. That both these broader blessings may also be granted by the Lord is what this prayer covers in this verse.

There is the added blessing of length of days inserted into the verse by a modifying phrase—"all the days of your life," implying that they are not to be few in number. The next verse carries this thought into a more colorful picture, where the man previously spoken of is envisioned as a grandfather, seeing generation after generation come upon the scene, all enjoying the same blessings that have just been enumerated. The broadest scope of the prayer is reached in a sort of concluding benediction: "Peace be upon Israel." In this connection one cannot help but think of passages like Zech. 8:4.

NOTES

2. When this verse introduces the second person ("your hand," etc.), this is best regarded as the so-called "ideal" second person, which is the equivalent of "anyone" or the German *man*. The word for "surely" (ki) carries a measure of reassurance; see *KS* 4151 and 351c.

5. The sequence of the verb forms used is: imperfect and two imperatives. The imperatives serve to introduce a final clause in each case. See *KS* 364i.

Psalm 129

"THEY HAVE NOT PREVAILED AGAINST ME"

ISRAEL IS SPEAKING, not the individual. This psalm has much in common with Ps. 124: the same general theme, the same mode of treatment, even a similar form of repetition at the beginning.

To give the psalm a classification, we would list it among the psalms of trust, which in this case merges into a prayer for the overthrow of the enemy. It has two parts:
a) A confident affirmation that the enemy has not prevailed (vv. 1–4).
b) A definite conclusion drawn from this fact: Zion's enemies shall perish (vv. 5–8).

It is not warranted by the facts of the case to assign a definite liturgical character to the psalm, or to associate it with the New Year's Festival, or to make overmuch of the closing prayer that the enemy may be overthrown and thus to call this a psalm of vengeance or the like.

Neither is there enough of an indication within the psalm as to the circumstances which may have given occasion for composing it. It fits into any time from the Assyrian domination onward. But it most likely stems from postexilic days as do most of the psalms in this part of the Psalter. For then, too, there was occasion to reflect on the many times in which the enemies had sought to give the deathblow to the little, hated nation.

To classify it as a "pilgrimage psalm" is, nevertheless, suitable, for though it reflects no situation which would be encountered by pilgrim bands as they wended their way to the Holy City, it would still touch upon a subject which was of perennial interest to the nation and the subject of earnest reflection.

a) **A confident affirmation that the enemy has not prevailed (vv. 1–4)**
   A pilgrimage psalm
1. *"Much have they afflicted me from my youth,"*
   May Israel now say—
2. *"Much have they afflicted me from my youth;*
   Yet they have not prevailed against me.
3. *The plowers have plowed upon my back;*
   They made their furrows long.
4. *The Lord, who is righteous,*
   Has cut the cords of the wicked."

1. As to sentence structure, the direct discourse, introduced by, "May Israel now say," extends to the end of v. 4. That which is to be said begins like a sigh or complaint but terminates on two triumphant notes, v. 2b (which we have chosen as the caption of the whole), and v. 4, which also sounds the note of victory. By using the expression, "May Israel now say," the writer encourages the nation to make this both its complaint and its confession. The grief that afflicts the nation is to be put into words, but it is not to stay on that level; it should ultimately become a strong confession of the Lord's righteousness and faithfulness.

Examining these verses in detail, we find that the lament is a kind of summary of all the national disasters that have befallen the nation at the hand of her enemies. From her youth onward Israel has suffered "much" from the hostility of others. Strangely, she can still make this her very apt confession, for the afflictions have not yet come to an end. Israel's youth takes us back to the days of Egyptian bondage (cf., Hos. 2:15; Jer. 2:2; 22:21; Ezek. 23:3). Then nations like the Canaanites, Aramaeans, Ammonites, Edomites, Philistines, Assyrians, and Chaldeans successively bore down upon her. The "much" stands first with emphasis. What nation has suffered as this nation has? Yet the note of confidence that is reached: "They have not prevailed against me," is the luminous point of the psalm.

3. The figure used by way of comparison is one, an extreme one at that (cf. Is. 51:23): it is as though Israel had been compelled to lie face down on the ground, and that plowers had then run their plows over the back of the poor wretch. There seems to blend into this figure another that is merely implied. The assumption is that Israel is like an individual whose back has been bruised by a succession of bloody welts that were caused by a scourge. These stripes lie across the back like furrows across the field. Even without a detailed analysis of the figure used, the propriety of it and its colorful nature are immediately apparent. This one comparison aims to condense within itself the total measure of suffering that befell the poor nation.

4. There follows another figure, which is indicated so briefly that one is at a loss as to how to interpret it. It could mean that the cords that hitch the beast that plows to the plow have been cut. That puts an end to the plowing. It could mean that the poor nation is being regarded as a captive in bonds. These cords that tie her may be thought of as being cut away from arms and legs, and thus the prisoner is freed. Either approach is legitimate. In any case, it was the Lord who always gave the longed-for deliverance; and again the whole history is covered by this one figure. By so doing the Lord gave new evidence of the fact that He is "righteous." This means more than that He gives to each his proper due. It means specifically that He measures up to the demands which a given situation imposes upon Him, which demands in this case are the covenant obligations by which He bound Himself.

Victory and deliverance are the dominant notes of this section of the psalm. The faith manifested may not be of heroic proportions. It is sufficient for the needs of the case.

b) **A definite conclusion drawn from this fact—Zion's enemies shall perish (vv. 5-8)**

5. *All who hate Zion*
Will be put to shame and turned backward.
6. *They will be like the grass on the housetops,*
Which withers before a man plucks it out;
7. *With which the reaper does not fill his hand,*
Nor the binder of sheaves his bosom;
8. *Concerning which the passers-by have not said:*
"The blessing of the Lord be upon you; we have blessed you in the name of the Lord!"

5. Since Israel prevails, it is the enemies, not Israel, who shall perish. This is the conclusion that Israel draws from its confident utterance in the first half of the psalm. It must be conceded that the verbs employed may be rendered either as prayers: May they be put to shame, or as plain futures: They will be put to shame. Always to put the harsher construction upon verb forms of this sort is not charitable. Therefore we view the whole passage as being in the nature of a prediction of what will befall those who are "haters of Zion" without a cause. These haters are apparently identical with those who were mentioned in the first half as having afflicted Israel. Defeat and confusion will be their lot. It is implied that God will administer the defeat.

6. Even as two telling comparisons were used in the first half, so two equally effective figures are used in this section. The life of those who oppose God's people and thus God Himself will be utterly futile. It will amount to as little as do the tufts of grass that in spring shot up from the mud roofs of the typical Palestinian homes of days of old. They were bound to appear there from time to time. But even before the owner had determined to pluck them out, they had already withered away, due to lack of moisture. This is scarcely a picture of solid achievement or of a life that is worth while.

7. The second comparison is similar in character. The reaper never plans to gather such tufts at the time when he is reaping grain. They are not worth the effort. The isolated stalks will not fill the hand or add to the sheaf that he gathers in his bosom before tying it into a bundle.

8. We believe that the first part of this verse is still spoken with regard to the tufts of grass on the housetop. The passers-by pronounce no blessing upon them as they might upon their own grain or upon that of a friend or neighbor. Construing the verse thus, the point that is made by the whole section, v. 5–8, is made very emphatic. Lives that turned against God and His people represent the utmost of futility. The section as such merely makes this observation. It expresses no hostile thoughts. It simply concludes: Such people cannot thrive. *Maclaren,* referring to the section as a whole, remarks very appropriately: "It is something far nobler than selfish vengeance which desires and foresees the certain failure of attempts against (Zion)." For the justification of this construction of v. 8 see the Notes.

NOTES

3. "Furrows" is introduced by a *le* rather than by the customary sign of the accusative. Cf.*GK* 117n.

5. The two verbs "put to shame and turned backward" are not in

the customary construction with *waw* consecutive. The simple *waw* makes the two verbs stand out more prominently. *KS* 370s.

6. The verb *shalaph* is established in the meaning of "pluck up" by the translation of the *Septuagint*. Another possible rendering is "grow up" (*RSV*).

8. The words "concerning which" in our translation grow out of a definite possibility which is here involved, namely, that the relative (*she*) found at the beginning of v. 7 may reach over into v. 8 and introduce another relative clause (cf. *KS* 57). The perfect form *'ameru* is, perhaps, best explained as being a plain narrative perfect as *Kessler* suggests which is used because the situation described by the writer becomes so vivid in his mind that he narrates it in the customary manner by the use of the perfect.

Psalm 130

DE PROFUNDIS

THIS IS ONE of the so-called penitential psalms. Ever since *Delitzsch,* attention has also been drawn to the fact that on one occasion *Luther* ventured to classify it as *Pauline* in character, obviously because it stresses the thoughts that this great apostle specially emphasized. Luther made a hymn of it, one of the finest examples of evangelical hymnody, *Aus tiefer Not schrei ich zu dir*.

The unique feature of the psalm over against the others that are in a special way designated as penitential (i.e., Ps. 6, 32, 38, 51, 106, 130, 143) is, perhaps, the fact that it centers attention on sin itself, not so much on its results and consequences. No other psalm expresses quite so well what an evil sin itself is. At the same time, as already indicated above, the psalm has a distinct gospel emphasis. True, this is cast into Old Testament forms and language, though the language of the cultus is noticeably absent. This aspect of the case led *Luther* to remark: "It treats of the chief article of doctrine necessary for salvation, namely, justification." (St. Louis Ed. IV, 2032).

There seems to be some warrant for the attitude of some interpreters who claim that the speaker in the psalm is the congregation. However, even though vv. 7, 8 do bring Israel into the picture, there is nothing to indicate that, because she is referred to, Israel is also the speaker from the very outset. In fact, it is better to follow the first impression which suggests that an individual is giving expression to a particularly meaningful experience of his. Then toward the close of the psalm he shares his experience with his people and in that sense addresses them. *Vilmar* remarks that the psalm has proved especially helpful in pastoral work to reassure troubled consciences of the certainty of forgiveness and claims that the reliving of the experience here rcorded is essential to evangelical insight. *Kittel* says rather appropriately that to regard this as a congregational lament serves to impoverish the interpretation.

It is not easy to classify this psalm as being anything other than a penitential psalm. The newer categories (e.g., a cultic lament veering over into a confession) are less to the point. But how did it come to be classified as "a pilgrimage song"? That is a difficult question to answer. *Oesterley* suggests that this is an indication "in what a haphazard way this title has been used." It might be a bit more constructive to use the approach that it was suggested to be sung on pilgrimages by way of preparation for the festivals to be kept in the Holy City.

a) How the assurance of forgiveness was reached (vv. 1–4)
1. *Out of the depths*
   I cry to Thee, O Lord!
2. *Lord, hear my voice;*
   Let Thy ears be attentive to the voice of my supplications!
3. *If Thou, Lord, shouldest be on the watch for iniquities,*
   O Lord, who could stand?
4. *But with Thee there is forgiveness*
   That Thou mayest be feared.

1. On reading the first statement of the psalm the reaction of the reader is apt to be a question: What "depths"? It so happens that the usage of this word is confined to the figure of a man who is caught in dangerous and deep waters (cf., Ps. 40:2; 69:2, 14; Is. 51:10; Ezek. 27:34). The use of the term is certainly figurative, allowing the reader to think of any and every kind of extremity or danger in which the writer (or even his nation) may find himself, whether it is physical, mental, or spiritual. That very vagueness allows each reader to appropriate the words to himself when he is in a more or less extreme difficulty. When one is in a difficult situation crying unto the Lord is comparatively easy. *Maclaren* remarks most appropriately: "If out of the depths we cry, we shall cry ourselves out of the depths." Times will come when trouble is deep and threatens to overwhelm us completely.

A matter of the use of Hebrew tenses may be suggested. It seems difficult to determine which translation is to be followed, *KJ*, which renders, "have I cried" or *Luther*, *RSV*, etc., which translate, "I cry."

The perfect which is used is best regarded as expressing a regular procedure: I have cried in the past and still cry. The Hebrew perfect is often translated as a present or gnomic aorist. This consideration redeems the verse from that shallow attitude which would be ascribed to its author, that when danger is for once very extreme, he makes a single outcry. It seems much more in keeping with the tenor of the psalm to think of this man as having so much insight that what he does in the recent extreme case is what he has done all his days.

2. There follows the first part of his plea. Doubts so often plague a man as to whether God will deign to hear him. Behind that impression lies a sense of total unworthiness. The reiteration of the plea shows how serious the doubts and misgivings are. The plea grows quite strong when the "attentive" suggests that God may bend over solicitously to the poor man in his need and hear his petitions.

3. It should be noted that v. 1 did not say or imply that the speaker was in a state of distress over his sins. He is simply in great trouble; he pleads to be heard. This verse now indicates that he is aware of the fact that sin is deeply involved in his problem. He does not say that sin is the ultimate source and root of all his troubles, but he does seem to realize keenly that sin has much to do with his state. In fact, to him sin is so serious a business that he realizes that, if all his sins were to be recorded against him and dealt with as they deserve, his case would be quite hopeless. In making that statement he momentarily envisions what would happen if God were on the alert, watching what sins a man may commit. This is an indirect confession and admission of guilt, a guilt so great that, if strict justice were done, the sinner would be beyond hope of redemption.

4. But he knows also that there is an attitude on the part of God which expresses itself in forgiveness. That he has heard. That he believes to be a certainty. By stating it thus the speaker appeals to God to let him be the recipient of such forgiveness. The very indirect way in which the subject is broached may be regarded as a delicate and humble appeal that God may grant him forgiveness. The statement certainly suggests a measure of hope and faith on the speaker's part.

The expressed purpose that is stated as being the object of such forgiveness might for a moment give a reader pause because it seems to be in violation of logic. One might theorize that forgiveness freely bestowed might render the recipient of it careless regarding God, just because He seems so ready to forgive. One's reverence for Him might seem to be endangered. Such an approach is, however, pure theorizing. All who have sincerely craved pardon and become assured that God is ready to grant it to a penitent soul find that their reaction is the opposite of such theorizing. A truehearted man will all the more hold God in

Psalm 130

reverence and respect, just because God has been so gracious in bestowing pardon. Therefore the conclusion rightly reads thus: "that Thou mayest be feared." Pardon works as a check on carelessness unless, of course, pardon was sought as a mere formality, and man did not realize how serious the issues were.

So, then, though no confession was made and no absolution formally granted, this statement of the case is, nevertheless, the record of a deep-going experience in which the man who here prays was taken out of the depths into which he had fallen and was cleansed of his sin which was the root of all his difficulties.

b) **The writer's attitude after this experience and his counsel to Israel to adopt the same attitude (vv. 5–8)**

5. *I wait for the Lord, my soul waits;*
   And in His word I hope.
6. *My soul waits for the Lord*
   More than watchmen do for the morning,
   More than watchmen do for the morning.
7. *O Israel, hope in the Lord,*
   For with the Lord there is steadfast love,
   And with Him is plenteous redemption.
8. *And He will redeem Israel*
   From all its iniquities.

5. The experience through which the psalmist has gone leads to a certain attitude that he aims to cultivate consistently from now on. This attitude is one of patient waiting for the Lord. To understand his statement thus is much better than to relate it to what went before in the sense that the writer expects to wait that God may bestow forgiveness and the assurance that sin is forgiven. It seems that, though it is not thus stated, the certainty of forgiveness was already in the picture when v. 4 was spoken. Seeing how gracious God can be, and how completely we are dependent upon His mercy, we can never demand instant action as a result of our petitions. It rather behooves us to make our plea and then to wait every day in deep humility until it pleases the Lord to act in our behalf.

That more than plain waiting is involved appears from the fact that the verb could also be translated "hope." The repetition, "My soul waits," intensifies the thought of complete resignation. But that this hope is not of a vague sort appears from the concluding statement, "And in His word do I hope." Many a good word of promise made by prophets and holy writers was within reach of the people of God and known to them. On precious words such as these God's saints built their hope. We think of words such as Jer. 31:31–34; 33:8; Exod. 34:6f.; Mic.

7:18. With feet firmly planted on such promises, man's hope is not an empty gesture.

6. That an attitude is here being cultivated and suggested which is well thought through and thoroughly consistent appears from the various forms in which the thought is reiterated. For v. 6 now adds that this waiting for the Lord has a measure of anxiety in it much like that which those persons feel who have reason to look for the breaking of the morning because there was a long night of sickness, of pain, or of danger. The suggestion that the Levitical Temple watchmen are thought of should be regarded only as a valid example of what kind of waiting is meant. The repetition of the comparison adds a plaintive note.

It should again be noted that there is more hinted at than is actually expressed in vv. 5 and 6. What it is that a man is waiting for is not stated; neither relief from distress nor forgiveness of sins is mentioned. It seems enough to the writer to have said that his waiting is for the *Lord,* for He does not need to have our particular needs always spelled out for Him before He can tell what we need.

7. Vital religious experience such as this psalm has dealt with seeks to communicate itself to others. It does not isolate the individual. It draws him closer into the fellowship of other saints who have had the same experience. This explains why the writer now addresses his people, inviting them to adopt that same attitude of waiting on the Lord until it please Him to help in all manner of need. It is true that the synonym "hope" is here used for "wait" as it was in v. 5b. Two considerations are advanced as to why such hope is to be thought of as being well-grounded. One is that on the Lord's part there is "steadfast love," that covenant faithfulness that Israel has so often witnessed and seen in action. Then there is "plenteous redemption," readiness to deliver from all sorts of necessities, whether they afflict the mind or the body.

The closing note of the psalm indicates that the writer has come to one particular insight when he experienced what this psalm seeks to perpetuate: he had seen that "iniquities" lie at the bottom of all human disorders. But he has also come to recognize that the Lord is a God who will redeem His people from all their basic ills. On this positive note of hope the psalm rests its case.

NOTES

1. The use of the perfect *qara'thi* described above equates it with the Greek gnomic aorist.

2. The words *qashshubhoth* and *selichah* (v. 4) are late Hebrew and help to establish the postexilic date of the psalm, which, perhaps, fits

best with the days of Nehemiah, whose prayer in Neh. 1 may be compared with this psalm.

4. *Ki* is better taken in the sense of "but" than "for." On this meaning see *KW* and *BDB* p. 474, e.

5. *Luther's* rendering cannot be summarily brushed aside. He translated the latter part of the verse: *von einer Morgenwache bis zur andern,* i.e. "from one morning watch until the other." The *Greek,* the *Syriac,* and the *Vulgate* have much the same reading. *Briggs* prefers to come back to this approach. *Luther's* version then conveys the idea of patient waiting that continues night after night. The net result is much the same, no matter how the text is translated.

7. "Plenteous" is that familiar Hebrew construction which uses *Hiphil* infinitives adverbially, a construction that is best translated by the adjective in English. Cf. *GK* 113k.

Psalm 131

A PSALM OF TRUST AND HUMILITY

THIS PSALM, modest and reserved in character, is one of the great gems of the Psalter. Because of its very unpretentiousness it may easily be overlooked. Yet it throws light upon one of the cardinal Christian virtues, which is always intimately linked with trust, the virtue of humility. It is parallel to passages like Matt. 19:3; Jas. 4:6; I Pet. 5:5.

Though it sings the praises of humility it does not make the mistake of having the writer pride himself on his humility, a mistake that is made only too easily. It avoids doing this by its very simplicity, brevity, and deep insight.

We have here a record of the experience of an individual. In that sense there is something autobiographical about the psalm. The writer gives us a brief glimpse into his own soul and into what happened there. But when that story is completed, he cannot but share with his people what he has learned. For the nation needs this lesson as badly as does the individual. It may almost be said that the nation of the Jews was in special need of being reminded of this point. Yet if we were to say so we might miss the very point that the psalm would make by aiming the psalm at others rather than at ourselves.

Very few interpreters accept as valid the heading which ascribes the psalm to David. We need not in this case insist on the correctness of the assertion because the words "of David" are missing in a number of versions. Still to think of David as being the author does not seem to be so much beside the point. We have one specific instance on record when he spoke sentiments that are in the spirit of this psalm (cf., II Sam. 6:21f.). We know furthermore that he manfully controlled himself by refusing to snatch at things that were too high and too difficult for him in the days when Saul was king and David had to practice humility at court and in numerous other difficult situations. Nor did he later as king aspire to achieve greatness by attacking other kings and rulers. All his wars were defensive in character. Certainly, David exemplified what this psalm teaches more than did many another famous character on the pages of the Old Testament.

A pilgrimage song. Of David.
1. *O Lord, my heart is not haughty;*
   And my eyes are not proud;
   Nor am I engaged in things too great and too difficult for me.
2. *But rather I have stilled and quieted my soul;*
   As a weaned child rests at its mother's bosom,
   So my soul within me is weaned.
3. *O Israel, hope in the Lord*
   From henceforth and forevermore.

1. The writer records a result that he has achieved: he claims that pride has been put aside. Pride always has its seat deep in the heart. From that citadel it has been ousted as far as he is concerned. Pride expresses itself in the glance of the eye more clearly than in any other way. From that field it has been removed. Its goals are objectives that are great and difficult of achievement. These have been totally disavowed. In this category are things that a man should not aim at, things that the Almighty never destined him to have, but things after which the proud aspire whether it pleases their Maker or not.

One could read a tone of pride into this verse, but that would be as unwarranted as it is uncharitable. As far as the writer is concerned, he merely catalogues what things have been overcome in his life, and that victory extends from the inmost core of his being to the peripheral objectives that he might otherwise be pursuing. The verse has a similarity in spirit to the word addressed to Baruch, Jer. 45:5, admonishing him to let high-flying goals be abandoned.

2. Whereas the first verse mentioned results achieved, this one shows how they were attained. It was not without an inner struggle. The writer had to take himself in hand: he "stilled and quieted" his soul.

There may have been a time when great plans and mighty projects surged through his thoughts and drove him onward along the road of ambition. In some way he came to see that it is wrong for a man to seek great things for himself and to aim at that type of fame. When the wrongness of his course became apparent, he desisted from his former pursuits.

He takes a child as his model, and again we are reminded of the episode recorded in Matt. 18, where the Savior instructed His disciples to follow such a course. As the weaned child rests content at its mother's side, no longer clamoring for the breast, so he, weaned of his ambitions, rests content to be at the side of his God. Though God is not mentioned at this point, it is He that was addressed in the opening statement of the psalm just as it is He to whom the writer points His people as their sole refuge (v. 3). Godly experience has taught men that the soul will never desist from its unseemly worldly objectives until it has found its true rest and peace in God.

3. What follows is more than a loose appendage to the preceding. It is more than a practical application of the truth experienced personally. There is apparently a parallel between the writer and his situation and the nation and its situation. For the greater likelihood is that the psalm is postexilic in character. The prophets of the Restoration had promised great things to the returnees who had ventured back from Babylon. Many may have come back inspired in part by the glamor of the future that had been held before them. All these glorious goals seemed to fail of realization. What had in reality failed was the physical aspect of goals that had been conceived in too material a fashion. Outward objectives had to be cast aside. The true inner objectives had to be sought. The nation had to still and quiet its soul just as the individual in the psalm did. The psalmist's whole experience, recorded in the first two verses, may in part have been tied up with the renunciation of Israel's wordly ambitions. Having learned his lesson, he was the better qualified to teach it to his people, and that is what he does in this verse. By emphasizing that this virtue of true humility is to be cultivated—for what is hoping in the Lord other than the essence of true humility?—and cultivated "from henceforth and forevermore" the writer indicates that no one and no nation can arrive at the point where the need of humbleness of mind is outgrown.

By its very brevity and simplicity this psalm teaches its lesson all the more effectively.

NOTES

2. The initial '*im-lo*' is not to be construed conditionally (*KJ*) but in the sense of an adversative "but rather"; see *GK* 149e and *KS* 391t.

Psalm 132

PRAYER FOR THE LORD'S BLESSING
UPON THE SANCTUARY

FOR THE UNDERSTANDING of this psalm it is especially important to fit it into a situation where the various parts fall into their proper places. We have not been able to find a statement of time or a situation for this psalm that is better than the one *Luther* expressed in his day: "This is a prayer-psalm in which Solomon or the people pray that the priesthood and the kingdom may be upheld." We would attempt to be a little more precise by adding that the psalm seems to be designed for the dedication of the Temple in Solomon's day. Though there is some reason for believing that Solomon may be the writer, it is better to regard the people as the ones that offer this prayer. In the first ten verses the prayer, chiefly for the sanctuary, is presented; in the remaining verses the answer is recorded, an answer that reflects what the believing congregation may legitimately hope to receive from the Lord. In this connection we should like to remark that though v. 13 may be regarded as a thought that is interjected by the people it may be regarded as being spoken by the Lord Himself, for it is not unnatural for the Lord by way of variety to refer to Himself in the third person, a procedure that is found rather commonly in the Scriptures. Among more recent writers only *Maclaren* and *Delitzsch* date the psalm as we suggest.

Those who favor the postexilic dating of this psalm are moved to choose this date by the fact that the psalm appears in the collection of the psalms of pilgrimage, most of which without a doubt come from that period. But the exclusive reference to the situation as it prevailed in David's time would suggest that the psalm originated near the time of that outstanding king and near the great work of this king that is alluded to in the psalm. The fact that this poem appears among pilgrim psalms may well be explained by the incidence that it presents thoughts concerning the holy sanctuary which are of value to pilgrims perennially. We are not impressed by the arguments that lead some interpreters to claim for the psalm a late pre-exilic date such as the days of Hezekiah.

Somewhat intriguing is the contention of some recent writers who state that this was a psalm that was to be used on the occasion of the

New Year's Festival and to be sung in procession. The different parts of the psalm seem to fit readily into place (see *Leslie* and *Taylor,* also *Schmidt*). However, the doubtful character of this New Year's Festival of which these writers make so much and the Scriptures make so little; the equally dubious character of the festival of the enthronement of Yahweh, for which again they cite so many passages, none of which alone and all of which together cannot establish their case; and the quite dubious nature of the enthronement festival of the king of Judah, which is also—though not on good Scriptural grounds—assigned to the same day—all these together present a very doubtful case, and with the contentions involved fall all the high-sounding claims that are made for the interpretation of this psalm which calls it a processional psalm for this composite festival.

The one psalm that has a close kinship with this one is, Ps. 89 with this difference, that Ps. 89, especially toward the close, manifests a very depressing attitude whereas this Ps. 132 has a confident note running through the whole of it.

Another question which is vigorously debated in connection with the interpretation of the psalm is this: Is this psalm Messianic? The difference in opinion on this matter is sometimes due to differing definitions of what the term "Messianic" involves. If the claim is made that the psalm does not specifically refer to the Messiah, it may have to be allowed that taken literally that claim is true. On the other hand, since such glorious promises had been made with reference to the house of David and the glorious future of the seed of David; and since furthermore prayer for David in this sense appears to be made in this psalm, prayer which obviously reaches to the deepest implication of this promise, we cannot help but feel that in that sense the psalm is Messianic in its ultimate implications, and that the men who used it at the time it was written were not ignorant of these implications.

a) **The prayer itself that was offered at the dedication (vv. 1–10)**
   A pilgrimage song.
   1. Remember, O Lord, in David's behalf
      All the concern he displayed.
   2. How he swore to the Lord
      And vowed to the Mighty God of Jacob:
   3. "I will not enter the tent of my house,
      Nor lie down upon the resting place of my bed;
   4. I will not give sleep to my eyes,
      Nor slumber to my eyelids;
   5. Until I find a sanctuary for the Lord,
      An exalted dwelling for the Mighty God of Jacob."

6. *"Lo, we heard of it in Ephratha;*
   We found it in the fields of Jaar.
7. *Let us go up to His exalted dwelling;*
   Let us worship at His footstool!"
8. *Arise, O Lord, and go to Thy resting place,*
   Thou and the ark of Thy might.
9. *Let Thy priests be clothed with righteousness;*
   And let Thy saints shout for joy.
10. *For Thy servant David's sake*
    Do not reject the petition of Thy anointed one.

1. We remind ourselves: the Temple of Solomon is about to be dedicated or has already been dedicated. The congregation recalls prayerfully the course of events that led directly to this work of building, for it is most instructive; the Temple can scarcely be understood unless these facts are recalled. At that time David had manifested great "concern" about having a structure reared for the Lord. The prayer now being made is to the effect that all the things that David sought so eagerly at that time might be realized. God is asked to recall David's eagerness and his prayers.

2. For he made a vow at that time and swore an oath that he would do what his position as king of God's people demanded of him, that Israel might have a worthy sanctuary. The reference is apparently to II Sam. 7:2. To tell the truth, nothing is there said about his having sworn an oath. So we must regard the form of statement here made as a rather free recasting of the facts of that event. His solemn resolution deserves to be regarded as an oath. In effect the oath amounted to this, that he would do nothing, not even rest or eat, until he had put his plans into execution. In a kind of hyperbole he is represented as vowing not to take rest upon his bed or even enter his house, not even to sleep or slumber in any sense until a dwelling place for the "Mighty God of Jacob" has been provided. We could interpret this to mean that he would not relax until he had something tangible by way of results.

A few incidental explanations along the line of these five verses are in order. The plea that the Lord might remember what David did in his day reminds us of similar prayers that were offered by Nehemiah (cf., Neh. 5:19; 13:14, 22, 31), a similarity which, however, gives no warrant for dating this psalm at the time of Nehemiah. The name for God used here, "the Mighty God of Jacob," is unique and choice, appearing, however, as early as Gen. 49:24.

6. By reminding the Lord of what David did and recalling his efforts and prayers the nation makes these prayers her own and seeks God's blessings upon the new sanctuary which is even now being dedicated.

Psalm 132

There follows a distinct turn of the thought. In fact, vv. 6 and 7 are the most difficult verses in the psalm. Without attempting to explore all possibilities we present certain results as briefly as possible, incorporating what seems to us the most plausible interpretation.

The people are still speaking. They recall events that some of the older people of their time may have shared during David's earlier life. They recall what many who were minded as David was and under David's leadership said at that time. In Ephratha, another name for David's ancestral home, Bethlehem, (cf. Mic. 5:2) the report came to them that the ark was still in hiding, buried, as it were, and all but forgotten in Kirjath-jearim, in the house of Abinadad (I Sam. 7:1f.). The expression "fields of Jaar" may be regarded as another form of the name of the town just mentioned, Kirjath-jearim. When David and likeminded friends heard in Bethlehem that the ark could be located in Abinadab's house they went on a search and found that the report was true.

7. This verse seems to be a summary of the sentiments David and his friends expressed at that time and implied that their expedition was undertaken, not merely to verify a rumor or to satisfy their curiosity, but, as Israel had been told to do in Mosaic times, to worship at this place of God's manifestation that was marked by the symbol of the ark. Even though the tent-house that had been provided at Abinadab's home may have been quite insignificant, because of what it housed it is called "His exalted dwelling." For the fact that this at the same time represented God's throne among men is implied in the further name here given, "His footstool." Over the ark God sat enthroned, though invisibly.

8. After this prayer had recorded what good sentiments were stirring in the hearts of godly men it moves over into the area of petition. An old prayer is used with a new meaning. In the days of the wanderings in the wilderness the Israelites had a formulated prayer by the use of which they besought the Lord to go before them each time a new stretch of their journey was to be undertaken. According to Num. 10:35 this prayer read thus: "Arise, O Lord, and let Thy enemies be scattered!" Since this prayer always involved the removal of the ark of the covenant to a new site, it is quite appropriate to have the prayer used again at the time when the ark was to be transferred to its new location in Jerusalem. The fact that the ark is regarded as "the ark of Thy might" or "Thy mighty ark" reminds the readers of those instances when grave disasters befell men who ventured to treat the ark without due respect (I Sam. 5:3f., 9f.; 6:19; II Sam. 6:7).

9. The original prayer is given greater scope in that it is enlarged to ask special grace for the priests, who ministered before the ark, the

petition being that these priests might "be clothed with righteousness," that is to say, that an even better garb than proper priestly attire might be theirs, namely, the garb of unblamable behavior which would fit them all the better for faithful service before the Lord. Since the whole transaction was one that called forth the enthusiastic approval of all godly men or "saints," these are bidden to express their joy with exuberant shouts. Since in addition to all this David himself, no doubt, accompanied the whole transaction with earnest prayer (especially after the tragic incident recorded in II Sam. 6:7) that God might prosper the undertaking, and that all might be done in a manner that was worthy of the Lord, their God.

10. The prayer concludes with a request that David's petition may not be rejected. He is the "anointed one" that is being referred to. Prayers like these accompanied the undertaking of providing proper housing for the sacred ark of the covenant; they were made in connection with the building of the Temple of Solomon. Such undertakings were apparently understood in their spiritual import more adequately than we have usually supposed.

b) **The Lord's answer, as the pious mind conceives it (vv. 11–18)**

11. *The Lord swore to David a faithful oath, from which He will not turn:*
    "I will set one of your own sons on your throne.
12. *If your sons will keep My covenant and My testimonies, which I taught them,*
    Also their sons shall sit forever upon your throne."
13. *For the Lord has chosen Zion;*
    He has desired it for His dwelling place.
14. *"This is My resting place forever;*
    Here will I dwell, for I have desired it.
15. *I will abundantly bless her provisions;*
    I will satisfy her poor with bread.
16. *Her priests will I clothe with salvation;*
    And her saints shall shout aloud for joy.
17. *There will I make a horn to sprout for David;*
    I have prepared a lamp for My anointed one.
18. *His enemies will I clothe with shame;*
    And upon himself his crown will gleam."

11. This is the Lord's answer to the people's prayer for His holy house. It is a free reproduction and elaboration of the promise that the Lord gave to David in II Sam. 7:11b ff. with special emphasis on what that promise involved for the sanctuary, because if the special occasion involved is the dedication of the Temple, that issue would claim special

attention. According to v. 2 David made an oath to the Lord, here the Lord is represented as making a solemn oath to David. Yet the record of what God said (II Sam. 7:11b), does not present God as actually having made an oath. Yet a solemn assurance made by the Lord may to all intents and purposes be described by the term "oath." The substance of the promise made is briefly offered in vv. 11b and 12, namely, a statement to the effect that a dynastic line will be established for David, depending for its tenure on the keeping of the covenant and testimonies that God had taught the children of Israel. But since on this occasion the interest was less the dynasty and much rather the sanctuary, the center of emphasis shifts from the former to the latter in v. 13.

13. As indicated above, this verse may be regarded as the continuation of the words of the Lord that were addressed to David, which were based chiefly on the episode described in II Sam. 24:18ff. After the pestilence had been averted from Jerusalem, the fact that God wanted a sacrifice offered on the mount where he had appeared to David assured the king that this was the place that the Lord had chosen for His permanent residence among His people. Though it is more precisely called Mount Moriah, it is frequently designated by the better known name of Zion. God's choice of the site of the Temple is recalled by this verse.

14. This verse developes the thought still farther by relating it, as it were, to the petition uttered in v. 8. The people had implored the Lord to come to the place where He would desire to abide. This is God's assurance that He will be pleased to do so and His further assurance that it is by His own choice that this place is to be His.

15. To this is appended another promise that is described as conveying the will of the Lord in this connection. Although His people had not asked Him to do so, He promised that He would bless the very food and drink of His people and would have special regard for the needs of the poor.

16. This verse is obviously related to the prayer uttered in v. 9 by indicating that God will be pleased to grant what His people asked there. However, in each case God's assurance is quite a bit richer than is the blessing that was originally asked for. The petition had been that priests might be clothed with righteousness; God promises that He Himself will clothe them with "salvation"—a richer concept than "righteousness" and implying that He will make their ministrations rebound to the salvation of God's people. Whereas the prayer had been that God's saints might shout for joy, the response is that they shall be induced to "shout aloud" for joy. God is always more ready to give than His people are to ask.

17. The petition uttered in v. 10 had been to the effect that all these

blessings might be granted by God "for David's sake." Once again God's promises exceed what was asked for. The Hebrew mode of speech that He "will make a horn to sprout for David" means that God will make of the house of David a powerful, victorious set of rulers, for "horn" often signifies might and power or a mighty and powerful ruler (cf., Dan. 7:7f., 24; 8:5). Similarly the statement, "I have prepared a lamp for my anointed one," indicates the continuance of the line or house of David as I Kings 11:36; 15:4; and II Sam. 21:17 indicate.

In the light of the great things that God promised David in the original passage (II Sam. 7:11b ff.) all this must refer to much more than the mere fact that David's line shall not die out, and rulers that descended from him shall occupy the throne of Judah. The promise reached even to eternity, and so there is included in all this, as the Jews in the pre-Christian days clearly recognized, the outlook that includes none less than the Messiah Himself. That interpretation certainly adds rich luster to the statement that God has prepared a lamp for His anointed one, i.e., for David.

18. This verse indicates in what further ways God will place His blessing upon the line of David's descendants. He will be victorious over all his enemies. That "he" includes both David and his greater Son, who gained a remarkable victory over all His foes. Upon both together "his crown will gleam." To ignore the glorious climax which a word like this reaches in the Christ is to cut out the very heart of what is here implied. It may well be true that not all of those who lived in Solomon's day saw the deep implications of Messianic thought in this passage. But for the enlightened ones this passage must have meant all that we claim for it.

NOTES

5. *Maqom* may be translated "place." Since in some instances it may mean sanctuary as similar Arabic usage of our day indicates, the latter translation is not out of place here. The noun *mishkanoth*, a plural, would by the use of the plural form convey the impression of the unusual importance of the structure. Though it may have been merely a tent as indicated above, the plural may convey the impression of "exalted dwelling."

6. One of the difficulties of this verse is that the object suffix attached to the verb "heard" would usually have to be translated, "we heard it." But here the connection seems to demand: "we heard *of* it." The question then is: To what does "it" refer? V. 8 belatedly brings the noun to which the pronoun "it" refers. This is not without analogy and far from an impossible construction. The "it" in "we found it" is to be explained in the same way. Attempts to have Ephrathah refer to Kir-

jath-jearim by using Ephrathah in the root meaning of a fruitful place strike us as being somewhat unnatural.

10. The Hebrew idiom reads thus: "Do not turn away the face." Since a petition is being considered, we understand this to express the thought: "Do not reject the petition."

12. The form of the suffix on 'edhothi is the one used on singular nouns. But this is a plural. So the conjecture seems in place that the form should be read 'edhuthi (without changing a consonant in the text). Zo, the demonstrative, is here used as a relative; see *GK* 34b.

It may yet be added that Gunkel (*Einleitung in die Psalmen,* p. 411) regards the psalm as one that was sung annually at the commemoration of the bringing of the ark to the Holy City.

Psalm 133

IN PRAISE OF BROTHERLY UNITY

IN EVALUATING this psalm difficulty is caused by unduly limiting the unity described in it. One such limitation insists that the psalm aims to re-establish an old custom, which, it is asserted, was once quite common among the Israelites, that is to say, the custom of having two brothers, after they were married, dwell together under one roof, perhaps the old ancestral roof of the old homestead. Another such undue limitation of the unity described refers it exclusively to the congregating of the children of Israel at the sanctuary on the occasions of the high festivals when all tribes of Israel mingled in the Holy City. Still another such limitation thinks of the unity involved as being only that of having men preserve outward unity without obvious and visible disturbance of the peace. In the other direction it would be equally one-sided to think only in terms of some inner fellowship of the spirit, as though it alone could be under consideration.

We believe rather that any and every kind of unity that can be observed among brethren is here praised as being most commendable, chiefly, of course, the obvious outer unity which is based on true fellowship of the spirit. For the points of emphasis grammatically (v. 1) are the last two words—"in unity," *gam yachadh,* where *gam* is used "with stress on a particular word" (*BDB* sub verb.). The familiar *KJ* and *RSV* versions cover the case in point very nicely: "when brethren dwell together *in unity*." *Luther* conveys the same emphasis by the adverb *eintraechtiglich*. Such a translation covers all the possibilities enumerated above. The psalm attempts to sing the praise of unity in every form. It praises it where it exists; it indirectly commends seeking after it where it does not exist. From this latter point of view this psalm is didactic in purpose and may be classed among the wisdom psalms, which often involve something of the element of instruction.

When we come to the matter of authorship, it may be pointed out that Davidic authorship of the psalm is not impossible. The claim to the contrary (the use of the shortened relative *she* before the participle) is not convincing. This form appears, for example, in Judg. 5 and may also be found in earlier writings though it is more common in later Hebrew. Historically it must be admitted that the subject that this psalm stresses would have been most apt if it had come from the mouth of David, for prior to his time there had been altogether too little unity in Israel. Now that the blessings of unity were becoming apparent, it would have been most appropriate for him to remind North and South Israel to seek to cultivate true unity more extensively.

Yet we would not insist on Davidic authorship though textually the "of David" in the heading is the better attested reading. The fact that this heading is lacking in the *Targum* and in some manuscripts of the *Septuagint* shows that there was a question about its validity. We cannot seriously object to the claim of those who feel that the psalm would fit better historically into the days of Nehemiah when as Neh. 11:1f. shows efforts were being made to promote the dwelling together of more Israelites in Jerusalem.

We regard it as unfortunate that only one kind of unity enjoys favor with a larger number of commentators at the present. We refer to what has become the popular interpretation, alluded to above, the interpretation that *Schmidt* seems to have encouraged most though it had *Koenig's* sanction several decades earlier—this idea of persuading brothers to revive the old custom of having two families dwell under one roof. *Oesterley* argues so strongly for this interpretation that he actually makes the healthy family life of the nation depend on the revival of such an old custom. Experience has amply shown that even when relations are harmonious and friendly the dwelling together under one roof can put an intolerable strain on the best friendship. The natural trend the world over is not only for man to leave father and mother (Gen. 2:24) but also brother and sister and establish a separate household.

We can scarcely offer an outline of the psalm. Its structure is simply this: What it offers by way of praise of brotherly unity is made more attractive by two comparisons, one in v. 2, the other in v. 3.

A pilgrimage song. Of David.
1. Behold, how good and how pleasant it is
   When brothers dwell together in unity!
2. It is like the precious oil upon the head,
   That ran down upon the beard, Aaron's beard,
   That even ran down to the collar of his robe.
3. It is like the dew of Hermon
   That ran down on the mountains of Zion;
   For there the Lord has commanded the blessing, life forevermore.

It is true that, when Israel went on pilgrimage to the sanctuary, the nation would see the blessings of fraternal association beautifully exemplified. Therefore it would have been most apt to have this psalm sung on such pilgrimages.

1. The initial "behold" points the finger at the blessings of unity among brethren, no matter when and where it manifests itself. It is always "good," that is, beneficial and "pleasant," that is, delightful to encounter. "Dwell" apparently refers to social contacts of every description as they are to be met with in daily associations of men one with the other. This word praises it where it exists. It commends the establishment of it where it does not exist.

2. The first comparison used to establish the correctness of v. 1 strikes us as being a bit inept. That is due to the difference between the Oriental and the Occidental points of view. To the Israelites this was a meaningful and sanctified simile. Whether it was suggested by seeing the high priest function at sacrifices in the Temple during the high festivals, or whether it was a recalling of matters recorded in the sacred writings of Israel is quite unimportant. One is as possible as is the other. In any case, the children of Israel remembered the tradition of the anointing of Aaron with the holy oil (cf., Exod. 29:7; 30:22ff.), and that holy rite was impressive and instructive. As one at that time could have seen it as a bystander if one stood near enough, or as many had relived the scene in their imagination at a later day—it was a solemn moment when the holy oil was poured in abundance on the high priest's head. The oil symbolized the rich gifts of the Spirit. The abundant use of it would most likely recall only that constructive thought. One could easily visualize how the oil ran down the beard and even, for that matter, down to, and onto, the collar of his priestly vestments.

This seems to suggest that a parallel blessing is unity, when head and body are of one mind. The blessing of unity seems to drip down from the leading spirits in the nation to the members of less importance in the official and the social scale. The blessing drops down on all and infuses itself into them. The Spirit's blessings thrive so much more richly when brotherly unity prevails; it is so much more difficult to enjoy these blessings when discord tears men apart and sets them at variance with one another. The figure has a charm and a rich meaning all its own.

3. The second comparison, drawn from the realm of nature, seems to require less interpretation, except for the fact that the dew of Hermon is said to descend on Mt. Zion, several hundred miles to the south. As far as this problem is concerned, the likelihood is that Hermon dews were proverbially copious. This is not instruction in meteorology but a poetic figure. Just as heavy dews refresh and invigorate plant life, so the blessing of unity descends alike on all those that are within the church, and all godly virtues thrive and flourish. Discord disrupts, destroys, and kills all the finer things that could grow under the blessing of true unity. Or to use the words of the psalm: "For there the Lord has commanded the blessing, life forevermore." A proper emphasis is placed on the divine causation. When men cultivate harmony, it is not they who make things thrive and flourish in the kingdom of God. God can bestow His blessing there because man has not interposed obstacles that prevent that blessing from becoming a reality. All the blessings of God are summed up in "life" in the richest sense of the word. Thus life is to some extent, dependent on true unity.

In the last part of the third verse it becomes apparent that the author is speaking in terms of spiritual values when he traces the blessings resulting from unity to the creative blessing of God. The close puts a higher element into the whole interpertation of the psalm.

NOTES

2. It may be questioned whether in the last line of this verse the thought should not be that the *beard,* not the oil, runs down to the collar of Aaron's robe. This construction is possible by construing *sheyyoredh* with *zaqan* rather than with *shemen.* But to have the same participle twice in close succession refer in the one instance to one noun and a moment later to another is quite unlikely.

Psalm 134

AN EXHORTATION TO PRAISE THE LORD

IT IS OBVIOUSLY helpful toward interpretation to determine the circumstances out of which a given psalm grew. But there are psalms which do not aid the interpreter in arriving at definite conclusions. The psalm before us is such. Quite a few possibilities as to what the original purpose may have been have been suggested, almost all of them equally plausible. Every interpreter grants that vv. 1, 2 are of one piece, and that v. 3 is in the nature of a response. The first section has been regarded by quite a few writers as being spoken by the congregation of Israel which is exhorting the priests; it might be possible, however, that they were spoken by the high priest in exhortation of the other priests. These verses might be a summons that was addressed to all worshipers; they might with equal likelihood have been addressed to priests who constituted a Temple watch. These words might again have been spoken to a small band of watchers as they were making their rounds at night (cf., I Chron. 9:33). The occasion might have been some special festival (Is. 30:29). We may have here an exhortation to prayer or possibly to pronounce a blessing, for the verb involved is used in both senses. *Luther* thought this to be an exhortation that was addressed by the writer of the psalm to all priests of all times to attend faithfully to their priestly duties, whatever they may be.

Though the precise origin and purpose of the psalm cannot be determined with any measure of finality, the manifold uses to which it may be put are obvious. It no doubt lay within the intention of those who incorporated the psalm into the Psalter to have it applied in whatever way men saw that it could be used.

As a matter of convenience we shall follow *Oesterley* who seems to have given as feasible an explanation as any we have encountered. He calls this "an exhortation to the priests sung by the high priest before the beginning of the service; the last verse is a response by the priestly choir .... It is a vigil service."

The psalm certainly lent itself to use by pilgrims, and thus its presence among the pilgrim songs may be justified. The pilgrims may have used it as a parting salutation to the priests, either during the last night service when there were such, or in the early morning hours when they left for their home before the dawn had broken.

A pilgrimage song.
1. Lo, bless the Lord, all you servants of the Lord,
Who stand in the house of the Lord by night!
2. Lift up your hands toward the sanctuary
And bless the Lord.
3. May the Lord bless you from Zion,
He who made heaven and earth.

1. The word "lo" usually draws attention to some significant item that is liable to be underestimated or overlooked. Blessing God is one of the sacred obligations that is frequently not given due attention, no matter how one understands the psalm. "Servants of the Lord" may clearly be laymen as well as priests. There is nothing in the psalm that points to the one or the other with unmistakable clearness. For either of the two may stand before the Lord also in worship services that were conducted during the night. Yet it must be admitted that to "stand" before the Lord is a technical expression which signifies some type of official service of God in the sanctuary (cf., Deut. 10:8; 18:7; I Chron. 23:30; II Chron. 29:11). It may yet be remarked that the expression "bless the Lord" means about as much as to "praise" Him, that is to say, to tell of His mighty acts.

3. In this verse an individual blessing is spoken on the worshipers. It is true that officially only the priests were permitted to pronounce a blessing in public worship. But who would deny the possibility of a pious wish being uttered by any man in behalf of another in the words: "May the Lord bless you from Zion?" Zion is mentioned to recall to mind that that is the place where He has chosen to have His dwelling among His people. What He appoints He honors; there we should seek Him (cf., Ps. 9:11; 76:2). In order that no man may think too lightly of Him whose blessing is involved the words are added, "He who made heaven and earth."

Psalm 135

PRAISE OF THE LORD, THE ONLY TRUE GOD, FOR HIS MERCY SHOWN TO ISRAEL

FROM ITS PLACE in the Psalter and from its general tone we may conclude that this psalm is of a postexilic date; Neh. 9:4, 5 seems to describe an analogous situation. This psalm may also be regarded as a sort of expansion of the one that precedes it. Beyond this very little can be said.

On closer investigation it becomes apparent that the psalm quotes frequently from earlier psalms and should, therefore, be called a mosaic. Lest this designation seem to involve an unwarranted criticism, we add the words of *Maclaren:* "The flowers are arranged in a new bouquet, because the poet had long delighted in their fragrance." In the process of inspiring men for the sacred writings the Spirit of God used manifold approaches.

The fact that the psalm may from the very outset have been designed for liturgical use, and that of a responsive character, in the Temple worship of Israel can scarcely be questioned. But to attempt to divide the psalm into parts from this point of view and to assign these parts to the various voices or groups is quite difficult. We must admit that too many possibilities confront us in such an effort. The words of *Oesterley* deserve to be heeded: "That it was designed for use in the worship of the Temple is obvious; and that it was sung antiphonally is also clear; but to assign the different parts to the respective singers is a somewhat precarious proceeding."

Before we proceed we may list the verses in the psalm that are quotations. With v. 1 cf. Ps. 113:1; with v. 2, Ps. 134:1; with v. 4, Exod. 19:5; Deut. 7:6; with v. 5, Exod. 19:5; 18:11; with v. 7, Jer. 10:13; vv. 10–12 are parallel with Ps 136:17–22 (without our being able to tell which of these psalms deserves priority in point of time); vv. 13–18 are to be compared with Is. 44:12–20; Jer. 10:6–10; vv. 15–20 are a slight readaptation of Ps. 115:4–11.

a) A summons to praise the Lord (vv. 1–4)
   1. *Praise the Lord!*
   Praise the name of the Lord, praise, O you servants of the Lord,

2. *You that stand in the house of the Lord,*
   In the courts of the house of our God!
3. *Praise the Lord, for the Lord is good;*
   Sing praises to His name, for that is pleasant!
4. *For the Lord has chosen Jacob for Himself,*
   Israel for His valued property.

1. In this summons to praise it is difficult to determine who is to be thought of as exhorting or to whom he addresses his exhortation. For practical purposes it matters little. The ultimate purpose may have been to incorporate the psalm into the divine Word, and when we say: "God's Word exhorts us to praise," it in fact exhorts all men to praise. Yet it is quite likely that, when the servants of the Lord who "stand in the house of the Lord" are specially addressed, we cannot help but think of men who were engaged officially in some form of Temple service. But here again, as was noted in the interpretation of Ps. 134, the expression used could be applied to all worshipers in God's house. If this praise is to center upon "the name of the Lord," that implies the totality of God's blessed works for His people that the mere mention of His name calls to remembrance.

3. Another summary is contained in the words "for He is good." Although this is quite general in character it is still a notably correct statement of all that God's people can at any time predicate about the Lord. The further motivation supplied for praising the Lord vocally in song is that this is a very pleasant occupation. This construction of the thought deserves preference over the two other possibilities. God's name is pleasant, or He is pleasant. The last named is somewhat artificial, to say the least.

4. In this summons to praise this verse is no longer a summons but assigns a major reason for praise, which is, however, not out of place. The nation of Israel was bound frequently to reflect upon the fact that she stood in a very special relation to God by virtue of her election. God has elevated her above other nations by choosing her for Himself and making her "His valued property," which may also be rendered, "His prized possession," an expression which dates back to Exod. 19:4; Deut. 7:6.

b) **He is to be blessed for His works in nature (vv. 5–7)**

5. *I know indeed that the Lord is great,*
   And that our Lord is above all gods.
6. *The Lord does whatever He pleases*
   In heaven and in earth, in the sea and in all the deeps.

7. *He makes the clouds to rise at the ends of the earth;*
He makes lightnings for the rain;
He brings forth the wind out of His storehouses.

5. Attention is first drawn to the realm of nature where the Lord is known to do works that would almost involuntarily lead men to praise Him as they give thought to what He does. When the pronoun of the first person suddenly appears at this point, one may be tempted to view the verse in question as some interpreters do as a solo which was spoken, let us say, by a priest. Equally to the point is the assumption that the individual who spoke the original summons to praise (vv. 1-4) here speaks in his own name and in his own person as is in part indicated by the use of the pronoun, which equals the English construction, "I for my part know." He has some strong convictions of his own on the matter. In the Hebrew "to know" usually refers to a matter regarding which a man has some measure of experience. The conviction of God's greatness has been driven home to this man's consciousness, in fact, to the point where he knows that the Lord is immeasurably "above all gods." By stating the case thus he is not granting that the gods of the heathen have existence; in fact, vv. 15ff. of this psalm prove the very contrary. The word itself reminds the reader of Exod. 15:11; 18:11.

6. The speaker moves on to give obvious proof of his claim by references to phenomena in the realm of nature. Many more could have been mentioned. All those that are referred to are striking. In a general way it may be claimed in this area that "the Lord does whatever He pleases." He is a law unto Himself. He asks permission of no man. He consults with none, for none can advise Him. Four areas in which mighty works of His are in evidence are mentioned: heaven, earth, sea, and the deeps. That is to say: Look wherever you will and striking works of God's sovereign rule stand out prominently.

7. Do you want examples? There is the eternal mystery of the clouds which seem to originate at almost any point on the horizon and move in on us. God makes them. There are the lightnings which are so commonly attendants upon the rainstorms, making the latter glorious in a somewhat terrifying way. God makes these lightnings. There are the winds of varying intensity, sometimes gentle and pleasant, sometimes horrifying in their fury. They stem from the Lord. Frequently, as here, the Old Testament Scriptures very properly dwell on the awe-inspiring character of the manifestations of God's glory. Viewed with a devout mind, all these works of the Lord call forth our praises.

c) **He is to be blessed for His works done for His people (vv. 8-14)**

8. *He it is who smote the first-born of Egypt,*
Both man and beast.

9. *He sent signs and wonders into your midst, O Egypt,*
   Upon Pharaoh and upon all his servants.
10. *He it is who smote many nations*
    And slew mighty kings,
11. *Sihon, king of the Amorites, and Og, king of Bashan,*
    And all the kingdoms of the Canaanites.
12. *And gave their land as a heritage,*
    A heritage for Israel, His people.
13. *O Lord, Thy name endures forever,*
    And Thy remembrance, O Lord, throughout all generations.
14. *For the Lord will execute judgment for His people*
    And will show mercy to His servants.

8. The second major area where God is known to work is His church or, to speak the language of the Old Testament, His people. The mighty works that He has done in their behalf should induce men to praise Him. Two special areas of this activity are brought to our attention in this connection: the deliverance from the bondage of Egypt and the occupation of the land of Canaan. Mighty works did shine forth with unusual splendor in this period of history.

9. First of all, there was that imposing climax of the Lord's judgments upon Egypt, the slaying of the first-born of man and beast. Signs and wonders of an appalling sort were done in the land, which the psalmist here apostrophizes. Especially was the Pharaoh himself involved in these signs, for he had ventured to challenge the Lord, and his servants had, no doubt, in a large measure shared this spirit of impudence.

10. In the matter of the occupation of the land of Canaan two events stood out with unusual clearness: the defeat of Sihon and the defeat of Og; Num. 21:21ff., 33ff.; Deut. 2:30ff.; 3:1ff. record the details of these events. Each of these accounts is comparatively brief. Thus the original record cannot be charged with glorifying warlike events overmuch. But we sense that the battle for Israel was in each case one that was waged against overwhelming odds. Yet the Lord gave a speedy and glorious victory to His people.

Thus He also gave into their hands "all the kingdoms of the Canaanites," that is, the territory west of the Jordan. As pleasantly as a heritage comes unearned into the hands of him who receives it, so did these lands fall to Israel's lot; and it was a pleasant experience. In doing these things the Lord made a name for Himself (v. 13), established a reputation, the remembrance of which would not soon be lost by His people.

14. To sum it all up, since in all these doings of His, the Lord was protecting the rights of His own people, this experience of theirs may

be expressed in the form of a general principle: "The Lord will execute judgment for His people." On this rule Deut. 32:36 may be compared. The other side of the matter is another form of a general rule which is that He "will show mercy to His servants," a reminder that His people have never merited such favors. They have been bestowed because the Lord is so good and so kind.

d) The utter vanity of the idols (vv. 15–18)

15. The idols of the nations are silver and gold,
    The work of man's hands.
16. They have mouths, but they do not speak;
    They have eyes, but they do not see.
17. They have ears, but they do not hear;
    Neither is there any breath in their mouths.
18. They that make them are like them;
    So is everyone that trusts in them.

This description of the utter vanity of the idols is in contrast to the glorious supremacy of the God of Israel, who so richly deserves the praises of His people. This picture of the idols serves to enhance the glory of Israel's Lord. The passage is the same as Ps. 115:4–8, with the exception of v. 7 of this latter section, which contains a few additional thoughts in the same vein. For the fuller interpretation of this section as well as of v. 6 of our psalm which serves as a preface to this section we refer to our treatment above (see Ps. 115:4–8).

e) A concluding summons to praise the Lord (vv. 19–21)

19. O House of Israel, praise the Lord;
    O house of Aaron, praise the Lord!
20. O house of Levi, praise the Lord;
    You that fear the Lord, praise the Lord!
21. Blessed be the Lord from Zion,
    He who dwells in Jerusalem!
    O praise the Lord!

The connection of thought is the fact that, if the Lord is so far above all the idols of the heathen, He more than ever deserves the praise which is the theme of this psalm. In a similar spirit Ps. 115:9–11 could exhort various groups to *trust* in the Lord. The enumeration of the various classes, here as there, apparently aims at reaching all men lest they fail to take their part in this grand work of praise. Ps. 118:2–4 has a similar approach. The nation, the priests, the Levites, as chief servants of the priests, and every last believer in the Lord are separately enumerated.

The last verse breathes the consciousness that God's dwelling among

His people at Jerusalem is no idle fiction. Where He dwells, it is particularly appropriate to praise Him.

NOTES

1. The long form (*Yahweh*) and the short form (*Yah*) of the divine name alternate in this verse, a difference which cannot be indicated in translation as can the difference between LORD for *Yahweh* and Lord for *Adhonay*.

5. The initial *ki* is best translated as the affirmative "indeed."

7. The construction begins with a participle and goes over into the finite verb. Cf. *KS* 4131. The participle *motse'* ("brings forth") has *e* instead of the usual *i* because the accent has been drawn back. Cf. *GK* 530.

9. The form *bethokhekhi* has an archaic *i* added to the feminine second person singular suffix.

10. *Weharagh* does not follow the usual *waw* consecutive construction because the verbs used are synonymns. Cf. *KS* 370k.

11. Sihon and Og have *le*, usually the sign of the dative but here introducing a direct object. *KS* 289i.

Psalm 136

HIS KINDNESS ENDURES FOREVER

WE LEAVE A PSALM of praise and come to a psalm of thanksgiving. As to structure this psalm is unique in the Psalter. Its refrain runs through the whole psalm and is always the same. Without the refrain the text would be in strict continuity; in fact, in some instances the refrain breaks into the midst of a statement.

One is quite involuntarily led to the conclusion that an arrangement such as this psalm has was originally designed for liturgical use, responsive or antiphonal. But here as in all similar cases it is impossible to determine exactly what the original pattern of the rendering of the psalm in public worship was. The first line of each verse could have been rendered by a solo voice or by a chorus. The second line, the refrain, was more than likely rendered by a chorus which very likely was the voice of the whole body of worshipers.

Special attention should be given to the key word of the refrain, which we have rendered "kindness." It is the Hebrew word *chésedh,*

Psalm 136

for which no single English or other language equivalent can be found. *KJ* translates "mercy." *RSV* prefers "steadfast love." *Taylor,* in *Interpreter's Bible,* has "kindness" as we have but adds that the term implies "fidelity" or "loyalty." We believe with *Koenig* that "covenant-faithfulness" comes close to catching the exact flavor of the word. But this is too cumbersome and seems to require an additional bit of explanation. So we use "kindness" as being the simplest of the possible equivalents.

All things point to a late date for the composition of the psalm. In Jewish tradition this psalm was called "the great Hallel" in distinction from the Hallel of Egypt. (Ps. 113–118).

a) **A threefold summons to give thanks (vv. 1–3)**
1. *O give thanks unto the Lord, for He is good;*
   For His kindness endures forever.
2. *O give thanks unto the God of gods;*
   For His kindness endures forever.
3. *O give thanks unto the Lord of lords;*
   For His kindness endures forever.

Basic to all thanksgiving is the conviction concerning the Lord that "He is good." But the significant experience that the people of God have concerning His goodness is in the area of His "kindness" to His people. In that respect the Lord is unwaveringly loyal because He is bound to His people by a solemn covenant which He entered into with their fathers (Gen. 15:18, etc.) as well as with the nation as a whole (Exod. 24:8). This psalm emphasizes that, in the last analysis, all the favors that God, the Lord, bestowed upon His people are traceable to this covenant. The exalted nature of Him who made the covenant is indicated by two superlatives: "God of gods" and "Lord of lords."

b) **The first motivation for thanks: God's work as Creator (vv. 4–9)**
4. *To Him who alone does great wonders;*
   For His kindness endures forever.
5. *To Him who with understanding made the heavens;*
   For His kindness endures forever.
6. *To Him who spread out the earth higher than the waters;*
   For His kindness endures forever.
7. *To Him who made the great lights;*
   For His kindness endures forever.
8. *The sun to rule the day;*
   For His kindness endures forever.
9. *The moon and the stars to rule the night;*
   For His kindness endures forever.

God's work as Creator of the world is under consideration. Though that work lies far in the past, its marvels and its benefits to us are so outstanding as to call for endless thanks. All of this work of His is presented under the category: He "alone does great wonders." Since the heavens are so uniquely marvelous, the modifying phrase is attached to the verb, "with understanding," a thought that occurs also in Prov. 3:19. For it surely required deep insight, such as man can never fathom, to accomplish so mighty a work. We believe that in v. 6 the translation may help the general reader by using "higher than" rather than "above" to show the relation of dry land to water. For to translate the simple Hebrew preposition "above" seems to argue for some strange notion that Israel and the ancients had about this relationship. Naturally sun, moon, and stars do in an unusual manner show forth the works of the Creator with unusual clearness and thus are mentioned separately. We frequently fail to thank God for these basic gifts that contribute so much to our well-being.

c) **The second motivation for thanks: His control of the realm of nature (vv. 10–15)**

10. *To Him who smote Egypt in their first-born;*
    For His kindness endures forever.
11. *And brought out Israel from among them;*
    For His kindness endures forever.
12. *With a strong hand and outstretched arm;*
    For His kindness endures forever.
13. *To Him who cut the Red Sea apart;*
    For His kindness endures forever.
14. *And led Israel across through the midst of it;*
    For His kindness endures forever.
15. *And tossed Pharaoh and his host into the Red Sea;*
    For His kindness endures forever.

The Lord's control that was manifested in the area of nature is also viewed from the point of view of having been exercised because of His "kindness" toward Israel. Here, if anywhere, the fact that it was "covenant faithfulness" that was meant appears in that a seeming paradox is involved: He manifested His kindness by smiting the first-born of Egypt. The deliverance from Egypt was so great an achievement that it deserved to be commemorated again and again. The descriptive phrase "with a strong hand and an outstretched arm" appears also in Deut. 4:34, which is the first use of this statement. Several exceptionally colorful verbs are used in this section: the Red Sea is said to have

Psalm 136 931

been "cut apart." Pharaoh is said to have "been tossed" into the Red Sea (literally "shaken").

d) The third motivation: His deliverance of His people (vv. 11-24)
16. *To Him who led His people through the wilderness;*
    For His kindness endures forever.
17. *To Him who smote great kings;*
    For His kindness endures forever;
18. *And slew famous kings;*
    For His kindness endures forever.
19. *Sihon, king of the Amorites,*
    For His kindness endures forever;
20. *And Og, king of Bashan;*
    For His kindness endures forever;
21. *And gave their land as a heritage;*
    For His kindness endures forever;
22. *A heritage to Israel forever;*
    For His kindness endures forever;
23. *Who remembered us when we were brought low;*
    For His kindness endures forever;
24. *And delivered us from our enemies;*
    For His kindness endures forever.

Various instances of great deliverance in Israel's glorious past are cited. The wilderness wanderings are mentioned, the occupation of the land, and the whole period of the monarchy and the captivity. Verse 23 covers all the instances when the nation was brought low by foes from near by or by foes from afar off. In the many instances when they "were brought low," the deliverance was solely the work of the Lord, who was faithful to His people because of the strong covenant that He had made with them. Then in a single verse the Lord's universal providence is alluded to, for Israel is not ignorant of the wideness in God's mercies:

e) The fourth motivation: His universal providence (v. 25)
25. *He who gives food to all flesh;*
    For His kindness endures forever.

This verse is simply a brief reminder that the kindness of the Lord is in no wise limited to Israel. It does not quite constitute the climax of the psalm; nor is it as has also been claimed an obviously later addition, which has no vital connection with what went before.

The psalm closes with v. 26, which is almost a repetition of v. 1 and rounds out the close by tying it up with the beginning.

f) The original summons reiterated (v. 26)
26. *O give thanks unto the God of heaven;*
For His kindness endures forever.

The new element in the verse is the designation of the Lord as "the God of heaven," an expression which is found only in the later books (Ezra 1:2; Neh. 1:4; II Chron. 36:23; Jonah 1:9; Dan. 2:18). The title is a reminder of the exalted nature of Him who did for His people all the mighty works which have been enumerated in the psalm.

NOTES

2. The expression "God of gods" is a typical Hebrew superlative (cf. *KS* 309i). The same holds true with regard to "Lord of lords" (v. 3). In the first expression the term gods does not admit that beings other than the Lord have a divine nature. It simply means: such as are called gods.

21. In the Hebrew the expression "and gave" would lead one to expect an imperfect form with *waw* conversive instead of the perfect here offered. The reason for this is that the strict continuity is in this instance broken by the refrain. Cf. *KS* 370n.

Psalm 137

THE EXILES IN BABYLONIAN CAPTIVITY

THE PRESENT-DAY READER is apt to find himself torn between conflicting emotions when reading this psalm. Strong sympathy wells up in his heart for the sorry lot of the captives in Babylon; a shock of horror at the almost implacable hatred that one seems to find expressed in the concluding verse. This latter impression may have to be modified slightly before a reader can say that he has entered fully into the spirit of the psalm on this point. It does, indeed, seem almost unthinkable that one and the same heart should be able to harbor such conflicting sentiments, the one so praiseworthy and deserving of imitation, and the other so utterly lacking in pity. This should give us pause. A charitable judgment would conclude that, if the love for the Holy City is as strong as it is here represented, it is so fine a godly virtue that it must have some sanctifying influence on the whole of a man's thinking. But let the further investigation into this problem be postponed till the last part of the psalm is being studied.

The time in which the psalm was composed must be determined somewhat more accurately. The past tenses used in the first two verses naturally lead to the conclusion that the Babylonian Captivity is a thing of the past, the comparatively recent past, because the memory of the grief of the captivity seems still quite fresh at the time of the composition of the psalm. Therefore, shortly after the captives had returned to Jerusalem, and while Babylon was still standing, this touching and challenging psalm was composed.

1. *By the rivers of Babylonia, there we sat and wept*
   When we remembered Zion.
2. *Upon the poplars there*
   We hung up our harps.
3. *For there our captors demanded of us songs,*
   And our oppressors something joyful,
   Saying: Sing us one of the songs of Zion!"

1. The psalm begins with an indication as to how deeply the love of the Holy City had taken root in the hearts of those who were in Babylonia as exiles. These poor Israelites would on occasion and by preference gather by the rivers of Babylonia (not merely of Babylon, the city; for there were other rivers that were more distant from Babylon where the captives also were stationed). Many suggestions have been offered as to why they should have been in the habit of gathering at the "rivers." The best one offered is the suggestion that the presence of water facilitated the ceremonial ablutions which were also a mark of the Hebrew religion (cf., Matt. 15:20; Mark 7:2, 5). Besides, there may have been comparative quiet along these streams, an atmosphere of quiet that was conducive to meditation and worship, cf. also Acts 16:13. The rivers of Babylon were more than the Euphrates and the Tigris; for many canals, a whole system of them in fact, were known to have connected these two major rivers for the purpose of extensive irrigation. There may, therefore, have been many spots that witnessed scenes like those here described.

The grief described is not the ordinary longing for the homeland, a longing which displaced persons may always have felt. It was rather occasioned by the fact that they remembered Zion and all that that ancient capital stood for: the Temple, its services, the remembrance of godly men that dwelt there, the mighty deliverances that God had wrought, the dynasty of David that had had its seat there, and the Holy City as the object of sacred pilgrimages during high festivals. All these facts would flood through the minds of captives and move them to bitter tears, which we cannot help but believe were frequently the tears of repentance.

2. These captives may often have brought their harps along, intending to beguile the sad hours with worldly or sacred music. The mood of the occasion usually did not allow them to resort to any kind of singing; and so they hung up their harps, often perhaps upon the very poplars that grew alongside these streams. For writers who have probed into the matter have concluded that a kind of Euphrates poplar, which flourished also along the Jordan, is the tree here described, a tree which does bear some resemblance to the willows we know.

3. In this verse one incident is described that may have been typical of these sorrowful gatherings and may have made the Hebrews all the more disinclined to play upon their harps. From time to time the captors of Israel, having heard of the unique character of the Hebrew melodies, may have requested, not necessarily in a rigorous demand, that the captives furnish them a sample of these plaintive melodies of which they had heard. "Songs of Zion" the oppressors called them. But the fact that the ones who were asking for a demonstration of what these songs were like are called "captors" and "oppressors" shows that the experience must have been a painful one. More likely than not a tone of tolerant amusement may have been heard in this request.

b) **Malediction upon him who forgets Jerusalem (vv. 4–6)**

4. *How could we sing the songs of the Lord*
   In a foreign land?
5. *If I forget you, O Jerusalem,*
   May my right hand fail me.
6. *May my tongue cleave to the roof of my mouth if I do not*
   remember you;
   If I do not set Jerusalem above my highest joy.

Although this malediction is spoken as though referring only to the writer himself, the thought quite obviously implied is that anyone who could remove the remembrance of the Holy City and what it stood for from his heart deserved punishment, severe punishment. The writer uses the first person to indicate that he does not exempt himself.

4. This verse could have been regarded as the conclusion of the preceding section which presents the reaction to the request of the "captors." In any case, it marks the transition from the one section to the other. The answer to the question raised by this verse could be an affirmative: Why should the Lord's songs not be proper in a foreign land? But the abstract possibility of the singing of them is apparently not the matter under consideration but rather the singing of them under

Psalm 137

circumstances such as those just described. To sing the Lord's holy songs for the amusement of the scoffing foreigner would be to degrade them; it would be an indication that that love of which v. 1 spoke was absent. This leads naturally to the thought expressed in v. 5.

5. This is the first of two self-imprecations. This fact should be borne in mind. The writer whom men charge with being all too ready to speak imprecations upon the heads of others does not spare himself or invite a less stringent measure of judgment when he evaluates his own attitude. For one thing, if he should forget Jerusalem and all that God has made it to stand for in the sight of His people he fully deserves that some judgment, such as the paralyzing of his right hand, be visited upon him. The propriety of this judgment is indicated by letting the forgetter be visited by a judgment of his right hand's forgetting, that is, failing to respond to his attempt to use it. This seems to be the simplest and most appropriate interpretation of this somewhat difficult passage, where the object of the verb is not stated (aposiopesis). But whom would the right hand fail (or forget) if not its owner? This involves the invoking of a heavy curse.

6. Analogous to this curse is the second one. This could be interpreted to mean, "May my vocal organs suffer paralysis; may the ability to speak forsake me." It would again be retribution for having failed to bear in mind all that the Holy City should have meant to a faithful and grateful man. The parallel statement interprets in its own way what such forgetting would involve: It would be losing sight of the fact that God's city is the "highest joy" of His people because of all that it stands for or because of all that God has associated with it in the past. Or more precisely stated, it would mean attaching a higher value to some other object in life than to the Holy City and its importance.

c) **Curse upon Edom (v. 7) and Babylonia (vv. 8, 9)**

7. *Remember, O Lord, against the children of Edom the day of Jerusalem; How they said: "Down with it, down with it to the very foundations!"*
8. *O daughter of Babylon, you devastator, Happy shall he be who repays you what you have dealt out to us!*
9. *Happy shall he be who takes your young children And dashes them against a rock!*

7. We have grouped these two curses together. Strictly speaking, these are not curses, except indirectly. In the one instance God is called on to remember the wickedness that was done, in the other a benediction is pronounced upon him who requites the evildoer.

That Edom had done much spiteful evil to Israel was a matter of historical record. Note the instances that may be cited: Amos 1:11;

Obad. 10ff.; Joel 3:19; Ezek. 25:12ff.; Is. 34:5ff.; Ezek. 35:2ff. The "day of Jerusalem" that the Edomites gloated over was the day of the fall of Jerusalem; see Jer. 52:12ff. How Edom felt is drastically illustrated by the one instance cited. The Edomites cried: "Down with it, down with it to the very foundations!" Nothing short of total devastation of the ancient rival city would satisfy them. Jealously over a brother nation apparently motivated this attitude. A high measure of guilt is incurred by such behavior. A man may harbor a mere feeling of revenge over against one who has taken so cruel an attitude. It cannot be denied that a man could also think in terms of just retribution and be desirous to have justice done to the guilty one.

In this connection we should like to point out a possibility of interpreting this and similar passages that, it seems to us, has not been sufficiently appreciated. When such thoughts are voiced in prayer, is not the issue committed to the hands of the Almighty? And did not the children of Israel know the principle: "Vengeance is Mine, I will repay, saith the Lord"? (Jer. 11:20; Ps. 94:1, etc.). By putting just vengeance into the hands of God they allowed Him to determine what was to be done, for He knew much better than they did. Or is retribution a thing about which we are so calmly indifferent that we do not care whether it is visited upon the guilty or not?

8. This verse indicates why Babylon deserves to be taken in hand. She merited the title "you devastator." Many were the towns and nations that she had ruthlessly devastated in the process of her conquests. "Daughter of Babylon" is a collective personification of all her inhabitants. Whoever has the task of dealing with her as she has dealt with others will be doing a good work; for which he shall justly be praised or called "blessed" or "happy." Justice is out of balance until just retribution has been visited upon the guilty. Our generation somehow has difficulty in understanding this and would pass all such instances by as not calling for intervention.

9. In order to understand the last verse rightly, we must recall everything that had just been said on the subject of retribution. It should also be recalled that all the neighboring nations round about Israel were in the habit of dealing thus with infants when they engaged in their many wars. Never a trace of indignation seems to be kindled in writers in regard to the outside nations. Note the following instances of this kind of behavior: II Kings 8:12; Hos. 10:14; 13:16; Nah. 3:10. In addition, Is. 13:16 had prophesied specifically with regard to Babylon that this cruel fate should befall her according to the verdict of the Almighty. The writer of the psalm may have known of this prediction and may have here sought to express the thought that what the Almighty has decreed he on his part would also like to see executed.

If a man takes such an attitude, is he more cruel than the Lord? Considerations of this sort have not been sufficiently weighed, but unwarranted and thoughtless criticisms have been quickly allowed to be just and have been endlessly repeated.

NOTES

3. "Oppressors" is a word that appears only here. Its root is difficult to determine. The meaning we offer is quite reasonable.
5. "Fail me"—the object is suppressed. See *KS*, p. 342, footnote 1.
7. After translating '*aru* (piel imperfect of 'arah) as we have, we discovered that the *Prayer Book* version has done the same.
8. *Shedhudhah* as a feminine passive participle is perfectly possible, implying that Babylon is already destroyed. That would make the curse involved meaningless. An active form may be gained for this word by a change of vowels to *shadhodah*.

Psalm 138

THANKSGIVING FOR THE LORD'S LOVING-KINDNESS

THIS IS A PSALM in which some unknown individual praises the Lord for some unmentioned mercy that has been bestowed upon him; or the nation is praising the Lord for restoration from Babylonian captivity; or David is offering praise to God for the unusual honor that was bestowed upon his house by the promises recorded in II Sam. 7. Though the third possibility is almost universally rejected as bordering on the impossible, it seems to offer the most satisfactory solution of the question regarding the distinct meaning of the psalm.

If this third possibility is accepted, everything quite obviously, turns on the question of authorship by David. The Hebrew text ascribes the psalm to him. True, the *Septuagint* text suggests that *Zechariah* had something to do with this psalm. But the Greek tradition is usually less reliable than is the Hebrew. Up to this point we have found the Hebrew headings to be at least defensible. We believe that in this instance a safe and reliable tradition is presented by what the Hebrew heading offers.

The objectors to this view suggest that in this last part of the Psalter Davidic psalms would not occur. That is an instance of prejudging the issue. The fact that a mixed style—thanksgiving mingled with lament—appears in the psalm is assumed to be indicative of late composition. We know too little about such issues as to the form in which the psalms are cast to give warrant to such conclusions. Psalms are sometimes denied Davidic authorship merely on the assumption that David wrote few if any psalms. That view denies the historical evidence provided by the Scriptures in passages like II Sam. 23:1.

A major difficulty connected with the acceptance of the suggestion that David wrote the psalm to thank God for having singled him out to be the founder of a dynasty that would endure forever is the fact that no specific mention of this grand prospect for David is made in the psalm. Yet, going on the reasonable assumption that David's contemporaries knew what rare things God had promised David as surely the contemporaries of Jesus were well aware of these promises, we may note that David did not need to specify the obvious which was common knowledge in his day. Statements like v. 2, "Thou hast magnified Thy promise [or, word] above all Thy name" would quite obviously point to some unique statement that had at one time been spoken to David; and what was more unique than II Sam. 7? We may likewise, point out that v. 4 points to an issue of such magnitude that kings of the earth could well feel moved to join their praises to those of David whereas some unknown experience of some unknown person would scarcely be thought of as arousing universal interest unless the writer were speaking in almost absurd hyperbole. In like manner it may justly be claimed that some great project that God has in store for the writer must be involved in a statement like that of v. 8: "The Lord will complete His purposes in my behalf." When men speak thus, great things are in prospect but are not yet realized.

It may also be pointed out that echoes of psalms written by David are clearly indicated in this psalm. Compare Ps. 9:1 with v. 1; or Ps. 5:7 with v. 2 or Ps. 113:5–9 with v. 6; or Ps. 23:4 with v. 7; and Ps. 57:3 with v. 8. Such echoes of Davidic thought are scarcely accidental.

We may yet add the following consideration: the promise that was made to David was of such a scope that it scarcely seems likely that David will have reflected on it but once as is written in II Sam. 7:18ff. A singer of David's ability would have found occasion for further treatment of the issue, especially in the psalms that he loved to write. Besides, the issue deserved to be treated time and again in public pronouncements, for it was a matter of interest and concern to the whole nation and even to succeeding generations.

1. *I will give thanks to Thee with my whole heart;*
   In the presence of the gods will I sing praise to Thee.

Psalm 138

2. *I will bow down facing Thy holy temple;*
   And I will give thanks to Thy name for Thy
      loving-kindness and for Thy faithfulness.
3. *In the day when I called Thou didst answer me;*
   Thou didst embolden me with strength in my soul.

1. We may well suppose that David is returning to a subject which has before this time elicited his thankful praise. The subject is so grand that it warrants repeated treatment. It is as though the writer were again bestirring himself to offer praise when an abundance of praise is obviously called for.

It has often been pointed out in connection with this opening verse that its author states neither for what he is giving thanks nor directly mentions Him whom he thanks. It may be rightly claimed that both issues are so obvious as to allow the writer to assume that his readers will readily supply the missing features. Whom do you thank for great benefits but the Lord? What was the one great blessing in David's life that far exceeded all others? Such as issue calls for praise with one's "whole heart," putting every last ounce of ability into it.

We may at first be a bit startled by the phrase "in the presence of the gods." But the mention of the gods does not necessarily imply that their existence is granted. An expression like this may mean: those that are commonly called gods. The point at issue is that in the experience of God's people there has arisen a notable prospect the like of which is not to be found in the religion of the nations round about Israel nor is under the influence and power of their supposed deities.

2. Already in David's day the fact of God's dwelling among His people at the sanctuary which He had appointed was well known (cf., Exod. 40:34). For this reason true worshipers quite naturally turned toward the official sanctuary, which can with all propriety be called "temple" whether it referred to a tent sanctuary or to the later shrine erected by Solomon (cf., I Sam. 1:9). This praise to be offered rightly involves humble adoration ("bow down") and fervent thanks ("I will give thanks"). Two attributes of the Lord have been made prominent by this recent experience of David's. His "loving-kindness" and His "faithfulness." Man can never comprehend the full magnitude of these divine attributes.

The last part of the verse is to be interpreted thus: God's "name" is the totality of that which God has up to the present made known to David concerning Himself. The present promise (Hebrew, "word") has been made so vast by the Lord that it exceeds all that David had heretofore believed to be the scope of the divine attributes. We might paraphrase it with the familiar words: "Thou hast given us a new revelation of Thy glory."

3. Though the historical books of the Old Testament do not indicate that God's unique promise to David was made as an answer to prayer, yet Ps. 21:2, 4; 61:5 point in that direction. See our comments on those passages. Whether David had ventured to ask for a blessing that was of the magnitude of the one God bestowed upon him may well be questioned. But after the promise had been given it did surge through the thoughts and consciousness of David in a manner that can scarcely be expressed too strongly. He describes it thus: "Thou didst embolden me with strength in my soul." The verb involved is to be translated, "Thou didst make me arrogant" (RSV margin) or better: "Thou didst make me proud" (*BDB*) in the good sense of the word; Is. 40:29 is a good parallel.

b) **The prospect of having the kings of the earth share in this praise (vv. 4–6)**

4. *All the kings of the earth shall praise Thee, O Lord;*
   For they shall hear the words of Thy mouth.
5. *And they shall sing of the ways of the Lord,*
   That the glory of the Lord is Great.
6. *For though the Lord is high He regards the lowly;*
   But the haughty He knows afar off.

This whole section has a close parallel in Ps. 102:15ff.

4. Everything centers about the prospect of having the kings of the earth offer their praises to the Lord for what He had done to David. The propriety of our approach is particularly evident on this point. The thought involved is somewhat like that expressed in Deut. 4:8, where God's revelation to Israel is thought of as being something which no other nation can boast of. Thus this promise about the eternal kingdom to come from David's line is without parallel among the nations. From the ideal point of view, poetically, so to speak, the thought is entertained that the kings of the earth shall learn of this glorious promise to David and shall recognize that they may come and worship the same eternal Lord (cf. the Magi) and sing His praises. This is more in the nature of a happy anticipation than in the nature of a strict prophecy. It is also much in the spirit of Is. 2:2–4. What will in such instances particularly intrigue the ones who are praising God are the "ways of the Lord," how marvelously he does things, and how strangely He deals with the nations (cf., Is. 55:9). For in what He does and what He reveals step by step in His progressive revelation it becomes apparent "that the glory of the Lord is great."

6. An additional point of special interest will also become rather

clear to all those who have gained insight into the Lord's ways, especially the kings of the earth. It will be an ancient rule that is emphasized throughout sacred Scripture, the rule that the exalted Lord stoops with special interest to the lowly and has regard for them. On the other hand, He knows the haughty afar off for what they are: persons who are self-sufficient and believe that they can well do without the Almighty. Obviously parallel are passages such as I Sam. 2:2–8; Is. 66:2; Luke 1:51, 52.

c) **The certainty of God's faithfulness in performing His promise (vv. 7, 8)**

> 7. Though I walk in the midst of distress, Thou dost preserve my life in spite of the wrath of my enemies;
> Thou dost stretch forth Thy hand, and Thy right hand delivers me.
> 8. The Lord will complete His purposes in my behalf;
> Thy loving-kindness, O Lord, endures forever;
> Forsake not the works of Thy hands!

7. In spite of all the greatness that was promised the line of David, he himself still had many a difficult situation to face; he finds himself "in the midst of distress." But He sees the providential care of God watching over him in spite of all that the enemies may do against him. Time after time he has had the experience of remarkable deliverance from danger. God has virtually reached down from high heaven to save him (cf. Ps. 18) and has, so to speak, stretched forth His right hand to deliver the man of His choice. All this argues for a firm hope for the future and for the fulfillment of all that is still unfulfilled in God's purposes.

8. Therefore the statement: "The Lord will complete His purposes in my behalf." Any enlightened observer could detect that the greater part of what God had in mind for David still had to be done. But the assurance is firm that it will come in due season. Another way of stating the case is: "Thy loving-kindness endures forever." God's faithfulness to His covenant obligations cannot be shaken. For this David fervently prays in the words: "Forsake not the works of Thy hands."

NOTES

4. Another feasible translation of the second half of the verse would be to begin: "When they shall have heard." The initial *ki* may be construed either way. In our translation above we could have used the future perfect: "For they shall have heard."

6. "Knows," *yeyeda'*, with a double prefix for the imperfect is an alternate form. Cf. *GK* 70b, Remark 2.

7. The preposition *'al* may be taken in the sense of "in spite of" as *BDB*, p. 754, indicates.

8. Some manuscripts and versions regard *ma'asey* as ending on an *h* and thus construe it as a singular, which seems at first glance to make the statement apply to David more aptly. But the plural construct form may well be allowed to stand. David then prays not only for himself but also remembers all to whom promises in one form or another may have been given.

The attempt to make the basis of the psalm a cultic experience (*Weiser*) stresses a favorite theory to the utmost, beyond what the facts warrant.

Psalm 139

A DEVOUT CONTEMPLATION OF GOD, THE OMNIPRESENT AND OMNIPOTENT ONE

THOUGH THIS PSALM is ascribed to David in the Hebrew text it does not have the same ascription in the Greek, where it is specifically associated with Zechariah in the Captivity. Besides, it must be admitted that it has a distinct Aramaic coloring, which does, indeed, point to a later date. But for all that it seems best with *Taylor* to leave the issue of dating the psalm open, chiefly because we have not the slightest indication into what period of Israel's history it may be fitted. If it is claimed that contemplative thinking about God did not originate before Jeremiah's time, that assertion is quite arbitrary. In fact, since the devout character of the many psalms which are rightly ascribed to David is obvious, it could be possible that the ascription to David is meant in that loose sense—a psalm in the spirit of David.

Though it is obviously a devout meditation, the thinking in evidence in this psalm is not formulated in theological abstractions but in terms of personal religious experience: the psalm throbs with warm emotion and deep feeling. Seldom has any man ventured to expose himself so fully to the searching gaze of the Almighty or meditated so fittingly on His nature and being. It is true that only two major divine attributes are considered; but these are dealt with all the more exhaustively. Both grow on the reader, for nowhere else are they set forth so effectively and tellingly.

Psalm 139

The symmetry of the psalm is obvious as is the clear-cut division into parts. It is true that vv. 19ff. introduce an unexpected turn of thought. Must writers, secular or sacred, follow only the line of thought that we happen to anticipate? As shall be shown later, an approach such as these last six verses make agrees well with what preceded. Deeper reflection often reveals deeper latent coherence.

Here, as so often in previous instances, the text is not as sorely in need of correction as is commonly asserted. A few minor adjustments are admissible.

In the Hebrew text the heading reads thus: *To the Choir Director; a psalm of David.*

a) **Man in the face of God's omniscience (vv. 1–6)**

1. *O Lord, Thou hast searched me and known me.*
2. *Thou hast known when I sit down and when I rise up;*
   Thou hast discerned all my thoughts from afar.
3. *Thou hast scrutinized my wandering and my encamping;*
   Thou hast been intimately acquainted with all my ways.
4. *For there is not a word on my tongue—*
   Behold, O Lord, Thou hast known it all!
5. *Thou hast closed me in behind and before;*
   And Thou hast laid Thy hand upon me.
6. *To understand this is too wonderful for me;*
   It is lofty—I cannot attain to it.

1. This opening statement of the psalm is its theme. For this reason it is repeated at the close. The writer is telling what he has experienced. It is for this reason that he uses a historical perfect. This matter of the tenses should not be overlooked. These perfects continue through v. 5. They are all of the same sort. The psalmist is not saying that God continually puts men to the test, probes into their thinking, and thus knows what goes on in their inmost minds, true as this is. He is recording that, as far as his own experience goes, God has let the full force of His Omniscience play upon every thought and activity of the psalmist and therefore has always known him more intimately than he knows himself. There are other Scripture passages that speak in a similar vein; see Jer. 23:23f.; Ps. 44:21.

2. The writer makes this clearer by citing specific instances. Whatever activity he may engage in, whether it is more passive, like sitting down, or more active, like rising up, God is always immediately aware of what he is doing. Even his most secret thoughts are not hidden from God. If He knows them afar off, that seems to imply more than that He can detect them although He is high up in His heaven. It would seem rather to imply that even before the thoughts are fully present

to him that thinks them, God is aware of what they are going to be before they are fully formed.

3. Or to use other colorful illustrations, the Lord has carefully scrutinized what the writer does when he journeys along the way or when he stops off at any place to lie down to rest. All this God fully discerns. As a result there is more than a superficial acquaintance with what is being done: the Lord is "intimately acquainted with all (his) ways."

4. Moving on to things that are still more wonderful: not a word that he ventures to speak escapes the Almighty. The form of the statement of the first half of the verse seems to imply that, before the thought has taken shape to the point where it can be cast into the appropriate word, God knows what it is going to be. This is knowledge superlative.

5. Or to advance from striking examples to all-embracing activity, the psalmist says that wherever he may happen to turn, behind him or before him, God has closed him in; wherever he turns he is in God's power. It is now precisely said whether this terrifies the author or whether it merely rouses his wonder and prayerful adoration. In the light of the next verse it would seem that the latter result is the one we are to regard as correct. There is no denying the fact that a reverent awe goes hand in hand with such an insight into the nature of God's dealings with man.

6. In this verse the emphasis is chiefly on the fact that a God who has all of man's doings and thinking so completely in His power is so far above the finite comprehension of the small being called man that man must admit that this is "too wonderful" and too utterly "lofty." Our little mind just cannot begin to fathom the depth of the mind of God, to put it mildly. If the familiar translation of this verse is retained, "such knowledge is too wonderful for me," the expression "such knowledge" refers to *God's* knowledge, i.e., how can He know and control things so absolutely and so effectively? Rom. 11:33 may be aptly compared.

b) **Man in the face of God's omnipresence (vv. 7–12)**

7. *Whither could I go from Thy Spirit?*
    Or whither could I flee from Thy presence?
8. *If I were to ascend up into heaven; Thou art there;*
    If I were to spread my couch in Sheol, lo, Thou art there.
9. *If I were to take the wings of the dawn*
    And were to dwell in the uttermost parts of the sea,
10. *Even there Thy hand would lead me,*
    And Thy right hand would hold me.

11. Then I said: "Total darkness shall press me down;
And the night shall be the light round about me."
12. Even darkness is not too dark for Thee;
And the night is as bright as the day;
The darkness is like the light.

7. Never has the pen of man more effectively described the omnipresence of God. One feels at the same time that this is more than beautiful poetry. This is the writer's inmost experience. He has not even in his thinking been able to put himself beyond the reach of the Almighty. It seems a bit misleading to begin: "Whither *shall* I go," etc.? He is not attempting to flee from God. The writer is rather visualizing what might happen if one were to attempt to get beyond the reach of God. This thought would seem to be conveyed more effectively by saying: "Whither *could* I go?" The writer is not oppressed with a sense of guilt. His problem is more theoretical. This approach reaches down through v. 9. Instead of God His Spirit is mentioned, perhaps, as being the more pervasive aspect of His being. The writer is still thinking of God Himself, though at this point in the Old Testament scarcely in the precise sense of the third person of the Holy Trinity. "Presence" is synonymous with God Himself, being, in a sense, the equivalent of His personality.

8. Several possibilities are considered. When heaven and Sheol are mentioned, that is an instance of the wider use of these terms, when they signify not a specific place but two possible extremes—the physically highest versus the physically lowest. Amos 9:2 is much in the same spirit. Therefore: If I were to ascend as high as I could; I could not escape Thee, nor could I if I went to the lowest thinkable depth. To translate, "If I make my bed in hell," is quite misleading.

9. Or, carrying this approach still farther, "If I were to take the wings of the dawn"—the lightning-like rapidity with which the light of the morning flashes all over the utmost reaches of the horizon after it has once cleared to eastern bounds, is the point of the comparison. For this light flashes to the utmost reaches of the sea faster than the eye can follow. Were this light to be my chariot, so to speak, I still could not get away from Thee.

10. For I should even then find that Thy hand is exercising its kindly control over all my steps, and Thy right hand would still be there to afford that support that I need every hour of the day. That is the psalmist's confession. The marvel of God's presence everywhere does not repel and frighten the writer. It is God's *gracious* presence that has impressed him.

11. One more possibility is to be considered that has not yet been

fully evaluated (v. 11, 12), and that is to try to hide in total darkness, wherever it may be found. One may think of deep caves of the earth where absolutely no light is able to penetrate. But though he were wrapped in such darkness, the writer knows that, as far as the all-seeing eye of God is concerned, such night would become light round about him. Even the thickest gloom is penetrated by God's penetrating gaze. Before Him who is light everything is continually light.

c) **Man as the work of God's hands (vv. 13–18)**

13. *For Thou holdest my vital parts in Thy power;*
    Thou didst weave me together in my mother's womb.
14. *I will praise Thee, for I am made in a tremendously wonderful fashion;*
    Wonderful are Thy works, and that my soul knoweth right well.
15. *My potentialities were not hidden from Thee*
    When I was made in secret, when I was skillfully wrought in the depths of the earth.
16. *Thy eyes beheld my unformed substance;*
    In Thy book it was all written,
    Days which were to be prepared when as yet there was not one of them.
17. *But as for me, how precious are Thy thoughts, O God!*
    How mighty is the sum of them!
18. *I shall count them; they are more than the sand;*
    I have awaked and am still with Thee.

13. When man is now regarded as the work of God's hands, this is at the same time a further unfolding of the preceding line of thought, for what is being demonstrated is the fact that in his very being man shows both the omniscience and the omnipresence of God. The beginning is made by showing how it was God who controlled the very inception of life as well as the deepest evidences of life. On the latter the Hebrew says: "Thou holdest my reins (or kidneys) in Thy power." The most deep-seated of all the organs is obviously referred to, whose activity cannot even be detected as the heart can by its throbbing. But it was not mother nature mysteriously at work when the human being began to take shape and form in the body of the mother. God was at work there, weaving together the substances that go to make up a human being.

14. At this point the psalmist cannot let the marvel of it all be passed by without due recognition. He must praise God for the remarkable way in which He wrought at the time when all this took place. There is something awe-inspiring about God's designs and modes of operation just as all His works are "wonderful." This the writer ac-

knowledges as one of his most vital and positive insights: "that my soul knoweth right well" as the inimitable *KJ* has so aptly rendered the statement.

15. This verse has its difficulties. What we have rendered "potentiality" is really "strength" and could refer to the sturdy part of the human frame, the bones. It could be considered more in the nature of an abstract noun and so refer to all the potentialities that lay latent in this human being which is just beginning to take shape and form. The latter thought is more graphic. The Creator knew the capabilities that this human being would carry within it, seeing that He Himself gave it all that it has.

All this was going on "in secret," when no man could tell what the hidden processes of life in its inception were. When it is said that this was being done "when I was being skillfully wrought in the depths of the earth" this may, perhaps, be best explained as a reference to the original formation of the first man, who was, indeed, compounded of the dust of the ground. Every one whose life is brought into being may be said, with some measure of poetic license, as being made by the same Creator in a way that is analogous to the first creation. The same skill—here lies the emphasis—that made Adam makes every son of Adam. As God's work was then hidden from the eyes of men, so it is now.

16. The all-seeing eye of God rested upon this new life which was far from ready to be seen by man; it rested upon even the unseen days that this being should live and beheld all that should transpire within those days. This touches upon the deep mystery of the divine foreknowledge, which our little minds can never begin to grasp. In this case the book of God is not the book of life or of the record of the deeds of men (Exod. 32:32f.; Ps. 56:8; 69:28; Dan. 7:10) but the book of divine foreknowledge, where, as it were, the days are known as to their number, and a blank page is provided for each.

17. Rather than lose himself in the abstractions of God's foreknowledge the writer asserts how precious it is to him that God should already then have concerned Himself about this being which was scarcely a complete thing. It is a precious thing that God should have had concern for him from that time onward. And how mighty must be the sum of thoughts that the Maker has concerning the work of His hands! Perish the thought that God's notice of us consists of occasional bits of attention in a passing mood!

18. If one should venture to count how many these thoughts are he would rather find that they are more than the sand of the sea. I may at times be unimportant in my own sight but I am never thus in the

sight of the Almighty, says the psalmist, for His thoughts concerning me cannot even be numbered.
The second half of the verse has its difficulties. Most commentators go on the assumption that the writer was overwhelmed by the magnitude of the subject that engaged his attention and either actually fell asleep or at least became all but entranced by the great things that passed through his mind. He comes to with a start and quite in the spirit of the whole psalm comes to the realization that now as always he is still in the presence of his God, who will never be separated from him.

d) **Prayer that God might overthrow the wicked and test the sincerity of the writer (vv. 19–24)**

19. *O that Thou wouldest slay the wicked, O God!*
    And you bloodthirsty men, depart from me!
20. *Who speak against Thee wickedly;*
    They have taken (Thy name) in vain.
21. *Do I not hate them that hate Thee, O Lord?*
    And do I not loathe them that rise up against Thee?
22. *I hate them with perfect hatred;*
    I count them my enemies.
23. *Search me, O God, and know my heart;*
    Test me and know my thoughts.
24. *And see if there be any way in me that leads to pain;*
    And lead me in the way everlasting!

In a connection such as this the prayer for the overthrow of the wicked must refer to those who refuse to acknowledge the providential care of God that watches over them, to those who refuse to be God-related in their thinking and doing though God stands so closely related to them. What the writer feels keenly is that such persons spurn so much of the grace of God that their sin borders on the heinous. Such persons deserve to be overthrown. Though their basic sin is a wrong attitude against God, the manifestations of that sin as they are here enumerated include the following: they are "wicked"; they are "bloodthirsty"; they even "speak wickedly against (God)"; they have taken His "name in vain." It is certainly less in the nature of hatred when the psalmist speaks thus and more in the nature of the vindication of the honor of his Lord. Yet in the words that follow hatred of a certain kind is claimed by the writer and obviously in the sense in which Jesus demanded hatred of wicked things of His followers and also called it hatred of the persons that exemplified these wicked things (Luke 14: 26). Vv. 21 and 22 are a complete disavowal of those persons who disavow God. Even *Kittel,* who is very strong in his denunciation of

Psalm 139

what may be inadequate about this sort of imprecation, cannot close the subject without remarking that the motive is "not a spirit of revenge, but grief over the presence of wickedness." *Oesterley* characterizes this as a "justifiable outburst."

Neither the verses just touched upon nor the rest of the psalm are to be thought of apart from the two closing verses. For if the writer would have God search and know his heart he without a doubt thinks first of the presence of any unhallowed thought that might have wormed its way into his thinking as he denounced and prayed for the overthrow of the wicked. All such thoughts demand a never-ending scrutiny lest they degenerate into something that is utterly unwholesome. Here if anywhere the dividing line between right and wrong is a very sharp one. Thus the concluding verse offers the thought, if there is anything that is in the least unwholesome, may God help him to see it, remove it, and walk in the way of life, which is the "way everlasting," and keep him from "every way that leads to pain," which is, of course, the way of sin.

There seems to be a broader purpose behind this closing prayer. Should the psalmist have harbored *any* thoughts that were not worthy of the noble subject that engaged his utterance, the prayer is that God might pardon such shortcomings and lead him to more wholesome insight.

NOTES

3. We have in this verse a typical instance of how the Hebrew loves to touch upon the two extremes of a given concept, implying that everything that lies between these two is also to be included (*KS* 92c).

8. The verb "spread" has the lengthened form with added *ah* (*jaqtul gravatum*) in a conditional clause—a not so very uncommon procedure (*KS* 201c).

9. The "if" ('*im*) of v. 8 still applies to this verse. See *KS* 381i.

14. Something of the distinctive character of this verse is lost if changes in the text are resorted to: cf. *RSV:* "I praise Thee, for Thou art fearful and wonderful." It should be noted that *nora'oth* is used adverbially (*KS* 344d). We have sought to catch its force by using the adverb "tremendously." The *KJ* rendering can well be defended from the grammatical point of view.

16. *Yikkathebhu* is one of the many instances when the *waw* consecutive is separated from the imperfect form of the verb which belongs to it. See *KS* 368i. The plural of the verb seems to anticipate the word following—"days."

20. The expression, "they have taken in vain," we believe is rightly considered to be in the nature of an abbreviated familiar expression, which stated in its entirety is "to take the name of the Lord in vain,"

cited from Exod. 20:7. The word "Thy enemies" is a loose apposition. In *nasu'* the *aleph* and the *u* appear to have been interchanged.

22. For "perfect" the Hebrew uses *takhlith* ("completeness") which, being in a sense an indication of the superlative, may well be translated as the adjective "perfect." Cf. *KS* 309g.

Psalm 140

PRAYER FOR PROTECTION AGAINST PERSECUTORS

THE POSSIBILITY of the Davidic authorship of this psalm must not be entirely disregarded. What makes such an assumption difficult is that certain forms in vv. 9 and 10 seem to have an Aramaic flavor, in any case they are unusual and difficult forms. For that reason we could favor the opinion of some that the psalm is "cast in the Davidic manner" and does represent quite a number of turns of thought that have been commonly noted in the valid psalms of David. We have in mind such factors as that the writer has been bitterly assailed or slandered; he casts himself without reserve into the arms of God; he strongly hopes for the overthrow of his adversaries.

But one scarcely deals fairly with the psalm when one claims that "its cry is only for vengeance." Far more sober is the evaluation that says that "there is no hint of the desire of any personal retaliation against the vindictive enemies of the psalmist; all is left in the hands of God." On the question as to whether the issues involved in this psalm are in the nature of factional strife between parties among the Jews at a later date, we feel that those interpreters are more in the right who see nothing of that element in the psalm.

a) **Prayer for deliverance from unprincipled slanders (vv. 1–5)**

To the Choir Director, A psalm. Of David.

1. Deliver me, O Lord, from wicked men;
   Protect me from violent men,
2. Who devise evil things in their heart,
   Who continually stir up wars.
3. They make their tongue sharp like that of a serpent;
   The poison of adders is under their lips. Selah.
4. Guard me, O Lord, from the hands of the wicked;
   Protect me from violent men, who devise how to trip up my steps.

Psalm 140

> 5. *Arrogant men lay a trap for me and lines;*
> *They spread a net by the wayside;*
> *They set snares for me. Selah.*

Even as in earlier psalms of David there are wicked men who are in opposition to the good king of Israel, so the writer is troubled by the same problem. The opponents are wicked and violent. Their assaults are such that the writer needs protection. All the thinking of these men is a devising of evil, or to use a more drastic figure, they "continually stir up wars." From that point onward the description of these men resorts to figures in which the slanders that these men indulge in are likened to the sharpening of the tongue even as weapons are sharpened. Similar passages are Ps. 55:21; 59:7; 64:3. The figure of the sharp weapon blends with that of poison which, like that of the serpent, seems to lodge under the tongue. Deadly as such poison may be, so are the words of these slanderers. Another set of figures is then resorted to, that of the hunter who seeks to ensnare his prey. Dangerous traps are hidden from sight to catch the unsuspecting victim: snares, nets, lines, and traps. This, too, is a relatively familiar figure. See Ps. 31:4; 57:6; 64:5; 142:3.

b) A similar prayer in a tone of great confidence (vv. 6–8)

> 6. *I said unto the Lord: Thou art my God;*
> *Give ear, O Lord, to the voice of my supplications.*
> 7. *O Lord, my Lord, my strong deliverance,*
> *Thou hast covered my head in the day of battle.*
> 8. *O Lord, do not grant the things the wicked desire;*
> *Do not prosper his devices.*

As is so often the case, prayer gains assurance as it proceeds. The situation in which the writer finds himself has not changed, but a stronger confidence floods the heart. By claiming the Lord for his God the psalmist fortifies himself to believe more wholeheartedly that God will give ear to his petitions. Such claims as that God is the writer's "strong deliverance" are based on previous experience. If a reassuring way to depict what this means is sought, it is as if a man held a sturdy protection over the head of the other, a helmet or a shield. This God is appealed to to foil the wicked purpose of these evil men and their unwholesome desires. God can make the unholy plans of the evildoer miscarry and come to naught.

c) A prayer for the overthrow of the slanderers (vv. 9–11)

> 9. *When they who surround me lift up their head,*
> *Let the mischief of their lips press them down!*

10. *Let hot coals be cast upon them;*
    Let them fall into fire, yea, into deep pits and not rise again.
11. *Let not the slanderer be established in the land;*
    As for the violent man, let evil pursue him thrust upon thrust,

The first thought expressed is that those who surround the psalmist may be at the point of lifting up their heads. The thought is apparently that they are bestirring themselves to act. Whenever they do that, the prayer here voiced asks that the evil that their own lips have devised may fall on them rather than on those for whom it was intended. Throughout this prayer for the overthrow of the wicked it should be borne in mind that the purpose of it is not that these persons may suffer and their suffering delight the man who makes this prayer, but rather that they may be dealt with in such a manner that the evil which they plot may not be successful. The figures used are, we admit, full of color and vigor: may hot coals be cast upon them; may they fall into the fire which they have prepared for others; may they fall into the deep pits which have been dug for others. There is a fairness about such an outcome.

The particular issue that is involved is formulated more precisely in v. 11. It is the slanderers who are gaining control in the land. The psalmist asks that such an eventuality may not come to pass. Who could find any fault with such a prayer? As for the violent man, the psalmist prays that "evil may pursue him thrust upon thrust" but scarcely even after he has been turned aside from his evil designs. We regard this entire verse as still belonging to the prayer begun two verses earlier even though as to the verb forms used it might seem to express a firm confidence that this result will be attained. That note of confidence does not seem to be reached before the next verse.

d) Renewed assurance of deliverance for the upright (vv. 12, 13)

12. *I know that the Lord will maintain the cause of the afflicted,*
    The rights of the poor.
13. *Surely, the righteous will give thanks to Thy name;*
    The upright will dwell in Thy presence.

The psalm has mounted to successive levels of confidence, the highest being reached in these last two verses. Faith grows with prayer. The new confidence now arrived at is expressed in terms that are practically generalizations. Not only with reference to himself but also with regard to all afflicted and poor persons who cast their burden upon the Lord it is true that the Lord maintains the cause of all such. That the psalmist "knows," that is to say, has acquired as a new and deeper experience. From that point the writer mounts to the higher plateau where he sees righteous men the world over being delivered from their affliction and giving thanks to the name of the Lord. In fact, he dares to venture to rise even one step higher: he sees the upright dwelling in the very presence of the Lord. Not only are they delivered; they are admitted to close fellowship with their God. By the time this thought is reached the tone of the psalm has become calm and serene. The affliction that had previously beset the psalmist has vanquished.

NOTES

2. The fact that the plural appears in this verse indicates that the singular of v. 1 is thought of as a collective. We have, therefore, translated v. 1 accordingly: "wicked men" and "violent men."

7. Two words for "Lord" are used, a difference which is indicated in our versions by large capitals (for *Yahweh*) and small capitals (for *adhonay*).

9. The *Kittel* text may well be followed at this point. The Selah is apparently misplaced. The initial imperfect represents a temporal clause. See also *KS* 352v.

11. *Madhchephoth*, rendered by *BDB* and *Koehler* "thrust upon thrust," is rendered *Abgrund* (*KW*), i.e., "into the abyss."

Psalm 141

AN EVENING PRAYER
FOR SANCTIFICATION AND PROTECTION

FROM DAYS of old this has been regarded as the evening prayer by the church as v. 2 which is used in the Vespers indicates; Ps. 63 was the corresponding morning prayer.

The particular difficulty that is to be encountered in connection with the interpretation of this psalm is the fact that vv. 6, 7 or 5–7 are beset with unusual problems. It may be possible that the text has suffered impairment to some degree. In any case, many commentators despair utterly of ever arriving at a unified interpretation of the psalm or begin to conjecture as to how the text is to be reconstructed. In proof of the latter procedure it may be noted that the conjectural marginal material in the Kittel text is more extensive than is given for any other psalm; and yet these conjectures yield anything but a unified approach.

A bewildering array of possibilities confronts the interpreter who considers possible emendations of the text. This psalm is the prayer of a penitent, though this is but vaguely indicated; or the speaker is a youth who is to be subjected to the discipline of rigorous religionists; or he is a youth of unusual spiritual maturity; or the speaker is a man of rare discernment in regard to spiritual values, especially in the area of worship.

The heading, which attributes the psalm to David, is consistently ignored and not regarded as even worthy of refutation. *Delitzsch* somewhat timidly admits that this suggestion has possibilities. Yet we see no serious objection to authorship by David on any score: the language argument can scarcely be employed although a few phrases are not strictly like the known expressions of David; no historical fact in the psalm clashes with known facts of David's life. We are, therefore, content to allow for the possibility that this psalm may have been written by David and be thought of as belonging, perhaps, in the period of Absalom's rebellion.

It would not occur to us to deny the difficulties that are to be encountered in the interpretation of the psalm. We shall attempt to show that a unified approach is at least possible. The caption that we have chosen above is taken from *ARV*.

a) **A plea to be heard (vv. 1, 2)**

1. *O Lord, I have called unto Thee, make haste unto me;*
   Give ear to my voice when I call unto Thee.
2. *Let my prayer be presented before Thee as incense*
   And the lifting up of my hands as an evening sacrifice.

1. The opening of the psalm gives utterance to that urgency that godly men feel over against God when they are in peril and almost desperately need divine help; when they have cried long and have met no response. Behind it all lies the deep need of help as well as the feeling that God alone can help even though the individual who prays in no wise deserves to be heard.

2. The second verse indicates that at least among the more enlightened saints of the Old Testament there was an understanding of the ritual observances of the current worship, particularly of such facts as that the essence of the offering of incense was prayer, or that prayer is the true incense which rises up to God like a sweet and acceptable odor. The second half of the verse would seem to indicate that this prayer was presented in the sanctuary at the time of the evening sacrifice although it would not be impossible to have prayed thus at the time of the evening sacrifice without being actually present at the Temple in Jerusalem as I Kings 18:36 would seem to indicate. The fact that the

Psalm 141

use of incense typifies prayer is stated with abundant clearness in the New Testament as Rev. 5:8 indicates. On the use of incense in the sanctuary see Exod. 30:7ff.; Exod. 29:41 shows that the evening sacrifice was appointed early in Israel's history. That it should be mentioned exclusively without a reference to the morning sacrifice appears to indicate that the evening sacrifice had somehow gained a certain popularity in the course of years; cf., Dan. 9:21; Ezra 9:4, 5. In any case, a spiritual conception of the forms of worship is clearly indicated in the verse; and according to our approach we believe that such deeper spiritual insights were not unknown in the days of David. On the whole we have here an earnest petition that God may give ear to the cry of His child.

b) A petition to be guarded against ill-advised words and wicked deeds (vv. 3–7)

3. *Set a guard, O Lord, over my mouth;*
   Keep watch at the door of my lips.
4. *Let not my heart incline to any evil thing,*
   to launch into deeds done iniquitously
   together with men who practice wrong;
   And let me not eat of their dainties.
5. *If a righteous man smite me and rebuke me with kindness,*
   Let not my head refuse the oil upon my head;
   For yet even my prayer shall arise for them for their evil deeds.
6. *The judges among them shall be dashed down by the side of the cliffs;*
   Then shall they hear that my words are sweet.
7. *As when a man plows in the earth and breaks it up,*
   So our bones lie scattered at the mouth of Sheol.

3. Since this section is, first of all, a petition to be kept from ill-advised words and wicked deeds, and since it follows upon the petition to be heard in some form of grave difficulty, the connection may well be this, that the trouble in which the psalmist finds himself is such that he may under the circumstances be tempted to speak rashly and act foolishly. This would clearly motivate the prayer of this verse which may be paraphrased: "Keep me, O Lord, from uncontrolled utterances; do not let impatient and foolish remarks well up from my lips." Cf. Ps. 39:1.

4. Closely allied to this is the danger of rushing into some wicked deeds that may be done because the situation in which men find themselves at a given time almost seems to force them into such deeds. "Men who practice wrong" outline such a wicked course for themselves. A certain measure of impetus is built up. The whole crowd is of one mind. The momentum or at least the pressure exerted seems irresistible. Be-

fore he knows it, a man finds himself swept along with the rest. When in this verse the writer prays to be kept from "eating the dainties" of such persons, it would appear that the issue is that he is being invited to the feasts in which these persons share, and the social fellowship seems to be a method of winning the reluctant over to run with the throng. Table fellowship constitutes a sort of bribe to which there is danger of succumbing.

5. If this verse has any connection with the preceding, it would be reasonable to understand it to mean that some righteous person with good spiritual insight might notice the danger in which the psalmist happens to be and address an admonition to him in the spirit of the prayer that he himself has just made. Since too often, when men admonish us, even justly, our pride forbids our accepting the admonition, the writer in this case prays that grace may be given him to be humble enough under such circumstances to let himself be admonished, all the more so since righteous men will, as a rule, administer the needed admonition "with kindness." In the next words this rebuke is likened to the perfume that Orientals in days of old were in the habit of pouring upon their guests at banquets, and the writer reiterates his prayer that he may regard the rebuke as such a sweet-smelling perfume and may cheerfully accept it. In line with this humility he makes mention of another virtue which he aims to put into practice at this time: unselfish intercessory prayer with which he hopes graciously to repay these evildoers. Though they aim to bring him to fall and to inveigle him into becoming an accessory to their evil deeds, he hopes by this means to repay them in a God-pleasing manner.

6. At this point the writer falls back upon an ancient principle, the validity of which has long been known among God's people, the principle of just retribution. Though he well knows that it does not always work out with such regularity as we might wish to see in the course of a man's lifetime, yet evidence of its being a firmly established principle is rather abundant. This verse and the next one are spoken in the spirit of Ps. 1. For a reason that is not now obvious he mentions particularly "the judges among them," apparently an influential group who may have been the ringleaders in the whole movement they represent. These shall come to a drastic overthrow in that they "shall be dashed down by the side of the cliffs." The writer may be thinking of such instances as II Chron. 25:12, without necessarily prophesying that this very type of judgment must befall them. He may imply that this or any similar judgment will be their lot in the just judgment of God. The last line of the verse may be fitted into the picture in various ways—"Then shall they hear that my words are sweet." We prefer the construction which has this statement refer to the intercessory prayer mentioned in the pre-

ceding verse. When the calamity of these wicked men breaks in upon them, they will find that the psalmist continues to do as he has done all along: he speaks no harsh words in gloating over their misfortune; he still prays for them.

7. There are two major approaches to this verse: one states that the verse does nothing more than describe the bitter lot of the writer and the group that he represents—the remains of their dead bodies (their bones) lie scattered abroad with no man to bury them. A hard lot indeed! The other prefers to consider this a statement of the *hopeful* lot of the oppressed righteous men, and thus it is a statement that is in direct opposition to the preceding verse. We favor this interpretation, for then the first half of the verse makes good sense. For when one "plows in the earth and breaks it up," that is work which is done in anticipation of things to be sown and harvested. On the plowed earth that has been prepared for the sowing lie the bones of God's saints, scattered right at the mouth of the grave where they are buried, but not buried in utter hopelessness. Though buried, they are a seed sown unto a new life. This verse then appears like a statement of a belief in the resurrection. It is not as clear as Is. 26:19 or, in another sense, Ezek. 37, but still a statement that has an outlook of hope for the children of God.

Thus the petition to be kept from rash words and wicked deeds is motivated by a look into the future which serves both as a deterrent and as a wholesome encouragement. The sad overthrow of the wicked is briefly recalled, only to be contrasted with the hopeful outlook of the righteous.

c) **A final plea for protection and for the downfall of the wicked (vv. 8–10)**

8. *For unto Thee, O Lord God, are my eyes;*
   In Thee have I taken refuge; Do not cast out my soul!
9. *Keep me from the trap they have laid for me*
   And from the snares of evildoers.
10. *Let the wicked fall, each into his own net,*
    While I at the same time forever escape.

8. Though the psalmist may have become somewhat more reassured by the time this point of his prayer is reached, he is yet not free from danger. He stills feels the need of an earnest cry for protection. He feels that the fact that he keeps directing his eyes toward the Lord is a matter that the Lord cannot disregard. Or what amounts to the same thing— "In Thee have I taken refuge." When the Lord sees men sitting down, so to speak, on His doorstep and waiting for Him to deliver them, that is a token of trust that moves Him to action. If one adds the pitiful

cry "Do not cast out my soul," he may well hope to be heard right soon. The plea for help is amplified in that the situation involved is described as that of a being for whom traps have been set as also in Ps. 140:4, 5 and many other instances.

10. Whereas this is the positive side of the matter, the negative is the overthrow of the wicked, for whose overthrow he now asks. The fact that it is a very just and righteous thing to have men fall into the trap that they have wickedly set for others has long been acknowledged. When that happens, not only has the righteous man been vindicated but the wicked man has also experienced just retribution. Once more in a ringing note of confidence the hope of ultimate and total deliverance is clearly voiced. And thus the psalm closes.

NOTES

5. *Chesedh* is used adverbially, cf. *KS* 332e. The form *yani* is a hiphil from the root nô' in which the quiescent aleph is not written as *GK* 74k explains.

7. This verse offers a double instance of the somewhat indefinite use of participles when the subject has to be supplied; cf. *KS* 324n.

9. After *pach* the relative is omitted; our English translation imitates the Hebrew at this point. Cf. *KS* 337v. The second object of the preposition "from" does not repeat the preposition; *KS* 319m.

On the question of the spiritual aspect of outward forms of worship this psalm has a measure of similarity with Ps. 40, 50, 51, 69, 71.

Psalm 142

A CRY FOR HELP IN THE MIDST OF TROUBLE

WHAT WAS the situation of the writer of this psalm? The heading calls the psalm a "didactic poem" (*maskil*). This is scarcely a worthless suggestion. The psalm would, therefore, convey some helpful instruction on the basis of the experience out of which it grew. The writer is quite obviously a man who is in trouble. There are treacherous men with whom he is dealing; there are persecutors who make life bitter for him. There apparently is no man to help him. This is at least the feeling voiced in v. 4; but by the time the end of the psalm is reached, it becomes obvious that there is a company of saints who are vitally interested in what befalls this man of God. We cannot be sure that the man was in prison even though v. 7 says: "Bring me out of prison." It must be allowed that such expression may be used figuratively although the possibility of an actual imprisonment dare not be completely ruled out.

But was it David as the heading claims? Since we have found the headings conveying a reliable tradition, that may also be the case in this instance. It is too much to expect some reference in the psalm to furnish absolutely convincing proof of Davidic authorship. Suffice it to say that there is nothing in the psalm that conflicts with the ancient tradition that David wrote it. To point to certain words as being distinctly Aramaic and therefore proof of late origin overlooks the fact that the late character of the words referred to has not been too clearly established —"complaint" (v. 2), "faints away" (v. 3), and "throng around" (v. 7).

The distinctive feature of the psalm is a pathetic cry of an individual in trouble—as our title of the psalm also indicates. In this unhappy situation the only thing that is left the writer is to clasp the hand of God. That he does in a way that is almost touching. In this respect the psalm has thoughts in common with Ps. 64, 120, 140. There is not enough material in the psalm to warrant the conclusion that the writer is the victim of the party strife of his time, a misfortune that was much in evidence in the last two centuries of the Old Testament era. Neither can we be sure that the reference to the "hidden trap" (v. 3) is to slanders that have been uttered about the psalmist. It is enough to know that a man in deep distress cries out unto the Lord and expects to be helped.

The heading reads thus: *A didactic poem. Of David. When he was in the cave. A prayer.* The designation "didactic poem" was discussed above. The term "prayer" may have a technical designation that we do not appear to be able to determine. If an actual "cave" was referred to it would have been either the cave of Adullam (I Sam. 22) or the cave near Engedi (I Sam. 24). But as little as the term "prison" dare not be pressed, so little the term "cave." Either in a cave or in one of life's distressful situations the writer had thoughts like the ones here recorded, which he presents for whatever use they may have for others in times to come.

a) **A cry to God for help (vv. 1, 2)**

1. *I cry aloud to the Lord;*
I make supplication aloud to the Lord.
2. *I pour out my complaint before Him;*
I declare my distress before Him.

Each of the four statements of this cry to the Lord says practically the same thing. It is not spoken to furnish information to the Lord as has been aptly remarked, but for the relief of the petitioner. The Hebrew idiom has a somewhat unusual way of saying, "I cry aloud." It says, "With my voice I cry." The implied contrast is: Not only in my inmost heart. Nor is a special emphasis to be attached to the "aloud" as if some particular volume of voice were involved. It simply implies: I have put my petition into precise words that I address to God. There seems to be some advantage in putting trouble into words: it then seems less threatening; we have its measure after we have stated it. All God's saints have found this to be the case with regard to their prayers. When v. 2 speaks of "pouring out a complaint," this implies nothing more than providing relief from the inward pressure as *Oesterley* says: "the gushing forth of words from an overfull heart."

b) **Confidence in the midst of distress (vv. 3–5)**

3. *When my spirit faints away within me, yet Thou knowest my way;*
   In the path where I walk they have hidden a trap for me.
4. *I look to the right and see, but there is no one who takes note of me;*
   No refuge is to be found, no one cares for me.
5. *I have cried unto Thee, O Lord;*
   I have said: "Thou art my refuge, my portion in the land of the living."

3. Whereas the preceding section was a pure outcry of pain, when the case is being reviewed a bit more fully, at least toward the end, and to a lesser degree already at the beginning, a note of confidence creeps in. The descriptive expression that speaks of the "spirit fainting away" is quite readily understood. But the expression "Thou knowest my way" has occasioned much comment. The difficulty in determining exactly what this suggests may stem from the fact that the word "way" is circumscribed too much. It can allow for the situation in which the man finds himself at the moment as well as for the things that may yet develop as he progresses along life's way. God obviously knows both, and there is comfort in that fact. What concerns the writer at the moment is that a trap has been hidden for him in the path where he is walking. That is again an expression that allows for a great variety of possibilities. It involves something that may bring the man to fall. There is treachery involved. But his comfort is that God knows what is in the offing and can protect him against it.

4. At the moment, however, there is no human help on which he can depend. As he turns to one side he sees nothing. This seems to imply that the situation is the same as he looks to the other. The case is so desperate that no one even "takes note of him." And when he says that "no refuge is found," the Hebrew says that refuge has perished. Though

the Hebrew reads, "No man cared for my soul," (*KJ*) that does not mean, as might be assumed, that it was a matter of indifference to men whether he was among the saved or the damned. The idiom implies no more than: "No one cares for me."

5. It seems more to the point to translate the Hebrew verb at the beginning of this verse as a perfect, which it is: "I have cried"—implying that this has gone on for some time and is still in progress. In this verse the note of confidence becomes very positive. God is the writer's refuge and portion in the land of the living. He builds all his hope on Him. The term "portion" always implies one's highest good or prized possession. It occurs also in Ps. 16:5; 73:26; Lam. 3:24. For "in the land of the living" we would use a less colorful expression, "as long as I live." A clear-cut resolve of faith is indicated by the words, "I have said." This is what the psalmist purposes to do consistently and without wavering.

c) A renewed and more hopeful cry (vv. 6, 7)

6. *Give attention to my cry, for I am brought very low!*
Deliver me from my persecutors, for they are stronger than I.
7. *Bring me out of prison that I may praise Thy name!*
The righteous will throng around me, for Thou wilt deal bountifully with me.

6. This last cry for help ends on a very hopeful note. There is still some measure of lament involved: "I am brought very low." The full deliverance is not yet in sight. The "persecutors" are still hot on his heels and still have greater strength than he has, but God can deliver him from their hand.

7. When the motivation for deliverance from prison is suggested, "that I may praise Thy name," that is more than a resolve to offer such praise. It is based on the supposition that such praise will also delight the Lord, for all praise is comely; nor should anyone feel that this is an unworthy motivation. Selfishness does not enter into these vows made before the Lord by His saints. By this time the writer has recalled what he had momentarily forgotten, namely, that the righteous have an interest in their fellow saints. They will, if he is delivered, gather around him and reassure him that they had never forgotten him in his distress and rejoice now in the help that he has received.

NOTES

3. The "yet" in the second clause of the verse is a *waw* similar to the one found in I Kings 8:36 as *Delitzsch* has pointed out.
7. For "bring *me* out" the Hebrew says: "Bring my soul out of prison" (*KJ*). Though this does mean a bit more than plain "me" it,

nevertheless, does not signify deliver my *soul* from some spiritual affliction. Thus our translation is less likely to be misconstrued. In like manner the clause following says: "That *she* (the soul) may praise Thy name." Again "that *I* may praise Thee" comes closest to the original expression. The verb "throng around" is not too clearly established as to its meaning. "Surround me" (*RSV*) says the same.

Psalm 143

PRAYER FOR DELIVERANCE
FROM ENEMIES AND FOR GUIDANCE

THE LINE of thought of this psalm may be described as follows: vv. 1–6, complaint; vv. 7–12, prayer. The writer describes the situation in which he finds himself (vv. 1–3) and follows this with a description of his reaction (vv. 4–6). Then, though there was a brief initial prayer for help, the prayer for deliverance is voiced in vv. 7–9; there follows an earnest petition for rehabilitation (vv. 10–12).

The precise situation that called forth this prayer is not too easy to determine. The writer is in some grievous trouble, which he describes in v. 3 as a dwelling in dark regions. There is one enemy in particular who has borne down hard upon him and dashed him to the ground (v. 3). He feels this affliction very painfully and is sorely depressed. But beyond the fact that his situation is desperate, we cannot outline the difficulty more sharply. This is quite in keeping with much that is found in the psalms, where a sort of generalization is attempted so as to make the psalms usable by people in all manner of similar situations.

May the psalm have been written by David? Commentators with almost one voice say No. Aside from the prejudging of the case because the psalm is found in the latter part of the Psalter, the most common reason for denying the possibility of Davidic authorship is that there are so many direct quotations from or at least allusions to other psalms. Since most of these psalms are Davidic, it would seem equally logical to conclude that the psalm is Davidic because of the frequent use of phrases that are characteristically Davidic. If in a few instances there appear to be quotations from psalms that were not written by David, there is still the possibility that these psalms may also have borrowed

Psalm 143 963

from psalms that are to be attributed to David. In any case, we see no serious obstacle to the assumption that David is the author.

We find no good basis for the claim that the psalm does not voice the plaint of an individual but expresses the distress of the nation in exilic or postexilic days. To us the tenor of the psalm is far too personal to allow for such an approach. Whether those texts of the *Septuagint* are correct which assign the psalm to the days when David fled before Absalom may well be questioned.

The most distinctive feature of the psalm is v. 2, which voices the conviction that the writer cannot stand before God in judgment and expect vindication on the basis of his merits. He has sinned much and, indeed, deserved nothing but punishment. By classifying himself thus the writer indicates that he well knows that such is the common lot of all men. If he is, therefore, obliged to suffer affliction he knows it to be well deserved. He still pleads for help. With good reason, therefore, this has always been regarded in the church as a penitential psalm, one that is proper for Ash Wednesday. This verse reminds the reader of Ps. 51:5; Job 9:2; 14:4; 25:4; 130:3; Rom. 3:20.

To have the "dark regions" (v. 3) refer clearly to imprisonment and to have the writer's apprehensiveness result from his fear of the impending trial must be classified as conjectures.

The heading says: *A Psalm of David.*

1. *O Lord, hear my prayer;*
   Give ear to my supplications in Thy faithfulness;
   Answer me in Thy righteousness.
2. *And enter not into judgment with Thy servant,*
   For in Thy sight no man living can be righteous.
3. *For the enemy has pursued me;*
   He has dashed my life to the ground;
   He has made me to dwell in dark regions like those eternally dead.

1. When men begin to cry out as this man does they have a feeling that they have not been heard, that God has closed His ears to their petitions. They quite naturally seek some reason for being heard. In this case the psalmist appeals to God's "faithfulness" and to His "righteousness." His saints have long known that He can be absolutely depended upon; He is faithful. They also know well that He vindicates the right: He is "righteous." To these well-known attributes of God the psalmist directs his appeal.

2. That which makes his present situation especially painful is the deep-seated knowledge that, if desert and merit were to be the determining factors whether or not God will help, his case would be hope-

less. He therefore pleads that God would not make an issue of what he does or does not deserve. He who as a "servant" of God should have been engaged in doing God's will faithfully has been utterly remiss. In that respect he is like all others, none of whom can claim to have done better than he has. But the writer is not dealing in abstract truth. When he asks God not to make a test case of his situation he implies that God would exercise the opposite prerogative and vindicate him in His mercy. Nor is he content with the gloomy fact that no man can be righteous in God's sight. Implied in that statement is the request that God would grant him that righteousness which He alone can impart out of pure grace. Therefore the connection between vv. 1 and 2 might be stated thus: v. 1—help me; v. 2—justify me so that those things that stand in the way of my receiving help may be removed from Thy sight. The negative expressed in v. 2 must result in a positive plea for justification.

3. The writer now presents the details of his case more fully. He describes his situation. When he does that in the sight of the Lord, his thought is not to inform God concerning things of which He has no knowledge, but rather the wholesome conviction that God cannot view with complacency the anguish that His pardoned children suffer without going into action.

Rather desperate is the case of the psalmist in this instance. He has been hounded by an enemy. This enemy is a person of some influence who has been able to dash his life to the ground, which surely implies some harsh treatment that might have resulted in death. He has been able to bring about a situation which wraps the psalmist in deepest gloom and makes him appear almost like those that have been laid into the grave. For the familiar translation, "like those long dead," is not as strong as the original Hebrew states it. For there is written "the dead men of eternity." Here, as so often in the Old Testament, the hope of resurrection does not shine through. Yet for all that, the writer is saying nothing more than: I am already as good as dead. His is, therefore, a very unhappy lot due to the assault of a particular enemy.

4. *And my spirit fainted away within me;*
   And my heart within me was appalled.
5. *I remembered the days of old;*
   I meditated upon all Thy works;
   I mused upon the works of Thy hands.
6. *I spread forth my hands to Thee;*
   My soul thirsteth for Thee as parched land. Selah.

4. In these words the psalmist goes on to describe how the affliction that has befallen him has affected him. The approach is purely histori-

cal: he reports what he did. In the Hebrew all the verbs are past tenses, not presents. There was first an utter fainting away in weakness so that no courage was left. His spirit did not stand up manfully in bearing the shock. The stroke was almost too much for him. At the same time his heart within him was appalled. The greatness of the grief that had come upon him amazed him. This could not have been a trivial affliction. In casting about how to meet the emergency he did what so many saints of God have done, he "remembered the days of old."

5. What help was to be gained from reflecting upon those things which God had done in the past? As they give the record of the past, beginning with creation, the sacred Scriptures list a vast array of mighty works that God did, works of power and deeds of deliverance. Upon these the psalmist "meditated" and "mused." That is an effective way of getting one's bearings. God does not change. His works reveal adequately what an attitude He has toward His people.

6. Such meditation resulted in prayer: "I spread forth my hands to Thee" in the characteristic gesture of prayer of Old Testament times. Without indicating what it was that he asked for, by these words he seems to tell of the outreach of his soul to God; for that is the spirit of the next line: "My soul thirsteth for Thee as parched land." His meditation upon the past caused the realization of the need of God to come to him forcibly. The thirst for God was awakened (cf. Ps. 28:2), which is effectively stated as being like that of "parched land;" cf. also Ps. 63:1.

7. *Answer me soon, O Lord, my spirit fails!*
Hide not Thy face from me lest I become like those that go down to the pit.
8. *Let me hear of Thy kindness in the morning, for in Thee have I trusted;*
Reveal to me the way in which I should go, for to Thee I have lifted up my soul.
9. *Deliver me from my enemies, O Lord;*
In Thee have I taken refuge.

7. The prayer which began in v. 1 but was interrupted by the sense of guilt as well as by the anguish which the writer's soul felt in its present plight is now unfolded at length. His first thought is about help as soon as possible. He cannot bear up much longer. If, instead of showing a gracious countenance, God were to turn His face away from His servant in displeasure, that alone would be more than he could bear. He would perish and become like all those that have gone down into death, which is here described as "the pit," the vast realm into which all the

dead of bygone ages have sunk. Again the hope of the hereafter and of a resurrection doth not lighten the writer's path as was often the case in the times of the Old Covenant. Cf. Ps. 28:1.

8. Analogous to the prayer that he might be heard "soon" is the prayer that a report of God's "kindness" may come to him in the "morning," which is another way of saying, as soon as the next day breaks, or, if the night spoken of was a figurative expression for his affliction, this could be interpreted with *Delitzsch* to mean that "with the next morning's dawn the night of affliction may have an end." In addition to having God's kindness toward him manifested again the writer seeks from God that He may "reveal to (him) the way in which (he) should go." This could be interpreted to mean the way of salvation, especially if one compares the analogous statement made in Ps. 25:4. But this, which would be the way in the higher sense of the word, becomes the object of his prayer in v. 10. So it seems preferable to interpret this to mean the course which leads out of the present difficulty. As a motivating plea he adds: "for to Thee I have lifted up my soul." That is to say, if a man approaches God for help he need never fear that he will be turned down. He has turned to God; help will come.

At this point we may indicate how numerous the quotations are that are taken from other psalms. With the first half of the verse we may compare Ps. 69:17; 27:9; 102:2; and with the second part Ps. 28:1; 88:4. In like manner on v. 8 we might compare Ps. 90:14; 25:2; 25:4; 142:3; 25:1; 86:4. Here particularly the mosaic character of the psalm becomes apparent.

9. The last part of this prayer makes special reference to the enemies who are to a large extent the source of the difficulty that troubles him; and thus the psalmist asks to be delivered from them. The motivation advanced is like that found at the close of the preceding verse: "In Thee I have taken refuge." The very fact that a man has cast himself upon God's mercy gives warrant for the hope that he shall not have appealed to God in vain.

10. *Teach me to do what pleaseth Thee, for Thou art my God;*
    Let Thy good Spirit lead me in a level land.
11. *For Thy name's sake, O Lord, revive me;*
    In Thy righteousness bring me out of trouble.
12. *In Thy steadfast love put an end to my enemies*
    And destroy all my adversaries,
    For I am Thy servant.

10. We have labelled this a prayer for rehabilitation. Whereas trouble has brought the psalmist low, he asks that God may set him on his feet and enable him to go steadfastly on his way. He offers the

prayer to be enabled to live a God-pleasing life or to walk in the way of God's commandments, chief of which is the commandment of faith. The needed power will be supplied by none other than God's "Spirit," who is very appropriately called "good" because of the good work which He does. To walk in the course in which He directs men always means to be walking "in a level land." It is not a path that is tortuous and difficult but the clear-cut path of right and truth.

11. Analogous is the plea to be "revived," that is, reinvigorated, which implies to be equipped with the strength that is needed for this holy pilgrimage. The modifying phrase "for Thy name's sake" means that God has a reputation for dealing thus with His saints; may He in this case make the heart of His servant glad by dealing with him as He has dealt with so many others. Cf. Ps. 23:3; 25:11; 31:3; 109:21. The negative side of the matter is, "bring me out of trouble." Deliverance and the equipping with fresh strength go hand in hand.

12. The concluding verse is directed against the enemies and asks that an end be put to them, and that they may be destroyed. This prayer is scarcely thinkable unless the psalmist is keenly aware of the fact that his enemies are at the same time the enemies of the Lord's cause, who as long as they oppose His "servant" are opposing the Lord. There is nothing of petty malice behind this prayer. As long as they oppose God, their devices must be overthrown, and they as well. This does not eliminate the possibility of his still desiring their conversion. But more likely than not he clearly understands that they will not experience a change of heart.

NOTES

1. In the expression "in Thy righteousness" the initial *beth* may be regarded as a *beth normae* and thus, "according to Thy righteousness." Cf. *KS* 332r.

4. The verb "was appalled," *yishtomem,* is to be construed as involving a *waw* consecutive from which the verb has been separated. Therefore we have translated it as a perfect. Cf. *KS* 368i.

10. The adjective "good" is attributive and not predicative as *AV* has rendered it. *KS* discusses this in 334m, and *GK* explains why the *tobhah* has no article (126z).

Psalm 144

A KING AT HIS PRAYERS

IS THIS PSALM a compilation, and, perhaps, a none too happy compilation at that? The majority of commentators are pretty well agreed that such is the case though some will allow that the final result is a poem that deserves to be classed as a forceful production. Their conclusion is based chiefly on the fact that so many quotations from earlier psalms appear—from Ps. 18 in particular, also from Ps. 8, 33, 102, 103, 104. Under the influence of the thought that all is compilation, the last section, vv. 12–15, is claimed to be an addition from some unknown psalm. Nothing original! However, as was the case regarding the preceding psalm, we would indicate that ample use of Davidic material can be an argument for Davidic authorship as well as for the contrary.

Is the psalm a liturgy as the more recent writers suggest? Such a conclusion rests upon subjective feelings as well as upon the presupposition that liturgies preponderate in the Psalter. This theory about the prevalence of liturgies is not so well established as to allow for operating freely with this presupposition. Does the psalm bear marks of being connected with the festival of the enthronement of Yahweh? Nothing even remotely suggests such a conclusion unless one reads into this and into many other of the psalms ideas borrowed from Babylon which do not happen to be native to Israel.

Shall we despair of fixing a time for the psalm, except that it must needs be a very late date like that of Nehemiah or even beyond his time? Suffice it to say that *Oesterley* would prefer the age of Hezekiah, in fact, he regards Hezekiah as the king who speaks here.

By almost common consent the possibility of authorship by David is almost derided except by a writer like *Delitzsch,* who is not of very recent date. Yet we believe that the tradition which the heading embodies has much to commend it. The *Septuagint* felt thus, for it added the words "in reference to Goliath" to the heading. We have already suggested that the prevalence of quotations does not rule out Davidic authorship. The use of late words (which we shall list later) is no infallible criterion of a late date. For as *Weiser* has pointed out, these words indicate merely that the psalm may have been freely used at a later time (when Aramaic was beginning to supersede the Hebrew) and thus may have acquired an Aramaic coloring—a possibility that has not yet been sufficiently explored. Aside from these two, which are the major current objections, the contents of the psalm agree well with the life and spirit of David, especially if one note what I Sam. 17:47 records. The psalm is certainly composed in the spirit of the man who encountered Goliath though it may have been written at a later date with the Goliath incident as a general background.

In place of the idea that the psalm is an inferior piece of patchwork it might be well to consider the possibility that *Schmidt* suggests that we have here *ein originales Kunstwerk,* "an original work of art."

a) **A grateful prayer for deliverance uttered by the king (vv. 1–8)**
1. *Blessed be the Lord, my rock,*
   Who imparts skill to my hands for war and to my fingers for battle,
2. *The source of loving-kindness for me and my fortress,*
   My citadel and my deliverer, my shield and He in whom I have taken refuge,
   Who subdues my people under me.
3. *O Lord, what was man that Thou didst take note of him,*
   The son of man, that Thou didst take account of him?
4. *Man has (always) been like a mere breath,*
   His days like a fleeting shadow.
5. *Bow the heavens, O Lord, and come down;*
   Touch the mountains that they smoke.
6. *Flash Thy lightnings and scatter them;*
   Send forth Thy arrows and rout them.
7. *Stretch forth Thy hand from on high;*
   Snatch me away and deliver me out of the mighty waters,
   From the hand of aliens,
8. *Whose mouth speaks falsehood;*
   And whose right hand is a right hand of lies.

1. When we labeled this "a grateful prayer for deliverance" we sought to indicate that, though it is largely petition, it begins with thanksgiving for what God is and has done for the psalmist. It begins with a resounding bit of praise which is voiced in a sort of exuberant exclamation. A point of similarity with Ps. 18:46 at once becomes apparent; cf. also v. 35. Apart from this, the terminology of the first two verses is distinctly martial in character. In fact, it has been said that this "opening ascription . . . does not present a very edifying conception of Yahweh" but rather reflects that "ancient Semitic belief that the deities played a leading part in war." This is arm-chair criticism of sentiments that are born out of bitter conflict. He who has been ruler of a people

in time of war and was compelled to lead them in battle in a just cause and has experienced the potent help of the living God could write words like these in an entirely worthy conception of the God who helped him in the day of battle. Whatever skill he had in the use of weapons is not attributed to his prowess or exceptional strength but to those abilities which God gave. "Hands" are, perhaps, referred to as the agents for throwing the spear and "fingers" as used for shooting the arrow.

2. This verse multiplies metaphors that are descriptive of what God has meant to the psalmist, again mostly in the terminology of warfare. The first of these, not martial, however, is striking, for it says literally "my goodness" (*KJ*) or as *RSV* margin translates, "my steadfast love." This could be translated "the source of loving-kindness for me," for that is about what it means. A similar use of the word appears in Jonah 2:8 and Ps. 59:17. There is no need to remove the word in order to establish an agreement with Ps. 18:2 as *RSV* does. Then follow the terms: fortress, citadel, shield, and—in a more personal strain—deliverer. But still more personally He is the one in whom the psalmist has always taken refuge, not just now—always. If one reads Ps. 18:42–44 with care one notices that the writer very properly designates those whom he has enabled to conquer as his people. So here "my people" refers to all over whom he was given dominion. Again there is no need of amending the text as *RSV* does. The psalmist claims that he is a ruler by virtue of the victory which the Lord has granted him.

3. Success has not gone to the writer's head. He is fully aware of the fact that he has deserved nothing of this sort, neither he nor any other man. When the Lord deals thus with the children of men, it is on His part undeserved condescension pure and simple. Much in the spirit of Ps. 8 and almost in its very words he describes the innate insignificance of man. The statement is cast into terms of the past: "What was man?" implying that this has always been man's situation.

4. Positively stated, man's existence has always been a very fleeting thing, "mere breath" or " a fleeting shadow." By thoughts such as these the success that has come to him in his lifetime is kept in wholesome check and all incipient pride is squelched. The fact that David also in other instances gave expression to thoughts like this appears from II Sam. 7:18ff., a striking parallel.

5. The plea for direct divine intervention is now voiced. A man must be distinctly conscious of a certain high destiny to feel that his deliverance is important enough to presume to call upon God directly to come down from the heights of heaven and take his case in hand. Such was the certainty that David had on the basis of divine assurances that he as

head of God's chosen people had a high mission. "Bow the heavens" implies that He who sits enthroned above the clouds would on the chariot of His clouds come down to the emergency situation in which the petitioner finds himself. It scarcely implies that some sort of ramp be made from heaven down to earth upon which He might conveniently descend as *Schmidt* inappropriately suggests. If He comes down to the earth, in this instance to the land of promise itself, which is mountainous, the very mountains will begin to smoke at His sublime presence as they did at Sinai (Exod. 19:18). Cf. also Ps. 104:32. He is such a great God that in His presence the eternal hills are all but consumed.

6. The effect upon the enemies that need to be restrained is this that He will from the cloud of His appearing flash forth His lightnings upon them and scatter them. For this the psalmist confidently prays. He shall also send forth His arrows and rout them—a parallel statement in another figure, much as He did at the Red Sea cf. Exod. 14:24. That is the negative side of His activity in reference to the enemies.

7. On the positive side prayer is made to Him that He may in person reach forth after He has come down and "stretch forth (His) hand" from His superior position and "snatch away and deliver" His servant that calls upon Him even as Ps. 18:16 voiced the same thought. "Mighty waters" could in this case be a figure of speech that seeks to include all forms of danger that beset David at that time.

There follows a more complete description of those who were the opposition. First of all, they are aliens, people of another race. Besides, they seem to have engaged in the customary forms of diplomacy which even in those days consisted of "speaking falsehood." Similarly, any pledges that they might have given with a solemn grasping of the hand were idle gestures. For their "right hand was a right hand of lies." If treachery motivated all their doings, it is not expecting too much to have them dealt with severely according to their falsehood.

b) A vow to praise the Deliverer (vv. 9–11)

9. *I will sing a new song to Thee, O God;*
   Upon a harp of ten strings will I play unto Thee.
10. *O Thou, who didst give victory to kings,*
    Who didst deliver David, Thy servant, from the wicked sword,
11. *Snatch me away and deliver me from the hand of aliens,*
    Whose mouth speaks falsehood, and whose right hand is a right hand of lies.

This section is mostly a vow to praise the Deliverer when He shall have saved the psalmist. A new deliverance is anticipated, something that is so new as to call forth a new effort of praise (cf., Ps. 32:2, 3).

The harp of ten strings would seem to allow for full-toned music and thus suggests that an effort to match the greatness of the mercy received is going to be made.

Two things support the writer in this confident assertion: one is that God has in the past often functioned as a one who gave "victory to kings." By this statement the psalmist does not necessarily limit himself to the kings of His chosen people. From Him stems all government; all rulers who sought to defend a just cause were sustained by Him. The second source of confidence is that God has in the past delivered His servant David from the wicked sword. Why should He not do so again when this man legitimately calls upon Him in time of trouble?

The help from on high has not yet come. So the vow to praise naturally terminates in a plea for help. This plea again makes it plain that the treacherous aliens involved were a grave peril, for in a refrain the same plea that was voiced above is heard a second time (cf. vv. 7b and 8). Since this is a refrain, and since refrains are used to stress important issues, we are at this point made to feel that the danger represented by these enemies was the major one at this time.

The fact that David refers to himself (v. 10) in the third person need not be regarded as an obstacle to the claim that he wrote this psalm. There are similar objective statements in other psalms: cf., 61:6; 63:11; 18:50; II Sam. 7:26.

c) **A prayer for the prosperity of the nation (vv. 12–15)**

12. *That our sons in their youth may be like plants full grown;*
    Our daughters like corner pillars carved fit for a palace;
13. *That our garners may be full, yielding all sorts of store;*
    That our flocks may multiply by thousands and by tens of
        thousands in our fields;
14. *That our oxen may be heavily laden;*
    That there be no mishap or exile and no outcry in our streets.
15. *Happy the people that is in such a state;*
    Happy the people whose God is the Lord!

12. This is thought to be the later addition to the psalm that can only artificially be appended to what precedes. We feel quite otherwise. Since we regard the psalm as a unit prayer by the king of Israel we feel that he very appropriately broadens his prayer from the narrower concerns which are largely his own to the larger issues that involve the nation as a whole though it cannot be denied that in the first part of the psalm the welfare of the nation was also deeply involved. Why should a king be thought of as being concerned merely about his private and personal issues? The welfare of the king and of the nation go hand in hand.

It cannot, however, be denied that there are some unusual difficulties of translation and interpretation, especially in v. 14. We shall present what seems to us the more acceptable interpretation without attempting to offer a criticism of all others.

The nation consists of persons, very important among whom is the coming generation. Therefore prayer is first made for the coming generation, the sons and the daughters. For them prayer is made that they may be healthy and strong and comely. If the sons are like "plants full grown" they have not been stunted in their growth by wartime famine. Similarly the daughters are thought of as having enjoyed a healthy development and as being, so says the choice figure, "like corner pillars carved fit for a palace." This would connote a slim beauty and a sturdy strength. The caryatids of Greek architecture do not seem to be the thought; they stem from a later age, especially as far as Israel is concerned.

13. In addition abundance of grain in the granaries and prospering herds may be the objects of prayer inasmuch as all physical blessings come from the Lord; and bread and meat are still staples of diet.

14. In this verse there is listed a wide assortment of blessings that mark times of peace and prosperity. If oxen are "heavily laden," that expression would regard them as beasts of burden, which they sometimes are, and would picture them as transporting the various types of goods that a prosperous nation deals in commercially. The "mishap" here spoken of means "breach" and could refer to a breach in the wall that was made by the enemy in a time of siege. We prefer to regard it in the broader sense of "mishap." "Exile" is plain enough though it happens to be a word that in its root meaning involved only "going forth." We borrowed this thought from *Kautzsch,* who renders the word *Auszug.* Thus also "outcry" may be taken in the broadest sense as involving any exclamation of pain or alarm; *RSV* translates appropriately "cry of distress." This broad assortment of physical blessings does not argue for the thought that the writer was obsessed with the importance of things physical. He rightly regards material goods as only fine tokens of the Lord's favor, which may properly be sought; for God delights to bestow them upon His faithful children.

15. However, the fact that spiritual issues are fundamental is well indicated by the psalmist, who brings his psalm to a full-toned, ringing climax by stressing that "such a state" as he has just described can be realized in any measure of perfection only if the people are a "people whose God is the Lord." That means so much more than merely that He is regarded as the national God. It surely means nothing less than that the people build their life and thinking on Him and cheerfully

walk in His ways. The psalmist has laid his finger on the true source of success and lasting happiness for a nation.

NOTES

2. The difficulty regarding the word *chasdi* is solved when it is understood in the sense of "the *source* of loving-kindness for me." The verb *chasithi* is a perfect and should be translated as such. It is best construed as a gromic aorist, "I have always in the past taken refuge in Him." The fact that *mephalti* is followed by a dative helps to make the possessive idea more emphatic.

3. By the use of the *waw* consecutive the whole verse is cast into the past tense (*KS* 363c) in like manner as in the preceding verse. Man's past record is being considered. The same holds true for *damah* (v. 4), which is also in the perfect.

6. For the suffix in the expression "scatter them" there is no expressed antecedent. Therefore the "logical object" must be drawn on; the "them" refers to the enemies to be mentioned later.

10. Following the lead of the *Septuagint* and of the *Kittel* text "from the wicked sword" could be considered the beginning of v. 11. Nothing is particularly gained by the emendation. Since the participle (here *potseh*) takes its tense from its context, and the reference is obviously to the past, it must be translated by a past tense.

12. "Fit for a palace" involves an adverbial accusative of norm (*tabhnith*); see *KS* 332p and *GK* 118q.

Psalm 145

"GREAT IS THE LORD
AND GREATLY TO BE PRAISED"

As TO ITS FORM this psalm is an acrostic, that is to say, each successive verse begins with a new letter of the Hebrew alphabet. It has much in common with two other acrostics, Pss. 111 and 112. One Hebrew letter fails to receive consideration or has been inadvertantly omitted, the letter *Nun*. The *Septuagint* restores the missing verse, but with a dubious effort; for the verse produced to fill in the gap is like v. 17, with the exception of the first word.

It should be noted that this psalm is of a kindred spirit with the others that close the book as *Kirkpatrick* nicely points out. They all develop the theme, "For Thine is the kingdom, and the power, and the glory forever and ever. Amen."

A note of universalism is particularly noticeable in this psalm. It thinks in terms of all of God's works and all of those that dwell on the face of the earth by seeing them as also coming to the knowledge of the God of Israel and singing His praises.

All of which raises the question, Is the speaker in the psalm an individual or is he the personified nation, Israel? There does not appear to be anything that indicates a particularly personal character of the psalm. On the other hand, nothing seems to compel the reader to think in terms of the nation. The speaker is continually transferring himself into the situation of the nation as a whole. One may be inclined at least to say that the collective "I" might be the speaker in the psalm.

The psalm has a history. In the old Jewish church it was assigned to be used twice in the morning service and once in the evening service. Vv. 15 and 16 have since times immemorial been used in colleges as well as in countless homes in Christendom as a table prayer. Besides it is regarded as a proper psalm for Whitsunday.

It seems that only those interpreters who are under the impression that the enthronement of Yahweh festival fills a most prominent place in the services of Israel are inclined to associate this psalm with that festival. The psalm as such suggests no such use.

On the question of authorship by David, which the heading claims, the situation is practically the same as it was regarding the preceding psalm, except that no special occasion in the life of David could be cited as agreeing with this claim. The Aramaic words that are said to prove a late date are listed in *BDB* and *Koehler* as also being used in the Aramaic, but that does not prove them to have been distinctly Aramaic words.

a) **Resolve to bless the Lord forever (vv. 1, 2)**

   A song of praise. Of David
   1. *I will exalt Thee, my God, O King;*
      And I will bless Thy name forever and ever.
   2. *Every day will I bless Thee*
      And praise Thy name forever and ever.

In this resolve to bless the Lord it immediately becomes apparent that the psalmist stands in a personal relationship to the Lord: He is both his God and his King. When one has come to the point of knowing the Lord in a personal way, the desire to sing His praise and sing it often becomes very strong. In fact, when the writer says, "I will bless Thy name forever and ever," it is not so much the literal meaning of the phrase expressing the duration that is to be pressed. The psalmist apparently means nothing more than that he intends to praise the Lord as long as he has any being. He was scarcely thinking consciously of the life after death when he wrote thus. The verse is reminiscent of Ps. 34:1. Here as always the "name" of God connotes His revealed character; it is the summary of all that God has disclosed of Himself or of what the writer has experienced. It would also seem that the words "every day" are a comment on "forever and ever." This verse reminds the reader of Ps. 69:30. Taken together, the verses express an ardent desire to praise God worthily and continuously.

b) **His incomparable greatness the theme for all generations to come** (vv. 3-7)

3. *Great is the Lord and greatly to be praised;*
   and His greatness is unsearchable.
4. *One generation shall tell the other the praises of Thy works*
   And shall declare Thy heroic acts.
5. *Upon the glorious splendor of Thy majesty*
   And upon Thy wonderful works will I meditate.
6. *And men shall speak of the might of Thy awe-inspiring acts;*
   And as for Thy greatness, I shall declare it.
7. *They shall pour forth the remembrance of Thy great goodness;*
   And they shall exult over Thy righteousness.

3. God's incomparable greatness in its broadest aspects is thought of as being the theme that shall occupy generations to come. God's acts, thought of in a general way rather than His specific acts for the salvation of men, are under consideration.

The opening statement concerns itself with the fact that the Lord is great and greatly deserving of praise. Yet for all that, the subject of God's greatness can never be sufficiently fathomed by any man; for that matter, it is "unsearchable." Echoes of Ps. 8:1 and 40:5 are heard. In a certain kind of holy relay one generation is thought of as passing on to the next (cf. Ps. 19:2) the marvelous story of the works that God is known to have done, like His works of creation and preservation. In addition there will be the theme of "His heroic acts," deeds which He undertook in the spirit of the great heroes of old and achieved right marvelously.

5. By the building up of phrases and expressions the unique glory of God through His works is described: the Hebrew says: "the glory of the splendor of the majesty." In addition those works of God which have throughout the ages aroused great wonder are spoken of as being the subject of meditation. In addition there may be enumerated God's

"awe-inspiring acts," which have been done times without number. All these are worthy themes for the devout mind. All this adds up to the "greatness" (v. 6) of His being, which can never be sufficiently declared.

7. With a rather expressive verb that speaks of words flowing forth as waters well up from a fountain (cf. Ps. 119:171) all these generations together are described as extolling the Lord. Another summary term that covers this whole area is God's "righteousness," which includes all those things that He has actively engaged in to maintain the covenant relationship with the children of Israel. *Briggs* quite appropriately designates this as God's "saving righteousness."

c) **His grace and mercy is especially to be praised (vv. 8, 9)**

8. *Gracious and merciful is the Lord,*
Slow to anger and of great kindness.
9. *The Lord is good to all;*
And His compassion is over all His works.

8. When the psalmist emphasizes that the Lord's grace and mercy are to be especially praised he advances from the works to the basic attributes. Till now God's power and might have been indirectly under consideration. It has been rightly observed that the psalmist mounts to ever greater heights. He who recognizes that God is merciful understands God much more completely than does he who merely recognizes how mighty He is. The words are practically the same as Ps. 103:8, and both verses are a quotation from the famous declaration in which God revealed the depth of His character to Moses in Exod. 34:6. "Gracious" stresses the undeserved favor that God bestows; "merciful" lays the finger of compassion on the deep need of man. He that has been forgiven cannot help but make mention of the fact that God is also "slow to anger" and does not punish us as we so richly merit. The "great kindness" spoken of has to do with that quality which is so commonly translated "steadfast love" in the *RSV*, a term for which our language has no equivalent that is quite big enough to express all that is involved.

9. At this point a new turn is introduced into the thought of the psalm which keeps reappearing down to the very end. It is the universality of outlook that finds expression in the words: "The Lord is good to all." Since the second half of the verse speaks of the works of God, "all" would by contrast seem to imply all persons. Israel was often so preoccupied with itself that it forgot or overlooked the fact that God was concerned about all that were His creatures. It redounds to His rich praise that His interest is of such a universal breadth. One

cannot comprehend this broad scope of which divine goodness is capable, but one can regard this as an inspiring article of faith; and for it the Lord deserves to be praised abundantly.

d) The kingdom of the Lord the object of praise of all His works (vv. 10–16)

10. *All Thy works give thanks to Thee, O Lord;*
    And Thy saints bless Thee.
11. *They speak of the glory of Thy kingdom*
    And tell of Thy heroic deeds;
12. *To make known to the sons of men His heroic deeds*
    And the glorious splendor of His kingdom.
13. *Thy kingdom is an everlasting kingdom;*
    And Thy dominion endures throughout all generations.
14. *The Lord sustains all who are falling*
    And raises up all who are bowed down.
15. *The eyes of all wait upon Thee;*
    And Thou givest them their food in due season.
16. *Thou openest Thy hand*
    And satisfiest the desire of every living thing.

10. The subject of the "kingdom of the Lord" comes prominently to the forefront as being the object of praise by all His works. First of all, the works of God and His saints (i.e., those who are loyal to the covenant that He has made with His people) are listed as constituting one great chorus in the praise to be rendered. We have intentionally used a different translation and a permissible one for the verbs here involved, thus indicating that this praise is not to be throught of as lying only in the future. The insight of people in the psalmist's day was concerned about rendering this thanks properly. The use of the future tense would imply the very proper thought that, as time goes on and insight grows, this praise will be tendered ever more effectively. Both thoughts are in place.

11. The new theme is announced—not merely "the kingdom" but "the glory of Thy kingdom." In the maintenance of this kingdom and in the support of its advance the Lord has achieved many "heroic deeds," (cf. v. 4); therefore both are mentioned in one breath. The kingdom without a doubt appears here in its broadest aspects as a kingdom of grace as well as a kingdom of might. The glory aspect of the kingdom of eternity was only faintly apprehended in the Old Testament. The object of the praises uttered in this case is specifically stated as being to make these heroic deeds known to the "sons of men" that they, too, may see what a glorious thing this kingdom is and may aspire to enter into it.

The claim that the mere fact of the mention of the kingdom of God indicates a rather late date in Old Testament thinking is not warranted. Already in David's day the subject was broached (cf. I Chron. 17:14; Ps. 2, etc.). Broader aspects of truth may flash upon certain generations without entering fully into the thinking of the men of that age. David could well have uttered thoughts such as these.

13. One characteristic of this kingdom is especially stressed in this connection—it is "everlasting," and it "endures throughout all generations." In that respect it is so utterly unlike the kingdoms of this world, of which David may have seen quite a few come and go. This verse appears in Dan. 4:3, 34, indeed in words uttered by Nebuchadnezzar, but words which Daniel may have taught him.

14. A more intimate and attractive side of the kingdom of the Lord is to be dwelt upon through the rest of this section: the kindliness of the Lord of this kingdom toward those that stand in need of help. When men are about to fall or are already falling, the Lord sustains them; when they are bowed down with grief ar adversity, He raises them up. Besides, He provides for all His subjects by providing for all of them the food they need. In a very striking manner all living creatures are represented as being aware of what the Lord does and so trustingly lifting up their eyes to Him that, when they hunger, He may supply their need. Waiting on their part connotes trusting. For countless centuries the record that God has achieved is this: "Thou givest them their food (meat *KJ* is Old English for food) in due season" without undue delay. The few exceptions to this rule that men could cite vanish in contrast with the countless instances of its fulfilment every day. The picture is drawn out a bit more fully: God is represented as opening His hand and then giving to each, man or beast, as much as may be required to satisfy what they need and desire. He then passes on to the next and does the same. What a kingdom, where its Lord has time and ability to proceed thus!

e) **God's readiness to hear prayer especially comforting (vv. 17–21)**

17. The Lord is just in all His ways
    And kind in all His works.
18. The Lord is near to all that call upon Him,
    To all who call upon Him sincerely.
19. He will fulfil the desire of those who fear Him;
    He also will hear their cry and will save them.
20. The Lord preserves all those that love Him;
    But all the wicked will He destroy.
21. My mouth shall speak the praise of the Lord;
    And all flesh shall bless His holy name forever and ever.

In this last section of the psalm the emphasis lies on the fact that the Lord's readiness to hear prayer is especially comforting. The broad aspects of His work and being are grand and inspiring. They have been given due attention. The psalm now comes closer to the special needs of the individual. These are again not considered in a narrow and exclusive way. This comforting truth is thought of in relation to all His creatures. The broad universalism of the psalm is evident also in this point.

17. The starting point is God's justice and kindness. It again becomes apparent that "justice" did not connote sternness and punishment exclusively as it usually does with us. A man could derive comfort from the fact that God was just. It reminded him of the energy with which God maintained His side of the covenant for His people. These two attributes are akin—"just" and "kind." They extend in an infinite scope over "all His works" and are manifest "in all His ways."

18. The special adaptation of this truth that is now made concerns the prayers of men: this same God is near to all who call upon Him as long as they call "sincerely." Though the Hebrew says "in truth" for "sincerely," the implied contrast must be mere formalistic prayers that are spoken but are not really prayers. Most commentators agree completely with Luther who translated, *mit Ernst,* which is either earnestly or sincerely. The first part of the verse should not be lost sight of. It gives the comforting assurance that, as soon as a man begins to call upon the Lord, the Lord is near (cf. Ps. 34:18; 119:151).

19. Something in the nature of a blanket promise is now given. But lest all caution be thrown to the winds, there is the necessary phrase which limits the promise to those "who fear Him." True fear of God gives direction and limitation to prayers and prevents men from asking for things rashly, forgetting the nature of the Lord and His wholesome restraints. We have the same approach in Ps. 34:15 and 37:39. In this connection "save" means "deliver" in the broadest sense.

20. This thought of God's readiness to hear His children is again repeated with the further suggestion that He may also at times be pleased to keep His own in such a manner that they do not even come into the anticipated danger. What a wholesome thing the "fear" of v. 19 is appears from the fact that the parallel expression is "love." The two go hand in hand most beautifully. But a contrasting thought is expressed to round out this verse, and that is the thought: "All the wicked will He destroy." This contrast, so often met with in the Old Testament, expressed what all of God's saints had abundantly observed. For before the Great Commission was given and men in greater numbers repented and turned to the Lord, the wicked quite uniformly continued in their wickedness and went down to destruction. Men

should not find undue fault or any at all, for that matter, with so true and correct an observation. To inject the further thought that Old Testament saints gloried in such an overthrow of the wicked is quite unjust.

21. By way of an appropriate conclusion the psalmist sums up both his own reaction to these manifold operations of divine grace which he has enumerated as well as the reaction of "all flesh," that is, all animated beings that benefit from the gracious government of the earth by its Sovereign Lord. He for his part shall speak the praises of the Lord. He exhorts all beings to bless that Holy name forever and ever.

Though it is cast into the somewhat stiff mold of an acrostic this psalm has, with singular flexibility of thought, built up a well-rounded picture of the manifold works of God, for which He should be abundantly praised. Both the breadth and the warmth of the psalm deserve special notice.

NOTES

5. The *Septuagint* read *wedhibhrey* as *yedhabberu,* "they shall speak." This relieves a somewhat unusual sentence structure. Even *RSV* did not regard such a change as necessary.

6. One is apt to overlook the object suffix on the verb "declare." Translating it merely preserves the somewhat unusual construction and affords a bit of variety.

14. *Hannophelim* as a participle may be translated "are falling" or "about to fall," a potential participle as *Buttenwieser* suggests. On the two objects introduced by *le* see *GK* 117n.

16. *Ratson,* "goodwill" or "desire," raises the question as to whose goodwill is involved—God's or man's. By the translation "desire" the English versions eliminate the difficulty and arrive at the simple conclusion: Man is given what he so strongly desires. This seems to be the best interpretation.

19. "Will save" is not in the usual construction, *waw* consecutive with perfect, but is an unconverted imperfect. *KS* explains this as an attempt to let the two consecutive acts stand out more prominently by contrast, 370 3.

Psalm 146

BLESSED THE MAN WHO HOPES IN THE LORD

IN ADDITION to Ps. 113–118, the Ps. 146–150 constitute a Hallel in the Jewish tradition (Talmud).

One is somewhat at a loss to determine the special emphasis of this psalm. It is without a doubt a psalm of praise, beginning and ending as all the last five do, "Praise the Lord." It clearly counsels the reader to refrain from putting confidence in what man can do, a fact which has led some interpreters to maintain that this is its theme. But it also puts emphasis upon trusting in the Lord, which is a positive over against the preceding negative. We might state the case thus: We have, therefore, a psalm of praise which has the didactic purpose to urge men to put their trust in the Lord.

Its place in the Psalter, the heading found in some manuscripts of the *Septuagint*, and the absence of any reference to earlier occasions as well as the frequent quotations from other late psalms suggest that it is of comparatively late date. The heading in the *Septuagint* referred to reads: "Of Haggai and Zechariah." That could mean that the psalm may come from the time of these prophets. It certainly would fit well into the days of Nehemiah.

The occasion which may have given rise to the psalm cannot be determined. It is a guess that the writer had had a sad experience by putting his trust in some prominent personage. It is another guess to claim that Jewish rulers had recently committed some egregious blunder. We have just as little warrant to claim that this is a part of the ritual of paying a vow in the sanctuary. It is true that significant utterances are sometimes the outgrowth of special experiences. It is equally true that deeper insights come as a result of reflection.

A somewhat unique factor in the psalm is its distinctive social emphasis—God's concern for the helpless and needy. This is not too unique in the Psalter. As *Taylor* has pointed out, the following psalms sound something of the same note: 10, 15, 24, 37, 72, 103.

It has also been remarked that especially in v. 7–9 the psalm has something that would correspond to what we call rhyme—in this case the ending of a number of lines on the Hebrew syllable *im*. To us this appears purely accidental, of no significance whatever, because it happens to be the regular Hebrew masculine plural ending, and quite a few masculine plural nouns are demanded by the context.

Though it abounds in allusions and more especially in somewhat free quotations from earlier psalms, this resultant poem is, nevertheless, rather fresh in tone and content. The quotations come so naturally and have been so thoroughly absorbed by the writer that the resultant psalm seems anything but a string of familiar quotations. This is good, fresh poetry.

a) A summons to praise God (vv. 1, 2)

1. *Praise the Lord!*
Praise the Lord, O my soul!
2. *I will praise the Lord as long as I live;*
I will sing praise to my God as long as I have any being.

1. The first line is a translation of the familiar Hebrew word Alleluiah (or Hallelujah). It is a call that is addressed to all to engage in this holy business. It may be understood liturgically. It may be a mere summons to all who hear or read this word to act accordingly. But he who here summons others to engage in this delightful task at the same time exhorts himself or his inmost soul to have a part in it all. The resemblance to Ps. 104:1 is obvious.

2. The exhortation addressed to himself has taken fire, for it has already grown to the proportion where he resolves to praise the Lord as long as he lives. The theme is so great that it calls for great efforts to do justice to it. Such perpetual preoccupation with so great a subject does not strike the psalmist as involving any growing weary of the theme or of its losing its freshness. He is sure that its possibilities and resources are endless. So he repeats his self-exhortation in even more general terms, "as long as I have any being." Those individuals who have made derisive remarks about the monotony of eternal praise of God know not whereof they speak. The similarity between v. 2 and Ps. 104:33 is plain.

It will be noted that the writer who is about to exhort and instruct others first exhorts himself. That is one of the appealing touches of the psalm.

b) Negative counsel: put no trust in princes (vv. 3, 4)

3. *Put no trust in princes,*
Nor in mere man, in whom there is no help.
4. *When his spirit expires, he returns to his earth;*
In that day all his devisings will have perished.

3. One is intrigued a bit as to how this thought quite unexpectedly comes into the picture, this warning men against putting their hopes

in men of high standing. It may be only a point of departure from the positive that follows and is injected to constitute some sort of contrast. Of the many objects in which a man may place confidence certainly prominent personages are one of the outstanding. For this reason other Scripture passages give the same counsel; see Ps. 118:8, 9; Jer. 17: 5ff. According to the root meaning of the term, the princes are persons who are in a position to make their own decisions as to what they shall do. To bank on such is always uncertain, for as the second line suggests, they are "mere man." The Hebrew says, "son of man," which, however, in this instance has no further connotation than that such a one is descended from that being which was originally compounded from earth. Though such beings have been known at times to have been of some help to those that appealed to them, yet strictly speaking, in them "there is no help." They do not have resources which enable them always to deliver those who turn to them.

4. This thought of their native incapacity is developed a bit farther. The time will come when the spirit that animates such a one "goes out" (so the Hebrew) and returns to his own earth from which he was taken (cf., Gen. 2:7; 3:19). Whatever he may have been devising up to that time, whatever unfinished plans there are, by that time all these "will have perished." This affords sufficient proof of the frailty of princes and of the vanity of pinning one's hopes on them. This last verse is referred to in I Macc. 2:63.

c) **Positive counsel: hope in the Lord (vv. 5–9)**

5. *Blessed is the man whose help is the God of Jacob,*
   Whose hope is in the Lord his God,
6. *Who made heaven and earth, the sea and all that is in them,*
   Who keeps faith forever,
7. *Who upholds justice for the oppressed,*
   Who gives food to the hungry;
   The Lord sets the prisoners free.
8. *The Lord opens the eyes of the blind;*
   The Lord raises up those that are bowed down;
   The Lord loves the righteous.
9. *The Lord watches over the strangers;*
   The Lord restores the orphan and the widow
   And makes the way of the wicked crooked.

5. It required but a few arguments to establish the thesis that princes are vain as a basis of confidence. Much more could have been adduced by way of proof. But any man can grasp the point involved without lengthy argumentation. But the positive side of the matter, that the man

is blessed "whose help is the God of Jacob," invites more abundant illustration, we prefer not to say "proof" because so many things are known that the Lord does and has always done. The somewhat condensed expression that the God of Jacob is such a person's help certainly means that such a one is in the habit of seeking his help at this source, or as the next line states it, he keeps pinning his "hope in the Lord his God." Such a man does not merely have a correct theory about what God can do; he puts his theory into practice. "Jacob" rather than Israel may be used as the less frequent and therefore more choice expression.

6. The manifold evidences of what God can do may be grouped into two classes: there are, first of all, the great works that God is known to have done; then there are the kindly works that He loves to do for the children of men. The first group extends from vv. 5—7b.

These are quite effectively listed by a participial construction, with the participle always standing first and so placing emphasis on both the action and the continuance of that action. These are works that the Lord continually performs. There are, first of all, certain fundamental works that God once did in a creative way. This whole theatre of action in which man moves and has his being originated with God who made "heaven and earth, the sea and all that is in them." It must be quite obvious that He who made can control what He made. This is in the nature of a quotation; cf. Ps. 115:15; 121:2, etc. An equally stable thing to build confidence on is the further fact that He "keeps faith forever." No one of His saints has as yet found Him unreliable. His is a long record of dependability.

7. All that He does is at the same time governed by a principle, and the governing principle is that He "upholds justice for the oppressed." A point of this sort would be urged by those that have suffered oppression. Wherever men may try to override justice, the Almighty overrides their injustice. The fact that from this point onward the works of the Lord done for the helpless and insignificant stand in the forefront would again seem to indicate that at the time the psalm was written Israel's lot was a depressing and unhappy one. The last item mentioned is that He "gives food to the hungry." According to its nature this work would seem to belong among those in the next class, but according to the grammatical construction it is listed in the first group. It rightly belongs there. For all grow hungry, man and beast, and it is God who satisfies their hunger, not the independent operations of the laws of nature (cf. Ps. 145:15, 16). On v. 7a, cf. Ps. 103:6.

Among the kindly things that the Lord does for the benefit of men the first mentioned is that He "sets the prisoners free." The context demands some limitations such as freeing those who are innocently imprisoned or those who have served their sentence and deserve to be liberated. Since the expression occurs also in Is. 42:7 and 61:1, and there in reference to the deliverance from Babylonian Captivity, perhaps the figurative interpretation is the one to be preferred here. Otherwise Joseph in Egypt might well be thought of.

8. He is then said to "open the eyes of the blind." Is. 35:5 makes the same claim. Since there is no instance on record in the Old Testament that a physical healing of blind eyes took place, this, too, had, perhaps, rather be understood in the spiritual sense of enlightenment although there is no doubt that God's ability to cure blindness must surely be included in the expression. The fact that God "raises up those that are bowed down" (found also in Ps. 145:14) calls for the broadest application. God has at numberless times lifted up the discouraged and those who were physically bowed down and given them fresh hope.

The next turn of thought, however, strikes some interpreters as being out of proper sequence and they insert it after v. 9b. We feel that enough may be said for its place at this point to permit our keeping it here. The fact that God "loves the righteous" is inserted in order to convey the needed reminder that those whose suffering is alleviated must be righteous persons in the sight of the Lord. Not every evildoer, least of all the impenitent one, may comfort himself with the hope of kindly deliverance.

9. A few more acts of mercy on the Lord's part are enumerated. He "watches over the strangers." Ever since Israel herself was a stranger in the land of Egypt, the remembrance of that fact is kept alive, and the nation is taught to show kindness to those from without the nation who for the time being dwelt in its midst. The Lord Himself is thought of as having the same consideration for these, whose rights might so easily be violated. In a similar class are the orphans and the widows (cf. Ps. 68:5, 6). The Lord champions their rights as well. God is a God of the weak and helpless.

There follows an unanticipated turn of the thought: "He makes the way of the wicked crooked." We are reminded of 1:6. The thought is the familiar one that God is the one who must punish the individual who is consistently hostile to him and refuses to walk in His ways. This is not a thought that grows out of limited insight but an emphasis on one of the Lord's consistent and admirable qualities. If God's strict judgment upon wickedness is overlooked, a vital divine attribute is neglected, and a distorted picture of God results. All these works of the Lord were enumerated in order to foster trust in Him as the One on whom man can and should always lean. "Making the way crooked" turns a man aside from his goal and may lead him to destruction.

d) The Lord's unending kingship (v. 10)

10. *The Lord shall reign forever,*
    Thy God, O Zion, to all generations.
    Praise the Lord!

Lest the worshiper lose sight of the fact that all that was thus far spoken is said in the spirit of jubilant praise, the concluding verse specifically rings the note of praise with a statement on the Lord's unending kingship, based on Exod. 15:18, where the hymn of Miriam closes with the same words. The reminder is added that this eternal king is Zion's God. Happy is the nation that can claim this God for her own! Therefore a final victorious Alleluiah.

NOTES

3. On "mere man" see *KS* 306i. "Son of man" may even be disturbing because of its New Testament use with reference to the Lord. The German *Menschenkind* conveys the proper impression. The plural "children of men" has the same connotation in English.

4. An imperfect like *tetse'* may be used to express a conditional or temporal clause. See *KS* 193b. The perfect *'abhedu* had better be rendered as a future perfect rather than as a plain present. The force of the Hebrew tenses is regarded all too little.

5. The noun that is dependent of *'ashrey* is omitted but easily supplied; we have used "the man" in order to round out the construction. Cf. *KS* 337w. The *be* before *'ezro* may be the result of dittography. It is best to omit it.

Psalm 147

PRAISE THE LORD WHO GOVERNS HIS PEOPLE AND THE WHOLE EARTH

If a time may be suggested as being favorable to the composition of this psalm, none would seem to fit better than the situation in the days of Nehemiah, when the walls had finally been successfully rebuilt, and the people greatly rejoiced because of the resultant sense of security and prosperity (see Neh. 12:27–43). To this event the words of v. 1 may be an allusion when the Lord is praised as the one who "builds up Jerusalem." For all building that was undertaken up to the time of the completion of the walls was of a very unsatisfactory kind.

There are two psalms to which this one has unusual affinity. First there is Ps. 145, the points of contact with which may be readily detected without enumerating them. Then there is Ps. 33, which has been likened to a preexilic treatment of the same subject. Here, too, the points of similarity are quite obvious. Yet each of these three has its distinctive character.

Because of an inclination to draw heavily upon earlier psalms and Scripture passages this psalm is faulted even to the point where it is claimed that it "does not rank high either spiritually or poetically" (*Buttenwieser*). Many interpreters would at least concede that it is lacking in logical build-up. However, as we hope to show, when instances are cited in proof of a certain contention, anything that serves as a good illustration has good logic by virtue of its very aptness. If these illustrations are chosen from a wide area of possibilities, that merely proves the broad outlook of the writer. No man would care to claim that the psalm lacks warmth and fervor. In fact, it is a very excellent psalm that is abundantly grounded in earlier Scripture passages and enriched by the use of them.

Because our psalm may be divided into two, even three, parts, some interpreters immediately question its unity and would claim that it was later combined into one. However, it would seem quite reasonable, since each of the two or three portions are decidedly similar in character and approach, that they could have been composed by one and the same man and put together by him in the sequence in which we now have them. The *Septuagint* offers vv. 12–20 as a separate psalm and so evens out the count which had departed from the Hebrew since Ps. 9 and 10, which had been combined into one.

When we come to outlining the psalm we find that almost all writers find three parts, each of which begins with an exhortation to praise. Because of the wealth of thought contained, we will not attempt to outline all the separate thoughts offered under each head.

a) **Praise the Lord who builds Jerusalem and controls the heavens (vv. 1–6)**

1. *Praise the Lord!*
   For it is good to sing praises to our God;
   For it is pleasant, and praise is befitting.
2. *The Lord builds up Jerusalem;*
   He gathers together those in Israel who have been pushed aside;
3. *He heals the brokenhearted;*
   And He binds up their wounds.

4. *He assigns the number of the stars;*
   He calls all of them by names.
5. *Great is our sovereign Lord and of great strength;*
   There is no limit to His understanding.
6. *The Lord raises up the meek;*
   He casts the wicked down to the ground.

1. The motivation for praise regularly includes two areas in each of the three sections of the psalm—what the Lord does in His universal government of the world as well as what He does for His people. In this section both are well blended. The idea is first reinforced that praise itself is a pleasant and most delightful and proper occupation. It may be possible that the sequence of the clauses is not as smooth as is the case elsewhere. They are marked by an almost choppy brevity. But the familiar rendering is clear and appropriate, and there is no good reason for resorting to alterations. The style of even the best of writers may at times be devoid of a smooth flow. Reminiscences of Ps. 92:2; 135:3; 33:1 are blended in this verse, which offers a fresh and acceptable thought.

2. That Jerusalem and the fact that it has seen building activity are brought into the picture would argue for the fact that this was a subject which was uppermost in the minds of men at the time, a situation which certainly prevailed in the days of Nehemiah (ca. 444 B.C.). The participial form of the verb used suggests that the Lord is continually at work building up the holy city (cf. Ps. 51:18; 102:16). Of an analogous nature is the next work attributed to Him: "He gathers together in Israel those who have been pushed aside." This statement may include a number of possibilities. It may include those who have in the course of perhaps 75 years been brought back to the Holy Land from captivity. It may refer to those commonly classed as "outcasts," (*KJ*), whom others reject, but whom the Lord accepts. It may refer to all who have been "pushed aside," which the verb basically means. When the lowly and all persons who are in need of help are thought of as the ones whom the Lord loves to support, we might remember that many men are usually in such unfortunate situations. This constitutes an argument for a date in the days of Nehemiah. The next verse has a similar emphasis.

3. The healing of the "brokenhearted" is to be taken in the broadest sense by including those who grieve over their sins as well as those who are afflicted by life's manifold adversities. Similar is the thought of the binding up of wounds. In either case the gentle pity of the Lord is beautifully depicted as He stands by to comfort or to act the part of the kindly physician.

4. This verse seems to describe a work that is of much vaster scope. But are the care and control of the stars really greater than is the help bestowed upon needy souls? The approach seems to be that certain mighty works that are rightly to be attributed to the Lord guarantee that He will be able to care adequately for the helpless. Is. 40:26 compared with v. 27 argues in the same manner. There is then, first of all, this work of His: He "assigns the number of the stars"; He has control as to how many there shall be, for He is the creator of them all. He also appoints them for their various functions, for that is what "calling them by names" seems to signify. For "name" designates "character," and each star fills its own particular place by divine appointment.

5. From the assorted works thus far enumerated the conclusion is now drawn with regard to Him who does them all: "Great is the Lord and of great strength; there is no limit to His understanding." He has the insight that is required for the planning and devising of all these creatures of His; He has the strength to create them; He is the Lord. Similar is the thought expressed in Job 37:23. In our translation we used the expression "sovereign Lord" to catch the force of the Hebrew plural, a sort of plural of majesty.

6. Only for a moment the psalmist dwells on the things that transpire in the vastness of space. He is concerned about more intimate works of the Lord that lie closer to the hearts of His people, and evidences of which have recently been seen in great number. Two works that hold one another in balance are considered. On the one hand, the Lord "raises up the meek." Those are the ones who have bowed under the blows of adversity and have accepted them as coming from the Lord's hand and have meekly agreed that the will of their sovereign Lord was good. Cf. also Ps. 146:9. But as is so often the case in the sacred Scriptures, the Lord's work of deliverance of the righteous is presented in the same breath with His judgment upon the wicked, of whom it is here asserted that He casts them down to the ground. One group experiences help, the other defeat.

b) **Praise the Lord who governs the earth and helps those who fear Him (vv. 7–11)**

7. *Sing to the Lord with thanksgiving;*
   Sing praises to our God with the harp.
8. *He covers the heavens with clouds;*
   He prepares rain for the earth; He makes grass to grow upon the mountains.
9. *He gives to the cattle its food,*
   To the young ravens that cry.

10. *He takes no particular delight in the strength of a horse;
Nor does He take delight in the strong thighs of a man.*
11. *The Lord takes delight in those who fear Him,
In those that hope in His mercy.*

7. What we have inadequately rendered "sing" is really "respond," i.e., to the Lord for what He has done. His goodness to us calls for appropriate response. But if this response is done with thanksgiving, it may be thought of as responsive singing. The parallel expression brings instrumental music into the picture. Again some obviously mighty work of the Lord is taken under consideration, beginning, as above, in the high heavens, in this instance with the clouds. The heavens often continue cloudless day for day, but God causes clouds to form so that He may prepare rain for the earth. The grass that then springs up from the earth is, therefore, directly attributable to Him. It is not the processes of nature that produce these things. All such forces are directly under the control of the Lord. Ps. 104:13f. expressed the same thought.

9. Among those that are the recipients of His bounty the cattle are mentioned, which term may here be used in the very broad sense of all beasts. In a specific instance by way of colorful illustration the "young ravens that cry" are then specifically mentioned. These birds are singled out because their raucous cawing certainly has nothing attractive about it so as to make them candidates for God's benefits in a particular sense. The expression does not go quite so far in this instance as some statements do in which (cf. Ps. 104:27, 28) the creatures are said to appeal to God directly for help—a fact which led *Luther* to translate: *die ihn anrufen* ("that cry to *Him*").

10. The thought takes a particular turn at this point, reminding us that it is no merit or worthiness of any of His creatures that causes the Lord to take note of them. It cannot be "the strength of a horse" that impresses Him, for He supplied the strength that the horse has. By the same token the "strong thighs of a man" cannot be a source of special delight to Him, for He gave man his strength. In fact, these two illustrations may have been used largely to furnish a darker background for the thought about to be expressed. What God does delight in is a man who either has the true "fear" of Him in his heart or, what always goes hand in hand with such reverent fear, who "hopes in His mercy." These are the qualities that all His dealings with the sons of men try to arouse in their hearts. Those who have these qualities may look with confidence for His help. All this serves as a personal reminder to the reader as to what attitude the individual should seek to cultivate.

c) **Praise the Lord for what He has done for Zion (vv. 12-20)**

12. Praise the Lord, O Jerusalem;
    Praise your God, O Zion.
13. For He has strengthened the bars of your gates;
    He has blessed your children in the midst of you.
14. He makes peace your boundary;
    He satisfies you with the finest of the wheat.
15. He sends forth His command to the earth;
    His word runs very swiftly.
16. He gives snow like wool;
    He scatters the hoarfrost like ashes.
17. He casts forth His ice like chunks;
    Who can stand before His cold?
18. He sends forth His word and melts them;
    He makes His wind to blow, and the waters flow.
19. He makes His word known to Jacob;
    His statutes and ordinances to Israel.
20. He has not dealt so with any nation;
    And as for His ordinances, they have not known them.
    Praise the Lord!

12. Whereas in the preceding note was taken of what God has done and is able to do for individuals, the emphasis now lies upon what He achieves for His people as a whole, here referred to by the capital city as so often and merely called Jerusalem or Zion. This people owes a large debt of gratitude to its sovereign Lord. A particular item is singled out as marking the blessings that God has so abundantly bestowed, the fact, namely, that the bars of her gates are now made strong by Him. At no time was that an issue to the extent that it was in the days of Nehemiah, where for the first time after more than a century there were gates that could be shut and effectively barred, and thus the city could have a sense of security such as many had never experienced.

Note how these very bars and gates figure in the historical report of Neh. 3:3, 6, 13, 14, 15. This achievement meant for parents a feeling of security for their children that had long been painfully lacking. It is for this reason that the thought turns to the children and calls them blessed for being able to live in a place and at a time when security was a cherished reality. It should not be overlooked in this connection that the Hebrew in a way that is analogous to the English way of stating things uses the perfect form of the verb whereas throughout the section a participial construction prevails. This construction says in effect that the well-barred gates and the children blessed with peace lie within the realm of accomplished facts, long hoped for and now to be enjoyed.

14. What a great factor this had to be for the achievement of peace can readily be understood: the enemy is not going to dash its head against strong gates and bars. As a result the whole land benefited by the security of the city. Again the psalmist states the issue very effectively when he says that God has made peace the boundary, perhaps a sort of personification where peace is thought of as being entrenched round about the land as a better boundary than one that is marked by stones and fences and fortifications. Peace is the protecting angel. "He makes peace in your borders" (*RSV*) robs the statement of some of its strength. The progression of thought to the second member of the verse suggests the result that grows out of the situation just described. Crops can grow, and if they grow under divine benediction with sufficient rains, the outcome is "the finest of wheat" with which their hunger is amply satisfied.

15. Though the next four verses (15–18) describe a group of physical phenomena, especially in the area of winter phenomena, they are not only of one piece, but they are not as is usually assumed on the same level as the works of God in nature that have thus far been presented in the psalm. Till now the other works—the creation and control of the stars and the formation of clouds in the skies for rain—have demonstrated God's control over nature in order to emphasize His ability to govern His people in difficult circumstances. Here the making of snow, the spreading of hoarfrost, the making of cold, the melting of ice and snow are not thought of as great works but especially as works which display God's power in the creation of the unusual, which was greatly feared and had been known to be used by God for the destruction of the enemies of the people of God (see Josh. 10:11; Job 38:22, 23). Ice and snow and hoarfrost are quite infrequent in the Holy Land and are, therefore, thought of as evidences of the unusual which God is able to perform for the good of His people and as a destructive force against His enemies. *Briggs* seems to have been the first to clinch this point.

There is another emphasis which should not be minimized—the making of these items (hail, frost, snow) as well as the removal of them from the scene is clearly traceable to one agency, which man does not sufficiently appreciate, and that agency is the *word* of the Lord. He sends forth this word or command of His (v. 15), and it goes into action like an efficient and promptly obedient servant and brings into being what the Lord intends to use: the snow while like wool; the hoarfrost evenly scattered like ashes; the chunks of ice, surprisingly large and hard; the cold, which because of its infrequent appearance seems irresistible. Does this, especially the last of these, refer also to the harsh experiences like the Exile, which Israel had been exposed to?

The other side of the matter is that these forces of nature do not by some law of readjustment remove themselves off the scene. It is not certain laws of nature that work automatically and remove what was strangely formed. The same word that brought these matters into being is again sent forth with a command to bring them to an end. The means employed is the wind that this creative word calls forth. This wind blows, and the waters flow. Certainly words like these are calculated to instil a reverence for the mighty word of the Lord, which was operative in creation (Gen. 1:3, 6, 9, etc.) and has been equally operative ever since, more so than men are inclined to believe.

19. In fact, the word dominates the scene of the entire section under consideration, being mentioned not only in vv. 15 and 18 but now, from another point of view, in v. 19. Now it is the revealed Word, a synonymn for which is "statutes"—definite, authoritative pronouncements from the Almighty—and "ordinances"—judicial verdicts of His, governing cases that are difficult for men to evaluate. In other words, the Word here spoken of is the written Word of the law as it had been given to Israel, law being practically synonymous with the Pentateuch. It pleased the Lord in days of old to let some of that Word be pronounced at Mt. Sinai and to be offered in greater detail through Moses in the days of the wilderness. It further pleased Him to let it be given by the mouth of prophets through the centuries as a further elucidation of the law that was originally laid down for Jacob.

The point that was becoming particularly apparent to Israel, especially after its contacts with Babylon during the captivity, was the fact that no nation had anything that could remotely compare with such a Word of the Lord (cf. Deut. 4:8; Ps. 119:98). Never did the Lord show the same favor to any other nation. As a result, none of the nations had such a wise set of directives to guide its footsteps, and Israel was therefore singularly favored. What responsibility that entailed is at best only hinted at in this statement. But a wholesome and well-balanced statement has been made of the fact that Israel is blessed above measure by having the Word of the Lord in its midst. An obvious responsibility laid upon the Israelites by such a gift is that God be worthily praised for what He has given to His own. Therefore the psalm appropriately closes with the injunction: "Praise the Lord."

NOTES

1. The Piel infinitive *zammerah,* with a feminine ending, which is explained *GK* 52p. See also *KS* 226c and 251a. On the two coordinated causal closes beginning with *ki* see *KS* 373d.

8. The *Septuagint* adds a further member to this verse, at least in some of its manuscripts: "and grass for the service of man."

Psalm 148

LET THE WHOLE CREATION PRAISE THE LORD
FOR HIS MERCY TO ISRAEL

THIS PSALM has the somewhat unusual arrangement of beginning with a number of urgent calls to praise—through about twelve verses. Then it begins to assign the special reason for which this praise is to be offered: The Lord "has exalted the horn of His people." Precisely what this means is not immediately clear. That a major blessing has been bestowed upon Israel is evident. Nothing seems to be quite so appropriate as an occasion for such a call to praise as is the Restoration of Israel from Captivity. The offering up of praise in the days of Nehemiah (Neh. 9:5, 6) would seem to be the most fitting Scripture passage to suggest as a possible occasion for the writing of this psalm. It should, of course, always be borne in mind that the writers of the psalms seem to make a point of trying to cast each psalm into a more general form that will allow for its use under a broad variety of occasions.

An apocryphal booklet, "The Song of the Three Holy Children," which is in effect an appendix to Dan. 3, is an expansion of this psalm and usually goes under the name of the Benedicite.

The claim that this psalm was designed for use in connection with the so-called New Year's Festival in fall, when God is supposed to have been praised especially as Creator, does not find sufficient warrant in the text or in the facts of the case.

The psalm reflects a unified view of the whole realm of nature. All things in this realm are to be traced to the almighty Creator and owe so much to Him that they ought to unite with one another in singing His praise. One may very appropriately ask the question, in what sense dumb and inanimate creatures may be expected to sing their Maker's praise. Is this mere poetry, beautiful personification? Is it a beautiful and somewhat exuberant play of sentiment and fancy?

It appears that we should say it is more than this. In line with what is written in Rom. 8:18ff. and what Isaiah and other prophets and the book of Revelation say on the subject, the animate and the inanimate creatures are bound together into a sort of common fellowship of sympathetic suffering. The dumb creature world was made to suffer some of the effects of the fall of man into sin. When man is finally and completely redeemed from all these disastrous effects, then also the whole creation shall in some way share in the glorious liberty of the sons of God. For this all wait with earnest expectation. This psalm takes us one step farther in that it represents the goal as being practically achieved and the whole realm of nature as offering praise to God, except, of course, that that is not the occasion for praise here specified—as already indicated above. Israel's Restoration may apparently be regarded as a guaranty of the final restoration of all things.

a) A summons to the heavens and all that is in them to praise the Lord (vv. 1–6)

1. *Praise the Lord!*
   Praise the Lord from the heavens;
   Praise Him in the heights!
2. *Praise Him, all His angels;*
   Praise Him, all His host!
3. *Praise Him, sun and moon;*
   Praise Him, all you shining stars!
4. *Praise Him, you highest heavens*
   And you waters which are above the heavens!
5. *Let them praise the name of the Lord!*
   For He commanded, and they were created.
6. *And He established them forever and ever;*
   He appointed an ordinance which cannot be violated.

1. Like the last of the psalms from 146 onward, this one begins and ends with an Alleluiah. The first group to be summoned to praise is then indicated: they are the ones that will praise "from the heavens," the parallel expression for which is the "heights." Most prominent among those that can offer praise in this area are "His angels," who are elsewhere also exhorted to present their praises before the Almighty (cf., Ps. 29:1; 89:5; 103:20f.). When men address the angels thus, it is done because of a deep sense of the fact that the church above and that below constitute but one communion. We would not admonish them as though they were reluctant. We would merely express our sense of common purpose.

2. When the "host" is also mentioned, it seems most in keeping with the parallelism of the verse at this point to regard this as a parallel expression for "angels," though we well know that the term at times includes the heavenly bodies. Here the usage is that of Josh. 5:14f. and of I Kings 22:19 and not that of Deut. 4:19. This is all the more likely because in the next verse the stars are specifically referred to.

3. Of the heavenly bodies sun and moon are mentioned as being the more prominent, and the stars are mentioned separately as being the

more numerous. When the "highest heavens" are separately called upon in v. 4, in the light of Deut. 10:14, this would seem to refer to the heavens in so far as they are the dwelling place of God Himself. Whether this refers to a mode of thinking which was later more fully developed as the seven heavens is very hard to determine (cf. also II Cor. 12:2). In this connection the psalmist refers to a fact that all thinking men still observe, namely, that there are water sources above the heavens or the clouds which seem illimitable and are here described as the "waters which are above the heavens." At times there seems to be no water in these regions; then vast amounts seem to be available up there. This does not necessitate our subscribing to the belief that the old Israelites believed in a siderial ocean, where waters were always stored up in quantity as they are in the seven seas. That would mean to draw unwarranted inferences from language that is largely poetic.

5. There comes a turn in the expression in which the author, after having addressed all these mighty works of God, continues in the third person to express the wish that all these might jointly praise the Lord. The preliminary reason assigned for such praise is that they were all created by God, and created in a manner that particularly redounds to their Maker's glory. According to the whole pattern of the psalm he still has in mind to share in praise of the event which is to be specified later and is the major cause for praise. What they are to praise first is the remarkable manner of their creation: God commanded, and they were created as Gen. 1 so eloquently and clearly testifies. It is the permanence of that creation which is of especial moment to the psalmist.

6. By creating them He also established them forever and ever. This is a helpful description of what we sometimes call the "continuous creation," that work in which the power of the original word of creation still sustains and vitalizes all things and continues them in being. This latter thought is the one expressed by the words: "He appointed an ordinance which cannot be violated." That is to say: He gave them being, and no man can cancel that being. This is in line with words of Scripture like Jer. 31:55f.; 33:25. The "ordinance" is something analogous to what we call the "laws of nature" though, strictly speaking, the Scriptures know of no laws that operate as natural forces apart from God. The fact that they continue operative is due to the continual sustaining power of God. Gen. 8:22 is also in line with the thought expressed here.

b) A summons to the earth similarly to praise the Lord (vv. 7–12)

7. *Praise the Lord from the earth,*
    You sea monsters and all oceans;
8. *Fire and hail, snow and mists,*
    Stormy wind fulfilling His word;

9. *Mountains and all hills,*
    Fruit trees and all cedars;
10. *Beasts and all cattle,*
    Creeping things and winged creatures;
11. *You kings of the earth and all peoples,*
    Princes and all rulers of the earth;
12. *Young men and also maidens,*
    Old men together with children.

7. The summons to praise the Lord is addressed to those who are upon the earth; and if those creatures called upon above were the highest imaginable, the psalmist now begins with those that are the lowest on earth, beginning, one might say, with the very ocean depths. The chief and most impressive forms of life in the ocean are the sea monsters—whales, sharks, and others that are impressive because of their size. God has given them so much that they ought to offer praise. The vast oceans are appropriately included at this point. Then in fine order are listed all those things that fill the atmosphere. There fire burns, that mysterious power to which man owes so much. There hail, snow, and mists have their origin. There the stormy winds become agitated, not only to wreak destruction upon the works of men, but also to accomplish the manifold things that they are bidden to do by the Almighty, for they are continually "fulfilling His word."

9. Another vast area of God's creation is that which is filled by the mountains in which the Holy Land especially abounded, whether the high or the low, each having its peculiar majesty. They are summoned to join the mighty chorus as well as the regular trees of the forest and the fruit trees that may dot the hillside. Then there is the vast realm of animated beings apart from man: the wild "beasts" and the domesticated "cattle" and the other great realms of animal life of a smaller sort where creatures swarm and amaze us by their prolific increase. Then lastly there are the manifold "winged creatures," which term apparently includes all animal life that has wings.

11. Aside from the angels who were mentioned early in this mighty catalogue of created things all those called upon to praise God were of the kind that we call inanimate, or if they were animate they were below the level of man. In a swift summary all the children of men are now called upon to do their part. The highest of mankind, at least from the point of view of the authority that they universally enjoyed, were the "kings of the earth." Grouped together with these is all the rest of mankind. Then follow princes and rulers, high and low, wherever they may be upon the earth. And lastly, to make it clear that no group is to be excluded, young men and maidens, old men and children are brought

into the picture. Though this is a somewhat long enumeration, its ingenuity and the effective manner in which various classes are grouped together enhance the interest. In fact, a sense of awe at the magnitude of the grand chorus that is being invoked creeps over man as he reads attentively. We may have heard impressive choruses; none could compare with this one.

Two thoughts may be considered before we go on to the conclusion. One involves a kind of inference that grows out of v. 3. For if the heavenly bodies are called on to acknowledge their Creator, and if that is one of their major functions, then they do not have an independent existence. Israel did not worship the stars as the Babylonians did. Israel called upon the stars to adore their Maker. Second, to attribute some kind of "remnants of animistic" notions to the psalmist because he calls upon these various classes to offer praise to the Lord is not a valid conclusion. Otherwise poetic personifications would point in the same direction, which, as far as we know, no man has ever claimed.

c) **The chief reason for praise in the present instance (vv. 13, 14)**

13. *Let them praise the name of the Lord,*
    For His name is exalted;
    His praise is above earth and heaven.
14. *And He has exalted the horn of His people;*
    Praise for all His saints, for the children of Israel, a people close to Him.
    Praise the Lord!

As was the case in v. 5, the form of statement now shifts from the second person, direct address, to the third by grouping together all those that have been enumerated in vv. 7–12 as well as those that were first called upon to sing the praises of the Lord. That which is the object of their praise is here designated by the comprehensive term "name." That means the sum total of all the things that He has achieved, or which are known concerning Him—popularly stated: His reputation. For the reputation that He has among His saints is so far above everything that any other being can achieve that the statement, "for His name alone is exalted," is very much in order. Besides, whenever His "praise" is worthily rendered it is "above heaven and earth."

14. But it is not these generalities that the psalmist has specially in mind. They would scarcely seem to warrant calling together so mighty a chorus to offer praise. The one thing that he has in mind is the special benefit conferred, apparently recently, upon Israel, and that is, "He has exalted the horn of His people." But God's mercies so obviously intertwine that not one of them can be considered in total isolation from the others. It is for this reason that all that His name stands for is first

brought into the picture. This for us somewhat unique statement about the exalting of the horn of His people must start with the thought that horn connotes strength. On this use of the term see Deut. 33:17; I Sam. 2:1; Ps. 132:17. Israel had been almost completely deprived of strength during the captivity. She could achieve nothing; she had been brought very low. New strength for living and achievement had again been instilled. This was an occasion for "praise for all His saints." This word "praise" is apparently in apposition to the whole preceding clause, a connection which is not immediately apparent to the reader. "Saints" is, of course, a choice name for the "children of Israel, a people close to Him." The term implies loyalty to the obligations of the faithful covenant that the Lord had established with His people.

The basic thought is this. The destiny of Israel is so important, and what God had recently done for His people in their Restoration is of such vital importance to all nations and creatures that, if they grasped what it involved, they would be glad to add their praises to Israel's praises. Thus the psalm closes with a jubilant "Alleluiah."

NOTES

6. We have translated the word *ya'abhor* in the sense in which it is used when it is connected with nouns such as "ordinances." It appears to be the impersonal use of the third person singular. In meaning it is, therefore, the same as if the impersonal third person plural were used. Oftentimes such forms are best translated as passives as we have done. The word means, "which are not violated" or" which cannot be violated." See *KS* 3371.

14. To regard the word "praise" as being at this point a sort of liturgical or musical footnote, indicating into what category this psalm falls, does not strike us as being particularly happy. Is the character of this psalm so dubious as to require such a footnote? The expression "a people close to Him" reads literally, "a people of His nearness," an expression which does not so much state how Israel customarily behaved but what, by God's grace, was the dignity that God had assigned to this people.

Psalm 149

PRAISE FOR PRESENT AND FUTURE VICTORY

THERE IS historical evidence that this psalm has been put to unholy uses. As *Delitzsch* has pointed out, Catholic princes were incited to warlike fervor at the beginning of the Thirty Years' War by reference to it; and in the Protestant camp by use of it Thomas Muenzer incited the peasants to rebellion at the beginning of the Peasants' War. These will scarcely have been the only instances when the psalm was wrongly used. These facts seem to have encouraged a hostile attitude toward this psalm as though anything said in defense of it were reprehensible.

Many commentators make mention of the fact that the criticism of this psalm has been too sharp. Some of the misunderstandings involved have grown out of wrong motives that were attributed to the psalmist, motives for which no solid ground can be found. Because a man may have bloodthirsty ambitions and then expresses them by the use of this psalm does not necessarily indicate that the author must be thought of as belonging in the same category.

All the needs of the case are fully met if a situation like the following is assumed: In a time of grave peril the children of Israel have been granted a great victory; they rejoice over it; more battles are yet to be fought; their very existence trembles in the balance; they hope that, as they go out to fight, God may again grant them victory; arms must be used; home and family must be fought for; in the Lord's name they hope to take up their arms again and achieve a further victory; to share in it will be a noble distinction for all of His people who participate. To be in such a situation and to hope to use arms successfully—is that bloodthirstiness? Can nothing be said in defense of such an attitude? Was it unholy business when Joshua fought the Amalakites (Exod. 17:11–13)? Or when Gideon took up the sword against the Midianites (Judg. 7:20)? Or when Asa had to fight the Ethiopians (II Chron. 14:10f)? Or when Nehemiah had the builders of the wall gird on their weapons as they built (Neh. 4:16)? With these situations in mind, we shall feel reluctant to attribute to the persons here involved anything bloodthirsty or unwholesome. Why not put the best construction on things Biblical?

It is true that we seem to be under necessity of assigning a late date to the psalm, perhaps the age of Nehemiah. It is also true that there seems to be no historical occasion known to us that would meet the needs of this case. But the psalm as such gives the impression that those for whom it was first written had the same incident in mind and understood right well what was involved. A newer explanation (*Gunkel, Einleitung in die Psalmen,* p. 63) of the reference in v. 6 to the swords in the hands of those that are praising the Lord seems to relieve some of the possible tension involved. It is pointed out that we have a reference to some type of sword dance, where the warriors, before going out to battle, appear at a solemn service in the sanctuary, where they wave their swords as they chant their praises. There appears to be nothing too unholy about that under certain circumstances.

Staying close to the material offered by the psalm itself, we should also point out that those who are exhorted to share in this manifestation of the praises of the Lord are three times called God's "pious" ones (also translated "saints" and "faithful"). This does not appear to be a reference to the later Jewish sect of the *Chasidim* although the word used is the same. For here the word seems still to be used in its general connotation. Without a doubt the ones addressed are, therefore, the sincere and truehearted Israelites. Of them it may be expected that they will have understood the call to praise and the use of the sword in a truly spiritual sense.

The close of v. 1 ("His praise in the assembly of the pious") and the close of Ps. 148:14 connect these two psalms outwardly.

a) **The faithful are exhorted to praise God for victory achieved (vv. 1–4)**

1. *Praise the Lord!*
   Sing unto the Lord a new song,
   His praise in the assembly of the pious!
2. *Let Israel be glad in its Maker;*
   Let the sons of Zion rejoice in their King!
3. *Let them praise His name in the solemn dance;*
   Let them make music to Him with timbrel and harp!
4. *For the Lord takes pleasure in His people;*
   He adorns the meek with victory.

1. The reason for this exhortation to praise appears in v. 4. "A new song" is called for, for new mercies make us feel the inadequacy of our past efforts at praise (cf. Ps. 33:3; 96:1). The song is to be "praise" offered in the assembly of the pious because there it is done well, there the desire to praise the Lord flourishes best. Whenever praise is offered for an individual mercy of God, it is well to couple with it the remembrance of manifold other mercies, for God's favors to us are never iso-

lated. Therefore the writer goes on to recall that God is the "Maker" of the nation: He brought it into being. But He also successfully governs what He has created. Therefore He is to be praised as "their King."

3. With this as a background, the psalmist goes on to show in what traditional way this praise of the Lord is to be manifested. The solemn dance may well serve its purpose as it did in Exod. 15:20; Judg. 11:34; Sam. 6:14; Jer. 31:4. Instrumental music, percussive and stringed, may be added. Since the psalm has undertones of the martial, the percussive instruments have a special place.

4. Special mention is now made of the particular occasion that calls forth the praise that is enjoined: it is the general statement which allows for a wide range of possibilities that the Lord "takes pleasure in His people." Since the verb is in the participial form, we may regard that fact as an indication that the uninterrupted stream of divine favor now flows forth upon His people. Men speak thus when they were for a time denied this blessing. The parallel statement says that "He adorns the meek with victory." The designation "meek" implies that recent adversity had produced a frame of mind in which men bowed down under the will of God and accepted it as being well merited.

The "victory" could include any aspect of the restoration from captivity, to which this term may be a reference. The word is often translated "salvation," but since the purely spiritual connotation of this term predominates in our thinking, we translated the word "victory" as coming closer to what we should use. The people, once stigmatized and besmirched by God's harsh judgment upon them, are now free from that ugly blot and are gaily decorated with the great deliverance that the Lord has wrought. There appears to be no indication that we must select a Maccabean date to find a situation that would correspond to the case as here outlined.

b) **The faithful are exhorted to praise God for victory anticipated (vv. 5–9)**

5. *Let the pious exult in glory;*
   Let them shout for joy upon their couches.
6. *Let the high praises of God be in their mouth*
   And a two-edged sword in their hand;
7. *To execute vengeance upon the nations,*
   Chastisements upon the peoples;
8. *To bind their kings with chains*
   And their dignitaries with fetters of iron;
9. *To execute upon them the judgment written.*
   Such honor have all His pious ones.
   Praise the Lord!

5. It need only be assumed as indicated above that the Israelites had a war upon their hands, in which they had to participate or be destroyed. They had already achieved a victory. They now hoped for more. They were not forcing themselves into the situation. They were not anxious to share in the carrying out of God's judgments in a cruel and bloodthirsty manner. They hoped that the victory attained would be in fulfilment of things that God had promised. Was not something of that spirit found in the armies under Gustavus Adolphus in the Thirty Years' War?

The section begins by tying back to the situation described in the first section. The victory there referred to had created a state of "glory," in which the pious are now bidden to exult. A paraphrase of what the last clause means is well covered by the somewhat free translation: "Let the devout exult at the glory that has come." That such exultation is not to be confined to the public services at the sanctuary is indicated by the next line, which suggests the possibility of continuing it, each man for himself, upon his couch at home, during the night or before he falls asleep. A little practical readjustment of thought will spare a man the agony of the literalists who feel that the psalmist is here suggesting that men should on their couches sing praises and wave swords. The "couches" are appropriately mentioned, for certain Scripture passages suggest that there the pain of one's affliction was often felt during sleepless nights (cf. Ps. 4:4; 6:6; Hos. 7:14); here there is a valid contrast to that situation.

6. Under very special circumstances as indicated above it is quite possible that one may have the high praises of God upon his mouth (the Hebrew uses "throat" in its idiom) and a two-edged sword in one's hand. If our taste would not favor a sword dance, it would for that matter favor no religious dances at all. Yet the Israelites had a different approach on this score.

7. As we go on we note that the swords are thought of as executing vengeance on hostile nations. Nothing indicates that this vengeance is undeserved. Since the "pious" execute it, the greater likelihood is that the opposite is the case. The parallelism suggests the same. For "chastisements" always have wholesome objectives.

8. This verse then thinks in terms of total victory achieved. For when kings are bound, their armies are first vanquished. The binding of the kings takes us to the point of the total triumph of the victors.

9. This verse helps to establish the approach that we have used in that the last formulation of the purpose that what those who participate in this war have in mind is this: "to execute upon them the judgment written." Exactly what passages are in the writer's mind it may be difficult to determine, but it seems quite clear that he wants no other judg-

ment inflicted than that which God had indicated in His sure Word as being the infallible outcome. General passages on the subject of the defeat of the enemies of God's people seem to be under consideration, passages like Deut. 32:42ff.; Is. 41:15ff.; Ezek. 38 and 39; Mic. 4:13). The psalmist wants to have only those results reached that the Lord has sanctioned. Looked at from this point of view, the stern necesstiy of war, which is utterly unavoidable, may then be regarded as a privilege to participate in.

When we claim this we do not deny that other points of view may be stressed just as legitimately. But we feel that we can grasp why such a task as vv. 5–8 outlined may also be described in the words: "Such honor have all His pious ones." Such was at least the case in this particular instance out of which the psalm grew. That men must carefully search their souls before they can with pure purpose engage in any venture that may be thought similar to the one just described cannot be emphasized too strongly. We cannot feel that we should take an apologetic attitude with reference to this psalm.

NOTES

2. "Maker" is an emphatic plural. Cf. *GK* 124k.
3. We translated the simple word "dance" as "solemn dance" to indicate that only a religious dance was under consideration.

Psalm 150

LET EVERYTHING THAT HAS BREATH PRAISE THE LORD!

BETWEEN EVEN these last two psalms there is some word or phrase that associates them outwardly: here it is the expression "timbrel and dance" (cf. Ps. 149:3 with 150:4).

One can at a glance recognize the propriety of having this psalm serve as the conclusion of the Psalter. The note of praise swells out more and more strongly toward the close of the book, finally to break out in this crescendo which is full-toned and jubilant. Each of the four preceding books was concluded by a doxology (see Ps. 41:13; 72:18–20; etc.). What is more appropriate than to have a very special doxology for the final conclusion? But there is more to it than that. *Maclaren* has a word to this effect in classic style: "The psalm is more than an artistic close of the Psalter; it is a prophecy of the last result of the devout life, and in its unclouded sunniness, as well as in its universality, it proclaims the certain end of the weary years for the individual and for the world." A book of hymns and prayers like the Psalter should end on a note of triumph and victory.

There are a few minor difficulties of interpretation, but on the whole the psalm is clear as to its structure and purpose. One is practically compelled to agree with those commentators who assert that a type of liturgical use is assumed for this psalm. It is even possible that as each instrument is named, it set in and joined the chorus of praise, action being supplied by those who engaged in the sacred dance. The vocal background consisted in the loudly chanted praises of the Lord, which were called forth by the opening and especially the closing summons. One difficulty is involved here: Musical instruments did not seem to be used to accompany human voices.

The outline of the psalm is surprisingly simple. It begins by indicating who is to praise (v. 1); it continues with the why (v. 2); then follows the how (vv. 3–5); the last verse reverts to the who again. But in v. 1 the ones exhorted to praise are different from those appealed to in v. 6.

1. *Praise the Lord!*
   Praise God in His sanctuary;
   Praise Him in His mighty firmament!
2. *Praise Him according to His mighty acts;*
   Praise Him according to His excellent greatness!
3. *Praise Him with the blast of the trumpet;*
   Praise Him with lute and harp!
4. *Praise Him with timbrel and dance;*
   Praise Him with stringed instruments and pipes!
5. *Praise Him with sharp-sounding cymbals;*
   Praise Him with crashing cymbals!
6. *Let everything that has breath praise the Lord!*
   Praise the Lord!

1. Though the issue has been much debated, we feel strongly that the sanctuary referred to in v. 1 is the heavenly one. The phrase "in His sanctuary" does not modify the noun "God" but the verb "praise." The parallelism of the second member of the verse supports this view. Those who are to be found in the heavenly sanctuary who are capable of singing God's praises are the holy angels, who are here addressed as they were in Ps. 103:20; they are part of the same communion of

saints; we feel that kinship as a very real one. Those that are to be found in "His mighty firmament" are the stars of the heavens (cf. Job 38:7). Animate and inanimate beings have thus been summoned to the praise of God, i.e., 'El in the Hebrew. He who was in the opening statement designated as Lord is now called God, the Strong One, according to the more likely meaning of the term. He is, therefore, being thought of both as the covenant Lord of Israel and as the Strong Ruler of the universe.

2. This verse indicates in brief what kind of works of His are to be borne in mind. There are His "mighty acts" which demonstrate His illimitable power; there is "His excellent greatness," which draws attention to the superior being that He Himself is. These two terms are general enough in sweep to cover everything for which God may be praised.

3. As the instruments to be used are listed, it is of more than passing interest to note that almost all that are known to have been in use in Israel, except two, are referred to. But it is more to the point to be reminded that "trumpets" seem to have been reserved for the use of priests (Josh. 6:4) and "harps, lutes, and cymbals" for the Levites (Neh. 12:27; I Chron. 15:16; II Chron. 29:25). The remaining instruments seem to have been in use among the laity generally. To the typical Israelite the mention of the instruments involved might readily bring before his mind's eye these various groups. It also appears that, though the resultant music would have nothing in common with the harmony pattern familiar to our ears but rather be a weird blending of many types of sound, it could in its own way be a very effective accompaniment of the text and serve to give expression to its spirit.

We should, perhaps, again have substituted the expression "solemn dance" for "dance" to recall the distinctive nature of this type of liturgical action. Sound and action were blended in this picture. A mighty symphony orchestra is involved as it was in Ps. 148.

Until this point mankind had not been specifically mentioned by name. To be very literalistic about it, one might conclude that only angels and stars had been addressed, and they were the ones who were to take hold of the various instruments listed and use them to praise the Mighty One. But it need scarcely be pointed out that beginning with v. 3 one quite naturally thinks in terms of man as using the instruments suggested.

6. What has thus far then been taken for granted is now specifically stated. In fact, not only man is called upon but every being that "has breath." Let them all employ the breath they have for the most holy use to which it can be put—the praise of the Lord. The universal sweep of that thought is most attractive.

Thus the Book of Praises, as the Hebrew Bible calls it, comes to a fitting close; and almost every writer feels impelled to add his personal wish and admonition that he and all who read may follow this fine injunction now and all the days of their life.

NOTES

2. Many interpreters translate, "Praise Him *for* His mighty deeds." The parallel expression suggests that the *be* is to be regarded as a *beth normae,* "*according to* His mighty acts." See *KS* 332r.

Index of Subjects

acrostic 108, 226, 278, 821, 974ff.
afterlife 26f., 319
allegory 796
angels 245f, 250, 654f., 721
anger (of God) 48, 69, 84, 309, 557, 654
anointed 41, 46, 187
Aramaism 8, 57, 942, 969
ark of covenant 215f., 221, 872
assurance 458f.
Assyrian 362, 365, 368, 378, 415f., 479, 548, 600
avenger of blood 112, 116

Babylon(ian) 91, 533, 609, 793, 797, 932f.
Baca (valley of) 608

captivity (bring back) 615
caravansary 211
Cherub 580
confession 267
corruption (of text) 381
cosmology (semitic) 218
criticism 40
curses 333

dance 256
degrees 862
doctrines (of the Psalms) 22

Egypt(ian) 134, 624, 723, 793
enemies 108, 201, 284, 615, 661
enthronement of Yahweh 11, 222, 272, 374, 715, 774
eternity 250
evening prayer 953ff.

faith 553ff.
father 50
fear of God 281f., 294, 413, 647, 895

forgiveness 263ff.
formalism 142

gittith 101, 105, 603
glory 61
gods 22
guilt 406

Hallel 982
heart 316, 327
hereafter 86, 151, 160, 530
higgaion 114
history 24, 733ff.
holiness 198
house of God 77f., 603ff., 667

I, collective 12, 124, 129, 236, 313, 345, 448, 612, 803, 898
idolatry 588, 749ff., 799
immorality 642
imprecations 18, 79, 93, 131, 261, 285f., 422, 440ff., 467, 507, 597, 601f., 736ff., 932ff., 948, 967

judges (elohim) 592ff.
judgment 38, 95f., 97, 155, 517, 542ff., 550, 567, 592, 691, 703ff.

king (God) 677, 680ff., 685ff., 695ff., 978f.
king (man) 968
kiss 55

lament 307, 344, 421, 453
law 32, 35, 176, 181ff., 305, 565, 823, 834
laws of nature 23
leviathan 538
liturgy 146, 185, 194, 217, 228, 265, 322, 329, 374, 479, 548, 642, 698, 733, 743, 790, 797, 867, 923, 928

1009

love, steadfast 411

Maccabean period 9
maskil 9, 265, 346, 353, 372, 417, 421, 561, 632, 958
Messiah 20, 42f., 44, 56, 100, 174, 189, 194ff., 215, 322, 330, 351ff., 454, 501, 515ff., 627, 690, 687, 770ff., 812ff., 911
morning psalm 463, 975
miktam 9, 147
music director 71
mythology 604

name (of God) 102, 418, 976
nature psalms 100, 244ff., 476f., 663ff., 722ff., 925, 929, 992ff., 996

old age 510ff.
omnipresence 942ff.

parallels (Babylonian and Egyptian) 16
penitence 6, 263, 307, 398ff., 742ff., 902ff., 963ff.
Phoenician 57
pilgrimage psalms 862ff.
poetry, Hebrew 14
praise 87, 108, 162, 173f., 243, 251f., 262, 271, 278, 289, 465f., 472ff., 484, 485, 508, 577, 675ff., 691ff., 715ff., 762ff., 779ff., 784, 789ff., 810, 921ff., 923ff., 961, 974, 998, 1001, 1005
problem psalms 522ff.
prophecy 195
prosperity (of wicked) 298ff., 522ff.
providence 276
punishment 25, 308

reformers 5
repentance 408
restoration from Captivity 753ff., 887
retribution 264
rewards 25
righteous(ness) 18, 212, 301, 305, 326, 407, 518, 614, 636, 717, 786, 817, 914f.

river (Euphrates) 519
rod 213

saints 17, 148, 391, 1002
sacrifices 23, 69, 393, 407, 419
salvation 235, 287, 683, 1003
scepter 52
selah 9, 61
self-righteousness 82, 154, 228ff.
shadow of death 212ff.
sheminith 129
sheol 90, 151, 385, 621
shiggaion 91
sin (doctrine of) 25, 266, 270, 401, 403, 415ff., 474, 560, 646
sickness 257, 270, 400
sinners 17, 34
Sitz im Leben 13
son of man 101
sorcerers 17
soul (nephesh) 202, 239, 291, 332, 386, 418
spirit (of man) 259
spirit (of God) 273, 944
staff 213
style 15
synagogue 536

text (Hebrew) 15
thanksgiving 190ff.
titles 6, 256
transitoriness 641ff., 719
trust 650ff., 657ff., 907ff.
types (of psalms) 10

Ugaritic 251, 778
unity 917ff.
universalism 24, 472, 693, 940, 987ff.

value (of Psalms) 27ff.
vengeance 668f.
victory 491ff.
vows 807

wadis 889
wicked 120f., 127, 159, 527
wisdom 382
worship 23, 389ff., 497, 508, 607, 658ff., 698ff.
wrath 551, 782